INVESTIGATIVE CRIMINAL PROCEDURE

Third Edition

■ ■ ■

Sam Kamin
Professor of Law
University of Denver, Sturm College of Law

Ricardo J. Bascuas
Professor of Law
University of Miami School of Law

AMERICAN CASEBOOK SERIES®

WEST ACADEMIC PUBLISHING

444 Cedar Street, Suite 700
St. Paul, MN 55101
1-877-888-1330

Printed in the United States of America

ISBN: 978-1-64242-493-5

PREFACE

This Third Edition of Investigative Criminal Procedure benefits from the valuable suggestions of the law professors across the country who have used the first two editions in their courses. Each of our home institutions, the University of Denver College of Law and the University of Miami School of Law, afforded us the resources—through summer research grants as well as administrative and research assistance and support—that have allowed us to continue to improve the book.

Our focus in the Third Edition remains on the seminal decisions of the United States Supreme Court interpreting the Fourth, Fifth, Sixth, and Fourteenth Amendments to the Constitution. We have also increased the number of cases dealing with the enforcement of these rights through the remedy of exclusion. These cases define the permissible scope of criminal investigation and have important things to say about the relationship between the state and its citizens more generally. Placing these materials within a broader historical and theoretical context enables students to reflect on larger questions, such as how crime control and due process are balanced, how power is allocated between the courts and the political branches, and how a constitutional text adapts to an ever-changing society.

To this end, we made the editorial choice to present, where possible, all of the justices' views in each case. Concurrences and dissents help students develop critical reasoning skills by testing the assumptions, reasoning, and wisdom supporting the majority's view. Every opinion has been carefully edited to communicate fully but concisely its signatories' views; we have tried not to use the editorial process to express our own views on the soundness or persuasiveness of any particular opinion. This approach also affords students a window into how perspectives on constitutional provisions are shaped by the course of the nation's history and by changes in the Court's makeup. The value of a long view of constitutional thought is exemplified by cases like *United States v. Jones*, 565 U.S. 400 (2012), and *Florida v. Jardines*, 568 U.S. 1 (2013), which show that even long-neglected views of the Constitution's meaning can be suddenly revivified. In the rare case where we omitted an opinion entirely, it was only because that opinion was limited to an alternative ground of decision not germane to the topics covered in the book.

New in this edition are the Supreme Court's recent cases including those dealing with technology and the Fourth Amendment (*Carpenter v. United States*, 138 S.Ct. 2206 (2018) and *Riley v. California*, 573 U.S. 373 (2014)), *Terry* Stops (*Prado Navarette v. California*, 572 U.S. 393 (2014), *Heien v. North Carolina*, 574 U.S. 54 (2014), and *Rodriguez v. United*

States, 135 S.Ct. 1609 (2015)), and the exclusionary rule (*Utah v. Strieff*, 136 S.Ct. 2056 (2016)). In addition to updating the book through the Supreme Court's October 2018 term, there are also some format changes. Gone are the text boxes and cross-references that were present in previous editions. Some of this content has been moved to the Points for Discussion while most has been eliminated entirely. We believe these changes make the book more streamlined and keep the students' focus on the cases at hand. Users of previous editions will find the cases and topics they are used to nearly fully intact.

We welcome feedback from students as well as from faculty using this book.

SAM KAMIN
(skamin@law.du.edu)

RICARDO BASCUAS
(rbascuas@law.miami.edu)

Sept. 2019

SUMMARY OF CONTENTS

PART III. REMEDY

TABLE OF CONTENTS

PART II. POLICE QUESTIONING

PART III. REMEDY

Table of Cases

The principal cases are in bold type.

INVESTIGATIVE CRIMINAL PROCEDURE

Third Edition

INTRODUCTION

LITIGATING CRIMINAL PROCEDURE

■ ■ ■

The basic Criminal Procedure course in the United States explores the provisions of the Bill of Rights that delineate crucial aspects of the relationship between the government and its citizens and the relationships among the three branches of government. Specifically, it focuses on the protections that the federal Constitution affords against the official gathering of evidence before a person is tried on criminal charges. It deals with searches, seizures, interrogations, and some aspects of the right to counsel. In other words, Criminal Procedure is a constitutional law course. It is an introduction to the Fourth Amendment, the Fifth Amendment's Self-Incrimination Clause, and some aspects of the Sixth Amendment's Assistance of Counsel Clause.

All of the cases in this textbook are Supreme Court cases dating only as far back as the Prohibition era. This is because, before Prohibition, the federal government's involvement in criminal law enforcement was extremely limited relative to modern times.

> Fourth and Fifth Amendment law was not terribly important during America's first century. Federal criminal prosecutions were rare, and federal prosecutions were the only ones to which the Fourth and Fifth Amendments applied.

William Stuntz, *The Substantive Origins of Criminal Procedure*, 105 YALE L. J. 393, 419 (1995).

As Professor Stuntz notes, the Supreme Court determined very early in the nation's history that the Bill of Rights restrained only the federal government and not the states. *See, e.g., Barron v. Baltimore*, 32 U.S. 243 (1833). Because the federal government played only a small role in the enforcement of the criminal laws during the nineteenth century, the Supreme Court did not have many opportunities to rule on Fourth and Fifth Amendment questions until the twentieth century.

> As a subfield of constitutional law, constitutional criminal procedure stands as an anomaly. In many other areas of constitutional law, major Marshall Court opinions stand out and continue to frame debate both in courts and beyond. . . . But no comparable Marshall Court landmarks dot the plain of constitutional criminal procedure.

* * *

> . . . [F]or virtually the entire first century of the Bill of Rights, the United States Supreme Court lacked general appellate jurisdiction over federal criminal cases. This little-known fact helps explain why, for example, the Sedition Act Prosecutions in the late 1790s—which raised the most important and far-reaching constitutional issues of their day—never reached the Supreme Court for ultimate judicial resolution.

Akhil Reed Amar, *The Future of Constitutional Criminal Procedure*, 33 AM. CRIM. L. REV. 1123, 1123–24 (1996). Beginning in 1891 the Supreme Court was given broad appellate jurisdiction over criminal cases, creating at least one avenue for the adjudication of criminal procedure questions. Not long thereafter, the Court began to rule that the Fourteenth Amendment's Due Process Clause made provisions in the Bill of Rights enforceable against state and local governments. The Prohibition era, from 1920 to 1933, forced the Supreme Court to contend with a rapidly expanding federal bureaucracy that sprang up to deal with the impossible challenge of enforcing the National Prohibition Act.

> The brief constitutionalization of prohibition . . . forced Justices on both the right and the left to stop debating whether there should be an American administrative state, and required them instead to reconstruct their judicial philosophy on the assumption that the administrative state was an unalterable reality. . . . Prohibition also forced a rethinking of the appropriate limits of national power, as well as fundamental developments in the meaning of Fourth Amendment limitations on law enforcement.

Robert Post, *Federalism, Positive Law, and the Emergence of the American Administrative State: Prohibition in the Taft Court Era*, 48 WM. & MARY L. REV. 1, 3 (2006).

Between 1953 and 1969, the Warren Court applied most of the clauses in the first eight amendments to the states through selective incorporation. The Supreme Court recently described that process:

> In the late 19th century, the Court began to consider whether the Due Process Clause prohibits the States from infringing rights set out in the Bill of Rights. Five features of the approach taken during the ensuing era should be noted.
>
> First, the Court viewed the due process question as entirely separate from the question whether a right was a privilege or immunity of national citizenship.
>
> Second, the Court explained that the only rights protected against state infringement by the Due Process Clause were those rights "of such a nature that they are included in the conception

of due process of law." While it was "possible that some of the personal rights safeguarded by the first eight Amendments against National action [might] also be safeguarded against state action," the Court stated, this was "not because those rights are enumerated in the first eight Amendments."

* * *

Third, in some cases decided during this era the Court "can be seen as having asked, when inquiring into whether some particular procedural safeguard was required of a State, if a civilized system could be imagined that would not accord the particular protection." Thus, in holding that due process prohibits a State from taking private property without just compensation, the Court described the right as "a principle of natural equity, recognized by all temperate and civilized governments, from a deep and universal sense of its justice." Similarly, the Court found that due process did not provide a right against compelled incrimination in part because this right "has no place in the jurisprudence of civilized and free countries outside the domain of the common law."

Fourth, the Court during this era was not hesitant to hold that a right set out in the Bill of Rights failed to meet the test for inclusion within the protection of the Due Process Clause. The Court found that some such rights qualified. But others did not.

Finally, even when a right set out in the Bill of Rights was held to fall within the conception of due process, the protection or remedies afforded against state infringement sometimes differed from the protection or remedies provided against abridgment by the Federal Government. . . .

An alternative theory regarding the relationship between the Bill of Rights and § 1 of the Fourteenth Amendment was championed by Justice Black. This theory held that § 1 of the Fourteenth Amendment totally incorporated all of the provisions of the Bill of Rights. As Justice Black noted, the chief congressional proponents of the Fourteenth Amendment espoused the view that the Amendment made the Bill of Rights applicable to the States . . . . Nonetheless, the Court never has embraced Justice Black's "total incorporation" theory.

While Justice Black's theory was never adopted, the Court eventually moved in that direction by initiating what has been called a process of "selective incorporation," i.e., the Court began to hold that the Due Process Clause fully incorporates particular rights contained in the first eight Amendments.

> The decisions during this time abandoned three of the previously noted characteristics of the earlier period. The Court made it clear that the governing standard is not whether any "civilized system [can] be imagined that would not accord the particular protection." Instead, the Court inquired whether a particular Bill of Rights guarantee is fundamental to our scheme of ordered liberty and system of justice.
>
> The Court also shed any reluctance to hold that rights guaranteed by the Bill of Rights met the requirements for protection under the Due Process Clause. The Court eventually incorporated almost all of the provisions of the Bill of Rights. Only a handful of the Bill of Rights protections remain unincorporated.[13]
>
> Finally, the Court abandoned "the notion that the Fourteenth Amendment applies to the States only a watered-down, subjective version of the individual guarantees of the Bill of Rights," stating that it would be "incongruous" to apply different standards "depending on whether the claim was asserted in a state or federal court." Instead, the Court decisively held that incorporated Bill of Rights protections "are all to be enforced against the States under the Fourteenth Amendment according to the same standards that protect those personal rights against federal encroachment."

McDonald v. City of Chicago, 561 U.S. 742, 759–765 (2010) (holding that the right to keep and bear arms is applicable against the states).

Selective incorporation led to an explosion of litigation as criminal defendants used the newly applicable rights to challenge state as well as federal convictions. "With many, many more state criminal cases fueling its docket, the Warren Court proceeded to build up, in short order, a remarkable doctrinal edifice of Fourth Amendment, Fifth Amendment, and Sixth Amendment rules—the foundations of modern constitutional criminal procedure." Amar, *The Future of Constitutional Criminal Procedure*, 33 AM. CRIM. L. REV. at 1125. That edifice forms the raw material of this book.

---

[13] In addition to the right to keep and bear arms (and the Sixth Amendment right to a unanimous jury verdict), the only rights not fully incorporated are (1) the Third Amendment's protection against quartering of soldiers; (2) the Fifth Amendment's grand jury indictment requirement; (3) the Seventh Amendment right to a jury trial in civil cases; and (4) the Eighth Amendment's prohibition on excessive fines.

We never have decided whether the Third Amendment or the Eighth Amendment's prohibition of excessive fines applies to the States through the Due Process Clause.

Our governing decisions regarding the Grand Jury Clause of the Fifth Amendment and the Seventh Amendment's civil jury requirement long predate the era of selective incorporation.

PART I

THE FOURTH AMENDMENT

■ ■ ■

CHAPTER 1

THE REASONABLENESS CLAUSE

■ ■ ■

This chapter focuses on the terms used in the Fourth Amendment's Reasonableness Clause. It looks at the judicial debate over whether the Fourth Amendment's protection of "persons, houses, papers, and effects" should be read narrowly or broadly in light of the amendment's purposes. It also examines the Supreme Court's efforts to define what actions constitute a "search" or a "seizure."

A. "PERSONS, HOUSES, PAPERS, AND EFFECTS"

Most of the cases in this book concern the Fourth Amendment's protection "against unreasonable searches and seizures. . . ." Though the Fourth Amendment is now implicated in an enormous range of encounters between government employees and individuals, scholars generally agree that the founders were concerned primarily with generalized or suspicionless searches and seizures. The Framers drafted the Fourth Amendment in direct response to the English practice of searching homes under general warrants—warrants that did not specify what was to be searched or seized—to uncover evidence of seditious libel. Despite these modest origins, scholars and jurists generally agree today that the Fourth Amendment regulates a wide array of searches and seizures; in the modern world of organized, professional police forces and extensive government regulation of everyday life through criminal and administrative regimes, an expansive reading of the Amendment provides a powerful check on official discretion.

How the Amendment should be read to afford this protection remains the source of much debate, however. Early Supreme Court decisions closely tied the Fourth Amendment's protections to property rights—compliance with the Fourth Amendment was generally litigated as a defense to a trespass action against government agents. The Warren Court's shift to interpreting the Amendment as guaranteeing a "right to privacy" was intended to broaden its protections beyond tangible items. Recently, the court has reemphasized the significance of property concepts. This chapter introduces the Fourth Amendment and traces the shift from the protection of tangible property to the protection of intangible privacy.

SAM KAMIN, *THE PRIVATE IS PUBLIC: THE RELEVANCE OF PRIVATE ACTORS IN DEFINING THE FOURTH AMENDMENT*

46 BOSTON COLLEGE LAW REVIEW 83, 87 (2004)

Although a general right to privacy has been read into a number of the guarantees of the bill of rights, the privacy rights of the people vis-à-vis the government are protected most fundamentally by the Fourth Amendment of the Constitution which provides:

> The right of the people to be secure in their persons, houses, papers, and effects, against unreasonable searches and seizures, shall not be violated, and no Warrants shall issue, but upon probable cause, supported by Oath or affirmation, and particularly describing the place to be searched, and the persons or things to be seized.

The Amendment is generally thought of as containing two clauses, one speaking to unreasonable searches and seizures, and the other discussing the requirements for the issuance of warrants. The relationship between these two clauses is murky at best and has been the topic of much controversy in the two-hundred-plus years since their drafting.[22]

Faced with an essentially inscrutable text, the Supreme Court has generated a number of interpretive rules that find varying degrees of support in the text of the Amendment: the Amendment expresses a strong preference for searches conducted pursuant to judicially approved warrants; all searches, whether subject to the warrant requirement or not, must generally be supported by probable cause; and the ultimate constitutional test for every search is reasonableness. Although each of these interpretations is now taken more or less as orthodoxy, the heuristics are inherently inconsistent and none of them is entirely free from controversy.

Thus, at its most fundamental levels—the relationship between the Amendment's two clauses, the degree of suspicion that must be shown before a warrantless search may be conducted, and so on—it becomes clear

---

[22] *See, e.g.*, NELSON LASSON, THE HISTORY AND DEVELOPMENT OF THE FOURTH AMENDMENT TO THE UNITED STATES CONSTITUTION 100–103 (1937). Lasson writes that the confusion regarding the two clauses is essentially a result of misreporting by one of the drafters. He writes that the House of Representatives originally approved a draft of what would become the Fourth Amendment that read:

> The rights of the people to be secured in their persons, their houses, their papers, and their other property, from all unreasonable searches and seizures, *shall not be violated by warrants issued without probable cause*, supported by oath or affirmation, or not particularly describing the places to be searched, or the persons or things to be seized. (emphasis added).

While the relationship between the two clauses is relatively straightforward in this draft, the House's reporting committee reported that the House had approved the version we are now familiar with, which contained amendments the House had in fact rejected. *But see* Thomas Y. Davies, *Recovering the Original Fourth Amendment*, 98 MICH. L. REV. 547, 718–19 (1999) (arguing that the evidence that the current version of the Fourth Amendment is not the one that was approved by the House of Representatives is "inconsistent.").

that the Fourth Amendment is hardly self-defining in its terms. These problems of construction are compounded by the fact that at the time of the Amendment's drafting, conceptions of privacy, crime, and policing were fundamentally different than they are today. For example, there were no organized police forces during the founding period. Rather, law enforcement was handled exclusively by part-timers and amateurs. Although clearly crime as we know it today existed in colonial times, the physical fear of crime as a social phenomenon and as a political issue simply did not. Today the primary conundrum of crime in the United States is generally seen as the importance of protecting the public from predation while protecting individuals from the invasive power of the state. By contrast, crime in colonial times was feared not so much as a threat to individual safety, but as a threat to the moral and social order. Furthermore, the main privacy concern of the founders generally was not searches by police officers in pursuit of criminal prosecutions, but rather wide-ranging and unfettered searches by custom and tax inspectors or by officials of the crown looking for materials deemed seditious. Similarly, Nelson Lasson cites as the main impetus for the protections of the Fourth Amendment and its state analogues a number of cases, both from the colonies and England, involving the enforcement of unpopular tax and sedition laws. In fact, during the founding period, Fourth Amendment claims were rarely even raised in the criminal context. At that time, the legality of a search usually was contested as a defense to a civil trespass action rather than in the course of a criminal prosecution. One primary reason for this, of course, is the fact that the exclusionary rule is entirely an invention of the twentieth century; it likely would have come as a surprise to the founders that otherwise competent evidence would not be admitted in court because of the means by which it was obtained.

Even if the text of the Fourth Amendment were clear in its terms (and it is not), applying in contemporary times a document written in a very different context and addressing very different concerns is a task necessarily requiring a certain amount of inventiveness on the part of jurists. For example, how is one to determine, parsing the 54 words of the Amendment, whether or not police officers may conduct a warrantless search of a paper bag contained in the trunk of a suspicious automobile, whether federal officers may "massage" a duffle bag in the luggage compartment of a bus, or whether law enforcement officials may fly over private property in a borrowed aircraft to peer through the semi-opaque roof of a shed. The short answer, of course, is that neither the text of the Amendment nor founding-era understandings of its meaning is likely to provide consistent answers to these questions. Rather, judges must turn elsewhere to determine the scope of the Amendment's protections in contemporary society.

The two clauses of the Fourth Amendment and the relationship between them are obscure at best. Two competing theories have arisen to explain the relationship of the Warrant Clause and the Reasonableness Clause. The Warrant Preference Theory posits that the Fourth Amendment's Warrant Clause modifies its Reasonableness Clause. Searches are generally unreasonable unless authorized in advance by a warrant. Warrantless searches are permitted only when so-called "exigent circumstances" or "special needs" make it impossible or impracticable to obtain a warrant in advance. These are the "well-defined exceptions" to the warrant requirement referred to toward the end of the *Katz* majority opinion. As the text of the Amendment makes clear, warrants must be supported by probable cause and particularly describe what is to be searched or seized. They provide a neutral judicial determination of whether probable cause exists as well as notice of the scope of the police's authority.

The Reasonableness Theory, on the other hand, postulates that the Reasonableness Clause is grammatically independent of the Warrant Clause. Under this reading, the Fourth Amendment requires at bottom that all searches and seizures be reasonable. "Reasonable," in turn, is defined on a contextual and *ad hoc* basis. Some searches, primarily those of a home, are in fact reasonable only when authorized by a warrant, but this warrant requirement is not a general rule. Nor are warrants intended primarily to provide any notice to the target of the search or seizure. The Reasonableness Theory seems to conceive of warrants as a way for judges to supervise policework, as it permits even searches based on invalid warrants, so long as the officers reasonably relied on the warrant's validity. *See, e.g.*, *United States v. Leon*, 468 U.S. 897 (1986). Some searches are reasonable without probable cause while others never are, depending on whether privacy interests outweigh government objectives. In other words, the Reasonableness Theory evaluates every search with the balancing test that the Warrant Preference Theory reserves for "special needs" cases.

The Justices have dueled and continue to duel over which theory should guide Fourth Amendment jurisprudence. The cases in this section show the Court working to apply the Fourth Amendment's protection of "houses, persons, papers, and effects" to a changing society. They show the justices grappling over whether "houses, persons, papers, and effects" should be read literally or liberally. In the Prohibition era, a literal reading won over a majority of the Court. By mid-century, the Court had repudiated that view. Most recently, the Court has adopted an amalgamated approach that purports to combine its 1928 Fourth Amendment test with the test that replaced it in 1967. The question that pervades these cases is how far beyond the words in the text the Court can legitimately go to give effect to the Fourth Amendment's fundamental purpose and guarantee.

OLMSTEAD V. UNITED STATES

277 U.S. 438 (1928)

MR. CHIEF JUSTICE TAFT delivered the opinion of the court.

* * *

The petitioners were convicted in the District Court for the Western District of Washington of a conspiracy to violate the National Prohibition Act by unlawfully possessing, transporting and importing intoxicating liquors and maintaining nuisances, and by selling intoxicating liquors. Seventy-two others, in addition to the petitioners, were indicted. Some were not apprehended, some were acquitted, and others pleaded guilty.

The evidence in the records discloses a conspiracy of amazing magnitude to import, possess, and sell liquor unlawfully. It involved the employment of not less than 50 persons, of two sea-going vessels for the transportation of liquor to British Columbia, of smaller vessels for coastwise transportation to the state of Washington, the purchase and use of a branch beyond the suburban limits of Seattle, with a large underground cache for storage and a number of smaller caches in that city, the maintenance of a central office manned with operators, and the employment of executives, salesmen, deliverymen dispatchers, scouts, bookkeepers, collectors, and an attorney. In a bad month sales amounted to $176,000; the aggregate for a year must have exceeded $2,000,000.

Olmstead was the leading conspirator and the general manager of the business. He made a contribution of $10,000 to the capital; 11 others contributed $1,000 each. The profits were divided, one-half to Olmstead and the remainder to the other 11. Of the several offices in Seattle, the chief one was in a large office building. In this there were three telephones on three different lines. There were telephones in an office of the manager in his own home, at the homes of his associates, and at other places in the city. Communication was had frequently with Vancouver, British Columbia. Times were fixed for the deliveries of the "stuff" to places along Puget Sound near Seattle, and from there the liquor was removed and deposited in the caches already referred to. One of the chief men was always on duty at the main office to receive orders by the telephones and to direct their filling by a corps of men stationed in another room—the "bull pen." The call numbers of the telephones were given to those known to be likely customers. At times the sales amounted to 200 cases of liquor per day.

The information which led to the discovery of the conspiracy and its nature and extent was largely obtained by intercepting messages on the telephones of the conspirators by four federal prohibition officers. Small wires were inserted along the ordinary telephone wires from the residences of four of the petitioners and those leading from the chief office. The insertions were made without trespass upon any property of the defendants. They were made in the basement of the large office building. The taps from house lines were made in the streets near the houses.

The gathering of evidence continued for many months. Conversations of the conspirators, of which refreshing stenographic notes were currently made, were testified to by the government witnesses. They revealed the large business transactions of the partners and their subordinates. Men at the wires heard the orders given for liquor by customers and the acceptances; they became auditors of the conversations between the partners. All this disclosed the conspiracy charged in the indictment. Many of the intercepted conversations were not merely reports, but parts of the criminal acts. The evidence also disclosed the difficulties to which the conspirators were subjected, the reported news of the capture of vessels, the arrest of their men, and the seizure of cases of liquor in garages and other places. It showed the dealing by Olmstead, the chief conspirator, with members of the Seattle police, the messages to them which secured the release of arrested members of the conspiracy, and also direct promises to officers of payments as soon as opportunity offered.

* * *

The amendment itself shows that the search is to be of material things—the person, the house, his papers, or his effects. The description of the warrant necessary to make the proceeding lawful is that it must specify the place to be searched and the person or things to be seized.

. . . The Fourth Amendment may have proper application to a sealed letter in the mail, because of the constitutional provision for the Postoffice Department and the relations between the government and those who pay to secure protection of their sealed letters. It is plainly within the words of the amendment to say that the unlawful rifling by a government agent of a sealed letter is a search and seizure of the sender's papers of effects. The letter is a paper, an effect, and in the custody of a government that forbids carriage, except under its protection.

The United States takes no such care of telegraph or telephone messages as of mailed sealed letters. The amendment does not forbid what was done here. There was no searching. There was no seizure. The evidence was secured by the use of the sense of hearing and that only. There was no entry of the houses or offices of the defendants.

By the invention of the telephone 50 years ago, and its application for the purpose of extending communications, one can talk with another at a far distant place.

The language of the amendment cannot be extended and expanded to include telephone wires, reaching to the whole world from the defendant's house or office. The intervening wires are not part of his house or office, any more than are the highways along which they are stretched.

* * *

Congress may, of course, protect the secrecy of telephone messages by making them, when intercepted, inadmissible in evidence in federal criminal trials, by direct legislation, and thus depart from the common law of evidence. But the courts may not adopt such a policy by attributing an enlarged and unusual meaning to the Fourth Amendment.

The reasonable view is that one who installs in his house a telephone instrument with connecting wires intends to project his voice to those quite outside, and that the wires beyond his house, and messages while passing over them, are not within the protection of the Fourth Amendment. Here those who intercepted the projected voices were not in the house of either party to the conversation.

Neither the cases we have cited nor any of the many federal decisions brought to our attention hold the Fourth Amendment to have been violated as against a defendant, unless there has been an official search and seizure of his person or such a seizure of his papers or his tangible material effects or an actual physical invasion of his house "or curtilage" for the purpose of making a seizure.

We think, therefore, that the wire tapping here disclosed did not amount to a search or seizure within the meaning of the Fourth Amendment.

What has been said disposes of the only question that comes within the terms of our order granting certiorari in these cases. But some of our number, departing from that order, have concluded that there is merit in the twofold objection, overruled in both courts below, that evidence obtained through intercepting of telephone messages by government agents was inadmissible, because the mode of obtaining it was unethical and a misdemeanor under the law of Washington. To avoid any misapprehension of our views of that objection we shall deal with it in both of its phases.

* * *

[We cannot], without the sanction of congressional enactment, subscribe to the suggestion that the courts have a discretion to exclude evidence, the admission of which is not unconstitutional, because unethically secured. This would be at variance with the common-law doctrine generally supported by authority. There is no case that sustains, nor any recognized text-book that gives color to, such a view. Our general experience shows that much evidence has always been receivable, although not obtained by conformity to the highest ethics. The history of criminal trials shows numerous cases of prosecutions of oathbound conspiracies for murder, robbery, and other crimes, where officers of the law have disguised themselves and joined the organizations, taken the oaths, and given themselves every appearance of active members engaged in the promotion of crime for the purpose of securing evidence. Evidence secured by such means has always been received.

A standard which would forbid the reception of evidence, if obtained by other than nice ethical conduct by government officials, would make society suffer and give criminals greater immunity than has been known heretofore. In the absence of controlling legislation by Congress, those who realize the difficulties in bringing offenders to justice may well deem it wise that the exclusion of evidence should be confined to cases where rights under the Constitution would be violated by admitting it.

* * *

MR. JUSTICE BRANDEIS (dissenting).

The defendants were convicted of conspiring to violate the National Prohibition Act. Before any of the persons now charged had been arrested or indicted, the telephones by means of which they habitually communicated with one another and with others had been tapped by federal officers. To this end, a lineman of long experience in wire tapping was employed, on behalf of the government and at its expense. He tapped eight telephones, some in the homes of the persons charged, some in their offices. Acting on behalf of the government and in their official capacity, at least six other prohibition agents listened over the tapped wires and reported the messages taken. Their operations extended over a period of nearly five months. The typewritten record of the notes of conversations overheard occupies 775 typewritten pages. By objections seasonably made and persistently renewed, the defendants objected to the admission of the evidence obtained by wire tapping, on the ground that the government's wire tapping constituted an unreasonable search and seizure, in violation of the Fourth Amendment, and that the use as evidence of the conversations overheard compelled the defendants to be witnesses against themselves, in violation of the Fifth Amendment.

The government makes no attempt to defend the methods employed by its officers. Indeed, it concedes that, if wire tapping can be deemed a search and seizure within the Fourth Amendment, such wire tapping as was practiced in the case at bar was an unreasonable search and seizure, and that the evidence thus obtained was inadmissible. But it relies on the language of the amendment, and it claims that the protection given thereby cannot properly be held to include a telephone conversation.

* * *

When the Fourth and Fifth Amendments were adopted, "the form that evil had theretofore taken" had been necessarily simple. Force and violence were then the only means known to man by which a government could directly effect self-incrimination. It could compel the individual to testify—a compulsion effected, if need be, by torture. It could secure possession of his papers and other articles incident to his private life—a seizure effected, if need be, by breaking and entry. Protection against such invasion of "the sanctities of a man's home and the privacies of life" was provided in the Fourth and Fifth Amendments by specific language. But "time works changes, brings into existence new conditions and purposes." Subtler and more far-reaching means of invading privacy have become available to the government. Discovery and invention have made it possible for the government, by means far more effective than stretching upon the rack, to obtain disclosure in court of what is whispered in the closet.

Moreover, "in the application of a Constitution, our contemplation cannot be only of what has been, but of what may be." The progress of science in furnishing the government with means of espionage is not likely to stop with wire tapping. Ways may some day be developed by which the government, without removing papers from secret drawers, can reproduce them in court, and by which it will be enabled to expose to a jury the most intimate occurrences of the home. Advances in the psychic and related sciences may bring means of exploring unexpressed beliefs, thoughts and emotions. "That places the liberty of every man in the hands of every petty officer" was said by James Otis of much lesser intrusions than these. To Lord Camden a far slighter intrusion seemed "subversive of all the comforts of society." Can it be that the Constitution affords no protection against such invasions of individual security?

* * *

In *Ex parte Jackson*, 96 U.S. 727 (1878), it was held that a sealed letter intrusted to the mail is protected by the amendments. The mail is a public service furnished by the government. The telephone is a public service furnished by its authority. There is, in essence, no difference between the sealed letter and the private telephone message. As Judge Rudkin said below: "True, the one is visible, the other invisible; the one is tangible, the other intangible; the one is sealed, and the other unsealed; but these are distinctions without a difference." The evil incident to invasion of the privacy of the telephone is far greater than that involved in tampering with the mails. Whenever a telephone line is tapped, the privacy of the persons at both ends of the line is invaded, and all conversations between them upon any subject, and although proper, confidential, and privileged, may be overheard. Moreover, the tapping of one man's telephone line involves the tapping of the telephone of every other person whom he may call, or who may call him. As a means of espionage, writs of assistance and general warrants are but puny instruments of tyranny and oppression when compared with wire tapping.

* * *

. . . The makers of our Constitution undertook to secure conditions favorable to the pursuit of happiness. They recognized the significance of man's spiritual nature, of his feelings and of his intellect. They knew that only a part of the pain, pleasure and satisfactions of life are to be found in material things. They sought to protect Americans in their beliefs, their thoughts, their emotions and their sensations. They conferred, as against the government, the right to be let alone—the most comprehensive of rights and the right most valued by civilized men. To protect that right, every unjustifiable intrusion by the government upon the privacy of the individual, whatever the means employed, must be deemed a violation of the Fourth Amendment. And the use, as evidence in a criminal proceeding, of facts ascertained by such intrusion must be deemed a violation of the Fifth.

Applying to the Fourth and Fifth Amendments the established rule of construction, the defendants' objections to the evidence obtained by wire tapping must, in my opinion, be sustained. It is, of course, immaterial where the physical connection with the telephone wires leading into the defendants' premises was made. And it is also immaterial that the intrusion was in aid of law enforcement. Experience should teach us to be most on our guard to protect liberty when the government's purposes are beneficent. Men born to freedom are naturally alert to repel invasion of their liberty by evil-minded rulers. The greatest dangers to liberty lurk in insidious encroachment by men of zeal, well-meaning but without understanding.[12]

Independently of the constitutional question, I am of opinion that the judgment should be reversed. By the laws of Washington, wire tapping is a crime. To prove its case, the government was obliged to lay bare the crimes committed by its officers on its behalf. A federal court should not permit such a prosecution to continue.

* * *

Decency, security, and liberty alike demand that government officials shall be subjected to the same rules of conduct that are commands to the citizen. In a government of laws, existence of the government will be imperiled if it fails to observe the law scrupulously. Our government is the potent, the omnipresent teacher. For good or for ill, it teaches the whole people by its example. Crime is contagious. If the government becomes a lawbreaker, it breeds contempt for law; it invites every man to become a law unto himself; it invites anarchy. To declare that in the administration of the criminal law the end justifies the means—to declare that the government may commit crimes in order to secure the conviction of a

---

[12] The point is thus stated by counsel for the telephone companies, who have filed a brief as *amici curiae*: "Criminals will not escape detection and conviction merely because evidence obtained by tapping wires of a public telephone system is inadmissible, if it should be so held; but, in any event, it is better that a few criminals escape than that the privacies of life of all the people be exposed to the agents of the government, who will act at their own discretion, the honest and the dishonest, unauthorized and unrestrained by the courts. Legislation making wire tapping a crime will not suffice if the courts nevertheless hold the evidence to be lawful."

private criminal—would bring terrible retribution. Against that pernicious doctrine this court should resolutely set its face.

MR. JUSTICE HOLMES (dissenting).

My brother Brandeis has given this case so exhaustive an examination that I desire to add but a few words. While I do not deny it I am not prepared to say that the penumbra of the Fourth and Fifth Amendments covers the defendant, although I fully agree that courts are apt to err by sticking too closely to the words of a law where those words import a policy that goes beyond them. But I think, as Mr. Justice Brandeis says, that apart from the Constitution the government ought not to use evidence obtained and only obtainable by a criminal act. There is no body of precedents by which we are bound, and which confines us to logical deduction from established rules. Therefore we must consider the two objects of desire both of which we cannot have and make up our minds which to choose. It is desirable that criminals should be detected, and to that end that all available evidence should be used. It also is desirable that the government should not itself foster and pay for other crimes, when they are the means by which the evidence is to be obtained. If it pays its officers for having got evidence by crime I do not see why it may not as well pay them for getting it in the same way, and I can attach no importance to protestations of disapproval if it knowingly accepts and pays and announces that in future it will pay for the fruits. We have to choose, and for my part I think it a less evil that some criminals should escape than that the government should play an ignoble part.

For those who agree with me no distinction can be taken between the government as prosecutor and the government as judge. If the existing code does not permit district attorneys to have a hand in such dirty business it does not permit the judge to allow such iniquities to succeed. And if all that I have said so far be accepted it makes no difference that in this case wire tapping is made a crime by the law of the state, not by the law of the United States. It is true that a state cannot make rules of evidence for courts of the United States, but the state has authority over the conduct in question, and I hardly think that the United States would appear to greater advantage when paying for an odious crime against state law than when inciting to the disregard of its own. I am aware of the often-repeated statement that in a criminal proceeding the court will not take notice of the manner in which papers offered in evidence have been obtained. But that somewhat rudimentary mode of disposing of the question has been overthrown by *Weeks v. United States*, 232 U.S. 383 (1914), and the cases that have followed it. I have said that we are free to choose between two principles of policy. But if we are to confine ourselves to precedent and logic the reason for excluding evidence obtained by violating the Constitution seems to me logically to lead to excluding evidence obtained by a crime of the officers of the law.

MR. JUSTICE BUTLER (dissenting).

* * *

Telephones are used generally for transmission of messages concerning official, social, business and personal affairs including communications that are private and privileged—those between physician and patient, lawyer and client, parent and child, husband and wife. The contracts between telephone companies and users contemplate the private use of the facilities employed in the service. The communications belong to the parties between whom they pass. During their transmission the exclusive use of the wire belongs to the persons served by it. Wire tapping involves interference with the wire while being used. Tapping the wires and listening in by the officers literally constituted a search for evidence. As the communications passed, they were heard and taken down.

* * *

This court has always construed the Constitution in the light of the principles upon which it was founded. The direct operation or literal meaning of the words used do not measure the purpose or scope of its provisions. Under the principles established and applied by this court, the Fourth Amendment safeguards against all evils that are like and equivalent to those embraced within the ordinary meaning of its words. . . .

When the facts in these cases are truly estimated, a fair application of that principle decides the constitutional question in favor of the petitioners. With great deference, I think they should be given a new trial.

MR. JUSTICE STONE (dissenting).

I concur in the opinions of Mr. Justice Holmes and Mr. Justice Brandeis. I agree also with that of Mr. Justice Butler so far as it deals with the merits. . . .

Points for Discussion

1. Justice Brandeis' *Olmstead* dissent proved more enduring than the majority's opinion. *See* Carol S. Steiker, *Brandeis In* Olmstead: *"Our Government Is the Potent, the Omnipresent Teacher"*, 79 MISS. L.J. 149 (2009). Brandeis writes, "The door of a court is not barred because the plaintiff has committed a crime." In fact, most Fourth Amendment claims are brought by criminal defendants who seek to keep prosecutors from introducing allegedly unconstitutionally seized evidence against them at trial. Because the contested evidence is usually probative of guilt, it is nearly always the case that the defendant seeking the suppression of evidence from her case is guilty of at least some crime, if not of exactly the crime charged. Why does Brandeis argue that these claims should be cognizable in a federal court, notwithstanding the defendant's apparent guilt of the crime charged? Today, the other principal means for vindicating Fourth Amendment rights is through a civil suit against

the offending officers and their employers. *See, e.g.*, *Atwater v. City of Lago Vista*, 532 U.S. 318 (2001). Should it be relevant in such a suit whether incriminating evidence was found on the party asserting a violation of the Constitution?

2. How compelling is the majority's reading of the Fourth Amendment as protecting only persons, houses, papers, and effects? Isn't it true none of these categories includes conversations, which are consequently not protected? Under this reading of the Constitution, what else that we might seek to keep private might not be entitled to Fourth Amendment protection?

3. Justice Holmes writes separately to emphasize that evidence obtained by federal agents in violation of *state* law should be inadmissible just as evidence obtained in violation of the Fourth Amendment had been held inadmissible in *Weeks v. United States*, 232 U.S. 383 (1914). How is Justice Holmes' justification for excluding evidence obtained by criminal means—"no distinction can be taken between the government as prosecutor and the government as judge"—different from Justice Brandeis'—"[t]he court protects itself"?

4. The majority and the principal dissent both deploy some staggering numbers in setting forth the facts of the case, but they emphasize different statistics. These facts are technically irrelevant to the outcome. Why, then, did Chief Justice Taft and Justice Brandeis bother to tell us how much money the conspirators made or how many pages of transcript the government compiled?

5. As Justice Brandeis' footnote 12 observes, the Bell telephone companies filed an *amicus curiae* brief supporting the bootleggers. In their brief, they argued:

> When the lines of two "parties" are connected at the central office, they are intended to be devoted to the exclusive use, and in that sense to be turned over to the exclusive possession, of the parties. A third person who taps the lines violates the property rights of both persons then using the telephone, and of the telephone company as well.

Justice Butler's dissent endorsed much of the telephone companies' argument. Why did the telephone companies file a brief in the case and why did they side with the conspirators?

Justice Brandeis' impassioned *Olmstead* dissent memorably wedded the Fourth Amendment's protections to the notion of privacy. At the time, the Court's Fourth Amendment decisions, beginning with *Boyd v. United States*, 116 U.S. 616 (1886), had closely tied the Amendment's protection to property rights. *Boyd* was a forfeiture action in which the claimants objected to an order of the trial court requiring them to produce certain invoices to be used as evidence against them. Extensively quoting from the English case *Entick v. Carrington*, (1765) 19 How. St. Tri. 1029, *reprinted in* (1765) 95 Eng. Rep. 807 (K.B.) (partial reprint), the Court held that the search violated the Fourth and Fifth Amendments because the order to produce the papers invaded the "indefeasible right of personal security, personal liberty, and private property." The Court's reliance on *Entick*, which was undergirded by a great solicitude for property rights, fostered the conception that the Fourth Amendment's protections were delineated by property interests.

Entick was a trespass action against messengers of the Crown who ransacked Entick's house in a search for seditious writings. Lord Camden's celebrated opinion upheld the jury's verdict for Entick, stating: "The great end for which men entered into society was to secure their property. . . . By the laws of England, every invasion of private property, be it ever so minute, is a trespass." Relying on this reasoning, *Boyd* held that the government could seize only forfeitable property, i.e. items of contraband or the fruits and instrumentalities of crime, and not items of mere evidentiary value.

The pressure to scrap *Boyd*'s restriction of the government's ability to seize mere evidence of a crime led to the collapse of the Fourth Amendment's strict connection to property rights and the elevation instead of privacy as the Amendment's core concern. In *Warden, Maryland Penitentiary v. Hayden*, 387 U.S. 294 (1967), the Court held that the government could constitutionally seize items of purely evidentiary value, such as clothing described by witnesses to an armed robbery. Justice Brennan's opinion for the Court emphasized "that the principal object of the Fourth Amendment is the protection of privacy rather than property." The decision declared *Boyd*'s substantive limitation on searches and seizures to the fruits and instrumentalities of crime and contraband to be a legal fiction. Later that same term, the Fourth Amendment's concern with privacy, which had gradually risen in prominence since *Olmstead*, achieved preeminence in *Katz v. United States*.

KATZ V. UNITED STATES

389 U.S. 347 (1967)

MR. JUSTICE STEWART delivered the opinion of the court.

The petitioner was convicted in the District Court for the Southern District of California under an eight-count indictment charging him with transmitting wagering information by telephone from Los Angeles to Miami and Boston in violation of a federal statute. At trial the Government was permitted, over the petitioner's objection, to introduce evidence of the petitioner's end of telephone conversations, overheard by FBI agents who had attached an electronic listening and recording device to the outside of the public telephone booth from which he had placed his calls. In affirming his conviction, the Court of Appeals rejected the contention that the recordings had been obtained in violation of the Fourth Amendment, because "(t)here was no physical entrance into the area occupied by, (the petitioner)." We granted certiorari in order to consider the constitutional questions thus presented.

* * *

The petitioner had phrased those questions as follows:

> A. Whether a public telephone booth is a constitutionally protected area so that evidence obtained by attaching an electronic listening recording device to the top of such a booth is obtained in violation of the right to privacy of the user of the booth.
>
> B. Whether physical penetration of a constitutionally protected area is necessary before a search and seizure can be said to be violative of the Fourth Amendment to the United States Constitution.

We decline to adopt this formulation of the issues. In the first place the correct solution of Fourth Amendment problems is not necessarily promoted by incantation of the phrase "constitutionally protected area." Secondly, the Fourth Amendment cannot be translated into a general constitutional "right to privacy." That Amendment protects individual privacy against certain kinds of governmental intrusion, but its protections go further, and often have nothing to do with privacy at all. Other provisions of the Constitution protect personal privacy from other forms of governmental invasion. But the protection of a person's general right to privacy—his right to be let alone by other people—is, like the protection of his property and of his very life, left largely to the law of the individual States.

Because of the misleading way the issues have been formulated, the parties have attached great significance to the characterization of the telephone booth from which the petitioner placed his calls. The petitioner has strenuously argued that the booth was a "constitutionally protected area." The Government has maintained with equal vigor that it was not. But this effort to decide whether or not a given "area," viewed in the abstract, is "constitutionally protected" deflects attention from the problem presented by this case. For the Fourth Amendment protects people, not places. What a person knowingly exposes to the public, even in his own home or office, is not a subject of Fourth Amendment protection.

The Government stresses the fact that the telephone booth from which the petitioner made his calls was constructed partly of glass, so that he was as visible after he entered it as he would have been if he had remained outside. But what he sought to exclude when he entered the booth was not the intruding eye—it was the uninvited ear. He did not shed his right to do so simply because he made his calls from a place where he might be seen. No less than an individual in a business office, in a friend's apartment, or in a taxicab, a person in a telephone booth may rely upon the protection of the Fourth Amendment. One who occupies it, shuts the door behind him, and pays the toll that permits him to place a call is surely entitled to assume that the words he utters into the mouthpiece will not be broadcast to the world. To read the Constitution more narrowly is to ignore the vital role that the public telephone has come to play in private communication.

The Government contends, however, that the activities of its agents in this case should not be tested by Fourth Amendment requirements, for the surveillance technique they employed involved no physical penetration of the telephone booth from which the petitioner placed his calls. It is true that the absence of such penetration was at one time thought to foreclose further Fourth Amendment inquiry, *Olmstead v. United States*, 277 U.S. 438, 457; *Goldman v. United States*, 316 U.S. 129, 134–36, for that Amendment was thought to limit only searches and seizures of tangible property. But "(t)he premise that property interests control the right of the Government to search and seize has been discredited." *Warden, Md. Penitentiary v. Hayden*, 387 U.S. 294, 304. Thus, although a closely divided Court supposed in *Olmstead* that surveillance without any trespass and without the seizure of any material object fell outside the ambit of the Constitution, we have since departed from the narrow view on which that decision rested. Indeed, we have expressly held that the Fourth Amendment governs not only the seizure of tangible items, but extends as well to the recording of oral statements overheard without any "technical trespass under * * * local property law." *Silverman v. United States*, 365 U.S. 505, 511. Once this much is acknowledged, and once it is recognized that the Fourth Amendment protects people—and not simply "areas"—against unreasonable searches and seizures it becomes clear that the reach of that Amendment cannot turn upon the presence or absence of a physical intrusion into any given enclosure.

We conclude that the underpinnings of *Olmstead* and *Goldman* have been so eroded by our subsequent decisions that the "trespass" doctrine there enunciated can no longer be regarded as controlling. The Government's activities in electronically listening to and recording the petitioner's words violated the privacy upon which he justifiably relied while using the telephone booth and thus constituted a "search and seizure" within the meaning of the Fourth Amendment. The fact that the electronic device employed to achieve that end did not happen to penetrate the wall of the booth can have no constitutional significance.

The question remaining for decision, then, is whether the search and seizure conducted in this case complied with constitutional standards. In that regard, the Government's position is that its agents acted in an entirely defensible manner: They did not begin their electronic surveillance until investigation of the petitioner's activities had established a strong probability that he was using the telephone in question to transmit gambling information to persons in other States, in violation of federal law. Moreover, the surveillance was limited, both in scope and in duration, to the specific purpose of establishing the contents of the petitioner's unlawful telephonic communications. The agents confined their surveillance to the brief periods during which he used the telephone booth,[14] and they took great care to overhear only the conversations of the petitioner himself.

Accepting this account of the Government's actions as accurate, it is clear that this surveillance was so narrowly circumscribed that a duly authorized magistrate, properly notified of the need for such investigation, specifically informed of the basis on which it was to proceed, and clearly apprised of the precise intrusion it would entail, could constitutionally have authorized, with appropriate safeguards, the very limited search and seizure that the Government asserts in fact took place. . . .

* * *

The Government urges that, because its agents relied upon the decisions in *Olmstead* and *Goldman*, and because they did no more here than they might properly have done with prior judicial sanction, we should retroactively validate their conduct. That we cannot do. It is apparent that the agents in this case acted with restraint. Yet the inescapable fact is that this restraint was imposed by the agents themselves, not by a judicial officer. They were not required, before commencing the search, to present their estimate of probable cause for detached scrutiny by a neutral magistrate. They were not compelled, during the conduct of the search itself, to observe precise limits established in advance by a specific court order. Nor were they directed, after the search had been completed, to notify the authorizing magistrate in detail of all that had been seized. In the absence of such safeguards, this Court has never sustained a search upon the sole ground that officers reasonably expected to find evidence of a particular crime and voluntarily confined their activities to the least intrusive means consistent with that end. Searches conducted without warrants have been held unlawful "notwithstanding facts unquestionably showing probable cause," for the Constitution requires "that the deliberate, impartial judgment of a judicial officer * * * be interposed between the citizen and the police * * *." "Over and again this Court has emphasized that the mandate of the (Fourth) Amendment requires adherence to judicial processes," and that searches conducted outside the judicial process, without prior approval by judge or magistrate, are *per se* unreasonable under the Fourth Amendment—subject only to a few specifically established and well-delineated exceptions.

* * *

[14] Based upon their previous visual observations of the petitioner, the agents correctly predicted that he would use the telephone booth for several minutes at approximately the same time each morning. The petitioner was subjected to electronic surveillance only during this predetermined period. Six recordings, averaging some three minutes each, were obtained and admitted in evidence. They preserved the petitioner's end of conversations concerning the placing of bets and the receipt of wagering information.

The Government does not question these basic principles. Rather, it urges the creation of a new exception to cover this case. It argues that surveillance of a telephone booth should be exempted from the usual requirement of advance authorization by a magistrate upon a showing of probable cause. We cannot agree. Omission of such authorization

> bypasses the safeguards provided by an objective predetermination of probable cause, and substitutes instead the far less reliable procedure of an after-the-event justification for the * * * search, too likely to be subtly influenced by the familiar shortcomings of hindsight judgment.

Beck v. State of Ohio, 379 U.S. 89, 96. And bypassing a neutral predetermination of the scope of a search leaves individuals secure from Fourth Amendment violations "only in the discretion of the police."

These considerations do not vanish when the search in question is transferred from the setting of a home, an office, or a hotel room to that of a telephone booth. Wherever a man may be, he is entitled to know that he will remain free from unreasonable searches and seizures. The government agents here ignored "the procedure of antecedent justification * * * that is central to the Fourth Amendment," a procedure that we hold to be a constitutional precondition of the kind of electronic surveillance involved in this case. Because the surveillance here failed to meet that condition, and because it led to the petitioner's conviction, the judgment must be reversed.

MR. JUSTICE MARSHALL took no part in the consideration or decision of this case.

MR. JUSTICE DOUGLAS, with whom MR. JUSTICE BRENNAN joins, concurring.

While I join the opinion of the Court, I feel compelled to reply to the separate concurring opinion of my Brother White, which I view as a wholly unwarranted green light for the Executive Branch to resort to electronic eavesdropping without a warrant in cases which the Executive Branch itself labels "national security" matters.

Neither the President nor the Attorney General is a magistrate. In matters where they believe national security may be involved they are not detached, disinterested, and neutral as a court or magistrate must be. Under the separation of powers created by the Constitution, the Executive Branch is not supposed to be neutral and disinterested. Rather it should vigorously investigate and prevent breaches of national security and prosecute those who violate the pertinent federal laws. The President and Attorney General are properly interested parties, cast in the role of adversary, in national security cases. They may even be the intended victims of subversive action. Since spies and saboteurs are as entitled to the protection of the Fourth Amendment as suspected gamblers like petitioner, I cannot agree that where spies and saboteurs are involved adequate protection of Fourth Amendment rights is assured when the President and Attorney General assume both the position of adversary-and-prosecutor and disinterested, neutral magistrate.

* * *

MR. JUSTICE HARLAN, concurring.

I join the opinion of the Court, which I read to hold only (a) that an enclosed telephone booth is an area where, like a home, and unlike a field, a person has a constitutionally protected reasonable expectation of privacy; (b) that electronic as well as physical intrusion into a place that is in this sense private may constitute a violation of the Fourth Amendment; and (c) that the invasion of a constitutionally protected area by federal authorities is, as the Court has long held, presumptively unreasonable in the absence of a search warrant.

As the Court's opinion states, "the Fourth Amendment protects people, not places." The question, however, is what protection it affords to those people. Generally, as here, the answer to that question requires reference to a "place." My understanding of the rule that has emerged from prior decisions is that there is a twofold requirement, first that a person have exhibited an actual (subjective) expectation of privacy and, second, that the expectation be one that society is prepared to recognize as "reasonable." Thus a man's home is, for most purposes, a place where he expects privacy, but objects, activities, or statements that he exposes to the "plain view" of outsiders are not "protected" because no intention to keep them to himself has been exhibited. On the other hand, conversations in the open would not be protected against being overheard, for the expectation of privacy under the circumstances would be unreasonable.

The critical fact in this case is that "(o)ne who occupies it, (a telephone booth) shuts the door behind him, and pays the toll that permits him to place a call is surely entitled to assume" that his conversation is not being intercepted. The point is not that the booth is "accessible to the public" at other times, but that it is a temporarily private place whose momentary occupants' expectations of freedom from intrusion are recognized as reasonable.

* * *

Finally, I do not read the Court's opinion to declare that no interception of a conversation one-half of which occurs in a public telephone booth can be reasonable in the absence of a warrant. As elsewhere under the Fourth Amendment, warrants are the general rule, to which the legitimate needs of law enforcement may demand specific exceptions. It will be time enough to consider any such exceptions when an appropriate occasion presents itself, and I agree with the Court that this is not one.

MR. JUSTICE WHITE, concurring.

I agree that the official surveillance of petitioner's telephone conversations in a public booth must be subjected to the test of reasonableness under the Fourth Amendment and that on the record now before us the particular surveillance undertaken was unreasonable absent a warrant properly authorizing it. This application of the Fourth Amendment need not interfere with legitimate needs of law enforcement.*

In joining the Court's opinion, I note the Court's acknowledgment that there are circumstances in which it is reasonable to search without a warrant. . . . Wiretapping to protect the security of the Nation has been authorized by successive Presidents. The present Administration would apparently save national security cases from restrictions against wiretapping. We should not require the warrant procedure and the magistrate's judgment if the President of the United States or his chief legal officer, the Attorney General, has considered the requirements of national security and authorized electronic surveillance as reasonable.

MR. JUSTICE BLACK, dissenting.

* * *

My basic objection is twofold: (1) I do not believe that the words of the Amendment will bear the meaning given them by today's decision, and (2) I do not believe that it is the proper role of this Court to rewrite the Amendment in order "to bring it into harmony with the times" and thus reach a result that many people believe to be desirable.

While I realize that an argument based on the meaning of words lacks the scope, and no doubt the appeal, of broad policy discussions and philosophical discourses on such nebulous subjects as privacy, for me the language of the Amendment is the crucial place to look in construing a written document such as our Constitution. The Fourth Amendment says that

> The right of the people to be secure in their persons, houses, papers, and effects, against unreasonable searches and seizures,

* In previous cases, which are undisturbed by today's decision, the Court has upheld, as reasonable under the Fourth Amendment, admission at trial of evidence obtained (1) by an undercover police agent to whom a defendant speaks without knowledge that he is in the employ of the police, *Hoffa v. United States*, 385 U.S. 293 (1966); (2) by a recording device hidden on the person of such an informant, *Lopez v. United States*, 373 U.S. 427 (1963); *Osborn v. United States*, 385 U.S. 323 (1966); and (3) by a policeman listening to the secret micro-wave transmissions of an agent conversing with the defendant in another location, *On Lee v. United States*, 343 U.S. 747 (1952). When one man speaks to another he takes all the risks ordinarily inherent in so doing, including the risk that the man to whom he speaks will make public what he has heard. The Fourth Amendment does not protect against unreliable (or law-abiding) associates. It is but a logical and reasonable extension of this principle that a man take the risk that his hearer, free to memorize what he hears for later verbatim repetitions, is instead recording it or transmitting it to another. The present case deals with an entirely different situation, for as the Court emphasizes the petitioner "sought to exclude * * * the uninvited ear," and spoke under circumstances in which a reasonable person would assume that uninvited ears were not listening.

> shall not be violated, and no Warrants shall issue, but upon probable cause, supported by Oath or affirmation, and particularly describing the place to be searched, and the persons or things to be seized.

The first clause protects "persons, houses, papers, and effects, against unreasonable searches and seizures * * *." These words connote the idea of tangible things with size, form, and weight, things capable of being searched, seized, or both. The second clause of the Amendment still further establishes its Framers' purpose to limit its protection to tangible things by providing that no warrants shall issue but those "particularly describing the place to be searched, and the persons or things to be seized." A conversation overheard by eavesdropping, whether by plain snooping or wiretapping, is not tangible and, under the normally accepted meanings of the words, can neither be searched nor seized. In addition the language of the second clause indicates that the Amendment refers not only to something tangible so it can be seized but to something already in existence so it can be described. Yet the Court's interpretation would have the Amendment apply to overhearing future conversations which by their very nature are nonexistent until they take place. How can one "describe" a future conversation, and, if one cannot, how can a magistrate issue a warrant to eavesdrop one in the future? It is argued that information showing what is expected to be said is sufficient to limit the boundaries of what later can be admitted into evidence; but does such general information really meet the specific language of the Amendment which says "particularly describing"? Rather than using language in a completely artificial way, I must conclude that the Fourth Amendment simply does not apply to eavesdropping.

Tapping telephone wires, of course, was an unknown possibility at the time the Fourth Amendment was adopted. But eavesdropping (and wiretapping is nothing more than eavesdropping by telephone) was, as even the majority opinion in *Berger*, recognized, "an ancient practice which at common law was condemned as a nuisance. IV Blackstone, COMMENTARIES § 168. In those days the eavesdropper listened by naked ear under the eaves of houses or their windows, or beyond their walls seeking out private discourse." [*Berger v. State of New York*, 388 U.S. 41, 45 (1967)]. There can be no doubt that the Framers were aware of this practice, and if they had desired to outlaw or restrict the use of evidence obtained by eavesdropping, I believe that they would have used the appropriate language to do so in the Fourth Amendment. They certainly would not have left such a task to the ingenuity of language-stretching judges. No one, it seems to me, can read the debates on the Bill of Rights without reaching the conclusion that its Framers and critics well knew the meaning of the words they used, what they would be understood to mean by others, their scope and their limitations. Under these circumstances it strikes me as a charge against their scholarship, their common sense and their candor to give to the Fourth Amendment's language the eavesdropping meaning the Court imputes to it today.

I do not deny that common sense requires and that this Court often has said that the Bill of Rights' safeguards should be given a liberal construction. This principle, however, does not justify construing the search and seizure amendment as applying to eavesdropping or the "seizure" of conversations. The Fourth Amendment was aimed directly at the abhorred practice of breaking in, ransacking and searching homes and other buildings and seizing people's personal belongings without warrants issued by magistrates. The Amendment deserves, and this Court has given it, a liberal construction in order to protect against warrantless searches of buildings and seizures of tangible personal effects. But until today this Court has refused to say that eavesdropping comes within the ambit of Fourth Amendment restrictions.

* * *

Since I see no way in which the words of the Fourth Amendment can be construed to apply to eavesdropping, that closes the matter for me. In interpreting the Bill of Rights, I willingly go as far as a liberal construction of the language takes me, but I simply cannot in good conscience give a meaning to words which they have never before been thought to have and which they certainly do not have in common ordinary usage. I will not distort the words of the Amendment in order to "keep the Constitution up to date" or "to bring it into harmony with the times." It was never meant that this Court have such power, which in effect would make us a continuously functioning constitutional convention.

With this decision the Court has completed, I hope, its rewriting of the Fourth Amendment, which started only recently when the Court began referring incessantly to the Fourth Amendment not so much as a law against unreasonable searches and seizures as one to protect an individual's privacy. By clever word juggling the Court finds it plausible to argue that language aimed specifically at searches and seizures of things that can be searched and seized may, to protect privacy, be applied to eavesdropped evidence of conversations that can neither be searched nor seized. Few things happen to an individual that do not affect his privacy in one way or another. Thus, by arbitrarily substituting the Court's language, designed to protect privacy, for the Constitution's language, designed to protect against unreasonable searches and seizures, the Court has made the Fourth Amendment its vehicle for holding all laws violative of the Constitution which offend the Court's broadest concept of privacy. As I said in *Griswold v. State of Connecticut*, 381 U.S. 479 [(1965)], "The Court talks about a constitutional 'right of privacy' as though there is some constitutional provision or provisions forbidding any law ever to be passed which might abridge the 'privacy' of individuals. But there is not." I made clear in that dissent my fear of the dangers involved when this Court uses the "broad, abstract and ambiguous concept" of "privacy" as a "comprehensive substitute for the Fourth Amendment's guarantee against "unreasonable searches and seizures."

The Fourth Amendment protects privacy only to the extent that it prohibits unreasonable searches and seizures of "persons, houses, papers, and effects." No general right is created by the Amendment so as to give this Court the unlimited power to hold unconstitutional everything which affects privacy. Certainly the Framers, well acquainted as they were with the excesses of governmental power, did not intend to grant this Court such omnipotent lawmaking authority as that. The history of governments proves that it is dangerous to freedom to repose such powers in courts.

Points for Discussion

1. The *Katz* Court first concluded that the Fourth Amendment applied to the government conduct in question—electronic eavesdropping. It then concluded that the wiretap was unconstitutional because the authorities did not have a warrant to record Katz's calls. This two-step process—determining first whether the Constitution applies and then whether it was violated—is used throughout the Court's criminal procedure decisions. If the Constitution does apply and was violated by the challenged act, the Court now makes a third inquiry into what remedy is due the person whose rights were violated. See *United States v. Leon* 468 U.S. 897 (1984), and *Herring v. United States*, 555 U.S. 135 (2009), which appear in chapter 10.

2. Although it appeared in a concurrence, Justice Harlan's formulation of the Court's holding has come to be the rule cited in later decisions applying *Katz*:

> My understanding of the rule that has emerged from prior decisions is that there is a twofold requirement, first that a person have exhibited an actual (subjective) expectation of privacy and, second, that the expectation be one that society is prepared to recognize as "reasonable."

This language does not completely account for the Court's pronouncements that "the Fourth Amendment cannot be translated into a general constitutional 'right to privacy' " and that its "protections often have nothing to do with privacy at all." Why might lower courts and the Supreme Court apply Justice Harlan's *Katz* opinion in later cases rather than the majority's? Consider this:

> The *Olmstead* decision was very divisive, and the government's use of wiretaps continued to be controversial. In 1967, after a series of cases had begun to cast doubt on the continued constitutional viability of governmental wiretapping, the Supreme Court granted certiorari in *Katz v. United States*. In *Katz*, the Ninth Circuit affirmed a conviction obtained through the use of FBI interceptions of the defendant's telephone conversations involving interstate betting. On

the initial petition for certiorari, Chief Justice Warren and Justices Brennan, Fortas, and Douglas voted to grant review of the lower court's decision, while Justices Stewart, Clark, Harlan, White, and Black opposed it. Justice Clark resigned on June 12, 1967, and was replaced by then Solicitor General Thurgood Marshall. Marshall recused himself from the case . . . . When the eight remaining justices conferred after oral argument on October 20, 1967, they split 4–4 along the same lines as their votes on certiorari—a split which would ordinarily mean that the underlying decision would be summarily affirmed. However, two weeks later, Justice Stewart changed his mind and joined the justices voting to reverse.

Justice Stewart circulated a proposed draft opinion and a short memorandum to explain his change of mind, both of which appear to have been initially composed by Professor Laurence Tribe who at the time was one of Justice Stewart's law clerks. According to the memorandum, Justice Stewart's change of mind appears to have come about in part because of the Wiretap Act that was debated in Congress at the time. If the tie vote had persisted, the Court's views on the constitutionality of electronic surveillance would not have been available to Congress as it worked on this important legislation. Justice Stewart also appeared to have been concerned that the Court's recent decision in *Berger v. New York* cast some doubt on the constitutionality of electronic surveillance, even when authorized by a warrant. In *Berger*, the Court struck down a state wiretapping statute on the ground that the wiretapping constituted a "general search." The facts of *Katz* were close, and reasonable people could argue it either way.

Accordingly, Justice Stewart appears to have changed his vote so the Court's views about the constitutional parameters of electronic surveillance could help inform the legislative debate. In response to Justice Stewart's memo, the justices who initially voted in favor of reversal signed onto the draft opinion. Justices White and Harlan, initially voting for affirmance, followed Stewart's lead and changed their positions. This left Justice Black as the lone dissenter in a 7–1 decision to reverse. Although several minor changes were made to the draft opinion, the final opinion of the Court appears to have remained substantially as it was when Justice Stewart's law clerk originally drafted it.

The majority opinion adopts the magisterial language, "the Fourth Amendment protects people, not places," and at first glance, appears to sweep away *Olmstead*'s property-based regime, replacing it with a regime based on a right of privacy. But at the same time, the opinion has a reassuring conservative side, rejecting the view that wiretapping constituted an illegal "general search"; the Court explicitly held that under the facts of the *Katz* case, where the agents took extensive steps to minimize the interception of non-relevant conversations, the electronic surveillance would have passed constitutional muster if only the FBI had obtained a warrant from a judge before beginning surveillance. The opinion also rejected the argument that the lack of notice inherent in the wiretapping presented an insurmountable hurdle to its lawfulness. *Katz* thus bears the marks of a quintessential political compromise, with both sides getting something they wanted—one side, the overthrow of the overly restrictive *Olmstead* decision; the other, a clear statement of the essential legality of electronic surveillance.

Although the majority opinion is a masterful example of judicial politics, and presents a reasoned defense of the result, it is not without its flaws. It begins with a highly unusual attack on counsel—both the petitioner's attorneys as well as the government's—criticizing them for framing the issue as "whether a public telephone booth is a constitutionally protected area so that evidence obtained by attaching an electronic listening recording device to the top of such a booth is obtained in violation of the right to privacy of the user of the booth." However, this judicial "frame" was not invented by the lawyers, but had been used explicitly by the Court itself in numerous earlier Fourth Amendment cases—many of them written by some of the very justices who signed the majority opinion. Furthermore, when the Court granted certiorari, it framed the issues in precisely this manner, presumably because it was comfortable with the issues in the petition for certiorari and saw no need to reformulate them. Once the Court accepted this formulation, the parties would be expected to address only those issues in their briefs and argument. . . .

* * *

There is an even more surprising mistake in the majority opinion: When one listens to the oral argument or reads the transcript, one recognizes that it was counsel for the petitioner who first took the position that the manner in which the issues had been framed (by reference to a "constitutionally protected area") needed to be altered, and who reformulated the issues into exactly the manner ultimately adopted by the Court. It appears that the oral argument persuaded the Court to reformulate the issues. However, instead of acknowledging flaws in the earlier cases and correcting the analysis, the Court's opinion blames counsel for getting it wrong.

* * *

In addition to its embarrassing attack on counsel, the majority opinion contains an important weakness in its legal analysis. The opinion creates the impression of a revolutionary upheaval of the previous regime, while using criticism of counsel to sidestep the otherwise difficult job of addressing prior inconsistent case law with candor. By dismissing precedent without adequate analysis, it loses the ballast of history. While announcing a new understanding of the

> Fourth Amendment based on a right of privacy, it says nothing about how this newfound right is to be determined. In eliminating the trespass standard of *Olmstead*, it offers nothing by way of a standard to replace it. How then, has a Supreme Court case, which contains so many mistakes and which promised a legal revolution that it ultimately could never deliver, come to occupy such an unchallenged position in the modern legal Pantheon? The short answer is that the majority opinion has been largely ignored.

Peter Winn, Katz *and the Origins of the "Reasonable Expectation of Privacy" Test*, 40 MCGEORGE L. REV. 1, 2–6 (2009).

3. Justice Black criticizes the majority for deviating from the text of the Fourth Amendment in an attempt to keep the Constitution up to date. How valid is this criticism? How might the move from unreasonable searches and seizures to reasonable expectations of privacy fail to inure to the benefit of criminal defendants?

OLIVER V. UNITED STATES

466 U.S. 170 (1984)[a]

JUSTICE POWELL delivered the opinion of the court.

The "open fields" doctrine, first enunciated by this Court in *Hester v. United States*, 265 U.S. 57 (1924), permits police officers to enter and search a field without a warrant. We granted certiorari in these cases to clarify confusion that has arisen as to the continued vitality of the doctrine.

I

No. 82-15. Acting on reports that marihuana was being raised on the farm of petitioner Oliver, two narcotics agents of the Kentucky State Police went to the farm to investigate.[1]

Arriving at the farm, they drove past petitioner's house to a locked gate with a "No Trespassing" sign. A footpath led around one side of the gate. The agents walked around the gate and along the road for several hundred yards, passing a barn and a parked camper. At that point, someone standing in front of the camper shouted: "No hunting is allowed, come back up here." The officers shouted back that they were Kentucky State Police officers, but found no one when they returned to the camper. The officers resumed their investigation of the farm and found a field of marihuana over a mile from petitioner's home.

* * *

[a] The Court refers to the two cases consolidated for decision—*Oliver v. United States* and *Maine v. Thornton*—by their Supreme Court filing numbers.—Eds.

[1] It is conceded that the police did not have a warrant authorizing the search, that there was no probable cause for the search, and that no exception to the warrant requirement is applicable.

No. 82-1273. After receiving an anonymous tip that marihuana was being grown in the woods behind respondent Thornton's residence, two police officers entered the woods by a path between this residence and a neighboring house. They followed a footpath through the woods until they reached two marihuana patches fenced with chicken wire. Later, the officers determined that the patches were on the property of respondent, obtained a warrant to search the property, and seized the marihuana. On the basis of this evidence, respondent was arrested and indicted.

The trial court granted respondent's motion to suppress the fruits of the second search. The warrant for this search was premised on information that the police had obtained during their previous warrantless search, that the court found to be unreasonable. "No Trespassing" signs and the secluded location of the marihuana patches evinced a reasonable expectation of privacy. Therefore, the court held, the open fields doctrine did not apply.

* * *

II

The rule announced in *Hester v. United States* was founded upon the explicit language of the Fourth Amendment. That Amendment indicates with some precision the places and things encompassed by its protections. As Justice Holmes explained for the Court in his characteristically laconic style: "[T]he special protection accorded by the Fourth Amendment to the people in their 'persons, houses, papers, and effects,' is not extended to the open fields. The distinction between the latter and the house is as old as the common law."

Nor are the open fields "effects" within the meaning of the Fourth Amendment. In this respect, it is suggestive that James Madison's proposed draft of what became the Fourth Amendment preserves "[t]he rights of the people to be secured in their persons, their houses, their papers, and their other property, from all unreasonable searches and seizures . . . ." See N. LASSON, THE HISTORY AND DEVELOPMENT OF THE FOURTH AMENDMENT TO THE UNITED STATES CONSTITUTION 100, n. 77 (1937). Although Congress' revisions of Madison's proposal broadened the scope of the Amendment in some respects, the term "effects" is less inclusive than "property" and cannot be said to encompass open fields. We conclude, as did the Court in deciding *Hester v. United States*, that the government's intrusion upon the open fields is not one of those "unreasonable searches" proscribed by the text of the Fourth Amendment.

III

* * *

A

No single factor determines whether an individual legitimately may claim under the Fourth Amendment that a place should be free of government intrusion not authorized by warrant. In assessing the degree to which a search infringes upon individual privacy, the Court has given weight to such factors as the intention of the Framers of the Fourth Amendment, the uses to which the individual has put a location, and our societal understanding that certain areas deserve the most scrupulous protection from government invasion. These factors are equally relevant to determining whether the government's intrusion upon open fields without a warrant or probable cause violates reasonable expectations of privacy and is therefore a search proscribed by the Amendment.

In this light, the rule of *Hester v. United States*, that we reaffirm today, may be understood as providing that an individual may not legitimately demand privacy for activities conducted out of doors in fields, except in the area immediately surrounding the home. This rule is true to the conception of the right to privacy embodied in the Fourth Amendment. The Amendment reflects the recognition of the Framers that certain enclaves should be free from arbitrary government interference. For example, the Court since the enactment of the Fourth Amendment has stressed "the overriding respect for the sanctity of the home that has been embedded in our traditions since the origins of the Republic."

In contrast, open fields do not provide the setting for those intimate activities that the Amendment is intended to shelter from government interference or surveillance. There is no societal interest in protecting the privacy of those activities, such as the cultivation of crops, that occur in open fields. Moreover, as a practical matter these lands usually are accessible to the public and the police in ways that a home, an office, or commercial structure would not be. It is not generally true that fences or "No Trespassing" signs effectively bar the public from viewing open fields in rural areas. And both petitioner Oliver and respondent Thornton concede that the public and police lawfully may survey lands from the air. For these reasons, the asserted expectation of privacy in open fields is not an expectation that "society recognizes as reasonable."

The historical underpinnings of the open fields doctrine also demonstrate that the doctrine is consistent with respect for "reasonable expectations of privacy." As Justice Holmes, writing for the Court, observed in *Hester*, the common law distinguished "open fields" from the "curtilage," the land immediately surrounding and associated with the home. The distinction implies that only the curtilage, not the neighboring open fields, warrants the Fourth Amendment protections that attach to the home. At common law, the curtilage is the area to which extends the intimate activity associated with the "sanctity of a man's home and the privacies of life," *Boyd v. United States*, 116 U.S. 616, 630 (1886), and therefore has been considered part of home itself for Fourth Amendment purposes. Thus, courts have extended Fourth Amendment protection to the curtilage; and they have defined the curtilage, as did the common law, by reference to the factors that determine whether an individual reasonably may expect that an area immediately adjacent to the home will remain private. Conversely, the common law implies, as we reaffirm today, that no expectation of privacy legitimately attaches to open fields.

We conclude, from the text of the Fourth Amendment and from the historical and contemporary understanding of its purposes, that an individual has no legitimate expectation that open fields will remain free from warrantless intrusion by government officers.

B

Petitioner Oliver and respondent Thornton contend, to the contrary, that the circumstances of a search sometimes may indicate that reasonable expectations of privacy were violated; and that courts therefore should analyze these circumstances on a case-by-case basis. The language of the Fourth Amendment itself answers their contention.

Nor would a case-by-case approach provide a workable accommodation between the needs of law enforcement and the interests protected by the Fourth Amendment. Under this approach, police officers would have to guess before every search whether landowners had erected fences sufficiently high, posted a sufficient number of warning signs, or located contraband in an area sufficiently secluded to establish a right of privacy. The lawfulness of a search would turn on "[a] highly sophisticated set of rules, qualified by all sorts of ifs, ands, and buts and requiring the drawing of subtle nuances and hairline distinctions . . . ." This Court repeatedly has acknowledged the difficulties created for courts, police, and citizens by an ad hoc, case-by-case definition of Fourth Amendment standards to be applied in differing factual circumstances. The ad hoc approach not only makes it difficult for the policeman to discern the scope of his authority; it also creates a danger that constitutional rights will be arbitrarily and inequitably enforced.

IV

In any event, while the factors that petitioner Oliver and respondent Thornton urge the courts to consider may be relevant to Fourth Amendment analysis in some contexts, these factors cannot be decisive on the question whether the search of an open field is subject to the Amendment. Initially, we reject the suggestion that steps taken to protect privacy establish that expectations of privacy in an open field are legitimate. It is true, of course, that petitioner Oliver and respondent

Thornton, in order to conceal their criminal activities, planted the marihuana upon secluded land and erected fences and "No Trespassing" signs around the property. And it may be that because of such precautions, few members of the public stumbled upon the marihuana crops seized by the police. Neither of these suppositions demonstrates, however, that the expectation of privacy was legitimate in the sense required by the Fourth Amendment. The test of legitimacy is not whether the individual chooses to conceal assertedly "private" activity. Rather, the correct inquiry is whether the government's intrusion infringes upon the personal and societal values protected by the Fourth Amendment. As we have explained, we find no basis for concluding that a police inspection of open fields accomplishes such an infringement.

Nor is the government's intrusion upon an open field a "search" in the constitutional sense because that intrusion is a trespass at common law. The existence of a property right is but one element in determining whether expectations of privacy are legitimate. " 'The premise that property interests control the right of the Government to search and seize has been discredited.' " *Katz*, 389 U.S., at 353 (quoting *Warden v. Hayden*, 387 U.S. 294, 304 (1967)). "[E]ven a property interest in premises may not be sufficient to establish a legitimate expectation of privacy with respect to particular items located on the premises or activity conducted thereon."

The common law may guide consideration of what areas are protected by the Fourth Amendment by defining areas whose invasion by others is wrongful. The law of trespass, however, forbids intrusions upon land that the Fourth Amendment would not proscribe. For trespass law extends to instances where the exercise of the right to exclude vindicates no legitimate privacy interest.[15] Thus, in the case of open fields, the general rights of property protected by the common law of trespass have little or no relevance to the applicability of the Fourth Amendment.

V

We conclude that the open fields doctrine, as enunciated in *Hester*, is consistent with the plain language of the Fourth Amendment and its historical purposes. Moreover, Justice Holmes' interpretation of the Amendment in *Hester* accords with the "reasonable expectation of privacy"

[15] The law of trespass recognizes the interest in possession and control of one's property and for that reason permits exclusion of unwanted intruders. But it does not follow that the right to exclude conferred by trespass law embodies a privacy interest also protected by the Fourth Amendment. To the contrary, the common law of trespass furthers a range of interests that have nothing to do with privacy and that would not be served by applying the strictures of trespass law to public officers. Criminal laws against trespass are prophylactic: they protect against intruders who poach, steal livestock and crops, or vandalize property. And the civil action of trespass serves the important function of authorizing an owner to defeat claims of prescription by asserting his own title. *See, e.g.*, O. HOLMES, THE COMMON LAW 98–100, 244–246 (1881). In any event, unlicensed use of property by others is presumptively unjustified, as anyone who wishes to use the property is free to bargain for the right to do so with the property owner. For these reasons, the law of trespass confers protections from intrusion by others far broader than those required by Fourth Amendment interests.

analysis developed in subsequent decisions of this Court. We therefore affirm *Oliver v. United States*; *Maine v. Thornton* is reversed and remanded for further proceedings not inconsistent with this opinion.

JUSTICE WHITE, concurring in part and concurring in the judgment.

I concur in the judgment and join Parts I and II of the Court's opinion. These Parts dispose of the issue before us; there is no need to go further and deal with the expectation of privacy matter. However reasonable a landowner's expectations of privacy may be, those expectations cannot convert a field into a "house" or an "effect."

JUSTICE MARSHALL, with whom JUSTICE BRENNAN and JUSTICE STEVENS join, dissenting.

In each of these consolidated cases, police officers, ignoring clearly visible "No Trespassing" signs, entered upon private land in search of evidence of a crime. At a spot that could not be seen from any vantage point accessible to the public, the police discovered contraband, which was subsequently used to incriminate the owner of the land. In neither case did the police have a warrant authorizing their activities.

The Court holds that police conduct of this sort does not constitute an "unreasonable search" within the meaning of the Fourth Amendment. The Court reaches that startling conclusion by two independent analytical routes. First, the Court argues that, because the Fourth Amendment by its terms renders people secure in their "persons, houses, papers, and effects," it is inapplicable to trespasses upon land not lying within the curtilage of a dwelling. Second, the Court contends that "an individual may not legitimately demand privacy for activities conducted out of doors in fields, except in the area immediately surrounding the home." Because I cannot agree with either of these propositions, I dissent.

I

The first ground on which the Court rests its decision is that the Fourth Amendment "indicates with some precision the places and things encompassed by its protections," and that real property is not included in the list of protected spaces and possessions. This line of argument has several flaws. Most obviously, it is inconsistent with the results of many of our previous decisions, none of which the Court purports to overrule. For example, neither a public telephone booth nor a conversation conducted therein can fairly be described as a person, house, paper, or effect; yet we have held that the Fourth Amendment forbids the police without a warrant to eavesdrop on such a conversation. *Katz v. United States*, 389 U.S. 347 (1967). Nor can it plausibly be argued that an office or commercial establishment is covered by the plain language of the Amendment; yet we have held that such premises are entitled to constitutional protection if they are marked in a fashion that alerts the public to the fact that they are private.[2]

Indeed, the Court's reading of the plain language of the Fourth Amendment is incapable of explaining even its own holding in this case. The Court rules that the curtilage, a zone of real property surrounding a dwelling, is entitled to constitutional protection. We are not told, however, whether the curtilage is a "house" or an "effect"—or why, if the curtilage can be incorporated into the list of things and spaces shielded by the Amendment, a field cannot.

The Court's inability to reconcile its parsimonious reading of the phrase "persons, houses, papers, and effects" with our prior decisions or even its own holding is a symptom of a more fundamental infirmity in the Court's reasoning. The Fourth Amendment, like the other central provisions of the Bill of Rights that loom large in our modern jurisprudence, was designed, not to prescribe with "precision" permissible and impermissible activities, but to identify a fundamental human liberty that should be shielded forever from government intrusion. We do not construe constitutional provisions of this sort the way we do statutes, whose drafters can be expected to indicate with some comprehensiveness and exactitude the conduct they wish to forbid or control and to change those prescriptions when they become obsolete. Rather, we strive, when interpreting these seminal constitutional provisions, to effectuate their purposes—to lend them meanings that ensure that the liberties the Framers sought to protect are not undermined by the changing activities of government officials.[5]

The liberty shielded by the Fourth Amendment, as we have often acknowledged, is freedom "from unreasonable government intrusions into . . . legitimate expectations of privacy." That freedom would be incompletely protected if only government conduct that impinged upon a person, house, paper, or effect were subject to constitutional scrutiny. Accordingly, we have repudiated the proposition that the Fourth Amendment applies only to a limited set of locales or kinds of property. In *Katz v. United States*, we expressly rejected a proffered locational theory of the coverage of the Amendment, holding that it "protects people, not places." Since that time we have consistently adhered to the view that the applicability of the provision depends solely upon "whether the person

[2] On the other hand, an automobile surely does constitute an "effect." Under the Court's theory, cars should therefore stand on the same constitutional footing as houses. Our cases establish, however, that car owners' diminished expectations that their cars will remain free from prying eyes warrants a corresponding reduction in the constitutional protection accorded cars.

[5] Our rejection of the mode of interpretation appropriate for statutes is perhaps clearest in our treatment of the First Amendment. That Amendment provides, in pertinent part, that "Congress shall make no law . . . abridging the freedom of speech, or of the press" but says nothing, for example, about restrictions on expressive behavior or about access to the courts. Yet, to give effect to the purpose of the Amendment, we have applied it to regulations of conduct designed to convey a message and have accorded constitutional protection to the public's "right of access to criminal trials."

invoking its protection can claim a 'justifiable,' a 'reasonable,' or a 'legitimate expectation of privacy' that has been invaded by government action." *Smith v. Maryland*, 442 U.S. 735, 740 (1979). The Court's contention that, because a field is not a house or effect, it is not covered by the Fourth Amendment is inconsistent with this line of cases and with the understanding of the nature of constitutional adjudication from which it derives.

* * *

II

The second ground for the Court's decision is its contention that any interest a landowner might have in the privacy of his woods and fields is not one that "society is prepared to recognize as 'reasonable.' " The mode of analysis that underlies this assertion is certainly more consistent with our prior decisions than that discussed above. But the Court's conclusion cannot withstand scrutiny.

* * *

A

We have frequently acknowledged that privacy interests are not coterminous with property rights. However, because "property rights reflect society's explicit recognition of a person's authority to act as he wishes in certain areas, [they] should be considered in determining whether an individual's expectations of privacy are reasonable."[10] Indeed, the Court has suggested that, insofar as "[o]ne of the main rights attaching to property is the right to exclude others, . . . one who owns or lawfully possesses or controls property will in all likelihood have a legitimate expectation of privacy by virtue of this right to exclude."

It is undisputed that Oliver and Thornton each owned the land into which the police intruded. That fact alone provides considerable support for their assertion of legitimate privacy interests in their woods and fields. But even more telling is the nature of the sanctions that Oliver and Thornton could invoke, under local law, for violation of their property rights. In Kentucky, a knowing entry upon fenced or otherwise enclosed land, or upon unenclosed land conspicuously posted with signs excluding the public, constitutes criminal trespass. The law in Maine is similar. An

[10] The Court today seeks to evade the force of this principle by contending that the law of property is designed to serve various "prophylactic" and "economic" purposes unrelated to the protection of privacy. Such efforts to rationalize the distribution of entitlements under state law are interesting and may have some explanatory power, but cannot support the weight the Court seeks to place upon them. The Court surely must concede that one of the purposes of the law of real property (and specifically the law of criminal trespass) is to define and enforce privacy interests—to empower some people to make whatever use they wish of certain tracts of land without fear that other people will intrude upon their activities. The views of commentators, old and new, as to other functions served by positive law are thus insufficient to support the Court's sweeping assertion that "in the case of open fields, the general rights of property . . . have little or no relevance to the applicability of the Fourth Amendment."

intrusion into "any place from which [the intruder] may lawfully be excluded and which is posted in a manner prescribed by law or in a manner reasonably likely to come to the attention of intruders or which is fenced or otherwise enclosed" is a crime. Thus, positive law not only recognizes the legitimacy of Oliver's and Thornton's insistence that strangers keep off their land, but subjects those who refuse to respect their wishes to the most severe of penalties—criminal liability. Under these circumstances, it is hard to credit the Court's assertion that Oliver's and Thornton's expectations of privacy were not of a sort that society is prepared to recognize as reasonable.

B

The uses to which a place is put are highly relevant to the assessment of a privacy interest asserted therein. If, in light of our shared sensibilities, those activities are of a kind in which people should be able to engage without fear of intrusion by private persons or government officials, we extend the protection of the Fourth Amendment to the space in question, even in the absence of any entitlement derived from positive law.

Privately owned woods and fields that are not exposed to public view regularly are employed in a variety of ways that society acknowledges deserve privacy. Many landowners like to take solitary walks on their property, confident that they will not be confronted in their rambles by strangers or policemen. Others conduct agricultural businesses on their property.[14] Some landowners use their secluded spaces to meet lovers, others to gather together with fellow worshippers, still others to engage in sustained creative endeavor. Private land is sometimes used as a refuge for wildlife, where flora and fauna are protected from human intervention of any kind.[15] Our respect for the freedom of landowners to use their posted "open fields" in ways such as these partially explains the seriousness with which the positive law regards deliberate invasions of such spaces and substantially reinforces the landowners' contention that their expectations of privacy are "reasonable."

C

Whether a person "took normal precautions to maintain his privacy" in a given space affects whether his interest is one protected by the Fourth Amendment. The reason why such precautions are relevant is that we do not insist that a person who has a right to exclude others exercise that

---

[14] We accord constitutional protection to businesses conducted in office buildings; it is not apparent why businesses conducted in fields that are not open to the public are less deserving of the benefit of the Fourth Amendment.

[15] This last-mentioned use implicates a kind of privacy interest somewhat different from those to which we are accustomed. It involves neither a person's interest in immunity from observation nor a person's interest in shielding from scrutiny the residues and manifestations of his personal life. It derives, rather, from a person's desire to preserve inviolate a portion of his world. The idiosyncracy of this interest does not, however, render it less deserving of constitutional protection.

right. A claim to privacy is therefore strengthened by the fact that the claimant somehow manifested to other people his desire that they keep their distance.

Certain spaces are so presumptively private that signals of this sort are unnecessary; a homeowner need not post a "Do Not Enter" sign on his door in order to deny entrance to uninvited guests. Privacy interests in other spaces are more ambiguous, and the taking of precautions is consequently more important; placing a lock on one's footlocker strengthens one's claim that an examination of its contents is impermissible. Still other spaces are, by positive law and social convention, presumed accessible to members of the public unless the owner manifests his intention to exclude them.

Undeveloped land falls into the last-mentioned category. If a person has not marked the boundaries of his fields or woods in a way that informs passersby that they are not welcome, he cannot object if members of the public enter onto the property. There is no reason why he should have any greater rights as against government officials. Accordingly, we have held that an official may, without a warrant, enter private land from which the public is not excluded and make observations from that vantage point. Fairly read, the case on which the majority so heavily relies, *Hester v. United States*, 265 U.S. 57 (1924), affirms little more than the foregoing unremarkable proposition. From aught that appears in the opinion in that case, the defendants, fleeing from revenue agents who had observed them committing a crime, abandoned incriminating evidence on private land from which the public had not been excluded. Under such circumstances, it is not surprising that the Court was unpersuaded by the defendants' argument that the entry onto their fields by the agents violated the Fourth Amendment.

* * *

A very different case is presented when the owner of undeveloped land has taken precautions to exclude the public. As indicated above, a deliberate entry by a private citizen onto private property marked with "No Trespassing" signs will expose him to criminal liability. I see no reason why a government official should not be obliged to respect such unequivocal and universally understood manifestations of a landowner's desire for privacy.

* * *

III

A clear, easily administrable rule emerges from the analysis set forth above: Private land marked in a fashion sufficient to render entry thereon a criminal trespass under the law of the State in which the land lies is protected by the Fourth Amendment's proscription of unreasonable searches and seizures. One of the advantages of the foregoing rule is that it draws upon a doctrine already familiar to both citizens and government officials. In each jurisdiction, a substantial body of statutory and case law defines the precautions a landowner must take in order to avail himself of the sanctions of the criminal law. The police know that body of law, because they are entrusted with responsibility for enforcing it against the public; it therefore would not be difficult for the police to abide by it themselves.

By contrast, the doctrine announced by the Court today is incapable of determinate application. Police officers, making warrantless entries upon private land, will be obliged in the future to make on-the-spot judgments as to how far the curtilage extends, and to stay outside that zone. In addition, we may expect to see a spate of litigation over the question of how much improvement is necessary to remove private land from the category of "unoccupied or undeveloped area" to which the "open fields exception" is now deemed applicable.

* * *

Points for Discussion

1. The Court writes in *Oliver* that the government's intrusion upon the open fields is not one of those 'unreasonable searches' proscribed by the text of the Fourth Amendment." Does the majority mean that what the police did was not a search or that it was not unreasonable? Does it matter?

2. In part III.B of its opinion, the Court holds not only that Oliver and Thornton failed to demonstrate a reasonable expectation of privacy in their fields, but that *no* homeowner can reasonably expect privacy in such areas. The Court justifies this conclusion with reference to the Fourth Amendment's text and on the ground that an "ad hoc approach not only makes it difficult for the policeman to discern the scope of his authority; it also creates a danger that constitutional rights will be arbitrarily and inequitably enforced." What are the comparative advantages of a bright-line rule versus case-by-case adjudication guided by general principles?

3. What is the appropriate role of property rights in determining whether or not a particular government action infringes upon a reasonable expectation of privacy? How does Justice Marshall's conception of the interplay between property law and the protection of privacy differ from the majority's?

UNITED STATES V. JONES

565 U.S. 400 (2012)

JUSTICE SCALIA delivered the opinion of the court.

* * *

I

In 2004 respondent Antoine Jones, owner and operator of a nightclub in the District of Columbia, came under suspicion of trafficking in narcotics and was made the target of an investigation by a joint FBI and Metropolitan Police Department task force. Officers employed various investigative techniques, including visual surveillance of the nightclub, installation of a camera focused on the front door of the club, and a pen register and wiretap covering Jones's cellular phone.

Based in part on information gathered from these sources, in 2005 the Government applied to the United States District Court for the District of Columbia for a warrant authorizing the use of an electronic tracking device on the Jeep Grand Cherokee registered to Jones's wife. A warrant issued, authorizing installation of the device in the District of Columbia and within 10 days.

On the 11th day, and not in the District of Columbia but in Maryland, agents installed a GPS tracking device on the undercarriage of the Jeep while it was parked in a public parking lot. Over the next 28 days, the Government used the device to track the vehicle's movements, and once had to replace the device's battery when the vehicle was parked in a different public lot in Maryland. By means of signals from multiple satellites, the device established the vehicle's location within 50 to 100 feet, and communicated that location by cellular phone to a Government computer. It relayed more than 2,000 pages of data over the 4-week period.

The Government ultimately obtained a multiple-count indictment charging Jones and several alleged co-conspirators with, as relevant here, conspiracy to distribute and possess with intent to distribute five kilograms or more of cocaine and 50 grams or more of cocaine base, in violation of 21 U.S.C. §§ 841 and 846. Before trial, Jones filed a motion to suppress evidence obtained through the GPS device. The District Court granted the motion only in part, suppressing the data obtained while the vehicle was parked in the garage adjoining Jones's residence. It held the remaining data admissible, because " '[a] person traveling in an automobile on public thoroughfares has no reasonable expectation of privacy in his movements from one place to another.' " Jones's trial in October 2006 produced a hung jury on the conspiracy count.

In March 2007, a grand jury returned another indictment, charging Jones and others with the same conspiracy. The Government introduced at trial the same GPS-derived locational data admitted in the first trial, which connected Jones to the alleged conspirators' stash house that contained $850,000 in cash, 97 kilograms of cocaine, and 1 kilogram of cocaine base. The jury returned a guilty verdict, and the District Court sentenced Jones to life imprisonment.

* * *

II

A

The Fourth Amendment provides in relevant part that "[t]he right of the people to be secure in their persons, houses, papers, and effects, against unreasonable searches and seizures, shall not be violated." It is beyond dispute that a vehicle is an "effect" as that term is used in the Amendment. We hold that the Government's installation of a GPS device on a target's vehicle,[2] and its use of that device to monitor the vehicle's movements, constitutes a "search."

It is important to be clear about what occurred in this case: The Government physically occupied private property for the purpose of obtaining information. We have no doubt that such a physical intrusion would have been considered a "search" within the meaning of the Fourth Amendment when it was adopted. *Entick v. Carrington,* 95 Eng. Rep. 807 (C.P. 1765), is a "case we have described as a 'monument of English freedom' 'undoubtedly familiar' to 'every American statesman' at the time the Constitution was adopted, and considered to be 'the true and ultimate expression of constitutional law' " with regard to search and seizure. In that case, Lord Camden expressed in plain terms the significance of property rights in search-and-seizure analysis:

> [O]ur law holds the property of every man so sacred, that no man can set his foot upon his neighbour's close without his leave; if he does he is a trespasser, though he does no damage at all; if he will tread upon his neighbour's ground, he must justify it by law.

The text of the Fourth Amendment reflects its close connection to property, since otherwise it would have referred simply to "the right of the people to be secure against unreasonable searches and seizures"; the phrase "in their persons, houses, papers, and effects" would have been superfluous.

Consistent with this understanding, our Fourth Amendment jurisprudence was tied to common-law trespass, at least until the latter half of the 20th century. Thus, in *Olmstead v. United States,* 277 U.S. 438 (1928), we held that wiretaps attached to telephone wires on the public streets did not constitute a Fourth Amendment search because "[t]here was no entry of the houses or offices of the defendants."

Our later cases, of course, have deviated from that exclusively property-based approach. In *Katz v. United States,* 389 U.S. 347, 351 (1967), we said that "the Fourth Amendment protects people, not places,"

---

[2] As we have noted, the Jeep was registered to Jones's wife. The Government acknowledged, however, that Jones was "the exclusive driver." If Jones was not the owner he had at least the property rights of a bailee. The Court of Appeals concluded that the vehicle's registration did not affect his ability to make a Fourth Amendment objection, and the Government has not challenged that determination here. We therefore do not consider the Fourth Amendment significance of Jones's status.

and found a violation in attachment of an eavesdropping device to a public telephone booth. Our later cases have applied the analysis of Justice Harlan's concurrence in that case, which said that a violation occurs when government officers violate a person's "reasonable expectation of privacy."

The Government contends that the Harlan standard shows that no search occurred here, since Jones had no "reasonable expectation of privacy" in the area of the Jeep accessed by Government agents (its underbody) and in the locations of the Jeep on the public roads, which were visible to all. But we need not address the Government's contentions, because Jones's Fourth Amendment rights do not rise or fall with the *Katz* formulation. At bottom, we must "assure preservation of that degree of privacy against government that existed when the Fourth Amendment was adopted." As explained, for most of our history the Fourth Amendment was understood to embody a particular concern for government trespass upon the areas ("persons, houses, papers, and effects") it enumerates.[3]

Katz did not repudiate that understanding. Less than two years later the Court upheld defendants' contention that the Government could not introduce against them conversations between *other* people obtained by warrantless placement of electronic surveillance devices in their homes. The opinion rejected the dissent's contention that there was no Fourth Amendment violation "unless the conversational privacy of the homeowner himself is invaded." "We do not believe that *Katz,* by holding that the Fourth Amendment protects persons and their private conversations, was intended to withdraw any of the protection which the Amendment extends to the home . . . ."

More recently, in *Soldal v. Cook County,* 506 U.S. 56 (1992), the Court unanimously rejected the argument that although a "seizure" had occurred "in a 'technical' sense" when a trailer home was forcibly removed, no Fourth Amendment violation occurred because law enforcement had not invaded the individuals' privacy. *Katz,* the Court explained, established that "property rights are not the sole measure of Fourth Amendment violations," but did not "snuff out the previously recognized protection for property." . . . We have embodied that preservation of past rights in our very definition of "reasonable expectation of privacy" which we have said to be an expectation "that has a source outside of the Fourth Amendment,

[3] Justice ALITO's concurrence (hereinafter concurrence) doubts the wisdom of our approach because "it is almost impossible to think of late-18th-century situations that are analogous to what took place in this case." But in fact it posits a situation that is not far afield—a constable's concealing himself in the target's coach in order to track its movements. There is no doubt that the information gained by that trespassory activity would be the product of an unlawful search—whether that information consisted of the conversations occurring in the coach, or of the destinations to which the coach traveled.

In any case, it is quite irrelevant whether there was an 18th-century analog. Whatever new methods of investigation may be devised, our task, *at a minimum,* is to decide whether the action in question would have constituted a "search" within the original meaning of the Fourth Amendment. Where, as here, the Government obtains information by physically intruding on a constitutionally protected area, such a search has undoubtedly occurred.

either by reference to concepts of real or personal property law or to understandings that are recognized and permitted by society." *Katz* did not narrow the Fourth Amendment's scope.[5]

Related to this, and similarly irrelevant, is the concurrence's point that, if analyzed separately, neither the installation of the device nor its use would constitute a Fourth Amendment search. Of course not. A trespass on "houses" or "effects," or a *Katz* invasion of privacy, is not alone a search unless it is done to obtain information; and the obtaining of information is not alone a search unless it is achieved by such a trespass or invasion of privacy.

The Government contends that several of our post-*Katz* cases foreclose the conclusion that what occurred here constituted a search. It relies principally on two cases in which we rejected Fourth Amendment challenges to "beepers," electronic tracking devices that represent another form of electronic monitoring. The first case, [*United States v. Knotts,* 460 U.S. 276 (1983),] upheld against Fourth Amendment challenge the use of a "beeper" that had been placed in a container of chloroform, allowing law enforcement to monitor the location of the container. We said that there had been no infringement of Knotts' reasonable expectation of privacy since the information obtained—the location of the automobile carrying the container on public roads, and the location of the off-loaded container in open fields near Knotts' cabin—had been voluntarily conveyed to the public. But as we have discussed, the *Katz* reasonable-expectation-of-privacy test has been *added to,* not *substituted for,* the common-law trespassory test. The holding in *Knotts* addressed only the former, since the latter was not at issue. The beeper had been placed in the container before it came into Knotts' possession, with the consent of the then-owner. Knotts did not challenge that installation, and we specifically declined to consider its effect on the Fourth Amendment analysis. *Knotts* would be relevant, perhaps, if the Government were making the argument that what would otherwise be an unconstitutional search is not such where it produces only public information. The Government does not make that argument, and we know of no case that would support it.

The second "beeper" case, *United States v. Karo,* 468 U.S. 705 (1984), does not suggest a different conclusion. There we addressed the question left open by *Knotts,* whether the installation of a beeper in a container amounted to a search or seizure. As in *Knotts,* at the time the beeper was installed the container belonged to a third party, and it did not come into

[5] The concurrence notes that post-*Katz* we have explained that " 'an actual trespass is neither necessary *nor sufficient* to establish a constitutional violation.' " (quoting *United States v. Karo,* 468 U.S. 705, 713 (1984)). That is undoubtedly true, and undoubtedly irrelevant. *Karo* was considering whether a seizure occurred, and as the concurrence explains, a seizure of property occurs, not when there is a trespass, but "when there is some meaningful interference with an individual's possessory interests in that property." Likewise with a search. Trespass alone does not qualify, but there must be conjoined with that what was present here: an attempt to find something or to obtain information.

possession of the defendant until later. Thus, the specific question we considered was whether the installation "*with the consent of the original owner* constitute[d] a search or seizure . . . when the container is delivered to a buyer having no knowledge of the presence of the beeper." We held not. The Government, we said, came into physical contact with the container only before it belonged to the defendant Karo; and the transfer of the container with the unmonitored beeper inside did not convey any information and thus did not invade Karo's privacy. That conclusion is perfectly consistent with the one we reach here. Karo accepted the container as it came to him, beeper and all, and was therefore not entitled to object to the beeper's presence, even though it was used to monitor the container's location. Jones, who possessed the Jeep at the time the Government trespassorily inserted the information-gathering device, is on much different footing.

The Government also points to our exposition in *New York v. Class,* 475 U.S. 106 (1986), that "the exterior of a car . . . is thrust into the public eye, and thus to examine it does not constitute a 'search.'" That statement is of marginal relevance here since, as the Government acknowledges, "the officers in this case did *more* than conduct a visual inspection of respondent's vehicle." By attaching the device to the Jeep, officers encroached on a protected area. In *Class* itself we suggested that this would make a difference, for we concluded that an officer's momentary reaching into the interior of a vehicle did constitute a search.

Finally, the Government's position gains little support from our conclusion in *Oliver v. United States,* 466 U.S. 170 (1984), that officers' information-gathering intrusion on an "open field" did not constitute a Fourth Amendment search even though it was a trespass at common law. Quite simply, an open field, unlike the curtilage of a home, is not one of those protected areas enumerated in the Fourth Amendment. The Government's physical intrusion on such an area—unlike its intrusion on the "effect" at issue here—is of no Fourth Amendment significance.

B

The concurrence begins by accusing us of applying "18th-century tort law." That is a distortion. What we apply is an 18th-century guarantee against unreasonable searches, which we believe must provide *at a minimum* the degree of protection it afforded when it was adopted. The concurrence does not share that belief. It would apply *exclusively Katz*'s reasonable-expectation-of-privacy test, even when that eliminates rights that previously existed.

The concurrence faults our approach for "present[ing] particularly vexing problems" in cases that do not involve physical contact, such as those that involve the transmission of electronic signals. We entirely fail to understand that point. For unlike the concurrence, which would make *Katz* the *exclusive* test, we do not make trespass the exclusive test. Situations involving merely the transmission of electronic signals without trespass would *remain* subject to *Katz* analysis.

In fact, it is the concurrence's insistence on the exclusivity of the *Katz* test that needlessly leads us into "particularly vexing problems" in the present case. This Court has to date not deviated from the understanding that mere visual observation does not constitute a search. We accordingly held in *Knotts* that "[a] person traveling in an automobile on public thoroughfares has no reasonable expectation of privacy in his movements from one place to another." Thus, even assuming that the concurrence is correct to say that "[t]raditional surveillance" of Jones for a 4-week period "would have required a large team of agents, multiple vehicles, and perhaps aerial assistance," our cases suggest that such visual observation is constitutionally permissible. It may be that achieving the same result through electronic means, without an accompanying trespass, is an unconstitutional invasion of privacy, but the present case does not require us to answer that question.

And answering it affirmatively leads us needlessly into additional thorny problems. The concurrence posits that "relatively short-term monitoring of a person's movements on public streets" is okay, but that "the use of longer term GPS monitoring in investigations *of most offenses*" is no good. That introduces yet another novelty into our jurisprudence. There is no precedent for the proposition that whether a search has occurred depends on the nature of the crime being investigated. And even accepting that novelty, it remains unexplained why a 4-week investigation is "surely" too long and why a drug-trafficking conspiracy involving substantial amounts of cash and narcotics is not an "extraordinary offense" which may permit longer observation. What of a 2-day monitoring of a suspected purveyor of stolen electronics? Or of a 6-month monitoring of a suspected terrorist? We may have to grapple with these "vexing problems" in some future case where a classic trespassory search is not involved and resort must be had to *Katz* analysis; but there is no reason for rushing forward to resolve them here.

* * *

JUSTICE SOTOMAYOR, concurring.

I join the Court's opinion because I agree that a search within the meaning of the Fourth Amendment occurs, at a minimum, "[w]here, as here, the Government obtains information by physically intruding on a constitutionally protected area." In this case, the Government installed a Global Positioning System tracking device on respondent Antoine Jones' Jeep without a valid warrant and without Jones' consent, then used that device to monitor the Jeep's movements over the course of four weeks. The Government usurped Jones' property for the purpose of conducting surveillance on him, thereby invading privacy interests long afforded, and undoubtedly entitled to, Fourth Amendment protection.

* * *

In cases involving even short-term monitoring, some unique attributes of GPS surveillance relevant to the *Katz* analysis will require particular attention. GPS monitoring generates a precise, comprehensive record of a person's public movements that reflects a wealth of detail about her familial, political, professional, religious, and sexual associations. The Government can store such records and efficiently mine them for information years into the future. And because GPS monitoring is cheap in comparison to conventional surveillance techniques and, by design, proceeds surreptitiously, it evades the ordinary checks that constrain abusive law enforcement practices: "limited police resources and community hostility."

Awareness that the Government may be watching chills associational and expressive freedoms. And the Government's unrestrained power to assemble data that reveal private aspects of identity is susceptible to abuse. The net result is that GPS monitoring—by making available at a relatively low cost such a substantial quantum of intimate information about any person whom the Government, in its unfettered discretion, chooses to track—may "alter the relationship between citizen and government in a way that is inimical to democratic society."

I would take these attributes of GPS monitoring into account when considering the existence of a reasonable societal expectation of privacy in the sum of one's public movements. I would ask whether people reasonably expect that their movements will be recorded and aggregated in a manner that enables the Government to ascertain, more or less at will, their political and religious beliefs, sexual habits, and so on. I do not regard as dispositive the fact that the Government might obtain the fruits of GPS monitoring through lawful conventional surveillance techniques. I would also consider the appropriateness of entrusting to the Executive, in the absence of any oversight from a coordinate branch, a tool so amenable to misuse, especially in light of the Fourth Amendment's goal to curb arbitrary exercises of police power to and prevent "a too permeating police surveillance."

* * *

JUSTICE ALITO, with whom JUSTICE GINSBURG, JUSTICE BREYER, and JUSTICE KAGAN join, concurring in the judgment.

This case requires us to apply the Fourth Amendment's prohibition of unreasonable searches and seizures to a 21st-century surveillance technique, the use of a Global Positioning System device to monitor a vehicle's movements for an extended period of time. Ironically, the Court has chosen to decide this case based on 18th-century tort law. By attaching a small GPS device to the underside of the vehicle that respondent drove, the law enforcement officers in this case engaged in conduct that might have provided grounds in 1791 for a suit for trespass to chattels. And for this reason, the Court concludes, the installation and use of the GPS device constituted a search.

This holding, in my judgment, is unwise. It strains the language of the Fourth Amendment; it has little if any support in current Fourth Amendment case law; and it is highly artificial.

I would analyze the question presented in this case by asking whether respondent's reasonable expectations of privacy were violated by the long-term monitoring of the movements of the vehicle he drove.

I

A

The Fourth Amendment prohibits "unreasonable searches and seizures," and the Court makes very little effort to explain how the attachment or use of the GPS device fits within these terms. The Court does not contend that there was a seizure. A seizure of property occurs when there is "some meaningful interference with an individual's possessory interests in that property," *United States v. Jacobsen,* 466 U.S. 109, 113(1984), and here there was none. Indeed, the success of the surveillance technique that the officers employed was dependent on the fact that the GPS did not interfere in any way with the operation of the vehicle, for if any such interference had been detected, the device might have been discovered.

The Court does claim that the installation and use of the GPS constituted a search, but this conclusion is dependent on the questionable proposition that these two procedures cannot be separated for purposes of Fourth Amendment analysis. If these two procedures are analyzed separately, it is not at all clear from the Court's opinion why either should be regarded as a search. It is clear that the attachment of the GPS device was not itself a search; if the device had not functioned or if the officers had not used it, no information would have been obtained. And the Court does not contend that the use of the device constituted a search either. On the contrary, the Court accepts the holding in *United States v. Knotts,* 460 U.S. 276 (1983), that the use of a surreptitiously planted electronic device to monitor a vehicle's movements on public roads did not amount to a search.

The Court argues—and I agree—that "we must 'assur[e] preservation of that degree of privacy against government that existed when the Fourth Amendment was adopted.'" But it is almost impossible to think of late-18th-century situations that are analogous to what took place in this case. (Is it possible to imagine a case in which a constable secreted himself somewhere in a coach and remained there for a period of time in order to monitor the movements of the coach's owner?[3]) The Court's theory seems to be that the concept of a search, as originally understood, comprehended any technical trespass that led to the gathering of evidence, but we know that this is incorrect. At common law, any unauthorized intrusion on private property was actionable, but a trespass on open fields, as opposed to the "curtilage" of a home, does not fall within the scope of the Fourth Amendment because private property outside the curtilageis not part of a "house" within the meaning of the Fourth Amendment.

B

The Court's reasoning in this case is very similar to that in the Court's early decisions involving wiretapping and electronic eavesdropping, namely, that a technical trespass followed by the gathering of evidence constitutes a search. In the early electronic surveillance cases, the Court concluded that a Fourth Amendment search occurred when private conversations were monitored as a result of an "unauthorized physical penetration into the premises occupied" by the defendant. *Silverman v. United States,* 365 U.S. 505, 509 (1961). In *Silverman,* police officers listened to conversations in an attached home by inserting a "spike mike" through the wall that this house shared with the vacant house next door. This procedure was held to be a search because the mike made contact with a heating duct on the other side of the wall and thus "usurped . . . an integral part of the premises."

* * *

Katz v. United States, 389 U.S. 347 (1967), finally did away with the old approach, holding that a trespass was not required for a Fourth Amendment violation. *Katz* involved the use of a listening device that was attached to the outside of a public telephone booth and that allowed police officers to eavesdrop on one end of the target's phone conversation. This procedure did not physically intrude on the area occupied by the target, but the *Katz* Court, repudiated the old doctrine and held that "[t]he fact that the electronic device employed . . . did not happen to penetrate the wall of the booth can have no constitutional significance." What mattered, the Court now held, was whether the conduct at issue "violated the privacy upon which [the defendant] justifiably relied while using the telephone booth."

Under this approach, as the Court later put it when addressing the relevance of a technical trespass, "an actual trespass is neither necessary *nor sufficient* to establish a constitutional violation." *United States v. Karo,* 468 U.S. 705, 713 (1984). . . .

[3] The Court suggests that something like this might have occurred in 1791, but this would have required either a gigantic coach, a very tiny constable, or both—not to mention a constable with incredible fortitude and patience.

* * *

III

Disharmony with a substantial body of existing case law is only one of the problems with the Court's approach in this case.

I will briefly note four others. First, the Court's reasoning largely disregards what is really important (the *use* of a GPS for the purpose of long-term tracking) and instead attaches great significance to something that most would view as relatively minor (attaching to the bottom of a car a small, light object that does not interfere in any way with the car's operation). Attaching such an object is generally regarded as so trivial that it does not provide a basis for recovery under modern tort law. But under the Court's reasoning, this conduct may violate the Fourth Amendment. By contrast, if long-term monitoring can be accomplished without committing a technical trespass—suppose, for example, that the Federal Government required or persuaded auto manufacturers to include a GPS tracking device in every car—the Court's theory would provide no protection.

Second, the Court's approach leads to incongruous results. If the police attach a GPS device to a car and use the device to follow the car for even a brief time, under the Court's theory, the Fourth Amendment applies. But if the police follow the same car for a much longer period using unmarked cars and aerial assistance, this tracking is not subject to any Fourth Amendment constraints.

In the present case, the Fourth Amendment applies, the Court concludes, because the officers installed the GPS device after respondent's wife, to whom the car was registered, turned it over to respondent for his exclusive use. But if the GPS had been attached prior to that time, the Court's theory would lead to a different result. The Court proceeds on the assumption that respondent "had at least the property rights of a bailee," but a bailee may sue for a trespass to chattel only if the injury occurs during the term of the bailment. So if the GPS device had been installed before respondent's wife gave him the keys, respondent would have no claim for trespass—and, presumably, no Fourth Amendment claim either.

Third, under the Court's theory, the coverage of the Fourth Amendment may vary from State to State. If the events at issue here had occurred in a community property State or a State that has adopted the Uniform Marital Property Act, respondent would likely be an owner of the vehicle, and it would not matter whether the GPS was installed before or after his wife turned over the keys. In non-community-property States, on the other hand, the registration of the vehicle in the name of respondent's wife would generally be regarded as presumptive evidence that she was the sole owner.

Fourth, the Court's reliance on the law of trespass will present particularly vexing problems in cases involving surveillance that is carried out by making electronic, as opposed to physical, contact with the item to be tracked. For example, suppose that the officers in the present case had followed respondent by surreptitiously activating a stolen vehicle detection system that came with the car when it was purchased. Would the sending of a radio signal to activate this system constitute a trespass to chattels? Trespass to chattels has traditionally required a physical touching of the property. In recent years, courts have wrestled with the application of this old tort in cases involving unwanted electronic contact with computer systems, and some have held that even the transmission of electrons that occurs when a communication is sent from one computer to another is enough. But may such decisions be followed in applying the Court's trespass theory? Assuming that what matters under the Court's theory is the law of trespass as it existed at the time of the adoption of the Fourth Amendment, do these recent decisions represent a change in the law or simply the application of the old tort to new situations?

IV

A

The *Katz* expectation-of-privacy test avoids the problems and complications noted above, but it is not without its own difficulties. It involves a degree of circularity, and judges are apt to confuse their own expectations of privacy with those of the hypothetical reasonable person to which the *Katz* test looks. In addition, the *Katz* test rests on the assumption that this hypothetical reasonable person has a well-developed and stable set of privacy expectations. But technology can change those expectations. Dramatic technological change may lead to periods in which popular expectations are in flux and may ultimately produce significant changes in popular attitudes. New technology may provide increased convenience or security at the expense of privacy, and many people may find the tradeoff worthwhile. And even if the public does not welcome the diminution of privacy that new technology entails, they may eventually reconcile themselves to this development as inevitable.

* * *

B

Recent years have seen the emergence of many new devices that permit the monitoring of a person's movements. In some locales, closed-circuit television video monitoring is becoming ubiquitous. On toll roads, automatic toll collection systems create a precise record of the movements of motorists who choose to make use of that convenience. Many motorists purchase cars that are equipped with devices that permit a central station to ascertain the car's location at any time so that roadside assistance may be provided if needed and the car may be found if it is stolen.

Perhaps most significant, cell phones and other wireless devices now permit wireless carriers to track and record the location of users—and as of June 2011, it has been reported, there were more than 322 million wireless devices in use in the United States. For older phones, the accuracy of the location information depends on the density of the tower network, but new "smart phones," which are equipped with a GPS device, permit more precise tracking. For example, when a user activates the GPS on such a phone, a provider is able to monitor the phone's location and speed of movement and can then report back real-time traffic conditions after combining ("crowdsourcing") the speed of all such phones on any particular road. Similarly, phone-location-tracking services are offered as "social" tools, allowing consumers to find (or to avoid) others who enroll in these services. The availability and use of these and other new devices will continue to shape the average person's expectations about the privacy of his or her daily movements.

V

In the pre-computer age, the greatest protections of privacy were neither constitutional nor statutory, but practical. Traditional surveillance for any extended period of time was difficult and costly and therefore rarely undertaken. The surveillance at issue in this case—constant monitoring of the location of a vehicle for four weeks—would have required a large team of agents, multiple vehicles, and perhaps aerial assistance. Only an investigation of unusual importance could have justified such an expenditure of law enforcement resources. Devices like the one used in the present case, however, make long-term monitoring relatively easy and cheap. In circumstances involving dramatic technological change, the best solution to privacy concerns may be legislative. A legislative body is well situated to gauge changing public attitudes, to draw detailed lines, and to balance privacy and public safety in a comprehensive way.

To date, however, Congress and most States have not enacted statutes regulating the use of GPS tracking technology for law enforcement purposes. The best that we can do in this case is to apply existing Fourth Amendment doctrine and to ask whether the use of GPS tracking in a particular case involved a degree of intrusion that a reasonable person would not have anticipated.

Under this approach, relatively short-term monitoring of a person's movements on public streets accords with expectations of privacy that our society has recognized as reasonable. But the use of longer term GPS monitoring in investigations of most offenses impinges on expectations of privacy. For such offenses, society's expectation has been that law enforcement agents and others would not—and indeed, in the main, simply could not—secretly monitor and catalogue every single movement of an individual's car for a very long period. In this case, for four weeks, law enforcement agents tracked every movement that respondent made in the vehicle he was driving. We need not identify with precision the point at which the tracking of this vehicle became a search, for the line was surely crossed before the 4-week mark. Other cases may present more difficult questions. But where uncertainty exists with respect to whether a certain period of GPS surveillance is long enough to constitute a Fourth Amendment search, the police may always seek a warrant. We also need not consider whether prolonged GPS monitoring in the context of investigations involving extraordinary offenses would similarly intrude on a constitutionally protected sphere of privacy. In such cases, long-term tracking might have been mounted using previously available techniques.

For these reasons, I conclude that the lengthy monitoring that occurred in this case constituted a search under the Fourth Amendment. I therefore agree with the majority that the decision of the Court of Appeals must be affirmed.

Points for Discussion

1. The *Jones* Court unanimously agreed that the police violated the Fourth Amendment when they attached a tracking device to Antoine Jones' Jeep. They divided, however, over why. Four justices would have held that GPS tracking infringed on "expectations of privacy." A bare majority invoked the pre-*Katz* property framework, claiming that "the *Katz* reasonable-expectation-of-privacy test has been *added to*, not *substituted for*, the common-law trespassory test." Yet, nearly every justice to sit on the Court since *Katz*—including every justice on the *Jones* Court except the recently confirmed Justice Elena Kagan—had written or joined an opinion that expressly said that *Katz* overruled *Olmstead*. For example, the majority opinion in *Kyllo v. United States*, also by Justice Scalia, stated that the Court had "decoupled violation of a person's Fourth Amendment rights from trespassory violation of his property . . . ." 533 U.S. 27, 32 (2001). Until *Jones*, *Katz*'s overruling of *Olmstead* was such a foregone certainty that *The Bluebook*, the most influential legal style manual, used *Olmstead* to illustrate how to cite an overruled case. *The Bluebook*, Rule 10.7.1(c)(i) at 102 (19th ed.). Why, then, would the majority choose to re- (or mis-) characterize *Katz* rather than simply announce a new rule?

2. Between the decisions in *Katz* and *Jones*, "expectations of privacy" supplanted trespass as the dominant concept in Fourth Amendment search cases. Justice Sotomayor's concurrence strongly suggests that she agreed with the other four concurring justices that the GPS tracking infringed on "expectations of privacy." It is possible that one or more justices in the majority did so as well. So, there were almost certainly at least five—and possibly more—justices who agreed that the GPS tracking ran afoul of *Katz*. Why, then, did the majority vote to take the relatively radical step of reviving a long-abandoned trespass notion in a case in which it made no difference which of the two tests was used?

3. *Jones* returned property conceptions to the center of Fourth Amendment analysis. The *Jones* Court, however, accepted that there was no "seizure" of Antoine Jones' Jeep. Using a definition of a property seizure from

United States v. Jacobsen, both the *Jones* majority and Justice Alito's concurrence reasoned that the GPS device did not "meaningfully interfere" with the Jeep's operation. Does every trespass require "meaningful interference"? When a car is deliberately keyed, dinged, or dented, does property law consider that a trespass even if the car remains fully operational? Should the Fourth Amendment trespass test be different? Part IV of the *Oliver* majority is relevant to these considerations.

B. "SEARCHES"

As all three opinions in *Jones* either state or imply, the *Katz* test for determining what amounts to a "search" has been less than a complete success. While the *Katz* test provided a framework for determining whether a search occurred, it merely focused the Court's attention on a different difficult question: whether the government's conduct impinged on a reasonable expectation of privacy. Whether privacy is invaded may depend upon whether personal information is uncovered, whether possessions are touched or moved, whether information from inside a home or other location is discovered, or whether intrusive means were used to obtain information. This section surveys the Court's experience using the *Katz* framework to define the word "search" for Fourth Amendment purposes.

UNITED STATES V. WHITE

401 U.S. 745 (1971)

MR. JUSTICE WHITE announced the judgment of the court and an opinion in which THE CHIEF JUSTICE, MR. JUSTICE STEWART, and MR. JUSTICE BLACKMUN join.

In 1966, respondent James A. White was tried and convicted under two consolidated indictments charging various illegal transactions in narcotics violative of 26 U.S.C. § 4705(a) and 21 U.S.C. § 174. He was fined and sentenced as a second offender to 25-year concurrent sentences. The issue before us is whether the Fourth Amendment bars from evidence the testimony of governmental agents who related certain conversations which had occurred between defendant White and a government informant, Harvey Jackson, and which the agents overheard by monitoring the frequency of a radio transmitter carried by Jackson and concealed on his person. On four occasions the conversations took place in Jackson's home; each of these conversations was overheard by an agent concealed in a kitchen closet with Jackson's consent and by a second agent outside the house using a radio receiver. Four other conversations—one in respondent's home, one in a restaurant, and two in Jackson's car—were overheard by the use of radio equipment. The prosecution was unable to locate and produce Jackson at the trial and the trial court overruled objections to the testimony of the agents who conducted the electronic surveillance. The jury returned a guilty verdict and defendant appealed.

* * *

I

Until *Katz v. United States*, neither wiretapping nor electronic eavesdropping violated a defendant's Fourth Amendment rights "unless there has been an official search and seizure of his person, or such a seizure of his papers or his tangible material effects, or an actual physical invasion of his house 'or curtilage' for the purpose of making a seizure." *Olmstead v. United States*, 277 U.S. 438, 466 (1928). But where "eavesdropping was accomplished by means of an unauthorized physical penetration into the premises occupied" by the defendant, although falling short of a "technical trespass under the local property law," the Fourth Amendment was violated and any evidence of what was seen and heard, as well as tangible objects seized, was considered the inadmissible fruit of an unlawful invasion.

* * *

Hoffa v. United States, 385 U.S. 293 (1966), which was left undisturbed by *Katz*, held that however strongly a defendant may trust an apparent colleague, his expectations in this respect are not protected by the Fourth Amendment when it turns out that the colleague is a government agent regularly communicating with the authorities. In these circumstances, "no interest legitimately protected by the Fourth Amendment is involved," for that amendment affords no protection to "a wrongdoer's misplaced belief that a person to whom he voluntarily confides his wrongdoing will not reveal it." No warrant to "search and seize" is required in such circumstances, nor is it when the Government sends to defendant's home a secret agent who conceals his identity and makes a purchase of narcotics from the accused, *Lewis v. United States*, 385 U.S. 206 (1966), or when the same agent, unbeknown to the defendant, carries electronic equipment to record the defendant's words and the evidence so gathered is later offered in evidence. *Lopez v. United States*, 373 U.S. 427 (1963).

* * *

Concededly a police agent who conceals his police connections may write down for official use his conversations with a defendant and testify concerning them, without a warrant authorizing his encounters with the defendant and without otherwise violating the latter's Fourth Amendment rights. For constitutional purposes, no different result is required if the agent instead of immediately reporting and transcribing his conversations with defendant, either (1) simultaneously records them with electronic equipment which he is carrying on his person, *Lopez v. United States*; (2) or carries radio equipment which simultaneously transmits the conversations either to recording equipment located elsewhere or to other agents monitoring the transmitting frequency, *On Lee v. United States*, [343 U.S. 747 (1952)]. If the conduct and revelations of an agent operating without electronic equipment do not invade the defendant's constitutionally justifiable expectations of privacy, neither does a simultaneous recording of the same conversations made by the agent or by others from transmissions received from the agent to whom the defendant is talking and whose trustworthiness the defendant necessarily risks.

Our problem is not what the privacy expectations of particular defendants in particular situations may be or the extent to which they may in fact have relied on the discretion of their companions. Very probably, individual defendants neither know nor suspect that their colleagues have gone or will go to the police or are carrying recorders or transmitters. Otherwise, conversation would cease and our problem with these encounters would be nonexistent or far different from those now before us. Our problem, in terms of the principles announced in *Katz*, is what expectations of privacy are constitutionally "justifiable"—what expectations the Fourth Amendment will protect in the absence of a warrant. So far, the law permits the frustration of actual expectations of privacy by permitting authorities to use the testimony of those associates who for one reason or another have determined to turn to the police, as well as by authorizing the use of informants in the manner exemplified by *Hoffa* and *Lewis*. If the law gives no protection to the wrongdoer whose trusted accomplice is or becomes a police agent, neither should it protect him when that same agent has recorded or transmitted the conversations which are later offered in evidence to prove the State's case.

Inescapably, one contemplating illegal activities must realize and risk that his companions may be reporting to the police. If he sufficiently doubts their trustworthiness, the association will very probably end or never materialize. But if he has no doubts, or allays them, or risks what doubt he has, the risk is his. In terms of what his course will be, what he will or will not do or say, we are unpersuaded that he would distinguish between probable informers on the one hand and probable informers with transmitters on the other. Given the possibility or probability that one of his colleagues is cooperating with the police, it is only speculation to assert that the defendant's utterances would be substantially different or his sense of security any less if he also thought it possible that the suspected colleague is wired for sound. At least there is no persuasive evidence that the difference in this respect between the electronically equipped and the unequipped agent is substantial enough to require discrete constitutional recognition, particularly under the Fourth Amendment which is ruled by fluid concepts of 'reasonableness.'

Nor should we be too ready to erect constitutional barriers to relevant and probative evidence which is also accurate and reliable. An electronic recording will many times produce a more reliable rendition of what a defendant has said than will the unaided memory of a police agent. It may also be that with the recording in existence it is less likely that the informant will change his mind, less chance that threat or injury will suppress unfavorable evidence and less chance that cross-examination will confound the testimony. Considerations like these obviously do not favor the defendant, but we are not prepared to hold that a defendant who has no constitutional right to exclude the informer's unaided testimony nevertheless has a Fourth Amendment privilege against a more accurate version of the events in question.

* * *

II

The Court of Appeals was in error for another reason. In *Desist v. United States*, 394 U.S. 244 (1969), we held that our decision in *Katz v. United States* applied only to those electronic surveillances that occurred subsequent to the date of that decision. Here the events in question took place in late 1965 and early 1966, long prior to *Katz*. We adhere to the rationale of *Desist*. It was error for the Court of Appeals to dispose of this case based on its understanding of the principles announced in the *Katz* case. The court should have judged this case by the pre-*Katz* law and under that law, as *On Lee* clearly holds, the electronic surveillance here involved did not violate White's rights to be free from unreasonable searches and seizures.

MR. JUSTICE BLACK . . . concurs in the judgment of the court for the reasons set forth in his dissent in Katz v. United States.

MR. JUSTICE BRENNAN, concurring in the result.

I agree that *Desist v. United States*, 394 U.S. 244 (1969), requires reversal of the judgment of the Court of Appeals. Therefore, a majority of the Court supports disposition of this case on that ground. . . . [I]t is my view that current Fourth Amendment jurisprudence interposes a warrant requirement not only in cases of third-party electronic monitoring (the situation in *On Lee* and in this case) but also in cases of electronic recording by a government agent of a face-to-face conversation with a criminal suspect, which was the situation in *Lopez*. . . .

MR. JUSTICE DOUGLAS, dissenting.

I

The issue in this case is clouded and concealed by the very discussion of it in legalistic terms. What the ancients knew as "eavesdropping," we now call "electronic surveillance"; but to equate the two is to treat man's first gunpowder on the same level as the nuclear bomb. Electronic surveillance is the greatest leveler of human privacy ever known. How most forms of it can be held "reasonable" within the meaning of the Fourth Amendment is a mystery. To be sure, the Constitution and Bill of Rights are not to be read as covering only the technology known in the 18th century. Otherwise its concept of "commerce" would be hopeless when it comes to the management of modern affairs. At the same time the concepts of privacy which the Founders enshrined in the Fourth Amendment vanish completely when we slavishly allow an all-powerful government, proclaiming law and order, efficiency, and other benign purposes, to penetrate all the walls and doors which men need to shield them from the pressures of a turbulent life around them and give them the health and strength to carry on.

That is why a "strict construction" of the Fourth Amendment is necessary if every man's liberty and privacy are to be constitutionally honored.

* * *

II

* * *

The threads of thought running through our recent decisions are that these extensive intrusions into privacy made by electronic surveillance make self-restraint by law enforcement officials an inadequate protection, that the requirement of warrants under the Fourth Amendment is essential to a free society.

Monitoring, if prevalent, certainly kills free discourse and spontaneous utterances. Free discourse—a First Amendment value—may be frivolous or serious, humble or defiant, reactionary or revolutionary, profane or in good taste; but it is not free if there is surveillance. Free discourse liberates the spirit, though it may produce only froth. The individual must keep some facts concerning his thoughts within a small zone of people. At the same time he must be free to pour out his woes or inspirations or dreams to others. He remains the sole judge as to what must be said and what must remain unspoken. This is the essence of the idea of privacy implicit in the First and Fifth Amendments as well as in the Fourth.

The philosophy of the value of privacy reflected in the Fourth Amendment's ban on "unreasonable searches and seizures" has been forcefully stated by a former Attorney General of the United States:

> Privacy is the basis of individuality. To be alone and be let alone, to be with chosen company, to say what you think, or don't think, but to say what you will, is to be yourself. Solitude is imperative, even in a high rise apartment. Personality develops from within. To reflect is to know yourself. Character is formed through years of self-examination. Without this opportunity, character will be formed largely by uncontrolled external social stimulations. Americans are excessively homogenized already.
>
> Few conversations would be what they are if the speakers thought others were listening. Silly, secret, thoughtless and thoughtful statements would all be affected. The sheer numbers

> in our lives, the anonymity of urban living and the inability to influence things that are important are depersonalizing and dehumanizing factors of modern life. To penetrate the last refuge of the individual, the precious little privacy that remains, the basis of individual dignity, can have meaning to the quality of our lives that we cannot foresee. In terms of present values, that meaning cannot be good.
>
> Invasions of privacy demean the individual. Can a society be better than the people composing it? When a government degrades its citizens, or permits them to degrade each other, however beneficent the specific purpose, it limits opportunities for individual fulfillment and national accomplishment. If America permits fear and its failure to make basic social reforms to excuse police use of secret electronic surveillance, the price will be dear indeed. The practice is incompatible with a free society.

R. CLARK, CRIME IN AMERICA 287 (1970).

* * *

MR. JUSTICE HARLAN, dissenting.

* * *

I

Before turning to matters of precedent and policy, several preliminary observations should be made. We deal here with the constitutional validity of instantaneous third-party electronic eavesdropping, conducted by federal law enforcement officers, without any prior judicial approval of the technique utilized, but with the consent and cooperation of a participant in the conversation, and where the substance of the matter electronically overheard is related in a federal criminal trial by those who eavesdropped as direct, not merely corroborative, evidence of the guilt of the nonconsenting party. The magnitude of the issue at hand is evidenced not simply by the obvious doctrinal difficulty of weighing such activity in the Fourth Amendment balance, but also, and more importantly, by the prevalence of police utilization of this technique. Professor Westin has documented in careful detail the numerous devices that make technologically feasible the Orwellian Big Brother. Of immediate relevance is his observation that " 'participant recording,' in which one participant in a conversation or meeting, either a police officer or a co-operating party, wears a concealed device that records the conversation or broadcasts it to others nearby * * * is used tens of thousands of times each year throughout the country, particularly in cases involving extortion, conspiracy, narcotics, gambling, prostitution, corruption by police officials * * * and similar crimes." A. WESTIN, PRIVACY AND FREEDOM 131 (1967).

* * *

Finally, given the importance of electronic eavesdropping as a technique for coping with the more deep-seated kinds of criminal activity, and the complexities that are encountered in striking a workable constitutional balance between the public and private interests at stake, I believe that the courts should proceed with specially measured steps in this field. More particularly, I think this Court should not foreclose itself from reconsidering doctrines that would prevent the States from seeking, independently of the niceties of federal restrictions as they may develop, solutions to such vexing problems. I also think that in the adjudication of federal cases, the Court should leave ample room for congressional developments.

* * *

III

A

* * *

The plurality opinion seeks to erase the crucial distinction between the facts before us and these holdings by the following reasoning: if A can relay verbally what is revealed to him by B (as in *Lewis* and *Hoffa*), or record and later divulge it (as in *Lopez*), what difference does it make if A conspires with another to betray B by contemporaneously transmitting to the other all that is said? The contention is, in essence, an argument that the distinction between third-party monitoring and other undercover techniques is one of form and not substance. The force of the contention depends on the evaluation of two separable but intertwined assumptions: first, that there is no greater invasion of privacy in the third-party situation, and, second, that uncontrolled consensual surveillance in an electronic age is a tolerable technique of law enforcement, given the values and goals of our political system.

* * *

Since it is the task of the law to form and project, as well as mirror and reflect, we should not, as judges, merely recite the expectations and risks without examining the desirability of saddling them upon society. The critical question, therefore, is whether under our system of government, as reflected in the Constitution, we should impose on our citizens the risks of the electronic listener or observer without at least the protection of a warrant requirement.

This question must, in my view, be answered by assessing the nature of a particular practice and the likely extent of its impact on the individual's sense of security balanced against the utility of the conduct as a technique of law enforcement. For those more extensive intrusions that significantly jeopardize the sense of security which is the paramount concern of Fourth Amendment liberties, I am of the view that more than self-restraint by law enforcement officials is required and at the least warrants should be necessary.

B

The impact of the practice of third-party bugging, must, I think, be considered such as to undermine that confidence and sense of security in dealing with one another that is characteristic of individual relationships between citizens in a free society. It goes beyond the impact on privacy occasioned by the ordinary type of "informer" investigation upheld in *Lewis* and *Hoffa*. The argument of the plurality opinion, to the effect that it is irrelevant whether secrets are revealed by the mere tattletale or the transistor, ignores the differences occasioned by third-party monitoring and recording which insures full and accurate disclosure of all that is said, free of the possibility of error and oversight that inheres in human reporting.

Authority is hardly required to support the proposition that words would be measured a good deal more carefully and communication inhibited if one suspected his conversations were being transmitted and transcribed. Were third-party bugging a prevalent practice, it might well smother that spontaneity—reflected in frivolous, impetuous, sacrilegious, and defiant discourse—that liberates daily life. Much offhand exchange is easily forgotten and one may count on the obscurity of his remarks, protected by the very fact of a limited audience, and the likelihood that the listener will either overlook or forget what is said, as well as the listener's inability to reformulate a conversation without having to contend with a documented record. All these values are sacrificed by a rule of law that permits official monitoring of private discourse limited only by the need to locate a willing assistant.

* * *

MR. JUSTICE MARSHALL, dissenting.

I am convinced that the correct view of the Fourth Amendment in the area of electronic surveillance is one that brings the safeguards of the warrant requirement to bear on the investigatory activity involved in this case. In this regard I agree with the dissents of Mr. Justice Douglas and Mr. Justice Harlan. . . .

Points for Discussion

1. How does the reasoning of *White* affect *Katz*? Didn't Katz run the risk that his bookie on the other end of the line would record their conversation? Doesn't this mean that he had no reasonable expectation of privacy in that conversation? If so, how can he object when the government tapes that conversation?

2. In *On Lee v. United States*, 343 U.S. 747 (1952), the petitioner challenged a government agent's testimony regarding a conversation between On Lee and an informant that was broadcast to the agent by a concealed transmitter. As Justice Jackson suggested in his opinion for the Court, the agent was called to testify rather than the informant because the informant likely had an unsavory past that would have been exposed on cross-examination. Among the many arguments the petitioner raised was that the Court should overrule *Olmstead*'s holding that wiretapping was not within the scope of the Fourth Amendment:

> We need not consider this, however, for success in this attempt, which failed in *Goldman v. United States*, 316 U.S. 129, would be of no aid to petitioner unless he can show that his situation should be treated as wiretapping. The presence of a radio set is not sufficient to suggest more than the most attenuated analogy to wiretapping. Petitioner was talking confidentially and indiscreetly with one he trusted, and he was overheard. This was due to aid from a transmitter and receiver, to be sure, but with the same effect on his privacy as if agent Lee had been eavesdropping outside an open window. The use of bifocals, field glasses or the telescope to magnify the object of a witness' vision is not a forbidden search or seizure, even if they focus without his knowledge or consent upon what one supposes to be private indiscretions. It would be a dubious service to the genuine liberties protected by the Fourth Amendment to make them bedfellows with spurious liberties improvised by farfetched analogies which would liken eavesdropping on a conversation, with the connivance of one of the parties, to an unreasonable search or seizure. We find no violation of the Fourth Amendment here.

On Lee, 343 U.S. at 753–54.

3. Justice Black concurs in the outcome on the ground that the Fourth Amendment does not apply to wiretapping at all, as he wrote in his dissent in *Katz*. The justices other than Justice Black are evenly divided over whether the police should have been required to obtain a warrant for the radio surveillance they made of James White's conversations with the informant. The four justices in the plurality believe that radio surveillance of an informant's conversation with a target is not a search at all, even if wiretapping is. The other four justices believe this surveillance was a Fourth Amendment search under *Katz*. Which side's position seems more logical?

4. Whether the use of sense-enhancing technology—such as the bifocals, field glasses, or the telescope that Justice Jackson mentions in *On Lee*—transforms observation into a Fourth Amendment search is a difficult and recurring question. The Court, in an opinion by Justice Scalia, attempted to draw a line in the sand in *Kyllo v. United States*, 533 U.S. 27, 34 (2001). That case held "that obtaining by sense-enhancing technology any information regarding the interior of the home that could not otherwise have been obtained without physical 'intrusion into a constitutionally protected area,' constitutes a search—at least where (as here) the technology in question is not in general

public use." As Justice Stevens' dissent in that case suggests, however, the problem is not so easily solved.

UNITED STATES V. MILLER

425 U.S. 435 (1976)

MR. JUSTICE POWELL delivered the opinion of the court.

Respondent was convicted of possessing an unregistered still, carrying on the business of a distiller without giving bond and with intent to defraud the Government of whiskey tax, possessing 175 gallons of whiskey upon which no taxes had been paid, and conspiring to defraud the United States of tax revenues. Prior to trial respondent moved to suppress copies of checks and other bank records obtained by means of allegedly defective subpoenas duces tecum served upon two banks at which he had accounts. The records had been maintained by the banks in compliance with the requirements of the Bank Secrecy Act of 1970, 12 U.S.C. § 1829b(d).

The District Court overruled respondent's motion to suppress, and the evidence was admitted. The Court of Appeals for the Fifth Circuit reversed on the ground that a depositor's Fourth Amendment rights are violated when bank records maintained pursuant to the Bank Secrecy Act are obtained by means of a defective subpoena. It held that any evidence so obtained must be suppressed. Since we find that respondent had no protectable Fourth Amendment interest in the subpoenaed documents, we reverse the decision below.

I

On December 18, 1972, in response to an informant's tip, a deputy sheriff from Houston County, Ga., stopped a van-type truck occupied by two of respondent's alleged co-conspirators. The truck contained distillery apparatus and raw material. On January 9, 1973, a fire broke out in a Kathleen, Ga., warehouse rented to respondent. During the blaze firemen and sheriff department officials discovered a 7,500-gallon-capacity distillery, 175 gallons of nontax-paid whiskey, and related paraphernalia.

Two weeks later agents from the Treasury Department's Alcohol, Tobacco and Firearms Bureau presented grand jury subpoenas issued in blank by the clerk of the District Court, and completed by the United States Attorney's office, to the presidents of the Citizens & Southern National Bank of Warner Robins and the Bank of Byron, where respondent maintained accounts. The subpoenas required the two presidents to appear on January 24, 1973, and to produce

> all records of accounts, i.e., savings, checking, loan or otherwise, in the name of Mr. Mitch Miller (respondent), 3859 Mathis Street, Macon, Ga. and/or Mitch Miller Associates, 100 Executive Terrace, Warner Robins, Ga., from October, 1972, through the

present date (January 22, 1973, in the case of the Bank of Byron, and January 23, 1973, in the case of the Citizens & Southern National Bank of Warner Robins).[b]

The banks did not advise respondent that the subpoenas had been served but ordered their employees to make the records available and to provide copies of any documents the agents desired. At the Bank of Byron, an agent was shown microfilm records of the relevant account and provided with copies of one deposit slip and one or two checks. At the Citizens & Southern National Bank microfilm records also were shown to the agent, and he was given copies of the records of respondent's account during the applicable period. These included all checks, deposit slips, two financial statements, and three monthly statements. The bank presidents were then told that it would not be necessary to appear in person before the grand jury.

The grand jury met on February 12, 1973, 19 days after the return date on the subpoenas. Respondent and four others were indicted. The overt acts alleged to have been committed in furtherance of the conspiracy included three financial transactions—the rental by respondent of the van-type truck, the purchase by respondent of radio equipment, and the purchase by respondent of a quantity of sheet metal and metal pipe. The record does not indicate whether any of the bank records were in fact presented to the grand jury. They were used in the investigation and provided "one or two" investigatory leads. Copies of the checks also were introduced at trial to establish the overt acts described above.

* * *

II

On their face, the documents subpoenaed here are not respondent's "private papers." Unlike the claimant in *Boyd* [*v. United States*, 116 U.S. 616 (1886)], respondent can assert neither ownership nor possession. Instead, these are the business records of the banks. As we said in *California Bankers Assn. v. Shultz*, [416 U.S. 21 (1974)], "(b)anks are . . . not . . . neutrals in transactions involving negotiable instruments, but parties to the instruments with a substantial stake in their continued availability and acceptance." The records of respondent's accounts, like "all of the records (which are required to be kept pursuant to the Bank Secrecy Act,) pertain to transactions to which the bank was itself a party."

Respondent argues, however, that the Bank Secrecy Act introduces a factor that makes the subpoena in this case the functional equivalent of a search and seizure of the depositor's "private papers." We have held, in *California Bankers Assn. v. Shultz*, that the mere maintenance of records

[b] A grand jury subpoena is an investigatory tool used by prosecutors to prepare a case. The subpoena directs the recipient to furnish certain documents under penalty of contempt; the word subpoena literally translates as "under penalty".—Eds.

pursuant to the requirements of the Act "invade(s) no Fourth Amendment right of any depositor." But respondent contends that the combination of the recordkeeping requirements of the Act and the issuance of a subpoena to obtain those records permits the Government to circumvent the requirements of the Fourth Amendment by allowing it to obtain a depositor's private records without complying with the legal requirements that would be applicable had it proceeded against him directly. Therefore, we must address the question whether the compulsion embodied in the Bank Secrecy Act as exercised in this case creates a Fourth Amendment interest in the depositor where none existed before. This question was expressly reserved in *California Bankers Assn.*

* * *

Even if we direct our attention to the original checks and deposit slips, rather than to the microfilm copies actually viewed and obtained by means of the subpoena, we perceive no legitimate "expectation of privacy" in their contents. The checks are not confidential communications but negotiable instruments to be used in commercial transactions. All of the documents obtained, including financial statements and deposit slips, contain only information voluntarily conveyed to the banks and exposed to their employees in the ordinary course of business. The lack of any legitimate expectation of privacy concerning the information kept in bank records was assumed by Congress in enacting the Bank Secrecy Act, the expressed purpose of which is to require records to be maintained because they "have a high degree of usefulness in criminal tax, and regulatory investigations and proceedings."

The depositor takes the risk, in revealing his affairs to another, that the information will be conveyed by that person to the Government. *United States v. White*, 401 U.S. 745, 751–752 (1971). This Court has held repeatedly that the Fourth Amendment does not prohibit the obtaining of information revealed to a third party and conveyed by him to Government authorities, even if the information is revealed on the assumption that it will be used only for a limited purpose and the confidence placed in the third party will not be betrayed. *Id.*, at 752; *Hoffa v. United States*, 385 U.S. at 302; *Lopez v. United States*, 373 U.S. 427 (1963).

This analysis is not changed by the mandate of the Bank Secrecy Act that records of depositors' transactions be maintained by banks. In *California Bankers Assn. v. Shultz*, we rejected the contention that banks, when keeping records of their depositors' transactions pursuant to the Act, are acting solely as agents of the Government. But, even if the banks could be said to have been acting solely as Government agents in transcribing the necessary information and complying without protest[5] with the

[5] Nor did the banks notify respondent, a neglect without legal consequences here, however unattractive it may be.

requirements of the subpoenas, there would be no intrusion upon the depositors' Fourth Amendment rights.

III

Since no Fourth Amendment interests of the depositor are implicated here, this case is governed by the general rule that the issuance of a subpoena to a third party to obtain the records of that party does not violate the rights of a defendant, even if a criminal prosecution is contemplated at the time of the subpoena is issued. Under these principles, it was firmly settled, before the passage of the Bank Secrecy Act, that an Internal Revenue Service summons directed to a third-party bank does not violate the Fourth Amendment rights of a depositor under investigation.

Many banks traditionally kept permanent records of their depositors' accounts, although not all banks did so and the practice was declining in recent years. By requiring that such records be kept by all banks, the Bank Secrecy Act is not a novel means designed to circumvent established Fourth Amendment rights. It is merely an attempt to facilitate the use of a proper and long-standing law enforcement technique by insuring that records are available when they are needed.

* * *

MR. JUSTICE BRENNAN, dissenting.

* * *

In *Burrows v. Superior Court*, 529 P.2d 590 (1974), the question was whether bank statements or copies thereof relating to an accused's bank accounts obtained by the sheriff and prosecutor without benefit of legal process, but with the consent of the bank, were acquired as a result of an illegal search and seizure. The California Supreme Court held that the accused had a reasonable expectation of privacy in his bank statements and records, that the voluntary relinquishment of such records by the bank at the request of the sheriff and prosecutor did not constitute a valid consent by the accused, and that the acquisition by the officers of the records therefore was the result of an illegal search and seizure. In my view the same conclusion, for the reasons stated by the California Supreme Court, is compelled in this case under the practically identical phrasing of the Fourth Amendment. Addressing the threshold question whether the accused's right of privacy was invaded, and relying in part on the decision of the Court of Appeals in this case, Mr. Justice Mosk stated in his excellent opinion for a unanimous court:

* * *

> It cannot be gainsaid that the customer of a bank expects that the documents, such as checks, which he transmits to the bank in the course of his business operations, will remain private, and that such an expectation is reasonable. The prosecution concedes

as much, although it asserts that this expectation is not constitutionally cognizable. Representatives of several banks testified at the suppression hearing that information in their possession regarding a customer's account is deemed by them to be confidential.

* * *

The underlying dilemma in this and related cases is that the bank, a detached and disinterested entity, relinquished the records voluntarily. But that circumstance should not be crucial. For all practical purposes, the disclosure by individuals or business firms of their financial affairs to a bank is not entirely volitional, since it is impossible to participate in the economic life of contemporary society without maintaining a bank account. In the course of such dealings, a depositor reveals many aspects of his personal affairs, opinions, habits and associations. Indeed, the totality of bank records provides a virtual current biography. While we are concerned in the present case only with bank statements, the logical extension of the contention that the bank's ownership of records permits free access to them by any police officer extends far beyond such statements to checks, savings, bonds, loan applications, loan guarantees, and all papers which the customer has supplied to the bank to facilitate the conduct of his financial affairs upon the reasonable assumption that the information would remain confidential. To permit a police officer access to these records merely upon his request, without any judicial control as to relevancy or other traditional requirements of legal process, and to allow the evidence to be used in any subsequent criminal prosecution against a defendant, opens the door to a vast and unlimited range of very real abuses of police power.

Cases are legion that condemn violent searches and invasions of an individual's right to the privacy of his dwelling. The imposition upon privacy, although perhaps not so dramatic, may be equally devastating when other methods are employed. Development of photocopying machines, electronic computers and other sophisticated instruments have accelerated the ability of government to intrude into areas which a person normally chooses to exclude from prying eyes and inquisitive minds. Consequently judicial interpretations of the reach of the constitutional protection of individual privacy must keep pace with the perils created by these new devices.

* * *

I would therefore affirm the judgment of the Court of Appeals. I add only that *Burrows* strikingly illustrates the emerging trend among high state courts of relying upon state constitutional protections of individual liberties protections pervading counterpart provisions of the United States Constitution, but increasingly being ignored by decisions of this Court. . . .

MR. JUSTICE MARSHALL, dissenting.

In *California Bankers Assn. v. Shultz*, 416 U.S. 21 (1974), the Court upheld the constitutionality of the recordkeeping requirements of the Bank Secrecy Act. I dissented, finding the required maintenance of bank customers' records to be a seizure within the meaning of the Fourth Amendment and unlawful in the absence of a warrant and probable cause. While the Court in *California Bankers Assn.* did not then purport to decide whether a customer could later challenge the bank's delivery of his records to the Government pursuant to subpoena, I warned:

> (I)t is ironic that although the majority deems the bank customers' Fourth Amendment claims premature, it also intimates that once the bank has made copies of a customer's checks, the customer no longer has standing to invoke his Fourth Amendment rights when a demand is made on the bank by the Government for the records. . . . By accepting the Government's bifurcated approach to the recordkeeping requirement and the acquisition of the records, the majority engages in a hollow charade whereby Fourth Amendment claims are to be labeled premature until such time as they can be deemed too late.

Today, not surprisingly, the Court finds respondent's claims to be made too late. Since the Court in *California Bankers Assn.* held that a bank, in complying with the requirement that it keep copies of the checks written by its customers, "neither searches nor seizes records in which the depositor has a Fourth Amendment right," there is nothing new in today's holding that respondent has no protected Fourth Amendment interest in such records. A fortiori, he does not have standing to contest the Government's subpoena to the bank.

I wash my hands of today's extended redundancy by the Court. Because the recordkeeping requirements of the Act order the seizure of customers' bank records without a warrant and probable cause, I believe the Act is unconstitutional and that respondent has standing to raise that claim. Since the Act is unconstitutional, the Government cannot rely on records kept pursuant to it in prosecuting bank customers. The Government relied on such records in this case and, because of that, I would affirm the Court of Appeals' reversal of respondent's conviction. I respectfully dissent.

Points for Discussion

1. The *Miller* majority distinguished *Boyd v. United States*, 116 U.S. 616 (1886), stating that the depositor in this case could "assert neither ownership nor possession. Instead, these are the business records of the bank." Is the question of ownership of the records in fact so cut-and-dried? Furthermore, after *Katz*, why should the defendant's property interest in the thing searched or seized be dispositive?

2. Applying *Katz*, *Miller* held that the bank's records were not protected by a privacy interest. The Court reasoned that the Fourth Amendment does not prohibit a third party from conveying even supposedly confidential information to government authorities. This proposition was supported by three cases, all dealing with information revealed to an undercover agent or confidential informant. *See United States v. White*, 401 U.S. 745 (1971) (holding that conversations with a bugged informant were not protected by Fourth Amendment); *Hoffa v. United States*, 385 U.S. 293 (1966) (holding that use of a defendant's conversations with an informant did not violate the Fourth Amendment); *Lopez v. United States*, 373 U.S. 427 (1963) (holding that use of an undercover agent's testimony did not violate the Fourth Amendment)). Do these cases, which were decided on the idea that one assumes the risk of betrayal, support the holding in *Miller*? Are there not significant differences between the relationships created by trusting a false friend and the relationships created by opening a bank account?

3. In direct response to *Miller,* Congress enacted the Right to Financial Privacy Act of 1968, sharply limiting the federal government's ability to obtain information concerning individuals from their financial institutions. What impact should legislation like this have on the question of whether a reasonable expectation of privacy exists in a particular context?

4. *Miller* stands for the proposition that any information shared with another entity loses constitutional protection because it is no longer private. This is implicit in the Court having adopted a definition of "private" in these cases that is essentially synonymous with "secret". However, privacy and secrecy are not necessarily the same thing; there can be such a thing as a shared but private space. *See Minnesota v. Carter*, 525 U.S. 83, 107 (1998) (Ginsburg, J., dissenting). Is equating privacy with secrecy faithful to what Justice Brandeis had in mind in his *Olmstead* dissent or what the *Katz* majority intended? For an extensive analysis of the Court's "knowing exposure" cases, *see* Sherry F. Colb, *What Is a Search? Two Conceptual Flaws in Fourth Amendment Doctrine and Some Hints of a Remedy*, 55 STAN. L. REV. 119 (2002).

5. Justice Marshall's dissent reasons that when the government legislatively mandates the creation of records and later serves a subpoena demanding those records a seizure has occurred. To be constitutional, that seizure must be supported by both probable cause and a warrant. To understand Justice Marshall's point in today's world, consider that Congress now requires telecommunications and technology companies "to circumvent the privacy protections they have built into their products and insert

backdoors—adding new features, the sole purpose of which is to violate the privacy of the customer." Christopher Soghoian, *Caught In The Cloud: Privacy, Encryption, and Government Back Doors In the Web 2.0 Era*, 8 J. Telecomm. & High Tech. L. 359, 400 (2010). If Congress requires companies like Google, Apple, Facebook, AT&T, and Verizon to design their products and services in a way that makes government surveillance possible, is the Fourth Amendment implicated? Is there something about the way Justice Marshall reasons in *Miller* that allows his opinion to anticipate technologies he could not have imagined in 1976?

CALIFORNIA V. GREENWOOD

486 U.S. 35 (1988)

JUSTICE WHITE delivered the opinion of the court.

The issue here is whether the Fourth Amendment prohibits the warrantless search and seizure of garbage left for collection outside the curtilage of a home. We conclude, in accordance with the vast majority of lower courts that have addressed the issue, that it does not.

I

In early 1984, Investigator Jenny Stracner of the Laguna Beach Police Department received information indicating that respondent Greenwood might be engaged in narcotics trafficking. Stracner learned that a criminal suspect had informed a federal drug enforcement agent in February 1984 that a truck filled with illegal drugs was en route to the Laguna Beach address at which Greenwood resided. In addition, a neighbor complained of heavy vehicular traffic late at night in front of Greenwood's single-family home. The neighbor reported that the vehicles remained at Greenwood's house for only a few minutes.

Stracner sought to investigate this information by conducting a surveillance of Greenwood's home. She observed several vehicles make brief stops at the house during the late-night and early morning hours, and she followed a truck from the house to a residence that had previously been under investigation as a narcotics-trafficking location.

On April 6, 1984, Stracner asked the neighborhood's regular trash collector to pick up the plastic garbage bags that Greenwood had left on the curb in front of his house and to turn the bags over to her without mixing their contents with garbage from other houses. The trash collector cleaned his truck bin of other refuse, collected the garbage bags from the street in front of Greenwood's house, and turned the bags over to Stracner. The officer searched through the rubbish and found items indicative of narcotics use. She recited the information that she had gleaned from the trash search in an affidavit in support of a warrant to search Greenwood's home.

Police officers encountered both respondents at the house later that day when they arrived to execute the warrant. The police discovered quantities of cocaine and hashish during their search of the house. Respondents were arrested on felony narcotics charges. They subsequently posted bail.

The police continued to receive reports of many late-night visitors to the Greenwood house. On May 4, Investigator Robert Rahaeuser obtained Greenwood's garbage from the regular trash collector in the same manner as had Stracner. The garbage again contained evidence of narcotics use.

Rahaeuser secured another search warrant for Greenwood's home based on the information from the second trash search. The police found more narcotics and evidence of narcotics trafficking when they executed the warrant. Greenwood was again arrested.

* * *

II

The warrantless search and seizure of the garbage bags left at the curb outside the Greenwood house would violate the Fourth Amendment only if respondents manifested a subjective expectation of privacy in their garbage that society accepts as objectively reasonable. Respondents do not disagree with this standard.

They assert, however, that they had, and exhibited, an expectation of privacy with respect to the trash that was searched by the police: The trash, which was placed on the street for collection at a fixed time, was contained in opaque plastic bags, which the garbage collector was expected to pick up, mingle with the trash of others, and deposit at the garbage dump. The trash was only temporarily on the street, and there was little likelihood that it would be inspected by anyone.

It may well be that respondents did not expect that the contents of their garbage bags would become known to the police or other members of the public. An expectation of privacy does not give rise to Fourth Amendment protection, however, unless society is prepared to accept that expectation as objectively reasonable.

Here, we conclude that respondents exposed their garbage to the public sufficiently to defeat their claim to Fourth Amendment protection. It is common knowledge that plastic garbage bags left on or at the side of a public street are readily accessible to animals,[2] children, scavengers,[3]

[2] For example, *State v. Ronngren,* 361 N.W.2d 224 (N.D.1985), involved the search of a garbage bag that a dog, acting "at the behest of no one," had dragged from the defendants' yard into the yard of a neighbor. The neighbor deposited the bag in his own trash can, which he later permitted the police to search. The North Dakota Supreme Court held that the search of the garbage bag did not violate the defendants' Fourth Amendment rights.

[3] It is not only the homeless of the Nation's cities who make use of others' refuse. For example, a nationally syndicated consumer columnist has suggested that apartment dwellers obtain cents-off coupons by "mak[ing] friends with the fellow who handles the trash" in their buildings, and has recounted the tale of "the 'Rich lady' from Westmont who once a week puts on rubber gloves and hip boots and wades into the town garbage dump looking for labels and other

snoops,[4] and other members of the public. Moreover, respondents placed their refuse at the curb for the express purpose of conveying it to a third party, the trash collector, who might himself have sorted through respondents' trash or permitted others, such as the police, to do so. Accordingly, having deposited their garbage "in an area particularly suited for public inspection and, in a manner of speaking, public consumption, for the express purpose of having strangers take it," respondents could have had no reasonable expectation of privacy in the inculpatory items that they discarded.

Furthermore, as we have held, the police cannot reasonably be expected to avert their eyes from evidence of criminal activity that could have been observed by any member of the public. Hence, "[w]hat a person knowingly exposes to the public, even in his own home or office, is not a subject of Fourth Amendment protection." *Katz v. United States*, 389 U.S. at 351. We held in *Smith v. Maryland*, 442 U.S. 735 (1979), for example, that the police did not violate the Fourth Amendment by causing a pen register to be installed at the telephone company's offices to record the telephone numbers dialed by a criminal suspect. An individual has no legitimate expectation of privacy in the numbers dialed on his telephone, we reasoned, because he voluntarily conveys those numbers to the telephone company when he uses the telephone. Again, we observed that "a person has no legitimate expectation of privacy in information he voluntarily turns over to third parties."

Similarly, we held in *California v. Ciraolo*, [476 U.S. 207 (1986),] that the police were not required by the Fourth Amendment to obtain a warrant before conducting surveillance of the respondent's fenced backyard from a private plane flying at an altitude of 1,000 feet. We concluded that the respondent's expectation that his yard was protected from such surveillance was unreasonable because "[a]ny member of the public flying in this airspace who glanced down could have seen everything that these officers observed."

* * *

III

We reject respondent Greenwood's alternative argument for affirmance: that his expectation of privacy in his garbage should be deemed reasonable as a matter of federal constitutional law because the warrantless search and seizure of his garbage was impermissible as a

proofs of purchase" needed to obtain manufacturers' refunds. M. Sloane, "The Supermarket Shopper's" 1980 Guide to Coupons and Refunds 74, 161 (1980).

[4] Even the refuse of prominent Americans has not been invulnerable. In 1975, for example, a reporter for a weekly tabloid seized five bags of garbage from the sidewalk outside the home of Secretary of State Henry Kissinger. A newspaper editorial criticizing this journalistic "trash-picking" observed that "[e]vidently . . . 'everybody does it.'" Washington Post, July 10, 1975, p. A18, col. 1. We of course do not, as the dissent implies, "bas[e] [our] conclusion" that individuals have no reasonable expectation of privacy in their garbage on this "sole incident."

matter of California law. He urges that the state-law right of Californians to privacy in their garbage, announced by the California Supreme Court in [*People v.*] *Krivda* 5 Cal.3d 367 (1971), survived the subsequent state constitutional amendment eliminating the suppression remedy as a means of enforcing that right. Hence, he argues that the Fourth Amendment should itself vindicate that right.

Individual States may surely construe their own constitutions as imposing more stringent constraints on police conduct than does the Federal Constitution. We have never intimated, however, that whether or not a search is reasonable within the meaning of the Fourth Amendment depends on the law of the particular State in which the search occurs. We have emphasized instead that the Fourth Amendment analysis must turn on such factors as "our *societal* understanding that certain areas deserve the most scrupulous protection from government invasion." *Oliver v. United States*, 466 U.S., at 178 (emphasis added). We have already concluded that society as a whole possesses no such understanding with regard to garbage left for collection at the side of a public street. Respondent's argument is no less than a suggestion that concepts of privacy under the laws of each State are to determine the reach of the Fourth Amendment. We do not accept this submission.

* * *

JUSTICE KENNEDY took no part in the consideration or decision of this case.

JUSTICE BRENNAN, with whom JUSTICE MARSHALL joins, dissenting.

Every week for two months, and at least once more a month later, the Laguna Beach police clawed through the trash that respondent Greenwood left in opaque, sealed bags on the curb outside his home. Complete strangers minutely scrutinized their bounty, undoubtedly dredging up intimate details of Greenwood's private life and habits. The intrusions proceeded without a warrant, and no court before or since has concluded that the police acted on probable cause to believe Greenwood was engaged in any criminal activity.

Scrutiny of another's trash is contrary to commonly accepted notions of civilized behavior. I suspect, therefore, that members of our society will be shocked to learn that the Court, the ultimate guarantor of liberty, deems unreasonable our expectation that the aspects of our private lives that are concealed safely in a trash bag will not become public.

I

* * *

Our precedent . . . leaves no room to doubt that had respondents been carrying their personal effects in opaque, sealed plastic bags—identical to the ones they placed on the curb—their privacy would have been protected from warrantless police intrusion. So far as Fourth Amendment protection is concerned, opaque plastic bags are every bit as worthy as "packages wrapped in green opaque plastic" and "double-locked footlocker[s]."

II

Respondents deserve no less protection just because Greenwood used the bags to discard rather than to transport his personal effects. Their contents are not inherently any less private, and Greenwood's decision to discard them, at least in the manner in which he did, does not diminish his expectation of privacy.

A trash bag, like any of the above-mentioned containers, "is a common repository for one's personal effects" and, even more than many of them, is "therefore . . . inevitably associated with the expectation of privacy." [*Arkansas v. Sanders*, 442 U.S. 753, 762 (1979) (citing [*United States v. Chadwick*, 433 U.S. 1, 13 (1977)]). "[A]lmost every human activity ultimately manifests itself in waste products. . . ." A single bag of trash testifies eloquently to the eating, reading, and recreational habits of the person who produced it. A search of trash, like a search of the bedroom, can relate intimate details about sexual practices, health, and personal hygiene. Like rifling through desk drawers or intercepting phone calls, rummaging through trash can divulge the target's financial and professional status, political affiliations and inclinations, private thoughts, personal relationships, and romantic interests. It cannot be doubted that a sealed trash bag harbors telling evidence of the "intimate activity associated with the 'sanctity of a man's home and the privacies of life,'" which the Fourth Amendment is designed to protect. *Oliver v. United States*, 466 U.S. 170, 180 (1984) (quoting *Boyd v. United States*, 116 U.S. 616, 630 (1886)).

The Court properly rejects the State's attempt to distinguish trash searches from other searches on the theory that trash is abandoned and therefore not entitled to an expectation of privacy. As the author of the Court's opinion observed last Term, a defendant's "property interest [in trash] does not settle the matter for Fourth Amendment purposes, for the reach of the Fourth Amendment is not determined by state property law." [*California v. Rooney*, 483 U.S. 307, 320 (1987)] (White, J., dissenting).

In evaluating the reasonableness of Greenwood's expectation that his sealed trash bags would not be invaded, the Court has held that we must look to "understandings that are recognized and permitted by society." Most of us, I believe, would be incensed to discover a meddler—whether a neighbor, a reporter, or a detective—scrutinizing our sealed trash containers to discover some detail of our personal lives. That was, quite naturally, the reaction to the sole incident on which the Court bases its conclusion that "snoops" and the like defeat the expectation of privacy in trash. When a tabloid reporter examined then-Secretary of State Henry Kissinger's trash and published his findings, Kissinger was "really revolted" by the intrusion and his wife suffered "grave anguish." N.Y. TIMES, July 9, 1975, p. A1, col. 8. The public response roundly condemning the reporter demonstrates that society not only recognized those reactions as reasonable, but shared them as well. Commentators variously characterized his conduct as "a disgusting invasion of personal privacy," Flieger, *Investigative Trash*, U.S. NEWS & WORLD REPORT, July 28, 1975, p. 72 (editor's page); "indefensible . . . as civilized behavior," WASHINGTON POST, July 10, 1975, A18, col. 1 (editorial); and contrary to "the way decent people behave in relation to each other."

Beyond a generalized expectation of privacy, many municipalities, whether for reasons of privacy, sanitation, or both, reinforce confidence in the integrity of sealed trash containers by "prohibit[ing] anyone, except authorized employees of the Town . . ., to rummage into, pick up, collect, move or otherwise interfere with articles or materials placed on . . . any public street for collection." In fact, the California Constitution, as interpreted by the State's highest court, guarantees a right of privacy in trash vis-à-vis government officials.

That is not to deny that isolated intrusions into opaque, sealed trash containers occur. When, acting on their own, "animals, children, scavengers, snoops, [or] other members of the public," *actually* rummage through a bag of trash and expose its contents to plain view, "police cannot reasonably be expected to avert their eyes from evidence of criminal activity that could have been observed by any member of the public." That much follows from cases like [*United States v. Jacobsen*, 466 U.S. 109, 117, 120 n.17 (1984)] (emphasis added), which held that police may constitutionally inspect a package whose "integrity" a private carrier has *already* "compromised," because "[t]he Fourth Amendment is implicated only if the authorities use information with respect to which the expectation of privacy has not *already* been frustrated;" and *California v. Ciraolo*, 476 U.S. 207, 213–14 (1986) (emphasis added), which held that the Fourth Amendment does not prohibit police from observing what "[a]ny member of the public flying in this airspace who glanced down *could* have seen."

* * *

The mere *possibility* that unwelcome meddlers *might* open and rummage through the containers does not negate the expectation of privacy in their contents any more than the possibility of a burglary negates an expectation of privacy in the home; or the possibility of a private intrusion negates an expectation of privacy in an unopened package; or the possibility that an operator will listen in on a telephone conversation negates an expectation of privacy in the words spoken on the telephone. "What a person . . . seeks to preserve as private, *even in an area accessible to the public*, may be constitutionally protected." *Katz*, 389 U.S., at 351–52. We have therefore repeatedly rejected attempts to justify a State's invasion of privacy on the ground that the privacy is not absolute. As Justice Scalia aptly put it, the Fourth Amendment protects "privacy . . . not solitude." *O'Connor* [*v. Ortega*, 480 U.S. 709, 730 (1987)] (opinion concurring in judgment).

Nor is it dispositive that "respondents placed their refuse at the curb for the express purpose of conveying it to a third party, . . . who might himself have sorted through respondents' trash or permitted others, such as the police, to do so." In the first place, Greenwood can hardly be faulted for leaving trash on his curb when a county ordinance commanded him to do so and prohibited him from disposing of it in any other way. Unlike in other circumstances where privacy is compromised, Greenwood could not "avoid exposing personal belongings . . . by simply leaving them at home." *O'Connor*, at 725. More importantly, even the voluntary relinquishment of possession or control over an effect does not necessarily amount to a relinquishment of a privacy expectation in it. Were it otherwise, a letter or package would lose all Fourth Amendment protection when placed in a mailbox or other depository with the "express purpose" of entrusting it to the postal officer or a private carrier; those bailees are just as likely as trash collectors (and certainly have greater incentive) to "sor[t] through" the personal effects entrusted to them, "or permi[t] others, such as police to do so." Yet, it has been clear for at least 110 years that the possibility of such an intrusion does not justify a warrantless search by police in the first instance.

* * *

Points for Discussion

1. The Court states in *Greenwood* that the police cannot reasonably be expected to avert their eyes from evidence of criminal wrongdoing. Were the actions of the Laguna Beach Police Department here merely a failure to avert their eyes?

2. How appropriate is the "assumption of risk" argument to the facts of Greenwood's case? On the one hand, it seems clear that Greenwood placed his trash on the street where anyone could go through it. On the other, as the dissent points out, this was the only legal way for him to dispose of his trash.

3. Citing *United States v. Jacobsen*, Justice Brennan writes that, if an animal or vandal ripped open Greenwood's garbage bags and spilled their contents into the street, police inspection of the trash would not be a Fourth Amendment search. What difference does it make whether the police open the trash bags or a raccoon does? How does Justice Brennan's position parallel the plurality's in *United States v. White* regarding the use of informants to record conversations?

FLORIDA V. RILEY

488 U.S. 445 (1989)

JUSTICE WHITE announced the judgment of the court and delivered an opinion, in which THE CHIEF JUSTICE, JUSTICE SCALIA, and JUSTICE KENNEDY join.

* * *

Respondent Riley lived in a mobile home located on five acres of rural property. A greenhouse was located 10 to 20 feet behind the mobile home. Two sides of the greenhouse were enclosed. The other two sides were not enclosed but the contents of the greenhouse were obscured from view from surrounding property by trees, shrubs, and the mobile home. The greenhouse was covered by corrugated roofing panels, some translucent and some opaque. At the time relevant to this case, two of the panels, amounting to approximately 10% of the roof area, were missing. A wire fence surrounded the mobile home and the greenhouse, and the property was posted with a "DO NOT ENTER" sign.

This case originated with an anonymous tip to the Pasco County Sheriff's office that marijuana was being grown on respondent's property. When an investigating officer discovered that he could not see the contents of the greenhouse from the road, he circled twice over respondent's property in a helicopter at the height of 400 feet. With his naked eye, he was able to see through the openings in the roof and one or more of the open sides of the greenhouse and to identify what he thought was marijuana growing in the structure. A warrant was obtained based on these observations, and the ensuing search revealed marijuana growing in the greenhouse. Respondent was charged with possession of marijuana under Florida law. The trial court granted his motion to suppress; the Florida Court of Appeals reversed but certified the case to the Florida Supreme Court, which quashed the decision of the Court of Appeals and reinstated the trial court's suppression order.

We agree with the State's submission that our decision in *California v. Ciraolo,* 476 U.S. 207 (1986), controls this case. There, acting on a tip, the police inspected the back-yard of a particular house while flying in a fixed-wing aircraft at 1,000 feet. With the naked eye the officers saw what they concluded was marijuana growing in the yard. A search warrant was obtained on the strength of this airborne inspection, and marijuana plants were found. The trial court refused to suppress this evidence, but a state appellate court held that the inspection violated the Fourth and Fourteenth Amendments to the United States Constitution, and that the warrant was therefore invalid. We in turn reversed, holding that the inspection was not a search subject to the Fourth Amendment. We recognized that the yard was within the curtilage of the house, that a fence shielded the yard from observation from the street, and that the occupant had a subjective expectation of privacy. We held, however, that such an expectation was not reasonable and not one "that society is prepared to honor." Our reasoning was that the home and its curtilage are not necessarily protected from inspection that involves no physical invasion. " 'What a person knowingly exposes to the public, even in his own home or office, is not a subject of Fourth Amendment protection.' " As a general proposition, the police may see what may be seen "from a public vantage point where [they have] a right to be." Thus the police, like the public, would have been free to inspect the backyard garden from the street if their view had been unobstructed. They were likewise free to inspect the yard from the vantage point of an aircraft flying in the navigable airspace as this plane was. "In an age where private and commercial flight in the public airways is routine, it is unreasonable for respondent to expect that his marijuana plants were constitutionally protected from being observed with the naked eye from an altitude of 1,000 feet. The Fourth Amendment simply does not require the police traveling in the public airways at this altitude to obtain a warrant in order to observe what is visible to the naked eye."

We arrive at the same conclusion in the present case. In this case, as in *Ciraolo,* the property surveyed was within the curtilage of respondent's home. Riley no doubt intended and expected that his greenhouse would not be open to public inspection, and the precautions he took protected against ground-level observation. Because the sides and roof of his greenhouse were left partially open, however, what was growing in the greenhouse was subject to viewing from the air. Under the holding in *Ciraolo,* Riley could not reasonably have expected the contents of his greenhouse to be immune from examination by an officer seated in a fixed-wing aircraft flying in navigable airspace at an altitude of 1,000 feet or, as the Florida Supreme Court seemed to recognize, at an altitude of 500 feet, the lower limit of the navigable airspace for such an aircraft. Here, the inspection was made from a helicopter, but as is the case with fixed-wing planes, "private and commercial flight [by helicopter] in the public airways is routine" in this country, *Ciraolo,* 476 U.S., at 215, and there is no indication that such flights are unheard of in Pasco County, Florida. Riley could not reasonably have expected that his greenhouse was protected from public or official observation from a helicopter had it been flying within the navigable airspace for fixed-wing aircraft.

Nor on the facts before us, does it make a difference for Fourth Amendment purposes that the helicopter was flying at 400 feet when the officer saw what was growing in the greenhouse through the partially open roof and sides of the structure. We would have a different case if flying at that altitude had been contrary to law or regulation. But helicopters are not bound by the lower limits of the navigable airspace allowed to other aircraft.[3] Any member of the public could legally have been flying over Riley's property in a helicopter at the altitude of 400 feet and could have observed Riley's greenhouse. The police officer did no more. This is not to say that an inspection of the curtilage of a house from an aircraft will always pass muster under the Fourth Amendment simply because the plane is within the navigable airspace specified by law. But it is of obvious importance that the helicopter in this case was *not* violating the law, and there is nothing in the record or before us to suggest that helicopters flying at 400 feet are sufficiently rare in this country to lend substance to respondent's claim that he reasonably anticipated that his greenhouse would not be subject to observation from that altitude. Neither is there any intimation here that the helicopter interfered with respondent's normal use of the greenhouse or of other parts of the curtilage. As far as this record reveals, no intimate details connected with the use of the home or curtilage were observed, and there was no undue noise, and no wind, dust, or threat of injury. In these circumstances, there was no violation of the Fourth Amendment.

JUSTICE O'CONNOR, concurring in the judgment.

I concur in the judgment reversing the Supreme Court of Florida because I agree that police observation of the greenhouse in Riley's curtilage from a helicopter passing at an altitude of 400 feet did not violate an expectation of privacy "that society is prepared to recognize as 'reasonable.'" *Katz v. United States,* 389 U.S. 347, 361 (1967) (Harlan, J., concurring). I write separately, however, to clarify the standard I believe follows from *California v. Ciraolo,* 476 U.S. 207 (1986). In my view, the plurality's approach rests the scope of Fourth Amendment protection too heavily on compliance with FAA regulations whose purpose is to promote air safety, not to protect "[t]he right of the people to be secure in their persons, houses, papers, and effects, against unreasonable searches and seizures." U.S. Const., Amdt. 4.

* * *

Ciraolo's expectation of privacy was unreasonable not because the airplane was operating where it had a "right to be," but because public air travel at 1,000 feet is a sufficiently routine part of modern life that it is unreasonable for persons on the ground to expect that their curtilage will not be observed from the air at that altitude. Although "helicopters are not bound by the lower limits of the navigable airspace allowed to other aircraft," there is no reason to assume that compliance with FAA

[3] While Federal Aviation Administration regulations permit fixed-wing-aircraft to be operated at an altitude of 1,000 feet while flying over congested areas and at an altitude of 500 feet above the surface in other than congested areas, helicopters may be operated at less than the minimums for fixed-wing-aircraft "if the operation is conducted without hazard to persons or property on the surface. In addition, each person operating a helicopter shall comply with routes or altitudes specifically prescribed for helicopters by the [FAA] Administrator." 14 CFR § 91.79 (1988).

regulations alone determines " 'whether the government's intrusion infringes upon the personal and societal values protected by the Fourth Amendment.' " *Ciraolo,* at 212 (quoting *Oliver v. United States,* 466 U.S. 170, 182–183 (1984)). Because the FAA has decided that helicopters can lawfully operate at virtually any altitude so long as they pose no safety hazard, it does not follow that the expectations of privacy "society is prepared to recognize as 'reasonable' " simply mirror the FAA's safety concerns.

Observations of curtilage from helicopters at very low altitudes are not perfectly analogous to ground-level observations from public roads or sidewalks. While in both cases the police may have a legal right to occupy the physical space from which their observations are made, the two situations are not necessarily comparable in terms of whether expectations of privacy from such vantage points should be considered reasonable. Public roads, even those less traveled by, are clearly demarked public thoroughfares. Individuals who seek privacy can take precautions, tailored to the location of the road, to avoid disclosing private activities to those who pass by. They can build a tall fence, for example, and thus ensure private enjoyment of the curtilage without risking public observation from the road or sidewalk. If they do not take such precautions, they cannot reasonably expect privacy from public observation. In contrast, even individuals who have taken effective precautions to ensure against ground-level observations cannot block off all conceivable aerial views of their outdoor patios and yards without entirely giving up their enjoyment of those areas. To require individuals to completely cover and enclose their curtilage is to demand more than the "precautions customarily taken by those seeking privacy." The fact that a helicopter could conceivably observe the curtilage at virtually any altitude or angle, without violating FAA regulations, does not in itself mean that an individual has no reasonable expectation of privacy from such observation.

In determining whether Riley had a reasonable expectation of privacy from aerial observation, the relevant inquiry after *Ciraolo* is not whether the helicopter was where it had a right to be under FAA regulations. Rather, consistent with *Katz,* we must ask whether the helicopter was in the public airways at an altitude at which members of the public travel with sufficient regularity that Riley's expectation of privacy from aerial observation was not "one that society is prepared to recognize as 'reasonable.' " Thus, in determining "whether the government's intrusion infringes upon the personal and societal values protected by the Fourth Amendment," it is not conclusive to observe, as the plurality does, that "[a]ny member of the public could legally have been flying over Riley's property in a helicopter at the altitude of 400 feet and could have observed Riley's greenhouse." Nor is it conclusive that police helicopters may often fly at 400 feet. If the public rarely, if ever, travels overhead at such altitudes, the observation cannot be said to be from a vantage point generally used by the public and Riley cannot be said to have "knowingly expose[d]" his greenhouse to public view. However, if the public can generally be expected to travel over residential backyards at an altitude of 400 feet, Riley cannot reasonably expect his curtilage to be free from such aerial observation.

In my view, the defendant must bear the burden of proving that his expectation of privacy was a reasonable one, and thus that a "search" within the meaning of the Fourth Amendment even took place.

Because there is reason to believe that there is considerable public use of airspace at altitudes of 400 feet and above, and because Riley introduced no evidence to the contrary before the Florida courts, I conclude that Riley's expectation that his curtilage was protected from naked-eye aerial observation from that altitude was not a reasonable one. However, public use of altitudes lower than that—particularly public observations from helicopters circling over the curtilage of a home—may be sufficiently rare that police surveillance from such altitudes would violate reasonable expectations of privacy, despite compliance with FAA air safety regulations.

JUSTICE BRENNAN, with whom JUSTICE MARSHALL and JUSTICE STEVENS, join, dissenting.

The Court holds today that police officers need not obtain a warrant based on probable cause before circling in a helicopter 400 feet above a home in order to investigate what is taking place behind the walls of the curtilage. I cannot agree that the Fourth Amendment to the Constitution, which safeguards "[t]he right of the people to be secure in their persons, houses, papers, and effects, against unreasonable searches and seizures," tolerates such an intrusion on privacy and personal security.

I

* * *

I agree, of course, that "[w]hat a person knowingly exposes to the public . . . is not a subject of Fourth Amendment protection." But I cannot agree that one "knowingly exposes [an area] to the public" solely because a helicopter may legally fly above it. Under the plurality's exceedingly grudging Fourth Amendment theory, the expectation of privacy is defeated if a single member of the public could conceivably position herself to see into the area in question without doing anything illegal. It is defeated whatever the difficulty a person would have in so positioning herself, and however infrequently anyone would in fact do so. In taking this view the plurality ignores the very essence of *Katz*. The reason why there is no reasonable expectation of privacy in an area that is exposed to the public is that little diminution in "the amount of privacy and freedom remaining to citizens" will result from police surveillance of something that any passerby readily sees. To pretend, as the plurality opinion does, that the same is true when the police use a helicopter to peer over high fences is, at best, disingenuous. Notwithstanding the plurality's statistics about the number of helicopters registered in this country, can it seriously be questioned that Riley enjoyed virtually complete privacy in his backyard greenhouse, and that that privacy was invaded solely by police helicopter surveillance? Is the theoretical possibility that any member of the public (with sufficient means) could also have hired a helicopter and looked over Riley's fence of any relevance at all in determining whether Riley suffered a serious loss of privacy and personal security through the police action?

* * *

It is a curious notion that the reach of the Fourth Amendment can be so largely defined by administrative regulations issued for purposes of flight safety. It is more curious still that the plurality relies to such an extent on the legality of the officer's act, when we have consistently refused to equate police violation of the law with infringement of the Fourth Amendment. But the plurality's willingness to end its inquiry when it finds that the officer was in a position he had a right to be in is misguided for an even more fundamental reason. Finding determinative the fact that the officer was where he had a right to be is, at bottom, an attempt to analogize surveillance from a helicopter to surveillance by a police officer standing on a public road and viewing evidence of crime through an open window or a gap in a fence. In such a situation, the occupant of the home may be said to lack any reasonable expectation of privacy in what can be seen from that road—even if, in fact, people rarely pass that way.

The police officer positioned 400 feet above Riley's backyard was not, however, standing on a public road. The vantage point he enjoyed was not one any citizen could readily share. His ability to see over Riley's fence depended on his use of a very expensive and sophisticated piece of machinery to which few ordinary citizens have access. In such circumstances it makes no more sense to rely on the legality of the officer's position in the skies than it would to judge the constitutionality of the wiretap in *Katz* by the legality of the officer's position outside the telephone booth. The simple inquiry whether the police officer had the legal right to be in the position from which he made his observations cannot suffice, for we cannot assume that Riley's curtilage was so open to the observations of passersby in the skies that he retained little privacy or personal security to be lost to police surveillance. The question before us must be not whether the police were where they had a right to be, but whether public observation of Riley's curtilage was so commonplace that Riley's expectation of privacy in his backyard could not be considered reasonable. To say that an invasion of Riley's privacy from the skies was not impossible is most emphatically not the same as saying that his expectation of privacy within his enclosed curtilage was not "one that society is prepared to recognize as 'reasonable.'" *Katz,* 389 U.S., at 361 (Harlan, J., concurring).

While, as we held in *Ciraolo,* air traffic at elevations of 1,000 feet or more may be so common that whatever could be seen with the naked eye from that elevation is unprotected by the Fourth Amendment, it is a large step from there to say that the Amendment offers no protection against low-level helicopter surveillance of enclosed curtilage areas. To take this step is error enough. That the plurality does so with little analysis beyond its determination that the police complied with FAA regulations is particularly unfortunate.

II

Equally disconcerting is the lack of any meaningful limit to the plurality's holding. It is worth reiterating that the FAA regulations the plurality relies on as establishing that the officer was where he had a right to be set no minimum flight altitude for helicopters. It is difficult, therefore, to see what, if any, helicopter surveillance would run afoul of the plurality's rule that there exists no reasonable expectation of privacy as long as the helicopter is where it has a right to be.

* * *

III

Perhaps the most remarkable passage in the plurality opinion is its suggestion that the case might be a different one had any "intimate details connected with the use of the home or curtilage [been] observed." What, one wonders, is meant by "intimate details"? If the police had observed Riley embracing his wife in the backyard greenhouse, would we then say that his reasonable expectation of privacy had been infringed? Where in the Fourth Amendment or in our cases is there any warrant for imposing a requirement that the activity observed must be "intimate" in order to be protected by the Constitution?

It is difficult to avoid the conclusion that the plurality has allowed its analysis of Riley's expectation of privacy to be colored by its distaste for the activity in which he was engaged. It is indeed easy to forget, especially in view of current concern over drug trafficking, that the scope of the Fourth Amendment's protection does not turn on whether the activity disclosed by a search is illegal or innocuous. But we dismiss this as a "drug case" only at the peril of our own liberties. Justice Frankfurter once noted that "[i]t is a fair summary of history to say that the safeguards of liberty have frequently been forged in controversies involving not very nice people," *United States v. Rabinowitz,* 339 U.S. 56, 69 (1950) (dissenting opinion), and nowhere is this observation more apt than in the area of the Fourth Amendment, whose words have necessarily been given meaning largely through decisions suppressing evidence of criminal activity. The principle enunciated in this case determines what limits the Fourth Amendment imposes on aerial surveillance of any person, for any reason. If the Constitution does not protect Riley's marijuana garden against such surveillance, it is hard to see how it will prohibit the government from aerial spying on the activities of a law-abiding citizen on her fully enclosed outdoor patio. As Professor Amsterdam has eloquently written: "The question is not whether you or I must draw the blinds before we commit a crime. It is whether you and I must discipline ourselves to draw the blinds every time we enter a room, under pain of surveillance if we do not."

* * *

V

The issue in this case is, ultimately, "how tightly the Fourth Amendment permits people to be driven back into the recesses of their lives by the risk of surveillance." Amsterdam, at 402. The Court today approves warrantless helicopter surveillance from an altitude of 400 feet. While Justice O'Connor's opinion gives reason to hope that this altitude may constitute a lower limit, I find considerable cause for concern in the fact that a plurality of four Justices would remove virtually all constitutional barriers to police surveillance from the vantage point of helicopters. The Fourth Amendment demands that we temper our efforts to apprehend criminals with a concern for the impact on our fundamental liberties of the methods we use. I hope it will be a matter of concern to my colleagues that the police surveillance methods they would sanction were among those described 40 years ago in George Orwell's dread vision of life in the 1980's:

> The black-mustachio'd face gazed down from every commanding corner. There was one on the house front immediately opposite. BIG BROTHER IS WATCHING YOU, the caption said. . . . In the far distance a helicopter skimmed down between the roofs, hovered for an instant like a bluebottle, and darted away again with a curving flight. It was the Police Patrol, snooping into people's windows.

NINETEEN EIGHTY-FOUR 4 (1949).

Who can read this passage without a shudder, and without the instinctive reaction that it depicts life in some country other than ours? I respectfully dissent.

JUSTICE BLACKMUN, dissenting.

The question before the Court is whether the helicopter surveillance over Riley's property constituted a "search" within the meaning of the Fourth Amendment. Like Justice Brennan, Justice Marshall, Justice Stevens, and Justice O'Connor, I believe that answering this question depends upon whether Riley has a "reasonable expectation of privacy" that no such surveillance would occur, and does not depend upon the fact that the helicopter was flying at a lawful altitude under FAA regulations. A majority of this Court thus agrees to at least this much.

The inquiry then becomes how to determine whether Riley's expectation was a reasonable one. Justice Brennan, the two Justices who have joined him, and Justice O'Connor all believe that the reasonableness of Riley's expectation depends, in large measure, on the frequency of nonpolice helicopter flights at an altitude of 400 feet. Again, I agree.

* * *

. . . In the absence of precedent on the point, it is appropriate for us to take into account our estimation of the frequency of nonpolice helicopter flights. Thus, because I believe that private helicopters rarely fly over curtilages at an altitude of 400 feet, I would impose upon the prosecution the burden of proving contrary facts necessary to show that Riley lacked a reasonable expectation of privacy. Indeed, I would establish this burden of proof for any helicopter surveillance case in which the flight occurred below 1,000 feet—in other words, for any aerial surveillance case not governed by the Court's decision in *California v. Ciraolo,* 476 U.S. 207 (1986).

* * *

Points for Discussion

1. In *California v. Ciraolo* the Supreme Court held that observation from a plane flying within FAA-approved airspace was not a search for Fourth Amendment purposes. The plurality seems convinced that that holding disposes of Riley's claim. Why does this position not command a majority of the Court?

2. Justice Blackmun would require the government to prove not just that members of the public could do what the police did, but that they do so regularly enough that the defendant cannot claim a reasonable expectation of privacy. Is this a sensible approach to the *Katz* framework? How might it affect the result in *White*? In *Greenwood*? In *Oliver*?

3. The principal dissent quotes from George Orwell's cautionary novel, *Nineteen Eighty-Four*. Is that mere hyperbole here, or does the use of helicopters to view private property signal a significant change in the balance between privacy and government power?

CARPENTER V. UNITED STATES

138 S.Ct. 2206 (2018)

CHIEF JUSTICE ROBERTS delivered the opinion of the court.

This case presents the question whether the Government conducts a search under the Fourth Amendment when it accesses historical cell phone records that provide a comprehensive chronicle of the user's past movements.

I

A

There are 396 million cell phone service accounts in the United States—for a Nation of 326 million people. Cell phones perform their wide and growing variety of functions by connecting to a set of radio antennas called "cell sites." Although cell sites are usually mounted on a tower, they can also be found on light posts, flagpoles, church steeples, or the sides of buildings. Cell sites typically have several directional antennas that divide the covered area into sectors.

Cell phones continuously scan their environment looking for the best signal, which generally comes from the closest cell site. Most modern devices, such as smartphones, tap into the wireless network several times a minute whenever their signal is on, even if the owner is not using one of the phone's features. Each time the phone connects to a cell site, it generates a time-stamped record known as cell-site location information (CSLI). The precision of this information depends on the size of the geographic area covered by the cell site. The greater the concentration of cell sites, the smaller the coverage area. As data usage from cell phones has increased, wireless carriers have installed more cell sites to handle the traffic. That has led to increasingly compact coverage areas, especially in urban areas.

Wireless carriers collect and store CSLI for their own business purposes, including finding weak spots in their network and applying "roaming" charges when another carrier routes data through their cell sites. In addition, wireless carriers often sell aggregated location records to data brokers, without individual identifying information of the sort at issue here. While carriers have long retained CSLI for the start and end of incoming calls, in recent years phone companies have also collected location information from the transmission of text messages and routine data connections. Accordingly, modern cell phones generate increasingly vast amounts of increasingly precise CSLI.

B

In 2011, police officers arrested four men suspected of robbing a series of Radio Shack and (ironically enough) T-Mobile stores in Detroit. One of the men confessed that, over the previous four months, the group (along with a rotating cast of getaway drivers and lookouts) had robbed nine different stores in Michigan and Ohio. The suspect identified 15 accomplices who had participated in the heists and gave the FBI some of their cell phone numbers; the FBI then reviewed his call records to identify additional numbers that he had called around the time of the robberies.

Based on that information, the prosecutors applied for court orders under the Stored Communications Act to obtain cell phone records for petitioner Timothy Carpenter and several other suspects. That statute, as amended in 1994, permits the Government to compel the disclosure of certain telecommunications records when it "offers specific and articulable facts showing that there are reasonable grounds to believe" that the records sought "are relevant and material to an ongoing criminal investigation." 18 U.S.C. § 2703(d). Federal Magistrate Judges issued two orders directing Carpenter's wireless carriers—MetroPCS and Sprint—to disclose "cell/site sector information for Carpenter's telephone at call origination and at call termination for incoming and outgoing calls" during the four-month period when the string of robberies occurred. The first order sought 152 days of cell-site records from MetroPCS, which produced records spanning 127 days. The second order requested seven days of CSLI from Sprint, which produced two days of records covering the period when Carpenter's phone was "roaming" in northeastern Ohio. Altogether the Government obtained 12,898 location points cataloging Carpenter's movements—an average of 101 data points per day.

Carpenter was charged with six counts of robbery and an additional six counts of carrying a firearm during a federal crime of violence. Prior to trial, Carpenter moved to suppress the cell-site data provided by the wireless carriers. He argued that the Government's seizure of the records violated the Fourth Amendment because they had been obtained without a warrant supported by probable cause. The District Court denied the motion.

At trial, seven of Carpenter's confederates pegged him as the leader of the operation. In addition, FBI agent Christopher Hess offered expert testimony about the cell-site data. Hess explained that each time a cell phone taps into the wireless network, the carrier logs a time-stamped record of the cell site and particular sector that were used. With this information, Hess produced maps that placed Carpenter's phone near four of the charged robberies. In the Government's view, the location records clinched the case: They confirmed that Carpenter was "right where the . . . robbery was at the exact time of the robbery." Carpenter was convicted on all but one of the firearm counts and sentenced to more than 100 years in prison.

The Court of Appeals for the Sixth Circuit affirmed. The court held that Carpenter lacked a reasonable expectation of privacy in the location information collected by the FBI because he had shared that information with his wireless carriers. Given that cell phone users voluntarily convey cell-site data to their carriers as "a means of establishing communication," the court concluded that the resulting business records are not entitled to Fourth Amendment protection.

We granted certiorari.

II

* * *

B

The case before us involves the Government's acquisition of wireless carrier cell-site records revealing the location of Carpenter's cell phone whenever it made or received calls. This sort of digital data—personal location information maintained by a third party—does not fit neatly under existing precedents. Instead, requests for cell-site records lie at the intersection of two lines of cases, both of which inform our understanding of the privacy interests at stake.

The first set of cases addresses a person's expectation of privacy in his physical location and movements. In *United States v. Knotts*, 460 U.S. 276 (1983), we considered the Government's use of a "beeper" to aid in tracking a vehicle through traffic. Police officers in that case planted a beeper in a container of chloroform before it was purchased by one of Knotts's co-conspirators. The officers (with intermittent aerial assistance) then followed the automobile carrying the container from Minneapolis to Knotts's cabin in Wisconsin, relying on the beeper's signal to help keep the vehicle in view. The Court concluded that the "augment[ed]" visual surveillance did not constitute a search because "[a] person traveling in an automobile on public thoroughfares has no reasonable expectation of privacy in his movements from one place to another." Since the movements of the vehicle and its final destination had been "voluntarily conveyed to anyone who wanted to look," Knotts could not assert a privacy interest in the information obtained.

This Court in *Knotts*, however, was careful to distinguish between the rudimentary tracking facilitated by the beeper and more sweeping modes of surveillance. The Court emphasized the "limited use which the government made of the signals from this particular beeper" during a discrete "automotive journey." Significantly, the Court reserved the question whether "different constitutional principles may be applicable" if "twenty-four hour surveillance of any citizen of this country [were] possible."

Three decades later, the Court considered more sophisticated surveillance of the sort envisioned in *Knotts* and found that different principles did indeed apply. In *United States v. Jones*, FBI agents installed a GPS tracking device on Jones's vehicle and remotely monitored the vehicle's movements for 28 days. The Court decided the case based on the Government's physical trespass of the vehicle. At the same time, five Justices agreed that related privacy concerns would be raised by, for example, "surreptitiously activating a stolen vehicle detection system" in Jones's car to track Jones himself, or conducting GPS tracking of his cell phone. Since GPS monitoring of a vehicle tracks "every movement" a person makes in that vehicle, the concurring Justices concluded that "longer term GPS monitoring in investigations of most offenses impinges on expectations of privacy"—regardless whether those movements were disclosed to the public at large.

In a second set of decisions, the Court has drawn a line between what a person keeps to himself and what he shares with others. We have previously held that "a person has no legitimate expectation of privacy in information he voluntarily turns over to third parties." [*Smith v. Maryland*, 442 U.S. 735, 743–44 (1979)]. That remains true "even if the information is revealed on the assumption that it will be used only for a limited purpose." *United States v. Miller*, 425 U.S. 435, 443 (1976). As a result, the Government is typically free to obtain such information from the recipient without triggering Fourth Amendment protections.

This third-party doctrine largely traces its roots to *Miller*. While investigating Miller for tax evasion, the Government subpoenaed his banks, seeking several months of canceled checks, deposit slips, and monthly statements. The Court rejected a Fourth Amendment challenge to the records collection. For one, Miller could "assert neither ownership nor possession" of the documents; they were "business records of the banks." For another, the nature of those records confirmed Miller's limited expectation of privacy, because the checks were "not confidential communications but negotiable instruments to be used in commercial transactions," and the bank statements contained information "exposed to [bank] employees in the ordinary course of business." The Court thus concluded that Miller had "take[n] the risk, in revealing his affairs to another, that the information [would] be conveyed by that person to the Government."

Three years later, *Smith* applied the same principles in the context of information conveyed to a telephone company. The Court ruled that the Government's use of a pen register—a device that recorded the outgoing phone numbers dialed on a landline telephone—was not a search. Noting the pen register's "limited capabilities," the Court "doubt[ed] that people in general entertain any actual expectation of privacy in the numbers they dial." Telephone subscribers know, after all, that the numbers are used by the telephone company "for a variety of legitimate business purposes," including routing calls. And at any rate, the Court explained, such an expectation "is not one that society is prepared to recognize as reasonable." When Smith placed a call, he "voluntarily conveyed" the dialed numbers to the phone company by "expos[ing] that information to its equipment in the ordinary course of business." Once again, we held that the defendant "assumed the risk" that the company's records "would be divulged to police."

III

The question we confront today is how to apply the Fourth Amendment to a new phenomenon: the ability to chronicle a person's past movements through the record of his cell phone signals. Such tracking partakes of many of the qualities of the GPS monitoring we considered in *Jones*. Much like GPS tracking of a vehicle, cell phone location information is detailed, encyclopedic, and effortlessly compiled.

At the same time, the fact that the individual continuously reveals his location to his wireless carrier implicates the third-party principle of *Smith* and *Miller*. But while the third-party doctrine applies to telephone numbers and bank records, it is not clear whether its logic extends to the qualitatively different category of cell-site records. After all, when *Smith* was decided in 1979, few could have imagined a society in which a phone goes wherever its owner goes, conveying to the wireless carrier not just dialed digits, but a detailed and comprehensive record of the person's movements.

We decline to extend *Smith* and *Miller* to cover these novel circumstances. Given the unique nature of cell phone location records, the fact that the information is held by a third party does not by itself overcome the user's claim to Fourth Amendment protection. Whether the Government employs its own surveillance technology as in *Jones* or leverages the technology of a wireless carrier, we hold that an individual maintains a legitimate expectation of privacy in the record of his physical movements as captured through CSLI. The location information obtained from Carpenter's wireless carriers was the product of a search.[3]

A

A person does not surrender all Fourth Amendment protection by venturing into the public sphere. To the contrary, "what [one] seeks to preserve as private, even in an area accessible to the public, may be constitutionally protected." *Katz*, 389 U.S., at 351–352. A majority of this Court has already recognized that individuals have a reasonable expectation of privacy in the whole of their physical movements. *Jones*, 565 U.S., at 430 (Alito, J., concurring in judgment); *id.*, at 415 (Sotomayor, J., concurring). Prior to the digital age, law enforcement might have pursued a suspect for a brief stretch, but doing so "for any extended period of time was difficult and costly and therefore rarely undertaken." *Id.*, at 429 (opinion of Alito, J.). For that reason, "society's expectation has been that

[3] The parties suggest as an alternative to their primary submissions that the acquisition of CSLI becomes a search only if it extends beyond a limited period. As part of its argument, the Government treats the seven days of CSLI requested from Sprint as the pertinent period, even though Sprint produced only two days of records. Contrary to Justice Kennedy's assertion, we need not decide whether there is a limited period for which the Government may obtain an individual's historical CSLI free from Fourth Amendment scrutiny, and if so, how long that period might be. It is sufficient for our purposes today to hold that accessing seven days of CSLI constitutes a Fourth Amendment search.

law enforcement agents and others would not—and indeed, in the main, simply could not—secretly monitor and catalogue every single movement of an individual's car for a very long period." *Id.*, at 430.

Allowing government access to cell-site records contravenes that expectation. Although such records are generated for commercial purposes, that distinction does not negate Carpenter's anticipation of privacy in his physical location. Mapping a cell phone's location over the course of 127 days provides an all-encompassing record of the holder's whereabouts. As with GPS information, the time-stamped data provides an intimate window into a person's life, revealing not only his particular movements, but through them his "familial, political, professional, religious, and sexual associations." *Id.*, at 415 (opinion of Sotomayor, J.). These location records "hold for many Americans the 'privacies of life.' " And like GPS monitoring, cell phone tracking is remarkably easy, cheap, and efficient compared to traditional investigative tools. With just the click of a button, the Government can access each carrier's deep repository of historical location information at practically no expense.

* * *

Moreover, the retrospective quality of the data here gives police access to a category of information otherwise unknowable. In the past, attempts to reconstruct a person's movements were limited by a dearth of records and the frailties of recollection. With access to CSLI, the Government can now travel back in time to retrace a person's whereabouts, subject only to the retention polices of the wireless carriers, which currently maintain records for up to five years. Critically, because location information is continually logged for all of the 400 million devices in the United States—not just those belonging to persons who might happen to come under investigation—this newfound tracking capacity runs against everyone. Unlike with the GPS device in *Jones*, police need not even know in advance whether they want to follow a particular individual, or when.

Whoever the suspect turns out to be, he has effectively been tailed every moment of every day for five years, and the police may—in the Government's view—call upon the results of that surveillance without regard to the constraints of the Fourth Amendment. Only the few without cell phones could escape this tireless and absolute surveillance.

The Government and Justice Kennedy contend, however, that the collection of CSLI should be permitted because the data is less precise than GPS information. Not to worry, they maintain, because the location records did "not on their own suffice to place [Carpenter] at the crime scene"; they placed him within a wedge-shaped sector ranging from one-eighth to four square miles. Yet the Court has already rejected the proposition that "inference insulates a search." [*Kyllo v. United States*, 533 U.S. 27, 36 (2001)]. From the 127 days of location data it received, the Government could, in combination with other information, deduce a detailed log of Carpenter's movements, including when he was at the site of the robberies. And the Government thought the CSLI accurate enough to highlight it during the closing argument of his trial.

At any rate, the rule the Court adopts "must take account of more sophisticated systems that are already in use or in development." *Kyllo*, 533 U.S., at 36. While the records in this case reflect the state of technology at the start of the decade, the accuracy of CSLI is rapidly approaching GPS-level precision. As the number of cell sites has proliferated, the geographic area covered by each cell sector has shrunk, particularly in urban areas. In addition, with new technology measuring the time and angle of signals hitting their towers, wireless carriers already have the capability to pinpoint a phone's location within 50 meters.

Accordingly, when the Government accessed CSLI from the wireless carriers, it invaded Carpenter's reasonable expectation of privacy in the whole of his physical movements.

B

The Government's primary contention to the contrary is that the third-party doctrine governs this case. In its view, cell-site records are fair game because they are "business records" created and maintained by the wireless carriers. The Government (along with Justice Kennedy) recognizes that this case features new technology, but asserts that the legal question nonetheless turns on a garden-variety request for information from a third-party witness.

The Government's position fails to contend with the seismic shifts in digital technology that made possible the tracking of not only Carpenter's location but also everyone else's, not for a short period but for years and years. Sprint Corporation and its competitors are not your typical witnesses. Unlike the nosy neighbor who keeps an eye on comings and goings, they are ever alert, and their memory is nearly infallible. There is a world of difference between the limited types of personal information addressed in *Smith* and *Miller* and the exhaustive chronicle of location information casually collected by wireless carriers today. The Government thus is not asking for a straightforward application of the third-party doctrine, but instead a significant extension of it to a distinct category of information.

The third-party doctrine partly stems from the notion that an individual has a reduced expectation of privacy in information knowingly shared with another. But the fact of "diminished privacy interests does not mean that the Fourth Amendment falls out of the picture entirely." [*Riley v. California*, 134 S.Ct. 2473, 2494 (2014)]. *Smith* and *Miller*, after all, did not rely solely on the act of sharing. Instead, they considered "the nature of the particular documents sought" to determine whether "there is a legitimate 'expectation of privacy' concerning their contents." *Miller*, 425 U.S., at 442. *Smith* pointed out the limited capabilities of a pen register; as explained in *Riley*, telephone call logs reveal little in the way of "identifying information." *Miller* likewise noted that checks were "not confidential communications but negotiable instruments to be used in commercial transactions." 425 U.S., at 442. In mechanically applying the third-party doctrine to this case, the Government fails to appreciate that there are no comparable limitations on the revealing nature of CSLI.

The Court has in fact already shown special solicitude for location information in the third-party context. In *Knotts*, the Court relied on *Smith* to hold that an individual has no reasonable expectation of privacy in public movements that he "voluntarily conveyed to anyone who wanted to look." But when confronted with more pervasive tracking, five Justices agreed that longer term GPS monitoring of even a vehicle traveling on public streets constitutes a search. Justice Gorsuch wonders why "someone's location when using a phone" is sensitive, and Justice Kennedy assumes that a person's discrete movements "are not particularly private." Yet this case is not about "using a phone" or a person's movement at a particular time. It is about a detailed chronicle of a person's physical presence compiled every day, every moment, over several years. Such a chronicle implicates privacy concerns far beyond those considered in *Smith* and *Miller*.

Neither does the second rationale underlying the third-party doctrine—voluntary exposure—hold up when it comes to CSLI. Cell phone location information is not truly "shared" as one normally understands the term. In the first place, cell phones and the services they provide are "such a pervasive and insistent part of daily life" that carrying one is indispensable to participation in modern society. *Riley*, 134 S.Ct., at 2484. Second, a cell phone logs a cell-site record by dint of its operation, without any affirmative act on the part of the user beyond powering up. Virtually any activity on the phone generates CSLI, including incoming calls, texts, or e-mails and countless other data connections that a phone automatically makes when checking for news, weather, or social media updates. Apart from disconnecting the phone from the network, there is no way to avoid leaving behind a trail of location data. As a result, in no meaningful sense does the user voluntarily "assume the risk" of turning over a comprehensive dossier of his physical movements.

We therefore decline to extend *Smith* and *Miller* to the collection of CSLI. Given the unique nature of cell phone location information, the fact that the Government obtained the information from a third party does not overcome Carpenter's claim to Fourth Amendment protection. The Government's acquisition of the cell-site records was a search within the meaning of the Fourth Amendment.

* * *

Our decision today is a narrow one. We do not express a view on matters not before us: real-time CSLI or "tower dumps" (a download of information on all the devices that connected to a particular cell site during a particular interval). We do not disturb the application of *Smith* and *Miller* or call into question conventional surveillance techniques and tools, such as security cameras. Nor do we address other business records that might incidentally reveal location information. Further, our opinion does not consider other collection techniques involving foreign affairs or national security. As Justice Frankfurter noted when considering new innovations in airplanes and radios, the Court must tread carefully in such cases, to ensure that we do not "embarrass the future." *Northwest Airlines, Inc. v. Minnesota*, 322 U.S. 292, 300 (1944).

IV

Having found that the acquisition of Carpenter's CSLI was a search, we also conclude that the Government must generally obtain a warrant supported by probable cause before acquiring such records. Although the "ultimate measure of the constitutionality of a governmental search is 'reasonableness,'" our cases establish that warrantless searches are typically unreasonable where "a search is undertaken by law enforcement officials to discover evidence of criminal wrongdoing." *Vernonia School Dist. 47J v. Acton*, 515 U.S. 646, 652–53 (1995). Thus, "in the absence of a warrant, a search is reasonable only if it falls within a specific exception to the warrant requirement." *Riley*, 134 S.Ct., at 2482.

The Government acquired the cell-site records pursuant to a court order issued under the Stored Communications Act, which required the Government to show "reasonable grounds" for believing that the records were "relevant and material to an ongoing investigation." 18 U.S.C. § 2703(d). That showing falls well short of the probable cause required for a warrant. The Court usually requires "some quantum of individualized suspicion" before a search or seizure may take place. *United States v. Martinez-Fuerte*, 428 U.S. 543, 560–61 (1976). Under the standard in the Stored Communications Act, however, law enforcement need only show that the cell-site evidence might be pertinent to an ongoing investigation—a "gigantic" departure from the probable cause rule, as the Government explained below. Consequently, an order issued under Section 2703(d) of the Act is not a permissible mechanism for accessing historical cell-site records. Before compelling a wireless carrier to turn over a subscriber's CSLI, the Government's obligation is a familiar one—get a warrant.

* * *

JUSTICE KENNEDY, with whom JUSTICE THOMAS and JUSTICE ALITO join, dissenting.

* * *

The new rule the Court seems to formulate puts needed, reasonable, accepted, lawful, and congressionally authorized criminal investigations at serious risk in serious cases, often when law enforcement seeks to prevent the threat of violent crimes. And it places undue restrictions on the lawful and necessary enforcement powers exercised not only by the Federal Government, but also by law enforcement in every State and locality throughout the Nation. Adherence to this Court's longstanding precedents and analytic framework would have been the proper and prudent way to resolve this case.

The Court has twice held that individuals have no Fourth Amendment interests in business records which are possessed, owned, and controlled by a third party. *United States v. Miller*, 425 U.S. 435 (1976); *Smith v. Maryland*, 442 U.S. 735 (1979). This is true even when the records contain personal and sensitive information. So when the Government uses a subpoena to obtain, for example, bank records, telephone records, and credit card statements from the businesses that create and keep these records, the Government does not engage in a search of the business's customers within the meaning of the Fourth Amendment.

In this case petitioner challenges the Government's right to use compulsory process to obtain a now-common kind of business record: cell-site records held by cell phone service providers. The Government acquired the records through an investigative process enacted by Congress. Upon approval by a neutral magistrate, and based on the Government's duty to show reasonable necessity, it authorizes the disclosure of records and information that are under the control and ownership of the cell phone service provider, not its customer. Petitioner acknowledges that the Government may obtain a wide variety of business records using compulsory process, and he does not ask the Court to revisit its precedents. Yet he argues that, under those same precedents, the Government searched his records when it used court-approved compulsory process to obtain the cell-site information at issue here.

Cell-site records, however, are no different from the many other kinds of business records the Government has a lawful right to obtain by compulsory process. Customers like petitioner do not own, possess, control, or use the records, and for that reason have no reasonable expectation that they cannot be disclosed pursuant to lawful compulsory process.

. . .

In concluding that the Government engaged in a search, the Court unhinges Fourth Amendment doctrine from the property-based concepts that have long grounded the analytic framework that pertains in these cases. In doing so it draws an unprincipled and unworkable line between cell-site records on the one hand and financial and telephonic records on the other. According to today's majority opinion, the Government can acquire a record of every credit card purchase and phone call a person makes over months or years without upsetting a legitimate expectation of privacy. But, in the Court's view, the Government crosses a constitutional line when it obtains a court's approval to issue a subpoena for more than six days of cell-site records in order to determine whether a person was within several hundred city blocks of a crime scene. That distinction is illogical and will frustrate principled application of the Fourth Amendment in many routine yet vital law enforcement operations.

* * *

II

* * *

Here the only question necessary to decide is whether the Government searched anything of Carpenter's when it used compulsory process to obtain cell-site records from Carpenter's cell phone service providers. This Court's decisions in *Miller* and *Smith* dictate that the answer is no, as every Court of Appeals to have considered the question has recognized.

A

Miller and *Smith* hold that individuals lack any protected Fourth Amendment interests in records that are possessed, owned, and controlled only by a third party. In *Miller* federal law enforcement officers obtained four months of the defendant's banking records. And in *Smith* state police obtained records of the phone numbers dialed from the defendant's home phone. The Court held in both cases that the officers did not search anything belonging to the defendants within the meaning of the Fourth Amendment. The defendants could "assert neither ownership nor possession" of the records because the records were created, owned, and controlled by the companies. And the defendants had no reasonable expectation of privacy in information they "voluntarily conveyed to the [companies] and exposed to their employees in the ordinary course of business." Rather, the defendants "assumed the risk that the information would be divulged to police."

Miller and *Smith* have been criticized as being based on too narrow a view of reasonable expectations of privacy. Those criticisms, however, are unwarranted. The principle established in *Miller* and *Smith* is correct for two reasons, the first relating to a defendant's attenuated interest in property owned by another, and the second relating to the safeguards inherent in the use of compulsory process.

* * *

Miller and *Smith* set forth an important and necessary limitation on the *Katz* framework. They rest upon the commonsense principle that the absence of property law analogues can be dispositive of privacy expectations. The defendants in those cases could expect that the third-party businesses could use the records the companies collected, stored, and classified as their own for any number of business and commercial purposes. The businesses were not bailees or custodians of the records, with a duty to hold the records for the defendants' use. The defendants could make no argument that the records were their own papers or effects. The records were the business entities' records, plain and simple. The defendants had no reason to believe the records were owned or controlled by them and so could not assert a reasonable expectation of privacy in the records.

* * *

B

* * *

Carpenter argues that he has Fourth Amendment interests in the cell-site records because they are in essence his personal papers by operation of 47 U.S.C. § 222. That statute imposes certain restrictions on how providers may use "customer proprietary network information"—a term that encompasses cell-site records. §§ 222(c), (h)(1)(A). The statute in general prohibits providers from disclosing personally identifiable cell-site records to private third parties. And it allows customers to request cell-site records from the provider.

Carpenter's argument is unpersuasive, however, for § 222 does not grant cell phone customers any meaningful interest in cell-site records. The statute's confidentiality protections may be overridden by the interests of the providers or the Government. The providers may disclose the records "to protect the[ir] rights or property" or to "initiate, render, bill, and collect for telecommunications services." They also may disclose the records "as required by law"—which, of course, is how they were disclosed in this case. Nor does the statute provide customers any practical control over the records. Customers do not create the records; they have no say in whether or for how long the records are stored; and they cannot require the records to be modified or destroyed. Even their right to request access to the records is limited, for the statute "does not preclude a carrier from being reimbursed by the customers . . . for the costs associated with making such disclosures." H.R.Rep. No. 104–204, pt. 1, p. 90 (1995). So in every legal and practical sense the "network information" regulated by § 222 is, under that statute, "proprietary" to the service providers, not Carpenter. The Court does not argue otherwise.

Because Carpenter lacks a requisite connection to the cell-site records, he also may not claim a reasonable expectation of privacy in them. He could expect that a third party—the cell phone service provider—could use the information it collected, stored, and classified as its own for a variety of business and commercial purposes.

All this is not to say that *Miller* and *Smith* are without limits. *Miller* and *Smith* may not apply when the Government obtains the modern-day equivalents of an individual's own "papers" or "effects," even when those papers or effects are held by a third party. As already discussed, however, this case does not involve property or a bailment of that sort. Here the Government's acquisition of cell-site records falls within the heartland of *Miller* and *Smith*.

* * *

III

The Court rejects a straightforward application of *Miller* and *Smith*. It concludes instead that applying those cases to cell-site records would work a "significant extension" of the principles underlying them and holds that the acquisition of more than six days of cell-site records constitutes a search.

* * *

B

* * *

The Court appears, in my respectful view, to read *Miller* and *Smith* to establish a balancing test. For each "qualitatively different category" of information, the Court suggests, the privacy interests at stake must be weighed against the fact that the information has been disclosed to a third party. When the privacy interests are weighty enough to "overcome" the third-party disclosure, the Fourth Amendment's protections apply.

That is an untenable reading of *Miller* and *Smith*. As already discussed, the fact that information was relinquished to a third party was the entire basis for concluding that the defendants in those cases lacked a reasonable expectation of privacy. *Miller* and *Smith* do not establish the kind of category-by-category balancing the Court today prescribes.

But suppose the Court were correct to say that *Miller* and *Smith* rest on so imprecise a foundation. Still the Court errs, in my submission, when it concludes that cell-site records implicate greater privacy interests—and thus deserve greater Fourth Amendment protection—than financial records and telephone records.

Indeed, the opposite is true. A person's movements are not particularly private. As the Court recognized in *Knotts*, when the defendant there "traveled over the public streets he voluntarily conveyed to anyone who wanted to look the fact that he was traveling over particular roads in a particular direction, the fact of whatever stops he made, and the fact of his final destination." 460 U.S., at 281–82. Today expectations of privacy in one's location are, if anything, even less reasonable than when the Court decided *Knotts* over 30 years ago. Millions of Americans choose to share their location on a daily basis, whether by using a variety of location-based services on their phones, or by sharing their location with friends and the public at large via social media.

* * *

Still, the Court maintains, cell-site records are "unique" because they are "comprehensive" in their reach; allow for retrospective collection; are "easy, cheap, and efficient compared to traditional investigative tools"; and are not exposed to cell phone service providers in a meaningfully voluntary manner. But many other kinds of business records can be so described. Financial records are of vast scope. Banks and credit card companies keep a comprehensive account of almost every transaction an individual makes on a daily basis. "With just the click of a button, the Government can access each [company's] deep repository of historical [financial] information at practically no expense." And the decision whether to transact with banks and credit card companies is no more or less voluntary than the decision whether to use a cell phone. Today, just as when *Miller* was decided, " 'it is impossible to participate in the economic life of contemporary society without maintaining a bank account.' " 425 U.S., at 451 (Brennan, J., dissenting). But this Court, nevertheless, has held that individuals do not have a reasonable expectation of privacy in financial records.

* * *

Having concluded, however, that the Government searched Carpenter when it obtained cell-site records from his cell phone service providers, the proper resolution of this case should have been to remand for the Court of Appeals to determine in the first instance whether the search was reasonable. Most courts of appeals, believing themselves bound by *Miller* and *Smith*, have not grappled with this question. And the Court's reflexive imposition of the warrant requirement obscures important and difficult issues, such as the scope of Congress' power to authorize the Government to collect new forms of information using processes that deviate from traditional warrant procedures, and how the Fourth Amendment's reasonableness requirement should apply when the Government uses compulsory process instead of engaging in an actual, physical search.

JUSTICE THOMAS, dissenting.

* * *

B

The word "privacy" does not appear in the Fourth Amendment (or anywhere else in the Constitution for that matter). Instead, the Fourth Amendment references "[t]he right of the people to be secure." It then qualifies that right by limiting it to "persons" and three specific types of property: "houses, papers, and effects." By connecting the right to be secure to these four specific objects, "[t]he text of the Fourth Amendment reflects its close connection to property." *Jones*, *supra*, at 405. . . .

Those who ratified the Fourth Amendment were quite familiar with the notion of security in property. Security in property was a prominent concept in English law. See, *e.g.*, 3 W. Blackstone, Commentaries on the Laws of England 288 (1768) ("[E]very man's house is looked upon by the law to be his castle"); 3 E. Coke, Institutes of Laws of England 162 (6th ed. 1680) ("For a man's house is his Castle, & domus sua cuique est tutissimum refugium [each man's home is his safest refuge]"). The political philosophy of John Locke, moreover, permeated the 18th-century political scene in America. For Locke, every individual had a property right "in his own person" and in anything he "removed from the common state [of] Nature" and "mixed his labour with." Second Treatise of Civil Government § 27 (1690). Because property is "very unsecure" in the state of nature, individuals form governments to obtain "a secure enjoyment of their properties." Once a government is formed, however, it cannot be given "a power to destroy that which every one designs to secure"; it cannot legitimately "endeavour to take away, and destroy the property of the people," or exercise "an absolute power over [their] lives, liberties, and estates."

* * *

Of course, the founding generation understood that, by securing their property, the Fourth Amendment would often protect their privacy as well. But the Fourth Amendment's attendant protection of privacy does not justify *Katz*'s elevation of privacy as the *sine qua non* of the Amendment. As the majority opinion in *Katz* recognized, the Fourth Amendment "cannot be translated into a general constitutional 'right to privacy,'" as its protections "often have nothing to do with privacy at all." Justice Harlan's focus on privacy in his concurrence—an opinion that was issued between *Griswold v. Connecticut*, 381 U.S. 479 (1965), and *Roe v. Wade*, 410 U.S. 113 (1973)—reflects privacy's status as the organizing constitutional idea of the 1960's and 1970's. The organizing constitutional idea of the founding era, by contrast, was property.

C

In shifting the focus of the Fourth Amendment from property to privacy, the *Katz* test also reads the words "persons, houses, papers, and effects" out of the text. At its broadest formulation, the *Katz* test would find a search "*wherever* an individual may harbor a reasonable 'expectation of privacy.'" *Terry*, 392 U.S., at 9 (emphasis added). The Court today, for example, does not ask whether cell-site location records are "persons, houses, papers, [or] effects" within the meaning of the Fourth Amendment.

Yet "persons, houses, papers, and effects" cannot mean "anywhere" or "anything." *Katz's* catchphrase that "the Fourth Amendment protects people, not places," is not a serious attempt to reconcile the constitutional text. The Fourth Amendment obviously protects people; "[t]he question . . . is what protection it affords to those people." *Katz*, 389 U.S., at 361 (Harlan, J., concurring). The Founders decided to protect the people from unreasonable searches and seizures of four specific things—persons, houses, papers, and effects. They identified those four categories as "the objects of privacy protection to which the *Constitution* would extend, leaving further expansion to the good judgment . . . of the people through their representatives in the legislature." *Carter*, *supra*, at 97–98 (opinion of Scalia, J.).

This limiting language was important to the founders. Madison's first draft of the Fourth Amendment used a different phrase: "their persons, their houses, their papers, and their *other property*." 1 Annals of Cong. 452 (1789) (emphasis added). In one of the few changes made to Madison's draft, the House Committee of Eleven changed "other property" to "effects." This change might have narrowed the Fourth Amendment by clarifying that it does not protect real property (other than houses). See *Oliver v. United States*, 466 U.S. 170, 177, and n. 7 (1984). Or the change might have broadened the Fourth Amendment by clarifying that it protects commercial goods, not just personal possessions. Or it might have done both. Whatever its ultimate effect, the change reveals that the Founders understood the phrase "persons, houses, papers, and effects" to be an important measure of the Fourth Amendment's overall scope. The *Katz* test, however, displaces and renders that phrase entirely superfluous.

* * *

E

The *Katz* test comes closer to the text of the Fourth Amendment when it asks whether an expectation of privacy is "reasonable," but it ultimately distorts that term as well. The Fourth Amendment forbids "unreasonable searches." In other words, reasonableness determines the legality of a search, not "whether a search . . . within the meaning of the Constitution has *occurred*." *Carter*, 525 U.S., at 97 (opinion of Scalia, J.).

Moreover, the *Katz* test invokes the concept of reasonableness in a way that would be foreign to the ratifiers of the Fourth Amendment. Originally, the word "unreasonable" in the Fourth Amendment likely meant "against reason"—as in "against the reason of the common law." At the founding, searches and seizures were regulated by a robust body of common-law rules. The search-and-seizure practices that the Founders feared most—such as general warrants—were already illegal under the common law, and jurists such as Lord Coke described violations of the common law as "against reason." Locke, Blackstone, Adams, and other influential figures shortened the phrase "against reason" to "unreasonable." Thus, by prohibiting "unreasonable" searches and seizures in the Fourth Amendment, the Founders ensured that the newly created Congress could not use legislation to abolish the established common-law rules of search and seizure.

* * *

III

That the *Katz* test departs so far from the text of the Fourth Amendment is reason enough to reject it. But the *Katz* test also has proved unworkable in practice. Jurists and commentators tasked with deciphering our jurisprudence have described the *Katz* regime as "an unpredictable jumble," "a mass of contradictions and obscurities," "all over the map," "riddled with inconsistency and incoherence," "a series of inconsistent and bizarre results that [the Court] has left entirely undefended," "unstable," "chameleon-like," " 'notoriously unhelpful,' " "a conclusion rather than a starting point for analysis," "distressingly unmanageable," "a dismal failure," "flawed to the core," "unadorned fiat," and "inspired by the kind of logic that produced Rube Goldberg's bizarre contraptions." Even Justice Harlan, four years after penning his concurrence in *Katz*, confessed that the test encouraged "the substitution of words for analysis." *United States v. White*, 401 U.S. 745, 786 (1971) (dissenting opinion).

After 50 years, it is still unclear what question the *Katz* test is even asking. This Court has steadfastly declined to elaborate the relevant considerations or identify any meaningful constraints.

* * *

In several recent decisions, this Court has declined to apply the *Katz* test because it threatened to narrow the original scope of the Fourth Amendment. But as today's decision demonstrates, *Katz* can also be invoked to expand the Fourth Amendment beyond its original scope. This Court should not tolerate errors in either direction. The People, through ratification, have already weighed the policy tradeoffs that constitutional rights entail. Whether the rights they ratified are too broad or too narrow by modern lights, this Court has no authority to unilaterally alter the document they approved.

Because the *Katz* test is a failed experiment, this Court is dutybound to reconsider it. Until it does, I agree with my dissenting colleagues' reading of our precedents. Accordingly, I respectfully dissent.

JUSTICE ALITO, with whom JUSTICE THOMAS joins, dissenting.

I share the Court's concern about the effect of new technology on personal privacy, but I fear that today's decision will do far more harm than good. The Court's reasoning fractures two fundamental pillars of Fourth Amendment law, and in doing so, it guarantees a blizzard of litigation while threatening many legitimate and valuable investigative practices upon which law enforcement has rightfully come to rely.

* * *

I

Today the majority holds that a court order requiring the production of cell-site records may be issued only after the Government demonstrates probable cause. That is a serious and consequential mistake. The Court's holding is based on the premise that the order issued in this case was an actual "search" within the meaning of the Fourth Amendment, but that premise is inconsistent with the original meaning of the Fourth Amendment and with more than a century of precedent.

A

The order in this case was the functional equivalent of a subpoena for documents, and there is no evidence that these writs were regarded as "searches" at the time of the founding. Subpoenas *duces tecum* and other forms of compulsory document production were well known to the founding generation. Blackstone dated the first writ of subpoena to the reign of King Richard II in the late 14th century, and by the end of the 15th century, the use of such writs had "become the daily practice of the [Chancery] court." 3 W. Blackstone, Commentaries on the Laws of England 53 (G. Tucker ed. 1803). Over the next 200 years, subpoenas would grow in prominence and power in tandem with the Court of Chancery, and by the end of Charles II's reign in 1685, two important innovations had occurred.

* * *

B

Talk of kings and common-law writs may seem out of place in a case about cell-site records and the protections afforded by the Fourth Amendment in the modern age. But this history matters, not least because it tells us what was on the minds of those who ratified the Fourth Amendment and how they understood its scope. That history makes it abundantly clear that the Fourth Amendment, as originally understood, did not apply to the compulsory production of documents at all.

The Fourth Amendment does not regulate all methods by which the Government obtains documents. Rather, it prohibits only those "searches and seizures" of "persons, houses, papers, and effects" that are "unreasonable." Consistent with that language, "at least until the latter half of the 20th century" "our Fourth Amendment jurisprudence was tied to common-law trespass." *United States v. Jones*, 565 U.S. 400, 405 (2012). So by its terms, the Fourth Amendment does not apply to the compulsory production of documents, a practice that involves neither any physical intrusion into private space nor any taking of property by agents of the state. Even Justice Brandeis—a stalwart proponent of construing the

Fourth Amendment liberally—acknowledged that "under any ordinary construction of language," "there is no 'search' or 'seizure' when a defendant is required to produce a document in the orderly process of a court's procedure." *Olmstead v. United States*, 277 U.S. 438, 476 (1928) (dissenting opinion).

Nor is there any reason to believe that the Founders intended the Fourth Amendment to regulate courts' use of compulsory process. American colonists rebelled against the Crown's physical invasions of their persons and their property, not against its acquisition of information by any and all means. As Justice Black once put it, "[t]he Fourth Amendment was aimed directly at the abhorred practice of breaking in, ransacking and searching homes and other buildings and seizing people's personal belongings without warrants issued by magistrates." *Katz*, 389 U.S., at 367 (dissenting opinion). More recently, we have acknowledged that "the Fourth Amendment was the founding generation's response to the reviled 'general warrants' and 'writs of assistance' of the colonial era, which allowed British officers to rummage through homes in an unrestrained search for evidence of criminal activity." *Riley v. California*, 134 S.Ct. 2473, 2494 (2014).

General warrants and writs of assistance were noxious not because they allowed the Government to acquire evidence in criminal investigations, but because of the means by which they permitted the Government to acquire that evidence. Then, as today, searches could be quite invasive. Searches generally begin with officers "mak[ing] nonconsensual entries into areas not open to the public." *Donovan v. Lone Steer, Inc.*, 464 U.S. 408, 414 (1984). Once there, officers are necessarily in a position to observe private spaces generally shielded from the public and discernible only with the owner's consent. Private area after private area becomes exposed to the officers' eyes as they rummage through the owner's property in their hunt for the object or objects of the search. If they are searching for documents, officers may additionally have to rifle through many other papers—potentially filled with the most intimate details of a person's thoughts and life—before they find the specific information they are seeking. If anything sufficiently incriminating comes into view, officers seize it. Physical destruction always lurks as an underlying possibility; "officers executing search warrants on occasion must damage property in order to perform their duty." *Dalia v. United States*, 441 U.S. 238, 258 (1979).

Compliance with a subpoena *duces tecum* requires none of that. A subpoena *duces tecum* permits a subpoenaed individual to conduct the search for the relevant documents himself, without law enforcement officers entering his home or rooting through his papers and effects. As a result, subpoenas avoid the many incidental invasions of privacy that necessarily accompany any actual search. And it was *those* invasions of privacy—which, although incidental, could often be extremely intrusive and damaging—that led to the adoption of the Fourth Amendment.

* * *

C

Of course, our jurisprudence has not stood still since 1791. We now evaluate subpoenas *duces tecum* and other forms of compulsory document production under the Fourth Amendment, although we employ a reasonableness standard that is less demanding than the requirements for a warrant. But the road to that doctrinal destination was anything but smooth, and our initial missteps—and the subsequent struggle to extricate ourselves from their consequences—should provide an object lesson for today's majority about the dangers of holding compulsory process to the same standard as actual searches and seizures.

* * *

All of this is unnecessary. In the Stored Communications Act, Congress addressed the specific problem at issue in this case. The Act restricts the misuse of cell-site records by cell service providers, something that the Fourth Amendment cannot do. The Act also goes beyond current Fourth Amendment case law in restricting access by law enforcement. It permits law enforcement officers to acquire cell-site records only if they meet a heightened standard and obtain a court order. If the American people now think that the Act is inadequate or needs updating, they can turn to their elected representatives to adopt more protective provisions. Because the collection and storage of cell-site records affects nearly every American, it is unlikely that the question whether the current law requires strengthening will escape Congress's notice.

Legislation is much preferable to the development of an entirely new body of Fourth Amendment caselaw for many reasons, including the enormous complexity of the subject, the need to respond to rapidly changing technology, and the Fourth Amendment's limited scope. The Fourth Amendment restricts the conduct of the Federal Government and the States; it does not apply to private actors. But today, some of the greatest threats to individual privacy may come from powerful private companies that collect and sometimes misuse vast quantities of data about the lives of ordinary Americans. If today's decision encourages the public to think that this Court can protect them from this looming threat to their privacy, the decision will mislead as well as disrupt. And if holding a provision of the Stored Communications Act to be unconstitutional dissuades Congress from further legislation in this field, the goal of protecting privacy will be greatly disserved.

The desire to make a statement about privacy in the digital age does not justify the consequences that today's decision is likely to produce.

JUSTICE GORSUCH, dissenting.

In the late 1960s this Court suggested for the first time that a search triggering the Fourth Amendment occurs when the government violates an "expectation of privacy" that "society is prepared to recognize as 'reasonable.'" *Katz v. United States*, 389 U.S. 347, 361 (1967) (Harlan, J., concurring). Then, in a pair of decisions in the 1970s applying the *Katz* test, the Court held that a "reasonable expectation of privacy" doesn't attach to information shared with "third parties." By these steps, the Court came to conclude, the Constitution does nothing to limit investigators from searching records you've entrusted to your bank, accountant, and maybe even your doctor.

What's left of the Fourth Amendment? Today we use the Internet to do most everything. Smartphones make it easy to keep a calendar, correspond with friends, make calls, conduct banking, and even watch the game. Countless Internet companies maintain records about us and, increasingly, *for* us. Even our most private documents—those that, in other eras, we would have locked safely in a desk drawer or destroyed—now reside on third party servers. *Smith* and *Miller* teach that the police can review all of this material, on the theory that no one reasonably expects any of it will be kept private. But no one believes that, if they ever did.

* * *

There is another way. From the founding until the 1960s, the right to assert a Fourth Amendment claim didn't depend on your ability to appeal to a judge's personal sensibilities about the "reasonableness" of your expectations or privacy. It was tied to the law. The Fourth Amendment protects "the right of the people to be secure in their persons, houses, papers and effects, against unreasonable searches and seizures." True to those words and their original understanding, the traditional approach asked if a house, paper or effect was yours under law. No more was needed to trigger the Fourth Amendment. Though now often lost in *Katz*'s shadow, this traditional understanding persists. *Katz* only supplements, rather than displaces the traditional property-based understanding of the Fourth Amendment.

Beyond its provenance in the text and original understanding of the Amendment, this traditional approach comes with other advantages. Judges are supposed to decide cases based on "democratically legitimate sources of law"—like positive law or analogies to items protected by the enacted Constitution—rather than "their own biases or personal policy preferences." A Fourth Amendment model based on positive legal rights "carves out significant room for legislative participation in the Fourth Amendment context," too, by asking judges to consult what the people's representatives have to say about their rights. Nor is this approach hobbled by *Smith* and *Miller*, for those cases are just *limitations* on *Katz*, addressing only the question whether individuals have a reasonable expectation of privacy in materials they share with third parties. Under this more traditional approach, Fourth Amendment protections for your papers and effects do not automatically disappear just because you share them with third parties.

Given the prominence *Katz* has claimed in our doctrine, American courts are pretty rusty at applying the traditional approach to the Fourth Amendment. We know that if a house, paper, or effect is yours, you have a Fourth Amendment interest in its protection. But what kind of legal interest is sufficient to make something *yours*? And what source of law determines that? Current positive law? The common law at 1791, extended by analogy to modern times? Both? Much work is needed to revitalize this area and answer these questions. I do not begin to claim all the answers today, but (unlike with *Katz*) at least I have a pretty good idea what the questions *are*. And it seems to me a few things can be said.

First, the fact that a third party has access to or possession of your papers and effects does not necessarily eliminate your interest in them. Ever hand a private document to a friend to be returned? Toss your keys to a valet at a restaurant? Ask your neighbor to look after your dog while you travel? You would not expect the friend to share the document with others; the valet to lend your car to his buddy; or the neighbor to put Fido up for adoption. Entrusting your stuff to others is a *bailment*. A bailment is the "delivery of personal property by one person (the *bailor*) to another (the *bailee*) who holds the property for a certain purpose." Black's Law Dictionary 169 (10th ed. 2014). A bailee normally owes a legal duty to keep the item safe, according to the terms of the parties' contract if they have one, and according to the implications from their conduct if they don't. A bailee who uses the item in a different way than he's supposed to, or against the bailor's instructions, is liable for conversion. This approach is quite different from *Smith* and *Miller*'s (counter)-intuitive approach to reasonable expectations of privacy; where those cases extinguish Fourth Amendment interests once records are given to a third party, property law may preserve them.

Our Fourth Amendment jurisprudence already reflects this truth. In *Ex parte Jackson*, 96 U.S. 727 (1878), this Court held that sealed letters placed in the mail are "as fully guarded from examination and inspection, except as to their outward form and weight, as if they were retained by the parties forwarding them in their own domiciles." The reason, drawn from the Fourth Amendment's text, was that "[t]he constitutional guaranty of the right of the people to be secure in their papers against unreasonable searches and seizures extends to *their papers*, thus closed against inspection, *wherever they may be*." *Ibid.* (emphasis added). It did not matter that letters were bailed to a third party (the government, no less). The sender enjoyed the same Fourth Amendment protection as he does "when papers are subjected to search in one's own household."

These ancient principles may help us address modern data cases too. Just because you entrust your data—in some cases, your modern-day papers and effects—to a third party may not mean you lose any Fourth Amendment interest in its contents. Whatever may be left of *Smith* and *Miller*, few doubt that e-mail should be treated much like the traditional mail it has largely supplanted—as a bailment in which the owner retains a vital and protected legal interest. See *United States v. Warshak*, 631 F.3d 266, 285–286 (C.A.6 2010) (relying on an analogy to *Jackson* to extend Fourth Amendment protection to e-mail held by a third party service provider).

Second, I doubt that complete ownership or exclusive control of property is always a necessary condition to the assertion of a Fourth Amendment right. Where houses are concerned, for example, individuals can enjoy Fourth Amendment protection without fee simple title. Both the text of the Amendment and the common law rule support that conclusion. "People call a house 'their' home when legal title is in the bank, when they rent it, and even when they merely occupy it rent free." *Carter*, 525 U.S., at 95–96 (Scalia, J., concurring). That rule derives from the common law. *Oystead v. Shed*, 13 Mass. 520, 523 (1816) (explaining, citing "[t]he very learned judges, *Foster*, *Hale*, and *Coke*," that the law "would be as much disturbed by a forcible entry to arrest a boarder or a servant, who had acquired, by contract, express or implied, a right to enter the house at all times, and to remain in it as long as they please, as if the object were to arrest the master of the house or his children"). That is why tenants and resident family members—though they have no legal title—have standing to complain about searches of the houses in which they live.

* * *

Third, positive law may help provide detailed guidance on evolving technologies without resort to judicial intuition. State (or sometimes federal) law often creates rights in both tangible and intangible things. In the context of the Takings Clause we often ask whether those state-created rights are sufficient to make something someone's property for constitutional purposes. A similar inquiry may be appropriate for the Fourth Amendment. Both the States and federal government are actively legislating in the area of third party data storage and the rights users enjoy. State courts are busy expounding common law property principles in this area as well. If state legislators or state courts say that a digital record has the attributes that normally make something property, that may supply a sounder basis for judicial decisionmaking than judicial guesswork about societal expectations.

Fourth, while positive law may help establish a person's Fourth Amendment interest there may be some circumstances where positive law cannot be used to defeat it. *Ex parte Jackson* reflects that understanding. There this Court said that "[n]o law of Congress" could authorize letter carriers "to invade the secrecy of letters." So the post office couldn't impose a regulation dictating that those mailing letters surrender all legal interests in them once they're deposited in a mailbox. If that is right, *Jackson* suggests the existence of a constitutional floor below which Fourth Amendment rights may not descend. Legislatures cannot pass laws declaring your house or papers to be your property except to the extent the police wish to search them without cause. As the Court has previously explained, "we must 'assure preservation of that degree of privacy against government that existed when the Fourth Amendment was adopted.'" *Jones*, 565 U.S., at 406 (quoting *Kyllo v. United States*, 533 U.S. 27, 34 (2001)). Nor does this mean protecting only the specific rights known at the founding; it means protecting their modern analogues too. So, for example, while thermal imaging was unknown in 1791, this Court has recognized that using that technology to look inside a home constitutes a Fourth Amendment "search" of that "home" no less than a physical inspection might. *Id.*, at 40.

Fifth, this constitutional floor may, in some instances, bar efforts to circumvent the Fourth Amendment's protection through the use of subpoenas. No one thinks the government can evade *Jackson*'s prohibition on opening sealed letters without a warrant simply by issuing a subpoena to a postmaster for "all letters sent by John Smith" or, worse, "all letters sent by John Smith concerning a particular transaction." So the question courts will confront will be this: What other kinds of records are sufficiently similar to letters in the mail that the same rule should apply?

It may be that, as an original matter, a subpoena requiring the recipient to produce records wasn't thought of as a "search or seizure" by the government implicating the Fourth Amendment, but instead as an act of compelled self-incrimination implicating the Fifth Amendment. But the common law of searches and seizures does not appear to have confronted a case where private documents equivalent to a mailed letter were entrusted to a bailee and then subpoenaed. As a result, the common-law rule regarding subpoenas for documents held by third parties entrusted with information from the target is . . . unknown and perhaps unknowable. Given that (perhaps insoluble) uncertainty, I am content to adhere to *Jackson* and its implications for now.

* * *

What does all this mean for the case before us? To start, I cannot fault the Sixth Circuit for holding that *Smith* and *Miller* extinguish any *Katz*-based Fourth Amendment interest in third party cell-site data. That is the plain effect of their categorical holdings. Nor can I fault the Court today for its implicit but unmistakable conclusion that the rationale of *Smith* and *Miller* is wrong; indeed, I agree with that. The Sixth Circuit was powerless to say so, but this Court can and should. At the same time, I do not agree with the Court's decision today to keep *Smith* and *Miller* on life support and supplement them with a new and multilayered inquiry that seems to be only *Katz*-squared. Returning there, I worry, promises more trouble than help. Instead, I would look to a more traditional Fourth Amendment approach. Even if *Katz* may still supply one way to prove a Fourth Amendment interest, it has never been the only way. Neglecting more traditional approaches may mean failing to vindicate the full protections of the Fourth Amendment.

Our case offers a cautionary example. It seems to me entirely possible a person's cell-site data could qualify as *his* papers or effects under existing law. Yes, the telephone carrier holds the information. But 47 U.S.C. § 222 designates a customer's cell-site location information as "customer proprietary network information" (CPNI), § 222(h)(1)(A), and gives customers certain rights to control use of and access to CPNI about themselves. The statute generally forbids a carrier to "use, disclose, or permit access to individually identifiable" CPNI without the customer's consent, except as needed to provide the customer's telecommunications services. § 222(c)(1). It also requires the carrier to disclose CPNI "upon affirmative written request by the customer, to any person designated by the customer." § 222(c)(2). Congress even afforded customers a private cause of action for damages against carriers who violate the Act's terms. § 207. Plainly, customers have substantial legal interests in this information, including at least some right to include, exclude, and control its use. Those interests might even rise to the level of a property right.

* * *

Points for Discussion

1. The majority states that it will not "extend" the third party doctrine to cover the facts of this case. The principal dissent states that this case can be resolved in the government's favor with a "straightforward" application of the third party doctrine. Who has the better of the argument on this point?

2. Do the decisions in *Smith* and *Miller*, referred to in all of the opinions, survive the Court's decision in *Carpenter*? If so, is it clear when the third party doctrine applies and when it does not? Is the law clarified or muddled by the Court's decision in this case?

3. The majority opinion refers extensively to the *Karo* and *Knotts* opinions. In both, the Supreme Court found that there is no reasonable expectation of privacy in one's location in public because one has knowingly exposed that information to public view. Why do those precedents not resolve this in the government's favor? Do *Knotts* and *Karo* survive Carpenter?

4. In his separate dissent, Justice Gorsuch suggests an alternative both to the majority's approach and a strict application of the third party doctrine. How would Justice Gorsuch resolve questions like the one presented in *Carpenter*? Is his approach an improvement upon the way the Court resolved this case?

UNITED STATES V. JACOBSEN

466 U.S. 109 (1984)

JUSTICE STEVENS delivered the opinion of the court.

During their examination of a damaged package, the employees of a private freight carrier observed a white powdery substance, originally concealed within eight layers of wrappings. They summoned a federal agent, who removed a trace of the powder, subjected it to a chemical test and determined that it was cocaine. The question presented is whether the Fourth Amendment required the agent to obtain a warrant before he did so.

The relevant facts are not in dispute. Early in the morning of May 1, 1981, a supervisor at the Minneapolis-St. Paul airport Federal Express office asked the office manager to look at a package that had been damaged and torn by a forklift. They then opened the package in order to examine its contents pursuant to a written company policy regarding insurance claims.

The container was an ordinary cardboard box wrapped in brown paper. Inside the box five or six pieces of crumpled newspaper covered a tube about 10 inches long; the tube was made of the silver tape used on basement ducts. The supervisor and office manager cut open the tube, and found a series of four zip-lock plastic bags, the outermost enclosing the other three and the innermost containing about six and a half ounces of white powder. When they observed the white powder in the innermost bag, they notified the Drug Enforcement Administration. Before the first DEA agent arrived, they replaced the plastic bags in the tube and put the tube and the newspapers back into the box.

When the first federal agent arrived, the box, still wrapped in brown paper, but with a hole punched in its side and the top open, was placed on a desk. The agent saw that one end of the tube had been slit open; he removed the four plastic bags from the tube and saw the white powder. He then opened each of the four bags and removed a trace of the white substance with a knife blade. A field test made on the spot identified the substance as cocaine.

In due course, other agents arrived, made a second field test, rewrapped the package, obtained a warrant to search the place to which it was addressed, executed the warrant, and arrested respondents. After they were indicted for the crime of possessing an illegal substance with intent to distribute, their motion to suppress the evidence on the ground that the warrant was the product of an illegal search and seizure was denied; they were tried and convicted, and appealed. The Court of Appeals reversed. It held that the validity of the search warrant depended on the validity of the agents' warrantless test of the white powder, that the testing constituted a significant expansion of the earlier private search, and that a warrant was required.

* * *

I

The first clause of the Fourth Amendment provides that the "right of the people to be secure in their persons, houses, papers and effects, against unreasonable searches and seizures, shall not be violated . . . ." This text protects two types of expectations, one involving "searches," the other "seizures." A "search" occurs when an expectation of privacy that society is prepared to consider reasonable is infringed. A "seizure" of property occurs when there is some meaningful interference with an individual's possessory interests in that property.[5] This Court has also consistently construed this protection as proscribing only governmental action; it is wholly inapplicable "to a search or seizure, even an unreasonable one, effected by a private individual not acting as an agent of the Government or with the participation or knowledge of any governmental official."

When the wrapped parcel involved in this case was delivered to the private freight carrier, it was unquestionably an "effect" within the meaning of the Fourth Amendment. Letters and other sealed packages are in the general class of effects in which the public at large has a legitimate expectation of privacy; warrantless searches of such effects are presumptively unreasonable. Even when government agents may lawfully seize such a package to prevent loss or destruction of suspected contraband, the Fourth Amendment requires that they obtain a warrant before examining the contents of such a package. Such a warrantless search could not be characterized as reasonable simply because, after the official invasion of privacy occurred, contraband is discovered. Conversely, in this case the fact that agents of the private carrier independently opened the package and made an examination that might have been impermissible for a government agent cannot render otherwise reasonable official conduct unreasonable. The reasonableness of an official invasion of the citizen's privacy must be appraised on the basis of the facts as they existed at the time that invasion occurred.

The initial invasions of respondents' package were occasioned by private action. Those invasions revealed that the package contained only

[5] While the concept of a "seizure" of property is not much discussed in our cases, this definition follows from our oft-repeated definition of the "seizure" of a person within the meaning of the Fourth Amendment—meaningful interference, however brief, with an individual's freedom of movement.

one significant item, a suspicious looking tape tube. Cutting the end of the tube and extracting its contents revealed a suspicious looking plastic bag of white powder. Whether those invasions were accidental or deliberate,[10] and whether they were reasonable or unreasonable, they did not violate the Fourth Amendment because of their private character.

* * *

In this case, the federal agents' invasions of respondents' privacy involved two steps: first, they removed the tube from the box, the plastic bags from the tube and a trace of powder from the innermost bag; second, they made a chemical test of the powder. Although we ultimately conclude that both actions were reasonable for essentially the same reason, it is useful to discuss them separately.

II

When the first federal agent on the scene initially saw the package, he knew it contained nothing of significance except a tube containing plastic bags and, ultimately, white powder. It is not entirely clear that the powder was visible to him before he removed the tube from the box. Even if the white powder was not itself in "plain view" because it was still enclosed in so many containers and covered with papers, there was a virtual certainty that nothing else of significance was in the package and that a manual inspection of the tube and its contents would not tell him anything more than he already had been told. Respondents do not dispute that the Government could utilize the Federal Express employees' testimony concerning the contents of the package. If that is the case, it hardly infringed respondents' privacy for the agents to reexamine the contents of the open package by brushing aside a crumpled newspaper and picking up the tube. The advantage the Government gained thereby was merely avoiding the risk of a flaw in the employees' recollection, rather than in further infringing respondents' privacy. Protecting the risk of misdescription hardly enhances any legitimate privacy interest, and is not protected by the Fourth Amendment. Respondents could have no privacy interest in the contents of the package, since it remained unsealed and since the Federal Express employees had just examined the package and had, of their own accord, invited the federal agent to their offices for the express purpose of viewing its contents. The agent's viewing of what a private party had freely made available for his inspection did not violate the Fourth Amendment.

Similarly, the removal of the plastic bags from the tube and the agent's visual inspection of their contents enabled the agent to learn nothing that

[10] A post-trial affidavit indicates that an agent of Federal Express may have opened the package because he was suspicious about its contents, and not because of damage from a forklift. However, the lower courts found no governmental involvement in the private search, a finding not challenged by respondents. The affidavit thus is of no relevance to the issue we decide.

had not previously been learned during the private search.[17] It infringed no legitimate expectation of privacy and hence was not a "search" within the meaning of the Fourth Amendment.

While the agents' assertion of dominion and control over the package and its contents did constitute a "seizure," that seizure was not unreasonable. The fact that, prior to the field test, respondents' privacy interest in the contents of the package had been largely compromised, is highly relevant to the reasonableness of the agents' conduct in this respect. The agents had already learned a great deal about the contents of the package from the Federal Express employees, all of which was consistent with what they could see. The package itself, which had previously been opened, remained unsealed, and the Federal Express employees had invited the agents to examine its contents. Under these circumstances, the package could no longer support any expectation of privacy; it was just like a balloon "the distinctive character [of which] spoke volumes as to its contents, particularly to the trained eye of the officer," *Texas v. Brown,* 460 U.S. [730, 743] (1983) (plurality opinion); or the hypothetical gun case in *Arkansas v. Sanders,* 442 U.S. 753, 764–765, n. 13 (1979). Such containers may be seized, at least temporarily, without a warrant. Accordingly, since it was apparent that the tube and plastic bags contained contraband and little else, this warrantless seizure was reasonable for it is well-settled that it is constitutionally reasonable for law enforcement officials to seize "effects" that cannot support a justifiable expectation of privacy without a warrant, based on probable cause to believe they contain contraband.

III

The question remains whether the additional intrusion occasioned by the field test, which had not been conducted by the Federal Express agents and therefore exceeded the scope of the private search, was an unlawful "search" or "seizure" within the meaning of the Fourth Amendment.

The field test at issue could disclose only one fact previously unknown to the agent—whether or not a suspicious white powder was cocaine. It

[17] We reject Justice White's suggestion that this case is indistinguishable from one in which the police simply learn from a private party that a container contains contraband, seize it from its owner, and conduct a warrantless search which, as Justice White properly observes, would be unconstitutional. Here, the Federal Express employees who were lawfully in possession of the package invited the agent to examine its contents; the governmental conduct was made possible only because private parties had compromised the integrity of this container. Justice White would have this case turn on the fortuity of whether the Federal Express agents placed the tube back into the box. But in the context of their previous examination of the package, their communication of what they had learned to the agent, and their offer to have the agent inspect it, that act surely could not create any privacy interest with respect to the package that would not otherwise exist. Thus the precise character of the white powder's visibility to the naked eye is far less significant than the facts that the container could no longer support any expectation of privacy, and that it was virtually certain that it contained nothing but contraband. Contrary to Justice White's suggestion, we do not "sanction[ ] warrantless searches of closed or covered containers or packages whenever probable cause exists as a result of a prior private search." A container which can support a reasonable expectation of privacy may not be searched, even on probable cause, without a warrant.

could tell him nothing more, not even whether the substance was sugar or talcum powder. We must first determine whether this can be considered a "search" subject to the Fourth Amendment—did it infringe an expectation of privacy that society is prepared to consider reasonable?

The concept of an interest in privacy that society is prepared to recognize as reasonable is, by its very nature, critically different from the mere expectation, however well justified, that certain facts will not come to the attention of the authorities. Indeed, this distinction underlies the rule that Government may utilize information voluntarily disclosed to a governmental informant, despite the criminal's reasonable expectation that his associates would not disclose confidential information to the authorities.

A chemical test that merely discloses whether or not a particular substance is cocaine does not compromise any legitimate interest in privacy. This conclusion is not dependent on the result of any particular test. It is probably safe to assume that virtually all of the tests conducted under circumstances comparable to those disclosed by this record would result in a positive finding; in such cases, no legitimate interest has been compromised. But even if the results are negative—merely disclosing that the substance is something other than cocaine—such a result reveals nothing of special interest. Congress has decided—and there is no question about its power to do so—to treat the interest in "privately" possessing cocaine as illegitimate; thus governmental conduct that can reveal whether a substance is cocaine, and no other arguably "private" fact, compromises no legitimate privacy interest.

This conclusion is dictated by *United States v. Place,* 462 U.S. 696 (1983), in which the Court held that subjecting luggage to a "sniff test" by a trained narcotics detection dog was not a "search" within the meaning of the Fourth Amendment:

> A "canine sniff" by a well-trained narcotics detection dog, however, does not require opening of the luggage. It does not expose noncontraband items that otherwise would remain hidden from public view, as does, for example, an officer's rummaging through the contents of the luggage. Thus, the manner in which information is obtained through this investigative technique is much less intrusive than a typical search. Moreover, the sniff discloses only the presence or absence of narcotics, a contraband item. Thus, despite the fact that the sniff tells the authorities something about the contents of the luggage, the information obtained is limited.[24]

[24] Respondents attempt to distinguish *Place* arguing that it involved no physical invasion of Place's effects, unlike the conduct at issue here. However, as the quotation makes clear, the *reason* this did not intrude upon any legitimate privacy interest was that the governmental conduct could reveal nothing about noncontraband items. That rationale is fully applicable here.

Here, as in *Place,* the likelihood that official conduct of the kind disclosed by the record will actually compromise any legitimate interest in privacy seems much too remote to characterize the testing as a search subject to the Fourth Amendment.

We have concluded, in Part II, that the initial "seizure" of the package and its contents was reasonable. Nevertheless, as *Place* also holds, a seizure lawful at its inception can nevertheless violate the Fourth Amendment because its manner of execution unreasonably infringes possessory interests protected by the Fourth Amendment's prohibition on "unreasonable seizures." Here, the field test did affect respondents' possessory interests protected by the Amendment, since by destroying a quantity of the powder it converted what had been only a temporary deprivation of possessory interests into a permanent one. To assess the reasonableness of this conduct, "[w] e must balance the nature and quality of the intrusion on the individual's Fourth Amendment interests against the importance of the governmental interests alleged to justify the intrusion."

Applying this test, we conclude that the destruction of the powder during the course of the field test was reasonable. The law enforcement interests justifying the procedure were substantial; the suspicious nature of the material made it virtually certain that the substance tested was in fact contraband. Conversely, because only a trace amount of material was involved, the loss of which appears to have gone unnoticed by respondents, and since the property had already been lawfully detained, the "seizure" could, at most, have only a *de minimis* impact on any protected property interest. Under these circumstances, the safeguards of a warrant would only minimally advance Fourth Amendment interests. This warrantless "seizure" was reasonable.

* * *

JUSTICE WHITE, concurring in part and concurring in the judgment.

* * *

The governing principles with respect to the constitutional protection afforded closed containers and packages may be readily discerned from our cases. The Court has consistently rejected proposed distinctions between worthy and unworthy containers and packages and has made clear that "the Fourth Amendment provides protection to the owner of every container that conceals its contents from plain view" and does not otherwise unmistakably reveal its contents. Although law-enforcement officers may sometimes seize such containers and packages pending issuance of warrants to examine their contents, the mere existence of probable cause to believe that a container or package contains contraband plainly cannot justify a warrantless examination of its contents.

This well-established prohibition of warrantless searches has applied notwithstanding the manner in which the police obtained probable cause. The Court now for the first time sanctions warrantless searches of closed or covered containers or packages whenever probable cause exists as a result of a prior private search. It declares, in fact, that governmental inspections following on the heels of private searches are not searches at all as long as the police do no more than the private parties have already done. In reaching this conclusion, the Court excessively expands our prior decisions recognizing that the Fourth Amendment proscribes only governmental action.

* * *

Undoubtedly, the fact that a private party has conducted a search "that might have been impermissible for a government agent cannot render otherwise reasonable official conduct unreasonable." But the fact that a repository of personal property previously was searched by a private party has never been used to legitimize *governmental conduct* that otherwise would be subject to challenge under the Fourth Amendment. If government agents are unwilling or unable to rely on information or testimony provided by a private party concerning the results of a private search and that search has not left incriminating evidence in plain view, the agents may wish to duplicate the private search to observe first-hand what the private party has related to them or to examine and seize the suspected contraband the existence of which has been reported. The information provided by the private party clearly would give the agents probable cause to secure a warrant authorizing such actions. Nothing in our previous cases suggests, however, that the agents may proceed to conduct their own search of the same or lesser scope as the private search without first obtaining a warrant.

* * *

Today's decision also is not supported by the majority's reference to cases involving the transmission of previously private information to the police by a third party who has been made privy to that information. The police may, to be sure, use confidences revealed to them by a third party to establish probable cause or for other purposes, and the third party may testify about those confidences at trial without violating the Fourth Amendment. But we have never intimated until now that an individual who reveals that he stores contraband in a particular container or location to an acquaintance who later betrays his confidence has no expectation of privacy in that container or location and that the police may thus search it without a warrant.

That, I believe, is the effect of the Court's opinion. If a private party breaks into a locked suitcase, a locked car, or even a locked house, observes incriminating information, returns the object of his search to its prior locked condition, and then reports his findings to the police, the majority apparently would allow the police to duplicate the prior search on the ground that the private search vitiated the owner's expectation of privacy. As Justice Stevens has previously observed, this conclusion cannot rest on the proposition that the owner no longer has a subjective expectation of privacy since a person's expectation of privacy cannot be altered by subsequent events of which he was unaware.

* * *

The majority opinion is particularly troubling when one considers its logical implications. I would be hard-pressed to distinguish this case, which involves a private search, from (1) one in which the private party's knowledge, later communicated to the government, that a particular container concealed contraband and nothing else arose from his presence at the time the container was sealed; (2) one in which the private party learned that a container concealed contraband and nothing else when it was previously opened in his presence; or (3) one in which the private party knew to a certainty that a container concealed contraband and nothing else as a result of conversations with its owner. In each of these cases, the approach adopted by the Court today would seem to suggest that the owner of the container has no legitimate expectation of privacy in its contents and that government agents opening that container without a warrant on the strength of information provided by the private party would not violate the Fourth Amendment.

Because I cannot accept the majority's novel extension of the private-search doctrine and its implications for the entire concept of legitimate expectations of privacy, I concur only in Part III of its opinion and in the judgment.

JUSTICE BRENNAN, with whom JUSTICE MARSHALL joins, dissenting.

This case presents two questions: first whether law enforcement officers may conduct a warrantless search of the contents of a container merely because a private party has previously examined the container's contents and informed the officers of its suspicious nature; and second, whether law enforcement officers may conduct a chemical field test of a substance once the officers have legitimately located the substance. Because I disagree with the Court's treatment of each of these issues, I respectfully dissent.

I

I agree entirely with Justice White that the Court has expanded the reach of the private-search doctrine far beyond its logical bounds. It is difficult to understand how respondents can be said to have no expectation of privacy in a closed container simply because a private party has previously opened the container and viewed its contents. I also agree with Justice White, however, that if the private party presents the contents of a container to a law enforcement officer in such a manner that the contents are plainly visible, the officer's visual inspection of the contents does not constitute a "search" within the meaning of the Fourth Amendment. Because the record in this case is unclear on the question whether the contents of respondents' package were plainly visible when the Federal Express employee showed the package to the DEA officer, I would remand the case for further factfinding on this central issue.

II

As noted, I am not persuaded that the DEA officer actually came upon respondents' cocaine without violating the Fourth Amendment and accordingly, I need not address the legality of the chemical field test. Since the Court has done so, however, I too will address the question, assuming, *arguendo,* that the officer committed neither an unconstitutional search nor an unconstitutional seizure prior to the point at which he took the sample of cocaine out of the plastic bags to conduct the test.

A

* * *

It is certainly true that a surveillance technique that identifies only the presence or absence of contraband is less intrusive than a technique that reveals the precise nature of an item regardless of whether it is contraband. But by seizing upon this distinction alone to conclude that the first type of technique, as a general matter, is not a search, the Court has foreclosed any consideration of the circumstances under which the technique is used, and may very well have paved the way for technology to override the limits of law in the area of criminal investigation.

For example, under the Court's analysis in these cases, law enforcement officers could release a trained cocaine-sensitive dog—to paraphrase the California Court of Appeal, a "canine cocaine connoisseur"—to roam the streets at random, alerting the officers to people carrying cocaine. Or, if a device were developed that, when aimed at a person, would detect instantaneously whether the person is carrying cocaine, there would be no Fourth Amendment bar, under the Court's approach, to the police setting up such a device on a street corner and scanning all passersby. In fact, the Court's analysis is so unbounded that if a device were developed that could detect, from the outside of a building, the presence of cocaine inside, there would be no constitutional obstacle to the police cruising through a residential neighborhood and using the device to identify all homes in which the drug is present. In short, under the interpretation of the Fourth Amendment first suggested in *Place* and first applied in this case, these surveillance techniques would not constitute searches and therefore could be freely pursued whenever and wherever law enforcement officers desire. Hence, at some point in the future, if the Court stands by the theory it has adopted today, search warrants, probable cause, and even "reasonable suspicion" may very well become notions of the past. Fortunately, we know from precedents such as *Katz v. United States* that this Court ultimately stands ready to prevent this Orwellian world from coming to pass.

* * *

B

* * *

In this case, the chemical field test was used to determine whether certain white powder was cocaine. Upon visual inspection of the powder in isolation, one could not identify it as cocaine. In the abstract, therefore, it is possible that an individual could keep the powder in such a way as to preserve a reasonable expectation of privacy in its identity. For instance, it might be kept in a transparent pharmaceutical vial and disguised as legitimate medicine. Under those circumstances, the use of a chemical field test would constitute a search. However, in this case, as hypothesized above, the context in which the powder was found could not support a reasonable expectation of privacy. In particular, the substance was found in four plastic bags, which had been inside a tube wrapped with tape and sent to respondents via Federal Express. It was essentially inconceivable that a legal substance would be packaged in this manner for transport by a common carrier. Thus, viewing the powder as they did at the offices of Federal Express, the DEA agent could identify it with "virtual certainty"; it was essentially as though the chemical identity of the powder was plainly visible. Under these circumstances, therefore, respondents had no reasonable expectation of privacy in the identity of the powder, and the use of the chemical field test did not constitute a "search" violative of the Fourth Amendment.

Points for Discussion

1. The majority and dissent disagree about the following assertion: "A chemical test that merely discloses whether or not a particular substance is cocaine does not compromise any legitimate interest in privacy." Who has the better of the argument here?

2. Relatedly, what do you make of Justice Brennan's assertion that "the Court's analysis is so unbounded that if a device were developed that could detect, from the outside of a building, the presence of cocaine inside, there would be no constitutional obstacle to the police cruising through a residential neighborhood and using the device to identify all homes in which the drug is present"? Does that conclusion follow directly from the Court's opinion in *Jacobsen*? As a matter of constitutional law, what should be the status of such a device? *See, e.g.*, Sam Kamin, *Law and Technology: The Case for a Smart Gun Detector*, 59 L. AND CONTEMP. PROBS 221 (1996) (arguing for the constitutionality of such a device).

3. Justice Stevens writes for the Court that "it is well-settled that it is constitutionally reasonable for law enforcement officials to seize 'effects' that cannot support a justifiable expectation of privacy without a warrant, based on probable cause to believe they contain contraband." More than two decades later, the Court in another majority opinion by Justice Stevens relied on *Jacobsen* for the proposition that "any interest in possessing contraband cannot be deemed 'legitimate.'" *Illinois v. Caballes*, 543 U.S. 405 (2005). The effect of this conclusion is to predicate what constitutes a search at least in part on what government action reveals. Given that the Fourth Amendment was a reaction against general searches for seditious libels, how defensible is the claim that the Fourth Amendment's protection can be withdrawn by the government declaring an object contraband?

ARIZONA V. HICKS

480 U.S. 321 (1987)

JUSTICE SCALIA delivered the opinion of the court.

In *Coolidge v. New Hampshire*, 403 U.S. 443 (1971), we said that in certain circumstances a warrantless seizure by police of an item that comes within plain view during their lawful search of a private area may be reasonable under the Fourth Amendment. We granted certiorari in the present case to decide whether this "plain view" doctrine may be invoked when the police have less than probable cause to believe that the item in question is evidence of a crime or is contraband.

I

On April 18, 1984, a bullet was fired through the floor of respondent's apartment, striking and injuring a man in the apartment below. Police officers arrived and entered respondent's apartment to search for the shooter, for other victims, and for weapons. They found and seized three weapons, including a sawed-off rifle, and in the course of their search also discovered a stocking-cap mask.

One of the policemen, Officer Nelson, noticed two sets of expensive stereo components, which seemed out of place in the squalid and otherwise ill-appointed four-room apartment. Suspecting that they were stolen, he read and recorded their serial numbers-moving some of the components, including a Bang and Olufsen turntable, in order to do so-which he then reported by phone to his headquarters. On being advised that the turntable had been taken in an armed robbery, he seized it immediately. It was later determined that some of the other serial numbers matched those on other stereo equipment taken in the same armed robbery, and a warrant was obtained and executed to seize that equipment as well. Respondent was subsequently indicted for the robbery.

The state trial court granted respondent's motion to suppress the evidence that had been seized. The Court of Appeals of Arizona affirmed.

It was conceded that the initial entry and search, although warrantless, were justified by the exigent circumstance of the shooting. The Court of Appeals viewed the obtaining of the serial numbers, however, as an additional search, unrelated to that exigency. Relying upon a statement in *Mincey v. Arizona,* 437 U.S. 385 (1978), that a "warrantless search must be 'strictly circumscribed by the exigencies which justify its initiation,' " *id.,* at 393 (citation omitted), the Court of Appeals held that the police conduct violated the Fourth Amendment, requiring the evidence derived from that conduct to be excluded. Both courts—the trial court explicitly and the Court of Appeals by necessary implication—rejected the State's contention that Officer Nelson's actions were justified under the "plain view" doctrine of *Coolidge v. New Hampshire, supra.* The Arizona Supreme Court denied review, and the State filed this petition.

II

As an initial matter, the State argues that Officer Nelson's actions constituted neither a "search" nor a "seizure" within the meaning of the Fourth Amendment. We agree that the mere recording of the serial numbers did not constitute a seizure. To be sure, that was the first step in a process by which respondent was eventually deprived of the stereo equipment. In and of itself, however, it did not "meaningfully interfere" with respondent's possessory interest in either the serial numbers or the equipment, and therefore did not amount to a seizure. See *Maryland v. Macon,* 472 U.S. 463, 469 (1985).

Officer Nelson's moving of the equipment, however, did constitute a "search" separate and apart from the search for the shooter, victims, and weapons that was the lawful objective of his entry into the apartment. Merely inspecting those parts of the turntable that came into view during the latter search would not have constituted an independent search, because it would have produced no additional invasion of respondent's privacy interest. But taking action, unrelated to the objectives of the authorized intrusion, which exposed to view concealed portions of the apartment or its contents, did produce a new invasion of respondent's privacy unjustified by the exigent circumstance that validated the entry. This is why, contrary to Justice Powell's suggestion, the "distinction between 'looking' at a suspicious object in plain view and 'moving' it even a few inches" is much more than trivial for purposes of the Fourth Amendment. It matters not that the search uncovered nothing of any great personal value to respondent—serial numbers rather than (what might conceivably have been hidden behind or under the equipment) letters or photographs. A search is a search, even if it happens to disclose nothing but the bottom of a turntable.

III

The remaining question is whether the search was "reasonable" under the Fourth Amendment.

On this aspect of the case we reject, at the outset, the apparent position of the Arizona Court of Appeals that because the officers' action directed to the stereo equipment was unrelated to the justification for their entry into respondent's apartment, it was *ipso facto* unreasonable. That lack of relationship *always* exists with regard to action validated under the "plain view" doctrine; where action is taken for the purpose justifying the entry, invocation of the doctrine is superfluous. *Mincey v. Arizona, supra,* in saying that a warrantless search must be "strictly circumscribed by the exigencies which justify its initiation,"437 U.S., at 393 (citation omitted), was addressing only the scope of the primary search itself, and was not overruling by implication the many cases acknowledging that the "plain view" doctrine can legitimate action beyond that scope.

We turn, then, to application of the doctrine to the facts of this case. "It is well established that under certain circumstances the police may *seize* evidence in plain view without a warrant," *Coolidge v. New Hampshire,* 403 U.S., at 465 (plurality opinion) (emphasis added). Those circumstances include situations "[w]here the initial intrusion that brings the police within plain view of such [evidence] is supported . . . by one of the recognized exceptions to the warrant requirement," *ibid.,* such as the exigent-circumstances intrusion here. It would be absurd to say that an object could lawfully be seized and taken from the premises, but could not be moved for closer examination. It is clear, therefore, that the search here was valid if the "plain view" doctrine would have sustained a seizure of the equipment.

There is no doubt it would have done so if Officer Nelson had probable cause to believe that the equipment was stolen. The State has conceded, however, that he had only a "reasonable suspicion," by which it means something less than probable cause. We have not ruled on the question whether probable cause is required in order to invoke the "plain view" doctrine. Dicta in *Payton v. New York,* 445 U.S. 573, 587 (1980), suggested that the standard of probable cause must be met, but our later opinions in *Texas v. Brown,* 460 U.S. 730 (1983), explicitly regarded the issue as unresolved, see *id.,* at 742, n. 7 (plurality opinion); *id.,* at 746 (STEVENS, J., concurring in judgment).

We now hold that probable cause is required. To say otherwise would be to cut the "plain view" doctrine loose from its theoretical and practical moorings. The theory of that doctrine consists of extending to nonpublic places such as the home, where searches and seizures without a warrant are presumptively unreasonable, the police's longstanding authority to make warrantless seizures in public places of such objects as weapons and contraband. And the practical justification for that extension is the desirability of sparing police, whose viewing of the object in the course of a lawful search is as legitimate as it would have been in a public place, the inconvenience and the risk-to themselves or to preservation of the evidence-of going to obtain a warrant. Dispensing with the need for a warrant is worlds apart from permitting a lesser standard of *cause* for the seizure than a warrant would require, *i.e.,* the standard of probable cause. No reason is apparent why an object should routinely be seizable on lesser grounds, during an unrelated search and seizure, than would have been needed to obtain a warrant for that same object if it had been known to be on the premises.

We do not say, of course, that a seizure can never be justified on less than probable cause. We have held that it can—where, for example, the seizure is minimally intrusive and operational necessities render it the only practicable means of detecting certain types of crime. No special operational necessities are relied on here, however-but rather the mere fact that the items in question came lawfully within the officer's plain view. That alone cannot supplant the requirement of probable cause.

The same considerations preclude us from holding that, even though probable cause would have been necessary for a *seizure,* the *search* of objects in plain view that occurred here could be sustained on lesser grounds. A dwelling-place search, no less than a dwelling-place seizure, requires probable cause, and there is no reason in theory or practicality why application of the "plain view" doctrine would supplant that requirement. Although the interest protected by the Fourth Amendment injunction against unreasonable searches is quite different from that protected by its injunction against unreasonable seizures, neither the one nor the other is of inferior worth or necessarily requires only lesser protection. We have not elsewhere drawn a categorical distinction between the two insofar as concerns the degree of justification needed to establish the reasonableness of police action, and we see no reason for a distinction in the particular circumstances before us here. Indeed, to treat searches more liberally would especially erode the plurality's warning in *Coolidge* that "the 'plain view' doctrine may not be used to extend a general exploratory search from one object to another until something incriminating at last emerges." 403 U.S., at 466. In short, whether legal authority to move the equipment could be found only as an inevitable concomitant of the authority to seize it, or also as a consequence of some independent power to search certain objects in plain view, probable cause to believe the equipment was stolen was required.

Justice O'Connor's dissent suggests that we uphold the action here on the ground that it was a "cursory inspection" rather than a "full-blown search," and could therefore be justified by reasonable suspicion instead of probable cause. As already noted, a truly cursory inspection—one that involves merely looking at what is already exposed to view, without disturbing it—is not a "search" for Fourth Amendment purposes, and therefore does not even require reasonable suspicion. We are unwilling to send police and judges into a new thicket of Fourth Amendment law, to seek a creature of uncertain description that is neither a "plain view" inspection nor yet a "full-blown search." Nothing in the prior opinions of this Court supports such a distinction, not even the dictum from Justice Stewart's concurrence in *Stanley v. Georgia,* 394 U.S. 557, 571 (1969), whose reference to a "mere inspection" describes, in our view, close observation of what lies in plain sight.

Justice Powell's dissent reasonably asks what it is we would have had Officer Nelson do in these circumstances. The answer depends, of course, upon whether he had probable cause to conduct a search, a question that was not preserved in this case. If he had, then he should have done precisely what he did. If not, then he should have followed up his suspicions, if possible, by means other than a search—just as he would have had to do if, while walking along the street, he had noticed the same suspicious stereo equipment sitting inside a house a few feet away from him, beneath an open window. It may well be that, in such circumstances, no effective means short of a search exist. But there is nothing new in the realization that the Constitution sometimes insulates the criminality of a few in order to protect the privacy of us all. Our disagreement with the dissenters pertains to where the proper balance should be struck; we choose to adhere to the textual and traditional standard of probable cause.

JUSTICE WHITE, concurring.

I write only to emphasize that this case does not present, and we have no occasion to address, the so-called "inadvertent discovery" prong of the plain-view exception to the Warrant Clause. See *Coolidge v. New Hampshire,* 403 U.S. 443, 469–471 (1971) (plurality opinion). This "requirement" of the plain-view doctrine has never been accepted by a judgment supported by a majority of this Court, and I therefore do not accept Justice O'Connor's dissent's assertion that evidence seized in plain view must have been inadvertently discovered in order to satisfy the dictates of the Fourth Amendment. I join the majority opinion today without regard to the inadvertence of the officers' discovery of the stereo components' serial numbers. The police officers conducted a search of respondent's stereo equipment absent probable cause that the equipment was stolen. It is for this reason that the judgment of the Court of Appeals of Arizona must be affirmed.

JUSTICE POWELL, with whom THE CHIEF JUSTICE and JUSTICE O'CONNOR join, dissenting.

I join Justice O'Connor's dissenting opinion, and write briefly to highlight what seem to me the unfortunate consequences of the Court's decision.

Today the Court holds for the first time that the requirement of probable cause operates as a separate limitation on the application of the plain-view doctrine. The plurality opinion in *Coolidge v. New Hampshire,*

403 U.S. 443 (1971), required only that it be "immediately apparent to the police that they have evidence before them; the 'plain view' doctrine may not be used to extend a general exploratory search from one object to another until something incriminating at last emerges." *Id.*, at 466 (citation omitted). There was no general exploratory search in this case, and I would not approve such a search. All the pertinent objects were in plain view and could be identified as objects frequently stolen. There was no looking into closets, opening of drawers or trunks, or other "rummaging around." Justice O'Connor properly emphasizes that the moving of a suspicious object in plain view results in a minimal invasion of privacy. The Court nevertheless holds that "merely looking at" an object in plain view is lawful, but "moving" or "disturbing" the object to investigate a reasonable suspicion is not. The facts of this case well illustrate the unreasonableness of this distinction.

The officers' suspicion that the stereo components at issue were stolen was both reasonable and based on specific, articulable facts. Indeed, the State was unwise to concede the absence of probable cause. The police lawfully entered respondent's apartment under exigent circumstances that arose when a bullet fired through the floor of the apartment struck a man in the apartment below. What they saw in the apartment hardly suggested that it was occupied by law-abiding citizens. A .25-caliber automatic pistol lay in plain view on the living room floor. During a concededly lawful search, the officers found a .45-caliber automatic, a .22-caliber, sawed-off rifle, and a stocking-cap mask. The apartment was littered with drug paraphernalia. The officers also observed two sets of expensive stereo components of a type that frequently was stolen.

It is fair to ask what Officer Nelson should have done in these circumstances. Accepting the State's concession that he lacked probable cause, he could not have obtained a warrant to seize the stereo components. Neither could he have remained on the premises and forcibly prevented their removal. Officer Nelson's testimony indicates that he was able to read some of the serial numbers without moving the components. To read the serial number on a Bang and Olufsen turntable, however, he had to "turn it around or turn it upside down." Officer Nelson noted the serial numbers on the stereo components and telephoned the National Crime Information Center to check them against the Center's computerized listing of stolen property. The computer confirmed his suspicion that at least the Bang and Olufsen turntable had been stolen. On the basis of this information, the officers obtained a warrant to seize the turntable and other stereo components that also proved to be stolen.

The Court holds that there was an unlawful search of the turntable. It agrees that the "mere recording of the serial numbers did not constitute a seizure." Thus, if the computer had identified as stolen property a component with a visible serial number, the evidence would have been admissible. But the Court further holds that "Officer Nelson's moving of the equipment ... did constitute a 'search'. . . ." It perceives a constitutional distinction between reading a serial number on an object and moving or picking up an identical object to see its serial number. To make its position unmistakably clear, the Court concludes that a "search is a search, even if it happens to disclose nothing but the bottom of a turntable." With all respect, this distinction between "looking" at a suspicious object in plain view and "moving" it even a few inches trivializes the Fourth Amendment. The Court's new rule will cause uncertainty, and could deter conscientious police officers from lawfully obtaining evidence necessary to convict guilty persons. Apart from the importance of rationality in the interpretation of the Fourth Amendment, today's decision may handicap law enforcement without enhancing privacy interests. Accordingly, I dissent.

JUSTICE O'CONNOR, with whom THE CHIEF JUSTICE and JUSTICE POWELL join, dissenting.

The Court today gives the right answer to the wrong question. The Court asks whether the police must have probable cause before either seizing an object in plain view or conducting a full-blown search of that object, and concludes that they must. I agree. In my view, however, this case presents a different question: whether police must have probable cause before conducting a cursory inspection of an item in plain view. Because I conclude that such an inspection is reasonable if the police are aware of facts or circumstances that justify a reasonable suspicion that the item is evidence of a crime, I would reverse the judgment of the Arizona Court of Appeals, and therefore dissent.

In *Coolidge v. New Hampshire,* 403 U.S. 443 (1971), Justice Stewart summarized three requirements that the plurality thought must be satisfied for a plain-view search or seizure. First, the police must lawfully make an initial intrusion or otherwise be in a position from which they can view a particular area. Second, the officer must discover incriminating evidence "inadvertently." Third, it must be "immediately apparent" to the police that the items they observe may be evidence of a crime, contraband, or otherwise subject to seizure. As another plurality observed in *Texas v. Brown,* 460 U.S. 730, 737 (1983), these three requirements have never been expressly adopted by a majority of this Court, but "as the considered opinion of four Members of this Court [the *Coolidge* plurality] should obviously be the point of reference for further discussion of the issue." There is no dispute in this case that the first two requirements have been satisfied. The officers were lawfully in the apartment pursuant to exigent circumstances, and the discovery of the stereo was inadvertent—the officers did not " 'know in advance the location of [certain] evidence and intend to seize it,' relying on the plain-view doctrine only as a pretext." Instead, the dispute in this case focuses on the application of the "immediately apparent" requirement; at issue is whether a police officer's reasonable suspicion is adequate to justify a cursory examination of an item in plain view.

The purpose of the "immediately apparent" requirement is to prevent "general, exploratory rummaging in a person's belongings." *Coolidge v. New Hampshire,* 403 U.S., at 467. If an officer could indiscriminately search every item in plain view, a search justified by a limited purpose—such as exigent circumstances—could be used to eviscerate the protections of the Fourth Amendment. In order to prevent such a general search, therefore, we require that the relevance of the item be "immediately apparent." . . .

Thus, I agree with the Court that even under the plain-view doctrine, probable cause is required before the police seize an item, or conduct a full-blown search of evidence in plain view. Such a requirement of probable cause will prevent the plain-view doctrine from authorizing general searches. This is not to say, however, that even a mere inspection of a suspicious item must be supported by probable cause. When a police officer makes a cursory inspection of a suspicious item in plain view in order to determine whether it is indeed evidence of a crime, there is no "exploratory rummaging." Only those items that the police officer "reasonably suspects" as evidence of a crime may be inspected, and perhaps more importantly, the scope of such an inspection is quite limited. In short, if police officers have a reasonable, articulable suspicion that an object they come across during the course of a lawful search is evidence of crime, in my view they may make a cursory examination of the object to verify their suspicion. If the officers wish to go beyond such a cursory examination of the object, however, they must have probable cause.

* * *

In my view, the balance of the governmental and privacy interests strongly supports a reasonable-suspicion standard for the cursory examination of items in plain view. The additional intrusion caused by an inspection of an item in plain view for its serial number is miniscule. Indeed, the intrusion in this case was even more transitory and less intrusive than the seizure of luggage from a suspected drug dealer in *United States v. Place,* [462 U.S. 696 (1983)] and the "severe, though brief, intrusion upon cherished personal security" in *Terry v. Ohio, supra,* at 24–25.

Weighed against this minimal additional invasion of privacy are rather major gains in law enforcement. The use of identification numbers in tracing stolen property is a powerful law enforcement tool. Serial numbers are far more helpful and accurate in detecting stolen property than simple police recollection of the evidence. Given the prevalence of mass produced goods in our national economy, a serial number is often the only sure method of detecting stolen property. The balance of governmental and private interests strongly supports the view accepted by a majority of courts that a standard of reasonable suspicion meets the requirements of the Fourth Amendment.

Unfortunately, in its desire to establish a "bright-line" test, the Court has taken a step that ignores a substantial body of precedent and that places serious roadblocks to reasonable law enforcement practices. Indeed, in this case no warrant to search the stereo equipment for its serial number could have been obtained by the officers based on reasonable suspicion alone, and in the Court's view the officers may not even move the stereo turntable to examine its serial number. The theoretical advantages of the "search is a search" approach adopted by the Court today are simply too remote to justify the tangible and severe damage it inflicts on legitimate and effective law enforcement.

Even if probable cause were the appropriate standard, I have little doubt that it was satisfied here. When police officers, during the course of a search inquiring into grievously unlawful activity, discover the tools of a thief (a sawed-off rifle and a stocking mask) and observe in a small apartment *two* sets of stereo equipment that are both inordinately expensive in relation to their surroundings and known to be favored targets of larcenous activity, the "flexible, common-sense standard" of probable cause has been satisfied.

Because the Court today ignores the existence of probable cause, and in doing so upsets a widely accepted body of precedent on the standard of reasonableness for the cursory examination of evidence in plain view, I respectfully dissent.

Points for Discussion

1. Justice White summarized the Court's rationale for holding the police's actions unconstitutional thusly: "The police officers conducted a search of respondent's stereo equipment absent probable cause [to believe] that the equipment was stolen." Justice O'Connor's dissent claimed that this straightforward holding would yield only "theoretical advantages" and speculated about the "severe damage it inflicts on legitimate and effective law enforcement." The majority's response is that "there is nothing new in the realization that the Constitution sometimes insulates the criminality of a few in order to protect the privacy of us all." Who has the better of the argument?

2. The dissent's citation to *United States v. Place* is telling. In *Place*, the Court held that it was unconstitutional to take a traveler's luggage from him at LaGuardia Airport and transport it to Kennedy Airport so that a dog could sniff it for narcotics. Although it was dicta, the Court then went on to remark more generally on drug interdiction at airports. After balancing its estimation of the privacy interests against the government's interest in intercepting drugs, the Court held that luggage could be "briefly" seized without probable

cause to have a dog sniff it for drugs. The Court also concluded—although the issue was not raised by the parties—that having a dog take a whiff of luggage is not a 'search' under the Fourth Amendment because it detects only contraband. Is such a conclusion consistent with the text and history of the Fourth Amendment?

C. "SEIZURES"

The previous section discussed the way the Court defines a search, focusing on the two-part test that Justice Harlan devised in *Katz v. United States*: whether a defendant has a subjective expectation of privacy and whether society is willing to validate that expectation of privacy as reasonable. In this section we look at the Court's definition of the other kind of government action policed by the Fourth Amendment: seizures.

The cases in this section all involve seizures of persons rather than property. That is because, as Justice Stevens' majority noted in footnote 5 of *United States v. Jacobsen*, relatively few of the Court's cases have analyzed property seizures. Since *Katz,* alleged Fourth Amendment violations involving property have generally been analyzed using *Katz*'s expectations-of-privacy framework.

CALIFORNIA V. HODARI D.

499 U.S. 621 (1991)

JUSTICE SCALIA delivered the opinion of the court.

Late one evening in April 1988, Officers Brian McColgin and Jerry Pertoso were on patrol in a high-crime area of Oakland, California. They were dressed in street clothes but wearing jackets with "Police" embossed on both front and back. Their unmarked car proceeded west on Foothill Boulevard, and turned south onto 63rd Avenue. As they rounded the corner, they saw four or five youths huddled around a small red car parked at the curb. When the youths saw the officers' car approaching they apparently panicked, and took flight. The respondent here, Hodari D., and one companion ran west through an alley; the others fled south. The red car also headed south, at a high rate of speed.

The officers were suspicious and gave chase. McColgin remained in the car and continued south on 63rd Avenue; Pertoso left the car, ran back north along 63rd, then west on Foothill Boulevard, and turned south on 62nd Avenue. Hodari, meanwhile, emerged from the alley onto 62nd and ran north. Looking behind as he ran, he did not turn and see Pertoso until the officer was almost upon him, whereupon he tossed away what appeared to be a small rock. A moment later, Pertoso tackled Hodari, handcuffed him, and radioed for assistance. Hodari was found to be carrying $130 in cash and a pager; and the rock he had discarded was found to be crack cocaine.

* * *

As this case comes to us, the only issue presented is whether, at the time he dropped the drugs, Hodari had been "seized" within the meaning of the Fourth Amendment.[1] If so, respondent argues, the drugs were the fruit of that seizure and the evidence concerning them was properly excluded. If not, the drugs were abandoned by Hodari and lawfully recovered by the police, and the evidence should have been admitted. (In addition, of course, Pertoso's seeing the rock of cocaine, at least if he recognized it as such, would provide reasonable suspicion for the unquestioned seizure that occurred when he tackled Hodari.

We have long understood that the Fourth Amendment's protection against "unreasonable . . . seizures" includes seizure of the person. From the time of the founding to the present, the word "seizure" has meant a "taking possession," 2 N. Webster, An American Dictionary of the English Language 67 (1828).

For most purposes at common law, the word connoted not merely grasping, or applying physical force to, the animate or inanimate object in question, but actually bringing it within physical control. A ship still fleeing, even though under attack, would not be considered to have been seized as a war prize. A res capable of manual delivery was not seized until "tak[en] into custody." *Pelham v. Rose,* 9 Wall. 103, 106 (1870). To constitute an arrest, however—the quintessential "seizure of the person" under our Fourth Amendment jurisprudence—the mere grasping or application of physical force with lawful authority, whether or not it succeeded in subduing the arrestee, was sufficient. As one commentator has described it:

> There can be constructive detention, which will constitute an arrest, although the party is never actually brought within the physical control of the party making an arrest. This is accomplished by merely touching, however slightly, the body of the accused, by the party making the arrest and for that purpose, although he does not succeed in stopping or holding him even for an instant; as where the bailiff had tried to arrest one who fought him off by a fork, the court said, "If the bailiff had touched him, that had been an arrest. . . ."

A. Cornelius, Search and Seizure 163–164 (2d ed. 1930) (footnote omitted).

To say that an arrest is effected by the slightest application of physical force, despite the arrestee's escape, is not to say that for Fourth

---

[1] California conceded below that Officer Pertoso did not have the "reasonable suspicion" required to justify stopping Hodari, see *Terry v. Ohio,* 392 U.S. 1 (1968). That it would be unreasonable to stop, for brief inquiry, young men who scatter in panic upon the mere sighting of the police is not self-evident, and arguably contradicts proverbial common sense. See Proverbs 28:1 ("The wicked flee when no man pursueth"). We do not decide that point here, but rely entirely upon the State's concession.

Amendment purposes there is a *continuing* arrest during the period of fugitivity. If, for example, Pertoso had laid his hands upon Hodari to arrest him, but Hodari had broken away and had *then* cast away the cocaine, it would hardly be realistic to say that that disclosure had been made during the course of an arrest. Cf. *Thompson v. Whitman,* 18 Wall. 457, 471 (1874) ("A seizure is a single act, and not a continuous fact"). The present case, however, is even one step further removed. It does not involve the application of any physical force; Hodari was untouched by Officer Pertoso at the time he discarded the cocaine. His defense relies instead upon the proposition that a seizure occurs "when the officer, by means of physical force *or show of authority,* has in some way restrained the liberty of a citizen." *Terry v. Ohio,* 392 U.S. 1, 19, n. 16 (1968) (emphasis added). Hodari contends (and we accept as true for purposes of this decision) that Pertoso's pursuit qualified as a "show of authority" calling upon Hodari to halt. The narrow question before us is whether, with respect to a show of authority as with respect to application of physical force, a seizure occurs even though the subject does not yield. We hold that it does not.

The language of the Fourth Amendment, of course, cannot sustain respondent's contention. The word "seizure" readily bears the meaning of a laying on of hands or application of physical force to restrain movement, even when it is ultimately unsuccessful. ("She seized the purse-snatcher, but he broke out of her grasp.") It does not remotely apply, however, to the prospect of a policeman yelling "Stop, in the name of the law!" at a fleeing form that continues to flee. That is no seizure. Nor can the result respondent wishes to achieve be produced—indirectly, as it were—by suggesting that Pertoso's uncomplied-with show of authority was a common-law arrest, and then appealing to the principle that all common-law arrests are seizures. An arrest requires *either* physical force (as described above) *or,* where that is absent, *submission* to the assertion of authority.

We do not think it desirable, even as a policy matter, to stretch the Fourth Amendment beyond its words and beyond the meaning of arrest, as respondent urges. Street pursuits always place the public at some risk, and compliance with police orders to stop should therefore be encouraged. Only a few of those orders, we must presume, will be without adequate basis, and since the addressee has no ready means of identifying the deficient ones it almost invariably is the responsible course to comply. Unlawful orders will not be deterred, moreover, by sanctioning through the exclusionary rule those of them that are *not* obeyed. Since policemen do not command "Stop!" expecting to be ignored, or give chase hoping to be outrun, it fully suffices to apply the deterrent to their genuine, successful seizures.

Respondent contends that his position is sustained by the so-called *Mendenhall* test, formulated by Justice Stewart's opinion in *United States v. Mendenhall,* 446 U.S. 544, 554 (1980), and adopted by the Court in later cases see: "[A] person has been 'seized' within the meaning of the Fourth Amendment only if, in view of all the circumstances surrounding the incident, a reasonable person would have believed that he was not free to leave." In seeking to rely upon that test here, respondent fails to read it carefully. It says that a person has been seized "only if," not that he has been seized "whenever"; it states a *necessary,* but not a *sufficient,* condition for seizure—or, more precisely, for seizure effected through a "show of authority." *Mendenhall* establishes that the test for existence of a "show of authority" is an objective one: not whether the citizen perceived that he was being ordered to restrict his movement, but whether the officer's words and actions would have conveyed that to a reasonable person. Application of this objective test was the basis for our decision in the other case principally relied upon by respondent, [*Michigan v. Chesternut,* 486 U.S. 567 (1988)], where we concluded that the police cruiser's slow following of the defendant did not convey the message that he was not free to disregard the police and go about his business. We did not address in *Chesternut,* however, the question whether, if the *Mendenhall* test was met—if the message that the defendant was not free to leave *had* been conveyed—a Fourth Amendment seizure would have occurred.

Quite relevant to the present case, however, was our decision in *Brower v. Inyo County,* 489 U.S. 593, 596 (1989). In that case, police cars with flashing lights had chased the decedent for 20 miles—surely an adequate "show of authority"—but he did not stop until his fatal crash into a police-erected blockade. The issue was whether his death could be held to be the consequence of an unreasonable seizure in violation of the Fourth Amendment. We did not even consider the possibility that a seizure could have occurred during the course of the chase because, as we explained, that "show of authority" did not produce his stop. And we discussed an opinion of Justice Holmes, involving a situation not much different from the present case, where revenue agents had picked up containers dropped by moonshiners whom they were pursuing without adequate warrant. The containers were not excluded as the product of an unlawful seizure because "[t]he defendant's own acts, and those of his associates, disclosed the jug, the jar and the bottle—and there was no seizure in the sense of the law when the officers examined the contents of each after they had been abandoned." *Hester v. United States,* 265 U.S. 57, 58 (1924). The same is true here.

In sum, assuming that Pertoso's pursuit in the present case constituted a "show of authority" enjoining Hodari to halt, since Hodari did not comply with that injunction he was not seized until he was tackled. The cocaine abandoned while he was running was in this case not the fruit of a seizure, and his motion to exclude evidence of it was properly denied.

JUSTICE STEVENS, with whom JUSTICE MARSHALL joins, dissenting.

* * *

For the purposes of decision, the following propositions are not in dispute. First, when Officer Pertoso began his pursuit of respondent,[4] the officer did not have a lawful basis for either stopping or arresting respondent. Second, the officer's chase amounted to a "show of authority" as soon as respondent saw the officer nearly upon him. Third, the act of discarding the rock of cocaine was the direct consequence of the show of authority. Fourth, as the Court correctly demonstrates, no common-law arrest occurred until the officer tackled respondent. Thus, the Court is quite right in concluding that the abandonment of the rock was not the fruit of a common-law arrest.

It is equally clear, however, that if the officer had succeeded in touching respondent before he dropped the rock—even if he did not subdue him—an arrest would have occurred. In that event (assuming the touching precipitated the abandonment), the evidence would have been the fruit of an unlawful common-law arrest. The distinction between the actual case and the hypothetical case is the same as the distinction between the common-law torts of assault and battery—a touching converts the former into the latter. Although the distinction between assault and battery was important for pleading purposes, the distinction should not take on constitutional dimensions. The Court mistakenly allows this common-law distinction to define its interpretation of the Fourth Amendment.

At the same time, the Court fails to recognize the existence of another, more telling, common-law distinction—the distinction between an arrest and an attempted arrest. As the Court teaches us, the distinction between battery and assault was critical to a correct understanding of the common law of arrest. However, the facts of this case do not describe an actual arrest, but rather an unlawful *attempt* to take a presumptively innocent person into custody. Such an attempt was unlawful at common law. Thus, if the Court wants to define the scope of the Fourth Amendment based on the common law, it should look, not to the common law of arrest, but to the common law of attempted arrest, according to the facts of this case.

* * *

In *United States v. Mendenhall,* 446 U.S. 544 (1980), the Court "adhere[d] to the view that a person is 'seized' only when, by means of

[4] The Court's gratuitous quotation from Proverbs 28:1 mistakenly assumes that innocent residents have no reason to fear the sudden approach of strangers. We have previously considered, and rejected, this ivory-towered analysis of the real world for it fails to describe the experience of many residents, particularly if they are members of a minority. It has long been "a matter of common knowledge that men who are entirely innocent do sometimes fly from the scene of a crime through fear of being apprehended as the guilty parties, or from an unwillingness to appear as witnesses. Nor is it true as an accepted axiom of criminal law that 'the wicked flee when no man pursueth, but the righteous are as bold as a lion.'" *Alberty v. United States,* 162 U.S. 499, 511 (1896).

physical force or a show of authority, his freedom of movement is restrained." The Court looked to whether the citizen who is questioned "remains free to disregard the questions and walk away," and if he or she is able to do so, then "there has been no intrusion upon that person's liberty or privacy" that would require some "particularized and objective justification" under the Constitution. The test for a "seizure," as formulated by the Court in *Mendenhall,* was whether, "in view of all of the circumstances surrounding the incident, a reasonable person would have believed that he was not free to leave." Examples of seizures include "the threatening presence of several officers, the display of a weapon by an officer, some physical touching of the person of the citizen, or the use of language or tone of voice indicating that compliance with the officer's request might be compelled." The Court's unwillingness today to adhere to the "reasonable person" standard, as formulated by Justice Stewart in *Mendenhall,* marks an unnecessary departure from Fourth Amendment case law.

* * *

More importantly, in *Florida v. Royer,* 460 U.S. 491 (1983), a plurality of the Court adopted Justice Stewart's formulation in *Mendenhall* as the appropriate standard for determining when police questioning crosses the threshold from a consensual encounter to a forcible stop. In *Royer,* the Court held that an illegal seizure had occurred. As a predicate for that holding, Justice White, in his opinion for the plurality, explained that the citizen "may not be detained *even momentarily* without reasonable, objective grounds for doing so; and his refusal to listen or answer does not, without more, furnish those grounds." The rule looks, not to the subjective perceptions of the person questioned, but rather, to the objective characteristics of the encounter that may suggest whether a reasonable person would have felt free to leave.

* * *

Finally, it is noteworthy that in *Michigan v. Chesternut,* 486 U.S. 567 (1988), the State asked us to repudiate the reasonable person standard developed in *Terry, Mendenhall, Delgado,* and *Royer.* We decided, however, to "adhere to our traditional contextual approach." In our opinion, we described Justice Stewart's analysis in *Mendenhall* as "a test to be applied in determining whether 'a person has been "seized" within the meaning of the Fourth Amendment' " and noted that "[t]he Court has since embraced this test." Moreover, in commenting on the virtues of the test, we explained that it focused on the police officer's conduct:

> The test's objective standard—looking to the reasonable man's interpretation of the conduct in question—allows the police to determine in advance whether the conduct contemplated will implicate the Fourth Amendment.

* * *

III

* * *

Because the facts of this case are somewhat unusual, it is appropriate to note that the same issue would arise if the show of force took the form of a command to "freeze," a warning shot, or the sound of sirens accompanied by a patrol car's flashing lights. In any of these situations, there may be a significant time interval between the initiation of the officer's show of force and the complete submission by the citizen. At least on the facts of this case, the Court concludes that the timing of the seizure is governed by the citizen's reaction, rather than by the officer's conduct. One consequence of this conclusion is that the point at which the interaction between citizen and police officer becomes a seizure occurs, not when a reasonable citizen believes he or she is no longer free to go, but, rather, only after the officer exercises control over the citizen.

In my view, our interests in effective law enforcement and in personal liberty would be better served by adhering to a standard that "allows the police to determine in advance whether the conduct contemplated will implicate the Fourth Amendment." The range of possible responses to a police show of force, and the multitude of problems that may arise in determining whether, and at which moment, there has been "submission," can only create uncertainty and generate litigation.

* * *

It seems equally clear to me that the constitutionality of a police officer's show of force should be measured by the conditions that exist at the time of the officer's action. A search must be justified on the basis of the facts available at the time it is initiated; the subsequent discovery of evidence does not retroactively validate an unconstitutional search. The same approach should apply to seizures; the character of the citizen's response should not govern the constitutionality of the officer's conduct.

If an officer effects an arrest by touching a citizen, apparently the Court would accept the fact that a seizure occurred, even if the arrestee should thereafter break loose and flee. In such a case, the constitutionality of the seizure would be evaluated as of the time the officer acted. That category of seizures would then be analyzed in the same way as searches, namely, was the police action justified when it took place? It is anomalous, at best, to fashion a different rule for the subcategory of "show of force" arrests.

In cases within this new subcategory, there will be a period of time during which the citizen's liberty has been restrained, but he or she has not yet completely submitted to the show of force. A motorist pulled over by a highway patrol car cannot come to an immediate stop, even if the motorist intends to obey the patrol car's signal. If an officer decides to make the kind of random stop forbidden by *Delaware v. Prouse,* 440 U.S. 648 (1979), and, after flashing his lights, but before the vehicle comes to a complete stop, sees that the license plate has expired, can he justify his action on the ground that the seizure became lawful after it was initiated but before it was completed? In an airport setting, may a drug enforcement agent now approach a group of passengers with his gun drawn, announce a "baggage search," and rely on the passengers' reactions to justify his investigative stops? The holding of today's majority fails to recognize the coercive and intimidating nature of such behavior and creates a rule that may allow such behavior to go unchecked.

The deterrent purposes of the exclusionary rule focus on the conduct of law enforcement officers and on discouraging improper behavior on their part, and not on the reaction of the citizen to the show of force. In the present case, if Officer Pertoso had succeeded in tackling respondent before he dropped the rock of cocaine, the rock unquestionably would have been excluded as the fruit of the officer's unlawful seizure. Instead, under the Court's logic-chopping analysis, the exclusionary rule has no application because an attempt to make an unconstitutional seizure is beyond the coverage of the Fourth Amendment, no matter how outrageous or unreasonable the officer's conduct may be.

* * *

Points for Discussion

1. If the Court were to apply the *Mendenhall* test in this case—whether a reasonable person would feel free to ignore the officers and leave—the outcome would appear clear. A reasonable person in Hodari D's position would have felt compelled to stop when ordered to do so by Officer Petroso. As a result, a seizure would have occurred, a seizure which the state conceded would have violated the Fourth Amendment for lack of reasonable suspicion. Why is the *Mendenhall* test not sufficient to resolve this case?

2. Are you convinced by the Court's assertion that *Mendenhall* set forth a necessary, but not a sufficient condition for a seizure?

3. Why does it matter when the seizure actually occurred if, as the dissent points out, Officer Petroso's attempt to seize Hodari D. would have been unreasonable if successful? Why should that not be enough to dispose of the case?

4. In another case decided the same term as *Hodari D.*, the Court rejected the Florida Supreme Court's "*per se* rule prohibiting the police from randomly boarding buses as a means of drug interdiction." *Florida v. Bostick*, 501 U.S. 429 (1991). The majority opinion by Justice O'Connor reasoned that Bostick may not have felt free to leave once the police boarded the bus but only because the bus was scheduled to depart. "He would not have felt free to leave

the bus even if the police had not been present. Bostick's movements were 'confined' in a sense, but this was the natural result of his decision to take the bus; it says nothing about whether or not the police conduct at issue was coercive." The Court remanded for the Florida Supreme Court "to determine whether the police conduct would have communicated to a reasonable person that the person was not free to decline the officers' requests or otherwise terminate the encounter." Justice Marshall's dissent, joined by Justice Blackmun and Justice Stevens, argued that "officers who conduct suspicionless, dragnet-style sweeps put passengers to the choice of cooperating or of exiting their buses and possibly being stranded in unfamiliar locations. It is exactly because this 'choice' is no 'choice' at all that police engage this technique." The Court returned to the issue of drug interdiction on buses in the following case.

UNITED STATES V. DRAYTON

536 U.S. 194 (2002)

JUSTICE KENNEDY delivered the opinion of the court.

The Fourth Amendment permits police officers to approach bus passengers at random to ask questions and to request their consent to searches, provided a reasonable person would understand that he or she is free to refuse. *Florida v. Bostick,* 501 U.S. 429 (1991). This case requires us to determine whether officers must advise bus passengers during these encounters of their right not to cooperate.

I

On February 4, 1999, respondents Christopher Drayton and Clifton Brown, Jr., were traveling on a Greyhound bus en route from Ft. Lauderdale, Florida, to Detroit, Michigan. The bus made a scheduled stop in Tallahassee, Florida. The passengers were required to disembark so the bus could be refueled and cleaned. As the passengers reboarded, the driver checked their tickets and then left to complete paperwork inside the terminal. As he left, the driver allowed three members of the Tallahassee Police Department to board the bus as part of a routine drug and weapons interdiction effort. The officers were dressed in plain clothes and carried concealed weapons and visible badges.

Once onboard Officer Hoover knelt on the driver's seat and faced the rear of the bus. He could observe the passengers and ensure the safety of the two other officers without blocking the aisle or otherwise obstructing the bus exit. Officers Lang and Blackburn went to the rear of the bus. Blackburn remained stationed there, facing forward. Lang worked his way toward the front of the bus, speaking with individual passengers as he went. He asked the passengers about their travel plans and sought to match passengers with luggage in the overhead racks. To avoid blocking the aisle, Lang stood next to or just behind each passenger with whom he spoke.

According to Lang's testimony, passengers who declined to cooperate with him or who chose to exit the bus at any time would have been allowed to do so without argument. In Lang's experience, however, most people are willing to cooperate. Some passengers go so far as to commend the police for their efforts to ensure the safety of their travel. Lang could recall five to six instances in the previous year in which passengers had declined to have their luggage searched. It also was common for passengers to leave the bus for a cigarette or a snack while the officers were on board. Lang sometimes informed passengers of their right to refuse to cooperate. On the day in question, however, he did not.

Respondents were seated next to each other on the bus. Drayton was in the aisle seat, Brown in the seat next to the window. Lang approached respondents from the rear and leaned over Drayton's shoulder. He held up his badge long enough for respondents to identify him as a police officer. With his face 12- to 18-inches away from Drayton's, Lang spoke in a voice just loud enough for respondents to hear: "I'm Investigator Lang with the Tallahassee Police Department. We're conducting bus interdiction *[sic]*, attempting to deter drugs and illegal weapons being transported on the bus. Do you have any bags on the bus?" Both respondents pointed to a single green bag in the overhead luggage rack. Lang asked, "Do you mind if I check it?," and Brown responded, "Go ahead." Lang handed the bag to Officer Blackburn to check. The bag contained no contraband.

Officer Lang noticed that both respondents were wearing heavy jackets and baggy pants despite the warm weather. In Lang's experience drug traffickers often use baggy clothing to conceal weapons or narcotics. The officer thus asked Brown if he had any weapons or drugs in his possession. And he asked Brown: "Do you mind if I check your person?" Brown answered, "Sure," and cooperated by leaning up in his seat, pulling a cell phone out of his pocket, and opening up his jacket. Lang reached across Drayton and patted down Brown's jacket and pockets, including his waist area, sides, and upper thighs. In both thigh areas, Lang detected hard objects similar to drug packages detected on other occasions. Lang arrested and handcuffed Brown. Officer Hoover escorted Brown from the bus.

Lang then asked Drayton, "Mind if I check you?" Drayton responded by lifting his hands about eight inches from his legs. Lang conducted a patdown of Drayton's thighs and detected hard objects similar to those found on Brown. He arrested Drayton and escorted him from the bus. A further search revealed that respondents had duct-taped plastic bundles of powder cocaine between several pairs of their boxer shorts. Brown possessed three bundles containing 483 grams of cocaine. Drayton possessed two bundles containing 295 grams of cocaine.

* * *

II

Law enforcement officers do not violate the Fourth Amendment's prohibition of unreasonable seizures merely by approaching individuals on the street or in other public places and putting questions to them if they are willing to listen. Even when law enforcement officers have no basis for suspecting a particular individual, they may pose questions, ask for identification, and request consent to search luggage—provided they do not induce cooperation by coercive means. If a reasonable person would feel free to terminate the encounter, then he or she has not been seized.

The Court has addressed on a previous occasion the specific question of drug interdiction efforts on buses. In *Bostick,* two police officers requested a bus passenger's consent to a search of his luggage. The passenger agreed, and the resulting search revealed cocaine in his suitcase. The Florida Supreme Court suppressed the cocaine. In doing so it adopted a *per se* rule that due to the cramped confines onboard a bus the act of questioning would deprive a person of his or her freedom of movement and so constitute a seizure under the Fourth Amendment.

This Court reversed. *Bostick* first made it clear that for the most part *per se* rules are inappropriate in the Fourth Amendment context. The proper inquiry necessitates a consideration of "all the circumstances surrounding the encounter." The Court noted next that the traditional rule, which states that a seizure does not occur so long as a reasonable person would feel free "to disregard the police and go about his business," *California v. Hodari D.,* 499 U.S. 621, 628 (1991), is not an accurate measure of the coercive effect of a bus encounter. A passenger may not want to get off a bus if there is a risk it will depart before the opportunity to reboard. A bus rider's movements are confined in this sense, but this is the natural result of choosing to take the bus; it says nothing about whether the police conduct is coercive. The proper inquiry "is whether a reasonable person would feel free to decline the officers' requests or otherwise terminate the encounter." Finally, the Court rejected Bostick's argument that he must have been seized because no reasonable person would consent to a search of luggage containing drugs. The reasonable person test, the Court explained, is objective and "presupposes an *innocent* person."

* * *

Applying the *Bostick* framework to the facts of this particular case, we conclude that the police did not seize respondents when they boarded the bus and began questioning passengers. The officers gave the passengers no reason to believe that they were required to answer the officers' questions. When Officer Lang approached respondents, he did not brandish a weapon or make any intimidating movements. He left the aisle free so that respondents could exit. He spoke to passengers one by one and in a polite, quiet voice. Nothing he said would suggest to a reasonable person that he or she was barred from leaving the bus or otherwise terminating the encounter.

There were ample grounds for the District Court to conclude that "everything that took place between Officer Lang and [respondents] suggests that it was cooperative" and that there "was nothing coercive [or] confrontational" about the encounter. There was no application of force, no intimidating movement, no overwhelming show of force, no brandishing of weapons, no blocking of exits, no threat, no command, not even an authoritative tone of voice. It is beyond question that had this encounter occurred on the street, it would be constitutional. The fact that an encounter takes place on a bus does not on its own transform standard police questioning of citizens into an illegal seizure. Indeed, because many fellow passengers are present to witness officers' conduct, a reasonable person may feel even more secure in his or her decision not to cooperate with police on a bus than in other circumstances.

* * *

Drayton contends that even if Brown's cooperation with the officers was consensual, Drayton was seized because no reasonable person would feel free to terminate the encounter with the officers after Brown had been arrested. The Court of Appeals did not address this claim; and in any event the argument fails. The arrest of one person does not mean that everyone around him has been seized by police. If anything, Brown's arrest should have put Drayton on notice of the consequences of continuing the encounter by answering the officers' questions. Even after arresting Brown, Lang addressed Drayton in a polite manner and provided him with no indication that he was required to answer Lang's questions.

We turn now from the question whether respondents were seized to whether they were subjected to an unreasonable search, *i.e.*, whether their consent to the suspicionless search was involuntary. In circumstances such as these, where the question of voluntariness pervades both the search and seizure inquiries, the respective analyses turn on very similar facts. And, as the facts above suggest, respondents' consent to the search of their luggage and their persons was voluntary. Nothing Officer Lang said indicated a command to consent to the search. Rather, when respondents informed Lang that they had a bag on the bus, he asked for their permission to check it. And when Lang requested to search Brown and Drayton's persons, he asked first if they objected, thus indicating to a reasonable person that he or she was free to refuse. Even after arresting Brown, Lang provided Drayton with no indication that he was required to consent to a search. To the contrary, Lang asked for Drayton's permission to search him ("Mind if I check you?"), and Drayton agreed.

The Court has rejected in specific terms the suggestion that police officers must always inform citizens of their right to refuse when seeking permission to conduct a warrantless consent search. "While knowledge of the right to refuse consent is one factor to be taken into account, the government need not establish such knowledge as the *sine qua non* of an effective consent." *Schneckloth* v. *Bustamonte,* 412 U. S. 218, 227 (1973). Nor do this Court's decisions suggest that even though there are no *per se* rules, a presumption of invalidity attaches if a citizen consented without explicit notification that he or she was free to refuse to cooperate. Instead, the Court has repeated that the totality of the circumstances must control, without giving extra weight to the absence of this type of warning. Although Officer Lang did not inform respondents of their right to refuse the search, he did request permission to search, and the totality of the circumstances indicates that their consent was voluntary, so the searches were reasonable.

* * *

JUSTICE SOUTER, with whom JUSTICE STEVENS and JUSTICE GINSBURG join, dissenting.

* * *

Florida v. Bostick, 501 U.S. 429 (1991), established the framework for determining whether the bus passengers were seized in the constitutional sense. In that case, we rejected the position that police questioning of bus passengers was a *per se* seizure, and held instead that the issue of seizure was to be resolved under an objective test considering all circumstances: whether a reasonable passenger would have felt "free to decline the officers' requests or otherwise terminate the encounter." We thus applied to a bus passenger the more general criterion, whether the person questioned was free "to ignore the police presence and go about his business."

Before applying the standard in this case, it may be worth getting some perspective from different sets of facts. A perfect example of police conduct that supports no colorable claim of seizure is the act of an officer who simply goes up to a pedestrian on the street and asks him a question. A pair of officers questioning a pedestrian, without more, would presumably support the same conclusion. Now consider three officers, one of whom stands behind the pedestrian, another at his side toward the open sidewalk, with the third addressing questions to the pedestrian a foot or two from his face. Finally, consider the same scene in a narrow alley. On such barebones facts, one may not be able to say a seizure occurred, even in the last case, but one can say without qualification that the atmosphere of the encounters differed significantly from the first to the last examples. In the final instance there is every reason to believe that the pedestrian would have understood, to his considerable discomfort, what Justice Stewart described as the "threatening presence of several officers," *United States v. Mendenhall,* 446 U.S. 544, 554 (1980) (opinion of Stewart, J.). The police not only carry legitimate authority but also exercise power free from immediate check, and when the attention of several officers is brought to bear on one civilian the imbalance of immediate power is unmistakable. We all understand this, as well as we understand that a display of power rising to Justice Stewart's "threatening" level may overbear a normal person's ability to act freely, even in the absence of explicit commands or the formalities of detention. As common as this understanding is, however, there is little sign of it in the Court's opinion. My own understanding of the relevant facts and their significance follows.

When the bus in question made its scheduled stop in Tallahassee, the passengers were required to disembark while the vehicle was cleaned and refueled. When the passengers returned, they gave their tickets to the driver, who kept them and then left himself, after giving three police officers permission to board the bus in his absence. Although they were not in uniform, the officers displayed badges and identified themselves as police. One stationed himself in the driver's seat by the door at the front, facing back to observe the passengers. The two others went to the rear, from which they worked their way forward, with one of them speaking to passengers, the other backing him up. They necessarily addressed the passengers at very close range; the aisle was only 15 inches wide, and each seat only 18. The quarters were cramped further by the overhead rack, 19 inches above the top of the passenger seats. The passenger by the window could not have stood up straight and the face of the nearest officer was only a foot or 18 inches from the face of the nearest passenger being addressed. During the exchanges, the officers looked down, and the passengers had to look up if they were to face the police. The officer asking the questions spoke quietly. He prefaced his requests for permission to search luggage and do a body patdown by identifying himself by name as a police investigator "conducting bus interdiction" and saying, " 'We would like for your cooperation. Do you have any luggage on the bus?' "

Thus, for reasons unexplained, the driver with the tickets entitling the passengers to travel had yielded his custody of the bus and its seated travelers to three police officers, whose authority apparently superseded the driver's own. The officers took control of the entire passenger compartment, one stationed at the door keeping surveillance of all the occupants, the others working forward from the back. With one officer right behind him and the other one forward, a third officer accosted each passenger at quarters extremely close and so cramped that as many as half the passengers could not even have stood to face the speaker. None was asked whether he was willing to converse with the police or to take part in the enquiry. Instead the officer said the police were "conducting bus interdiction," in the course of which they "would like . . . cooperation." The reasonable inference was that the "interdiction" was not a consensual exercise, but one the police would carry out whatever the circumstances; that they would prefer " cooperation" but would not let the lack of it stand in their way. There was no contrary indication that day, since no passenger had refused the cooperation requested, and there was no reason for any passenger to believe that the driver would return and the trip resume until the police were satisfied. The scene was set and an atmosphere of obligatory participation was established by this introduction. Later requests to search prefaced with "Do you mind . . ." would naturally have been understood in the terms with which the encounter began.

It is very hard to imagine that either Brown or Drayton would have believed that he stood to lose nothing if he refused to cooperate with the police, or that he had any free choice to ignore the police altogether. No reasonable passenger could have believed that, only an uncomprehending one. It is neither here nor there that the interdiction was conducted by three officers, not one, as a safety precaution. The fact was that there were three, and when Brown and Drayton were called upon to respond, each one was presumably conscious of an officer in front watching, one at his side questioning him, and one behind for cover, in case he became unruly, perhaps, or "cooperation" was not forthcoming. The situation is much like the one in the alley, with civilians in close quarters, unable to move effectively, being told their cooperation is expected. While I am not prepared to say that no bus interrogation and search can pass the *Bostick* test without a warning that passengers are free to say no, the facts here surely required more from the officers than a quiet tone of voice. A police officer who is certain to get his way has no need to shout.

* * *

Points for Discussion

1. The dissent discusses situations that clearly are, and clearly are not, Fourth Amendment seizures. Where along the following continuum do you believe a seizure occurs?

   a. Officer greets passerby.

   b. Officer asks passerby his name.

   c. Officer asks passerby where he's going.

   d. Officer asks passerby why he's going there.

   e. Officer asks passerby what he's carrying.

   f. Officer asks passerby if he can look in his bag.

   g. Officer asks passerby if he can frisk him.

   h. Officer asks passerby to accompany him to the police station.

Does it matter how many officers are present? Where the encounter takes place? The race, gender, education, and age of the officers? Of the passerby? How helpful is the Court's test in answering these questions?

2. Justice Kennedy's majority opinion and Justice Souter's dissent do not disagree on the objective facts—the space in the bus, the words that were used, the sequence of events. Nor do they disagree on the law to be applied—the *Mendenhall* reasonable-person test. Nonetheless, they arrive at disparate legal conclusions as to whether a seizure occurred. In what sense is the *Mendenhall* test "objective" if reasonable people can arrive at divergent conclusions after starting from many of the same premises? What, in the end, are the premises—whether stated expressly or merely implied—that the majority and the dissent disagree about?

BRENDLIN V. CALIFORNIA

551 U.S. 249 (2007)

JUSTICE SOUTER delivered the opinion of the court.

When a police officer makes a traffic stop, the driver of the car is seized within the meaning of the Fourth Amendment. The question in this case is whether the same is true of a passenger. We hold that a passenger is seized as well and so may challenge the constitutionality of the stop.

I

Early in the morning of November 27, 2001, Deputy Sheriff Robert Brokenbrough and his partner saw a parked Buick with expired registration tags. In his ensuing conversation with the police dispatcher, Brokenbrough learned that an application for renewal of registration was being processed. The officers saw the car again on the road, and this time Brokenbrough noticed its display of a temporary operating permit with the number "11," indicating it was legal to drive the car through November. The officers decided to pull the Buick over to verify that the permit matched the vehicle, even though, as Brokenbrough admitted later, there was nothing unusual about the permit or the way it was affixed. Brokenbrough asked the driver, Karen Simeroth, for her license and saw a passenger in the front seat, petitioner Bruce Brendlin, whom he recognized as "one of the Brendlin brothers." He recalled that either Scott or Bruce Brendlin had dropped out of parole supervision and asked Brendlin to identify himself. Brokenbrough returned to his cruiser, called for backup, and verified that Brendlin was a parole violator with an outstanding no-bail warrant for his arrest. While he was in the patrol car, Brokenbrough saw Brendlin briefly open and then close the passenger door of the Buick. Once reinforcements arrived, Brokenbrough went to the passenger side of the Buick, ordered him out of the car at gunpoint, and declared him under arrest. When the police searched Brendlin incident to arrest, they found an orange syringe cap on his person. A patdown search of Simeroth revealed syringes and a plastic bag of a green leafy substance, and she was also formally arrested. Officers then searched the car and found tubing, a scale, and other things used to produce methamphetamine.

Brendlin was charged with possession and manufacture of methamphetamine, and he moved to suppress the evidence obtained in the searches of his person and the car as fruits of an unconstitutional seizure, arguing that the officers lacked probable cause or reasonable suspicion to make the traffic stop. He did not assert that his Fourth Amendment rights were violated by the search of Simeroth's vehicle but claimed only that the traffic stop was an unlawful seizure of his person. The trial court denied the suppression motion after finding that the stop was lawful and Brendlin was not seized until Brokenbrough ordered him out of the car and formally arrested him. Brendlin pleaded guilty, subject to appeal on the suppression issue, and was sentenced to four years in prison.

* * *

II

A

A person is seized by the police and thus entitled to challenge the government's action under the Fourth Amendment when the officer, " 'by means of physical force or show of authority,' " terminates or restrains his freedom of movement, *Florida v. Bostick,* 501 U.S. 429, 434 (1991) (quoting *Terry v. Ohio,* 392 U.S. 1, 19, n. 16 (1968)), "*through means intentionally applied,*" *Brower v. County of Inyo,* 489 U.S. 593, 597 (1989) (emphasis in original). Thus, an "unintended person . . . [may be] the object of the detention," so long as the detention is "willful" and not merely the consequence of "an unknowing act." A police officer may make a seizure by a show of authority and without the use of physical force, but there is no seizure without actual submission; otherwise, there is at most an attempted seizure, so far as the Fourth Amendment is concerned.

When the actions of the police do not show an unambiguous intent to restrain or when an individual's submission to a show of governmental authority takes the form of passive acquiescence, there needs to be some test for telling when a seizure occurs in response to authority, and when it does not. The test was devised by Justice Stewart in *United States v. Mendenhall,* 446 U.S. 544 (1980), who wrote that a seizure occurs if "in view of all of the circumstances surrounding the incident, a reasonable person would have believed that he was not free to leave." Later on, the Court adopted Justice Stewart's touchstone but added that when a person "has no desire to leave" for reasons unrelated to the police presence, the "coercive effect of the encounter" can be measured better by asking whether "a reasonable person would feel free to decline the officers' requests or otherwise terminate the encounter."

* * *

B

The State concedes that the police had no adequate justification to pull the car over but argues that the passenger was not seized and thus cannot claim that the evidence was tainted by an unconstitutional stop. We resolve this question by asking whether a reasonable person in Brendlin's position when the car stopped would have believed himself free to "terminate the encounter" between the police and himself. We think that in these circumstances any reasonable passenger would have understood the police officers to be exercising control to the point that no one in the car was free to depart without police permission.

A traffic stop necessarily curtails the travel a passenger has chosen just as much as it halts the driver, diverting both from the stream of traffic to the side of the road, and the police activity that normally amounts to intrusion on "privacy and personal security" does not normally (and did not here) distinguish between passenger and driver. An officer who orders one particular car to pull over acts with an implicit claim of right based on fault of some sort, and a sensible person would not expect a police officer to allow people to come and go freely from the physical focal point of an investigation into faulty behavior or wrongdoing. If the likely wrongdoing is not the driving, the passenger will reasonably feel subject to suspicion owing to close association; but even when the wrongdoing is only bad driving, the passenger will expect to be subject to some scrutiny, and his attempt to leave the scene would be so obviously likely to prompt an objection from the officer that no passenger would feel free to leave in the first place.

It is also reasonable for passengers to expect that a police officer at the scene of a crime, arrest, or investigation will not let people move around in ways that could jeopardize his safety. In *Maryland v. Wilson,* 519 U.S. 408 (1997), we held that during a lawful traffic stop an officer may order a passenger out of the car as a precautionary measure, without reasonable suspicion that the passenger poses a safety risk. In fashioning this rule, we invoked our earlier statement that "[t] he risk of harm to both the police and the occupants is minimized if the officers routinely exercise unquestioned command of the situation." What we have said in these opinions probably reflects a societal expectation of "unquestioned [police] command" at odds with any notion that a passenger would feel free to leave, or to terminate the personal encounter any other way, without advance permission.[4]

* * *

[4] Although the State Supreme Court inferred from Brendlin's decision to open and close the passenger door during the traffic stop that he was "awar[e] of the available options," this conduct could equally be taken to indicate that Brendlin felt compelled to remain inside the car. In any event, the test is not what Brendlin felt but what a reasonable passenger would have understood.

C

The contrary conclusion drawn by the Supreme Court of California, that seizure came only with formal arrest, reflects three premises as to which we respectfully disagree. First, the State Supreme Court reasoned that Brendlin was not seized by the stop because Deputy Sheriff Brokenbrough only intended to investigate Simeroth and did not direct a show of authority toward Brendlin. The court saw Brokenbrough's "flashing lights [as] directed at the driver," and pointed to the lack of record evidence that Brokenbrough "was even aware [Brendlin] was in the car prior to the vehicle stop." But that view of the facts ignores the objective *Mendenhall* test of what a reasonable passenger would understand. To the extent that there is anything ambiguous in the show of force (was it fairly seen as directed only at the driver or at the car and its occupants?), the test resolves the ambiguity, and here it leads to the intuitive conclusion that all the occupants were subject to like control by the successful display of authority. The State Supreme Court's approach, on the contrary, shifts the issue from the intent of the police as objectively manifested to the motive of the police for taking the intentional action to stop the car, and we have repeatedly rejected attempts to introduce this kind of subjectivity into Fourth Amendment analysis.

* * *

Second, the Supreme Court of California assumed that Brendlin, "as the passenger, had no ability to submit to the deputy's show of authority" because only the driver was in control of the moving vehicle. But what may amount to submission depends on what a person was doing before the show of authority: a fleeing man is not seized until he is physically overpowered, but one sitting in a chair may submit to authority by not getting up to run away. Here, Brendlin had no effective way to signal submission while the car was still moving on the roadway, but once it came to a stop he could, and apparently did, submit by staying inside.

Third, the State Supreme Court shied away from the rule we apply today for fear that it "would encompass even those motorists following the vehicle subject to the traffic stop who, by virtue of the original detention, are forced to slow down and perhaps even come to a halt in order to accommodate that vehicle's submission to police authority." But an occupant of a car who knows that he is stuck in traffic because another car has been pulled over (like the motorist who can't even make out why the road is suddenly clogged) would not perceive a show of authority as directed at him or his car. Such incidental restrictions on freedom of movement would not tend to affect an individual's "sense of security and privacy in traveling in an automobile." [*Delaware v. Prouse,* 440 U.S. 648, 662 (1979)]. Nor would the consequential blockage call for a precautionary rule to avoid the kind of "arbitrary and oppressive interference by [law] enforcement officials with the privacy and personal security of individuals" that the

Fourth Amendment was intended to limit. [*United States v. Martinez-Fuerte*, 428 U.S. 543, 554 (1976)].[6]

Indeed, the consequence to worry about would not flow from our conclusion, but from the rule that almost all courts have rejected. Holding that the passenger in a private car is not (without more) seized in a traffic stop would invite police officers to stop cars with passengers regardless of probable cause or reasonable suspicion of anything illegal. The fact that evidence uncovered as a result of an arbitrary traffic stop would still be admissible against any passengers would be a powerful incentive to run the kind of "roving patrols" that would still violate the driver's Fourth Amendment right.

* * *

Points for Discussion

1. Do you agree with the Court that Brendlin was seized along with Simeroth? Did the police have any reason to suspect Brendlin of misbehavior? Did they have any basis to hold him if he had chosen to leave?

2. Justice Souter's dissent in *Drayton* emphasized the fact that "[t]he officers took control of the entire passenger compartment, one stationed at the door keeping surveillance of all the occupants, the others working forward from the back." His opinion for a unanimous Court in *Brendlin* held that the passenger was seized because "any reasonable passenger would have understood the police officers to be exercising control to the point that no one in the car was free to depart without police permission." Is the *Drayton* majority opinion consistent with the apparent view in *Brendlin* that the degree of "control" is determinative? Are there significant factual differences between the two scenarios that might explain any inconsistency?

NOTE: THE EXCLUSIONARY RULE AND ILLEGAL SEIZURES

Hodari D., Drayton, and *Brendlin* all involve attempts by defendants to invoke the exclusionary rule and the "fruit of the poisonous tree" doctrine. Under these doctrines, evidence seized in violation of the Fourth Amendment—and evidence that derives from a Fourth Amendment violation—must be suppressed from the government's case in chief at trial. Thus, all three defendants argued that the evidence found in their possession was found after they were unreasonably seized and should therefore be suppressed as the fruit of the poisonous tree. In *Hodari D.* and *Drayton*, a majority of the Court held that there was no seizure and therefore no violation of the Fourth Amendment. In *Brendlin*, the Court agreed that Brendlin had

[6] California claims that, under today's rule, "all taxi cab and bus passengers would be 'seized' under the Fourth Amendment when the cab or bus driver is pulled over by the police for running a red light." But the relationship between driver and passenger is not the same in a common carrier as it is in a private vehicle, and the expectations of police officers and passengers differ accordingly. In those cases, as here, the crucial question would be whether a reasonable person in the passenger's position would feel free to take steps to terminate the encounter.

been seized. Because the state admitted that there was no reasonable suspicion to support such a seizure, the Fourth Amendment was violated and the drug evidence found in the car could not be used. We return to the exclusionary rule and the "fruit of the poisonous tree" doctrine in chapter 10.

CHAPTER 2

THE WARRANT CLAUSE

■ ■ ■

A. "PROBABLE CAUSE"

Once a court decides whether government action implicates the Fourth Amendment—i.e., whether there has been a "search" or a "seizure" of a person, house, paper, or other effect—the court must decide whether the search was unreasonable and, thus, unconstitutional. Two of the historically important factors in the reasonableness analysis are found in the Warrant Clause: whether the search or seizure was supported by "probable cause" and whether the authorities obtained a judicial warrant prior to acting. The cases in this chapter discuss these two considerations.

Although probable cause is mentioned only in the Fourth Amendment's Warrant Clause, the Supreme Court repeatedly held prior to *Terry v. Ohio*, 392 U.S. 1 (1968), that all searches and seizures, whether conducted with or without a warrant, required probable cause. Even after *Terry* allowed some searches and seizures to be made on mere "reasonable suspicion," the Court maintained that probable cause is generally required even when a warrant is not. *See, e.g., Chambers v. Maroney*, 399 U.S. 42, 51 (1970) ("In enforcing the Fourth Amendment's prohibition against unreasonable searches and seizures, the Court has insisted upon probable cause as a minimum requirement for a reasonable search permitted by the Constitution.").

Unlike proof to a preponderance of the evidence (which requires demonstrating that some fact is more likely true than not), courts have been loath to associate probable cause with a discrete numerical probability. However, that is not to say the term has no meaning. As Chief Justice Marshall implied early in the 19th century, the term existed in law before the Constitution was ratified: "[T]he term 'probable cause,' according to its usual acceptation, means less than evidence which would justify condemnation; and, in all cases of seizure, has a fixed and well known meaning. It imports a seizure made under circumstances which warrant suspicion." *Locke v. United States*, 11 U.S. (7 Cranch) 339, 348 (1813). In numerous cases since at least the late 19th century (including *Brinegar v. United States*, the first case excerpted in this section), the Supreme Court has used essentially this definition for "probable cause": "If the facts and circumstances before the officer are such as to warrant a man of prudence and caution in believing that the offence has been committed, it is sufficient." *Stacey v. Emery*, 97 U.S. 642, 645 (1878).

Given the imprecise nature of probable cause, it may make sense to think about the following issues as you read the cases in this section: How much suspicion should the police be required to demonstrate before they deprive an individual of her liberty—that is, before they arrest or search her or seize her property? Does it matter how the police came to suspect the individual—whether they observed her suspicious behavior themselves, heard about it from a known source, or heard about it from an anonymous source? What if the police paid the person who provided them with their information?

BRINEGAR V. UNITED STATES

338 U.S. 160 (1949)

MR. JUSTICE RUTLEDGE delivered the opinion of the court.

Brinegar was convicted of importing intoxicating liquor into Oklahoma from Missouri in violation of the federal statute which forbids such importation contrary to the laws of any state. His conviction was based in part on the use in evidence against him of liquor seized from his automobile in the course of the alleged unlawful importation.

Prior to the trial Brinegar moved to suppress this evidence as having been secured through an unlawful search and seizure. The motion was denied, as was a renewal of the objection at the trial.

The Court of Appeals affirmed the conviction and certiorari was sought solely on the ground that the search and seizure contravened the Fourth Amendment and therefore the use of the liquor in evidence vitiated the conviction. We granted the writ to determine this question.

The facts are substantially undisputed. At about six o'clock on the evening of March 3, 1947, Malsed, an investigator of the Alcohol Tax Unit, and Creehan, a special investigator, were parked in a car beside a highway near the Quapaw Bridge in northeastern Oklahoma. The point was about five miles west of the Missouri-Oklahoma line. Brinegar drove past headed west in his Ford coupe. Malsed had arrested him about five months earlier for illegally transporting liquor; had seen him loading liquor into a car or truck in Joplin, Missouri, on at least two occasions during the preceding six months; and knew him to have a reputation for hauling liquor. As Brinegar passed, Malsed recognized both him and the Ford. He told Creehan, who was driving the officers' car, that Brinegar was the driver of the passing car. Both agents later testified that the car, but not especially its rear end, appeared to be "heavily loaded" and "weighted down with something." Brinegar increased his speed as he passed the officers. They gave chase. After pursuing him for about a mile at top speed, they gained on him as his car skidded on a curve, sounded their siren, overtook him, and crowded his car to the side of the road by pulling across in front of it.

The highway was one leading from Joplin, Missouri, toward Vinita, Oklahoma, Brinegar's home.

As the agents got out of their car and walked back toward petitioner, Malsed said, "Hello, Brinegar, how much liquor have you got in the car?" or "How much liquor have you got in the car this time?" Petitioner replied, "Not too much," or "Not so much." After further questioning he admitted that he had twelve cases in the car. Malsed testified that one case, which was on the front seat, was visible from outside the car, but petitioner testified that it was covered by a lap robe. Twelve more cases were found under and behind the front seat. The agents then placed Brinegar under arrest and seized the liquor.

* * *

The crucial question is whether there was probable cause for Brinegar's arrest, in the light of prior adjudications on this problem, more particularly *Carroll v. United States*, 267 U.S. 132 [(1925)], which on its face most closely approximates the situation presented here. The *Carroll* decision held that, under the Fourth Amendment, a valid search of a vehicle moving on a public highway may be had without a warrant, but only if probable cause for the search exists. The court then went on to rule that the facts presented amounted to probable cause for the search of the automobile there involved.

In the *Carroll* case three federal prohibition agents and a state officer stopped and searched the defendants' car on a highway leading from Detroit to Grand Rapids, Michigan, and seized a quantity of liquor discovered in the search. About three months before the search, the two defendants and another man called on two of the agents at an apartment in Grand Rapids and, unaware that they were dealing with federal agents, agreed to sell one of the agents three cases of liquor. Both agents noticed the Oldsmobile roadster in which the three men came to the apartment and its license number. Presumably because the official capacity of the proposed purchaser was suspected by the defendants, the liquor was never delivered.

About a week later the same two agents, while patrolling the road between Grand Rapids and Detroit on the lookout for violations of the National Prohibition Act, were passed by the defendants, who were proceeding in a direction from Grand Rapids toward Detroit in the same Oldsmobile roadster. The agents followed the defendants for some distance but lost trace of them. Still later, on the occasion of the search, while the officers were patrolling the same highway, they met and passed the defendants, who were in the same roadster, going in a direction from Detroit toward Grand Rapids. Recognizing the defendants, the agents turned around, pursued them, stopped them about sixteen miles outside Grand Rapids, searched their car and seized the liquor it carried.

This Court ruled that the information held by the agents, together with the judicially noticed fact that Detroit was "one of the most active centers for introducing illegally into this country spirituous liquors for distribution into the interior," constituted probable cause for the search.

I

Obviously the basic facts held to constitute probable cause in the *Carroll* case were very similar to the basic facts here. In each case the search was of an automobile moving on a public highway and was made without a warrant by federal officers charged with enforcing federal statutes outlawing the transportation of intoxicating liquors (except under conditions not complied with). In each instance the officers were patrolling the highway in the discharge of their duty. And in each before stopping the car or starting to pursue it they recognized both the driver and the car, from recent personal contact and observation, as having been lately engaged in illicit liquor dealings. Finally, each driver was proceeding in his identified car in a direction from a known source of liquor supply toward a probable illegal market, under circumstances indicating no other probable purpose than to carry on his illegal adventure.

These are the ultimate facts. Necessarily the concrete, subordinate facts on which they were grounded in the two cases differed somewhat in detail. The more important of the variations in details of the proof are as follows:

In *Carroll* the agent's knowledge of the primary and ultimate fact that the accused were engaged in liquor running was derived from the defendants' offer to sell liquor to the agents some three months prior to the search, while here that knowledge was derived largely from Malsed's personal observation, reinforced by hearsay; the officers when they bargained for the liquor in *Carroll* saw the number of the defendants' car, whereas no such fact is shown in this record; and in *Carroll* the Court took judicial notice that Detroit was on the international boundary and an active center for illegal importation of spirituous liquors for distribution into the interior, while in this case the facts that Joplin, Missouri, was a ready source of supply for liquor and Oklahoma a place of likely illegal market were known to the agent Malsed from his personal observation and experience as well as from facts of common knowledge.

* * *

In this case, the record shows that Brinegar had used Joplin, Missouri, to Malsed's personal knowledge derived from direct observation, not merely from hearsay as seems to be suggested, as a source of supply on other occasions within the preceding six months. It also discloses that Brinegar's home was in Vinita, Oklahoma, and that Brinegar when apprehended was traveling in a direction leading from Joplin to Vinita, at a point about four or five miles west of the Missouri-Oklahoma line.

Joplin, like Detroit in the *Carroll* case, was a ready source of supply. But unlike Detroit it was not an illegal source. So far as appears, Brinegar's purchases there were entirely legal. And so, we may assume for present purposes, was his transportation of the liquor in Missouri, until he reached and crossed the state line into Oklahoma.

This difference, however, is insubstantial. For the important thing here is not whether Joplin was an illegal source of a supply; it is rather that Joplin was a ready, convenient and probable one for persons disposed to violate the Oklahoma and federal statutes. That fact was demonstrated fully, not only by the geographic facts, but by Malsed's direct and undisputed testimony of his personal observation of Brinegar's use of liquor dispensing establishments in Joplin for procuring his whiskey. Such direct evidence was lacking in *Carroll* as to Detroit, and for that reason the Court resorted to judicial notice of the commonly known facts to supply that deficiency. Malsed's direct testimony, based on his personal observation, dispensed with that necessity in this case.

The situation relating to the probable place of market, as bearing on the probability of unlawful importation, is somewhat different. Broadly on the facts this may well have been taken to be the State of Oklahoma as a whole or its populous northeastern region. From the facts of record we know, as the agents knew, that Oklahoma was a "dry" state. At the time of the search, its law forbade the importation of intoxicating liquors from other states, except under a permit not generally procurable and which there is no pretense Brinegar had secured or attempted to secure. This fact, taken in connection with the known "wet" status of Missouri and the location of Joplin close to the Oklahoma line, affords a very natural situation for persons inclined to violate the Oklahoma and federal statutes to ply their trade. The proof therefore concerning the source of supply, the place of probable destination and illegal market, and hence the probability that Brinegar was using the highway for the forbidden transportation, was certainly no less strong than the showing in these respects in the *Carroll* case.

Finally, as for the most important potential distinction, namely, that concerning the primary and ultimate fact that the petitioner was engaging in liquor running, Malsed's personal observation of Brinegar's recent activities established that he was so engaged quite as effectively as did the agent's prior bargaining with the defendants in the *Carroll* case. He saw Brinegar loading liquor, in larger quantities than would be normal for personal consumption, into a car or a truck in Joplin on other occasions during the six months prior to the search. He saw the car Brinegar was using in this case in use by him at least once in Joplin within that period and followed it. And several months prior to the search he had arrested Brinegar for unlawful transportation of liquor and this arrest had resulted in an indictment which was pending at the time of this trial. Moreover

Malsed instantly recognized Brinegar's Ford coupe and Brinegar as the driver when he passed the parked police car. And at that time Brinegar was moving in a direction from Joplin toward Vinita only a short distance inside Oklahoma from the state line.

All these facts are undisputed. Wholly apart from Malsed's knowledge that Brinegar bore the general reputation of being engaged in liquor running, they constitute positive and convincing evidence that Brinegar was engaged in that activity, no less convincing than the evidence in *Carroll* that the defendants had offered to sell liquor to the officers. The evidence here is undisputed, is admissible on the issue of probable cause, and clearly establishes that the agent had good ground for believing that Brinegar was engaged regularly throughout the period in illicit liquor running and dealing.

* * *

II

* * *

In dealing with probable cause . . ., as the very name implies, we deal with probabilities. These are not technical; they are the factual and practical considerations of everyday life on which reasonable and prudent men, not legal technicians, act. The standard of proof is accordingly correlative to what must be proved.

"The substance of all the definitions" of probable cause "is a reasonable ground for belief of guilt." *McCarthy v. De Armit*, 99 Pa. 63, 69 [(1881)], quoted with approval in the *Carroll* opinion. And this "means less than evidence which would justify condemnation" or conviction, as Marshall, C.J., said for the Court more than a century ago in *Locke v. United States*, 7 Cranch 339, 348 [(1813)]. Since Marshall's time, at any rate, it has come to mean more than bare suspicion: Probable cause exists where "the facts and circumstances within their (the officers') knowledge and of which they had reasonably trustworthy information (are) sufficient in themselves to warrant a man of reasonable caution in the belief that" an offense has been or is being committed. *Carroll v. United States*, 267 U.S. 132, 162 [(1925)].

These long-prevailing standards seek to safeguard citizens from rash and unreasonable interferences with privacy and from unfounded charges of crime. They also seek to give fair leeway for enforcing the law in the community's protection. Because many situations which confront officers in the course of executing their duties are more or less ambiguous, room must be allowed for some mistakes on their part. But the mistakes must be those of reasonable men, acting on facts leading sensibly to their conclusions of probability. The rule of probable cause is a practical, nontechnical conception affording the best compromise that has been found for accommodating these often opposing interests. Requiring more would unduly hamper law enforcement. To allow less would be to leave law-abiding citizens at the mercy of the officers' whim or caprice.

The troublesome line posed by the facts in the *Carroll* case and this case is one between mere suspicion and probable cause. That line necessarily must be drawn by an act of judgment formed in the light of the particular situation and with account taken of all the circumstances. No problem of searching the home or any other place of privacy was presented either in *Carroll* or here. Both cases involve freedom to use public highways in swiftly moving vehicles for dealing in contraband, and to be unmolested by investigation and search in those movements. In such a case the citizen who has given no good cause for believing he is engaged in that sort of activity is entitled to proceed on his way without interference. But one who recently and repeatedly has given substantial ground for believing that he is engaging in the forbidden transportation in the area of his usual operations has no such immunity, if the officer who intercepts him in that region knows that fact at the time he makes the interception and the circumstances under which it is made are not such as to indicate the suspect going about legitimate affairs.

This does not mean, as seems to be assumed, that every traveler along the public highways may be stopped and searched at the officers' whim, caprice or mere suspicion. The question presented in the *Carroll* case lay on the border between suspicion and probable cause. But the Court carefully considered that problem and resolved it by concluding that the facts within the officers' knowledge when they intercepted the *Carroll* defendants amounted to more than mere suspicion and constituted probable cause for their action. We cannot say this conclusion was wrong, or was so lacking in reason and consistency with the Fourth Amendment's purposes that it should now be overridden. Nor, as we have said, can we find in the present facts any substantial basis for distinguishing this case from the *Carroll* case.

MR. JUSTICE MURPHY dissents.

MR. JUSTICE BURTON, concurring.

I join in the opinion of the Court that there was probable cause for the search within the standards established in *Carroll v. United States*, 267 U.S. 132 [(1925)].

Whether or not the necessary probable cause for a search of the petitioner's car existed before the government agents caught up with him and said to him, "How much liquor have you got in the car this time?" and he replied, "Not too much," it is clear, and each of the lower courts found, that, under all of the circumstances of this case, the necessary probable cause for the search of the petitioner's car then existed. If probable cause for the search existed at that point, the search which then was begun was lawful without a search warrant as is demonstrated in the opinion of the

Court. That search disclosed that a crime was in the course of its commission in the presence of the arresting officers, precisely as those officers had good reason to believe was the fact. The ensuing arrest of the petitioner was lawful and the subsequent denial of his motion to suppress the evidence obtained by the search was properly sustained.

It is my view that it is not necessary, for the purposes of this case, to establish probable cause for the search at any point earlier than that of the above colloquy. The earlier events, recited in the opinion of the Court, disclose at least ample grounds to justify the chase and official interrogation of the petitioner by the government agents in the manner adopted. This interrogation quickly disclosed indisputable probable cause for the search and for the arrest. In my view, these earlier events not only justified the steps taken by the government agents but those events imposed upon the government agents a positive duty to investigate further, in some such manner as they adopted. It is only by alertness to proper occasions for prompt inquiries and investigations that effective prevention of crime and enforcement of law is possible. Government agents are commissioned to represent the interests of the public in the enforcement of the law and this requires affirmative action not only when there is reasonable ground for an arrest or probable cause for a search but when there is reasonable ground for an investigation. This is increasingly true when the facts point directly to a crime in the course of commission in the presence of the agent. Prompt investigation may then not only discover but, what is still more important, may interrupt the crime and prevent some or all of its damaging consequences.

* * *

MR. JUSTICE JACKSON, dissenting.

When this Court recently has promulgated a philosophy that some rights derived from the Constitution are entitled to "a preferred position," *Murdock v. Pennsylvania*, 319 U.S. 105, 115, dissent at page 166 [(1943)], I have not agreed. We cannot give some constitutional rights a preferred position without relegating others to a deferred position; we can establish no firsts without thereby establishing seconds. Indications are not wanting that Fourth Amendment freedoms are tacitly marked as secondary rights, to be relegated to a deferred position.

* * *

These, I protest, are not mere second-class rights but belong in the catalog of indispensable freedoms. Among deprivations of rights, none is so effective in cowing a population, crushing the spirit of the individual and putting terror in every heart. Uncontrolled search and seizure is one of the first and most effective weapons in the arsenal of every arbitrary government. And one need only briefly to have dwelt and worked among a people possessed of many admirable qualities but deprived of these rights to know that the human personality deteriorates and dignity and self-reliance disappear where homes, persons and possessions are subject at any hour to unheralded search and seizure by the police.

But the right to be secure against searches and seizures is one of the most difficult to protect. Since the officers are themselves the chief invaders, there is no enforcement outside of court.

Only occasional and more flagrant abuses come to the attention of the courts, and then only those where the search and seizure yields incriminating evidence and the defendant is at least sufficiently compromised to be indicted. If the officers raid a home, an office, or stop and search an automobile but find nothing incriminating, this invasion of the personal liberty of the innocent too often finds no practical redress. There may be, and I am convinced that there are, many unlawful searches of homes and automobiles of innocent people which turn up nothing incriminating, in which no arrest is made, and about which we never hear.

Courts can protect the innocent against such invasions indirectly and through the medium of excluding evidence obtained against those who frequently are guilty. Federal courts have used this method of enforcement of the Amendment, in spite of its unfortunate consequences on law enforcement, although many state courts do not. This inconsistency does not disturb me, for local excesses or invasions of liberty are more amenable to political correction, the Amendment was directed only against the new and centralized government, and any really dangerous threat to the general liberties of the people can come only from this source. We must therefore look upon the exclusion of evidence in federal prosecutions if obtained in violation of the Amendment as a means of extending protection against the central government's agencies. So a search against Brinegar's car must be regarded as a search of the car of Everyman.

We must remember that the extent of any privilege of search and seizure without warrant which we sustain, the officers interpret and apply themselves and will push to the limit. We must remember, too, that freedom from unreasonable search differs from some of the other rights of the Constitution in that there is no way the innocent citizen can invoke advance protection. For example, any effective interference with freedom of the press, or free speech, or religion, usually requires a course of suppressions against which the citizen can and often does go to the court and obtain an injunction. Other rights, such as that to an impartial jury or the aid of counsel, are within the supervisory power of the courts themselves. Such a right as just compensation for the taking of private property may be vindicated after the act in terms of money.

But an illegal search and seizure usually is a single incident, perpetrated by surprise, conducted in haste, kept purposely beyond the court's supervision and limited only by the judgment and moderation of officers whose own interests and records are often at stake in the search.

There is no opportunity for injunction or appeal to disinterested intervention. The citizen's choice is quietly to submit to whatever the officers undertake or to resist at risk of arrest or immediate violence.

And we must remember that the authority which we concede to conduct searches and seizures without warrant may be exercised by the most unfit and ruthless officers as well as by the fit and responsible, and resorted to in case of petty misdemeanors as well as in the case of the gravest felonies.

With this prologue I come to the case of Brinegar. His automobile was one of his "effects" and hence within the express protection of the Fourth Amendment. Undoubtedly the automobile presents peculiar problems for enforcement agencies, is frequently a facility for the perpetration of crime and an aid in the escape of criminals. But if we are to make judicial exceptions to the Fourth Amendment for these reasons, it seems to me they should depend somewhat upon the gravity of the offense. If we assume, for example, that a child is kidnapped and the officers throw a roadblock about the neighborhood and search every outgoing car, it would be a drastic and undiscriminating use of the search. The officers might be unable to show probable cause for searching any particular car. However, I should candidly strive hard to sustain such an action, executed fairly and in good faith, because it might be reasonable to subject travelers to that indignity if it was the only way to save a threatened life and detect a vicious crime. But I should not strain to sustain such a roadblock and universal search to salvage a few bottles of bourbon and catch a bootlegger.

The Court sustains this search as an application of *Carroll v. United States*, 267 U.S. 132 [(1925)]. I dissent because I regard it as an extension of the *Carroll* case, which already has been too much taken by enforcement officers as blanket authority to stop and search cars on suspicion. I shall confine this opinion to showing the several ways in which this decision seems to expand the already expansive right to stop and search automobiles.

* * *

While the Court sustained the search without warrant in the *Carroll* case, it emphatically declined to dispense with the necessity for evidence of probable cause for making such a search. It said: "It would be intolerable and unreasonable if a prohibition agent were authorized to stop every automobile on the chance of finding liquor, and thus subject all persons lawfully using the highways to the inconvenience and indignity of such a search. Travelers may be so stopped in crossing an international boundary because of national self-protection reasonably requiring one entering the country to identify himself as entitled to come in, and his belongings as effects which may be lawfully brought in. But those lawfully within the country, entitled to use the public highways, have a right to free passage without interruption or search unless there is known to a competent official, authorized to search, probable cause for believing that their vehicles are carrying contraband or illegal merchandise."

* * *

I think we cannot say the lower courts were wrong as matter of law in holding that there was no probable cause up to the time the car was put off the road and stopped, and that we cannot say it was proper to consider the deficiency supplied by what followed. When these officers engaged in a chase at speeds dangerous to those who participated, and to other lawful wayfarers, and ditched the defendant's car, they were either taking the initial steps in arrest, search and seizure, or they were committing a completely lawless and unjustifiable act. That they intended to set out on a search is unquestioned, and there seems no reason to doubt that in their own minds they thought there was cause and right to search. They have done exactly what they would have done, and done rightfully, if they had been executing a warrant. At all events, whatever it may have lacked technically of arrest, search and seizure, it was a form of coercion and duress under color of official authority—and a very formidable type of duress at that.

* * *

MR. JUSTICE FRANKFURTER and MR. JUSTICE MURPHY join in this opinion.

Points for Discussion

1. The majority concludes that the officers had probable cause and thus were entitled to pull over Brinegar's car without a warrant. What facts led the Court to that holding? Should these facts be sufficient to deprive a person of his liberty in a free society? Justice Burton and Justice Jackson, joined by Justices Frankfurter and Murphy, would have held that there was no probable cause until Brinegar was run off the road and admitted to having alcohol. The concurring and dissenting justices disagree among themselves as to whether the police needed to have probable cause to force Brinegar to stop. Can you articulate the precise disagreement between Justice Burton and the dissenting justices?

2. When Justice Jackson writes that "the human personality deteriorates and dignity and self-reliance disappear where homes, persons and possessions are subject at any hour to unheralded search and seizure by the police" he is drawing upon his experience the United States' chief prosecutor of Nazi war criminals at the International Military Tribunal. Thus, while *Brinegar* is ostensibly about liquor trafficking, Justice Jackson, emphasizes that the protections the Court applies even to common criminals differentiate an open society from a totalitarian one. Nonetheless, he attempts to draw a distinction between a roadblock "executed fairly and in good faith" to catch a

kidnapper and one to catch a bootlegger. Is this distinction a principled one? Had it been the Court's holding, how could courts hope to apply this reasoning evenhandedly in future cases?

DRAPER V. UNITED STATES

358 U.S. 307 (1959)

MR. JUSTICE WHITTAKER delivered the opinion of the court.

Petitioner was convicted of knowingly concealing and transporting narcotic drugs in Denver, Colorado, in violation of 21 U.S.C. § 174. His conviction was based in part on the use in evidence against him of two "envelopes containing 865 grams of heroin" and a hypodermic syringe that had been taken from his person, following his arrest, by the arresting officer. Before the trial, he moved to suppress that evidence as having been secured through an unlawful search and seizure. . . .

The evidence offered at the hearing on the motion to suppress was not substantially disputed. It established that one Marsh, a federal narcotic agent with 29 years' experience, was stationed at Denver; that one Hereford had been engaged as a "special employee" of the Bureau of Narcotics at Denver for about six months, and from time to time gave information to Marsh regarding violations of the narcotic laws, for which Hereford was paid small sums of money, and that Marsh had always found the information given by Hereford to be accurate and reliable. On September 3, 1956, Hereford told Marsh that James Draper (petitioner) recently had taken up abode at a stated address in Denver and "was peddling narcotics to several addicts" in that city. Four days later, on September 7, Hereford told Marsh "that Draper had gone to Chicago the day before [September 6] by train and that he was going to bring back three ounces of heroin and that he would return to Denver either on the morning of the 8th of September or the morning of the 9th of September also by train." Hereford also gave Marsh a detailed physical description of Draper and of the clothing he was wearing,[2] and said that he would be carrying "a tan zipper bag," and that he habitually "walked real fast."

On the morning of September 8, Marsh and a Denver police officer went to the Denver Union Station and kept watch over all incoming trains from Chicago, but they did not see anyone fitting the description that Hereford had given. Repeating the process on the morning of September 9, they saw a person, having the exact physical attributes and wearing the precise clothing described by Hereford, alight from an incoming Chicago train and start walking "fast" toward the exit. He was carrying a tan zipper bag in his right hand and the left was thrust in his raincoat pocket. Marsh, accompanied by the police officer, overtook, stopped and arrested him. They

[2] Hereford told Marsh that Draper was a Negro of light brown complexion, 27 years of age, 5 feet 8 inches tall, weighed about 160 pounds, and that he was wearing a light colored raincoat, brown slacks and black shoes.

then searched him and found the two "envelopes containing heroin" clutched in his left hand in his raincoat pocket, and found the syringe in the tan zipper bag. Marsh then took him (petitioner) into custody. Hereford died four days after the arrest and therefore did not testify at the hearing on the motion.

* * *

[We cannot agree with the] contention that Marsh's information was insufficient to show probable cause and reasonable grounds to believe that petitioner had violated or was violating the narcotic laws and to justify his arrest without a warrant. The information given to narcotic agent Marsh by "special employee" Hereford may have been hearsay to Marsh, but coming from one employed for that purpose and whose information had always been found accurate and reliable, it is clear that Marsh would have been derelict in his duties had he not pursued it. And when, in pursuing that information, he saw a man, having the exact physical attributes and wearing the precise clothing and carrying the tan zipper bag that Hereford had described, alight from one of the very trains from the very place stated by Hereford and start to walk at a "fast" pace toward the station exit, Marsh had personally verified every facet of the information given him by Hereford except whether petitioner had accomplished his mission and had the three ounces of heroin on his person or in his bag. And surely, with every other bit of Hereford's information being thus personally verified, Marsh had "reasonable grounds" to believe that the remaining unverified bit of Hereford's information—that Draper would have the heroin with him—was likewise true.

"In dealing with probable cause, * * * as the very name implies, we deal with probabilities. These are not technical; they are the factual and practical considerations of everyday life on which reasonable and prudent men, not legal technicians, act." *Brinegar v. United States*, 338 U.S. at page 175. Probable cause exists where "the facts and circumstances within their [the arresting officers'] knowledge and of which they had reasonably trustworthy information [are] sufficient in themselves to warrant a man of reasonable caution in the belief that" an offense has been or is being committed. *Carroll v. United States*, 267 U.S. 132, 162.

We believe that, under the facts and circumstances here, Marsh had probable cause and reasonable grounds to believe that petitioner was committing a violation of the laws of the United States relating to narcotic drugs at the time he arrested him. The arrest was therefore lawful, and the subsequent search and seizure, having been made incident to that lawful arrest, were likewise valid. It follows that petitioner's motion to suppress was properly denied and that the seized heroin was competent evidence lawfully received at the trial.

THE CHIEF JUSTICE and MR. JUSTICE FRANKFURTER took no part in the consideration or decision of this case.

MR. JUSTICE DOUGLAS, dissenting.

Decisions under the Fourth Amendment, taken in the long view, have not given the protection to the citizen which the letter and spirit of the Amendment would seem to require. One reason, I think, is that wherever a culprit is caught red-handed, as in leading Fourth Amendment cases, it is difficult to adopt and enforce a rule that would turn him loose. A rule protective of law-abiding citizens is not apt to flourish where its advocates are usually criminals. Yet the rule we fashion is for the innocent and guilty alike. If the word of the informer on which the present arrest was made is sufficient to make the arrest legal, his word would also protect the police who, acting on it, hauled the innocent citizen off to jail.

Of course, the education we receive from mystery stories and television shows teaches that what happened in this case is efficient police work. The police are tipped off that a man carrying narcotics will step off the morning train. A man meeting the precise description does alight from the train. No warrant for his arrest has been—or, as I see it, could then be—obtained. Yet he is arrested; and narcotics are found in his pocket and a syringe in the bag he carried. This is the familiar pattern of crime detection which has been dinned into public consciousness as the correct and efficient one. It is, however, a distorted reflection of the constitutional system under which we are supposed to live.

With all due deference, the arrest made here on the mere word of an informer violated the spirit of the Fourth Amendment and the requirement of the law governing arrests in narcotics cases. If an arrest is made without a warrant, the offense must be committed in the presence of the officer or the officer must have "reasonable grounds to believe that the person to be arrested has committed or is committing" a violation of the narcotics law. The arresting officers did not have a bit of evidence, known to them and as to which they could take an oath had they gone to a magistrate for a warrant, that petitioner had committed any crime. The arresting officers did not know the grounds on which the informer based his conclusion; nor did they seek to find out what they were. They acted solely on the informer's word. In my view that was not enough.

* * *

Here the officers had no evidence—apart from the mere word of an informer—that petitioner was committing a crime. The fact that petitioner walked fast and carried a tan zipper bag was not evidence of any crime. The officers knew nothing except what they had been told by the informer. If they went to a magistrate to get a warrant of arrest and relied solely on the report of the informer, it is not conceivable to me that one would be granted. For they could not present to the magistrate any of the facts which the informer may have had. They could swear only to the fact that the informer had made the accusation. They could swear to no evidence that lay in their own knowledge. They could present, on information and belief, no facts which the informer disclosed. No magistrate could issue a warrant on the mere word of an officer, without more. We are not justified in lowering the standard when an arrest is made without a warrant and allowing the officers more leeway than we grant the magistrate.

With all deference I think we break with tradition when we sustain this arrest. We said in *United States v. Di Re*, 332 U.S. at page 229, "* * * a search is not to be made legal by what it turns up. In law it is good or bad when it starts and does not change character from its success." In this case it was only after the arrest and search were made that there was a shred of evidence known to the officers that a crime was in the process of being committed.

Points for Discussion

1. Does *Brinegar* or *Draper* make a stronger case for the existence of probable cause? What do you make of the fact that the suspicion in *Draper* came from an informant rather than primarily from the officer's own observations? What does Justice Douglas have to say on this point?

2. Justice Douglas argues that the "familiar pattern of crime detection which has been dinned into public consciousness as the correct and efficient one" is "a distorted reflection" of what the Constitution requires. What, in Justice Douglas' opinion, is unconstitutional about the police catching a drug trafficker by acting on an informant's tip?

3. Justice Douglas here, like Justice Jackson before him in *Brinegar*, notes in dissent that it will often be proven criminals who bring the cases that define the scope of Constitutional rights. Do you think the majorities in these cases ignored the admonition of *Di Re* that "a search is not to be made legal by what it turns up"?

NOTE: THE AGUILAR-SPINELLI TEST

Draper was hardly the Court's last word on the use of police informants. In *Aguilar v. Texas*, 378 U.S. 108 (1964), the Supreme Court held that, in passing upon a warrant based in part on details supplied by an informant, "the magistrate must be informed of some of the underlying circumstances from which the informant concluded that the narcotics were where he claimed they were, and some of the underlying circumstances from which the officer concluded that the informant, whose identity need not be disclosed was 'credible' or his information 'reliable.' " In *Spinelli v. United States*, 393 U.S. 410 (1969), the Supreme Court added to *Aguilar*'s requirements: "In the absence of a statement detailing the manner in which the information was gathered, it is especially important that the [informant's] tip describe the accused's criminal activity in sufficient detail that the magistrate may know that he is relying on something more substantial than a casual rumor circulating in the underworld or an accusation based merely on an individual's general reputation." Together these cases came to enunciate a two-part test for determining whether or not sufficient evidence was presented to a magistrate to support a showing of probable cause: 1) Did the officer requesting the warrant make clear why the information supplied to him was reliable or trustworthy? 2) Was the magistrate told the basis for the informant's information? Many courts interpreted these cases to mean that probable cause was not established unless both of these prongs were satisfied. In *Illinois v. Gates* the Supreme Court examined whether rigid adherence to the two-prong test is necessary.

ILLINOIS V. GATES

462 U.S. 213 (1983)

JUSTICE REHNQUIST delivered the opinion of the court.

Respondents Lance and Susan Gates were indicted for violation of state drug laws after police officers, executing a search warrant, discovered marijuana and other contraband in their automobile and home. Prior to trial the Gates' moved to suppress evidence seized during this search. The Illinois Supreme Court affirmed the decisions of lower state courts granting the motion. It held that the affidavit submitted in support of the State's application for a warrant to search the Gates' property was inadequate under this Court's decisions in *Aguilar v. Texas,* 378 U.S. 108 (1964) and *Spinelli v. United States,* 393 U.S. 410 (1969).

* * *

II

We . . . turn to the question presented in the State's original petition for certiorari, which requires us to decide whether respondents' rights under the Fourth and Fourteenth Amendments were violated by the search of their car and house. A chronological statement of events usefully introduces the issues at stake. Bloomingdale, Ill., is a suburb of Chicago located in DuPage County. On May 3, 1978, the Bloomingdale Police Department received by mail an anonymous handwritten letter which read as follows:

> This letter is to inform you that you have a couple in your town who strictly make their living on selling drugs. They are Sue and Lance Gates, they live on Greenway, off Bloomingdale Rd. in the condominiums. Most of their buys are done in Florida. Sue his wife drives their car to Florida, where she leaves it to be loaded up with drugs, then Lance flys down and drives it back. Sue flys back after she drops the car off in Florida. May 3 she is driving down there again and Lance will be flying down in a few days to drive it back. At the time Lance drives the car back he has the trunk loaded

> with over $100,000.00 in drugs. Presently they have over $100,000.00 worth of drugs in their basement.
>
> They brag about the fact they never have to work, and make their entire living on pushers.
>
> I guarantee if you watch them carefully you will make a big catch. They are friends with some big drugs dealers, who visit their house often.
>
> Lance & Susan Gates
> Greenway in Condominiums

The letter was referred by the Chief of Police of the Bloomingdale Police Department to Detective Mader, who decided to pursue the tip. Mader learned, from the office of the Illinois Secretary of State, that an Illinois driver's license had been issued to one Lance Gates, residing at a stated address in Bloomingdale. He contacted a confidential informant, whose examination of certain financial records revealed a more recent address for the Gates, and he also learned from a police officer assigned to O'Hare Airport that "L. Gates" had made a reservation on Eastern Airlines flight 245 to West Palm Beach, Fla., scheduled to depart from Chicago on May 5 at 4:15 p.m.

Mader then made arrangements with an agent of the Drug Enforcement Administration for surveillance of the May 5 Eastern Airlines flight. The agent later reported to Mader that Gates had boarded the flight, and that federal agents in Florida had observed him arrive in West Palm Beach and take a taxi to the nearby Holiday Inn. They also reported that Gates went to a room registered to one Susan Gates and that, at 7:00 a.m. the next morning, Gates and an unidentified woman left the motel in a Mercury bearing Illinois license plates and drove northbound on an interstate frequently used by travelers to the Chicago area. In addition, the DEA agent informed Mader that the license plate number on the Mercury registered to a Hornet station wagon owned by Gates. The agent also advised Mader that the driving time between West Palm Beach and Bloomingdale was approximately 22 to 24 hours.

Mader signed an affidavit setting forth the foregoing facts, and submitted it to a judge of the Circuit Court of DuPage County, together with a copy of the anonymous letter. The judge of that court thereupon issued a search warrant for the Gates' residence and for their automobile. The judge, in deciding to issue the warrant, could have determined that the *modus operandi* of the Gates had been substantially corroborated. As the anonymous letter predicted, Lance Gates had flown from Chicago to West Palm Beach late in the afternoon of May 5th, had checked into a hotel room registered in the name of his wife, and, at 7:00 a.m. the following morning, had headed north, accompanied by an unidentified woman, out of West

Palm Beach on an interstate highway used by travelers from South Florida to Chicago in an automobile bearing a license plate issued to him.

At 5:15 a.m. on March 7th, only 36 hours after he had flown out of Chicago, Lance Gates, and his wife, returned to their home in Bloomingdale, driving the car in which they had left West Palm Beach some 22 hours earlier. The Bloomingdale police were awaiting them, searched the trunk of the Mercury, and uncovered approximately 350 pounds of marijuana. A search of the Gates' home revealed marijuana, weapons, and other contraband. The Illinois Circuit Court ordered suppression of all these items, on the ground that the affidavit submitted to the Circuit Judge failed to support the necessary determination of probable cause to believe that the Gates' automobile and home contained the contraband in question. This decision was affirmed in turn by the Illinois Appellate Court and by a divided vote of the Supreme Court of Illinois.

The Illinois Supreme Court concluded—and we are inclined to agree—that, standing alone, the anonymous letter sent to the Bloomingdale Police Department would not provide the basis for a magistrate's determination that there was probable cause to believe contraband would be found in the Gates' car and home. The letter provides virtually nothing from which one might conclude that its author is either honest or his information reliable; likewise, the letter gives absolutely no indication of the basis for the writer's predictions regarding the Gates' criminal activities. Something more was required, then, before a magistrate could conclude that there was probable cause to believe that contraband would be found in the Gates' home and car.

The Illinois Supreme Court also properly recognized that Detective Mader's affidavit might be capable of supplementing the anonymous letter with information sufficient to permit a determination of probable cause. In holding that the affidavit in fact did not contain sufficient additional information to sustain a determination of probable cause, the Illinois court applied a "two-pronged test," derived from our decision in *Spinelli v. United States,* 393 U.S. 410 (1969). The Illinois Supreme Court, like some others, apparently understood *Spinelli* as requiring that the anonymous letter satisfy each of two independent requirements before it could be relied on. According to this view, the letter, as supplemented by Mader's affidavit, first had to adequately reveal the "basis of knowledge" of the letter writer—the particular means by which he came by the information given in his report. Second, it had to provide facts sufficiently establishing either the "veracity" of the affiant's informant, or, alternatively, the "reliability" of the informant's report in this particular case.

* * *

We agree with the Illinois Supreme Court that an informant's "veracity," "reliability" and "basis of knowledge" are all highly relevant in determining the value of his report. We do not agree, however, that these elements should be understood as entirely separate and independent requirements to be rigidly exacted in every case, which the opinion of the Supreme Court of Illinois would imply. Rather, as detailed below, they should be understood simply as closely intertwined issues that may usefully illuminate the commonsense, practical question whether there is "probable cause" to believe that contraband or evidence is located in a particular place.

III

This totality-of-the-circumstances approach is far more consistent with our prior treatment of probable cause than is any rigid demand that specific "tests" be satisfied by every informant's tip. Perhaps the central teaching of our decisions bearing on the probable cause standard is that it is a "practical, nontechnical conception." *Brinegar v. United States,* 338 U.S. 160, 176 (1949). "In dealing with probable cause, . . . as the very name implies, we deal with probabilities. These are not technical; they are the factual and practical considerations of everyday life on which reasonable and prudent men, not legal technicians, act." Our observation in *United States v. Cortez,* 449 U.S. 411, 418 (1981), regarding "particularized suspicion," is also applicable to the probable cause standard:

> The process does not deal with hard certainties, but with probabilities. Long before the law of probabilities was articulated as such, practical people formulated certain common-sense conclusions about human behavior; jurors as factfinders are permitted to do the same—and so are law enforcement officers. Finally, the evidence thus collected must be seen and weighed not in terms of library analysis by scholars, but as understood by those versed in the field of law enforcement.

As these comments illustrate, probable cause is a fluid concept—turning on the assessment of probabilities in particular factual contexts—not readily, or even usefully, reduced to a neat set of legal rules. Informants' tips doubtless come in many shapes and sizes from many different types of persons. As we said in *Adams v. Williams,* 407 U.S. 143, 147 (1972), "Informants' tips, like all other clues and evidence coming to a policeman on the scene may vary greatly in their value and reliability." Rigid legal rules are ill-suited to an area of such diversity. "One simple rule will not cover every situation."

Moreover, the "two-pronged test" directs analysis into two largely independent channels—the informant's "veracity" or "reliability" and his "basis of knowledge." There are persuasive arguments against according these two elements such independent status. Instead, they are better understood as relevant considerations in the totality-of-the-circumstances analysis that traditionally has guided probable cause determinations: a deficiency in one may be compensated for, in determining the overall reliability of a tip, by a strong showing as to the other, or by some other indicia of reliability.

If, for example, a particular informant is known for the unusual reliability of his predictions of certain types of criminal activities in a locality, his failure, in a particular case, to thoroughly set forth the basis of his knowledge surely should not serve as an absolute bar to a finding of probable cause based on his tip. Likewise, if an unquestionably honest citizen comes forward with a report of criminal activity—which if fabricated would subject him to criminal liability—we have found rigorous scrutiny of the basis of his knowledge unnecessary. Conversely, even if we entertain some doubt as to an informant's motives, his explicit and detailed description of alleged wrongdoing, along with a statement that the event was observed first-hand, entitles his tip to greater weight than might otherwise be the case. Unlike a totality-of-the-circumstances analysis, which permits a balanced assessment of the relative weights of all the various indicia of reliability (and unreliability) attending an informant's tip, the "two-pronged test" has encouraged an excessively technical dissection of informants' tips, with undue attention being focused on isolated issues that cannot sensibly be divorced from the other facts presented to the magistrate.

* * *

If the affidavits submitted by police officers are subjected to the type of scrutiny some courts have deemed appropriate, police might well resort to warrantless searches, with the hope of relying on consent or some other exception to the warrant clause that might develop at the time of the search. In addition, the possession of a warrant by officers conducting an arrest or search greatly reduces the perception of unlawful or intrusive police conduct, by assuring "the individual whose property is searched or seized of the lawful authority of the executing officer, his need to search, and the limits of his power to search." Reflecting this preference for the warrant process, the traditional standard for review of an issuing magistrate's probable cause determination has been that so long as the magistrate had a "substantial basis for . . . conclud[ing]" that a search would uncover evidence of wrongdoing, the Fourth Amendment requires no more. We think reaffirmation of this standard better serves the purpose of encouraging recourse to the warrant procedure and is more consistent with our traditional deference to the probable cause determinations of magistrates than is the "two-pronged test."

* * *

For all these reasons, we conclude that it is wiser to abandon the "two-pronged test" established by our decisions in *Aguilar* and *Spinelli*. In its place we reaffirm the totality-of-the-circumstances analysis that traditionally has informed probable cause determinations. The task of the issuing magistrate is simply to make a practical, common-sense decision whether, given all the circumstances set forth in the affidavit before him, including the "veracity" and "basis of knowledge" of persons supplying hearsay information, there is a fair probability that contraband or evidence of a crime will be found in a particular place. And the duty of a reviewing court is simply to ensure that the magistrate had a "substantial basis for . . . conclud[ing]" that probable cause existed. We are convinced that this flexible, easily applied standard will better achieve the accommodation of public and private interests that the Fourth Amendment requires than does the approach that has developed from *Aguilar* and *Spinelli*.

* * *

Our earlier cases illustrate the limits beyond which a magistrate may not venture in issuing a warrant. A sworn statement of an affiant that "he has cause to suspect and does believe that" liquor illegally brought into the United States is located on certain premises will not do. *Nathanson v. United States,* 290 U.S. 41 (1933). An affidavit must provide the magistrate with a substantial basis for determining the existence of probable cause, and the wholly conclusory statement at issue in *Nathanson* failed to meet this requirement. An officer's statement that "affiants have received reliable information from a credible person and believe" that heroin is stored in a home, is likewise inadequate. *Aguilar v. Texas,* 378 U.S. 108 (1964). As in *Nathanson,* this is a mere conclusory statement that gives the magistrate virtually no basis at all for making a judgment regarding probable cause. Sufficient information must be presented to the magistrate to allow that official to determine probable cause; his action cannot be a mere ratification of the bare conclusions of others. In order to ensure that such an abdication of the magistrate's duty does not occur, courts must continue to conscientiously review the sufficiency of affidavits on which warrants are issued. But when we move beyond the "bare bones" affidavits present in cases such as *Nathanson* and *Aguilar,* this area simply does not lend itself to a prescribed set of rules, like that which had developed from *Spinelli*. Instead, the flexible, common-sense standard . . . better serves the purposes of the Fourth Amendment's probable cause requirement.

* * *

IV

Our decisions applying the totality-of-the-circumstances analysis outlined above have consistently recognized the value of corroboration of details of an informant's tip by independent police work. In *Jones v. United States,* 362 U.S. [257,] 269 [(1960)], we held that an affidavit relying on hearsay "is not to be deemed insufficient on that score, so long as a substantial basis for crediting the hearsay is presented." We went on to say that even in making a warrantless arrest an officer "may rely upon information received through an informant, rather than upon his direct observations, so long as the informant's statement is reasonably corroborated by other matters within the officer's knowledge." Likewise, we recognized the probative value of corroborative efforts of police officials in *Aguilar*—the source of the "two-pronged test"—by observing that if the police had made some effort to corroborate the informant's report at issue, "an entirely different case" would have been presented.

* * *

The showing of probable cause in the present case was fully as compelling as that in *Draper*. Even standing alone, the facts obtained through the independent investigation of Mader and the DEA at least suggested that the Gates were involved in drug trafficking. In addition to being a popular vacation site, Florida is well-known as a source of narcotics and other illegal drugs. Lance Gates' flight to Palm Beach, his brief, overnight stay in a motel, and apparent immediate return north to Chicago in the family car, conveniently awaiting him in West Palm Beach, is as suggestive of a pre-arranged drug run, as it is of an ordinary vacation trip.

In addition, the magistrate could rely on the anonymous letter, which had been corroborated in major part by Mader's efforts—just as had occurred in *Draper*. The Supreme Court of Illinois reasoned that *Draper* involved an informant who had given reliable information on previous occasions, while the honesty and reliability of the anonymous informant in this case were unknown to the Bloomingdale police. While this distinction might be an apt one at the time the police department received the anonymous letter, it became far less significant after Mader's independent investigative work occurred. The corroboration of the letter's predictions that the Gates' car would be in Florida, that Lance Gates would fly to Florida in the next day or so, and that he would drive the car north toward Bloomingdale all indicated, albeit not with certainty, that the informant's other assertions also were true. "Because an informant is right about some things, he is more probably right about other facts," *Spinelli,* 393 U.S., at 427 (White, J., concurring)—including the claim regarding the Gates' illegal activity. This may well not be the type of "reliability" or "veracity" necessary to satisfy some views of the "veracity prong" of *Spinelli,* but we think it suffices for the practical, common-sense judgment called for in making a probable cause determination. It is enough, for purposes of assessing probable cause, that "corroboration through other sources of information reduced the chances of a reckless or prevaricating tale," thus providing "a substantial basis for crediting the hearsay."

Finally, the anonymous letter contained a range of details relating not just to easily obtained facts and conditions existing at the time of the tip, but to future actions of third parties ordinarily not easily predicted. The letter writer's accurate information as to the travel plans of each of the

Gates was of a character likely obtained only from the Gates themselves, or from someone familiar with their not entirely ordinary travel plans. If the informant had access to accurate information of this type a magistrate could properly conclude that it was not unlikely that he also had access to reliable information of the Gates' alleged illegal activities. Of course, the Gates' travel plans might have been learned from a talkative neighbor or travel agent; under the "two-pronged test" developed from *Spinelli,* the character of the details in the anonymous letter might well not permit a sufficiently clear inference regarding the letter writer's "basis of knowledge." But, as discussed previously, probable cause does not demand the certainty we associate with formal trials. It is enough that there was a fair probability that the writer of the anonymous letter had obtained his entire story either from the Gates or someone they trusted. And corroboration of major portions of the letter's predictions provides just this probability. It is apparent, therefore, that the judge issuing the warrant had a "substantial basis for . . . conclud[ing]" that probable cause to search the Gates' home and car existed. The judgment of the Supreme Court of Illinois therefore must be reversed.

JUSTICE WHITE, concurring in the judgment.

* * *

A

For present purposes, the *Aguilar-Spinelli* rules can be summed up as follows. First, an affidavit based on an informer's tip, standing alone, cannot provide probable cause for issuance of a warrant unless the tip includes information that apprises the magistrate of the informant's basis for concluding that the contraband is where he claims it is (the "basis of knowledge" prong), and the affiant informs the magistrate of his basis for believing that the informant is credible (the "veracity" prong). Second, if a tip fails under either or both of the two prongs, probable cause may yet be established by independent police investigatory work that corroborates the tip to such an extent that it supports "both the inference that the informer was generally trustworthy and that he made his charge on the basis of information obtained in a reliable way." In instances where the officers rely on corroboration, the ultimate question is whether the corroborated tip "is as trustworthy as a tip which would pass *Aguilar*'s tests without independent corroboration."

* * *

In my view, the lower court's characterization of the Gates' activity here as totally "innocent" is dubious. In fact, the behavior was quite suspicious. I agree with the Court that Lance Gates' flight to Palm Beach, an area known to be a source of narcotics, the brief overnight stay in a motel, and apparent immediate return North, suggest a pattern that trained law-enforcement officers have recognized as indicative of illicit drug-dealing activity. Even, however, had the corroboration related only to completely innocuous activities, this fact alone would not preclude the issuance of a valid warrant. The critical issue is not whether the activities observed by the police are innocent or suspicious. Instead, the proper focus should be on whether the actions of the suspects, whatever their nature, give rise to an inference that the informant is credible and that he obtained his information in a reliable manner.

* * *

B

The Court agrees that the warrant was valid, but, in the process of reaching this conclusion, it overrules the *Aguilar-Spinelli* tests and replaces them with a "totality of the circumstances" standard. As shown above, it is not at all necessary to overrule *Aguilar-Spinelli* in order to reverse the judgment below. Therefore, because I am inclined to believe that, when applied properly, the *Aguilar-Spinelli* rules play an appropriate role in probable cause determinations, and because the Court's holding may foretell an evisceration of the probable cause standard, I do not join the Court's holding.

* * *

Thus, as I read the majority opinion, it appears that the question whether the probable cause standard is to be diluted is left to the common-sense judgments of issuing magistrates. I am reluctant to approve any standard that does not expressly require, as a prerequisite to issuance of a warrant, some showing of facts from which an inference may be drawn that the informant is credible and that his information was obtained in a reliable way. The Court is correctly concerned with the fact that some lower courts have been applying *Aguilar-Spinelli* in an unduly rigid manner. I believe, however, that with clarification of the rule of corroborating information, the lower courts are fully able to properly interpret *Aguilar-Spinelli* and avoid such unduly-rigid applications. I may be wrong; it ultimately may prove to be the case that the only profitable instruction we can provide to magistrates is to rely on common sense. But the question whether a particular anonymous tip provides the basis for issuance of a warrant will often be a difficult one, and I would at least attempt to provide more precise guidance by clarifying *Aguilar-Spinelli* and the relationship of those cases with *Draper* before totally abdicating our responsibility in this area. Hence, I do not join the Court's opinion rejecting the *Aguilar-Spinelli* rules.

JUSTICE BRENNAN, with whom JUSTICE MARSHALL joins, dissenting.

Although I join Justice Stevens' dissenting opinion and agree with him that the warrant is invalid even under the Court's newly announced "totality of the circumstances" test, I write separately to dissent from the Court's unjustified and ill-advised rejection of the two-prong test for evaluating the validity of a warrant based on hearsay announced in *Aguilar v. Texas,* 378 U.S. 108 (1964), and refined in *Spinelli v. United States,* 393 U.S. 410 (1969).

I

* * *

Until today the Court has never squarely addressed the application of the *Aguilar* and *Spinelli* standards to tips from anonymous informants. Both *Aguilar* and *Spinelli* dealt with tips from informants known at least to the police. And surely there is even more reason to subject anonymous informants' tips to the tests established by *Aguilar* and *Spinelli.* By definition nothing is known about an anonymous informant's identity, honesty, or reliability. One commentator has suggested that anonymous informants should be treated as presumptively unreliable. In any event, there certainly is no basis for treating anonymous informants as presumptively reliable. Nor is there any basis for assuming that the information provided by an anonymous informant has been obtained in a reliable way. If we are unwilling to accept conclusory allegations from the police, who are presumptively reliable, or from informants who are known, at least to the police, there cannot possibly be any rational basis for accepting conclusory allegations from anonymous informants.

To suggest that anonymous informants' tips are subject to the tests established by *Aguilar* and *Spinelli* is not to suggest that they can never provide a basis for a finding of probable cause. It is conceivable that police corroboration of the details of the tip might establish the reliability of the informant under *Aguilar*'s veracity prong, as refined in *Spinelli,* and that the details in the tip might be sufficient to qualify under the "self-verifying detail" test established by *Spinelli* as a means of satisfying *Aguilar*'s basis of knowledge prong. The *Aguilar* and *Spinelli* tests must be applied to anonymous informants' tips, however, if we are to continue to insure that findings of probable cause, and attendant intrusions, are based on information provided by an honest or credible person who has acquired the information in a reliable way.

In cases in which the police rely on information obtained from an anonymous informant, the police, by hypothesis, cannot obtain further information from the informant regarding the facts and circumstances on which the informant based his conclusion. When the police seek a warrant based solely on an anonymous informants' tip, therefore, they are providing the magistrate with all the information on which they have based their conclusion. In this respect, the command of *Aguilar* and *Spinelli* has been met and the process value identified above has been served. But *Aguilar* and *Spinelli* advance other values which argue for their application even to anonymous informants' tips. They structure the magistrate's probable cause inquiry and, more importantly, they guard against findings of probable cause, and attendant intrusions, based on anything other than information which magistrates reasonably can conclude has been obtained in a reliable way by an honest or credible person.

* * *

JUSTICE STEVENS, with whom JUSTICE BRENNAN joins, dissenting.

The fact that Lance and Sue Gates made a 22-hour nonstop drive from West Palm Beach, Florida, to Bloomingdale, Illinois, only a few hours after Lance had flown to Florida provided persuasive evidence that they were engaged in illicit activity. That fact, however, was not known to the magistrate when he issued the warrant to search their home.

What the magistrate did know at that time was that the anonymous informant had not been completely accurate in his or her predictions. The informant had indicated that "Sue drives their car to Florida *where she leaves it to be loaded up with drugs. . . . Sue flies back after she drops the car off in Florida.*" Yet Detective Mader's affidavit reported that she "left the West Palm Beach area driving the Mercury northbound."

The discrepancy between the informant's predictions and the facts known to Detective Mader is significant for three reasons. First, it cast doubt on the informant's hypothesis that the Gates already had "over $100,000 worth of drugs in their basement," The informant had predicted an itinerary that always kept one spouse in Bloomingdale, suggesting that the Gates did not want to leave their home unguarded because something valuable was hidden within. That inference obviously could not be drawn when it was known that the pair was actually together over a thousand miles from home.

Second, the discrepancy made the Gates' conduct seem substantially less unusual than the informant had predicted it would be. It would have been odd if, as predicted, Sue had driven down to Florida on Wednesday, left the car, and flown right back to Illinois. But the mere facts that Sue was in West Palm Beach with the car,[1] that she was joined by her husband at the Holiday Inn on Friday, and that the couple drove north together the next morning[3] are neither unusual nor probative of criminal activity.

Third, the fact that the anonymous letter contained a material mistake undermines the reasonableness of relying on it as a basis for making a forcible entry into a private home.

---

[1] The anonymous note suggested that she was going down on Wednesday, but for all the officers knew she had been in Florida for a month.

[3] Detective Mader's affidavit hinted darkly that the couple had set out upon "that interstate highway commonly used by travelers to the Chicago area." But the same highway is also commonly used by travelers to Disney World, Sea World, and Ringling Brothers and Barnum and Bailey Circus World. It is also the road to Cocoa Beach, Cape Canaveral, and Washington, D.C. I would venture that each year dozens of perfectly innocent people fly to Florida, meet a waiting spouse, and drive off together in the family car.

Of course, the activities in this case did not stop when the magistrate issued the warrant. The Gates drove all night to Bloomingdale, the officers searched the car and found 400 pounds of marijuana, and then they searched the house. However, none of these subsequent events may be considered in evaluating the warrant, and the search of the house was legal only if the warrant was valid. I cannot accept the Court's casual conclusion that, *before the Gates arrived in Bloomingdale,* there was probable cause to justify a valid entry and search of a private home. No one knows who the informant in this case was, or what motivated him or her to write the note. Given that the note's predictions were faulty in one significant respect, and were corroborated by nothing except ordinary innocent activity, I must surmise that the Court's evaluation of the warrant's validity has been colored by subsequent events.

* * *

Points for Discussion

1. How would the facts of *Brinegar* or *Draper* fare under the two-prong *Aguilar-Spinelli* test? Under the *Gates* totality of the circumstances test?

2. The majority and the dissents disagree, at length, about whether a rule—like *Aguilar-Spinelli*—or a standard—like *Gates*—best serves the goals of the Fourth Amendment. For a thoughtful discussion of the issue, see, Wayne R. LaFave, *"Case-by-Case Adjudication" v. "Standardized Procedures": The Robinson Dilemma*, 1974 S. CT. REV. 127 (1974).

3. Consider the following search warrant affidavit:

> Affidavit in Support of a U.S. Commissioners Search Warrant for Premises 1436 Meridian Place, N.W., Washington, D.C., apartment 36, including window spaces of said apartment. Occupied by Cecil Jones and Earline Richardson.
>
> In the late afternoon of Tuesday, August 20, 1957, I, Detective Thomas Didone, Jr., received information that Cecil Jones and Earline Richardson were involved in the illicit narcotic traffic and that they kept a ready supply of heroin on hand in the above mentioned apartment. The source of information also relates that the two aforementioned persons kept these same narcotics either on their person, under a pillow, on a dresser or on a window ledge in said apartment. The source of information goes on to relate that on many occasions the source of information has gone to said apartment and purchased narcotic drugs from the abovementioned persons and that the narcotics were secreated (sic) in the above mentioned places. The last time being August 20, 1957.
>
> Both the aforementioned persons are familiar to the undersigned and other members of the Narcotic Squad. Both have admitted to the use of narcotic drugs and display needle marks as evidence of same.

> This same information, regarding the illicit narcotic traffic, conducted by Cecil Jones and Earline Richardson, has been given to the undersigned and to other officers of the narcotic squad by other sources of information.
>
> Because the source of information mentioned in the opening paragraph has given information to the undersigned on previous occasion and which was correct, and because this same information is given by other sources does believe that there is now illicit narcotic drugs being secreated (sic) in the above apartment by Cecil Jones and Earline Richardson.

Do you think it supplies sufficient information to provide probable cause? *See Jones v. United States*, 362 U.S. 257 (1960).

4. *Spinelli v. United States* was decided by a vote of 5–3, Justice Marshall not having participated in the case. Justice Harlan's opinion for the Court specifically rejected the approach that *Gates* later adopted:

> It is true, of course, that the magistrate is obligated to render a judgment based upon a common-sense reading of the entire affidavit. We believe, however, that the "totality of circumstances" approach taken by the Court of Appeals paints with too broad a brush. Where, as here, the informer's tip is a necessary element in a finding of probable cause, its proper weight must be determined by a more precise analysis.

393 U.S. 410, 415 (1969). Justice Black wrote that he "dissented as vigorously I can" because "the Court is moving rapidly, through complex analyses and obfuscatory language, toward the holding that no magistrate can issue a warrant unless according to some unknown standard of proof he can be persuaded that the suspect defendant is actually guilty of a crime."

FLORIDA V. HARRIS

568 U.S. 237 (2013)

JUSTICE KAGAN delivered the opinion of the court.

In this case, we consider how a court should determine if the "alert" of a drug-detection dog during a traffic stop provides probable cause to search a vehicle. The Florida Supreme Court held that the State must in every case present an exhaustive set of records, including a log of the dog's performance in the field, to establish the dog's reliability. We think that demand inconsistent with the "flexible, common-sense standard" of probable cause. *Illinois v. Gates,* 462 U.S. 213, 239 (1983).

I

William Wheetley is a K-9 Officer in the Liberty County, Florida, Sheriff's Office. On June 24, 2006, he was on a routine patrol with Aldo, a German shepherd trained to detect certain narcotics (methamphetamine, marijuana, cocaine, heroin, and ecstasy). Wheetley pulled over respondent

Clayton Harris's truck because it had an expired license plate. On approaching the driver's-side door, Wheetley saw that Harris was "visibly nervous," unable to sit still, shaking, and breathing rapidly. Wheetley also noticed an open can of beer in the truck's cup holder. Wheetley asked Harris for consent to search the truck, but Harris refused. At that point, Wheetley retrieved Aldo from the patrol car and walked him around Harris's truck for a "free air sniff." Aldo alerted at the driver's-side door handle—signaling, through a distinctive set of behaviors, that he smelled drugs there.

Wheetley concluded, based principally on Aldo's alert, that he had probable cause to search the truck. His search did not turn up any of the drugs Aldo was trained to detect. But it did reveal 200 loose pseudoephedrine pills, 8,000 matches, a bottle of hydrochloric acid, two containers of antifreeze, and a coffee filter full of iodine crystals—all ingredients for making methamphetamine. Wheetley accordingly arrested Harris, who admitted after proper Miranda warnings that he routinely "cooked" methamphetamine at his house and could not go "more than a few days without using" it. The State charged Harris with possessing pseudoephedrine for use in manufacturing methamphetamine.

While out on bail, Harris had another run-in with Wheetley and Aldo. This time, Wheetley pulled Harris over for a broken brake light. Aldo again sniffed the truck's exterior, and again alerted at the driver's-side door handle. Wheetley once more searched the truck, but on this occasion discovered nothing of interest.

Harris moved to suppress the evidence found in his truck on the ground that Aldo's alert had not given Wheetley probable cause for a search. At the hearing on that motion, Wheetley testified about both his and Aldo's training in drug detection. In 2004, Wheetley (and a different dog) completed a 160-hour course in narcotics detection offered by the Dothan, Alabama, Police Department, while Aldo (and a different handler) completed a similar, 120-hour course given by the Apopka, Florida, Police Department. That same year, Aldo received a one-year certification from Drug Beat, a private company that specializes in testing and certifying K-9 dogs. Wheetley and Aldo teamed up in 2005 and went through another, 40-hour refresher course in Dothan together. They also did four hours of training exercises each week to maintain their skills. Wheetley would hide drugs in certain vehicles or buildings while leaving others "blank" to determine whether Aldo alerted at the right places. According to Wheetley, Aldo's performance in those exercises was "really good." The State introduced "Monthly Canine Detection Training Logs" consistent with that testimony: They showed that Aldo always found hidden drugs and that he performed "satisfactorily" (the higher of two possible assessments) on each day of training.

On cross-examination, Harris's attorney chose not to contest the quality of Aldo's or Wheetley's training. She focused instead on Aldo's certification and his performance in the field, particularly the two stops of Harris's truck. Wheetley conceded that the certification (which, he noted, Florida law did not require) had expired the year before he pulled Harris over. Wheetley also acknowledged that he did not keep complete records of Aldo's performance in traffic stops or other field work; instead, he maintained records only of alerts resulting in arrests. But Wheetley defended Aldo's two alerts to Harris's seemingly narcotics-free truck: According to Wheetley, Harris probably transferred the odor of methamphetamine to the door handle, and Aldo responded to that "residual odor."

The trial court concluded that Wheetley had probable cause to search Harris's truck and so denied the motion to suppress. Harris then entered a no-contest plea while reserving the right to appeal the trial court's ruling. . . .

* * *

II

A police officer has probable cause to conduct a search when "the facts available to [him] would 'warrant a [person] of reasonable caution in the belief' " that contraband or evidence of a crime is present. *Texas v. Brown*, 460 U.S. 730, 742 (1983) (plurality opinion) (quoting *Carroll v. United States*, 267 U.S. 132, 162 (1925)). The test for probable cause is not reducible to "precise definition or quantification." *Maryland v. Pringle*, 540 U.S. 366, 371 (2003). "Finely tuned standards such as proof beyond a reasonable doubt or by a preponderance of the evidence . . . have no place in the [probable-cause] decision." *Gates*, 462 U.S. at 235. All we have required is the kind of "fair probability" on which "reasonable and prudent [people,] not legal technicians, act." *Id.* at 238, 231.

* * *

The Florida Supreme Court flouted this established approach to determining probable cause. To assess the reliability of a drug-detection dog, the court created a strict evidentiary checklist, whose every item the State must tick off. Most prominently, an alert cannot establish probable cause under the Florida court's decision unless the State introduces comprehensive documentation of the dog's prior "hits" and "misses" in the field. (One wonders how the court would apply its test to a rookie dog.) No matter how much other proof the State offers of the dog's reliability, the absent field performance records will preclude a finding of probable cause. That is the antithesis of a totality-of-the-circumstances analysis. It is, indeed, the very thing we criticized in Gates when we overhauled our method for assessing the trustworthiness of an informant's tip. A gap as to any one matter, we explained, should not sink the State's case; rather, that "deficiency . . . may be compensated for, in determining the overall reliability of a tip, by a strong showing as to . . . other indicia of reliability." So too here, a finding of a drug-detection dog's reliability cannot depend on the State's satisfaction of multiple, independent evidentiary requirements. No more for dogs than for human informants is such an inflexible checklist the way to prove reliability, and thus establish probable cause.

Making matters worse, the decision below treats records of a dog's field performance as the gold standard in evidence, when in most cases they have relatively limited import. Errors may abound in such records. If a dog on patrol fails to alert to a car containing drugs, the mistake usually will go undetected because the officer will not initiate a search. Field data thus may not capture a dog's false negatives. Conversely (and more relevant here), if the dog alerts to a car in which the officer finds no narcotics, the dog may not have made a mistake at all. The dog may have detected substances that were too well hidden or present in quantities too small for the officer to locate. Or the dog may have smelled the residual odor of drugs previously in the vehicle or on the driver's person.[2]

Field data thus may markedly overstate a dog's real false positives. By contrast, those inaccuracies—in either direction—do not taint records of a dog's performance in standard training and certification settings. There, the designers of an assessment know where drugs are hidden and where they are not—and so where a dog should alert and where he should not. The better measure of a dog's reliability thus comes away from the field, in controlled testing environments.

For that reason, evidence of a dog's satisfactory performance in a certification or training program can itself provide sufficient reason to trust his alert. If a bona fide organization has certified a dog after testing his reliability in a controlled setting, a court can presume (subject to any conflicting evidence offered) that the dog's alert provides probable cause to search. The same is true, even in the absence of formal certification, if the dog has recently and successfully completed a training program that evaluated his proficiency in locating drugs. After all, law enforcement units have their own strong incentive to use effective training and certification

---

[2] See U.S. Dept. of Army, Military Working Dog Program 30 (Pamphlet 190–12, 1993) ("The odor of a substance may be present in enough concentration to cause the dog to respond even after the substance has been removed. Therefore, when a detector dog responds and no drug or explosive is found, do not assume the dog has made an error"); S. Bryson, Police Dog Tactics 257 (2d ed. 2000) ("Four skiers toke up in the parking lot before going up the mountain. Five minutes later a narcotic detector dog alerts to the car. There is no dope inside. However, the dog has performed correctly"). The Florida Supreme Court treated a dog's response to residual odor as an error, referring to the "inability to distinguish between [such] odors and actual drugs" as a "facto[r] that call[s] into question Aldo's reliability." But that statement reflects a misunderstanding. A detection dog recognizes an odor, not a drug, and should alert whenever the scent is present, even if the substance is gone (just as a police officer's much inferior nose detects the odor of marijuana for some time after a joint has been smoked). In the usual case, the mere chance that the substance might no longer be at the location does not matter; a well-trained dog's alert establishes a fair probability—all that is required for probable cause—that either drugs or evidence of a drug crime (like the precursor chemicals in Harris's truck) will be found.

programs, because only accurate drug-detection dogs enable officers to locate contraband without incurring unnecessary risks or wasting limited time and resources.

A defendant, however, must have an opportunity to challenge such evidence of a dog's reliability, whether by cross-examining the testifying officer or by introducing his own fact or expert witnesses. The defendant, for example, may contest the adequacy of a certification or training program, perhaps asserting that its standards are too lax or its methods faulty. So too, the defendant may examine how the dog (or handler) performed in the assessments made in those settings. Indeed, evidence of the dog's (or handler's) history in the field, although susceptible to the kind of misinterpretation we have discussed, may sometimes be relevant, as the Solicitor General acknowledged at oral argument. See Tr. of Oral Arg. 23–24 ("[T]he defendant can ask the handler, if the handler is on the stand, about field performance, and then the court can give that answer whatever weight is appropriate"). And even assuming a dog is generally reliable, circumstances surrounding a particular alert may undermine the case for probable cause—if, say, the officer cued the dog (consciously or not), or if the team was working under unfamiliar conditions.

In short, a probable-cause hearing focusing on a dog's alert should proceed much like any other. The court should allow the parties to make their best case, consistent with the usual rules of criminal procedure. And the court should then evaluate the proffered evidence to decide what all the circumstances demonstrate. If the State has produced proof from controlled settings that a dog performs reliably in detecting drugs, and the defendant has not contested that showing, then the court should find probable cause. If, in contrast, the defendant has challenged the State's case (by disputing the reliability of the dog overall or of a particular alert), then the court should weigh the competing evidence. In all events, the court should not prescribe, as the Florida Supreme Court did, an inflexible set of evidentiary requirements. The question—similar to every inquiry into probable cause—is whether all the facts surrounding a dog's alert, viewed through the lens of common sense, would make a reasonably prudent person think that a search would reveal contraband or evidence of a crime. A sniff is up to snuff when it meets that test.

III

And here, Aldo's did. The record in this case amply supported the trial court's determination that Aldo's alert gave Wheetley probable cause to search Harris's truck.

The State, as earlier described, introduced substantial evidence of Aldo's training and his proficiency in finding drugs. The State showed that two years before alerting to Harris's truck, Aldo had successfully completed a 120-hour program in narcotics detection, and separately obtained a certification from an independent company. And although the certification expired after a year, the Sheriff's Office required continuing training for Aldo and Wheetley. The two satisfied the requirements of another, 40-hour training program one year prior to the search at issue. And Wheetley worked with Aldo for four hours each week on exercises designed to keep their skills sharp. Wheetley testified, and written records confirmed, that in those settings Aldo always performed at the highest level.

Harris, as also noted above, declined to challenge in the trial court any aspect of Aldo's training. To be sure, Harris's briefs in this Court raise questions about that training's adequacy—for example, whether the programs simulated sufficiently diverse environments and whether they used enough blind testing (in which the handler does not know the location of drugs and so cannot cue the dog). Similarly, Harris here queries just how well Aldo performed in controlled testing. But Harris never voiced those doubts in the trial court, and cannot do so for the first time here. As the case came to the trial court, Aldo had successfully completed two recent drug-detection courses and maintained his proficiency through weekly training exercises. Viewed alone, that training record—with or without the prior certification—sufficed to establish Aldo's reliability.

And Harris's cross-examination of Wheetley, which focused on Aldo's field performance, failed to rebut the State's case. Harris principally contended in the trial court that because Wheetley did not find any of the substances Aldo was trained to detect, Aldo's two alerts must have been false. But we have already described the hazards of inferring too much from the failure of a dog's alert to lead to drugs; and here we doubt that Harris's logic does justice to Aldo's skills. Harris cooked and used methamphetamine on a regular basis; so as Wheetley later surmised, Aldo likely responded to odors that Harris had transferred to the driver's-side door handle of his truck. A well-trained drug-detection dog should alert to such odors; his response to them might appear a mistake, but in fact is not. And still more fundamentally, we do not evaluate probable cause in hindsight, based on what a search does or does not turn up. For the reasons already stated, Wheetley had good cause to view Aldo as a reliable detector of drugs. And no special circumstance here gave Wheetley reason to discount Aldo's usual dependability or distrust his response to Harris's truck.

Because training records established Aldo's reliability in detecting drugs and Harris failed to undermine that showing, we agree with the trial court that Wheetley had probable cause to search Harris's truck. We accordingly reverse the judgment of the Florida Supreme Court.

Points for Discussion

1. The Florida Supreme Court held below "that evidence that the dog has been trained and certified to detect narcotics, standing alone, is not sufficient to establish the dog's reliability for purposes of determining probable

cause—especially since training and certification in this state are not standardized and thus each training and certification program may differ with no meaningful way to assess them." *Harris v. Florida*, 71 So.3d 756, 759 (Fla. 2011). That standard would have required the state to show not only that the dog was "certified" but also to detail what the training program entailed and to maintain and present records of the dog's performance in the field. The reason for this was that a dog cannot be cross-examined as to why it alerted to a particular car: "Because the State bears the burden of establishing probable cause, if the courts are to make determinations of probable cause based on the alerts of dogs, who can neither be cross-examined nor otherwise independently assessed as to their reliability, it is appropriate to place the burden on the State to ensure uniformity in the way dogs are evaluated for reliability of their alerts." *Id.* at 772. Why do you think the Supreme Court unanimously rejected this standard?

2. Because none of the drugs that Aldo was trained to detect were actually found in Harris' truck either time he was stopped, the Supreme Court cites in footnote 2 a number of publications to support the idea that Aldo must have alerted to "residual odors" on the car door. Is citing to these authorities persuasive? When cross-examined by the defendant as to how long "residual odors" linger on a car door, Officer Wheetley said he could not answer the question. He simply insisted that the fact that Aldo alerted proved that there was a "residual odor" on the door. Does Harris make it too easy for police to search a car? Without any information as to a given dog's performance in the field, how can a defendant show that the alert was either false or instigated by the handler?

MARYLAND V. PRINGLE

540 U.S. 366 (2003)

CHIEF JUSTICE REHNQUIST delivered the opinion of the court.

In the early morning hours a passenger car occupied by three men was stopped for speeding by a police officer. The officer, upon searching the car, seized $763 of rolled-up cash from the glove compartment and five glassine baggies of cocaine from between the back-seat armrest and the back seat. After all three men denied ownership of the cocaine and money, the officer arrested each of them. We hold that the officer had probable cause to arrest Pringle—one of the three men.

At 3:16 a.m. on August 7, 1999, a Baltimore County Police officer stopped a Nissan Maxima for speeding. There were three occupants in the car: Donte Partlow, the driver and owner, respondent Pringle, the front-seat passenger, and Otis Smith, the back-seat passenger. The officer asked Partlow for his license and registration. When Partlow opened the glove compartment to retrieve the vehicle registration, the officer observed a large amount of rolled-up money in the glove compartment. The officer returned to his patrol car with Partlow's license and registration to check the computer system for outstanding violations. The computer check did not reveal any violations. The officer returned to the stopped car, had Partlow get out, and issued him an oral warning.

After a second patrol car arrived, the officer asked Partlow if he had any weapons or narcotics in the vehicle. Partlow indicated that he did not. Partlow then consented to a search of the vehicle. The search yielded $763 from the glove compartment and five plastic glassine baggies containing cocaine from behind the back-seat armrest. When the officer began the search the armrest was in the upright position flat against the rear seat. The officer pulled down the armrest and found the drugs, which had been placed between the armrest and the back seat of the car.

The officer questioned all three men about the ownership of the drugs and money, and told them that if no one admitted to ownership of the drugs he was going to arrest them all. The men offered no information regarding the ownership of the drugs or money. All three were placed under arrest and transported to the police station.

Later that morning, Pringle waived his rights under *Miranda v. Arizona*, 384 U.S. 436 (1966), and gave an oral and written confession in which he acknowledged that the cocaine belonged to him, that he and his friends were going to a party, and that he intended to sell the cocaine or "[u]se it for sex." Pringle maintained that the other occupants of the car did not know about the drugs, and they were released.

The trial court denied Pringle's motion to suppress his confession as the fruit of an illegal arrest, holding that the officer had probable cause to arrest Pringle. A jury convicted Pringle of possession with intent to distribute cocaine and possession of cocaine. He was sentenced to 10 years' incarceration without the possibility of parole. The Court of Special Appeals of Maryland affirmed.

* * *

It is uncontested in the present case that the officer, upon recovering the five plastic glassine baggies containing suspected cocaine, had probable cause to believe a felony had been committed. The sole question is whether the officer had probable cause to believe that Pringle committed that crime.

* * *

In this case, Pringle was one of three men riding in a Nissan Maxima at 3:16 a.m. There was $763 of rolled-up cash in the glove compartment directly in front of Pringle. Five plastic glassine baggies of cocaine were behind the back-seat armrest and accessible to all three men. Upon questioning, the three men failed to offer any information with respect to the ownership of the cocaine or the money.

We think it an entirely reasonable inference from these facts that any or all three of the occupants had knowledge of, and exercised dominion and control over, the cocaine. Thus a reasonable officer could conclude that there was probable cause to believe Pringle committed the crime of possession of cocaine, either solely or jointly.

Pringle's attempt to characterize this case as a guilt-by-association case is unavailing. His reliance on *Ybarra v. Illinois*, [444 U.S. 85 (1978),] and *United States v. Di Re,* 332 U.S. 581 (1948), is misplaced. In *Ybarra,* police officers obtained a warrant to search a tavern and its bartender for evidence of possession of a controlled substance. Upon entering the tavern, the officers conducted patdown searches of the customers present in the tavern, including Ybarra. Inside a cigarette pack retrieved from Ybarra's pocket, an officer found six tinfoil packets containing heroin. We stated:

> [A] person's mere propinquity to others independently suspected of criminal activity does not, without more, give rise to probable cause to search that person. Where the standard is probable cause, a search or seizure of a person must be supported by probable cause particularized with respect to that person. This requirement cannot be undercut or avoided by simply pointing to the fact that coincidentally there exists probable cause to search or seize another or to search the premises where the person may happen to be.

We held that the search warrant did not permit body searches of all of the tavern's patrons and that the police could not pat down the patrons for weapons, absent individualized suspicion.

This case is quite different from *Ybarra*. Pringle and his two companions were in a relatively small automobile, not a public tavern. In *Wyoming v. Houghton,* 526 U.S. 295 (1999), we noted that "a car passenger—unlike the unwitting tavern patron in *Ybarra*—will often be engaged in a common enterprise with the driver, and have the same interest in concealing the fruits or the evidence of their wrongdoing."

Here we think it was reasonable for the officer to infer a common enterprise among the three men. The quantity of drugs and cash in the car indicated the likelihood of drug dealing, an enterprise to which a dealer would be unlikely to admit an innocent person with the potential to furnish evidence against him.

In *Di Re*, a federal investigator had been told by an informant, Reed, that he was to receive counterfeit gasoline ration coupons from a certain Buttitta at a particular place. The investigator went to the appointed place and saw Reed, the sole occupant of the rear seat of the car, holding gasoline ration coupons. There were two other occupants in the car: Buttitta in the driver's seat and Di Re in the front passenger's seat. Reed informed the investigator that Buttitta had given him counterfeit coupons. Thereupon, all three men were arrested and searched. After noting that the officers had no information implicating Di Re and no information pointing to Di Re's possession of coupons, unless presence in the car warranted that inference, we concluded that the officer lacked probable cause to believe that Di Re was involved in the crime. We said "[a]ny inference that everyone on the scene of a crime is a party to it must disappear if the Government informer singles out the guilty person." No such singling out occurred in this case; none of the three men provided information with respect to the ownership of the cocaine or money.

We hold that the officer had probable cause to believe that Pringle had committed the crime of possession of a controlled substance. Pringle's arrest therefore did not contravene the Fourth and Fourteenth Amendments. Accordingly, the judgment of the Court of Appeals of Maryland is reversed, and the case is remanded for further proceedings not inconsistent with this opinion.

Points for Discussion

1. The Court unanimously decides that there was probable cause to support Pringle's arrest. But doesn't his arrest come dangerously close to the guilt-by-association cases that the Court attempts to distinguish? How valid is the Court's premise that car passengers "will often be engaged in a common enterprise with the driver"? Is it true, as the Court supposes, that drug dealers are unlikely to deal drugs in the presence of an innocent friend or relative?

2. Can we conclude from the Court's approval of the arrest in this case that probable cause can be established by a probability of one in three? From the police's point of view, wasn't the likelihood of Pringle's guilt no greater than that?

B. "WARRANTS"

Rhetoric in Supreme Court opinions stretching back to the early 20th century insists that a judicial warrant, issued in advance of a government search or seizure, is the gold standard for determining the reasonableness of the government intrusion: " 'Over and again this Court has emphasized that the mandate of the (Fourth) Amendment requires adherence to judicial processes,' and that searches conducted outside the judicial process, without prior approval by judge or magistrate, are per se unreasonable under the Fourth Amendment—subject only to a few specifically established and well-delineated exceptions." *Katz v. United States*, 389 U.S. 347, 356–57 (1967) (quoting *United States v. Jeffers*, 342 U.S. 48, 51 (1951)). The Court has quoted *Katz*'s claim that the exceptions to the so-called warrant requirement are "well-delineated" and "few" many times since, including in some of its recent decisions. *See, e.g.*, *City of Ontario v. Quon*, 130 S.Ct. 2619, 2630 (2010); *Arizona v. Gant*, 556 U.S. 332, 338 (2009).

The judicial warrant is so prominently discussed in search-and-seizure cases (as well as in movies and television shows) that it is easy to forget that the vast majority of legal government searches and seizures fall within one of the many "exceptions" to the supposed warrant requirement. As Justice Scalia noted in *California v. Acevedo*: "Even before today's decision, the 'warrant requirement' had become so riddled with exceptions that it was basically unrecognizable. In 1985, one commentator cataloged nearly 20 such exceptions, including 'searches incident to arrest . . . automobile searches . . . border searches . . . administrative searches of regulated businesses . . . exigent circumstances . . . search[es] incident to nonarrest when there is probable cause to arrest . . . boat boarding for document checks . . . welfare searches . . . inventory searches . . . airport searches . . . school search[es]. . . .' " 500 U.S. 565, 583 (1991) (Scalia, J., concurring). A decade later, Justice Thomas wrote, "The Court has most frequently held that warrantless searches are presumptively unreasonable but has also found a plethora of exceptions to presumptive unreasonableness." *Groh v. Ramirez*, 540 U.S. 551, 573 (2004) (Thomas, J., dissenting).

The Warrant Clause provides that "no Warrants shall issue, but upon probable cause, supported by Oath or affirmation, and particularly describing the place to be searched, and the persons or things to be seized." Putting aside the matter of whether this clause requires a warrant in advance of any given search or seizure, it does impose certain attributes for a valid warrant. It requires a specific description of what the government is after, which reinforces the probable-cause requirement and also limits the scope of a search. The word "warrants" itself is understood to mean *judicial* warrants—those issued by a common-law judicial officer—one who is theoretically neutral as to the outcome of a case and whose only duty is to uphold the law's requirements. The oath requirement is satisfied in practice by an affidavit, typically from a law enforcement officer, setting forth enough information to establish probable cause. The affidavit and the draft warrant are both prepared by prosecutors and presented to a judicial officer for evaluation and approval. Probable cause must be evident from the affidavits accompanying the warrant request. "Under the cases of this Court, an otherwise insufficient affidavit cannot be rehabilitated by testimony concerning information possessed by the affiant when he sought the warrant but not disclosed to the issuing magistrate." *Whitney v. Warden*, 401 U.S. 560 (1971). This section explores these requirements in detail.

1. PARTICULARITY

By its terms, the Fourth Amendment requires particularity with regard to both the place to be searched and the persons or things to be seized. To understand the reasons for the particularity requirement, it is important to remember exactly what it was the Founders were reacting to in enacting the Amendment. In *Marron v. United States*, 275 U.S. 192, 195–96 (1927), Justice Butler recounted some of this history:

General searches have long been deemed to violate fundamental rights. It is plain that the amendment forbids them. In *Boyd v. United States*, 116 U.S. 616, 624 (1886), Mr. Justice Bradley, writing for the court, said:

> In order to ascertain the nature of the proceedings intended by the Fourth Amendment to the Constitution under the terms "unreasonable searches and seizures," it is only necessary to recall the contemporary or then recent history of the controversies on the subject, both in this country and in England. The practice had obtained in the colonies of issuing writs of assistance to the revenue officers, empowering them, in this discretion, to search suspected places for smuggled goods, which James Otis pronounced "the worst instrument of arbitrary power, the most destructive of English liberty, and the fundamental principles of law, that ever was found in an English law book," since they placed "the liberty of every man in the hands of every petty officer."

And in *Weeks v. United States*, 232 U.S. 383, 391 (1914), Mr. Justice Day, writing for the court, said:

> The effect of the 4th Amendment is to put the courts of the United States and federal officials, in the exercise of their power and authority, under limitations and restraints as to the exercise of such power and authority, and to forever secure the people, their persons, houses, papers, and effects, against all unreasonable searches and seizures under the guise of law. This protection reaches all alike, whether accused of crime or not, and the duty of giving to it force and effect is obligatory upon all intrusted under our federal system with the enforcement of the laws. The tendency of those who execute the criminal laws of the country to obtain conviction by means of unlawful seizures and enforced confessions * * * should find no sanction in the judgments of the courts, which are charged at all times with the support of the Constitution, and to which people of all conditions have a right to appeal for the maintenance of such fundamental rights.

The requirement that warrants shall particularly describe the things to be seized makes general searches under them impossible and prevents the seizure of one thing under a warrant describing another. As to what is to be taken, nothing is left to the discretion of the officer executing the warrant.

In other words, the Founders' principal concern about both general warrants and writs of assistance was the discretion that they left to the officer in the field. The officer was often allowed to choose where to search, whom to arrest, and what to seize. The particularity requirement of the warrant clause was aimed directly at this concern.

MARYLAND V. GARRISON

480 U.S. 79 (1987)

JUSTICE STEVENS delivered the opinion of the court.

Baltimore police officers obtained and executed a warrant to search the person of Lawrence McWebb and "the premises known as 2036 Park Avenue third floor apartment." When the police applied for the warrant and when they conducted the search pursuant to the warrant, they reasonably believed that there was only one apartment on the premises described in the warrant. In fact, the third floor was divided into two apartments, one occupied by McWebb and one by respondent Garrison. Before the officers executing the warrant became aware that they were in a separate apartment occupied by respondent, they had discovered the contraband that provided the basis for respondent's conviction for violating Maryland's Controlled Substances Act. The question presented is whether the seizure of that contraband was prohibited by the Fourth Amendment.

* * *

There is no question that the warrant was valid and was supported by probable cause. The trial court found, and the two appellate courts did not dispute, that after making a reasonable investigation, including a verification of information obtained from a reliable informant, an exterior examination of the three-story building at 2036 Park Avenue, and an inquiry of the utility company, the officer who obtained the warrant reasonably concluded that there was only one apartment on the third floor and that it was occupied by McWebb. When six Baltimore police officers executed the warrant, they fortuitously encountered McWebb in front of the building and used his key to gain admittance to the first-floor hallway and to the locked door at the top of the stairs to the third floor. As they entered the vestibule on the third floor, they encountered respondent, who was standing in the hallway area. The police could see into the interior of both McWebb's apartment to the left and respondent's to the right, for the doors to both were open. Only after respondent's apartment had been entered and heroin, cash, and drug paraphernalia had been found did any of the officers realize that the third floor contained two apartments. As soon as they became aware of that fact, the search was discontinued. All of the officers reasonably believed that they were searching McWebb's apartment. No further search of respondent's apartment was made.

The matter on which there is a difference of opinion concerns the proper interpretation of the warrant. A literal reading of its plain language, as well as the language used in the application for the warrant, indicates that it was intended to authorize a search of the entire third floor.

* * *

I

The Warrant Clause of the Fourth Amendment categorically prohibits the issuance of any warrant except one "particularly describing the place to be searched and the persons or things to be seized." The manifest purpose of this particularity requirement was to prevent general searches. By limiting the authorization to search to the specific areas and things for which there is probable cause to search, the requirement ensures that the search will be carefully tailored to its justifications, and will not take on the character of the wide-ranging exploratory searches the Framers intended to prohibit. Thus, the scope of a lawful search is "defined by the object of the search and the places in which there is probable cause to believe that it may be found. Just as probable cause to believe that a stolen lawnmower may be found in a garage will not support a warrant to search an upstairs bedroom, probable cause to believe that undocumented aliens are being transported in a van will not justify a warrantless search of a suitcase."

In this case there is no claim that the "persons or things to be seized" were inadequately described or that there was no probable cause to believe that those things might be found in "the place to be searched" as it was described in the warrant. With the benefit of hindsight, however, we now know that the description of that place was broader than appropriate because it was based on the mistaken belief that there was only one apartment on the third floor of the building at 2036 Park Avenue. The question is whether that factual mistake invalidated a warrant that undoubtedly would have been valid if it had reflected a completely accurate understanding of the building's floor plan.

Plainly, if the officers had known, or even if they should have known, that there were two separate dwelling units on the third floor of 2036 Park Avenue, they would have been obligated to exclude respondent's apartment from the scope of the requested warrant. But we must judge the constitutionality of their conduct in light of the information available to them at the time they acted. Those items of evidence that emerge after the warrant is issued have no bearing on whether or not a warrant was validly issued. Just as the discovery of contraband cannot validate a warrant invalid when issued, so is it equally clear that the discovery of facts demonstrating that a valid warrant was unnecessarily broad does not retroactively invalidate the warrant. The validity of the warrant must be assessed on the basis of the information that the officers disclosed, or had a duty to discover and to disclose, to the issuing Magistrate. On the basis of that information, we agree with the conclusion of all three Maryland courts that the warrant, insofar as it authorized a search that turned out to be ambiguous in scope, was valid when it issued.

II

The question whether the execution of the warrant violated respondent's constitutional right to be secure in his home is somewhat less clear. We have no difficulty concluding that the officers' entry into the third-floor common area was legal; they carried a warrant for those premises, and they were accompanied by McWebb, who provided the key that they used to open the door giving access to the third-floor common area. If the officers had known, or should have known, that the third floor contained two apartments before they entered the living quarters on the third floor, and thus had been aware of the error in the warrant, they would have been obligated to limit their search to McWebb's apartment. Moreover, as the officers recognized, they were required to discontinue the search of respondent's apartment as soon as they discovered that there were two separate units on the third floor and therefore were put on notice of the risk that they might be in a unit erroneously included within the terms of the warrant. The officers' conduct and the limits of the search were based on the information available as the search proceeded. While the purposes justifying a police search strictly limit the permissible extent of the search, the Court has also recognized the need to allow some latitude for honest mistakes that are made by officers in the dangerous and difficult process of making arrests and executing search warrants.[11]

In *Hill v. California*, 401 U.S. 797 (1971), we considered the validity of the arrest of a man named Miller based on the mistaken belief that he was Hill. The police had probable cause to arrest Hill and they in good faith believed that Miller was Hill when they found him in Hill's apartment. As we explained:

> The upshot was that the officers in good faith believed Miller was Hill and arrested him. They were quite wrong as it turned out, and subjective good-faith belief would not in itself justify either the arrest or the subsequent search. But sufficient probability, not certainty, is the touchstone of reasonableness under the Fourth Amendment and on the record before us the officers' mistake was understandable and the arrest a reasonable response to the situation facing them at the time.

While *Hill* involved an arrest without a warrant, its underlying rationale that an officer's reasonable misidentification of a person does not invalidate a valid arrest is equally applicable to an officer's reasonable failure to appreciate that a valid warrant describes too broadly the premises to be searched. Under the reasoning in *Hill*, the validity of the search of respondent's apartment pursuant to a warrant authorizing the

[11] "Because many situations which confront officers in the course of executing their duties are more or less ambiguous, room must be allowed for some mistakes on their part. But the mistakes must be those of reasonable men, acting on facts leading sensibly to their conclusions of probability." *Brinegar v. United States*, 338 U.S. 160, 176 (1949).

search of the entire third floor depends on whether the officers' failure to realize the overbreadth of the warrant was objectively understandable and reasonable. Here it unquestionably was. The objective facts available to the officers at the time suggested no distinction between McWebb's apartment and the third-floor premises.[12]

For that reason, the officers properly responded to the command contained in a valid warrant even if the warrant is interpreted as authorizing a search limited to McWebb's apartment rather than the entire third floor. Prior to the officers' discovery of the factual mistake, they perceived McWebb's apartment and the third-floor premises as one and the same; therefore their execution of the warrant reasonably included the entire third floor.[13]

Under either interpretation of the warrant, the officers' conduct was consistent with a reasonable effort to ascertain and identify the place intended to be searched within the meaning of the Fourth Amendment.

JUSTICE BLACKMUN, with whom JUSTICE BRENNAN and JUSTICE MARSHALL join, dissenting.

Under this Court's precedents, the search of respondent Garrison's apartment violated the Fourth Amendment. While executing a warrant specifically limited to McWebb's residence, the officers expanded their search to include respondent's adjacent apartment, an expansion made without a warrant and in the absence of exigent circumstances. In my view, Maryland's highest court correctly concluded that the trial judge should have granted respondent's motion to suppress the evidence seized as a result of this warrantless search of his apartment. Moreover, even if I were to accept the majority's analysis of this case as one involving a mistake on the part of the police officers, I would find that the officers' error, either in obtaining or in executing the warrant, was not reasonable under the circumstances.

I

The home always has received special protection in analysis under the Fourth Amendment, which protects the "right of the people to be secure in their persons, *houses*, papers, and effects, against unreasonable searches and seizures" (emphasis added). The Fourth Amendment, in fact, was a

---

[12] Nothing McWebb did or said after he was detained outside 2036 Park Avenue would have suggested to the police that there were two apartments on the third floor. McWebb provided the key that opened the doors on the first floor and on the third floor. The police could reasonably have believed that McWebb was admitting them to an undivided apartment on the third floor. When the officers entered the foyer on the third floor, neither McWebb nor Garrison informed them that they lived in separate apartments.

[13] We expressly distinguish the facts of this case from a situation in which the police know there are two apartments on a certain floor of a building, and have probable cause to believe that drugs are being sold out of that floor, but do not know in which of the two apartments the illegal transactions are taking place. A search pursuant to a warrant authorizing a search of the entire floor under those circumstances would present quite different issues from the ones before us in this case.

direct response to the colonists' objection to searches of homes under general warrants or without warrants. In today's society, the protection of the Amendment of course is extended to the equivalent of the traditional single-family house, such as an apartment.

* * *

The Fourth Amendment also states that "no Warrants shall issue, but upon probable cause, supported by Oath or affirmation, and *particularly describing* the place to be searched, and the persons or things to be seized" (emphasis added). The particularity-of-description requirement is satisfied where "the description is such that the officer with a search warrant can with reasonable effort ascertain and identify the place intended." In applying this requirement to searches aimed at residences within multiunit buildings, such as the search in the present case, courts have declared invalid those warrants that fail to describe the targeted unit with enough specificity to prevent a search of all the units. Courts have used different criteria to determine whether a warrant has identified a unit with sufficient particularity.

Applying the above principles to this case, I conclude that the search of respondent's apartment was improper. The words of the warrant were plain and distinctive: the warrant directed the officers to seize marijuana and drug paraphernalia on the person of McWebb and in McWebb's apartment, i.e., "on the premises known as 2036 Park Avenue third floor apartment." As the Court of Appeals observed, this warrant specifically authorized a search only of McWebb's—not respondent's residence. In its interpretation of the warrant, the majority suggests that the language of this document, as well as that in the supporting affidavit, permitted a search of the entire third floor. It escapes me why the language in question, "third floor apartment," when used with reference to a single unit in a multiple-occupancy building and in the context of one person's residence, plainly has the meaning the majority discerns, rather than its apparent and, indeed, obvious signification—one apartment located on the third floor. Accordingly, if, as appears to be the case, the warrant was limited in its description to the third floor apartment of McWebb, then the search of an additional apartment—respondent's—was warrantless and is presumed unreasonable "in the absence of some one of a number of well defined 'exigent circumstances.'" Because the State has not advanced any such exception to the warrant requirement, the evidence obtained as a result of this search should have been excluded.

II

* * *

Even if one accepts the majority's view that there is no Fourth Amendment violation where the officers' mistake is reasonable, it is questionable whether that standard was met in this case. To repeat Justice

Harlan's observation, although the proper question in Fourth Amendment analysis is "what protection it affords to . . . people, . . . that question requires reference to a 'place.'" *Katz v. United States*, 389 U.S., at 361 (concurring opinion). The "place" at issue here is a small multiple-occupancy building. Such forms of habitation are now common in this country, particularly in neighborhoods with changing populations and of declining affluence. Accordingly, any analysis of the "reasonableness" of the officers' behavior here must be done with this context in mind

* * *

In my view . . . the "objective facts" should have made the officers aware that there were two different apartments on the third floor well before they discovered the incriminating evidence in respondent's apartment. Before McWebb happened to drive up while the search party was preparing to execute the warrant, one of the officers, Detective Shea, somewhat disguised as a construction worker, was already on the porch of the row house and was seeking to gain access to the locked first-floor door that permitted entrance into the building. From this vantage point he had time to observe the seven mailboxes and bells; indeed, he rang all seven bells, apparently in an effort to summon some resident to open the front door to the search party. A reasonable officer in Detective Shea's position, already aware that this was a multiunit building and now armed with further knowledge of the number of units in the structure, would have conducted at that time more investigation to specify the exact location of McWebb's apartment before proceeding further. For example, he might have questioned another resident of the building.

* * *

Accordingly, even if a reasonable error on the part of police officers prevents a Fourth Amendment violation, the mistakes here, both with respect to obtaining and executing the warrant, are not reasonable and could easily have been avoided.

Points for Discussion

1. The Court concludes that this was a reasonable search and thus that no Fourth Amendment violation occurred. From the point of view of Garrison, how is this explicable? The officers did not have probable cause to believe anything would be found in *his* apartment, the warrant authorized the searching only of McWebb's apartment, and no exigency justified a warrantless search of Garrison's apartment. The officer's reasonable belief that they were in Webb's apartment when they discovered evidence used against Garrison is nonetheless deemed sufficient to make the search constitutional. What does this tell us about the Court's views about the relationship between the reasonableness and warrant clauses?

2. As we shall see in chapter 10, there is another way the Court could have come to a similar result in this case: It could have concluded that, although the Fourth Amendment was violated because there was not probable cause to search Garrison's apartment, the exclusionary rule should not apply because the officers' conduct was reasonable. *See, e.g.*, *Herring v. United States*, 555 U.S. 135, 144 (2009) ("To trigger the exclusionary rule, police conduct must be sufficiently deliberate that exclusion can meaningfully deter it, and sufficiently culpable that such deterrence is worth the price paid by the justice system.").

GROH V. RAMIREZ

540 U.S. 551 (2004)

JUSTICE STEVENS delivered the opinion of the court.

Petitioner conducted a search of respondents' home pursuant to a warrant that failed to describe the "persons or things to be seized." U.S. Const., Amdt. 4. The questions presented are (1) whether the search violated the Fourth Amendment, and (2) if so, whether petitioner nevertheless is entitled to qualified immunity, given that a Magistrate Judge (Magistrate), relying on an affidavit that particularly described the items in question, found probable cause to conduct the search.

I

Respondents, Joseph Ramirez and members of his family, live on a large ranch in Butte-Silver Bow County, Montana. Petitioner, Jeff Groh, has been a Special Agent for the Bureau of Alcohol, Tobacco and Firearms (ATF) since 1989. In February 1997, a concerned citizen informed petitioner that on a number of visits to respondents' ranch the visitor had seen a large stock of weaponry, including an automatic rifle, grenades, a grenade launcher, and a rocket launcher. Based on that information, petitioner prepared and signed an application for a warrant to search the ranch. The application stated that the search was for "any automatic firearms or parts to automatic weapons, destructive devices to include but not limited to grenades, grenade launchers, rocket launchers, and any and all receipts pertaining to the purchase or manufacture of automatic weapons or explosive devices or launchers." Petitioner supported the application with a detailed affidavit, which he also prepared and executed, that set forth the basis for his belief that the listed items were concealed on the ranch. Petitioner then presented these documents to a Magistrate, along with a warrant form that petitioner also had completed. The Magistrate signed the warrant form.

Although the application particularly described the place to be searched and the contraband petitioner expected to find, the warrant itself was less specific; it failed to identify any of the items that petitioner intended to seize. In the portion of the form that called for a description of the "person or property" to be seized, petitioner typed a description of respondents' two-story blue house rather than the alleged stockpile of firearms.[2] The warrant did not incorporate by reference the itemized list contained in the application. It did, however, recite that the Magistrate was satisfied the affidavit established probable cause to believe that contraband was concealed on the premises, and that sufficient grounds existed for the warrant's issuance.

The day after the Magistrate issued the warrant, petitioner led a team of law enforcement officers, including both federal agents and members of the local sheriff's department, in the search of respondents' premises. Although respondent Joseph Ramirez was not home, his wife and children were. Petitioner states that he orally described the objects of the search to Mrs. Ramirez in person and to Mr. Ramirez by telephone. According to Mrs. Ramirez, however, petitioner explained only that he was searching for "an explosive device in a box." At any rate, the officers' search uncovered no illegal weapons or explosives. When the officers left, petitioner gave Mrs. Ramirez a copy of the search warrant, but not a copy of the application, which had been sealed. The following day, in response to a request from respondents' attorney, petitioner faxed the attorney a copy of the page of the application that listed the items to be seized. No charges were filed against the Ramirezes.

Respondents sued petitioner and the other officers under *Bivens v. Six Unknown Fed. Narcotics Agents,* 403 U.S. 388 (1971), and Rev. Stat. § 1979, 42 U.S.C. § 1983, raising eight claims, including violation of the Fourth Amendment. The District Court entered summary judgment for all defendants. The court found no Fourth Amendment violation, because it considered the case comparable to one in which the warrant contained an inaccurate address, and in such a case, the court reasoned, the warrant is sufficiently detailed if the executing officers can locate the correct house. The court added that even if a constitutional violation occurred, the defendants were entitled to qualified immunity because the failure of the warrant to describe the objects of the search amounted to a mere "typographical error."

* * *

II

The warrant was plainly invalid. The Fourth Amendment states unambiguously that "no Warrants shall issue, but upon probable cause, supported by Oath or affirmation, and *particularly describing* the place to be searched, and *the persons or things to be seized.*" (Emphasis added.) The warrant in this case complied with the first three of these requirements: It

[2] The warrant stated: "[T]here is now concealed [on the specified premises] a certain person or property, namely [a] single dwelling residence two story in height which is blue in color and has two additions attached to the east. The front entrance to the residence faces in a southerly direction."

was based on probable cause and supported by a sworn affidavit, and it described particularly the place of the search. On the fourth requirement, however, the warrant failed altogether. Indeed, petitioner concedes that "the warrant . . . was deficient in particularity because it provided no description of the type of evidence sought."

The fact that the *application* adequately described the "things to be seized" does not save the *warrant* from its facial invalidity. The Fourth Amendment by its terms requires particularity in the warrant, not in the supporting documents. And for good reason: "The presence of a search warrant serves a high function," *McDonald v. United States,* 335 U.S. 451, 455 (1948), and that high function is not necessarily vindicated when some other document, somewhere, says something about the objects of the search, but the contents of that document are neither known to the person whose home is being searched nor available for her inspection. We do not say that the Fourth Amendment prohibits a warrant from cross-referencing other documents. Indeed, most Courts of Appeals have held that a court may construe a warrant with reference to a supporting application or affidavit if the warrant uses appropriate words of incorporation, and if the supporting document accompanies the warrant. But in this case the warrant did not incorporate other documents by reference, nor did either the affidavit or the application (which had been placed under seal) accompany the warrant. Hence, we need not further explore the matter of incorporation.

Petitioner argues that even though the warrant was invalid, the search nevertheless was "reasonable" within the meaning of the Fourth Amendment. He notes that a Magistrate authorized the search on the basis of adequate evidence of probable cause, that petitioner orally described to respondents the items to be seized, and that the search did not exceed the limits intended by the Magistrate and described by petitioner. Thus, petitioner maintains, his search of respondents' ranch was functionally equivalent to a search authorized by a valid warrant.

We disagree. This warrant did not simply omit a few items from a list of many to be seized, or misdescribe a few of several items. Nor did it make what fairly could be characterized as a mere technical mistake or typographical error. Rather, in the space set aside for a description of the items to be seized, the warrant stated that the items consisted of a "single dwelling residence . . . blue in color." In other words, the warrant did not describe the items to be seized *at all.* In this respect the warrant was so obviously deficient that we must regard the search as "warrantless" within the meaning of our case law. "We are not dealing with formalities." Because " 'the right of a man to retreat into his own home and there be free from unreasonable governmental intrusion' " stands " '[a]t the very core' of the Fourth Amendment," our cases have firmly established the " 'basic principle of Fourth Amendment law' that searches and seizures inside a home without a warrant are presumptively unreasonable." Thus, "absent exigent circumstances, a warrantless entry to search for weapons or contraband is unconstitutional even when a felony has been committed and there is probable cause to believe that incriminating evidence will be found within."

We have clearly stated that the presumptive rule against warrantless searches applies with equal force to searches whose only defect is a lack of particularity in the warrant. In [*Massachusetts v.*] *Sheppard,* for instance, the petitioner argued that even though the warrant was invalid for lack of particularity, "the search was constitutional because it was reasonable within the meaning of the Fourth Amendment." 468 U.S. [981, 988, n. 5 (1984)]. In squarely rejecting that position, we explained:

> The uniformly applied rule is that a search conducted pursuant to a warrant that fails to conform to the particularity requirement of the Fourth Amendment is unconstitutional. That rule is in keeping with the well-established principle that "except in certain carefully defined classes of cases, a search of private property without proper consent is 'unreasonable' unless it has been authorized by a valid search warrant."

Petitioner asks us to hold that a search conducted pursuant to a warrant lacking particularity should be exempt from the presumption of unreasonableness if the goals served by the particularity requirement are otherwise satisfied. He maintains that the search in this case satisfied those goals—which he says are "to prevent general searches, to prevent the seizure of one thing under a warrant describing another, and to prevent warrants from being issued on vague or dubious information"—because the scope of the search did not exceed the limits set forth in the application. But unless the particular items described in the affidavit are also set forth in the warrant itself (or at least incorporated by reference, and the affidavit present at the search), there can be no written assurance that the Magistrate actually found probable cause to search for, and to seize, every item mentioned in the affidavit. In this case, for example, it is at least theoretically possible that the Magistrate was satisfied that the search for weapons and explosives was justified by the showing in the affidavit, but not convinced that any evidentiary basis existed for rummaging through respondents' files and papers for receipts pertaining to the purchase or manufacture of such items. Or, conceivably, the Magistrate might have believed that some of the weapons mentioned in the affidavit could have been lawfully possessed and therefore should not be seized. The mere fact that the Magistrate issued a warrant does not necessarily establish that he agreed that the scope of the search should be as broad as the affiant's request. Even though petitioner acted with restraint in conducting the search, "the inescapable fact is that this restraint was imposed by the agents themselves, not by a judicial officer." *Katz v. United States,* 389 U.S. 347, 356 (1967).[4]

We have long held, moreover, that the purpose of the particularity requirement is not limited to the prevention of general searches. A particular warrant also "assures the individual whose property is searched or seized of the lawful authority of the executing officer, his need to search, and the limits of his power to search."[5]

* * *

It is incumbent on the officer executing a search warrant to ensure the search is lawfully authorized and lawfully conducted. Because petitioner did not have in his possession a warrant particularly describing the things he intended to seize, proceeding with the search was clearly "unreasonable" under the Fourth Amendment. The Court of Appeals correctly held that the search was unconstitutional.

III

Having concluded that a constitutional violation occurred, we turn to the question whether petitioner is entitled to qualified immunity despite that violation. The answer depends on whether the right that was transgressed was "clearly established"—that is, "whether it would be clear to a reasonable officer that his conduct was unlawful in the situation he confronted."[a]

* * *

---

[4] For this reason petitioner's argument that any constitutional error was committed by the Magistrate, not petitioner, is misplaced. In *Massachusetts v. Sheppard*, 468 U.S. 981 (1984), we suggested that "the judge, not the police officers," may have committed "[a]n error of constitutional dimension" because the judge had assured the officers requesting the warrant that he would take the steps necessary to conform the warrant to constitutional requirements. Thus, "it was not unreasonable for the police in [that] case to rely on the judge's assurances that the warrant authorized the search they had requested." In this case, by contrast, petitioner did not alert the Magistrate to the defect in the warrant that petitioner had drafted, and we therefore cannot know whether the Magistrate was aware of the scope of the search he was authorizing. Nor would it have been reasonable for petitioner to rely on a warrant that was so patently defective, even if the Magistrate was aware of the deficiency.

[5] It is true, as petitioner points out, that neither the Fourth Amendment nor Rule 41 of the Federal Rules of Criminal Procedure requires the executing officer to serve the warrant on the owner before commencing the search. Rule 41(f)(3) provides that "[t]he officer executing the warrant must: (A) give a copy of the warrant and a receipt for the property taken to the person from whom, or from whose premises, the property was taken; or (B) leave a copy of the warrant and receipt at the place where the officer took the property." Quite obviously, in some circumstances—a surreptitious search by means of a wiretap, for example, or the search of empty or abandoned premises—it will be impracticable or imprudent for the officers to show the warrant in advance. Whether it would be unreasonable to refuse a request to furnish the warrant at the outset of the search when, as in this case, an occupant of the premises is present and poses no threat to the officers' safe and effective performance of their mission, is a question that this case does not present.

[a] Officers have qualified immunity from suit "insofar as their conduct does not violate clearly established statutory or constitutional rights of which a reasonable person would have known." *Harlow v. Fitzgerald*, 457 U.S. 800, 818 (1982).—Eds.

Petitioner contends that the search in this case was the product, at worst, of a lack of due care, and that our case law requires more than negligent behavior before depriving an official of qualified immunity. But as we observed in the companion case to *Sheppard,* "a warrant may be so facially deficient—*i.e.,* in failing to particularize the place to be searched or the things to be seized—that the executing officers cannot reasonably presume it to be valid." *Leon,* 468 U.S., at 923. This is such a case.

* * *

JUSTICE KENNEDY, with whom the CHIEF JUSTICE joins, dissenting.

I agree with the Court that the Fourth Amendment was violated in this case. The Fourth Amendment states that "no Warrants shall issue, but upon probable cause, supported by Oath or affirmation, and particularly describing the place to be searched, and the persons or things to be seized." The warrant issued in this case did not particularly describe the things to be seized, and so did not comply with the Fourth Amendment. I disagree with the Court on whether the officer who obtained the warrant and led the search team is entitled to qualified immunity for his role in the search. In my view, the officer should receive qualified immunity.

* * *

JUSTICE THOMAS, with whom JUSTICE SCALIA joins, and with whom THE CHIEF JUSTICE joins as to Part III, dissenting.

The Fourth Amendment provides: "The right of the people to be secure in their persons, houses, papers, and effects, against unreasonable searches and seizures, shall not be violated, and no Warrants shall issue, but upon probable cause, supported by Oath or affirmation, and particularly describing the place to be searched, and the persons or things to be seized." The precise relationship between the Amendment's Warrant Clause and Unreasonableness Clause is unclear. But neither Clause explicitly requires a warrant. While "it is of course textually possible to consider [a warrant requirement] implicit within the requirement of reasonableness," *California v. Acevedo,* 500 U.S. 565, 582 (1991) (Scalia, J., concurring in judgment), the text of the Fourth Amendment certainly does not mandate this result. Nor does the Amendment's history, which is clear as to the Amendment's principal target (general warrants), but not as clear with respect to when warrants were required, if ever. Indeed, because of the very different nature and scope of federal authority and ability to conduct searches and arrests at the founding, it is possible that neither the history of the Fourth Amendment nor the common law provides much guidance.

As a result, the Court has vacillated between imposing a categorical warrant requirement and applying a general reasonableness standard. The Court has most frequently held that warrantless searches are presumptively unreasonable, see, *e.g., Katz v. United States,* 389 U.S. 347,

357 (1967); *Payton v. New York,* 445 U.S. 573, 583 (1980), but has also found a plethora of exceptions to presumptive unreasonableness, see, *e.g.,* *Chimel v. California,* 395 U.S. 752, 762–763 (1969) (searches incident to arrest); *United States v. Ross,* 456 U.S. 798, 800 (1982) (automobile searches); *United States v. Biswell,* 406 U.S. 311, 315–317 (1972) (searches of "pervasively regulated" businesses); *Camara v. Municipal Court of City and County of San Francisco,* 387 U.S. 523, 534–539 (1967) (administrative searches); *Warden, Md. Penitentiary v. Hayden,* 387 U.S. 294, 298 (1967) (exigent circumstances); *California v. Carney,* 471 U.S. 386, 390–394 (1985) (mobile home searches); *Illinois v. Lafayette,* 462 U.S. 640, 648 (1983) (inventory searches); *Almeida-Sanchez v. United States,* 413 U.S. 266, 272 (1973) (border searches). That is, our cases stand for the illuminating proposition that warrantless searches are *per se* unreasonable, except, of course, when they are not.

Today the Court holds that the warrant in this case was "so obviously deficient" that the ensuing search must be regarded as a warrantless search and thus presumptively unreasonable. However, the text of the Fourth Amendment, its history, and the sheer number of exceptions to the Court's categorical warrant requirement seriously undermine the bases upon which the Court today rests its holding. Instead of adding to this confusing jurisprudence, as the Court has done, I would turn to first principles in order to determine the relationship between the Warrant Clause and the Unreasonableness Clause. But even within the Court's current framework, a search conducted pursuant to a defective warrant is constitutionally different from a "warrantless search." Consequently, despite the defective warrant, I would still ask whether this search was unreasonable and would conclude that it was not. Furthermore, even if the Court were correct that this search violated the Constitution (and in particular, respondents' Fourth Amendment rights), given the confused state of our Fourth Amendment jurisprudence and the reasonableness of petitioner's actions, I cannot agree with the Court's conclusion that petitioner is not entitled to qualified immunity. For these reasons, I respectfully dissent.

I

"[A]ny Fourth Amendment case may present two separate questions: whether the search was conducted pursuant to a warrant issued in accordance with the second Clause, and, if not, whether it was nevertheless 'reasonable' within the meaning of the first." *United States v. Leon,* 468 U.S. 897, 961 (1984) (Stevens, J., dissenting). By categorizing the search here to be a "warrantless" one, the Court declines to perform a reasonableness inquiry and ignores the fact that this search is quite different from searches that the Court has considered to be "warrantless" in the past. Our cases involving "warrantless" searches do not generally involve situations in which an officer has obtained a warrant that is later determined to be facially defective, but rather involve situations in which the officers neither sought nor obtained a warrant. By simply treating this case as if no warrant had even been sought or issued, the Court glosses over what should be the key inquiry: whether it is always appropriate to treat a search made pursuant to a warrant that fails to describe particularly the things to be seized as presumptively unreasonable.

The Court bases its holding that a defect in the particularity of the warrant by itself renders a search "warrantless" on a citation of a single footnote in *Massachusetts v. Sheppard,* 468 U.S. 981 (1984). In *Sheppard,* the Court, after noting that "the sole issue . . . in th[e] case is whether the officers reasonably believed that the search they conducted was authorized by a valid warrant," rejected the petitioner's argument that despite the invalid warrant, the otherwise reasonable search was constitutional. The Court recognized that under its case law a reasonableness inquiry would be appropriate if one of the exceptions to the warrant requirement applied. But the Court declined to consider whether such an exception applied and whether the search actually violated the Fourth Amendment because that question presented merely a "fact-bound issue of little importance." Because the Court in *Sheppard* did not conduct any sort of inquiry into whether a Fourth Amendment violation actually occurred, it is clear that the Court assumed a violation for the purposes of its analysis. Rather than rely on dicta buried in a footnote in *Sheppard,* the Court should actually analyze the arguably dispositive issue in this case.

The Court also rejects the argument that the details of the warrant application and affidavit save the warrant, because " '[t]he presence of a search warrant serves a high function.' " But it is not only the physical existence of the warrant and its typewritten contents that serve this high function. The Warrant Clause's principal protection lies in the fact that the " 'Fourth Amendment has interposed a magistrate between the citizen and the police . . . so that an objective mind might weigh the need to invade [the searchee's] privacy in order to enforce the law.' " The Court has further explained:

> The point of the Fourth Amendment . . . is not that it denies law enforcement the support of the usual inferences which reasonable men draw from evidence. Its protection consists in requiring that those inferences be drawn by a neutral and detached magistrate instead of being judged by the officer engaged in the often competitive enterprise of ferreting out crime. Any assumption that evidence sufficient to support a magistrate's disinterested determination to issue a search warrant will justify the officers in making a search without a warrant would reduce the Amendment to a nullity and leave the people's homes secure only in the discretion of police officers . . . . When the right of privacy must reasonably yield to the right of search is, as a rule, to be decided

> by a judicial officer, not by a policeman or government enforcement agent.

Johnson v. United States, 333 U.S. 10, 13–14 (1948) (footnotes omitted).

But the actual contents of the warrant are simply manifestations of this protection. Hence, in contrast to the case of a truly warrantless search, where a warrant (due to a mistake) does not specify on its face the particular items to be seized but the warrant application passed on by the magistrate judge contains such details, a searchee still has the benefit of a determination by a neutral magistrate that there is probable cause to search a particular place and to seize particular items. In such a circumstance, the principal justification for applying a rule of presumptive unreasonableness falls away.

In the instant case, the items to be seized were clearly specified in the warrant application and set forth in the affidavit, both of which were given to the Judge (Magistrate). The Magistrate reviewed all of the documents and signed the warrant application and made no adjustment or correction to this application. It is clear that respondents here received the protection of the Warrant Clause, as described in *Johnson* and *McDonald*. Under these circumstances, I would not hold that any ensuing search constitutes a presumptively unreasonable warrantless search. Instead, I would determine whether, despite the invalid warrant, the resulting search was reasonable and hence constitutional.

II

Because the search was not unreasonable, I would conclude that it was constitutional. Prior to execution of the warrant, petitioner briefed the search team and provided a copy of the search warrant application, the supporting affidavit, and the warrant for the officers to review. Petitioner orally reviewed the terms of the warrant with the officers, including the specific items for which the officers were authorized to search. Petitioner and his search team then conducted the search entirely within the scope of the warrant application and warrant; that is, within the scope of what the Magistrate had authorized. Finding no illegal weapons or explosives, the search team seized nothing. When petitioner left, he gave respondents a copy of the search warrant. Upon request the next day, petitioner faxed respondents a copy of the more detailed warrant application. Indeed, putting aside the technical defect in the warrant, it is hard to imagine how the actual search could have been carried out any more reasonably.

The Court argues that this eminently reasonable search is nonetheless unreasonable because "there can be no written assurance that the Magistrate actually found probable cause to search for, and to seize, every item mentioned in the affidavit" "unless the particular items described in the affidavit are also set forth in the warrant itself." The Court argues that it was at least possible that the Magistrate intended to authorize a much more limited search than the one petitioner requested. As a theoretical matter, this may be true. But the more reasonable inference is that the Magistrate intended to authorize everything in the warrant application, as he signed the application and did not make any written adjustments to the application or the warrant itself.

The Court also attempts to bolster its focus on the faulty warrant by arguing that the purpose of the particularity requirement is not only to prevent general searches, but also to assure the searchee of the lawful authority for the search. But as the Court recognizes, neither the Fourth Amendment nor Federal Rule of Criminal Procedure 41 requires an officer to serve the warrant on the searchee before the search. Thus, a search should not be considered *per se* unreasonable for failing to apprise the searchee of the lawful authority prior to the search, especially where, as here, the officer promptly provides the requisite information when the defect in the papers is detected. Additionally, unless the Court adopts the Court of Appeals' view that the Constitution protects a searchee's ability to "be on the lookout and to challenge officers," while the officers are actually carrying out the search, petitioner's provision of the requisite information the following day is sufficient to satisfy this interest.

* * *

Points for Discussion

1. The Court begins by acknowledging that the warrant was supported by probable cause, was applied for under oath, and particularly described the place to be searched. What, then, is the problem with the warrant that the magistrate issued? Would that constitutional infirmity have been remedied simply by incorporating the affidavit into the warrant by reference? That is, would the warrant be valid if it explicitly authorized a search for all of the items described in the application?

2. The Court treats a search conducted pursuant to a defective warrant as equivalent to a search conducted without one. Is this a sensible equation? Isn't Justice Thomas correct that the requisite neutral evaluation of probable cause occurred here?

3. The dissenters would hold that because the officers' conduct was reasonable, their conduct does not violate the Fourth Amendment. Isn't this how the Court resolved the issue in *Garrison*? Why does it not do the same here?

4. A fact left out of the Supreme Court's decision is that the Ramirezes operated a shelter for victims of domestic abuse. The Ramirezes' brief stated:

> Respondents Joseph, Julia, Joshua and Regina Ramirez are members of the Tehinnah Apostolic ministry, a non-mainstream religion. They resided on the Moose Creek Ranch in Silverbow County, Montana. The ministry provides refuge to abused women and children which

> results in outrageous reports to law enforcement from estranged husbands. The Moose Creek Ranch includes several hundred acres. Its buildings, including the blue two story house, are all readily visible to persons driving by on Interstate Highway 15.

In light of these facts, consider that the majority and the dissent disagree about the purposes a warrant serves. Justice Stevens' majority opinion imposes a duty on law enforcement officers to ensure that a warrant meets some minimal standard of facial validity. Justice Thomas, on the other hand, argues that the principal purpose of the warrant requirement is to have a judicial officer determine in advance of any search or seizure that it is justified by probable cause.

2. NEUTRAL AND DETACHED MAGISTRATE

One professed benefit of the warrant process is that it reviews, prior to a search or seizure, the probable cause determinations of police officers whose judgment may be compromised by their role as law enforcers. *See United States v. Chadwick*, 433 U.S. 1, 9 (1977) ("The judicial warrant has a significant role to play in that it provides the detached scrutiny of a neutral magistrate, which is a more reliable safeguard against improper searches than the hurried judgment of a law enforcement officer 'engaged in the often competitive enterprise of ferreting out crime.' "). However, as Professor Abraham Goldstein has pointed out, because judges lack the information and the motivation needed to scrutinize a warrant request effectively, the interposition of a judicial officer may have little practical effect. *See* Abraham S. Goldstein, *Reflections on Two Models: Inquisitorial Themes in American Criminal Procedure*, 26 STAN. L. REV. 1009, 1024–25 (1974) (arguing "that judges 'rubber stamp' warrant applications and barely supervise the process."). Also, because judges review warrant applications *ex parte* with only the prosecution making itself heard, judicial scrutiny is limited. As the Court once put it,

> [T]he usual reliance of our legal system on adversary proceedings itself should be an indication that an *ex parte* inquiry is likely to be less vigorous. The magistrate has no acquaintance with the information that may contradict the good faith and reasonable basis of the affiant's allegations. The pre-search proceeding will frequently be marked by haste, because of the understandable desire to act before the evidence disappears; this urgency will not always permit the magistrate to make an extended independent examination of the affiant or other witnesses.

Franks v. Delaware, 438 U.S. 154, 169 (1978).

This section examines what it means to be a "neutral and detached" magistrate. But, as two cases excerpted in chapter 10—*Murray v. United States*, 487 U.S. 533, 543–44 (1988), and *United States v. Leon*, 468 U.S. 897, 916 (1984)—show, even perfectly neutral judicial review may not deliver the benefits it promises. One problem is that warrants are issued based on limited information. The Supreme Court has held that a warrant affidavit is sufficient even if it is based only on inadmissible hearsay—including statements of undisclosed informants—as long as there is a "substantial basis" for believing the hearsay. *Illinois v. Gates*, 462 U.S. 213, 239–40 (1983). The Court also countenances surreptitious, illegal searches by law enforcement officers and even outright lies in the warrant affidavit, as long as probable cause independent of the police misconduct justifies the search. *See Murray*, 487 U.S. at 543–44; *Franks*, 438 U.S. at 155–56. Compounding the inherent difficulties of an *ex parte* process, the Court has said that warrant affidavits carry a "presumption of validity," thus relaxing the government's burden of establishing probable cause. *Franks*, 438 U.S. at 171. When a judge erroneously finds that there is probable cause and issues a warrant, the Supreme Court has held that evidence should not be excluded so long as the officers acted in good faith reliance on the warrant. This "good faith" exception to the exclusionary rule is premised on the idea that excluding evidence in such circumstances would only "punish the errors of judges and magistrates." *Leon*, 468 U.S. at 916.

SHADWICK V. CITY OF TAMPA

407 U.S. 345 (1972)

MR. JUSTICE POWELL delivered the opinion for a unanimous court.

The charter of Tampa, Florida, authorizes the issuance of certain arrest warrants by clerks of the Tampa Municipal Court. The sole question in this case is whether these clerks qualify as neutral and detached magistrates for purposes of the Fourth Amendment. We hold that they do.

Appellant was arrested for impaired driving on a warrant issued by a clerk of the municipal court. He moved the court to quash the warrant on the ground that it was issued by a nonjudicial officer in violation of the Fourth and Fourteenth Amendments. When the motion was denied, he initiated proceedings in the Florida courts by means of that State's writ of common-law certiorari. The state proceedings culminated in the holding of the Florida Supreme Court that "(t)he clerk and deputy clerks of the municipal court of the City of Tampa are neutral and detached 'magistrates' . . . for the purpose of issuing arrest warrants within the requirements of the United States Constitution . . ." We noted probable jurisdiction.

I

A clerk of the municipal court is appointed by the city clerk from a classified list of civil servants and assigned to work in the municipal court. The statute does not specify the qualifications necessary for this job, but no law degree or special legal training is required. The clerk's duties are to receive traffic fines, prepare the court's dockets and records, fill out commitment papers and perform other routine clerical tasks. Apparently he may issue subpoenas. He may not, however, sit as a judge, and he may not issue a search warrant or even a felony or misdemeanor arrest warrant for violations of state laws. The only warrants he may issue are for the arrest of those charged with having breached municipal ordinances of the city of Tampa.

* * *

II

Past decisions of the Court have mentioned review by a "judicial officer" prior to issuance of a warrant. In some cases the term "judicial officer" appears to have been used interchangeably with that of "magistrate." In others, it was intended simply to underscore the now accepted fact that someone independent of the police and prosecution must determine probable cause. The very term "judicial officer" implies, of course, some connection with the judicial branch. But it has never been held that only a lawyer or judge could grant a warrant, regardless of the court system or the type of warrant involved. In *Jones [v. United States,* 362 U.S. 257,] 270–271 (1960), the Court implied that United States Commissioners, many of whom were not lawyers or judges, were nonetheless "independent judicial officers."

The Court frequently has employed the term "magistrate" to denote those who may issue warrants. Historically, a magistrate has been defined broadly as "a public civil officer, possessing such power—legislative, executive, or judicial—as the government appointing him may ordain," *Compton v. Alabama*, 214 U.S. 1, 7 (1909), or, in a narrower sense "an inferior judicial officer, such as a justice of the peace." More recent definitions have not much changed.[7]

An examination of the Court's decisions reveals that the terms "magistrate" and "judicial officer" have been used interchangeably. Little attempt was made to define either term, to distinguish the one from the other, or to advance one as the definitive Fourth Amendment requirement. We find no commendment in either term, however, that all warrant authority must reside exclusively in a lawyer or judge. Such a requirement

[7] In *Compton*, a notary public was deemed a "magistrate," but the Court has nowhere indicated that the term denotes solely a lawyer or judge. Webster's Dictionary (2d ed. 1957), defines magistrate as "(a) person clothed with power as a public civil officer; a public civil officer invested with executive or judicial powers . . ." or, more narrowly, "(a) magistrate of a class having summary, often criminal, jurisdiction, as a justice of the peace, or one of certain officials having a similar jurisdiction . . ." Random House Dictionary (1966) defines magistrate as (1) "a civil officer charged with the administration of the law" and (2) "a minor judicial officer, as a justice of the peace or a police justice, having jurisdiction to try minor criminal cases and to conduct preliminary examinations of persons charged with serious crimes."

would have been incongruous when even within the federal system warrants were until recently widely issued by nonlawyers.[8]

To attempt to extract further significance from the above terminology would be both unnecessary and futile. The substance of the Constitution's warrant requirements does not turn on the labeling of the issuing party. The warrant traditionally has represented an independent assurance that a search and arrest will not proceed without probable cause to believe that a crime has been committed and that the person or place named in the warrant is involved in the crime. Thus, an issuing magistrate must meet two tests. He must be neutral and detached, and he must be capable of determining whether probable cause exists for the requested arrest or search. This Court long has insisted that inferences of probable cause be drawn by "a neutral and detached magistrate instead of being judged by the officer engaged in the often competitive enterprise of ferreting out crime." In *Coolidge v. New Hampshire*, [403 U.S. 443 (1971),] the Court last Term voided a search warrant issued by the state attorney general "who was actively in charge of the investigation and later was to be chief prosecutor at trial." If, on the other hand, detachment and capacity do conjoin, the magistrate has satisfied the Fourth Amendment's purpose.

III

The requisite detachment is present in the case at hand. Whatever else neutrality and detachment might entail, it is clear that they require severance and disengagement from activities of law enforcement. There has been no showing whatever here of partiality, or affiliation of these clerks with prosecutors or police. The record shows no connection with any law enforcement activity or authority which would distort the independent judgment the Fourth Amendment requires. Appellant himself expressly refused to allege anything to that effect. The municipal court clerk is assigned not to the police or prosecutor but to the municipal court judge for whom he does much of his work. In this sense, he may well be termed a "judicial officer." While a statutorily specified term of office and appointment by someone other than 'an executive authority' might be desirable, the absence of such features is hardly disqualifying. Judges themselves take office under differing circumstances. Some are appointed, but many are elected by legislative bodies or by the people. Many enjoy but limited terms and are subject to re-appointment or re-election. Most depend for their salary level upon the legislative branch. We will not elevate requirements for the independence of a municipal clerk to a level higher than that prevailing with respect to many judges. The clerk's neutrality has not been impeached: he is removed from prosecutor or police

[8] United States Commissioners were not required to be lawyers until passage of the Federal Magistrates Act of 1968. Even under this Act, a limited exception to lawyer's status is afforded part-time magistrates. 28 U.S.C. § 631(b)(1).

and works within the judicial branch subject to the supervision of the municipal court judge.

Appellant likewise has failed to demonstrate that these clerks lack capacity to determine probable cause. The clerk's authority extends only to the issuance of arrest warrants for breach of municipal ordinances. We presume from the nature of the clerk's position that he would be able to deduce from the facts on an affidavit before him whether there was probable cause to believe a citizen guilty of impaired driving, breach of peace, drunkenness, trespass, or the multiple other common offenses covered by a municipal code. There has been no showing that this is too difficult a task for a clerk to accomplish. Our legal system has long entrusted nonlawyers to evaluate more complex and significant factual data than that in the case at hand. Grand juries daily determine probable cause prior to rendering indictments, and trial juries assess whether guilt is proved beyond a reasonable doubt. The significance and responsibility of these lay judgments betray any belief that the Tampa clerks could not determine probable cause for arrest.

We decide today only that clerks of the municipal court may constitutionally issue the warrants in question. We have not considered whether the actual issuance was based upon an adequate showing of probable cause. Appellant did not submit this question to the courts below, and we will not decide it here initially. The single question is whether power has been lawfully vested, not whether it has been constitutionally exercised.

Nor need we determine whether a State may lodge warrant authority in someone entirely outside the sphere of the judicial branch. Many persons may not qualify as the kind of "public civil officers" we have come to associate with the term "magistrate." Had the Tampa clerk been entirely divorced from a judicial position, this case would have presented different considerations. Here, however, the clerk is an employee of the judicial branch of the city of Tampa, disassociated from the role of law enforcement. On the record in this case, the independent status of the clerk cannot be questioned.

What we do reject today is any per se invalidation of a state or local warrant system on the ground that the issuing magistrate is not a lawyer or judge. Communities may have sound reasons for delegating the responsibility of issuing warrants to competent personnel other than judges or lawyers.[10]

* * *

[10] Some communities, such as those in rural or sparsely settled areas, may have a shortage of available lawyers and judges and must entrust responsibility for issuing warrants to other qualified persons. The Federal Magistrates Act, for example, explicitly makes provision for nonlawyers to be appointed in those communities where members of the bar are not available. 28 U.S.C. § 631(b)(1).

Points for Discussion

1. As *Shadwick* notes, there are essentially two requirements of magistrates: They must be neutral and detached and they must be capable of making the probable cause determination. The defendant here challenges only the magistrate's capacity. Are you satisfied with the Court's analysis of whether a layperson is able to determine whether probable cause is present? How useful is the analogy to grand and petit juries?

MCCOMMON V. MISSISSIPPI

474 U.S. 984 (1985)

JUSTICE BRENNAN, with whom JUSTICE MARSHALL joins, dissenting from the denial of a petition for a writ of certiorari.

It is well recognized that the Fourth Amendment "imposes substantive standards for searches and seizures; but with them one of the important safeguards it establishes is a procedure; and [that] central to this procedure is an independent control over the actions of officers effecting searches of private premises." *Abel v. United States,* 362 U.S. 217, 251–252 (1960) (Brennan, J., dissenting). Thus this Court has long insisted that the determination whether probable cause exists to support a search warrant be made by "a *neutral* and *detached* magistrate instead of being judged by the officer engaged in the often competitive enterprise of ferreting out crime." *Johnson v. United States*, 333 U.S. 10, 14 (1948) (emphasis added). Just two Terms ago in *United States v. Leon,* [488 U.S. 897 (1984)], the Court vigorously reaffirmed that the probable-cause decision must be made by a neutral and detached magistrate, stating that "the courts must . . . insist that the magistrate purport to 'perform his "neutral and detached" function and not serve merely as a rubber stamp for the police.' " And, as we explained in *Shadwick v. City of Tampa*, 407 U.S., at 350, "[w]hatever else neutrality and detachment might entail, it is clear that they require severance and disengagement from activities of law enforcement." Today the Court refuses to act on its convictions, denying certiorari in a case in which the judge who issued the search warrant indisputably "rubber-stamped" the police request.

In this case, a large quantity of marijuana was discovered in the trunk of petitioner's automobile when it was searched pursuant to a warrant. Petitioner challenged the validity of the warrant at a pretrial suppression hearing, arguing that it was not supported by probable cause. The judge who granted the warrant testified at the hearing. With remarkable candor, he explained that he had relied principally on the fact that *police officers* had asked for the warrant, rather than on the underlying facts and circumstances set forth in the affidavit. The pertinent portion of the judge's testimony on cross-examination follows:

Q. You would have issued [the search warrant even if a certain statement in the affidavit either had not been included or the judge had known it not to be true]?

A. Certainly, because the officer—you've got to have enough faith and confidence in the officer that's asking for the search warrant to warrant it for him and then if it proves it's invalid, well, or whatever, there's nothing there what they're hunting—that's not the first time I ever made a Search Warrant.

Q. So, you were relying on the fact that these officers were of the law—

A. Of the law sworn—

Q. —and they were in there—they were sworn officers—

A. That's right.

Q. —they were in there telling you that this fellow was a drug dealer and they wanted to search his car—

A. That's exactly right.

Q. —and you relied on that rather than any particulars of this thing?

A. That's right.

* * *

Q. So, you really issued the Search Warrant because you were asked for it by two sworn officers of law rather than any particular thing they told you?

A. Well, I based my decision not primarily on that, but because—if Sheriff Jones walked in there and said, "Judge, I need a Search Warrant to search John Doe for Marijuana," drugs or whatever—liquor or whatever it might be, I'm going to go on his word because he's—I take him to be an honest law enforcement officer and he needs help to get in to search these places and it's my duty to help him to fulfill that.

Q. Okay. And it's really based on the request other than any particular thing he might tell you?

A. That's right. That's right.

Q. And that's what the situation was here?

A. Well, if I didn't feel like it was warranted, now, then, naturally, I wouldn't issue it.

Q. Okay, but . . . the swaying fact was that this was two sworn officers of the law rather than anything they told you in these Underlying Facts and Circumstances?

A. That's right. They were officers of the Narcotics.

The trial court rejected petitioner's arguments and admitted the evidence. The Mississippi Supreme Court affirmed petitioner's conviction, holding both that the warrant was supported by probable cause and that the conduct of the judge who signed the warrant, although not a model of judicial deportment, had satisfied the constitutional requirements of detachment and neutrality.

Respondent argues before this Court that even if the judge failed to evaluate the request for the warrant in a neutral and detached fashion, the warrant was nonetheless valid because it was, in fact, supported by probable cause. This attempt to evade review of the judge's lack of independence should not succeed. In *Coolidge v. New Hampshire,* 403 U.S., at 450–451, we firmly rejected the argument that "the existence of probable cause renders noncompliance with the warrant procedure an irrelevance." Indeed, in *Coolidge* the Court declared that because the warrant was not issued by "the neutral and detached magistrate required by the Constitution, the search stands on no firmer ground than if there had been no warrant at all."

As the transcript of the suppression hearing clearly demonstrates, the judge who issued the warrant to search petitioner's automobile, although formally separate from law enforcement officials, viewed himself as a facilitator of police investigations and simply acquiesced in police requests, without giving serious and independent consideration to the facts set forth in supporting affidavits. The Court's failure to grant certiorari in this case suggests that our admonitions that probable cause must be determined by a neutral and detached magistrate are hollow pronouncements.

I find the Court's refusal to take this case particularly disturbing in light of the good faith exception to the Fourth-Amendment exclusionary rule created by *United States v. Leon,* 468 U.S. 897 (1984).

In *Leon,* the Court held that physical evidence seized by police officers reasonably relying upon a warrant issued by a detached and neutral magistrate is admissible in the prosecution's case in chief, even though a reviewing court has subsequently determined that the warrant was defective or that the officers failed to demonstrate when applying for the warrant that there was probable cause to conduct the search. The Court justified its holding to a large extent on the special protective role that a neutral and detached magistrate plays in safeguarding the Fourth Amendment right against unreasonable searches and seizures. In fact, the Court indicated that suppression of evidence is appropriate where "the magistrate [has] abandoned his detached and neutral role." In my dissent, I warned that creation of a good-faith exception implicitly tells magistrates that they need not take much care in reviewing warrant applications, since their mistakes will have virtually no consequence. Today the Court tacitly informs magistrates that not only need they not worry about mistakes, they also need no longer be neutral and detached in their review of supporting affidavits. The combined message of *Leon* and the Court's refusal to grant certiorari in this case is that the police may rely on the magistrates and the magistrates may rely on the police. On whom may citizens rely to protect their Fourth Amendment rights?

Points for Discussion

1. Unlike *Shadwick*, which deals with a magistrate's capacity to determine probable cause, *McCommon* confronts what it means for a magistrate to be neutral and detached. McCommon's challenge is not the typical one that the magistrate is employed by or answerable to law enforcement officials. Rather, he argues that the magistrate abdicated his neutral role and unduly deferred to the officers. Seven justices, apparently, believed that the absence of an obvious conflict satisfies the requirement of neutrality. Justices Brennan and Marshall, by contrast, were willing to look beyond the formality of who employs the magistrate and how she is compensated to examine how carefully she considered the evidence presented. Is their critique really one of neutrality?

2. In the absence of the kind of testimonial evidence available in this case, how would a defendant demonstrate that the magistrate who considered the search warrant in her case was not neutral and detached? Would statistical evidence be relevant? What percentage of search warrant applications would a magistrate have to approve before we could conclude that she was not neutral and detached? See, e.g., RICHARD VAN DUIZEND ET AL., THE SEARCH WARRANT PROCESS: PRECONCEPTIONS, PERCEPTIONS, PRACTICES (1985) (finding that magistrates approved more than 90% of warrant applications submitted to them and that nearly 90% of warrant applications were reviewed for less than five minutes before a decision was reached).

3. NEED FOR A WARRANT

Whether a search warrant or an arrest warrant is required under particular circumstances depends in part on what purpose a warrant serves. Adherents of the Warrant Preference view of the Fourth Amendment believe, as some of the cases earlier in this chapter show, that warrants are presumptively required and provide both a neutral determination of whether probable cause exists and notice to the target of the scope of the police's authority. The Reasonableness Theory, on the other hand, does not take for granted that warrants need to be served on the target at the time of the search. This theory conceives of warrants primarily (if not exclusively) as a check on law enforcement. The Reasonableness Theory posits that some searches, primarily those of a home, are "reasonable" only when authorized by a warrant, but that warrants are not generally necessary so long as police act "reasonably." The lack of consensus regarding the purposes served by warrants is evident in the Court's decisions below.

PAYTON V. NEW YORK

445 U.S. 573 (1980)

MR. JUSTICE STEVENS delivered the opinion of the court.

These appeals challenge the constitutionality of New York statutes that authorize police officers to enter a private residence without a warrant and with force, if necessary, to make a routine felony arrest.

* * *

I

On January 14, 1970, after two days of intensive investigation, New York detectives had assembled evidence sufficient to establish probable cause to believe that Theodore Payton had murdered the manager of a gas station two days earlier. At about 7:30 a. m. on January 15, six officers went to Payton's apartment in the Bronx, intending to arrest him. They had not obtained a warrant. Although light and music emanated from the apartment, there was no response to their knock on the metal door. They summoned emergency assistance and, about 30 minutes later, used crowbars to break open the door and enter the apartment. No one was there. In plain view, however, was a .30-caliber shell casing that was seized and later admitted into evidence at Payton's murder trial.

In due course Payton surrendered to the police, was indicted for murder, and moved to suppress the evidence taken from his apartment. The trial judge held that the warrantless and forcible entry was authorized by the New York Code of Criminal Procedure, and that the evidence in plain view was properly seized. He found that exigent circumstances justified the officers' failure to announce their purpose before entering the apartment as required by the statute. He had no occasion, however, to decide whether those circumstances also would have justified the failure to obtain a warrant, because he concluded that the warrantless entry was adequately supported by the statute without regard to the circumstances. The Appellate Division, First Department, summarily affirmed.

* * *

II

* * *

It is a "basic principle of Fourth Amendment law" that searches and seizures inside a home without a warrant are presumptively unreasonable. Yet it is also well settled that objects such as weapons or contraband found in a public place may be seized by the police without a warrant. The seizure of property in plain view involves no invasion of privacy and is presumptively reasonable, assuming that there is probable cause to associate the property with criminal activity. The distinction between a warrantless seizure in an open area and such a seizure on private premises was plainly stated in *G.M. Leasing Corp. v. United States*, 429 U.S. 338, 354:

> It is one thing to seize without a warrant property resting in an open area or seizable by levy without an intrusion into privacy, and it is quite another thing to effect a warrantless seizure of property, even that owned by a corporation, situated on private premises to which access is not otherwise available for the seizing officer.

As the late Judge Leventhal recognized, this distinction has equal force when the seizure of a person is involved. Writing on the constitutional issue now before us for the United States Court of Appeals for the District of Columbia Circuit sitting en banc, *Dorman v. United States*, 140 U.S.App.D.C. 313, 435 F.2d 385 (1970), Judge Leventhal first noted the settled rule that warrantless arrests in public places are valid. He immediately recognized, however, that "[a] greater burden is placed . . . on officials who enter a home or dwelling without consent. Freedom from intrusion into the home or dwelling is the archetype of the privacy protection secured by the Fourth Amendment."

His analysis of this question then focused on the long-settled premise that, absent exigent circumstances, a warrantless entry to search for weapons or contraband is unconstitutional even when a felony has been committed and there is probable cause to believe that incriminating evidence will be found within. He reasoned that the constitutional protection afforded to the individual's interest in the privacy of his own home is equally applicable to a warrantless entry for the purpose of arresting a resident of the house; for it is inherent in such an entry that a search for the suspect may be required before he can be apprehended. Judge Leventhal concluded that an entry to arrest and an entry to search for and to seize property implicate the same interest in preserving the privacy and the sanctity of the home, and justify the same level of constitutional protection.

* * *

The majority of the New York Court of Appeals, however, suggested that there is a substantial difference in the relative intrusiveness of an entry to search for property and an entry to search for a person. It is true that the area that may legally be searched is broader when executing a search warrant than when executing an arrest warrant in the home. This difference may be more theoretical than real, however, because the police may need to check the entire premises for safety reasons, and sometimes they ignore the restrictions on searches incident to arrest.

But the critical point is that any differences in the intrusiveness of entries to search and entries to arrest are merely ones of degree rather than kind. The two intrusions share this fundamental characteristic: the breach of the entrance to an individual's home. The Fourth Amendment protects the individual's privacy in a variety of settings. In none is the zone of privacy more clearly defined than when bounded by the unambiguous physical dimensions of an individual's home—a zone that finds its roots in clear and specific constitutional terms: "The right of the people to be secure in their . . . houses . . . shall not be violated." That language unequivocally establishes the proposition that "[a]t the very core [of the Fourth Amendment] stands the right of a man to retreat into his own home and there be free from unreasonable governmental intrusion." *Silverman v. United States*, 365 U.S. 505, 511. In terms that apply equally to seizures of property and to seizures of persons, the Fourth Amendment has drawn a firm line at the entrance to the house. Absent exigent circumstances, that threshold may not reasonably be crossed without a warrant.

III

Without contending that *United States v. Watson*, [423 U.S. 411 (1976),] decided the question presented by these appeals, New York argues that the reasons that support the *Watson* holding require a similar result here. In *Watson* the Court relied on (a) the well-settled common-law rule that a warrantless arrest in a public place is valid if the arresting officer had probable cause to believe the suspect is a felon; (b) the clear consensus among the States adhering to that well-settled common-law rule; and (c) the expression of the judgment of Congress that such an arrest is "reasonable." We consider each of these reasons as it applies to a warrantless entry into a home for the purpose of making a routine felony arrest.

A

An examination of the common-law understanding of an officer's authority to arrest sheds light on the obviously relevant, if not entirely dispositive, consideration of what the Framers of the Amendment might have thought to be reasonable. Initially, it should be noted that the common-law rules of arrest developed in legal contexts that substantially differ from the cases now before us. In these cases, which involve application of the exclusionary rule, the issue is whether certain evidence is admissible at trial.[34]

At common law, the question whether an arrest was authorized typically arose in civil damages actions for trespass or false arrest, in which a constable's authority to make the arrest was a defense. Additionally, if an officer was killed while attempting to effect an arrest, the question whether the person resisting the arrest was guilty of murder or manslaughter turned on whether the officer was acting within the bounds of his authority.

---

[34] The issue is not whether a defendant must stand trial, because he must do so even if the arrest is illegal.

A study of the common law on the question whether a constable had the authority to make warrantless arrests in the home on mere suspicion of a felony—as distinguished from an officer's right to arrest for a crime committed in his presence—reveals a surprising lack of judicial decisions and a deep divergence among scholars.

* * *

It is obvious that the common-law rule on warrantless home arrests was not as clear as the rule on arrests in public places. Indeed, particularly considering the prominence of Lord Coke, the weight of authority as it appeared to the Framers was to the effect that a warrant was required, or at the minimum that there were substantial risks in proceeding without one. The common-law sources display a sensitivity to privacy interests that could not have been lost on the Framers. The zealous and frequent repetition of the adage that a "man's house is his castle," made it abundantly clear that both in England and in the Colonies "the freedom of one's house" was one of the most vital elements of English liberty.

Thus, our study of the relevant common law does not provide the same guidance that was present in *Watson*. Whereas the rule concerning the validity of an arrest in a public place was supported by cases directly in point and by the unanimous views of the commentators, we have found no direct authority supporting forcible entries into a home to make a routine arrest and the weight of the scholarly opinion is somewhat to the contrary. Indeed, the absence of any 17th- or 18th-century English cases directly in point, together with the unequivocal endorsement of the tenet that "a man's house is his castle," strongly suggests that the prevailing practice was not to make such arrests except in hot pursuit or when authorized by a warrant. In all events, the issue is not one that can be said to have been definitively settled by the common law at the time the Fourth Amendment was adopted.

B

A majority of the States that have taken a position on the question permit warrantless entry into the home to arrest even in the absence of exigent circumstances. At this time, 24 States permit such warrantless entries; 15 States clearly prohibit them, though 3 States do so on federal constitutional grounds alone; and 11 States have apparently taken no position on the question. But these current figures reflect a significant decline during the last decade in the number of States permitting warrantless entries for arrest. Recent dicta in this Court raising questions about the practice, and Federal Courts of Appeals' decisions on point have led state courts to focus on the issue. Virtually all of the state courts that have had to confront the constitutional issue directly have held warrantless entries into the home to arrest to be invalid in the absence of exigent circumstances. Three state courts have relied on Fourth Amendment grounds alone, while seven have squarely placed their decisions on both federal and state constitutional grounds. A number of other state courts, though not having had to confront the issue directly, have recognized the serious nature of the constitutional question. Apparently, only the Supreme Court of Florida and the New York Court of Appeals in this case have expressly upheld warrantless entries to arrest in the face of a constitutional challenge.

A longstanding, widespread practice is not immune from constitutional scrutiny. But neither is it to be lightly brushed aside. This is particularly so when the constitutional standard is as amorphous as the word "reasonable," and when custom and contemporary norms necessarily play such a large role in the constitutional analysis. In this case, although the weight of state-law authority is clear, there is by no means the kind of virtual unanimity on this question that was present in *United States v. Watson*, with regard to warrantless arrests in public places. Only 24 of the 50 States currently sanction warrantless entries into the home to arrest, and there is an obvious declining trend. Further, the strength of the trend is greater than the numbers alone indicate. Seven state courts have recently held that warrantless home arrests violate their respective *State* Constitutions. That is significant because by invoking a state constitutional provision, a state court immunizes its decision from review by this Court. This heightened degree of immutability underscores the depth of the principle underlying the result.

* * *

IV

The parties have argued at some length about the practical consequences of a warrant requirement as a precondition to a felony arrest in the home. In the absence of any evidence that effective law enforcement has suffered in those States that already have such a requirement, we are inclined to view such arguments with skepticism. More fundamentally, however, such arguments of policy must give way to a constitutional command that we consider to be unequivocal.

Finally, we note the State's suggestion that only a search warrant based on probable cause to believe the suspect is at home at a given time can adequately protect the privacy interests at stake, and since such a warrant requirement is manifestly impractical, there need be no warrant of any kind. We find this ingenious argument unpersuasive. It is true that an arrest warrant requirement may afford less protection than a search warrant requirement, but it will suffice to interpose the magistrate's determination of probable cause between the zealous officer and the citizen. If there is sufficient evidence of a citizen's participation in a felony to persuade a judicial officer that his arrest is justified, it is constitutionally reasonable to require him to open his doors to the officers of the law. Thus, for Fourth Amendment purposes, an arrest warrant founded on probable cause implicitly carries with it the limited authority to enter a dwelling in which the suspect lives when there is reason to believe the suspect is within.

MR. JUSTICE BLACKMUN, concurring.

I joined the Court's opinion in *United States v. Watson*, 423 U.S. 411 (1976), upholding, on probable cause, the warrantless arrest in a public place. I, of course, am still of the view that the decision in *Watson* is correct. The Court's balancing of the competing governmental and individual interests properly occasioned that result. Where, however, the warrantless arrest is in the suspect's home, that same balancing requires that, absent exigent circumstances, the result be the other way. The suspect's interest in the sanctity of his home then outweighs the governmental interests.

I therefore join the Court's opinion, firm in the conviction that the result in *Watson* and the result here, although opposite, are fully justified by history and by the Fourth Amendment.

MR. JUSTICE WHITE, with whom THE CHIEF JUSTICE and MR. JUSTICE REHNQUIST join, dissenting.

The Court today holds that absent exigent circumstances officers may never enter a home during the daytime to arrest for a dangerous felony unless they have first obtained a warrant. This hard-and-fast rule, founded on erroneous assumptions concerning the intrusiveness of home arrest entries, finds little or no support in the common law or in the text and history of the Fourth Amendment. I respectfully dissent.

* * *

II

A

* * *

Today's decision ignores the carefully crafted restrictions on the common-law power of arrest entry and thereby overestimates the dangers inherent in that practice. At common law, absent exigent circumstances, entries to arrest could be made only for felony. Even in cases of felony, the officers were required to announce their presence, demand admission, and be refused entry before they were entitled to break doors. Further, it seems generally accepted that entries could be made only during daylight hours. And, in my view, the officer entering to arrest must have reasonable grounds to believe, not only that the arrestee has committed a crime, but also that the person suspected is present in the house at the time of the entry.

These four restrictions on home arrests—felony, knock and announce, daytime, and stringent probable cause—constitute powerful and complementary protections for the privacy interests associated with the home. The felony requirement guards against abusive or arbitrary enforcement and ensures that invasions of the home occur only in case of the most serious crimes. The knock-and-announce and daytime requirements protect individuals against the fear, humiliation, and embarrassment of being aroused from their beds in states of partial or complete undress. And these requirements allow the arrestee to surrender at his front door, thereby maintaining his dignity and preventing the officers from entering other rooms of the dwelling. The stringent probable-cause requirement would help ensure against the possibility that the police would enter when the suspect was not home, and, in searching for him, frighten members of the family or ransack parts of the house, seizing items in plain view. In short, these requirements, taken together, permit an individual suspected of a serious crime to surrender at the front door of his dwelling and thereby avoid most of the humiliation and indignity that the Court seems to believe necessarily accompany a house arrest entry. Such a front-door arrest, in my view, is no more intrusive on personal privacy than the public warrantless arrests which we found to pass constitutional muster in *Watson*.

All of these limitations on warrantless arrest entries are satisfied on the facts of the present cases. The arrests here were for serious felonies—murder and armed robbery—and both occurred during daylight hours. The authorizing statutes required that the police announce their business and demand entry; neither Payton nor Riddick makes any contention that these statutory requirements were not fulfilled. And it is not argued that the police had no probable cause to believe that both Payton and Riddick were in their dwellings at the time of the entries. Today's decision, therefore, sweeps away any possibility that warrantless home entries might be permitted in some limited situations other than those in which exigent circumstances are present. The Court substitutes, in one sweeping decision, a rigid constitutional rule in place of the common-law approach, evolved over hundreds of years, which achieved a flexible accommodation between the demands of personal privacy and the legitimate needs of law enforcement.

A rule permitting warrantless arrest entries would not pose a danger that officers would use their entry power as a pretext to justify an otherwise invalid warrantless search. A search pursuant to a warrantless arrest entry will rarely, if ever, be as complete as one under authority of a search warrant. If the suspect surrenders at the door, the officers may not enter other rooms. Of course, the suspect may flee or hide, or may not be at home, but the officers cannot anticipate the first two of these possibilities and the last is unlikely given the requirement of probable cause to believe that the suspect is at home. Even when officers are justified in searching other rooms, they may seize only items within the arrestee's position or immediate control or items in plain view discovered during the course of a search reasonably directed at discovering a hiding suspect. Hence a warrantless home entry is likely to uncover far less evidence than a search conducted under authority of a search warrant. Furthermore, an arrest entry will inevitably tip off the suspects and likely result in destruction or removal of evidence not uncovered during the arrest. I therefore cannot believe that the police would take the risk of losing valuable evidence through a pretextual arrest entry rather than applying to a magistrate for a search warrant.

B

While exaggerating the invasion of personal privacy involved in home arrests, the Court fails to account for the danger that its rule will "severely hamper effective law enforcement," *United States v. Watson*, 423 U.S., at 431 (Powell, J., concurring). The policeman on his beat must now make subtle discriminations that perplex even judges in their chambers. As Mr. Justice Powell noted, concurring in *United States v. Watson,* police will sometimes delay making an arrest, even after probable cause is established, in order to be sure that they have enough evidence to convict. Then, if they suddenly have to arrest, they run the risk that the subsequent exigency will not excuse their prior failure to obtain a warrant. This problem cannot effectively be cured by obtaining a warrant as soon as probable cause is established because of the chance that the warrant will go stale before the arrest is made.

* * *

Our cases establish that the ultimate test under the Fourth Amendment is one of "reasonableness." I cannot join the Court in declaring unreasonable a practice which has been thought entirely reasonable by so many for so long. It would be far preferable to adopt a clear and simple rule: after knocking and announcing their presence, police may enter the home to make a daytime arrest without a warrant when there is probable cause to believe that the person to be arrested committed a felony and is present in the house. This rule would best comport with the common-law background, with the traditional practice in the States, and with the history and policies of the Fourth Amendment. Accordingly, I respectfully dissent.

MR. JUSTICE REHNQUIST, dissenting.

* * *

I fully concur in and join the dissenting opinion of Mr. Justice White. There is significant historical evidence that we have over the years misread the history of the Fourth Amendment in connection with searches, elevating the warrant requirement over the necessity for probable cause in a way which the Framers of that Amendment did not intend. But one may accept all of that as *stare decisis*, and still feel deeply troubled by the transposition of these same errors into the area of actual arrests of felons within their houses with respect to whom there is probable cause to suspect guilt of the offense in question.

Points for Discussion

1. Why does the Court decide here that arrests within a home generally require an arrest warrant when it had held in *United States v. Watson* that arrests in public do not?

2. What is required to obtain an arrest warrant for an individual? How does this showing protect the sanctity of the home? Is it meant to?

3. In determining whether a warrantless arrest in a defendant's home is constitutional, why does the Court consider how many states permit such a practice? How can the popularity of a procedure bear on its constitutionality?

4. Justice Stevens' opinion makes clear at the outset that there are no exigent circumstances in this case. He calls the arrest a "routine" one and points out that the police had been investigating for "two days" before establishing probable cause to arrest Payton. Nonetheless, Justice White objects to the majority's substituting "a rigid constitutional rule in place of the common law approach." Justice Rehnquist's related contention that the Court has effectively elevated form over substance by insisting on warrants foreshadowed the approach the Court would increasingly take following his elevation to Chief Justice in 1986. Does the holding impose a "rigid" rule?

STEAGALD V. UNITED STATES

451 U.S. 204 (1981)

JUSTICE MARSHALL delivered the opinion of the court.

* * *

I

In early January 1978, an agent of the Drug Enforcement Administration was contacted in Detroit, Mich., by a confidential informant who suggested that he might be able to locate Ricky Lyons, a federal fugitive wanted on drug charges. On January 14, 1978, the informant called the agent again, and gave him a telephone number in the Atlanta, Ga., area where, according to the informant, Ricky Lyons could be reached during the next 24 hours. On January 16, 1978, the agent called fellow DEA Agent Kelly Goodowens in Atlanta and relayed the information he had obtained from the informant. Goodowens contacted Southern Bell Telephone Co., and secured the address corresponding to the telephone number obtained by the informant. Goodowens also discovered that Lyons was the subject of a 6-month-old arrest warrant.

Two days later, Goodowens and 11 other officers drove to the address supplied by the telephone company to search for Lyons. The officers observed two men standing outside the house to be searched. These men were Hoyt Gaultney and petitioner Gary Steagald. The officers approached with guns drawn, frisked both men, and, after demanding identification, determined that neither man was Lyons. Several agents proceeded to the house. Gaultney's wife answered the door, and informed the agents that she was alone in the house. She was told to place her hands against the wall and was guarded in that position while one agent searched the house. Ricky Lyons was not found, but during the search of the house the agent observed what he believed to be cocaine. Upon being informed of this discovery, Agent Goodowens sent an officer to obtain a search warrant and in the meantime conducted a second search of the house, which uncovered additional incriminating evidence. During a third search conducted pursuant to a search warrant, the agents uncovered 43 pounds of cocaine. Petitioner was arrested and indicted on federal drug charges.

* * *

III

The question before us is a narrow one.[6]

The search at issue here took place in the absence of consent or exigent circumstances. Except in such special situations, we have consistently held that the entry into a home to conduct a search or make an arrest is unreasonable under the Fourth Amendment unless done pursuant to a warrant. Thus, as we recently observed: "In terms that apply equally to seizures of property and to seizures of persons, the Fourth Amendment has drawn a firm line at the entrance to the house. Absent exigent circumstances, that threshold may not reasonably be crossed without a warrant." *Payton v. New York,* 445 U.S., at 590. Here, of course, the agents had a warrant—one authorizing the arrest of Ricky Lyons. However, the Fourth Amendment claim here is not being raised by Ricky Lyons. Instead, the challenge to the search is asserted by a person not named in the warrant who was convicted on the basis of evidence uncovered during a search of his residence for Ricky Lyons. Thus, the narrow issue before us is whether an arrest warrant—as opposed to a search warrant—is adequate to protect the Fourth Amendment interests of persons not named in the warrant, when their homes are searched without their consent and in the absence of exigent circumstances.

The purpose of a warrant is to allow a neutral judicial officer to assess whether the police have probable cause to make an arrest or conduct a search. As we have often explained, the placement of this checkpoint between the Government and the citizen implicitly acknowledges that an "officer engaged in the often competitive enterprise of ferreting out crime," *Johnson v. United States,* 333 U.S. at 14, may lack sufficient objectivity to

[6] Initially, we assume without deciding that the information relayed to Agent Goodowens concerning the whereabouts of Ricky Lyons would have been sufficient to establish probable cause to believe that Lyons was at the house searched by the agents.

weigh correctly the strength of the evidence supporting the contemplated action against the individual's interests in protecting his own liberty and the privacy of his home. However, while an arrest warrant and a search warrant both serve to subject the probable-cause determination of the police to judicial review, the interests protected by the two warrants differ. An arrest warrant is issued by a magistrate upon a showing that probable cause exists to believe that the subject of the warrant has committed an offense and thus the warrant primarily serves to protect an individual from an unreasonable seizure. A search warrant, in contrast is issued upon a showing of probable cause to believe that the legitimate object of a search is located in a particular place, and therefore safeguards an individual's interest in the privacy of his home and possessions against the unjustified intrusion of the police.

Thus, whether the arrest warrant issued in this case adequately safeguarded the interests protected by the Fourth Amendment depends upon what the warrant authorized the agents to do. To be sure, the warrant embodied a judicial finding that there was probable cause to believe the Ricky Lyons had committed a felony, and the warrant therefore authorized the officers to seize Lyons. However, the agents sought to do more than use the warrant to arrest Lyons in a public place or in his home; instead, they relied on the warrant as legal authority to enter the home of a third person based on their belief that Ricky Lyons might be a guest there. Regardless of how reasonable this belief might have been, it was never subjected to the detached scrutiny of a judicial officer. Thus, while the warrant in this case may have protected Lyons from an unreasonable seizure, it did absolutely nothing to protect petitioner's privacy interest in being free from an unreasonable invasion and search of his home. Instead, petitioner's only protection from an illegal entry and search was the agent's personal determination of probable cause. In the absence of exigent circumstances, we have consistently held that such judicially untested determinations are not reliable enough to justify an entry into a person's home to arrest him without a warrant, or a search of a home for objects in the absence of a search warrant. We see no reason to depart from this settled course when the search of a home is for a person rather than an object.

* * *

A contrary conclusion—that the police, acting alone and in the absence of exigent circumstances, may decide when there is sufficient justification for searching the home of a third party for the subject of an arrest warrant—would create a significant potential for abuse. Armed solely with an arrest warrant for a single person, the police could search all the homes of that individual's friends and acquaintances. Moreover, an arrest warrant may serve as the pretext for entering a home in which the police have a suspicion, but not probable cause to believe, that illegal activity is taking place. The Government recognizes the potential for such abuses, but contends that existing remedies—such as motions to suppress illegally procured evidence and damages actions for Fourth Amendment violations—provide adequate means of redress. We do not agree. As we observed on a previous occasion, "[t]he [Fourth] Amendment is designed to prevent, not simply to redress, unlawful police action." *Chimel v. California,* [395 U.S. 752, 766, n. 12 (1969)]. Indeed, if suppression motions and damages actions were sufficient to implement the Fourth Amendment's prohibition against unreasonable searches and seizures, there would be no need for the constitutional requirement that in the absence of exigent circumstances a warrant must be obtained for a home arrest or a search of a home for objects. We have instead concluded that in such cases the participation of a detached magistrate in the probable-cause determination is an essential element of a reasonable search or seizure, and we believe that the same conclusion should apply here.

In sum, two distinct interests were implicated by the search at issue here—Ricky Lyons' interest in being free from an unreasonable seizure and petitioner's interest in being free from an unreasonable search of his home. Because the arrest warrant for Lyons addressed only the former interest, the search of petitioner's home was no more reasonable from petitioner's perspective than it would have been if conducted in the absence of any warrant. Since warrantless searches of a home are impermissible absent consent or exigent circumstances, we conclude that the instant search violated the Fourth Amendment.

IV

* * *

B

The Government also suggests that practical problems might arise if law enforcement officers are required to obtain a search warrant before entering the home of a third party to make an arrest. The basis of this concern is that persons, as opposed to objects, are inherently mobile, and thus officers seeking to effect an arrest may be forced to return to the magistrate several times as the subject of the arrest warrant moves from place to place. We are convinced, however, that a search warrant requirement will not significantly impede effective law enforcement efforts.

First, the situations in which a search warrant will be necessary are few. As noted in *Payton v. New York,* an arrest warrant alone will suffice to enter a suspect's own residence to effect his arrest. Furthermore, if probable cause exists, no warrant is required to apprehend a suspected felon in a public place. Thus, the subject of an arrest warrant can be readily seized before entering or after leaving the home of a third party. Finally, the exigent-circumstances doctrine significantly limits the situations in which a search warrant would be needed. For example, a warrantless entry of a home would be justified if the police were in "hot pursuit" of a fugitive.

Thus, to the extent that searches for persons pose special problems, we believe that the exigent-circumstances doctrine is adequate to accommodate legitimate law enforcement needs.

Moreover, in those situations in which a search warrant is necessary, the inconvenience incurred by the police is simply not that significant. First, if the police know of the location of the felon when they obtain an arrest warrant, the additional burden of obtaining a search warrant at the same time is miniscule. The inconvenience of obtaining such a warrant does not increase significantly when an outstanding arrest warrant already exists. In this case, for example, Agent Goodowens knew the address of the house to be searched two days in advance, and planned the raid from the federal courthouse in Atlanta where, we are informed, three full-time magistrates were on duty. In routine search cases such as this, the short time required to obtain a search warrant from a magistrate will seldom hinder efforts to apprehend a felon. Finally, if a magistrate is not nearby, a telephonic search warrant can usually be obtained.

Whatever practical problems remain, however, cannot outweigh the constitutional interests at stake. Any warrant requirement impedes to some extent the vigor with which the Government can seek to enforce its laws, yet the Fourth Amendment recognizes that this restraint is necessary in some cases to protect against unreasonable searches and seizures. We conclude that this is such a case. The additional burden imposed on the police by a warrant requirement is minimal. In contrast, the right protected—that of presumptively innocent people to be secure in their homes from unjustified, forcible intrusions by the Government—is weighty. Thus, in order to render the instant search reasonable under the Fourth Amendment, a search warrant was required.

THE CHIEF JUSTICE concurs in the judgment.

JUSTICE REHNQUIST, with whom justice white joins, dissenting.

* * *

The government's interests in the warrantless entry of a third-party dwelling to execute an arrest warrant are compelling. The basic problem confronting police in such situations is the inherent mobility of the fugitive. By definition, the police have probable cause to believe that the fugitive is in a dwelling which is not his home. He may stay there for a week, a day, or 10 minutes. Fugitives from justice tend to be mobile, and police officers will generally have no way of knowing whether the subject of an arrest warrant will be at the dwelling when they return from seeking a search warrant. Imposition of a search warrant requirement in such circumstances will frustrate the compelling interests of the government and indeed the public in the apprehension of those subject to outstanding arrest warrants.

The Court's responses to these very real concerns are singularly unpersuasive. It first downplays them by stating that "the situations in which a search warrant will be necessary are few," because no search warrant is necessary to arrest a suspect at his home and, if the suspect is at another's home, the police need only wait until he leaves, since no search warrant is needed to arrest him in a public place. These beguilingly simple answers to a serious law enforcement problem simply will not wash. Criminals who know or suspect they are subject to arrest warrants would not be likely to return to their homes, and while "[t]he police could reduce the likelihood of escape by staking out all possible exits . . . the costs of such a stakeout seems excessive in an era of rising crime and scarce police resources." *Payton v. New York*, [445 U.S.] at 619 (White, J., dissenting). The Court's ivory tower misconception of the realities of the apprehension of fugitives from justice reaches its apogee when it states: "In routine search cases such as this, the short time required to obtain a search warrant from a magistrate will seldom hinder efforts to apprehend a felon." The cases we are considering are *not* "routine search cases." They are cases of attempted arrest, pursuant to a warrant, when the object of the arrest may flee at any time—including the "short time" during which the police are endeavoring to obtain a search warrant.

At the same time the interference with the Fourth Amendment privacy interests of those whose homes are entered to apprehend the felon is not nearly as significant as suggested by the Court. The arrest warrant serves some of the functions a separate search warrant would. It assures the occupants that the police officer is present on official business. The arrest warrant also limits the scope of the search, specifying what the police may search for—*i.e.*, the subject of the arrest warrant. No general search is permitted, but only a search of those areas in which the object of the search might hide. Indeed there may be no intrusion on the occupant's privacy at all, since if present the suspect will have the opportunity to voluntarily surrender at the door. Even if the suspect does not surrender but secretes himself within the house, the occupant can limit the search by pointing him out to the police. It is important to remember that the contraband discovered during the entry and search for Lyons was in plain view, and was discovered during a "sweep search" for Lyons, not a probing of drawers or cabinets for contraband.

Because the burden on law enforcement officers to obtain a separate search warrant before entering the dwelling of a third party to execute a concededly valid arrest warrant is great, and carries with it a high possibility that the fugitive named in the arrest warrant will escape apprehension, I would conclude that the application of the traditional "reasonableness" standard of the Fourth Amendment does not require a separate search warrant in a case such as this.

* * *

Points for Discussion

1. The officers had a warrant for Lyons' arrest and, as the Court notes in a footnote, probable cause to believe that Lyons was at Steagald's home. Why does the Court conclude that these facts are insufficient to satisfy the Fourth Amendment?

2. For whose protection is the search warrant required here? Had Lyons been arrested inside Steagald's home without a search warrant would Lyons have been able to challenge the officers' entry into the home? If the officers had had a search warrant for Steagald's home but not an arrest warrant for Lyons, would Steagald be able to challenge the officers' entry?

WILSON V. ARKANSAS

514 U.S. 927 (1995)

JUSTICE THOMAS delivered the opinion of the court.

At the time of the framing, the common law of search and seizure recognized a law enforcement officer's authority to break open the doors of a dwelling, but generally indicated that he first ought to announce his presence and authority. In this case, we hold that this common-law "knock and announce" principle forms a part of the reasonableness inquiry under the Fourth Amendment.

I

During November and December 1992, petitioner Sharlene Wilson made a series of narcotics sales to an informant acting at the direction of the Arkansas State Police. In late November, the informant purchased marijuana and methamphetamine at the home that petitioner shared with Bryson Jacobs. On December 30, the informant telephoned petitioner at her home and arranged to meet her at a local store to buy some marijuana. According to testimony presented below, petitioner produced a semiautomatic pistol at this meeting and waved it in the informant's face, threatening to kill her if she turned out to be working for the police. Petitioner then sold the informant a bag of marijuana.

The next day, police officers applied for and obtained warrants to search petitioner's home and to arrest both petitioner and Jacobs. Affidavits filed in support of the warrants set forth the details of the narcotics transactions and stated that Jacobs had previously been convicted of arson and firebombing. The search was conducted later that afternoon. Police officers found the main door to petitioner's home open. While opening an unlocked screen door and entering the residence, they identified themselves as police officers and stated that they had a warrant. Once inside the home, the officers seized marijuana, methamphetamine, valium, narcotics paraphernalia, a gun, and ammunition. They also found petitioner in the bathroom, flushing marijuana down the toilet. Petitioner and Jacobs were arrested and charged with delivery of marijuana, delivery of methamphetamine, possession of drug paraphernalia, and possession of marijuana.

* * *

II

* * *

The common-law knock and announce principle was woven quickly into the fabric of early American law. Most of the States that ratified the Fourth Amendment had enacted constitutional provisions or statutes generally incorporating English common law, and a few States had enacted statutes specifically embracing the common-law view that the breaking of the door of a dwelling was permitted once admittance was refused. Early American courts similarly embraced the common-law knock and announce principle.

Our own cases have acknowledged that the common law principle of announcement is "embedded in Anglo-American law," but we have never squarely held that this principle is an element of the reasonableness inquiry under the Fourth Amendment. We now so hold. Given the longstanding common-law endorsement of the practice of announcement, we have little doubt that the Framers of the Fourth Amendment thought that the method of an officer's entry into a dwelling was among the factors to be considered in assessing the reasonableness of a search or seizure. Contrary to the decision below, we hold that in some circumstances an officer's unannounced entry into a home might be unreasonable under the Fourth Amendment.

This is not to say, of course, that every entry must be preceded by an announcement. The Fourth Amendment's flexible requirement of reasonableness should not be read to mandate a rigid rule of announcement that ignores countervailing law enforcement interests. As even petitioner concedes, the common-law principle of announcement was never stated as an inflexible rule requiring announcement under all circumstances.

* * *

Thus, because the common-law rule was justified in part by the belief that announcement generally would avoid "the destruction or breaking of any house . . . by which great damage and inconvenience might ensue," courts acknowledged that the presumption in favor of announcement would yield under circumstances presenting a threat of physical violence. Similarly, courts held that an officer may dispense with announcement in cases where a prisoner escapes from him and retreats to his dwelling. Proof of "demand and refusal" was deemed unnecessary in such cases because it would be a "senseless ceremony" to require an officer in pursuit of a recently escaped arrestee to make an announcement prior to breaking the door to retake him. Finally, courts have indicated that unannounced entry may be justified where police officers have reason to believe that evidence would likely be destroyed if advance notice were given.

* * *

III

Respondent contends that the judgment below should be affirmed because the unannounced entry in this case was justified for two reasons. First, respondent argues that police officers reasonably believed that a prior announcement would have placed them in peril, given their knowledge that petitioner had threatened a government informant with a semiautomatic weapon and that Mr. Jacobs had previously been convicted of arson and firebombing. Second, respondent suggests that prior announcement would have produced an unreasonable risk that petitioner would destroy easily disposable narcotics evidence.

These considerations may well provide the necessary justification for the unannounced entry in this case. Because the Arkansas Supreme Court did not address their sufficiency, however, we remand to allow the state courts to make any necessary findings of fact and to make the determination of reasonableness in the first instance. The judgment of the Arkansas Supreme Court is reversed, and the case is remanded for further proceedings not inconsistent with this opinion.

Points for Discussion

1. Notice that here there is nothing wrong with the warrant the police obtained in this case; there is no allegation that it failed any of the requirements imposed by the Fourth Amendment. The Court nonetheless concludes that the entry into the home was invalid. What does this tell us about the relationship between the Reasonableness and Warrant Clauses of the Fourth Amendment?

2. The holding in *Wilson* is a major addition to the protection afforded home-owners. The Court holds that a suspect whom the police have a warrant to arrest may choose to surrender at the threshold, denying the officers entry to the home. In chapter 10, however, we see that the Court's holding in this case is significantly weakened by the Court's unwillingness to apply the exclusionary rule in this context. *See Hudson v. Michigan,* 547 U.S. 586 (2006).

CHAPTER 3

THE FOURTH AMENDMENT IN CONTEXT

■ ■ ■

Notwithstanding the Court's pithy dictum in *Katz v. United States* that "the Fourth Amendment protects people, not places," the protection the amendment affords those people has long varied with the circumstances. Even the most devoted adherents of the Warrant Preference Theory have acknowledged the needs for exceptions to the warrant requirement. For example, the Reasonableness Theory has, at least since *Carroll v. United States* was decided in 1925, recognized that many searches are constitutionally reasonable without a warrant. This chapter examines how the Fourth Amendment protections accorded to people and effects vary with the place and circumstance.

In large part as an accommodation of the realities of law enforcement, the Court has built over the years a sort of hierarchy of Fourth Amendment protection, a process that *Katz*'s expectations-of-privacy framework facilitated. Persons and houses are widely acknowledged as receiving the greatest degree of constitutional solicitude. For dubious reasons, automobiles receive comparatively weak protection.

A. SEARCHES OF PERSONS INCIDENT TO ARREST

Many years ago, Columbia law professor Telford Taylor observed that "it is abundantly apparent that searches of persons and premises incident to an arrest outnumber manifold searches covered by warrants." TELFORD TAYLOR, TWO STUDIES IN CONSTITUTIONAL INTERPRETATION, 48 (1969). Because warrantless searches of people being arrested are so numerous, it is important that they be limited by the rationale that justifies them.

CHIMEL V. CALIFORNIA

395 U.S. 752 (1969)

MR. JUSTICE STEWART delivered the opinion of the court.

search incident to arrest

This case raises basic questions concerning the permissible scope under the Fourth Amendment of a search incident to a lawful arrest.

The relevant facts are essentially undisputed. Late in the afternoon of September 13, 1965, three police officers arrived at the Santa Ana, California, home of the petitioner with a warrant authorizing his arrest for the burglary of a coin shop. The officers knocked on the door, identified themselves to the petitioner's wife, and asked if they might come inside. She ushered them into the house, where they waited 10 or 15 minutes until the petitioner returned home from work. When the petitioner entered the house, one of the officers handed him the arrest warrant and asked for permission to "look around." The petitioner objected, but was advised that "on the basis of the lawful arrest," the officers would nonetheless conduct a search. No search warrant had been issued.

Accompanied by the petitioner's wife, the officers then looked through the entire three-bedroom house, including the attic, the garage, and a small workshop. In some rooms the search was relatively cursory. In the master bedroom and sewing room, however, the officers directed the petitioner's wife to open drawers and "to physically move contents of the drawers from side to side so that (they) might view any items that would have come from (the) burglary." After completing the search, they seized numerous items—primarily coins, but also several medals, tokens, and a few other objects. The entire search took between 45 minutes and an hour.

* * *

Without deciding the question, we proceed on the hypothesis that the California courts were correct in holding that the arrest of the petitioner was valid under the Constitution. This brings us directly to the question whether the warrantless search of the petitioner's entire house can be constitutionally justified as incident to that arrest. The decisions of this Court bearing upon that question have been far from consistent, as even the most cursory review makes evident.

* * *

Only last Term in *Terry v. Ohio*, 392 U.S. 1, we emphasized that "the police must, whenever practicable, obtain advance judicial approval of searches and seizures through the warrant procedure," and that "(t)he scope of (a) search must be 'strictly tied to and justified by' the circumstances which rendered its initiation permissible." The search undertaken by the officer in that "stop and frisk" case was sustained under that test, because it was no more than a "protective * * * search for weapons." But in a companion case, *Sibron v. New York*, 392 U.S. 40, we applied the same standard to another set of facts and reached a contrary result, holding that a policeman's action in thrusting his hand into a suspect's pocket had been neither motivated by nor limited to the objective of protection. Rather, the search had been made in order to find narcotics, which were in fact found.

A similar analysis underlies the "search incident to arrest" principle, and marks its proper extent. When an arrest is made, it is reasonable for the arresting officer to search the person arrested in order to remove any weapons that the latter might seek to use in order to resist arrest or effect his escape. Otherwise, the officer's safety might well be endangered, and the arrest itself frustrated. In addition, it is entirely reasonable for the arresting officer to search for and seize any evidence on the arrestee's person in order to prevent its concealment or destruction. And the area into which an arrestee might reach in order to grab a weapon or evidentiary items must, of course, be governed by a like rule. A gun on a table or in a drawer in front of one who is arrested can be as dangerous to the arresting officer as one concealed in the clothing of the person arrested. There is ample justification, therefore, for a search of the arrestee's person and the area "within his immediate control"—construing that phrase to mean the area from within which he might gain possession of a weapon or destructible evidence.

There is no comparable justification, however, for routinely searching any room other than that in which an arrest occurs—or, for that matter, for searching through all the desk drawers or other closed or concealed areas in that room itself. Such searches, in the absence of well-recognized exceptions, may be made only under the authority of a search warrant. The "adherence to judicial processes" mandated by the Fourth Amendment requires no less.

* * *

It is argued in the present case that it is "reasonable" to search a man's house when he is arrested in it. But that argument is founded on little more than a subjective view regarding the acceptability of certain sorts of police conduct, and not on consideration relevant to Fourth Amendment interests. Under such an unconfined analysis, Fourth Amendment protection in this area would approach the evaporation point. It is not easy to explain why, for instance, it is less subjectively "reasonable" to search a man's house when he is arrested on his front lawn—or just down the street—than it is when he happens to be in the house at the time of arrest. As Mr. Justice Frankfurter put it:

> To say that the search must be reasonable is to require some criterion of reason. It is no guide at all either for a jury or for district judges or the police to say that an "unreasonable search" is forbidden—that the search must be reasonable. What is the test of reason which makes a search reasonable? The test is the reason underlying and expressed by the Fourth Amendment: the history and experience which it embodies and the safeguards afforded by it against the evils to which it was a response.

United States v. *Robinowitz*, [339 US. 56, 83 (1950)]. Thus, although "(t)he recurring questions of the reasonableness of searches" depend upon "the facts and circumstances—the total atmosphere of the case," those facts and circumstances must be viewed in the light of established Fourth Amendment principles.

* * *

The petitioner correctly points out that one result of decisions such as *Rabinowitz* and *Harris* [*v. United States*, 331 U.S. 145 (1947),] is to give law enforcement officials the opportunity to engage in searches not justified by probable cause, by the simple expedient of arranging to arrest suspects at home rather than elsewhere. We do not suggest that the petitioner is necessarily correct in his assertion that such a strategy was utilized here, but the fact remains that had he been arrested earlier in the day, at his place of employment rather than at home, no search of his house could have been made without a search warrant. In any event, even apart from the possibility of such police tactics, the general point so forcefully made by Judge Learned Hand in *United States v. Kirschenblatt*, 2 Cir., 16 F.2d 202, remains:

> After arresting a man in his house, to rummage at will among his papers in search of whatever will convict him, appears to us to be indistinguishable from what might be done under a general warrant; indeed, the warrant would give more protection, for presumably it must be issued by a magistrate. True, by hypothesis the power would not exist, if the supposed offender were not found on the premises; but it is small consolation to know that one's papers are safe only so long as one is not at home.

* * *

Application of sound Fourth Amendment principles to the facts of this case produces a clear result. The search here went far beyond the petitioner's person and the area from within which he might have obtained either a weapon or something that could have been used as evidence against him. There was no constitutional justification, in the absence of a search warrant, for extending the search beyond that area. The scope of the search was, therefore, "unreasonable" under the Fourth and Fourteenth Amendments and the petitioner's conviction cannot stand.

MR. JUSTICE HARLAN, concurring.

I join the Court's opinion with these remarks concerning a factor to which the Court has not alluded.

The only thing that has given me pause in voting to overrule *Harris* and *Rabinowitz* is that as a result of *Mapp v. Ohio*, 367 U.S. 643 (1961), and *Ker v. California*, 374 U.S. 23 (1963), every change in Fourth Amendment law must now be obeyed by state officials facing widely different problems of local law enforcement. We simply do not know the extent to which cities and towns across the Nation are prepared to administer the greatly expanded warrant system which will be required by today's decision; nor can we say with assurance that in each and every local situation, the warrant requirement plays an essential role in the protection of those fundamental liberties protected against state infringement by the Fourteenth Amendment.

* * *

This federal-state factor has not been an easy one for me to resolve, but in the last analysis I cannot in good conscience vote to perpetuate bad Fourth Amendment law.

MR. JUSTICE WHITE, with whom MR. JUSTICE BLACK joins, dissenting.

Few areas of the law have been as subject to shifting constitutional standards over the last 50 years as that of the search "incident to an arrest." There has been a remarkable instability in this whole area, which has seen at least four major shifts in emphasis. Today's opinion makes an untimely fifth. In my view, the Court should not now abandon the old rule.

* * *

II

The rule which has prevailed, but for very brief or doubtful periods of aberration, is that a search incident to an arrest may extend to those areas under the control of the defendant and where items subject to constitutional seizure may be found. The justification for this rule must, under the language of the Fourth Amendment, lie in the reasonableness of the rule. . . .

In terms, then, the Court must decide whether a given search is reasonable. The Amendment does not proscribe "warrantless searches" but instead it proscribes "unreasonable searches" and this Court has never held nor does the majority today assert that warrantless searches are necessarily unreasonable.

Applying this reasonableness test to the area of searches incident to arrests, one thing is clear at the outset. Search of an arrested man and of the items within his immediate reach must in almost every case be reasonable. There is always a danger that the suspect will try to escape, seizing concealed weapons with which to overpower and injure the arresting officers, and there is a danger that he may destroy evidence vital to the prosecution. Circumstances in which these justifications would not apply are sufficiently rare that inquiry is not made into searches of this scope, which have been considered reasonable throughout.

The justifications which make such a search reasonable obviously do not apply to the search of areas to which the accused does not have ready physical access. This is not enough, however, to prove such searches unconstitutional. The Court has always held, and does not today deny, that when there is probable cause to search and it is "impracticable" for one reason or another to get a search warrant, then a warrantless search may be reasonable. This is the case whether an arrest was made at the time of the search or not.

This is not to say that a search can be reasonable without regard to the probable cause to believe that seizable items are on the premises. But when there are exigent circumstances, and probable cause, then the search may be made without a warrant, reasonably. An arrest itself may often create an emergency situation making it impracticable to obtain a warrant before embarking on a related search. Again assuming that there is probable cause to search premises at the spot where a suspect is arrested, it seems to me unreasonable to require the police to leave the scene in order to obtain a search warrant when they are already legally there to make a valid arrest, and when there must almost always be a strong possibility that confederates of the arrested man will in the meanwhile remove the items for which the police have probable cause to search. This must so often be the case that it seems to me as unreasonable to require a warrant for a search of the premises as to require a warrant for search of the person and his very immediate surroundings.

This case provides a good illustration of my point that it is unreasonable to require police to leave the scene of an arrest in order to obtain a search warrant when they already have probable cause to search and there is a clear danger that the items for which they may reasonably search will be removed before they return with a warrant. Petitioner was arrested in his home after an arrest whose validity will be explored below, but which I will now assume was valid. There was doubtless probable cause not only to arrest petitioner, but also to search his house. He had obliquely admitted, both to a neighbor and to the owner of the burglarized store, that he had committed the burglary. In light of this, and the fact that the neighbor had seen other admittedly stolen property in petitioner's house, there was surely probable cause on which a warrant could have issued to search the house for the stolen coins. Moreover, had the police simply arrested petitioner, taken him off to the station house, and later returned with a warrant,[5] it seems very likely that petitioner's wife, who in view of petitioner's generally garrulous nature must have known of the robbery, would have removed the coins. For the police to search the house while the evidence they had probable cause to search out and seize was still there cannot be considered unreasonable.

* * *

[5] There were three officers at the scene of the arrest, one from the city where the coin burglary had occurred, and two from the city where the arrest was made. Assuming that one policeman from each city would be needed to bring the petitioner in and obtain a search warrant, one policeman could have been left to guard the house. However, if he not only could have remained in the house against petitioner's wife's will, but followed her about to assure that no evidence was being tampered with, the invasion of her privacy would be almost as great as that accompanying an actual search. Moreover, had the wife summoned an accomplice, one officer could not have watched them both.

IV

If circumstances so often require the warrantless arrest that the law generally permits it, the typical situation will find the arresting officers lawfully on the premises without arrest or search warrant. Like the majority, I would permit the police to search the person of a suspect and the area under his immediate control either to assure the safety of the officers or to prevent the destruction of evidence. And like the majority, I see nothing in the arrest alone furnishing probable cause for a search of any broader scope. However, where as here the existence of probable cause is independently established and would justify a warrant for a broader search for evidence, I would follow past cases and permit such a search to be carried out without a warrant, since the fact of arrest supplies an exigent circumstance justifying police action before the evidence can be removed, and also alerts the suspect to the fact of the search so that he can immediately seek judicial determination of probable cause in an adversary proceeding, and appropriate redress.

This view, consistent with past cases, would not authorize the general search against which the Fourth Amendment was meant to guard, nor would it broaden or render uncertain in any way whatsoever the scope of searches permitted under the Fourth Amendment. The issue in this case is not the breadth of the search, since there was clearly probable cause for the search which was carried out. No broader search than if the officers had a warrant would be permitted. The only issue is whether a search warrant was required as a precondition to that search. It is agreed that such a warrant would be required absent exigent circumstances. I would hold that the fact of arrest supplies such an exigent circumstance, since the police had lawfully gained entry to the premises to effect the arrest and since delaying the search to secure a warrant would have involved the risk of not recovering the fruits of the crime.

The majority today proscribes searches for which there is probable cause and which may prove fruitless unless carried out immediately. This rule will have no added effect whatsoever in protecting the rights of the criminal accused at trial against introduction of evidence seized without probable cause. Such evidence could not be introduced under the old rule. Nor does the majority today give any added protection to the right of privacy of those whose houses there is probable cause to search. A warrant would still be sworn out for those houses, and the privacy of their owners invaded. The only possible justification for the majority's rule is that in some instances arresting officers may search when they have no probable cause to do so and that such unlawful searches might be prevented if the officers first sought a warrant from a magistrate. Against the possible protection of privacy in that class of cases, in which the privacy of the house has already been invaded by entry to make the arrest—an entry for which the majority does not assert that any warrant is necessary—must be weighed the risk of destruction of evidence for which there is probable cause to search, as a result of delays in obtaining a search warrant. Without more basis for radical change than the Court's opinion reveals, I would not upset the balance of these interests which has been struck by the former decisions of this Court.

* * *

An arrested man, by definition conscious of the police interest in him, and provided almost immediately with a lawyer and a judge, is in an excellent position to dispute the reasonableness of his arrest and contemporaneous search in a full adversary proceeding. I would uphold the constitutionality of this search contemporaneous with an arrest since there were probable cause both for the search and for the arrest, exigent circumstances involving the removal or destruction of evidence, and satisfactory opportunity to dispute the issues of probable cause shortly thereafter. In this case, the search was reasonable.

Points for Discussion

1. The search-incident-to-arrest doctrine that the Court describes in *Chimel* permits a limited search that can be conducted only in a manner consistent with its justifications. What is the justification for the search in *Chimel*? What are the resulting limits on the search? Why did the search conducted in this case violate those limits?

2. In what circumstances would the police be unable to get a warrant to search the home of a person whom they have a warrant to arrest? How much of a limitation is the *Chimel* doctrine on the authority of police to search the house of someone arrested at home?

3. *Chimel* showcases the clash between adherents of the Warrant Preference Theory and adherents of the Reasonableness Theory. Justice Stewart's opinion for the Court disavows the Reasonableness Theory, with help from one of Justice Frankfurter's dissents. The majority criticizes the Reasonableness Theory for doing nothing more than validating the "subjective view[s]" of some justices "regarding the acceptability of certain sorts of police conduct." Justice White's dissent just as pointedly states that the Fourth Amendment "does not proscribe 'warrantless searches' but instead it proscribes 'unreasonable searches' . . . ."

UNITED STATES V. ROBINSON

414 U.S. 218 (1973)

MR. JUSTICE REHNQUIST delivered the opinion of the court.

* * *

On April 23, 1968, at approximately 11 p.m., Officer Richard Jenks, a 15-year veteran of the District of Columbia Metropolitan Police

Department, observed the respondent driving a 1965 Cadillac near the intersection of 8th and C Streets, N.E., in the District of Columbia. Jenks, as a result of previous investigation following a check of respondent's operator's permit four days earlier, determined there was reason to believe that respondent was operating a motor vehicle after the revocation of his operator's permit. This is an offense defined by statute in the District of Columbia which carries a mandatory minimum jail term, a mandatory minimum fine, or both.

Jenks signaled respondent to stop the automobile, which respondent did, and all three of the occupants emerged from the car. At that point Jenks informed respondent that he was under arrest for "operating after revocation and obtaining a permit by misrepresentation." It was assumed by the Court of Appeals, and is conceded by the respondent here, that Jenks had probable cause to arrest respondent, and that he effected a full custody arrest.

In accordance with procedures prescribed in police department instructions, Jenks then began to search respondent. He explained at a subsequent hearing that he was "face-to-face" with the respondent, and "placed (his) hands on (the respondent), my right-hand to his left breast like this (demonstrating) and proceeded to pat him down thus (with the right hand)." During this patdown, Jenks felt an object in the left breast pocket of the heavy coat respondent was wearing, but testified that he "couldn't tell what it was" and also that he "couldn't actually tell the size of it." Jenks then reached into the pocket and pulled out the object, which turned out to be a "crumpled up cigarette package." Jenks testified that at this point he still did not know what was in the package: "As I felt the package I could feel objects in the package but I couldn't tell what they were. . . . I knew they weren't cigarettes."

The officer then opened the cigarette pack and found 14 gelatin capsules of white powder which he thought to be, and which later analysis proved to be, heroin. Jenks then continued his search of respondent to completion, feeling around his waist and trouser legs, and examining the remaining pockets. The heroin seized from the respondent was admitted into evidence at the trial which resulted in his conviction in the District Court.

* * *

II

In its decision of this case, the Court of Appeals decided that even after a police officer lawfully places a suspect under arrest for the purpose of taking him into custody, he may not ordinarily proceed to fully search the prisoner. He must, instead, conduct a limited frisk of the outer clothing and remove such weapons that he may, as a result of that limited frisk, reasonably believe and ascertain that the suspect has in his possession.

While recognizing that *Terry v. Ohio*, 392 U.S. 1 (1968), dealt with a permissible "frisk" incident to an investigative stop based on less than probable cause to arrest, the Court of Appeals felt that the principles of that case should be carried over to this probable-cause arrest for driving while one's license is revoked. Since there would be no further evidence of such a crime to be obtained in a search of the arrestee, the court held that only a search for weapons could be justified.

* * *

III

* * *

The justification or reason for the authority to search incident to a lawful arrest rests quite as much on the need to disarm the suspect in order to take him into custody as it does on the need to preserve evidence on his person for later use at trial. The standards traditionally governing a search incident to lawful arrest are not, therefore, commuted to the stricter *Terry* standards by the absence of probable fruits or further evidence of the particular crime for which the arrest is made.

Nor are we inclined, on the basis of what seems to us to be a rather speculative judgment, to qualify the breadth of the general authority to search incident to a lawful custodial arrest on an assumption that persons arrested for the offense of driving while their licenses have been revoked are less likely to possess dangerous weapons than are those arrested for other crimes. It is scarcely open to doubt that the danger to an officer is far greater in the case of the extended exposure which follows the taking of a suspect into custody and transporting him to the police station than in the case of the relatively fleeting contact resulting from the typical *Terry*-type stop. This is an adequate basis for treating all custodial arrests alike for purposes of search justification.

But quite apart from these distinctions, our more fundamental disagreement with the Court of Appeals arises from its suggestion that there must be litigated in each case the issue of whether or not there was present one of the reasons supporting the authority for a search of the person incident to a lawful arrest. We do not think the long line of authorities of this Court dating back to *Weeks*, or what we can glean from the history of practice in this country and in England, requires such a case-by-case adjudication. A police officer's determination as to how and where to search the person of a suspect whom he has arrested is necessarily a quick ad hoc judgment which the Fourth Amendment does not require to be broken down in each instance into an analysis of each step in the search. The authority to search the person incident to a lawful custodial arrest, while based upon the need to disarm and to discover evidence, does not depend on what a court may later decide was the probability in a particular arrest situation that weapons or evidence would in fact be found upon the person of the suspect. A custodial arrest of a suspect based on probable cause is a reasonable intrusion under the Fourth Amendment; that intrusion being lawful, a search incident to the arrest requires no additional justification. It is the fact of the lawful arrest which establishes the authority to search, and we hold that in the case of a lawful custodial arrest a full search of the person is not only an exception to the warrant requirement of the Fourth Amendment, but is also a "reasonable" search under that Amendment.

IV

The search of respondent's person conducted by Officer Jenks in this case and the seizure from him of the heroin, were permissible under established Fourth Amendment law. While thorough, the search partook of none of the extreme or patently abusive characteristics which were held to violate the Due Process Clause of the Fourteenth Amendment in *Rochin v. California*, 342 U.S. 165 (1952). Since it is the fact of custodial arrest which gives rise to the authority to search, it is of no moment that Jenks did not indicate any subjective fear of the respondent or that he did not himself suspect that respondent was armed. Having in the course of a lawful search come upon the crumpled package of cigarettes, he was entitled to inspect it; and when his inspection revealed the heroin capsules, he was entitled to seize them as "fruits, instrumentalities, or contraband" probative of criminal conduct.

MR. JUSTICE MARSHALL, with whom MR. JUSTICE DOUGLAS and MR. JUSTICE BRENNAN join, dissenting.

* * *

II

The majority's attempt to avoid case-by-case adjudication of Fourth Amendment issues is not only misguided as a matter of principle, but is also doomed to fail as a matter of practical application. As the majority itself is well aware, the powers granted the police in this case are strong ones, subject to potential abuse. Although, in this particular case, Officer Jenks was required by police department regulations to make an in-custody arrest rather than to issue a citation, in most jurisdictions and for most traffic offenses the determination of whether to issue a citation or effect a full arrest is discretionary with the officer. There is always the possibility that a police officer, lacking probable cause to obtain a search warrant, will use a traffic arrest as a pretext to conduct a search. I suggest this possibility not to impugn the integrity of our police, but merely to point out that case-by-case adjudication will always be necessary to determine whether a full arrest was effected for purely legitimate reasons or, rather, as a pretext for searching the arrestee. "An arrest may not be used as a pretext to search for evidence." *United States v. Lefkowitz*, 285 U.S. 452, 467 (1932).

III

The majority states that "(a) police officer's determination as to how and where to search the person of a suspect whom he has arrested is necessarily a quick ad hoc judgment which the Fourth Amendment does not require to be broken down in each instance into an analysis of each step in the search." No precedent is cited for this broad assertion—not surprisingly, since there is none. Indeed, we only recently rejected such "a rigid all-or-nothing model of justification and regulation under the Amendment, (for) it obscures the utility of limitations upon the scope, as well as the initiation, of police action as a means of constitutional regulation. This Court has held in the past that a search which is reasonable at its inception may violate the Fourth Amendment by virtue of its intolerable intensity and scope." *Terry v. Ohio*, [392 U.S. 1, 17–18 (1968)]. As we there concluded, "in determining whether the seizure and search were 'unreasonable' our inquiry is a dual one—whether the officer's action was justified at its inception, and whether it was reasonably related in scope to the circumstances which justified the interference in the first place."

As I view the matter, the search in this case divides into three distinct phases: the patdown of respondent's coat pocket; the removal of the unknown object from the pocket; and the opening of the crumpled-up cigarette package.

A

No question is raised here concerning the lawfulness of the patdown of respondent's coat pocket. . . .

* * *

B

* * *

It appears to have been conceded by the Government below that the removal of the object from respondent's coat pocket exceeded the scope of a Terry frisk for weapons, since, under *Terry*, an officer may not remove an object from the suspect's pockets unless he has reason to believe it to be a dangerous weapon.

In the present case, however, Officer Jenks had no reason to believe and did not in fact believe that the object in respondent's coat pocket was a weapon. He admitted later that the object did not feel like a gun. In fact, he did not really have any thoughts one way or another about what was in the pocket. As Jenks himself testified, "I just searched him. I didn't think about what I was looking for. I just searched him." Since the removal of the object from the pocket cannot be justified as part of a limited *Terry* weapons frisk, the question arises whether it is reasonable for a police officer, when effecting an in-custody arrest of a traffic offender, to make a fuller search of the person than is permitted pursuant to *Terry*.

The underlying rationale of a search incident to arrest of a traffic offender initially suggests as reasonable a search whose scope is similar to the protective weapons frisk permitted in *Terry*. A search incident to arrest, as the majority indicates, has two basic functions: the removal of weapons the arrestee might use to resist arrest or effect an escape, and the seizure of evidence or fruits of the crime for which the arrest is made, so as to prevent their concealment or destruction.

The Government does not now contend that the search of respondent's pocket can be justified by any need to find and seize evidence in order to prevent its concealment or destruction, for, as the Court of Appeals found, there is no evidence or fruits of the offense with which respondent was charged. The only rationale for a search in this case, then, is the removal of weapons which the arrestee might use to harm the officer and attempt an escape. This rationale, of course, is identical to the rationale of the search permitted in *Terry*. As we said there, "The sole justification of the search in the present situation is the protection of the police officer and others nearby, and it must therefore be confined in scope to an intrusion reasonably designed to discover guns, knives, clubs, or other hidden instruments for the assault of the police officer." Since the underlying rationale of a *Terry* search and the search of a traffic violator are identical, the Court of Appeals held that the scope of the searches must be the same. And in view of its conclusion that the removal of the object from respondent's coat pocket exceeded the scope of a lawful *Terry* frisk, a conclusion not disputed by the Government or challenged by the majority here, the plurality of the Court of Appeals held that the removal of the package exceeded the scope of a lawful search incident to arrest of a traffic violator.

The problem with this approach, however, is that it ignores several significant differences between the context in which a search incident to arrest for a traffic violation is made, and the situation presented in *Terry*. Some of these differences would appear to suggest permitting a more thorough search in this case than was permitted in *Terry*; other differences suggest a narrower, more limited right to search than was there recognized.

The most obvious difference between the two contexts relates to whether the officer has cause to believe that the individual he is dealing with possesses weapons which might be used against him. *Terry* did not permit an officer to conduct a weapons frisk of anyone he lawfully stopped on the street, but rather, only where "he has reason to believe that he is dealing with an armed and dangerous individual. . . ." While the policeman who arrests a suspected rapist or robber may well have reason to believe he is dealing with an armed and dangerous person, certainly this does not hold true with equal force with respect to a person arrested for a motor vehicle violation of the sort involved in this case.

Nor was there any particular reason in this case to believe that respondent was dangerous. He had not attempted to evade arrest, but had quickly complied with the police both in bringing his car to a stop after being signaled to do so and in producing the documents Officer Jenks requested. In fact, Jenks admitted that he searched respondent face to face rather than in spread-eagle fashion because he had no reason to believe respondent would be violent.

* * *

C

The majority opinion fails to recognize that the search conducted by Officer Jenks did not merely involve a search of respondent's person. It also included a separate search of effects found on his person. And even were we to assume, arguendo, that it was reasonable for Jenks to remove the object he felt in respondent's pocket, clearly there was no justification consistent with the Fourth Amendment which would authorize his opening the package and looking inside.

* * *

The Government argues that it is difficult to see what constitutionally protected "expectation of privacy" a prisoner has in the interior of a cigarette pack. One wonders if the result in this case would have been the same were respondent a businessman who was lawfully taken into custody for driving without a license and whose wallet was taken from him by the police. Would it be reasonable for the police officer, because of the possibility that a razor blade was hidden somewhere in the wallet, to open it, remove all the contents, and examine each item carefully? Or suppose a lawyer lawfully arrested for a traffic offense is found to have a sealed envelope on his person. Would it be permissible for the arresting officer to tear open the envelope in order to make sure that it did not contain a clandestine weapon—perhaps a pin or a razor blade? Would it not be more consonant with the purpose of the Fourth Amendment and the legitimate needs of the police to require the officer, if he has any question whatsoever about what the wallet or letter contains, to hold on to it until the arrestee is brought to the precinct station?

Second, even had it become necessary to place respondent in confinement, it is still doubtful whether one could justify opening up the cigarette package and examining its contents. The purposes of preventing the introduction of weapons or contraband into the jail facility are fully served simply by removing the package from the prisoner. It is argued that the police must inventory effects found on the prisoner in order to avoid a later claim by the prisoner that jail personnel stole his property. But as the Court of Appeals noted in Mills, the police can protect themselves against such claims by means involving a less extreme intrusion on privacy than would be entailed in opening up and examining the contents of all effects found on the person. As an example, the Court of Appeals suggested that the prisoner be given "an opportunity, like that accorded someone given a bathhouse locker for temporary use, to 'check' his belongings in a sealed envelope, perhaps upon executing a waiver releasing the officer of any responsibility."

* * *

The search conducted by Officer Jenks in this case went far beyond what was reasonably necessary to protect him from harm or to ensure that respondent would not effect an escape from custody. In my view, it therefore fell outside the scope of a properly drawn "search incident to arrest" exception to the Fourth Amendment's warrant requirement. I would affirm the judgment of the Court of Appeals holding that the fruits of the search should have been suppressed at respondent's trial.

Points for Discussion

1. *Robinson* makes clear what the Court hinted at in *Chimel*—that a search incident to arrest is permissible *whenever* the police make a custodial arrest. Does the fact that there is no reason to suspect that Robinson was armed have any bearing on whether the search of his person is reasonable? If the only justification for the search is the protection of the officers, isn't the dissent correct that the *Terry* test has already been crafted for that purpose?

2. Do you agree with the dissent that the search of Robinson might have been valid at its inception but that it was excessive in its scope? Is the dissent persuasive in claiming that a warrant was required to open the cigarette pack even if its discovery was lawful?

RILEY V. CALIFORNIA

573 U.S. 373 (2014)

CHIEF JUSTICE ROBERTS delivered the opinion of the court.

These two cases raise a common question: whether the police may, without a warrant, search digital information on a cell phone seized from an individual who has been arrested.

I

A

In the first case, petitioner David Riley was stopped by a police officer for driving with expired registration tags. In the course of the stop, the officer also learned that Riley's license had been suspended. The officer impounded Riley's car, pursuant to department policy, and another officer conducted an inventory search of the car. Riley was arrested for possession of concealed and loaded firearms when that search turned up two handguns under the car's hood.

An officer searched Riley incident to the arrest and found items associated with the "Bloods" street gang. He also seized a cell phone from Riley's pants pocket. According to Riley's uncontradicted assertion, the phone was a "smart phone," a cell phone with a broad range of other functions based on advanced computing capability, large storage capacity, and Internet connectivity. The officer accessed information on the phone and noticed that some words (presumably in text messages or a contacts list) were preceded by the letters "CK"—a label that, he believed, stood for "Crip Killers," a slang term for members of the Bloods gang.

At the police station about two hours after the arrest, a detective specializing in gangs further examined the contents of the phone. The detective testified that he "went through" Riley's phone "looking for evidence, because . . . gang members will often video themselves with guns or take pictures of themselves with the guns." Although there was "a lot of stuff" on the phone, particular files that "caught [the detective's] eye" included videos of young men sparring while someone yelled encouragement using the moniker "Blood." The police also found photographs of Riley standing in front of a car they suspected had been involved in a shooting a few weeks earlier.

Riley was ultimately charged, in connection with that earlier shooting, with firing at an occupied vehicle, assault with a semiautomatic firearm, and attempted murder. The State alleged that Riley had committed those crimes for the benefit of a criminal street gang, an aggravating factor that carries an enhanced sentence. Prior to trial, Riley moved to suppress all evidence that the police had obtained from his cell phone. He contended that the searches of his phone violated the Fourth Amendment, because they had been performed without a warrant and were not otherwise justified by exigent circumstances. The trial court rejected that argument. At Riley's trial, police officers testified about the photographs and videos found on the phone, and some of the photographs were admitted into evidence. Riley was convicted on all three counts and received an enhanced sentence of 15 years to life in prison.

* * *

B

In the second case, a police officer performing routine surveillance observed respondent Brima Wurie make an apparent drug sale from a car. Officers subsequently arrested Wurie and took him to the police station. At the station, the officers seized two cell phones from Wurie's person. The one at issue here was a "flip phone," a kind of phone that is flipped open for use and that generally has a smaller range of features than a smart phone. Five to ten minutes after arriving at the station, the officers noticed that the phone was repeatedly receiving calls from a source identified as "my house" on the phone's external screen. A few minutes later, they opened the phone and saw a photograph of a woman and a baby set as the phone's wallpaper. They pressed one button on the phone to access its call log, then another button to determine the phone number associated with the "my house" label. They next used an online phone directory to trace that phone number to an apartment building.

When the officers went to the building, they saw Wurie's name on a mailbox and observed through a window a woman who resembled the woman in the photograph on Wurie's phone. They secured the apartment while obtaining a search warrant and, upon later executing the warrant, found and seized 215 grams of crack cocaine, marijuana, drug paraphernalia, a firearm and ammunition, and cash.

Wurie was charged with distributing crack cocaine, possessing crack cocaine with intent to distribute, and being a felon in possession of a firearm and ammunition. He moved to suppress the evidence obtained from the search of the apartment, arguing that it was the fruit of an unconstitutional search of his cell phone. The District Court denied the motion. Wurie was convicted on all three counts and sentenced to 262 months in prison.

* * *

II

* * *

The two cases before us concern the reasonableness of a warrantless search incident to a lawful arrest. In 1914, this Court first acknowledged in dictum "the right on the part of the Government, always recognized under English and American law, to search the person of the accused when legally arrested to discover and seize the fruits or evidences of crime." *Weeks v. United States*, 232 U.S. 383, 392. Since that time, it has been well accepted that such a search constitutes an exception to the warrant requirement. Indeed, the label "exception" is something of a misnomer in this context, as warrantless searches incident to arrest occur with far greater frequency than searches conducted pursuant to a warrant.

Although the existence of the exception for such searches has been recognized for a century, its scope has been debated for nearly as long. That debate has focused on the extent to which officers may search property found on or near the arrestee. Three related precedents set forth the rules governing such searches:

The first, *Chimel v. California*, 395 U.S. 752 (1969), laid the groundwork for most of the existing search incident to arrest doctrine. Police officers in that case arrested Chimel inside his home and proceeded to search his entire three-bedroom house, including the attic and garage. In particular rooms, they also looked through the contents of drawers.

The Court crafted the following rule for assessing the reasonableness of a search incident to arrest:

> When an arrest is made, it is reasonable for the arresting officer to search the person arrested in order to remove any weapons that the latter might seek to use in order to resist arrest or effect his escape. Otherwise, the officer's safety might well be endangered, and the arrest itself frustrated. In addition, it is entirely reasonable for the arresting officer to search for and seize any evidence on the arrestee's person in order to prevent its concealment or destruction. . . . There is ample justification, therefore, for a search of the arrestee's person and the area 'within his immediate control'—construing that phrase to mean the area from within which he might gain possession of a weapon or destructible evidence.

Id., at 762–63. The extensive warrantless search of Chimel's home did not fit within this exception, because it was not needed to protect officer safety or to preserve evidence.

Four years later, in *United States v. Robinson*, 414 U.S. 218 (1973), the Court applied the *Chimel* analysis in the context of a search of the arrestee's person. A police officer had arrested Robinson for driving with a revoked license. The officer conducted a patdown search and felt an object that he could not identify in Robinson's coat pocket. He removed the object, which turned out to be a crumpled cigarette package, and opened it. Inside were 14 capsules of heroin.

The Court of Appeals concluded that the search was unreasonable because Robinson was unlikely to have evidence of the crime of arrest on his person, and because it believed that extracting the cigarette package and opening it could not be justified as part of a protective search for weapons. This Court reversed, rejecting the notion that "case-by-case adjudication" was required to determine "whether or not there was present one of the reasons supporting the authority for a search of the person incident to a lawful arrest." As the Court explained, "[t]he authority to search the person incident to a lawful custodial arrest, while based upon the need to disarm and to discover evidence, does not depend on what a court may later decide was the probability in a particular arrest situation that weapons or evidence would in fact be found upon the person of the suspect." Instead, a "custodial arrest of a suspect based on probable cause is a reasonable intrusion under the Fourth Amendment; that intrusion being lawful, a search incident to the arrest requires no additional justification."

The Court thus concluded that the search of Robinson was reasonable even though there was no concern about the loss of evidence, and the arresting officer had no specific concern that Robinson might be armed. In doing so, the Court did not draw a line between a search of Robinson's person and a further examination of the cigarette pack found during that search. It merely noted that, "[h]aving in the course of a lawful search come upon the crumpled package of cigarettes, [the officer] was entitled to inspect it." A few years later, the Court clarified that this exception was limited to "personal property . . . immediately associated with the person of the arrestee." *United States v. Chadwick*, 433 U.S. 1, 15 (1977) (200-pound, locked footlocker could not be searched incident to arrest), *abrogated on other grounds by California v. Acevedo*, 500 U.S. 565 (1991).

The search incident to arrest trilogy concludes with [*Arizona v. Gant*, 556 U.S. 332 (2009)], which analyzed searches of an arrestee's vehicle. *Gant*, like *Robinson*, recognized that the *Chimel* concerns for officer safety and evidence preservation underlie the search incident to arrest exception. As a result, the Court concluded that *Chimel* could authorize police to search a vehicle "only when the arrestee is unsecured and within reaching distance of the passenger compartment at the time of the search." *Gant* added, however, an independent exception for a warrantless search of a vehicle's passenger compartment "when it is 'reasonable to believe evidence relevant to the crime of arrest might be found in the vehicle.'" *Ibid.* (quoting *Thornton v. United States*, 541 U.S. 615, 632 (2004) (Scalia, J., concurring in judgment)). That exception stems not from *Chimel*, the Court explained, but from "circumstances unique to the vehicle context." 556 U.S., at 343.

III

These cases require us to decide how the search incident to arrest doctrine applies to modern cell phones, which are now such a pervasive and insistent part of daily life that the proverbial visitor from Mars might conclude they were an important feature of human anatomy. A smart phone of the sort taken from Riley was unheard of ten years ago; a significant majority of American adults now own such phones. Even less sophisticated phones like Wurie's, which have already faded in popularity since Wurie was arrested in 2007, have been around for less than 15 years. Both phones are based on technology nearly inconceivable just a few decades ago, when *Chimel* and *Robinson* were decided.

Absent more precise guidance from the founding era, we generally determine whether to exempt a given type of search from the warrant requirement "by assessing, on the one hand, the degree to which it intrudes upon an individual's privacy and, on the other, the degree to which it is needed for the promotion of legitimate governmental interests." *Wyoming v. Houghton*, 526 U.S. 295, 300 (1999). Such a balancing of interests supported the search incident to arrest exception in *Robinson*, and a mechanical application of *Robinson* might well support the warrantless searches at issue here.

But while *Robinson*'s categorical rule strikes the appropriate balance in the context of physical objects, neither of its rationales has much force with respect to digital content on cell phones. On the government interest side, *Robinson* concluded that the two risks identified in *Chimel*—harm to officers and destruction of evidence—are present in all custodial arrests. There are no comparable risks when the search is of digital data. In addition, *Robinson* regarded any privacy interests retained by an individual after arrest as significantly diminished by the fact of the arrest itself. Cell phones, however, place vast quantities of personal information literally in the hands of individuals. A search of the information on a cell phone bears little resemblance to the type of brief physical search considered in *Robinson.*

We therefore decline to extend *Robinson* to searches of data on cell phones, and hold instead that officers must generally secure a warrant before conducting such a search.

A

We first consider each *Chimel* concern in turn. In doing so, we do not overlook *Robinson*'s admonition that searches of a person incident to arrest, "while based upon the need to disarm and to discover evidence," are reasonable regardless of "the probability in a particular arrest situation that weapons or evidence would in fact be found." Rather than requiring the "case-by-case adjudication" that *Robinson* rejected, we ask instead whether application of the search incident to arrest doctrine to this particular category of effects would "untether the rule from the justifications underlying the *Chimel* exception," *Gant, supra*, at 343. See also *Knowles v. Iowa*, 525 U.S. 113, 119 (1998) (declining to extend *Robinson* to the issuance of citations, "a situation where the concern for officer safety is not present to the same extent and the concern for destruction or loss of evidence is not present at all").

1

Digital data stored on a cell phone cannot itself be used as a weapon to harm an arresting officer or to effectuate the arrestee's escape. Law enforcement officers remain free to examine the physical aspects of a phone to ensure that it will not be used as a weapon—say, to determine whether there is a razor blade hidden between the phone and its case. Once an officer has secured a phone and eliminated any potential physical threats, however, data on the phone can endanger no one.

Perhaps the same might have been said of the cigarette pack seized from Robinson's pocket. Once an officer gained control of the pack, it was unlikely that Robinson could have accessed the pack's contents. But unknown physical objects may always pose risks, no matter how slight, during the tense atmosphere of a custodial arrest. The officer in *Robinson* testified that he could not identify the objects in the cigarette pack but knew they were not cigarettes. Given that, a further search was a reasonable protective measure. No such unknowns exist with respect to digital data. As the First Circuit explained, the officers who searched Wurie's cell phone "knew exactly what they would find therein: data. They also knew that the data could not harm them."

The United States and California both suggest that a search of cell phone data might help ensure officer safety in more indirect ways, for example by alerting officers that confederates of the arrestee are headed to the scene. There is undoubtedly a strong government interest in warning officers about such possibilities, but neither the United States nor California offers evidence to suggest that their concerns are based on actual experience. The proposed consideration would also represent a broadening of *Chimel's* concern that an *arrestee himself* might grab a weapon and use it against an officer "to resist arrest or effect his escape." And any such threats from outside the arrest scene do not "lurk in all custodial arrests." Accordingly, the interest in protecting officer safety does not justify dispensing with the warrant requirement across the board. To the extent dangers to arresting officers may be implicated in a particular way in a particular case, they are better addressed through consideration of case-specific exceptions to the warrant requirement, such as the one for exigent circumstances.

2

The United States and California focus primarily on the second *Chimel* rationale: preventing the destruction of evidence.

Both Riley and Wurie concede that officers could have seized and secured their cell phones to prevent destruction of evidence while seeking a warrant. That is a sensible concession. And once law enforcement officers have secured a cell phone, there is no longer any risk that the arrestee himself will be able to delete incriminating data from the phone.

The United States and California argue that information on a cell phone may nevertheless be vulnerable to two types of evidence destruction unique to digital data—remote wiping and data encryption. Remote wiping occurs when a phone, connected to a wireless network, receives a signal that erases stored data. This can happen when a third party sends a remote signal or when a phone is preprogrammed to delete data upon entering or leaving certain geographic areas (so-called "geofencing"). Encryption is a security feature that some modern cell phones use in addition to password protection. When such phones lock, data becomes protected by sophisticated encryption that renders a phone all but "unbreakable" unless police know the password.

As an initial matter, these broader concerns about the loss of evidence are distinct from *Chimel*'s focus on a defendant who responds to arrest by trying to conceal or destroy evidence within his reach. With respect to remote wiping, the Government's primary concern turns on the actions of third parties who are not present at the scene of arrest. And data encryption is even further afield. There, the Government focuses on the ordinary operation of a phone's security features, apart from *any* active attempt by a defendant or his associates to conceal or destroy evidence upon arrest.

We have also been given little reason to believe that either problem is prevalent. The briefing reveals only a couple of anecdotal examples of remote wiping triggered by an arrest. Similarly, the opportunities for officers to search a password-protected phone before data becomes encrypted are quite limited. Law enforcement officers are very unlikely to come upon such a phone in an unlocked state because most phones lock at the touch of a button or, as a default, after some very short period of inactivity. This may explain why the encryption argument was not made until the merits stage in this Court, and has never been considered by the Courts of Appeals.

Moreover, in situations in which an arrest might trigger a remote-wipe attempt or an officer discovers an unlocked phone, it is not clear that the ability to conduct a warrantless search would make much of a difference. The need to effect the arrest, secure the scene, and tend to other pressing matters means that law enforcement officers may well not be able to turn their attention to a cell phone right away. Cell phone data would be vulnerable to remote wiping from the time an individual anticipates arrest to the time any eventual search of the phone is completed, which might be at the station house hours later. Likewise, an officer who seizes a phone in an unlocked state might not be able to begin his search in the short time remaining before the phone locks and data becomes encrypted.

In any event, as to remote wiping, law enforcement is not without specific means to address the threat. Remote wiping can be fully prevented by disconnecting a phone from the network. There are at least two simple ways to do this: First, law enforcement officers can turn the phone off or remove its battery. Second, if they are concerned about encryption or other potential problems, they can leave a phone powered on and place it in an enclosure that isolates the phone from radio waves. Such devices are commonly called "Faraday bags," after the English scientist Michael Faraday. They are essentially sandwich bags made of aluminum foil: cheap, lightweight, and easy to use. They may not be a complete answer to the problem, but at least for now they provide a reasonable response. In fact, a number of law enforcement agencies around the country already encourage the use of Faraday bags.

* * *

B

The search incident to arrest exception rests not only on the heightened government interests at stake in a volatile arrest situation, but also on an arrestee's reduced privacy interests upon being taken into police custody. *Robinson* focused primarily on the first of those rationales. But it also quoted with approval then-Judge Cardozo's account of the historical basis for the search incident to arrest exception: "Search of the person becomes lawful when grounds for arrest and accusation have been discovered, and the law is in the act of subjecting the body of the accused to its physical dominion." 414 U.S., at 232 (quoting *People v. Chiagles*, 237 N.Y. 193, 197, 142 N.E. 583, 584 (1923)). Put simply, a patdown of Robinson's clothing and an inspection of the cigarette pack found in his pocket constituted only minor additional intrusions compared to the substantial government authority exercised in taking Robinson into custody.

The fact that an arrestee has diminished privacy interests does not mean that the Fourth Amendment falls out of the picture entirely. Not every search "is acceptable solely because a person is in custody." *Maryland v. King*, 569 U.S. 435, 463 (2013). To the contrary, when "privacy-related concerns are weighty enough" a "search may require a warrant, notwithstanding the diminished expectations of privacy of the arrestee." *Ibid.* One such example, of course, is *Chimel*. *Chimel* refused to "characterize the invasion of privacy that results from a top-to-bottom search of a man's house as 'minor.'" Because a search of the arrestee's entire house was a substantial invasion beyond the arrest itself, the Court concluded that a warrant was required.

Robinson is the only decision from this Court applying *Chimel* to a search of the contents of an item found on an arrestee's person. In an earlier case, this Court had approved a search of a zipper bag carried by an arrestee, but the Court analyzed only the validity of the arrest itself. See *Draper v. United States*, 358 U.S. 307, 310–311 (1959). Lower courts applying *Robinson* and *Chimel*, however, have approved searches of a variety of personal items carried by an arrestee.

The United States asserts that a search of all data stored on a cell phone is "materially indistinguishable" from searches of these sorts of physical items. That is like saying a ride on horseback is materially indistinguishable from a flight to the moon. Both are ways of getting from point A to point B, but little else justifies lumping them together. Modern cell phones, as a category, implicate privacy concerns far beyond those implicated by the search of a cigarette pack, a wallet, or a purse. A conclusion that inspecting the contents of an arrestee's pockets works no substantial additional intrusion on privacy beyond the arrest itself may make sense as applied to physical items, but any extension of that reasoning to digital data has to rest on its own bottom.

1

Cell phones differ in both a quantitative and a qualitative sense from other objects that might be kept on an arrestee's person. The term "cell phone" is itself misleading shorthand; many of these devices are in fact minicomputers that also happen to have the capacity to be used as a telephone. They could just as easily be called cameras, video players, rolodexes, calendars, tape recorders, libraries, diaries, albums, televisions, maps, or newspapers.

One of the most notable distinguishing features of modern cell phones is their immense storage capacity. Before cell phones, a search of a person was limited by physical realities and tended as a general matter to constitute only a narrow intrusion on privacy. Most people cannot lug around every piece of mail they have received for the past several months, every picture they have taken, or every book or article they have read—nor would they have any reason to attempt to do so. And if they did, they would have to drag behind them a trunk of the sort held to require a search warrant in *Chadwick*, rather than a container the size of the cigarette package in *Robinson*.

* * *

The storage capacity of cell phones has several interrelated consequences for privacy. First, a cell phone collects in one place many distinct types of information—an address, a note, a prescription, a bank statement, a video—that reveal much more in combination than any isolated record. Second, a cell phone's capacity allows even just one type of information to convey far more than previously possible. The sum of an individual's private life can be reconstructed through a thousand photographs labeled with dates, locations, and descriptions; the same cannot be said of a photograph or two of loved ones tucked into a wallet. Third, the data on a phone can date back to the purchase of the phone, or even earlier. A person might carry in his pocket a slip of paper reminding him to call Mr. Jones; he would not carry a record of all his communications with Mr. Jones for the past several months, as would routinely be kept on a phone.

Finally, there is an element of pervasiveness that characterizes cell phones but not physical records. Prior to the digital age, people did not typically carry a cache of sensitive personal information with them as they went about their day. Now it is the person who is not carrying a cell phone, with all that it contains, who is the exception. According to one poll, nearly three-quarters of smart phone users report being within five feet of their phones most of the time, with 12% admitting that they even use their phones in the shower. A decade ago police officers searching an arrestee might have occasionally stumbled across a highly personal item such as a diary. But those discoveries were likely to be few and far between. Today, by contrast, it is no exaggeration to say that many of the more than 90% of American adults who own a cell phone keep on their person a digital record of nearly every aspect of their lives—from the mundane to the intimate. Allowing the police to scrutinize such records on a routine basis is quite different from allowing them to search a personal item or two in the occasional case.

Although the data stored on a cell phone is distinguished from physical records by quantity alone, certain types of data are also qualitatively different. An Internet search and browsing history, for example, can be found on an Internet-enabled phone and could reveal an individual's private interests or concerns—perhaps a search for certain symptoms of disease, coupled with frequent visits to WebMD. Data on a cell phone can also reveal where a person has been. Historic location information is a standard feature on many smart phones and can reconstruct someone's specific movements down to the minute, not only around town but also within a particular building.

* * *

In 1926, Learned Hand observed (in an opinion later quoted in *Chimel*) that it is "a totally different thing to search a man's pockets and use against him what they contain, from ransacking his house for everything which may incriminate him." *United States v. Kirschenblatt*, 16 F.2d 202, 203 (C.A.2). If his pockets contain a cell phone, however, that is no longer true. Indeed, a cell phone search would typically expose to the government far *more* than the most exhaustive search of a house: A phone not only contains in digital form many sensitive records previously found in the home; it also contains a broad array of private information never found in a home in any form—unless the phone is.

2

To further complicate the scope of the privacy interests at stake, the data a user views on many modern cell phones may not in fact be stored on the device itself. Treating a cell phone as a container whose contents may be searched incident to an arrest is a bit strained as an initial matter. But the analogy crumbles entirely when a cell phone is used to access data located elsewhere, at the tap of a screen. That is what cell phones, with increasing frequency, are designed to do by taking advantage of "cloud computing." Cloud computing is the capacity of Internet-connected devices to display data stored on remote servers rather than on the device itself. Cell phone users often may not know whether particular information is stored on the device or in the cloud, and it generally makes little difference. Moreover, the same type of data may be stored locally on the device for one user and in the cloud for another.

The United States concedes that the search incident to arrest exception may not be stretched to cover a search of files accessed remotely—that is, a search of files stored in the cloud. Such a search would be like finding a key in a suspect's pocket and arguing that it allowed law enforcement to unlock and search a house. But officers searching a phone's data would not typically know whether the information they are viewing was stored locally at the time of the arrest or has been pulled from the cloud.

Although the Government recognizes the problem, its proposed solutions are unclear. It suggests that officers could disconnect a phone from the network before searching the device—the very solution whose feasibility it contested with respect to the threat of remote wiping. Alternatively, the Government proposes that law enforcement agencies "develop protocols to address" concerns raised by cloud computing. Probably a good idea, but the Founders did not fight a revolution to gain the right to government agency protocols. The possibility that a search might extend well beyond papers and effects in the physical proximity of an arrestee is yet another reason that the privacy interests here dwarf those in *Robinson*.

C

Apart from their arguments for a direct extension of *Robinson*, the United States and California offer various fallback options for permitting warrantless cell phone searches under certain circumstances. Each of the proposals is flawed and contravenes our general preference to provide clear guidance to law enforcement through categorical rules. "[I]f police are to have workable rules, the balancing of the competing interests . . . 'must in large part be done on a categorical basis—not in an ad hoc, case-by-case fashion by individual police officers.' " *Michigan v. Summers*, 452 U.S. 692, 705, n. 19 (1981) (quoting *Dunaway v. New York*, 442 U.S. 200, 219–20 (1979) (White, J., concurring)).

The United States first proposes that the *Gant* standard be imported from the vehicle context, allowing a warrantless search of an arrestee's cell phone whenever it is reasonable to believe that the phone contains evidence of the crime of arrest. But *Gant* relied on "circumstances unique to the vehicle context" to endorse a search solely for the purpose of gathering evidence. Justice Scalia's *Thornton* opinion, on which *Gant* was based, explained that those unique circumstances are "a reduced expectation of privacy" and "heightened law enforcement needs" when it comes to motor vehicles. For reasons that we have explained, cell phone searches bear neither of those characteristics.

At any rate, a *Gant* standard would prove no practical limit at all when it comes to cell phone searches. In the vehicle context, *Gant* generally protects against searches for evidence of past crimes. In the cell phone context, however, it is reasonable to expect that incriminating information will be found on a phone regardless of when the crime occurred. Similarly, in the vehicle context *Gant* restricts broad searches resulting from minor crimes such as traffic violations. That would not necessarily be true for cell phones. It would be a particularly inexperienced or unimaginative law enforcement officer who could not come up with several reasons to suppose evidence of just about any crime could be found on a cell phone. Even an individual pulled over for something as basic as speeding might well have locational data dispositive of guilt on his phone. An individual pulled over for reckless driving might have evidence on the phone that shows whether he was texting while driving. The sources of potential pertinent information are virtually unlimited, so applying the *Gant* standard to cell phones would in effect give "police officers unbridled discretion to rummage at will among a person's private effects."

The United States also proposes a rule that would restrict the scope of a cell phone search to those areas of the phone where an officer reasonably believes that information relevant to the crime, the arrestee's identity, or officer safety will be discovered. This approach would again impose few meaningful constraints on officers. The proposed categories would sweep in a great deal of information, and officers would not always be able to discern in advance what information would be found where.

We also reject the United States' final suggestion that officers should always be able to search a phone's call log, as they did in Wurie's case. The Government relies on *Smith v. Maryland*, 442 U.S. 735 (1979), which held that no warrant was required to use a pen register at telephone company premises to identify numbers dialed by a particular caller. The Court in that case, however, concluded that the use of a pen register was not a "search" at all under the Fourth Amendment. There is no dispute here that the officers engaged in a search of Wurie's cell phone. Moreover, call logs typically contain more than just phone numbers; they include any identifying information that an individual might add, such as the label "my house" in Wurie's case.

Finally, at oral argument California suggested a different limiting principle, under which officers could search cell phone data if they could have obtained the same information from a pre-digital counterpart. But the fact that a search in the pre-digital era could have turned up a photograph or two in a wallet does not justify a search of thousands of photos in a digital gallery. The fact that someone could have tucked a paper bank statement in a pocket does not justify a search of every bank statement from the last five years. And to make matters worse, such an analogue test would allow law enforcement to search a range of items contained on a phone, even though people would be unlikely to carry such a variety of information in physical form. In Riley's case, for example, it is implausible that he would have strolled around with video tapes, photo albums, and an address book all crammed into his pockets. But because each of those items has a pre-digital analogue, police under California's proposal would be able to search a phone for all of those items—a significant diminution of privacy.

In addition, an analogue test would launch courts on a difficult line-drawing expedition to determine which digital files are comparable to physical records. Is an e-mail equivalent to a letter? Is a voicemail equivalent to a phone message slip? It is not clear how officers could make these kinds of decisions before conducting a search, or how courts would apply the proposed rule after the fact. An analogue test would "keep defendants and judges guessing for years to come." *Sykes v. United States*, 564 U.S. 1, 34 (2011) (Scalia, J., dissenting).

IV

We cannot deny that our decision today will have an impact on the ability of law enforcement to combat crime. Cell phones have become important tools in facilitating coordination and communication among members of criminal enterprises, and can provide valuable incriminating information about dangerous criminals. Privacy comes at a cost.

Our holding, of course, is not that the information on a cell phone is immune from search; it is instead that a warrant is generally required before such a search, even when a cell phone is seized incident to arrest. Our cases have historically recognized that the warrant requirement is "an important working part of our machinery of government," not merely "an inconvenience to be somehow 'weighed' against the claims of police efficiency." *Coolidge v. New Hampshire*, 403 U.S. 443, 481 (1971). Recent technological advances similar to those discussed here have, in addition, made the process of obtaining a warrant itself more efficient. See *McNeely*, 569 U.S., at 173 (Roberts, C.J., concurring in part and dissenting in part) (describing jurisdiction where "police officers can e-mail warrant requests to judges' iPads [and] judges have signed such warrants and e-mailed them back to officers in less than 15 minutes").

Moreover, even though the search incident to arrest exception does not apply to cell phones, other case-specific exceptions may still justify a warrantless search of a particular phone. "One well-recognized exception applies when " 'the exigencies of the situation" make the needs of law enforcement so compelling that [a] warrantless search is objectively reasonable under the Fourth Amendment.' " *Kentucky v. King*, 563 U.S., at 460 (quoting *Mincey v. Arizona*, 437 U.S. 385, 394 (1978)). Such exigencies could include the need to prevent the imminent destruction of evidence in individual cases, to pursue a fleeing suspect, and to assist persons who are seriously injured or are threatened with imminent injury. In *Chadwick*, for example, the Court held that the exception for searches incident to arrest did not justify a search of the trunk at issue, but noted that "if officers have reason to believe that luggage contains some immediately dangerous instrumentality, such as explosives, it would be foolhardy to transport it to the station house without opening the luggage." 433 U.S., at 15, n. 9.

* * *

Modern cell phones are not just another technological convenience. With all they contain and all they may reveal, they hold for many Americans "the privacies of life." The fact that technology now allows an individual to carry such information in his hand does not make the information any less worthy of the protection for which the Founders fought. Our answer to the question of what police must do before searching a cell phone seized incident to an arrest is accordingly simple—get a warrant.

* * *

JUSTICE ALITO, concurring in part and concurring in the judgment.

I agree with the Court that law enforcement officers, in conducting a lawful search incident to arrest, must generally obtain a warrant before searching information stored or accessible on a cell phone. I write separately to address two points.

I

A

First, I am not convinced at this time that the ancient rule on searches incident to arrest is based exclusively (or even primarily) on the need to protect the safety of arresting officers and the need to prevent the destruction of evidence. This rule antedates the adoption of the Fourth Amendment by at least a century. In *Weeks v. United States*, 232 U.S. 383, 392 (1914), we held that the Fourth Amendment did not disturb this rule. And neither in *Weeks* nor in any of the authorities discussing the old common-law rule have I found any suggestion that it was based exclusively or primarily on the need to protect arresting officers or to prevent the destruction of evidence.

* * *

The idea that officer safety and the preservation of evidence are the sole reasons for allowing a warrantless search incident to arrest appears to derive from the Court's reasoning in *Chimel v. California*, 395 U.S. 752 (1969), a case that involved the lawfulness of a search of the scene of an arrest, not the person of an arrestee. As I have explained, *Chimel*'s reasoning is questionable, see *Arizona v. Gant*, 556 U.S. 332, 361–363 (2009) (Alito, J., dissenting), and I think it is a mistake to allow that reasoning to affect cases like these that concern the search of the person of arrestees.

B

Despite my view on the point discussed above, I agree that we should not mechanically apply the rule used in the predigital era to the search of a cell phone. Many cell phones now in use are capable of storing and accessing a quantity of information, some highly personal, that no person would ever have had on his person in hard-copy form. This calls for a new balancing of law enforcement and privacy interests.

The Court strikes this balance in favor of privacy interests with respect to all cell phones and all information found in them, and this approach leads to anomalies. For example, the Court's broad holding favors information in digital form over information in hard-copy form. Suppose that two suspects are arrested. Suspect number one has in his pocket a monthly bill for his land-line phone, and the bill lists an incriminating call to a long-distance number. He also has in his a wallet a few snapshots, and one of these is incriminating. Suspect number two has in his pocket a cell phone, the call log of which shows a call to the same incriminating number. In addition, a number of photos are stored in the memory of the cell phone, and one of these is incriminating. Under established law, the police may seize and examine the phone bill and the snapshots in the wallet without obtaining a warrant, but under the Court's holding today, the information stored in the cell phone is out.

* * *

II

This brings me to my second point. While I agree with the holding of the Court, I would reconsider the question presented here if either Congress or state legislatures, after assessing the legitimate needs of law enforcement and the privacy interests of cell phone owners, enact legislation that draws reasonable distinctions based on categories of information or perhaps other variables.

The regulation of electronic surveillance provides an instructive example. After this Court held that electronic surveillance constitutes a search even when no property interest is invaded, see *Katz v. United States*, 389 U.S. 347, 353–359 (1967), Congress responded by enacting Title III of the Omnibus Crime Control and Safe Streets Act of 1968, 82 Stat. 211. Since that time, electronic surveillance has been governed primarily, not by decisions of this Court, but by the statute, which authorizes but imposes detailed restrictions on electronic surveillance.

* * *

In light of these developments, it would be very unfortunate if privacy protection in the 21st century were left primarily to the federal courts using the blunt instrument of the Fourth Amendment. Legislatures, elected by the people, are in a better position than we are to assess and respond to the changes that have already occurred and those that almost certainly will take place in the future.

Points for Discussion

1. Recall that in *Olmstead* federal agents tapped telephone lines and AT&T and other leading telephone companies filed an important amicus brief in support of Olmstead's position. No telephone manufacturers or service providers filed a brief in *Riley*. What changed? For one thing, encryption means that telephone manufacturers and service providers do not need to rely on the courts to protect information anymore; they can do it themselves. Extracting data from an encrypted device in the early 21st century is much more difficult than tapping physical telephone lines was in the early 20th century. This fact has pitted the FBI against Apple, which markets its iPhone as a secure storage place for personal or intimate data. See Leander Kahney, *The FBI Wanted a Backdoor to the iPhone. Tim Cook Said No*, Wired Magazine, April 16, 2019.

2. *Riley* holds that the police can seize a mobile phone while they obtain a warrant to search it. So, what practical protection, if any, does this decision provide? How is this inquiry informed by the Court's assertion that "[i]t would be a particularly inexperienced or unimaginative law enforcement officer who could not come up with several reasons to suppose evidence of just about any crime could be found on a cell phone."

3. There has been plenty of criticism leveled at Congress for not updating federal privacy laws to take account of rapid technological change. What is the proper role of the Court in dealing with technological advances in the way information is generated, stored, and communicated? How is Congress' role different?

WINSTON V. LEE

470 U.S. 753 (1985)

JUSTICE BRENNAN delivered the opinion of the court.

Schmerber v. California, 384 U.S. 757 (1966), held, *inter alia*, that a State may, over the suspect's protest, have a physician extract blood from a person suspected of drunken driving without violation of the suspect's right secured by the Fourth Amendment not to be subjected to unreasonable searches and seizures. However, *Schmerber* cautioned: "That we today hold that the Constitution does not forbid the States['] minor intrusions into an individual's body under stringently limited conditions in no way indicates that it permits more substantial intrusions, or intrusions under other conditions." In this case, the Commonwealth of Virginia seeks to compel the respondent Rudolph Lee, who is suspected of attempting to commit armed robbery, to undergo a surgical procedure under a general anesthetic for removal of a bullet lodged in his chest. Petitioners allege that the bullet will provide evidence of respondent's guilt or innocence. We conclude that the procedure sought here is an example of the "more substantial intrusion" cautioned against in *Schmerber*, and hold that to permit the procedure would violate respondent's right to be secure in his person guaranteed by the Fourth Amendment.

I

A

At approximately 1 a.m. on July 18, 1982, Ralph E. Watkinson was closing his shop for the night. As he was locking the door, he observed someone armed with a gun coming toward him from across the street. Watkinson was also armed and when he drew his gun, the other person told him to freeze. Watkinson then fired at the other person, who returned his fire. Watkinson was hit in the legs, while the other individual, who appeared to be wounded in his left side, ran from the scene. The police arrived on the scene shortly thereafter, and Watkinson was taken by ambulance to the emergency room of the Medical College of Virginia (MCV) Hospital.

Approximately 20 minutes later, police officers responding to another call found respondent eight blocks from where the earlier shooting occurred. Respondent was suffering from a gunshot wound to his left chest area and told the police that he had been shot when two individuals attempted to rob him. An ambulance took respondent to the MCV Hospital. Watkinson was still in the MCV emergency room and, when respondent entered that room, said "[t]hat's the man that shot me." After an investigation, the police decided that respondent's story of having been himself the victim of a robbery was untrue and charged respondent with attempted robbery, malicious wounding, and two counts of using a firearm in the commission of a felony.

B

The Commonwealth shortly thereafter moved in state court for an order directing respondent to undergo surgery to remove an object thought to be a bullet lodged under his left collarbone. The court conducted several evidentiary hearings on the motion. At the first hearing, the Commonwealth's expert testified that the surgical procedure would take 45 minutes and would involve a three to four percent chance of temporary nerve damage, a one percent chance of permanent nerve damage, and a one-tenth of one percent chance of death. At the second hearing, the expert testified that on reexamination of respondent, he discovered that the bullet was not "back inside close to the nerves and arteries as he originally had thought. Instead, he now believed the bullet to be located "just beneath the skin." He testified that the surgery would require an incision of only one and one-half centimeters (slightly more than one-half inch), could be performed under local anesthesia, and would result in "no danger on the basis that there's no general anesthesia employed."

The state trial judge granted the motion to compel surgery. Respondent petitioned the Virginia Supreme Court for a writ of prohibition and/or a writ of habeas corpus, both of which were denied. Respondent then brought an action in the United States District Court for the Eastern District of Virginia to enjoin the pending operation on Fourth Amendment grounds. The court refused to issue a preliminary injunction, holding that respondent's cause had little likelihood of success on the merits.

On October 18, 1982, just before the surgery was scheduled, the surgeon ordered that X rays be taken of respondent's chest. The X rays revealed that the bullet was in fact lodged two and one-half to three centimeters (approximately one inch) deep in muscular tissue in respondent's chest, substantially deeper than had been thought when the state court granted the motion to compel surgery. The surgeon now believed that a general anesthetic would be desirable for medical reasons.

* * *

II

The Fourth Amendment protects "expectations of privacy"—the individual's legitimate expectations that in certain places and at certain times he has "the right to be let alone—the most comprehensive of rights and the right most valued by civilized men." *Olmstead v. United States,* 277 U.S. 438, 478 (1928) (Brandeis, J., dissenting). Putting to one side the procedural protections of the warrant requirement, the Fourth Amendment generally protects the "security" of "persons, houses, papers, and effects" against official intrusions up to the point where the community's need for evidence surmounts a specified standard, ordinarily "probable cause." Beyond this point, it is ordinarily justifiable for the community to demand that the individual give up some part of his interest in privacy and security to advance the community's vital interests in law enforcement; such a search is generally "reasonable" in the Amendment's terms.

A compelled surgical intrusion into an individual's body for evidence, however, implicates expectations of privacy and security of such magnitude that the intrusion may be "unreasonable" even if likely to produce evidence of a crime. In *Schmerber v. California,* 384 U.S. 757 (1966), we addressed a claim that the State had breached the Fourth Amendment's protection of the "right of the people to be secure in their *persons* . . . against unreasonable searches and seizures" (emphasis added) when it compelled an individual suspected of drunken driving to undergo a blood test. Schmerber had been arrested at a hospital while receiving treatment for injuries suffered when the automobile he was driving struck a tree. Despite Schmerber's objection, a police officer at the hospital had directed a physician to take a blood sample from him. Schmerber subsequently objected to the introduction at trial of evidence obtained as a result of the blood test.

The authorities in *Schmerber* clearly had probable cause to believe that he had been driving while intoxicated, and to believe that a blood test would provide evidence that was exceptionally probative in confirming this belief. Because the case fell within the exigent-circumstances exception to the warrant requirement, no warrant was necessary. The search was not more intrusive than reasonably necessary to accomplish its goals. Nonetheless, Schmerber argued that the Fourth Amendment prohibited the authorities from intruding into his body to extract the blood that was needed as evidence.

* * *

The reasonableness of surgical intrusions beneath the skin depends on a case-by-case approach, in which the individual's interests in privacy and security are weighed against society's interests in conducting the procedure. In a given case, the question whether the community's need for evidence outweighs the substantial privacy interests at stake is a delicate one admitting of few categorical answers. We believe that *Schmerber,* however, provides the appropriate framework of analysis for such cases.

Schmerber recognized that the ordinary requirements of the Fourth Amendment would be the threshold requirements for conducting this kind of surgical search and seizure. We noted the importance of probable cause. And we pointed out: "Search warrants are ordinarily required for searches of dwellings, and, absent an emergency, no less could be required where intrusions into the human body are concerned. . . . The importance of informed, detached and deliberate determinations of the issue whether or not to invade another's body in search of evidence of guilt is indisputable and great."

Beyond these standards, *Schmerber*'s inquiry considered a number of other factors in determining the "reasonableness" of the blood test. A crucial factor in analyzing the magnitude of the intrusion in *Schmerber* is the extent to which the procedure may threaten the safety or health of the individual. "[F]or most people [a blood test] involves virtually no risk, trauma, or pain." Moreover, all reasonable medical precautions were taken and no unusual or untested procedures were employed in *Schmerber;* the procedure was performed "by a physician in a hospital environment according to accepted medical practices." *Ibid.* Notwithstanding the existence of probable cause, a search for evidence of a crime may be unjustifiable if it endangers the life or health of the suspect.

Another factor is the extent of intrusion upon the individual's dignitary interests in personal privacy and bodily integrity. Intruding into an individual's living room, eavesdropping upon an individual's telephone conversations, or forcing an individual to accompany police officers to the police station, typically do not injure the physical person of the individual. Such intrusions do, however, damage the individual's sense of personal privacy and security and are thus subject to the Fourth Amendment's dictates. In noting that a blood test was "a commonplace in these days of periodic physical examinations," *Schmerber* recognized society's judgment that blood tests do not constitute an unduly extensive imposition on an individual's personal privacy and bodily integrity.

Weighed against these individual interests is the community's interest in fairly and accurately determining guilt or innocence. This interest is of course of great importance. We noted in *Schmerber* that a blood test is "a highly effective means of determining the degree to which a person is under the influence of alcohol." Moreover, there was "a clear indication that in fact [desired] evidence [would] be found" if the blood test were undertaken. Especially given the difficulty of proving drunkenness by other means, these considerations showed that results of the blood test were of vital importance if the State were to enforce its drunken driving laws. In *Schmerber,* we concluded that this state interest was sufficient to justify the intrusion, and the compelled blood test was thus "reasonable" for Fourth Amendment purposes.

III

Applying the *Schmerber* balancing test in this case, we believe that the Court of Appeals reached the correct result. The Commonwealth plainly had probable cause to conduct the search. In addition, all parties apparently agree that respondent has had a full measure of procedural protections and has been able fully to litigate the difficult medical and legal questions necessarily involved in analyzing the reasonableness of a surgical incision of this magnitude. Our inquiry therefore must focus on the extent of the intrusion on respondent's privacy interests and on the State's need for the evidence.

The threats to the health or safety of respondent posed by the surgery are the subject of sharp dispute between the parties. Before the new revelations of October 18, the District Court found that the procedure could be carried out "with virtually no risk to [respondent]." On rehearing, however, with new evidence before it, the District Court held that "the risks previously involved have increased in magnitude even as new risks are being added."

The Court of Appeals examined the medical evidence in the record and found that respondent would suffer some risks associated with the surgical procedure. One surgeon had testified that the difficulty of discovering the exact location of the bullet "could require extensive probing and retracting of the muscle tissue," carrying with it "the concomitant risks of injury to the muscle as well as injury to the nerves, blood vessels and other tissue in the chest and pleural cavity." The court further noted that "the greater intrusion and the larger incisions increase the risks of infection." Moreover, there was conflict in the testimony concerning the nature and the scope of the operation. One surgeon stated that it would take 15–20 minutes, while another predicted the procedure could take up to two and one-half hours. The court properly took the resulting uncertainty about the medical risks into account.

Both lower courts in this case believed that the proposed surgery, which for purely medical reasons required the use of a general anesthetic, would be an "extensive" intrusion on respondent's personal privacy and bodily integrity. When conducted with the consent of the patient, surgery requiring general anesthesia is not necessarily demeaning or intrusive. In such a case, the surgeon is carrying out the patient's own will concerning the patient's body and the patient's right to privacy is therefore preserved. In this case, however, the Court of Appeals noted that the Commonwealth proposes to take control of respondent's body, to "drug this citizen—not yet convicted of a criminal offense—with narcotics and barbiturates into a state of unconsciousness," and then to search beneath his skin for evidence of a crime. This kind of surgery involves a virtually total divestment of respondent's ordinary control over surgical probing beneath his skin.

The other part of the balance concerns the Commonwealth's need to intrude into respondent's body to retrieve the bullet. The Commonwealth claims to need the bullet to demonstrate that it was fired from Watkinson's gun, which in turn would show that respondent was the robber who confronted Watkinson. However, although we recognize the difficulty of making determinations in advance as to the strength of the case against respondent, petitioners' assertions of a compelling need for the bullet are hardly persuasive. The very circumstances relied on in this case to demonstrate probable cause to believe that evidence will be found tend to vitiate the Commonwealth's need to compel respondent to undergo surgery. The Commonwealth has available substantial additional evidence that respondent was the individual who accosted Watkinson on the night of the robbery. No party in this case suggests that Watkinson's entirely spontaneous identification of respondent at the hospital would be inadmissible. In addition, petitioners can no doubt prove that Watkinson was found a few blocks from Watkinson's store shortly after the incident took place. And petitioners can certainly show that the location of the bullet (under respondent's left collarbone) seems to correlate with Watkinson's report that the robber "jerked" to the left. The fact that the Commonwealth has available such substantial evidence of the origin of the bullet restricts the need for the Commonwealth to compel respondent to undergo the contemplated surgery.

In weighing the various factors in this case, we therefore reach the same conclusion as the courts below. The operation sought will intrude substantially on respondent's protected interests. The medical risks of the operation, although apparently not extremely severe, are a subject of considerable dispute; the very uncertainty militates against finding the operation to be "reasonable." In addition, the intrusion on respondent's privacy interests entailed by the operation can only be characterized as severe. On the other hand, although the bullet may turn out to be useful to the Commonwealth in prosecuting respondent, the Commonwealth has failed to demonstrate a compelling need for it. We believe that in these circumstances the Commonwealth has failed to demonstrate that it would be "reasonable" under the terms of the Fourth Amendment to search for evidence of this crime by means of the contemplated surgery.

IV

The Fourth Amendment is a vital safeguard of the right of the citizen to be free from unreasonable governmental intrusions into any area in which he has a reasonable expectation of privacy. Where the Court has found a lesser expectation of privacy or where the search involves a minimal intrusion on privacy interests, the Court has held that the Fourth Amendment's protections are correspondingly less stringent. Conversely, however, the Fourth Amendment's command that searches be "reasonable" requires that when the State seeks to intrude upon an area in which our society recognizes a significantly heightened privacy interest, a more substantial justification is required to make the search "reasonable." Applying these principles, we hold that the proposed search in this case would be "unreasonable" under the Fourth Amendment.

JUSTICE BLACKMUN and JUSTICE REHNQUIST concur in the judgment.

CHIEF JUSTICE BURGER, concurring.

I join because I read the Court's opinion as not preventing detention of an individual if there are reasonable grounds to believe that natural bodily functions will disclose the presence of contraband materials secreted internally.

Points for Discussion

1. *Schmerber* upheld the drawing of blood from a suspect to determine whether he had been driving while intoxicated. Here, the government's interest is greater (the crime of which Lee is accused is more serious) and the intrusion on the defendant's bodily integrity is greater as well. How does the Court conclude that the balance here tips in favor of the individual?

2. Although the Court cites it here as a Fourth Amendment case, *Schmerber* is an important precedent in the Court's Fifth Amendment jurisprudence as well. In that case, the Court held that forcibly withdrawing blood from the defendant's veins does not compel him to be a witness against himself. We discuss *Schmerber* and its progeny in chapter 8.

3. In *United States v. Montoya de Hernandez*, 473 U.S. 531 (1985), the defendant was suspected of smuggling drugs on Avianca Flight 080 from Bogota, Colombia. The Court set forth the facts as follows:

[The] inspector suspected that respondent was a "balloon swallower," one who attempts to smuggle narcotics into this country hidden in her alimentary canal. Over the years Inspector Talamantes had apprehended dozens of alimentary canal smugglers arriving on Avianca Flight 080.

The inspectors requested a female customs inspector to take respondent to a private area and conduct a patdown and strip search. During the search the female inspector felt respondent's abdomen area and noticed a firm fullness, as if respondent were wearing a girdle. The search revealed no contraband, but the inspector noticed that respondent was wearing two pairs of elastic underpants with a paper towel lining the crotch area.

When respondent returned to the customs area and the female inspector reported her discoveries, the inspector in charge told respondent that he suspected she was smuggling drugs in her alimentary canal. Respondent agreed to the inspector's request that she be x-rayed at a hospital but in answer to the inspector's query stated that she was pregnant. She agreed to a pregnancy test before the x ray. Respondent withdrew the consent for an x ray when she learned that she would have to be handcuffed en route to the hospital. The inspector then gave respondent the option of returning to Colombia on the next available flight, agreeing to an x ray, or remaining in detention until she produced a monitored bowel movement that would confirm or rebut the inspectors' suspicions. Respondent chose the first option and was placed in a customs office under observation. She was told that if she went to the toilet she would have to use a wastebasket in the women's restroom, in order that female customs inspectors could inspect her stool for balloons or capsules carrying narcotics. The inspectors refused respondent's request to place a telephone call.

Respondent sat in the customs office, under observation, for the remainder of the night. During the night customs officials attempted to place respondent on a Mexican airline that was flying to Bogota via Mexico City in the morning. The airline refused to transport respondent because she lacked a Mexican visa necessary to land in Mexico City. Respondent was not permitted to leave, and was informed that she would be detained until she agreed to an x ray or her bowels moved. She remained detained in the customs office under observation, for most of the time curled up in a chair leaning to one side. She refused all offers of food and drink, and refused to use the toilet facilities. The Court of Appeals noted that she exhibited symptoms of discomfort consistent with "heroic efforts to resist the usual calls of nature."

At the shift change at 4 o'clock the next afternoon, almost 16 hours after her flight had landed, respondent still had not defecated or urinated or partaken of food or drink. At that time customs officials

> sought a court order authorizing a pregnancy test, an x ray, and a rectal examination. The Federal Magistrate issued an order just before midnight that evening, which authorized a rectal examination and involuntary x ray, provided that the physician in charge considered respondent's claim of pregnancy. Respondent was taken to a hospital and given a pregnancy test, which later turned out to be negative. Before the results of the pregnancy test were known, a physician conducted a rectal examination and removed from respondent's rectum a balloon containing a foreign substance. Respondent was then placed formally under arrest. By 4:10 a.m. respondent had passed 6 similar balloons; over the next four days she passed 88 balloons containing a total of 528 grams of 80% pure cocaine hydrochloride.

Montoya de Hernandez maintained that her detention and search were unreasonable under the Fourth Amendment. The Court, in an opinion by then-Justice Rehnquist, rejected her claim.

MISSOURI V. MCNEELY

569 U.S. 141 (2013)

JUSTICE SOTOMAYOR announced the judgment of the court and delivered the opinion of the court with respect to Parts I, II-A, II-B, and IV, and an opinion with respect to Parts II-C and III, in which JUSTICE SCALIA, JUSTICE GINSBURG, and JUSTICE KAGAN join.

In *Schmerber v. California*, 384 U.S. 757 (1966), this Court upheld a warrantless blood test of an individual arrested for driving under the influence of alcohol because the officer "might reasonably have believed that he was confronted with an emergency, in which the delay necessary to obtain a warrant, under the circumstances, threatened the destruction of evidence." The question presented here is whether the natural metabolization of alcohol in the bloodstream presents a *per se* exigency that justifies an exception to the Fourth Amendment's warrant requirement for nonconsensual blood testing in all drunk-driving cases. We conclude that it does not, and we hold, consistent with general Fourth Amendment principles, that exigency in this context must be determined case by case based on the totality of the circumstances.

I

While on highway patrol at approximately 2:08 a.m., a Missouri police officer stopped Tyler McNeely's truck after observing it exceed the posted speed limit and repeatedly cross the centerline. The officer noticed several signs that McNeely was intoxicated, including McNeely's bloodshot eyes, his slurred speech, and the smell of alcohol on his breath. McNeely acknowledged to the officer that he had consumed "a couple of beers" at a bar, and he appeared unsteady on his feet when he exited the truck. After McNeely performed poorly on a battery of field-sobriety tests and declined to use a portable breath-test device to measure his blood alcohol concentration, the officer placed him under arrest.

The officer began to transport McNeely to the station house. But when McNeely indicated that he would again refuse to provide a breath sample, the officer changed course and took McNeely to a nearby hospital for blood testing. The officer did not attempt to secure a warrant. Upon arrival at the hospital, the officer asked McNeely whether he would consent to a blood test. Reading from a standard implied consent form, the officer explained to McNeely that under state law refusal to submit voluntarily to the test would lead to the immediate revocation of his driver's license for one year and could be used against him in a future prosecution. McNeely nonetheless refused. The officer then directed a hospital lab technician to take a blood sample, and the sample was secured at approximately 2:35 a.m. Subsequent laboratory testing measured McNeely's BAC at 0.154 percent, which was well above the legal limit of 0.08 percent.

* * *

We granted certiorari to resolve a split of authority on the question whether the natural dissipation of alcohol in the bloodstream establishes a *per se* exigency that suffices on its own to justify an exception to the warrant requirement for nonconsensual blood testing in drunk-driving investigations.

II

A

* * *

To determine whether a law enforcement officer faced an emergency that justified acting without a warrant, this Court looks to the totality of circumstances. We apply this "finely tuned approach" to Fourth Amendment reasonableness in this context because the police action at issue lacks "the traditional justification that . . . a warrant . . . provides." Absent that established justification, "the fact-specific nature of the reasonableness inquiry," demands that we evaluate each case of alleged exigency based "on its own facts and circumstances."

Our decision in *Schmerber* applied this totality of the circumstances approach. In that case, the petitioner had suffered injuries in an automobile accident and was taken to the hospital. While he was there receiving treatment, a police officer arrested the petitioner for driving while under the influence of alcohol and ordered a blood test over his objection. After explaining that the warrant requirement applied generally to searches that intrude into the human body, we concluded that the warrantless blood test "in the present case" was nonetheless permissible because the officer "might reasonably have believed that he was confronted with an emergency, in which the delay necessary to obtain a warrant, under the circumstances, threatened 'the destruction of evidence.' "

In support of that conclusion, we observed that evidence could have been lost because "the percentage of alcohol in the blood begins to diminish shortly after drinking stops, as the body functions to eliminate it from the system." We added that "[p]articularly in a case such as this, where time had to be taken to bring the accused to a hospital and to investigate the scene of the accident, there was no time to seek out a magistrate and secure a warrant." "Given these special facts," we found that it was appropriate for the police to act without a warrant. We further held that the blood test at issue was a reasonable way to recover the evidence because it was highly effective, "involve[d] virtually no risk, trauma, or pain," and was conducted in a reasonable fashion "by a physician in a hospital environment according to accepted medical practices." And in conclusion, we noted that our judgment that there had been no Fourth Amendment violation was strictly based "on the facts of the present record."

Thus, our analysis in *Schmerber* fits comfortably within our case law applying the exigent circumstances exception. In finding the warrantless blood test reasonable in *Schmerber*, we considered all of the facts and circumstances of the particular case and carefully based our holding on those specific facts.

B

The State properly recognizes that the reasonableness of a warrantless search under the exigency exception to the warrant requirement must be evaluated based on the totality of the circumstances. But the State nevertheless seeks a *per se* rule for blood testing in drunk-driving cases. The State contends that whenever an officer has probable cause to believe an individual has been driving under the influence of alcohol, exigent circumstances will necessarily exist because BAC evidence is inherently evanescent. As a result, the State claims that so long as the officer has probable cause and the blood test is conducted in a reasonable manner, it is categorically reasonable for law enforcement to obtain the blood sample without a warrant.

It is true that as a result of the human body's natural metabolic processes, the alcohol level in a person's blood begins to dissipate once the alcohol is fully absorbed and continues to decline until the alcohol is eliminated. Testimony before the trial court in this case indicated that the percentage of alcohol in an individual's blood typically decreases by approximately 0.015 percent to 0.02 percent per hour once the alcohol has been fully absorbed. More precise calculations of the rate at which alcohol dissipates depend on various individual characteristics (such as weight, gender, and alcohol tolerance) and the circumstances in which the alcohol was consumed. Regardless of the exact elimination rate, it is sufficient for our purposes to note that because an individual's alcohol level gradually declines soon after he stops drinking, a significant delay in testing will negatively affect the probative value of the results. This fact was essential to our holding in *Schmerber*, as we recognized that, under the circumstances, further delay in order to secure a warrant after the time spent investigating the scene of the accident and transporting the injured suspect to the hospital to receive treatment would have threatened the destruction of evidence.

But it does not follow that we should depart from careful case-by-case assessment of exigency and adopt the categorical rule proposed by the State and its *amici*. In those drunk-driving investigations where police officers can reasonably obtain a warrant before a blood sample can be drawn without significantly undermining the efficacy of the search, the Fourth Amendment mandates that they do so. We do not doubt that some circumstances will make obtaining a warrant impractical such that the dissipation of alcohol from the bloodstream will support an exigency justifying a properly conducted warrantless blood test. That, however, is a reason to decide each case on its facts, as we did in *Schmerber*, not to accept the "considerable overgeneralization" that a *per se* rule would reflect.

The context of blood testing is different in critical respects from other destruction-of-evidence cases in which the police are truly confronted with a " 'now or never' " situation. In contrast to, for example, circumstances in which the suspect has control over easily disposable evidence, BAC evidence from a drunk-driving suspect naturally dissipates over time in a gradual and relatively predictable manner. Moreover, because a police officer must typically transport a drunk-driving suspect to a medical facility and obtain the assistance of someone with appropriate medical training before conducting a blood test, some delay between the time of the arrest or accident and the time of the test is inevitable regardless of whether police officers are required to obtain a warrant. This reality undermines the force of the State's contention, endorsed by the dissent, that we should recognize a categorical exception to the warrant requirement because BAC evidence "is actively being destroyed with every minute that passes." Consider, for example, a situation in which the warrant process will not significantly increase the delay before the blood test is conducted because an officer can take steps to secure a warrant while the suspect is being transported to a medical facility by another officer. In such a circumstance, there would be no plausible justification for an exception to the warrant requirement.

The State's proposed *per se* rule also fails to account for advances in the 47 years since *Schmerber* was decided that allow for the more expeditious processing of warrant applications, particularly in contexts like drunk-driving investigations where the evidence offered to establish probable cause is simple. The Federal Rules of Criminal Procedure were amended in 1977 to permit federal magistrate judges to issue a warrant based on sworn testimony communicated by telephone. As amended, the law now allows a federal magistrate judge to consider "information communicated by telephone or other reliable electronic means." States have also innovated. Well over a majority of States allow police officers or prosecutors to apply for search warrants remotely through various means, including telephonic or radio communication, electronic communication such as e-mail, and video conferencing. And in addition to technology-based developments, jurisdictions have found other ways to streamline the warrant process, such as by using standard-form warrant applications for drunk-driving investigations.

We by no means claim that telecommunications innovations have, will, or should eliminate all delay from the warrant-application process. Warrants inevitably take some time for police officers or prosecutors to complete and for magistrate judges to review. Telephonic and electronic warrants may still require officers to follow time-consuming formalities designed to create an adequate record, such as preparing a duplicate warrant before calling the magistrate judge. And improvements in communications technology do not guarantee that a magistrate judge will be available when an officer needs a warrant after making a late-night arrest. But technological developments that enable police officers to secure warrants more quickly, and do so without undermining the neutral magistrate judge's essential role as a check on police discretion, are relevant to an assessment of exigency. That is particularly so in this context, where BAC evidence is lost gradually and relatively predictably.

* * *

In short, while the natural dissipation of alcohol in the blood may support a finding of exigency in a specific case, as it did in *Schmerber*, it does not do so categorically. Whether a warrantless blood test of a drunk-driving suspect is reasonable must be determined case by case based on the totality of the circumstances.

C

In an opinion concurring in part and dissenting in part, the Chief Justice agrees that the State's proposed *per se* rule is overbroad because "[f]or exigent circumstances to justify a warrantless search . . . there must . . . be 'no time to secure a warrant.' " But the Chief Justice then goes on to suggest his own categorical rule under which a warrantless blood draw is permissible if the officer could not secure a warrant (or reasonably believed he could not secure a warrant) in the time it takes to transport the suspect to a hospital or similar facility and obtain medical assistance. Although we agree that delay inherent to the blood-testing process is relevant to evaluating exigency, we decline to substitute the Chief Justice's modified *per se* rule for our traditional totality of the circumstances analysis.

For one thing, making exigency completely dependent on the window of time between an arrest and a blood test produces odd consequences. Under the Chief Justice's rule, if a police officer serendipitously stops a suspect near an emergency room, the officer may conduct a nonconsensual warrantless blood draw even if all agree that a warrant could be obtained with very little delay under the circumstances (perhaps with far less delay than an average ride to the hospital in the jurisdiction). The rule would also distort law enforcement incentives. As with the State's *per se* rule, the Chief Justice's rule might discourage efforts to expedite the warrant process because it categorically authorizes warrantless blood draws so long as it takes more time to secure a warrant than to obtain medical assistance. On the flip side, making the requirement of independent judicial oversight turn exclusively on the amount of time that elapses between an arrest and BAC testing could induce police departments and individual officers to minimize testing delay to the detriment of other values. The Chief Justice correctly observes that "[t]his case involves medical personnel drawing blood at a medical facility, not police officers doing so by the side of the road." But the Chief Justice does not say that roadside blood draws are necessarily unreasonable, and if we accepted the Chief Justice's approach, they would become a more attractive option for the police.

III

The remaining arguments advanced in support of a *per se* exigency rule are unpersuasive.

The State and several of its *amici*, including the United States, express concern that a case-by-case approach to exigency will not provide adequate guidance to law enforcement officers deciding whether to conduct a blood test of a drunk-driving suspect without a warrant. The Chief Justice and the dissent also raise this concern. While the desire for a bright-line rule is understandable, the Fourth Amendment will not tolerate adoption of an overly broad categorical approach that would dilute the warrant requirement in a context where significant privacy interests are at stake. Moreover, a case-by-case approach is hardly unique within our Fourth Amendment jurisprudence. Numerous police actions are judged based on fact-intensive, totality of the circumstances analyses rather than according to categorical rules, including in situations that are more likely to require police officers to make difficult split-second judgments.

Next, the State and the United States contend that the privacy interest implicated by blood draws of drunk-driving suspects is relatively minimal. That is so, they claim, both because motorists have a diminished expectation of privacy and because our cases have repeatedly indicated that blood testing is commonplace in society and typically involves "virtually no risk, trauma, or pain."

But the fact that people are "accorded less privacy in . . . automobiles because of th[e] compelling governmental need for regulation," does not diminish a motorist's privacy interest in preventing an agent of the government from piercing his skin. As to the nature of a blood test conducted in a medical setting by trained personnel, it is concededly less intrusive than other bodily invasions we have found unreasonable. For that reason, we have held that medically drawn blood tests are reasonable in appropriate circumstances. We have never retreated, however, from our recognition that any compelled intrusion into the human body implicates significant, constitutionally protected privacy interests.

Finally, the State and its *amici* point to the compelling governmental interest in combating drunk driving and contend that prompt BAC testing, including through blood testing, is vital to pursuit of that interest. They argue that is particularly so because, in addition to laws that make it illegal to operate a motor vehicle under the influence of alcohol, all 50 States and the District of Columbia have enacted laws that make it *per se* unlawful to operate a motor vehicle with a BAC of over 0.08 percent. See National Highway Traffic Safety Admin., Alcohol and Highway Safety: A Review of the State of Knowledge 167 (No. 811374, Mar. 2011).[8] To enforce these provisions, they reasonably assert, accurate BAC evidence is critical.

* * *

But the general importance of the government's interest in this area does not justify departing from the warrant requirement without showing exigent circumstances that make securing a warrant impractical in a particular case. To the extent that the State and its *amici* contend that applying the traditional Fourth Amendment totality-of-the-circumstances analysis to determine whether an exigency justified a warrantless search will undermine the governmental interest in preventing and prosecuting drunk-driving offenses, we are not convinced.

* * *

IV

* * *

Because this case was argued on the broad proposition that drunk-driving cases present a *per se* exigency, the arguments and the record do not provide the Court with an adequate analytic framework for a detailed discussion of all the relevant factors that can be taken into account in determining the reasonableness of acting without a warrant. It suffices to say that the metabolization of alcohol in the bloodstream and the ensuing loss of evidence are among the factors that must be considered in deciding

[8] Pursuant to congressional directive, the NHTSA conditions federal highway grants on States' adoption of laws making it a per se offense to operate a motor vehicle with a BAC of 0.08 percent or greater. In addition, 32 States and the District of Columbia have adopted laws that impose heightened penalties for operating a motor vehicle at or above a BAC of 0.15 percent.

whether a warrant is required. No doubt, given the large number of arrests for this offense in different jurisdictions nationwide, cases will arise when anticipated delays in obtaining a warrant will justify a blood test without judicial authorization, for in every case the law must be concerned that evidence is being destroyed. But that inquiry ought not to be pursued here where the question is not properly before this Court. Having rejected the sole argument presented to us challenging the Missouri Supreme Court's decision, we affirm its judgment.

* * *

JUSTICE KENNEDY, concurring in part.

I join Parts I, II-A, II-B, and IV of the opinion for the Court.

* * *

As the opinion of the Court is correct to note, the instant case, by reason of the way in which it was presented and decided in the state courts, does not provide a framework where it is prudent to hold any more than that always dispensing with a warrant for a blood test when a driver is arrested for being under the influence of alcohol is inconsistent with the Fourth Amendment.

CHIEF JUSTICE ROBERTS, with whom JUSTICE BREYER and JUSTICE ALITO join, concurring in part and dissenting in part.

A police officer reading this Court's opinion would have no idea—no idea—what the Fourth Amendment requires of him, once he decides to obtain a blood sample from a drunk driving suspect who has refused a breathalyzer test. I have no quarrel with the Court's "totality of the circumstances" approach as a general matter; that is what our cases require. But the circumstances in drunk driving cases are often typical, and the Court should be able to offer guidance on how police should handle cases like the one before us.

In my view, the proper rule is straightforward. Our cases establish that there is an exigent circumstances exception to the warrant requirement. That exception applies when there is a compelling need to prevent the imminent destruction of important evidence, and there is no time to obtain a warrant. The natural dissipation of alcohol in the bloodstream constitutes not only the imminent but ongoing destruction of critical evidence. That would qualify as an exigent circumstance, except that there may be time to secure a warrant before blood can be drawn. If there is, an officer must seek a warrant. If an officer could reasonably conclude that there is not, the exigent circumstances exception applies by its terms, and the blood may be drawn without a warrant.

* * *

II

A

The reasonable belief that critical evidence is being destroyed gives rise to a compelling need for blood draws in cases like this one. Here, in fact, there is not simply a belief that any alcohol in the bloodstream will be destroyed; it is a biological certainty. Alcohol dissipates from the bloodstream at a rate of 0.01 percent to 0.025 percent per hour. Evidence is literally disappearing by the minute. That certainty makes this case an even stronger one than usual for application of the exigent circumstances exception.

And that evidence is important. A serious and deadly crime is at issue. According to the Department of Transportation, in 2011, one person died every 53 minutes due to drinking and driving. National Highway Traffic Safety Admin., Traffic Safety Facts, 2011 Data 1 (No. 811700, Dec. 2012). No surprise then that drinking and driving is punished severely, including with jail time. McNeely, for instance, faces up to four years in prison.

Evidence of a driver's blood alcohol concentration is crucial to obtain convictions for such crimes. All 50 States and the District of Columbia have laws providing that it is *per se* illegal to drive with a BAC of 0.08 percent or higher. Most States also have laws establishing additional penalties for drivers who drive with a "high BAC," often defined as 0.15 percent or above. NHTSA, Digest of Impaired Driving and Selected Beverage Control Laws, pp. vii, x–xviii (No. 811673, Oct. 2012). BAC evidence clearly matters. And when drivers refuse breathalyzers, as McNeely did here, a blood draw becomes necessary to obtain that evidence.

* * *

McNeely contends that there is no compelling need for a warrantless blood draw, because if there is some alcohol left in the blood by the time a warrant is obtained, the State can use math and science to work backwards and identify a defendant's BAC at the time he was driving. But that's not good enough. We have indicated that exigent circumstances justify warrantless entry when drugs are about to be flushed down the toilet. We have not said that, because there could well be drug paraphernalia elsewhere in the home, or because a defendant's co-conspirator might testify to the amount of drugs involved, the drugs themselves are not crucial and there is no compelling need for warrantless entry.

The same approach should govern here. There is a compelling need to search because alcohol—the nearly conclusive evidence of a serious crime—is dissipating from the bloodstream. The need is no less compelling because the police might be able to acquire second-best evidence some other way.

B

For exigent circumstances to justify a warrantless search, however, there must also be "no time to secure a warrant." In this respect, obtaining a blood sample from a suspected drunk driver differs from other exigent circumstances cases.

Importantly, there is typically delay between the moment a drunk driver is stopped and the time his blood can be drawn. Drunk drivers often end up in an emergency room, but they are not usually pulled over in front of one. In most exigent circumstances situations, police are just outside the door to a home. Inside, evidence is about to be destroyed, a person is about to be injured, or a fire has broken out. Police can enter promptly and must do so to respond effectively to the emergency. But when police pull a person over on suspicion of drinking and driving, they cannot test his blood right away. There is a time-consuming obstacle to their search, in the form of a trip to the hospital and perhaps a wait to see a medical professional. In this case, for example, approximately 25 minutes elapsed between the time the police stopped McNeely and the time his blood was drawn.

As noted, the fact that alcohol dissipates gradually from the bloodstream does not diminish the compelling need for a search—critical evidence is still disappearing. But the fact that the dissipation persists for some time means that the police—although they may not be able to do anything about it right away—may still be able to respond to the ongoing destruction of evidence later on.

There might, therefore, be time to obtain a warrant in many cases. As the Court explains, police can often request warrants rather quickly these days. At least 30 States provide for electronic warrant applications. In many States, a police officer can call a judge, convey the necessary information, and be authorized to affix the judge's signature to a warrant. Utah has an e-warrant procedure where a police officer enters information into a system, the system notifies a prosecutor, and upon approval the officer forwards the information to a magistrate, who can electronically return a warrant to the officer. Judges have been known to issue warrants in as little as five minutes. And in one county in Kansas, police officers can e-mail warrant requests to judges' iPads; judges have signed such warrants and e-mailed them back to officers in less than 15 minutes. The police are presumably familiar with the mechanics and time involved in the warrant process in their particular jurisdiction.

III

A

In a case such as this, applying the exigent circumstances exception to the general warrant requirement of the Fourth Amendment seems straightforward: If there is time to secure a warrant before blood can be drawn, the police must seek one. If an officer could reasonably conclude that there is not sufficient time to seek and receive a warrant, or he applies for one but does not receive a response before blood can be drawn, a warrantless blood draw may ensue.

Requiring police to apply for a warrant if practicable increases the likelihood that a neutral, detached judicial officer will review the case, helping to ensure that there is probable cause for any search and that any search is reasonable. We have already held that forced blood draws can be constitutional—that such searches can be reasonable—but that does not change the fact that they are significant bodily intrusions. See *Schmerber*, 384 U.S., at 770 (upholding a warrantless forced blood draw but noting the "importance of informed, detached and deliberate determinations of the issue whether or not to invade another's body in search of evidence of guilt" as "indisputable and great"). Requiring a warrant whenever practicable helps ensure that when blood draws occur, they are indeed justified.

At the same time, permitting the police to act without a warrant to prevent the imminent destruction of evidence is well established in Fourth Amendment law. There is no reason to preclude application of that exception in drunk driving cases simply because it may take the police some time to be able to respond to the undoubted destruction of evidence, or because the destruction occurs continuously over an uncertain period.

And that is so even in situations where police have requested a warrant but do not receive a timely response. An officer who reasonably concluded there was no time to secure a warrant may have blood drawn from a suspect upon arrival at a medical facility. There is no reason an officer should be in a worse position, simply because he sought a warrant prior to his arrival at the hospital.

B

The Court resists the foregoing, contending that the question presented somehow inhibits such a focused analysis in this case. It does not. The question presented is whether a warrantless blood draw is permissible under the Fourth Amendment "based upon the natural dissipation of alcohol in the bloodstream." The majority answers "It depends," and so do I. The difference is that the majority offers no additional guidance, merely instructing courts and police officers to consider the totality of the circumstances. I believe more meaningful guidance can be provided about how to handle the typical cases, and nothing about the question presented prohibits affording that guidance.

A plurality of the Court also expresses concern that my approach will discourage state and local efforts to expedite the warrant application process. That is not plausible: Police and prosecutors need warrants in a wide variety of situations, and often need them quickly. They certainly would not prefer a slower process, just because that might obviate the need to ask for a warrant in the occasional drunk driving case in which a blood draw is necessary. The plurality's suggestion also overlooks the interest of law enforcement in the protection a warrant provides.

The Court is correct when it says that every case must be considered on its particular facts. But the pertinent facts in drunk driving cases are often the same, and the police should know how to act in recurring factual situations. Simply put, when a drunk driving suspect fails field sobriety tests and refuses a breathalyzer, whether a warrant is required for a blood draw should come down to whether there is time to secure one.

* * *

JUSTICE THOMAS, dissenting.

This case requires the Court to decide whether the Fourth Amendment prohibits an officer from obtaining a blood sample without a warrant when there is probable cause to believe that a suspect has been driving under the influence of alcohol. Because the body's natural metabolization of alcohol inevitably destroys evidence of the crime, it constitutes an exigent circumstance. As a result, I would hold that a warrantless blood draw does not violate the Fourth Amendment.

I

* * *

B

* * *

The rapid destruction of evidence acknowledged by the parties, the majority, and *Schmerber*'s exigency determination occurs in *every* situation where police have probable cause to arrest a drunk driver. In turn, that destruction of evidence implicates the exigent-circumstances doctrine. See *Cupp v. Murphy*, 412 U.S. 291 (1973). In *Cupp*, officers questioning a murder suspect observed a spot on the suspect's finger that they believed might be dried blood. After the suspect began making obvious efforts to remove the spots from his hands, the officers took samples without obtaining either his consent or a warrant. Following a Fourth Amendment challenge to this search, the Court held that the "ready destructibility of the evidence" and the suspect's observed efforts to destroy it "justified the police in subjecting him to the very limited search necessary to preserve the highly evanescent evidence they found under his fingernails."

In this case, a similar exigency is present. Just as the suspect's efforts to destroy "highly evanescent evidence" gave rise to the exigency in *Cupp*, the natural metabolization of blood alcohol concentration creates an exigency once police have probable cause to believe the driver is drunk. It naturally follows that police may conduct a search in these circumstances.

* * *

II

In today's decision, the Court elides the certainty of evidence destruction in drunk-driving cases and focuses primarily on the time necessary for destruction. In doing so, it turns the exigency inquiry into a question about the amount of evidentiary destruction police must permit before they may act without a warrant. That inquiry is inconsistent with the actual exigency at issue: the uncontested destruction of evidence due to metabolization of alcohol. Moreover, the Court's facts-and-circumstances analysis will be difficult to administer, a particularly important concern in the Fourth Amendment context.

The Court's judgment reflects nothing more than a vague notion that everything will come out right most of the time so long as the delay is not too lengthy. But hard percentage lines have meaningful legal consequences in the drunk-driving context. The fact that police will be able to retrieve *some* evidence before it is all destroyed is simply not relevant to the exigency inquiry.

* * *

Further, the Court nowhere explains how an officer in the field is to apply the facts-and-circumstances test it adopts. First, officers do not have the facts needed to assess how much time can pass before too little evidence remains. They will never know how intoxicated a suspect is at the time of arrest. Otherwise, there would be no need for testing. Second, they will not know how long it will take to roust a magistrate from his bed, reach the hospital, or obtain a blood sample once there. As the Minnesota Supreme Court recognized in rejecting arguments like those adopted by the Court today:

> [T]he officer has no control over how long it would take to travel to a judge or the judge's availability. The officer also may not know the time of the suspect's last drink, the amount of alcohol consumed, or the rate at which the suspect will metabolize alcohol. Finally, an officer cannot know how long it will take to obtain the blood sample once the suspect is brought to the hospital. Under a totality of the circumstances test, an officer would be called upon to speculate on each of these considerations and predict how long the most probative evidence of the defendant's blood-alcohol level would continue to exist before a blood sample was no longer reliable.

State v. Shriner, 751 N.W.2d 538, 549 (2008) (footnote omitted).

The Court should not adopt a rule that requires police to guess whether they will be able to obtain a warrant before "too much" evidence is destroyed, for the police lack reliable information concerning the relevant variables.

* * *

The availability of telephonic warrant applications is not an answer to this conundrum. For one thing, Missouri still requires written warrant applications and affidavits, rendering the Court's 50-State survey irrelevant to the actual disposition of this case. But even if telephonic applications were available in Missouri, the same difficulties would arise. As the majority correctly recognizes, "[w]arrants inevitably take some time for police officers or prosecutors to complete and for magistrate judges to review." During that time, evidence is destroyed, and police who have probable cause to believe a crime has been committed should not have to guess how long it will take to secure a warrant.

* * *

Points for Discussion

1. Part III of Justice Sotomayor's opinion (which is not part of the majority opinion) notes that the states all made driving with a .08% BAC illegal *per se* because the federal government conditioned highway funds on the passage of such legislation. Why is it important to point that out? How does the fact that the development of state law in this area was prompted by the promise of federal money affect adjudication of this issue? Relatedly, what is the relevance of the dissent's ominous observation that drunk driving is a "serious and deadly crime"? Is it that the Fourth Amendment's protections need to be relaxed to allow the government to thwart certain serious crimes? Do you think the principal dissent would support a rule that the headquarters of tobacco companies or oil companies can be raided without a warrant because smoking and climate change are both serious and deadly? Is "obtaining convictions" the only (or best) way to reduce drunk driving?

2. The principal dissent claims that the plurality "overlooks the interest of law enforcement in the protection a warrant provides." Aren't warrants supposed to protect people *from* law enforcement officers? What protection is the dissent referring to? What assumption is the dissent making about the purpose warrants serve in the constitutional scheme? What purpose does the plurality seem to believe warrants serve?

3. The testing of drunk driving suspects has occupied a disproportionate amount of the Court's time of late. In 2016, the Court held in *Birchfield v. North Dakota*, 136 S.Ct. 2160, that the states may compel suspected drunk drivers to take warrantless breath tests, but not warrantless blood tests. In 2019, the Court held in *Mitchell v. Wisconsin*, 139 S.Ct. 2525 that exigent circumstances permitted the extraction of blood from an unconscious suspect who could neither take a breath test nor consent to a blood test.

B. HOUSES

One of the principal evils the Fourth Amendment was designed to remedy was the breaking and entering of homes by public officials. In this section we step behind the Court's repeated pronouncements about the sanctity of the home and examine how the privacy of the home is treated in practice.

WELSH V. WISCONSIN

466 U.S. 740 (1984)

JUSTICE BRENNAN delivered the opinion of the court.

Payton v. New York, 445 U.S. 573 (1980), held that, absent probable cause and exigent circumstances, warrantless arrests in the home are prohibited by the Fourth Amendment. But the Court in that case explicitly refused "to consider the sort of emergency or dangerous situation, described in our cases as 'exigent circumstances,' that would justify a warrantless entry into a home for the purpose of either arrest or search." Certiorari was granted in this case to decide at least one aspect of the unresolved question: whether, and if so under what circumstances, the Fourth Amendment prohibits the police from making a warrantless night entry of a person's home in order to arrest him for a nonjailable traffic offense.

I

A

Shortly before 9 o'clock on the rainy night of April 24, 1978, a lone witness, Randy Jablonic, observed a car being driven erratically. After changing speeds and veering from side to side, the car eventually swerved off the road and came to a stop in an open field. No damage to any person or property occurred. Concerned about the driver and fearing that the car would get back on the highway, Jablonic drove his truck up behind the car so as to block it from returning to the road. Another passerby also stopped at the scene, and Jablonic asked her to call the police. Before the police arrived, however, the driver of the car emerged from his vehicle, approached Jablonic's truck, and asked Jablonic for a ride home. Jablonic instead suggested that they wait for assistance in removing or repairing the car. Ignoring Jablonic's suggestion, the driver walked away from the scene.

A few minutes later, the police arrived and questioned Jablonic. He told one officer what he had seen, specifically noting that the driver was either very inebriated or very sick. The officer checked the motor vehicle registration of the abandoned car and learned that it was registered to the petitioner, Edward G. Welsh. In addition, the officer noted that the petitioner's residence was a short distance from the scene, and therefore easily within walking distance.

Without securing any type of warrant, the police proceeded to the petitioner's home, arriving about 9 p.m. When the petitioner's stepdaughter answered the door, the police gained entry into the house. Proceeding upstairs to the petitioner's bedroom, they found him lying naked in bed. At this point, the petitioner was placed under arrest for driving or operating a motor vehicle while under the influence of an intoxicant, in violation of Wis. Stat. § 346.63(1) (1977). The petitioner was taken to the police station, where he refused to submit to a breath-analysis test.

* * *

C

As noted, in this case the petitioner refused to submit to a breath test; he subsequently filed a timely request for a refusal hearing. Before that hearing was held, however, the State filed a criminal complaint against the petitioner for driving while intoxicated. The petitioner responded by filing a motion to dismiss the complaint, relying on his contention that the underlying arrest was invalid. After receiving evidence at a hearing on this motion in July 1980, the trial court concluded that the criminal complaint would not be dismissed because the existence of both probable cause and exigent circumstances justified the warrantless arrest. The decision at the refusal hearing, which was not held until September 1980, was therefore preordained. In fact, the primary issue at the refusal hearing—whether the petitioner acted reasonably in refusing to submit to a breath test because he was unlawfully placed under arrest—had already been determined two months earlier by the same trial court.

As expected, after the refusal hearing, the trial court concluded that the arrest of the petitioner was lawful and that the petitioner's refusal to take the breath test was therefore unreasonable. Accordingly, the court issued an order suspending the petitioner's operating license for 60 days. On appeal, the suspension order was vacated by the Wisconsin Court of Appeals. Contrary to the trial court, the appellate court concluded that the warrantless arrest of the petitioner in his home violated the Fourth Amendment because the State, although demonstrating probable cause to arrest, had not established the existence of exigent circumstances. The petitioner's refusal to submit to a breath test was therefore reasonable. The Supreme Court of Wisconsin in turn reversed the Court of Appeals, relying on the existence of three factors that it believed constituted exigent circumstances: the need for "hot pursuit" of a suspect, the need to prevent physical harm to the offender and the public, and the need to prevent destruction of evidence. Because of the important Fourth Amendment implications of the decision below, we granted certiorari.

* * *

II

* * *

Our hesitation in finding exigent circumstances, especially when warrantless arrests in the home are at issue, is particularly appropriate when the underlying offense for which there is probable cause to arrest is relatively minor. Before agents of the government may invade the sanctity of the home, the burden is on the government to demonstrate exigent circumstances that overcome the presumption of unreasonableness that attaches to all warrantless home entries. When the government's interest is only to arrest for a minor offense, that presumption of unreasonableness is difficult to rebut, and the government usually should be allowed to make such arrests only with a warrant issued upon probable cause by a neutral and detached magistrate.

* * *

Application of this principle to the facts of the present case is relatively straightforward. The petitioner was arrested in the privacy of his own bedroom for a noncriminal, traffic offense. The State attempts to justify the arrest by relying on the hot-pursuit doctrine, on the threat to public safety, and on the need to preserve evidence of the petitioner's blood-alcohol level. On the facts of this case, however, the claim of hot pursuit is unconvincing because there was no immediate or continuous pursuit of the petitioner from the scene of a crime. Moreover, because the petitioner had already arrived home, and had abandoned his car at the scene of the accident, there was little remaining threat to the public safety. Hence, the only potential emergency claimed by the State was the need to ascertain the petitioner's blood-alcohol level.

Even assuming, however, that the underlying facts would support a finding of this exigent circumstance, mere similarity to other cases involving the imminent destruction of evidence is not sufficient. The State of Wisconsin has chosen to classify the first offense for driving while intoxicated as a noncriminal, civil forfeiture offense for which no imprisonment is possible. This is the best indication of the State's interest in precipitating an arrest, and is one that can be easily identified both by the courts and by officers faced with a decision to arrest. See n. 6, supra. Given this expression of the State's interest, a warrantless home arrest cannot be upheld simply because evidence of the petitioner's blood-alcohol level might have dissipated while the police obtained a warrant. To allow a warrantless home entry on these facts would be to approve unreasonable police behavior that the principles of the Fourth Amendment will not sanction.

III

The Supreme Court of Wisconsin let stand a warrantless, nighttime entry into the petitioner's home to arrest him for a civil traffic offense. Such an arrest, however, is clearly prohibited by the special protection afforded the individual in his home by the Fourth Amendment. The petitioner's arrest was therefore invalid, the judgment of the Supreme Court of Wisconsin is vacated, and the case is remanded for further proceedings not inconsistent with this opinion.

THE CHIEF JUSTICE would dismiss the writ as having been improvidently granted and defer resolution of the question presented to a more appropriate case.

JUSTICE BLACKMUN, concurring.

* * *

[I]t is amazing to me that one of our great States—one which, by its highway signs, proclaims to be diligent and emphatic in its prosecution of the drunken driver—still classifies driving while intoxicated as a civil violation that allows only a money forfeiture of not more than $300 so long as it is a first offense. The State, like the indulgent parent, hesitates to discipline the spoiled child very much, even though the child is engaging in an act that is dangerous to others who are law abiding and helpless in the face of the child's act. Our personal convenience still weighs heavily in the balance, and the highway deaths and injuries continue. But if Wisconsin and other States choose by legislation thus to regulate their penalty structure, there is, unfortunately, nothing in the United States Constitution that says they may not do so.

JUSTICE WHITE, with whom JUSTICE REHNQUIST joins, dissenting.

* * *

First, it is not at all clear to me that the important constitutional question decided today should be resolved in a case such as this. Although Welsh argues vigorously that the State violated his federal constitutional rights, he at no point relied on the exclusionary rule, and he does not contend that the Federal Constitution or federal law provides the remedy he seeks. As a general rule, this Court "reviews judgments, not statements in opinions." *Black v. Cutter Laboratories*, 351 U.S. 292, 297 (1956). Because the Court does not purport to hold that federal law requires the conclusion that Welsh's refusal to submit to a sobriety test was reasonable, it is not clear to me how the judgment of the Supreme Court of Wisconsin offends federal law.

It is true that under the Wisconsin statutory scheme, an arrestee's refusal to take a breath or blood test would be reasonable and would not justify revocation of operating privileges if the underlying arrest violated the Fourth Amendment or was otherwise unlawful. What the State has done, however, is to attach consequences to an arrest found unlawful under the Federal Constitution that we have never decided federal law itself would attach. The Court has occasionally taken jurisdiction over cases in which the States have provided remedies for violations of federally defined obligations. But it has done so in contexts where state remedies are employed to further federal policies. The Fourth Amendment of course applies to the police conduct at issue here. In providing that a driver may reasonably refuse to submit to a sobriety test if he was unlawfully arrested, Wisconsin's Legislature and courts are pursuing a course that they apparently hope will reduce police illegality and safeguard their citizens' rights. Although the State is entitled to draw this conclusion and to implement it as a matter of state law, I am very doubtful that the policies underlying the Fourth Amendment would require exclusion of the fruits of an illegal arrest in a civil proceeding to remove from the highways a person who insists on driving while under the influence of alcohol. If that is the case—if it would violate no federal policy to revoke Welsh's license even if his arrest was illegal—there is no satisfactory reason for us to review the Supreme Court of Wisconsin's judgment affirming the revocation, even if that court mistakenly applied the Fourth Amendment. For me, this is ample reason not to disturb the judgment.

In any event, I believe that the state court properly construed the Fourth Amendment. It follows from *Payton v. New York*, 445 U.S. 573 (1980), that warrantless nonfelony arrests in the home are prohibited by the Fourth Amendment absent probable cause and exigent circumstances. Although I continue to believe that the Court erred in *Payton* in requiring exigent circumstances to justify warrantless in-home felony arrests, I do not reject the obvious logical implication of the Court's decision. But I see little to commend an approach that looks to "the nature of the underlying offense as an important factor to be considered in the exigent-circumstances calculus."

The gravity of the underlying offense is, I concede, a factor to be considered in determining whether the delay that attends the warrant-issuance process will endanger officers or other persons. The seriousness of the offense with which a suspect may be charged also bears on the likelihood that he will flee and escape apprehension if not arrested immediately. But if, under all the circumstances of a particular case, an officer has probable cause to believe that the delay involved in procuring an arrest warrant will gravely endanger the officer or other persons or will result in the suspect's escape, I perceive no reason to disregard those exigencies on the ground that the offense for which the suspect is sought is a "minor" one.

* * *

A warrantless home entry to arrest is no more intrusive when the crime is "minor" than when the suspect is sought in connection with a serious felony. The variable factor, if there is one, is the governmental interest that will be served by the warrantless entry. Wisconsin's Legislature and its Supreme Court have both concluded that warrantless in-home arrests under circumstances like those present here promote valid and substantial state interests. In determining whether the challenged governmental conduct was reasonable, we are not bound by these determinations. But nothing in our previous decisions suggests that the fact that a State has defined an offense as a misdemeanor for a variety of social, cultural, and political reasons necessarily requires the conclusion that warrantless in-home arrests designed to prevent the imminent destruction or removal of evidence of that offense are always impermissible. If anything, the Court's prior decisions support the opposite conclusion.

* * *

Even if the Court were correct in concluding that the gravity of the offense is an important factor to consider in determining whether a warrantless in-home arrest is justified by exigent circumstances, it has erred in assessing the seriousness of the civil-forfeiture offense for which the officers thought they were arresting Welsh. As the Court observes, the statutory scheme in force at the time of Welsh's arrest provided that the first offense for driving under the influence of alcohol involved no potential incarceration. Nevertheless, this Court has long recognized the compelling state interest in highway safety, the Supreme Court of Wisconsin identified a number of factors suggesting a substantial and growing governmental interest in apprehending and convicting intoxicated drivers and in deterring alcohol-related offenses, and recent actions of the Wisconsin Legislature evince its "belief that significant benefits, in the reduction of the costs attributable to drunk driving, may be achieved by the increased apprehension and conviction of even first time . . . offenders." Note, 1983 Wis. L. Rev. 1023, 1053.

* * *

Points for Discussion

1. Note that *Welsh* raises the same concerns about exigency and the dissipation of evidence that are raised in *McNeely*, *Birchfield*, and *Mitchell.* What does the disposition of this case tell us about the relative intrusions of entering the home and testing a suspect's breath or blood?

2. The dissent argues that this case should not have been decided because no constitutional issue was at stake. Because a state is not required to apply the exclusionary rule to civil proceedings (*see, e.g., I.N.S. v. Lopez-Mendoza*, 468 U.S. 1032, 1050 (1984)), the dissenters argue that whether the Fourth Amendment was violated was simply irrelevant to the Wisconsin state courts' proceedings.

ILLINOIS V. MCARTHUR

531 U.S. 326 (2001)

JUSTICE BREYER delivered the opinion of the court.

Police officers, with probable cause to believe that a man had hidden marijuana in his home, prevented that man from entering the home for about two hours while they obtained a search warrant. We must decide whether those officers violated the Fourth Amendment. We conclude that the officers acted reasonably. They did not violate the Amendment's requirements. And we reverse an Illinois court's holding to the contrary.

I

A

On April 2, 1997, Tera McArthur asked two police officers to accompany her to the trailer where she lived with her husband, Charles, so that they could keep the peace while she removed her belongings. The two officers, Assistant Chief John Love and Officer Richard Skidis, arrived with Tera at the trailer at about 3:15 p.m. Tera went inside, where Charles was present. The officers remained outside.

When Tera emerged after collecting her possessions, she spoke to Chief Love, who was then on the porch. She suggested he check the trailer because "Chuck had dope in there." She added (in Love's words) that she had seen Chuck "slid[e] some dope underneath the couch."

Love knocked on the trailer door, told Charles what Tera had said, and asked for permission to search the trailer, which Charles denied. Love then sent Officer Skidis with Tera to get a search warrant.

Love told Charles, who by this time was also on the porch, that he could not reenter the trailer unless a police officer accompanied him. Charles subsequently reentered the trailer two or three times (to get cigarettes and to make phone calls), and each time Love stood just inside the door to observe what Charles did.

Officer Skidis obtained the warrant by about 5 p.m. He returned to the trailer and, along with other officers, searched it. The officers found under the sofa a marijuana pipe, a box for marijuana (called a "one-hitter" box), and a small amount of marijuana. They then arrested Charles.

* * *

II

A

* * *

We conclude that the restriction at issue was reasonable, and hence lawful, in light of the following circumstances, which we consider in combination. First, the police had probable cause to believe that McArthur's trailer home contained evidence of a crime and contraband, namely, unlawful drugs. The police had had an opportunity to speak with Tera McArthur and make at least a very rough assessment of her reliability. They knew she had had a firsthand opportunity to observe her husband's behavior, in particular with respect to the drugs at issue. And they thought, with good reason, that her report to them reflected that opportunity.

Second, the police had good reason to fear that, unless restrained, McArthur would destroy the drugs before they could return with a warrant. They reasonably might have thought that McArthur realized that his wife knew about his marijuana stash; observed that she was angry or frightened enough to ask the police to accompany her; saw that after leaving the trailer she had spoken with the police; and noticed that she had walked off with one policeman while leaving the other outside to observe the trailer. They reasonably could have concluded that McArthur, consequently suspecting an imminent search, would, if given the chance, get rid of the drugs fast.

Third, the police made reasonable efforts to reconcile their law enforcement needs with the demands of personal privacy. They neither searched the trailer nor arrested McArthur before obtaining a warrant. Rather, they imposed a significantly less restrictive restraint, preventing McArthur only from entering the trailer unaccompanied. They left his home and his belongings intact—until a neutral Magistrate, finding probable cause, issued a warrant.

Fourth, the police imposed the restraint for a limited period of time, namely, two hours. As far as the record reveals, this time period was no longer than reasonably necessary for the police, acting with diligence, to obtain the warrant. Given the nature of the intrusion and the law enforcement interest at stake, this brief seizure of the premises was permissible.

* * *

C

Nor are we persuaded by the countervailing considerations that the parties or lower courts have raised. McArthur argues that the police proceeded without probable cause. But McArthur has waived this argument. And, in any event, it is without merit.

The Appellate Court of Illinois concluded that the police could not order McArthur to stay outside his home because McArthur's porch, where he stood at the time, was part of his home; hence the order "amounted to a constructive eviction" of McArthur from his residence. This Court has held, however, that a person standing in the doorway of a house is "in a 'public' place," and hence subject to arrest without a warrant permitting entry of the home. Regardless, we do not believe the difference to which the Appellate Court points—porch versus, *e.g.,* front walk—could make a significant difference here as to the reasonableness of the police restraint; and that, from the Fourth Amendment's perspective, is what matters.

The Appellate Court also found negatively significant the fact that Chief Love, with McArthur's consent, stepped inside the trailer's doorway to observe McArthur when McArthur reentered the trailer on two or three occasions. McArthur, however, reentered simply for his own convenience, to make phone calls and to obtain cigarettes. Under these circumstances, the reasonableness of the greater restriction (preventing reentry) implies the reasonableness of the lesser (permitting reentry conditioned on observation).

Finally, McArthur points to a case (and we believe it is the only case) that he believes offers direct support, namely, *Welsh v. Wisconsin.* In *Welsh,* this Court held that police could not enter a home without a warrant in order to prevent the loss of evidence (namely, the defendant's blood alcohol level) of the "nonjailable traffic offense" of driving while intoxicated. McArthur notes that his two convictions are for misdemeanors, which, he says, are as minor, and he adds that the restraint, keeping him out of his home, was nearly as serious.

We nonetheless find significant distinctions. The evidence at issue here was of crimes that were "jailable," not "nonjailable." In *Welsh,* we noted that, "[g]iven that the classification of state crimes differs widely among the States, the penalty that may attach to any particular offense seems to provide the clearest and most consistent indication of the State's interest in arresting individuals suspected of committing that offense." The same reasoning applies here, where class C misdemeanors include such widely diverse offenses as drag racing, drinking alcohol in a railroad car or on a railroad platform, bribery by a candidate for public office, and assault.

And the restriction at issue here is less serious. Temporarily keeping a person from entering his home, a consequence whenever police stop a person on the street, is considerably less intrusive than police entry into the home itself in order to make a warrantless arrest or conduct a search.

We have explained above why we believe that the need to preserve evidence of a "jailable" offense was sufficiently urgent or pressing to justify the restriction upon entry that the police imposed. We need not decide whether the circumstances before us would have justified a greater restriction for this type of offense or the same restriction were only a "nonjailable" offense at issue.

III

In sum, the police officers in this case had probable cause to believe that a home contained contraband, which was evidence of a crime. They reasonably believed that the home's resident, if left free of any restraint, would destroy that evidence. And they imposed a restraint that was both limited and tailored reasonably to secure law enforcement needs while protecting privacy interests. In our view, the restraint met the Fourth Amendment's demands.

JUSTICE SOUTER, concurring.

I join the Court's opinion subject to this afterword on two points: the constitutionality of a greater intrusion than the one here and the permissibility of choosing impoundment over immediate search. Respondent McArthur's location made the difference between the exigency that justified temporarily barring him from his own dwelling and circumstances that would have supported a greater interference with his privacy and property. As long as he was inside his trailer, the police had probable cause to believe that he had illegal drugs stashed as his wife had reported and that with any sense he would flush them down the drain before the police could get a warrant to enter and search. This probability of destruction in anticipation of a warrant exemplifies the kind of present risk that undergirds the accepted exigent circumstances exception to the general warrant requirement. That risk would have justified the police in entering McArthur's trailer promptly to make a lawful, warrantless search. When McArthur stepped outside and left the trailer uninhabited, the risk abated and so did the reasonableness of entry by the police for as long as he was outside. This is so because the only justification claimed for warrantless action here is the immediate risk, and the limit of reasonable response by the police is set by the scope of the risk.

Since, however, McArthur wished to go back in, why was it reasonable to keep him out when the police could perfectly well have let him do as he chose, and then enjoyed the ensuing opportunity to follow him and make a warrantless search justified by the renewed danger of destruction? The answer is not that the law officiously insists on safeguarding a suspect's privacy from search, in preference to respecting the suspect's liberty to enter his own dwelling. Instead, the legitimacy of the decision to impound the dwelling follows from the law's strong preference for warrants, which underlies the rule that a search with a warrant has a stronger claim to justification on later, judicial review than a search without one. The law can hardly raise incentives to obtain a warrant without giving the police a fair chance to take their probable cause to a magistrate and get one.

JUSTICE STEVENS, dissenting.

The Illinois General Assembly has decided that the possession of less than 2.5 grams of marijuana is a class C misdemeanor. In so classifying the offense, the legislature made a concerted policy judgment that the possession of small amounts of marijuana for personal use does not constitute a particularly significant public policy concern. While it is true that this offense—like feeding livestock on a public highway or offering a movie for rent without clearly displaying its rating—may warrant a jail sentence of up to 30 days, the detection and prosecution of possessors of small quantities of this substance is by no means a law enforcement priority in the State of Illinois.

Because the governmental interest implicated by the particular criminal prohibition at issue in this case is so slight, this is a poor vehicle for probing the boundaries of the government's power to limit an individual's possessory interest in his or her home pending the arrival of a search warrant. Given my preference, I would, therefore, dismiss the writ of certiorari as improvidently granted.

Compelled by the vote of my colleagues to reach the merits, I would affirm. As the majority explains, the essential inquiry in this case involves a balancing of the "privacy-related and law enforcement-related concerns to determine if the intrusion was reasonable." Under the specific facts of this case, I believe the majority gets the balance wrong. Each of the Illinois jurists who participated in the decision of this case placed a higher value on the sanctity of the ordinary citizen's home than on the prosecution of this petty offense. They correctly viewed that interest—whether the home be a humble cottage, a secondhand trailer, or a stately mansion—as one meriting the most serious constitutional protection. Following their analysis and the reasoning in our decision in *Welsh v. Wisconsin,* 466 U.S. 740 (1984) (holding that some offenses may be so minor as to make it unreasonable for police to undertake searches that would be constitutionally permissible if graver offenses were suspected), I would affirm.

Points for Discussion

1. The question of whether the seriousness of the offense under investigation should be considered in the constitutional calculus is one that divides the Court here and throughout the book. For which Fourth Amendment questions should the seriousness of the offense be relevant: Determining whether a warrant is required? Whether probable cause is? Whether the scope of a search or seizure was reasonable?

KENTUCKY V. KING

563 U.S. 452 (2011)

JUSTICE ALITO delivered the opinion of the court.

It is well established that "exigent circumstances," including the need to prevent the destruction of evidence, permit police officers to conduct an otherwise permissible search without first obtaining a warrant. In this case, we consider whether this rule applies when police, by knocking on the door of a residence and announcing their presence, cause the occupants to attempt to destroy evidence. The Kentucky Supreme Court held that the exigent circumstances rule does not apply in the case at hand because the police should have foreseen that their conduct would prompt the occupants to attempt to destroy evidence. We reject this interpretation of the exigent circumstances rule. The conduct of the police prior to their entry into the apartment was entirely lawful. They did not violate the Fourth Amendment or threaten to do so. In such a situation, the exigent circumstances rule applies.

I

A

This case concerns the search of an apartment in Lexington, Kentucky. Police officers set up a controlled buy of crack cocaine outside an apartment complex. Undercover Officer Gibbons watched the deal take place from an unmarked car in a nearby parking lot. After the deal occurred, Gibbons radioed uniformed officers to move in on the suspect. He told the officers that the suspect was moving quickly toward the breezeway of an apartment building, and he urged them to "hurry up and get there" before the suspect entered an apartment.

In response to the radio alert, the uniformed officers drove into the nearby parking lot, left their vehicles, and ran to the breezeway. Just as they entered the breezeway, they heard a door shut and detected a very strong odor of burnt marijuana. At the end of the breezeway, the officers saw two apartments, one on the left and one on the right, and they did not know which apartment the suspect had entered. Gibbons had radioed that the suspect was running into the apartment on the right, but the officers did not hear this statement because they had already left their vehicles. Because they smelled marijuana smoke emanating from the apartment on the left, they approached the door of that apartment.

Officer Steven Cobb, one of the uniformed officers who approached the door, testified that the officers banged on the left apartment door "as loud as [they] could" and announced, "This is the police" or "Police, police, police." Cobb said that "[a]s soon as [the officers] started banging on the door," they "could hear people inside moving," and "[i]t sounded as [though] things were being moved inside the apartment." These noises, Cobb testified, led the officers to believe that drug-related evidence was about to be destroyed.

At that point, the officers announced that they "were going to make entry inside the apartment." Cobb then kicked in the door, the officers entered the apartment, and they found three people in the front room: respondent Hollis King, respondent's girlfriend, and a guest who was smoking marijuana. The officers performed a protective sweep of the apartment during which they saw marijuana and powder cocaine in plain view. In a subsequent search, they also discovered crack cocaine, cash, and drug paraphernalia.

Police eventually entered the apartment on the right. Inside, they found the suspected drug dealer who was the initial target of their investigation.

* * *

II

A

* * *

Although the text of the Fourth Amendment does not specify when a search warrant must be obtained, this Court has inferred that a warrant must generally be secured. "It is a 'basic principle of Fourth Amendment law,' " we have often said, " 'that searches and seizures inside a home without a warrant are presumptively unreasonable.' " *Brigham City v. Stuart,* 547 U.S. 398, 403 (2006) (quoting *Groh v. Ramirez,* 540 U.S. 551, 559 (2004)). But we have also recognized that this presumption may be overcome in some circumstances because "[t]he ultimate touchstone of the Fourth Amendment is 'reasonableness.' " *Brigham City,* at 403. Accordingly, the warrant requirement is subject to certain reasonable exceptions.

One well-recognized exception applies when " 'the exigencies of the situation' make the needs of law enforcement so compelling that [a] warrantless search is objectively reasonable under the Fourth Amendment." *Mincey v. Arizona,* 437 U.S. 385, 394 (1978).

This Court has identified several exigencies that may justify a warrantless search of a home. Under the "emergency aid" exception, for example, "officers may enter a home without a warrant to render emergency assistance to an injured occupant or to protect an occupant from imminent injury." Police officers may enter premises without a warrant when they are in hot pursuit of a fleeing suspect. And—what is relevant here—the need "to prevent the imminent destruction of evidence" has long been recognized as a sufficient justification for a warrantless search.

B

Over the years, lower courts have developed an exception to the exigent circumstances rule, the so-called "police-created exigency" doctrine. Under this doctrine, police may not rely on the need to prevent destruction of evidence when that exigency was "created" or "manufactured" by the conduct of the police.

In applying this exception for the "creation" or "manufacturing" of an exigency by the police, courts require something more than mere proof that fear of detection by the police caused the destruction of evidence. An additional showing is obviously needed because, as the Eighth Circuit has recognized, "in some sense the police always create the exigent circumstances." That is to say, in the vast majority of cases in which evidence is destroyed by persons who are engaged in illegal conduct, the reason for the destruction is fear that the evidence will fall into the hands of law enforcement. Destruction of evidence issues probably occur most frequently in drug cases because drugs may be easily destroyed by flushing them down a toilet or rinsing them down a drain. Persons in possession of valuable drugs are unlikely to destroy them unless they fear discovery by the police. Consequently, a rule that precludes the police from making a warrantless entry to prevent the destruction of evidence whenever their conduct causes the exigency would unreasonably shrink the reach of this well-established exception to the warrant requirement.

Presumably for the purpose of avoiding such a result, the lower courts have held that the police-created exigency doctrine requires more than simple causation, but the lower courts have not agreed on the test to be applied. Indeed, the petition in this case maintains that "[t]here are currently five different tests being used by the United States Courts of Appeals" and that some state courts have crafted additional tests.

III

A

Despite the welter of tests devised by the lower courts, the answer to the question presented in this case follows directly and clearly from the principle that permits warrantless searches in the first place. As previously noted, warrantless searches are allowed when the circumstances make it reasonable, within the meaning of the Fourth Amendment, to dispense with the warrant requirement. Therefore, the answer to the question before us is that the exigent circumstances rule justifies a warrantless search when the conduct of the police preceding the exigency is reasonable in the same sense. Where, as here, the police did not create the exigency by engaging or threatening to engage in conduct that violates the Fourth Amendment, warrantless entry to prevent the destruction of evidence is reasonable and thus allowed.

We have taken a similar approach in other cases involving warrantless searches. For example, we have held that law enforcement officers may seize evidence in plain view, provided that they have not violated the Fourth Amendment in arriving at the spot from which the observation of the evidence is made. See *Horton v. California,* 496 U.S. 128, 136–140 (1990). As we put it in *Horton,* "[i]t is . . . an essential predicate to any valid warrantless seizure of incriminating evidence that the officer did not violate the Fourth Amendment in arriving at the place from which the evidence could be plainly viewed." So long as this prerequisite is satisfied, however, it does not matter that the officer who makes the observation may have gone to the spot from which the evidence was seen with the hope of being able to view and seize the evidence. Instead, the Fourth Amendment requires only that the steps preceding the seizure be lawful.

* * *

B

Some lower courts have adopted a rule that is similar to the one that we recognize today. But others, including the Kentucky Supreme Court, have imposed additional requirements that are unsound and that we now reject.

Bad faith. Some courts, including the Kentucky Supreme Court, ask whether law enforcement officers " 'deliberately created the exigent circumstances with the bad faith intent to avoid the warrant requirement.' " This approach is fundamentally inconsistent with our Fourth Amendment jurisprudence. "Our cases have repeatedly rejected" a subjective approach, asking only whether "the circumstances, viewed *objectively*, justify the action.' "

The reasons for looking to objective factors, rather than subjective intent, are clear. Legal tests based on reasonableness are generally objective, and this Court has long taken the view that "evenhanded law enforcement is best achieved by the application of objective standards of conduct, rather than standards that depend upon the subjective state of mind of the officer."

Reasonable foreseeability. Some courts, again including the Kentucky Supreme Court, hold that police may not rely on an exigency if " 'it was reasonably foreseeable that the investigative tactics employed by the police would create the exigent circumstances.' " Courts applying this test have invalidated warrantless home searches on the ground that it was reasonably foreseeable that police officers, by knocking on the door and announcing their presence, would lead a drug suspect to destroy evidence.

* * *

We have noted that "[t]he calculus of reasonableness must embody allowance for the fact that police officers are often forced to make split-second judgments—in circumstances that are tense, uncertain, and rapidly evolving." The reasonable foreseeability test would create unacceptable and unwarranted difficulties for law enforcement officers who must make quick decisions in the field, as well as for judges who would be required to determine after the fact whether the destruction of evidence in response to a knock on the door was reasonably foreseeable based on what the officers knew at the time.

Probable cause and time to secure a warrant. Some courts, in applying the police-created exigency doctrine, fault law enforcement officers if, after acquiring evidence that is sufficient to establish probable cause to search particular premises, the officers do not seek a warrant but instead knock on the door and seek either to speak with an occupant or to obtain consent to search.

This approach unjustifiably interferes with legitimate law enforcement strategies. There are many entirely proper reasons why police may not want to seek a search warrant as soon as the bare minimum of evidence needed to establish probable cause is acquired. Without attempting to provide a comprehensive list of these reasons, we note a few.

First, the police may wish to speak with the occupants of a dwelling before deciding whether it is worthwhile to seek authorization for a search. They may think that a short and simple conversation may obviate the need to apply for and execute a warrant. Second, the police may want to ask an occupant of the premises for consent to search because doing so is simpler, faster, and less burdensome than applying for a warrant. A consensual search also "may result in considerably less inconvenience" and embarrassment to the occupants than a search conducted pursuant to a warrant. Third, law enforcement officers may wish to obtain more evidence before submitting what might otherwise be considered a marginal warrant application. Fourth, prosecutors may wish to wait until they acquire evidence that can justify a search that is broader in scope than the search that a judicial officer is likely to authorize based on the evidence then available. And finally, in many cases, law enforcement may not want to execute a search that will disclose the existence of an investigation because doing so may interfere with the acquisition of additional evidence against those already under suspicion or evidence about additional but as yet unknown participants in a criminal scheme.

* * *

Standard or good investigative tactics. Finally, some lower court cases suggest that law enforcement officers may be found to have created or manufactured an exigency if the court concludes that the course of their investigation was "contrary to standard or good law enforcement practices (or to the policies or practices of their jurisdictions)." This approach fails to provide clear guidance for law enforcement officers and authorizes courts to make judgments on matters that are the province of those who are responsible for federal and state law enforcement agencies.

C

Respondent argues for a rule that differs from those discussed above, but his rule is also flawed. Respondent contends that law enforcement officers impermissibly create an exigency when they "engage in conduct that would cause a reasonable person to believe that entry is imminent and inevitable." In respondent's view, relevant factors include the officers' tone of voice in announcing their presence and the forcefulness of their knocks. But the ability of law enforcement officers to respond to an exigency cannot turn on such subtleties.

Police officers may have a very good reason to announce their presence loudly and to knock on the door with some force. A forceful knock may be necessary to alert the occupants that someone is at the door. Furthermore, unless police officers identify themselves loudly enough, occupants may not know who is at their doorstep. Officers are permitted—indeed, encouraged—to identify themselves to citizens, and "in many circumstances this is cause for assurance, not discomfort." *United States v. Drayton,* 536 U.S. 194, 204 (2002). Citizens who are startled by an unexpected knock on the door or by the sight of unknown persons in plain clothes on their doorstep may be relieved to learn that these persons are police officers. Others may appreciate the opportunity to make an informed decision about whether to answer the door to the police.

If respondent's test were adopted, it would be extremely difficult for police officers to know how loudly they may announce their presence or how forcefully they may knock on a door without running afoul of the police-created exigency rule. And in most cases, it would be nearly impossible for a court to determine whether that threshold had been passed. The Fourth Amendment does not require the nebulous and impractical test that respondent proposes.

D

* * *

When law enforcement officers who are not armed with a warrant knock on a door, they do no more than any private citizen might do. And whether the person who knocks on the door and requests the opportunity to speak is a police officer or a private citizen, the occupant has no obligation to open the door or to speak. Cf. *Florida v. Royer,* 460 U.S. 491, 497–498 (1983). ("[H]e may decline to listen to the questions at all and may go on his way"). When the police knock on a door but the occupants choose not to respond or to speak, "the investigation will have reached a conspicuously low point," and the occupants "will have the kind of warning that even the most elaborate security system cannot provide." And even if an occupant chooses to open the door and speak with the officers, the occupant need not allow the officers to enter the premises and may refuse to answer any questions at any time.

Occupants who choose not to stand on their constitutional rights but instead elect to attempt to destroy evidence have only themselves to blame for the warrantless exigent-circumstances search that may ensue.

IV

* * *

In this case, we see no evidence that the officers either violated the Fourth Amendment or threatened to do so prior to the point when they entered the apartment. Officer Cobb testified without contradiction that the officers "banged on the door as loud as [they] could" and announced either " 'Police, police, police' " or " 'This is the police.' " This conduct was entirely consistent with the Fourth Amendment, and we are aware of no other evidence that might show that the officers either violated the Fourth Amendment or threatened to do so (for example, by announcing that they would break down the door if the occupants did not open the door voluntarily).

Respondent argues that the officers "demanded" entry to the apartment, but he has not pointed to any evidence in the record that supports this assertion. . . . There is no evidence of a "demand" of any sort, much less a demand that amounts to a threat to violate the Fourth Amendment. If there is contradictory evidence that has not been brought to our attention, the state court may elect to address that matter on remand.

* * *

Like the court below, we assume for purposes of argument that an exigency existed. Because the officers in this case did not violate or threaten to violate the Fourth Amendment prior to the exigency, we hold that the exigency justified the warrantless search of the apartment.

JUSTICE GINSBURG, dissenting.

The Court today arms the police with a way routinely to dishonor the Fourth Amendment's warrant requirement in drug cases. In lieu of presenting their evidence to a neutral magistrate, police officers may now knock, listen, then break the door down, nevermind that they had ample time to obtain a warrant. I dissent from the Court's reduction of the Fourth Amendment's force.

* * *

This case involves a principal exception to the warrant requirement, the exception applicable in "exigent circumstances." "[C]arefully delineated," the exception should govern only in genuine emergency situations. Circumstances qualify as "exigent" when there is an imminent risk of death or serious injury, or danger that evidence will be immediately destroyed, or that a suspect will escape. *Brigham City v. Stuart,* 547 U.S. 398, 403 (2006). The question presented: May police, who could pause to gain the approval of a neutral magistrate, dispense with the need to get a warrant by themselves creating exigent circumstances? I would answer no, as did the Kentucky Supreme Court. The urgency must exist, I would rule, when the police come on the scene, not subsequent to their arrival, prompted by their own conduct.

I

Two pillars of our Fourth Amendment jurisprudence should have controlled the Court's ruling: First, "whenever practical, [the police must] obtain advance judicial approval of searches and seizures through the warrant procedure," *Terry v. Ohio,* 392 U.S. 1, 20 (1968); second, unwarranted "searches and seizures inside a home" bear heightened scrutiny, *Payton v. New York,* 445 U.S. 573, 586 (1980). The warrant requirement, Justice Jackson observed, ranks among the "fundamental distinctions between our form of government, where officers are under the law, and the police-state where they are the law." *Johnson v. United States,* 333 U.S. 10, 17 (1948). The Court has accordingly declared warrantless searches, in the main, "*per se* unreasonable." *Mincey v. Arizona,* 437 U.S. 385, 390 (1978). "[T]he police bear a heavy burden," the Court has cautioned, "when attempting to demonstrate an urgent need that might justify warrantless searches." *Welsh v. Wisconsin,* 466 U.S. 740, 749–750 (1984).

That heavy burden has not been carried here. There was little risk that drug-related evidence would have been destroyed had the police delayed the search pending a magistrate's authorization. As the Court recognizes, "[p]ersons in possession of valuable drugs are unlikely to destroy them unless they fear discovery by the police." Nothing in the record shows that, prior to the knock at the apartment door, the occupants were apprehensive about police proximity.

In no quarter does the Fourth Amendment apply with greater force than in our homes, our most private space which, for centuries, has been regarded as " 'entitled to special protection.' " Home intrusions, the Court has said, are indeed "the chief evil against which . . . the Fourth Amendment is directed." " '[S]earches and seizures inside a home without a warrant are [therefore] presumptively unreasonable.' " How "secure" do our homes remain if police, armed with no warrant, can pound on doors at will and, on hearing sounds indicative of things moving, forcibly enter and search for evidence of unlawful activity?

II

* * *

Under an appropriately reined-in "emergency" or "exigent circumstances" exception, the result in this case should not be in doubt. The target of the investigation's entry into the building, and the smell of marijuana seeping under the apartment door into the hallway, the Kentucky Supreme Court rightly determined, gave the police "probable cause . . . sufficient . . . to obtain a warrant to search the . . . apartment." As that court observed, nothing made it impracticable for the police to post officers on the premises while proceeding to obtain a warrant authorizing their entry. Before this Court, Kentucky does not urge otherwise.

* * *

Points for Discussion

1. The majority notes that there is some doubt as to whether the police "demanded" entry to the apartment and implies that the outcome might be different if they had. On the other hand, the court has no problem with the police knocking forcefully and announcing themselves loudly. Citing *Drayton*, the court suggests that such steps might be reassuring, particularly if the police are not in uniform. How do the concerns expressed in Justice Souter's dissent in *Drayton* counter this reasoning? Does encouraging plain-clothed officers to yell and bang on doors before kicking them down seem either wise or consonant with the Court's earlier decisions?

2. Justice Ginsburg's dissent reasons that in this particular case the police had time to get a warrant. Her dissent, however, does not explain why the police should have refrained from knocking on the door and instead repaired to a judge for a warrant. If what the officers here did comported with the Fourth Amendment, why would, or should, they have applied for a warrant instead?

KYLLO V. UNITED STATES

533 U.S. 27 (2001)

JUSTICE SCALIA delivered the opinion of the court.

This case presents the question whether the use of a thermal-imaging device aimed at a private home from a public street to detect relative amounts of heat within the home constitutes a "search" within the meaning of the Fourth Amendment.

I

In 1991 Agent William Elliott of the United States Department of the Interior came to suspect that marijuana was being grown in the home belonging to petitioner Danny Kyllo, part of a triplex on Rhododendron Drive in Florence, Oregon. Indoor marijuana growth typically requires high-intensity lamps. In order to determine whether an amount of heat was emanating from petitioner's home consistent with the use of such lamps, at 3:20 a.m. on January 16, 1992, Agent Elliott and Dan Haas used an Agema Thermovision 210 thermal imager to scan the triplex. Thermal imagers detect infrared radiation, which virtually all objects emit but which is not visible to the naked eye. The imager converts radiation into images based on relative warmth—black is cool, white is hot, shades of gray connote relative differences; in that respect, it operates somewhat like a video camera showing heat images. The scan of Kyllo's home took only a few minutes and was performed from the passenger seat of Agent Elliott's vehicle across the street from the front of the house and also from the street in back of the house. The scan showed that the roof over the garage and a side wall of petitioner's home were relatively hot compared to the rest of the home and substantially warmer than neighboring homes in the triplex.

Agent Elliott concluded that petitioner was using halide lights to grow marijuana in his house, which indeed he was. Based on tips from informants, utility bills, and the thermal imaging, a Federal Magistrate Judge issued a warrant authorizing a search of petitioner's home, and the agents found an indoor growing operation involving more than 100 plants. Petitioner was indicted on one count of manufacturing marijuana, in violation of 21 U.S.C. § 841(a)(1). He unsuccessfully moved to suppress the evidence seized from his home and then entered a conditional guilty plea.

* * *

II

* * *

The present case involves officers on a public street engaged in more than naked-eye surveillance of a home. We have previously reserved judgment as to how much technological enhancement of ordinary perception from such a vantage point, if any, is too much. While we upheld enhanced aerial photography of an industrial complex in *Dow Chemical v. United States*, 476 U.S. 227 (1986), we noted that we found "it important that this is *not* an area immediately adjacent to a private home, where privacy expectations are most heightened."

III

* * *

The *Katz* test—whether the individual has an expectation of privacy that society is prepared to recognize as reasonable—has often been criticized as circular, and hence subjective and unpredictable. While it may be difficult to refine *Katz* when the search of areas such as telephone booths, automobiles, or even the curtilage and uncovered portions of residences is at issue, in the case of the search of the interior of homes—the prototypical and hence most commonly litigated area of protected privacy—there is a ready criterion, with roots deep in the common law, of the minimal expectation of privacy that *exists,* and that is acknowledged to be *reasonable.* To withdraw protection of this minimum expectation would be to permit police technology to erode the privacy guaranteed by the Fourth Amendment. We think that obtaining by sense-enhancing technology any information regarding the interior of the home that could not otherwise have been obtained without physical "intrusion into a constitutionally protected area," *Silverman* [*v. United States,* 365 U.S. 505, 512 (1961)] constitutes a search—at least where (as here) the technology in question is not in general public use. This assures preservation of that degree of privacy against government that existed when the Fourth

Amendment was adopted. On the basis of this criterion, the information obtained by the thermal imager in this case was the product of a search.[2]

The Government maintains, however, that the thermal imaging must be upheld because it detected "only heat radiating from the external surface of the house." The dissent makes this its leading point, contending that there is a fundamental difference between what it calls "off-the-wall" observations and "through-the-wall surveillance." But just as a thermal imager captures only heat emanating from a house, so also a powerful directional microphone picks up only sound emanating from a house—and a satellite capable of scanning from many miles away would pick up only visible light emanating from a house. We rejected such a mechanical interpretation of the Fourth Amendment in *Katz,* where the eavesdropping device picked up only sound waves that reached the exterior of the phone booth. Reversing that approach would leave the homeowner at the mercy of advancing technology—including imaging technology that could discern all human activity in the home. While the technology used in the present case was relatively crude, the rule we adopt must take account of more sophisticated systems that are already in use or in development.[3]

The dissent's reliance on the distinction between "off-the-wall" and "through-the-wall" observation is entirely incompatible with the dissent's belief, which we discuss below, that thermal-imaging observations of the intimate details of a home are impermissible. The most sophisticated thermal-imaging devices continue to measure heat "off-the-wall" rather than "through-the-wall"; the dissent's disapproval of those more sophisticated thermal-imaging devices is an acknowledgement that there is no substance to this distinction. As for the dissent's extraordinary assertion that anything learned through "an inference" cannot be a search, that would validate even the "through-the-wall" technologies that the dissent purports to disapprove. Surely the dissent does not believe that the

[2] The dissent's repeated assertion that the thermal imaging did not obtain information regarding the interior of the home is simply inaccurate. A thermal imager reveals the relative heat of various rooms in the home. The dissent may not find that information particularly private or important, but there is no basis for saying it is not information regarding the interior of the home. The dissent's comparison of the thermal imaging to various circumstances in which outside observers might be able to perceive, without technology, the heat of the home—for example, by observing snowmelt on the roof—is quite irrelevant. The fact that equivalent information could sometimes be obtained by other means does not make lawful the use of means that violate the Fourth Amendment. The police might, for example, learn how many people are in a particular house by setting up year-round surveillance; but that does not make breaking and entering to find out the same information lawful. In any event, on the night of January 16, 1992, no outside observer could have discerned the relative heat of Kyllo's home without thermal imaging.

[3] The ability to "see" through walls and other opaque barriers is a clear, and scientifically feasible, goal of law enforcement research and development. The National Law Enforcement and Corrections Technology Center, a program within the United States Department of Justice, features on its Internet Website projects that include a "Radar-Based Through-the-Wall Surveillance System," "Handheld Ultrasound Through the Wall Surveillance," and a "Radar Flashlight" that "will enable law enforcement officers to detect individuals through interior building walls." www.nlectc.org/techproj/ (visited May 3, 2001). Some devices may emit low levels of radiation that travel "through-the-wall," but others, such as more sophisticated thermal-imaging devices, are entirely passive, or "off-the-wall" as the dissent puts it.

through-the-wall radar or ultrasound technology produces an 8-by-10 Kodak glossy that needs no analysis (*i.e.,* the making of inferences). And, of course, the novel proposition that inference insulates a search is blatantly contrary to *United States v. Karo,* 468 U.S. 705 (1984), where the police "inferred" from the activation of a beeper that a certain can of ether was in the home. The police activity was held to be a search, and the search was held unlawful.

The Government also contends that the thermal imaging was constitutional because it did not "detect private activities occurring in private areas." It points out that in *Dow Chemical* we observed that the enhanced aerial photography did not reveal any "intimate details." *Dow Chemical,* however, involved enhanced aerial photography of an industrial complex, which does not share the Fourth Amendment sanctity of the home. The Fourth Amendment's protection of the home has never been tied to measurement of the quality or quantity of information obtained. In *Silverman,* for example, we made clear that any physical invasion of the structure of the home, "by even a fraction of an inch," was too much, and there is certainly no exception to the warrant requirement for the officer who barely cracks open the front door and sees nothing but the nonintimate rug on the vestibule floor. In the home, our cases show, *all* details are intimate details, because the entire area is held safe from prying government eyes. Thus, in *Karo* the only thing detected was a can of ether in the home; and in *Arizona v. Hicks,* 480 U.S. 321 (1987), the only thing detected by a physical search that went beyond what officers lawfully present could observe in "plain view" was the registration number of a phonograph turntable. These were intimate details because they were details of the home, just as was the detail of how warm—or even how relatively warm—Kyllo was heating his residence.

Limiting the prohibition of thermal imaging to "intimate details" would not only be wrong in principle; it would be impractical in application, failing to provide "a workable accommodation between the needs of law enforcement and the interests protected by the Fourth Amendment," *Oliver v. United States,* 466 U.S. 170, 181 (1984). To begin with, there is no necessary connection between the sophistication of the surveillance equipment and the "intimacy" of the details that it observes—which means that one cannot say (and the police cannot be assured) that use of the relatively crude equipment at issue here will always be lawful. The Agema Thermovision 210 might disclose, for example, at what hour each night the lady of the house takes her daily sauna and bath—a detail that many would consider "intimate"; and a much more sophisticated system might detect nothing more intimate than the fact that someone left a closet light on. We could not, in other words, develop a rule approving only that through-the-wall surveillance which identifies objects no smaller than 36 by 36 inches, but would have to develop a jurisprudence specifying which home activities are "intimate" and which are not. And even when (if ever) that jurisprudence were fully developed, no police officer would be able to know *in advance* whether his through-the-wall surveillance picks up "intimate" details—and thus would be unable to know in advance whether it is constitutional.

The dissent's proposed standard—whether the technology offers the "functional equivalent of actual presence in the area being searched,"—would seem quite similar to our own at first blush. The dissent concludes that *Katz* was such a case, but then inexplicably asserts that if the same listening device only revealed the volume of the conversation, the surveillance would be permissible. Yet if, without technology, the police could not discern volume without being actually present in the phone booth, Justice Stevens should conclude a search has occurred. The same should hold for the interior heat of the home if only a person present in the home could discern the heat. Thus the driving force of the dissent, despite its recitation of the above standard, appears to be a distinction among different types of information—whether the "homeowner would even care if anybody noticed." The dissent offers no practical guidance for the application of this standard, and for reasons already discussed, we believe there can be none. The people in their houses, as well as the police, deserve more precision.[6]

We have said that the Fourth Amendment draws "a firm line at the entrance to the house." That line, we think, must be not only firm but also bright—which requires clear specification of those methods of surveillance that require a warrant. While it is certainly possible to conclude from the videotape of the thermal imaging that occurred in this case that no "significant" compromise of the homeowner's privacy has occurred, we must take the long view, from the original meaning of the Fourth Amendment forward.

* * *

Where, as here, the Government uses a device that is not in general public use, to explore details of the home that would previously have been unknowable without physical intrusion, the surveillance is a "search" and is presumptively unreasonable without a warrant.

Since we hold the Thermovision imaging to have been an unlawful search, it will remain for the District Court to determine whether, without the evidence it provided, the search warrant issued in this case was supported by probable cause—and if not, whether there is any other basis

---

[6] The dissent argues that we have injected potential uncertainty into the constitutional analysis by noting that whether or not the technology is in general public use may be a factor. That quarrel, however, is not with us but with this Court's precedent. See *Ciraolo*, at 215 ("In an age where private and commercial flight in the public airways is routine, it is unreasonable for respondent to expect that his marijuana plants were constitutionally protected from being observed with the naked eye from an altitude of 1,000 feet"). Given that we can quite confidently say that thermal imaging is not "routine," we decline in this case to reexamine that factor.

for supporting admission of the evidence that the search pursuant to the warrant produced.

JUSTICE STEVENS, with whom THE CHIEF JUSTICE, JUSTICE O'CONNOR, and JUSTICE KENNEDY join, dissenting.

There is, in my judgment, a distinction of constitutional magnitude between "through-the-wall surveillance" that gives the observer or listener direct access to information in a private area, on the one hand, and the thought processes used to draw inferences from information in the public domain, on the other hand. The Court has crafted a rule that purports to deal with direct observations of the inside of the home, but the case before us merely involves indirect deductions from "off-the-wall" surveillance, that is, observations of the exterior of the home. Those observations were made with a fairly primitive thermal imager that gathered data exposed on the outside of petitioner's home but did not invade any constitutionally protected interest in privacy. Moreover, I believe that the supposedly "bright-line" rule the Court has created in response to its concerns about future technological developments is unnecessary, unwise, and inconsistent with the Fourth Amendment.

I

* * *

While the Court "take[s] the long view" and decides this case based largely on the potential of yet-to-be-developed technology that might allow "through-the-wall surveillance," this case involves nothing more than off-the-wall surveillance by law enforcement officers to gather information exposed to the general public from the outside of petitioner's home. All that the infrared camera did in this case was passively measure heat emitted from the exterior surfaces of petitioner's home; all that those measurements showed were relative differences in emission levels, vaguely indicating that some areas of the roof and outside walls were warmer than others. As still images from the infrared scans show, no details regarding the interior of petitioner's home were revealed. Unlike an x-ray scan, or other possible "through-the-wall" techniques, the detection of infrared radiation emanating from the home did not accomplish "an unauthorized physical penetration into the premises," nor did it "obtain information that it could not have obtained by observation from outside the curtilage of the house."

Indeed, the ordinary use of the senses might enable a neighbor or passerby to notice the heat emanating from a building, particularly if it is vented, as was the case here. Additionally, any member of the public might notice that one part of a house is warmer than another part or a nearby building if, for example, rainwater evaporates or snow melts at different rates across its surfaces. Such use of the senses would not convert into an unreasonable search if, instead, an adjoining neighbor allowed an officer onto her property to verify her perceptions with a sensitive thermometer. Nor, in my view, does such observation become an unreasonable search if made from a distance with the aid of a device that merely discloses that the exterior of one house, or one area of the house, is much warmer than another. Nothing more occurred in this case.

Thus, the notion that heat emissions from the outside of a dwelling are a private matter implicating the protections of the Fourth Amendment (the text of which guarantees the right of people "to be secure *in* their . . . houses" against unreasonable searches and seizures) is not only unprecedented but also quite difficult to take seriously. Heat waves, like aromas that are generated in a kitchen, or in a laboratory or opium den, enter the public domain if and when they leave a building. A subjective expectation that they would remain private is not only implausible but also surely not "one that society is prepared to recognize as 'reasonable.' "

To be sure, the homeowner has a reasonable expectation of privacy concerning what takes place within the home, and the Fourth Amendment's protection against physical invasions of the home should apply to their functional equivalent. But the equipment in this case did not penetrate the walls of petitioner's home, and while it did pick up "details of the home" that were exposed to the public, it did not obtain "any information regarding the *interior* of the home." In the Court's own words, based on what the thermal imager "showed" regarding the outside of petitioner's home, the officers "concluded" that petitioner was engaging in illegal activity inside the home. It would be quite absurd to characterize their thought processes as "searches," regardless of whether they inferred (rightly) that petitioner was growing marijuana in his house, or (wrongly) that "the lady of the house [was taking] her daily sauna and bath." In either case, the only conclusions the officers reached concerning the interior of the home were at least as indirect as those that might have been inferred from the contents of discarded garbage, see *California v. Greenwood,* 486 U.S. 35 (1988), or pen register data, see *Smith v. Maryland,* 442 U.S. 735 (1979), or, as in this case, subpoenaed utility records. For the first time in its history, the Court assumes that an inference can amount to a Fourth Amendment violation.

Notwithstanding the implications of today's decision, there is a strong public interest in avoiding constitutional litigation over the monitoring of emissions from homes, and over the inferences drawn from such monitoring. Just as "the police cannot reasonably be expected to avert their eyes from evidence of criminal activity that could have been observed by any member of the public," *Greenwood,* 486 U.S., at 41, so too public officials should not have to avert their senses or their equipment from detecting emissions in the public domain such as excessive heat, traces of smoke, suspicious odors, odorless gases, airborne particulates, or radioactive emissions, any of which could identify hazards to the community. In my judgment, monitoring such emissions with "sense-enhancing technology," and drawing useful conclusions from such monitoring, is an entirely reasonable public service.

On the other hand, the countervailing privacy interest is at best trivial. After all, homes generally are insulated to keep heat in, rather than to prevent the detection of heat going out, and it does not seem to me that society will suffer from a rule requiring the rare homeowner who both intends to engage in uncommon activities that produce extraordinary amounts of heat, and wishes to conceal that production from outsiders, to make sure that the surrounding area is well insulated. The interest in concealing the heat escaping from one's house pales in significance to "the chief evil against which the wording of the Fourth Amendment is directed," the "physical entry of the home," and it is hard to believe that it is an interest the Framers sought to protect in our Constitution.

Since what was involved in this case was nothing more than drawing inferences from off-the-wall surveillance, rather than any "through-the-wall" surveillance, the officers' conduct did not amount to a search and was perfectly reasonable.

II

Instead of trying to answer the question whether the use of the thermal imager in this case was even arguably unreasonable, the Court has fashioned a rule that is intended to provide essential guidance for the day when "more sophisticated systems" gain the "ability to 'see' through walls and other opaque barriers." The newly minted rule encompasses "obtaining [1] by sense-enhancing technology [2] any information regarding the interior of the home [3] that could not otherwise have been obtained without physical intrusion into a constitutionally protected area . . . [4] at least where (as here) the technology in question is not in general public use." In my judgment, the Court's new rule is at once too broad and too narrow, and is not justified by the Court's explanation for its adoption. As I have suggested, I would not erect a constitutional impediment to the use of sense-enhancing technology unless it provides its user with the functional equivalent of actual presence in the area being searched.

Despite the Court's attempt to draw a line that is "not only firm but also bright," the contours of its new rule are uncertain because its protection apparently dissipates as soon as the relevant technology is "in general public use." Yet how much use is general public use is not even hinted at by the Court's opinion, which makes the somewhat doubtful assumption that the thermal imager used in this case does not satisfy that criterion.[5] In any event, putting aside its lack of clarity, this criterion is

[5] The record describes a device that numbers close to a thousand manufactured units; that has a predecessor numbering in the neighborhood of 4,000 to 5,000 units; that competes with a similar product numbering from 5,000 to 6,000 units; and that is "readily available to the public" for commercial, personal, or law enforcement purposes, and is just an 800-number away from being

somewhat perverse because it seems likely that the threat to privacy will grow, rather than recede, as the use of intrusive equipment becomes more readily available.

It is clear, however, that the category of "sense-enhancing technology" covered by the new rule is far too broad. It would, for example, embrace potential mechanical substitutes for dogs trained to react when they sniff narcotics. But in *United States v. Place,* 462 U.S. 696, 707 (1983), we held that a dog sniff that "discloses only the presence or absence of narcotics" does "not constitute a 'search' within the meaning of the Fourth Amendment," and it must follow that sense-enhancing equipment that identifies nothing but illegal activity is not a search either. Nevertheless, the use of such a device would be unconstitutional under the Court's rule, as would the use of other new devices that might detect the odor of deadly bacteria or chemicals for making a new type of high explosive, even if the devices (like the dog sniffs) are "so limited both in the manner in which" they obtain information and "in the content of the information" they reveal. If nothing more than that sort of information could be obtained by using the devices in a public place to monitor emissions from a house, then their use would be no more objectionable than the use of the thermal imager in this case.

The application of the Court's new rule to "any information regarding the interior of the home," is also unnecessarily broad. If it takes sensitive equipment to detect an odor that identifies criminal conduct and nothing else, the fact that the odor emanates from the interior of a home should not provide it with constitutional protection. The criterion, moreover, is too sweeping in that information "regarding" the interior of a home apparently is not just information obtained through its walls, but also information concerning the outside of the building that could lead to (however many) inferences "regarding" what might be inside. Under that expansive view, I suppose, an officer using an infrared camera to observe a man silently entering the side door of a house at night carrying a pizza might conclude that its interior is now occupied by someone who likes pizza, and by doing so the officer would be guilty of conducting an unconstitutional "search" of the home.

Because the new rule applies to information regarding the "interior" of the home, it is too narrow as well as too broad. Clearly, a rule that is designed to protect individuals from the overly intrusive use of sense-enhancing equipment should not be limited to a home. If such equipment did provide its user with the functional equivalent of access to a private place—such as, for example, the telephone booth involved in *Katz,* or an

rented from "half a dozen national companies" by anyone who wants one. Since, by virtue of the Court's new rule, the issue is one of first impression, perhaps it should order an evidentiary hearing to determine whether these facts suffice to establish "general public use."

office building—then the rule should apply to such an area as well as to a home.

The final requirement of the Court's new rule, that the information "could not otherwise have been obtained without physical intrusion into a constitutionally protected area," also extends too far as the Court applies it. As noted, the Court effectively treats the mental process of analyzing data obtained from external sources as the equivalent of a physical intrusion into the home. As I have explained, however, the process of drawing inferences from data in the public domain should not be characterized as a search.

The two reasons advanced by the Court as justifications for the adoption of its new rule are both unpersuasive. First, the Court suggests that its rule is compelled by our holding in *Katz,* because in that case, as in this, the surveillance consisted of nothing more than the monitoring of waves emanating from a private area into the public domain. Yet there are critical differences between the cases. In *Katz,* the electronic listening device attached to the outside of the phone booth allowed the officers to pick up the content of the conversation inside the booth, making them the functional equivalent of intruders because they gathered information that was otherwise available only to someone inside the private area; it would be as if, in this case, the thermal imager presented a view of the heat-generating activity inside petitioner's home. By contrast, the thermal imager here disclosed only the relative amounts of heat radiating from the house; it would be as if, in *Katz,* the listening device disclosed only the relative volume of sound leaving the booth, which presumably was discernible in the public domain.[6] Surely, there is a significant difference between the general and well-settled expectation that strangers will not have direct access to the contents of private communications, on the one hand, and the rather theoretical expectation that an occasional homeowner would even care if anybody noticed the relative amounts of heat emanating from the walls of his house, on the other. It is pure hyperbole for the Court to suggest that refusing to extend the holding of *Katz* to this case would leave the homeowner at the mercy of "technology that could discern all human activity in the home."

Second, the Court argues that the permissibility of "through-the-wall surveillance" cannot depend on a distinction between observing "intimate details" such as "the lady of the house [taking] her daily sauna and bath," and noticing only "the nonintimate rug on the vestibule floor" or "objects no smaller than 36 by 36 inches." This entire argument assumes, of course, that the thermal imager in this case could or did perform "through-the-wall surveillance" that could identify any detail "that would previously have

[6] The use of the latter device would be constitutional given *Smith v. Maryland,* 442 U.S. 735, 741 (1979), which upheld the use of pen registers to record numbers dialed on a phone because, unlike "the listening device employed in *Katz* . . . pen registers do not acquire the *contents* of communications."

been unknowable without physical intrusion." In fact, the device could not and did not enable its user to identify either the lady of the house, the rug on the vestibule floor, or anything else inside the house, whether smaller or larger than 36 by 36 inches. Indeed, the vague thermal images of petitioner's home that are reproduced in the Appendix were submitted by him to the District Court as part of an expert report raising the question whether the device could even take "accurate, consistent infrared images" of the *outside* of his house. But even if the device could reliably show extraordinary differences in the amounts of heat leaving his home, drawing the inference that there was something suspicious occurring inside the residence—a conclusion that officers far less gifted than Sherlock Holmes would readily draw—does not qualify as "through-the-wall surveillance," much less a Fourth Amendment violation.

III

Although the Court is properly and commendably concerned about the threats to privacy that may flow from advances in the technology available to the law enforcement profession, it has unfortunately failed to heed the tried and true counsel of judicial restraint. Instead of concentrating on the rather mundane issue that is actually presented by the case before it, the Court has endeavored to craft an all-encompassing rule for the future. It would be far wiser to give legislators an unimpeded opportunity to grapple with these emerging issues rather than to shackle them with prematurely devised constitutional constraints.

Points for Discussion

1. Why does the Court employ "general public use" as a significant factor in its decision? The dissent wonders in a footnote how many units of a particular technology have to be shipped before it has entered public use. Does the majority provide an answer?

2. The issue in *Kyllo* was not whether the police could use the thermal imager but only whether they needed to obtain a warrant first. Because the majority held that use of the device was a "search" under the Fourth Amendment, its use without a warrant was presumed to be unconstitutional. A search warrant, however, would allow police to enter the home and presumably obviate the need for a thermal scan entirely. In 2004, for example, police in Carlsbad, California, obtained a search warrant based on high activity on the street, a positive alert by a drug dog during a walk-by, and a high utility bill which they believed signaled the use of heat lamps to grow marijuana. After an exhaustive search of the home, the police found that the high utility bill was attributable to nothing more than "doing laundry, operating a dishwasher, running four ceiling fans and three computers, and trying to keep up with three active children who leave the lights on." Deborah Schoch, *The State; Grass Stains, Not a Pot Farm, Blamed for Bills; Carlsbad homeowners*

say their high use of electricity reflects a busy but boring family life. Police suspected other possibilities, L.A. TIMES, Mar. 28, 2004, at B6.

3. As technology advances, more thorough methods of viewing the interior of a home without alerting its residents will surely develop. Whether the police should be able to search a home, even with a warrant, without alerting the owners depends in large measure on what purpose warrants serve under the Constitution. The Supreme Court used to assert that warrants reassured the person whose property was being searched and seized of the officers' authority and of the limits of that authority. *See, e.g.*, *Illinois v. Gates*, 462 U.S. 213, 236 (1983); *United States v. Chadwhick*, 433 U.S. 1, 9 (1977); *Camara v. Mun. Court*, 387 U.S. 523, 532 (1967). More recently, however, the Court has held that warrants are not meant to provide such notice. In *Groh v. Ramirez*, Justice Stevens' majority opinion noted that the Fourth Amendment does not require law enforcement "to serve notice on the owner before commencing the search." 540 U.S. 551, 562 n.5 (2004) ("Quite obviously, in some circumstances—a surreptitious search by means of a wiretap, for example, or the search of empty or abandoned premises—it will be impracticable or imprudent for the officers to show the warrant in advance.")

FLORIDA V. JARDINES

569 U.S. 1 (2013)

JUSTICE SCALIA delivered the opinion of the court.

We consider whether using a drug-sniffing dog on a homeowner's porch to investigate the contents of the home is a "search" within the meaning of the Fourth Amendment.

I

In 2006, Detective William Pedraja of the Miami-Dade Police Department received an unverified tip that marijuana was being grown in the home of respondent Joelis Jardines. One month later, the Department and the Drug Enforcement Administration sent a joint surveillance team to Jardines' home. Detective Pedraja was part of that team. He watched the home for fifteen minutes and saw no vehicles in the driveway or activity around the home, and could not see inside because the blinds were drawn. Detective Pedraja then approached Jardines' home accompanied by Detective Douglas Bartelt, a trained canine handler who had just arrived at the scene with his drug-sniffing dog. The dog was trained to detect the scent of marijuana, cocaine, heroin, and several other drugs, indicating the presence of any of these substances through particular behavioral changes recognizable by his handler.

Detective Bartelt had the dog on a six-foot leash, owing in part to the dog's "wild" nature, and tendency to dart around erratically while searching. As the dog approached Jardines' front porch, he apparently sensed one of the odors he had been trained to detect, and began energetically exploring the area for the strongest point source of that odor. As Detective Bartelt explained, the dog "began tracking that airborne odor by . . . tracking back and forth," engaging in what is called "bracketing," "back and forth, back and forth." Detective Bartelt gave the dog "the full six feet of the leash plus whatever safe distance [he could] give him" to do this—he testified that he needed to give the dog "as much distance as I can." And Detective Pedraja stood back while this was occurring, so that he would not "get knocked over" when the dog was "spinning around trying to find" the source.

After sniffing the base of the front door, the dog sat, which is the trained behavior upon discovering the odor's strongest point. Detective Bartelt then pulled the dog away from the door and returned to his vehicle. He left the scene after informing Detective Pedraja that there had been a positive alert for narcotics.

On the basis of what he had learned at the home, Detective Pedraja applied for and received a warrant to search the residence. When the warrant was executed later that day, Jardines attempted to flee and was arrested; the search revealed marijuana plants, and he was charged with trafficking in cannabis.

* * *

II

The Fourth Amendment provides in relevant part that the "right of the people to be secure in their persons, houses, papers, and effects, against unreasonable searches and seizures, shall not be violated." The Amendment establishes a simple baseline, one that for much of our history formed the exclusive basis for its protections: When "the Government obtains information by physically intruding" on persons, houses, papers, or effects, "a 'search' within the original meaning of the Fourth Amendment" has "undoubtedly occurred." *United States v. Jones,* 565 U.S. 400, 406, n. 3 (2012). By reason of our decision in *Katz v. United States,* 389 U.S. 347 (1967), property rights "are not the sole measure of Fourth Amendment violations," *Soldal v. Cook County,* 506 U.S. 56, 64 (1992)—but though *Katz* may add to the baseline, it does not subtract anything from the Amendment's protections "when the Government *does* engage in [a] physical intrusion of a constitutionally protected area," *United States v. Knotts,* 460 U.S. 276, 286 (1983) (Brennan, J., concurring in the judgment).

That principle renders this case a straightforward one. The officers were gathering information in an area belonging to Jardines and immediately surrounding his house—in the curtilage of the house, which we have held enjoys protection as part of the home itself. And they gathered that information by physically entering and occupying the area to engage in conduct not explicitly or implicitly permitted by the homeowner.

A

The Fourth Amendment "indicates with some precision the places and things encompassed by its protections": persons, houses, papers, and effects. *Oliver v. United States,* 466 U.S. 170, 176 (1984). The Fourth Amendment does not, therefore, prevent all investigations conducted on private property; for example, an officer may (subject to *Katz*) gather information in what we have called "open fields"—even if those fields are privately owned—because such fields are not enumerated in the Amendment's text. *Hester v. United States,* 265 U.S. 57 (1924).

But when it comes to the Fourth Amendment, the home is first among equals. At the Amendment's "very core" stands "the right of a man to retreat into his own home and there be free from unreasonable governmental intrusion." *Silverman v. United States,* 365 U.S. 505, 511 (1961). This right would be of little practical value if the State's agents could stand in a home's porch or side garden and trawl for evidence with impunity; the right to retreat would be significantly diminished if the police could enter a man's property to observe his repose from just outside the front window.

We therefore regard the area "immediately surrounding and associated with the home"—what our cases call the curtilage—as "part of the home itself for Fourth Amendment purposes." *Oliver,* at 180. That principle has ancient and durable roots. Just as the distinction between the home and the open fields is "as old as the common law," *Hester,* at 59, so too is the identity of home and what Blackstone called the "curtilage or homestall," for the "house protects and privileges all its branches and appurtenants." 4 W. Blackstone, Commentaries on the Laws of England 223, 225 (1769). This area around the home is "intimately linked to the home, both physically and psychologically," and is where "privacy expectations are most heightened." *California v. Ciraolo,* 476 U.S. 207, 213 (1986).

While the boundaries of the curtilage are generally "clearly marked," the "conception defining the curtilage" is at any rate familiar enough that it is "easily understood from our daily experience." *Oliver,* 466 U.S., at 182, n. 12. Here there is no doubt that the officers entered it: The front porch is the classic exemplar of an area adjacent to the home and "to which the activity of home life extends."

B

Since the officers' investigation took place in a constitutionally protected area, we turn to the question of whether it was accomplished through an unlicensed physical intrusion.[1] While law enforcement officers

[1] At oral argument, the State and its *amicus* the Solicitor General argued that Jardines conceded in the lower courts that the officers had a right to be where they were. This misstates the record. Jardines conceded nothing more than the unsurprising proposition that the officers

need not "shield their eyes" when passing by the home "on public thoroughfares," *Ciraolo,* 476 U.S., at 213, an officer's leave to gather information is sharply circumscribed when he steps off those thoroughfares and enters the Fourth Amendment's protected areas. In permitting, for example, visual observation of the home from "public navigable airspace," we were careful to note that it was done "in a physically nonintrusive manner." *Ibid. Entick v. Carrington,* 2 Wils. K.B. 275, 95 Eng. Rep. 807 (K.B.1765), a case "undoubtedly familiar" to "every American statesman" at the time of the Founding, states the general rule clearly: "[O]ur law holds the property of every man so sacred, that no man can set his foot upon his neighbour's close without his leave." 2 Wils. K. B., at 291, 95 Eng. Rep., at 817. As it is undisputed that the detectives had all four of their feet and all four of their companion's firmly planted on the constitutionally protected extension of Jardines' home, the only question is whether he had given his leave (even implicitly) for them to do so. He had not.

"A license may be implied from the habits of the country," notwithstanding the "strict rule of the English common law as to entry upon a close." *McKee v. Gratz,* 260 U.S. 127, 136 (1922) (Holmes, J.). We have accordingly recognized that "the knocker on the front door is treated as an invitation or license to attempt an entry, justifying ingress to the home by solicitors, hawkers and peddlers of all kinds." *Breard v. Alexandria,* 341 U.S. 622, 626 (1951). This implicit license typically permits the visitor to approach the home by the front path, knock promptly, wait briefly to be received, and then (absent invitation to linger longer) leave. Complying with the terms of that traditional invitation does not require fine-grained legal knowledge; it is generally managed without incident by the Nation's Girl Scouts and trick-or-treaters.[2] Thus, a police officer not armed with a warrant may approach a home and knock, precisely because that is "no more than any private citizen might do." *Kentucky v. King,* 563 U.S. 452, 469 (2011).

But introducing a trained police dog to explore the area around the home in hopes of discovering incriminating evidence is something else. There is no customary invitation to do *that.* An invitation to engage in canine forensic investigation assuredly does not inhere in the very act of hanging a knocker.[3] To find a visitor knocking on the door is routine (even

could have lawfully approached his home to knock on the front door in hopes of speaking with him. Of course, that is not what they did.

[2] With this much, the dissent seems to agree—it would inquire into " 'the appearance of things,' " *post,* at 5 (opinion of Alito, J.), what is "typica[l]" for a visitor, *ibid.,* what might cause "alarm" to a "resident of the premises," *ibid.,* what is "expected" of "ordinary visitors," *ibid.,* and what would be expected from a " 'reasonably respectful citizen,' " *post,* at 7. These are good questions. But their answers are incompatible with the dissent's outcome, which is presumably why the dissent does not even try to argue that it would be customary, usual, reasonable, respectful, ordinary, typical, nonalarming, etc., for a stranger to explore the curtilage of the home with trained drug dogs.

[3] The dissent insists that our argument must rest upon "the particular instrument that Detective Bartelt used to detect the odor of marijuana"—the dog. It is not the dog that is the

if sometimes unwelcome); to spot that same visitor exploring the front path with a metal detector, or marching his bloodhound into the garden before saying hello and asking permission, would inspire most of us to—well, call the police. The scope of a license—express or implied—is limited not only to a particular area but also to a specific purpose. Consent at a traffic stop to an officer's checking out an anonymous tip that there is a body in the trunk does not permit the officer to rummage through the trunk for narcotics. Here, the background social norms that invite a visitor to the front door do not invite him there to conduct a search.[4] The State points to our decisions holding that the subjective intent of the officer is irrelevant. But those cases merely hold that a stop or search *that is objectively reasonable* is not vitiated by the fact that the officer's real reason for making the stop or search has nothing to do with the validating reason. Thus, the defendant will not be heard to complain that although he was speeding the officer's real reason for the stop was racial harassment. Here, however, the question before the court is precisely *whether* the officer's conduct was an objectively reasonable search. As we have described, that depends upon whether the officers had an implied license to enter the porch, which in turn depends upon the purpose for which they entered. Here, their behavior objectively reveals a purpose to conduct a search, which is not what anyone would think he had license to do.

III

The State argues that investigation by a forensic narcotics dog by definition cannot implicate any legitimate privacy interest. The State cites for authority our decisions in *United States v. Place,* 462 U.S. 696 (1983), *United States v. Jacobsen,* 466 U.S. 109 (1984), and *Illinois v. Caballes,* 543 U.S. 405 (2005), which held, respectively, that canine inspection of luggage in an airport, chemical testing of a substance that had fallen from a parcel in transit, and canine inspection of an automobile during a lawful traffic stop, do not violate the "reasonable expectation of privacy" described in *Katz.*

* * *

problem, but the behavior that here involved use of the dog. We think a typical person would find it " 'a cause for great alarm' " (the kind of reaction the dissent quite rightly relies upon to justify its no-night-visits rule) to find a stranger snooping about his front porch *with or without* a dog. The dissent would let the police do whatever they want by way of gathering evidence so long as they stay on the base-path, to use a baseball analogy—so long as they "stick to the path that is typically used to approach a front door, such as a paved walkway." From that vantage point they can presumably peer into the house through binoculars with impunity. That is not the law, as even the State concedes.

[4] The dissent argues, citing *King,* that "gathering evidence—even damning evidence—is a lawful activity that falls within the scope of the license to approach." That is a false generalization. What *King* establishes is that it is not a Fourth Amendment search to approach the home in order to speak with the occupant, *because all are invited to do that.* The mere "purpose of discovering information," in the course of engaging in that permitted conduct does not cause it to violate the Fourth Amendment. But no one is impliedly invited to enter the protected premises of the home in order to do nothing but conduct a search.

[W]e need not decide whether the officers' investigation of Jardines' home violated his expectation of privacy under *Katz.* One virtue of the Fourth Amendment's property-rights baseline is that it keeps easy cases easy. That the officers learned what they learned only by physically intruding on Jardines' property to gather evidence is enough to establish that a search occurred.

For a related reason we find irrelevant the State's argument (echoed by the dissent) that forensic dogs have been commonly used by police for centuries. This argument is apparently directed to our holding in *Kyllo v. United States,* 533 U.S. 27 (2001), that surveillance of the home is a search where "the Government uses a device that is not in general public use" to "explore details of the home that would previously have been unknowable *without physical intrusion.*" But the implication of that statement (*inclusio unius est exclusio alterius*) is that when the government uses a physical intrusion to explore details of the home (including its curtilage), the antiquity of the tools that they bring along is irrelevant.

JUSTICE KAGAN, with whom JUSTICE GINSBURG and JUSTICE SOTOMAYOR join, concurring.

For me, a simple analogy clinches this case—and does so on privacy as well as property grounds. A stranger comes to the front door of your home carrying super-high-powered binoculars. He doesn't knock or say hello. Instead, he stands on the porch and uses the binoculars to peer through your windows, into your home's furthest corners. It doesn't take long (the binoculars are really very fine): In just a couple of minutes, his uncommon behavior allows him to learn details of your life you disclose to no one. Has your "visitor" trespassed on your property, exceeding the license you have granted to members of the public to, say, drop off the mail or distribute campaign flyers? Yes, he has. And has he also invaded your "reasonable expectation of privacy," by nosing into intimacies you sensibly thought protected from disclosure? *Katz v. United States,* 389 U.S. 347, 360 (1967) (Harlan, J., concurring). Yes, of course, he has done that too.

That case is this case in every way that matters. Here, police officers came to Joelis Jardines' door with a super-sensitive instrument, which they deployed to detect things inside that they could not perceive unassisted. The equipment they used was animal, not mineral. But contra the dissent, that is of no significance in determining whether a search occurred. Detective Bartelt's dog was not your neighbor's pet, come to your porch on a leisurely stroll. As this Court discussed earlier this Term, drug-detection dogs are highly trained tools of law enforcement, geared to respond in distinctive ways to specific scents so as to convey clear and reliable information to their human partners. They are to the poodle down the street as high-powered binoculars are to a piece of plain glass. Like the binoculars, a drug-detection dog is a specialized device for discovering objects not in plain view (or plain smell). And as in the hypothetical above, that device was aimed here at a home—the most private and inviolate (or so we expect) of all the places and things the Fourth Amendment protects. Was this activity a trespass? Yes, as the Court holds today. Was it also an invasion of privacy? Yes, that as well.

The Court today treats this case under a property rubric; I write separately to note that I could just as happily have decided it by looking to Jardines' privacy interests. A decision along those lines would have looked . . . well, much like this one. It would have talked about " 'the right of a man to retreat into his own home and there be free from unreasonable governmental intrusion.' " It would have insisted on maintaining the "practical value" of that right by preventing police officers from standing in an adjacent space and "trawl[ing] for evidence with impunity." It would have explained that " 'privacy expectations are most heightened' " in the home and the surrounding area. And it would have determined that police officers invade those shared expectations when they use trained canine assistants to reveal within the confines of a home what they could not otherwise have found there.

It is not surprising that in a case involving a search of a home, property concepts and privacy concepts should so align. The law of property "naturally enough influence[s]" our "shared social expectations" of what places should be free from governmental incursions. *Georgia v. Randolph,* 547 U.S. 103, 111 (2006). And so the sentiment "my home is my own," while originating in property law, now also denotes a common understanding—extending even beyond that law's formal protections—about an especially private sphere. Jardines' home was his property; it was also his most intimate and familiar space. The analysis proceeding from each of those facts, as today's decision reveals, runs mostly along the same path.

I can think of only one divergence: If we had decided this case on privacy grounds, we would have realized that *Kyllo v. United States,* 533 U.S. 27 (2001), already resolved it.[1] The *Kyllo* Court held that police officers conducted a search when they used a thermal-imaging device to detect heat emanating from a private home, even though they committed no trespass. Highlighting our intention to draw both a "firm" and a "bright" line at "the entrance to the house," we announced the following rule: "Where, as here, the Government uses a device that is not in general public use, to explore details of the home that would previously have been unknowable without physical intrusion, the surveillance is a 'search' and is presumptively unreasonable without a warrant."

That "firm" and "bright" rule governs this case: The police officers here conducted a search because they used a "device . . . not in general public

[1] The dissent claims, alternatively, that *Illinois v. Caballes,* 543 U.S. 405, 409–410 (2005), controls this case (or nearly does). But *Caballes* concerned a drug-detection dog's sniff of an automobile during a traffic stop. And we have held, over and over again, that people's expectations of privacy are much lower in their cars than in their homes.

use" (a trained drug-detection dog) to "explore details of the home" (the presence of certain substances) that they would not otherwise have discovered without entering the premises.

And again, the dissent's argument that the device is just a dog cannot change the equation. As *Kyllo* made clear, the "sense-enhancing" tool at issue may be "crude" or "sophisticated," may be old or new (drug-detection dogs actually go back not "12,000 years" or "centuries," but only a few decades), may be either smaller or bigger than a breadbox; still, "at least where (as here)" the device is not "in general public use," training it on a home violates our "minimal expectation of privacy"—an expectation "that *exists,* and that is acknowledged to be *reasonable.*"[2] That does not mean the device is off-limits, as the dissent implies; it just means police officers cannot use it to examine a home without a warrant or exigent circumstance.

With these further thoughts, suggesting that a focus on Jardines' privacy interests would make an "easy cas[e] easy" twice over, I join the Court's opinion in full.

JUSTICE ALITO, with whom THE CHIEF JUSTICE, JUSTICE KENNEDY, and JUSTICE BREYER join, dissenting.

The Court's decision in this important Fourth Amendment case is based on a putative rule of trespass law that is nowhere to be found in the annals of Anglo-American jurisprudence.

The law of trespass generally gives members of the public a license to use a walkway to approach the front door of a house and to remain there for a brief time. This license is not limited to persons who intend to speak to an occupant or who actually do so. (Mail carriers and persons delivering packages and flyers are examples of individuals who may lawfully approach a front door without intending to converse.) Nor is the license restricted to categories of visitors whom an occupant of the dwelling is likely to welcome; as the Court acknowledges, this license applies even to "solicitors, hawkers and peddlers of all kinds." And the license even extends to police officers who wish to gather evidence against an occupant (by asking potentially incriminating questions).

[2] The dissent's other principal reason for concluding that no violation of privacy occurred in this case—that police officers themselves might detect an aroma wafting from a house—works no better. If officers can smell drugs coming from a house, they can use that information; a human sniff is not a search, we can all agree. But it does not follow that a person loses his expectation of privacy in the many scents within his home that (his own nose capably tells him) are not usually detectible by humans standing outside. And indeed, *Kyllo* already decided as much. In response to an identical argument from the dissent in that case, the *Kyllo* Court stated: "The dissent's comparison of the thermal imaging to various circumstances in which outside observers might be able to perceive, without technology, the heat of the home . . . is quite irrelevant. The fact that equivalent information could sometimes be obtained by other means does not make lawful the use of means that violate the Fourth Amendment. . . . In any event, [at the time in question,] no outside observer could have discerned the relative heat of Kyllo's home without thermal imaging."

According to the Court, however, the police officer in this case, Detective Bartelt, committed a trespass because he was accompanied during his otherwise lawful visit to the front door of respondent's house by his dog, Franky.

Where is the authority evidencing such a rule? Dogs have been domesticated for about 12,000 years; they were ubiquitous in both this country and Britain at the time of the adoption of the Fourth Amendment; and their acute sense of smell has been used in law enforcement for centuries. Yet the Court has been unable to find a single case—from the United States or any other common-law nation—that supports the rule on which its decision is based. Thus, trespass law provides no support for the Court's holding today.

The Court's decision is also inconsistent with the reasonable-expectations-of-privacy test that the Court adopted in *Katz v. United States,* 389 U.S. 347 (1967). A reasonable person understands that odors emanating from a house may be detected from locations that are open to the public, and a reasonable person will not count on the strength of those odors remaining within the range that, while detectible by a dog, cannot be smelled by a human.

For these reasons, I would hold that no search within the meaning of the Fourth Amendment took place in this case, and I would reverse the decision below.

I

The opinion of the Court may leave a reader with the mistaken impression that Detective Bartelt and Franky remained on respondent's property for a prolonged period of time and conducted a far-flung exploration of the front yard. But that is not what happened.

Detective Bartelt and Franky approached the front door via the driveway and a paved path—the route that any visitor would customarily use—and Franky was on the kind of leash that any dog owner might employ. As Franky approached the door, he started to track an airborne odor. He held his head high and began "bracketing" the area (pacing back and forth) in order to determine the strongest source of the smell. Detective Bartelt knew "the minute [he] observed" this behavior that Franky had detected drugs. Upon locating the odor's strongest source, Franky sat at the base of the front door, and at this point, Detective Bartelt and Franky immediately returned to their patrol car.

A critical fact that the Court omits is that, as respondent's counsel explained at oral argument, this entire process—walking down the driveway and front path to the front door, waiting for Franky to find the strongest source of the odor, and walking back to the car—took approximately a minute or two. Thus, the amount of time that Franky and the detective remained at the front porch was even less. The Court also fails to mention that, while Detective Bartelt apparently did not personally smell the odor of marijuana coming from the house, another officer who subsequently stood on the front porch, Detective Pedraja, did notice that smell and was able to identify it.

II

The Court concludes that the conduct in this case was a search because Detective Bartelt exceeded the boundaries of the license to approach the house that is recognized by the law of trespass, but the Court's interpretation of the scope of that license is unfounded.

A

It is said that members of the public may lawfully proceed along a walkway leading to the front door of a house because custom grants them a license to do so. This rule encompasses categories of visitors whom most homeowners almost certainly wish to allow to approach their front doors—friends, relatives, mail carriers, persons making deliveries. But it also reaches categories of visitors who are less universally welcome—"solicitors," "hawkers," "peddlers," and the like. The law might attempt to draw fine lines between categories of welcome and unwelcome visitors, distinguishing, for example, between tolerable and intolerable door-to-door peddlers (Girl Scouts selling cookies versus adults selling aluminum siding) or between police officers on agreeable and disagreeable missions (gathering information about a bothersome neighbor versus asking potentially incriminating questions). But the law of trespass has not attempted such a difficult taxonomy.

Of course, this license has certain spatial and temporal limits. A visitor must stick to the path that is typically used to approach a front door, such as a paved walkway. A visitor cannot traipse through the garden, meander into the backyard, or take other circuitous detours that veer from the pathway that a visitor would customarily use.

Nor, as a general matter, may a visitor come to the front door in the middle of the night without an express invitation.

Similarly, a visitor may not linger at the front door for an extended period. The license is limited to the amount of time it would customarily take to approach the door, pause long enough to see if someone is home, and (if not expressly invited to stay longer), leave.

As I understand the law of trespass and the scope of the implied license, a visitor who adheres to these limitations is not necessarily required to ring the doorbell, knock on the door, or attempt to speak with an occupant. For example, mail carriers, persons making deliveries, and individuals distributing flyers may leave the items they are carrying and depart without making any attempt to converse. A pedestrian or motorist looking for a particular address may walk up to a front door in order to check a house number that is hard to see from the sidewalk or road. A neighbor who knows that the residents are away may approach the door to retrieve an accumulation of newspapers that might signal to a potential burglar that the house is unoccupied.

As the majority acknowledges, this implied license to approach the front door extends to the police. As we recognized in *Kentucky v. King,* 563 U.S. 452 (2011), police officers do not engage in a search when they approach the front door of a residence and seek to engage in what is termed a "knock and talk," *i.e.,* knocking on the door and seeking to speak to an occupant for the purpose of gathering evidence. Even when the objective of a "knock and talk" is to obtain evidence that will lead to the homeowner's arrest and prosecution, the license to approach still applies. In other words, gathering evidence—even damning evidence—is a lawful activity that falls within the scope of the license to approach. And when officers walk up to the front door of a house, they are permitted to see, hear, and smell whatever can be detected from a lawful vantage point.

B

Detective Bartelt did not exceed the scope of the license to approach respondent's front door. He adhered to the customary path; he did not approach in the middle of the night; and he remained at the front door for only a very short period (less than a minute or two).

The Court concludes that Detective Bartelt went too far because he had the "*objectiv[e] . . . purpose* to conduct a search." What this means, I take it, is that anyone aware of what Detective Bartelt did would infer that his subjective purpose was to gather evidence. But if this is the Court's point, then a standard "knock and talk" and most other police visits would likewise constitute searches. With the exception of visits to serve warrants or civil process, police almost always approach homes with a purpose of discovering information. That is certainly the objective of a "knock and talk." The Court offers no meaningful way of distinguishing the "objective purpose" of a "knock and talk" from the "objective purpose" of Detective Bartelt's conduct here.

The Court contends that a "knock and talk" is different because it involves talking, and "all are invited" to do that. But a police officer who approaches the front door of a house in accordance with the limitations already discussed may gather evidence by means other than talking. The officer may observe items in plain view and smell odors coming from the house. So the Court's "objective purpose" argument cannot stand.

What the Court must fall back on, then, is the particular instrument that Detective Bartelt used to detect the odor of marijuana, namely, his dog. But in the entire body of common-law decisions, the Court has not found a single case holding that a visitor to the front door of a home commits a trespass if the visitor is accompanied by a dog on a leash. On the contrary, the common law allowed even unleashed dogs to wander on private property without committing a trespass.

The Court responds that "[i]t is not the dog that is the problem, but the behavior that here involved use of the dog." But where is the support in the law of trespass for *this* proposition? Dogs' keen sense of smell has been used in law enforcement for centuries. The antiquity of this practice is evidenced by a Scottish law from 1318 that made it a crime to "disturb a tracking dog or the men coming with it for pursuing thieves or seizing malefactors." K. Brown et al., The Records of the Parliaments of Scotland to 1707, (St Andrews, 2007–2013), online at http://www.rps.ac.uk/mss/1318/9. If bringing a tracking dog to the front door of a home constituted a trespass, one would expect at least one case to have arisen during the past 800 years. But the Court has found none.

For these reasons, the real law of trespass provides no support for the Court's holding today. While the Court claims that its reasoning has "ancient and durable roots," its trespass rule is really a newly struck counterfeit.

III

The concurring opinion attempts to provide an alternative ground for today's decision, namely, that Detective Bartelt's conduct violated respondent's reasonable expectations of privacy. But we have already rejected a very similar, if not identical argument, see *Illinois v. Caballes,* 543 U.S. 405, 409–410 (2005), and in any event I see no basis for concluding that the occupants of a dwelling have a reasonable expectation of privacy in odors that emanate from the dwelling and reach spots where members of the public may lawfully stand.

It is clear that the occupant of a house has no reasonable expectation of privacy with respect to odors that can be smelled by human beings who are standing in such places. And I would not draw a line between odors that can be smelled by humans and those that are detectible only by dogs.

* * *

In an attempt to show that respondent had a reasonable expectation of privacy in the odor of marijuana wafting from his house, the concurrence argues that this case is just like *Kyllo v. United States,* 533 U.S. 27 (2001), which held that police officers conducted a search when they used a thermal imaging device to detect heat emanating from a house. This Court, however, has already rejected the argument that the use of a drug-sniffing dog is the same as the use of a thermal imaging device. The very argument now advanced by the concurrence appears in Justice Souter's *Caballes* dissent. But the Court was not persuaded.

Contrary to the interpretation propounded by the concurrence, *Kyllo* is best understood as a decision about the use of new technology. The *Kyllo*

Court focused on the fact that the thermal imaging device was a form of "sense-enhancing technology" that was "not in general public use," and it expressed concern that citizens would be "at the mercy of advancing technology" if its use was not restricted. A dog, however, is not a new form of "technology or a "device." And, as noted, the use of dogs' acute sense of smell in law enforcement dates back many centuries.

The concurrence suggests that a *Kyllo*-based decision would be "much like" the actual decision of the Court, but that is simply not so. The holding of the Court is based on what the Court sees as a " 'physical intrusion of a constitutionally protected area.' " As a result, it does not apply when a dog alerts while on a public sidewalk or street or in the corridor of a building to which the dog and handler have been lawfully admitted.

The concurrence's *Kyllo*-based approach would have a much wider reach. When the police used the thermal imaging device in *Kyllo,* they were on a public street and "committed no trespass." Therefore, if a dog's nose is just like a thermal imaging device for Fourth Amendment purposes, a search would occur if a dog alerted while on a public sidewalk or in the corridor of an apartment building. And the same would be true if the dog was trained to sniff, not for marijuana, but for more dangerous quarry, such as explosives or for a violent fugitive or kidnaped child. I see no ground for hampering legitimate law enforcement in this way.

* * *

Points for Discussion

1. The majority's property-based rationale for its holding states that "[i]t is not the dog that is the problem, but the behavior that here involved use of the dog"—i.e., the officers' approaching the house in order to search for incriminating evidence. The majority holds that the officers' adversarial purpose exceeded the scope of the implicit license to approach a house; hence, the officers trespassed the curtilage. *Katz*, of course, was meant to move Fourth Amendment analysis away from such technicalities of property law. Does the *Jones* approach actually keep "easy cases easy"? Doesn't the fact that this is a 5–4 decision show that this is *not* an easy case?

2. Justice Kagan's concurrence disputes the majority's assertion that the use of the dog is not what taints the police conduct here. Because a "trained drug-detection dog" is not in general public use, she argues, using it to learn what is inside a home violates the Fourth Amendment. However, her concurrence does not explain why people have an expectation of privacy in marijuana kept at home but not in luggage, FedEx packages, or cars (as *Place*, *Jacobsen*, and *Caballes* respectively held). One possibility is that the edict that there can be no reasonable expectation of privacy in contraband simply does not apply to the home. This is what the Florida Supreme Court concluded when it ruled (before *Jones* was decided) in favor of Jardines. Can the concurring opinion be reconciled with *Place*, *Jacobsen*, or *Caballes*? Is the dissent correct

that the concurrence's rationale means drug-detection dogs cannot be used in public places?

C. AUTOMOBILES

The Court sees the automobile as occupying a special place in Fourth Amendment jurisprudence. It is an effect, and therefore explicitly protected by the Fourth Amendment. However its inherent mobility, heavy regulation, and relative lack of privacy are all seen by the Court as calling for lesser constitutional protection than is afforded to persons or homes. In this section, we examine some of the enormous body of case law that the Supreme Court has created to deal with the automobile's unique status in American life.

1. THE AUTOMOBILE "EXCEPTION"

CHAMBERS V. MARONEY

399 U.S. 42 (1970)

MR. JUSTICE WHITE delivered the opinion of the court.

The principal question in this case concerns the admissibility of evidence seized from an automobile, in which petitioner was riding at the time of his arrest, after the automobile was taken to a police station and was there thoroughly searched without a warrant. The Court of Appeals for the Third Circuit found no violation of petitioner's Fourth Amendment rights. We affirm.

I

During the night of May 20, 1963, a Gulf service station in North Braddock, Pennsylvania, was robbed by two men, each of whom carried and displayed a gun. The robbers took the currency from the cash register; the service station attendant, one Stephen Kovacich, was directed to place the coins in his right-hand glove, which was then taken by the robbers. Two teen-agers, who had earlier noticed a blue compact station wagon circling the block in the vicinity of the Gulf station, then saw the station wagon speed away from a parking lot close to the Gulf station. About the same time, they learned that the Gulf station had been robbed. They reported to police, who arrived immediately, that four men were in the station wagon and one was wearing a green sweater. Kovacich told the police that one of the men who robbed him was wearing a green sweater and the other was wearing a trench coat. A description of the car and the two robbers was broadcast over the police radio. Within an hour, a light blue compact station wagon answering the description and carrying four men was stopped by the police about two miles from the Gulf station. Petitioner was one of the men in the station wagon. He was wearing a green sweater and there was a trench coat in the car. The occupants were arrested and the car was driven to the police station. In the course of a thorough search of the car at the station, the police found concealed in a compartment under the dashboard two .38-caliber revolvers (one loaded with dumdum bullets), a right-hand glove containing small change, and certain cards bearing the name of Raymond Havicon, the attendant at a Boron service station in McKeesport, Pennsylvania, who had been robbed at gunpoint on May 13, 1963. In the course of a warrant-authorized search of petitioner's home the day after petitioner's arrest, police found and seized certain .38-caliber ammunition, including some dumdum bullets similar to those found in one of the guns taken from the station wagon.

* * *

We pass quickly the claim that the search of the automobile was the fruit of an unlawful arrest. Both the courts below thought the arresting officers had probable cause to make the arrest. We agree. Having talked to the teen-age observers and to the victim Kovacich, the police had ample cause to stop a light blue compact station wagon carrying four men and to arrest the occupants, one of whom was wearing a green sweater and one of whom had a trench coat with him in the car.[6]

Even so, the search that produced the incriminating evidence was made at the police station some time after the arrest and cannot be justified as a search incident to an arrest: "Once an accused is under arrest and in custody, then a search made at another place, without a warrant, is simply not incident to the arrest." *Preston v. United States*, 376 U.S. 364, 367 (1964). *Dyke v. Taylor Implement Mfg. Co.*, 391 U.S. 216 (1968), is to the same effect; the reasons that have been thought sufficient to justify warrantless searches carried out in connection with an arrest no longer obtain when the accused is safely in custody at the station house.

There are, however alternative grounds arguably justifying the search of the car in this case. In *Preston*, the arrest was for vagrancy; it was apparent that the officers had no cause to believe that evidence of crime was concealed in the auto. In *Dyke*, the Court expressly rejected the suggestion that there was probable cause to search the car. Here the situation is different, for the police had probable cause to believe that the robbers, carrying guns and the fruits of the crime, had fled the scene in a light blue compact station wagon which would be carrying four men, one wearing a green sweater and another wearing a trench coat. As the state courts correctly held, there was probable cause to arrest the occupants of the station wagon that the officers stopped; just as obviously was there probable cause to search the car for guns and stolen money.

---

[6] In any event, as we point out below, the validity of an arrest is not necessarily determinative of the right to search a car if there is probable cause to make the search. Here as will be true in many cases, the circumstances justifying the arrest are also those furnishing probable cause for the search.

* * *

Neither *Carroll* [*v. United States*, 267 U.S. 132 (1925),] nor other cases in this Court require or suggest that in every conceivable circumstance the search of an auto even with probable cause may be made without the extra protection for privacy that a warrant affords. But the circumstances that furnish probable cause to search a particular auto for particular articles are most often unforeseeable; moreover, the opportunity to search is fleeting since a car is readily movable. Where this is true, as in *Carroll* and the case before us now, if an effective search is to be made at any time, either the search must be made immediately without a warrant or the car itself must be seized and held without a warrant for whatever period is necessary to obtain a warrant for the search.

In enforcing the Fourth Amendment's prohibition against unreasonable searches and seizures, the Court has insisted upon probable cause as a minimum requirement for a reasonable search permitted by the Constitution. As a general rule, it has also required the judgment of a magistrate on the probable-cause issue and the issuance of a warrant before a search is made. Only in exigent circumstances will the judgment of the police as to probable cause serve as a sufficient authorization for a search. *Carroll* holds a search warrant unnecessary where there is probable cause to search an automobile stopped on the highway; the car is movable, the occupants are alerted, and the car's contents may never be found again if a warrant must be obtained. Hence an immediate search is constitutionally permissible.

Arguably, because of the preference for a magistrate's judgment, only the immobilization of the car should be permitted until a search warrant is obtained; arguably, only the "lesser" intrusion is permissible until the magistrate authorizes the "greater." But which is the "greater" and which the "lesser" intrusion is itself a debatable question and the answer may depend on a variety of circumstances. For constitutional purposes, we see no difference between on the one hand seizing and holding a car before presenting the probable cause issue to a magistrate and on the other hand carrying out an immediate search without a warrant. Given probable cause to search, either course is reasonable under the Fourth Amendment.

On the facts before us, the blue station wagon could have been searched on the spot when it was stopped since there was probable cause to search and it was a fleeting target for a search. The probable-cause factor still obtained at the station house and so did the mobility of the car unless the Fourth Amendment permits a warrantless seizure of the car and the denial of its use to anyone until a warrant is secured. In that event there is little to choose in terms of practical consequences between an immediate search without a warrant and the car's immobilization until a warrant is obtained.[10] The same consequences may not follow where there is unforeseeable cause to search a house. But as *Carroll* held, for the purposes of the Fourth Amendment there is a constitutional difference between houses and cars.

* * *

MR. JUSTICE BLACKMUN took no part in the consideration or decision of this case.

MR. JUSTICE STEWART, concurring.

I adhere to the view that the admission at trial of evidence acquired in alleged violation of Fourth Amendment standards is not of itself sufficient ground for a collateral attack upon an otherwise valid criminal conviction, state or federal. But until the Court adopts that view, I regard myself as obligated to consider the merits of the Fourth and Fourteenth Amendment claims in a case of this kind. Upon that premise I join the opinion and judgment of the Court.

MR. JUSTICE HARLAN, concurring in part and dissenting in part.

* * *

In sustaining the search of the automobile I believe the Court ignores the framework of our past decisions circumscribing the scope of permissible search without a warrant. The Court has long read the Fourth Amendment's proscription of "unreasonable" searches as imposing a general principle that a search without a warrant is not justified by the mere knowledge by the searching officers of facts showing probable cause. The "general requirement that a search warrant be obtained" is basic to the Amendment's protection of privacy, and "the burden is on those seeking (an) exemption * * * to show the need for it." *E.g., Chimel v. California*, 395 U.S. 752, 762 (1969).

Fidelity to this established principle requires that, where exceptions are made to accommodate the exigencies of particular situations, those exceptions be no broader than necessitated by the circumstances presented. For example, the Court has recognized that an arrest creates an emergency situation justifying a warrantless search of the arrestee's person and of "the area from within which he might gain possession of a weapon or destructible evidence"; however, because the exigency giving rise to this exception extends only that far, the search may go no further. *Chimel v. California*, 395 U.S., at 763. Similarly we held in *Terry v. Ohio*, 392 U.S. 1 (1968), that a warrantless search in a "stop and frisk" situation must "be strictly circumscribed by the exigencies which justify its

[10] It was not unreasonable in this case to take the car to the station house. All occupants in the car were arrested in a dark parking lot in the middle of the night. A careful search at that point was impractical and perhaps not safe for the officers, and it would serve the owner's convenience and the safety of his car to have the vehicle and the keys together at the station house.

initiation." Any intrusion beyond what is necessary for the personal safety of the officer or others nearby is forbidden.

Where officers have probable cause to search a vehicle on a public way, a further limited exception to the warrant requirement is reasonable because "the vehicle can be quickly moved out of the locality or jurisdiction in which the warrant must be sought." *Carroll v. United States*, 267 U.S. 132, 153 (1925). Because the officers might be deprived of valuable evidence if required to obtain a warrant before effecting any search or seizure, I agree with the Court that they should be permitted to take the steps necessary to preserve evidence and to make a search possible.[6]

The Court holds that those steps include making a warrantless search of the entire vehicle on the highway—a conclusion reached by the Court in *Carroll* without discussion—and indeed appears to go further and to condone the removal of the car to the police station for a warrantless search there at the convenience of the police.[7] I cannot agree that this result is consistent with our insistence in other areas that departures from the warrant requirement strictly conform to the exigency presented.

The Court concedes that the police could prevent removal of the evidence by temporarily seizing the car for the time necessary to obtain a warrant. It does not dispute that such a course would fully protect the interests of effective law enforcement; rather it states that whether temporary seizure is a "lesser" intrusion than warrantless search "is itself a debatable question and the answer may depend on a variety of circumstances."[8] I believe it clear that a warrantless search involves the greater sacrifice of Fourth Amendment values.

The Fourth Amendment proscribes, to be sure, unreasonable "seizures" as well as "searches." However, in the circumstances in which this problem is likely to occur, the lesser intrusion will almost always be the simple seizure of the car for the period—perhaps a day—necessary to enable the officers to obtain a search warrant. In the first place, as this case shows, the very facts establishing probable cause to search will often

---

[6] Where a suspect is lawfully arrested in the automobile, the officers may, of course, perform a search within the limits prescribed by *Chimel* as an incident to the lawful arrest. However, as the Court recognizes, the search here exceeded those limits. Nor was the search here within the limits imposed by pre-*Chimel* law for searches incident to arrest; therefore, the retroactivity of *Chimel* is not drawn into question in this case.

[7] The Court disregards the fact that *Carroll*, and each of this Court's decisions upholding a warrantless vehicle search on its authority, involved a search for contraband. Although subsequent dicta have omitted this limitation, the *Carroll* decision has not until today been held to authorize a general search of a vehicle for evidence of crime, without a warrant, in every case where probable cause exists.

[8] The Court, unable to decide whether search or temporary seizure is the "lesser" intrusion, in this case authorizes both. The Court concludes that it was reasonable for the police to take the car to the station, where they searched it once to no avail. The searching officers then entered the station, interrogated petitioner and the car's owner, and returned later for another search of the car—this one successful. At all times the car and its contents were secure against removal or destruction. Nevertheless the Court approves the searches without even an inquiry into the officers' ability promptly to take their case before a magistrate.

also justify arrest of the occupants of the vehicle. Since the occupants themselves are to be taken into custody, they will suffer minimal further inconvenience from the temporary immobilization of their vehicle. Even where no arrests are made, persons who wish to avoid a search—either to protect their privacy or to conceal incriminating evidence—will almost certainly prefer a brief loss of the use of the vehicle in exchange for the opportunity to have a magistrate pass upon the justification for the search. To be sure, one can conceive of instances in which the occupant, having nothing to hide and lacking concern for the privacy of the automobile, would be more deeply offended by a temporary immobilization of his vehicle than by a prompt search of it. However, such a person always remains free to consent to an immediate search, thus avoiding any delay. Where consent is not forthcoming, the occupants of the car have an interest in privacy that is protected by the Fourth Amendment even where the circumstances justify a temporary seizure. The Court's endorsement of a warrantless invasion of that privacy where another course would suffice is simply inconsistent with our repeated stress on the Fourth Amendment's mandate of "adherence to judicial processes."[9]

* * *

Points for Discussion

1. *Chambers* cites *Carroll v. United States* for the proposition that an automobile may be searched based upon probable cause and without a warrant. Here, the Court holds that it was reasonable for the police to conduct a *Carroll* search at the stationhouse rather than at the scene of the stop. Does the *Carroll* reasoning readily apply to such a search?

2. The Court refuses to require the police to obtain a warrant before searching a seized car because it is unwilling to conclude that a warrantless search is a greater intrusion than a seizure pending a warrant. Do you agree? Does Justice Harlan?

3. In *California v. Carney*, 471 U.S. 386, 393 (1985), the Supreme Court upheld the warrantless search of a mobile home: "While it is true that respondent's vehicle possessed some, if not many of the attributes of a home, it is equally clear that the vehicle falls clearly within the scope of the exception laid down in *Carroll* and applied in succeeding cases."

[9] Circumstances might arise in which it would be impracticable to immobilize the car for the time required to obtain a warrant—for example, where a single police officer must take arrested suspects to the station, and has no way of protecting the suspects' car during his absence. In such situations it might be wholly reasonable to perform an on-the-spot search based on probable cause. However, where nothing in the situation makes impracticable the obtaining of a warrant, I cannot join the Court in shunting aside that vital Fourth Amendment safeguard.

2. CONTAINERS IN CARS

UNITED STATES V. CHADWICK

433 U.S. 1 (1977)

MR. CHIEF JUSTICE BURGER delivered the opinion of the court.

We granted certiorari in this case to decide whether a search warrant is required before federal agents may open a locked footlocker which they have lawfully seized at the time of the arrest of its owners, when there is probable cause to believe the footlocker contains contraband.

(1)

On May 8, 1973, Amtrak railroad officials in San Diego observed respondents Gregory Machado and Bridget Leary load a brown footlocker onto a train bound for Boston. Their suspicions were aroused when they noticed that the trunk was unusually heavy for its size, and that it was leaking talcum power, a substance often used to mask the odor of marihuana or hashish. Because Machado matched a profile used to spot drug traffickers, the railroad officials reported these circumstances to federal agents in San Diego, who in turn relayed the information, together with detailed descriptions of Machado and the footlocker, to their counterparts in Boston.

When the train arrived in Boston two days later, federal narcotics agents were on hand. Though the officers had not obtained an arrest or search warrant, they had with them a police dog trained to detect marihuana. The agents identified Machado and Leary and kept them under surveillance as they claimed their suitcases and the footlocker, which had been transported by baggage cart from the train to the departure area. Machado and Leary lifted the footlocker from the baggage cart, placed it on the floor and sat down on it.

The agents then released the dog near the footlocker. Without alerting respondents, the dog signaled the presence of a controlled substance inside. Respondent Chadwick then joined Machado and Leary, and they engaged an attendant to move the footlocker outside to Chadwick's waiting automobile. Machado, Chadwick, and the attendant together lifted the 200-pound footlocker into the trunk of the car, while Leary waited in the front seat. At that point, while the trunk of the car was still open and before the car engine had been started, the officers arrested all three. A search disclosed no weapons, but the keys to the footlocker were apparently taken from Machado.

Respondents were taken to the Federal Building in Boston; the agents followed with Chadwick's car and the footlocker. As the Government concedes, from the moment of respondents' arrests at about 9 p. m., the footlocker remained under the exclusive control of law enforcement officers at all times. The footlocker and luggage were placed in the Federal Building, where, as one of the agents later testified, "there was no risk that whatever was contained in the footlocker trunk would be removed by the defendants or their associates." The agents had no reason to believe that the footlocker contained explosives or other inherently dangerous items, or that it contained evidence which would lose its value unless the footlocker were opened at once. Facilities were readily available in which the footlocker could have been stored securely; it is not contended that there was any exigency calling for an immediate search.

At the Federal Building an hour and a half after the arrests, the agents opened the footlocker and luggage. They did not obtain respondents' consent; they did not secure a search warrant. The footlocker was locked with a padlock and a regular trunk lock. It is unclear whether it was opened with the keys taken from respondent Machado, or by other means. Large amounts of marihuana were found in the footlocker.

* * *

(2)

* * *

Drawing on its reading of history, the Government argues that only homes, offices, and private communications implicate interests which lie at the core of the Fourth Amendment. Accordingly, it is only in these contexts that the determination whether a search or seizure is reasonable should turn on whether a warrant has been obtained. In all other situations, the Government contends, less significant privacy values are at stake, and the reasonableness of a government intrusion should depend solely on whether there is probable cause to believe evidence of criminal conduct is present. Where personal effects are lawfully seized outside the home on probable cause, the Government would thus regard searches without a warrant as not "unreasonable."

We do not agree that the Warrant Clause protects only dwellings and other specifically designated locales. As we have noted before, the Fourth Amendment "protects people, not places," *Katz v. United States*, 389 U.S. 347, 351 (1967); more particularly, it protects people from unreasonable government intrusions into their legitimate expectations of privacy. In this case, the Warrant Clause makes a significant contribution to that protection. The question, then, is whether a warrantless search in these circumstances was unreasonable.

(3)

* * *

Although the searches and seizures which deeply concerned the colonists, and which were foremost in the minds of the Framers, were those involving invasions of the home, it would be a mistake to conclude, as the

Government contends, that the Warrant Clause was therefore intended to guard only against intrusions into the home. First, the Warrant Clause does not in terms distinguish between searches conducted in private homes and other searches. There is also a strong historical connection between the Warrant Clause and the initial clause of the Fourth Amendment, which draws no distinctions among "persons, houses, papers, and effects" in safeguarding against unreasonable searches and seizures.

Moreover, if there is little evidence that the Framers intended the Warrant Clause to operate outside the home, there is no evidence at all that they intended to exclude from protection of the Clause all searches occurring outside the home. The absence of a contemporary outcry against warrantless searches in public places was because, aside from searches incident to arrest, such warrantless searches were not a large issue in colonial America. Thus, silence in the historical record tells us little about the Framers' attitude toward application of the Warrant Clause to the search of respondents' footlocker.

* * *

In this case, important Fourth Amendment privacy interests were at stake. By placing personal effects inside a double-locked footlocker, respondents manifested an expectation that the contents would remain free from public examination. No less than one who locks the doors of his home against intruders, one who safeguards his personal possessions in this manner is due the protection of the Fourth Amendment Warrant Clause. There being no exigency, it was unreasonable for the Government to conduct this search without the safeguards a judicial warrant provides.

(4)

The Government does not contend that the footlocker's brief contact with Chadwick's car makes this an automobile search, but it is argued that the rationale of our automobile search cases demonstrates the reasonableness of permitting warrantless searches of luggage; the Government views such luggage as analogous to motor vehicles for Fourth Amendment purposes. It is true that, like the footlocker in issue here, automobiles are "effects" under the Fourth Amendment, and searches and seizures of automobiles are therefore subject to the constitutional standard of reasonableness. But this Court has recognized significant differences between motor vehicles and other property which permit warrantless searches of automobiles in circumstances in which warrantless searches would not be reasonable in other contexts.

* * *

The factors which diminish the privacy aspects of an automobile do not apply to respondents' footlocker. Luggage contents are not open to public view, except as a condition to a border entry or common carrier travel; nor is luggage subject to regular inspections and official scrutiny on a continuing basis. Unlike an automobile, whose primary function is transportation, luggage is intended as a repository of personal effects. In sum, a person's expectations of privacy in personal luggage are substantially greater than in an automobile.

Nor does the footlocker's mobility justify dispensing with the added protections of the Warrant Clause. Once the federal agents had seized it at the railroad station and had safely transferred it to the Boston Federal Building under their exclusive control, there was not the slightest danger that the footlocker or its contents could have been removed before a valid search warrant could be obtained. The initial seizure and detention of the footlocker, the validity of which respondents do not contest, were sufficient to guard against any risk that evidence might be lost. With the footlocker safely immobilized, it was unreasonable to undertake the additional and greater intrusion of a search without a warrant.[8]

Finally, the Government urges that the Constitution permits the warrantless search of any property in the possession of a person arrested in public, so long as there is probable cause to believe that the property contains contraband or evidence of crime. Although recognizing that the footlocker was not within respondents' immediate control, the Government insists that the search was reasonable because the footlocker was seized contemporaneously with respondents' arrests and was searched as soon thereafter as was practicable. The reasons justifying search in a custodial arrest are quite different. When a custodial arrest is made, there is always some danger that the person arrested may seek to use a weapon, or that evidence may be concealed or destroyed. To safeguard himself and others, and to prevent the loss of evidence, it has been held reasonable for the arresting officer to conduct a prompt, warrantless "search of the arrestee's person and the area 'within his immediate control' construing that phrase to mean the area from within which he might gain possession of a weapon or destructible evidence."

Such searches may be conducted without a warrant, and they may also be made whether or not there is probable cause to believe that the person arrested may have a weapon or is about to destroy evidence. The potential dangers lurking in all custodial arrests make warrantless searches of items within the "immediate control" area reasonable without requiring the arresting officer to calculate the probability that weapons or destructible

---

[8] Respondents' principal privacy interest in the footlocker was, of course, not in the container itself, which was exposed to public view, but in its contents. A search of the interior was therefore a far greater intrusion into Fourth Amendment values than the impoundment of the footlocker. Though surely a substantial infringement of respondents' use and possession, the seizure did not diminish respondents' legitimate expectation that the footlocker's contents would remain private.

It was the greatly reduced expectation of privacy in the automobile, coupled with the transportation function of the vehicle, which made the Court in Chambers unwilling to decide whether an immediate search of an automobile, or its seizure and indefinite immobilization, constituted a greater interference with the rights of the owner. This is clearly not the case with locked luggage.

evidence may be involved. However, warrantless searches of luggage or other property seized at the time of an arrest cannot be justified as incident to that arrest either if the "search is remote in time or place from the arrest," or no exigency exists. Once law enforcement officers have reduced luggage or other personal property not immediately associated with the person of the arrestee to their exclusive control, and there is no longer any danger that the arrestee might gain access to the property to seize a weapon or destroy evidence, a search of that property is no longer an incident of the arrest.[9]

Here the search was conducted more than an hour after federal agents had gained exclusive control of the footlocker and long after respondents were securely in custody; the search therefore cannot be viewed as incidental to the arrest or as justified by any other exigency. Even though on this record the issuance of a warrant by a judicial officer was reasonably predictable, a line must be drawn. In our view, when no exigency is shown to support the need for an immediate search, the Warrant Clause places the line at the point where the property to be searched comes under the exclusive dominion of police authority. Respondents were therefore entitled to the protection of the Warrant Clause with the evaluation of a neutral magistrate, before their privacy interests in the contents of the footlocker were invaded.[10]

MR. JUSTICE BRENNAN, concurring.

I fully join the Chief Justice's thorough opinion for the Court. I write only to comment upon two points made by my Brother Blackmun's dissent.

First, I agree wholeheartedly with my Brother Blackmun that it is "unfortunate" that the Government in this case "sought . . . to vindicate an extreme view of the Fourth Amendment." It is unfortunate, in my view, not because this argument somehow "distract(ed)" the Court from other more meritorious arguments made by the Government—these arguments are addressed and convincingly rejected in the Court's opinion—but because it is deeply distressing that the Department of Justice, whose mission is to protect the constitutional liberties of the people of the United States, should even appear to be seeking to subvert them by extreme and dubious legal arguments. It is gratifying that the Court today unanimously rejects the Government's position.

---

[9] Of course, there may be other justifications for a warrantless search of luggage taken from a suspect at the time of his arrest; for example, if officers have reason to believe that luggage contains some immediately dangerous instrumentality, such as explosives, it would be foolhardy to transport it to the station house without opening the luggage and disarming the weapon.

[10] Unlike searches of the person, *United States v. Robinson*, 414 U.S. 218 (1973); *United States v. Edwards*, 415 U.S. 800 (1974), searches of possessions within an arrestee's immediate control cannot be justified by any reduced expectations of privacy caused by the arrest. Respondents' privacy interest in the contents of the footlocker was not eliminated simply because they were under arrest.

Second, it should be noted that while Part II of the dissent suggests a number of possible alternative courses of action that the agents could have followed without violating the Constitution, no decision of this Court is cited to support the constitutionality of these courses, but only some decisions of Courts of Appeals. In my view, it is not at all obvious that the agents could legally have searched the footlocker had they seized it after Machado and Leary had driven away with it in their car or "at the time and place of the arrests."

MR. JUSTICE BLACKMUN, with whom MR. JUSTICE REHNQUIST joins, dissenting.

I think it somewhat unfortunate that the Government sought a reversal in this case primarily to vindicate an extreme view of the Fourth Amendment that would restrict the protection of the Warrant Clause to private dwellings and a few other "high privacy" areas. I reject this argument for the reasons stated in Parts (2) and (3) of the Court's opinion, with which I am in general agreement. The overbroad nature of the Government's principal argument, however, has served to distract the Court from the more important task of defining the proper scope of a search incident to an arrest. The Court fails to accept the opportunity this case presents to apply the rationale of recent decisions and develop a clear doctrine concerning the proper consequences of custodial arrest. Accordingly, I dissent from the judgment.

I

One line of recent decisions establishes that no warrant is required for the arresting officer to search the clothing and effects of one placed in custodial arrest. The rationale for this was explained in *United States v. Robinson*, 414 U.S. 218, 235 (1973):

> A police officer's determination as to how and where to search the person of a suspect whom he has arrested is necessarily a quick ad hoc judgment which the Fourth Amendment does not require to be broken down in each instance into an analysis of each step in the search. The authority to search the person incident to a lawful custodial arrest, while based upon the need to disarm and to discover evidence, does not depend on what a court may later decide was the probability in a particular arrest situation that weapons or evidence would in fact be found upon the person of the suspect. A custodial arrest of a suspect based on probable cause is a reasonable intrusion under the Fourth Amendment; that intrusion being lawful, a search incident to the arrest requires no additional justification. It is the fact of the lawful arrest which establishes the authority to search, and we hold that in the case of a lawful custodial arrest a full search of the person is not only an exception to the warrant requirement of the Fourth

Amendment, but is also a "reasonable" search under that Amendment.

Under this doctrine, a search of personal effects need not be contemporaneous with the arrest, and indeed may be delayed a number of hours while the suspect remains in lawful custody.

A second series of decisions concerns the consequences of custodial arrest of a person driving an automobile. The car may be impounded and, with probable cause, its contents (including locked compartments) subsequently examined without a warrant. *Texas v. White*, 423 U.S. 67 (1975). Moreover, once a car has been properly impounded for any reason, the police may follow a standard procedure of inventorying its contents without any showing of probable cause.

I would apply the rationale of these two lines of authority and hold generally that a warrant is not required to seize and search any movable property in the possession of a person properly arrested in a public place. A person arrested in a public place is likely to have various kinds of property with him: items inside his clothing, a briefcase or suitcase, packages, or a vehicle. In such instances the police cannot very well leave the property on the sidewalk or street while they go to get a warrant. The items may be stolen by a passer-by or removed by the suspect's confederates. Rather than requiring the police to "post a guard" over such property, I think it is surely reasonable for the police to take the items along to the station with the arrested person.

In the present case the Court of Appeals held, and respondents do not contest, that it was proper for the federal agents to seize the footlocker and take it to their office. Given the propriety of seizing the footlocker, there is some reason to believe that the subsequent search a fortiori was permissible. I acknowledge, however, that impounding the footlocker without searching it would have been a less intrusive alternative in this case. The police could have waited to conduct their search until after a warrant had been obtained. Nevertheless, the mere fact that a warrant could have been obtained while the footlocker was safely impounded does not necessarily make the warrantless search unreasonable.

As the Court in *Robinson* recognized, custodial arrest is such a serious deprivation that various lesser invasions of privacy may be fairly regarded as incidental. An arrested person, of course, has an additional privacy interest in the objects in his possession at the time of arrest. To be sure, allowing impoundment of those objects pursuant to arrest, but requiring a warrant for examination of their contents, would protect that incremental privacy interest in cases where the police assessment of probable cause is subsequently rejected by a magistrate. But a countervailing consideration is that a warrant would be routinely forthcoming in the vast majority of situations where the property has been seized in conjunction with the valid arrest of a person in a public place. I therefore doubt that requiring the authorities to go through the formality of obtaining a warrant in this situation would have much practical effect in protecting Fourth Amendment values.

* * *

II

The approach taken by the Court has the perverse result of allowing fortuitous circumstances to control the outcome of the present case. The agents probably could have avoided having the footlocker search held unconstitutional either by delaying the arrest for a few minutes or by conducting the search on the spot rather than back at their office. Probable cause for the arrest was present from the time respondents Machado and Leary were seated on the footlocker inside Boston's South Station and the agents' dog signalled the presence of marihuana. Rather than make an arrest at this moment, the agents commendably sought to determine the possible involvement of others in the illegal scheme. They waited a short time until respondent Chadwick arrived and the footlocker had been loaded into the trunk of his car, and then made the arrest. But if the agents had postponed the arrest just a few minutes longer until the respondents started to drive away, then the car could have been seized, taken to the agents' office, and all its contents including the footlocker searched without a warrant.

Alternatively, the agents could have made a search of the footlocker at the time and place of the arrests. Machado and Leary were standing next to an open automobile trunk containing the footlocker, and thus it was within the area of their "immediate control." And certainly the footlocker would have been properly subject to search at the time if the arrest had occurred a few minutes earlier while Machado and Leary were seated on it.

In many cases, of course, small variations in the facts are determinative of the legal outcome. Criminal law necessarily involves some line drawing. But I see no way that these alternative courses of conduct, which likely would have been held constitutional under the Fourth Amendment, would have been any more solicitous of the privacy or well-being of the respondents. Indeed, as Judge Thomsen observed in dissenting from this aspect of the Court of Appeals' decision that is today affirmed, the course of conduct followed by the agents in this case was good police procedure. It is decisions of the kind made by the Court today that make criminal law a trap for the unwary policeman and detract from the important activities of detecting criminal activity and protecting the public safety.

I might add that postponing the arrest until after the car was started would have increased the likelihood that respondents would attempt to evade arrest, possibly endangering innocent bystanders.

Points for Discussion

1. The Court states that the footlocker here could not be searched at the federal building, even with probable cause, unless a warrant was first obtained from a magistrate. Do you find the majority's attempt to distinguish its contrary holding regarding the impounded car in *Chambers* to be compelling? What is the difference between the footlocker and the car that explains the different results in the two cases?

2. Do you agree with the dissent's assertion that the footlocker could have been searched at the scene as a search incident to arrest? Was the double-locked footlocker within the defendants' immediate control at the time of arrest?

3. Justice Brennan chastises the government for advancing unfounded theories to support this search. But note that the government explicitly declined to argue that the footlocker's brief contact with the trunk somehow transformed this into an automobile search. As the next case shows, later prosecutors were not always so willing to forgo this argument.

CALIFORNIA V. ACEVEDO

500 U.S. 565 (1991)

JUSTICE BLACKMUN delivered the opinion of the court.

* * *

I

On October 28, 1987, Officer Coleman of the Santa Ana, Cal., Police Department received a telephone call from a federal drug enforcement agent in Hawaii. The agent informed Coleman that he had seized a package containing marijuana which was to have been delivered to the Federal Express Office in Santa Ana and which was addressed to J.R. Daza at 805 West Stevens Avenue in that city. The agent arranged to send the package to Coleman instead. Coleman then was to take the package to the Federal Express office and arrest the person who arrived to claim it.

Coleman received the package on October 29, verified its contents, and took it to the Senior Operations Manager at the Federal Express office. At about 10:30 a.m. on October 30, a man, who identified himself as Jamie Daza, arrived to claim the package. He accepted it and drove to his apartment on West Stevens. He carried the package into the apartment.

At 11:45 a.m., officers observed Daza leave the apartment and drop the box and paper that had contained the marijuana into a trash bin. Coleman at that point left the scene to get a search warrant. About 12:05 p.m., the officers saw Richard St. George leave the apartment carrying a blue knapsack which appeared to be half full. The officers stopped him as he was driving off, searched the knapsack, and found 1½ pounds of marijuana.

At 12:30 p.m., respondent Charles Steven Acevedo arrived. He entered Daza's apartment, stayed for about 10 minutes, and reappeared carrying a brown paper bag that looked full. The officers noticed that the bag was the size of one of the wrapped marijuana packages sent from Hawaii. Acevedo walked to a silver Honda in the parking lot. He placed the bag in the trunk of the car and started to drive away. Fearing the loss of evidence, officers in a marked police car stopped him. They opened the trunk and the bag, and found marijuana.[1]

* * *

II

The Fourth Amendment protects the "right of the people to be secure in their persons, houses, papers, and effects, against unreasonable searches and seizures." Contemporaneously with the adoption of the Fourth Amendment, the First Congress, and, later, the Second and Fourth Congresses, distinguished between the need for a warrant to search for contraband concealed in "a dwelling house or similar place" and the need for a warrant to search for contraband concealed in a movable vessel. See *Carroll v. United States,* 267 U.S. 132, 151 (1925). In *Carroll,* this Court established an exception to the warrant requirement for moving vehicles, for it recognized "a necessary difference between a search of a store, dwelling house or other structure in respect of which a proper official warrant readily may be obtained, and a search of a ship, motor boat, wagon or automobile, for contraband goods, where it is not practicable to secure a warrant because the vehicle can be quickly moved out of the locality or jurisdiction in which the warrant must be sought."

It therefore held that a warrantless search of an automobile, based upon probable cause to believe that the vehicle contained evidence of crime in the light of an exigency arising out of the likely disappearance of the vehicle, did not contravene the Warrant Clause of the Fourth Amendment.

The Court refined the exigency requirement in *Chambers v. Maroney,* 399 U.S. 42 (1970), when it held that the existence of exigent circumstances was to be determined at the time the automobile is seized. The car search at issue in *Chambers* took place at the police station, where the vehicle was immobilized, some time after the driver had been arrested. Given probable cause and exigent circumstances at the time the vehicle was first stopped, the Court held that the later warrantless search at the station passed constitutional muster. The validity of the later search derived from the ruling in *Carroll* that an immediate search without a warrant at the moment of seizure would have been permissible. The Court reasoned in *Chambers* that the police could search later whenever they could have

[1] When Officer Coleman returned with a warrant, the apartment was searched and bags of marijuana were found there. We are here concerned, of course, only with what was discovered in the automobile.

searched earlier, had they so chosen. Following *Chambers,* if the police have probable cause to justify a warrantless seizure of an automobile on a public roadway, they may conduct either an immediate or a delayed search of the vehicle.

In *United States v. Ross,* 456 U.S. 798, decided in 1982, we held that a warrantless search of an automobile under the *Carroll* doctrine could include a search of a container or package found inside the car when such a search was supported by probable cause. The warrantless search of Ross' car occurred after an informant told the police that he had seen Ross complete a drug transaction using drugs stored in the trunk of his car. The police stopped the car, searched it, and discovered in the trunk a brown paper bag containing drugs. We decided that the search of Ross' car was not unreasonable under the Fourth Amendment: "The scope of a warrantless search based on probable cause is no narrower—and no broader—than the scope of a search authorized by a warrant supported by probable cause." Thus, "[i]f probable cause justifies the search of a lawfully stopped vehicle, it justifies the search of every part of the vehicle and its contents that may conceal the object of the search." In *Ross,* therefore, we clarified the scope of the *Carroll* doctrine as properly including a "probing search" of compartments and containers within the automobile so long as the search is supported by probable cause.

In addition to this clarification, *Ross* distinguished the *Carroll* doctrine from the separate rule that governed the search of closed containers. The Court had announced this separate rule, unique to luggage and other closed packages, bags, and containers, in *United States v. Chadwick,* 433 U.S. 1 (1977). In *Chadwick,* federal narcotics agents had probable cause to believe that a 200-pound double-locked footlocker contained marijuana. The agents tracked the locker as the defendants removed it from a train and carried it through the station to a waiting car. As soon as the defendants lifted the locker into the trunk of the car, the agents arrested them, seized the locker, and searched it. In this Court, the United States did not contend that the locker's brief contact with the automobile's trunk sufficed to make the *Carroll* doctrine applicable. Rather, the United States urged that the search of movable luggage could be considered analogous to the search of an automobile.

The Court rejected this argument because, it reasoned, a person expects more privacy in his luggage and personal effects than he does in his automobile. Moreover, it concluded that as "may often not be the case when automobiles are seized," secure storage facilities are usually available when the police seize luggage.

In *Arkansas v. Sanders,* 442 U.S. 753 (1979), the Court extended *Chadwick*'s rule to apply to a suitcase actually being transported in the trunk of a car. In *Sanders,* the police had probable cause to believe a suitcase contained marijuana. They watched as the defendant placed the suitcase in the trunk of a taxi and was driven away. The police pursued the taxi for several blocks, stopped it, found the suitcase in the trunk, and searched it. Although the Court had applied the *Carroll* doctrine to searches of integral parts of the automobile itself, (indeed, in *Carroll,* contraband whiskey was in the upholstery of the seats), it did not extend the doctrine to the warrantless search of personal luggage "merely because it was located in an automobile lawfully stopped by the police." Again, the *Sanders* majority stressed the heightened privacy expectation in personal luggage and concluded that the presence of luggage in an automobile did not diminish the owner's expectation of privacy in his personal items.

In *Ross,* the Court endeavored to distinguish between *Carroll,* which governed the *Ross* automobile search, and *Chadwick,* which governed the *Sanders* automobile search. It held that the *Carroll* doctrine covered searches of automobiles when the police had probable cause to search an entire vehicle, but that the *Chadwick* doctrine governed searches of luggage when the officers had probable cause to search only a container within the vehicle. Thus, in a *Ross* situation, the police could conduct a reasonable search under the Fourth Amendment without obtaining a warrant, whereas in a *Sanders* situation, the police had to obtain a warrant before they searched.

* * *

III

The facts in this case closely resemble the facts in *Ross*. In *Ross,* the police had probable cause to believe that drugs were stored in the trunk of a particular car. Here, the California Court of Appeal concluded that the police had probable cause to believe that respondent was carrying marijuana in a bag in his car's trunk. Furthermore, for what it is worth, in *Ross,* as here, the drugs in the trunk were contained in a brown paper bag.

This Court in *Ross* rejected *Chadwick*'s distinction between containers and cars. It concluded that the expectation of privacy in one's vehicle is equal to one's expectation of privacy in the container, and noted that "the privacy interests in a car's trunk or glove compartment may be no less than those in a movable container." It also recognized that it was arguable that the same exigent circumstances that permit a warrantless search of an automobile would justify the warrantless search of a movable container. In deference to the rule of *Chadwick* and *Sanders,* however, the Court put that question to one side. It concluded that the time and expense of the warrant process would be misdirected if the police could search every cubic inch of an automobile until they discovered a paper sack, at which point the Fourth Amendment required them to take the sack to a magistrate for permission to look inside. We now must decide the question deferred in *Ross:* whether the Fourth Amendment requires the police to obtain a warrant to open the sack in a movable vehicle simply because they lack probable cause to search the entire car. We conclude that it does not.

IV

Dissenters in *Ross* asked why the suitcase in *Sanders* was "more private, less difficult for police to seize and store, or in any other relevant respect more properly subject to the warrant requirement, than a container that police discover in a probable-cause search of an entire automobile?" We now agree that a container found after a general search of the automobile and a container found in a car after a limited search for the container are equally easy for the police to store and for the suspect to hide or destroy. In fact, we see no principled distinction in terms of either the privacy expectation or the exigent circumstances between the paper bag found by the police in *Ross* and the paper bag found by the police here. Furthermore, by attempting to distinguish between a container for which the police are specifically searching and a container which they come across in a car, we have provided only minimal protection for privacy and have impeded effective law enforcement.

The line between probable cause to search a vehicle and probable cause to search a package in that vehicle is not always clear, and separate rules that govern the two objects to be searched may enable the police to broaden their power to make warrantless searches and disserve privacy interests. We noted this in *Ross* in the context of a search of an entire vehicle. Recognizing that under *Carroll,* the "entire vehicle itself . . . could be searched without a warrant," we concluded that "prohibiting police from opening immediately a container in which the object of the search is most likely to be found and instead forcing them first to comb the entire vehicle would actually exacerbate the intrusion on privacy interests." At the moment when officers stop an automobile, it may be less than clear whether they suspect with a high degree of certainty that the vehicle contains drugs in a bag or simply contains drugs. If the police know that they may open a bag only if they are actually searching the entire car, they may search more extensively than they otherwise would in order to establish the general probable cause required by *Ross*.

* * *

To the extent that the *Chadwick-Sanders* rule protects privacy, its protection is minimal. Law enforcement officers may seize a container and hold it until they obtain a search warrant. "Since the police, by hypothesis, have probable cause to seize the property, we can assume that a warrant will be routinely forthcoming in the overwhelming majority of cases." And the police often will be able to search containers without a warrant, despite the *Chadwick-Sanders* rule, as a search incident to a lawful arrest. . . .

* * *

V

The *Chadwick-Sanders* rule not only has failed to protect privacy but also has confused courts and police officers and impeded effective law enforcement. The conflict between the *Carroll* doctrine cases and the *Chadwick-Sanders* line has been criticized in academic commentary. One leading authority on the Fourth Amendment, after comparing *Chadwick* and *Sanders* with *Carroll* and its progeny, observed: "These two lines of authority cannot be completely reconciled, and thus how one comes out in the container-in-the-car situation depends upon which line of authority is used as a point of departure." 3 W. LaFave, SEARCH AND SEIZURE 53 (2d ed. 1987).

* * *

Although we have recognized firmly that the doctrine of *stare decisis* serves profoundly important purposes in our legal system, this Court has overruled a prior case on the comparatively rare occasion when it has bred confusion or been a derelict or led to anomalous results. *Sanders* was explicitly undermined in *Ross,* and the existence of the dual regimes for automobile searches that uncover containers has proved as confusing as the *Chadwick* and *Sanders* dissenters predicted. We conclude that it is better to adopt one clear-cut rule to govern automobile searches and eliminate the warrant requirement for closed containers set forth in *Sanders*.

VI

The interpretation of the *Carroll* doctrine set forth in *Ross* now applies to all searches of containers found in an automobile. In other words, the police may search without a warrant if their search is supported by probable cause. The Court in *Ross* put it this way:

> The scope of a warrantless search of an automobile . . . is not defined by the nature of the container in which the contraband is secreted. Rather, it is defined by the object of the search and the places in which there is probable cause to believe that it may be found.

It went on to note: "Probable cause to believe that a container placed in the trunk of a taxi contains contraband or evidence does not justify a search of the entire cab." We reaffirm that principle. In the case before us, the police had probable cause to believe that the paper bag in the automobile's trunk contained marijuana. That probable cause now allows a warrantless search of the paper bag. The facts in the record reveal that the police did not have probable cause to believe that contraband was hidden in any other part of the automobile and a search of the entire vehicle would have been without probable cause and unreasonable under the Fourth Amendment.

* * *

Until today, this Court has drawn a curious line between the search of an automobile that coincidentally turns up a container and the search of a container that coincidentally turns up in an automobile. The protections of the Fourth Amendment must not turn on such coincidences. We therefore interpret *Carroll* as providing one rule to govern all automobile searches. The police may search an automobile and the containers within it where they have probable cause to believe contraband or evidence is contained.

JUSTICE SCALIA, concurring in the judgment.

I agree with the dissent that it is anomalous for a briefcase to be protected by the "general requirement" of a prior warrant when it is being carried along the street, but for that same briefcase to become unprotected as soon as it is carried into an automobile. On the other hand, I agree with the Court that it would be anomalous for a locked compartment in an automobile to be unprotected by the "general requirement" of a prior warrant, but for an unlocked briefcase within the automobile to be protected. I join in the judgment of the Court because I think its holding is more faithful to the text and tradition of the Fourth Amendment, and if these anomalies in our jurisprudence are ever to be eliminated that is the direction in which we should travel.

The Fourth Amendment does not by its terms require a prior warrant for searches and seizures; it merely prohibits searches and seizures that are "unreasonable." What it explicitly states regarding warrants is by way of limitation upon their issuance rather than requirement of their use. For the warrant was a means of insulating officials from personal liability assessed by colonial juries. An officer who searched or seized without a warrant did so at his own risk; he would be liable for trespass, including exemplary damages, unless the jury found that his action was "reasonable." Amar, *The Bill of Rights as a Constitution*, 100 YALE L.J. 1131, 1178–1180 (1991). If, however, the officer acted pursuant to a proper warrant, he would be absolutely immune. By restricting the issuance of warrants, the Framers endeavored to preserve the jury's role in regulating searches and seizures. Amar, *supra*; Posner, *Rethinking the Fourth Amendment*, 1981 S.CT.REV. 49, 72–73; see also T. Taylor, TWO STUDIES IN CONSTITUTIONAL INTERPRETATION 41 (1969).

Although the Fourth Amendment does not explicitly impose the requirement of a warrant, it is of course textually possible to consider that implicit within the requirement of reasonableness. For some years after the (still continuing) explosion in Fourth Amendment litigation that followed our announcement of the exclusionary rule in *Weeks v. United States,* 232 U.S. 383 (1914), our jurisprudence lurched back and forth between imposing a categorical warrant requirement and looking to reasonableness alone. (The opinions preferring a warrant involved searches of structures.) By the late 1960's, the preference for a warrant had won out, at least rhetorically.

The victory was illusory. Even before today's decision, the "warrant requirement" had become so riddled with exceptions that it was basically unrecognizable. In 1985, one commentator cataloged nearly 20 such exceptions, including "searches incident to arrest . . . automobile searches . . . border searches . . . administrative searches of regulated businesses . . . exigent circumstances . . . search[es] incident to nonarrest when there is probable cause to arrest . . . boat boarding for document checks . . . welfare searches . . . inventory searches . . . airport searches . . . school search[es]. . . ." Bradley, *Two Models of the Fourth Amendment*, 83 MICH. L. REV. 1468, 1473–1474. Since then, we have added at least two more. *California v. Carney,* 471 U.S. 386 (1985) (searches of mobile homes); *O'Connor v. Ortega,* 480 U.S. 709 (1987) (searches of offices of government employees). Our intricate body of law regarding "reasonable expectation of privacy" has been developed largely as a means of creating these exceptions, enabling a search to be denominated not a Fourth Amendment "search" and therefore not subject to the general warrant requirement.

Unlike the dissent, therefore, I do not regard today's holding as some momentous departure, but rather as merely the continuation of an inconsistent jurisprudence that has been with us for years. Cases like *United States v. Chadwick,* 433 U.S. 1 (1977), and *Arkansas v. Sanders,* 442 U.S. 753 (1979), have taken the "preference for a warrant" seriously, while cases like *United States v. Ross,* 456 U.S. 798 (1982), and *Carroll v. United States,* 267 U.S. 132 (1925), have not. There can be no clarity in this area unless we make up our minds, and unless the principles we express comport with the actions we take.

In my view, the path out of this confusion should be sought by returning to the first principle that the "reasonableness" requirement of the Fourth Amendment affords the protection that the common law afforded. I have no difficulty with the proposition that that includes the requirement of a warrant, where the common law required a warrant; and it may even be that changes in the surrounding legal rules (for example, elimination of the common-law rule that reasonable, good-faith belief was no defense to absolute liability for trespass), may make a warrant indispensable to reasonableness where it once was not. But the supposed "general rule" that a warrant is always required does not appear to have any basis in the common law and confuses rather than facilitates any attempt to develop rules of reasonableness in light of changed legal circumstances, as the anomaly eliminated and the anomaly created by today's holding both demonstrate.

And there are more anomalies still. Under our precedents (as at common law), a person may be arrested outside the home on the basis of probable cause, without an arrest warrant. *United States v. Watson,* 423

U.S. 411, 418–421 (1976). Upon arrest, the person, as well as the area within his grasp, may be searched for evidence related to the crime. Under these principles, if a known drug dealer is carrying a briefcase reasonably believed to contain marijuana (the unauthorized possession of which is a crime), the police may arrest him and search his person on the basis of probable cause alone. And, under our precedents, upon arrival at the station house, the police may inventory his possessions, including the briefcase, even if there is no reason to suspect that they contain contraband. According to our current law, however, the police may not, on the basis of the same probable cause, take the less intrusive step of stopping the individual on the street and demanding to see the contents of his briefcase. That makes no sense *a priori,* and in the absence of any common-law tradition supporting such a distinction, I see no reason to continue it.

* * *

I would reverse the judgment in the present case, not because a closed container carried inside a car becomes subject to the "automobile" exception to the general warrant requirement, but because the search of a closed container, outside a privately owned building, with probable cause to believe that the container contains contraband, and when it in fact does contain contraband, is not one of those searches whose Fourth Amendment reasonableness depends upon a warrant. For that reason I concur in the judgment of the Court.

JUSTICE WHITE, dissenting.

Agreeing as I do with most of Justice Stevens' opinion and with the result he reaches, I dissent and would affirm the judgment below.

JUSTICE STEVENS, with whom JUSTICE MARSHALL joins, dissenting.

* * *

I

The Fourth Amendment is a restraint on Executive power. The Amendment constitutes the Framers' direct constitutional response to the unreasonable law enforcement practices employed by agents of the British Crown. Over the years—particularly in the period immediately after World War II and particularly in opinions authored by Justice Jackson after his service as a special prosecutor at the Nuremburg trials—the Court has recognized the importance of this restraint as a bulwark against police practices that prevail in totalitarian regimes.

This history is, however, only part of the explanation for the warrant requirement. The requirement also reflects the sound policy judgment that, absent exceptional circumstances, the decision to invade the privacy of an individual's personal effects should be made by a neutral magistrate rather than an agent of the Executive. In his opinion for the Court in *Johnson v. United States* [333 U.S. 10 (1948)], Justice Jackson explained:

> The point of the Fourth Amendment, which often is not grasped by zealous officers, is not that it denies law enforcement the support of the usual inferences which reasonable men draw from evidence. Its protection consists in requiring that those inferences be drawn by a neutral and detached magistrate instead of being judged by the officer engaged in the often competitive enterprise of ferreting out crime.

Our decisions have always acknowledged that the warrant requirement imposes a burden on law enforcement. And our cases have not questioned that trained professionals normally make reliable assessments of the existence of probable cause to conduct a search. We have repeatedly held, however, that these factors are outweighed by the individual interest in privacy that is protected by advance judicial approval. The Fourth Amendment dictates that the privacy interest is paramount, no matter how marginal the risk of error might be if the legality of warrantless searches were judged only after the fact.

* * *

II

In its opinion today, the Court recognizes that the police did not have probable cause to search respondent's vehicle and that a search of anything but the paper bag that respondent had carried from Daza's apartment and placed in the trunk of his car would have been unconstitutional. Moreover, as I read the opinion, the Court assumes that the police could not have made a warrantless inspection of the bag before it was placed in the car. Finally, the Court also does not question the fact that, under our prior cases, it would have been lawful for the police to seize the container and detain it (and respondent) until they obtained a search warrant. Thus, all of the relevant facts that governed our decisions in *Chadwick* and *Sanders* are present here whereas the relevant fact that justified the vehicle search in *Ross* is not present.

The Court does not attempt to identify any exigent circumstances that would justify its refusal to apply the general rule against warrantless searches. Instead, it advances these three arguments: First, the rules identified in the foregoing cases are confusing and anomalous. Second, the rules do not protect any significant interest in privacy. And, third, the rules impede effective law enforcement. None of these arguments withstands scrutiny.

* * *

The Court summarizes the alleged "anomaly" created by the coexistence of *Ross, Chadwick,* and *Sanders* with the statement that "the more likely the police are to discover drugs in a container, the less authority they have to search it." This juxtaposition is only anomalous, however, if one accepts the flawed premise that the degree to which the police are likely to discover contraband is correlated with their authority to search without a warrant. Yet, even proof beyond a reasonable doubt will not justify a warrantless search that is not supported by one of the exceptions to the warrant requirement. And, even when the police have a warrant or an exception applies, once the police possess probable cause, the extent to which they are more or less certain of the contents of a container has no bearing on their authority to search it.

To the extent there was any "anomaly" in our prior jurisprudence, the Court has "cured" it at the expense of creating a more serious paradox. For surely it is anomalous to prohibit a search of a briefcase while the owner is carrying it exposed on a public street yet to permit a search once the owner has placed the briefcase in the locked trunk of his car. One's privacy interest in one's luggage can certainly not be diminished by one's removing it from a public thoroughfare and placing it—out of sight—in a privately owned vehicle. Nor is the danger that evidence will escape increased if the luggage is in a car rather than on the street. In either location, if the police have probable cause, they are authorized to seize the luggage and to detain it until they obtain judicial approval for a search. Any line demarking an exception to the warrant requirement will appear blurred at the edges, but the Court has certainly erred if it believes that, by erasing one line and drawing another, it has drawn a clearer boundary.

* * *

Despite repeated claims that *Chadwick* and *Sanders* have "impeded effective law enforcement," the Court cites no authority for its contentions. Moreover, all evidence that does exist points to the contrary conclusion. In the years since *Ross* was decided, the Court has heard argument in 30 Fourth Amendment cases involving narcotics. In all but one, the government was the petitioner. All save two involved a search or seizure without a warrant or with a defective warrant. And, in all except three, the Court upheld the constitutionality of the search or seizure.

In the meantime, the flow of narcotics cases through the courts has steadily and dramatically increased. No impartial observer could criticize this Court for hindering the progress of the war on drugs. On the contrary, decisions like the one the Court makes today will support the conclusion that this Court has become a loyal foot soldier in the Executive's fight against crime.

* * *

It is too early to know how much freedom America has lost today. The magnitude of the loss is, however, not nearly as significant as the Court's willingness to inflict it without even a colorable basis for its rejection of prior law.

Points for Discussion

1. It is important to see how four cases—*Chadwick*, *Ross*, *Sanders*, and *Acevedo*—work together in this context. How does the Supreme Court see the relationship among these cases? What is left of what the Court calls the *Chadwick-Sanders* line after *Acevedo*?

2. As Justice Scalia points out in his concurrence, if they had probable cause the police could have arrested Acevedo as he left Daza's house and could have searched his paper bag pursuant to that arrest. If this is correct, what does *Acevedo* add to the state of the law?

3. Justice Stevens would have required the police to observe the "general rule" and obtain a warrant. Justice Scalia believed it was "reasonable" to search the bag as the "general rule" is general in name only. He agreed with Justice Stevens, however, that it was anomalous to require a warrant to search the bag while Acevedo was walking down the street with it but to dispense with the warrant requirement once Acevedo put the bag in his car.

4. Whether a warrant should be required in *Acevedo* hinges on whether warrants are meant to deter only intentional constitutional violations or inadvertent transgressions as well. If warrants serve only to keep the police from deliberately making an unjustified search, a warrant is hardly necessary. (This is especially so given that, as the Court gratuitously notes, one officer "left the scene to get a search warrant" for the apartment, suggesting they were not deliberately flouting the law.) The police undoubtedly had probable cause to search the bag, and precedent allowed the search of the trunk. There is no hint that the police did anything to circumvent either the letter or spirit of the Fourth Amendment. The majority opinion thus seems to posit that complicating matters for well-meaning officers serves no purpose. If, however, as the dissenting justices believed, prior approval by a magistrate serves to ensure that people are not searched without probable cause *even by well-meaning police*, then requiring a warrant in these circumstances would make some sense.

WYOMING V. HOUGHTON

526 U.S. 295 (1999)

JUSTICE SCALIA delivered the opinion of the court.

This case presents the question whether police officers violate the Fourth Amendment when they search a passenger's personal belongings inside an automobile that they have probable cause to believe contains contraband.

I

In the early morning hours of July 23, 1995, a Wyoming Highway Patrol officer stopped an automobile for speeding and driving with a faulty brake light. There were three passengers in the front seat of the car: David Young (the driver), his girlfriend, and respondent. While questioning Young, the officer noticed a hypodermic syringe in Young's shirt pocket. He left the occupants under the supervision of two backup officers as he went to get gloves from his patrol car. Upon his return, he instructed Young to step out of the car and place the syringe on the hood. The officer then asked Young why he had a syringe; with refreshing candor, Young replied that he used it to take drugs.

At this point, the backup officers ordered the two female passengers out of the car and asked them for identification. Respondent falsely identified herself as "Sandra James" and stated that she did not have any identification. Meanwhile, in light of Young's admission, the officer searched the passenger compartment of the car for contraband. On the back seat, he found a purse, which respondent claimed as hers. He removed from the purse a wallet containing respondent's driver's license, identifying her properly as Sandra K. Houghton. When the officer asked her why she had lied about her name, she replied: "In case things went bad."

Continuing his search of the purse, the officer found a brown pouch and a black wallet-type container. Respondent denied that the former was hers, and claimed ignorance of how it came to be there; it was found to contain drug paraphernalia and a syringe with 60 ccs of methamphetamine. Respondent admitted ownership of the black container, which was also found to contain drug paraphernalia, and a syringe (which respondent acknowledged was hers) with 10 ccs of methamphetamine—an amount insufficient to support the felony conviction at issue in this case. The officer also found fresh needle-track marks on respondent's arms. He placed her under arrest.

The State of Wyoming charged respondent with felony possession of methamphetamine in a liquid amount greater than three-tenths of a gram. After a hearing, the trial court denied her motion to suppress all evidence obtained from the purse as the fruit of a violation of the Fourth and Fourteenth Amendments. The court held that the officer had probable cause to search the car for contraband, and, by extension, any containers therein that could hold such contraband. A jury convicted respondent as charged.

* * *

II

The Fourth Amendment protects "[t]he right of the people to be secure in their persons, houses, papers, and effects, against unreasonable searches and seizures." In determining whether a particular governmental action violates this provision, we inquire first whether the action was regarded as an unlawful search or seizure under the common law when the Amendment was framed. Where that inquiry yields no answer, we must evaluate the search or seizure under traditional standards of reasonableness by assessing, on the one hand, the degree to which it intrudes upon an individual's privacy and, on the other, the degree to which it is needed for the promotion of legitimate governmental interests.

It is uncontested in the present case that the police officers had probable cause to believe there were illegal drugs in the car. *Carroll v. United States,* 267 U.S. 132 (1925), similarly involved the warrantless search of a car that law enforcement officials had probable cause to believe contained contraband—in that case, bootleg liquor. The Court concluded that the Framers would have regarded such a search as reasonable in light of legislation enacted by Congress from 1789 through 1799—as well as subsequent legislation from the founding era and beyond—that empowered customs officials to search any ship or vessel without a warrant if they had probable cause to believe that it contained goods subject to a duty. Thus, the Court held that "contraband goods concealed and illegally transported in an automobile or other vehicle may be searched for without a warrant" where probable cause exists.

We have furthermore read the historical evidence to show that the Framers would have regarded as reasonable (if there was probable cause) the warrantless search of containers *within* an automobile. In *United States v. Ross*, 456 U.S. 798 (1982), we upheld as reasonable the warrantless search of a paper bag and leather pouch found in the trunk of the defendant's car by officers who had probable cause to believe that the trunk contained drugs. . . .

* * *

To be sure, there was no passenger in *Ross,* and it was not claimed that the package in the trunk belonged to anyone other than the driver. Even so, if the rule of law that *Ross* announced were limited to contents belonging to the driver, or contents other than those belonging to passengers, one would have expected that substantial limitation to be expressed. And, more importantly, one would have expected that limitation to be apparent in the historical evidence that formed the basis for *Ross's* holding. In fact, however, nothing in the statutes *Ross* relied upon, or in the practice under those statutes, would except from authorized warrantless search packages belonging to passengers on the suspect ship, horse-drawn carriage, or automobile.

Finally, we must observe that the analytical principle underlying the rule announced in *Ross* is fully consistent—as respondent's proposal is not—with the balance of our Fourth Amendment jurisprudence. *Ross* concluded from the historical evidence that the permissible scope of a warrantless car search "is defined by the object of the search and the places in which there is probable cause to believe that it may be found." The same principle is reflected in an earlier case involving the constitutionality of a search warrant directed at premises belonging to one who is not suspected of any crime: "The critical element in a reasonable search is not that the owner of the property is suspected of crime but that there is reasonable cause to believe that the specific 'things' to be searched for and seized are located on the property to which entry is sought." *Zurcher v. Stanford Daily,* 436 U.S. 547, 556 (1978). This statement was illustrated by citation and description of *Carroll,* 267 U.S., at 158–159, 167.

In sum, neither *Ross* itself nor the historical evidence it relied upon admits of a distinction among packages or containers based on ownership. When there is probable cause to search for contraband in a car, it is reasonable for police officers—like customs officials in the founding era—to examine packages and containers without a showing of individualized probable cause for each one. A passenger's personal belongings, just like the driver's belongings or containers attached to the car like a glove compartment, are "in" the car, and the officer has probable cause to search for contraband *in* the car.

Even if the historical evidence, as described by *Ross,* were thought to be equivocal, we would find that the balancing of the relative interests weighs decidedly in favor of allowing searches of a passenger's belongings. Passengers, no less than drivers, possess a reduced expectation of privacy with regard to the property that they transport in cars, which "trave[l] public thoroughfares," "seldom serv[e] as . . . the repository of personal effects," are subjected to police stop and examination to enforce "pervasive" governmental controls "[a]s an everyday occurrence," and, finally, are exposed to traffic accidents that may render all their contents open to public scrutiny.

In this regard—the degree of intrusiveness upon personal privacy and indeed even personal dignity—the two cases the Wyoming Supreme Court found dispositive differ substantially from the package search at issue here. *United States v. Di Re,* 332 U.S. 581 (1948), held that probable cause to search a car did not justify a body search of a passenger. And *Ybarra v. Illinois,* 444 U.S. 85 (1979), held that a search warrant for a tavern and its bartender did not permit body searches of all the bar's patrons. These cases turned on the unique, significantly heightened protection afforded against searches of one's person. "Even a limited search of the outer clothing . . . constitutes a severe, though brief, intrusion upon cherished personal security, and it must surely be an annoying, frightening, and perhaps humiliating experience." *Terry v. Ohio,* 392 U.S. 1, 24–25 (1968). Such traumatic consequences are not to be expected when the police examine an item of personal property found in a car.

Whereas the passenger's privacy expectations are, as we have described, considerably diminished, the governmental interests at stake are substantial. Effective law enforcement would be appreciably impaired without the ability to search a passenger's personal belongings when there is reason to believe contraband or evidence of criminal wrongdoing is hidden in the car. As in all car-search cases, the "ready mobility" of an automobile creates a risk that the evidence or contraband will be permanently lost while a warrant is obtained. *California v. Carney,* 471 U.S. 386, 390 (1985). In addition, a car passenger—unlike the unwitting tavern patron in *Ybarra*—will often be engaged in a common enterprise with the driver, and have the same interest in concealing the fruits or the evidence of their wrongdoing. A criminal might be able to hide contraband in a passenger's belongings as readily as in other containers in the car—perhaps even surreptitiously, without the passenger's knowledge or permission. (This last possibility provided the basis for respondent's defense at trial; she testified that most of the seized contraband must have been placed in her purse by her traveling companions at one or another of various times, including the time she was "half asleep" in the car.)

To be sure, these factors favoring a search will not always be present, but the balancing of interests must be conducted with an eye to the generality of cases. To require that the investigating officer have positive reason to believe that the passenger and driver were engaged in a common enterprise, or positive reason to believe that the driver had time and occasion to conceal the item in the passenger's belongings, surreptitiously or with friendly permission, is to impose requirements so seldom met that a "passenger's property" rule would dramatically reduce the ability to find and seize contraband and evidence of crime. Of course these requirements would not attach (under the Wyoming Supreme Court's rule) until the police officer knows or has reason to know that the container belongs to a passenger. But once a "passenger's property" exception to car searches became widely known, one would expect passenger-confederates to claim everything as their own. And one would anticipate a bog of litigation—in the form of both civil lawsuits and motions to suppress in criminal trials—involving such questions as whether the officer should have believed a passenger's claim of ownership, whether he should have inferred ownership from various objective factors, whether he had probable cause to believe that the passenger was a confederate, or to believe that the driver might have introduced the contraband into the package with or without the passenger's knowledge. When balancing the competing interests, our determinations of "reasonableness" under the Fourth Amendment must take account of these practical realities. We think they militate in favor of the needs of law enforcement, and against a personal-privacy interest that is ordinarily weak.

Finally, if we were to invent an exception from the historical practice that *Ross* accurately described and summarized, it is perplexing why that exception should protect only property belonging to a passenger, rather than (what seems much more logical) property belonging to *anyone* other than the driver. Surely Houghton's privacy would have been invaded to the same degree whether she was present or absent when her purse was searched. And surely her presence in the car with the driver provided more, rather than less, reason to believe that the two were in league. It may ordinarily be easier to identify the property as belonging to someone other than the driver when the purported owner is present to identify it—but in the many cases (like *Ross* itself) where the car is seized, that identification may occur later, at the station house; and even at the site of the stop one can readily imagine a package clearly marked with the owner's name and phone number, by which the officer can confirm the driver's denial of ownership. The sensible rule (and the one supported by history and case law) is that such a package may be searched, whether or not its owner is present as a passenger or otherwise, because it may contain the contraband that the officer has reason to believe is in the car.

* * *

We hold that police officers with probable cause to search a car may inspect passengers' belongings found in the car that are capable of concealing the object of the search. The judgment of the Wyoming Supreme Court is reversed.

JUSTICE BREYER, concurring.

I join the Court's opinion with the understanding that history is meant to inform, but not automatically to determine, the answer to a Fourth Amendment question. I also agree with the Court that when a police officer has probable cause to search a car, say, for drugs, it is reasonable for that officer also to search containers within the car. If the police must establish a container's ownership prior to the search of that container (whenever, for example, a passenger says "that's mine"), the resulting uncertainty will destroy the workability of the bright-line rule set forth in *United States v. Ross,* 456 U.S. 798 (1982). At the same time, police officers with probable cause to search a car for drugs would often have probable cause to search containers regardless. Hence a bright-line rule will authorize only a limited number of searches that the law would not otherwise justify.

At the same time, I would point out certain limitations upon the scope of the bright-line rule that the Court describes. Obviously, the rule applies only to automobile searches. Equally obviously, the rule applies only to containers found within automobiles. And it does not extend to the search of a person found in that automobile. As the Court notes, and as *United States v. Di Re,* 332 U.S. 581, 586–587 (1948), relied on heavily by Justice Stevens' dissent, makes clear, the search of a person, including even "a limited search of the outer clothing," is a very different matter in respect to which the law provides "significantly heightened protection."

Less obviously, but in my view also important, is the fact that the container here at issue, a woman's purse, was found at a considerable distance from its owner, who did not claim ownership until the officer discovered her identification while looking through it. Purses are special containers. They are repositories of especially personal items that people generally like to keep with them at all times. So I am tempted to say that a search of a purse involves an intrusion so similar to a search of one's person that the same rule should govern both. However, given this Court's prior cases, I cannot argue that the fact that the container was a purse *automatically* makes a legal difference, for the Court has warned against trying to make that kind of distinction. But I can say that it would matter if a woman's purse, like a man's billfold, were attached to her person. It might then amount to a kind of "outer clothing," which under the Court's cases would properly receive increased protection. In this case, the purse was separate from the person, and no one has claimed that, under those circumstances, the type of container makes a difference. For that reason, I join the Court's opinion.

JUSTICE STEVENS, with whom JUSTICE SOUTER and JUSTICE GINSBURG join, dissenting.

* * *

In all of our prior cases applying the automobile exception to the Fourth Amendment's warrant requirement, either the defendant was the operator of the vehicle and in custody of the object of the search, or no question was raised as to the defendant's ownership or custody. In the only automobile case confronting the search of a passenger defendant—*United States v. Di Re,* 332 U.S. 581 (1948)—the Court held that the exception to the warrant requirement did not apply. In *Di Re,* as here, the information prompting the search directly implicated the driver, not the passenger. Today, instead of adhering to the settled distinction between drivers and passengers, the Court fashions a new rule that is based on a distinction between property contained in clothing worn by a passenger and property contained in a passenger's briefcase or purse. In cases on both sides of the Court's newly minted test, the property is in a "container" (whether a pocket or a pouch) located in the vehicle. Moreover, unlike the Court, I think it quite plain that the search of a passenger's purse or briefcase involves an intrusion on privacy that may be just as serious as was the intrusion in *Di Re.*

Even apart from *Di Re,* the Court's rights-restrictive approach is not dictated by precedent. For example, in *United States v. Ross,* 456 U.S. 798 (1982), we were concerned with the interest of the driver in the integrity of "his automobile," and we categorically rejected the notion that the scope of a warrantless search of a vehicle might be "defined by the nature of the container in which the contraband is secreted." "Rather, it is defined by the object of the search and the places in which there is probable cause to believe that it may be found." We thus disapproved of a possible container-based distinction between a man's pocket and a woman's pocketbook. Ironically, while we concluded in *Ross* that "[p]robable cause to believe that a container placed in the trunk of a taxi contains contraband or evidence does not justify a search of the entire cab," *ibid.*, the rule the Court fashions would apparently permit a warrantless search of a passenger's briefcase if there is probable cause to believe the taxidriver had a syringe somewhere in his vehicle.

* * *

Finally, in my view, the State's legitimate interest in effective law enforcement does not outweigh the privacy concerns at issue.[3] I am as confident in a police officer's ability to apply a rule requiring a warrant or individualized probable cause to search belongings that are—as in this case—obviously owned by and in the custody of a passenger as is the Court in a "passenger-confederate[']s" ability to circumvent the rule. Certainly the ostensible clarity of the Court's rule is attractive. But that virtue is insufficient justification for its adoption. Moreover, a rule requiring a warrant or individualized probable cause to search passenger belongings is every bit as simple as the Court's rule; it simply protects more privacy.

I would decide this case in accord with what we *have* said about passengers and privacy, rather than what we *might have* said in cases where the issue was not squarely presented. What Justice Jackson wrote for the Court 50 years ago is just as sound today:

> The Government says it would not contend that, armed with a search warrant for a residence only, it could search all persons found in it. But an occupant of a house could be used to conceal this contraband on his person quite as readily as can an occupant of a car. Necessity, an argument advanced in support of this search, would seem as strong a reason for searching guests of a house for which a search warrant had issued as for search of guests in a car for which none had been issued. By a parity of reasoning with that on which the Government disclaims the right to search occupants of a house, we suppose the Government would not contend that if it had a valid search warrant for the car only it could search the occupants as an incident to its execution. How then could we say that the right to search a car without a warrant

[3] To my knowledge, we have never restricted ourselves to a two-step Fourth Amendment approach wherein the privacy and governmental interests at stake must be considered only if 18th-century common law "yields no answer." Neither the precedent cited by the Court, nor the majority's opinion in this case, mandate that approach. In a later discussion, the Court does attempt to address the contemporary privacy and governmental interests at issue in cases of this nature. Either the majority is unconvinced by its own recitation of the historical materials, or it has determined that considering additional factors is appropriate in any event. The Court does not admit the former; and of course the latter, standing alone, would not establish uncertainty in the common law as the prerequisite to looking beyond history in Fourth Amendment cases.

> confers greater latitude to search occupants than a search by warrant would permit?
>
> We see no ground for expanding the ruling in the *Carroll* case to justify this arrest and search as incident to the search of a car. We are not convinced that a person, by mere presence in a suspected car, loses immunities from search of his person to which he would otherwise be entitled.

Instead of applying ordinary Fourth Amendment principles to this case, the majority extends the automobile warrant exception to allow searches of passenger belongings based on the driver's misconduct. Thankfully, the Court's automobile-centered analysis limits the scope of its holding. But it does not justify the outcome in this case.

Points for Discussion

1. On what basis was Houghton searched in this case? If it was under the automobile exception of *Carroll* and *Chambers*, was there in fact probable cause to believe that there was contraband in the car?

2. The majority rejects the argument that a third-party's belongings cannot be searched even where, as here, it is obvious that the thing searched belongs to a passenger not otherwise suspected of wrongdoing. Is Houghton's proposed rule reasonably applicable by officers in the field?

3. INVENTORY SEARCHES

SOUTH DAKOTA V. OPPERMAN

428 U.S. 364 (1976)

MR. CHIEF JUSTICE BURGER delivered the opinion of the court.

We review the judgment of the Supreme Court of South Dakota, holding that local police violated the Fourth Amendment to the Federal Constitution, as applicable to the States under the Fourteenth Amendment, when they conducted a routine inventory search of an automobile lawfully impounded by police for violations of municipal parking ordinances.

(1)

Local ordinances prohibit parking in certain areas of downtown Vermillion, S.D., between the hours of 2 a.m. and 6 a.m. During the early morning hours of December 10, 1973, a Vermillion police officer observed respondent's unoccupied vehicle illegally parked in the restricted zone. At approximately 3 a. m., the officer issued an overtime parking ticket and placed it on the car's windshield. The citation warned: "Vehicles in violation of any parking ordinance may be towed from the area."

At approximately 10 o'clock on the same morning, another officer issued a second ticket for an overtime parking violation. These circumstances were routinely reported to police headquarters, and after the vehicle was inspected, the car was towed to the city impound lot.

From outside the car at the impound lot, a police officer observed a watch on the dashboard and other items of personal property located on the back seat and back floorboard. At the officer's direction, the car door was then unlocked and, using a standard inventory form pursuant to standard police procedures, the officer inventoried the contents of the car, including the contents of the glove compartment which was unlocked. There he found marihuana contained in a plastic bag. All items, including the contraband, were removed to the police department for safekeeping. During the late afternoon of December 10, respondent appeared at the police department to claim his property. The marihuana was retained by police.

Respondent was subsequently arrested on charges of possession of marihuana. His motion to suppress the evidence yielded by the inventory search was denied; he was convicted after a jury trial and sentenced to a fine of $100 and 14 days' incarceration in the county jail. On appeal, the Supreme Court of South Dakota reversed the conviction. The court concluded that the evidence had been obtained in violation of the Fourth Amendment prohibition against unreasonable searches and seizures. We granted certiorari and we reverse.

(2)

This Court has traditionally drawn a distinction between automobiles and homes or offices in relation to the Fourth Amendment. Although automobiles are "effects" and thus within the reach of the Fourth Amendment, warrantless examinations of automobiles have been upheld in circumstances in which a search of a home or office would not.

The reason for this well-settled distinction is twofold. First, the inherent mobility of automobiles creates circumstances of such exigency that, as a practical necessity, rigorous enforcement of the warrant requirement is impossible. But the Court has also upheld warrantless searches where no immediate danger was presented that the car would be removed from the jurisdiction. Besides the element of mobility, less rigorous warrant requirements govern because the expectation of privacy with respect to one's automobile is significantly less than that relating to one's home or office. In discharging their varied responsibilities for ensuring the public safety, law enforcement officials are necessarily brought into frequent contact with automobiles. Most of this contact is distinctly noncriminal in nature. Automobiles, unlike homes, are subjected to pervasive and continuing governmental regulation and controls, including periodic inspection and licensing requirements. As an everyday occurrence, police stop and examine vehicles when license plates or inspection stickers have expired, or if other violations, such as exhaust fumes or excessive noise, are noted, or if headlights or other safety equipment are not in proper working order.

The expectation of privacy as to automobiles is further diminished by the obviously public nature of automobile travel. Only two Terms ago, the Court noted:

> One has a lesser expectation of privacy in a motor vehicle because its function is transportation and it seldom serves as one's residence or as the repository of personal effects. . . . A car has little capacity for escaping public scrutiny. It travels public thoroughfares where both its occupants and its contents are in plain view.

* * *

When vehicles are impounded, local police departments generally follow a routine practice of securing and inventorying the automobiles' contents. These procedures developed in response to three distinct needs: the protection of the owner's property while it remains in police custody, the protection the police against claims or disputes over lost or stolen property, and the protection of the police from potential danger. The practice has been viewed as essential to respond to incidents of theft or vandalism. In addition, police frequently attempt to determine whether a vehicle has been stolen and thereafter abandoned.

* * *

(3)

* * *

The Vermillion police were indisputably engaged in a caretaking search of a lawfully impounded automobile. The inventory was conducted only after the car had been impounded for multiple parking violations. The owner, having left his car illegally parked for an extended period, and thus subject to impoundment, was not present to make other arrangements for the safekeeping of his belongings. The inventory itself was prompted by the presence in plain view of a number of valuables inside the car. As in *Cady [v. Dombrowski*, 413 U.S. 433 (1973)], there is no suggestion whatever that this standard procedure, essentially like that followed throughout the country, was a pretext concealing an investigatory police motive.[10]

[10] The inventory was not unreasonable in scope. Respondent's motion to suppress in state court challenged the inventory only as to items inside the car not in plain view. But once the policeman was lawfully inside the car to secure the personal property in plain view, it was not unreasonable to open the unlocked glove compartment, to which vandals would have had ready and unobstructed access once inside the car.

The "consent" theory advanced by the dissent rests on the assumption that the inventory is exclusively for the protection of the car owner. It is not. The protection of the municipality and

On this record we conclude that in following standard police procedures, prevailing throughout the country and approved by the overwhelming majority of courts, the conduct of the police was not "unreasonable" under the Fourth Amendment.

MR. JUSTICE POWELL, concurring.

* * *

The routine inventory search under consideration in this case does not fall within any of the established exceptions to the warrant requirement. But examination of the interests which are protected when searches are conditioned on warrants issued by a judicial officer reveals that none of these is implicated here. A warrant may issue only upon "probable cause." In the criminal context the requirement of a warrant protects the individual's legitimate expectation of privacy against the overzealous police officer. "Its protection consists in requiring that those inferences (concerning probable cause) be drawn by a neutral and detached magistrate instead of being judged by the officer engaged in the often competitive enterprise of ferreting out crime." *Johnson v. United States*, 333 U.S. 10, 14 (1948). Inventory searches, however, are not conducted in order to discover evidence of crime. The officer does not make a discretionary determination to search based on a judgment that certain conditions are present. Inventory searches are conducted in accordance with established police department rules or policy and occur whenever an automobile is seized. There are thus no special facts for a neutral magistrate to evaluate.

A related purpose of the warrant requirement is to prevent hindsight from affecting the evaluation of the reasonableness of a search. In the case of an inventory search conducted in accordance with standard police department procedures, there is no significant danger of hindsight justification. The absence of a warrant will not impair the effectiveness of post-search review of the reasonableness of a particular inventory search.

* * *

In the inventory search context these concerns are absent. The owner or prior occupant of the automobile is not present, nor, in many cases, is there any real likelihood that he could be located within a reasonable period of time. More importantly, no significant discretion is placed in the hands of the individual officer: he usually has no choice as to the subject of the search or its scope.

public officers from claims of lost or stolen property and the protection of the public from vandals who might find a firearm, *Cady v. Dombrowski*, or as here, contraband drugs, are also crucial.

MR. JUSTICE MARSHALL, with whom MR. JUSTICE BRENNAN and MR. JUSTICE STEWART join, dissenting.

The Court today holds that the Fourth Amendment permits a routine police inventory search of the closed glove compartment of a locked automobile impounded for ordinary traffic violations. Under the Court's holding, such a search may be made without attempting to secure the consent of the owner and without any particular reason to believe the impounded automobile contains contraband, evidence, or valuables, or presents any danger to its custodians or the public.[1] Because I believe this holding to be contrary to sound elaboration of established Fourth Amendment principles, I dissent.

* * *

To begin with, the Court appears to suggest by reference to a "diminished" expectation of privacy that a person's constitutional interest in protecting the integrity of closed compartments of his locked automobile may routinely be sacrificed to governmental interests requiring interference with that privacy that are less compelling than would be necessary to justify a search of similar scope of the person's home or office. This has never been the law. The Court correctly observes that some prior cases have drawn distinctions between automobiles and homes or offices in Fourth Amendment cases; but even as the Court's discussion makes clear, the reasons for distinction in those cases are not present here. Thus, *Chambers v. Maroney*, 399 U.S. 42 (1970), and *Carroll v. United States*, 267 U.S. 132 (1925), permitted certain probable-cause searches to be carried out without warrants in view of the exigencies created by the mobility of automobiles, but both decisions reaffirmed that the standard of probable cause necessary to authorize such a search was no less than the standard applicable to search of a home or office. In other contexts the Court has recognized that automobile travel sacrifices some privacy interests to the publicity of plain view. But this recognition, too, is inapposite here, for there is no question of plain view in this case. Nor does this case concern intrusions of the scope that the Court apparently assumes would ordinarily be permissible in order insure the running safety of a car. While it may be that privacy expectations associated with automobile travel are in some regards less than those associated with a home or office, it is equally clear that "(t)he word 'automobile' is not a talisman in whose presence the Fourth Amendment fades away . . . ." Thus, we have recognized that "(a) *search*, even of an automobile, is a substantial invasion of privacy," and accordingly our cases have consistently recognized that the nature and substantiality of interest required to justify a Search of private areas of an

[1] The Court does not consider, however, whether the police might open and search the glove compartment if it is locked, or whether the police might search a locked trunk or other compartment.

automobile is no less than that necessary to justify an intrusion of similar scope into a home or office.

* * *

First, this search cannot be justified in any way as a safety measure, for though the Court ignores it the sole purpose given by the State for the Vermillion police's inventory procedure was to secure valuables. Nor is there any indication that the officer's search in this case was tailored in any way to safety concerns, or that ordinarily it is so circumscribed. Even aside from the actual basis for the police practice in this case, however, I do not believe that any blanket safety argument could justify a program of routine searches of the scope permitted here. As Mr. Justice Powell recognizes, ordinarily "there is little danger associated with impounding unsearched automobiles." Thus, while the safety rationale may not be entirely discounted when it is actually relied upon, it surely cannot justify the search of every car upon the basis of undifferentiated possibility of harm; on the contrary, such an intrusion could ordinarily be justified only in those individual cases where the officer's inspection was prompted by specific circumstances indicating the possibility of a particular danger.

Second, the Court suggests that the search for valuables in the closed glove compartment might be justified as a measure to protect the police against lost property claims. Again, this suggestion is belied by the record, since although the Court declines to discuss it the South Dakota Supreme Court's interpretation of state law explicitly absolves the police, as "gratuitous depositors," from any obligation beyond inventorying objects in plain view and locking the car. Moreover, as Mr. Justice Powell notes, it may well be doubted that an inventory procedure would in any event work significantly to minimize the frustrations of false claims.[a]

Finally, the Court suggests that the public interest in protecting valuables that may be found inside a closed compartment of an impounded car may justify the inventory procedure. I recognize the genuineness of this governmental interest in protecting property from pilferage. But even if I assume that the posting of a guard would be fiscally impossible as an alternative means to the same protective end, I cannot agree with the Court's conclusion. The Court's result authorizes—indeed it appears to require—the routine search of nearly every car impounded. In my view, the Constitution does not permit such searches as a matter of routine; absent specific consent, such a search is permissible only in exceptional circumstances of particular necessity.

* * *

[a] According to South Dakota statute, a gratuitous deposit is one for which the depository, in this case, the police, "receives no consideration beyond the mere possession of the thing deposited; an involuntary deposit is gratuitous, the depository being entitled to no reward."—Eds.

Because the record in this case shows that the procedures followed by the Vermillion police in searching respondent's car fall far short of these standards, in my view the search was impermissible and its fruits must be suppressed. First, so far as the record shows, the police in this case had no reason to believe that the glove compartment of the impounded car contained particular property of any substantial value. Moreover, the owner had apparently thought it adequate to protect whatever he left in the car overnight on the street in a business area simply to lock the car, and there is nothing in the record to show that the impoundment lot would prove a less secure location against pilferage, particularly when it would seem likely that the owner would claim his car and its contents promptly, at least if it contained valuables worth protecting. Even if the police had cause to believe that the impounded car's glove compartment contained particular valuables, however, they made no effort to secure the owner's consent to the search. Although the Court relies, as it must, upon the fact that respondent was not present to make other arrangements for the care of his belongings, in my view that is not the end of the inquiry. Here the police readily ascertained the ownership of the vehicle, yet they searched it immediately without taking any steps to locate respondent and procure his consent to the inventory or advise him to make alternative arrangements to safeguard his property. Such a failure is inconsistent with the rationale that the inventory procedure is carried out for the benefit of the owner.

The Court's result in this case elevates the conservation of property interests indeed mere possibilities of property interests above the privacy and security interests protected by the Fourth Amendment. For this reason I dissent. On the remand it should be clear in any event that this Court's holding does not preclude a contrary resolution of this case or others involving the same issues under any applicable state law.

Statement of MR. JUSTICE WHITE.

Although I do not subscribe to all of my Brother Marshall's dissenting opinion, particularly some aspects of his discussion concerning the necessity for obtaining the consent of the car owner, I agree with most of his analysis and conclusions and consequently dissent from the judgment of the Court.

Points for Discussion

1. Doesn't the "inventory search" concept threaten to swallow the whole? If the police need merely point to a neutral procedure in place for inventorying every impounded car, they have the capacity to search an enormous number of cars without any suspicion. The possibility of an inventory search can also give the police leverage when they seek consent for a search.

2. The Supreme Court applied *Opperman* in the context of personal effects in *Illinois v. Lafayette*, 462 U.S. 640 (1983).

> [The officer] found respondent involved in an altercation with the theater manager. He arrested respondent for disturbing the peace, handcuffed him, and took him to the police station. Respondent carried a purse-type shoulder bag on the trip to the station.
>
> At the police station, respondent was taken to the booking room; there, Officer Mietzner removed the handcuffs from respondent and ordered him to empty his pockets and place the contents on the counter. After doing so, respondent took a package of cigarettes from his shoulder bag and placed the bag on the counter. Mietzner then removed the contents of the bag, and found 10 amphetamine pills inside the plastic wrap of a cigarette package.

Finding the search to be a reasonable one, the Court concluded that the state's interest in maintaining the safety of the local jail outweighed the defendant's interest in the privacy of his bag. The Court refused to order the state to use a less invasive means to maintain security, such as impounding the bag and issuing Lafayette a receipt for it.

4. SEARCHES INCIDENT TO ARREST

Recall that when an individual is arrested, the police may search her person and the area within her immediate control incident to that arrest. In this section, we examine the application of this doctrine to arrests that occur in, or near, automobiles.

ARIZONA V. GANT

556 U.S. 332 (2009)

JUSTICE STEVENS delivered the opinion of the court.

After Rodney Gant was arrested for driving with a suspended license, handcuffed, and locked in the back of a patrol car, police officers searched his car and discovered cocaine in the pocket of a jacket on the backseat. Because Gant could not have accessed his car to retrieve weapons or evidence at the time of the search, the Arizona Supreme Court held that the search-incident-to-arrest exception to the Fourth Amendment's warrant requirement, as defined in *Chimel v. California,* 395 U.S. 752 (1969), and applied to vehicle searches in *New York v. Belton,* 453 U.S. 454 (1981), did not justify the search in this case. We agree with that conclusion.

Under *Chimel,* police may search incident to arrest only the space within an arrestee's "immediate control," meaning "the area from within which he might gain possession of a weapon or destructible evidence." The safety and evidentiary justifications underlying *Chimel*'s reaching-distance rule determine *Belton*'s scope. Accordingly, we hold that *Belton* does not authorize a vehicle search incident to a recent occupant's arrest after the arrestee has been secured and cannot access the interior of the vehicle. Consistent with the holding in *Thornton v. United States,* 541 U.S. 615 (2004), and following the suggestion in Justice Scalia's opinion concurring in the judgment in that case, we also conclude that circumstances unique to the automobile context justify a search incident to arrest when it is reasonable to believe that evidence of the offense of arrest might be found in the vehicle.

I

On August 25, 1999, acting on an anonymous tip that the residence at 2524 North Walnut Avenue was being used to sell drugs, Tucson police officers Griffith and Reed knocked on the front door and asked to speak to the owner. Gant answered the door and, after identifying himself, stated that he expected the owner to return later. The officers left the residence and conducted a records check, which revealed that Gant's driver's license had been suspended and there was an outstanding warrant for his arrest for driving with a suspended license.

When the officers returned to the house that evening, they found a man near the back of the house and a woman in a car parked in front of it. After a third officer arrived, they arrested the man for providing a false name and the woman for possessing drug paraphernalia. Both arrestees were handcuffed and secured in separate patrol cars when Gant arrived. The officers recognized his car as it entered the driveway, and Officer Griffith confirmed that Gant was the driver by shining a flashlight into the car as it drove by him. Gant parked at the end of the driveway, got out of his car, and shut the door. Griffith, who was about 30 feet away, called to Gant, and they approached each other, meeting 10-to-12 feet from Gant's car. Griffith immediately arrested Gant and handcuffed him.

Because the other arrestees were secured in the only patrol cars at the scene, Griffith called for backup. When two more officers arrived, they locked Gant in the backseat of their vehicle. After Gant had been handcuffed and placed in the back of a patrol car, two officers searched his car: One of them found a gun, and the other discovered a bag of cocaine in the pocket of a jacket on the backseat.

Gant was charged with two offenses—possession of a narcotic drug for sale and possession of drug paraphernalia (*i.e.,* the plastic bag in which the cocaine was found). He moved to suppress the evidence seized from his car on the ground that the warrantless search violated the Fourth Amendment. Among other things, Gant argued that *Belton* did not authorize the search of his vehicle because he posed no threat to the officers after he was handcuffed in the patrol car and because he was arrested for a traffic offense for which no evidence could be found in his vehicle. When asked at the suppression hearing why the search was conducted, Officer Griffith responded: "Because the law says we can do it."

* * *

II

Consistent with our precedent, our analysis begins, as it should in every case addressing the reasonableness of a warrantless search, with the basic rule that "searches conducted outside the judicial process, without prior approval by judge or magistrate, are *per se* unreasonable under the Fourth Amendment-subject only to a few specifically established and well-delineated exceptions." *Katz v. United States,* 389 U.S. 347, 357 (1967) (footnote omitted). Among the exceptions to the warrant requirement is a search incident to a lawful arrest. The exception derives from interests in officer safety and evidence preservation that are typically implicated in arrest situations.

In *Chimel,* we held that a search incident to arrest may only include "the arrestee's person and the area 'within his immediate control'—construing that phrase to mean the area from within which he might gain possession of a weapon or destructible evidence." That limitation, which continues to define the boundaries of the exception, ensures that the scope of a search incident to arrest is commensurate with its purposes of protecting arresting officers and safeguarding any evidence of the offense of arrest that an arrestee might conceal or destroy. If there is no possibility that an arrestee could reach into the area that law enforcement officers seek to search, both justifications for the search-incident-to-arrest exception are absent and the rule does not apply.

In *Belton,* we considered *Chimel*'s application to the automobile context. A lone police officer in that case stopped a speeding car in which Belton was one of four occupants. While asking for the driver's license and registration, the officer smelled burnt marijuana and observed an envelope on the car floor marked "Supergold"—a name he associated with marijuana. Thus having probable cause to believe the occupants had committed a drug offense, the officer ordered them out of the vehicle, placed them under arrest, and patted them down. Without handcuffing the arrestees, the officer " 'split them up into four separate areas of the Thruway . . . so they would not be in physical touching area of each other' " and searched the vehicle, including the pocket of a jacket on the backseat, in which he found cocaine.

* * *

[W]e held that when an officer lawfully arrests "the occupant of an automobile, he may, as a contemporaneous incident of that arrest, search the passenger compartment of the automobile" and any containers therein. That holding was based in large part on our assumption "that articles inside the relatively narrow compass of the passenger compartment of an automobile are in fact generally, even if not inevitably, within 'the area into which an arrestee might reach.' "

The Arizona Supreme Court read our decision in *Belton* as merely delineating "the proper scope of a search of the interior of an automobile" incident to an arrest. That is, *when* the passenger compartment is within an arrestee's reaching distance, *Belton* supplies the generalization that the entire compartment and any containers therein may be reached. On that view of *Belton,* the state court concluded that the search of Gant's car was unreasonable because Gant clearly could not have accessed his car at the time of the search. It also found that no other exception to the warrant requirement applied in this case.

Gant now urges us to adopt the reading of *Belton* followed by the Arizona Supreme Court.

III

Despite the textual and evidentiary support for the Arizona Supreme Court's reading of *Belton,* our opinion has been widely understood to allow a vehicle search incident to the arrest of a recent occupant even if there is no possibility the arrestee could gain access to the vehicle at the time of the search. This reading may be attributable to Justice Brennan's dissent in *Belton,* in which he characterized the Court's holding as resting on the "fiction . . . that the interior of a car is *always* within the immediate control of an arrestee who has recently been in the car." Under the majority's approach, he argued, "the result would presumably be the same even if [the officer] had handcuffed Belton and his companions in the patrol car" before conducting the search.

Since we decided *Belton,* Courts of Appeals have given different answers to the question whether a vehicle must be within an arrestee's reach to justify a vehicle search incident to arrest, but Justice Brennan's reading of the Court's opinion has predominated. As Justice O'Connor observed, "lower court decisions seem now to treat the ability to search a vehicle incident to the arrest of a recent occupant as a police entitlement rather than as an exception justified by the twin rationales of *Chimel.*" *Thornton,* 541 U.S., at 624 (opinion concurring in part). Justice Scalia has similarly noted that, although it is improbable that an arrestee could gain access to weapons stored in his vehicle after he has been handcuffed and secured in the backseat of a patrol car, cases allowing a search in "this precise factual scenario . . . are legion." *Id.,* at 628 (opinion concurring in judgment) (collecting cases). Indeed, some courts have upheld searches under *Belton* "even when . . . the handcuffed arrestee has already left the scene."

Under this broad reading of *Belton,* a vehicle search would be authorized incident to every arrest of a recent occupant notwithstanding that in most cases the vehicle's passenger compartment will not be within the arrestee's reach at the time of the search. To read *Belton* as authorizing a vehicle search incident to every recent occupant's arrest would thus untether the rule from the justifications underlying the *Chimel* exception—

a result clearly incompatible with our statement in *Belton* that it "in no way alters the fundamental principles established in the *Chimel* case regarding the basic scope of searches incident to lawful custodial arrests." Accordingly, we reject this reading of *Belton* and hold that the *Chimel* rationale authorizes police to search a vehicle incident to a recent occupant's arrest only when the arrestee is unsecured and within reaching distance of the passenger compartment at the time of the search.

Although it does not follow from *Chimel,* we also conclude that circumstances unique to the vehicle context justify a search incident to a lawful arrest when it is "reasonable to believe evidence relevant to the crime of arrest might be found in the vehicle." *Thornton,* 541 U.S., at 632 (Scalia, J., concurring in judgment). In many cases, as when a recent occupant is arrested for a traffic violation, there will be no reasonable basis to believe the vehicle contains relevant evidence. But in others, including *Belton* and *Thornton,* the offense of arrest will supply a basis for searching the passenger compartment of an arrestee's vehicle and any containers therein.

Neither the possibility of access nor the likelihood of discovering offense-related evidence authorized the search in this case. Unlike in *Belton,* which involved a single officer confronted with four unsecured arrestees, the five officers in this case outnumbered the three arrestees, all of whom had been handcuffed and secured in separate patrol cars before the officers searched Gant's car. Under those circumstances, Gant clearly was not within reaching distance of his car at the time of the search. An evidentiary basis for the search was also lacking in this case. Whereas Belton and Thornton were arrested for drug offenses, Gant was arrested for driving with a suspended license—an offense for which police could not expect to find evidence in the passenger compartment of Gant's car. Because police could not reasonably have believed either that Gant could have accessed his car at the time of the search or that evidence of the offense for which he was arrested might have been found therein, the search in this case was unreasonable.

IV

The State does not seriously disagree with the Arizona Supreme Court's conclusion that Gant could not have accessed his vehicle at the time of the search, but it nevertheless asks us to uphold the search of his vehicle under the broad reading of *Belton* discussed above. The State argues that *Belton* searches are reasonable regardless of the possibility of access in a given case because that expansive rule correctly balances law enforcement interests, including the interest in a bright-line rule, with an arrestee's limited privacy interest in his vehicle.

For several reasons, we reject the State's argument. First, the State seriously undervalues the privacy interests at stake. Although we have recognized that a motorist's privacy interest in his vehicle is less substantial than in his home, the former interest is nevertheless important and deserving of constitutional protection. It is particularly significant that *Belton* searches authorize police officers to search not just the passenger compartment but every purse, briefcase, or other container within that space. A rule that gives police the power to conduct such a search whenever an individual is caught committing a traffic offense, when there is no basis for believing evidence of the offense might be found in the vehicle, creates a serious and recurring threat to the privacy of countless individuals. Indeed, the character of that threat implicates the central concern underlying the Fourth Amendment—the concern about giving police officers unbridled discretion to rummage at will among a person's private effects.

At the same time as it undervalues these privacy concerns, the State exaggerates the clarity that its reading of *Belton* provides. Courts that have read *Belton* expansively are at odds regarding how close in time to the arrest and how proximate to the arrestee's vehicle an officer's first contact with the arrestee must be to bring the encounter within *Belton*'s purview and whether a search is reasonable when it commences or continues after the arrestee has been removed from the scene. The rule has thus generated a great deal of uncertainty, particularly for a rule touted as providing a "bright line."

Contrary to the State's suggestion, a broad reading of *Belton* is also unnecessary to protect law enforcement safety and evidentiary interests. Under our view, *Belton* and *Thornton* permit an officer to conduct a vehicle search when an arrestee is within reaching distance of the vehicle or it is reasonable to believe the vehicle contains evidence of the offense of arrest. Other established exceptions to the warrant requirement authorize a vehicle search under additional circumstances when safety or evidentiary concerns demand. For instance, *Michigan v. Long,* 463 U.S. 1032 (1983), permits an officer to search a vehicle's passenger compartment when he has reasonable suspicion that an individual, whether or not the arrestee, is "dangerous" and might access the vehicle to "gain immediate control of weapons." If there is probable cause to believe a vehicle contains evidence of criminal activity, *United States v. Ross,* 456 U.S. 798, 820–821 (1982), authorizes a search of any area of the vehicle in which the evidence might be found. Unlike the searches permitted by Justice Scalia's opinion concurring in the judgment in *Thornton,* which we conclude today are reasonable for purposes of the Fourth Amendment, *Ross* allows searches for evidence relevant to offenses other than the offense of arrest, and the scope of the search authorized is broader. Finally, there may be still other circumstances in which safety or evidentiary interests would justify a search.

These exceptions together ensure that officers may search a vehicle when genuine safety or evidentiary concerns encountered during the arrest of a vehicle's recent occupant justify a search. Construing *Belton* broadly to allow vehicle searches incident to any arrest would serve no purpose except to provide a police entitlement, and it is anathema to the Fourth Amendment to permit a warrantless search on that basis. For these reasons, we are unpersuaded by the State's arguments that a broad reading of *Belton* would meaningfully further law enforcement interests and justify a substantial intrusion on individuals' privacy.

V

Our dissenting colleagues argue that the doctrine of *stare decisis* requires adherence to a broad reading of *Belton* even though the justifications for searching a vehicle incident to arrest are in most cases absent. The doctrine of *stare decisis* is of course "essential to the respect accorded to the judgments of the Court and to the stability of the law," but it does not compel us to follow a past decision when its rationale no longer withstands "careful analysis." *Lawrence v. Texas,* 539 U.S. 558, 577 (2003).

We have never relied on *stare decisis* to justify the continuance of an unconstitutional police practice. And we would be particularly loath to uphold an unconstitutional result in a case that is so easily distinguished from the decisions that arguably compel it. The safety and evidentiary interests that supported the search in *Belton* simply are not present in this case. Indeed, it is hard to imagine two cases that are factually more distinct, as *Belton* involved one officer confronted by four unsecured arrestees suspected of committing a drug offense and this case involves several officers confronted with a securely detained arrestee apprehended for driving with a suspended license. This case is also distinguishable from *Thornton,* in which the petitioner was arrested for a drug offense. It is thus unsurprising that Members of this Court who concurred in the judgments in *Belton* and *Thornton* also concur in the decision in this case.

We do not agree with the contention in Justice Alito's dissent (hereinafter dissent) that consideration of police reliance interests requires a different result. Although it appears that the State's reading of *Belton* has been widely taught in police academies and that law enforcement officers have relied on the rule in conducting vehicle searches during the past 28 years, many of these searches were not justified by the reasons underlying the *Chimel* exception. Countless individuals guilty of nothing more serious than a traffic violation have had their constitutional right to the security of their private effects violated as a result. The fact that the law enforcement community may view the State's version of the *Belton* rule as an entitlement does not establish the sort of reliance interest that could outweigh the countervailing interest that all individuals share in having their constitutional rights fully protected. If it is clear that a practice is unlawful, individuals' interest in its discontinuance clearly outweighs any law enforcement "entitlement" to its persistence. The dissent's reference in this regard to the reliance interests cited in *Dickerson v. United States,* 530

U.S. 428 (2000), is misplaced. In observing that "*Miranda* has become embedded in routine police practice to the point where the warnings have become part of our national culture," 530 U.S., at 443, the Court was referring not to police reliance on a rule requiring them to provide warnings but to the broader societal reliance on that individual right.

* * *

The experience of the 28 years since we decided *Belton* has shown that the generalization underpinning the broad reading of that decision is unfounded. We now know that articles inside the passenger compartment are rarely "within 'the area into which an arrestee might reach,' " 453 U.S., at 460, and blind adherence to *Belton*'s faulty assumption would authorize myriad unconstitutional searches. The doctrine of *stare decisis* does not require us to approve routine constitutional violations.

VI

Police may search a vehicle incident to a recent occupant's arrest only if the arrestee is within reaching distance of the passenger compartment at the time of the search or it is reasonable to believe the vehicle contains evidence of the offense of arrest. When these justifications are absent, a search of an arrestee's vehicle will be unreasonable unless police obtain a warrant or show that another exception to the warrant requirement applies. The Arizona Supreme Court correctly held that this case involved an unreasonable search. Accordingly, the judgment of the State Supreme Court is affirmed.

JUSTICE SCALIA, concurring.

To determine what is an "unreasonable" search within the meaning of the Fourth Amendment, we look first to the historical practices the Framers sought to preserve; if those provide inadequate guidance, we apply traditional standards of reasonableness. Since the historical scope of officers' authority to search vehicles incident to arrest is uncertain, traditional standards of reasonableness govern. It is abundantly clear that those standards do not justify what I take to be the rule set forth in *New York v. Belton,* 453 U.S. 454 (1981), and *Thornton:* that arresting officers may always search an arrestee's vehicle in order to protect themselves from hidden weapons. When an arrest is made in connection with a roadside stop, police virtually always have a less intrusive and more effective means of ensuring their safety—and a means that is virtually always employed: ordering the arrestee away from the vehicle, patting him down in the open, handcuffing him, and placing him in the squad car.

Law enforcement officers face a risk of being shot whenever they pull a car over. But that risk is at its height at the time of the initial confrontation; and it is *not at all* reduced by allowing a search of the stopped vehicle after the driver has been arrested and placed in the squad car. I observed in *Thornton* that the government had failed to provide a single instance in which a formerly restrained arrestee escaped to retrieve a weapon from his own vehicle, Arizona and its *amici* have not remedied that significant deficiency in the present case.

It must be borne in mind that we are speaking here only of a rule automatically permitting a search when the driver or an occupant is arrested. Where no arrest is made, we have held that officers may search the car if they reasonably believe "the suspect is dangerous and . . . may gain immediate control of weapons." *Michigan v. Long,* 463 U.S. 1032, 1049 (1983). In the no-arrest case, the possibility of access to weapons in the vehicle always exists, since the driver or passenger will be allowed to return to the vehicle when the interrogation is completed. The rule of *Michigan v. Long* is not at issue here.

Justice Stevens acknowledges that an officer-safety rationale cannot justify all vehicle searches incident to arrest, but asserts that that is not the rule *Belton* and *Thornton* adopted. (As described above, I read those cases differently). Justice Stevens would therefore retain the application of *Chimel v. California,* 395 U.S. 752 (1969), in the car-search context but would apply in the future what he believes our cases held in the past: that officers making a roadside stop may search the vehicle so long as the "arrestee is within reaching distance of the passenger compartment at the time of the search." I believe that this standard fails to provide the needed guidance to arresting officers and also leaves much room for manipulation, inviting officers to leave the scene unsecured (at least where dangerous suspects are not involved) in order to conduct a vehicle search. In my view we should simply abandon the *Belton-Thornton* charade of officer safety and overrule those cases. I would hold that a vehicle search incident to arrest is *ipso facto* "reasonable" only when the object of the search is evidence of the crime for which the arrest was made, or of another crime that the officer has probable cause to believe occurred. Because respondent was arrested for driving without a license (a crime for which no evidence could be expected to be found in the vehicle), I would hold in the present case that the search was unlawful.

Justice Alito insists that the Court must demand a good reason for abandoning prior precedent. That is true enough, but it seems to me ample reason that the precedent was badly reasoned and produces erroneous (in this case unconstitutional) results. We should recognize *Belton*'s fanciful reliance upon officer safety for what it was: "a return to the broader sort of [evidence-gathering] search incident to arrest that we allowed before *Chimel*."

Justice Alito argues that there is no reason to adopt a rule limiting automobile-arrest searches to those cases where the search's object is evidence of the crime of arrest. I disagree. This formulation of officers' authority both preserves the outcomes of our prior cases and tethers the scope and rationale of the doctrine to the triggering event. *Belton,* by contrast, allowed searches precisely when its exigency-based rationale was least applicable: The fact of the arrest in the automobile context makes searches on exigency grounds *less* reasonable, not more. I also disagree with Justice Alito's conclusory assertion that this standard will be difficult to administer in practice; the ease of its application in this case would suggest otherwise.

No other Justice, however, shares my view that application of *Chimel* in this context should be entirely abandoned. It seems to me unacceptable for the Court to come forth with a 4-to-1-to-4 opinion that leaves the governing rule uncertain.

I am therefore confronted with the choice of either leaving the current understanding of *Belton* and *Thornton* in effect, or acceding to what seems to me the artificial narrowing of those cases adopted by Justice Stevens. The latter, as I have said, does not provide the degree of certainty I think desirable in this field; but the former opens the field to what I think are plainly unconstitutional searches—which is the greater evil. I therefore join the opinion of the Court.

JUSTICE BREYER, dissenting.

I agree with Justice Alito that *New York v. Belton,* 453 U.S. 454 (1981), is best read as setting forth a bright-line rule that permits a warrantless search of the passenger compartment of an automobile incident to the lawful arrest of an occupant-regardless of the danger the arrested individual in fact poses. I also agree with Justice Stevens, however, that the rule can produce results divorced from its underlying Fourth Amendment rationale. For that reason I would look for a better rule—were the question before us one of first impression.

The matter, however, is not one of first impression, and that fact makes a substantial difference. The *Belton* rule has been followed not only by this Court in *Thornton v. United States,* 541 U.S. 615 (2004), but also by numerous other courts. Principles of *stare decisis* must apply, and those who wish this Court to change a well-established legal precedent-where, as here, there has been considerable reliance on the legal rule in question-bear a heavy burden. I have not found that burden met. Nor do I believe that the other considerations ordinarily relevant when determining whether to overrule a case are satisfied. I consequently join Justice Alito's dissenting opinion with the exception of Part II-E.

JUSTICE ALITO, with whom THE CHIEF JUSTICE and JUSTICE KENNEDY join, and with whom JUSTICE BREYER joins except as to Part II-E, dissenting.

Twenty-eight years ago, in *New York v. Belton,* 453 U.S. 454, 460 (1981), this Court held that "when a policeman has made a lawful custodial arrest of the occupant of an automobile, he may, as a contemporaneous incident of that arrest, search the passenger compartment of that automobile." (Footnote omitted.) Five years ago, in *Thornton v. United States,* 541 U.S. 615 (2004)—a case involving a situation not materially distinguishable from the situation here—the Court not only reaffirmed but extended the holding of *Belton,* making it applicable to recent occupants. Today's decision effectively overrules those important decisions, even though respondent Gant has not asked us to do so.

To take the place of the overruled precedents, the Court adopts a new two-part rule under which a police officer who arrests a vehicle occupant or recent occupant may search the passenger compartment if (1) the arrestee is within reaching distance of the vehicle at the time of the search or (2) the officer has reason to believe that the vehicle contains evidence of the offense of arrest. The first part of this new rule may endanger arresting officers and is truly endorsed by only four Justices; Justice Scalia joins solely for the purpose of avoiding a "4-to-1-to-4 opinion." The second part of the new rule is taken from Justice Scalia's separate opinion in *Thornton* without any independent explanation of its origin or justification and is virtually certain to confuse law enforcement officers and judges for some time to come. The Court's decision will cause the suppression of evidence gathered in many searches carried out in good-faith reliance on well-settled case law, and although the Court purports to base its analysis on the landmark decision in *Chimel v. California,* 395 U.S. 752 (1969), the Court's reasoning undermines *Chimel.* I would follow *Belton,* and I therefore respectfully dissent.

* * *

Points for Discussion

1. By its terms, *Gant* applies only to automobile searches. But doesn't its logic apply in other contexts as well? After *Gant,* can the area where a defendant was recently arrested be searched after he has been handcuffed and led from the area? For a discussion of how courts have dealt with the issue, see Anthony M. Ruiz, *Defining Gant's Reach: The Search Incident to Arrest Doctrine Following* Arizona v. Gant, 89 NYU L. REV. 337 (2014).

2. Justice Scalia says that he joins the majority opinion with which he disagrees in order to avoid a 4–1–4 split. But doesn't his statement that he disagrees with the Court's opinion weaken its precedential value? More fundamentally, what does it mean when a Justice signs an opinion he expressly disavows?

KNOWLES V. IOWA

525 U.S. 113 (1998)

CHIEF JUSTICE REHNQUIST delivered the opinion of the court.

An Iowa police officer stopped petitioner Knowles for speeding, but issued him a citation rather than arresting him. The question presented is whether such a procedure authorizes the officer, consistently with the Fourth Amendment, to conduct a full search of the car. We answer this question "no."

Knowles was stopped in Newton, Iowa, after having been clocked driving 43 miles per hour on a road where the speed limit was 25 miles per hour. The police officer issued a citation to Knowles, although under Iowa law he might have arrested him. The officer then conducted a full search of the car, and under the driver's seat he found a bag of marijuana and a "pot pipe." Knowles was then arrested and charged with violation of state laws dealing with controlled substances.

Before trial, Knowles moved to suppress the evidence so obtained. He argued that the search could not be sustained under the "search incident to arrest" exception recognized in *United States v. Robinson,* [412 U.S. 218 (1973),] because he had not been placed under arrest. At the hearing on the motion to suppress, the police officer conceded that he had neither Knowles' consent nor probable cause to conduct the search. He relied on Iowa law dealing with such searches.

* * *

In *Robinson,* we noted the two historical rationales for the "search incident to arrest" exception: (1) the need to disarm the suspect in order to take him into custody, and (2) the need to preserve evidence for later use at trial. But neither of these underlying rationales for the search incident to arrest exception is sufficient to justify the search in the present case.

We have recognized that the first rationale—officer safety—is "both legitimate and weighty." The threat to officer safety from issuing a traffic citation, however, is a good deal less than in the case of a custodial arrest. In *Robinson,* we stated that a custodial arrest involves "danger to an officer" because of "the extended exposure which follows the taking of a suspect into custody and transporting him to the police station." We recognized that "[t]he danger to the police officer flows from the fact of the arrest, and its attendant proximity, stress, and uncertainty, and not from the grounds for arrest." A routine traffic stop, on the other hand, is a relatively brief encounter and "is more analogous to a so-called '*Terry* stop' . . . than to a formal arrest." *Berkemer v. McCarty,* 468 U.S. 420, 439 (1984).

This is not to say that the concern for officer safety is absent in the case of a routine traffic stop. It plainly is not. But while the concern for officer safety in this context may justify the "minimal" additional intrusion of ordering a driver and passengers out of the car, it does not by itself justify the often considerably greater intrusion attending a full field-type search. Even without the search authority Iowa urges, officers have other, independent bases to search for weapons and protect themselves from danger. For example, they may order out of a vehicle both the driver and any passengers, perform a "patdown" of a driver and any passengers upon reasonable suspicion that they may be armed and dangerous, conduct a "*Terry* patdown" of the passenger compartment of a vehicle upon reasonable suspicion that an occupant is dangerous and may gain immediate control of a weapon, and even conduct a full search of the passenger compartment, including any containers therein, pursuant to a custodial arrest.

Nor has Iowa shown the second justification for the authority to search incident to arrest—the need to discover and preserve evidence. Once Knowles was stopped for speeding and issued a citation, all the evidence necessary to prosecute that offense had been obtained. No further evidence of excessive speed was going to be found either on the person of the offender or in the passenger compartment of the car.

Iowa nevertheless argues that a "search incident to citation" is justified because a suspect who is subject to a routine traffic stop may attempt to hide or destroy evidence related to his identity (*e.g.,* a driver's license or vehicle registration), or destroy evidence of another, as yet undetected crime. As for the destruction of evidence relating to identity, if a police officer is not satisfied with the identification furnished by the driver, this may be a basis for arresting him rather than merely issuing a citation. As for destroying evidence of other crimes, the possibility that an officer would stumble onto evidence wholly unrelated to the speeding offense seems remote.

In *Robinson,* we held that the authority to conduct a full field search as incident to an arrest was a "bright-line rule," which was based on the concern for officer safety and destruction or loss of evidence, but which did not depend in every case upon the existence of either concern. Here we are asked to extend that "bright-line rule" to a situation where the concern for officer safety is not present to the same extent and the concern for destruction or loss of evidence is not present at all. We decline to do so. The judgment of the Supreme Court of Iowa is reversed, and the cause is remanded for further proceedings not inconsistent with this opinion.

Points for Discussion

1. *Knowles* makes clear that if an officer wishes to conduct a full search of a car without consent or probable cause to believe the car contains contraband, she must make a full custodial arrest. Could the officer present the driver with a choice: either a full custodial arrest and a search or the issuance of a citation and *consent* to search? The constitutionality of consent searches is discussed in chapter 4.

2. In *Virginia v. Moore*, 553 U.S. 164 (2008), the defendant was arrested for the misdemeanor of driving with a suspended license. A search incident to the arrest uncovered 16 grams of crack cocaine on him. Moore challenged the arrest, arguing that under state law the officer was required to issue a summons to appear rather than making a custodial arrest for driving with a

suspended license. The Court held that whether state law authorized the arrest was irrelevant to the constitutionality of the search:

> [L]inking Fourth Amendment protections to state law would cause them to "vary from place to place and from time to time." Even at the same place and time, the Fourth Amendment's protections might vary if federal officers were not subject to the same statutory constraints as state officers. . . .
>
> We conclude that warrantless arrests for crimes committed in the presence of an arresting officer are reasonable under the Constitution, and that while States are free to regulate such arrests however they desire, state restrictions do not alter the Fourth Amendment's protections.

Does *Moore* give the police an incentive to arrest people so that they can search them?

CHAPTER 4

SEARCHES AND SEIZURES WITHOUT PROBABLE CAUSE

■ ■ ■

Chapter 2 introduced the probable cause concept—what it means, how it is proven, and so forth. As we saw in that chapter, the Supreme Court has held that probable cause is the presumptive level of suspicion required for all searches and seizures, whether conducted with a warrant or without. *See, e.g.*, *United States v. Knights,* 534 U.S. 112, 121 (2001) ("Although the Fourth Amendment ordinarily requires the degree of probability embodied in the term 'probable cause,' a lesser degree satisfies the Constitution when the balance of governmental and private interests makes such a standard reasonable."). However, like the Court's assertion that searches conducted without a warrant are presumptively unreasonable with only certain, limited exceptions, the probable cause requirement is disregarded far more often than it is observed. "The reality experienced by American citizens today is that they are searched and seized on a regular basis, and for the vast majority of these searches (e.g., airport searches, street stops, DUI checkpoints, urine testing of government employees), the constitutionality seems to turn not on probable cause, but on the reasonableness of the search, factoring in the degree of the intrusion and the gravity of the investigated offense." Craig S. Lerner, *The Reasonableness of Probable Cause*, 81 TEXAS L. REV. 951 (2003).

In this chapter, we investigate searches and seizures that the Supreme Court has determined may be conducted with *less* than probable cause. We begin with the so-called *Terry* stop, the Supreme Court's acknowledgement that the police may sometimes intervene in the affairs of suspects at a point prior to the development of probable cause to search or arrest. We then turn to searches based upon the consent of the party being searched and the so-called special-needs searches. While this list is not exhaustive, it provides an opportunity to examine the bases on which the Court has been willing to depart from the probable cause requirement.

A. *TERRY* STOPS

In the first case of this section, *Terry v. Ohio*, the Supreme Court holds that under some circumstances a suspect can be briefly stopped and, if need be, frisked based on less than probable cause. *Terry* is one of the most important of the Court's Fourth Amendment decisions; it takes an enormous amount of street investigation outside of the probable cause presumption. What is more, *Terry* has entered the lexicon; within law enforcement reference to a "*Terry* stop" is almost as ubiquitous as talk of "*Miranda* warnings."

1. "REASONABLE SUSPICION"

TERRY V. OHIO

392 U.S. 1 (1968)

MR. CHIEF JUSTICE WARREN delivered the opinion of the court.

This case presents serious questions concerning the role of the Fourth Amendment in the confrontation on the street between the citizen and the policeman investigating suspicious circumstances.

Petitioner Terry was convicted of carrying a concealed weapon and sentenced to the statutorily prescribed term of one to three years in the penitentiary. Following the denial of a pretrial motion to suppress, the prosecution introduced in evidence two revolvers and a number of bullets seized from Terry and a codefendant, Richard Chilton,[2] by Cleveland Police Detective Martin McFadden. At the hearing on the motion to suppress this evidence, Officer McFadden testified that while he was patrolling in plain clothes in downtown Cleveland at approximately 2:30 in the afternoon of October 31, 1963, his attention was attracted by two men, Chilton and Terry, standing on the corner of Huron Road and Euclid Avenue. He had never seen the two men before, and he was unable to say precisely what first drew his eye to them. However, he testified that he had been a policeman for 39 years and a detective for 35 and that he had been assigned to patrol this vicinity of downtown Cleveland for shoplifters and pickpockets for 30 years. He explained that he had developed routine habits of observation over the years and that he would "stand and watch people or walk and watch people at many intervals of the day." He added: "Now, in this case when I looked over they didn't look right to me at the time."

His interest aroused, Officer McFadden took up a post of observation in the entrance to a store 300 to 400 feet away from the two men. "I get more purpose to watch them when I seen their movements," he testified. He saw one of the men leave the other one and walk southwest on Huron Road, past some stores. The man paused for a moment and looked in a store

---

[2] Terry and Chilton were arrested, indicted, tried and convicted together. They were represented by the same attorney, and they made a joint motion to suppress the guns. After the motion was denied, evidence was taken in the case against Chilton. This evidence consisted of the testimony of the arresting officer and of Chilton. It was then stipulated that this testimony would be applied to the case against Terry, and no further evidence was introduced in that case. The trial judge considered the two cases together, rendered the decisions at the same time and sentenced the two men at the same time. They prosecuted their state court appeals together through the same attorney, and they petitioned this Court for certiorari together. Following the grant of the writ upon this joint petition, Chilton died. Thus, only Terry's conviction is here for review.

window, then walked on a short distance, turned around and walked back toward the corner, pausing once again to look in the same store window. He rejoined his companion at the corner, and the two conferred briefly. Then the second man went through the same series of motions, strolling down Huron Road, looking in the same window, walking on a short distance, turning back, peering in the store window again, and returning to confer with the first man at the corner. The two men repeated this ritual alternately between five and six times apiece—in all, roughly a dozen trips. At one point, while the two were standing together on the corner, a third man approached them and engaged them briefly in conversation. This man then left the two others and walked west on Euclid Avenue. Chilton and Terry resumed their measured pacing, peering and conferring. After this had gone on for 10 to 12 minutes, the two men walked off together, heading west on Euclid Avenue, following the path taken earlier by the third man.

By this time Officer McFadden had become thoroughly suspicious. He testified that after observing their elaborately casual and oft-repeated reconnaissance of the store window on Huron Road, he suspected the two men of "casing a job, a stick-up," and that he considered it his duty as a police officer to investigate further. He added that he feared "they may have a gun." Thus, Officer McFadden followed Chilton and Terry and saw them stop in front of Zucker's store to talk to the same man who had conferred with them earlier on the street corner. Deciding that the situation was ripe for direct action, Officer McFadden approached the three men, identified himself as a police officer and asked for their names. At this point his knowledge was confined to what he had observed. He was not acquainted with any of the three men by name or by sight, and he had received no information concerning them from any other source. When the men "mumbled something" in response to his inquiries, Officer McFadden grabbed petitioner Terry, spun him around so that they were facing the other two, with Terry between McFadden and the others, and patted down the outside of his clothing. In the left breast pocket of Terry's overcoat Officer McFadden felt a pistol. He reached inside the overcoat pocket, but was unable to remove the gun. At this point, keeping Terry between himself and the others, the officer ordered all three men to enter Zucker's store. As they went in, he removed Terry's overcoat completely, removed a .38-caliber revolver from the pocket and ordered all three men to face the wall with their hands raised. Officer McFadden proceeded to pat down the outer clothing of Chilton and the third man, Katz. He discovered another revolver in the outer pocket of Chilton's overcoat, but no weapons were found on Katz. The officer testified that he only patted the men down to see whether they had weapons, and that he did not put his hands beneath the outer garments of either Terry or Chilton until he felt their guns. So far as appears from the record, he never placed his hands beneath Katz' outer garments. Officer McFadden seized Chilton's gun, asked the proprietor of the store to call a police wagon, and took all three men to the station, where Chilton and Terry were formally charged with carrying concealed weapons.

On the motion to suppress the guns the prosecution took the position that they had been seized following a search incident to a lawful arrest. The trial court rejected this theory, stating that it "would be stretching the facts beyond reasonable comprehension" to find that Officer McFadden had had probable cause to arrest the men before he patted them down for weapons. However, the court denied the defendants' motion on the ground that Officer McFadden, on the basis of his experience, "had reasonable cause to believe * * * that the defendants were conducting themselves suspiciously, and some interrogation should be made of their action." Purely for his own protection, the court held, the officer had the right to pat down the outer clothing of these men, who he had reasonable cause to believe might be armed. The court distinguished between an investigatory "stop" and an arrest, and between a "frisk" of the outer clothing for weapons and a full-blown search for evidence of crime. The frisk, it held, was essential to the proper performance of the officer's investigatory duties, for without it "the answer to the police officer may be a bullet, and a loaded pistol discovered during the frisk is admissible."

* * *

I

* * *

We would be less than candid if we did not acknowledge that this question thrusts to the fore difficult and troublesome issues regarding a sensitive area of police activity—issues which have never before been squarely presented to this Court. Reflective of the tensions involved are the practical and constitutional arguments pressed with great vigor on both sides of the public debate over the power of the police to "stop and frisk"—as it is sometimes euphemistically termed—suspicious persons.

On the one hand, it is frequently argued that in dealing with the rapidly unfolding and often dangerous situations on city streets the police are in need of an escalating set of flexible responses, graduated in relation to the amount of information they possess. For this purpose it is urged that distinctions should be made between a "stop" and an "arrest" (or a "seizure" of a person), and between a "frisk" and a "search." Thus, it is argued, the police should be allowed to "stop" a person and detain him briefly for questioning upon suspicion that he may be connected with criminal activity. Upon suspicion that the person may be armed, the police should have the power to "frisk" him for weapons. If the "stop" and the "frisk" give rise to probable cause to believe that the suspect has committed a crime, then the police should be empowered to make a formal "arrest," and a full incident "search" of the person. This scheme is justified in part upon the notion that a "stop" and a "frisk" amount to a mere "minor inconvenience

and petty indignity," which can properly be imposed upon the citizen in the interest of effective law enforcement on the basis of a police officer's suspicion.

On the other side the argument is made that the authority of the police must be strictly circumscribed by the law of arrest and search as it has developed to date in the traditional jurisprudence of the Fourth Amendment. It is contended with some force that there is not—and cannot be—a variety of police activity which does not depend solely upon the voluntary cooperation of the citizen and yet which stops short of an arrest based upon probable cause to make such an arrest. The heart of the Fourth Amendment, the argument runs, is a severe requirement of specific justification for any intrusion upon protected personal security, coupled with a highly developed system of judicial controls to enforce upon the agents of the State the commands of the Constitution. Acquiescence by the courts in the compulsion inherent in the field interrogation practices at issue here, it is urged, would constitute an abdication of judicial control over, and indeed an encouragement of, substantial interference with liberty and personal security by police officers whose judgment is necessarily colored by their primary involvement in "the often competitive enterprise of ferreting out crime." *Johnson v. United States*, 333 U.S. 10, 14 (1948). This, it is argued, can only serve to exacerbate police-community tensions in the crowded centers of our Nation's cities.

In this context we approach the issues in this case mindful of the limitations of the judicial function in controlling the myriad daily situations in which policemen and citizens confront each other on the street. The State has characterized the issue here as "the right of a police officer * * * to make an on-the-street stop, interrogate and pat down for weapons (known in street vernacular as 'stop and frisk')." But this is only partly accurate. For the issue is not the abstract propriety of the police conduct, but the admissibility against petitioner of the evidence uncovered by the search and seizure. Ever since its inception, the rule excluding evidence seized in violation of the Fourth Amendment has been recognized as a principal mode of discouraging lawless police conduct. Thus its major thrust is a deterrent one, and experience has taught that it is the only effective deterrent to police misconduct in the criminal context, and that without it the constitutional guarantee against unreasonable searches and seizures would be a mere "form of words." *Mapp v. Ohio*, 367 U.S. 643, 655 (1961). The rule also serves another vital function—"the imperative of judicial integrity." *Elkins v. United States*, 364 U.S. 206, 222 (1960). Courts which sit under our Constitution cannot and will not be made party to lawless invasions of the constitutional rights of citizens by permitting unhindered governmental use of the fruits of such invasions. Thus in our system evidentiary rulings provide the context in which the judicial process of inclusion and exclusion approves some conduct as comporting with constitutional guarantees and disapproves other actions by state agents. A ruling admitting evidence in a criminal trial, we recognize, has the necessary effect of legitimizing the conduct which produced the evidence, while an application of the exclusionary rule withholds the constitutional imprimatur.

The exclusionary rule has its limitations, however, as a tool of judicial control. It cannot properly be invoked to exclude the products of legitimate police investigative techniques on the ground that much conduct which is closely similar involves unwarranted intrusions upon constitutional protections. Moreover, in some contexts the rule is ineffective as a deterrent. Street encounters between citizens and police officers are incredibly rich in diversity. They range from wholly friendly exchanges of pleasantries or mutually useful information to hostile confrontations of armed men involving arrests, or injuries, or loss of life. Moreover, hostile confrontations are not all of a piece. Some of them begin in a friendly enough manner, only to take a different turn upon the injection of some unexpected element into the conversation. Encounters are initiated by the police for a wide variety of purposes, some of which are wholly unrelated to a desire to prosecute for crime. Doubtless some police "field interrogation" conduct violates the Fourth Amendment. But a stern refusal by this Court to condone such activity does not necessarily render it responsive to the exclusionary rule. Regardless of how effective the rule may be where obtaining convictions is an important objective of the police, it is powerless to deter invasions of constitutionally guaranteed rights where the police either have no interest in prosecuting or are willing to forgo successful prosecution in the interest of serving some other goal.

Proper adjudication of cases in which the exclusionary rule is invoked demands a constant awareness of these limitations. The wholesale harassment by certain elements of the police community, of which minority groups, particularly Negroes, frequently complain, will not be stopped by the exclusion of any evidence from any criminal trial.

Yet a rigid and unthinking application of the exclusionary rule, in futile protest against practices which it can never be used effectively to control, may exact a high toll in human injury and frustration of efforts to prevent crime. No judicial opinion can comprehend the protean variety of the street encounter, and we can only judge the facts of the case before us. Nothing we say today is to be taken as indicating approval of police conduct outside the legitimate investigative sphere. Under our decision, courts still retain their traditional responsibility to guard against police conduct which is over-bearing or harassing, or which trenches upon personal security without the objective evidentiary justification which the Constitution requires. When such conduct is identified, it must be condemned by the judiciary and its fruits must be excluded from evidence in criminal trials. And, of course, our approval of legitimate and restrained investigative conduct undertaken on the basis of ample factual justification should in no

required for a search or seizure and attempted to carefully circumscribe when and how a stop based on "reasonable suspicion" could occur. Why did the Court feel that these on-the-street encounters should be subject to constitutional regulation? Answering this question requires an understanding of race relations in the United States at the time and why the Court somewhat obliquely referred to "[t] he wholesale harassment by certain elements of the police community, of which minority groups, particularly Negroes, frequently complain."

ADAMS V. WILLIAMS

407 U.S. 143 (1972)

MR. JUSTICE REHNQUIST delivered the opinion of the court.

* * *

Police Sgt. John Connolly was alone early in the morning on car patrol duty in a high-crime area of Bridgeport, Connecticut. At approximately 2:15 a.m. a person known to Sgt. Connolly approached his cruiser and informed him that an individual seated in a nearby vehicle was carrying narcotics and had a gun at his waist.

After calling for assistance on his car radio, Sgt. Connolly approached the vehicle to investigate the informant's report. Connolly tapped on the car window and asked the occupant, Robert Williams to open the door. When Williams rolled down the window instead, the sergeant reached into the car and removed a fully loaded revolver from Williams' waistband. The gun had not been visible to Connolly from outside the car, but it was in precisely the place indicated by the informant. Williams was then arrested by Connolly for unlawful possession of the pistol. A search incident to that arrest was conducted after other officers arrived. They found substantial quantities of heroin on Williams' person and in the car, and they found a machete and a second revolver hidden in the automobile.

Respondent contends that the initial seizure of his pistol, upon which rested the later search and seizure of other weapons and narcotics, was not justified by the informant's tip to Sgt. Connolly. He claims that absent a more reliable informant, or some corroboration of the tip, the policeman's actions were unreasonable under the standards set forth in *Terry v. Ohio*.

In *Terry* this Court recognized that "a police officer may in appropriate circumstances and in an appropriate manner approach a person for purposes of investigating possibly criminal behavior even though there is no probable cause to make an arrest." The Fourth Amendment does not require a policeman who lacks the precise level of information necessary for probable cause to arrest to simply shrug his shoulders and allow a crime to occur or a criminal to escape. On the contrary, *Terry* recognizes that it may be the essence of good police work to adopt an intermediate response. A brief stop of a suspicious individual, in order to determine his identity or to maintain the status quo momentarily while obtaining more information, may be most reasonable in light of the facts known to the officer at the time.

The Court recognized in *Terry* that "the policeman making a reasonable investigatory stop should not be denied the opportunity to protect himself from attack by a hostile suspect. When an officer is justified in believing that the individual whose suspicious behavior he is investigating at close range is armed and presently dangerous to the officer or to others," he may conduct a limited protective search for concealed weapons. The purpose of this limited search is not to discover evidence of crime, but to allow the officer to pursue his investigation without fear of violence, and thus the frisk for weapons might be equally necessary and reasonable, whether or not carrying a concealed weapon violated any applicable state law. So long as the officer is entitled to make a forcible stop, and has reason to believe that the suspect is armed and dangerous, he may conduct a weapons search limited in scope to this protective purpose.

Applying these principles to the present case, we believe that Sgt. Connolly acted justifiably in responding to his informant's tip. The informant was known to him personally and had provided him with information in the past. This is a stronger case than obtains in the case of an anonymous telephone tip. The informant here came forward personally to give information that was immediately verifiable at the scene. Indeed, under Connecticut law, the informant might have been subject to immediate arrest for making a false complaint had Sgt. Connolly's investigation proved the tip incorrect. Thus, while the Court's decisions indicate that this informant's unverified tip may have been insufficient for a narcotics arrest or search warrant, the information carried enough indicia of reliability to justify the officer's forcible stop of Williams.

In reaching this conclusion, we reject respondent's argument that reasonable cause for a stop and frisk can only be based on the officer's personal observation, rather than on information supplied by another person. Informants' tips, like all other clues and evidence coming to a policeman on the scene, may vary greatly in their value and reliability. One simple rule will not cover every situation. Some tips, completely lacking in indicia of reliability, would either warrant no police response or require further investigation before a forcible stop of a suspect would be authorized. But in some situations—for example, when the victim of a street crime seeks immediate police aid and gives a description of his assailant, or when a credible informant warns of a specific impending crime—the subtleties of the hearsay rule should not thwart an appropriate police response.

While properly investigating the activity of a person who was reported to be carrying narcotics and a concealed weapon and who was sitting alone in a car in a high-crime area at 2:15 in the morning, Sgt. Connolly had ample reason to fear for his safety. When Williams rolled down his window, rather than complying with the policeman's request to step out of the car so that his movements could more easily be seen, the revolver allegedly at Williams' waist became an even greater threat. Under these circumstances the policeman's action in reaching to the spot where the gun was thought to be hidden constituted a limited intrusion designed to insure his safety, and we conclude that it was reasonable. The loaded gun seized as a result of this intrusion was therefore admissible at Williams' trial.

Once Sgt. Connolly had found the gun precisely where the informant had predicted, probable cause existed to arrest Williams for unlawful possession of the weapon. Probable cause to arrest depends "upon whether, at the moment the arrest was made . . . the facts and circumstances within (the arresting officers') knowledge and of which they had reasonably trustworthy information were sufficient to warrant a prudent man in believing that the (suspect) had committed or was committing an offense." In the present case the policeman found Williams in possession of a gun in precisely the place predicted by the informant. This tended to corroborate the reliability of the informant's further report of narcotics and, together with the surrounding circumstances, certainly suggested no lawful explanation for possession of the gun. Probable cause does not require the same type of specific evidence of each element of the offense as would be needed to support a conviction. Rather, the court will evaluate generally the circumstances at the time of the arrest to decide if the officer had probable cause for his action:

> In dealing with probable cause, however, as the very name implies, we deal with probabilities. These are not technical; they are the factual and practical considerations of everyday life on which reasonable and prudent men, not legal technicians, act.

Brinegar v. United States, 338 U.S. 160, 175 (1949).

Under the circumstances surrounding Williams' possession of the gun seized by Sgt. Connolly, the arrest on the weapons charge was supported by probable cause, and the search of his person and of the car incident to that arrest was lawful. The fruits of the search were therefore properly admitted at Williams' trial, and the Court of Appeals erred in reaching a contrary conclusion.

MR. JUSTICE DOUGLAS, with whom MR. JUSTICE MARSHALL concurs, dissenting.

. . . Connecticut allows its citizens to carry weapons, concealed or otherwise, at will, provided they have a permit. Connecticut law gives its police no authority to frisk a person for a permit. Yet the arrest was for illegal possession of a gun. The only basis for that arrest was the informer's tip on the narcotics. Can it be said that a man in possession of narcotics will not have a permit for his gun? Is that why the arrest for possession of a gun in the free-and-easy State of Connecticut becomes constitutional?

* * *

There is under our decisions no reason why stiff state laws governing the purchase and possession of pistols may not be enacted. There is no reason why pistols may not be barred from anyone with a police record. There is no reason why a State may not require a purchaser of a pistol to pass a psychiatric test. There is no reason why all pistols should not be barred to everyone except the police.

* * *

Critics say that proposals like this water down the Second Amendment. Our decisions belie that argument, for the Second Amendment, as noted, was designed to keep alive the militia. But if watering-down is the mood of the day, I would prefer to water down the Second rather than the Fourth Amendment. I share with Judge Friendly a concern that the easy extension of *Terry v. Ohio*, 392 U.S. 1, to "possessory offenses" is a serious intrusion on Fourth Amendment safeguards. "If it is to be extended to the latter at all, this should be only where observation by the officer himself or well authenticated information shows 'that criminal activity may be afoot.' "[a]

MR. JUSTICE BRENNAN, dissenting.

The crucial question on which this case turns, as the Court concedes, is whether, there being no contention that Williams acted voluntarily in rolling down the window of his car, the State had shown sufficient cause to justify Sgt. Connolly's "forcible" stop. I would affirm, believing, for the following reasons stated by Judge, now Chief Judge, Friendly, dissenting, that the State did not make that showing:

* * *

> *Terry v. Ohio* was intended to free a police officer from the rigidity of a rule that would prevent his doing anything to a man reasonably suspected of being about to commit or having just committed a crime of violence, no matter how grave the problem or impelling the need for swift action, unless the officer had what a court would later determine to be probable cause for arrest. It was meant for the serious cases of imminent danger or of harm recently perpetrated to persons or property, not the conventional ones of possessory offenses. If it is to be extended to the latter at

[a] Although the view that Justice Douglas expresses regarding the Second Amendment—that it was designed to regulate the militia, not to create an individual right to bear arms—was for many years Supreme Court orthodoxy, the Court changed direction in 2008. *District of Columbia v. Heller*, 554 U.S. 570, 595 ("There seems to us no doubt, on the basis of both text and history, that the Second Amendment conferred an individual right to keep and bear arms.")—Eds.

all, this should be only where observation by the officer himself or well authenticated information shows "that criminal activity may be afoot." I greatly fear that if the (contrary view) should be followed, *Terry* will have opened the sluicegates for serious and unintended erosion of the protection of the Fourth Amendment.

MR. JUSTICE MARSHALL, with whom MR. JUSTICE DOUGLAS joins, dissenting.

* * *

In today's decision the Court ignores the fact that *Terry* begrudgingly accepted the necessity for creating an exception from the warrant requirement of the Fourth Amendment and treats this case as if warrantless searches were the rule rather than the "narrowly drawn" exception. This decision betrays the careful balance that *Terry* sought to strike between a citizen's right to privacy and his government's responsibility for effective law enforcement and expands the concept of warrantless searches far beyond anything heretofore recognized as legitimate. I dissent.

I

A. The Court's opinion states the facts and I repeat only those that appear to me to be relevant to the Fourth Amendment issues presented.

Respondent was sitting on the passenger side of the front seat of a car parked on the street in a "high crime area" in Bridgeport, Connecticut, at 2:15 a.m. when a police officer approached his car. During a conversation that had just taken place nearby, the officer was told by an informant that respondent had narcotics on his person and that he had a gun in his waistband. The officer saw that the motor was not running, that respondent was seated peacefully in the car, and that there was no indication that he was about to leave the scene. After the officer asked respondent to open the door, respondent rolled down his window instead and the officer reached into the car and pulled a gun from respondent's waistband. The officer immediately placed respondent under arrest for carrying the weapon and searched him, finding heroin in his coat. More heroin was found in a later search of the automobile. Respondent moved to suppress both the gun and the heroin prior to trial. His motion was denied and he was convicted of possessing both items.

B. The Court erroneously attempts to describe the search for the gun as a protective search incident to a reasonable investigatory stop. But, as in *Terry*, . . . there is no occasion in this case to determine whether or not police officers have a right to seize and to restrain a citizen in order to interrogate him. The facts are clear that the officer intended to make the search as soon as he approached the respondent. He asked no questions; he made no investigation; he simply searched. There was nothing apart from the information supplied by the informant to cause the officer to search. Our inquiry must focus, therefore, as it did in *Terry* on whether the officer had sufficient facts from which he could reasonably infer that respondent was not only engaging in illegal activity, but also that he was armed and dangerous. The focus falls on the informant.

The only information that the informant had previously given the officer involved homosexual conduct in the local railroad station. The following colloquy took place between respondent's counsel and the officer at the hearing on respondent's motion to suppress the evidence that had been seized from him.

> Q. Now, with respect to the information that was given you about homosexuals in the Bridgeport Police Station (sic), did that lead to an arrest? A. No.
>
> Q. An arrest was not made. A. No. There was no substantiating evidence.
>
> Q. There was no substantiating evidence? A. No.
>
> Q. And what do you mean by that? A. I didn't have occasion to witness these individuals committing any crime of any nature.
>
> Q. In other words, after this person gave you the information, you checked for corroboration before you made an arrest. Is that right? A. Well, I checked to determine the possibility of homosexual activity.
>
> Q. And since an arrest was made, I take it you didn't find any substantiating information. A. I'm sorry counselor, you say since an arrest was made.
>
> Q. Was not made. Since an arrest was not made, I presume you didn't find any substantiating information. A. No.
>
> Q. So that, you don't recall any other specific information given you about the commission of crimes by this informant. A. No.
>
> Q. And you still thought this person was reliable. A. Yes.

* * *

Assuming, arguendo, that this case truly involves, not an arrest and a search incident thereto, but a stop and frisk, we must decide whether or not the information possessed by the officer justified this interference with respondent's liberty. *Terry*, our only case to actually uphold a stop and frisk,[3] is not directly in point, because the police officer in that case acted on the basis of his own personal observations. No informant was involved.

[3] In *Sibron v. New York*, 392 U.S. 40 (1968), the Court held that the action of the policeman could not be justified as a stop and frisk. In *Peters v. New York*, 392 U.S. 40 (1968), the Court sustained the validity of a search and seizure by holding that it was incident to a legal arrest.

But the rationale of *Terry* is still controlling, and it requires that we condemn the conduct of the police officer in encountering the respondent.

Terry did not hold that whenever a policeman has a hunch that a citizen is engaging in criminal activity, he may engage in a stop and frisk. It held that if police officers want to stop and frisk, they must have specific facts from which they can reasonably infer that an individual is engaged in criminal activity and is armed and dangerous. It was central to our decision in *Terry* that the police officer acted on the basis of his own personal observations and that he carefully scrutinized the conduct of his suspects before interfering with them in any way. When we legitimated the conduct of the officer in *Terry* we did so because of the substantial reliability of the information on which the officer based his decision to act.

If the Court does not ignore the care with which we examined the knowledge possessed by the officer in *Terry* when he acted, then I cannot see how the actions of the officer in this case can be upheld. The Court explains what the officer knew about respondent before accosting him. But what is more significant is what he did not know. With respect to the scene generally, the officer had no idea how long respondent had been in the car, how long the car had been parked, or to whom the car belonged. With respect to the gun,[5] the officer did not know if or when the informant had ever seen the gun, or whether the gun was carried legally, as Connecticut law permitted, or illegally. And with respect to the narcotics, the officer did not know what kind of narcotics respondent allegedly had, whether they were legally or illegally possessed, what the basis of the informant's knowledge was, or even whether the informant was capable of distinguishing narcotics from other substances.

Unable to answer any of these questions, the officer nevertheless determined that it was necessary to intrude on respondent's liberty. I believe that his determination was totally unreasonable. As I read *Terry*, an officer may act on the basis of reliable information short of probable cause to make a stop, and ultimately a frisk, if necessary; but the officer may not use unreliable, unsubstantiated, conclusory hearsay to justify an invasion of liberty. *Terry* never meant to approve the kind of knee-jerk police reaction that we have before us in this case.

Even assuming that the officer had some legitimate reason for relying on the informant, *Terry* requires, before any stop and frisk is made, that the reliable information in the officer's possession demonstrate that the suspect is both armed and dangerous. The fact remains that Connecticut specifically authorizes persons to carry guns so long as they have a permit. Thus, there was no reason for the officer to infer from anything that the

[5] The fact that the respondent carried his gun in a high-crime area is irrelevant. In such areas it is more probable than not that citizens would be more likely to carry weapons authorized by the State to protect themselves.

informant said that the respondent was dangerous. His frisk was, therefore, illegal under *Terry*.

II

Even if I could agree with the Court that the stop and frisk in this case was proper, I could not go further and sustain the arrest and the subsequent searches. It takes probable cause to justify an arrest and search and seizure incident thereto. Probable cause means that the "facts and circumstances before the officer are such as to warrant a man of prudence and caution in believing that the offence has been committed . . ." "(G)ood faith is not enough to constitute probable cause."

Once the officer seized the gun from respondent, it is uncontradicted that he did not ask whether respondent had a license to carry it, or whether respondent carried it for any other legal reason under Connecticut law. Rather, the officer placed him under arrest immediately and hastened to search his person. Since Connecticut has not made it illegal for private citizens to carry guns, there is nothing in the facts of this case to warrant a man "of prudence and caution" to believe that any offense had been committed merely because respondent had a gun on his person.[9] Any implication that respondent's silence was some sort of a tacit admission of guilt would be utterly absurd.

It is simply not reasonable to expect someone to protest that he is not acting illegally before he is told that he is suspected of criminal activity. It would have been a simple matter for the officer to ask whether respondent had a permit, but he chose not to do so. In making this choice, he clearly violated the Fourth Amendment.

* * *

III

Mr. Justice Douglas was the sole dissenter in *Terry*. He warned of the "powerful hydraulic pressures throughout our history that bear heavily on the Court to water down constitutional guarantees . . . ." While I took the position then that we were not watering down rights, but were hesitantly and cautiously striking a necessary balance between the rights of American citizens to be free from government intrusion into their privacy and their government's urgent need for a narrow exception to the warrant

---

[9] The Court appears to rely on the fact that the existence of the gun corroborated the information supplied to the officer by the informant. It cannot be disputed that there is minimal corroboration here, but the fact remains that the officer still lacked any knowledge that respondent had done anything illegal. Since carrying a gun is not per se illegal in Connecticut, the fact that respondent carried a gun is no more relevant to probable cause than the fact that his shirt may have been blue, or that he was wearing a jacket. Moreover, the fact that the informant can identify a gun on sight does not indicate an ability to do the same with narcotics. The corroboration of this one fact is a far cry from the corroboration that the Court found sufficient to sustain an arrest in *Draper v. United States*, 358 U.S. 307 (1959).

requirement of the Fourth Amendment, today's decision demonstrates just how prescient Mr. Justice Douglas was.

It seems that the delicate balance that *Terry* struck was simply too delicate, too susceptible to the "hydraulic pressures" of the day. As a result of today's decision, the balance struck in *Terry* is now heavily weighted in favor of the government. And the Fourth Amendment, which was included in the Bill of Rights to prevent the kind of arbitrary and oppressive police action involved herein, is dealt a serious blow. Today's decision invokes the specter of a society in which innocent citizens may be stopped, searched, and arrested at the whim of police officers who have only the slightest suspicion of improper conduct.

Points for Discussion

1. Notice that the *Adams* Court, like later Courts, reads *Terry* as creating two different tests: one for brief investigative stops and one for frisks for weapons. What suspicion is required to conduct a stop under *Terry*? To conduct a frisk? It is important to see that these two tests are different, although courts will not always treat them as such.

2. This case demonstrates how criminal procedure and substantive criminal law interact. Justice Douglas dissents on the ground that the officer, having found a gun in Adams' waist, still did not have probable cause to arrest him. Based on what you learned in previous chapters about probable cause do you agree with his assertion?

3. This case arises out of a petition for writ of habeas corpus. A habeas petition is a civil proceeding brought against a warden by an inmate who asserts that his conviction and continuing custody violate the federal constitution. In *Stone v. Powell*, the Supreme Court concluded that where a defendant has had a fair opportunity to litigate a Fourth Amendment claim in the state courts, he may not bring such a claim in a petition for habeas corpus. In other words, Adams would not be able to bring this claim in federal court today.

PRADO NAVARETTE V. CALIFORNIA

572 U.S. 393 (2014)

JUSTICE THOMAS delivered the opinion of the court.

After a 911 caller reported that a vehicle had run her off the road, a police officer located the vehicle she identified during the call and executed a traffic stop. We hold that the stop complied with the Fourth Amendment because, under the totality of the circumstances, the officer had reasonable suspicion that the driver was intoxicated.

I

On August 23, 2008, a Mendocino County 911 dispatch team for the California Highway Patrol received a call from another CHP dispatcher in neighboring Humboldt County. The Humboldt County dispatcher relayed a tip from a 911 caller, which the Mendocino County team recorded as follows: " 'Showing southbound Highway 1 at mile marker 88, Silver Ford 150 pickup. Plate of 8-David-94925. Ran the reporting party off the roadway and was last seen approximately five [minutes] ago.' " The Mendocino County team then broadcast that information to CHP officers at 3:47 p.m.

A CHP officer heading northbound toward the reported vehicle responded to the broadcast. At 4:00 p.m., the officer passed the truck near mile marker 69. At about 4:05 p.m., after making a U-turn, he pulled the truck over. A second officer, who had separately responded to the broadcast, also arrived on the scene. As the two officers approached the truck, they smelled marijuana. A search of the truck bed revealed 30 pounds of marijuana. The officers arrested the driver, petitioner Lorenzo Prado Navarette, and the passenger, petitioner José Prado Navarette.

Petitioners moved to suppress the evidence, arguing that the traffic stop violated the Fourth Amendment because the officer lacked reasonable suspicion of criminal activity. Both the magistrate who presided over the suppression hearing and the Superior Court disagreed.[1] Petitioners pleaded guilty to transporting marijuana and were sentenced to 90 days in jail plus three years of probation.

* * *

II

The Fourth Amendment permits brief investigative stops—such as the traffic stop in this case—when a law enforcement officer has "a particularized and objective basis for suspecting the particular person stopped of criminal activity." *United States v. Cortez*, 449 U. S. 411–418 (1981). The "reasonable suspicion" necessary to justify such a stop "is dependent upon both the content of information possessed by police and its degree of reliability." *Alabama v. White*, 496 U. S. 325, 330 (1990). The standard takes into account "the totality of the circumstances—the whole picture." Although a mere " 'hunch' " does not create reasonable suspicion, the level of suspicion the standard requires is "considerably less than proof of wrongdoing by a preponderance of the evidence," and "obviously less"

1 At the suppression hearing, counsel for petitioners did not dispute that the reporting party identified herself by name in the 911 call recording. Because neither the caller nor the Humboldt County dispatcher who received the call was present at the hearing, however, the prosecution did not introduce the recording into evidence. The prosecution proceeded to treat the tip as anonymous, and the lower courts followed suit.

than is necessary for probable cause, *United States v. Sokolow*, 490 U. S. 1, 7 (1989).

A

These principles apply with full force to investigative stops based on information from anonymous tips. We have firmly rejected the argument "that reasonable cause for a[n investigative stop] can only be based on the officer's personal observation, rather than on information supplied by another person." *Adams v. Williams*, 407 U. S. 143, 147 (1972). Of course, "an anonymous tip alone seldom demonstrates the informant's basis of knowledge or veracity." *White*, 496 U. S., at 329 (emphasis added). That is because "ordinary citizens generally do not provide extensive recitations of the basis of their everyday observations," and an anonymous tipster's veracity is " 'by hypothesis largely unknown, and unknowable.' " *Ibid.* But under appropriate circumstances, an anonymous tip can demonstrate "sufficient indicia of reliability to provide reasonable suspicion to make [an] investigatory stop."

Our decisions in *Alabama v. White*, 496 U. S. 325 (1990) and *Florida v. J. L.*, 529 U. S. 266 (2000) are useful guides. In *White*, an anonymous tipster told the police that a woman would drive from a particular apartment building to a particular motel in a brown Plymouth station wagon with a broken right tail light. The tipster further asserted that the woman would be transporting cocaine. After confirming the innocent details, officers stopped the station wagon as it neared the motel and found cocaine in the vehicle. *Id.*, at 331. We held that the officers' corroboration of certain details made the anonymous tip sufficiently reliable to create reasonable suspicion of criminal activity. By accurately predicting future behavior, the tipster demonstrated "a special familiarity with respondent's affairs," which in turn implied that the tipster had "access to reliable information about that individual's illegal activities." We also recognized that an informant who is proved to tell the truth about some things is more likely to tell the truth about other things, "including the claim that the object of the tip is engaged in criminal activity."

In *J. L.*, by contrast, we determined that no reasonable suspicion arose from a bare-bones tip that a young black male in a plaid shirt standing at a bus stop was carrying a gun. The tipster did not explain how he knew about the gun, nor did he suggest that he had any special familiarity with the young man's affairs. As a result, police had no basis for believing "that the tipster ha[d] knowledge of concealed criminal activity." Furthermore, the tip included no predictions of future behavior that could be corroborated to assess the tipster's credibility. We accordingly concluded that the tip was insufficiently reliable to justify a stop and frisk.

B

The initial question in this case is whether the 911 call was sufficiently reliable to credit the allegation that petitioners' truck "ran the [caller] off the roadway." Even assuming for present purposes that the 911 call was anonymous, see n. 1, *supra,* we conclude that the call bore adequate indicia of reliability for the officer to credit the caller's account. The officer was therefore justified in proceeding from the premise that the truck had, in fact, caused the caller's car to be dangerously diverted from the highway.

By reporting that she had been run off the road by a specific vehicle—a silver Ford F-150 pickup, license plate 8D94925—the caller necessarily claimed eyewitness knowledge of the alleged dangerous driving. That basis of knowledge lends significant support to the tip's reliability. This is in contrast to [*Florida v. J. L.*, 529 U.S. 266 (2000)], where the tip provided no basis for concluding that the tipster had actually seen the gun. [529 U.S. 266, 271 (2000)]. Even in [*Alabama v. White,* 496 U.S. 325 (1990)], where we upheld the stop, there was scant evidence that the tipster had actually observed cocaine in the station wagon. We called *White* a " 'close case' " because "[k]nowledge about a person's future movements indicates some familiarity with that person's affairs, but having such knowledge does not necessarily imply that the informant knows, in particular, whether that person is carrying hidden contraband." A driver's claim that another vehicle ran her off the road, however, necessarily implies that the informant knows the other car was driven dangerously.

There is also reason to think that the 911 caller in this case was telling the truth. Police confirmed the truck's location near mile marker 69 (roughly 19 highway miles south of the location reported in the 911 call) at 4:00 p.m. (roughly 18 minutes after the 911 call). That timeline of events suggests that the caller reported the incident soon after she was run off the road. That sort of contemporaneous report has long been treated as especially reliable. In evidence law, we generally credit the proposition that statements about an event and made soon after perceiving that event are especially trustworthy because "substantial contemporaneity of event and statement negate the likelihood of deliberate or conscious misrepresentation." Advisory Committee's Notes on Fed. Rule Evid. 803(1), 28 U.S.C.App., p. 371 (describing the rationale for the hearsay exception for "present sense impression[s]"). A similar rationale applies to a "statement relating to a startling event"—such as getting run off the road—"made while the declarant was under the stress of excitement that it caused." Fed. Rule Evid. 803(2) (hearsay exception for "excited utterances"). Unsurprisingly, 911 calls that would otherwise be inadmissible hearsay have often been admitted on those grounds. There was no indication that the tip in *J.L.* (or even in *White*) was contemporaneous with the observation of criminal activity or made under the stress of excitement caused by a startling event, but those considerations weigh in favor of the caller's veracity here.

Another indicator of veracity is the caller's use of the 911 emergency system. A 911 call has some features that allow for identifying and tracing callers, and thus provide some safeguards against making false reports with immunity. As this case illustrates, 911 calls can be recorded, which provides victims with an opportunity to identify the false tipster's voice and subject him to prosecution. The 911 system also permits law enforcement to verify important information about the caller. In 1998, the Federal Communications Commission began to require cellular carriers to relay the caller's phone number to 911 dispatchers. Beginning in 2001, carriers have been required to identify the caller's geographic location with increasing specificity. And although callers may ordinarily block call recipients from obtaining their identifying information, FCC regulations exempt 911 calls from that privilege. None of this is to suggest that tips in 911 calls are *per se* reliable. Given the foregoing technological and regulatory developments, however, a reasonable officer could conclude that a false tipster would think twice before using such a system. The caller's use of the 911 system is therefore one of the relevant circumstances that, taken together, justified the officer's reliance on the information reported in the 911 call.

C

Even a reliable tip will justify an investigative stop only if it creates reasonable suspicion that "criminal activity may be afoot." *Terry,* 392 U.S., at 30. We must therefore determine whether the 911 caller's report of being run off the roadway created reasonable suspicion of an ongoing crime such as drunk driving as opposed to an isolated episode of past recklessness. We conclude that the behavior alleged by the 911 caller, "viewed from the standpoint of an objectively reasonable police officer, amount[s] to reasonable suspicion" of drunk driving. *Ornelas v. United States,* 517 U.S. 690, 696 (1996). The stop was therefore proper.

Reasonable suspicion depends on "the factual and practical considerations of everyday life on which reasonable and prudent men, not legal technicians, act." *Id.,* at 695. Under that commonsense approach, we can appropriately recognize certain driving behaviors as sound indicia of drunk driving. Indeed, the accumulated experience of thousands of officers suggests that these sorts of erratic behaviors are strongly correlated with drunk driving. Of course, not all traffic infractions imply intoxication. Unconfirmed reports of driving without a seatbelt or slightly over the speed limit, for example, are so tenuously connected to drunk driving that a stop on those grounds alone would be constitutionally suspect. But a reliable tip alleging the dangerous behaviors discussed above generally would justify a traffic stop on suspicion of drunk driving.

The 911 caller in this case reported more than a minor traffic infraction and more than a conclusory allegation of drunk or reckless driving. Instead, she alleged a specific and dangerous result of the driver's conduct: running another car off the highway. That conduct bears too great a resemblance to paradigmatic manifestations of drunk driving to be dismissed as an isolated example of recklessness. Running another vehicle off the road suggests lane-positioning problems, decreased vigilance, impaired judgment, or some combination of those recognized drunk driving cues. And the experience of many officers suggests that a driver who almost strikes a vehicle or another object—the exact scenario that ordinarily causes "running [another vehicle] off the roadway"—is likely intoxicated. As a result, we cannot say that the officer acted unreasonably under these circumstances in stopping a driver whose alleged conduct was a significant indicator of drunk driving.

Petitioners' attempts to second-guess the officer's reasonable suspicion of drunk driving are unavailing. It is true that the reported behavior might also be explained by, for example, a driver responding to "an unruly child or other distraction." But we have consistently recognized that reasonable suspicion "need not rule out the possibility of innocent conduct."

Nor did the absence of additional suspicious conduct, after the vehicle was first spotted by an officer, dispel the reasonable suspicion of drunk driving. It is hardly surprising that the appearance of a marked police car would inspire more careful driving for a time. Extended observation of an allegedly drunk driver might eventually dispel a reasonable suspicion of intoxication, but the 5-minute period in this case hardly sufficed in that regard. Of course, an officer who already has such a reasonable suspicion need not surveil a vehicle at length in order to personally observe suspicious driving. Once reasonable suspicion of drunk driving arises, "[t]he reasonableness of the officer's decision to stop a suspect does not turn on the availability of less intrusive investigatory techniques." This would be a particularly inappropriate context to depart from that settled rule, because allowing a drunk driver a second chance for dangerous conduct could have disastrous consequences.

III

Like *White,* this is a "close case." As in that case, the indicia of the 911 caller's reliability here are stronger than those in *J.L.,* where we held that a bare-bones tip was unreliable. Although the indicia present here are different from those we found sufficient in *White,* there is more than one way to demonstrate "a particularized and objective basis for suspecting the particular person stopped of criminal activity." Under the totality of the circumstances, we find the indicia of reliability in this case sufficient to provide the officer with reasonable suspicion that the driver of the reported vehicle had run another vehicle off the road. That made it reasonable under the circumstances for the officer to execute a traffic stop. We accordingly affirm.

JUSTICE SCALIA, with whom JUSTICE GINSBURG, JUSTICE SOTOMAYOR, and JUSTICE KAGAN join, dissenting.

The California Court of Appeal in this case relied on jurisprudence from the California Supreme Court (adopted as well by other courts) to the effect that "an anonymous and uncorroborated tip regarding a possibly intoxicated highway driver" provides without more the reasonable suspicion necessary to justify a stop. Today's opinion does not explicitly adopt such a departure from our normal Fourth Amendment requirement that anonymous tips must be corroborated; it purports to adhere to our prior cases, such as *Florida v. J. L.,* 529 U.S. 266 (2000), and *Alabama v. White,* 496 U.S. 325 (1990). Be not deceived.

Law enforcement agencies follow closely our judgments on matters such as this, and they will identify at once our new rule: So long as the caller identifies where the car is, anonymous claims of a single instance of possibly careless or reckless driving, called in to 911, will support a traffic stop. This is not my concept, and I am sure would not be the Framers', of a people secure from unreasonable searches and seizures. I would reverse the judgment of the Court of Appeal of California.

I

The California Highway Patrol in this case knew nothing about the tipster on whose word—and that alone—they seized Lorenzo and José Prado Navarette. They did not know her name.[1] They did not know her phone number or address. They did not even know where she called from (she may have dialed in from a neighboring county).

The tipster said the truck had "[run her] off the roadway," but the police had no reason to credit that charge and many reasons to doubt it, beginning with the peculiar fact that the accusation was anonymous. "[E]liminating accountability . . . is ordinarily the very purpose of anonymity." The unnamed tipster "can lie with impunity," *J. L., supra,* at 275 (Kennedy, J., concurring). Anonymity is especially suspicious with respect to the call that is the subject of the present case. When does a victim complain to the police about an arguably criminal act (running the victim off the road) without giving his identity, so that he can accuse and testify when the culprit is caught?

The question before us, the Court agrees, is whether the "content of information possessed by police and its degree of reliability," gave the officers reasonable suspicion that the driver of the truck (Lorenzo) was committing an ongoing crime. When the only source of the government's information is an informant's tip, we ask whether the tip bears sufficient

[1] There was some indication below that the tipster was a woman. Beyond that detail, we must, as the Court notes, assume that the identity of the tipster was unknown.

" 'indicia of reliability,' " to establish "a particularized and objective basis for suspecting the particular person stopped of criminal activity."

The most extreme case, before this one, in which an anonymous tip was found to meet this standard was *White, supra*. There the reliability of the tip was established by the fact that it predicted the target's behavior in the finest detail—a detail that could be known only by someone familiar with the target's business: She would, the tipster said, leave a particular apartment building, get into a brown Plymouth station wagon with a broken right tail light, and drive immediately to a particular motel. Very few persons would have such intimate knowledge, and hence knowledge of the unobservable fact that the woman was carrying unlawful drugs was plausible. Here the Court makes a big deal of the fact that the tipster was dead right about the fact that a silver Ford F-150 truck (license plate 8D94925) was traveling south on Highway 1 somewhere near mile marker 88. But everyone in the world who saw the car would have that knowledge, and anyone who wanted the car stopped would have to provide that information. Unlike the situation in *White,* that generally available knowledge in no way makes it plausible that the tipster saw the car run someone off the road.

The Court says that "[b]y reporting that she had been run off the road by a specific vehicle . . . the caller necessarily claimed eyewitness knowledge." So what? The issue is not how she claimed to know, but whether what she claimed to know was true. The claim to "eyewitness knowledge" of being run off the road supports *not at all* its veracity; nor does the amazing, mystifying prediction (so far short of what existed in *White*) that the petitioners' truck *would be heading south on Highway 1.*

The Court finds "reason to think" that the informant "was telling the truth" in the fact that police observation confirmed that the truck had been driving near the spot at which, and at the approximate time at which, the tipster alleged she had been run off the road. According to the Court, the statement therefore qualifies as a " 'present sense impression' " or " 'excited utterance,' " kinds of hearsay that the law deems categorically admissible given their low likelihood of reflecting " 'deliberate or conscious misrepresentation.' " So, the Court says, we can fairly suppose that the accusation was true.

No, we cannot. To begin with, it is questionable whether either the "present sense impression" or the "excited utterance" exception to the hearsay rule applies here. The classic "present sense impression" is the recounting of an event that is occurring before the declarant's eyes, as the declarant is speaking ("I am watching the Hindenburg explode!"). And the classic "excited utterance" is a statement elicited, almost involuntarily, by the shock of what the declarant is immediately witnessing ("My God, those people will be killed!"). It is the immediacy that gives the statement some credibility; the declarant has not had time to dissemble or embellish. There is no such immediacy here. The declarant had time to observe the license number of the offending vehicle, 8D94925 (a difficult task if she was forced off the road and the vehicle was speeding away), to bring her car to a halt, to copy down the observed license number (presumably), and (if she was using her own cell phone) to dial a call to the police from the stopped car. Plenty of time to dissemble or embellish.

Moreover, even assuming that less than true immediacy will suffice for these hearsay exceptions to apply, the tipster's statement would run into additional barriers to admissibility and acceptance. According to the very Advisory Committee's Notes from which the Court quotes, cases addressing an unidentified declarant's present sense impression "indicate hesitancy in upholding the statement alone as sufficient" proof of the reported event. For excited utterances as well, the "knotty theoretical" question of statement-alone admissibility persists—seemingly even when the declarant is known. "Some courts . . . have taken the position that an excited utterance is admissible only if other proof is presented which supports a finding of fact that the exciting event did occur. The issue has not yet been resolved under the Federal Rules." It is even unsettled whether excited utterances of an unknown declarant are *ever* admissible. A leading treatise reports that "the courts have been reluctant to admit such statements, principally because of uncertainty that foundational requirements, including the impact of the event on the declarant, have been satisfied." In sum, it is unlikely that the law of evidence would deem the mystery caller in this case "especially trustworthy."

Finally, and least tenably, the Court says that another "indicator of veracity" is the anonymous tipster's mere "use of the 911 emergency system." Because, you see, recent "technological and regulatory developments" suggest that the identities of unnamed 911 callers are increasingly less likely to remain unknown. Indeed, the systems are able to identify "the caller's geographic location with increasing specificity." *Amici* disagree with this, see Brief for National Association of Criminal Defense Lawyers et al. 8–12, and the present case surely suggests that *amici* are right—since we know neither the identity of the tipster nor even the county from which the call was made. But assuming the Court is right about the ease of identifying 911 callers, it proves absolutely nothing in the present case unless the anonymous caller was *aware* of that fact. "It is the tipster's *belief* in anonymity, not its *reality,* that will control his behavior." There is no reason to believe that your average anonymous 911 tipster is aware that 911 callers are readily identifiable.

II

All that has been said up to now assumes that the anonymous caller made, at least in effect, an accusation of drunken driving. But in fact she did not. She said that the petitioners' truck " '[r]an [me] off the roadway.' " That neither asserts that the driver was drunk nor even raises the *likelihood* that the driver was drunk. The most it conveys is that the truck did some apparently nontypical thing that forced the tipster off the roadway, whether partly or fully, temporarily or permanently. Who really knows what (if anything) happened? The truck might have swerved to avoid an animal, a pothole, or a jaywalking pedestrian.

But let us assume the worst of the many possibilities: that it was a careless, reckless, or even intentional maneuver that forced the tipster off the road. Lorenzo might have been distracted by his use of a hands-free cell phone, or distracted by an intense sports argument with Jose. Or, indeed, he might have intentionally forced the tipster off the road because of some personal animus, or hostility to her "Make Love, Not War" bumper sticker. I fail to see how reasonable suspicion of a *discrete instance* of irregular or hazardous driving generates a reasonable suspicion of *ongoing intoxicated driving*. What proportion of the hundreds of thousands—perhaps millions—of careless, reckless, or intentional traffic violations committed each day is attributable to drunken drivers? I say 0.1 percent. I have no basis for that except my own guesswork. But unless the Court has some basis in reality to believe that the proportion is many orders of magnitude above that—say 1 in 10 or at least 1 in 20—it has no grounds for its unsupported assertion that the tipster's report in this case gave rise to a *reasonable suspicion* of drunken driving.

Bear in mind that that is the only basis for the stop that has been asserted in this litigation. The stop required suspicion of an ongoing crime, not merely suspicion of having run someone off the road earlier. And driving while being a careless or reckless person, unlike driving while being a drunk person, is not an ongoing crime. In other words, in order to stop the petitioners the officers here not only had to assume without basis the accuracy of the anonymous accusation but also had to posit an unlikely reason (drunkenness) for the accused behavior.

In sum, at the moment the police spotted the truck, it was more than merely "*possib[le]*" that the petitioners were not committing an ongoing traffic crime. It was overwhelmingly likely that they were not.

III

It gets worse. Not only, it turns out, did the police have no good reason *at first* to believe that Lorenzo was driving drunk, they had very good reason *at last* to know that he was not. The Court concludes that the tip, plus confirmation of the truck's location, produced reasonable suspicion that the truck not only had been *but still was* barreling dangerously and drunkenly down Highway 1. In fact, alas, it was not, and the officers knew it. They followed the truck for five minutes, presumably to see if it was being operated recklessly. And *that* was good police work. While the anonymous tip was not enough to support a stop for drunken driving under *Terry v. Ohio,* 392 U.S. 1 (1968), it was surely enough to counsel observation of the truck to see if it was driven by a drunken driver. But the pesky little detail left out of the Court's reasonable-suspicion equation is that, for the five minutes that the truck was being followed (five minutes is a *long* time), Lorenzo's driving was irreproachable. Had the officers witnessed the petitioners violate a single traffic law, they would have had cause to stop the truck, *Whren v. United States,* 517 U.S. 806, 810 (1996), and this case would not be before us. And not only was the driving *irreproachable,* but the State offers no evidence to suggest that the petitioners even did anything *suspicious,* such as suddenly slowing down, pulling off to the side of the road, or turning somewhere to see whether they were being followed. Consequently, the tip's suggestion of ongoing drunken driving (if it could be deemed to suggest that) not only went uncorroborated; it was affirmatively undermined.

* * *

The Court's opinion serves up a freedom-destroying cocktail consisting of two parts patent falsity: (1) that anonymous 911 reports of traffic violations are reliable so long as they correctly identify a car and its location, and (2) that a single instance of careless or reckless driving necessarily supports a reasonable suspicion of drunkenness. All the malevolent 911 caller need do is assert a traffic violation, and the targeted car will be stopped, forcibly if necessary, by the police. If the driver turns out not to be drunk (which will almost always be the case), the caller need fear no consequences, even if 911 knows his identity. After all, he never alleged drunkenness, but merely called in a traffic violation—and on that point his word is as good as his victim's.

Points for Discussion

1. In 2009, the Supreme Court declined to review a decision of the Virginia Supreme Court applying *J.L.* to anonymous reports of drunk driving. *Harris v. Virginia*, 668 S.E.2d 141 (Va. 2008), *cert. denied*, 558 U.S. 978 (Oct. 20, 2009). Dissenting from the denial of the writ of certiorari, Chief Justice Roberts, joined by Justice Scalia, suggested that *J.L.*'s rationale would not apply to such tips:

> The majority of courts examining the question have upheld investigative stops of allegedly drunk or erratic drivers, even when the police did not personally witness any traffic violations before conducting the stops. These courts have typically distinguished *J.L.*'s general rule based on some combination of (1) the especially grave and imminent dangers posed by drunk driving; (2) the enhanced reliability of tips alleging illegal activity in public, to which the tipster was presumably an eyewitness; (3) the fact that traffic stops are typically less invasive than searches or seizures of individuals on foot; and (4) the diminished expectation of privacy enjoyed by individuals driving their cars on public roads. A minority of jurisdictions, meanwhile, take the same position as the Virginia

> Supreme Court, requiring that officers first confirm an anonymous tip of drunk or erratic driving through their own independent observation.

Justices Roberts and Scalia ended up taking conflicting positions when the issue arrived before the Court in *Prado Navarette.* Their disagreement centers on whether to treat the call in this case as anonymous. The majority, like the state courts, treats the tip as though it were anonymous even though it was not, as the first footnote makes clear. Is this an actual case or controversy over whether an anonymous tip gives rise to reasonable suspicion or is it an advisory opinion on what the law would be if a tip in a situation like this had been anonymous?

2. Justice Scalia's dissent in *Prado Navarette* notes that "[l]aw enforcement agencies follow closely our judgments on matters such as this, and they will identify at once our new rule . . . ." As the Court often observes, police officers need to know what the law is so that they can conform their behavior to it. There is no practical way to train officers in the nuances of every Supreme Court majority opinion, e.g., that *Prado Navarette* was a "close case" that did *not* hold that "911 calls are *per se* reliable" but held only that *some* anonymous tips can support of finding of reasonable suspicion of drunk driving. Are the dissenters correct in warning readers to not be "deceived" by the majority's claim that it is adhering to *J.L.*?

ILLINOIS V. WARDLOW

528 U.S. 119 (2000)

CHIEF JUSTICE REHNQUIST delivered the opinion of the court.

Respondent Wardlow fled upon seeing police officers patrolling an area known for heavy narcotics trafficking. Two of the officers caught up with him, stopped him and conducted a protective patdown search for weapons. Discovering a .38-caliber handgun, the officers arrested Wardlow. We hold that the officers' stop did not violate the Fourth Amendment to the United States Constitution.

On September 9, 1995, Officers Nolan and Harvey were working as uniformed officers in the special operations section of the Chicago Police Department. The officers were driving the last car of a four car caravan converging on an area known for heavy narcotics trafficking in order to investigate drug transactions. The officers were traveling together because they expected to find a crowd of people in the area, including lookouts and customers.

As the caravan passed 4035 West Van Buren, Officer Nolan observed respondent Wardlow standing next to the building holding an opaque bag. Respondent looked in the direction of the officers and fled. Nolan and Harvey turned their car southbound, watched him as he ran through the gangway and an alley, and eventually cornered him on the street. Nolan then exited his car and stopped respondent. He immediately conducted a protective patdown search for weapons because in his experience it was common for there to be weapons in the near vicinity of narcotics transactions. During the frisk, Officer Nolan squeezed the bag respondent was carrying and felt a heavy, hard object similar to the shape of a gun. The officer then opened the bag and discovered a .38-caliber handgun with five live rounds of ammunition. The officers arrested Wardlow.

* * *

Nolan and Harvey were among eight officers in a four-car caravan that was converging on an area known for heavy narcotics trafficking, and the officers anticipated encountering a large number of people in the area, including drug customers and individuals serving as lookouts. It was in this context that Officer Nolan decided to investigate Wardlow after observing him flee. An individual's presence in an area of expected criminal activity, standing alone, is not enough to support a reasonable, particularized suspicion that the person is committing a crime. But officers are not required to ignore the relevant characteristics of a location in determining whether the circumstances are sufficiently suspicious to warrant further investigation. Accordingly, we have previously noted the fact that the stop occurred in a "high crime area" among the relevant contextual considerations in a *Terry* analysis. *Adams v. Williams,* 407 U.S. 143, 144, 147–48 (1972).

In this case, moreover, it was not merely respondent's presence in an area of heavy narcotics trafficking that aroused the officers' suspicion, but his unprovoked flight upon noticing the police. Our cases have also recognized that nervous, evasive behavior is a pertinent factor in determining reasonable suspicion.

Headlong flight—wherever it occurs—is the consummate act of evasion: It is not necessarily indicative of wrongdoing, but it is certainly suggestive of such. In reviewing the propriety of an officer's conduct, courts do not have available empirical studies dealing with inferences drawn from suspicious behavior, and we cannot reasonably demand scientific certainty from judges or law enforcement officers where none exists. Thus, the determination of reasonable suspicion must be based on commonsense judgments and inferences about human behavior. We conclude Officer Nolan was justified in suspecting that Wardlow was involved in criminal activity, and, therefore, in investigating further.

Such a holding is entirely consistent with our decision in *Florida v. Royer,* 460 U.S. 491 (1983), where we held that when an officer, without reasonable suspicion or probable cause, approaches an individual, the individual has a right to ignore the police and go about his business. And any "refusal to cooperate, without more, does not furnish the minimal level of objective justification needed for a detention or seizure." *Florida v. Bostick,* 501 U.S. 429, 437 (1991). But unprovoked flight is simply not a mere refusal to cooperate. Flight, by its very nature, is not "going about one's business"; in fact, it is just the opposite. Allowing officers confronted with such flight to stop the fugitive and investigate further is quite consistent with the individual's right to go about his business or to stay put and remain silent in the face of police questioning.

Respondent and *amici* also argue that there are innocent reasons for flight from police and that, therefore, flight is not necessarily indicative of ongoing criminal activity. This fact is undoubtedly true, but does not establish a violation of the Fourth Amendment. Even in *Terry,* the conduct justifying the stop was ambiguous and susceptible of an innocent explanation. The officer observed two individuals pacing back and forth in front of a store, peering into the window and periodically conferring. All of this conduct was by itself lawful, but it also suggested that the individuals were casing the store for a planned robbery. *Terry* recognized that the officers could detain the individuals to resolve the ambiguity.

In allowing such detentions, *Terry* accepts the risk that officers may stop innocent people. Indeed, the Fourth Amendment accepts that risk in connection with more drastic police action; persons arrested and detained on probable cause to believe they have committed a crime may turn out to be innocent. The *Terry* stop is a far more minimal intrusion, simply allowing the officer to briefly investigate further. If the officer does not learn facts rising to the level of probable cause, the individual must be allowed to go on his way. But in this case the officers found respondent in possession of a handgun, and arrested him for violation of an Illinois firearms statute. No question of the propriety of the arrest itself is before us.

JUSTICE STEVENS, with whom JUSTICE SOUTER, JUSTICE GINSBURG, and JUSTICE BREYER join, concurring in part and dissenting in part.

The State of Illinois asks this Court to announce a "bright-line rule" authorizing the temporary detention of anyone who flees at the mere sight of a police officer. Respondent counters by asking us to adopt the opposite *per se* rule—that the fact that a person flees upon seeing the police can never, by itself, be sufficient to justify a temporary investigative stop of the kind authorized by *Terry v. Ohio,* 392 U.S. 1 (1968).

The Court today wisely endorses neither *per se* rule. Instead, it rejects the proposition that "flight is . . . necessarily indicative of ongoing criminal activity," adhering to the view that "[t]he concept of reasonable suspicion . . . is not readily, or even usefully, reduced to a neat set of legal rules," but must be determined by looking to "the totality of the circumstances—the whole picture." Abiding by this framework, the Court concludes that "Officer Nolan was justified in suspecting that Wardlow was involved in criminal activity."

Although I agree with the Court's rejection of the *per se* rules proffered by the parties, unlike the Court, I am persuaded that in this case the brief testimony of the officer who seized respondent does not justify the conclusion that he had reasonable suspicion to make the stop. Before discussing the specific facts of this case, I shall comment on the parties' requests for a *per se* rule.

I

* * *

The question in this case concerns "the degree of suspicion that attaches to" a person's flight—or, more precisely, what "commonsense conclusions" can be drawn respecting the motives behind that flight. A pedestrian may break into a run for a variety of reasons—to catch up with a friend a block or two away, to seek shelter from an impending storm, to arrive at a bus stop before the bus leaves, to get home in time for dinner, to resume jogging after a pause for rest, to avoid contact with a bore or a bully, or simply to answer the call of nature—any of which might coincide with the arrival of an officer in the vicinity. A pedestrian might also run because he or she has just sighted one or more police officers. In the latter instance, the State properly points out "that the fleeing person may be, inter alia, (1) an escapee from jail; (2) wanted on a warrant; (3) in possession of contraband, (i.e. drugs, weapons, stolen goods, etc.); or (4) someone who has just committed another type of crime." In short, there are unquestionably circumstances in which a person's flight is suspicious, and undeniably instances in which a person runs for entirely innocent reasons.

Given the diversity and frequency of possible motivations for flight, it would be profoundly unwise to endorse either *per se* rule. The inference we can reasonably draw about the motivation for a person's flight, rather, will depend on a number of different circumstances. Factors such as the time of day, the number of people in the area, the character of the neighborhood, whether the officer was in uniform, the way the runner was dressed, the direction and speed of the flight, and whether the person's behavior was otherwise unusual might be relevant in specific cases. This number of variables is surely sufficient to preclude either a bright-line rule that always justifies, or that never justifies, an investigative stop based on the sole fact that flight began after a police officer appeared nearby.

* * *

In addition to these concerns, a reasonable person may conclude that an officer's sudden appearance indicates nearby criminal activity. And where there is criminal activity there is also a substantial element of danger—either from the criminal or from a confrontation between the criminal and the police. These considerations can lead to an innocent and understandable desire to quit the vicinity with all speed.

Among some citizens, particularly minorities and those residing in high crime areas, there is also the possibility that the fleeing person is entirely innocent, but, with or without justification, believes that contact with the police can itself be dangerous, apart from any criminal activity associated with the officer's sudden presence. For such a person, unprovoked flight is neither "aberrant" nor "abnormal." Moreover, these concerns and fears are known to the police officers themselves, and are validated by law enforcement investigations into their own practices. Accordingly, the evidence supporting the reasonableness of these beliefs is too pervasive to be dismissed as random or rare, and too persuasive to be disparaged as inconclusive or insufficient. In any event, just as we do not require "scientific certainty" for our commonsense conclusion that unprovoked flight can sometimes indicate suspicious motives, neither do we require scientific certainty to conclude that unprovoked flight can occur for other, innocent reasons.

* * *

"Unprovoked flight," in short, describes a category of activity too broad and varied to permit a *per se* reasonable inference regarding the motivation for the activity. While the innocent explanations surely do not establish that the Fourth Amendment is always violated whenever someone is stopped solely on the basis of an unprovoked flight, neither do the suspicious motivations establish that the Fourth Amendment is never violated when a *Terry* stop is predicated on that fact alone. For these reasons, the Court is surely correct in refusing to embrace either *per se* rule advocated by the parties. The totality of the circumstances, as always, must dictate the result.

II

Guided by that totality-of-the-circumstances test, the Court concludes that Officer Nolan had reasonable suspicion to stop respondent. In this respect, my view differs from the Court's. The entire justification for the stop is articulated in the brief testimony of Officer Nolan. Some facts are perfectly clear; others are not. This factual insufficiency leads me to conclude that the Court's judgment is mistaken.

Respondent Wardlow was arrested a few minutes after noon on September 9, 1995. Nolan was part of an eight-officer, four-car caravan patrol team. The officers were headed for "one of the areas in the 11th District [of Chicago] that's high [in] narcotics traffic." The reason why four cars were in the caravan was that "[n]ormally in these different areas there's an enormous amount of people, sometimes lookouts, customers." Officer Nolan testified that he was in uniform on that day, but he did not recall whether he was driving a marked or an unmarked car.

No other factors sufficiently support a finding of reasonable suspicion. Though respondent was carrying a white, opaque bag under his arm, there is nothing at all suspicious about that. Certainly the time of day—shortly after noon—does not support Illinois' argument. Nor were the officers "responding to any call or report of suspicious activity in the area." Officer Nolan did testify that he expected to find "an enormous amount of people," including drug customers or lookouts, and the Court points out that "[i]t was in this context that Officer Nolan decided to investigate Wardlow after observing him flee." This observation, in my view, lends insufficient weight to the reasonable suspicion analysis; indeed, in light of the absence of testimony that anyone else was nearby when respondent began to run, this observation points in the opposite direction.

The State, along with the majority of the Court, relies as well on the assumption that this flight occurred in a high crime area. Even if that assumption is accurate, it is insufficient because even in a high crime neighborhood unprovoked flight does not invariably lead to reasonable suspicion. On the contrary, because many factors providing innocent motivations for unprovoked flight are concentrated in high crime areas, the character of the neighborhood arguably makes an inference of guilt less appropriate, rather than more so. Like unprovoked flight itself, presence in a high crime neighborhood is a fact too generic and susceptible to innocent explanation to satisfy the reasonable suspicion inquiry.

* * *

Points for Discussion

1. Bear in mind that in *Hodari D.* the state declined to make the claim that Hodari's flight from the police was sufficient to give the police reasonable suspicion to believe that he was up to no good. If similar facts arose today, do you think the state would make the same concession?

2. As the dissent points out, there are a number of reasons that one might flee the police. For this reason, the dissent, like the majority, rejects both of the *per se* rules suggested by the parties. But do these multiple explanations for flight mean that flight can never give the police reasonable suspicion to believe that a crime has been committed?

3. What do you make of the fact that this encounter took place in what the Court describes as a high crime neighborhood? Should an individual's rights depend on the milieu in which she finds herself? *See*, David Seawell, Wardlow*'s Case: A Call to Broaden the Perspective of American Criminal Law*, 78 DENVER U. L. REV. 1119, 1125 (2001) ("The high-crime area label should be stricken from the totality of the circumstances analysis in *Terry* decisions as not cognizable in a legitimate manner. It is open to racial manipulation by the officers who utilize it and injurious to the communities which receive the label.")

4. Justice Stevens' opinion does not propose a different legal rule than Justice Rehnquist's. Rather, the two disagree about whether the facts gave rise to "reasonable suspicion". If the Supreme Court justices split by the narrowest

of margins on whether these circumstances allowed the police to make a seizure, it can hardly be said that this case provides any practical guidance to police, lawyers, or other courts. Why did the court reject—unanimously—both *per se* rules pressed by the parties? What effect does that rejection have on police-citizen interactions as a practical matter?

5. The decision in *Wardlow* came four years after a national controversy erupted over U.S. District Judge Harold Baer Jr.'s suppression of a confession, 34 kilograms of cocaine, and two kilograms of heroin in *United States v. Bayless,* 913 F. Supp. 232 (S.D.N.Y.), *vacated*, 921 F. Supp. 211 (S.D.N.Y. 1996). Prior to his appointment to the federal bench, Judge Baer served on the Mollen Commission, tasked in 1992 by the mayor of New York City with investigating police corruption. Judge Baer held that police stopped Carol Bayless' car without reasonable suspicion. An officer testified that Bayless drove slowly through a high-crime Manhattan neighborhood at 5 a.m. in a rented car with out-of-state plates and that four men put two duffle bags in the trunk and then scattered upon seeing the police. Judge Bear's opinion stated:

> [E]ven assuming that one or more of the males ran from the corner once they were aware of the officers' presence, it is hard to characterize this as evasive conduct. Police officers, even those travelling in unmarked vehicles, are easily recognized, particularly, in this area of Manhattan. In fact, the same United States Attorney's Office which brought this prosecution enjoyed more success in their prosecution of a corrupt police officer of an anti-crime unit operating in this very neighborhood. Even before this prosecution and the public hearing and final report of the Mollen Commission, residents in this neighborhood tended to regard police officers as corrupt, abusive and violent. After the attendant publicity surrounding the above events, had the men not run when the cops began to stare at them, it would have been unusual.

The New York Times reported the decision under the headline, "Not Suspicious To Flee Police, Judge Declares." The decision—particularly the premise that flight from police is not necessarily suspicious—became an issue in the 1996 presidential campaign. President Clinton, who had appointed Baer to the federal bench, called the ruling "wrong." Senator Bob Dole, the Republican candidate, called for Judge Baer's impeachment and used the case to criticize President Clinton's judicial appointees. After hearing additional testimony at a second hearing, Judge Baer reversed his initial ruling and determined that there was reasonable suspicion for the stop. How does knowledge of *Bayless* impact your reading of Part I of Justice Stevens' dissent?

HEIEN V. NORTH CAROLINA

574 U.S. 54 (2014)

CHIEF JUSTICE ROBERTS delivered the opinion of the court.

The Fourth Amendment prohibits "unreasonable searches and seizures." Under this standard, a search or seizure may be permissible even though the justification for the action includes a reasonable factual mistake. An officer might, for example, stop a motorist for traveling alone in a high-occupancy vehicle lane, only to discover upon approaching the car that two children are slumped over asleep in the back seat. The driver has not violated the law, but neither has the officer violated the Fourth Amendment.

But what if the police officer's reasonable mistake is not one of fact but of law? In this case, an officer stopped a vehicle because one of its two brake lights was out, but a court later determined that a single working brake light was all the law required. The question presented is whether such a mistake of law can nonetheless give rise to the reasonable suspicion necessary to uphold the seizure under the Fourth Amendment. We hold that it can. Because the officer's mistake about the brake-light law was reasonable, the stop in this case was lawful under the Fourth Amendment.

I

On the morning of April 29, 2009, Sergeant Matt Darisse of the Surry County Sheriff's Department sat in his patrol car near Dobson, North Carolina, observing northbound traffic on Interstate 77. Shortly before 8 a.m., a Ford Escort passed by. Darisse thought the driver looked "very stiff and nervous," so he pulled onto the interstate and began following the Escort. A few miles down the road, the Escort braked as it approached a slower vehicle, but only the left brake light came on. Noting the faulty right brake light, Darisse activated his vehicle's lights and pulled the Escort over.

Two men were in the car: Maynor Javier Vasquez sat behind the wheel, and petitioner Nicholas Brady Heien lay across the rear seat. Sergeant Darisse explained to Vasquez that as long as his license and registration checked out, he would receive only a warning ticket for the broken brake light. A records check revealed no problems with the documents, and Darisse gave Vasquez the warning ticket. But Darisse had become suspicious during the course of the stop—Vasquez appeared nervous, Heien remained lying down the entire time, and the two gave inconsistent answers about their destination. Darisse asked Vasquez if he would be willing to answer some questions. Vasquez assented, and Darisse asked whether the men were transporting various types of contraband. Told no, Darisse asked whether he could search the Escort. Vasquez said he had no objection, but told Darisse he should ask Heien, because Heien owned the car. Heien gave his consent, and Darisse, aided by a fellow officer who had since arrived, began a thorough search of the vehicle. In the side compartment of a duffle bag, Darisse found a sandwich bag containing cocaine. The officers arrested both men.

The State charged Heien with attempted trafficking in cocaine. Heien moved to suppress the evidence seized from the car, contending that the stop and search had violated the Fourth Amendment of the United States

Constitution. After a hearing at which both officers testified and the State played a video recording of the stop, the trial court denied the suppression motion, concluding that the faulty brake light had given Sergeant Darisse reasonable suspicion to initiate the stop, and that Heien's subsequent consent to the search was valid. Heien pleaded guilty but reserved his right to appeal the suppression decision.

* * *

II

* * *

As the text indicates and we have repeatedly affirmed, "the ultimate touchstone of the Fourth Amendment is 'reasonableness.'" *Riley v. California*, 134 S.Ct. 2473, 2482 (2014). To be reasonable is not to be perfect, and so the Fourth Amendment allows for some mistakes on the part of government officials, giving them "fair leeway for enforcing the law in the community's protection." *Brinegar v. United States*, 338 U.S. 160, 176 (1949). We have recognized that searches and seizures based on mistakes of fact can be reasonable. The warrantless search of a home, for instance, is reasonable if undertaken with the consent of a resident, and remains lawful when officers obtain the consent of someone who reasonably appears to be but is not in fact a resident. See *Illinois v. Rodriguez*, 497 U.S. 177, 183–86 (1990). By the same token, if officers with probable cause to arrest a suspect mistakenly arrest an individual matching the suspect's description, neither the seizure nor an accompanying search of the arrestee would be unlawful. See *Hill v. California*, 401 U.S. 797, 802–805 (1971). The limit is that "the mistakes must be those of reasonable men." *Brinegar*, *supra*, at 176.

But reasonable men make mistakes of law, too, and such mistakes are no less compatible with the concept of reasonable suspicion. Reasonable suspicion arises from the combination of an officer's understanding of the facts and his understanding of the relevant law. The officer may be reasonably mistaken on either ground. Whether the facts turn out to be not what was thought, or the law turns out to be not what was thought, the result is the same: the facts are outside the scope of the law. There is no reason, under the text of the Fourth Amendment or our precedents, why this same result should be acceptable when reached by way of a reasonable mistake of fact, but not when reached by way of a similarly reasonable mistake of law.

The dissent counters that our cases discussing probable cause and reasonable suspicion, most notably *Ornelas v. United States*, 517 U.S. 690, 696–97 (1996), have contained "scarcely a peep" about mistakes of law. It would have been surprising, of course, if they had, since none of those cases involved a mistake of law.

Although such recent cases did not address mistakes of law, older precedents did. In fact, cases dating back two centuries support treating legal and factual errors alike in this context. Customs statutes enacted by Congress not long after the founding authorized courts to issue certificates indemnifying customs officers against damages suits premised on unlawful seizures. See, *e.g.*, Act of Mar. 2, 1799, ch. 22, § 89, 1 Stat. 695–696. Courts were to issue such certificates on a showing that the officer had "reasonable cause"—a synonym for "probable cause"—for the challenged seizure. In *United States v. Riddle*, a customs officer seized goods on the ground that the English shipper had violated the customs laws by preparing an invoice that undervalued the merchandise, even though the American consignee declared the true value to the customs collector. Chief Justice Marshall held that there had been no violation of the customs law because, whatever the shipper's intention, the consignee had not actually attempted to defraud the Government. Nevertheless, because "the construction of the law was liable to some question," he affirmed the issuance of a certificate of probable cause: "A doubt as to the true construction of the *law* is as reasonable a cause for seizure as a doubt respecting the fact."

This holding—that reasonable mistakes of law, like those of fact, would justify certificates of probable cause—was reiterated in a number of 19th-century decisions. By the Civil War, there had been "numerous cases in which [a] captured vessel was in no fault, and had not, under a true construction of the law, presented even ground of suspicion, and yet the captor was exonerated because he acted under an honest mistake of the law." *The La Manche*, 14 F.Cas. 965, 972 (No. 8,004) (D.Mass.1863).

Riddle and its progeny are not directly on point. Chief Justice Marshall was not construing the Fourth Amendment, and a certificate of probable cause functioned much like a modern-day finding of qualified immunity, which depends on an inquiry distinct from whether an officer has committed a constitutional violation. But Chief Justice Marshall was nevertheless explaining the concept of probable cause, which, he noted elsewhere, "in all cases of seizure, has a fixed and well known meaning. It imports a seizure made under circumstances which warrant suspicion." *Locke v. United States*, 7 Cranch 339, 348 (1813). We have said the phrase "probable cause" bore this "fixed and well known meaning" in the Fourth Amendment, and *Riddle* illustrates that it encompassed suspicion based on reasonable mistakes of both fact and law. No decision of this Court in the two centuries since has undermined that understanding.

The contrary conclusion would be hard to reconcile with a much more recent precedent. In *Michigan v. DeFillippo*, 443 U.S. 31 (1979), we addressed the validity of an arrest made under a criminal law later declared unconstitutional. A Detroit ordinance that authorized police officers to stop and question individuals suspected of criminal activity also made it an offense for such an individual "to refuse to identify himself and produce evidence of his identity." Detroit police officers sent to investigate a report of public intoxication arrested Gary DeFillippo after he failed to identify himself. A search incident to arrest uncovered drugs, and DeFillippo was charged with possession of a controlled substance. The Michigan Court of Appeals ordered the suppression of the drugs, concluding that the identification ordinance was unconstitutionally vague and that DeFillippo's arrest was therefore invalid.

Accepting the unconstitutionality of the ordinance as a given, we nonetheless reversed. At the time the officers arrested DeFillippo, we explained, "there was no controlling precedent that this ordinance was or was not constitutional, and hence the conduct observed violated a presumptively valid ordinance." Acknowledging that the outcome might have been different had the ordinance been "grossly and flagrantly unconstitutional," we concluded that under the circumstances "there was abundant probable cause to satisfy the constitutional prerequisite for an arrest."

The officers were wrong in concluding that DeFillippo was guilty of a criminal offense when he declined to identify himself. That a court only *later* declared the ordinance unconstitutional does not change the fact that DeFillippo's conduct was lawful when the officers observed it. But the officers' assumption that the law was valid was reasonable, and their observations gave them "abundant probable cause" to arrest DeFillippo. Although DeFillippo could not be prosecuted under the identification ordinance, the search that turned up the drugs was constitutional.

* * *

Heien also contends that the reasons the Fourth Amendment allows some errors of fact do not extend to errors of law. Officers in the field must make factual assessments on the fly, Heien notes, and so deserve a margin of error. In Heien's view, no such margin is appropriate for questions of law: The statute here either requires one working brake light or two, and the answer does not turn on anything "an officer might suddenly confront in the field." Brief for Petitioner 21. But Heien's point does not consider the reality that an officer may "suddenly confront" a situation in the field as to which the application of a statute is unclear—however clear it may later become. A law prohibiting "vehicles" in the park either covers Segways or not, but an officer will nevertheless have to make a quick decision on the law the first time one whizzes by.

Contrary to the suggestion of Heien and *amici*, our decision does not discourage officers from learning the law. The Fourth Amendment tolerates only *reasonable* mistakes, and those mistakes—whether of fact or of law—must be *objectively* reasonable. We do not examine the subjective understanding of the particular officer involved. And the inquiry is not as forgiving as the one employed in the distinct context of deciding whether an officer is entitled to qualified immunity for a constitutional or statutory violation. Thus, an officer can gain no Fourth Amendment advantage through a sloppy study of the laws he is duty-bound to enforce.

Finally, Heien and *amici* point to the well-known maxim, "Ignorance of the law is no excuse," and contend that it is fundamentally unfair to let police officers get away with mistakes of law when the citizenry is accorded no such leeway. Though this argument has a certain rhetorical appeal, it misconceives the implication of the maxim. The true symmetry is this: Just as an individual generally cannot escape criminal liability based on a mistaken understanding of the law, so too the government cannot impose criminal liability based on a mistaken understanding of the law. If the law required two working brake lights, Heien could not escape a ticket by claiming he reasonably thought he needed only one; if the law required only one, Sergeant Darisse could not issue a valid ticket by claiming he reasonably thought drivers needed two. But just because mistakes of law cannot justify either the imposition or the avoidance of criminal liability, it does not follow that they cannot justify an investigatory stop. And Heien is not appealing a brake-light ticket; he is appealing a cocaine-trafficking conviction as to which there is no asserted mistake of fact or law.

III

Here we have little difficulty concluding that the officer's error of law was reasonable. Although the North Carolina statute at issue refers to "*a* stop lamp," suggesting the need for only a single working brake light, it also provides that "[t]he stop lamp may be incorporated into a unit with one or more *other* rear lamps." N.C. Gen.Stat. Ann. § 20–129(g) (emphasis added). The use of "other" suggests to the everyday reader of English that a "stop lamp" is a type of "rear lamp." And another subsection of the same provision requires that vehicles "have all originally equipped rear lamps or the equivalent in good working order," § 20–129(d), arguably indicating that if a vehicle has multiple "stop lamp[s]," all must be functional.

The North Carolina Court of Appeals concluded that the "rear lamps" discussed in subsection (d) do not include brake lights, but, given the "other," it would at least have been reasonable to think they did. Both the majority and the dissent in the North Carolina Supreme Court so concluded, and we agree. This "stop lamp" provision, moreover, had never been previously construed by North Carolina's appellate courts. It was thus objectively reasonable for an officer in Sergeant Darisse's position to think that Heien's faulty right brake light was a violation of North Carolina law. And because the mistake of law was reasonable, there was reasonable suspicion justifying the stop.

JUSTICE KAGAN, with whom JUSTICE GINSBURG joins, concurring.

I concur in full in the Court's opinion, which explains why certain mistakes of law can support the reasonable suspicion needed to stop a vehicle under the Fourth Amendment. In doing so, the Court correctly emphasizes that the "Fourth Amendment tolerates only . . . *objectively* reasonable" mistakes of law. And the Court makes clear that the inquiry into whether an officer's mistake of law counts as objectively reasonable "is not as forgiving as the one employed in the distinct context of deciding whether an officer is entitled to qualified immunity." I write separately to elaborate briefly on those important limitations.[1]

First, an officer's "subjective understanding" is irrelevant: As the Court notes, "[w]e do not examine" it at all. That means the government cannot defend an officer's mistaken legal interpretation on the ground that the officer was unaware of or untrained in the law. And it means that, contrary to the dissenting opinion in the court below, an officer's reliance on "an incorrect memo or training program from the police department" makes no difference to the analysis. Those considerations pertain to the officer's subjective understanding of the law and thus cannot help to justify a seizure.

Second, the inquiry the Court permits today is more demanding than the one courts undertake before awarding qualified immunity. Our modern qualified immunity doctrine protects "all but the plainly incompetent or those who knowingly violate the law." *Ashcroft v. al-Kidd*, 131 S.Ct. 2074, 2085 (2011) (quoting *Malley v. Briggs*, 475 U.S. 335, 341 (1986)). By contrast, Justice Story's opinion in *The Friendship*, 9 F.Cas. 825, 826 (No. 5,125) (C.C.D.Mass.1812), suggests the appropriate standard for deciding when a legal error can support a seizure: when an officer takes a reasonable view of a "vexata questio" on which different judges "hold opposite opinions." Or to make the same point without the Latin, the test is satisfied when the law at issue is "so doubtful in construction" that a reasonable judge could agree with the officer's view.

A court tasked with deciding whether an officer's mistake of law can support a seizure thus faces a straightforward question of statutory construction. If the statute is genuinely ambiguous, such that overturning the officer's judgment requires hard interpretive work, then the officer has made a reasonable mistake. But if not, not. As the Solicitor General made the point at oral argument, the statute must pose a "really difficult" or "very hard question of statutory interpretation." And indeed, both North Carolina and the Solicitor General agreed that such cases will be "exceedingly rare."

* * *

[1] I note in addition, as does the Court, that one kind of mistaken legal judgment—an error about the contours of the Fourth Amendment itself—can never support a search or seizure. See *ante* ("An officer's mistaken view that" conduct does "*not* give rise to" a Fourth Amendment violation, "no matter how reasonable," cannot change a court's "ultimate conclusion" that such a violation has occurred). As the Solicitor General has explained, mistakes about the requirements of the Fourth Amendment "violate the Fourth Amendment even when they are reasonable." Brief for United States as *Amicus Curiae* 30, n. 3.

JUSTICE SOTOMAYOR, dissenting.

* * *

I

It is common ground that Heien was seized within the meaning of the Fourth Amendment. Such a seizure comports with the Constitution only if the officers had articulable and reasonable suspicion that Heien was breaking the law. In *Ornelas v. United States*, 517 U.S. 690, 696 (1996), we explained that the "principal components" of that determination "will be the events which occurred leading up to the stop or search, and then the decision whether these historical facts, viewed from the standpoint of an objectively reasonable police officer, amount to reasonable suspicion or to probable cause." We described this kind of determination as "a mixed question of law and fact": " '[T]he issue is whether the facts satisfy the [relevant] statutory [or constitutional] standard, or to put it another way, whether the rule of law as applied to the established facts is or is not violated.' " What matters, we said, are the facts as viewed by an objectively reasonable officer, and the rule of law—not an officer's conception of the rule of law, and not even an officer's reasonable misunderstanding about the law, but the law.

* * *

Both our enunciation of the reasonableness inquiry and our justification for it thus have always turned on an officer's factual conclusions and an officer's expertise with respect to those factual conclusions. Neither has hinted at taking into account an officer's understanding of the law, reasonable or otherwise.

II

Departing from this tradition means further eroding the Fourth Amendment's protection of civil liberties in a context where that protection has already been worn down. Traffic stops like those at issue here can be "annoying, frightening, and perhaps humiliating." *Terry v. Ohio*, 392 U.S. 1, 25 (1968). We have nevertheless held that an officer's subjective motivations do not render a traffic stop unlawful. *Whren v. United States*, 517 U.S. 806 (1996). But we assumed in *Whren* that when an officer acts on pretext, at least that pretext would be the violation of an actual law. Giving officers license to effect seizures so long as they can attach to their reasonable view of the facts some reasonable legal interpretation (or misinterpretation) that suggests a law has been violated significantly expands this authority. One wonders how a citizen seeking to be law-abiding and to structure his or her behavior to avoid these invasive, frightening, and humiliating encounters could do so.

In addition to these human consequences—including those for communities and for their relationships with the police—permitting mistakes of law to justify seizures has the perverse effect of preventing or delaying the clarification of the law. Under such an approach, courts need not interpret statutory language but can instead simply decide whether an officer's interpretation was reasonable. Indeed, had this very case arisen after the North Carolina Supreme Court announced its rule, the North Carolina Court of Appeals would not have had the occasion to interpret the statute at issue. Similarly, courts in the Eighth Circuit, which has been the only Circuit to include police mistakes of law in the reasonableness inquiry, have observed that they need not decide interpretive questions under their approach. This result is bad for citizens, who need to know their rights and responsibilities, and it is bad for police, who would benefit from clearer direction.

Of course, if the law enforcement system could not function without permitting mistakes of law to justify seizures, one could at least argue that permitting as much is a necessary evil. But I have not seen any persuasive argument that law enforcement will be unduly hampered by a rule that precludes consideration of mistakes of law in the reasonableness inquiry. After all, there is no indication that excluding an officer's mistake of law from the reasonableness inquiry has created a problem for law enforcement in the overwhelming number of Circuits which have adopted that approach. If an officer makes a stop in good faith but it turns out that, as in this case, the officer was wrong about what the law proscribed or required, I know of no penalty that the officer would suffer. Moreover, such an officer would likely have a defense to any civil suit on the basis of qualified immunity.

Nor will it often be the case that any evidence that may be seized during the stop will be suppressed, thanks to the exception to the exclusionary rule for good-faith police errors. It is true that, unlike most States, North Carolina does not provide a good-faith exception as a matter of state law, but North Carolina recognizes that it may solve any remedial problems it may perceive on its own.[2] More fundamentally, that is a remedial concern, and the protections offered by the Fourth Amendment are not meant to yield to accommodate remedial concerns. Our jurisprudence draws a sharp "analytica[l] distinction" between the existence of a Fourth Amendment violation and the remedy for that violation.

In short, there is nothing in our case law requiring us to hold that a reasonable mistake of law can justify a seizure under the Fourth Amendment, and quite a bit suggesting just the opposite. I also see nothing to be gained from such a holding, and much to be lost.

[2] In addition to North Carolina, it appears that 13 States do not provide a good-faith exception.

III

In reaching the contrary conclusion, the Court makes both serious legal and practical errors. On the legal side, the Court barely addresses *Ornelas* and the other cases that frame the reasonableness inquiry around factual determinations. Instead, in support of its conclusion that reasonable suspicion "arises from the *combination* of an officer's understanding of the facts *and* his understanding of the relevant law," the Court first reaches to founding-era customs statutes and cases applying those statutes. It concedes, however, that these cases are "not directly on point" because they say nothing about the scope of the Fourth Amendment and are instead equivalents of our modern-day qualified immunity jurisprudence for civil damages.

The only link in the tenuous chain the Court constructs between those cases and this one that has anything to say about the Fourth Amendment is *Brinegar v. United States*, 338 U.S. 160 (1949). But all that our opinion in *Brinegar* actually says is that probable cause exists where " 'the facts and circumstances within [the officers'] knowledge and of which they had reasonably trustworthy information [are] sufficient in themselves to warrant a man of reasonable caution in the belief that' an offense has been or is being committed." 338 U.S., at 175–76 (quoting *Carroll v. United States*, 267 U.S. 132, 162 (1925)). It thus states the uncontroversial proposition that the probable-cause inquiry looks to the reasonableness of an officer's understanding of the facts. Indeed, *Brinegar* is an odd case for the Court to rely on given that, like the cases I discussed above, it subsequently emphasizes that "the mistakes must be those of reasonable men, acting on *facts* leading sensibly to their conclusions of probability." 338 U.S., at 176 (emphasis added). Again, reasonable understandings of the facts, not reasonable understandings of what the law says.

Further, the Court looks to our decision in *Michigan v. DeFillippo*, 443 U.S. 31 (1979). This is a Fourth Amendment case, but the Court's reading of it imagines a holding that is not rooted in the logic of the opinion. We held in *DeFillippo* that an officer had probable cause to support an arrest even though the ordinance that had allegedly been violated was later held by the Michigan Court of Appeals to be unconstitutional. This was so, we explained, because the officer conducted an arrest after having observed conduct that was criminalized by a presumptively valid law at the time of that conduct. We noted that it would have been wrong for that officer not to enforce the law in that situation.

DeFillippo thus did not involve any police "mistake" at all. Rather, *DeFillippo* involved a police officer correctly applying the law that was then in existence and that carried with it a presumption of validity. Here, by contrast, police stopped Heien on suspicion of committing an offense that never actually existed. Given that our holding in *DeFillippo* relied so squarely on the existence of a law criminalizing the defendant's conduct, and on the presumption of validity that attends actual laws, it can hardly be said to control where, as here, no law ever actually criminalized Heien's conduct.

On the practical side, the Court primarily contends that an officer may confront "a situation in the field as to which the application of a statute is unclear." One is left to wonder, however, why an innocent citizen should be made to shoulder the burden of being seized whenever the law may be susceptible to an interpretive question. Moreover, the Court fails to reconcile its belief that the Fourth Amendment gives officers leeway to address situations where the application of a criminal statute may be unclear with our prior assumption that the Fourth Amendment does not give officers such leeway where they rely on a statute that authorizes police conduct that may violate the Fourth Amendment. Nor does it engage with the analytic consequences of North Carolina's similar concession that it does not mean to claim "that an officer's mistaken understanding of the Fourth Amendment itself can support a seizure if that understanding was reasonable." It is not clear why an officer's mistaken understanding of other laws should be viewed differently.

* * *

Points for Discussion

1. The court rejects Heien's argument that its ruling will discourage officers from learning the law (or from admitting they knowingly acted illegally). Instead, it states that mistakes must be objectively reasonable and italicizes the word objectively to imply that this qualifier imposes a significant hurdle. The court further claims that the mistake in this case was objectively reasonable because the statute prescribing the number of brake lights a car must have in North Carolina was, in the majority's view, ambiguous. But, the majority refuses to clarify whether statutory ambiguity is a necessary or merely a sufficient condition to make a mistake of law "*objectively* reasonable."

2. Given that the majority apparently disagrees with the concurrence's narrow view of what counts as "*objectively* reasonable," in what instances is the majority's view of what counts as "*objectively* reasonable" likely to differ from the concurrence's? What clues to the majority's likely view does Justice Sotomayor's dissent give?

3. At least one state supreme court has rejected the holding of *Heien*. In *Iowa v. Coleman*, 890 N.W.2d 284 (2017), the Supreme Court of Iowa held that *Heien* had no effect on its state law because it had previously ruled in *Iowa v. Tyler*, 830 N.W.2d 288 (2013), that a stop is not reasonable if it is based on the officer's mistake about what the law allows. "Further, the approach in *Heien* would be very difficult to square with our rejection of the good-faith exception to the exclusionary rule under article I, section 8 of the Iowa Constitution in [*Iowa v. Cline*, 617 N.W.2d 277, 293 (2000)]." In Chapter 10 we examine the Supreme Court's decision in *United States v. Leon*, 468 U.S. 897 (1984) which

created a good faith exception to the exclusionary rule: If officers rely in good faith on a facially valid warrant, the exclusionary rule will not apply even if the warrant is later determined to be defective.

2. SCOPE OF A *TERRY* STOP

UNITED STATES V. SHARPE

470 U.S. 675 (1985)

CHIEF JUSTICE BURGER delivered the opinion of the court.

We granted certiorari to decide whether an individual reasonably suspected of engaging in criminal activity may be detained for a period of 20 minutes, when the detention is necessary for law enforcement officers to conduct a limited investigation of the suspected criminal activity.

I

A

On the morning of June 9, 1978, Agent Cooke of the Drug Enforcement Administration (DEA) was on patrol in an unmarked vehicle on a coastal road near Sunset Beach, North Carolina, an area under surveillance for suspected drug trafficking. At approximately 6:30 a.m., Cooke noticed a blue pickup truck with an attached camper shell traveling on the highway in tandem with a blue Pontiac Bonneville. Respondent Savage was driving the pickup, and respondent Sharpe was driving the Pontiac. The Pontiac also carried a passenger, Davis, the charges against whom were later dropped. Observing that the truck was riding low in the rear and that the camper did not bounce or sway appreciably when the truck drove over bumps or around curves, Agent Cooke concluded that it was heavily loaded. A quilted material covered the rear and side windows of the camper.

Cooke's suspicions were sufficiently aroused to follow the two vehicles for approximately 20 miles as they proceeded south into South Carolina. He then decided to make an "investigative stop" and radioed the State Highway Patrol for assistance. Officer Thrasher, driving a marked patrol car, responded to the call. Almost immediately after Thrasher caught up with the procession, the Pontiac and the pickup turned off the highway and onto a campground road. Cooke and Thrasher followed the two vehicles as the latter drove along the road at 55 to 60 miles an hour, exceeding the speed limit of 35 miles an hour. The road eventually looped back to the highway, onto which Savage and Sharpe turned and continued to drive south.

At this point, all four vehicles were in the middle lane of the three right-hand lanes of the highway. Agent Cooke asked Officer Thrasher to signal both vehicles to stop. Thrasher pulled alongside the Pontiac, which was in the lead, turned on his flashing light, and motioned for the driver of the Pontiac to stop. As Sharpe moved the Pontiac into the right lane, the pickup truck cut between the Pontiac and Thrasher's patrol car, nearly hitting the patrol car, and continued down the highway. Thrasher pursued the truck while Cooke pulled up behind the Pontiac.

Cooke approached the Pontiac and identified himself. He requested identification, and Sharpe produced a Georgia driver's license bearing the name of Raymond J. Pavlovich. Cooke then attempted to radio Thrasher to determine whether he had been successful in stopping the pickup truck, but he was unable to make contact for several minutes, apparently because Thrasher was not in his patrol car. Cooke radioed the local police for assistance, and two officers from the Myrtle Beach Police Department arrived about 10 minutes later. Asking the two officers to "maintain the situation," Cooke left to join Thrasher.

In the meantime, Thrasher had stopped the pickup truck about one-half mile down the road. After stopping the truck, Thrasher had approached it with his revolver drawn, ordered the driver, Savage, to get out and assume a "spread eagled" position against the side of the truck, and patted him down. Thrasher then holstered his gun and asked Savage for his driver's license and the truck's vehicle registration. Savage produced his own Florida driver's license and a bill of sale for the truck bearing the name of Pavlovich. In response to questions from Thrasher concerning the ownership of the truck, Savage said that the truck belonged to a friend and that he was taking it to have its shock absorbers repaired. When Thrasher told Savage that he would be held until the arrival of Cooke, whom Thrasher identified as a dea agent, Savage became nervous, said that he wanted to leave, and requested the return of his driver's license. Thrasher replied that Savage was not free to leave at that time.

Agent Cooke arrived at the scene approximately 15 minutes after the truck had been stopped. Thrasher handed Cooke Savage's license and the bill of sale for the truck; Cooke noted that the bill of sale bore the same name as Sharpe's license. Cooke identified himself to Savage as a dea agent and said that he thought the truck was loaded with marihuana. Cooke twice sought permission to search the camper, but Savage declined to give it, explaining that he was not the owner of the truck. Cooke then stepped on the rear of the truck and, observing that it did not sink any lower, confirmed his suspicion that it was probably overloaded. He put his nose against the rear window, which was covered from the inside, and reported that he could smell marihuana. Without seeking Savage's permission, Cooke removed the keys from the ignition, opened the rear of the camper, and observed a large number of burlap-wrapped bales resembling bales of marihuana that Cooke had seen in previous investigations. Agent Cooke then placed Savage under arrest and left him with Thrasher.

Cooke returned to the Pontiac and arrested Sharpe and Davis. Approximately 30 to 40 minutes had elapsed between the time Cooke stopped the Pontiac and the time he returned to arrest Sharpe and Davis.

Cooke assembled the various parties and vehicles and led them to the Myrtle Beach police station. That evening, dea agents took the truck to the Federal Building in Charleston, South Carolina. Several days later, Cooke supervised the unloading of the truck, which contained 43 bales weighing a total of 2,629 pounds. Acting without a search warrant, Cooke had eight randomly selected bales opened and sampled. Chemical tests showed that the samples were marihuana.

II

A

The Fourth Amendment is not, of course, a guarantee against *all* searches and seizures, but only against *unreasonable* searches and seizures. The authority and limits of the Amendment apply to investigative stops of vehicles such as occurred here. In *Terry v. Ohio,* 392 U.S. 1 (1968), we adopted a dual inquiry for evaluating the reasonableness of an investigative stop. Under this approach, we examine "whether the officer's action was justified at its inception, and whether it was reasonably related in scope to the circumstances which justified the interference in the first place."

As to the first part of this inquiry, the Court of Appeals assumed that the police had an articulable and reasonable suspicion that Sharpe and Savage were engaged in marihuana trafficking, given the setting and all the circumstances when the police attempted to stop the Pontiac and the pickup. That assumption is abundantly supported by the record. As to the second part of the inquiry, however, the court concluded that the 30- to 40-minute detention of Sharpe and the 20-minute detention of Savage "failed to meet the [Fourth Amendment's] requirement of brevity."

It is not necessary for us to decide whether the length of Sharpe's detention was unreasonable, because that detention bears no causal relation to Agent Cooke's discovery of the marihuana. The marihuana was in Savage's pickup, not in Sharpe's Pontiac; the contraband introduced at respondents' trial cannot logically be considered the "fruit" of Sharpe's detention. The only issue in this case, then, is whether it was reasonable under the circumstances facing Agent Cooke and Officer Thrasher to detain Savage, whose vehicle contained the challenged evidence, for approximately 20 minutes. We conclude that the detention of Savage clearly meets the Fourth Amendment's standard of reasonableness.

* * *

The Court of Appeals' decision would effectively establish a *per se* rule that a 20-minute detention is too long to be justified under the *Terry* doctrine. Such a result is clearly and fundamentally at odds with our approach in this area.

B

In assessing whether a detention is too long in duration to be justified as an investigative stop, we consider it appropriate to examine whether the police diligently pursued a means of investigation that was likely to confirm or dispel their suspicions quickly, during which time it was necessary to detain the defendant. A court making this assessment should take care to consider whether the police are acting in a swiftly developing situation, and in such cases the court should not indulge in unrealistic second-guessing. A creative judge engaged in *post hoc* evaluation of police conduct can almost always imagine some alternative means by which the objectives of the police might have been accomplished. But "[t]he fact that the protection of the public might, in the abstract, have been accomplished by 'less intrusive' means does not, itself, render the search unreasonable." The question is not simply whether some other alternative was available, but whether the police acted unreasonably in failing to recognize or to pursue it.

We readily conclude that, given the circumstances facing him, Agent Cooke pursued his investigation in a diligent and reasonable manner. During most of Savage's 20-minute detention, Cooke was attempting to contact Thrasher and enlisting the help of the local police who remained with Sharpe while Cooke left to pursue Officer Thrasher and the pickup. Once Cooke reached Officer Thrasher and Savage,[5] he proceeded expeditiously: within the space of a few minutes, he examined Savage's driver's license and the truck's bill of sale, requested (and was denied) permission to search the truck, stepped on the rear bumper and noted that the truck did not move, confirming his suspicion that it was probably overloaded. He then detected the odor of marihuana.

Clearly this case does not involve any delay unnecessary to the legitimate investigation of the law enforcement officers. Respondents presented no evidence that the officers were dilatory in their investigation. The delay in this case was attributable almost entirely to the evasive actions of Savage, who sought to elude the police as Sharpe moved his Pontiac to the side of the road.[6]

---

[5] It was appropriate for Officer Thrasher to hold Savage for the brief period pending Cooke's arrival. Thrasher could not be certain that he was aware of all of the facts that had aroused Cooke's suspicions; and, as a highway patrolman, he lacked Cooke's training and experience in dealing with narcotics investigations. In this situation, it cannot realistically be said that Thrasher, a state patrolman called in to assist a federal agent in making a stop, acted unreasonably because he did not release Savage based solely on his own limited investigation of the situation and without the consent of Agent Cooke.

[6] Even if it could be inferred that Savage was not attempting to elude the police when he drove his car *between* Thrasher's patrol car and Sharpe's Pontiac—in the process nearly hitting the patrol car—such an assumption would not alter our analysis or our conclusion. The significance of Savage's actions is that, whether innocent or purposeful, they made it necessary for Thrasher and Cooke to split up, placed Thrasher and Cooke out of contact with each other, and required Cooke to enlist the assistance of local police before he could join Thrasher and Savage.

* * *

We reject the contention that a 20-minute stop is unreasonable when the police have acted diligently and a suspect's actions contribute to the added delay about which he complains. The judgment of the Court of Appeals is reversed, and the case is remanded for further proceedings consistent with this opinion.

JUSTICE BLACKMUN, concurring.

In view of respondents' fugitive status I would have vacated the judgment of the Court of Appeals and remanded the case to that court with directions to dismiss the respondents' appeal from the District Court's judgment to the Court of Appeals.

This Court, however, does not follow that path, and chooses to decide the case on the merits. I therefore also reach the merits and join the Court's opinion.

JUSTICE MARSHALL, concurring in the judgment.

I join the result in this case because only the evasive actions of the defendants here turned what otherwise would have been a permissibly brief *Terry* stop into the prolonged encounter now at issue. I write separately, however, because in my view the Court understates the importance of *Terry*'s brevity requirement to the constitutionality of *Terry* stops.

I

* * *

To those who rank zealous law enforcement above all other values, it may be tempting to divorce *Terry* from its rationales and merge the two prongs of *Terry* into the single requirement that the police act reasonably under all the circumstances when they stop and investigate on less than probable cause. As long as the police are acting diligently to complete their investigation, it is difficult to maintain that law enforcement goals would better be served by releasing an individual after a brief stop than by continuing to detain him for as long as necessary to discover whether probable cause can be established. But while the preservation of order is important to any society, the "needs of law enforcement stand in constant tension with the Constitution's protections of the individual against certain exercises of official power. It is precisely the predictability of these pressures that counsels a resolute loyalty to constitutional safeguards." *Terry* must be justified, not because it makes law enforcement easier, but because a *Terry* stop does not constitute the sort of arrest that the Constitution requires be made only upon probable cause.

For this reason, in reviewing any *Terry* stop, the "critical threshold issue is the intrusiveness of the seizure." Regardless how efficient it may be for law enforcement officials to engage in prolonged questioning to investigate a crime, or how reasonable in light of law enforcement objectives it may be to detain a suspect until various inquiries can be made and answered, a seizure that in duration, scope, or means goes beyond the bounds of *Terry* cannot be reconciled with the Fourth Amendment in the absence of probable cause. Legitimate law enforcement interests that do not rise to the level of probable cause simply cannot turn an overly intrusive seizure into a constitutionally permissible one.

In my view, the length of the stop in and of itself may make the stop sufficiently intrusive to be unjustifiable in the absence of probable cause to arrest. *Terry* "stops" are justified, in part, because they are *stops,* rather than prolonged seizures. "[A] stopping differs from an arrest not in the incompleteness of the seizure but in the brevity of it." 1 W. LaFave & J. Israel, CRIMINAL PROCEDURE § 3.8, p. 297 (1984).

* * *

III

In light of these principles, I cannot join the Court's opinion. The Court offers a hodgepodge of reasons to explain why the 20-minute stop at issue here was permissible. At points we are told that the stop was no longer than "necessary" and that the police acted "diligently" in pursuing their investigation, all of which seems to suggest that, as long as a stop is no longer than necessary to the "legitimate investigation of the law enforcement officers," the stop is perfectly lawful. As I have just argued, such reasoning puts the horse before the cart by failing to focus on the critical threshold question of the intrusiveness of the stop, particularly its length. With respect to that question, the Court seems in one breath to chastise the Court of Appeals for concluding that the length of a detention alone can transform a *Terry* stop into a *de facto* arrest, while in another breath the Court acknowledges that, "if an investigative stop continues indefinitely, at some point it can no longer be justified as an investigative stop."

Fortunately, it is unnecessary to try to sort all of this out, for another rationale offered by the Court adequately disposes of this case. As the Court recognizes: "The delay in this case was attributable almost entirely to the evasive actions of Savage, who sought to elude the police as Sharpe moved his Pontiac to the side of the road. Except for Savage's maneuvers, only a short and certainly permissible pre-arrest detention would likely have taken place." With that holding I agree. Had Savage pulled over when signaled to, as did Sharpe, Savage and Sharpe both would have been subjected to only a permissibly brief *Terry* stop before the odor of the marihuana would have given the officers probable cause to arrest. Once Cooke caught back up with Savage, only a few minutes passed before Cooke smelled the marihuana. During these few brief minutes, Savage was subjected to no more than the identification request and minimal questioning, designed to confirm or dispel the reasonable suspicion causing the stop, that is legitimate under *Terry*. While a 20-minute stop would, under most circumstances, be longer than the limited intrusion entailed by the brief stop that *Terry* allows, I believe such a stop is permissible when a suspect's own actions are the primary cause for prolonging an encounter beyond the bounds to which *Terry's* brevity requirement ordinarily limits such stops. Nothing more is necessary to decide this case, and any further suggestions in the Court's opinion I find unwarranted, confusing, and potentially corrosive of the principles upon which *Terry* is grounded.

* * *

JUSTICE BRENNAN, dissenting.

* * *

I

* * *

If the facts are as the Court relates them, it is not readily apparent why the Court insists on using this case as a vehicle for expanding the outer bounds of *Terry* investigative stops. I had thought it rather well established that where police officers reasonably suspect that an individual may be engaged in criminal activity, and the individual deliberately takes flight when the officers attempt to stop and question him, the officers generally no longer have mere reasonable suspicion, but probable cause to arrest.

Of course, flight *alone* cannot give rise to probable cause; it must be coupled with pre-existing reasonable and articulable suspicion. And the act of flight must reasonably appear to be in response to the presence of the authorities. Here, however, the Court accepts the questionable premise that the officers already had reasonable suspicion when they decided to stop the vehicles, and it boldly concludes that Sharpe and Savage "started speeding" at Thrasher's approach, that Savage "sought to elude the police" when Thrasher attempted the stop, and that Savage took "evasive actions."

Thus if the facts were as the Court describes them, I would be inclined to view this as a probable-cause detention, and the reasonableness of these stops under *Terry* would not appear to be before us. The Court's failure even to consider this question of probable cause is baffling, but ultimately in keeping with its recent practice in *Terry* cases of reaching out far beyond what is required to resolve the cases at hand so as more immediately to impose its views without the bother of abiding by the necessarily gradual pace of case-by-case decisionmaking.

II

The Court's opinion is flawed in another critical respect: its discussion of Savage's purported attempt "to elude the police" amounts to nothing more than a *de novo* factual finding made on a record that is, at best, hopelessly ambiguous. Neither the District Court nor the Court of Appeals ever found that Savage's actions constituted evasion or flight. If we are nevertheless to engage in *de novo* factfinding, I submit the Court has taken insufficient account of several factors.

* * *

JUSTICE STEVENS, dissenting.

* * *

The correct disposition of this case, I believe, is to treat it as though the respondents' escape had mooted the appeal. If we vacate the judgment of the Court of Appeals, and if we direct that the appeal from the judgment of the District Court be dismissed, the consequences would be the same as if the escape had occurred in advance of the Court of Appeals' decision. Moreover, by vacating that court's judgment, the Government's interest in eliminating the precedent that it has challenged in its certiorari petition would be vindicated. Finally, such a disposition would make it unnecessary for this Court to decide the constitutional question that is presented. That, for me, is a matter of paramount importance.

There is one adverse consequence of the disposition I propose. It would deprive the Court of the opportunity to write an opinion in a Fourth Amendment case. The summary disposition of this case would not serve the interest of providing additional guidance to the law-enforcement community. But regarding that interest as paramount would support the wholesale adoption of a practice of rendering advisory opinions at the request of the Executive—a practice the Court abjured at the beginning of our history. We have, instead, opted for a policy of judicial restraint—of studiously avoiding the unnecessary adjudication of constitutional questions. The correct implementation of that policy, I submit, requires that we predicate the disposition of this case on the respondents' fugitive status.

Points for Discussion

1. *Sharpe* draws an important line between brief investigative stops—which may be supported by mere reasonable suspicion—and full-blown arrests—which must be supported by probable cause. Do you believe the line the Court drew in this case is a sensible one? What could the Court have done to draw that line more clearly? Are there advantages to the *per se* twenty-minute rule that the lower court adopted?

2. Justice Marshall's concurrence disagrees with the majority over whether the appropriate measure of the reasonableness of an investigative stop is objective or subjective. In Justice Marshall's reading of the majority opinion, the principal question is whether the investigating agents were "diligent" in their investigation, not whether, objectively, their investigation

went on too long to be fairly described as a brief investigative stop. Is this a fair reading of the majority opinion and, if so, who has the better of the argument here?

RODRIGUEZ V. UNITED STATES

135 S.Ct. 1609 (2015)

JUSTICE GINSBURG delivered the opinion of the court.

In *Illinois v. Caballes*, 543 U.S. 405 (2005), this Court held that a dog sniff conducted during a lawful traffic stop does not violate the Fourth Amendment's proscription of unreasonable seizures. This case presents the question whether the Fourth Amendment tolerates a dog sniff conducted after completion of a traffic stop. We hold that a police stop exceeding the time needed to handle the matter for which the stop was made violates the Constitution's shield against unreasonable seizures. A seizure justified only by a police-observed traffic violation, therefore, "become[s] unlawful if it is prolonged beyond the time reasonably required to complete th[e] mission" of issuing a ticket for the violation. The Court so recognized in *Caballes*, and we adhere to the line drawn in that decision.

I

Just after midnight on March 27, 2012, police officer Morgan Struble observed a Mercury Mountaineer veer slowly onto the shoulder of Nebraska State Highway 275 for one or two seconds and then jerk back onto the road. Nebraska law prohibits driving on highway shoulders and, on that basis, Struble pulled the Mountaineer over at 12:06 a.m. Struble is a K-9 officer with the Valley Police Department in Nebraska, and his dog Floyd was in his patrol car that night. Two men were in the Mountaineer: the driver, Dennys Rodriguez, and a front-seat passenger, Scott Pollman.

Struble approached the Mountaineer on the passenger's side. After Rodriguez identified himself, Struble asked him why he had driven onto the shoulder. Rodriguez replied that he had swerved to avoid a pothole. Struble then gathered Rodriguez's license, registration, and proof of insurance, and asked Rodriguez to accompany him to the patrol car. Rodriguez asked if he was required to do so, and Struble answered that he was not. Rodriguez decided to wait in his own vehicle.

After running a records check on Rodriguez, Struble returned to the Mountaineer. Struble asked passenger Pollman for his driver's license and began to question him about where the two men were coming from and where they were going. Pollman replied that they had traveled to Omaha, Nebraska, to look at a Ford Mustang that was for sale and that they were returning to Norfolk, Nebraska. Struble returned again to his patrol car, where he completed a records check on Pollman, and called for a second officer. Struble then began writing a warning ticket for Rodriguez for driving on the shoulder of the road.

Struble returned to Rodriguez's vehicle a third time to issue the written warning. By 12:27 or 12:28 a.m., Struble had finished explaining the warning to Rodriguez, and had given back to Rodriguez and Pollman the documents obtained from them. As Struble later testified, at that point, Rodriguez and Pollman "had all their documents back and a copy of the written warning. I got all the reason[s] for the stop out of the way[,] . . . took care of all the business."

Nevertheless, Struble did not consider Rodriguez "free to leave." Although justification for the traffic stop was "out of the way," Struble asked for permission to walk his dog around Rodriguez's vehicle. Rodriguez said no. Struble then instructed Rodriguez to turn off the ignition, exit the vehicle, and stand in front of the patrol car to wait for the second officer. Rodriguez complied. At 12:33 a.m., a deputy sheriff arrived. Struble retrieved his dog and led him twice around the Mountaineer. The dog alerted to the presence of drugs halfway through Struble's second pass. All told, seven or eight minutes had elapsed from the time Struble issued the written warning until the dog indicated the presence of drugs. A search of the vehicle revealed a large bag of methamphetamine.

Rodriguez was indicted in the United States District Court for the District of Nebraska on one count of possession with intent to distribute 50 grams or more of methamphetamine, in violation of 21 U.S.C. §§ 841(a)(1) and (b)(1). He moved to suppress the evidence seized from his car on the ground, among others, that Struble had prolonged the traffic stop without reasonable suspicion in order to conduct the dog sniff.

After receiving evidence, a Magistrate Judge recommended that the motion be denied. The Magistrate Judge found no probable cause to search the vehicle independent of the dog alert. He further found that no reasonable suspicion supported the detention once Struble issued the written warning. He concluded, however, that under Eighth Circuit precedent, extension of the stop by "seven to eight minutes" for the dog sniff was only a *de minimis* intrusion on Rodriguez's Fourth Amendment rights and was therefore permissible.

* * *

We granted certiorari to resolve a division among lower courts on the question whether police routinely may extend an otherwise-completed traffic stop, absent reasonable suspicion, in order to conduct a dog sniff.

* * *

II

A seizure for a traffic violation justifies a police investigation of that violation. "[A] relatively brief encounter," a routine traffic stop is "more analogous to a so-called '*Terry* stop' . . . than to a formal arrest." *Knowles v. Iowa*, 525 U.S. 113, 117 (1998). Like a *Terry* stop, the tolerable duration of police inquiries in the traffic-stop context is determined by the seizure's "mission"—to address the traffic violation that warranted the stop and attend to related safety concerns. Because addressing the infraction is the purpose of the stop, it may "last no longer than is necessary to effectuate that purpose." Authority for the seizure thus ends when tasks tied to the traffic infraction are—or reasonably should have been—completed.

Our decisions in *Caballes* and *Johnson* heed these constraints. In both cases, we concluded that the Fourth Amendment tolerated certain unrelated investigations that did not lengthen the roadside detention. *Johnson*, 555 U.S., at 327–328 (questioning); *Caballes*, 543 U.S., at 406, 408 (dog sniff). In *Caballes*, however, we cautioned that a traffic stop "can become unlawful if it is prolonged beyond the time reasonably required to complete th[e] mission" of issuing a warning ticket. And we repeated that admonition in *Johnson*: The seizure remains lawful only "so long as [unrelated] inquiries do not measurably extend the duration of the stop." An officer, in other words, may conduct certain unrelated checks during an otherwise lawful traffic stop. But contrary to Justice Alito's suggestion, he may not do so in a way that prolongs the stop, absent the reasonable suspicion ordinarily demanded to justify detaining an individual.

Beyond determining whether to issue a traffic ticket, an officer's mission includes "ordinary inquiries incident to [the traffic] stop." *Caballes*, 543 U.S., at 408. Typically such inquiries involve checking the driver's license, determining whether there are outstanding warrants against the driver, and inspecting the automobile's registration and proof of insurance. These checks serve the same objective as enforcement of the traffic code: ensuring that vehicles on the road are operated safely and responsibly.

A dog sniff, by contrast, is a measure aimed at "detect[ing] evidence of ordinary criminal wrongdoing." *Indianapolis v. Edmond*, 531 U.S. 32, 40–41 (2000). Candidly, the Government acknowledged at oral argument that a dog sniff, unlike the routine measures just mentioned, is not an ordinary incident of a traffic stop. Lacking the same close connection to roadway safety as the ordinary inquiries, a dog sniff is not fairly characterized as part of the officer's traffic mission.

In advancing its *de minimis* rule, the Eighth Circuit relied heavily on our decision in *Pennsylvania v. Mimms*, 434 U.S. 106 (1977) (*per curiam*). In *Mimms*, we reasoned that the government's "legitimate and weighty" interest in officer safety outweighs the "*de minimis*" additional intrusion of requiring a driver, already lawfully stopped, to exit the vehicle. See also *Maryland v. Wilson*, 519 U.S. 408, 413–15 (1997) (passengers may be required to exit vehicle stopped for traffic violation). The Eighth Circuit, echoed in Justice Thomas's dissent, believed that the imposition here similarly could be offset by the Government's "strong interest in interdicting the flow of illegal drugs along the nation's highways."

Unlike a general interest in criminal enforcement, however, the government's officer safety interest stems from the mission of the stop itself. Traffic stops are "especially fraught with danger to police officers," so an officer may need to take certain negligibly burdensome precautions in order to complete his mission safely. On-scene investigation into other crimes, however, detours from that mission. So too do safety precautions taken in order to facilitate such detours. Thus, even assuming that the imposition here was no more intrusive than the exit order in *Mimms*, the dog sniff could not be justified on the same basis. Highway and officer safety are interests different in kind from the Government's endeavor to detect crime in general or drug trafficking in particular.

The Government argues that an officer may "incremental[ly]" prolong a stop to conduct a dog sniff so long as the officer is reasonably diligent in pursuing the traffic-related purpose of the stop, and the overall duration of the stop remains reasonable in relation to the duration of other traffic stops involving similar circumstances. The Government's argument, in effect, is that by completing all traffic-related tasks expeditiously, an officer can earn bonus time to pursue an unrelated criminal investigation. The reasonableness of a seizure, however, depends on what the police in fact do. In this regard, the Government acknowledges that "an officer always has to be reasonably diligent." How could diligence be gauged other than by noting what the officer actually did and how he did it? If an officer can complete traffic-based inquiries expeditiously, then that is the amount of "time reasonably required to complete [the stop's] mission." *Caballes*, 543 U.S., at 407. As we said in *Caballes* and reiterate today, a traffic stop "prolonged beyond" that point is "unlawful." The critical question, then, is not whether the dog sniff occurs before or after the officer issues a ticket, as Justice Alito supposes, but whether conducting the sniff "prolongs"—*i.e.*, adds time to—"the stop."

III

The Magistrate Judge found that detention for the dog sniff in this case was not independently supported by individualized suspicion, and the District Court adopted the Magistrate Judge's findings. The Court of Appeals, however, did not review that determination. The question whether reasonable suspicion of criminal activity justified detaining Rodriguez beyond completion of the traffic infraction investigation, therefore, remains open for Eighth Circuit consideration on remand.

* * *

JUSTICE KENNEDY, dissenting.

My join in Justice Thomas' dissenting opinion does not extend to Part III. Although the issue discussed in that Part was argued here, the Court of Appeals has not addressed that aspect of the case in any detail. In my view the better course would be to allow that court to do so in the first instance.

JUSTICE THOMAS, with whom JUSTICE ALITO joins, and with whom JUSTICE KENNEDY joins as to all but Part III, dissenting.

Ten years ago, we explained that "conducting a dog sniff [does] not change the character of a traffic stop that is lawful at its inception and otherwise executed in a reasonable manner." *Illinois v. Caballes*, 543 U.S. 405, 408 (2005). The only question here is whether an officer executed a stop in a reasonable manner when he waited to conduct a dog sniff until after he had given the driver a written warning and a backup unit had arrived, bringing the overall duration of the stop to 29 minutes. Because the stop was reasonably executed, no Fourth Amendment violation occurred. The Court's holding to the contrary cannot be reconciled with our decision in *Caballes* or a number of common police practices. It was also unnecessary, as the officer possessed reasonable suspicion to continue to hold the driver to conduct the dog sniff. I respectfully dissent.

I

* * *

Because Rodriguez does not dispute that Officer Struble had probable cause to stop him, the only question is whether the stop was otherwise executed in a reasonable manner. I easily conclude that it was. Approximately 29 minutes passed from the time Officer Struble stopped Rodriguez until his narcotics-detection dog alerted to the presence of drugs. That amount of time is hardly out of the ordinary for a traffic stop by a single officer of a vehicle containing multiple occupants even when no dog sniff is involved. See, *e.g.*, *United States v. Ellis*, 497 F.3d 606 (C.A.6 2007) (22 minutes); *United States v. Barragan*, 379 F.3d 524 (C.A.8 2004) (approximately 30 minutes). During that time, Officer Struble conducted the ordinary activities of a traffic stop—he approached the vehicle, questioned Rodriguez about the observed violation, asked Pollman about their travel plans, ran serial warrant checks on Rodriguez and Pollman, and issued a written warning to Rodriguez. And when he decided to conduct a dog sniff, he took the precaution of calling for backup out of concern for his safety.

As *Caballes* makes clear, the fact that Officer Struble waited until after he gave Rodriguez the warning to conduct the dog sniff does not alter this analysis. Because "the use of a well-trained narcotics-detection dog . . . generally does not implicate legitimate privacy interests," "conducting a dog sniff would not change the character of a traffic stop that is lawful at its inception and otherwise executed in a reasonable manner." The stop here was "lawful at its inception and otherwise executed in a reasonable manner." As in *Caballes*, "conducting a dog sniff [did] not change the character of [the] traffic stop," and thus no Fourth Amendment violation occurred.

II

* * *

A

The majority's rule requires a traffic stop to "en[d] when tasks tied to the traffic infraction are—or reasonably should have been—completed." "If an officer can complete traffic-based inquiries expeditiously, then that is the amount of time reasonably required to complete the stop's mission" and he may hold the individual no longer. The majority's rule thus imposes a one-way ratchet for constitutional protection linked to the characteristics of the individual officer conducting the stop: If a driver is stopped by a particularly efficient officer, then he will be entitled to be released from the traffic stop after a shorter period of time than a driver stopped by a less efficient officer. Similarly, if a driver is stopped by an officer with access to technology that can shorten a records check, then he will be entitled to be released from the stop after a shorter period of time than an individual stopped by an officer without access to such technology.

I "cannot accept that the search and seizure protections of the Fourth Amendment are so variable and can be made to turn upon such trivialities." *Whren*, 517 U.S., at 815. We have repeatedly explained that the reasonableness inquiry must not hinge on the characteristics of the individual officer conducting the seizure. We have held, for example, that an officer's state of mind "does not invalidate [an] action taken as long as the circumstances, viewed objectively, justify that action." We have spurned theories that would make the Fourth Amendment "change with local law enforcement practices." And we have rejected a rule that would require the offense establishing probable cause to be "closely related to" the offense identified by the arresting officer, as such a rule would make "the constitutionality of an arrest . . . vary from place to place and from time to time, depending on whether the arresting officer states the reason for the detention and, if so, whether he correctly identifies a general class of offense for which probable cause exists." *Devenpeck v. Alford*, 543 U.S. 146, 154 (2004). In *Devenpeck*, a unanimous Court explained: "An arrest made by a knowledgeable, veteran officer would be valid, whereas an arrest made by a rookie *in precisely the same circumstances* would not. We see no reason to ascribe to the Fourth Amendment such arbitrarily variable protection."

The majority's logic would produce similarly arbitrary results. Under its reasoning, a traffic stop made by a rookie could be executed in a reasonable manner, whereas the same traffic stop made by a knowledgeable, veteran officer *in precisely the same circumstances* might not, if in fact his knowledge and experience made him capable of completing the stop faster. We have long rejected interpretations of the Fourth

Amendment that would produce such haphazard results, and I see no reason to depart from our consistent practice today.

B

As if that were not enough, the majority also limits the duration of the stop to the time it takes the officer to complete a narrow category of "traffic-based inquiries." According to the majority, these inquiries include those that "serve the same objective as enforcement of the traffic code: ensuring that vehicles on the road are operated safely and responsibly." Inquiries directed to "detecting evidence of ordinary criminal wrongdoing" are not traffic-related inquiries and thus cannot count toward the overall duration of the stop.

* * *

The majority's approach draws an artificial line between dog sniffs and other common police practices. The lower courts have routinely confirmed that warrant checks are a constitutionally permissible part of a traffic stop, and the majority confirms that it finds no fault in these measures. Yet its reasoning suggests the opposite. Such warrant checks look more like they are directed to "detecting evidence of ordinary criminal wrongdoing" than to "ensuring that vehicles on the road are operated safely and responsibly." Perhaps one could argue that the existence of an outstanding warrant might make a driver less likely to operate his vehicle safely and responsibly on the road, but the same could be said about a driver in possession of contraband. A driver confronted by the police in either case might try to flee or become violent toward the officer. But under the majority's analysis, a dog sniff, which is directed at uncovering that problem, is not treated as a traffic-based inquiry. Warrant checks, arguably, should fare no better. The majority suggests that a warrant check is an ordinary inquiry incident to a traffic stop because it can be used " 'to determine whether the apparent traffic violator is wanted for one or more previous traffic offenses.' " But as the very treatise on which the majority relies notes, such checks are a "manifest[ation of] the 'war on drugs' motivation so often underlying [routine traffic] stops," and thus are very much like the dog sniff in this case.

Investigative questioning rests on the same basis as the dog sniff. "Asking questions is an essential part of police investigations." *Hiibel v. Sixth Judicial Dist. Court of Nev., Humboldt Cty.*, 542 U.S. 177, 185 (2004). And the lower courts have routinely upheld such questioning during routine traffic stops. The majority's reasoning appears to allow officers to engage in *some* questioning aimed at detecting evidence of ordinary criminal wrongdoing. But it is hard to see how such inquiries fall within the "seizure's 'mission' [of] address[ing] the traffic violation that warranted the stop," or "attend[ing] to related safety concerns." Its reasoning appears to come down to the principle that dogs are different.

C

On a more fundamental level, the majority's inquiry elides the distinction between traffic stops based on probable cause and those based on reasonable suspicion. Probable cause is *the* "traditional justification" for the seizure of a person. *Whren*, 517 U.S., at 817. This Court created an exception to that rule in *Terry v. Ohio*, 392 U.S. 1 (1968), permitting "police officers who suspect criminal activity to make limited intrusions on an individual's personal security based on less than probable cause," *Michigan v. Summers*, 452 U.S. 692, 698 (1981). Reasonable suspicion is the justification for such seizures. *Prado Navarette v. California*, 572 U.S. 393 (2014).

* * *

Although all traffic stops must be executed reasonably, our precedents make clear that traffic stops justified by reasonable suspicion are subject to additional limitations that those justified by probable cause are not. A traffic stop based on reasonable suspicion, like all *Terry* stops, must be "justified at its inception" and "reasonably related in scope to the circumstances which justified the interference in the first place." *Hiibel*, 542 U.S., at 185. It also "cannot continue for an excessive period of time or resemble a traditional arrest." *Id.*, at 185–186. By contrast, a stop based on probable cause affords an officer considerably more leeway. In such seizures, an officer may engage in a warrantless arrest of the driver, a warrantless search incident to arrest of the driver, *Riley v. California*, 573 U.S. 373 (2014), and a warrantless search incident to arrest of the vehicle if it is reasonable to believe evidence relevant to the crime of arrest might be found there, *Arizona v. Gant*, 556 U.S. 332, 335 (2009).

The majority casually tosses this distinction aside. It asserts that the traffic stop in this case, which was undisputedly initiated on the basis of probable cause, can last no longer than is in fact necessary to effectuate the mission of the stop. And, it assumes that the mission of the stop was merely to write a traffic ticket, rather than to consider making a custodial arrest. In support of that durational requirement, it relies primarily on cases involving *Terry* stops.

The *only* case involving a traffic stop based on probable cause that the majority cites for its rule is *Caballes*. But, that decision provides no support for today's restructuring of our Fourth Amendment jurisprudence. In *Caballes*, the Court made clear that, in the context of a traffic stop supported by probable cause, "a dog sniff would not change the character of a traffic stop that is lawful at its inception and otherwise executed in a reasonable manner." 543 U.S., at 408. To be sure, *the dissent* in *Caballes* would have "appl[ied] *Terry*'s reasonable-relation test . . . to determine whether the canine sniff impermissibly expanded the scope of the initially valid seizure of *Caballes*." *Id.*, at 420 (Ginsburg, J., dissenting). But even it conceded that the *Caballes* majority had "implicitly [rejected] the application of *Terry* to a traffic stop converted, by calling in a dog, to a drug search." *Id.*, at 421.

By strictly limiting the tasks that define the durational scope of the traffic stop, the majority accomplishes today what the *Caballes* dissent could not: strictly limiting the scope of an officer's activities during a traffic stop justified by probable cause. In doing so, it renders the difference between probable cause and reasonable suspicion virtually meaningless in this context. That shift is supported neither by the Fourth Amendment nor by our precedents interpreting it. And, it results in a constitutional framework that lacks predictability. Had Officer Struble arrested, handcuffed, and taken Rodriguez to the police station for his traffic violation, he would have complied with the Fourth Amendment. But because he made Rodriguez wait for seven or eight extra minutes until a dog arrived, he evidently committed a constitutional violation. Such a view of the Fourth Amendment makes little sense.

III

Today's revision of our Fourth Amendment jurisprudence was also entirely unnecessary. Rodriguez suffered no Fourth Amendment violation here for an entirely independent reason: Officer Struble had reasonable suspicion to continue to hold him for investigative purposes. Our precedents make clear that the Fourth Amendment permits an officer to conduct an investigative traffic stop when that officer has "a particularized and objective basis for suspecting the particular person stopped of criminal activity." *Prado Navarette*, 572 U.S., at 396. Reasonable suspicion is determined by looking at "the whole picture," taking into account "the factual and practical considerations of everyday life on which reasonable and prudent men, not legal technicians, act."

Officer Struble testified that he first became suspicious that Rodriguez was engaged in criminal activity for a number of reasons. When he approached the vehicle, he smelled an "overwhelming odor of air freshener coming from the vehicle," which is, in his experience, "a common attempt to conceal an odor that [people] don't want . . . to be smelled by the police." He also observed, upon approaching the front window on the passenger side of the vehicle, that Rodriguez's passenger, Scott Pollman, appeared nervous. Pollman pulled his hat down low, puffed nervously on a cigarette, and refused to make eye contact with him. The officer thought he was "more nervous than your typical passenger" who "do[esn't] have anything to worry about because [t]hey didn't commit a [traffic] violation."

Officer Struble's interactions with the vehicle's occupants only increased his suspicions. When he asked Rodriguez why he had driven onto the shoulder, Rodriguez claimed that he swerved to avoid a pothole. But that story could not be squared with Officer Struble's observation of the vehicle slowly driving off the road before being jerked back onto it. And when Officer Struble asked Pollman where they were coming from and where they were going, Pollman told him they were traveling from Omaha, Nebraska, back to Norfolk, Nebraska, after looking at a vehicle they were considering purchasing. Pollman told the officer that he had neither seen pictures of the vehicle nor confirmed title before the trip. As Officer Struble explained, it "seemed suspicious" to him "to drive . . . approximately two hours . . . late at night to see a vehicle sight unseen to possibly buy it," and to go from Norfolk to Omaha to look at it because "[u]sually people leave Omaha to go get vehicles, not the other way around" due to higher Omaha taxes.

These facts, taken together, easily meet our standard for reasonable suspicion. "[N]ervous, evasive behavior is a pertinent factor in determining reasonable suspicion," *Illinois v. Wardlow*, 528 U.S. 119, 124 (2000), and both vehicle occupants were engaged in such conduct. The officer also recognized heavy use of air freshener, which, in his experience, indicated the presence of contraband in the vehicle. "[C]ommonsense judgments and inferences about human behavior" further support the officer's conclusion that Pollman's story about their trip was likely a cover story for illegal activity. Taking into account all the relevant facts, Officer Struble possessed reasonable suspicion of criminal activity to conduct the dog sniff.

* * *

JUSTICE ALITO, dissenting.

This is an unnecessary, impractical, and arbitrary decision. It addresses a purely hypothetical question: whether the traffic stop in this case *would be* unreasonable if the police officer, prior to leading a drug-sniffing dog around the exterior of petitioner's car, did not already have reasonable suspicion that the car contained drugs. In fact, however, the police officer *did have* reasonable suspicion, and, as a result, the officer was justified in detaining the occupants for the short period of time (seven or eight minutes) that is at issue.

* * *

Not only does the Court reach out to decide a question not really presented by the facts in this case, but the Court's answer to that question is arbitrary. The Court refuses to address the real Fourth Amendment question: whether the stop was unreasonably prolonged. Instead, the Court latches onto the fact that Officer Struble delivered the warning prior to the dog sniff and proclaims that the authority to detain based on a traffic stop ends when a citation or warning is handed over to the driver. The Court thus holds that the Fourth Amendment was violated, not because of the length of the stop, but simply because of the sequence in which Officer Struble chose to perform his tasks.

* * *

Points for Discussion

1. Officer Struble made clear that he had decided to issue a written warning and had gotten the paperwork out of the way before initiating the dog sniff. On this basis, the Court concluded that he exceeded the scope of the stop by needlessly prolonging it. What incentive does the Court's opinion create for future officers who wish to conduct drug sniffs?

2. Justice Thomas' dissent asserts that the Court's holding "cannot be reconciled with our decision in *Caballes* or a number of common police practices." Why should the Court reconcile its holding to "common police practices"? Are "common police practices" *ever* relevant to what the Constitution permits or requires? Does it seem that a 29-minute stop to issue a warning conforms to "common police practice" in enforcing traffic ordinances? Does Justice Thomas' citation to two federal appellate cases help establish how long a traffic typically lasts?

3. Justice Thomas states that "traffic stops justified by reasonable suspicion are subject to additional limitations that those justified by probable cause are not." Is his position that once the police have probable cause to believe a traffic infraction has occurred, they may take their time investigating *any* possible offense? What is the majority's response to this reasoning? Does the reasoning of *Terry v. Ohio* support Justice Thomas or the majority?

MINNESOTA V. DICKERSON

508 U.S. 366 (1993)

JUSTICE WHITE delivered the opinion of the court.

In this case, we consider whether the Fourth Amendment permits the seizure of contraband detected through a police officer's sense of touch during a protective patdown search.

I

On the evening of November 9, 1989, two Minneapolis police officers were patrolling an area on the city's north side in a marked squad car. At about 8:15 p.m., one of the officers observed respondent leaving a 12-unit apartment building on Morgan Avenue North. The officer, having previously responded to complaints of drug sales in the building's hallways and having executed several search warrants on the premises, considered the building to be a notorious "crack house." According to testimony credited by the trial court, respondent began walking toward the police but, upon spotting the squad car and making eye contact with one of the officers, abruptly halted and began walking in the opposite direction. His suspicion aroused, this officer watched as respondent turned and entered an alley on the other side of the apartment building. Based upon respondent's seemingly evasive actions and the fact that he had just left a building known for cocaine traffic, the officers decided to stop respondent and investigate further.

The officers pulled their squad car into the alley and ordered respondent to stop and submit to a patdown search. The search revealed no weapons, but the officer conducting the search did take an interest in a small lump in respondent's nylon jacket. The officer later testified: "[A]s I pat-searched the front of his body, I felt a lump, a small lump, in the front pocket. I examined it with my fingers and it slid and it felt to be a lump of crack cocaine in cellophane."

The officer then reached into respondent's pocket and retrieved a small plastic bag containing one fifth of one gram of crack cocaine. Respondent was arrested and charged in Hennepin County District Court with possession of a controlled substance.

Before trial, respondent moved to suppress the cocaine. The trial court first concluded that the officers were justified under *Terry v. Ohio,* 392 U.S. 1 (1968), in stopping respondent to investigate whether he might be engaged in criminal activity. The court further found that the officers were justified in frisking respondent to ensure that he was not carrying a weapon. Finally, analogizing to the "plain-view" doctrine, under which officers may make a warrantless seizure of contraband found in plain view during a lawful search for other items, the trial court ruled that the officers' seizure of the cocaine did not violate the Fourth Amendment:

> To this Court there is no distinction as to which sensory perception the officer uses to conclude that the material is contraband. An experienced officer may rely upon his sense of smell in DWI stops or in recognizing the smell of burning marijuana in an automobile. The sound of a shotgun being racked would clearly support certain reactions by an officer. The sense of touch, grounded in experience and training, is as reliable as perceptions drawn from other senses. "Plain feel," therefore, is no different than plain view and will equally support the seizure here.

His suppression motion having failed, respondent proceeded to trial and was found guilty.

* * *

II

* * *

B

We have already held that police officers, at least under certain circumstances, may seize contraband detected during the lawful execution of a *Terry* search. In *Michigan v. Long,* [436 U.S. 1032 (1983)], for example, police approached a man who had driven his car into a ditch and who appeared to be under the influence of some intoxicant. As the man moved to reenter the car from the roadside, police spotted a knife on the floorboard. The officers stopped the man, subjected him to a patdown search, and then inspected the interior of the vehicle for other weapons. During the search of the passenger compartment, the police discovered an open pouch containing marijuana and seized it. This Court upheld the validity of the search and seizure under *Terry*. The Court held first that, in the context of a roadside encounter, where police have reasonable suspicion based on specific and articulable facts to believe that a driver may be armed and dangerous, they may conduct a protective search for weapons not only of the driver's person but also of the passenger compartment of the automobile. Of course, the protective search of the vehicle, being justified solely by the danger that weapons stored there could be used against the officers or bystanders, must be "limited to those areas in which a weapon may be placed or hidden." The Court then held: "If, while conducting a legitimate *Terry* search of the interior of the automobile, the officer should, as here, discover contraband other than weapons, he clearly cannot be required to ignore the contraband, and the Fourth Amendment does not require its suppression in such circumstances."

The Court in *Long* justified this latter holding by reference to our cases under the "plain-view" doctrine. Under that doctrine, if police are lawfully in a position from which they view an object, if its incriminating character is immediately apparent, and if the officers have a lawful right of access to the object, they may seize it without a warrant. If, however, the police lack probable cause to believe that an object in plain view is contraband without conducting some further search of the object—*i.e.,* if "its incriminating character [is not] 'immediately apparent,' "—the plain-view doctrine cannot justify its seizure.

We think that this doctrine has an obvious application by analogy to cases in which an officer discovers contraband through the sense of touch during an otherwise lawful search. The rationale of the plain-view doctrine is that if contraband is left in open view and is observed by a police officer from a lawful vantage point, there has been no invasion of a legitimate expectation of privacy and thus no "search" within the meaning of the Fourth Amendment—or at least no search independent of the initial intrusion that gave the officers their vantage point. The warrantless seizure of contraband that presents itself in this manner is deemed justified by the realization that resort to a neutral magistrate under such circumstances would often be impracticable and would do little to promote the objectives of the Fourth Amendment. The same can be said of tactile discoveries of contraband. If a police officer lawfully pats down a suspect's outer clothing and feels an object whose contour or mass makes its identity immediately apparent, there has been no invasion of the suspect's privacy beyond that already authorized by the officer's search for weapons; if the object is contraband, its warrantless seizure would be justified by the same practical considerations that inhere in the plain-view context.

* * *

III

It remains to apply these principles to the facts of this case. Respondent has not challenged the finding made by the trial court and affirmed by both the Court of Appeals and the State Supreme Court that the police were justified under *Terry* in stopping him and frisking him for weapons. Thus, the dispositive question before this Court is whether the officer who conducted the search was acting within the lawful bounds marked by *Terry* at the time he gained probable cause to believe that the lump in respondent's jacket was contraband. The State District Court did not make precise findings on this point, instead finding simply that the officer, after feeling "a small, hard object wrapped in plastic" in respondent's pocket, "formed the opinion that the object . . . was crack . . . cocaine." The District Court also noted that the officer made "no claim that he suspected this object to be a weapon," a finding affirmed on appeal. The Minnesota Supreme Court, after "a close examination of the record," held that the officer's own testimony "belies any notion that he 'immediately' " recognized the lump as crack cocaine. Rather, the court concluded, the officer determined that the lump was contraband only after "squeezing, sliding and otherwise manipulating the contents of the defendant's pocket"—a pocket which the officer already knew contained no weapon.

Under the State Supreme Court's interpretation of the record before it, it is clear that the court was correct in holding that the police officer in this case overstepped the bounds of the "strictly circumscribed" search for weapons allowed under *Terry*. Where, as here, "an officer who is executing a valid search for one item seizes a different item," this Court rightly "has been sensitive to the danger . . . that officers will enlarge a specific authorization, furnished by a warrant or an exigency, into the equivalent of a general warrant to rummage and seize at will." Here, the officer's continued exploration of respondent's pocket after having concluded that it contained no weapon was unrelated to "[t]he sole justification of the search [under *Terry*:] . . . the protection of the police officer and others nearby." It therefore amounted to the sort of evidentiary search that *Terry* expressly refused to authorize and that we have condemned in subsequent cases.

Once again, the analogy to the plain-view doctrine is apt. In *Arizona v. Hicks,* 480 U.S. 321 (1987), this Court held invalid the seizure of stolen stereo equipment found by police while executing a valid search for other evidence. Although the police were lawfully on the premises, they obtained probable cause to believe that the stereo equipment was contraband only after moving the equipment to permit officers to read its serial numbers. The subsequent seizure of the equipment could not be justified by the plain-view doctrine, this Court explained, because the incriminating character of the stereo equipment was not immediately apparent; rather, probable cause to believe that the equipment was stolen arose only as a result of a further search—the moving of the equipment—that was not authorized by a search warrant or by any exception to the warrant requirement. The facts of this case are very similar. Although the officer was lawfully in a position to feel the lump in respondent's pocket, because *Terry* entitled him to place his hands upon respondent's jacket, the court below determined that the incriminating character of the object was not immediately apparent to him. Rather, the officer determined that the item was contraband only after conducting a further search, one not authorized by *Terry* or by any other exception to the warrant requirement. Because this further search of respondent's pocket was constitutionally invalid, the seizure of the cocaine that followed is likewise unconstitutional.

JUSTICE SCALIA, concurring.

* * *

My problem with the present case is that I am not entirely sure that the physical search—the "frisk"—that produced the evidence at issue here complied with that constitutional standard. The decision of ours that gave approval to such searches, *Terry v. Ohio,* 392 U.S. 1 (1968), made no serious attempt to determine compliance with traditional standards, but rather, according to the style of this Court at the time, simply adjudged that such a search was "reasonable" by current estimations.

There is good evidence, I think, that the "stop" portion of the *Terry* "stop-and-frisk" holding accords with the common law—that it had long been considered reasonable to detain suspicious persons for the purpose of demanding that they give an account of themselves. This is suggested, in particular, by the so-called night-walker statutes, and their common-law antecedents.

I am unaware, however, of any precedent for a physical search of a person thus temporarily detained for questioning. Sometimes, of course, the temporary detention of a suspicious character would be elevated to a full custodial arrest on probable cause—as, for instance, when a suspect was unable to provide a sufficient accounting of himself. At *that* point, it is clear that the common law would permit not just a protective "frisk," but a full physical search incident to the arrest. When, however, the detention did not rise to the level of a full-blown arrest (and was not supported by the degree of cause needful for that purpose), there appears to be no clear support at common law for physically searching the suspect.

I frankly doubt, moreover, whether the fiercely proud men who adopted our Fourth Amendment would have allowed themselves to be subjected, on mere *suspicion* of being armed and dangerous, to such indignity—which is described as follows in a police manual:

> Check the subject's neck and collar. A check should be made under the subject's arm. Next a check should be made of the upper back. The lower back should also be checked.

> A check should be made of the upper part of the man's chest and the lower region around the stomach. The belt, a favorite concealment spot, should be checked. The inside thigh and crotch area also should be searched. The legs should be checked for possible weapons. The last items to be checked are the shoes and cuffs of the subject. J. MOYNAHAN, POLICE SEARCHING PROCEDURES 7 (1963) (citations omitted).

On the other hand, even if a "frisk" prior to arrest would have been considered impermissible in 1791, perhaps it was considered permissible by 1868, when the Fourteenth Amendment (the basis for applying the Fourth Amendment to the States) was adopted. Or perhaps it is only since that time that concealed weapons capable of harming the interrogator quickly and from beyond arm's reach have become common—which might alter the judgment of what is "reasonable" under the original standard. But technological changes were no more discussed in *Terry* than was the original state of the law.

If I were of the view that *Terry* was (insofar as the power to "frisk" is concerned) incorrectly decided, I might—even if I felt bound to adhere to that case—vote to exclude the evidence incidentally discovered, on the theory that half a constitutional guarantee is better than none. I might also vote to exclude it if I agreed with the original-meaning-is-irrelevant, good-policy-is-constitutional-law school of jurisprudence that the *Terry* opinion represents. As a policy matter, it may be desirable to *permit* "frisks" for weapons, but not to *encourage* "frisks" for drugs by admitting evidence other than weapons.

I adhere to original meaning, however. And though I do not favor the mode of analysis in *Terry,* I cannot say that its result was wrong. Constitutionality of the "frisk" in the present case was neither challenged nor argued. Assuming, therefore, that the search was lawful, I agree with the Court's premise that any evidence incidentally discovered in the course of it would be admissible, and join the Court's opinion in its entirety.

CHIEF JUSTICE REHNQUIST, with whom JUSTICE BLACKMUN and JUSTICE THOMAS join, concurring in part and dissenting in part.

I join Parts I and II of the Court's opinion. Unlike the Court, however, I would vacate the judgment of the Supreme Court of Minnesota and remand the case to that court for further proceedings.

The Court, correctly in my view, states that "the dispositive question before this Court is whether the officer who conducted the search was acting within the lawful bounds marked by *Terry* at the time he gained probable cause to believe that the lump in respondent's jacket was contraband." The Court then goes on to point out that the state trial court did not make precise findings on this point, but accepts the appellate findings made by the Supreme Court of Minnesota. I believe that these findings, like those of the trial court, are imprecise and not directed expressly to the question of the officer's probable cause to believe that the lump was contraband. Because the Supreme Court of Minnesota employed a Fourth Amendment analysis which differs significantly from that now adopted by this Court, I would vacate its judgment and remand the case for further proceedings there in the light of this Court's opinion.

Points for Discussion

1. Although the Court focuses on the officer's manipulation of the object found in Dickerson's pocket, consider whether the earlier steps in this encounter complied with the Constitution. Did the officer have reasonable suspicion to believe that Dickerson was involved in criminal activity? Did the officer have reason to believe that Dickerson was armed and dangerous?

2. If a crack rock is not immediately identifiable as contraband through the sense of touch, what item is likely to be? Can you imagine any object that could be immediately apparent as contraband in a closed pocket?

3. Justice Scalia is strongly critical of the *Terry* opinion, saying it "made no serious attempt to determine compliance with traditional standards, but rather, according to the style of the Court at the time, simply adjudged that such a search was 'reasonable' by current estimates." What are the "traditional standards" to which Justice Scalia alludes? Does he say whether he believes that *Terry* stops-and-frisks are constitutional or unconstitutional?

BROWN V. TEXAS

443 U.S. 47 (1979)

MR. CHIEF JUSTICE BURGER delivered the opinion of the court.

This appeal presents the question whether appellant was validly convicted for refusing to comply with a policeman's demand that he identify himself pursuant to a provision of the Texas Penal Code which makes it a crime to refuse such identification on request.

I

At 12:45 in the afternoon of December 9, 1977, Officers Venegas and Sotelo of the El Paso Police Department were cruising in a patrol car. They observed appellant and another man walking in opposite directions away from one another in an alley. Although the two men were a few feet apart when they first were seen, Officer Venegas later testified that both officers believed the two had been together or were about to meet until the patrol car appeared.

The car entered the alley, and Officer Venegas got out and asked appellant to identify himself and explain what he was doing there. The other man was not questioned or detained. The officer testified that he stopped appellant because the situation "looked suspicious and we had never seen that subject in that area before." The area of El Paso where appellant was stopped has a high incidence of drug traffic. However, the officers did not claim to suspect appellant of any specific misconduct, nor did they have any reason to believe that he was armed.

Appellant refused to identify himself and angrily asserted that the officers had no right to stop him. Officer Venegas replied that he was in a "high drug problem area"; Officer Sotelo then "frisked" appellant, but found nothing.

When appellant continued to refuse to identify himself, he was arrested for violation of Texas Penal Code Ann. § 38.02(a) (1974), which makes it a criminal act for a person to refuse to give his name and address to an officer "who has lawfully stopped him and requested the information." Following the arrest the officers searched appellant; nothing untoward was found.

While being taken to the El Paso County Jail appellant identified himself. Nonetheless, he was held in custody and charged with violating § 38.02(a). When he was booked he was routinely searched a third time. Appellant was convicted in the El Paso Municipal Court and fined $20 plus court costs for violation of § 38.02. He then exercised his right under Texas law to a trial de novo in the El Paso County Court. There, he moved to set aside the information on the ground that § 38.02(a) of the Texas Penal Code violated the First, Fourth, and Fifth Amendments and was unconstitutionally vague in violation of the Fourteenth Amendment. The motion was denied. Appellant waived a jury, and the court convicted him and imposed a fine of $45 plus court costs.

* * *

II

* * *

The State does not contend that appellant was stopped pursuant to a practice embodying neutral criteria, but rather maintains that the officers were justified in stopping appellant because they had a "reasonable, articulable suspicion that a crime had just been, was being, or was about to be committed." We have recognized that in some circumstances an officer may detain a suspect briefly for questioning although he does not have "probable cause" to believe that the suspect is involved in criminal activity, as is required for a traditional arrest. However, we have required the officers to have a reasonable suspicion, based on objective facts, that the individual is involved in criminal activity.

The flaw in the State's case is that none of the circumstances preceding the officers' detention of appellant justified a reasonable suspicion that he was involved in criminal conduct. Officer Venegas testified at appellant's trial that the situation in the alley "looked suspicious," but he was unable to point to any facts supporting that conclusion. There is no indication in the record that it was unusual for people to be in the alley. The fact that appellant was in a neighborhood frequented by drug users, standing alone, is not a basis for concluding that appellant himself was engaged in criminal conduct. In short, the appellant's activity was no different from the activity of other pedestrians in that neighborhood. When pressed, Officer Venegas acknowledged that the only reason he stopped appellant was to ascertain his identity. The record suggests an understandable desire to assert a police presence; however, that purpose does not negate Fourth Amendment guarantees.

In the absence of any basis for suspecting appellant of misconduct, the balance between the public interest and appellant's right to personal security and privacy tilts in favor of freedom from police interference. The Texas statute under which appellant was stopped and required to identify himself is designed to advance a weighty social objective in large metropolitan centers: prevention of crime. But even assuming that purpose is served to some degree by stopping and demanding identification from an individual without any specific basis for believing he is involved in criminal activity, the guarantees of the Fourth Amendment do not allow it. When such a stop is not based on objective criteria, the risk of arbitrary and abusive police practices exceeds tolerable limits.

The application of Tex.Penal Code Ann., Tit. 8, § 38.02 (1974), to detain appellant and require him to identify himself violated the Fourth Amendment because the officers lacked any reasonable suspicion to believe appellant was engaged or had engaged in criminal conduct.[3] Accordingly, appellant may not be punished for refusing to identify himself, and the conviction is reversed.

Points for Discussion

1. If the Texas statute authorizes officers to request identification from those they encounter in the field, why does the Court conclude that an officer must have reasonable suspicion of criminal activity before he may ask Brown for his identification? Doesn't that statute provide sufficient neutral criteria to make any stops carried out in accordance with it reasonable?

2. In footnote 3 the Court makes clear that it is not deciding whether an individual may be punished for refusing to identify himself in the course of an otherwise lawful investigative stop. The Court answers this question in the next case.

---

[3] We need not decide whether an individual may be punished for refusing to identify himself in the context of a lawful investigatory stop which satisfies Fourth Amendment requirements. The County Court Judge who convicted appellant was troubled by this question, as shown by the colloquy set out in the Appendix to this opinion.

HIIBEL V. NEVADA

542 U.S. 177 (2004)

JUSTICE KENNEDY **delivered the opinion of the court.**

The petitioner was arrested and convicted for refusing to identify himself during a stop allowed by *Terry v. Ohio,* 392 U.S. 1 (1968). He challenges his conviction under the Fourth and Fifth Amendments to the United States Constitution, applicable to the States through the Fourteenth Amendment.

I

The sheriff's department in Humboldt County, Nevada, received an afternoon telephone call reporting an assault. The caller reported seeing a man assault a woman in a red and silver GMC truck on Grass Valley Road. Deputy Sheriff Lee Dove was dispatched to investigate. When the officer arrived at the scene, he found the truck parked on the side of the road. A man was standing by the truck, and a young woman was sitting inside it. The officer observed skid marks in the gravel behind the vehicle, leading him to believe it had come to a sudden stop.

The officer approached the man and explained that he was investigating a report of a fight. The man appeared to be intoxicated. The officer asked him if he had "any identification on [him]," which we understand as a request to produce a driver's license or some other form of written identification. The man refused and asked why the officer wanted to see identification. The officer responded that he was conducting an investigation and needed to see some identification. The unidentified man became agitated and insisted he had done nothing wrong. The officer explained that he wanted to find out who the man was and what he was doing there. After continued refusals to comply with the officer's request for identification, the man began to taunt the officer by placing his hands behind his back and telling the officer to arrest him and take him to jail. This routine kept up for several minutes: The officer asked for identification 11 times and was refused each time. After warning the man that he would be arrested if he continued to refuse to comply, the officer placed him under arrest.

We now know that the man arrested on Grass Valley Road is Larry Dudley Hiibel. Hiibel was charged with "willfully resist[ing], delay[ing] or obstruct [ing] a public officer in discharging or attempting to discharge any legal duty of his office" in violation of Nev.Rev.Stat. (NRS) § 199.280 (2003). The government reasoned that Hiibel had obstructed the officer in carrying out his duties under § 171.123, a Nevada statute that defines the legal rights and duties of a police officer in the context of an investigative stop. Section 171.123 provides in relevant part:

> 1. Any peace officer may detain any person whom the officer encounters under circumstances which reasonably indicate that

> the person has committed, is committing or is about to commit a crime.
>
> . . .
>
> 3. The officer may detain the person pursuant to this section only to ascertain his identity and the suspicious circumstances surrounding his presence abroad. Any person so detained shall identify himself, but may not be compelled to answer any other inquiry of any peace officer.

Hiibel was tried in the Justice Court of Union Township. The court agreed that Hiibel's refusal to identify himself as required by § 171.123 "obstructed and delayed Dove as a public officer in attempting to discharge his duty" in violation of § 199.280. Hiibel was convicted and fined $250. The Sixth Judicial District Court affirmed, rejecting Hiibel's argument that the application of § 171.123 to his case violated the Fourth and Fifth Amendments. On review the Supreme Court of Nevada rejected the Fourth Amendment challenge in a divided opinion. Hiibel petitioned for rehearing, seeking explicit resolution of his Fifth Amendment challenge. The petition was denied without opinion. We granted certiorari.

* * *

III

Hiibel argues that his conviction cannot stand because the officer's conduct violated his Fourth Amendment rights. We disagree.

Asking questions is an essential part of police investigations. In the ordinary course a police officer is free to ask a person for identification without implicating the Fourth Amendment. "[I]nterrogation relating to one's identity or a request for identification by the police does not, by itself, constitute a Fourth Amendment seizure." *INS v. Delgado,* 466 U.S. 210, 216 (1984). Beginning with *Terry v. Ohio,* 392 U.S. 1 (1968), the Court has recognized that a law enforcement officer's reasonable suspicion that a person may be involved in criminal activity permits the officer to stop the person for a brief time and take additional steps to investigate further. To ensure that the resulting seizure is constitutionally reasonable, a *Terry* stop must be limited. The officer's action must be " 'justified at its inception, and . . . reasonably related in scope to the circumstances which justified the interference in the first place.' " *United States v. Sharpe,* 470 U.S. 675 (1985) (quoting *Terry,* at 20). For example, the seizure can not continue for an excessive period of time, or resemble a traditional arrest.

* * *

Obtaining a suspect's name in the course of a *Terry* stop serves important government interests. Knowledge of identity may inform an officer that a suspect is wanted for another offense, or has a record of violence or mental disorder. On the other hand, knowing identity may help clear a suspect and allow the police to concentrate their efforts elsewhere. Identity may prove particularly important in cases such as this, where the police are investigating what appears to be a domestic assault. Officers called to investigate domestic disputes need to know whom they are dealing with in order to assess the situation, the threat to their own safety, and possible danger to the potential victim.

Although it is well established that an officer may ask a suspect to identify himself in the course of a *Terry* stop, it has been an open question whether the suspect can be arrested and prosecuted for refusal to answer. Petitioner draws our attention to statements in prior opinions that, according to him, answer the question in his favor. In *Terry,* Justice White stated in a concurring opinion that a person detained in an investigative stop can be questioned but is "not obliged to answer, answers may not be compelled, and refusal to answer furnishes no basis for an arrest." 392 U.S., at 34. The Court cited this opinion in dicta in *Berkemer v. McCarty,* 468 U.S. 420, 439 (1984), a decision holding that a routine traffic stop is not a custodial stop requiring the protections of *Miranda v. Arizona,* 384 U.S. 436 (1966). In the course of explaining why *Terry* stops have not been subject to *Miranda,* the Court suggested reasons why *Terry* stops have a "nonthreatening character," among them the fact that a suspect detained during a *Terry* stop "is not obliged to respond" to questions. According to petitioner, these statements establish a right to refuse to answer questions during a *Terry* stop.

We do not read these statements as controlling. The passages recognize that the Fourth Amendment does not impose obligations on the citizen but instead provides rights against the government. As a result, the Fourth Amendment itself cannot require a suspect to answer questions. This case concerns a different issue, however. Here, the source of the legal obligation arises from Nevada state law, not the Fourth Amendment. Further, the statutory obligation does not go beyond answering an officer's request to disclose a name. See NRS § 171.123(3) ("Any person so detained shall identify himself, but may not be compelled to answer any other inquiry of any peace officer"). As a result, we cannot view the dicta in *Berkemer* or Justice White's concurrence in *Terry* as answering the question whether a State can compel a suspect to disclose his name during a *Terry* stop.

The principles of *Terry* permit a State to require a suspect to disclose his name in the course of a *Terry* stop. The reasonableness of a seizure under the Fourth Amendment is determined "by balancing its intrusion on the individual's Fourth Amendment interests against its promotion of legitimate government interests." *Delaware v. Prouse,* 440 U.S. 648 (1979). The Nevada statute satisfies that standard. The request for identity has an immediate relation to the purpose, rationale, and practical demands of a *Terry* stop. The threat of criminal sanction helps ensure that the request for identity does not become a legal nullity. On the other hand, the Nevada statute does not alter the nature of the stop itself: it does not change its duration, or its location. A state law requiring a suspect to disclose his name in the course of a valid *Terry* stop is consistent with Fourth Amendment prohibitions against unreasonable searches and seizures.

Petitioner argues that the Nevada statute circumvents the probable-cause requirement, in effect allowing an officer to arrest a person for being suspicious. According to petitioner, this creates a risk of arbitrary police conduct that the Fourth Amendment does not permit. These are familiar concerns; they were central to the opinion in *Papachristou* [*v. Jacksonville*, 405 U.S. 156 (1972)], and also to the decisions limiting the operation of stop and identify statutes in *Kolender* [*v. Lawson*, 461 U.S. 352 (1983)], and *Brown* [*v. Texas*, 443 U.S. 47 (1979)]. Petitioner's concerns are met by the requirement that a *Terry* stop must be justified at its inception and "reasonably related in scope to the circumstances which justified" the initial stop. Under these principles, an officer may not arrest a suspect for failure to identify himself if the request for identification is not reasonably related to the circumstances justifying the stop. The Court noted a similar limitation in *Hayes,* where it suggested that *Terry* may permit an officer to determine a suspect's identity by compelling the suspect to submit to fingerprinting only if there is "a reasonable basis for believing that fingerprinting will establish or negate the suspect's connection with that crime." It is clear in this case that the request for identification was "reasonably related in scope to the circumstances which justified" the stop. The officer's request was a commonsense inquiry, not an effort to obtain an arrest for failure to identify after a *Terry* stop yielded insufficient evidence. The stop, the request, and the State's requirement of a response did not contravene the guarantees of the Fourth Amendment.

IV

Petitioner further contends that his conviction violates the Fifth Amendment's prohibition on compelled self-incrimination. The Fifth Amendment states that "[n]o person . . . shall be compelled in any criminal case to be a witness against himself." To qualify for the Fifth Amendment privilege, a communication must be testimonial, incriminating, and compelled.

* * *

In this case petitioner's refusal to disclose his name was not based on any articulated real and appreciable fear that his name would be used to incriminate him, or that it "would furnish a link in the chain of evidence needed to prosecute" him. As best we can tell, petitioner refused to identify himself only because he thought his name was none of the officer's business. Even today, petitioner does not explain how the disclosure of his name could have been used against him in a criminal case. While we recognize petitioner's strong belief that he should not have to disclose his identity, the Fifth Amendment does not override the Nevada Legislature's judgment to the contrary absent a reasonable belief that the disclosure would tend to incriminate him.

* * *

JUSTICE STEVENS, dissenting.

* * *

A person's identity obviously bears informational and incriminating worth, "even if the [name] itself is not inculpatory." *Hubbell [v. United States*, 530 U.S. 27, 38 (2000)]. A name can provide the key to a broad array of information about the person, particularly in the hands of a police officer with access to a range of law enforcement databases. And that information, in turn, can be tremendously useful in a criminal prosecution. It is therefore quite wrong to suggest that a person's identity provides a link in the chain to incriminating evidence "only in unusual circumstances."

The officer in this case told petitioner, in the Court's words, that "he was conducting an investigation and needed to see some identification." As the target of that investigation, petitioner, in my view, acted well within his rights when he opted to stand mute. Accordingly, I respectfully dissent.

JUSTICE BREYER, with whom JUSTICE SOUTER and JUSTICE GINSBURG join, dissenting.

* * *

In *Terry v. Ohio,* 392 U.S. 1 (1968), the Court considered whether police, in the absence of probable cause, can stop, question, or frisk an individual at all. The Court recognized that the Fourth Amendment protects the " 'right of every individual to the possession and control of his own person.' " At the same time, it recognized that in certain circumstances, public safety might require a limited "seizure," or stop, of an individual against his will. The Court consequently set forth conditions circumscribing when and how the police might conduct a *Terry* stop. They include what has become known as the "reasonable suspicion" standard. Justice White, in a separate concurring opinion, set forth further conditions. Justice White wrote: "Of course, the person stopped is not obliged to answer, answers may not be compelled, and refusal to answer furnishes no basis for an arrest, although it may alert the officer to the need for continued observation."

About 10 years later, the Court, in *Brown v. Texas,* 443 U.S. 47 (1979), held that police lacked "any reasonable suspicion" to detain the particular petitioner and require him to identify himself. The Court noted that the trial judge had asked the following: "I'm sure [officers conducting a *Terry* stop] should ask everything they possibly could find out. *What I'm asking is what's the State's interest in putting a man in jail because he doesn't want to answer. . . .*" The Court referred to Justice White's *Terry* concurrence. And it said that it "need not decide" the matter.

Then, five years later, the Court wrote that an "officer may ask the *[Terry]* detainee a moderate number of questions to determine his identity and to try to obtain information confirming or dispelling the officer's suspicions. *But the detainee is not obliged to respond.*" *Berkemer v. McCarty,* 468 U.S. 420, 439 (1984) (emphasis added).

This lengthy history—of concurring opinions, of references, and of clear explicit statements—means that the Court's statement in *Berkemer,* while technically dicta, is the kind of strong dicta that the legal community typically takes as a statement of the law. And that law has remained undisturbed for more than 20 years.

There is no good reason now to reject this generation-old statement of the law. There are sound reasons rooted in Fifth Amendment considerations for adhering to this Fourth Amendment legal condition circumscribing police authority to stop an individual against his will. Administrative considerations also militate against change. Can a State, in addition to requiring a stopped individual to answer "What's your name?" also require an answer to "What's your license number?" or "Where do you live?" Can a police officer, who must know how to make a *Terry* stop, keep track of the constitutional answers? After all, answers to any of these questions may, or may not, incriminate, depending upon the circumstances.

Indeed, as the Court points out, a name itself—even if it is not "Killer Bill" or "Rough 'em up Harry"—will sometimes provide the police with "a link in the chain of evidence needed to convict the individual of a separate offense." The majority reserves judgment about whether compulsion is permissible in such instances. How then is a police officer in the midst of a *Terry* stop to distinguish between the majority's ordinary case and this special case where the majority reserves judgment?

The majority presents no evidence that the rule enunciated by Justice White and then by the *Berkemer* Court, which for nearly a generation has set forth a settled *Terry* stop condition, has significantly interfered with law enforcement. Nor has the majority presented any other convincing justification for change. I would not begin to erode a clear rule with special exceptions.

Points for Discussion

1. Does the opinion in *Hiibel* overrule the decision in *Brown*? If not, how can the two opinions be reconciled?

2. How does the Court deal with Justice White's concurrence in *Terry* (arguing that a person stopped for investigation is not obligated to answer the officer's inquiries and that no negative inferences can be drawn from his

silence) and the Court's opinion in *Berkemer v. McCarty* (discussed in Chapter 9) that a *Terry* detainee is not obligated to answer any questions put to him?

3. In April 2010 the State of Arizona passed a law that permits law enforcement officers who have reasonable suspicion that an individual is an undocumented alien to demand proof of citizenship from that individual. Failure to produce documentation upon request is grounds for arrest. Is such a statute consistent with the Court's opinions in *Brown* and *Hiibel*? *See Arizona v. United States,* 567 U.S. 387, 411–13 (2012).

B. CONSENT SEARCHES

Another significant exception to the Court's assertion that searches conducted without probable cause are presumptively invalid is searches made with consent. This section investigates the contours of this exception, investigating why consensual searches are deemed valid.

1. VOLUNTARINESS

SCHNECKLOTH V. BUSTAMONTE

412 U.S. 218 (1973)

MR. JUSTICE STEWART delivered the opinion of the court.

It is well settled under the Fourth and Fourteenth Amendments that a search conducted without a warrant issued upon probable cause is "per se unreasonable . . . subject only to a few specifically established and well-delineated exceptions." *Katz v. United States*, 389 U.S. 347, 357. It is equally well settled that one of the specifically established exceptions to the requirements of both a warrant and probable cause is a search that is conducted pursuant to consent. The constitutional question in the present case concerns the definition of "consent" in this Fourth and Fourteenth Amendment context.

I

* * *

While on routine patrol in Sunnyvale, California, at approximately 2:40 in the morning, Police Officer James Rand stopped an automobile when he observed that one headlight and its license plate light were burned out. Six men were in the vehicle. Joe Alcala and the respondent, Robert Bustamonte, were in the front seat with Joe Gonzales, the driver. Three older men were seated in the rear. When, in response to the policeman's question, Gonzales could not produce a driver's license, Officer Rand asked if any of the other five had any evidence of identification. Only Alcala produced a license, and he explained that the car was his brother's. After the six occupants had stepped out of the car at the officer's request and after two additional policemen had arrived, Officer Rand asked Alcala if he could search the car. Alcala replied, "Sure, go ahead." Prior to the search no one was threatened with arrest and, according to Officer Rand's uncontradicted testimony, it "was all very congenial at this time." Gonzales testified that Alcala actually helped in the search of the car, by opening the trunk and glove compartment. In Gonzales' words: "(T)he police officer asked Joe (Alcala), he goes, 'Does the trunk open?' And Joe said, 'Yes.' He went to the car and got the keys and opened up the trunk." Wadded up under the left rear seat, the police officers found three checks that had previously been stolen from a car wash.

The trial judge denied the motion to suppress, and the checks in question were admitted in evidence at Bustamonte's trial. On the basis of this and other evidence he was convicted, and the California Court of Appeal for the First Appellate District affirmed the conviction. . . . The California Supreme Court denied review.

Thereafter, the respondent sought a writ of habeas corpus in a federal district court. It was denied. On appeal, the Court of Appeals for the Ninth Circuit . . . set aside the District Court's order. The appellate court reasoned that a consent was a waiver of a person's Fourth and Fourteenth Amendment rights, and that the State was under an obligation to demonstrate, not only that the consent had been uncoerced, but that it had been given with an understanding that it could be freely and effectively withheld. Consent could not be found, the court held, solely from the absence of coercion and a verbal expression of assent. Since the District Court had not determined that Alcala had known that his consent could have been withheld and that he could have refused to have his vehicle searched, the Court of Appeals vacated the order denying the writ and remanded the case for further proceedings. We granted certiorari to determine whether the Fourth and Fourteenth Amendments require the showing thought necessary by the Court of Appeals.

II

It is important to make it clear at the outset what is not involved in this case. The respondent concedes that a search conducted pursuant to a valid consent is constitutionally permissible. In *Katz v. United States*, 389 U.S., at 358, and more recently in *Vale v. Louisiana*, 399 U.S. 30, 35, we recognized that a search authorized by consent is wholly valid. And similarly the State concedes that "(w)hen a prosecutor seeks to rely upon consent to justify the lawfulness of a search, he has the burden of proving that the consent was, in fact, freely and voluntarily given." *Bumper v. North Carolina*, 391 U.S. 543, 548.

The precise question in this case, then, is what must the prosecution prove to demonstrate that a consent was "voluntarily" given. And upon that question there is a square conflict of views between the state and federal courts that have reviewed the search involved in the case before us. The Court of Appeals for the Ninth Circuit concluded that it is an essential part of the State's initial burden to prove that a person knows he has a right to refuse consent. The California courts have followed the rule that voluntariness is a question of fact to be determined from the totality of all the circumstances, and that the state of a defendant's knowledge is only one factor to be taken into account in assessing the voluntariness of a consent.

A

The most extensive judicial exposition of the meaning of "voluntariness" has been developed in those cases in which the Court has had to determine the "voluntariness" of a defendant's confession for purposes of the Fourteenth Amendment. . . .

Those cases yield no talismanic definition of "voluntariness," mechanically applicable to the host of situations where the question has arisen. "The notion of 'voluntariness,' " Mr. Justice Frankfurter once wrote, "is itself an amphibian." It cannot be taken literally to mean a "knowing" choice. "Except where a person is unconscious or drugged or otherwise lacks capacity for conscious choice, all incriminating statements—even those made under brutal treatment—are 'voluntary' in the sense of representing a choice of alternatives. On the other hand, if 'voluntariness' incorporates notions of 'but for' cause, the question should be whether the statement would have been made even absent inquiry or other official action. Under such a test, virtually no statement would be voluntary because very few people give incriminating statements in the absence of official action of some kind."

It is thus evident that neither linguistics nor epistemology will provide a ready definition of the meaning of "voluntariness."

Rather, "voluntariness" has reflected an accommodation of the complex of values implicated in police questioning of a suspect. At one end of the spectrum is the acknowledged need for police questioning as a tool for the effective enforcement of criminal laws. Without such investigation, those who were innocent might be falsely accused, those who were guilty might wholly escape prosecution, and many crimes would go unsolved. In short, the security of all would be diminished. At the other end of the spectrum is the set of values reflecting society's deeply felt belief that the criminal law cannot be used as an instrument of unfairness, and that the possibility of unfair and even brutal police tactics poses a real and serious threat to civilized notions of justice. "(I)n cases involving involuntary confessions, this Court enforces the strongly felt attitude of our society that important human values are sacrificed where an agency of the government, in the course of securing a conviction, wrings a confession out of an accused against his will."

This Court's decisions reflect a frank recognition that the Constitution requires the sacrifice of neither security nor liberty. The Due Process

Clause does not mandate that the police forgo all questioning, or that they be given carte blanche to extract what they can from a suspect. "The ultimate test remains that which has been the only clearly established test in Anglo-American courts for two hundred years: the test of voluntariness. Is the confession the product of an essentially free and unconstrained choice by its maker? If it is, if he has willed to confess, it may be used against him. If it is not, if his will has been overborne and his capacity for self-determination critically impaired, the use of his confession offends due process."

In determining whether a defendant's will was overborne in a particular case, the Court has assessed the totality of all the surrounding circumstances—both the characteristics of the accused and the details of the interrogation. Some of the factors taken into account have included the youth of the accused, his lack of education, or his low intelligence, the lack of any advice to the accused of his constitutional rights, the length of detention, the repeated and prolonged nature of the questioning, and the use of physical punishment such as the deprivation of food or sleep. In all of these cases, the Court determined the factual circumstances surrounding the confession, assessed the psychological impact on the accused, and evaluated the legal significance of how the accused reacted.

The significant fact about all of these decisions is that none of them turned on the presence or absence of a single controlling criterion; each reflected a careful scrutiny of all the surrounding circumstances. In none of them did the Court rule that the Due Process Clause required the prosecution to prove as part of its initial burden that the defendant knew he had a right to refuse to answer the questions that were put. While the state of the accused's mind, and the failure of the police to advise the accused of his rights, were certainly factors to be evaluated in assessing the "voluntariness" of an accused's responses, they were not in and of themselves determinative.

B

Similar considerations lead us to agree with the courts of California that the question whether a consent to a search was in fact "voluntary" or was the product of duress or coercion, express or implied, is a question of fact to be determined from the totality of all the circumstances. While knowledge of the right to refuse consent is one factor to be taken into account, the government need not establish such knowledge as the sine qua non of an effective consent. As with police questioning, two competing concerns must be accommodated in determining the meaning of a "voluntary" consent—the legitimate need for such searches and the equally important requirement of assuring the absence of coercion.

In situations where the police have some evidence of illicit activity, but lack probable cause to arrest or search, a search authorized by a valid consent may be the only means of obtaining important and reliable evidence. In the present case for example, while the police had reason to stop the car for traffic violations, the State does not contend that there was probable cause to search the vehicle or that the search was incident to a valid arrest of any of the occupants. Yet, the search yielded tangible evidence that served as a basis for a prosecution, and provided some assurance that others, wholly innocent of the crime, were not mistakenly brought to trial. And in those cases where there is probable cause to arrest or search, but where the police lack a warrant, a consent search may still be valuable. If the search is conducted and proves fruitless, that in itself may convince the police that an arrest with its possible stigma and embarrassment is unnecessary, or that a far more extensive search pursuant to a warrant is not justified. In short, a search pursuant to consent may result in considerably less inconvenience for the subject of the search, and, properly conducted, is a constitutionally permissible and wholly legitimate aspect of effective police activity.

* * *

The problem of reconciling the recognized legitimacy of consent searches with the requirement that they be free from any aspect of official coercion cannot be resolved by any infallible touchstone. To approve such searches without the most careful scrutiny would sanction the possibility of official coercion; to place artificial restrictions upon such searches would jeopardize their basic validity. Just as was true with confessions, the requirement of a "voluntary" consent reflects a fair accommodation of the constitutional requirements involved. In examining all the surrounding circumstances to determine if in fact the consent to search was coerced, account must be taken of subtly coercive police questions, as well as the possibly vulnerable subjective state of the person who consents. Those searches that are the product of police coercion can thus be filtered out without undermining the continuing validity of consent searches. In sum, there is no reason for us to depart in the area of consent searches, from the traditional definition of "voluntariness."

* * *

One alternative that would go far toward proving that the subject of a search did know he had a right to refuse consent would be to advise him of that right before eliciting his consent. That, however, is a suggestion that has been almost universally repudiated by both federal and state courts, and, we think, rightly so. For it would be thoroughly impractical to impose on the normal consent search the detailed requirements of an effective warning. Consent searches are part of the standard investigatory techniques of law enforcement agencies. They normally occur on the highway, or in a person's home or office, and under informal and unstructured conditions. The circumstances that prompt the initial request to search may develop quickly or be a logical extension of investigative police questioning. The police may seek to investigate further suspicious circumstances or to follow up leads developed in questioning persons at the scene of a crime. These situations are a far cry from the structured atmosphere of a trial where, assisted by counsel if he chooses, a defendant is informed of his trial rights. And, while surely a closer question, these situations are still immeasurably, far removed from "custodial interrogation" where, in *Miranda v. Arizona* we found that the Constitution required certain now familiar warnings as a prerequisite to police interrogation. Indeed, in language applicable to the typical consent search, we refused to extend the need for warnings:

> Our decision is not intended to hamper the traditional function of police officers in investigating crime. . . . When an individual is in custody on probable cause, the police may, of course, seek out evidence in the field to be used at trial against him. Such investigation may include inquiry of persons not under restraint. General on-the-scene questioning as to facts surrounding a crime or other general questioning of citizens in the fact-finding process is not affected by our holding. It is an act of responsible citizenship for individuals to give whatever information they may have to aid in law enforcement.

Consequently, we cannot accept the position of the Court of Appeals in this case that proof of knowledge of the right to refuse consent is a necessary prerequisite to demonstrating a "voluntary" consent. Rather it is only by analyzing all the circumstances of an individual consent that it can be ascertained whether in fact it was voluntary or coerced. It is this careful sifting of the unique facts and circumstances of each case that is evidenced in our prior decisions involving consent searches.

* * *

In short, neither this Court's prior cases, nor the traditional definition of "voluntariness" requires proof of knowledge of a right to refuse as the sine qua non of an effective consent to a search.

C

It is said, however, that a "consent" is a "waiver" of a person's rights under the Fourth and Fourteenth Amendments. The argument is that by allowing the police to conduct a search, a person "waives" whatever right he had to prevent the police from searching. It is argued that under the doctrine of *Johnson v. Zerbst*, 304 U.S. 458, 464, to establish such a "waiver" the State must demonstrate "an intentional relinquishment or abandonment of a known right or privilege."

But these standards were enunciated in *Johnson* in the context of the safeguards of a fair criminal trial. Our cases do not reflect an uncritical demand for a knowing and intelligent waiver in every situation where a person has failed to invoke a constitutional protection. As Mr. Justice Black once observed for the Court: "Waiver' is a vague term used for a great variety of purposes, good and bad, in the law." *Green v. United States*, 355 U.S. 184, 191. With respect to procedural due process, for example, the Court has acknowledged that waiver is possible, while explicitly leaving open the question whether a "knowing and intelligent" waiver need be shown.

* * *

Almost without exception, the requirement of a knowing and intelligent waiver has been applied only to those rights which the Constitution guarantees to a criminal defendant in order to preserve a fair trial. Hence, and hardly surprisingly in view of the facts of *Johnson* itself, the standard of a knowing and intelligent waiver has most often been applied to test the validity of a waiver of counsel, either at trial, or upon a guilty plea. And the Court has also applied the *Johnson* criteria to assess the effectiveness of a waiver of other trial rights such as the right to confrontation, to a jury trial, and to a speedy trial, and the right to be free from twice being placed in jeopardy. Guilty pleas have been carefully scrutinized to determine whether the accused knew and understood all the rights to which he would be entitled at trial, and that he had intentionally chosen to forgo them. And the Court has evaluated the knowing and intelligent nature of the waiver of trial rights in trial-type situations, such as the waiver of the privilege against compulsory self-incrimination before an administrative agency or a congressional committee, or the waiver of counsel in a juvenile proceeding.

* * *

The guarantees afforded a criminal defendant at trial also protect him at certain stages before the actual trial, and any alleged waiver must meet the strict standard of an intentional relinquishment of a "known" right. But the "trial" guarantees that have been applied to the "pretrial" stage of the criminal process are similarly designed to protect the fairness of the trial itself.

* * *

The protections of the Fourth Amendment are of a wholly different order, and have nothing whatever to do with promoting the fair ascertainment of truth at a criminal trial. Rather, as Mr. Justice Frankfurter's opinion for the Court put it in *Wolf v. Colorado*, 338 U.S. 25, 27, the Fourth Amendment protects the "security of one's privacy against arbitrary intrusion by the police . . . ." In declining to apply the exclusionary rule of *Mapp v. Ohio*, 367 U.S. 643, to convictions that had become final before rendition of that decision, the Court emphasized that "there is no likelihood of unreliability or coercion present in a search-and-seizure case," *Linkletter v. Walker*, 381 U.S. 618. In *Linkletter*, the Court indicated that those cases that had been given retroactive effect went to "the fairness of the trial—the very integrity of the fact-finding process.

Here . . . the fairness of the trial is not under attack." The Fourth Amendment "is not an adjunct to the ascertainment of truth." The guarantees of the Fourth Amendment stand "as a protection of quite different constitutional values—values reflecting the concern of our society for the right of each individual to be let alone. To recognize this is no more than to accord those values undiluted respect."

Nor can it even be said that a search, as opposed to an eventual trial, is somehow "unfair" if a person consents to a search. While the Fourth and Fourteenth Amendments limit the circumstances under which the police can conduct a search, there is nothing constitutionally suspect in a person's voluntarily allowing a search. The actual conduct of the search may be precisely the same as if the police had obtained a warrant. And, unlike those constitutional guarantees that protect a defendant at trial, it cannot be said every reasonable presumption ought to be indulged against voluntary relinquishment. We have only recently stated: "(I)t is no part of the policy underlying the Fourth and Fourteenth Amendments to discourage citizens from aiding to the utmost of their ability in the apprehension of criminals." Rather, the community has a real interest in encouraging consent, for the resulting search may yield necessary evidence for the solution and prosecution of crime, evidence that may insure that a wholly innocent person is not wrongly charged with a criminal offense.

* * *

It would be unrealistic to expect that in the informal, unstructured context of a consent search, a policeman, upon pain of tainting the evidence obtained, could make the detailed type of examination demanded by *Johnson*. And, if for this reason a diluted form of "waiver" were found acceptable, that would itself be ample recognition of the fact that there is no universal standard that must be applied in every situation where a person foregoes a constitutional right.

Similarly, a "waiver" approach to consent searches would be thoroughly inconsistent with our decisions that have approved "third party consents." In *Coolidge v. New Hampshire*, 403 U.S., at 487–490, where a wife surrendered to the police guns and clothing belonging to her husband, we found nothing constitutionally impermissible in the admission of that evidence at trial since the wife had not been coerced. *Frazier v. Cupp*, 394 U.S. 731, 740, held that evidence seized from the defendant's duffel bag in a search authorized by his cousin's consent was admissible at trial. We found that the defendant had assumed the risk that his cousin, with whom he shared the bag, would allow the police to search it. And in *Hill v. California*, 401 U.S. 797, 802–805, we held that the police had validly seized evidence from the petitioner's apartment incident to the arrest of a third party, since the police had probable cause to arrest the petitioner and reasonably, though mistakenly, believed the man they had arrested was he. Yet it is inconceivable that the Constitution could countenance the waiver of a defendant's right to counsel by a third party, or that a waiver could be found because a trial judge reasonably, though mistakenly, believed a defendant had waived his right to plead not guilty.[34]

* * *

D

* * *

It is also argued that the failure to require the Government to establish knowledge as a prerequisite to a valid consent, will relegate the Fourth Amendment to the special province of "the sophisticated, v. knowledgeable and the privileged." We cannot agree. The traditional definition of voluntariness we accept today has always taken into account evidence of minimal schooling, low intelligence, and the lack of any effective warnings to a person of his rights; and the voluntariness of any statement taken under those conditions has been carefully scrutinized to determine whether it was in fact voluntarily given.

E

Our decision today is a narrow one. We hold only that when the subject of a search is not in custody and the State attempts to justify a search on the basis of his consent, the Fourth and Fourteenth Amendments require that it demonstrate that the consent was in fact voluntarily given, and not the result of duress or coercion, express or implied. Voluntariness is a question of fact to be determined from all the circumstances, and while the subject's knowledge of a right to refuse is a factor to be taken into account, the prosecution is not required to demonstrate such knowledge as a prerequisite to establishing a voluntary consent.[38] Because the California court followed these principles in affirming the respondent's conviction, and because the Court of Appeals for the Ninth Circuit in remanding for an evidentiary hearing required more, its judgment must be reversed.

The concurring opinion of MR. JUSTICE BLACKMUN is omitted.

MR. JUSTICE POWELL, with whom THE CHIEF JUSTICE and MR. JUSTICE REHNQUIST join, concurring.

While I join the opinion of the Court, it does not address what seems to me the overriding issue briefed and argued in this case: the extent to which federal habeas corpus should be available to a state prisoner seeking to exclude evidence from an allegedly unlawful search and seizure. I would

[34] Our decision today is, of course, concerned with what constitutes a valid consent, not who can consent. But, the constitutional validity of third-party consents demonstrates the fundamentally different nature of a consent search from the waiver of a trial right.

[38] The State also urges us to hold that a violation of the exclusionary rule may not be raised by a state or federal prisoner in a collateral attack on his conviction, and thus asks us to overturn our contrary holdings in *Kaufman v. United States*, 394 U.S. 217; *Whiteley v. Warden*, 401 U.S. 560; *Harris v. Nelson*, 394 U.S. 286; and *Mancusi v. DeForte*, 392 U.S. 364. Since we have found no valid Fourth and Fourteenth Amendment claim in this case, we do not consider that question.

hold that federal collateral review of a state prisoner's Fourth Amendment claims—claims which rarely bear on innocence—should be confined solely to the question of whether the petitioner was provided a fair opportunity to raise and have adjudicated the question in state courts. In view of the importance of this issue to our system of criminal justice, I think it appropriate to express my views.

* * *

IV

* * *

Where there is no constitutional claim bearing on innocence, the inquiry of the federal court on habeas review of a state prisoner's Fourth Amendment claim should be confined solely to the question whether the defendant was provided a fair opportunity in the state courts to raise and have adjudicated the Fourth Amendment claim. Limiting the scope of habeas review in this manner would reduce the role of the federal courts in determining the merits of constitutional claims with no relation to a petitioner's innocence and contribute to the restoration of recently neglected values to their proper place in our criminal justice system.

* * *

MR. JUSTICE DOUGLAS, dissenting.

* * *

A considerable constitutional guarantee rides on this narrow issue. At the time of the search there was no probable cause to believe that the car contained contraband or other unlawful articles. The car was stopped only because a headlight and the license plate light were burned out. The car belonged to Alcala's brother, from whom it was borrowed, and Alcala had a driver's license. Traffic citations were appropriately issued. The car was searched, the present record showing that Alcala consented. But whether Alcala knew he had the right to refuse, we do not know. All the Court of Appeals did was to remand the case to the District Court for a finding—and if necessary, a hearing on that issue.

I would let the case go forward on that basis. The long, time-consuming contest in this Court might well wash out. At least we could be assured that, if it came back, we would not be rendering an advisory opinion. Had I voted to grant this petition, I would suggest we dismiss it as improvidently granted. But, being in the minority, I am bound by the Rule of Four.

MR. JUSTICE BRENNAN, dissenting.

. . . It wholly escapes me how our citizens can meaningfully be said to have waived something as precious as a constitutional guarantee without ever being aware of its existence. In my view, the Court's conclusion is supported neither by "linguistics," nor by "epistemology," nor, indeed, by "common sense." I respectfully dissent.

MR. JUSTICE MARSHALL, dissenting.

* * *

I

I believe that the Court misstates the true issue in this case. That issue is not, as the Court suggests whether the police overbore Alcala's will in eliciting his consent, but rather, whether a simple statement of assent to search, without more, should be sufficient to permit the police to search and thus act as a relinquishment of Alcala's constitutional right to exclude the police. This Court has always scrutinized with great care claims that a person has forgone the opportunity to assert constitutional rights. I see no reason to give the claim that a person consented to a search any less rigorous scrutiny. Every case in this Court involving this kind of search has heretofore spoken of consent as a waiver. Perhaps one skilled in linguistics or epistemology can disregard those comments, but I find them hard to ignore.

* * *

To begin, it is important to understand that the opinion of the Court is misleading in its treatment of the issue here in three ways. First, it derives its criterion for determining when a verbal statement of assent to search operates as a relinquishment of a person's right to preclude entry from a justification of consent searches that is inconsistent with our treatment in earlier cases of exceptions to the requirements of the Fourth Amendment, and that is not responsive to the unique nature of the consent-search exception. Second, it applies a standard of voluntariness that was developed in a very different context, where the standard was based on policies different from those involved in this case. Third, it mischaracterizes our prior cases involving consent searches.

A

The Court assumes that the issue in this case is: what are the standards by which courts are to determine that consent is voluntarily given? It then imports into the law of search and seizure standards developed to decide entirely different questions about coerced confessions.

The Fifth Amendment, in terms, provides that no person "shall be compelled in any criminal case to be a witness against himself." Nor is the interest protected by the Due Process Clause of the Fourteenth Amendment any different. The inquiry in a case where a confession is challenged as having been elicited in an unconstitutional manner is, therefore, whether the behavior of the police amounted to compulsion of the defendant. Because of the nature of the right to be free of compulsion, it would be pointless to ask whether a defendant knew of it before he made a statement; no sane person would knowingly relinquish a right to be free of compulsion. Thus, the questions of compulsion and of violation of the right itself are inextricably intertwined. The cases involving coerced confessions, therefore, pass over the question of knowledge of that right as irrelevant, and turn directly to the question of compulsion.

* * *

B

In contrast, this case deals not with "coercion," but with "consent," a subtly different concept to which different standards have been applied in the past. Freedom from coercion is a substantive right, guaranteed by the Fifth and Fourteenth Amendments. Consent, however, is a mechanism by which substantive requirements, otherwise applicable, are avoided. In the context of the Fourth Amendment, the relevant substantive requirements are that searches be conducted only after evidence justifying them has been submitted to an impartial magistrate for a determination of probable cause. There are, of course, exceptions to these requirements based on a variety of exigent circumstances that make it impractical to invalidate a search simply because the police failed to get a warrant. But none of the exceptions relating to the overriding needs of law enforcement are applicable when a search is justified solely by consent. On the contrary, the needs of law enforcement are significantly more attenuated, for probable cause to search may be lacking but a search permitted if the subject's consent has been obtained. Thus, consent searches are permitted, not because such an exception to the requirements of probable cause and warrant is essential to proper law enforcement, but because we permit our citizens to choose whether or not they wish to exercise their constitutional rights. Our prior decisions simply do not support the view that a meaningful choice has been made solely because no coercion was brought to bear on the subject.

* * *

For example, in *Bumper v. North Carolina*, 391 U.S. 543 (1968), four law enforcement officers went to the home of Bumper's grandmother. They announced that they had a search warrant, and she permitted them to enter. Subsequently, the prosecutor chose not to rely on the warrant, but attempted to justify the search by the woman's consent. We held that consent could not be established "by showing no more than acquiescence to a claim of lawful authority." We did not there inquire into all the circumstances, but focused on a single fact, the claim of authority, even though the grandmother testified that no threats were made. It may be that, on the facts of that case, her consent was under all the circumstances involuntary, but it is plain that we did not apply the test adopted by the Court today. And, whatever the posture of the case when it reached this Court, it could not be said that the police in *Bumper* acted in a threatening or coercive manner, for they did have the warrant they said they had; the decision not to rely on it was made long after the search, when the case came into court.

II

My approach to the case is straight-forward and, to me, obviously required by the notion of consent as a relinquishment of Fourth Amendment rights. I am at a loss to understand why consent "cannot be taken literally to mean a 'knowing' choice." In fact, I have difficulty in comprehending how a decision made without knowledge of available alternatives can be treated as a choice at all.

If consent to search means that a person has chosen to forgo his right to exclude the police from the place they seek to search, it follows that his consent cannot be considered a meaningful choice unless he knew that he could in fact exclude the police. The Court appears, however, to reject even the modest proposition that, if the subject of a search convinces the trier of fact that he did not know of his right to refuse assent to a police request for permission to search, the search must be held unconstitutional. For it says only that "knowledge of the right to refuse consent is one factor to be taken into account." I find this incomprehensible. I can think of no other situation in which we would say that a person agreed to some course of action if he convinced us that he did not know that there was some other course he might have pursued. I would therefore hold, at a minimum, that the prosecution may not rely on a purported consent to search if the subject of the search did not know that he could refuse to give consent. That, I think, is the import of *Bumper v. North Carolina*. Where the police claim authority to search yet in fact lack such authority, the subject does not know that he may permissibly refuse them entry, and it is this lack of knowledge that invalidates the consent.

If one accepts this view, the question then is a simple one: must the Government show that the subject knew of his rights, or must the subject show that he lacked such knowledge?

I think that any fair allocation of the burden would require that it be placed on the prosecution. On this question, the Court indulges in what might be called the "straw man" method of adjudication. The Court responds to this suggestion by overinflating the burden. And, when it is suggested that the prosecution's burden of proof could be easily satisfied if the police informed the subject of his rights, the Court responds by refusing to require the police to make a "detailed" inquiry. If the Court candidly faced the real question of allocating the burden of proof, neither of these maneuvers would be available to it.

If the burden is placed on the defendant, all the subject can do is to testify that he did not know of his rights. And I doubt that many trial judges will find for the defendant simply on the basis of that testimony.

Precisely because the evidence is very hard to come by, courts have traditionally been reluctant to require a party to prove negatives such as the lack of knowledge.

In contrast, there are several ways by which the subject's knowledge of his rights may be shown. The subject may affirmatively demonstrate such knowledge by his responses at the time the search took place, as in *United States v. Curiale*, 414 F.2d 744 (CA2 1969). Where, as in this case, the person giving consent is someone other than the defendant, the prosecution may require him to testify under oath. Denials of knowledge may be disproved by establishing that the subject had, in the recent past, demonstrated his knowledge of his rights, for example, by refusing entry when it was requested by the police. The prior experience or training of the subject might in some cases support an inference that he knew of his right to exclude the police.

The burden on the prosecutor would disappear, of course, if the police, at the time they requested consent to search, also told the subject that he had a right to refuse consent and that his decision to refuse would be respected. The Court's assertions to the contrary notwithstanding, there is nothing impractical about this method of satisfying the prosecution's burden of proof. It must be emphasized that the decision about informing the subject of his rights would lie with the officers seeking consent. If they believed that providing such information would impede their investigation, they might simply ask for consent, taking the risk that at some later date the prosecutor would be unable to prove that the subject knew of his rights or that some other basis for the search existed.

The Court contends that if an officer paused to inform the subject of his rights, the informality of the exchange would be destroyed. I doubt that a simple statement by an officer of an individual's right to refuse consent would do much to alter the informality of the exchange, except to alert the subject to a fact that he surely is entitled to know. It is not without significance that for many years the agents of the Federal Bureau of Investigation have routinely informed subjects of their right to refuse consent, when they request consent to search. The reported cases in which the police have informed subjects of their right to refuse consent show, also, that the information can be given without disrupting the casual flow of events. What evidence there is, then, rather strongly suggests that nothing disastrous would happen if the police, before requesting consent, informed the subject that he had a right to refuse consent and that his refusal would be respected.

I must conclude with some reluctance that when the Court speaks of practicality, what it really is talking of is the continued ability of the police to capitalize on the ignorance of citizens so as to accomplish by subterfuge what they could not achieve by relying only on the knowing relinquishment of constitutional rights. Of course it would be "practical" for the police to ignore the commands of the Fourth Amendment, if by practicality we mean that more criminals will be apprehended, even though the constitutional rights of innocent people also go by the board. But such a practical advantage is achieved only at the cost of permitting the police to disregard the limitations that the Constitution places on their behavior, a cost that a constitutional democracy cannot long absorb.

I find nothing in the opinion of the Court to dispel my belief that, in such a case, as the Court of Appeals for the Ninth Circuit said, "(u)nder many circumstances a reasonable person might read an officer's 'May I' as the courteous expression of a demand backed by force of law." Most cases, in my view, are akin to *Bumper v. North Carolina*, 391 U.S. 543 (1968): consent is ordinarily given as acquiescence in an implicit claim of authority to search. Permitting searches in such circumstances, without any assurance at all that the subject of the search knew that, by his consent, he was relinquishing his constitutional rights, is something that I cannot believe is sanctioned by the Constitution.

III

The proper resolution of this case turns, I believe, on a realistic assessment of the nature of the interchange between citizens and the police, and of the practical import of allocating the burden of proof in one way rather than another. The Court seeks to escape such assessments by escalating its rhetoric to unwarranted heights, but no matter how forceful the adjectives the Court uses, it cannot avoid being judged by how well its image of these interchanges accords with reality. Although the Court says without real elaboration that it "cannot agree," the holding today confines the protection of the Fourth Amendment against searches conducted without probable cause to the sophisticated, the knowledgeable, and, I might add, the few. In the final analysis, the Court now sanctions a game of blindman's buff, in which the police always have the upper hand, for the sake of nothing more than the convenience of the police. But the guarantees of the Fourth Amendment were never intended to shrink before such an ephemeral and changeable interest. The Framers of the Fourth Amendment struck the balance against this sort of convenience and in favor of certain basic civil rights. It is not for this Court to restrike that balance because of its own views of the needs of law enforcement officers. I fear that that is the effect of the Court's decision today.

It is regrettable that the obsession with validating searches like that conducted in this case, so evident in the Court's hyperbole, has obscured the Court's vision of how the Fourth Amendment was designed to govern the relationship between police and citizen in our society. I believe that experience and careful reflection show how narrow and inaccurate that vision is, and I respectfully dissent.

Points for Discussion

1. The Court analogizes the issue of whether consent has been voluntarily given to the issue of whether a confession has been voluntarily obtained. How analogous are these situations? How does Justice Marshall distinguish the two?

2. In the confession context, the Supreme Court has ruled that a confession is irrebuttably presumed to be coerced if it is not preceded by warnings, including the warning that the defendant has the right not to speak to the police unless he chooses to do so. *See Miranda v. Arizona*, 384 U.S. 436 (1966). Why did the Court not adopt a similar presumption with regard to consensual searches?

3. The Court quotes *Linkletter* for the proposition that "The Fourth Amendment 'is not an adjunct to the ascertainment of truth.'" Justice Powell—who would later write the Court's opinion in *Stone v. Powell* adopting his views—argues that the disconnect between the Fourth Amendment and the process of truth ascertainment counsels against adjudicating such claims on petitions for habeas corpus. How are Fourth Amendment rights less about ascertaining truth than Fifth or Sixth Amendment rights?

4. The majority opinion posits: "In situations where the police have some evidence of illicit activity, but lack probable cause to arrest a search, a search authorized by a valid consent may be the only means of obtaining important and reliable evidence." The Court then goes on to hold that advising targets that they have the right to refuse consent "would be thoroughly impractical." Justice Marshall counters, "Of course it would be 'practical' for the police to ignore the commands of the Fourth Amendment, if by practicality we mean that more criminals will be apprehended, even though the constitutional rights of innocent people also go by the board." Should courts weigh the "practicality" of enforcing any given rule when determining the scope of constitutional rights?

2. CAPACITY

While *Bustamonte* deals with the question of whether an individual's consent is valid, the cases in this section raise the question of *who* may validly consent to a search.

STONER V. CALIFORNIA

376 U.S. 483 (1964)

MR. JUSTICE STEWART delivered the opinion of the court.

The petitioner was convicted of armed robbery after a jury trial in the Superior Court of Los Angeles County, California. At the trial several articles which had been found by police officers in a search of the petitioner's hotel room during his absence were admitted into evidence over his objection. A District Court of Appeal of California affirmed the conviction, and the Supreme Court of California denied further review. We granted certiorari, limiting review "to the question of whether evidence was admitted which had been obtained by an unlawful search and seizure." For the reasons which follow, we conclude that the petitioner's conviction must be set aside.

The essential facts are not in dispute. On the night of October 25, 1960, the Budget Town Food Market in Monrovia, California, was robbed by two men, one of whom was described by eyewitnesses as carrying a gun and wearing hornrimmed glasses and a grey jacket. Soon after the robbery a checkbook belonging to the petitioner was found in an adjacent parking lot and turned over to the police. Two of the stubs in the checkbook indicated that checks had been drawn to the order of the Mayfair Hotel in Pomona, California. Pursuing this lead, the officers learned from the Police Department of Pomona that the petitioner had a previous criminal record, and they obtained from the Pomona police a photograph of the petitioner. They showed the photograph to the two eyewitnesses to the robbery, who both stated that the picture looked like the man who had carried the gun. On the basis of this information the officers went to the Mayfair Hotel in Pomona at about 10 o'clock on the night of October 27. They had neither search nor arrest warrants. There then transpired the following events, as later recounted by one of the officers:

> We approached the desk, the night clerk, and asked him if there was a party by the name of Joey L. Stoner living at the hotel. He checked his records and stated 'Yes, there is.' And we asked him what room he was in. He stated he was in Room 404 but he was out at this time.
>
> We asked him how he knew that he was out. He stated that the hotel regulations required that the key to the room would be placed in the mail box each time they left the hotel. The key was in the mail box, that he therefore knew he was out of the room.
>
> We asked him if he would give us permission to enter the room, explaining our reasons for this.
>
> Q. What reasons did you explain to the clerk?
>
> A. We explained that we were there to make an arrest of a man who had possibly committed a robbery in the City of Monrovia, and that we were concerned about the fact that he had a weapon. He stated 'In this case, I will be more than happy to give you permission and I will take you directly to the room.'
>
> Q. Is that what the clerk told you?
>
> A. Yes, sir.
>
> Q. What else happened?

> A. We left one detective in the lobby, and Detective Oliver, Officer Collins, and myself, along with the night clerk, got on the elevator and proceeded to the fourth floor, and went to Room 404. The night clerk placed a key in the lock, unlocked the door, and says, 'Be my guest.'

The officers entered and made a thorough search of the room and its contents. They found a pair of horn-rimmed glasses and a grey jacket in the room, and a .45-caliber automatic pistol with a clip and several cartridges in the bottom of a bureau drawer. The petitioner was arrested two days later in Las Vegas, Nevada. He waived extradition and was returned to California for trial on the charge of armed robbery. The gun, the cartridges and clip, the horn-rimmed glasses, and the grey jacket were all used as evidence against him at his trial.

The search of the petitioner's room by the police officers was conducted without a warrant of any kind, and it therefore "can survive constitutional inhibition only upon a showing that the surrounding facts brought it within one of the exceptions to the rule that a search must rest upon a search warrant." The District Court of Appeal thought the search was justified as an incident to a lawful arrest. But a search can be incident to an arrest only if it is substantially contemporaneous with the arrest and is confined to the immediate vicinity of the arrest. Whatever room for leeway there may be in these concepts, it is clear that the search of the petitioner's hotel room in Pomona, California, on October 27 was not incident to his arrest in Las Vegas, Nevada, on October 29. The search was completely unrelated to the arrest, both as to time and as to place.

* * *

Even if it be assumed that a state law which gave a hotel proprietor blanket authority to authorize the police to search the rooms of the hotel's guests could survive constitutional challenge, there is no intimation in the California cases cited by the respondent that California has any such law. Nor is there any substance to the claim that the search was reasonable because the police, relying upon the night clerk's expressions of consent, had a reasonable basis for the belief that the clerk had authority to consent to the search. Our decisions make clear that the rights protected by the Fourth Amendment are not to be eroded by strained applications of the law of agency or by unrealistic doctrines of "apparent authority."

As this Court has said,

> it is unnecessary and ill-advised to import into the law surrounding the constitutional right to be free from unreasonable searches and seizures subtle distinctions, developed and refined by the common law in evolving the body of private property law which, more than almost any other branch of law, has been shaped by distinctions whose validity is largely historical. * * * (W)e

ought not to bow to them in the fair administration of the criminal law. To do so would not comport with our justly proud claim of the procedural protections accorded to those charged with crime.

It is important to bear in mind that it was the petitioner's constitutional right which was at stake here, and not the night clerk's nor the hotel's. It was a right, therefore, which only the petitioner could waive by word or deed, either directly or through an agent. It is true that the night clerk clearly and unambiguously consented to the search. But there is nothing in the record to indicate that the police had any basis whatsoever to believe that the night clerk had been authorized by the petitioner to permit the police to search the petitioner's room.

At least twice this Court has explicitly refused to permit an otherwise unlawful police search of a hotel room to rest upon consent of the hotel proprietor. *Lustig v. United States*, 338 U.S. 74; *United States v. Jeffers*, 342 U.S. 48. In *Lustig* the manager of a hotel allowed police to enter and search a room without a warrant in the occupant's absence, and the search was held unconstitutional. In *Jeffers* the assistant manager allowed a similar search, and that search was likewise held unconstitutional.

It is true, as was said in *Jeffers*, that when a person engages a hotel room he undoubtedly gives "implied or express permission" to "such persons as maids, janitors or repairmen" to enter his room "in the performance of their duties." But the conduct of the night clerk and the police in the present case was of an entirely different order. In a closely analogous situation the Court has held that a search by police officers of a house occupied by a tenant invaded the tenant's constitutional right, even though the search was authorized by the owner of the house, who presumably had not only apparent but actual authority to enter the house for some purposes, such as to "view waste." The Court pointed out that the officers' purpose in entering was not to view waste but to search for distilling equipment, and concluded that to uphold such a search without a warrant would leave tenants' homes secure only in the discretion of their landlords.

No less than a tenant of a house, or the occupant of a room in a boarding house, a guest in a hotel room is entitled to constitutional protection against unreasonable searches and seizures. That protection would disappear if it were left to depend upon the unfettered discretion of an employee of the hotel. It follows that this search without a warrant was unlawful. Since evidence obtained through the search was admitted at the trial, the judgment must be reversed.

MR. JUSTICE HARLAN, concurring in part and dissenting in part.

I entirely agree with the Court's opinion, except as to its disposition of the case. I would remand the case to the California District Court of Appeal so that it may consider whether or not admission of the illegally seized evidence was harmless error. . . .

Points for Discussion

1. In *Miller v. United States* the Court held that one who shares financial information with his bank assumes the risk that the bank will surrender that information to the authorities. In *White v. United States* the Court held that one who confides in a friend runs the risk that the friend is recording the conversation and will turn it over to the police. Why does one who rents a hotel room not run the risk that the key that he leaves at the front desk will be handed over to the police for a search? Can *Stoner* be reconciled with the assumption of risk cases?

2. Because it was decided before *Katz v. United States, Stoner* relies on a property rationale rather than reasonable expectations of privacy. But did Stoner have a reasonable expectation of privacy in his hotel room? Do people treat their hotel rooms the way they treat their homes? Should the Court treat the two places as identical for privacy purposes? What are the consequences of treating renters and property owners differently for Fourth Amendment purposes?

UNITED STATES V. MATLOCK

415 U.S. 164 (1974)

MR. JUSTICE WHITE delivered the opinion of the court.

* * *

I

Respondent Matlock was indicted in February 1971 for the robbery of a federally insured bank in Wisconsin, in violation of 18 U.S.C. § 2113. A week later, he filed a motion to suppress evidence seized by law enforcement officers from a home in the town of Pardeeville, Wisconsin, in which he had been living. Suppression hearings followed. As found by the District Court, the facts were that respondent was arrested in the yard in front of the Pardeeville home on November 12, 1970. The home was leased from the owner by Mr. and Mrs. Marshall. Living in the home were Mrs. Marshall, several of her children, including her daughter Mrs. Gayle Graff, Gayle's three-year-old son, and respondent. Although the officers were aware at the time of the arrest that respondent lived in the house, they did not ask him which room he occupied or whether he would consent to a search. Three of the arresting officers went to the door of the house and were admitted by Mrs. Graff, who was dressed in a robe and was holding her son in her arms. The officers told her they were looking for money and a gun and asked if they could search the house. Although denied by Mrs. Graff at the suppression hearings, it was found that she consented voluntarily to the search of the house, including the east bedroom on the second floor which she said was jointly occupied by Matlock and herself. The east bedroom was searched and the evidence at issue here, $4,995 in cash, was found in a diaper bag in the only closet in the room. The issue came to be whether Mrs. Graff's relationship to the east bedroom was sufficient to make her consent to the search valid against respondent Matlock.

* * *

II

It has been assumed by the parties and the courts below that the voluntary consent of any joint occupant of a residence to search the premises jointly occupied is valid against the co-occupant, permitting evidence discovered in the search to be used against him at a criminal trial. This basic proposition was accepted by the Seventh Circuit in this case, as it had been in prior cases, and has generally been applied in similar circumstances by other courts of appeals, and various state courts. This Court left open, in *Amos v. United States*, 255 U.S. 313, 317 (1921), the question whether wife's permission to search the residence in which she lived with her husband could "waive his constitutional rights," but more recent authority here clearly indicates that the consent of one who possesses common authority over premises or effects is valid as against the absent, nonconsenting person with whom that authority is shared. In *Frazier v. Cupp*, 394 U.S. 731, 740 (1969), the Court "dismissed rather quickly" the contention that the consent of the petitioner's cousin to the search of a duffel bag, which was being used jointly by both men and had been left in the cousin's home, would not justify the seizure of petitioner's clothing found inside; joint use of the bag rendered the cousin's authority to consent to its search clear. Indeed, the Court was unwilling to engage in the "metaphysical subtleties" raised by Frazier's claim that his cousin only had permission to use one compartment within the bag. By allowing the cousin the use of the bag, and by leaving it in his house, Frazier was held to have assumed the risk that his cousin would allow someone else to look inside. More generally, in *Schneckloth v. Bustamonte*, [412 U.S. 218 (1972)], we noted that our prior recognition of the constitutional validity of "third party consent" searches in cases like *Frazier* and *Coolidge v. New Hampshire*, 403 U.S. 443, 487–490 (1971), supported the view that a consent search is fundamentally different in nature from the waiver of a trial right. These cases at least make clear that when the prosecution seeks to justify a warrantless search by proof of voluntary consent, it is not limited to proof that consent was given by the defendant, but may show that permission to search was obtained from a third party who possessed common authority over or other sufficient relationship to the premises or effects sought to be inspected.[7] The issue now before us is whether the Government made the requisite showing in this case.

* * *

IV

It appears to us, given the admissibility of Mrs. Graff's and respondent's out-of-court statements, that the Government sustained its burden of proving by the preponderance of the evidence that Mrs. Graff's voluntary consent to search the east bedroom was legally sufficient to warrant admitting into evidence the $4,995 found in the diaper bag.[14] But we prefer that the District Court first reconsider the sufficiency of the evidence in the light of this decision and opinion.

* * *

MR. JUSTICE DOUGLAS, dissenting.

* * *

Up to now, a police officer had a duty to secure a warrant when he had the opportunity to do so, even if substantial probable cause existed to justify a search. . . .

* * *

And, indeed, the provisions of the Fourth Amendment carefully and explicitly restricting the circumstances in which warrants can issue and the breadth of searches have become "empty phrases," when the Court sanctions this search conducted without any effort by the police to secure a valid search warrant. This was not a case where a grave emergency, such as the imminent loss of evidence or danger to human life, might excuse the failure to secure a warrant. Mrs. Graff's permission to the police to invade the house, simultaneously violating the privacy of Matlock and the Marshalls, provides a sorry and wholly inadequate substitute for the protections which inhere in a judicially granted warrant. It is inconceivable that a search conducted without a warrant can give more authority than a search conducted with a warrant. But here the police procured without a warrant all the authority which they had under the feared general warrants, hatred of which led to the passage of the Fourth Amendment.

---

[7] Common authority is, of course, not to be implied from the mere property interest a third party has in the property. The authority which justifies the third-party consent does not rest upon the law of property, with its attendant historical and legal refinements but rests rather on mutual use of the property by persons generally having joint access or control for most purposes, so that it is reasonable to recognize that any of the co-inhabitants has the right to permit the inspection in his own right and that the others have assumed the risk that one of their number might permit the common area to be searched.

[14] Accordingly, we do not reach another major contention of the United States in bringing this case here: that the Government in any event had only to satisfy the District Court that the searching officers reasonably believed that Mrs. Graff had sufficient authority over the premises to consent to the search.

Government agents are now free to rummage about the house, unconstrained by anything except their own desires. Even after finding items which they may have expected to find and which doubtless would have been specified in a valid warrant, they prolonged their exploratory search in pursuit of additional evidence. The judgment of whether the intrusion into the Marshalls' and Matlock's privacy was to be permitted was not made by an objective judicial officer respectful of the exacting demands of the Fourth Amendment; nor were the police limited by the need to make an initial showing of probable cause to invade the Marshall home. Since the Framers of the Amendment did not abolish the hated general warrants only to impose another oppressive regime on the people, I dissent.

MR. JUSTICE BRENNAN, with whom MR. JUSTICE MARSHALL joins, dissenting.

I would not limit the remand to the determination whether Mrs. Graff was in fact a joint occupant of the bedroom with sufficient authority to consent to the search. In my view the determination is also required that Mrs. Graff consented knowing that she was not required to consent. "It wholly escapes me how our citizens can meaningfully be said to have waived something as precious as a constitutional guarantee without ever being aware of its existence." *Schneckloth v. Bustamonte*, 412 U.S. 218, 277 (1973) (Brennan, J., dissenting). I would hold that an individual cannot effectively waive this right if he is totally ignorant of the fact that, in the absence of his consent, such invasions of privacy would be constitutionally prohibited.

Points for Discussion

1. How does this case differ from *Stoner*? In both *Stoner* and *Matlock*, the police asked for and received permission to search from someone, other than their target, who had the capacity to give it. Why is that capacity deemed legally sufficient in this case but not in the previous one?

2. The Court writes in footnote 7 that "common authority . . . rests on mutual use of the property by persons generally having joint access or control for most purposes . . . ." What are the facts here that indicate such common authority over the property searched in this case?

3. Assuming that Mrs. Graff was one who was legally entitled to give consent, was there something constitutionally suspect in the police's decision to seek consent from her rather than to obtain a warrant? Justice Douglas argues that in the absence of exigent circumstances, the authorities should seek to procure a warrant rather than permission to search. Why would this be so? Is a search supported by a warrant always more legitimate than one based on consent?

4. What is it about this search that makes it constitutional? Is it that Matlock had no reasonable expectation of privacy in the home he shared with Ms. Graff? Or is it that he had a reasonable expectation of privacy in his home,

but that the police entry was reasonable because they had the consent of his co-occupant?

ILLINOIS V. RODRIGUEZ

497 U.S. 177 (1990)

JUSTICE SCALIA delivered the opinion of the court.

In *United States v. Matlock,* 415 U.S. 164 (1974), this Court reaffirmed that a warrantless entry and search by law enforcement officers does not violate the Fourth Amendment's proscription of "unreasonable searches and seizures" if the officers have obtained the consent of a third party who possesses common authority over the premises. The present case presents an issue we expressly reserved in *Matlock*: Whether a warrantless entry is valid when based upon the consent of a third party whom the police, at the time of the entry, reasonably believe to possess common authority over the premises, but who in fact does not do so.

I

Respondent Edward Rodriguez was arrested in his apartment by law enforcement officers and charged with possession of illegal drugs. The police gained entry to the apartment with the consent and assistance of Gail Fischer, who had lived there with respondent for several months. The relevant facts leading to the arrest are as follows.

On July 26, 1985, police were summoned to the residence of Dorothy Jackson on South Wolcott in Chicago. They were met by Ms. Jackson's daughter, Gail Fischer, who showed signs of a severe beating. She told the officers that she had been assaulted by respondent Edward Rodriguez earlier that day in an apartment on South California. Fischer stated that Rodriguez was then asleep in the apartment, and she consented to travel there with the police in order to unlock the door with her key so that the officers could enter and arrest him. During this conversation, Fischer several times referred to the apartment on South California as "our" apartment, and said that she had clothes and furniture there. It is unclear whether she indicated that she currently lived at the apartment, or only that she used to live there.

The police officers drove to the apartment on South California, accompanied by Fischer. They did not obtain an arrest warrant for Rodriguez, nor did they seek a search warrant for the apartment. At the apartment, Fischer unlocked the door with her key and gave the officers permission to enter. They moved through the door into the living room, where they observed in plain view drug paraphernalia and containers filled with white powder that they believed (correctly, as later analysis showed) to be cocaine. They proceeded to the bedroom, where they found Rodriguez asleep and discovered additional containers of white powder in two open attaché cases. The officers arrested Rodriguez and seized the drugs and related paraphernalia.

* * *

II

* * *

As we stated in *Matlock*, "[c]ommon authority" rests "on mutual use of the property by persons generally having joint access or control for most purposes . . . ." The burden of establishing that common authority rests upon the State. On the basis of this record, it is clear that burden was not sustained. The evidence showed that although Fischer, with her two small children, had lived with Rodriguez beginning in December 1984, she had moved out on July 1, 1985, almost a month before the search at issue here, and had gone to live with her mother. She took her and her children's clothing with her, though leaving behind some furniture and household effects. During the period after July 1 she sometimes spent the night at Rodriguez's apartment, but never invited her friends there, and never went there herself when he was not home. Her name was not on the lease nor did she contribute to the rent. She had a key to the apartment, which she said at trial she had taken without Rodriguez's knowledge (though she testified at the preliminary hearing that Rodriguez had given her the key). On these facts the State has not established that, with respect to the South California apartment, Fischer had "joint access or control for most purposes." To the contrary, the Appellate Court's determination of no common authority over the apartment was obviously correct.

III

* * *

B

On the merits of the issue, respondent asserts that permitting a reasonable belief of common authority to validate an entry would cause a defendant's Fourth Amendment rights to be "vicariously waived." We disagree.

We have been unyielding in our insistence that a defendant's waiver of his trial rights cannot be given effect unless it is "knowing" and "intelligent." We would assuredly not permit, therefore, evidence seized in violation of the Fourth Amendment to be introduced on the basis of a trial court's mere "reasonable belief"—derived from statements by unauthorized persons—that the defendant has waived his objection. But one must make a distinction between, on the one hand, trial rights that *derive* from the violation of constitutional guarantees and, on the other hand, the nature of those constitutional guarantees themselves. As we said in *Schneckloth:*

> There is a vast difference between those rights that protect a fair criminal trial and the rights guaranteed under the Fourth Amendment. Nothing, either in the purposes behind requiring a "knowing" and "intelligent" waiver of trial rights, or in the practical application of such a requirement suggests that it ought to be extended to the constitutional guarantee against unreasonable searches and seizures.

What Rodriguez is assured by the trial right of the exclusionary rule, where it applies, is that no evidence seized in violation of the Fourth Amendment will be introduced at his trial unless he consents. What he is assured by the Fourth Amendment itself, however, is not that no government search of his house will occur unless he consents; but that no such search will occur that is "unreasonable." U.S. Const., Amdt. 4. There are various elements, of course, that can make a search of a person's house "reasonable"—one of which is the consent of the person or his cotenant. The essence of respondent's argument is that we should impose upon this element a requirement that we have not imposed upon other elements that regularly compel government officers to exercise judgment regarding the facts: namely, the requirement that their judgment be not only responsible but correct.

The fundamental objective that alone validates all unconsented government searches is, of course, the seizure of persons who have committed or are about to commit crimes, or of evidence related to crimes. But "reasonableness," with respect to this necessary element, does not demand that the government be factually correct in its assessment that that is what a search will produce. Warrants need only be supported by "probable cause," which demands no more than a proper "assessment of probabilities in particular factual contexts . . . ." *Illinois v. Gates,* 462 U.S. 213, 232 (1983). If a magistrate, based upon seemingly reliable but factually inaccurate information, issues a warrant for the search of a house in which the sought-after felon is not present, has never been present, and was never likely to have been present, the owner of that house suffers one of the inconveniences we all expose ourselves to as the cost of living in a safe society; he does not suffer a violation of the Fourth Amendment.

Another element often, though not invariably, required in order to render an unconsented search "reasonable" is, of course, that the officer be authorized by a valid warrant. Here also we have not held that "reasonableness" precludes error with respect to those factual judgments that law enforcement officials are expected to make. In *Maryland v. Garrison,* 480 U.S. 79 (1987), a warrant supported by probable cause with respect to one apartment was erroneously issued for an entire floor that was divided (though not clearly) into two apartments. We upheld the search of the apartment not properly covered by the warrant. We said:

> [T]he validity of the search of respondent's apartment pursuant to a warrant authorizing the search of the entire third floor depends on whether the officers' failure to realize the overbreadth of the warrant was objectively understandable and reasonable. Here it unquestionably was. The objective facts available to the officers at the time suggested no distinction between [the suspect's] apartment and the third-floor premises.

The ordinary requirement of a warrant is sometimes supplanted by other elements that render the unconsented search "reasonable." Here also we have not held that the Fourth Amendment requires factual accuracy. A warrant is not needed, for example, where the search is incident to an arrest. In *Hill v. California,* 401 U.S. 797 (1971), we upheld a search incident to an arrest, even though the arrest was made of the wrong person. We said:

> The upshot was that the officers in good faith believed Miller was Hill and arrested him. They were quite wrong as it turned out, and subjective good-faith belief would not in itself justify either the arrest or the subsequent search. But sufficient probability, not certainty, is the touchstone of reasonableness under the Fourth Amendment and on the record before us the officers' mistake was understandable and the arrest a reasonable response to the situation facing them at the time.

* * *

We see no reason to depart from this general rule with respect to facts bearing upon the authority to consent to a search. Whether the basis for such authority exists is the sort of recurring factual question to which law enforcement officials must be expected to apply their judgment; and all the Fourth Amendment requires is that they answer it reasonably. The Constitution is no more violated when officers enter without a warrant because they reasonably (though erroneously) believe that the person who has consented to their entry is a resident of the premises, than it is violated when they enter without a warrant because they reasonably (though erroneously) believe they are in pursuit of a violent felon who is about to escape.*

* Justice Marshall's dissent rests upon a rejection of the proposition that searches pursuant to valid third-party consent are "generally reasonable." Only a warrant or exigent circumstances, he contends, can produce "reasonableness"; consent validates the search only because the object of the search thereby "limit[s] his expectation of privacy," so that the search becomes not really a search at all. We see no basis for making such an artificial distinction. To describe a consented search as a noninvasion of privacy and thus a non-search is strange in the extreme. And while it must be admitted that this ingenious device can explain why consented searches are lawful, it cannot explain why seemingly consented searches are "unreasonable," which is all that the Constitution forbids. The only basis for contending that the constitutional standard could not possibly have been met here is the argument that reasonableness must be judged by the facts as they were, rather than by the facts as they were known. As we have discussed in text, that argument has long since been rejected.

* * *

In the present case, the Appellate Court found it unnecessary to determine whether the officers reasonably believed that Fischer had the authority to consent, because it ruled as a matter of law that a reasonable belief could not validate the entry. Since we find that ruling to be in error, we remand for consideration of that question. The judgment of the Illinois Appellate Court is reversed, and the case is remanded for further proceedings not inconsistent with this opinion.

JUSTICE MARSHALL, with whom JUSTICE BRENNAN and JUSTICE STEVENS join, dissenting.

Dorothy Jackson summoned police officers to her house to report that her daughter Gail Fischer had been beaten. Fischer told police that Ed Rodriguez, her boyfriend, was her assaulter. During an interview with Fischer, one of the officers asked if Rodriguez dealt in narcotics. Fischer did not respond. Fischer did agree, however, to the officers' request to let them into Rodriguez's apartment so that they could arrest him for battery. The police, without a warrant and despite the absence of an exigency, entered Rodriguez's home to arrest him. As a result of their entry, the police discovered narcotics that the State subsequently sought to introduce in a drug prosecution against Rodriguez.

The majority agrees with the Illinois Appellate Court's determination that Fischer did not have authority to consent to the officers' entry of Rodriguez's apartment. The Court holds that the warrantless entry into Rodriguez's home was nonetheless valid if the officers reasonably believed that Fischer had authority to consent. The majority's defense of this position rests on a misconception of the basis for third-party consent searches. That such searches do not give rise to claims of constitutional violations rests not on the premise that they are "reasonable" under the Fourth Amendment, but on the premise that a person may voluntarily limit his expectation of privacy by allowing others to exercise authority over his possessions. Thus, an individual's decision to permit another "joint access [to] or control [over the property] for most purposes," *United States v. Matlock,* 415 U.S. 164, 171, n. 7 (1974), limits that individual's reasonable expectation of privacy and to that extent limits his Fourth Amendment protections. If an individual has not so limited his expectation of privacy, the police may not dispense with the safeguards established by the Fourth Amendment.

The baseline for the reasonableness of a search or seizure in the home is the presence of a warrant. Indeed, "searches and seizures inside a home without a warrant are presumptively unreasonable." *Payton v. New York,* 445 U.S. 573, 586 (1980). Exceptions to the warrant requirement must therefore serve "compelling" law enforcement goals. Because the sole law enforcement purpose underlying third-party consent searches is avoiding the inconvenience of securing a warrant, a departure from the warrant requirement is not justified simply because an officer reasonably believes a third party has consented to a search of the defendant's home. In holding otherwise, the majority ignores our longstanding view that "the informed and deliberate determinations of magistrates . . . as to what searches and seizures are permissible under the Constitution are to be preferred over the hurried action of officers and others who may happen to make arrests."

I

* * *

The Court has tolerated departures from the warrant requirement only when an exigency makes a warrantless search imperative to the safety of the police and of the community. The Court has often heard, and steadfastly rejected, the invitation to carve out further exceptions to the warrant requirement for searches of the home because of the burdens on police investigation and prosecution of crime. Our rejection of such claims is not due to a lack of appreciation of the difficulty and importance of effective law enforcement, but rather to our firm commitment to "the view of those who wrote the Bill of Rights that the privacy of a person's home and property may not be totally sacrificed in the name of maximum simplicity in enforcement of the criminal law."

In the absence of an exigency, then, warrantless home searches and seizures are unreasonable under the Fourth Amendment. The weighty constitutional interest in preventing unauthorized intrusions into the home overrides any law enforcement interest in relying on the reasonable but potentially mistaken belief that a third party has authority to consent to such a search or seizure. Indeed, as the present case illustrates, only the minimal interest in avoiding the inconvenience of obtaining a warrant weighs in on the law enforcement side.

* * *

Unlike searches conducted pursuant to the recognized exceptions to the warrant requirement, third-party consent searches are not based on an exigency and therefore serve no compelling social goal. Police officers, when faced with the choice of relying on consent by a third party or securing a warrant, should secure a warrant and must therefore accept the risk of error should they instead choose to rely on consent.

II

Our prior cases discussing searches based on third-party consent have never suggested that such searches are "reasonable." In *United States v. Matlock,* this Court upheld a warrantless search conducted pursuant to the consent of a third party who was living with the defendant. The Court rejected the defendant's challenge to the search, stating that a person who permits others to have "joint access or control for most purposes . . .

assume[s] the risk that [such persons] might permit the common area to be searched." 415 U.S., at 171, n. 7; see also *Frazier v. Cupp,* 394 U.S. 731, 740 (1969) (holding that defendant who left a duffel bag at another's house and allowed joint use of the bag "assumed the risk that [the person] would allow someone else to look inside"). As the Court's assumption-of-risk analysis makes clear, third-party consent limits a person's ability to challenge the reasonableness of the search only because that person voluntarily has relinquished some of his expectation of privacy by sharing access or control over his property with another person.

A search conducted pursuant to an officer's reasonable but mistaken belief that a third party had authority to consent is thus on an entirely different constitutional footing from one based on the consent of a third party who in fact has such authority. Even if the officers reasonably believed that Fischer had authority to consent, she did not, and Rodriguez's expectation of privacy was therefore undiminished. Rodriguez accordingly can challenge the warrantless intrusion into his home as a violation of the Fourth Amendment. This conclusion flows directly from *Stoner v. California,* 376 U.S. 483 (1964). There, the Court required the suppression of evidence seized in reliance on a hotel clerk's consent to a warrantless search of a guest's room. The Court reasoned that the guest's right to be free of unwarranted intrusion "was a right . . . which only [he] could waive by word or deed, either directly or through an agent." Accordingly, the Court rejected resort to "unrealistic doctrines of 'apparent authority' " as a means of upholding the search to which the guest had not consented.[1]

III

Acknowledging that the third party in this case lacked authority to consent, the majority seeks to rely on cases suggesting that reasonable but

---

1 The majority insists that the rationale of *Stoner* is "ambiguous—and perhaps deliberately so" with respect to the permissibility of third-party searches where the suspect has not conferred actual authority on the third party. *Stoner* itself is clear, however; today's majority manufactures the ambiguity. When the *Stoner* Court stated that the Fourth Amendment is not to be eroded "by unrealistic doctrines of 'apparent authority,' " and that "only the petitioner could waive by word or deed" his freedom from a warrantless search, the Court rejected precisely the proposition that the majority today adopts.

The majority regards *Stoner*'s rejection of "unrealistic doctrines of 'apparent authority' " as ambiguous on the theory that the Court might have been referring only to unreasonable *applications* of such doctrines and not to the doctrines themselves. But *Stoner*'s express description of apparent authority *doctrines* as unrealistic cannot be viewed as mere happenstance. The Court in fact used the word "applications" in the same sentence to refer to misapplications of the *actual* authority doctrine: "Our decisions make clear that the rights protected by the Fourth Amendment are not to be eroded by strained applications of the law of agency *or* by unrealistic doctrines of 'apparent authority.' " (emphasis added). The full sentence thus unambiguously confirms that *Stoner* rejected any reliance on *apparent* authority doctrines.

Nor did the *Stoner* Court leave open the door for a police officer to rely on a reasonable but mistaken belief in a third party's authority to consent when it remarked that "there is nothing in the record to indicate that the police had any basis whatsoever to believe that the night clerk had been authorized by the petitioner to permit the police to search the petitioner's room." Stating that a defendant must "by word or deed" waive his rights is not inconsistent with noting that, in a particular case, the absence of actual waiver is confirmed by the police's inability to identify any basis for their contention that waiver had indeed occurred.

mistaken factual judgments by police will not invalidate otherwise reasonable searches. The majority reads these cases as establishing a "general rule" that "what is generally demanded of the many factual determinations that must regularly be made by agents of the government—whether the magistrate issuing a warrant, the police officer executing a warrant, or the police officer conducting a search or seizure under one of the exceptions to the warrant requirement—is not that they always be correct, but that they always be reasonable."

The majority's assertion, however, is premised on the erroneous assumption that third-party consent searches are generally reasonable. The cases the majority cites thus provide no support for its holding.

* * *

IV

Our cases demonstrate that third-party consent searches are free from constitutional challenge only to the extent that they rest on consent by a party empowered to do so. The majority's conclusion to the contrary ignores the legitimate expectations of privacy on which individuals are entitled to rely. That a person who allows another joint access to his property thereby limits his expectation of privacy does not justify trampling the rights of a person who has not similarly relinquished any of his privacy expectation.

* * *

Points for Discussion

1. Recall the question after *Matlock* regarding what makes a third party consent search constitutional. Which of the two views—assumption of risk or reasonableness—does the *Rodriguez* majority rely on? The dissent? Who has the stronger argument?

2. In *Rodriguez* the Court adopts the apparent authority doctrine—consent is valid if given by someone with apparent, but not actual authority—despite having apparently rejected it in *Stoner*. How convincing is the Court's attempt to distinguish the two cases?

3. Justice Scalia's majority opinion concludes that the search is "reasonable" because the police did not deliberately do anything wrong. This conclusion, however, is necessarily dependent on whether the police reasonably and actually believe that the person who consented had authority to do so. The majority's view that police officers' subjective mistakes should not be held against them any more than their subjectively bad motives may ultimately reflect a disagreement with the dissent over the purpose of warrants. Placing the burden on police to ensure that consent is actually, and not just apparently, valid makes little sense if exclusion is meant to deter deliberate police misconduct. If the police have good reason to believe they have permission to enter and search, punishing them if by some fluke they are wrong is pointless. However, the dissenters in *Rodriguez* would suppress

evidence not to punish the police but to vindicate Rodriguez' privacy right. Burdening the police with getting a warrant whenever possible, despite apparent consent, makes sense if warrants are meant to minimize even innocent mistakes and misunderstandings.

4. In *Georgia v. Randolph*, 547 U.S. 103 (2006), the Supreme Court held that the consent of one occupant of an apartment was not valid as against the objection of a present co-occupant. Mrs. Randolph offered to let police into the apartment she shared with her husband in order to show them evidence of his drug use; needless to say he objected. In holding that her permission to search was insufficient to overcome his objection the Court wrote "a caller standing at the door of shared premises would have no confidence that one occupant's invitation was a sufficiently good reason to enter when a fellow tenant stood there saying, 'stay out.' " How compelling is this analogy? Furthermore, how is the Court's holding reconcilable with the assumption of risk cases? Don't those cases hold exactly that Mr. Randolph runs the risk that Mrs. Randolph will betray him to the police? Why should it matter whether he is present for that betrayal?

5. In *Fernandez v. California*, 571 U.S. 292 (2014), the Court "refuse[d] to extend" *Randolph* to a case where the objecting co-habitant was arrested, removed from the scene, and the police later returned to the home and obtained consent to search from his purported victim. Holding that *Randolph* creates a narrow rule that "consent of one occupant is insufficient when another occupant is present and objects to the search," the court held that the consent in this case was valid. What incentives does such a holding create for law enforcement? How different are these facts from those of *Matlock*?

C. "SPECIAL NEEDS" SEARCHES

Terry v. Ohio's watershed holding that some searches and seizures are reasonable even if not supported by probable cause was presaged the previous year by *Camara v. Municipal Court of the City and County of San Francisco*, 387 U.S. 523 (1967). In *Camara*, the Court maintained a "probable cause" requirement for administrative searches but only by drastically redefining the term. *Terry*'s reasonable suspicion standard proved much more influential than *Camara*'s redefinition of probable cause.

Terry opened the door for the Court to decide suspicionless search cases on an *ad hoc* basis. The Court does this today by balancing government interests against privacy rights when the government can demonstrate "special needs," a label taken from Justice Blackmun's concurrence in *New Jersey v. T.L.O.*: "Only in those exceptional circumstances in which special needs, beyond the normal need for law enforcement, make the warrant and probable-cause requirement impracticable, is a court entitled to substitute its balancing of interests for that of the Framers." 469 U.S. 325, 351 (1985) (Blackmun, J., concurring). Thus, the "special needs" analysis requires the government to assert a reason, other than simply solving or preventing crimes, for conducting a search. The Court then determines the reasonableness of the government action by considering the strength of the privacy interest implicated, the character of the government intrusion, the nature and immediacy of the government's special needs, and the efficacy of the search.

1. ADMINISTRATIVE SEARCHES

CAMARA V. MUNICIPAL COURT OF THE CITY AND COUNTY OF SAN FRANCISCO

387 U.S. 523 (1967)

MR. JUSTICE WHITE delivered the opinion of the court.

* * *

Appellant brought this action in a California Superior Court alleging that he was awaiting trial on a criminal charge of violating the San Francisco Housing Code by refusing to permit a warrantless inspection of his residence, and that a writ of prohibition should issue to the criminal court because the ordinance authorizing such inspections is unconstitutional on its face. The Superior Court denied the writ, the District Court of Appeal affirmed, and the Supreme Court of California denied a petition for hearing. Appellant properly raised and had considered by the California courts the federal constitutional questions he now presents to this Court.

Though there were no judicial findings of fact in this prohibition proceeding, we shall set forth the parties' factual allegations. On November 6, 1963, an inspector of the Division of Housing Inspection of the San Francisco Department of Public Health entered an apartment building to make a routine annual inspection for possible violations of the city's Housing Code. The building's manager informed the inspector that appellant, lessee of the ground floor, was using the rear of his leasehold as a personal residence. Claiming that the building's occupancy permit did not allow residential use of the ground floor, the inspector confronted appellant and demanded that he permit an inspection of the premises. Appellant refused to allow the inspection because the inspector lacked a search warrant.

The inspector returned on November 8, again without a warrant, and appellant again refused to allow an inspection. A citation was then mailed ordering appellant to appear at the district attorney's office. When appellant failed to appear, two inspectors returned to his apartment on November 22. They informed appellant that he was required by law to permit an inspection under § 503 of the Housing Code:

> Sec. 503 RIGHT TO ENTER BUILDING. Authorized employees of the City departments or City agencies, so far as may be

> necessary for the performance of their duties, shall, upon presentation of proper credentials, have the right to enter, at reasonable times, any building, structure, or premises in the City to perform any duty imposed upon them by the Municipal Code.

Appellant nevertheless refused the inspectors access to his apartment without a search warrant. Thereafter, a complaint was filed charging him with refusing to permit a lawful inspection in violation of § 507 of the Code. Appellant was arrested on December 2 and released on bail. When his demurrer to the criminal complaint was denied, appellant filed this petition for a writ of prohibition.

* * *

I

* * *

Though there has been general agreement as to the fundamental purpose of the Fourth Amendment, translation of the abstract prohibition against "unreasonable searches and seizures" into workable guidelines for the decision of particular cases is a difficult task which has for many years divided the members of this Court. Nevertheless, one governing principle, justified by history and by current experience, has consistently been followed: except in certain carefully defined classes of cases, a search of private property without proper consent is "unreasonable" unless it has been authorized by a valid search warrant. . . .

In *Frank v. State of Maryland*, [359 U.S. 360 (1959),] this Court upheld the conviction of one who refused to permit a warrantless inspection of private premises for the purposes of locating and abating a suspected public nuisance. Although *Frank* can arguably be distinguished from this case on its facts, the *Frank* opinion has generally been interpreted as carving out an additional exception to the rule that warrantless searches are unreasonable under the Fourth Amendment. The District Court of Appeal so interpreted *Frank* in this case, and that ruling is the core of appellant's challenge here. We proceed to a re-examination of the factors which persuaded the *Frank* majority to adopt this construction of the Fourth Amendment's prohibition against unreasonable searches.

To the *Frank* majority, municipal fire, health, and housing inspection programs "touch at most upon the periphery of the important interests safeguarded by the Fourteenth Amendment's protection against official intrusion," because the inspections are merely to determine whether physical conditions exist which do not comply with minimum standards prescribed in local regulatory ordinances. Since the inspector does not ask that the property owner open his doors to a search for "evidence of criminal action" which may be used to secure the owner's criminal conviction, historic interests of "self-protection" jointly protected by the Fourth and

Fifth Amendments are said not to be involved, but only the less intense "right to be secure from intrusion into personal privacy."

We may agree that a routine inspection of the physical condition of private property is a less hostile intrusion than the typical policeman's search for the fruits and instrumentalities of crime. For this reason alone, *Frank* differed from the great bulk of Fourth Amendment cases which have been considered by this Court. But we cannot agree that the Fourth Amendment interests at stake in these inspection cases are merely "peripheral." It is surely anomalous to say that the individual and his private property are fully protected by the Fourth Amendment only when the individual is suspected of criminal behavior. For instance, even the most law-abiding citizen has a very tangible interest in limiting the circumstances under which the sanctity of his home may be broken by official authority, for the possibility of criminal entry under the guise of official sanction is a serious threat to personal and family security. And even accepting Frank's rather remarkable premise, inspections of the kind we are here considering do in fact jeopardize "self-protection" interests of the property owner. Like most regulatory laws, fire, health, and housing codes are enforced by criminal processes. In some cities, discovery of a violation by the inspector leads to a criminal complaint. Even in cities where discovery of a violation produces only an administrative compliance order, refusal to comply is a criminal offense, and the fact of compliance is verified by a second inspection, again without a warrant. Finally, as this case demonstrates, refusal to permit an inspection is itself a crime, punishable by fine or even by jail sentence.

The *Frank* majority suggested, and appellee reasserts, two other justifications for permitting administrative health and safety inspections without a warrant. First, it is argued that these inspections are "designed to make the least possible demand on the individual occupant." The ordinances authorizing inspections are hedged with safeguards, and at any rate the inspector's particular decision to enter must comply with the constitutional standard of reasonableness even if he may enter without a warrant. In addition, the argument proceeds, the warrant process could not function effectively in this field. The decision to inspect an entire municipal area is based upon legislative or administrative assessment of broad factors such as the area's age and condition. Unless the magistrate is to review such policy matters, he must issue a "rubber stamp" warrant which provides no protection at all to the property owner.

In our opinion, these arguments unduly discount the purposes behind the warrant machinery contemplated by the Fourth Amendment. Under the present system, when the inspector demands entry, the occupant has no way of knowing whether enforcement of the municipal code involved requires inspection of his premises, no way of knowing the lawful limits of the inspector's power to search, and no way of knowing whether the inspector himself is acting under proper authorization. These are questions which may be reviewed by a neutral magistrate without any reassessment of the basic agency decision to canvass an area. Yet, only by refusing entry and risking a criminal conviction can the occupant at present challenge the inspector's decision to search. And even if the occupant possesses sufficient fortitude to take this risk, as appellant did here, he may never learn any more about the reason for the inspection than that the law generally allows housing inspectors to gain entry. The practical effect of this system is to leave the occupant subject to the discretion of the official in the field. This is precisely the discretion to invade private property which we have consistently circumscribed by a requirement that a disinterested party warrant the need to search. We simply cannot say that the protections provided by the warrant procedure are not needed in this context; broad statutory safeguards are no substitute for individualized review, particularly when those safeguards may only be invoked at the risk of a criminal penalty.

The final justification suggested for warrantless administrative searches is that the public interest demands such a rule: it is vigorously argued that the health and safety of entire urban populations is dependent upon enforcement of minimum fire, housing, and sanitation standards, and that the only effective means of enforcing such codes is by routine systematized inspection of all physical structures. Of course, in applying any reasonableness standard, including one of constitutional dimension, an argument that the public interest demands a particular rule must receive careful consideration. But we think this argument misses the mark. The question is not, at this stage at least, whether these inspections may be made, but whether they may be made without a warrant. For example, to say that gambling raids may not be made at the discretion of the police without a warrant is not necessarily to say that gambling raids may never be made. In assessing whether the public interest demands creation of a general exception to the Fourth Amendment's warrant requirement, the question is not whether the public interest justifies the type of search in question, but whether the authority to search should be evidenced by a warrant, which in turn depends in part upon whether the burden of obtaining a warrant is likely to frustrate the governmental purpose behind the search. It has nowhere been urged that fire, health, and housing code inspection programs could not achieve their goals within the confines of a reasonable search warrant requirement. Thus, we do not find the public need argument dispositive.

In summary, we hold that administrative searches of the kind at issue here are significant intrusions upon the interests protected by the Fourth Amendment, that such searches when authorized and conducted without a warrant procedure lack the traditional safeguards which the Fourth Amendment guarantees to the individual, and that the reasons put forth in *Frank v. State of Maryland* and in other cases for upholding these warrantless searches are insufficient to justify so substantial a weakening of the Fourth Amendment's protections. Because of the nature of the municipal programs under consideration, however, these conclusions must be the beginning, not the end, of our inquiry. The *Frank* majority gave recognition to the unique character of these inspection programs by refusing to require search warrants; to reject that disposition does not justify ignoring the question whether some other accommodation between public need and individual rights is essential.

II

* * *

In cases in which the Fourth Amendment requires that a warrant to search be obtained, "probable cause" is the standard by which a particular decision to search is tested against the constitutional mandate of reasonableness. To apply this standard, it is obviously necessary first to focus upon the governmental interest which allegedly justifies official intrusion upon the constitutionally protected interests of the private citizen. For example, in a criminal investigation, the police may undertake to recover specific stolen or contraband goods. But that public interest would hardly justify a sweeping search of an entire city conducted in the hope that these goods might be found. Consequently, a search for these goods, even with a warrant, is "reasonable" only when there is "probable cause" to believe that they will be uncovered in a particular dwelling.

Unlike the search pursuant to a criminal investigation, the inspection programs at issue here are aimed at securing city-wide compliance with minimum physical standards for private property. The primary governmental interest at stake is to prevent even the unintentional development of conditions which are hazardous to public health and safety. Because fires and epidemics may ravage large urban areas, because unsightly conditions adversely affect the economic values of neighboring structures, numerous courts have upheld the police power of municipalities to impose and enforce such minimum standards even upon existing structures. In determining whether a particular inspection is reasonable—and thus in determining whether there is probable cause to issue a warrant for that inspection—the need for the inspection must be weighed in terms of these reasonable goals of code enforcement.

There is unanimous agreement among those most familiar with this field that the only effective way to seek universal compliance with the minimum standards required by municipal codes is through routine periodic inspections of all structures. It is here that the probable cause debate is focused, for the agency's decision to conduct an area inspection is unavoidably based on its appraisal of conditions in the area as a whole, not on its knowledge of conditions in each particular building. Appellee contends that, if the probable cause standard urged by appellant is adopted, the area inspection will be eliminated as a means of seeking compliance with code standards and the reasonable goals of code enforcement will be dealt a crushing blow.

In meeting this contention, appellant argues first, that his probable cause standard would not jeopardize area inspection programs because only a minute portion of the population will refuse to consent to such inspections, and second, that individual privacy in any event should be given preference to the public interest in conducting such inspections. The first argument, even if true, is irrelevant to the question whether the area inspection is reasonable within the meaning of the Fourth Amendment. The second argument is in effect an assertion that the area inspection is an unreasonable search. Unfortunately, there can be no ready test for determining reasonableness other than by balancing the need to search against the invasion which the search entails. But we think that a number of persuasive factors combine to support the reasonableness of area code-enforcement inspections. First, such programs have a long history of judicial and public acceptance. Second, the public interest demands that all dangerous conditions be prevented or abated, yet it is doubtful that any other canvassing technique would achieve acceptable results. Many such conditions—faulty wiring is an obvious example—are not observable from outside the building and indeed may not be apparent to the inexpert occupant himself. Finally, because the inspections are neither personal in nature nor aimed at the discovery of evidence of crime, they involve a relatively limited invasion of the urban citizen's privacy. . . .

* * *

Having concluded that the area inspection is a "reasonable" search of private property within the meaning of the Fourth Amendment, it is obvious that "probable cause" to issue a warrant to inspect must exist if reasonable legislative or administrative standards for conducting an area inspection are satisfied with respect to a particular dwelling. Such standards, which will vary with the municipal program being enforced, may be based upon the passage of time, the nature of the building (e.g., a multifamily apartment house), or the condition of the entire area, but they will not necessarily depend upon specific knowledge of the condition of the particular dwelling. It has been suggested that so to vary the probable cause test from the standard applied in criminal cases would be to authorize a "synthetic search warrant" and thereby to lessen the overall protections of the Fourth Amendment. But we do not agree. The warrant procedure is designed to guarantee that a decision to search private property is justified by a reasonable governmental interest. But reasonableness is still the ultimate standard. If a valid public interest justifies the intrusion contemplated, then there is probable cause to issue a suitably restricted search warrant. Such an approach neither endangers time-honored doctrines applicable to criminal investigations nor makes a nullity of the probable cause requirement in this area. It merely gives full recognition to the competing public and private interests here at stake and, in so doing, best fulfills the historic purpose behind the constitutional right to be free from unreasonable government invasions of privacy.

III

Since our holding emphasizes the controlling standard of reasonableness, nothing we say today is intended to foreclose prompt inspections, even without a warrant, that the law has traditionally upheld in emergency situations. On the other hand, in the case of most routine area inspections, there is no compelling urgency to inspect at a particular time or on a particular day. Moreover, most citizens allow inspections of their property without a warrant. Thus, as a practical matter and in light of the Fourth Amendment's requirement that a warrant specify the property to be searched, it seems likely that warrants should normally be sought only after entry is refused unless there has been a citizen complaint or there is other satisfactory reason for securing immediate entry. Similarly, the requirement of a warrant procedure does not suggest any change in what seems to be the prevailing local policy, in most situations, of authorizing entry, but not entry by force, to inspect.

* * *

Points for Discussion

1. Can the Court's conclusion in *Camara* be squared with the text of the Fourth Amendment? Did the Court authorize magistrates to issue warrants based on something other than probable cause? Notwithstanding its assertion to the contrary, doesn't the Court here authorize "synthetic" search warrants—warrants in name only?

2. What exactly is required to get an area warrant under *Camara*? What must law enforcement officials demonstrate before a magistrate is entitled to issue such a warrant?

3. The Court writes that "it seems likely that warrants should normally be sought only after entry is refused unless there has been a citizen complaint or there is other satisfactory reason for securing immediate entry." Is a request for consent made a condition precedent for the issuance of an administrative warrant? Should it be?

FERGUSON V. CITY OF CHARLESTON

532 U.S. 67 (2001)

JUSTICE STEVENS delivered the opinion of the court.

In this case, we must decide whether a state hospital's performance of a diagnostic test to obtain evidence of a patient's criminal conduct for law enforcement purposes is an unreasonable search if the patient has not consented to the procedure. More narrowly, the question is whether the interest in using the threat of criminal sanctions to deter pregnant women from using cocaine can justify a departure from the general rule that an official nonconsensual search is unconstitutional if not authorized by a valid warrant.

I

In the fall of 1988, staff members at the public hospital operated in the city of Charleston by the Medical University of South Carolina (MUSC) became concerned about an apparent increase in the use of cocaine by patients who were receiving prenatal treatment.[1] In response to this perceived increase, as of April 1989, MUSC began to order drug screens to be performed on urine samples from maternity patients who were suspected of using cocaine. If a patient tested positive, she was then referred by MUSC staff to the county substance abuse commission for counseling and treatment. However, despite the referrals, the incidence of cocaine use among the patients at MUSC did not appear to change.

Some four months later, Nurse Shirley Brown, the case manager for the MUSC obstetrics department, heard a news broadcast reporting that the police in Greenville, South Carolina, were arresting pregnant users of cocaine on the theory that such use harmed the fetus and was therefore child abuse.[2] Nurse Brown discussed the story with MUSC's general counsel, Joseph C. Good, Jr., who then contacted Charleston Solicitor Charles Condon in order to offer MUSC's cooperation in prosecuting mothers whose children tested positive for drugs at birth.

After receiving Good's letter, Solicitor Condon took the first steps in developing the policy at issue in this case. He organized the initial meetings, decided who would participate, and issued the invitations, in which he described his plan to prosecute women who tested positive for cocaine while pregnant. The task force that Condon formed included representatives of MUSC, the police, the County Substance Abuse Commission and the Department of Social Services. Their deliberations led to MUSC's adoption of a 12-page document entitled "POLICY M-7," dealing with the subject of "Management of Drug Abuse During Pregnancy."

The first three pages of Policy M-7 set forth the procedure to be followed by the hospital staff to "identify/assist pregnant patients suspected of drug abuse." The first section, entitled the "Identification of Drug Abusers," provided that a patient should be tested for cocaine through

---

1 As several witnesses testified at trial, the problem of "crack babies" was widely perceived in the late 1980's as a national epidemic, prompting considerable concern both in the medical community and among the general populace.

2 Under South Carolina law, a viable fetus has historically been regarded as a person; in 1995, the South Carolina Supreme Court held that the ingestion of cocaine during the third trimester of pregnancy constitutes criminal child neglect. *Whitner v. South Carolina,* 328 S.C. 1, 492 S.E.2d 777 (1997), cert. denied, 523 U.S. 1145 (1998).

a urine drug screen if she met one or more of nine criteria.[4] It also stated that a chain of custody should be followed when obtaining and testing urine samples, presumably to make sure that the results could be used in subsequent criminal proceedings. The policy also provided for education and referral to a substance abuse clinic for patients who tested positive. Most important, it added the threat of law enforcement intervention that "provided the necessary 'leverage' to make the [p]olicy effective." That threat was, as respondents candidly acknowledge, essential to the program's success in getting women into treatment and keeping them there.

The threat of law enforcement involvement was set forth in two protocols, the first dealing with the identification of drug use during pregnancy, and the second with identification of drug use after labor. Under the latter protocol, the police were to be notified without delay and the patient promptly arrested. Under the former, after the initial positive drug test, the police were to be notified (and the patient arrested) only if the patient tested positive for cocaine a second time or if she missed an appointment with a substance abuse counselor. In 1990, however, the policy was modified at the behest of the solicitor's office to give the patient who tested positive during labor, like the patient who tested positive during a prenatal care visit, an opportunity to avoid arrest by consenting to substance abuse treatment.

The last six pages of the policy contained forms for the patients to sign, as well as procedures for the police to follow when a patient was arrested. The policy also prescribed in detail the precise offenses with which a woman could be charged, depending on the stage of her pregnancy. If the pregnancy was 27 weeks or less, the patient was to be charged with simple possession. If it was 28 weeks or more, she was to be charged with possession and distribution to a person under the age of 18—in this case, the fetus. If she delivered "while testing positive for illegal drugs," she was also to be charged with unlawful neglect of a child. Under the policy, the police were instructed to interrogate the arrestee in order "to ascertain the identity of the subject who provided illegal drugs to the suspect." Other than the provisions describing the substance abuse treatment to be offered to women who tested positive, the policy made no mention of any change in

---

[4] Those criteria were as follows:

1. No prenatal care
2. Late prenatal care after 24 weeks gestation
3. Incomplete prenatal care
4. Abruptio placentae
5. Intrauterine fetal death
6. Preterm labor 'of no obvious cause'
7. IUGR [intrauterine growth retardation] 'of no obvious cause'
8. Previously known drug or alcohol abuse
9. Unexplained congenital anomalies.

the prenatal care of such patients, nor did it prescribe any special treatment for the newborns.

II

Petitioners are 10 women who received obstetrical care at MUSC and who were arrested after testing positive for cocaine. Four of them were arrested during the initial implementation of the policy; they were not offered the opportunity to receive drug treatment as an alternative to arrest. The others were arrested after the policy was modified in 1990; they either failed to comply with the terms of the drug treatment program or tested positive for a second time. Respondents include the city of Charleston, law enforcement officials who helped develop and enforce the policy, and representatives of MUSC.

* * *

III

Because MUSC is a state hospital, the members of its staff are government actors, subject to the strictures of the Fourth Amendment. *New Jersey v. T.L.O.,* 469 U.S. 325, 335–337 (1985). Moreover, the urine tests conducted by those staff members were indisputably searches within the meaning of the Fourth Amendment. Neither the District Court nor the Court of Appeals concluded that any of the nine criteria used to identify the women to be searched provided either probable cause to believe that they were using cocaine, or even the basis for a reasonable suspicion of such use. Rather, the District Court and the Court of Appeals viewed the case as one involving MUSC's right to conduct searches without warrants or probable cause. Furthermore, given the posture in which the case comes to us, we must assume for purposes of our decision that the tests were performed without the informed consent of the patients.[11]

* * *

In looking to the programmatic purpose, we consider all the available evidence in order to determine the relevant primary purpose. In this case, as Judge Blake put it in her dissent below, "it . . . is clear from the record that an initial and continuing focus of the policy was on the arrest and prosecution of drug-abusing mothers. . . ." Tellingly, the document codifying the policy incorporates the police's operational guidelines. It devotes its attention to the chain of custody, the range of possible criminal charges, and the logistics of police notification and arrests. Nowhere, however, does the document discuss different courses of medical treatment for either mother or infant, aside from treatment for the mother's addiction.

[11] The dissent would have us do otherwise and resolve the issue of consent in favor of respondents. Because the Court of Appeals did not discuss this issue, we think it more prudent to allow that court to resolve the legal and factual issues in the first instance, and we express no view on those issues.

Moreover, throughout the development and application of the policy, the Charleston prosecutors and police were extensively involved in the day-to-day administration of the policy. Police and prosecutors decided who would receive the reports of positive drug screens and what information would be included with those reports. Law enforcement officials also helped determine the procedures to be followed when performing the screens. In the course of the policy's administration, they had access to Nurse Brown's medical files on the women who tested positive, routinely attended the substance abuse team's meetings, and regularly received copies of team documents discussing the women's progress. Police took pains to coordinate the timing and circumstances of the arrests with MUSC staff, and, in particular, Nurse Brown.

While the ultimate goal of the program may well have been to get the women in question into substance abuse treatment and off of drugs, the immediate objective of the searches was to generate evidence *for law enforcement purposes* in order to reach that goal. The threat of law enforcement may ultimately have been intended as a means to an end, but the direct and primary purpose of MUSC's policy was to ensure the use of those means. In our opinion, this distinction is critical. Because law enforcement involvement always serves some broader social purpose or objective, under respondents' view, virtually any nonconsensual suspicionless search could be immunized under the special needs doctrine by defining the search solely in terms of its ultimate, rather than immediate, purpose. Such an approach is inconsistent with the Fourth Amendment. Given the primary purpose of the Charleston program, which was to use the threat of arrest and prosecution in order to force women into treatment, and given the extensive involvement of law enforcement officials at every stage of the policy, this case simply does not fit within the closely guarded category of "special needs."

The fact that positive test results were turned over to the police does not merely provide a basis for distinguishing our prior cases applying the "special needs" balancing approach to the determination of drug use. It also provides an affirmative reason for enforcing the strictures of the Fourth Amendment. While state hospital employees, like other citizens, may have a duty to provide the police with evidence of criminal conduct that they inadvertently acquire in the course of routine treatment, when they undertake to obtain such evidence from their patients *for the specific purpose of incriminating those patients,* they have a special obligation to make sure that the patients are fully informed about their constitutional rights, as standards of knowing waiver require.

As respondents have repeatedly insisted, their motive was benign rather than punitive. Such a motive, however, cannot justify a departure from Fourth Amendment protections, given the pervasive involvement of law enforcement with the development and application of the MUSC policy.

The stark and unique fact that characterizes this case is that Policy M-7 was designed to obtain evidence of criminal conduct by the tested patients that would be turned over to the police and that could be admissible in subsequent criminal prosecutions. While respondents are correct that drug abuse both was and is a serious problem, "the gravity of the threat alone cannot be dispositive of questions concerning what means law enforcement officers may employ to pursue a given purpose." The Fourth Amendment's general prohibition against nonconsensual, warrantless, and suspicionless searches necessarily applies to such a policy.

JUSTICE KENNEDY, concurring in the judgment.

I agree that the search procedure in issue cannot be sustained under the Fourth Amendment. My reasons for this conclusion differ somewhat from those set forth by the Court, however, leading to this separate opinion.

I

The Court does not dispute that the search policy at some level serves special needs, beyond those of ordinary law enforcement, such as the need to protect the health of mother and child when a pregnant mother uses cocaine. Instead, the majority characterizes these special needs as the "ultimate goal[s]" of the policy, as distinguished from the policy's "immediate purpose," the collection of evidence of drug use, which, the Court reasons, is the appropriate inquiry for the special needs analysis.

The majority views its distinction between the ultimate goal and immediate purpose of the policy as critical to its analysis. The distinction the Court makes, however, lacks foundation in our special needs cases. All of our special needs cases have turned upon what the majority terms the policy's ultimate goal. For example, in *Skinner v. Railway Labor Executives' Assn.,* 489 U.S. 602 (1989), had we employed the majority's distinction, we would have identified as the relevant need the collection of evidence of drug and alcohol use by railway employees. Instead, we identified the relevant need as "[t]he Government's interest in regulating the conduct of railroad employees to ensure [railroad] safety." In *Treasury Employees v. Von Raab,* 489 U.S. 656 (1989), the majority's distinction should have compelled us to isolate the relevant need as the gathering of evidence of drug abuse by would-be drug interdiction officers. Instead, the special needs the Court identified were the necessities "to deter drug use among those eligible for promotion to sensitive positions within the [United States Customs] Service and to prevent the promotion of drug users to those positions." In *Vernonia School Dist. 47J v. Acton,* 515 U.S. 646 (1995), the majority's distinction would have required us to identify the immediate purpose of gathering evidence of drug use by student-athletes as the relevant "need" for purposes of the special needs analysis. Instead, we sustained the policy as furthering what today's majority would have termed the policy's ultimate goal: "[d]eterring drug use by our Nation's schoolchildren," and particularly by student-athletes, because "the risk of immediate physical harm to the drug user or those with whom he is playing his sport is particularly high."

It is unsurprising that in our prior cases we have concentrated on what the majority terms a policy's ultimate goal, rather than its proximate purpose. By very definition, in almost every case the immediate purpose of a search policy will be to obtain evidence. The circumstance that a particular search, like all searches, is designed to collect evidence of some sort reveals nothing about the need it serves. Put a different way, although procuring evidence is the immediate result of a successful search, until today that procurement has not been identified as the special need which justifies the search.

II

While the majority's reasoning seems incorrect in the respects just discussed, I agree with the Court that the search policy cannot be sustained. As the majority demonstrates and well explains, there was substantial law enforcement involvement in the policy from its inception. None of our special needs precedents has sanctioned the routine inclusion of law enforcement, both in the design of the policy and in using arrests, either threatened or real, to implement the system designed for the special needs objectives. The special needs cases we have decided do not sustain the active use of law enforcement, including arrest and prosecutions, as an integral part of a program which seeks to achieve legitimate, civil objectives. The traditional warrant and probable-cause requirements are waived in our previous cases on the explicit assumption that the evidence obtained in the search is not intended to be used for law enforcement purposes. Most of those tested for drug use under the policy at issue here were not brought into direct contact with law enforcement. This does not change the fact, however, that, as a systemic matter, law enforcement was a part of the implementation of the search policy in each of its applications. Every individual who tested positive was given a letter explaining the policy not from the hospital but from the solicitor's office. Everyone who tested positive was told a second positive test or failure to undergo substance abuse treatment would result in arrest and prosecution. As the Court holds, the hospital acted, in some respects, as an institutional arm of law enforcement for purposes of the policy. Under these circumstances, while the policy may well have served legitimate needs unrelated to law enforcement, it had as well a penal character with a far greater connection to law enforcement than other searches sustained under our special needs rationale.

* * *

III

An essential, distinguishing feature of the special needs cases is that the person searched has consented, though the usual voluntariness analysis is altered because adverse consequences (*e.g.,* dismissal from employment or disqualification from playing on a high school sports team) will follow from refusal. The person searched has given consent, as defined to take into account that the consent was not voluntary in the full sense of the word. The consent, and the circumstances in which it was given, bear upon the reasonableness of the whole special needs program.

Here, on the other hand, the question of consent, even with the special connotation used in the special needs cases, has yet to be decided. Indeed, the Court finds it necessary to take the unreal step of assuming there was no voluntary consent at all. Thus, we have erected a strange world for deciding the case.

My discussion has endeavored to address the permissibility of a law enforcement purpose in this artificial context. The role played by consent might have affected our assessment of the issues. My concurrence in the judgment, furthermore, should not be interpreted as having considered or resolved the important questions raised by Justice Scalia with reference to whether limits might be imposed on the use of the evidence if in fact it were obtained with the patient's consent and in the context of the special needs program. Had we the prerogative to discuss the role played by consent, the case might have been quite a different one. All are in agreement, of course, that the Court of Appeals will address these issues in further proceedings on remand.

JUSTICE SCALIA, with whom THE CHIEF JUSTICE and JUSTICE THOMAS join as to Part II, dissenting.

There is always an unappealing aspect to the use of doctors and nurses, ministers of mercy, to obtain incriminating evidence against the supposed objects of their ministration—although here, it is correctly pointed out, the doctors and nurses were ministering not just to the mothers but also to the children whom their cooperation with the police was meant to protect. But whatever may be the correct social judgment concerning the desirability of what occurred here, that is not the issue in the present case. The Constitution does not resolve all difficult social questions, but leaves the vast majority of them to resolution by debate and the democratic process—which would produce a decision by the citizens of Charleston, through their elected representatives, to forbid or permit the police action at issue here. The question before us is a narrower one: whether, whatever the desirability of this police conduct, it violates the Fourth Amendment's prohibition of unreasonable searches and seizures. In my view, it plainly does not.

I

The first step in Fourth Amendment analysis is to identify the search or seizure at issue. What petitioners, the Court, and to a lesser extent the concurrence really object to is not the urine testing, but the hospital's reporting of positive drug-test results to police. But the latter is obviously not a search. At most it may be a "derivative use of the product of a past unlawful search," which, of course, "works no new Fourth Amendment wrong" and "presents a question, not of rights, but of remedies." There is only one act that could conceivably be regarded as a search of petitioners in the present case: the *taking* of the urine sample. I suppose the *testing* of that urine for traces of unlawful drugs could be considered a search of sorts, but the Fourth Amendment protects only against searches of citizens' "persons, houses, papers, and effects"; and it is entirely unrealistic to regard urine as one of the "effects" (*i.e.,* part of the property) of the person who has passed and abandoned it. Cf. *California v. Greenwood,* 486 U.S. 35 (1988) (garbage left at curb is not property protected by the Fourth Amendment). Some would argue, I suppose, that testing of the urine is prohibited by some generalized privacy right "emanating" from the "penumbras" of the Constitution (a question that is not before us); but it is not even arguable that the testing of urine that has been lawfully obtained is a Fourth Amendment search. (I may add that, even if it were, the factors legitimizing the taking of the sample, which I discuss below, would likewise legitimize the testing of it.)

It is rudimentary Fourth Amendment law that a search which has been consented to is not unreasonable. There is no contention in the present case that the urine samples were extracted forcibly. The only conceivable bases for saying that they were obtained without consent are the contentions (1) that the consent was coerced by the patients' need for medical treatment, (2) that the consent was uninformed because the patients were not told that the tests would include testing for drugs, and (3) that the consent was uninformed because the patients were not told that the results of the tests would be provided to the police.[1] (When the court below said that it was reserving the factual issue of consent, it was referring at most to these three—and perhaps just to the last two.)

* * *

Until today, we have *never* held—or even suggested—that material which a person voluntarily entrusts to someone else cannot be given by that person to the police, and used for whatever evidence it may contain. Without so much as discussing the point, the Court today opens a hole in our Fourth Amendment jurisprudence, the size and shape of which is entirely indeterminate. Today's holding would be remarkable enough if the confidential relationship violated by the police conduct were at least one

---

[1] The Court asserts that it is improper to "disaggregate the taking and testing of the urine sample from the reporting of the results to the police," because "in our special needs cases, we have routinely treated urine screens taken by state agents as searches within the meaning of the Fourth Amendment." But in all of those cases, the urine was obtained involuntarily. Where the taking of the urine sample is unconsented (and thus a Fourth Amendment search), the subsequent testing and reporting of the results to the police are obviously part of (or infected by) the same search; but where, as here, the taking of the sample was not a Fourth Amendment search, it is necessary to consider separately whether the testing and reporting were.

protected by state law. It would be surprising to learn, for example, that in a State which recognizes a spousal evidentiary privilege the police cannot use evidence obtained from a cooperating husband or wife. But today's holding goes even beyond that, since there does not exist any physician-patient privilege in South Carolina. Since the Court declines even to discuss the issue, it leaves law enforcement officials entirely in the dark as to when they can use incriminating evidence obtained from "trusted" sources. Presumably the lines will be drawn in the case-by-case development of a whole new branch of Fourth Amendment jurisprudence, taking yet another social judgment (which confidential relationships ought not be invaded by the police) out of democratic control, and confiding it to the uncontrolled judgment of this Court—uncontrolled because there is no common-law precedent to guide it. I would adhere to our established law, which says that information obtained through violation of a relationship of trust is obtained consensually, and is hence not a search.

There remains to be considered the first possible basis for invalidating this search, which is that the patients were coerced to produce their urine samples by their necessitous circumstances, to wit, their need for medical treatment of their pregnancy. If that was coercion, it was not coercion applied by the government—and if such nongovernmental coercion sufficed, the police would never be permitted to use the ballistic evidence obtained from treatment of a patient with a bullet wound. And the Fourth Amendment would invalidate those many state laws that require physicians to report gunshot wounds, evidence of spousal abuse, and (like the South Carolina law relevant here) evidence of child abuse.

II

I think it clear, therefore, that there is no basis for saying that obtaining of the urine sample was unconstitutional. The special-needs doctrine is thus quite irrelevant, since it operates only to validate searches and seizures that are otherwise unlawful. In the ensuing discussion, however, I shall assume (contrary to legal precedent) that the taking of the urine sample was (either because of the patients' necessitous circumstances, or because of failure to disclose that the urine would be tested for drugs, or because of failure to disclose that the results of the test would be given to the police) coerced. Indeed, I shall even assume (contrary to common sense) that the testing of the urine constituted an unconsented search of the patients' effects. On those assumptions, the special-needs doctrine *would* become relevant; and, properly applied, would validate what was done here.

* * *

The cocaine tests started in April 1989, *neither at police suggestion nor with police involvement*. Expectant mothers who tested positive were referred by hospital staff for substance-abuse treatment—an obvious health benefit to both mother and child. And, since "[i]nfants whose mothers abuse cocaine during pregnancy are born with a wide variety of physical and neurological abnormalities," which require medical attention, the tests were of additional medical benefit in predicting needed postnatal treatment for the child. Thus, in their origin—before the police were in any way involved—the tests had an immediate, not merely an "ultimate," purpose of improving maternal and infant health. Several months after the testing had been initiated, a nurse discovered that local police were arresting pregnant users of cocaine for child abuse, the hospital's general counsel wrote the county solicitor to ask "what, if anything, our Medical Center needs to do to assist you in this matter," the police suggested ways to avoid tainting evidence, and the hospital and police in conjunction used the testing program as a means of securing what the Court calls the "ultimate" health benefit of coercing drug-abusing mothers into drug treatment. Why would there be any reason to believe that, once this policy of using the drug tests for their "ultimate" health benefits had been adopted, use of them for their original, *immediate,* benefits somehow disappeared, and testing somehow became in its entirety nothing more than a "pretext" for obtaining grounds for arrest? On the face of it, this is incredible. The only evidence of the exclusively arrest-related purpose of the testing adduced by the Court is that the police-cooperation policy *itself* does not describe how to care for cocaine-exposed infants. But *of course* it does not, since that policy, adopted months after the cocaine testing was initiated, had as its only health object the "ultimate" goal of inducing drug treatment through threat of arrest. Does the Court really believe (or even *hope*) that, once invalidation of the program challenged here has been decreed, drug testing will cease?

In sum, there can be no basis for the Court's purported ability to "distinguis[h] this case from circumstances in which physicians or psychologists, in the course of ordinary medical procedures aimed at helping the patient herself, come across information that . . . is subject to reporting requirements," unless it is this: That the *addition* of a law-enforcement-related purpose *to* a legitimate medical purpose destroys applicability of the "special-needs" doctrine. But that is quite impossible, since the special-needs doctrine was developed, and is ordinarily employed, precisely to enable searches *by law enforcement officials* who, of course, ordinarily have a law enforcement objective. Thus, in *Griffin v. Wisconsin,* 483 U.S. 868 (1987), a probation officer received a tip from a detective that petitioner, a felon on probation, possessed a firearm. Accompanied by police, he conducted a warrantless search of petitioner's home. The weapon was found and used as evidence in the probationer's trial for unlawful possession of a firearm. Affirming denial of a motion to suppress, we concluded that the "special need" of assuring compliance with terms of release justified a warrantless search of petitioner's home. Notably, we observed that a probation officer is not

> the police officer who normally conducts searches against the ordinary citizen. He is an employee of the State Department of Health and Social Services who, while assuredly charged with protecting the public interest, is also supposed to have in mind the welfare of the probationer.... In such a setting, we think it reasonable to dispense with the warrant requirement.

Like the probation officer, the doctors here do not "ordinarily conduc[t] searches against the ordinary citizen," and they are "supposed to have in mind the welfare of the [mother and child]." That they have in mind in addition the provision of evidence to the police should make no difference. The Court suggests that if police involvement in this case was in some way incidental and after-the-fact, that would make a difference in the outcome. But in *Griffin,* even more than here, police were involved in the search from the very beginning; indeed, the initial tip about the gun came from a detective. Under the factors relied upon by the Court, the use of evidence approved in *Griffin* would have been permitted only if the parole officer had been untrained in chain-of-custody procedures, had not known of the possibility a gun was present, and had been unaccompanied by police when he simply happened upon the weapon. Why any or all of these is constitutionally significant is baffling.

* * *

The concurrence makes essentially the same basic error as the Court, though it puts the point somewhat differently: "The special needs cases we have decided," it says, "do not sustain the active use of law enforcement . . . as an integral part of a program which seeks to achieve legitimate, civil objectives." *Griffin* shows that is not true. Indeed, *Griffin* shows that there is not even any truth in the more limited proposition that our cases do not support application of the special-needs exception where the "legitimate, civil objectives" are sought only *through* the use of law enforcement means. (Surely the parole officer in *Griffin* was using threat of reincarceration to assure compliance with parole.) But even if this latter proposition *were* true, it would invalidate what occurred here only if the drug testing sought exclusively the "ultimate" health benefits achieved by coercing the mothers into drug treatment through threat of prosecution. But in fact the drug testing sought, independently of law enforcement involvement, the "immediate" health benefits of identifying drug-impaired mother and child for necessary medical treatment. The concurrence concedes that if the testing is conducted for medical reasons, the fact that "prosecuting authorities *then* adopt legitimate procedures to discover this information and prosecution follows . . . ought not to invalidate the testing." But here the police involvement in each case did *take place after* the testing was conducted for independent reasons. Surely the concurrence cannot mean that no police-suggested procedures (such as preserving the chain of custody of the urine sample) can be applied until *after* the testing; or that the police-suggested procedures must have been *designed* after the testing. The facts in *Griffin* (and common sense) show that this cannot be so. It seems to me that the only real distinction between what the concurrence must reasonably be thought to be approving, and what we have here, is that here the police took the lesser step of initially *threatening* prosecution rather than bringing it.

* * *

Points for Discussion

1. Is the Court's attempt to distinguish *Skinner*, *Vernonia*, and *Von Raab* persuasive? Was the hospital's testing policy created because of special needs or the normal needs of law enforcement? Does the involvement of the police or the possibility of criminal prosecution necessarily make this case something other than a "special needs" search?

2. What do you make of the concurrence's argument that this case is principally one about consent? Was the consent in this case voluntarily given? Also, is Justice Kennedy's assertion that the special needs cases are mostly about consent an accurate description of the Court's reasoning in those cases?

3. Although the issue did not explicitly figure into the Supreme Court's decision, the petitioners argued in their brief that the program disproportionately targeted African-Americans, noting that "of the thirty women arrested under the Policy, twenty-nine were African-American." The brief further stated: "The record demonstrates that Nurse Brown, who helped establish the Search Policy and was integral to its everyday implementation, held racist views. Nurse Brown admitted at trial that she believed that interracial relationships were 'against God's way' and noted in the charts of pregnant white women if their partners were black. She also raised the option of sterilization for black women testing positive for cocaine, but not for white women." The Court has held in cases such as *Whren v. United States*, 517 U.S. 806 (1996), that a police officer's subjective reasons for conducting a search are irrelevant; what matters is whether probable cause existed as an objective matter. In the "special needs" context, however, probable cause is by definition absent. Should Nurse Brown's subjective intentions have been considered in determining whether the drug-testing program was reasonable?

FLORENCE V. BOARD OF CHOSEN FREEHOLDERS OF BURLINGTON COUNTY

566 U.S. 318 (2012)

JUSTICE KENNEDY delivered the opinion of the court, except as to Part IV.[1]

Correctional officials have a legitimate interest, indeed a responsibility, to ensure that jails are not made less secure by reason of

[1] Justice Thomas joins all but Part IV of this opinion.

what new detainees may carry in on their bodies. Facility personnel, other inmates, and the new detainee himself or herself may be in danger if these threats are introduced into the jail population. This case presents the question of what rules, or limitations, the Constitution imposes on searches of arrested persons who are to be held in jail while their cases are being processed. The term "jail" is used here in a broad sense to include prisons and other detention facilities. The specific measures being challenged will be described in more detail; but, in broad terms, the controversy concerns whether every detainee who will be admitted to the general population may be required to undergo a close visual inspection while undressed.

The case turns in part on the extent to which this Court has sufficient expertise and information in the record to mandate, under the Constitution, the specific restrictions and limitations sought by those who challenge the visual search procedures at issue. In addressing this type of constitutional claim courts must defer to the judgment of correctional officials unless the record contains substantial evidence showing their policies are an unnecessary or unjustified response to problems of jail security. That necessary showing has not been made in this case.

I

In 1998, seven years before the incidents at issue, petitioner Albert Florence was arrested after fleeing from police officers in Essex County, New Jersey. He was charged with obstruction of justice and use of a deadly weapon. Petitioner entered a plea of guilty to two lesser offenses and was sentenced to pay a fine in monthly installments. In 2003, after he fell behind on his payments and failed to appear at an enforcement hearing, a bench warrant was issued for his arrest. He paid the outstanding balance less than a week later; but, for some unexplained reason, the warrant remained in a statewide computer database.

Two years later, in Burlington County, New Jersey, petitioner and his wife were stopped in their automobile by a state trooper. Based on the outstanding warrant in the computer system, the officer arrested petitioner and took him to the Burlington County Detention Center. He was held there for six days and then was transferred to the Essex County Correctional Facility. It is not the arrest or confinement but the search process at each jail that gives rise to the claims before the Court.

Burlington County jail procedures required every arrestee to shower with a delousing agent. Officers would check arrestees for scars, marks, gang tattoos, and contraband as they disrobed. Petitioner claims he was also instructed to open his mouth, lift his tongue, hold out his arms, turn around, and lift his genitals. (It is not clear whether this last step was part of the normal practice.) Petitioner shared a cell with at least one other person and interacted with other inmates following his admission to the jail.

The Essex County Correctional Facility, where petitioner was taken after six days, is the largest county jail in New Jersey. It admits more than 25,000 inmates each year and houses about 1,000 gang members at any given time. When petitioner was transferred there, all arriving detainees passed through a metal detector and waited in a group holding cell for a more thorough search. When they left the holding cell, they were instructed to remove their clothing while an officer looked for body markings, wounds, and contraband. Apparently without touching the detainees, an officer looked at their ears, nose, mouth, hair, scalp, fingers, hands, arms, armpits, and other body openings. This policy applied regardless of the circumstances of the arrest, the suspected offense, or the detainee's behavior, demeanor, or criminal history. Petitioner alleges he was required to lift his genitals, turn around, and cough in a squatting position as part of the process. After a mandatory shower, during which his clothes were inspected, petitioner was admitted to the facility. He was released the next day, when the charges against him were dismissed.

* * *

The Federal Courts of Appeals have come to differing conclusions as to whether the Fourth Amendment requires correctional officials to exempt some detainees who will be admitted to a jail's general population from the searches here at issue. This Court granted certiorari to address the question.

II

The difficulties of operating a detention center must not be underestimated by the courts. Jails (in the stricter sense of the term, excluding prison facilities) admit more than 13 million inmates a year. The largest facilities process hundreds of people every day; smaller jails may be crowded on weekend nights, after a large police operation, or because of detainees arriving from other jurisdictions. Maintaining safety and order at these institutions requires the expertise of correctional officials, who must have substantial discretion to devise reasonable solutions to the problems they face. The Court has confirmed the importance of deference to correctional officials and explained that a regulation impinging on an inmate's constitutional rights must be upheld "if it is reasonably related to legitimate penological interests."

* * *

In many jails officials seek to improve security by requiring some kind of strip search of everyone who is to be detained. These procedures have been used in different places throughout the country, from Cranston, Rhode Island, to Sapulpa, Oklahoma, to Idaho Falls, Idaho.

Persons arrested for minor offenses may be among the detainees processed at these facilities. This is, in part, a consequence of the exercise of state authority that was the subject of *Atwater v. Lago Vista,* 532 U.S.

318 (2001). *Atwater* addressed the perhaps more fundamental question of who may be deprived of liberty and taken to jail in the first place. The case involved a woman who was arrested after a police officer noticed neither she nor her children were wearing their seatbelts. The arrestee argued the Fourth Amendment prohibited her custodial arrest without a warrant when an offense could not result in jail time and there was no compelling need for immediate detention. The Court held that a Fourth Amendment restriction on this power would put officers in an "almost impossible spot." Their ability to arrest a suspect would depend in some cases on the precise weight of drugs in his pocket, whether he was a repeat offender, and the scope of what counted as a compelling need to detain someone. The Court rejected the proposition that the Fourth Amendment barred custodial arrests in a set of these cases as a matter of constitutional law. It ruled, based on established principles, that officers may make an arrest based upon probable cause to believe the person has committed a criminal offense in their presence. The Court stated that "a responsible Fourth Amendment balance is not well served by standards requiring sensitive, case-by-case determinations of government need, lest every discretionary judgment in the field be converted into an occasion for constitutional review."

Atwater did not address whether the Constitution imposes special restrictions on the searches of offenders suspected of committing minor offenses once they are taken to jail. Some Federal Courts of Appeals have held that corrections officials may not conduct a strip search of these detainees, even if no touching is involved, absent reasonable suspicion of concealed contraband. The Courts of Appeals to address this issue in the last decade, however, have come to the opposite conclusion.

III

The question here is whether undoubted security imperatives involved in jail supervision override the assertion that some detainees must be exempt from the more invasive search procedures at issue absent reasonable suspicion of a concealed weapon or other contraband. The Court has held that deference must be given to the officials in charge of the jail unless there is "substantial evidence" demonstrating their response to the situation is exaggerated. Petitioner has not met this standard, and the record provides full justifications for the procedures used.

A

Correctional officials have a significant interest in conducting a thorough search as a standard part of the intake process. The admission of inmates creates numerous risks for facility staff, for the existing detainee population, and for a new detainee himself or herself. The danger of introducing lice or contagious infections, for example, is well documented. The Federal Bureau of Prisons recommends that staff screen new detainees for these conditions. Persons just arrested may have wounds or other injuries requiring immediate medical attention. It may be difficult to identify and treat these problems until detainees remove their clothes for a visual inspection.

Jails and prisons also face grave threats posed by the increasing number of gang members who go through the intake process. . . .

Detecting contraband concealed by new detainees, furthermore, is a most serious responsibility. Weapons, drugs, and alcohol all disrupt the safe operation of a jail. Correctional officers have had to confront arrestees concealing knives, scissors, razor blades, glass shards, and other prohibited items on their person, including in their body cavities. They have also found crack, heroin, and marijuana. The use of drugs can embolden inmates in aggression toward officers or each other; and, even apart from their use, the trade in these substances can lead to violent confrontations.

* * *

Something as simple as an overlooked pen can pose a significant danger. Inmates commit more than 10,000 assaults on correctional staff every year and many more among themselves.

* * *

It is not surprising that correctional officials have sought to perform thorough searches at intake for disease, gang affiliation, and contraband. Jails are often crowded, unsanitary, and dangerous places. There is a substantial interest in preventing any new inmate, either of his own will or as a result of coercion, from putting all who live or work at these institutions at even greater risk when he is admitted to the general population.

B

* * *

1

People detained for minor offenses can turn out to be the most devious and dangerous criminals. Hours after the Oklahoma City bombing, Timothy McVeigh was stopped by a state trooper who noticed he was driving without a license plate. Police stopped serial killer Joel Rifkin for the same reason. One of the terrorists involved in the September 11 attacks was stopped and ticketed for speeding just two days before hijacking Flight 93. Reasonable correctional officials could conclude these uncertainties mean they must conduct the same thorough search of everyone who will be admitted to their facilities.

Experience shows that people arrested for minor offenses have tried to smuggle prohibited items into jail, sometimes by using their rectal cavities or genitals for the concealment. They may have some of the same incentives as a serious criminal to hide contraband. A detainee might risk carrying cash, cigarettes, or a penknife to survive in jail. Others may make a quick decision to hide unlawful substances to avoid getting in more trouble at the time of their arrest. This record has concrete examples. Officers at the Atlantic County Correctional Facility, for example, discovered that a man arrested for driving under the influence had "2 dime bags of weed, 1 pack of rolling papers, 20 matches, and 5 sleeping pills" taped under his scrotum. A person booked on a misdemeanor charge of disorderly conduct in Washington State managed to hide a lighter, tobacco, tattoo needles, and other prohibited items in his rectal cavity. San Francisco officials have discovered contraband hidden in body cavities of people arrested for trespassing, public nuisance, and shoplifting. There have been similar incidents at jails throughout the country.

Even if people arrested for a minor offense do not themselves wish to introduce contraband into a jail, they may be coerced into doing so by others. This could happen any time detainees are held in the same area, including in a van on the way to the station or in the holding cell of the jail. If, for example, a person arrested and detained for unpaid traffic citations is not subject to the same search as others, this will be well known to other detainees with jail experience. A hardened criminal or gang member can, in just a few minutes, approach the person and coerce him into hiding the fruits of a crime, a weapon, or some other contraband. As an expert in this case explained, "the interaction and mingling between misdemeanants and felons will only increase the amount of contraband in the facility if the jail can only conduct admission searches on felons." Exempting people arrested for minor offenses from a standard search protocol thus may put them at greater risk and result in more contraband being brought into the detention facility. This is a substantial reason not to mandate the exception petitioner seeks as a matter of constitutional law.

2

* * *

The laborious administration of prisons would become less effective, and likely less fair and evenhanded, were the practical problems inevitable from the rules suggested by petitioner to be imposed as a constitutional mandate. Even if they had accurate information about a detainee's current and prior arrests, officers, under petitioner's proposed regime, would encounter serious implementation difficulties. They would be required, in a few minutes, to determine whether any of the underlying offenses were serious enough to authorize the more invasive search protocol. Other possible classifications based on characteristics of individual detainees also might prove to be unworkable or even give rise to charges of discriminatory application. Most officers would not be well equipped to make any of these legal determinations during the pressures of the intake process. To avoid liability, officers might be inclined not to conduct a thorough search in any close case, thus creating unnecessary risk for the entire jail population.

The Court addressed an analogous problem in *Atwater*. The petitioner in that case argued the Fourth Amendment prohibited a warrantless arrest when being convicted of the suspected crime "could not ultimately carry any jail time" and there was "no compelling need for immediate detention." That rule "promise[d] very little in the way of administrability." Officers could not be expected to draw the proposed lines on a moment's notice, and the risk of violating the Constitution would have discouraged them from arresting criminals in any questionable circumstances. The Fourth Amendment did not compel this result in *Atwater*. The Court held that officers who have probable cause to believe even a minor criminal offense has been committed in their presence may arrest the offender. Individual jurisdictions can of course choose "to impose more restrictive safeguards through statutes limiting warrantless arrests for minor offenders."

One of the central principles in *Atwater* applies with equal force here. Officers who interact with those suspected of violating the law have an "essential interest in readily administrable rules." The officials in charge of the jails in this case urge the Court to reject any complicated constitutional scheme requiring them to conduct less thorough inspections of some detainees based on their behavior, suspected offense, criminal history, and other factors. They offer significant reasons why the Constitution must not prevent them from conducting the same search on any suspected offender who will be admitted to the general population in their facilities. The restrictions suggested by petitioner would limit the intrusion on the privacy of some detainees but at the risk of increased danger to everyone in the facility, including the less serious offenders themselves.

IV

This case does not require the Court to rule on the types of searches that would be reasonable in instances where, for example, a detainee will be held without assignment to the general jail population and without substantial contact with other detainees. This describes the circumstances in *Atwater*. The accommodations provided in these situations may diminish the need to conduct some aspects of the searches at issue. The circumstances before the Court, however, do not present the opportunity to consider a narrow exception of the sort Justice Alito describes, which might restrict whether an arrestee whose detention has not yet been reviewed by a magistrate or other judicial officer, and who can be held in available facilities removed from the general population, may be subjected to the types of searches at issue here.

* * *

CHIEF JUSTICE ROBERTS, concurring.

I join the opinion of the Court. As with Justice Alito, however, it is important for me that the Court does not foreclose the possibility of an exception to the rule it announces. Justice Kennedy explains that the circumstances before it do not afford an opportunity to consider that possibility. Those circumstances include the facts that Florence was detained not for a minor traffic offense but instead pursuant to a warrant for his arrest, and that there was apparently no alternative, if Florence were to be detained, to holding him in the general jail population.

Factual nuances have not played a significant role as this case has been presented to the Court. Both courts below regarded acknowledged factual disputes as "immaterial" to their conflicting dispositions, and before this Court Florence challenged suspicionless strip searches "no matter what the circumstances."

The Court makes a persuasive case for the general applicability of the rule it announces. The Court is nonetheless wise to leave open the possibility of exceptions, to ensure that we "not embarrass the future."

JUSTICE ALITO, concurring.

I join the opinion of the Court but emphasize the limits of today's holding. The Court holds that jail administrators may require all arrestees *who are committed to the general population of a jail* to undergo visual strip searches not involving physical contact by corrections officers. To perform the searches, officers may direct the arrestees to disrobe, shower, and submit to a visual inspection. As part of the inspection, the arrestees may be required to manipulate their bodies.

* * *

It is important to note, however, that the Court does not hold that it is *always* reasonable to conduct a full strip search of an arrestee whose detention has not been reviewed by a judicial officer and who could be held in available facilities apart from the general population. Most of those arrested for minor offenses are not dangerous, and most are released from custody prior to or at the time of their initial appearance before a magistrate. In some cases, the charges are dropped. In others, arrestees are released either on their own recognizance or on minimal bail. In the end, few are sentenced to incarceration. For these persons, admission to the general jail population, with the concomitant humiliation of a strip search, may not be reasonable, particularly if an alternative procedure is feasible. For example, the Federal Bureau of Prisons and possibly even some local jails appear to segregate temporary detainees who are minor offenders from the general population.

The Court does not address whether it is always reasonable, without regard to the offense or the reason for detention, to strip search an arrestee before the arrestee's detention has been reviewed by a judicial officer. The lead opinion explicitly reserves judgment on that question. In light of that limitation, I join the opinion of the Court in full.

JUSTICE BREYER, with whom JUSTICE GINSBURG, JUSTICE SOTOMAYOR, and JUSTICE KAGAN join, dissenting.

The petition for certiorari asks us to decide "[w]hether the Fourth Amendment permits a . . . suspicionless strip search of every individual arrested for any minor offense. . . ." This question is phrased more broadly than what is at issue. The case is limited to strip searches of those arrestees entering a jail's general population. And the kind of strip search in question involves more than undressing and taking a shower (even if guards monitor the shower area for threatened disorder). Rather, the searches here involve close observation of the private areas of a person's body and for that reason constitute a far more serious invasion of that person's privacy.

* * *

In my view, such a search of an individual arrested for a minor offense that does not involve drugs or violence—say a traffic offense, a regulatory offense, an essentially civil matter, or any other such misdemeanor—is an "unreasonable searc[h]" forbidden by the Fourth Amendment, unless prison authorities have reasonable suspicion to believe that the individual possesses drugs or other contraband. And I dissent from the Court's contrary determination.

* * *

II

A strip search that involves a stranger peering without consent at a naked individual, and in particular at the most private portions of that person's body, is a serious invasion of privacy. We have recently said, in respect to a schoolchild (and a less intrusive search), that the "meaning of such a search, and the degradation its subject may reasonably feel, place a search that intrusive in a category of its own demanding its own specific suspicions." *Safford Unified School Dist. # 1 v. Redding,* 557 U.S. 364, 377 (2009). The Courts of Appeals have more directly described the privacy interests at stake, writing, for example, that practices similar to those at issue here are "demeaning, dehumanizing, undignified, humiliating, terrifying, unpleasant, embarrassing, [and] repulsive, signifying degradation and submission." *Mary Beth G. v. Chicago,* 723 F.2d 1263, 1272 (C.A.7 1984). . . . Even when carried out in a respectful manner, and even absent any physical touching, such searches are inherently harmful, humiliating, and degrading. And the harm to privacy interests would seem particularly acute where the person searched may well have no expectation of being subject to such a search, say, because she had simply received a traffic ticket for failing to buckle a seatbelt, because he had not previously paid a civil fine, or because she had been arrested for a minor trespass.

In *Atwater v. Lago Vista,* 532 U.S. 318, 323–324 (2001), for example, police arrested a mother driving with her two children because their seat belts were not buckled. This Court held that the Constitution did not forbid an arrest for a minor seatbelt offense. But, in doing so, it pointed out that the woman was held for only an hour (before being taken to a magistrate and released on bond) and that the search—she had to remove her shoes, jewelry, and the contents of her pockets—was not " 'unusually harmful to [her] privacy or . . . physical interests.' " Would this Court have upheld the arrest had the magistrate not been immediately available, had the police housed her overnight in the jail, and had they subjected her to a search of the kind at issue here?

The petitioner, Albert W. Florence, states that his present arrest grew out of an (erroneous) report that he had failed to pay a minor civil fine previously assessed because he had hindered a prosecution (by fleeing police officers in his automobile). He alleges that he was held for six days in jail before being taken to a magistrate and that he was subjected to two strip searches of the kind in question.

Amicus briefs present other instances in which individuals arrested for minor offenses have been subjected to the humiliations of a visual strip search. They include a nun, a Sister of Divine Providence for 50 years, who was arrested for trespassing during an antiwar demonstration. They include women who were strip-searched during periods of lactation or menstruation. They include victims of sexual violence. They include individuals detained for such infractions as driving with a noisy muffler, driving with an inoperable headlight, failing to use a turn signal, or riding a bicycle without an audible bell. They include persons who perhaps should never have been placed in the general jail population in the first place.

I need not go on. I doubt that we seriously disagree about the nature of the strip search or about the serious affront to human dignity and to individual privacy that it presents. The basic question before us is whether such a search is nonetheless justified when an individual arrested for a minor offense is involuntarily placed in the general jail or prison population.

III

The majority, like the respondents, argues that strip searches are needed (1) to detect injuries or diseases, such as lice, that might spread in confinement, (2) to identify gang tattoos, which might reflect a need for special housing to avoid violence, and (3) to detect contraband, including drugs, guns, knives, and even pens or chewing gum, which might prove harmful or dangerous in prison. In evaluating this argument, I, like the majority, recognize: that managing a jail or prison is an "inordinately difficult undertaking;" that prison regulations that interfere with important constitutional interests are generally valid as long as they are "reasonably related to legitimate penological interests;" that finding injuries and preventing the spread of disease, minimizing the threat of gang violence, and detecting contraband are "legitimate penological interests;" and that we normally defer to the expertise of jail and prison administrators in such matters.

Nonetheless, the "particular" invasion of interests must be " 'reasonably related' " to the justifying "penological interest" and the need must not be " 'exaggerated.' " It is at this point that I must part company with the majority. I have found no convincing reason indicating that, in the absence of reasonable suspicion, involuntary strip searches of those arrested for minor offenses are necessary in order to further the penal interests mentioned. And there are strong reasons to believe they are not justified.

The lack of justification is fairly obvious with respect to the first two penological interests advanced. The searches already employed at Essex and Burlington include: (a) pat-frisking all inmates; (b) making inmates go through metal detectors (including the Body Orifice Screening System chair used at Essex County Correctional Facility that identifies metal hidden within the body); (c) making inmates shower and use particular delousing agents or bathing supplies; and (d) searching inmates' clothing. In addition, petitioner concedes that detainees could be lawfully subject to being viewed in their undergarments by jail officers or during showering (for security purposes). No one here has offered any reason, example, or empirical evidence suggesting the inadequacy of such practices for detecting injuries, diseases, or tattoos. In particular, there is no connection between the genital lift and the "squat and cough" that Florence was allegedly subjected to and health or gang concerns.

The lack of justification for such a strip search is less obvious but no less real in respect to the third interest, namely that of detecting contraband. The information demonstrating the lack of justification is of three kinds. First, there are empirically based conclusions reached in specific cases. The New York Federal District Court, [in *Dodge v. County of Orange*, 282 F. Supp.2d 41 (S.D. N.Y. 2003)], conducted a study of 23,000 persons admitted to the Orange County correctional facility between 1999 and 2003. These 23,000 persons underwent a strip search of the kind described, *supra,* at 1513. Of these 23,000 persons, the court wrote, "the County encountered three incidents of drugs recovered from an inmate's anal cavity and two incidents of drugs falling from an inmate's underwear during the course of a strip search." The court added that in four of these five instances there may have been "reasonable suspicion" to search, leaving only one instance in 23,000 in which the strip search policy "arguably" detected additional contraband. The study is imperfect, for search standards changed during the time it was conducted. But the large number of inmates, the small number of "incidents," and the District Court's own conclusions make the study probative though not conclusive.

Similarly, in *Shain v. Ellison,* 273 F.3d 56, 60 (C.A.2 2001), the court received data produced by the county jail showing that authorities conducted body-cavity strip searches, similar to those at issue here, of 75,000 new inmates over a period of five years. In 16 instances the searches led to the discovery of contraband. The record further showed that 13 of these 16 pieces of contraband would have been detected in a patdown or a search of shoes and outer-clothing. In the three instances in which contraband was found on the detainee's body or in a body cavity, there was a drug or felony history that would have justified a strip search on individualized reasonable suspicion.

Second, there is the plethora of recommendations of professional bodies, such as correctional associations, that have studied and thoughtfully considered the matter. . . .

Moreover, many correctional facilities apply a reasonable suspicion standard before strip searching inmates entering the general jail population, including the U.S. Marshals Service, the Immigration and Customs Service, and the Bureau of Indian Affairs. The Federal Bureau of Prisons itself forbids suspicionless strip searches for minor offenders, though it houses separately (and does not admit to the general jail population) a person who does not consent to such a search.

Third, there is general experience in areas where the law has forbidden here-relevant suspicionless searches. Laws in at least 10 States prohibit suspicionless strip searches. At the same time at least seven Courts of Appeals have considered the question and have required reasonable suspicion that an arrestee is concealing weapons or contraband before a strip search of one arrested for a minor offense can take place. Respondents have not presented convincing grounds to believe that administration of these legal standards has increased the smuggling of contraband into prison.

* * *

Points for Discussion

1. The majority puts the burden of proof on the plaintiffs, asserting that the outcome "turns in part on the extent to which this Court has sufficient expertise and information in the record to mandate, under the Constitution, the specific restrictions and limitations sought by [the plaintiffs]." It then ascribes a presumption of validity to the "judgment of correctional officials" regarding the degree to which they can afford to respect a constitutional right. Does this approach make sense? Don't government officials *always* claim that the decisions they make are necessary to achieve important governmental goals? How does this approach compare to that used in *Terry v. Ohio*? On the other hand, does it make a difference that this is a civil suit and that civil plaintiffs typically bear the burden of proof?

2. Are the dissent's statistics an effective response to the majority's presumption that the correctional officials acted constitutionally?

3. Recall that an individual can be arrested in public based on probable cause and without a warrant. Does learning about the kinds of invasive bodily searches authorized in *Florence* change your views about how high a standard probable cause should be?

MARYLAND V. KING

569 U.S. 435 (2013)

JUSTICE KENNEDY delivered the opinion of the court.

In 2003 a man concealing his face and armed with a gun broke into a woman's home in Salisbury, Maryland. He raped her. The police were unable to identify or apprehend the assailant based on any detailed description or other evidence they then had, but they did obtain from the victim a sample of the perpetrator's DNA.

In 2009 Alonzo King was arrested in Wicomico County, Maryland, and charged with first- and second-degree assault for menacing a group of people with a shotgun. As part of a routine booking procedure for serious offenses, his DNA sample was taken by applying a cotton swab or filter paper—known as a buccal swab—to the inside of his cheeks. The DNA was found to match the DNA taken from the Salisbury rape victim. King was tried and convicted for the rape. Additional DNA samples were taken from him and used in the rape trial, but there seems to be no doubt that it was the DNA from the cheek sample taken at the time he was booked in 2009 that led to his first having been linked to the rape and charged with its commission.

The Court of Appeals of Maryland, on review of King's rape conviction, ruled that the DNA taken when King was booked for the 2009 charge was an unlawful seizure because obtaining and using the cheek swab was an unreasonable search of the person. It set the rape conviction aside. This Court granted certiorari and now reverses the judgment of the Maryland court.

I

When King was arrested on April 10, 2009, for menacing a group of people with a shotgun and charged in state court with both first- and second-degree assault, he was processed for detention in custody at the Wicomico County Central Booking facility. Booking personnel used a cheek swab to take the DNA sample from him pursuant to provisions of the Maryland DNA Collection Act.

On July 13, 2009, King's DNA record was uploaded to the Maryland DNA database, and three weeks later, on August 4, 2009, his DNA profile was matched to the DNA sample collected in the unsolved 2003 rape case. Once the DNA was matched to King, detectives presented the forensic evidence to a grand jury, which indicted him for the rape. Detectives obtained a search warrant and took a second sample of DNA from King, which again matched the evidence from the rape. He moved to suppress the DNA match on the grounds that Maryland's DNA collection law violated the Fourth Amendment. The Circuit Court Judge upheld the statute as constitutional. King pleaded not guilty to the rape charges but was convicted and sentenced to life in prison without the possibility of parole.

* * *

Both federal and state courts have reached differing conclusions as to whether the Fourth Amendment prohibits the collection and analysis of a DNA sample from persons arrested, but not yet convicted, on felony charges. This Court granted certiorari to address the question. King is the respondent here.

II

* * *

A

The current standard for forensic DNA testing relies on an analysis of the chromosomes located within the nucleus of all human cells. "The DNA material in chromosomes is composed of 'coding' and 'noncoding' regions. The coding regions are known as *genes* and contain the information necessary for a cell to make proteins. . . . Non-protein-coding regions . . . are not related directly to making proteins, [and] have been referred to as 'junk' DNA." The adjective "junk" may mislead the layperson, for in fact this is the DNA region used with near certainty to identify a person. The term apparently is intended to indicate that this particular noncoding region, while useful and even dispositive for purposes like identity, does not show more far-reaching and complex characteristics like genetic traits.

Many of the patterns found in DNA are shared among all people, so forensic analysis focuses on "repeated DNA sequences scattered throughout the human genome," known as "short tandem repeats". The alternative possibilities for the size and frequency of these STRs at any given point along a strand of DNA are known as "alleles"; and multiple alleles are analyzed in order to ensure that a DNA profile matches only one individual. Future refinements may improve present technology, but even now STR analysis makes it "possible to determine whether a biological tissue matches a suspect with near certainty."

The Act authorizes Maryland law enforcement authorities to collect DNA samples from "an individual who is charged with . . . a crime of violence or an attempt to commit a crime of violence; or . . . burglary or an attempt to commit burglary." Maryland law defines a crime of violence to include murder, rape, first-degree assault, kidnaping, arson, sexual assault, and a variety of other serious crimes. Once taken, a DNA sample may not be processed or placed in a database before the individual is arraigned (unless the individual consents). It is at this point that a judicial officer ensures that there is probable cause to detain the arrestee on a qualifying serious offense. If "all qualifying criminal charges are determined to be unsupported by probable cause . . . the DNA sample shall be immediately destroyed." DNA samples are also destroyed if "a criminal action begun against the individual . . . does not result in a conviction," "the conviction is finally reversed or vacated and no new trial is permitted," or "the individual is granted an unconditional pardon."

The Act also limits the information added to a DNA database and how it may be used. Specifically, "[o]nly DNA records that directly relate to the identification of individuals shall be collected and stored." No purpose other than identification is permissible: "A person may not willfully test a DNA sample for information that does not relate to the identification of individuals as specified in this subtitle. Tests for familial matches are also prohibited. The officers involved in taking and analyzing respondent's DNA sample complied with the Act in all respects.

Respondent's DNA was collected in this case using a common procedure known as a "buccal swab." "Buccal cell collection involves wiping a small piece of filter paper or a cotton swab similar to a Q-tip against the inside cheek of an individual's mouth to collect some skin cells." The procedure is quick and painless. The swab touches inside an arrestee's mouth, but it requires no "surgical intrusio[n] beneath the skin," *Winston v. Lee,* 470 U.S. 753, 760 (1985), and it poses no "threa[t] to the health or safety" of arrestees, *id.,* at 763.

B

Respondent's identification as the rapist resulted in part through the operation of a national project to standardize collection and storage of DNA profiles. Authorized by Congress and supervised by the Federal Bureau of Investigation, the Combined DNA Index System connects DNA laboratories at the local, state, and national level. Since its authorization in 1994, the CODIS system has grown to include all 50 States and a number of federal agencies. CODIS collects DNA profiles provided by local laboratories taken from arrestees, convicted offenders, and forensic evidence found at crime scenes. To participate in CODIS, a local laboratory must sign a memorandum of understanding agreeing to adhere to quality standards and submit to audits to evaluate compliance with the federal standards for scientifically rigorous DNA testing.

One of the most significant aspects of CODIS is the standardization of the points of comparison in DNA analysis. The CODIS database is based on 13 loci at which the STR alleles are noted and compared. These loci make possible extreme accuracy in matching individual samples, with a "random match probability of approximately 1 in 100 trillion (assuming unrelated individuals)." The CODIS loci are from the non-protein coding junk regions of DNA, and "are not known to have any association with a genetic disease or any other genetic predisposition. Thus, the information in the database is only useful for human identity testing." STR information is recorded only as a "string of numbers"; and the DNA identification is accompanied only by information denoting the laboratory and the analyst responsible for the submission. In short, CODIS sets uniform national standards for DNA matching and then facilitates connections between local law enforcement agencies who can share more specific information about matched STR profiles.

All 50 States require the collection of DNA from felony convicts, and respondent does not dispute the validity of that practice. Twenty-eight States and the Federal Government have adopted laws similar to the Maryland Act authorizing the collection of DNA from some or all arrestees. Although those statutes vary in their particulars, such as what charges require a DNA sample, their similarity means that this case implicates more than the specific Maryland law. At issue is a standard, expanding technology already in widespread use throughout the Nation.

III

A

Although the DNA swab procedure used here presents a question the Court has not yet addressed, the framework for deciding the issue is well established. The Fourth Amendment, binding on the States by the Fourteenth Amendment, provides that "[t]he right of the people to be secure in their persons, houses, papers, and effects, against unreasonable searches and seizures, shall not be violated." It can be agreed that using a buccal swab on the inner tissues of a person's cheek in order to obtain DNA samples is a search. Virtually any "intrusio[n] into the human body," *Schmerber v. California,* 384 U.S. 757, 770 (1966), will work an invasion of " 'cherished personal security' that is subject to constitutional scrutiny," *Cupp v. Murphy,* 412 U.S. 291, 295 (1973) (quoting *Terry v. Ohio,* 392 U.S. 1, 24–25 (1968)). The Court has applied the Fourth Amendment to police efforts to draw blood, see *Schmerber, supra*; *Missouri v. McNeely,* 569 U.S. 141 (2013), scraping an arrestee's fingernails to obtain trace evidence, see *Cupp, supra,* and even to "a breathalyzer test, which generally requires the production of alveolar or 'deep lung' breath for chemical analysis," *Skinner v. Railway Labor Executives' Assn.,* 489 U.S. 602, 616 (1989).

A buccal swab is a far more gentle process than a venipuncture to draw blood. It involves but a light touch on the inside of the cheek; and although it can be deemed a search within the body of the arrestee, it requires no "surgical intrusions beneath the skin." *Winston,* 470 U.S., at 760. The fact than an intrusion is negligible is of central relevance to determining reasonableness, although it is still a search as the law defines that term.

B

To say that the Fourth Amendment applies here is the beginning point, not the end of the analysis. "[T]he Fourth Amendment's proper function is to constrain, not against all intrusions as such, but against intrusions which are not justified in the circumstances, or which are made in an improper manner." *Schmerber, supra,* at 768. "As the text of the Fourth Amendment indicates, the ultimate measure of the constitutionality of a governmental search is 'reasonableness.'" *Vernonia School Dist. 47J v. Acton,* 515 U.S. 646, 652 (1995). In giving content to the inquiry whether an intrusion is reasonable, the Court has preferred "some quantum of individualized suspicion . . . [as] a prerequisite to a constitutional search or seizure. But the Fourth Amendment imposes no irreducible requirement of such suspicion." *United States v. Martinez-Fuerte,* 428 U.S. 543, 560–61 (1976).

In some circumstances, such as "[w]hen faced with special law enforcement needs, diminished expectations of privacy, minimal intrusions, or the like, the Court has found that certain general, or individual, circumstances may render a warrantless search or seizure reasonable." *Illinois v. McArthur,* 531 U.S. 326, 330 (2001). Those circumstances diminish the need for a warrant, either because "the public interest is such that neither a warrant nor probable cause is required," *Maryland v. Buie,* 494 U.S. 325, 331 (1990), or because an individual is already on notice, for instance because of his employment, see *Skinner, supra,* or the conditions of his release from government custody, see *Samson v. California,* 547 U.S. 843 (2006), that some reasonable police intrusion on his privacy is to be expected. The need for a warrant is perhaps least when the search involves no discretion that could properly be limited by the "interpo[lation of] a neutral magistrate between the citizen and the law enforcement officer." *Treasury Employees v. Von Raab,* 489 U.S. 656, 667 (1989).

The instant case can be addressed with this background. The Maryland DNA Collection Act provides that, in order to obtain a DNA sample, all arrestees charged with serious crimes must furnish the sample on a buccal swab applied, as noted, to the inside of the cheeks. The arrestee is already in valid police custody for a serious offense supported by probable cause. The DNA collection is not subject to the judgment of officers whose perspective might be "colored by their primary involvement in 'the often competitive enterprise of ferreting out crime.'" *Terry, supra,* at 12. As noted by this Court in a different but still instructive context involving blood testing, "[b]oth the circumstances justifying toxicological testing and the permissible limits of such intrusions are defined narrowly and specifically in the regulations that authorize them. . . . Indeed, in light of the standardized nature of the tests and the minimal discretion vested in those charged with administering the program, there are virtually no facts for a neutral magistrate to evaluate." *Skinner, supra,* at 622. Here, the search effected by the buccal swab of respondent falls within the category of cases this Court has analyzed by reference to the proposition that the "touchstone of the Fourth Amendment is reasonableness, not individualized suspicion." *Samson, supra,* at 855, n.4.

Even if a warrant is not required, a search is not beyond Fourth Amendment scrutiny; for it must be reasonable in its scope and manner of execution. Urgent government interests are not a license for indiscriminate police behavior. To say that no warrant is required is merely to acknowledge that "rather than employing a *per se* rule of unreasonableness, we balance the privacy-related and law enforcement-related concerns to determine if the intrusion was reasonable." *McArthur, supra,* at 331. This application of "traditional standards of reasonableness" requires a court to weigh "the promotion of legitimate governmental interests" against "the degree to which [the search] intrudes upon an individual's privacy." *Wyoming v. Houghton,* 526 U.S. 295, 300 (1999). An assessment of reasonableness to determine the lawfulness of requiring this class of arrestees to provide a DNA sample is central to the instant case.

IV

A

The legitimate government interest served by the Maryland DNA Collection Act is one that is well established: the need for law enforcement officers in a safe and accurate way to process and identify the persons and possessions they must take into custody. It is beyond dispute that "probable cause provides legal justification for arresting a person suspected of crime, and for a brief period of detention to take the administrative steps incident to arrest." *Gerstein v. Pugh,* 420 U.S. 103, 113–14 (1975). Also uncontested is the "right on the part of the Government, always recognized under English and American law, to search the person of the accused when legally arrested." *Weeks v. United States,* 232 U.S. 383, 392 (1914), overruled on other grounds, *Mapp v. Ohio,* 367 U.S. 643 (1961). "The validity of the search of a person incident to a lawful arrest has been regarded as settled from its first enunciation, and has remained virtually unchallenged." *United States v. Robinson,* 414 U.S. 218, 224 (1973). Even in that context, the Court has been clear that individual suspicion is not necessary, because "[t]he constitutionality of a search incident to an arrest does not depend on whether there is any indication that the person arrested possesses weapons or evidence. The fact of a lawful arrest, standing alone, authorizes a search." *Michigan v. DeFillippo,* 443 U.S. 31, 35 (1979).

The "routine administrative procedure[s] at a police station house incident to booking and jailing the suspect" derive from different origins and have different constitutional justifications than, say, the search of a place, *Illinois v. Lafayette,* 462 U.S. 640, 643 (1983); for the search of a place not incident to an arrest depends on the "fair probability that contraband or evidence of a crime will be found in a particular place," *Illinois v. Gates,* 462 U.S. 213, 238 (1983). The interests are further different when an individual is formally processed into police custody. Then "the law is in the act of subjecting the body of the accused to its physical dominion." *People v. Chiagles,* 237 N.Y. 193, 197 (1923) (Cardozo, J.). When probable cause exists to remove an individual from the normal channels of society and hold him in legal custody, DNA identification plays a critical role in serving those interests.

First, "[i]n every criminal case, it is known and must be known who has been arrested and who is being tried." *Hiibel v. Sixth Judicial Dist. Court of Nev., Humboldt Cty.*, 542 U.S. 177, 191 (2004). An individual's identity is more than just his name or Social Security number, and the government's interest in identification goes beyond ensuring that the proper name is typed on the indictment. Identity has never been considered limited to the name on the arrestee's birth certificate. In fact, a name is of little value compared to the real interest in identification at stake when an individual is brought into custody. "It is a well recognized aspect of criminal conduct that the perpetrator will take unusual steps to conceal not only his conduct, but also his identity. Disguises used while committing a crime may be supplemented or replaced by changed names, and even changed physical features." *Jones v. Murray,* 962 F.2d 302, 307 (C.A.4 1992). An "arrestee may be carrying a false ID or lie about his identity," and "criminal history records . . . can be inaccurate or incomplete." *Florence v. Board of Chosen Freeholders of County of Burlington,* 566 U.S. 318, 336 (2012).

A suspect's criminal history is a critical part of his identity that officers should know when processing him for detention. It is a common occurrence that "[p]eople detained for minor offenses can turn out to be the most devious and dangerous criminals. Hours after the Oklahoma City bombing, Timothy McVeigh was stopped by a state trooper who noticed he was driving without a license plate. Police stopped serial killer Joel Rifkin for the same reason. One of the terrorists involved in the September 11 attacks was stopped and ticketed for speeding just two days before hijacking Flight 93." *Id.,* at 335. Police already seek this crucial identifying information. They use routine and accepted means as varied as comparing the suspect's booking photograph to sketch artists' depictions of persons of interest, showing his mugshot to potential witnesses, and of course making a computerized comparison of the arrestee's fingerprints against electronic databases of known criminals and unsolved crimes. In this respect the only difference between DNA analysis and the accepted use of fingerprint databases is the unparalleled accuracy DNA provides.

The task of identification necessarily entails searching public and police records based on the identifying information provided by the arrestee to see what is already known about him. The DNA collected from arrestees is an irrefutable identification of the person from whom it was taken. Like a fingerprint, the 13 CODIS loci are not themselves evidence of any particular crime, in the way that a drug test can by itself be evidence of illegal narcotics use. A DNA profile is useful to the police because it gives them a form of identification to search the records already in their valid possession. In this respect the use of DNA for identification is no different than matching an arrestee's face to a wanted poster of a previously unidentified suspect; or matching tattoos to known gang symbols to reveal a criminal affiliation; or matching the arrestee's fingerprints to those recovered from a crime scene. DNA is another metric of identification used to connect the arrestee with his or her public persona, as reflected in records of his or her actions that are available to the police. Those records may be linked to the arrestee by a variety of relevant forms of identification, including name, alias, date and time of previous convictions and the name then used, photograph, Social Security number, or CODIS profile. These data, found in official records, are checked as a routine matter to produce a more comprehensive record of the suspect's complete identity. Finding occurrences of the arrestee's CODIS profile in outstanding cases is consistent with this common practice. It uses a different form of identification than a name or fingerprint, but its function is the same.

Second, law enforcement officers bear a responsibility for ensuring that the custody of an arrestee does not create inordinate "risks for facility staff, for the existing detainee population, and for a new detainee." *Florence, supra,* at 330. DNA identification can provide untainted information to those charged with detaining suspects and detaining the property of any felon. For these purposes officers must know the type of person whom they are detaining, and DNA allows them to make critical choices about how to proceed.

"Knowledge of identity may inform an officer that a suspect is wanted for another offense, or has a record of violence or mental disorder. On the other hand, knowing identity may help clear a suspect and allow the police to concentrate their efforts elsewhere. Identity may prove particularly important in [certain cases, such as] where the police are investigating what appears to be a domestic assault. Officers called to investigate domestic disputes need to know whom they are dealing with in order to assess the situation, the threat to their own safety, and possible danger to the potential victim." *Hiibel, supra,* at 186.

Recognizing that a name alone cannot address this interest in identity, the Court has approved, for example, "a visual inspection for certain tattoos and other signs of gang affiliation as part of the intake process," because "[t]he identification and isolation of gang members before they are admitted protects everyone." *Florence, supra,* at 331, 132 S.Ct., at 1519.

Third, looking forward to future stages of criminal prosecution, "the Government has a substantial interest in ensuring that persons accused of crimes are available for trials." *Bell v. Wolfish,* 441 U.S. 520 (1979). A person who is arrested for one offense but knows that he has yet to answer for some past crime may be more inclined to flee the instant charges, lest continued contact with the criminal justice system expose one or more other serious offenses. For example, a defendant who had committed a prior sexual assault might be inclined to flee on a burglary charge, knowing that in every State a DNA sample would be taken from him after his conviction on the burglary charge that would tie him to the more serious charge of rape. In addition to subverting the administration of justice with respect to the crime of arrest, this ties back to the interest in safety; for a detainee who absconds from custody presents a risk to law enforcement officers, other detainees, victims of previous crimes, witnesses, and society at large.

Fourth, an arrestee's past conduct is essential to an assessment of the danger he poses to the public, and this will inform a court's determination whether the individual should be released on bail. "The government's interest in preventing crime by arrestees is both legitimate and compelling." *United States v. Salerno,* 481 U.S. 739, 749 (1987). DNA identification of a suspect in a violent crime provides critical information to the police and judicial officials in making a determination of the arrestee's future dangerousness. This inquiry always has entailed some scrutiny beyond the name on the defendant's driver's license. For example, Maryland law requires a judge to take into account not only "the nature and circumstances of the offense charged" but also "the defendant's family ties, employment status and history, financial resources, reputation, character and mental condition, length of residence in the community." Knowing that the defendant is wanted for a previous violent crime based on DNA identification is especially probative of the court's consideration of "the danger of the defendant to the alleged victim, another person, or the community."

* * *

B

DNA identification represents an important advance in the techniques used by law enforcement to serve legitimate police concerns for as long as there have been arrests, concerns the courts have acknowledged and approved for more than a century. Law enforcement agencies routinely have used scientific advancements in their standard procedures for the identification of arrestees. "Police had been using photography to capture the faces of criminals almost since its invention." S. Cole, Suspect Identities 20 (2001). Courts did not dispute that practice, concluding that a "sheriff in making an arrest for a felony on a warrant has the right to exercise a discretion . . ., [if] he should deem it necessary to the safe-keeping of a prisoner, and to prevent his escape, or to enable him the more readily to retake the prisoner if he should escape, to take his photograph." *State ex rel. Bruns v. Clausmier,* 154 Ind. 599, 601, 603 (1900). By the time that it had become "the daily practice of the police officers and detectives of crime to use photographic pictures for the discovery and identification of criminals," the courts likewise had come to the conclusion that "it would be [a] matter of regret to have its use unduly restricted upon any fanciful theory or constitutional privilege." *Shaffer v. United States,* 24 App.D.C. 417, 426 (1904).

Beginning in 1887, some police adopted more exacting means to identify arrestees, using the system of precise physical measurements pioneered by the French anthropologist Alphonse Bertillon. Bertillon identification consisted of 10 measurements of the arrestee's body, along with a "scientific analysis of the features of the face and an exact anatomical localization of the various scars, marks, &c., of the body." Defense of the Bertillon System, N.Y. Times, Jan. 20, 1896, p. 3. "[W]hen a prisoner was brought in, his photograph was taken according to the Bertillon system, and his body measurements were then made. The measurements were made . . . and noted down on the back of a card or a blotter, and the photograph of the prisoner was expected to be placed on the card. This card, therefore, furnished both the likeness and description of the prisoner, and was placed in the rogues' gallery, and copies were sent to various cities where similar records were kept." *People ex rel. Jones v. Diehl,* 65 N.Y.S. 801, 802 (1900). As in the present case, the point of taking this information about each arrestee was not limited to verifying that the proper name was on the indictment. These procedures were used to "facilitate the recapture of escaped prisoners," to aid "the investigation of their past records and personal history," and "to preserve the means of identification for . . . future supervision after discharge." *Hodgeman v. Olsen,* 86 Wash. 615, 619 (1915).

Perhaps the most direct historical analogue to the DNA technology used to identify respondent is the familiar practice of fingerprinting arrestees. From the advent of this technique, courts had no trouble determining that fingerprinting was a natural part of "the administrative steps incident to arrest." *County of Riverside v. McLaughlin,* 500 U.S. 44, 58 (1991). In the seminal case of *United States v. Kelly,* 55 F.2d 67 (C.A.2 1932), Judge Augustus Hand wrote that routine fingerprinting did not violate the Fourth Amendment precisely because it fit within the accepted means of processing an arrestee into custody:

> Finger printing seems to be no more than an extension of methods of identification long used in dealing with persons under arrest for real or supposed violations of the criminal laws. It is known to be a very certain means devised by modern science to reach the desired end, and has become especially important in a time when increased population and vast aggregations of people in urban

> centers have rendered the notoriety of the individual in the community no longer a ready means of identification.
>
> * * *
>
> We find no ground in reason or authority for interfering with a method of identifying persons charged with crime which has now become widely known and frequently practiced.

Id., at 69–70. By the middle of the 20th century, it was considered "elementary that a person in lawful custody may be required to submit to photographing and fingerprinting as part of routine identification processes." *Smith v. United States,* 324 F.2d 879, 882 (C.A.D.C.1963) (Burger, J.) (citations omitted).

DNA identification is an advanced technique superior to fingerprinting in many ways, so much so that to insist on fingerprints as the norm would make little sense to either the forensic expert or a layperson. The additional intrusion upon the arrestee's privacy beyond that associated with fingerprinting is not significant, and DNA is a markedly more accurate form of identifying arrestees. A suspect who has changed his facial features to evade photographic identification or even one who has undertaken the more arduous task of altering his fingerprints cannot escape the revealing power of his DNA.

* * *

V

A

* * *

The expectations of privacy of an individual taken into police custody "necessarily [are] of a diminished scope." *Bell,* 441 U.S., at 557. "[B]oth the person and the property in his immediate possession may be searched at the station house." *United States v. Edwards,* 415 U.S. 800, 803 (1974). A search of the detainee's person when he is booked into custody may " 'involve a relatively extensive exploration,' " *Robinson,* 414 U.S., at 227, including "requir[ing] at least some detainees to lift their genitals or cough in a squatting position," *Florence,* 566 U.S., at 334.

In this critical respect, the search here at issue differs from the sort of programmatic searches of either the public at large or a particular class of regulated but otherwise law-abiding citizens that the Court has previously labeled as " 'special needs' " searches. *Chandler v. Miller,* 520 U.S. 305, 314 (1997). When the police stop a motorist at a checkpoint, see *Indianapolis v. Edmond,* 531 U.S. 32 (2000), or test a political candidate for illegal narcotics, see *Chandler, supra,* they intrude upon substantial expectations of privacy. So the Court has insisted on some purpose other than "to detect evidence of ordinary criminal wrongdoing" to justify these searches in the absence of individualized suspicion. *Edmond, supra,* at 38. Once an individual has been arrested on probable cause for a dangerous offense that may require detention before trial, however, his or her expectations of privacy and freedom from police scrutiny are reduced. DNA identification like that at issue here thus does not require consideration of any unique needs that would be required to justify searching the average citizen. The special needs cases, though in full accord with the result reached here, do not have a direct bearing on the issues presented in this case, because unlike the search of a citizen who has not been suspected of a wrong, a detainee has a reduced expectation of privacy.

The reasonableness inquiry here considers two other circumstances in which the Court has held that particularized suspicion is not categorically required: "diminished expectations of privacy [and] minimal intrusions." *McArthur,* 531 U.S., at 330. This is not to suggest that any search is acceptable solely because a person is in custody. Some searches, such as invasive surgery, see *Winston,* 470 U.S. 753, or a search of the arrestee's home, see *Chimel v. California,* 395 U.S. 752 (1969), involve either greater intrusions or higher expectations of privacy than are present in this case. In those situations, when the Court must "balance the privacy-related and law enforcement-related concerns to determine if the intrusion was reasonable," *McArthur, supra,* at 331, the privacy-related concerns are weighty enough that the search may require a warrant, notwithstanding the diminished expectations of privacy of the arrestee.

* * *

B

In addition the processing of respondent's DNA sample's 13 CODIS loci did not intrude on respondent's privacy in a way that would make his DNA identification unconstitutional.

First, as already noted, the CODIS loci come from noncoding parts of the DNA that do not reveal the genetic traits of the arrestee. While science can always progress further, and those progressions may have Fourth Amendment consequences, alleles at the CODIS loci "are not at present revealing information beyond identification." Katsanis & Wagner, Characterization of the Standard and Recommended CODIS Markers, 58 J. Forensic Sci. S169, S171 (2013). The argument that the testing at issue in this case reveals any private medical information at all is open to dispute.

And even if non-coding alleles could provide some information, they are not in fact tested for that end. It is undisputed that law enforcement officers analyze DNA for the sole purpose of generating a unique identifying number against which future samples may be matched. This parallels a similar safeguard based on actual practice in the school drug-testing context, where the Court deemed it "significant that the tests at issue here look only for drugs, and not for whether the student is, for example, epileptic, pregnant, or diabetic." *Vernonia School Dist. 47J,* 515 U.S., at 658. If in the future police analyze samples to determine, for instance, an arrestee's predisposition for a particular disease or other hereditary factors not relevant to identity, that case would present additional privacy concerns not present here.

Finally, the Act provides statutory protections that guard against further invasion of privacy. As noted above, the Act requires that "[o]nly DNA records that directly relate to the identification of individuals shall be collected and stored." No purpose other than identification is permissible: "A person may not willfully test a DNA sample for information that does not relate to the identification of individuals as specified in this subtitle." This Court has noted often that "a 'statutory or regulatory duty to avoid unwarranted disclosures' generally allays . . . privacy concerns." *NASA v. Nelson,* 562 U.S. 134, 155 (2011). The Court need not speculate about the risks posed "by a system that did not contain comparable security provisions." In light of the scientific and statutory safeguards, once respondent's DNA was lawfully collected the STR analysis of respondent's DNA pursuant to CODIS procedures did not amount to a significant invasion of privacy that would render the DNA identification impermissible under the Fourth Amendment.

* * *

JUSTICE SCALIA, with whom JUSTICE GINSBURG, JUSTICE SOTOMAYOR, and JUSTICE KAGAN join, dissenting.

The Fourth Amendment forbids searching a person for evidence of a crime when there is no basis for believing the person is guilty of the crime or is in possession of incriminating evidence. That prohibition is categorical and without exception; it lies at the very heart of the Fourth Amendment. Whenever this Court has allowed a suspicionless search, it has insisted upon a justifying motive apart from the investigation of crime.

It is obvious that no such noninvestigative motive exists in this case. The Court's assertion that DNA is being taken, not to solve crimes, but to *identify* those in the State's custody, taxes the credulity of the credulous. And the Court's comparison of Maryland's DNA searches to other techniques, such as fingerprinting, can seem apt only to those who know no more than today's opinion has chosen to tell them about how those DNA searches actually work.

I

A

At the time of the Founding, Americans despised the British use of so-called "general warrants"—warrants not grounded upon a sworn oath of a specific infraction by a particular individual, and thus not limited in scope and application. The first Virginia Constitution declared that "general warrants, whereby any officer or messenger may be commanded to search suspected places without evidence of a fact committed," or to search a person "whose offence is not particularly described and supported by evidence," "are grievous and oppressive, and ought not be granted." Va. Declaration of Rights § 10 (1776), in 1 B. Schwartz, The Bill of Rights: A Documentary History 234, 235 (1971). The Maryland Declaration of Rights similarly provided that general warrants were "illegal." Md. Declaration of Rights § XXIII (1776), in *id.*, at 280, 282.

In the ratification debates, Antifederalists sarcastically predicted that the general, suspicionless warrant would be among the Constitution's "blessings." "Brutus" of New York asked why the Federal Constitution contained no provision like Maryland's, and Patrick Henry warned that the new Federal Constitution would expose the citizenry to searches and seizures "in the most arbitrary manner, without any evidence or reason."

Madison's draft of what became the Fourth Amendment answered these charges by providing that the "rights of the people to be secured in their persons . . . from all unreasonable searches and seizures, shall not be violated by warrants issued without probable cause . . . or not particularly describing the places to be searched." 1 Annals of Cong. 434–435 (1789). As ratified, the Fourth Amendment's Warrant Clause forbids a warrant to "issue" except "upon probable cause," and requires that it be "particula[r]" (which is to say, *individualized*) to "the place to be searched, and the persons or things to be seized." And we have held that, even when a warrant is not constitutionally necessary, the Fourth Amendment's general prohibition of "unreasonable" searches imports the same requirement of individualized suspicion. See *Chandler v. Miller,* 520 U.S. 305, 308 (1997).

Although there is a "closely guarded category of constitutionally permissible suspicionless searches," *id.,* at 309, that has never included searches designed to serve "the normal need for law enforcement," *Skinner v. Railway Labor Executives' Assn.,* 489 U.S. 602, 619 (1989). Even the common name for suspicionless searches—"special needs" searches—itself reflects that they must be justified, *always,* by concerns "other than crime detection." *Chandler, supra,* at 313–314. We have approved random drug tests of railroad employees, yes—but only because the Government's need to "regulat[e] the conduct of railroad employees to ensure safety" is distinct from "normal law enforcement." *Skinner, supra,* at 620. So too we have approved suspicionless searches in public schools—but only because there the government acts in furtherance of its "responsibilities . . . as guardian and tutor of children entrusted to its care." *Vernonia School Dist. 47J v. Acton,* 515 U.S. 646, 665 (1995).

So while the Court is correct to note that there are instances in which we have permitted searches without individualized suspicion, "[i]n none of these cases . . . did we indicate approval of a [search] whose primary purpose was to detect evidence of ordinary criminal wrongdoing." *Indianapolis v. Edmond,* 531 U.S. 32, 38 (2000). That limitation is crucial. It is only when a governmental purpose aside from crime-solving is at stake that we engage in the free-form "reasonableness" inquiry that the Court indulges at length today. To put it another way, both the legitimacy of the Court's method and the correctness of its outcome hinge entirely on the truth of a single proposition: that the primary purpose of these DNA searches is something other than simply discovering evidence of criminal wrongdoing. As I detail below, that proposition is wrong.

B

The Court alludes at several points to the fact that King was an arrestee, and arrestees may be validly searched incident to their arrest. But the Court does not really *rest* on this principle, and for good reason: The objects of a search incident to arrest must be either (1) weapons or evidence that might easily be destroyed, or (2) evidence relevant to the crime of arrest. See *Arizona v. Gant,* 556 U.S. 332, 343–344 (2009). Neither is the object of the search at issue here.

The Court hastens to clarify that it does not mean to approve invasive surgery on arrestees or warrantless searches of their homes. That the Court feels the need to disclaim these consequences is as damning a criticism of its suspicionless-search regime as any I can muster. And the Court's attempt to distinguish those hypothetical searches from this real one is unconvincing. We are told that the "privacy-related concerns" in the search of a home "are weighty enough that the search may require a warrant, notwithstanding the diminished expectations of privacy of the arrestee." But why are the "privacy-related concerns" not also "weighty" when an intrusion into the *body* is at stake? (The Fourth Amendment lists "persons" *first* among the entities protected against unreasonable searches and seizures.) And could the police engage, without any suspicion of wrongdoing, in a "brief and . . . minimal" intrusion into the home of an arrestee—perhaps just peeking around the curtilage a bit? Obviously not.

At any rate, all this discussion is beside the point. No matter the degree of invasiveness, suspicionless searches are *never* allowed if their principal end is ordinary crime-solving. A search incident to arrest either serves other ends (such as officer safety, in a search for weapons) or is not suspicionless (as when there is reason to believe the arrestee possesses evidence relevant to the crime of arrest).

Sensing (correctly) that it needs more, the Court elaborates at length the ways that the search here served the special purpose of "identifying" King.[1] But that seems to me quite wrong—unless what one means by

---

[1] The Court's insistence that our special-needs cases "do not have a direct bearing on the issues presented in this case" is perplexing. Why spill so much ink on the special need of identification if a special need is not required? Why not just come out and say that any

"identifying" someone is "searching for evidence that he has committed crimes unrelated to the crime of his arrest." At points the Court does appear to use "identifying" in that peculiar sense—claiming, for example, that knowing "an arrestee's past conduct is essential to an assessment of the danger he poses." If identifying someone means finding out what unsolved crimes he has committed, then identification is indistinguishable from the ordinary law-enforcement aims that have never been thought to justify a suspicionless search. Searching every lawfully stopped car, for example, might turn up information about unsolved crimes the driver had committed, but no one would say that such a search was aimed at "identifying" him, and no court would hold such a search lawful. I will therefore assume that the Court means that the DNA search at issue here was useful to "identify" King in the normal sense of that word—in the sense that would identify the author of Introduction to the Principles of Morals and Legislation as Jeremy Bentham.

1

The portion of the Court's opinion that explains the identification rationale is strangely silent on the actual workings of the DNA search at issue here. To know those facts is to be instantly disabused of the notion that what happened had anything to do with identifying King.

King was arrested on April 10, 2009, on charges unrelated to the case before us. That same day, April 10, the police searched him and seized the DNA evidence at issue here. What happened next? Reading the Court's opinion, particularly its insistence that the search was necessary to know "who [had] been arrested," one might guess that King's DNA was swiftly processed and his identity thereby confirmed—perhaps against some master database of known DNA profiles, as is done for fingerprints. After all, was not the suspicionless search here crucial to avoid "inordinate risks for facility staff" or to "existing detainee population"? Surely, then—*surely*—the State of Maryland got cracking on those grave risks immediately, by rushing to identify King with his DNA as soon as possible.

Nothing could be further from the truth. Maryland officials did not even begin the process of testing King's DNA that day. Or, actually, the next day. Or the day after that. And that was for a simple reason: Maryland law forbids them to do so. A "DNA sample collected from an individual charged with a crime . . . *may not* be tested or placed in the statewide DNA data base system prior to the first scheduled arraignment date." And King's first appearance in court was not until three days after his arrest. (I

suspicionless search of an arrestee is allowed if it will be useful to solve crimes? The Court does not say that because most Members of the Court do not believe it. So whatever the Court's major premise—the opinion does not really contain what you would call a rule of decision—the *minor* premise is "this search was used to identify King." The incorrectness of that minor premise will therefore suffice to demonstrate the error in the Court's result.

suspect, though, that they did not wait three days to ask his name or take his fingerprints.)

This places in a rather different light the Court's solemn declaration that the search here was necessary so that King could be identified at "every stage of the criminal process." I hope that the Maryland officials who read the Court's opinion do not take it seriously. Acting on the Court's misperception of Maryland law could lead to jail time. Does the Court really believe that Maryland did not know whom it was arraigning? The Court's response is to imagine that release on bail could take so long that the DNA results are returned in time, or perhaps that bail could be revoked if the DNA test turned up incriminating information. That is no answer at all. If the purpose of this Act is to assess "whether [King] should be released on bail," why would it *possibly* forbid the DNA testing process to *begin* until King was arraigned? Why would Maryland resign itself to simply hoping that the bail decision will drag out long enough that the "identification" can succeed before the arrestee is released? The truth, known to Maryland and increasingly to the reader: this search had nothing to do with establishing King's identity.

It gets worse. King's DNA sample was not received by the Maryland State Police's Forensic Sciences Division until April 23, 2009—two weeks after his arrest. It sat in that office, ripening in a storage area, until the custodians got around to mailing it to a lab for testing on June 25, 2009—two months after it was received, and nearly *three* since King's arrest. After it was mailed, the data from the lab tests were not available for several more weeks, until July 13, 2009, which is when the test results were entered into Maryland's DNA database, *together with information identifying the person from whom the sample was taken*. Meanwhile, bail had been set, King had engaged in discovery, and he had requested a speedy trial—presumably not a trial of John Doe. It was not until August 4, 2009—four months after King's arrest—that the forwarded sample transmitted (*without* identifying information) from the Maryland DNA database to the Federal Bureau of Investigation's national database was matched with a sample taken from the scene of an unrelated crime years earlier.

A more specific description of exactly what happened at this point illustrates why, by definition, King could not have been *identified* by this match. The FBI's DNA database (known as CODIS) consists of two distinct collections. One of them, the one to which King's DNA was submitted, consists of DNA samples taken from known convicts or arrestees. I will refer to this as the "Convict and Arrestee Collection." The other collection consists of samples taken from crime scenes; I will refer to this as the "Unsolved Crimes Collection." The Convict and Arrestee Collection stores "no names or other personal identifiers of the offenders, arrestees, or detainees." Rather, it contains only the DNA profile itself, the name of the agency that submitted it, the laboratory personnel who analyzed it, and an identification number for the specimen. This is because the submitting state laboratories are expected *already* to know the identities of the convicts and arrestees from whom samples are taken. (And, of course, they do.)

Moreover, the CODIS system works by checking to see whether any of the samples in the Unsolved Crimes Collection match any of the samples in the Convict and Arrestee Collection. That is sensible, if what one wants to do is solve those cold cases, but note what it requires: that the identity of the people whose DNA has been entered in the Convict and Arrestee Collection *already be known*. If one wanted to identify someone in custody using his DNA, the logical thing to do would be to compare that DNA against the Convict and Arrestee Collection: to search, in other words, the collection that could be used (by checking back with the submitting state agency) to identify people, rather than the collection of evidence from unsolved crimes, whose perpetrators are by definition unknown. But that is not what was done. And that is because this search had nothing to do with identification.

In fact, if anything was "identified" at the moment that the DNA database returned a match, it was not King—his identity was already known. (The docket for the original criminal charges lists his full name, his race, his sex, his height, his weight, his date of birth, and his address.) Rather, what the August 4 match "identified" was *the previously-taken sample from the earlier crime*. That sample was genuinely mysterious to Maryland; the State knew that it had probably been left by the victim's attacker, but nothing else. King was not identified by his association with the sample; rather, the sample was identified by its association with King. The Court effectively destroys its own "identification" theory when it acknowledges that the object of this search was "to see what [was] already known about [King]." King was who he was, and volumes of his biography could not make him any more or any less King. No minimally competent speaker of English would say, upon noticing a known arrestee's similarity "to a wanted poster of a previously unidentified suspect," that the *arrestee* had thereby been identified. It was the previously unidentified suspect who had been identified—just as, here, it was the previously unidentified rapist.

2

That taking DNA samples from arrestees has nothing to do with identifying them is confirmed not just by actual practice (which the Court ignores) but by the enabling statute itself (which the Court also ignores). The Maryland Act at issue has a section helpfully entitled "Purpose of collecting and testing DNA samples." (One would expect such a section to play a somewhat larger role in the Court's analysis of the Act's purpose—which is to say, at least *some* role.) That provision lists five purposes for which DNA samples may be tested. By this point, it will not surprise the reader to learn that the Court's imagined purpose is not among them.

* * *

More devastating still for the Court's "identification" theory, the statute *does* enumerate two instances in which a DNA sample may be tested for the purpose of identification: "to help identify *human remains,*" and "to help identify *missing individuals.*" No mention of identifying arrestees. *Inclusio unius est exclusio alterius.* And note again that Maryland forbids using DNA records "for any purposes other than those specified"—it is actually a crime to do so.

* * *

So, to review: DNA testing does not even begin until after arraignment and bail decisions are already made. The samples sit in storage for months, and take weeks to test. When they are tested, they are checked against the Unsolved Crimes Collection—rather than the Convict and Arrestee Collection, which could be used to identify them. The Act forbids the Court's purpose (identification), but prescribes as its purpose what our suspicionless-search cases forbid ("official investigation into a crime"). Against all of that, it is safe to say that if the Court's identification theory is not wrong, there is no such thing as error.

II

The Court also attempts to bolster its identification theory with a series of inapposite analogies. Is not taking DNA samples the same, asks the Court, as taking a person's photograph? No—because that is not a Fourth Amendment search at all. It does not involve a physical intrusion onto the person, see *Florida v. Jardines,* 569 U.S. 1, 3–5 (2013), and we have never held that merely taking a person's photograph invades any recognized "expectation of privacy," see *Katz v. United States,* 389 U.S. 347 (1967). Thus, it is unsurprising that the cases the Court cites as authorizing photo-taking do not even mention the Fourth Amendment.

But is not the practice of DNA searches, the Court asks, the same as taking "Bertillon" measurements—noting an arrestee's height, shoe size, and so on, on the back of a photograph? No, because that system was not, in the ordinary case, used to solve unsolved crimes. It is possible, I suppose, to imagine situations in which such measurements might be useful to generate leads. (If witnesses described a very tall burglar, all the "tall man" cards could then be pulled.) But the obvious primary purpose of such measurements, as the Court's description of them makes clear, was to verify that, for example, the person arrested today is the same person that was arrested a year ago. Which is to say, Bertillon measurements were *actually* used as a system of identification, and drew their primary usefulness from that task.

It is on the fingerprinting of arrestees, however, that the Court relies most heavily. The Court does not actually say whether it believes that taking a person's fingerprints is a Fourth Amendment search, and our cases provide no ready answer to that question. Even assuming so, however, law enforcement's post-arrest use of fingerprints could not be more different from its post-arrest use of DNA. Fingerprints of arrestees are taken primarily to identify them (though that process sometimes solves crimes); the DNA of arrestees is taken to solve crimes (and nothing else). Contrast CODIS, the FBI's nationwide DNA database, with IAFIS, the FBI's Integrated Automated Fingerprint Identification System.

Fingerprints	DNA Samples
The "average response time for an electronic criminal fingerprint submission is about 27 minutes." *IAFIS.*	DNA analysis can take months—far too long to be useful for identifying someone.
IAFIS includes detailed identification information, including "criminal histories; mug shots; scars and tattoo photos; physical characteristics like height, weight, and hair and eye color."	CODIS contains "[n]o names or other personal identifiers of the offenders, arrestees, or detainees." See CODIS and NDIS Fact Sheet.
"Latent prints" recovered from crime scenes are not systematically compared against the database of known fingerprints, since that requires further forensic work.	The entire *point* of the DNA database is to check crime scene evidence against the profiles of arrestees and convicts as they come in.

The Court asserts that the taking of fingerprints was "constitutional for generations prior to the introduction" of the FBI's rapid computer-matching system. This bold statement is bereft of citation to authority because there is none for it. The "great expansion in fingerprinting came before the modern era of Fourth Amendment jurisprudence," and so we were never asked to decide the legitimacy of the practice. *United States v. Kincade,* 379 F.3d 813, 874 (C.A.9 2004) (Kozinski, J., dissenting). As fingerprint databases expanded from convicted criminals, to arrestees, to civil servants, to immigrants, to everyone with a driver's license, Americans simply "became accustomed to having our fingerprints on file in some government database." *Ibid.* But it is wrong to suggest that this was uncontroversial at the time, or that this Court blessed universal fingerprinting for "generations" before it was possible to use it effectively for identification.

* * *

Today, it can fairly be said that fingerprints really are used to identify people—so well, in fact, that there would be no need for the expense of a separate, wholly redundant DNA confirmation of the same information. What DNA adds—what makes it a valuable weapon in the law-enforcement arsenal—is the ability to solve unsolved crimes, by matching old crime-scene evidence against the profiles of people whose identities are already known. That is what was going on when King's DNA was taken, and we should not disguise the fact. Solving unsolved crimes is a noble objective, but it occupies a lower place in the American pantheon of noble objectives than the protection of our people from suspicionless law-enforcement searches. The Fourth Amendment must prevail.

* * *

The Court disguises the vast (and scary) scope of its holding by promising a limitation it cannot deliver. The Court repeatedly says that DNA testing, and entry into a national DNA registry, will not befall thee and me, dear reader, but only those arrested for "serious offense[s]." I cannot imagine what principle could possibly justify this limitation, and the Court does not attempt to suggest any. If one believes that DNA will "identify" someone arrested for assault, he must believe that it will "identify" someone arrested for a traffic offense. This Court does not base its judgments on senseless distinctions. At the end of the day, *logic will out*. When there comes before us the taking of DNA from an arrestee for a traffic violation, the Court will predictably (and quite rightly) say, "We can find no significant difference between this case and *King*." Make no mistake about it: As an entirely predictable consequence of today's decision, your DNA can be taken and entered into a national DNA database if you are ever arrested, rightly or wrongly, and for whatever reason.

The most regrettable aspect of the suspicionless search that occurred here is that it proved to be quite unnecessary. All parties concede that it would have been entirely permissible, as far as the Fourth Amendment is concerned, for Maryland to take a sample of King's DNA as a consequence of his conviction for second-degree assault. So the ironic result of the Court's error is this: The only arrestees to whom the outcome here will ever make a difference are those who *have been acquitted* of the crime of arrest (so that their DNA could not have been taken upon conviction). In other words, this Act manages to burden uniquely the sole group for whom the Fourth Amendment's protections ought to be most jealously guarded: people who are innocent of the State's accusations.

Today's judgment will, to be sure, have the beneficial effect of solving more crimes; then again, so would the taking of DNA samples from anyone who flies on an airplane (surely the Transportation Security Administration needs to know the "identity" of the flying public), applies for a driver's license, or attends a public school. Perhaps the construction of such a genetic panopticon is wise. But I doubt that the proud men who wrote the charter of our liberties would have been so eager to open their mouths for royal inspection.

I therefore dissent, and hope that today's incursion upon the Fourth Amendment, like an earlier one,[6] will some day be repudiated.

Points for Discussion

1. In the first footnote to his dissent, Justice Scalia criticizes the majority opinion for lacking a major premise or a rule of decision because the Court does not make clear whether the taking of DNA is a search incident to arrest or a "special needs" search. Placing it in one category or the other would dictate the analysis to be applied, though the dissent argues that the routine collecting of DNA samples from every arrested person is invalid under either. Are the dissenters correct that the majority's analysis is predicated on nothing more than the conclusion that the search would be useful to law enforcement and entails only a "minimal intrusion"? Even if that is true, is it enough to justify this search that it helps solve some serious crimes?

2. SEARCHES BY PUBLIC SCHOOL ADMINISTRATORS

The constitutionality of searching public schoolchildren first came to the Court in the mid-1980s. At the time, the Reagan Administration significantly escalated the "war on drugs" by, among other things, pushing for vastly expanded law enforcement funding and for much harsher drug sentences. It was in this milieu that the Supreme Court undertook to review *New Jersey v. T.L.O.*, 469 U.S. 325 (1985).

> A teacher found T.L.O. and another student smoking in a school bathroom in violation of the school disciplinary code. The teacher sent T.L.O. to the assistant principal's office where T.L.O. denied smoking. The assistant principal then searched her purse and discovered a pack of cigarettes and rolling papers. Suspecting that T.L.O.'s purse might contain additional drug-related evidence, the assistant principal conducted a more thorough search of the purse. This search uncovered "a small amount of marihuana, a pipe, a number of empty plastic bags, a substantial quantity of money in one-dollar bills, an index card that appeared to be a list of students who owed T.L.O. money, and two letters that implicated T.L.O. in marihuana dealing." The assistant principal turned over this evidence to the police and the state charged T.L.O. as a juvenile delinquent. . . .

---

[6] Compare, *New York v. Belton,* 453 U.S. 454 (1981) (suspicionless search of a car permitted upon arrest of the driver), with *Arizona v. Gant,* 556 U.S. 332 (2009) (on second thought, no).

In 1985, state and federal courts approached school searches in three different ways. In those days, the only public officials found in public schools were teachers and administrators, so the question was whether the Fourth Amendment applied to those officials at all. Some states regarded school officials as beyond the Fourth Amendment's reach because they were private citizens acting *in loco parentis*. At the other end of the spectrum were states that required school officials to have probable cause before conducting in-school searches. However, a majority of states took the middle ground, which was the approach taken by New Jersey and ultimately adopted by the Supreme Court; under this approach, the Fourth Amendment applies to searches conducted by school officials but "the special needs of the school environment require[d] assessment of the legality of such searches against a standard less exacting than that of probable cause."

Therefore, on certiorari, the Court found that while the Fourth Amendment applies to school searches, probable cause is not required because it "is not an irreducible requirement of a valid search." Reasonableness is all the Fourth Amendment requires. To determine what was reasonable in the context of a public school, the Court balanced the students' interest in privacy against the "substantial interest of teachers and administrators in maintaining [school] discipline." Although the Court agreed that students have a legitimate expectation of privacy at school, "the school setting requires some easing of the restrictions to which searches by public authorities are ordinarily subject." . . .

T.L.O. is a significant turning point in Fourth Amendment jurisprudence because it was the first time the Court departed from the probable cause standard for full-scale searches. . . .

* * *

To some extent, *T.L.O.* was part of a broader trend in the narrowing of Fourth Amendment rights in response to the "war on drugs," a strategy that has been largely unsuccessful, and much decried but fueled by a powerful narrative that awakens deeply held, if often irrational, fears. Like the narrative of the "war on drugs," the narrative of the dangerous, potentially violent youngster roaming the halls of our public schools, ready to shoot and kill "has features of what sociologists describe as a moral panic, in which the media, politicians, and the public reinforce each other in an escalating pattern of alarmed reaction to a perceived social threat." In the immediate wake of *T.L.O.*, scholars and commentators saw the writing on the wall with regard to the Fourth Amendment rights of students and tried to suggest ways to limit its reach, but the holding inevitably created a slippery

> slope that, in the following years, the Court slid down and fell off. The unanswered questions of *T.L.O.*, including the role of law enforcement, its applicability to blanket searches without individualized suspicion (such as dog sniffs and metal detectors), and the extent to which students have a legitimate expectation of privacy in desks, lockers, and now cell phones, are not easily resolved. Meanwhile, the narrative of youth criminality as a serious threat to society remains a potent theme in American culture and a driving force of public policy.

Sarah Jane Forman, *Countering Criminalization: Toward a Youth Development Approach to School Searches*, 14 SCHOLAR 301, 309–11 (2011) (footnotes omitted).

In the 1980s, there were no drug dogs or random drug testing in America's schools, and teachers rather than police officers enforced school rules. As Professor Forman argues, the accord among all three branches of the federal government to make schools a front in the "war on drugs" resulted in a generation of children raised under suspicion:

> Metal detectors greet [students] as they enter the building. Once inside, they are not only under the watchful eye of uniformed and armed SROs but also under constant video surveillance. Schools conduct random sweeps for contraband. Dogs are brought to school, sniffing for drugs. And draconian zero-tolerance policies subject violators to harsh punishments such as suspension or expulsion regardless of the circumstances. In conjunction with the lowered expectations of privacy embodied in the reasonable suspicion standard, such policies foster an authoritarian environment that is more like a prison than a place of learning and where the lessons that are learned are ones of fear and control.

Id. at 330. Echoing the final observation of Justice Brandeis' *Olmstead* dissent, Justice Stevens' *T.L.O.* dissent predicted that surveillance of students would work to undermine the Fourth Amendment's guarantee:

> The schoolroom is the first opportunity most citizens have to experience the power of government. Through it passes every citizen and public official, from schoolteachers to policemen and prison guards. The values they learn there, they take with them in life. One of our most cherished ideals is the one contained in the Fourth Amendment: that the government may not intrude on the personal privacy of its citizens without a warrant or compelling circumstance. The Court's decision today is a curious moral for the Nation's youth. Although the search of T.L.O.'s purse does not trouble today's majority, I submit that we are not dealing with "matters relatively trivial to the welfare of the Nation. . . ."

469 U.S. at 385–86 (Stevens, J., dissenting) (quoting *West Virginia State Board of Education v. Barnette*, 319 U.S. 624, 638 (1943)).

BOARD OF EDUC. OF IND. SCHOOL DIST. NO. 92 OF POTTAWATOMIE COUNTY V. EARLS

536 U.S. 822 (2002)

JUSTICE THOMAS delivered the opinion of the court.

The Student Activities Drug Testing Policy implemented by the Board of Education of Independent School District No. 92 of Pottawatomie County (School District) requires all students who participate in competitive extracurricular activities to submit to drug testing. Because this Policy reasonably serves the School District's important interest in detecting and preventing drug use among its students, we hold that it is constitutional.

I

The city of Tecumseh, Oklahoma, is a rural community located approximately 40 miles southeast of Oklahoma City. The School District administers all Tecumseh public schools. In the fall of 1998, the School District adopted the Student Activities Drug Testing Policy (Policy), which requires all middle and high school students to consent to drug testing in order to participate in any extracurricular activity. In practice, the Policy has been applied only to competitive extracurricular activities sanctioned by the Oklahoma Secondary Schools Activities Association, such as the Academic Team, Future Farmers of America, Future Homemakers of America, band, choir, pom-pom, cheerleading, and athletics. Under the Policy, students are required to take a drug test before participating in an extracurricular activity, must submit to random drug testing while participating in that activity, and must agree to be tested at any time upon reasonable suspicion. The urinalysis tests are designed to detect only the use of illegal drugs, including amphetamines, marijuana, cocaine, opiates, and barbituates, not medical conditions or the presence of authorized prescription medications.

At the time of their suit, both respondents attended Tecumseh High School. Respondent Lindsay Earls was a member of the show choir, the marching band, the Academic Team, and the National Honor Society. Respondent Daniel James sought to participate in the Academic Team. Together with their parents, Earls and James brought a Rev. Stat. § 1979, 42 U.S.C. § 1983, action against the School District, challenging the Policy both on its face and as applied to their participation in extracurricular activities. They alleged that the Policy violates the Fourth Amendment as incorporated by the Fourteenth Amendment and requested injunctive and declarative relief. They also argued that the School District failed to identify a special need for testing students who participate in extracurricular activities, and that the "Drug Testing Policy neither addresses a proven problem nor promises to bring any benefit to students or the school."

* * *

II

* * *

In *Vernonia* [*School Dist. 47J v. Acton*, 515 U.S. 646 (1985)], this Court held that the suspicionless drug testing of athletes was constitutional. The Court, however, did not simply authorize all school drug testing, but rather conducted a fact-specific balancing of the intrusion on the children's Fourth Amendment rights against the promotion of legitimate governmental interests. Applying the principles of *Vernonia* to the somewhat different facts of this case, we conclude that Tecumseh's Policy is also constitutional.

A

We first consider the nature of the privacy interest allegedly compromised by the drug testing. As in *Vernonia,* the context of the public school environment serves as the backdrop for the analysis of the privacy interest at stake and the reasonableness of the drug testing policy in general.

A student's privacy interest is limited in a public school environment where the State is responsible for maintaining discipline, health, and safety. Schoolchildren are routinely required to submit to physical examinations and vaccinations against disease. Securing order in the school environment sometimes requires that students be subjected to greater controls than those appropriate for adults.

Respondents argue that because children participating in nonathletic extracurricular activities are not subject to regular physicals and communal undress, they have a stronger expectation of privacy than the athletes tested in *Vernonia*. This distinction, however, was not essential to our decision in *Vernonia,* which depended primarily upon the school's custodial responsibility and authority.

In any event, students who participate in competitive extracurricular activities voluntarily subject themselves to many of the same intrusions on their privacy as do athletes. Some of these clubs and activities require occasional off-campus travel and communal undress. All of them have their own rules and requirements for participating students that do not apply to the student body as a whole. For example, each of the competitive extracurricular activities governed by the Policy must abide by the rules of the Oklahoma Secondary Schools Activities Association, and a faculty sponsor monitors the students for compliance with the various rules dictated by the clubs and activities. This regulation of extracurricular activities further diminishes the expectation of privacy among schoolchildren. *Cf. Vernonia, supra,* at 657 ("Somewhat like adults who choose to participate in a closely regulated industry, students who voluntarily participate in school athletics have reason to expect intrusions upon normal rights and privileges, including privacy.").

We therefore conclude that the students affected by this Policy have a limited expectation of privacy.

B

Next, we consider the character of the intrusion imposed by the Policy. Urination is "an excretory function traditionally shielded by great privacy." But the "degree of intrusion" on one's privacy caused by collecting a urine sample "depends upon the manner in which production of the urine sample is monitored."

Under the Policy, a faculty monitor waits outside the closed restroom stall for the student to produce a sample and must "listen for the normal sounds of urination in order to guard against tampered specimens and to insure an accurate chain of custody." The monitor then pours the sample into two bottles that are sealed and placed into a mailing pouch along with a consent form signed by the student. This procedure is virtually identical to that reviewed in *Vernonia,* except that it additionally protects privacy by allowing male students to produce their samples behind a closed stall. Given that we considered the method of collection in *Vernonia* a "negligible" intrusion, the method here is even less problematic.

In addition, the Policy clearly requires that the test results be kept in confidential files separate from a student's other educational records and released to school personnel only on a "need to know" basis. Respondents nonetheless contend that the intrusion on students' privacy is significant because the Policy fails to protect effectively against the disclosure of confidential information and, specifically, that the school "has been careless in protecting that information: for example, the Choir teacher looked at students' prescription drug lists and left them where other students could see them." But the choir teacher is someone with a "need to know," because during off-campus trips she needs to know what medications are taken by her students. Even before the Policy was enacted the choir teacher had access to this information. In any event, there is no allegation that any other student did see such information. This one example of alleged carelessness hardly increases the character of the intrusion.

Moreover, the test results are not turned over to any law enforcement authority. Nor do the test results here lead to the imposition of discipline or have any academic consequences. Rather, the only consequence of a failed drug test is to limit the student's privilege of participating in extracurricular activities. Indeed, a student may test positive for drugs twice and still be allowed to participate in extracurricular activities. After the first positive test, the school contacts the student's parent or guardian for a meeting. The student may continue to participate in the activity if within five days of the meeting the student shows proof of receiving drug counseling and submits to a second drug test in two weeks. For the second positive test, the student is suspended from participation in all extracurricular activities for 14 days, must complete four hours of substance abuse counseling, and must submit to monthly drug tests. Only after a third positive test will the student be suspended from participating in any extracurricular activity for the remainder of the school year, or 88 school days, whichever is longer.

Given the minimally intrusive nature of the sample collection and the limited uses to which the test results are put, we conclude that the invasion of students' privacy is not significant.

C

Finally, this Court must consider the nature and immediacy of the government's concerns and the efficacy of the Policy in meeting them. This Court has already articulated in detail the importance of the governmental concern in preventing drug use by schoolchildren. The drug abuse problem among our Nation's youth has hardly abated since *Vernonia* was decided in 1995. In fact, evidence suggests that it has only grown worse. As in *Vernonia,* "the necessity for the State to act is magnified by the fact that this evil is being visited not just upon individuals at large, but upon children for whom it has undertaken a special responsibility of care and direction." The health and safety risks identified in *Vernonia* apply with equal force to Tecumseh's children. Indeed, the nationwide drug epidemic makes the war against drugs a pressing concern in every school.

Additionally, the School District in this case has presented specific evidence of drug use at Tecumseh schools. Teachers testified that they had seen students who appeared to be under the influence of drugs and that they had heard students speaking openly about using drugs. A drug dog found marijuana cigarettes near the school parking lot. Police officers once found drugs or drug paraphernalia in a car driven by a Future Farmers of America member. And the school board president reported that people in the community were calling the board to discuss the "drug situation." We decline to second-guess the finding of the District Court that "[v]iewing the evidence as a whole, it cannot be reasonably disputed that the [School District] was faced with a 'drug problem' when it adopted the Policy."

Respondents consider the proffered evidence insufficient and argue that there is no "real and immediate interest" to justify a policy of drug testing nonathletes. We have recognized, however, that "[a] demonstrated problem of drug abuse . . . [is] not in all cases necessary to the validity of a testing regime," but that some showing does "shore up an assertion of special need for a suspicionless general search program." The School District has provided sufficient evidence to shore up the need for its drug testing program.

Furthermore, this Court has not required a particularized or pervasive drug problem before allowing the government to conduct suspicionless drug testing. For instance, in *Von Raab* the Court upheld the drug testing of customs officials on a purely preventive basis, without any documented history of drug use by such officials. In response to the lack of evidence relating to drug use, the Court noted generally that "drug abuse is one of the most serious problems confronting our society today," and that programs to prevent and detect drug use among customs officials could not be deemed unreasonable. Likewise, the need to prevent and deter the substantial harm of childhood drug use provides the necessary immediacy for a school testing policy. Indeed, it would make little sense to require a school district to wait for a substantial portion of its students to begin using drugs before it was allowed to institute a drug testing program designed to deter drug use.

Given the nationwide epidemic of drug use, and the evidence of increased drug use in Tecumseh schools, it was entirely reasonable for the School District to enact this particular drug testing policy. We reject the Court of Appeals' novel test that "any district seeking to impose a random suspicionless drug testing policy as a condition to participation in a school activity must demonstrate that there is some identifiable drug abuse problem among a sufficient number of those subject to the testing, such that testing that group of students will actually redress its drug problem." Among other problems, it would be difficult to administer such a test. As we cannot articulate a threshold level of drug use that would suffice to justify a drug testing program for schoolchildren, we refuse to fashion what would in effect be a constitutional quantum of drug use necessary to show a "drug problem."

Respondents also argue that the testing of nonathletes does not implicate any safety concerns, and that safety is a "crucial factor" in applying the special needs framework. They contend that there must be "surpassing safety interests," *Skinner,* at 634, or "extraordinary safety and national security hazards," *Von Raab,* at 674, in order to override the usual protections of the Fourth Amendment. Respondents are correct that safety factors into the special needs analysis, but the safety interest furthered by drug testing is undoubtedly substantial for all children, athletes and nonathletes alike. We know all too well that drug use carries a variety of health risks for children, including death from overdose.

We also reject respondents' argument that drug testing must presumptively be based upon an individualized reasonable suspicion of wrongdoing because such a testing regime would be less intrusive. In this context, the Fourth Amendment does not require a finding of individualized suspicion, and we decline to impose such a requirement on schools attempting to prevent and detect drug use by students. Moreover, we question whether testing based on individualized suspicion in fact would be less intrusive. Such a regime would place an additional burden on public school teachers who are already tasked with the difficult job of maintaining order and discipline. A program of individualized suspicion might unfairly target members of unpopular groups. The fear of lawsuits resulting from such targeted searches may chill enforcement of the program, rendering it ineffective in combating drug use. In any case, this Court has repeatedly stated that reasonableness under the Fourth Amendment does not require employing the least intrusive means, because "[t]he logic of such elaborate less-restrictive-alternative arguments could raise insuperable barriers to the exercise of virtually all search-and-seizure powers."

Finally, we find that testing students who participate in extracurricular activities is a reasonably effective means of addressing the School District's legitimate concerns in preventing, deterring, and detecting drug use. While in *Vernonia* there might have been a closer fit between the testing of athletes and the trial court's finding that the drug problem was "fueled by the 'role model' effect of athletes' drug use," such a finding was not essential to the holding. *Vernonia* did not require the school to test the group of students most likely to use drugs, but rather considered the constitutionality of the program in the context of the public school's custodial responsibilities. Evaluating the Policy in this context, we conclude that the drug testing of Tecumseh students who participate in extracurricular activities effectively serves the School District's interest in protecting the safety and health of its students.

III

Within the limits of the Fourth Amendment, local school boards must assess the desirability of drug testing schoolchildren. In upholding the constitutionality of the Policy, we express no opinion as to its wisdom. Rather, we hold only that Tecumseh's Policy is a reasonable means of furthering the School District's important interest in preventing and deterring drug use among its schoolchildren. Accordingly, we reverse the judgment of the Court of Appeals.

JUSTICE BREYER, concurring.

I agree with the Court that *Vernonia School Dist. 47J v. Acton,* 515 U.S. 646 (1995), governs this case and requires reversal of the Tenth Circuit's decision. The school's drug testing program addresses a serious national problem by focusing upon demand, avoiding the use of criminal or disciplinary sanctions, and relying upon professional counseling and treatment. In my view, this program does not violate the Fourth Amendment's prohibition of "unreasonable searches and seizures." I reach this conclusion primarily for the reasons given by the Court, but I would emphasize several underlying considerations, which I understand to be consistent with the Court's opinion.

I

In respect to the school's need for the drug testing program, I would emphasize the following: First, the drug problem in our Nation's schools is serious in terms of size, the kinds of drugs being used, and the consequences of that use both for our children and the rest of us.

Second, the government's emphasis upon supply side interdiction apparently has not reduced teenage use in recent years.

Third, public school systems must find effective ways to deal with this problem. Today's public expects its schools not simply to teach the fundamentals, but "to shoulder the burden of feeding students breakfast and lunch, offering before and after school child care services, and providing medical and psychological services," all in a school environment that is safe and encourages learning. The law itself recognizes these responsibilities with the phrase *in loco parentis*—a phrase that draws its legal force primarily from the needs of younger students (who here are necessarily grouped together with older high school students) and which reflects, not that a child or adolescent lacks an interest in privacy, but that a child's or adolescent's school-related privacy interest, when compared to the privacy interests of an adult, has different dimensions. A public school system that fails adequately to carry out its responsibilities may well see parents send their children to private or parochial school instead—with help from the State.

Fourth, the program at issue here seeks to discourage demand for drugs by changing the school's environment in order to combat the single most important factor leading schoolchildren to take drugs, namely, peer pressure. It offers the adolescent a nonthreatening reason to decline his friend's drug-use invitations, namely, that he intends to play baseball, participate in debate, join the band, or engage in any one of half a dozen useful, interesting, and important activities.

II

In respect to the privacy-related burden that the drug testing program imposes upon students, I would emphasize the following: First, not everyone would agree with this Court's characterization of the privacy-related significance of urine sampling as "negligible." Some find the procedure no more intrusive than a routine medical examination, but others are seriously embarrassed by the need to provide a urine sample with someone listening "outside the closed restroom stall." When trying to resolve this kind of close question involving the interpretation of constitutional values, I believe it important that the school board provided an opportunity for the airing of these differences at public meetings designed to give the entire community "the opportunity to be able to participate" in developing the drug policy. The board used this democratic, participatory process to uncover and to resolve differences, giving weight to the fact that the process, in this instance, revealed little, if any, objection to the proposed testing program.

Second, the testing program avoids subjecting the entire school to testing. And it preserves an option for a conscientious objector. He can refuse testing while paying a price (nonparticipation) that is serious, but less severe than expulsion from the school.

Third, a contrary reading of the Constitution, as requiring "individualized suspicion" in this public school context, could well lead schools to push the boundaries of "individualized suspicion" to its outer limits, using subjective criteria that may "unfairly target members of unpopular groups," or leave those whose behavior is slightly abnormal stigmatized in the minds of others. If so, direct application of the Fourth Amendment's prohibition against "unreasonable searches and seizures" will further that Amendment's liberty-protecting objectives at least to the same extent as application of the mediating "individualized suspicion" test, where, as here, the testing program is neither criminal nor disciplinary in nature.

* * *

I cannot know whether the school's drug testing program will work. But, in my view, the Constitution does not prohibit the effort. Emphasizing the considerations I have mentioned, along with others to which the Court refers, I conclude that the school's drug testing program, constitutionally speaking, is not "unreasonable." And I join the Court's opinion.

JUSTICE O'CONNOR, with whom JUSTICE SOUTER joins, dissenting.

I dissented in *Vernonia School Dist. 47J v. Acton,* 515 U.S. 646 (1995), and continue to believe that case was wrongly decided. Because *Vernonia* is now this Court's precedent, and because I agree that petitioners' program fails even under the balancing approach adopted in that case, I join Justice Ginsburg's dissent.

JUSTICE GINSBURG, with whom JUSTICE STEVENS, JUSTICE O'CONNOR, and JUSTICE SOUTER join, dissenting.

Seven years ago, in *Vernonia School Dist. 47J v. Acton,* 515 U.S. 646 (1995), this Court determined that a school district's policy of randomly testing the urine of its student athletes for illicit drugs did not violate the Fourth Amendment. In so ruling, the Court emphasized that drug use "increase[d] the risk of sports-related injury" and that Vernonia's athletes were the "leaders" of an aggressive local "drug culture" that had reached " 'epidemic proportions.' " Today, the Court relies upon *Vernonia* to permit a school district with a drug problem its superintendent repeatedly described as "not . . . major," to test the urine of an academic team member solely by reason of her participation in a nonathletic, competitive extracurricular activity—participation associated with neither special dangers from, nor particular predilections for, drug use.

"[T]he legality of a search of a student," this Court has instructed, "should depend simply on the reasonableness, under all the circumstances, of the search." *New Jersey v. T.L.O.*, 469 U.S. 325, 341 (1985). Although " 'special needs' inhere in the public school context," those needs are not so expansive or malleable as to render reasonable any program of student drug testing a school district elects to install. The particular testing program upheld today is not reasonable; it is capricious, even perverse: Petitioners' policy targets for testing a student population least likely to be at risk from illicit drugs and their damaging effects. I therefore dissent.

I

A

* * *

This case presents circumstances dispositively different from those of *Vernonia*. True, as the Court stresses, Tecumseh students participating in competitive extracurricular activities other than athletics share two relevant characteristics with the athletes of *Vernonia*. First, both groups attend public schools. "[O]ur decision in *Vernonia*," the Court states, "depended primarily upon the school's custodial responsibility and authority." Concern for student health and safety is basic to the school's caretaking, and it is undeniable that "drug use carries a variety of health risks for children, including death from overdose."

Those risks, however, are present for *all* schoolchildren. *Vernonia* cannot be read to endorse invasive and suspicionless drug testing of all students upon any evidence of drug use, solely because drugs jeopardize the life and health of those who use them. Many children, like many adults, engage in dangerous activities on their own time; that the children are enrolled in school scarcely allows government to monitor all such activities. If a student has a reasonable subjective expectation of privacy in the personal items she brings to school, surely she has a similar expectation regarding the chemical composition of her urine. Had the *Vernonia* Court agreed that public school attendance, in and of itself, permitted the State to test each student's blood or urine for drugs, the opinion in *Vernonia* could have saved many words.

The second commonality to which the Court points is the voluntary character of both interscholastic athletics and other competitive extracurricular activities. "By choosing to 'go out for the team,' [school athletes] voluntarily subject themselves to a degree of regulation even higher than that imposed on students generally." Comparably, the Court today observes, "students who participate in competitive extracurricular activities voluntarily subject themselves to" additional rules not applicable to other students.

The comparison is enlightening. While extracurricular activities are "voluntary" in the sense that they are not required for graduation, they are part of the school's educational program; for that reason, the petitioner (hereinafter School District) is justified in expending public resources to make them available. Participation in such activities is a key component of school life, essential in reality for students applying to college, and, for all participants, a significant contributor to the breadth and quality of the educational experience. Students "volunteer" for extracurricular pursuits in the same way they might volunteer for honors classes: They subject themselves to additional requirements, but they do so in order to take full advantage of the education offered them.

Voluntary participation in athletics has a distinctly different dimension: Schools regulate student athletes discretely because competitive school sports by their nature require communal undress and, more important, expose students to physical risks that schools have a duty to mitigate. For the very reason that schools cannot offer a program of competitive athletics without intimately affecting the privacy of students, *Vernonia* reasonably analogized school athletes to "adults who choose to participate in a closely regulated industry." Industries fall within the closely regulated category when the nature of their activities requires substantial government oversight. Interscholastic athletics similarly require close safety and health regulation; a school's choir, band, and academic team do not.

In short, *Vernonia* applied, it did not repudiate, the principle that "the legality of a search of a student should depend simply on the reasonableness, *under all the circumstances,* of the search." Enrollment in a public school, and election to participate in school activities beyond the bare minimum that the curriculum requires, are indeed factors relevant to reasonableness, but they do not on their own justify intrusive, suspicionless searches. *Vernonia,* accordingly, did not rest upon these factors; instead, the Court performed what today's majority aptly describes as a "fact-specific balancing." Balancing of that order, applied to the facts now before the Court, should yield a result other than the one the Court announces today.

B

Vernonia initially considered "the nature of the privacy interest upon which the search [there] at issue intrude[d]." The Court emphasized that student athletes' expectations of privacy are necessarily attenuated . . . .

Competitive extracurricular activities other than athletics, however, serve students of all manner: the modest and shy along with the bold and uninhibited. Activities of the kind plaintiff-respondent Lindsay Earls pursued—choir, show choir, marching band, and academic team—afford opportunities to gain self-assurance, to "come to know faculty members in a less formal setting than the typical classroom," and to acquire "positive social supports and networks [that] play a critical role in periods of heightened stress."

On "occasional out-of-town trips," students like Lindsay Earls "must sleep together in communal settings and use communal bathrooms." But those situations are hardly equivalent to the routine communal undress associated with athletics; the School District itself admits that when such trips occur, "public-like restroom facilities," which presumably include enclosed stalls, are ordinarily available for changing, and that "more modest students" find other ways to maintain their privacy.[1]

* * *

Finally, the "nature and immediacy of the governmental concern," faced by the Vernonia School District dwarfed that confronting Tecumseh administrators. Vernonia initiated its drug testing policy in response to an alarming situation: "[A] large segment of the student body, particularly those involved in interscholastic athletics, was in a state of rebellion . . . fueled by alcohol and drug abuse as well as the student[s'] misperceptions about the drug culture." Tecumseh, by contrast, repeatedly reported to the Federal Government during the period leading up to the adoption of the policy that "types of drugs [other than alcohol and tobacco] including controlled dangerous substances, are present [in the schools] but have not identified themselves as major problems at this time." As the Tenth Circuit observed, "without a demonstrated drug abuse problem among the group being tested, the efficacy of the District's solution to its perceived problem is . . . greatly diminished."

* * *

Not only did the Vernonia and Tecumseh districts confront drug problems of distinctly different magnitudes, they also chose different solutions: Vernonia limited its policy to athletes; Tecumseh indiscriminately subjected to testing all participants in competitive extracurricular activities. Urging that "the safety interest furthered by drug testing is undoubtedly substantial for all children, athletes and nonathletes alike," the Court cuts out an element essential to the *Vernonia* judgment. Citing medical literature on the effects of combining illicit drug use with physical exertion, the *Vernonia* Court emphasized that "the particular drugs screened by [Vernonia's] Policy have been demonstrated to pose substantial physical risks to athletes."

At the margins, of course, no policy of *random* drug testing is perfectly tailored to the harms it seeks to address. The School District cites the dangers faced by members of the band, who must "perform extremely

[1] According to Tecumseh's choir teacher, choir participants who chose not to wear their choir uniforms to school on the days of competitions could change either in "a rest room in a building" or on the bus, where "[m]any of them have figured out how to [change] without having [anyone] . . . see anything."

precise routines with heavy equipment and instruments in close proximity to other students," and by Future Farmers of America, who "are required to individually control and restrain animals as large as 1500 pounds." For its part, the United States acknowledges that "the linebacker faces a greater risk of serious injury if he takes the field under the influence of drugs than the drummer in the halftime band," but parries that "the risk of injury to a student who is under the influence of drugs while playing golf, cross country, or volleyball (sports covered by the policy in *Vernonia*) is scarcely any greater than the risk of injury to a student . . . handling a 1500-pound steer (as [Future Farmers of America] members do) or working with cutlery or other sharp instruments (as [Future Homemakers of America] members do)." One can demur to the Government's view of the risks drug use poses to golfers, for golfers were surely as marginal among the linebackers, sprinters, and basketball players targeted for testing in Vernonia as steer-handlers are among the choristers, musicians, and academic-team members subject to urinalysis in Tecumseh. Notwithstanding nightmarish images of out-of-control flatware, livestock run amok, and colliding tubas disturbing the peace and quiet of Tecumseh, the great majority of students the School District seeks to test in truth are engaged in activities that are not safety sensitive to an unusual degree. There is a difference between imperfect tailoring and no tailoring at all.

The Vernonia district, in sum, had two good reasons for testing athletes: Sports team members faced special health risks and they "were the leaders of the drug culture." No similar reason, and no other tenable justification, explains Tecumseh's decision to target for testing all participants in every competitive extracurricular activity.

Nationwide, students who participate in extracurricular activities are significantly less likely to develop substance abuse problems than are their less-involved peers. Even if students might be deterred from drug use in order to preserve their extracurricular eligibility, it is at least as likely that other students might forgo their extracurricular involvement in order to avoid detection of their drug use. Tecumseh's policy thus falls short doubly if deterrence is its aim: It invades the privacy of students who need deterrence least, and risks steering students at greatest risk for substance abuse away from extracurricular involvement that potentially may palliate drug problems.

To summarize, this case resembles *Vernonia* only in that the School Districts in both cases conditioned engagement in activities outside the obligatory curriculum on random subjection to urinalysis. The defining characteristics of the two programs, however, are entirely dissimilar. The Vernonia district sought to test a subpopulation of students distinguished by their reduced expectation of privacy, their special susceptibility to drug-related injury, and their heavy involvement with drug use. The Tecumseh district seeks to test a much larger population associated with none of these factors. It does so, moreover, without carefully safeguarding student confidentiality and without regard to the program's untoward effects. A program so sweeping is not sheltered by *Vernonia;* its unreasonable reach renders it impermissible under the Fourth Amendment.

II

* * *

It is a sad irony that the petitioning School District seeks to justify its edict here by trumpeting "the schools' custodial and tutelary responsibility for children." In regulating an athletic program or endeavoring to combat an exploding drug epidemic, a school's custodial obligations may permit searches that would otherwise unacceptably abridge students' rights. When custodial duties are not ascendant, however, schools' tutelary obligations to their students require them to "teach by example" by avoiding symbolic measures that diminish constitutional protections. "That [schools] are educating the young for citizenship is reason for scrupulous protection of Constitutional freedoms of the individual, if we are not to strangle the free mind at its source and teach youth to discount important principles of our government as mere platitudes."

Points for Discussion

1. The Court repeatedly refers to *Vernonia School Dist. 47J v. Acton,* 515 U.S. 646 (1995). In that case the Supreme Court upheld the suspicionless drug testing of high school athletes. Does the Court do a good job of convincing you that the reasoning of that case applies to the student testing at issue in here?

2. Unlike in *Vernonia*, in *Earls* there is no evidence whatsoever of drug use by students in Tecumseh, Oklahoma—as the Court concedes. The Court's reasoning goes significantly further than *Vernonia* because it allows for suspicionless drug testing of students without any showing of a specific drug problem because "the need to prevent and deter the substantial harm of childhood drug use provides the necessary immediacy for a school testing policy." In addition, although the majority repeatedly describes the target of the testing as students engaged in "*competitive* extracurricular activities," the adjective would seem to be of nothing more than rhetorical effect.

3. Justice Ginsburg joined the majority opinion in *Vernonia* because the testing in that case was limited "to students who voluntarily participate in interscholastic athletics." Her dissent in *Earls* protests that the majority allows drug testing of students "least likely to be at risk from illicit drugs and their damaging effects." She complains that the testing reaches the "modest and shy" as well as the "bold and uninhibited." In addition, she asserts that extracurricular activities are "part of the school's educational program," "a key component of school life," and "essential in reality for students applying to college." Aren't all of these things at least equally true of sports? Are all athletes "bold and uninhibited"? What does showering with one's teammates

have to do with one's expectation of privacy in the chemical composition of one's urine? Can Justice Ginsburg's positions in the two cases be reconciled with one another?

SAFFORD UNIFIED SCHOOL DISTRICT NO. 1 V. REDDING

557 U.S. 364 (2009)

JUSTICE SOUTER delivered the opinion of the court.

The issue here is whether a 13-year-old student's Fourth Amendment right was violated when she was subjected to a search of her bra and underpants by school officials acting on reasonable suspicion that she had brought forbidden prescription and over-the-counter drugs to school. Because there were no reasons to suspect the drugs presented a danger or were concealed in her underwear, we hold that the search did violate the Constitution, but because there is reason to question the clarity with which the right was established, the official who ordered the unconstitutional search is entitled to qualified immunity from liability.

I

The events immediately prior to the search in question began in 13-year-old Savana Redding's math class at Safford Middle School one October day in 2003. The assistant principal of the school, Kerry Wilson, came into the room and asked Savana to go to his office. There, he showed her a day planner, unzipped and open flat on his desk, in which there were several knives, lighters, a permanent marker, and a cigarette. Wilson asked Savana whether the planner was hers; she said it was, but that a few days before she had lent it to her friend, Marissa Glines. Savana stated that none of the items in the planner belonged to her.

Wilson then showed Savana four white prescription-strength ibuprofen 400-mg pills, and one over-the-counter blue naproxen 200-mg pill, all used for pain and inflammation but banned under school rules without advance permission. He asked Savana if she knew anything about the pills. Savana answered that she did not. Wilson then told Savana that he had received a report that she was giving these pills to fellow students; Savana denied it and agreed to let Wilson search her belongings. Helen Romero, an administrative assistant, came into the office, and together with Wilson they searched Savana's backpack, finding nothing.

At that point, Wilson instructed Romero to take Savana to the school nurse's office to search her clothes for pills. Romero and the nurse, Peggy Schwallier, asked Savana to remove her jacket, socks, and shoes, leaving her in stretch pants and a T-shirt (both without pockets), which she was then asked to remove. Finally, Savana was told to pull her bra out and to the side and shake it, and to pull out the elastic on her underpants, thus exposing her breasts and pelvic area to some degree. No pills were found.

* * *

II

* * *

In [*New Jersey v. T.L.O.*, 469 U.S. 325 (1985)], we recognized that the school setting "requires some modification of the level of suspicion of illicit activity needed to justify a search," and held that for searches by school officials "a careful balancing of governmental and private interests suggests that the public interest is best served by a Fourth Amendment standard of reasonableness that stops short of probable cause." We have thus applied a standard of reasonable suspicion to determine the legality of a school administrator's search of a student and have held that a school search "will be permissible in its scope when the measures adopted are reasonably related to the objectives of the search and not excessively intrusive in light of the age and sex of the student and the nature of the infraction."

* * *

Perhaps the best that can be said generally about the required knowledge component of probable cause for a law enforcement officer's evidence search is that it raise a "fair probability," [*Illinois v. Gates*, 462 U.S. 213, 238 (1983)], or a "substantial chance," *id.*, at 244, n. 13, of discovering evidence of criminal activity. The lesser standard for school searches could as readily be described as a moderate chance of finding evidence of wrongdoing.

III

A

In this case, the school's policies strictly prohibit the nonmedical use, possession, or sale of any drug on school grounds, including "[a]ny prescription or over-the-counter drug, except those for which permission to use in school has been granted pursuant to Board policy." A week before Savana was searched, another student, Jordan Romero (no relation of the school's administrative assistant), told the principal and Assistant Principal Wilson that "certain students were bringing drugs and weapons on campus," and that he had been sick after taking some pills that "he got from a classmate." On the morning of October 8, the same boy handed Wilson a white pill that he said Marissa Glines had given him. He told Wilson that students were planning to take the pills at lunch.

Wilson learned from Peggy Schwallier, the school nurse, that the pill was Ibuprofen 400 mg, available only by prescription. Wilson then called Marissa out of class. Outside the classroom, Marissa's teacher handed Wilson the day planner, found within Marissa's reach, containing various contraband items. Wilson escorted Marissa back to his office.

In the presence of Helen Romero, Wilson requested Marissa to turn out her pockets and open her wallet. Marissa produced a blue pill, several white ones, and a razor blade. Wilson asked where the blue pill came from, and Marissa answered, " 'I guess it slipped in when *she* gave me the IBU 400s.' " When Wilson asked whom she meant, Marissa replied, " 'Savana Redding.' " Wilson then enquired about the day planner and its contents; Marissa denied knowing anything about them. Wilson did not ask Marissa any followup questions to determine whether there was any likelihood that Savana presently had pills: neither asking when Marissa received the pills from Savana nor where Savana might be hiding them.

Schwallier did not immediately recognize the blue pill, but information provided through a poison control hotline indicated that the pill was a 200-mg dose of an anti-inflammatory drug, generically called naproxen, available over the counter. At Wilson's direction, Marissa was then subjected to a search of her bra and underpants by Romero and Schwallier, as Savana was later on. The search revealed no additional pills.

It was at this juncture that Wilson called Savana into his office and showed her the day planner. Their conversation established that Savana and Marissa were on friendly terms: while she denied knowledge of the contraband, Savana admitted that the day planner was hers and that she had lent it to Marissa. Wilson had other reports of their friendship from staff members, who had identified Savana and Marissa as part of an unusually rowdy group at the school's opening dance in August, during which alcohol and cigarettes were found in the girls' bathroom. Wilson had reason to connect the girls with this contraband, for Wilson knew that Jordan Romero had told the principal that before the dance, he had been at a party at Savana's house where alcohol was served. Marissa's statement that the pills came from Savana was thus sufficiently plausible to warrant suspicion that Savana was involved in pill distribution.

This suspicion of Wilson's was enough to justify a search of Savana's backpack and outer clothing.[3] If a student is reasonably suspected of giving out contraband pills, she is reasonably suspected of carrying them on her person and in the carryall that has become an item of student uniform in most places today. If Wilson's reasonable suspicion of pill distribution were not understood to support searches of outer clothes and backpack, it would not justify any search worth making. And the look into Savana's bag, in her presence and in the relative privacy of Wilson's office, was not excessively intrusive, any more than Romero's subsequent search of her outer clothing.

[3] There is no question here that justification for the school officials' search was required in accordance with the *T.L.O.* standard of reasonable suspicion, for it is common ground that Savana had a reasonable expectation of privacy covering the personal things she chose to carry in her backpack and that Wilson's decision to look through it was a "search" within the meaning of the Fourth Amendment.

B

Here it is that the parties part company, with Savana's claim that extending the search at Wilson's behest to the point of making her pull out her underwear was constitutionally unreasonable. The exact label for this final step in the intrusion is not important, though strip search is a fair way to speak of it. Romero and Schwallier directed Savana to remove her clothes down to her underwear, and then "pull out" her bra and the elastic band on her underpants. Although Romero and Schwallier stated that they did not see anything when Savana followed their instructions, we would not define strip search and its Fourth Amendment consequences in a way that would guarantee litigation about who was looking and how much was seen. The very fact of Savana's pulling her underwear away from her body in the presence of the two officials who were able to see her necessarily exposed her breasts and pelvic area to some degree, and both subjective and reasonable societal expectations of personal privacy support the treatment of such a search as categorically distinct, requiring distinct elements of justification on the part of school authorities for going beyond a search of outer clothing and belongings.

Savana's subjective expectation of privacy against such a search is inherent in her account of it as embarrassing, frightening, and humiliating. The reasonableness of her expectation (required by the Fourth Amendment standard) is indicated by the consistent experiences of other young people similarly searched, whose adolescent vulnerability intensifies the patent intrusiveness of the exposure. The common reaction of these adolescents simply registers the obviously different meaning of a search exposing the body from the experience of nakedness or near undress in other school circumstances. Changing for gym is getting ready for play; exposing for a search is responding to an accusation reserved for suspected wrongdoers and fairly understood as so degrading that a number of communities have decided that strip searches in schools are never reasonable and have banned them no matter what the facts may be.

The indignity of the search does not, of course, outlaw it, but it does implicate the rule of reasonableness as stated in *T.L.O.,* that "the search as actually conducted [be] reasonably related in scope to the circumstances which justified the interference in the first place." The scope will be permissible, that is, when it is "not excessively intrusive in light of the age and sex of the student and the nature of the infraction."

Here, the content of the suspicion failed to match the degree of intrusion. Wilson knew beforehand that the pills were prescription-strength ibuprofen and over-the-counter naproxen, common pain relievers equivalent to two Advil, or one Aleve. He must have been aware of the nature and limited threat of the specific drugs he was searching for, and while just about anything can be taken in quantities that will do real harm, Wilson had no reason to suspect that large amounts of the drugs were being passed around, or that individual students were receiving great numbers of pills.

Nor could Wilson have suspected that Savana was hiding common painkillers in her underwear. Petitioners suggest, as a truth universally acknowledged, that "students . . . hid[e] contraband in or under their clothing," and cite a smattering of cases of students with contraband in their underwear. But when the categorically extreme intrusiveness of a search down to the body of an adolescent requires some justification in suspected facts, general background possibilities fall short; a reasonable search that extensive calls for suspicion that it will pay off. But nondangerous school contraband does not raise the specter of stashes in intimate places, and there is no evidence in the record of any general practice among Safford Middle School students of hiding that sort of thing in underwear; neither Jordan nor Marissa suggested to Wilson that Savana was doing that, and the preceding search of Marissa that Wilson ordered yielded nothing. Wilson never even determined when Marissa had received the pills from Savana; if it had been a few days before, that would weigh heavily against any reasonable conclusion that Savana presently had the pills on her person, much less in her underwear.

In sum, what was missing from the suspected facts that pointed to Savana was any indication of danger to the students from the power of the drugs or their quantity, and any reason to suppose that Savana was carrying pills in her underwear. We think that the combination of these deficiencies was fatal to finding the search reasonable.

In so holding, we mean to cast no ill reflection on the assistant principal, for the record raises no doubt that his motive throughout was to eliminate drugs from his school and protect students from what Jordan Romero had gone through. Parents are known to overreact to protect their children from danger, and a school official with responsibility for safety may tend to do the same. The difference is that the Fourth Amendment places limits on the official, even with the high degree of deference that courts must pay to the educator's professional judgment.

We do mean, though, to make it clear that the *T.L.O.* concern to limit a school search to reasonable scope requires the support of reasonable suspicion of danger or of resort to underwear for hiding evidence of wrongdoing before a search can reasonably make the quantum leap from outer clothes and backpacks to exposure of intimate parts. The meaning of such a search, and the degradation its subject may reasonably feel, place a search that intrusive in a category of its own demanding its own specific suspicions.

* * *

JUSTICE STEVENS, with whom JUSTICE GINSBURG joins, concurring in part and dissenting in part.

In *New Jersey v. T.L.O.,* 469 U.S. 325 (1985), the Court established a two-step inquiry for determining the reasonableness of a school official's decision to search a student. First, the Court explained, the search must be " 'justified at its inception' " by the presence of "reasonable grounds for suspecting that the search will turn up evidence that the student has violated or is violating either the law or the rules of the school." Second, the search must be "permissible in its scope," which is achieved "when the measures adopted are reasonably related to the objectives of the search and *not excessively intrusive in light of the age and sex of the student and the nature of the infraction.*"

Nothing the Court decides today alters this basic framework. It simply applies *T.L.O.* to declare unconstitutional a strip search of a 13-year-old honors student that was based on a groundless suspicion that she might be hiding medicine in her underwear. This is, in essence, a case in which clearly established law meets clearly outrageous conduct. I have long believed that " '[i]t does not require a constitutional scholar to conclude that a nude search of a 13-year-old child is an invasion of constitutional rights of some magnitude.' " The strip search of Savana Redding in this case was both more intrusive and less justified than the search of the student's purse in *T.L.O.* Therefore, while I join Parts I-III of the Court's opinion, I disagree with its decision to extend qualified immunity to the school official who authorized this unconstitutional search.

* * *

JUSTICE GINSBURG, concurring in part and dissenting in part.

I agree with the Court that Assistant Principal Wilson's subjection of 13-year-old Savana Redding to a humiliating stripdown search violated the Fourth Amendment. But I also agree with Justice Stevens that our opinion in *New Jersey v. T.L.O.,* 469 U.S. 325 (1985), "clearly established" the law governing this case.

Fellow student Marissa Glines, caught with pills in her pocket, accused Redding of supplying them. Asked where the blue pill among several white pills in Glines's pocket came from, Glines answered: "I guess it slipped in when she gave me the IBU 400s." Asked next "who is she?", Glines responded: "Savana Redding." As the Court observes, no followup questions were asked. Wilson did not test Glines's accusation for veracity by asking Glines when did Redding give her the pills, where, for what purpose. Any reasonable search for the pills would have ended when inspection of Redding's backpack and jacket pockets yielded nothing. Wilson had no cause to suspect, based on prior experience at the school or clues in this case, that Redding had hidden pills—containing the equivalent of two Advils or one Aleve—in her underwear or body. To make matters worse, Wilson did not release Redding, to return to class or to go home, after the search. Instead, he made her sit on a chair outside his office for over two hours. At no point did he attempt to call her parent. Abuse of authority of that order should not be shielded by official immunity.

* * *

JUSTICE THOMAS, concurring in the judgment in part and dissenting in part.

I agree with the Court that the judgment against the school officials with respect to qualified immunity should be reversed. Unlike the majority, however, I would hold that the search of Savana Redding did not violate the Fourth Amendment. The majority imposes a vague and amorphous standard on school administrators. It also grants judges sweeping authority to second-guess the measures that these officials take to maintain discipline in their schools and ensure the health and safety of the students in their charge. This deep intrusion into the administration of public schools exemplifies why the Court should return to the common-law doctrine of *in loco parentis* under which "the judiciary was reluctant to interfere in the routine business of school administration, allowing schools and teachers to set and enforce rules and to maintain order." *Morse v. Frederick,* 551 U.S. 393, 414 (2007) (Thomas, J., concurring). But even under the prevailing Fourth Amendment test established by *New Jersey v. T.L.O.,* 469 U.S. 325 (1985), all petitioners, including the school district, are entitled to judgment as a matter of law in their favor.

I

* * *

A

* * *

Here, petitioners had reasonable grounds to suspect that Redding was in possession of prescription and nonprescription drugs in violation of the school's prohibition of the "non-medical use, possession, or sale of a drug" on school property or at school events. As an initial matter, school officials were aware that a few years earlier, a student had become "seriously ill" and "spent several days in intensive care" after ingesting prescription medication obtained from a classmate. Fourth Amendment searches do not occur in a vacuum; rather, context must inform the judicial inquiry. In this instance, the suspicion of drug possession arose at a middle school that had "a history of problems with students using and distributing prohibited and illegal substances on campus."

The school's substance-abuse problems had not abated by the 2003–2004 school year, which is when the challenged search of Redding took place. School officials had found alcohol and cigarettes in the girls' bathroom during the first school dance of the year and noticed that a group of students including Redding and Marissa Glines smelled of alcohol. Several weeks later, another student, Jordan Romero, reported that Redding had hosted a party before the dance where she served whiskey, vodka, and tequila. Romero had provided this report to school officials as a result of a meeting his mother scheduled with the officials after Romero "bec[a]me violent" and "sick to his stomach" one night and admitted that "he had taken some pills that he had got[ten] from a classmate." At that meeting, Romero admitted that "certain students were bringing drugs and weapons on campus." One week later, Romero handed the assistant principal a white pill that he said he had received from Glines. He reported "that a group of students [were] planning on taking the pills at lunch."

School officials justifiably took quick action in light of the lunchtime deadline. The assistant principal took the pill to the school nurse who identified it as prescription-strength 400-mg Ibuprofen. A subsequent search of Glines and her belongings produced a razor blade, a Naproxen 200-mg pill, and several Ibuprofen 400-mg pills. When asked, Glines claimed that she had received the pills from Redding. A search of Redding's planner, which Glines had borrowed, then uncovered "several knives, several lighters, a cigarette, and a permanent marker." Thus, as the majority acknowledges, the totality of relevant circumstances justified a search of Redding for pills.

B

The remaining question is whether the search was reasonable in scope. Under *T.L.O.,* "a search will be permissible in its scope when the measures adopted are reasonably related to the objectives of the search and not excessively intrusive in light of the age and sex of the student and the nature of the infraction." The majority concludes that the school officials' search of Redding's underwear was not "reasonably related in scope to the circumstances which justified the interference in the first place," notwithstanding the officials' reasonable suspicion that Redding "was involved in pill distribution." According to the majority, to be reasonable, this school search required a showing of "danger to the students from the power of the drugs or their quantity" or a "reason to suppose that [Redding] was carrying pills in her underwear." Each of these additional requirements is an unjustifiable departure from bedrock Fourth Amendment law in the school setting, where this Court has heretofore read the Fourth Amendment to grant considerable leeway to school officials. Because the school officials searched in a location where the pills could have been hidden, the search was reasonable in scope under *T.L.O.*

1

* * *

The Court has generally held that the reasonableness of a search's scope depends only on whether it is limited to the area that is capable of concealing the object of the search. In keeping with this longstanding rule, the "nature of the infraction" referenced in *T.L.O.* delineates the proper scope of a search of students in a way that is identical to that permitted for searches outside the school—*i.e.,* the search must be limited to the areas where the object of that infraction could be concealed. A search of a student therefore is permissible in scope under *T.L.O.* so long as it is objectively reasonable to believe that the area searched could conceal the contraband. The dissenting opinion below correctly captured this Fourth Amendment standard, noting that "if a student brought a baseball bat on campus in violation of school policy, a search of that student's shirt pocket would be patently unjustified."

The analysis of whether the scope of the search here was permissible under that standard is straightforward. Indeed, the majority does not dispute that "general background possibilities" establish that students conceal "contraband in their underwear." It acknowledges that school officials had reasonable suspicion to look in Redding's backpack and outer clothing because if "Wilson's reasonable suspicion of pill distribution were not understood to support searches of outer clothes and backpack, it would not justify any search worth making." The majority nevertheless concludes that proceeding any further with the search was unreasonable. But there is no support for this conclusion. The reasonable suspicion that Redding possessed the pills for distribution purposes did not dissipate simply because the search of her backpack turned up nothing. It was eminently reasonable to conclude that the backpack was empty because Redding was secreting the pills in a place she thought no one would look.

Redding would not have been the first person to conceal pills in her undergarments. Nor will she be the last after today's decision, which announces the safest place to secrete contraband in school.

2

The majority compounds its error by reading the "nature of the infraction" aspect of the *T.L.O.* test as a license to limit searches based on a judge's assessment of a particular school policy. According to the majority, the scope of the search was impermissible because the school official "must have been aware of the nature and limited threat of the specific drugs he was searching for" and because he "had no reason to suspect that large amounts of the drugs were being passed around, or that individual students were receiving great numbers of pills." Thus, in order to locate a rationale for finding a Fourth Amendment violation in this case, the majority retreats from its observation that the school's firm no-drug policy "makes sense, and there is no basis to claim that the search was unreasonable owing to some defect or shortcoming of the rule it was aimed at enforcing."

Even accepting the majority's assurances that it is not attacking the rule's reasonableness, it certainly is attacking the rule's importance. This approach directly conflicts with *T.L.O.* in which the Court was "unwilling to adopt a standard under which the legality of a search is dependent upon a judge's evaluation of the relative importance of school rules." Indeed, the Court in *T.L.O.* expressly rejected the proposition that the majority seemingly endorses—that "some rules regarding student conduct are by nature too 'trivial' to justify a search based upon reasonable suspicion."

The majority's decision in this regard also departs from another basic principle of the Fourth Amendment: that law enforcement officials can enforce with the same vigor all rules and regulations irrespective of the perceived importance of any of those rules. "In a long line of cases, we have said that when an officer has probable cause to believe a person committed even a minor crime in his presence, the balancing of private and public interests is not in doubt. The arrest is constitutionally reasonable." The Fourth Amendment rule for searches is the same: Police officers are entitled to search regardless of the perceived triviality of the underlying law. As we have explained, requiring police to make "sensitive, case-by-case determinations of government need," for a particular prohibition before conducting a search would "place police in an almost impossible spot."

The majority has placed school officials in this "impossible spot" by questioning whether possession of Ibuprofen and Naproxen causes a severe enough threat to warrant investigation. Had the suspected infraction involved a street drug, the majority implies that it would have approved the scope of the search. In effect, then, the majority has replaced a school rule that draws no distinction among drugs with a new one that does. As a result, a full search of a student's person for prohibited drugs will be permitted only if the Court agrees that the drug in question was sufficiently dangerous. Such a test is unworkable and unsound. School officials cannot be expected to halt searches based on the possibility that a court might later find that the particular infraction at issue is not severe enough to warrant an intrusive investigation.

* * *

3

Even if this Court were authorized to second-guess the importance of school rules, the Court's assessment of the importance of this district's policy is flawed. It is a crime to possess or use prescription-strength Ibuprofen without a prescription. By prohibiting unauthorized prescription drugs on school grounds—and conducting a search to ensure students abide by that prohibition—the school rule here was consistent with a routine provision of the state criminal code. It hardly seems unreasonable for school officials to enforce a rule that, in effect, proscribes conduct that amounts to a crime.

* * *

II

By declaring the search unreasonable in this case, the majority has "surrender[ed] control of the American public school system to public school students" by invalidating school policies that treat all drugs equally and by second-guessing swift disciplinary decisions made by school officials. The Court's interference in these matters of great concern to teachers, parents, and students illustrates why the most constitutionally sound approach to the question of applying the Fourth Amendment in local public schools would in fact be the complete restoration of the common-law doctrine of *in loco parentis*.

"[I]n the early years of public schooling," courts applied the doctrine of *in loco parentis* to transfer to teachers the authority of a parent to "command obedience, to control stubbornness, to quicken diligence, and to reform bad habits." *Morse,* at 413–414 (Thomas, J., concurring). So empowered, schoolteachers and administrators had almost complete discretion to establish and enforce the rules they believed were necessary to maintain control over their classrooms. The perils of judicial policymaking inherent in applying Fourth Amendment protections to public schools counsel in favor of a return to the understanding that existed in this Nation's first public schools, which gave teachers discretion to craft the rules needed to carry out the disciplinary responsibilities delegated to them by parents.

If the common-law view that parents delegate to teachers their authority to discipline and maintain order were to be applied in this case, the search of Redding would stand. There can be no doubt that a parent would have had the authority to conduct the search at issue in this case. Parents have "immunity from the strictures of the Fourth Amendment" when it comes to searches of a child or that child's belongings. *T.L.O.,* 469 U.S., at 337 (A parent's authority is "not subject to the limits of the Fourth Amendment").

* * *

In the end, the task of implementing and amending public school policies is beyond this Court's function. Parents, teachers, school administrators, local politicians, and state officials are all better suited than judges to determine the appropriate limits on searches conducted by school officials. Preservation of order, discipline, and safety in public schools is simply not the domain of the Constitution. And, common sense is not a judicial monopoly or a Constitutional imperative.

* * *

Points for Discussion

1. In *New Jersey v. TLO*, 469 U.S. 325 (1985), the Court held that school officials may search students if they have a reasonable suspicion that there has been a violation of the law or of school rules. Didn't the school officials here have reasonable suspicion to believe that Redding was violating school rules? Why then does the Court invalidate their search?

2. Justice Thomas accuses the majority of instructing would-be high school drug dealers exactly how to transport their drugs on school property. How fair is this criticism?

3. Justice Souter's majority opinion states that getting undressed for gym class is categorically different than getting undressed to be searched. How does this reasoning undermine the rationale for the random drug testing the Court approved of in *Vernonia* and *Earls*?

3. SEARCHES BY THE GOVERNMENT AS EMPLOYER

NATIONAL TREASURY EMPLOYEES UNION V. VON RAAB

489 U.S. 656 (1989)

JUSTICE KENNEDY delivered the opinion of the court.

We granted certiorari to decide whether it violates the Fourth Amendment for the United States Customs Service to require a urinalysis test from employees who seek transfer or promotion to certain positions.

I

A

* * *

In December 1985, respondent, the Commissioner of Customs, established a Drug Screening Task Force to explore the possibility of implementing a drug-screening program within the Service. After extensive research and consultation with experts in the field, the task force concluded that "drug screening through urinalysis is technologically reliable, valid and accurate." Citing this conclusion, the Commissioner announced his intention to require drug tests of employees who applied for, or occupied, certain positions within the Service. The Commissioner stated his belief that "Customs is largely drug-free," but noted also that "unfortunately no segment of society is immune from the threat of illegal drug use." Drug interdiction has become the agency's primary enforcement mission, and the Commissioner stressed that "there is no room in the Customs Service for those who break the laws prohibiting the possession and use of illegal drugs."

In May 1986, the Commissioner announced implementation of the drug-testing program. Drug tests were made a condition of placement or employment for positions that meet one or more of three criteria. The first is direct involvement in drug interdiction or enforcement of related laws, an activity the Commissioner deemed fraught with obvious dangers to the mission of the agency and the lives of Customs agents. The second criterion is a requirement that the incumbent carry firearms, as the Commissioner concluded that "[p]ublic safety demands that employees who carry deadly arms and are prepared to make instant life or death decisions be drug free." The third criterion is a requirement for the incumbent to handle "classified" material, which the Commissioner determined might fall into the hands of smugglers if accessible to employees who, by reason of their own illegal drug use, are susceptible to bribery or blackmail.

After an employee qualifies for a position covered by the Customs testing program, the Service advises him by letter that his final selection is contingent upon successful completion of drug screening. An independent contractor contacts the employee to fix the time and place for collecting the sample. On reporting for the test, the employee must produce photographic identification and remove any outer garments, such as a coat or a jacket, and personal belongings. The employee may produce the sample behind a partition, or in the privacy of a bathroom stall if he so chooses. To ensure against adulteration of the specimen, or substitution of a sample from another person, a monitor of the same sex as the employee remains close at hand to listen for the normal sounds of urination. Dye is added to the toilet water to prevent the employee from using the water to adulterate the sample.

* * *

Customs employees who test positive for drugs and who can offer no satisfactory explanation are subject to dismissal from the Service. Test results may not, however, be turned over to any other agency, including criminal prosecutors, without the employee's written consent.

B

Petitioners, a union of federal employees and a union official, commenced this suit in the United States District Court for the Eastern District of Louisiana on behalf of current Customs Service employees who seek covered positions. Petitioners alleged that the Custom Service drug-testing program violated, *inter alia,* the Fourth Amendment. . . .

* * *

II

* * *

It is clear that the Customs Service's drug-testing program is not designed to serve the ordinary needs of law enforcement. Test results may not be used in a criminal prosecution of the employee without the employee's consent. The purposes of the program are to deter drug use among those eligible for promotion to sensitive positions within the Service and to prevent the promotion of drug users to those positions. These substantial interests, no less than the Government's concern for safe rail transportation at issue in [*Skinner v. Railway Labor Executives,* 489 U.S. 602 (1989)] present a special need that may justify departure from the ordinary warrant and probable-cause requirements.

A

Petitioners do not contend that a warrant is required by the balance of privacy and governmental interests in this context, nor could any such contention withstand scrutiny. We have recognized before that requiring the Government to procure a warrant for every work-related intrusion "would conflict with 'the common-sense realization that government offices could not function if every employment decision became a constitutional matter.' " Even if Customs Service employees are more likely to be familiar with the procedures required to obtain a warrant than most other Government workers, requiring a warrant in this context would serve only to divert valuable agency resources from the Service's primary mission. The Customs Service has been entrusted with pressing responsibilities, and its mission would be compromised if it were required to seek search warrants in connection with routine, yet sensitive, employment decisions.

Furthermore, a warrant would provide little or nothing in the way of additional protection of personal privacy. A warrant serves primarily to advise the citizen that an intrusion is authorized by law and limited in its permissible scope and to interpose a neutral magistrate between the citizen and the law enforcement officer "engaged in the often competitive enterprise of ferreting out crime." But in the present context, "the circumstances justifying toxicological testing and the permissible limits of such intrusions are defined narrowly and specifically . . ., and doubtless are well known to covered employees." Under the Customs program, every employee who seeks a transfer to a covered position knows that he must take a drug test, and is likewise aware of the procedures the Service must follow in administering the test. A covered employee is simply not subject "to the discretion of the official in the field." *Camara v. Municipal Court of San Francisco,* 387 U.S. 523, 532 (1967). The process becomes automatic when the employee elects to apply for, and thereafter pursue, a covered position. Because the Service does not make a discretionary determination to search based on a judgment that certain conditions are present, there are simply "no special facts for a neutral magistrate to evaluate."

B

Even where it is reasonable to dispense with the warrant requirement in the particular circumstances, a search ordinarily must be based on probable cause. Our cases teach, however, that the probable-cause standard " 'is peculiarly related to criminal investigations.' " In particular, the traditional probable-cause standard may be unhelpful in analyzing the reasonableness of routine administrative functions especially where the Government seeks to *prevent* the development of hazardous conditions or to detect violations that rarely generate articulable grounds for searching any particular place or person. Our precedents have settled that, in certain limited circumstances, the Government's need to discover such latent or hidden conditions, or to prevent their development, is sufficiently compelling to justify the intrusion on privacy entailed by conducting such searches without any measure of individualized suspicion. We think the Government's need to conduct the suspicionless searches required by the Customs program outweighs the privacy interests of employees engaged directly in drug interdiction, and of those who otherwise are required to carry firearms.

The Customs Service is our Nation's first line of defense against one of the greatest problems affecting the health and welfare of our population. We have adverted before to "the veritable national crisis in law enforcement caused by smuggling of illicit narcotics." Our cases also reflect the traffickers' seemingly inexhaustible repertoire of deceptive practices and elaborate schemes for importing narcotics. The record in this case confirms that, through the adroit selection of source locations, smuggling routes, and increasingly elaborate methods of concealment, drug traffickers have managed to bring into this country increasingly large quantities of illegal drugs. The record also indicates, and it is well known, that drug smugglers do not hesitate to use violence to protect their lucrative trade and avoid apprehension.

Many of the Service's employees are often exposed to this criminal element and to the controlled substances it seeks to smuggle into the country. The physical safety of these employees may be threatened, and many may be tempted not only by bribes from the traffickers with whom they deal, but also by their own access to vast sources of valuable contraband seized and controlled by the Service. The Commissioner indicated below that "Customs [o]fficers have been shot, stabbed, run over, dragged by automobiles, and assaulted with blunt objects while performing their duties." At least nine officers have died in the line of duty since 1974. He also noted that Customs officers have been the targets of bribery by drug smugglers on numerous occasions, and several have been removed from the Service for accepting bribes and for other integrity violations.

It is readily apparent that the Government has a compelling interest in ensuring that front-line interdiction personnel are physically fit, and have unimpeachable integrity and judgment. Indeed, the Government's interest here is at least as important as its interest in searching travelers entering the country. We have long held that travelers seeking to enter the country may be stopped and required to submit to a routine search without probable cause, or even founded suspicion, "because of national self protection reasonably requiring one entering the country to identify himself as entitled to come in, and his belongings as effects which may be lawfully brought in." *Carroll v. United States,* 267 U.S. 132, 154 (1925). This national interest in self-protection could be irreparably damaged if those charged with safeguarding it were, because of their own drug use, unsympathetic to their mission of interdicting narcotics. A drug user's indifference to the Service's basic mission or, even worse, his active complicity with the malefactors, can facilitate importation of sizable drug shipments or block apprehension of dangerous criminals. The public interest demands effective measures to bar drug users from positions directly involving the interdiction of illegal drugs.

* * *

Without disparaging the importance of the governmental interests that support the suspicionless searches of these employees, petitioners nevertheless contend that the Service's drug-testing program is unreasonable in two particulars. First, petitioners argue that the program is unjustified because it is not based on a belief that testing will reveal any drug use by covered employees. In pressing this argument, petitioners point out that the Service's testing scheme was not implemented in response to any perceived drug problem among Customs employees, and that the program actually has not led to the discovery of a significant number of drug users. Counsel for petitioners informed us at oral argument that no more than 5 employees out of 3,600 have tested positive for drugs. Second, petitioners contend that the Service's scheme is not a "sufficiently productive mechanism to justify [its] intrusion upon Fourth Amendment interests," *Delaware v. Prouse,* 440 U.S. 648, 658–659 (1979), because illegal drug users can avoid detection with ease by temporary abstinence or by surreptitious adulteration of their urine specimens. These contentions are unpersuasive.

Petitioners' first contention evinces an unduly narrow view of the context in which the Service's testing program was implemented. Petitioners do not dispute, nor can there be doubt, that drug abuse is one of the most serious problems confronting our society today. There is little reason to believe that American workplaces are immune from this pervasive social problem, as is amply illustrated by our decision in *Railway Labor Executives*. Detecting drug impairment on the part of employees can be a difficult task, especially where, as here, it is not feasible to subject employees and their work product to the kind of day-to-day scrutiny that is the norm in more traditional office environments. Indeed, the almost unique mission of the Service gives the Government a compelling interest in ensuring that many of these covered employees do not use drugs even off duty, for such use creates risks of bribery and blackmail against which the Government is entitled to guard. In light of the extraordinary safety and national security hazards that would attend the promotion of drug users to positions that require the carrying of firearms or the interdiction of controlled substances, the Service's policy of deterring drug users from seeking such promotions cannot be deemed unreasonable.

The mere circumstance that all but a few of the employees tested are entirely innocent of wrongdoing does not impugn the program's validity. The same is likely to be true of householders who are required to submit to suspicionless housing code inspections and of motorists who are stopped at the checkpoints we approved in *United States v. Martinez-Fuerte,* 428 U.S. 543 (1976). The Service's program is designed to prevent the promotion of drug users to sensitive positions as much as it is designed to detect those employees who use drugs. Where, as here, the possible harm against which the Government seeks to guard is substantial, the need to prevent its occurrence furnishes an ample justification for reasonable searches calculated to advance the Government's goal.[3]

We think petitioners' second argument—that the Service's testing program is ineffective because employees may attempt to deceive the test by a brief abstention before the test date, or by adulterating their urine specimens—overstates the case. As the Court of Appeals noted, addicts may be unable to abstain even for a limited period of time, or may be unaware of the "fade-away effect" of certain drugs. More importantly, the avoidance techniques suggested by petitioners are fraught with uncertainty and risks for those employees who venture to attempt them. A particular employee's pattern of elimination for a given drug cannot be predicted with perfect accuracy, and, in any event, this information is not

[3] The point is well illustrated also by the Federal Government's practice of requiring the search of all passengers seeking to board commercial airliners, as well as the search of their carry-on luggage, without any basis for suspecting any particular passenger of an untoward motive. Applying our precedents dealing with administrative searches, the lower courts that have considered the question have consistently concluded that such searches are reasonable under the Fourth Amendment. As Judge Friendly explained in a leading case upholding such searches:

> When the risk is the jeopardy to hundreds of human lives and millions of dollars of property inherent in the pirating or blowing up of a large airplane, that danger *alone* meets the test of reasonableness, so long as the search is conducted in good faith for the purpose of preventing hijacking or like damage and with reasonable scope and the passenger has been given advance notice of his liability to such a search so that he can avoid it by choosing not to travel by air.

It is true, as counsel for petitioners pointed out at oral argument, that these air piracy precautions were adopted in response to an observable national and international hijacking crisis. Yet we would not suppose that, if the validity of these searches be conceded, the Government would be precluded from conducting them absent a demonstration of danger as to any particular airport or airline. It is sufficient that the Government have a compelling interest in preventing an otherwise pervasive societal problem from spreading to the particular context.

Nor would we think, in view of the obvious deterrent purpose of these searches, that the validity of the Government's airport screening program necessarily turns on whether significant numbers of putative air pirates are actually discovered by the searches conducted under the program. In the 15 years the program has been in effect, more than 9.5 *billion* persons have been screened, and over 10 *billion* pieces of luggage have been inspected. By far the overwhelming majority of those persons who have been searched, like Customs employees who have been tested under the Service's drug-screening scheme, have proved entirely innocent—only 42,000 firearms have been detected during the same period. When the Government's interest lies in deterring highly hazardous conduct, a low incidence of such conduct, far from impugning the validity of the scheme for implementing this interest, is more logically viewed as a hallmark of success.

likely to be known or available to the employee. Petitioners' own expert indicated below that the time it takes for particular drugs to become undetectable in urine can vary widely depending on the individual, and may extend for as long as 22 days. Thus, contrary to petitioners' suggestion, no employee reasonably can expect to deceive the test by the simple expedient of abstaining after the test date is assigned. Nor can he expect attempts at adulteration to succeed, in view of the precautions taken by the sample collector to ensure the integrity of the sample. In all the circumstances, we are persuaded that the program bears a close and substantial relation to the Service's goal of deterring drug users from seeking promotion to sensitive positions.

* * *

III

Where the Government requires its employees to produce urine samples to be analyzed for evidence of illegal drug use, the collection and subsequent chemical analysis of such samples are searches that must meet the reasonableness requirement of the Fourth Amendment. Because the testing program adopted by the Customs Service is not designed to serve the ordinary needs of law enforcement, we have balanced the public interest in the Service's testing program against the privacy concerns implicated by the tests, without reference to our usual presumption in favor of the procedures specified in the Warrant Clause, to assess whether the tests required by Customs are reasonable.

We hold that the suspicionless testing of employees who apply for promotion to positions directly involving the interdiction of illegal drugs, or to positions that require the incumbent to carry a firearm, is reasonable. The Government's compelling interests in preventing the promotion of drug users to positions where they might endanger the integrity of our Nation's borders or the life of the citizenry outweigh the privacy interests of those who seek promotion to these positions, who enjoy a diminished expectation of privacy by virtue of the special, and obvious, physical and ethical demands of those positions. We do not decide whether testing those who apply for promotion to positions where they would handle "classified" information is reasonable because we find the record inadequate for this purpose.

JUSTICE MARSHALL, with whom JUSTICE BRENNAN joins, dissenting.

For the reasons stated in my dissenting opinion in *Skinner v. Railway Labor Executives' Assn.*, 489 U.S., at 635, I also dissent from the Court's decision in this case. Here, as in *Skinner*, the Court's abandonment of the Fourth Amendment's express requirement that searches of the person rest on probable cause is unprincipled and unjustifiable. But even if I believed that balancing analysis was appropriate under the Fourth Amendment, I would still dissent from today's judgment for the reasons stated by Justice

Scalia in his dissenting opinion and for the reasons noted by the dissenting judge below relating to the inadequate tailoring of the Customs Service's drug-testing plan.

JUSTICE SCALIA, with whom JUSTICE STEVENS joins, dissenting.

The issue in this case is not whether Customs Service employees can constitutionally be denied promotion, or even dismissed, for a single instance of unlawful drug use, at home or at work. They assuredly can. The issue here is what steps can constitutionally be taken to *detect* such drug use. The Government asserts it can demand that employees perform "an excretory function traditionally shielded by great privacy," *Skinner v. Railway Labor Executives' Assn.*, 489 U.S., at 626, while "a monitor of the same sex . . . remains close at hand to listen for the normal sounds," and that the excretion thus produced be turned over to the Government for chemical analysis. The Court agrees that this constitutes a search for purposes of the Fourth Amendment—and I think it obvious that it is a type of search particularly destructive of privacy and offensive to personal dignity.

Until today this Court had upheld a bodily search separate from arrest and without individualized suspicion of wrongdoing only with respect to prison inmates, relying upon the uniquely dangerous nature of that environment. Today, in *Skinner,* we allow a less intrusive bodily search of railroad employees involved in train accidents. I joined the Court's opinion there because the demonstrated frequency of drug and alcohol use by the targeted class of employees, and the demonstrated connection between such use and grave harm, rendered the search a reasonable means of protecting society. I decline to join the Court's opinion in the present case because neither frequency of use nor connection to harm is demonstrated or even likely. In my view the Customs Service rules are a kind of immolation of privacy and human dignity in symbolic opposition to drug use.

* * *

The Court's opinion in the present case . . . will be searched in vain for real evidence of a real problem that will be solved by urine testing of Customs Service employees. Instead, there are assurances that "[t]he Customs Service is our Nation's first line of defense against one of the greatest problems affecting the health and welfare of our population," that "[m]any of the Service's employees are often exposed to [drug smugglers] and to the controlled substances [they seek] to smuggle into the country," that "Customs officers have been the targets of bribery by drug smugglers on numerous occasions, and several have been removed from the Service for accepting bribes and other integrity violations," that "the Government has a compelling interest in ensuring that front-line interdiction personnel are physically fit, and have unimpeachable integrity and judgment," that the "national interest in self-protection could be irreparably damaged if those charged with safeguarding it were, because of their own drug use, unsympathetic to their mission of interdicting narcotics," and that "the public should not bear the risk that employees who may suffer from impaired perception and judgment will be promoted to positions where they may need to employ deadly force." To paraphrase Churchill, all this contains much that is obviously true, and much that is relevant; unfortunately, what is obviously true is not relevant, and what is relevant is not obviously true. The only pertinent points, it seems to me, are supported by nothing but speculation, and not very plausible speculation at that. It is not apparent to me that a Customs Service employee who uses drugs is significantly more likely to be bribed by a drug smuggler, any more than a Customs Service employee who wears diamonds is significantly more likely to be bribed by a diamond smuggler—unless, perhaps, the addiction to drugs is so severe, and requires so much money to maintain, that it would be detectable even without benefit of a urine test. Nor is it apparent to me that Customs officers who use drugs will be appreciably less "sympathetic" to their drug-interdiction mission, any more than police officers who exceed the speed limit in their private cars are appreciably less sympathetic to their mission of enforcing the traffic laws. (The only difference is that the Customs officer's individual efforts, if they are irreplaceable, can theoretically affect the availability of his own drug supply—a prospect so remote as to be an absurd basis of motivation.) Nor, finally, is it apparent to me that urine tests will be even marginally more effective in preventing gun-carrying agents from risking "impaired perception and judgment" than is their current knowledge that, if impaired, they may be shot dead in unequal combat with unimpaired smugglers—unless, again, their addiction is so severe that no urine test is needed for detection.

What is absent in the Government's justifications—notably absent, revealingly absent, and as far as I am concerned dispositively absent—is the recitation of *even a single instance* in which any of the speculated horribles actually occurred: an instance, that is, in which the cause of bribe-taking, or of poor aim, or of unsympathetic law enforcement, or of compromise of classified information, was drug use. Although the Court points out that several employees have in the past been removed from the Service for accepting bribes and other integrity violations, and that at least nine officers have died in the line of duty since 1974, there is no indication whatever that these incidents were related to drug use by Service employees. Perhaps concrete evidence of the severity of a problem is unnecessary when it is so well known that courts can almost take judicial notice of it; but that is surely not the case here. The Commissioner of Customs himself has stated that he "believe[s] that Customs is largely drug-free," that "[t]he extent of illegal drug use by Customs employees was not the reason for establishing this program," and that he "hope[s] and expect[s] to receive reports of very few positive findings through drug screening." The test results have fulfilled those hopes and expectations. According to the Service's counsel, out of 3,600 employees tested, no more than 5 tested positive for drugs.

* * *

Today's decision would be wrong, but at least of more limited effect, if its approval of drug testing were confined to that category of employees assigned specifically to drug interdiction duties. Relatively few public employees fit that description. But in extending approval of drug testing to that category consisting of employees who carry firearms, the Court exposes vast numbers of public employees to this needless indignity. Logically, of course, if those who carry guns can be treated in this fashion, so can all others whose work, if performed under the influence of drugs, may endanger others—automobile drivers, operators of other potentially dangerous equipment, construction workers, school crossing guards. A similarly broad scope attaches to the Court's approval of drug testing for those with access to "sensitive information." Since this category is not limited to Service employees with drug interdiction duties, nor to "sensitive information" specifically relating to drug traffic, today's holding apparently approves drug testing for all federal employees with security clearances—or, indeed, for all federal employees with valuable confidential information to impart. Since drug use is not a particular problem in the Customs Service, employees throughout the Government are no less likely to violate the public trust by taking bribes to feed their drug habit, or by yielding to blackmail. Moreover, there is no reason why this super-protection against harms arising from drug use must be limited to public employees; a law requiring similar testing of private citizens who use dangerous instruments such as guns or cars, or who have access to classified information, would also be constitutional.

There is only one apparent basis that sets the testing at issue here apart from all these other situations—but it is not a basis upon which the Court is willing to rely. I do not believe for a minute that the driving force behind these drug-testing rules was any of the feeble justifications put forward by counsel here and accepted by the Court. The only plausible explanation, in my view, is what the Commissioner himself offered in the concluding sentence of his memorandum to Customs Service employees announcing the program: "Implementation of the drug screening program would set an important example in our country's struggle with this most serious threat to our national health and security." Or as respondent's brief to this Court asserted: "[I]f a law enforcement agency and its employees do not take the law seriously, neither will the public on which the agency's effectiveness depends." What better way to show that the Government is serious about its "war on drugs" than to subject its employees on the front line of that war to this invasion of their privacy and affront to their dignity?

To be sure, there is only a slight chance that it will prevent some serious public harm resulting from Service employee drug use, but it will show to the world that the Service is "clean," and—most important of all—will demonstrate the determination of the Government to eliminate this scourge of our society! I think it obvious that this justification is unacceptable; that the impairment of individual liberties cannot be the means of making a point; that symbolism, even symbolism for so worthy a cause as the abolition of unlawful drugs, cannot validate an otherwise unreasonable search.

There is irony in the Government's citation, in support of its position, of Justice Brandeis' statement in *Olmstead v. United States,* 277 U.S. 438, 485 (1928) that "[f]or good or for ill, [our Government] teaches the whole people by its example." Brandeis was there *dissenting* from the Court's admission of evidence obtained through an unlawful Government wiretap. He was not praising the Government's example of vigor and enthusiasm in combatting crime, but condemning its example that "the end justifies the means." An even more apt quotation from that famous Brandeis dissent would have been the following:

> [I]t is . . . immaterial that the intrusion was in aid of law enforcement. Experience should teach us to be most on our guard to protect liberty when the Government's purposes are beneficent. Men born to freedom are naturally alert to repel invasion of their liberty by evil-minded rulers. The greatest dangers to liberty lurk in insidious encroachment by men of zeal, well-meaning but without understanding.

Those who lose because of the lack of understanding that begot the present exercise in symbolism are not just the Customs Service employees, whose dignity is thus offended, but all of us—who suffer a coarsening of our national manners that ultimately give the Fourth Amendment its content, and who become subject to the administration of federal officials whose respect for our privacy can hardly be greater than the small respect they have been taught to have for their own.

Points for Discussion

1. Why does the balancing of the government interests and the privacy interests of employees come out in the government's favor in this case? Isn't Justice Scalia correct that the majority is unable to point to a single example of drugs impairing a Customs Service employee's job performance?

2. Why does the Court not simply hold that the Customs Service employees in *Von Raab* as well as the railway employees in *Skinner v. Railway Labor Executives' Association*, 489 U.S. 602 (1989), consented to suspicionless drug testing as a condition of their employment or promotion?

3. Justice Scalia points out, with apparent relish, the irony of the government's quotation of Justice Brandeis' famous *Olmstead* dissent in a brief arguing in favor of suspicionless urine testing. Why do you think the solicitor general chose this quotation, among all of those available to him, to make his argument?

CITY OF ONTARIO V. QUON

560 U.S. 746 (2010)

JUSTICE KENNEDY delivered the opinion of the court.

This case involves the assertion by a government employer of the right, in circumstances to be described, to read text messages sent and received on a pager the employer owned and issued to an employee. The employee contends that the privacy of the messages is protected by the ban on "unreasonable searches and seizures" found in the Fourth Amendment to the United States Constitution, made applicable to the States by the Due Process Clause of the Fourteenth Amendment. Though the case touches issues of farreaching significance, the Court concludes it can be resolved by settled principles determining when a search is reasonable.

I

A

The City of Ontario is a political subdivision of the State of California. The case arose out of incidents in 2001 and 2002 when respondent Jeff Quon was employed by the Ontario Police Department. He was a police sergeant and member of OPD's Special Weapons and Tactics Team. The City, OPD, and OPD's Chief, Lloyd Scharf, are petitioners here. As will be discussed, two respondents share the last name Quon. In this opinion "Quon" refers to Jeff Quon, for the relevant events mostly revolve around him.

In October 2001, the City acquired 20 alphanumeric pagers capable of sending and receiving text messages. Arch Wireless Operating Company provided wireless service for the pagers. Under the City's service contract with Arch Wireless, each pager was allotted a limited number of characters sent or received each month. Usage in excess of that amount would result in an additional fee. The City issued pagers to Quon and other SWAT Team members in order to help the SWAT Team mobilize and respond to emergency situations.

Before acquiring the pagers, the City announced a "Computer Usage, Internet and E-Mail Policy" that applied to all employees. Among other provisions, it specified that the City "reserves the right to monitor and log all network activity including e-mail and Internet use, with or without notice. Users should have no expectation of privacy or confidentiality when using these resources." In March 2000, Quon signed a statement acknowledging that he had read and understood the Computer Policy.

* * *

Although the Computer Policy did not cover text messages by its explicit terms, the City made clear to employees, including Quon, that the City would treat text messages the same way as it treated e-mails. At an April 18, 2002, staff meeting at which Quon was present, Lieutenant Steven Duke, the OPD officer responsible for the City's contract with Arch Wireless, told officers that messages sent on the pagers "are considered e-mail messages. This means that [text] messages would fall under the City's policy as public information and [would be] eligible for auditing." Duke's comments were put in writing in a memorandum sent on April 29, 2002, by Chief Scharf to Quon and other City personnel.

Within the first or second billing cycle after the pagers were distributed, Quon exceeded his monthly text message character allotment. Duke told Quon about the overage, and reminded him that messages sent on the pagers were "considered e-mail and could be audited." Duke said, however, that "it was not his intent to audit [an] employee's text messages to see if the overage [was] due to work related transmissions." Duke suggested that Quon could reimburse the City for the overage fee rather than have Duke audit the messages. Quon wrote a check to the City for the overage. Duke offered the same arrangement to other employees who incurred overage fees.

Over the next few months, Quon exceeded his character limit three or four times. Each time he reimbursed the City. Quon and another officer again incurred overage fees for their pager usage in August 2002. At a meeting in October, Duke told Scharf that he had become " 'tired of being a bill collector.' " Scharf decided to determine whether the existing character limit was too low—that is, whether officers such as Quon were having to pay fees for sending work-related messages—or if the overages were for personal messages. Scharf told Duke to request transcripts of text messages sent in August and September by Quon and the other employee who had exceeded the character allowance.

At Duke's request, an administrative assistant employed by OPD contacted Arch Wireless. After verifying that the City was the subscriber on the accounts, Arch Wireless provided the desired transcripts. Duke reviewed the transcripts and discovered that many of the messages sent and received on Quon's pager were not work related, and some were sexually explicit. Duke reported his findings to Scharf, who, along with Quon's immediate supervisor, reviewed the transcripts himself. After his review, Scharf referred the matter to OPD's internal affairs division for an investigation into whether Quon was violating OPD rules by pursuing personal matters while on duty.

The officer in charge of the internal affairs review was Sergeant Patrick McMahon. Before conducting a review, McMahon used Quon's work schedule to redact the transcripts in order to eliminate any messages Quon sent while off duty. He then reviewed the content of the messages Quon sent during work hours. McMahon's report noted that Quon sent or received 456 messages during work hours in the month of August 2002, of which no more than 57 were work related; he sent as many as 80 messages during a single day at work; and on an average workday, Quon sent or received 28 messages, of which only 3 were related to police business. The report concluded that Quon had violated OPD rules. Quon was allegedly disciplined.

B

Raising claims under [42 U.S.C. § 1983, the Stored Communications Act,] and California law, Quon filed suit against petitioners in the United States District Court for the Central District of California. Arch Wireless and an individual not relevant here were also named as defendants. Quon was joined in his suit by another plaintiff who is not a party before this Court and by the other respondents, each of whom exchanged text messages with Quon during August and September 2002: Jerilyn Quon, Jeff Quon's then-wife, from whom he was separated; April Florio, an OPD employee with whom Jeff Quon was romantically involved; and Steve Trujillo, another member of the OPD SWAT Team. Among the allegations in the complaint was that petitioners violated respondents' Fourth Amendment rights and the SCA by obtaining and reviewing the transcript of Jeff Quon's pager messages and that Arch Wireless had violated the SCA by turning over the transcript to the City.

* * *

II

The Fourth Amendment states: "The right of the people to be secure in their persons, houses, papers, and effects, against unreasonable searches and seizures, shall not be violated . . . ." It is well settled that the Fourth Amendment's protection extends beyond the sphere of criminal investigations. *Camara v. Municipal Court of City and County of San Francisco,* 387 U.S. 523, 530 (1967). "The Amendment guarantees the privacy, dignity, and security of persons against certain arbitrary and invasive acts by officers of the Government," without regard to whether the government actor is investigating crime or performing another function. *Skinner v. Railway Labor Executives' Assn.,* 489 U.S. 602, 613–614 (1989). The Fourth Amendment applies as well when the Government acts in its capacity as an employer. *Treasury Employees v. Von Raab,* 489 U.S. 656, 665 (1989).

The Court discussed this principle in [*O'Connor v. Ortega,* 480 U.S. 709 (1987)]. There a physician employed by a state hospital alleged that hospital officials investigating workplace misconduct had violated his Fourth Amendment rights by searching his office and seizing personal items from his desk and filing cabinet. All Members of the Court agreed with the general principle that "[i]ndividuals do not lose Fourth Amendment rights merely because they work for the government instead of a private employer." A majority of the Court further agreed that " 'special needs, beyond the normal need for law enforcement,' " make the warrant and probable-cause requirement impracticable for government employers.

The *O'Connor* Court did disagree on the proper analytical framework for Fourth Amendment claims against government employers. A four-Justice plurality concluded that the correct analysis has two steps. First, because "some government offices may be so open to fellow employees or the public that no expectation of privacy is reasonable," a court must consider "[t]he operational realities of the workplace" in order to determine whether an employee's Fourth Amendment rights are implicated. On this view, "the question whether an employee has a reasonable expectation of privacy must be addressed on a case-by-case basis." Next, where an employee has a legitimate privacy expectation, an employer's intrusion on that expectation "for noninvestigatory, work-related purposes, as well as for investigations of work-related misconduct, should be judged by the standard of reasonableness under all the circumstances."

Justice Scalia, concurring in the judgment, outlined a different approach. His opinion would have dispensed with an inquiry into "operational realities" and would conclude "that the offices of government employees . . . are covered by Fourth Amendment protections as a general matter." But he would also have held "that government searches to retrieve work-related materials or to investigate violations of workplace rules—searches of the sort that are regarded as reasonable and normal in the private-employer context—do not violate the Fourth Amendment."

Later, in the *Von Raab* decision, the Court explained that "operational realities" could diminish an employee's privacy expectations, and that this diminution could be taken into consideration when assessing the reasonableness of a workplace search. In the two decades since *O'Connor,* however, the threshold test for determining the scope of an employee's Fourth Amendment rights has not been clarified further. Here, though they disagree on whether Quon had a reasonable expectation of privacy, both petitioners and respondents start from the premise that the *O'Connor* plurality controls. It is not necessary to resolve whether that premise is correct. The case can be decided by determining that the search was reasonable even assuming Quon had a reasonable expectation of privacy. The two *O'Connor* approaches—the plurality's and Justice Scalia's—therefore lead to the same result here.

III

A

Before turning to the reasonableness of the search, it is instructive to note the parties' disagreement over whether Quon had a reasonable expectation of privacy. The record does establish that OPD, at the outset, made it clear that pager messages were not considered private. The City's Computer Policy stated that "[u]sers should have no expectation of privacy or confidentiality when using" City computers. Chief Scharf's memo and Duke's statements made clear that this official policy extended to text messaging. The disagreement, at least as respondents see the case, is over whether Duke's later statements overrode the official policy. Respondents contend that because Duke told Quon that an audit would be unnecessary if Quon paid for the overage, Quon reasonably could expect that the contents of his messages would remain private.

At this point, were we to assume that inquiry into "operational realities" were called for, it would be necessary to ask whether Duke's statements could be taken as announcing a change in OPD policy, and if so, whether he had, in fact or appearance, the authority to make such a change and to guarantee the privacy of text messaging. It would also be necessary to consider whether a review of messages sent on police pagers, particularly those sent while officers are on duty, might be justified for other reasons, including performance evaluations, litigation concerning the lawfulness of police actions, and perhaps compliance with state open records laws. These matters would all bear on the legitimacy of an employee's privacy expectation.

The Court must proceed with care when considering the whole concept of privacy expectations in communications made on electronic equipment owned by a government employer. The judiciary risks error by elaborating too fully on the Fourth Amendment implications of emerging technology before its role in society has become clear. See, *e.g., Olmstead v. United States,* 277 U.S. 438 (1928), overruled by *Katz v. United States,* 389 U.S. 347, 353 (1967). In *Katz,* the Court relied on its own knowledge and experience to conclude that there is a reasonable expectation of privacy in a telephone booth. It is not so clear that courts at present are on so sure a ground. Prudence counsels caution before the facts in the instant case are used to establish far-reaching premises that define the existence, and extent, of privacy expectations enjoyed by employees when using employer-provided communication devices.

Rapid changes in the dynamics of communication and information transmission are evident not just in the technology itself but in what society accepts as proper behavior. As one *amici* brief notes, many employers expect or at least tolerate personal use of such equipment by employees because it often increases worker efficiency. Another *amicus* points out that the law is beginning to respond to these developments, as some States have recently passed statutes requiring employers to notify employees when monitoring their electronic communications. At present, it is uncertain how workplace norms, and the law's treatment of them, will evolve.

Even if the Court were certain that the *O'Connor* plurality's approach were the right one, the Court would have difficulty predicting how employees' privacy expectations will be shaped by those changes or the degree to which society will be prepared to recognize those expectations as reasonable. Cell phone and text message communications are so pervasive that some persons may consider them to be essential means or necessary instruments for self-expression, even self-identification. That might strengthen the case for an expectation of privacy. On the other hand, the ubiquity of those devices has made them generally affordable, so one could counter that employees who need cell phones or similar devices for personal matters can purchase and pay for their own. And employer policies concerning communications will of course shape the reasonable expectations of their employees, especially to the extent that such policies are clearly communicated.

A broad holding concerning employees' privacy expectations vis-à-vis employer-provided technological equipment might have implications for future cases that cannot be predicted. It is preferable to dispose of this case on narrower grounds. For present purposes we assume several propositions *arguendo:* First, Quon had a reasonable expectation of privacy in the text messages sent on the pager provided to him by the City; second, petitioners' review of the transcript constituted a search within the meaning of the Fourth Amendment; and third, the principles applicable to a government employer's search of an employee's physical office apply with at least the same force when the employer intrudes on the employee's privacy in the electronic sphere.

B

* * *

Under the approach of the *O'Connor* plurality, when conducted for a "noninvestigatory, work-related purpos[e]" or for the "investigatio[n] of work-related misconduct," a government employer's warrantless search is reasonable if it is " 'justified at its inception' " and if "the measures adopted are reasonably related to the objectives of the search and not excessively intrusive in light of" the circumstances giving rise to the search. The search here satisfied the standard of the *O'Connor* plurality and was reasonable under that approach.

The search was justified at its inception because there were "reasonable grounds for suspecting that the search [was] necessary for a noninvestigatory work-related purpose." As a jury found, Chief Scharf ordered the search in order to determine whether the character limit on the City's contract with Arch Wireless was sufficient to meet the City's needs. This was, as the Ninth Circuit noted, a "legitimate work-related rationale." The City and OPD had a legitimate interest in ensuring that employees were not being forced to pay out of their own pockets for work-related expenses, or on the other hand that the City was not paying for extensive personal communications.

As for the scope of the search, reviewing the transcripts was reasonable because it was an efficient and expedient way to determine whether Quon's overages were the result of work-related messaging or personal use. The review was also not "excessively intrusive." Although Quon had gone over his monthly allotment a number of times, OPD requested transcripts for only the months of August and September 2002. While it may have been reasonable as well for OPD to review transcripts of all the months in which Quon exceeded his allowance, it was certainly reasonable for OPD to review messages for just two months in order to obtain a large enough sample to decide whether the character limits were efficacious. And it is worth noting that during his internal affairs investigation, McMahon redacted all messages Quon sent while off duty, a measure which reduced the intrusiveness of any further review of the transcripts.

* * *

From OPD's perspective, the fact that Quon likely had only a limited privacy expectation, with boundaries that we need not here explore, lessened the risk that the review would intrude on highly private details of Quon's life. OPD's audit of messages on Quon's employer-provided pager was not nearly as intrusive as a search of his personal e-mail account or pager, or a wiretap on his home phone line, would have been. That the search did reveal intimate details of Quon's life does not make it unreasonable, for under the circumstances a reasonable employer would not expect that such a review would intrude on such matters. The search was permissible in its scope.

* * *

Respondents argue that the search was *per se* unreasonable in light of the Court of Appeals' conclusion that Arch Wireless violated the SCA by giving the City the transcripts of Quon's text messages. The merits of the SCA claim are not before us. But even if the Court of Appeals was correct to conclude that the SCA forbade Arch Wireless from turning over the transcripts, it does not follow that petitioners' actions were unreasonable. Respondents point to no authority for the proposition that the existence of statutory protection renders a search *per se* unreasonable under the Fourth Amendment. And the precedents counsel otherwise. See *Virginia v. Moore,* 553 U.S. 164, 168 (2008) (search incident to an arrest that was illegal under state law was reasonable); *California v. Greenwood,* 486 U.S. 35, 43 (1988) (rejecting argument that if state law forbade police search of individual's garbage the search would violate the Fourth Amendment). Furthermore, respondents do not maintain that any OPD employee either violated the law him- or herself or knew or should have known that Arch Wireless, by turning over the transcript, would have violated the law. The otherwise reasonable search by OPD is not rendered unreasonable by the assumption that Arch Wireless violated the SCA by turning over the transcripts.

Because the search was motivated by a legitimate work-related purpose, and because it was not excessive in scope, the search was reasonable under the approach of the *O'Connor* plurality. For these same reasons—that the employer had a legitimate reason for the search, and that the search was not excessively intrusive in light of that justification—the Court also concludes that the search would be "regarded as reasonable and normal in the private-employer context" and would satisfy the approach of Justice Scalia's concurrence. The search was reasonable, and the Court of Appeals erred by holding to the contrary. Petitioners did not violate Quon's Fourth Amendment rights.

C

Finally, the Court must consider whether the search violated the Fourth Amendment rights of Jerilyn Quon, Florio, and Trujillo, the respondents who sent text messages to Jeff Quon. Petitioners and respondents disagree whether a sender of a text message can have a reasonable expectation of privacy in a message he knowingly sends to someone's employer-provided pager. It is not necessary to resolve this question in order to dispose of the case, however. Respondents argue that because "the search was unreasonable as to Sergeant Quon, it was also unreasonable as to his correspondents." They make no corollary argument that the search, if reasonable as to Quon, could nonetheless be unreasonable as to Quon's correspondents. In light of this litigating position and the Court's conclusion that the search was reasonable as to Jeff Quon, it necessarily follows that these other respondents cannot prevail.

JUSTICE STEVENS, concurring.

Although I join the Court's opinion in full, I write separately to highlight that the Court has sensibly declined to resolve whether the plurality opinion in *O'Connor v. Ortega,* 480 U.S. 709 (1987), provides the correct approach to determining an employee's reasonable expectation of privacy. Justice Blackmun, writing for the four dissenting Justices in *O'Connor,* agreed with Justice Scalia that an employee enjoys a reasonable expectation of privacy in his office. But he advocated a third approach to the reasonable expectation of privacy inquiry, separate from those proposed by the *O'Connor* plurality and by Justice Scalia. Recognizing that it is particularly important to safeguard "a public employee's expectation of privacy in the workplace" in light of the "reality of work in modern time," which lacks "tidy distinctions" between workplace and private activities, Justice Blackmun argued that "the precise extent of an employee's expectation of privacy often turns on the nature of the search." And he emphasized that courts should determine this expectation in light of the specific facts of each particular search, rather than by announcing a categorical standard.

[I]t is clear that respondent Jeff Quon, as a law enforcement officer who served on a SWAT Team, should have understood that all of his work-related actions—including all of his communications on his official pager—were likely to be subject to public and legal scrutiny. He therefore had only a limited expectation of privacy in relation to this particular audit of his pager messages. Whether one applies the reasoning from Justice O'Connor's opinion, Justice Scalia's concurrence, or Justice Blackmun's dissent in *O'Connor,* the result is the same: The judgment of the Court of Appeals in this case must be reversed.

JUSTICE SCALIA, concurring in part and concurring in the judgment.

I join the Court's opinion except for Part III-A. I continue to believe that the "operational realities" rubric for determining the Fourth Amendment's application to public employees invented by the plurality in *O'Connor v. Ortega,* 480 U.S. 709, 717 (1987), is standardless and unsupported. In this case, the proper threshold inquiry should be not whether the Fourth Amendment applies to messages on *public* employees' employer-issued pagers, but whether it applies *in general* to such messages on employer-issued pagers.

Here, however, there is no need to answer that threshold question. Even accepting at face value Quon's and his co-plaintiffs' claims that the Fourth Amendment applies to their messages, the city's search was reasonable, and thus did not violate the Amendment. Since it is unnecessary to decide whether the Fourth Amendment applies, it is unnecessary to resolve which approach in *O'Connor* controls: the plurality's or mine. That should end the matter.

The Court concedes as much, yet it inexplicably interrupts its analysis with a recitation of the parties' arguments concerning, and an excursus on the complexity and consequences of answering, that admittedly irrelevant threshold question. That discussion is unnecessary. (To whom do we owe an *additional* explanation for declining to decide an issue, once we have explained that it makes no difference?) It also seems to me exaggerated. Applying the Fourth Amendment to new technologies may sometimes be difficult, but when it is necessary to decide a case we have no choice. The Court's implication, that where electronic privacy is concerned we should decide less than we otherwise would (that is, less than the principle of law necessary to resolve the case and guide private action)—or that we should hedge our bets by concocting case-specific standards or issuing opaque opinions—is in my view indefensible. The-times-they-are-a-changin' is a feeble excuse for disregard of duty.

Worse still, the digression is self-defeating. Despite the Court's insistence that it is agnostic about the proper test, lower courts will likely read the Court's self-described "instructive" expatiation on how the *O'Connor* plurality's approach would apply here (if it applied) as a heavy-handed hint about how *they* should proceed. Litigants will do likewise, using the threshold question whether the Fourth Amendment is even implicated as a basis for bombarding lower courts with arguments about employer policies, how they were communicated, and whether they were authorized, as well as the latest trends in employees' use of electronic media. In short, in saying why it is not saying more, the Court says much more than it should.

The Court's inadvertent boosting of the *O'Connor* plurality's standard is all the more ironic because, in fleshing out its fears that applying that test to new technologies will be too hard, the Court underscores the unworkability of that standard. Any rule that requires evaluating whether a given gadget is a "necessary instrumen[t] for self-expression, even self-identification," on top of assessing the degree to which "the law's treatment of [workplace norms has] evolve[d]," is (to put it mildly) unlikely to yield objective answers.

Points for Discussion

1. Do employees expect the emails they send and receive from their work-provided email accounts and computers to remain private? If so, is it reasonable to expect that privacy to be respected? Do students have an expectation of privacy in the emails they send and receive on their university-provided accounts? Should the analysis change depending on whether the employer or the university is public or private?

2. *Quon* failed to resolve the question *O'Connor* left unresolved in 1987—how to evaluate government employees' privacy expectations in the workplace. Eight justices in *Quon* stated that applying the *Katz* test to text messaging (hardly cutting-edge technology in 2010) was too difficult. Despite Justice Scalia's criticism, the Court frankly confessed that, with respect to new ways of transacting business and communicating, it can determine neither subjective privacy expectations nor "the degree to which society will be prepared to recognize those expectations as reasonable." Ironically, the Court explained that *Katz*'s expectations-of-privacy inquiry—which was meant to make the Fourth Amendment flexible enough to deal with technological change—necessitated moving slowly: "The judiciary risks error by elaborating too fully on the Fourth Amendment implications of emerging technology before its role in society has become clear." What does this say about the *Katz* test's utility? Does *Jones* resolve these problems?

4. HIGHWAY CHECKPOINTS

MICHIGAN DEPT. OF STATE POLICE V. SITZ

496 U.S. 444 (1990)

CHIEF JUSTICE REHNQUIST delivered the opinion of the court.

This case poses the question whether a State's use of highway sobriety checkpoints violates the Fourth and Fourteenth Amendments to the United States Constitution. We hold that it does not and therefore reverse the contrary holding of the Court of Appeals of Michigan.

Petitioners, the Michigan Department of State Police and its director, established a sobriety checkpoint pilot program in early 1986. The director appointed a Sobriety Checkpoint Advisory Committee comprising representatives of the State Police force, local police forces, state prosecutors, and the University of Michigan Transportation Research Institute. Pursuant to its charge, the advisory committee created guidelines setting forth procedures governing checkpoint operations, site selection, and publicity.

Under the guidelines, checkpoints would be set up at selected sites along state roads. All vehicles passing through a checkpoint would be stopped and their drivers briefly examined for signs of intoxication. In cases where a checkpoint officer detected signs of intoxication, the motorist would be directed to a location out of the traffic flow where an officer would check the motorist's driver's license and car registration and, if warranted, conduct further sobriety tests. Should the field tests and the officer's observations suggest that the driver was intoxicated, an arrest would be made. All other drivers would be permitted to resume their journey immediately.

The first—and to date the only—sobriety checkpoint operated under the program was conducted in Saginaw County with the assistance of the Saginaw County Sheriff's Department. During the 75-minute duration of the checkpoint's operation, 126 vehicles passed through the checkpoint. The average delay for each vehicle was approximately 25 seconds. Two drivers were detained for field sobriety testing, and one of the two was arrested for driving under the influence of alcohol. A third driver who drove through without stopping was pulled over by an officer in an observation vehicle and arrested for driving under the influence.

On the day before the operation of the Saginaw County checkpoint, respondents filed a complaint in the Circuit Court of Wayne County seeking declaratory and injunctive relief from potential subjection to the checkpoints. Each of the respondents "is a licensed driver in the State of Michigan . . . who regularly travels throughout the State in his automobile." During pretrial proceedings, petitioners agreed to delay further implementation of the checkpoint program pending the outcome of this litigation.

* * *

In this Court respondents seek to defend the judgment in their favor by insisting that the balancing test derived from *Brown v. Texas,* 443 U.S. 47 (1979) was not the proper method of analysis. Respondents maintain that the analysis must proceed from a basis of probable cause or reasonable suspicion, and rely for support on language from our decision last Term in *Treasury Employees v. Von Raab,* 489 U.S. 656 (1989). We said in *Von Raab:*

> [W]here a Fourth Amendment intrusion serves special governmental needs, beyond the normal need for law enforcement, it is necessary to balance the individual's privacy expectations against the Government's interests to determine whether it is impractical to require a warrant or some level of individualized suspicion in the particular context.

Respondents argue that there must be a showing of some special governmental need "beyond the normal need" for criminal law enforcement before a balancing analysis is appropriate, and that petitioners have demonstrated no such special need.

But it is perfectly plain from a reading of *Von Raab,* which cited and discussed with approval our earlier decision in *United States v. Martinez-Fuerte,* 428 U.S. 543 (1976), that it was in no way designed to repudiate our prior cases dealing with police stops of motorists on public highways. *Martinez-Fuerte,* which utilized a balancing analysis in approving highway checkpoints for detecting illegal aliens, and *Brown v. Texas,* are the relevant authorities here.

Petitioners concede, correctly in our view, that a Fourth Amendment "seizure" occurs when a vehicle is stopped at a checkpoint. The question thus becomes whether such seizures are "reasonable" under the Fourth Amendment.

It is important to recognize what our inquiry is *not* about. No allegations are before us of unreasonable treatment of any person after an actual detention at a particular checkpoint. As pursued in the lower courts, the instant action challenges only the use of sobriety checkpoints generally. We address only the initial stop of each motorist passing through a checkpoint and the associated preliminary questioning and observation by checkpoint officers. Detention of particular motorists for more extensive field sobriety testing may require satisfaction of an individualized suspicion standard.

No one can seriously dispute the magnitude of the drunken driving problem or the States' interest in eradicating it. Media reports of alcohol-related death and mutilation on the Nation's roads are legion. The anecdotal is confirmed by the statistical. "Drunk drivers cause an annual death toll of over 25,000* and in the same time span cause nearly one million personal injuries and more than five billion dollars in property damage." 4 W. LaFave, SEARCH AND SEIZURE: A TREATISE ON THE FOURTH AMENDMENT § 10.8(d), p. 71 (2d ed. 1987). For decades, this Court has "repeatedly lamented the tragedy."

Conversely, the weight bearing on the other scale—the measure of the intrusion on motorists stopped briefly at sobriety checkpoints—is slight. We reached a similar conclusion as to the intrusion on motorists subjected to a brief stop at a highway checkpoint for detecting illegal aliens. We see virtually no difference between the levels of intrusion on law-abiding motorists from the brief stops necessary to the effectuation of these two types of checkpoints, which to the average motorist would seem identical save for the nature of the questions the checkpoint officers might ask. The trial court and the Court of Appeals, thus, accurately gauged the "objective" intrusion, measured by the duration of the seizure and the intensity of the investigation, as minimal.

With respect to what it perceived to be the "subjective" intrusion on motorists, however, the Court of Appeals found such intrusion substantial. The court first affirmed the trial court's finding that the guidelines governing checkpoint operation minimize the discretion of the officers on the scene. But the court also agreed with the trial court's conclusion that the checkpoints have the potential to generate fear and surprise in motorists. This was so because the record failed to demonstrate that approaching motorists would be aware of their option to make U-turns or turnoffs to avoid the checkpoints. On that basis, the court deemed the subjective intrusion from the checkpoints unreasonable.

We believe the Michigan courts misread our cases concerning the degree of "subjective intrusion" and the potential for generating fear and surprise. The "fear and surprise" to be considered are not the natural fear of one who has been drinking over the prospect of being stopped at a sobriety checkpoint but, rather, the fear and surprise engendered in law-abiding motorists by the nature of the stop. . . . Here, checkpoints are selected pursuant to the guidelines, and uniformed police officers stop every approaching vehicle. The intrusion resulting from the brief stop at the sobriety checkpoint is for constitutional purposes indistinguishable from the checkpoint stops we upheld in *Martinez-Fuerte*.

* Statistical evidence incorporated in Justice Stevens' dissent suggests that this figure declined between 1982 and 1988. It was during this same period that police departments experimented with sobriety checkpoint systems. Petitioners, for instance, operated their checkpoint in May 1986, and the Maryland State Police checkpoint program, about which much testimony was given before the trial court, began in December 1982. Indeed, it is quite possible that jurisdictions which have recently decided to implement sobriety checkpoint systems have relied on such data from the 1980's in assessing the likely utility of such checkpoints.

The Court of Appeals went on to consider as part of the balancing analysis the "effectiveness" of the proposed checkpoint program. Based on extensive testimony in the trial record, the court concluded that the checkpoint program failed the "effectiveness" part of the test, and that this failure materially discounted petitioners' strong interest in implementing the program. We think the Court of Appeals was wrong on this point as well.

* * *

[T]his case involves neither a complete absence of empirical data nor a challenge to random highway stops. During the operation of the Saginaw County checkpoint, the detention of the 126 vehicles that entered the checkpoint resulted in the arrest of two drunken drivers. Stated as a percentage, approximately 1.6 percent of the drivers passing through the checkpoint were arrested for alcohol impairment. In addition, an expert witness testified at the trial that experience in other States demonstrated that, on the whole, sobriety checkpoints resulted in drunken driving arrests of around 1 percent of all motorists stopped. By way of comparison, the record from one of the consolidated cases in *Martinez-Fuerte* showed that in the associated checkpoint, illegal aliens were found in only 0.12 percent of the vehicles passing through the checkpoint. The ratio of illegal aliens detected to vehicles stopped (considering that on occasion two or more illegal aliens were found in a single vehicle) was approximately 0.5 percent. We concluded that this "record . . . provides a rather complete picture of the effectiveness of the San Clemente checkpoint," and we sustained its constitutionality. We see no justification for a different conclusion here.

In sum, the balance of the State's interest in preventing drunken driving, the extent to which this system can reasonably be said to advance that interest, and the degree of intrusion upon individual motorists who are briefly stopped, weighs in favor of the state program. We therefore hold that it is consistent with the Fourth Amendment.

The concurring opinion of JUSTICE BLACKMUN is omitted.

JUSTICE BRENNAN, with whom JUSTICE MARSHALL joins, dissenting.

* * *

The majority opinion creates the impression that the Court generally engages in a balancing test in order to determine the constitutionality of all seizures, or at least those "dealing with police stops of motorists on public highways." This is not the case. In most cases, the police must possess probable cause for a seizure to be judged reasonable. Only when a seizure is "*substantially* less intrusive," than a typical arrest is the general rule replaced by a balancing test. I agree with the Court that the initial stop of a car at a roadblock under the Michigan State Police sobriety checkpoint policy is sufficiently less intrusive than an arrest so that the reasonableness of the seizure may be judged, not by the presence of probable cause, but by balancing "the gravity of the public concerns served by the seizure, the degree to which the seizure advances the public interest, and the severity of the interference with individual liberty." *Brown v. Texas,* 443 U.S. 47, 51 (1979). But one searches the majority opinion in vain for any acknowledgment that the *reason* for employing the balancing test is that the seizure is minimally intrusive.

Indeed, the opinion reads as if the minimal nature of the seizure *ends* rather than begins the inquiry into reasonableness. Once the Court establishes that the seizure is "slight," it asserts without explanation that the balance "weighs in favor of the state program." The Court ignores the fact that in this class of minimally intrusive searches, we have generally required the Government to prove that it had reasonable suspicion for a minimally intrusive seizure to be considered reasonable. Some level of individualized suspicion is a core component of the protection the Fourth Amendment provides against arbitrary government action. By holding that no level of suspicion is necessary before the police may stop a car for the purpose of preventing drunken driving, the Court potentially subjects the general public to arbitrary or harassing conduct by the police. I would have hoped that before taking such a step, the Court would carefully explain how such a plan fits within our constitutional framework.

* * *

JUSTICE STEVENS, with whom JUSTICE BRENNAN and JUSTICE MARSHALL join as to Parts I and II, dissenting.

A sobriety checkpoint is usually operated at night at an unannounced location. Surprise is crucial to its method. The test operation conducted by the Michigan State Police and the Saginaw County Sheriff's Department began shortly after midnight and lasted until about 1 a.m. During that period, the 19 officers participating in the operation made two arrests and stopped and questioned 124 other unsuspecting and innocent drivers. It is, of course, not known how many arrests would have been made during that period if those officers had been engaged in normal patrol activities. However, the findings of the trial court, based on an extensive record and affirmed by the Michigan Court of Appeals, indicate that the net effect of sobriety checkpoints on traffic safety is infinitesimal and possibly negative.

Indeed, the record in this case makes clear that a decision holding these suspicionless seizures unconstitutional would not impede the law enforcement community's remarkable progress in reducing the death toll on our highways. Because the Michigan program was patterned after an older program in Maryland, the trial judge gave special attention to that State's experience. Over a period of several years, Maryland operated 125 checkpoints; of the 41,000 motorists passing through those checkpoints, only 143 persons (0.3%) were arrested. The number of man-hours devoted to these operations is not in the record, but it seems inconceivable that a higher arrest rate could not have been achieved by more conventional means. Yet, even if the 143 checkpoint arrests were assumed to involve a net increase in the number of drunken driving arrests per year, the figure would still be insignificant by comparison to the 71,000 such arrests made by Michigan State Police without checkpoints in 1984 alone.

Any relationship between sobriety checkpoints and an actual reduction in highway fatalities is even less substantial than the minimal impact on arrest rates. As the Michigan Court of Appeals pointed out: "Maryland had conducted a study comparing traffic statistics between a county using checkpoints and a control county. The results of the study showed that alcohol-related accidents in the checkpoint county decreased by ten percent, whereas the control county saw an eleven percent decrease; and while fatal accidents in the control county fell from sixteen to three, fatal accidents in the checkpoint county actually doubled from the prior year."

In light of these considerations, it seems evident that the Court today misapplies the balancing test announced in *Brown v. Texas,* 443 U.S. 47, 50–51 (1979). The Court overvalues the law enforcement interest in using sobriety checkpoints, undervalues the citizen's interest in freedom from random, unannounced investigatory seizures, and mistakenly assumes that there is "virtually no difference" between a routine stop at a permanent, fixed checkpoint and a surprise stop at a sobriety checkpoint. I believe this case is controlled by our several precedents condemning suspicionless random stops of motorists for investigatory purposes.

I

There is a critical difference between a seizure that is preceded by fair notice and one that is effected by surprise. That is one reason why a border search, or indeed any search at a permanent and fixed checkpoint, is much less intrusive than a random stop. A motorist with advance notice of the location of a permanent checkpoint has an opportunity to avoid the search entirely, or at least to prepare for, and limit, the intrusion on her privacy.

No such opportunity is available in the case of a random stop or a temporary checkpoint, which both depend for their effectiveness on the element of surprise. A driver who discovers an unexpected checkpoint on a familiar local road will be startled and distressed. She may infer, correctly, that the checkpoint is not simply "business as usual," and may likewise infer, again correctly, that the police have made a discretionary decision to focus their law enforcement efforts upon her and others who pass the chosen point.

This element of surprise is the most obvious distinction between the sobriety checkpoints permitted by today's majority and the interior border checkpoints approved by this Court in *Martinez-Fuerte.* The distinction casts immediate doubt upon the majority's argument, for *Martinez-Fuerte* is the only case in which we have upheld suspicionless seizures of motorists. But the difference between notice and surprise is only one of the important reasons for distinguishing between permanent and mobile checkpoints. With respect to the former, there is no room for discretion in either the timing or the location of the stop—it is a permanent part of the landscape. In the latter case, however, although the checkpoint is most frequently employed during the hours of darkness on weekends (because that is when drivers with alcohol in their blood are most apt to be found on the road), the police have extremely broad discretion in determining the exact timing and placement of the roadblock.

There is also a significant difference between the kind of discretion that the officer exercises after the stop is made. A check for a driver's license, or for identification papers at an immigration checkpoint, is far more easily standardized than is a search for evidence of intoxication. A Michigan officer who questions a motorist at a sobriety checkpoint has virtually unlimited discretion to detain the driver on the basis of the slightest suspicion. A ruddy complexion, an unbuttoned shirt, bloodshot eyes, or a speech impediment may suffice to prolong the detention. Any driver who had just consumed a glass of beer, or even a sip of wine, would almost certainly have the burden of demonstrating to the officer that his or her driving ability was not impaired.

Finally, it is significant that many of the stops at permanent checkpoints occur during daylight hours, whereas the sobriety checkpoints are almost invariably operated at night. A seizure followed by interrogation and even a cursory search at night is surely more offensive than a daytime stop that is almost as routine as going through a tollgate. Thus we thought it important to point out that the random stops at issue in [*United States v. Ortiz*, 422 U.S. 891 (1975)], frequently occurred at night.

These fears are not, as the Court would have it, solely the lot of the guilty. To be law abiding is not necessarily to be spotless, and even the most virtuous can be unlucky. Unwanted attention from the local police need not be less discomforting simply because one's secrets are not the stuff of criminal prosecutions. Moreover, those who have found—by reason of prejudice or misfortune—that encounters with the police may become adversarial or unpleasant without good cause will have grounds for worrying at any stop designed to elicit signs of suspicious behavior. Being stopped by the police is distressing even when it should not be terrifying, and what begins mildly may by happenstance turn severe.

* * *

II

* * *

As I have already explained, I believe the Court is quite wrong in blithely asserting that a sobriety checkpoint is no more intrusive than a permanent checkpoint. In my opinion, unannounced investigatory seizures are, particularly when they take place at night, the hallmark of regimes far different from ours; the surprise intrusion upon individual liberty is not minimal. On that issue, my difference with the Court may amount to nothing less than a difference in our respective evaluations of the importance of individual liberty, a serious, albeit inevitable, source of constitutional disagreement. On the degree to which the sobriety checkpoint seizures advance the public interest, however, the Court's position is wholly indefensible.

The Court's analysis of this issue resembles a business decision that measures profits by counting gross receipts and ignoring expenses. The evidence in this case indicates that sobriety checkpoints result in the arrest of a fraction of one percent of the drivers who are stopped, but there is absolutely no evidence that this figure represents an increase over the number of arrests that would have been made by using the same law enforcement resources in conventional patrols.[12] Thus, although the *gross* number of arrests is more than zero, there is a complete failure of proof on the question whether the wholesale seizures have produced any *net* advance in the public interest in arresting intoxicated drivers.

Indeed, the position adopted today by the Court is not one endorsed by any of the law enforcement authorities to whom the Court purports to defer. The Michigan police do not rely, as the Court does, on the *arrest rate* at sobriety checkpoints to justify the stops made there. Colonel Hough, the commander of the Michigan State Police and a leading proponent of the checkpoints, admitted at trial that the arrest rate at the checkpoints was "very low." Instead, Colonel Hough and the State have maintained that the mere *threat* of such arrests is sufficient to deter drunk-driving and so to reduce the accident rate. The Maryland police officer who testified at trial took the same position with respect to his State's program. There is, obviously, nothing wrong with a law enforcement technique that reduces crime by pure deterrence without punishing anybody; on the contrary, such an approach is highly commendable. One cannot, however, prove its efficacy by counting the arrests that were made. One must instead measure the number of crimes that were avoided. Perhaps because the record is wanting, the Court simply ignores this point.

---

[12] Indeed, a single officer in a patrol car parked at the same place as the sobriety checkpoint would no doubt have been able to make some of the arrests based on the officer's observation of the way the intoxicated driver was operating his vehicle.

The Court's sparse analysis of this issue differs markedly from Justice Powell's opinion for the Court in *Martinez-Fuerte.* He did not merely count the 17,000 arrests made at the San Clemente checkpoint in 1973; he also carefully explained why those arrests represented a net benefit to the law enforcement interest at stake. Common sense, moreover, suggests that immigration checkpoints are more necessary than sobriety checkpoints: There is no reason why smuggling illegal aliens should impair a motorist's driving ability, but if intoxication did not noticeably affect driving ability it would not be unlawful. Drunk-driving, unlike smuggling, may thus be detected absent any checkpoints. A program that produces thousands of otherwise impossible arrests is not a relevant precedent for a program that produces only a handful of arrests which would be more easily obtained without resort to suspicionless seizures of hundreds of innocent citizens.

III

The most disturbing aspect of the Court's decision today is that it appears to give no weight to the citizen's interest in freedom from suspicionless unannounced investigatory seizures. Although the author of the opinion does not reiterate his description of that interest as "diaphanous," see *Delaware v. Prouse,* 440 U.S., at 666 (REHNQUIST, J., dissenting), the Court's opinion implicitly adopts that characterization. On the other hand, the Court places a heavy thumb on the law enforcement interest by looking only at gross receipts instead of net benefits. Perhaps this tampering with the scales of justice can be explained by the Court's obvious concern about the slaughter on our highways and a resultant tolerance for policies designed to alleviate the problem by "setting an example" of a few motorists. This possibility prompts two observations.

First, my objections to random seizures or temporary checkpoints do not apply to a host of other investigatory procedures that do not depend upon surprise and are unquestionably permissible. These procedures have been used to address other threats to human life no less pressing than the threat posed by drunken drivers. It is, for example, common practice to require every prospective airline passenger, or every visitor to a public building, to pass through a metal detector that will reveal the presence of a firearm or an explosive. Permanent, nondiscretionary checkpoints could be used to control serious dangers at other publicly operated facilities. Because concealed weapons obviously represent one such substantial threat to public safety, I would suppose that all subway passengers could be required to pass through metal detectors, so long as the detectors were permanent and every passenger was subjected to the same search. Likewise, I would suppose that a State could condition access to its toll roads upon not only paying the toll but also taking a uniformly administered breathalyzer test. That requirement might well keep all drunken drivers off the highways that serve the fastest and most dangerous traffic. This procedure would not be subject to the constitutional objections that control this case: The checkpoints would be permanently fixed, the stopping procedure would apply to all users of the toll road in precisely the same way, and police officers would not be free to make arbitrary choices about which neighborhoods should be targeted or about which individuals should be more thoroughly searched. Random, suspicionless seizures designed to search for evidence of firearms, drugs, or intoxication belong, however, in a fundamentally different category. These seizures play upon the detained individual's reasonable expectations of privacy, injecting a suspicionless search into a context where none would normally occur. The imposition that seems diaphanous today may be intolerable tomorrow.

Second, sobriety checkpoints are elaborate, and disquieting, publicity stunts. The possibility that anybody, no matter how innocent, may be stopped for police inspection is nothing if not attention getting. The shock value of the checkpoint program may be its most effective feature: Lieutenant Cotten of the Maryland State Police, a defense witness, testified that "the media coverage . . . has been absolutely overwhelming. . . . Quite frankly we got benefits just from the controversy of the sobriety checkpoints." Insofar as the State seeks to justify its use of sobriety checkpoints on the basis that they dramatize the public interest in the prevention of alcohol-related accidents, the Court should heed Justice Scalia's comment upon a similar justification for a drug screening program:

> The only plausible explanation, in my view, is what the Commissioner himself offered in the concluding sentence of his memorandum to Customs Service employees announcing the program: "Implementation of the drug screening program would set an important example in our country's struggle with this most serious threat to our national health and security." Or as respondent's brief to this Court asserted: "if a law enforcement agency and its employees do not take the law seriously, neither will the public on which the agency's effectiveness depends." What better way to show that the Government is serious about its "war on drugs" than to subject its employees on the front line of that war to this invasion of their privacy and affront to their dignity? To be sure, there is only a slight chance that it will prevent some serious public harm resulting from Service employee drug use, but it will show to the world that the Service is "clean," and—most important of all—will demonstrate the determination of the Government to eliminate this scourge of our society! I think it obvious that this justification is unacceptable; that the impairment of individual liberties cannot be the means of making a point; that symbolism, even symbolism for so worthy a cause as the abolition of unlawful drugs, cannot validate an otherwise unreasonable search.

Treasury Employees v. Von Raab, 489 U.S. 656, 686–687 (1989) (dissenting opinion).

This is a case that is driven by nothing more than symbolic state action—an insufficient justification for an otherwise unreasonable program of random seizures. Unfortunately, the Court is transfixed by the wrong symbol—the illusory prospect of punishing countless intoxicated motorists—when it should keep its eyes on the road plainly marked by the Constitution.

Points for Discussion

1. How does the Court arrive at the conclusion that the balancing of the government's interest in preventing drunk driving and the individual's interest in being free from seizures weighs in favor of permitting sobriety checkpoints?

2. The evidence set forth in this case seems to indicate that sobriety checkpoints are not particularly effective at detecting drunk driving. To what extent should the effectiveness of a particular mode of law enforcement enter the Court's constitutional calculus? Is a foolish or inefficient law enforcement strategy necessarily unreasonable?

3. Supreme Court opinions are, of course, typically worded with exacting care. In this case Justice Brennan criticizes the majority for labeling the individual's interest in not being stopped at sobriety checkpoints as "slight" compared to the government's interest in preventing highway fatalities. In a bit of sarcastic wordplay, Justice Brennan ends by asserting, "nor do I slight the government's efforts to prevent such tragic losses." Justice Stevens' dissent also includes a small pun, ending with the claim, "This is a case driven by nothing more than symbolic state action . . . ." That last part of Justice Stevens' opinion is the only part not joined by Justices Brennan and Marshall. In addition to asserting that checkpoints are "elaborate, and disquieting, publicity stunts," that section of Justice Stevens' opinion also argues that permanent checkpoints "would not be subject to the constitutional objections" that, in Justice Stevens' view, doom temporary checkpoints. With which of the points in Part III do Justices Brennan and Marshall likely disagree?

4. Justice Stevens quotes Justice Scalia's dissent in *Von Raab* to support his point that the checkpoints in *Sitz* are mere "publicity stunts". Why does Justice Scalia not join Justice Stevens' opinion here? What distinction is there between Michigan's DUI checkpoints and the Customs Service's drug-testing program challenged in *Von Raab*?

INDIANAPOLIS V. EDMOND

531 U.S. 32 (2000)

JUSTICE O'CONNOR delivered the opinion of the court.

In *Michigan Dept. of State Police v. Sitz,* 496 U.S. 444 (1990), and *United States v. Martinez-Fuerte,* 428 U.S. 543 (1976), we held that brief, suspicionless seizures at highway checkpoints for the purposes of combating drunk driving and intercepting illegal immigrants were constitutional. We now consider the constitutionality of a highway checkpoint program whose primary purpose is the discovery and interdiction of illegal narcotics.

I

In August 1998, the city of Indianapolis began to operate vehicle checkpoints on Indianapolis roads in an effort to interdict unlawful drugs. The city conducted six such roadblocks between August and November that year, stopping 1,161 vehicles and arresting 104 motorists. Fifty-five arrests were for drug-related crimes, while 49 were for offenses unrelated to drugs. The overall "hit rate" of the program was thus approximately nine percent.

The parties stipulated to the facts concerning the operation of the checkpoints by the Indianapolis Police Department (IPD) for purposes of the preliminary injunction proceedings instituted below. At each checkpoint location, the police stop a predetermined number of vehicles. Approximately 30 officers are stationed at the checkpoint. Pursuant to written directives issued by the chief of police, at least one officer approaches the vehicle, advises the driver that he or she is being stopped briefly at a drug checkpoint, and asks the driver to produce a license and registration. The officer also looks for signs of impairment and conducts an open-view examination of the vehicle from the outside. A narcotics-detection dog walks around the outside of each stopped vehicle.

The directives instruct the officers that they may conduct a search only by consent or based on the appropriate quantum of particularized suspicion. The officers must conduct each stop in the same manner until particularized suspicion develops, and the officers have no discretion to stop any vehicle out of sequence. The city agreed in the stipulation to operate the checkpoints in such a way as to ensure that the total duration of each stop, absent reasonable suspicion or probable cause, would be five minutes or less.

The affidavit of Indianapolis Police Sergeant Marshall DePew, although it is technically outside the parties' stipulation, provides further insight concerning the operation of the checkpoints. According to Sergeant DePew, checkpoint locations are selected weeks in advance based on such considerations as area crime statistics and traffic flow. The checkpoints are generally operated during daylight hours and are identified with lighted signs reading, "'NARCOTICS CHECKPOINT ___ MILE AHEAD,

NARCOTICS K-9 IN USE, BE PREPARED TO STOP.' " Once a group of cars has been stopped, other traffic proceeds without interruption until all the stopped cars have been processed or diverted for further processing. Sergeant DePew also stated that the average stop for a vehicle not subject to further processing lasts two to three minutes or less.

Respondents James Edmond and Joell Palmer were each stopped at a narcotics checkpoint in late September 1998. Respondents then filed a lawsuit on behalf of themselves and the class of all motorists who had been stopped or were subject to being stopped in the future at the Indianapolis drug checkpoints. Respondents claimed that the roadblocks violated the Fourth Amendment of the United States Constitution and the search and seizure provision of the Indiana Constitution. Respondents requested declaratory and injunctive relief for the class, as well as damages and attorney's fees for themselves.

* * *

III

It is well established that a vehicle stop at a highway checkpoint effectuates a seizure within the meaning of the Fourth Amendment. The fact that officers walk a narcotics-detection dog around the exterior of each car at the Indianapolis checkpoints does not transform the seizure into a search. See *United States v. Place,* 462 U.S. 696, 707 (1983). Just as in *Place,* an exterior sniff of an automobile does not require entry into the car and is not designed to disclose any information other than the presence or absence of narcotics. Like the dog sniff in *Place,* a sniff by a dog that simply walks around a car is "much less intrusive than a typical search." *Ibid.* Rather, what principally distinguishes these checkpoints from those we have previously approved is their primary purpose.

* * *

We have never approved a checkpoint program whose primary purpose was to detect evidence of ordinary criminal wrongdoing. Rather, our checkpoint cases have recognized only limited exceptions to the general rule that a seizure must be accompanied by some measure of individualized suspicion. We suggested in *Prouse* that we would not credit the "general interest in crime control" as justification for a regime of suspicionless stops. Consistent with this suggestion, each of the checkpoint programs that we have approved was designed primarily to serve purposes closely related to the problems of policing the border or the necessity of ensuring roadway safety. Because the primary purpose of the Indianapolis narcotics checkpoint program is to uncover evidence of ordinary criminal wrongdoing, the program contravenes the Fourth Amendment.

Petitioners propose several ways in which the narcotics-detection purpose of the instant checkpoint program may instead resemble the primary purposes of the checkpoints in *Sitz* and *Martinez-Fuerte.*

Petitioners state that the checkpoints in those cases had the same ultimate purpose of arresting those suspected of committing crimes. Securing the border and apprehending drunk drivers are, of course, law enforcement activities, and law enforcement officers employ arrests and criminal prosecutions in pursuit of these goals. If we were to rest the case at this high level of generality, there would be little check on the ability of the authorities to construct roadblocks for almost any conceivable law enforcement purpose. Without drawing the line at roadblocks designed primarily to serve the general interest in crime control, the Fourth Amendment would do little to prevent such intrusions from becoming a routine part of American life.

Petitioners also emphasize the severe and intractable nature of the drug problem as justification for the checkpoint program. There is no doubt that traffic in illegal narcotics creates social harms of the first magnitude. The law enforcement problems that the drug trade creates likewise remain daunting and complex, particularly in light of the myriad forms of spin-off crime that it spawns. The same can be said of various other illegal activities, if only to a lesser degree. But the gravity of the threat alone cannot be dispositive of questions concerning what means law enforcement officers may employ to pursue a given purpose. Rather, in determining whether individualized suspicion is required, we must consider the nature of the interests threatened and their connection to the particular law enforcement practices at issue. We are particularly reluctant to recognize exceptions to the general rule of individualized suspicion where governmental authorities primarily pursue their general crime control ends.

Nor can the narcotics-interdiction purpose of the checkpoints be rationalized in terms of a highway safety concern similar to that present in *Sitz*. The detection and punishment of almost any criminal offense serves broadly the safety of the community, and our streets would no doubt be safer but for the scourge of illegal drugs. Only with respect to a smaller class of offenses, however, is society confronted with the type of immediate, vehicle-bound threat to life and limb that the sobriety checkpoint in *Sitz* was designed to eliminate.

Petitioners also liken the anticontraband agenda of the Indianapolis checkpoints to the antismuggling purpose of the checkpoints in *Martinez-Fuerte*. Petitioners cite this Court's conclusion in *Martinez-Fuerte* that the flow of traffic was too heavy to permit "particularized study of a given car that would enable it to be identified as a possible carrier of illegal aliens," and claim that this logic has even more force here. The problem with this argument is that the same logic prevails any time a vehicle is employed to conceal contraband or other evidence of a crime. This type of connection to the roadway is very different from the close connection to roadway safety that was present in *Sitz* and *Prouse*. Further, the Indianapolis checkpoints are far removed from the border context that was crucial in *Martinez-Fuerte*. While the difficulty of examining each passing car was an important factor in validating the law enforcement technique employed in *Martinez-Fuerte,* this factor alone cannot justify a regime of suspicionless searches or seizures. Rather, we must look more closely at the nature of the public interests that such a regime is designed principally to serve.

The primary purpose of the Indianapolis narcotics checkpoints is in the end to advance "the general interest in crime control." We decline to suspend the usual requirement of individualized suspicion where the police seek to employ a checkpoint primarily for the ordinary enterprise of investigating crimes. We cannot sanction stops justified only by the generalized and ever-present possibility that interrogation and inspection may reveal that any given motorist has committed some crime.

Of course, there are circumstances that may justify a law enforcement checkpoint where the primary purpose would otherwise, but for some emergency, relate to ordinary crime control. For example, as the Court of Appeals noted, the Fourth Amendment would almost certainly permit an appropriately tailored roadblock set up to thwart an imminent terrorist attack or to catch a dangerous criminal who is likely to flee by way of a particular route. The exigencies created by these scenarios are far removed from the circumstances under which authorities might simply stop cars as a matter of course to see if there just happens to be a felon leaving the jurisdiction. While we do not limit the purposes that may justify a checkpoint program to any rigid set of categories, we decline to approve a program whose primary purpose is ultimately indistinguishable from the general interest in crime control.[1]

Petitioners argue that our prior cases preclude an inquiry into the purposes of the checkpoint program. For example, they cite *Whren v. United States,* 517 U.S. 806 (1996), and *Bond v. United States,* 529 U.S. 334 (2000), to support the proposition that "where the government articulates and pursues a legitimate interest for a suspicionless stop, courts should not look behind that interest to determine whether the government's 'primary purpose' is valid." These cases, however, do not control the instant situation.

In *Whren,* we held that an individual officer's subjective intentions are irrelevant to the Fourth Amendment validity of a traffic stop that is

---

[1] The Chief Justice's dissent erroneously characterizes our opinion as resting on the application of a "non-law-enforcement primary purpose test." Our opinion nowhere describes the purposes of the *Sitz* and *Martinez-Fuerte* checkpoints as being "not primarily related to criminal law enforcement." Rather, our judgment turns on the fact that the primary purpose of the Indianapolis checkpoints is to advance the general interest in crime control.

The Chief Justice's dissent also erroneously characterizes our opinion as holding that the "use of a drug-sniffing dog . . . annuls what is otherwise plainly constitutional under our Fourth Amendment jurisprudence." Again, the constitutional defect of the program is that its primary purpose is to advance the general interest in crime control.

justified objectively by probable cause to believe that a traffic violation has occurred. We observed that our prior cases "foreclose any argument that the constitutional reasonableness of traffic stops depends on the actual motivations of the individual officers involved." In so holding, we expressly distinguished cases where we had addressed the validity of searches conducted in the absence of probable cause.

Whren therefore reinforces the principle that, while "[s]ubjective intentions play no role in ordinary, probable-cause Fourth Amendment analysis," programmatic purposes may be relevant to the validity of Fourth Amendment intrusions undertaken pursuant to a general scheme without individualized suspicion. Accordingly, *Whren* does not preclude an inquiry into programmatic purpose in such contexts. It likewise does not preclude an inquiry into programmatic purpose here.

Last term in *Bond,* we addressed the question whether a law enforcement officer violated a reasonable expectation of privacy in conducting a tactile examination of carry-on luggage in the overhead compartment of a bus. In doing so, we simply noted that the principle of *Whren* rendered the subjective intent of an officer irrelevant to this analysis. While, as petitioners correctly observe, the analytical rubric of *Bond* was not "ordinary, probable-cause Fourth Amendment analysis," nothing in *Bond* suggests that we would extend the principle of *Whren* to all situations where individualized suspicion was lacking. Rather, subjective intent was irrelevant in *Bond* because the inquiry that our precedents required focused on the objective effects of the actions of an individual officer. By contrast, our cases dealing with intrusions that occur pursuant to a general scheme absent individualized suspicion have often required an inquiry into purpose at the programmatic level.

Petitioners argue that the Indianapolis checkpoint program is justified by its lawful secondary purposes of keeping impaired motorists off the road and verifying licenses and registrations. If this were the case, however, law enforcement authorities would be able to establish checkpoints for virtually any purpose so long as they also included a license or sobriety check. For this reason, we examine the available evidence to determine the primary purpose of the checkpoint program. While we recognize the challenges inherent in a purpose inquiry, courts routinely engage in this enterprise in many areas of constitutional jurisprudence as a means of sifting abusive governmental conduct from that which is lawful. As a result, a program driven by an impermissible purpose may be proscribed while a program impelled by licit purposes is permitted, even though the challenged conduct may be outwardly similar. While reasonableness under the Fourth Amendment is predominantly an objective inquiry, our special needs and administrative search cases demonstrate that purpose is often relevant when suspicionless intrusions pursuant to a general scheme are at issue.[2]

It goes without saying that our holding today does nothing to alter the constitutional status of the sobriety and border checkpoints that we approved in *Sitz* and *Martinez-Fuerte,* or of the type of traffic checkpoint that we suggested would be lawful in *Prouse*. The constitutionality of such checkpoint programs still depends on a balancing of the competing interests at stake and the effectiveness of the program. When law enforcement authorities pursue primarily general crime control purposes at checkpoints such as here, however, stops can only be justified by some quantum of individualized suspicion.

Our holding also does not affect the validity of border searches or searches at places like airports and government buildings, where the need for such measures to ensure public safety can be particularly acute. Nor does our opinion speak to other intrusions aimed primarily at purposes beyond the general interest in crime control. Our holding also does not impair the ability of police officers to act appropriately upon information that they properly learn during a checkpoint stop justified by a lawful primary purpose, even where such action may result in the arrest of a motorist for an offense unrelated to that purpose. Finally, we caution that the purpose inquiry in this context is to be conducted only at the programmatic level and is not an invitation to probe the minds of individual officers acting at the scene.

Because the primary purpose of the Indianapolis checkpoint program is ultimately indistinguishable from the general interest in crime control, the checkpoints violate the Fourth Amendment. The judgment of the Court of Appeals is, accordingly, affirmed.

CHIEF JUSTICE REHNQUIST, with whom JUSTICE THOMAS joins, and with whom JUSTICE SCALIA joins as to Part I, dissenting.

The State's use of a drug-sniffing dog, according to the Court's holding, annuls what is otherwise plainly constitutional under our Fourth Amendment jurisprudence: brief, standardized, discretionless, roadblock seizures of automobiles, seizures which effectively serve a weighty state interest with only minimal intrusion on the privacy of their occupants. Because these seizures serve the State's accepted and significant interests of preventing drunken driving and checking for driver's licenses and vehicle registrations, and because there is nothing in the record to indicate

2 Because petitioners concede that the primary purpose of the Indianapolis checkpoints is narcotics detection, we need not decide whether the State may establish a checkpoint program with the primary purpose of checking licenses or driver sobriety and a secondary purpose of interdicting narcotics. Specifically, we express no view on the question whether police may expand the scope of a license or sobriety checkpoint seizure in order to detect the presence of drugs in a stopped car.

that the addition of the dog sniff lengthens these otherwise legitimate seizures, I dissent.

I

As it is nowhere to be found in the Court's opinion, I begin with blackletter roadblock seizure law. "The principal protection of Fourth Amendment rights at checkpoints lies in appropriate limitations on the scope of the stop." *United States v. Martinez-Fuerte,* 428 U.S. 543, 566–567 (1976). Roadblock seizures are consistent with the Fourth Amendment if they are "carried out pursuant to a plan embodying explicit, neutral limitations on the conduct of individual officers." *Brown v. Texas,* 443 U.S. 47, 51 (1979). Specifically, the constitutionality of a seizure turns upon "a weighing of the gravity of the public concerns served by the seizure, the degree to which the seizure advances the public interest, and the severity of the interference with individual liberty."

* * *

This case follows naturally from *Martinez-Fuerte* and *Sitz*. Petitioners acknowledge that the "primary purpose" of these roadblocks is to interdict illegal drugs, but this fact should not be controlling. Even accepting the Court's conclusion that the checkpoints at issue in *Martinez-Fuerte* and *Sitz* were not primarily related to criminal law enforcement,[2] the question whether a law enforcement purpose could support a roadblock seizure is not presented in this case. The District Court found that another "purpose of the checkpoints is to check driver's licenses and vehicle registrations," and the written directives state that the police officers are to "[l]ook for signs of impairment." The use of roadblocks to look for signs of impairment was validated by *Sitz,* and the use of roadblocks to check for driver's licenses and vehicle registrations was expressly recognized in *Delaware v. Prouse,* 440 U.S. 648, 663 (1979). That the roadblocks serve these legitimate state interests cannot be seriously disputed, as the 49 people arrested for offenses unrelated to drugs can attest. And it would be speculative to conclude—given the District Court's findings, the written directives, and the actual arrests—that petitioners would not have operated these roadblocks but for the State's interest in interdicting drugs.

* * *

With these checkpoints serving two important state interests, the remaining prongs of the *Brown v. Texas* balancing test are easily met. The seizure is objectively reasonable as it lasts, on average, two to three minutes and does not involve a search. The subjective intrusion is likewise

[2] This gloss is not at all obvious. The respondents in *Martinez-Fuerte* were criminally prosecuted for illegally transporting aliens, and the Court expressly noted that "[i]nterdicting the flow of illegal entrants from Mexico poses formidable law enforcement problems." And the *Sitz* Court recognized that if an "officer's observations suggest that the driver was intoxicated, an arrest would be made." But however persuasive the distinction, the Court's opinion does not impugn the continuing validity of *Martinez-Fuerte* and *Sitz.*

limited as the checkpoints are clearly marked and operated by uniformed officers who are directed to stop every vehicle in the same manner. The only difference between this case and *Sitz* is the presence of the dog. We have already held, however, that a "sniff test" by a trained narcotics dog is not a "search" within the meaning of the Fourth Amendment because it does not require physical intrusion of the object being sniffed and it does not expose anything other than the contraband items. *United States v. Place,* 462 U.S. 696, 706–707 (1983). And there is nothing in the record to indicate that the dog sniff lengthens the stop. Finally, the checkpoints' success rate—49 arrests for offenses unrelated to drugs—only confirms the State's legitimate interests in preventing drunken driving and ensuring the proper licensing of drivers and registration of their vehicles.

These stops effectively serve the State's legitimate interests; they are executed in a regularized and neutral manner; and they only minimally intrude upon the privacy of the motorists. They should therefore be constitutional.

II

The Court, unwilling to adopt the straightforward analysis that these precedents dictate, adds a new non-law-enforcement primary purpose test lifted from a distinct area of Fourth Amendment jurisprudence relating to the *searches* of homes and businesses. As discussed above, the question that the Court answers is not even posed in this case given the accepted reasons for the seizures. But more fundamentally, whatever sense a non-law-enforcement primary purpose test may make in the search setting, it is ill suited to brief roadblock seizures, where we have consistently looked at "the scope of the stop" in assessing a program's constitutionality.

* * *

The "special needs" doctrine, which has been used to uphold certain suspicionless searches performed for reasons unrelated to law enforcement, is an exception to the general rule that a search must be based on individualized suspicion of wrongdoing. The doctrine permits intrusions into a person's body and home, areas afforded the greatest Fourth Amendment protection. But there were no such intrusions here.

"[O]ne's expectation of privacy in an automobile and of freedom in its operation are significantly different from the traditional expectation of privacy and freedom in one's residence." *Martinez-Fuerte,* at 561. This is because "[a]utomobiles, unlike homes, are subjected to pervasive and continuing governmental regulation and controls." The lowered expectation of privacy in one's automobile is coupled with the limited nature of the intrusion: a brief, standardized, nonintrusive seizure. The brief seizure of an automobile can hardly be compared to the intrusive search of the body or the home. Thus, just as the "special needs" inquiry serves to both define and limit the permissible scope of those searches, the

Brown v. Texas balancing test serves to define and limit the permissible scope of automobile seizures.

Because of these extrinsic limitations upon roadblock seizures, the Court's newfound non-law-enforcement primary purpose test is both unnecessary to secure Fourth Amendment rights and bound to produce wide-ranging litigation over the "purpose" of any given seizure. Police designing highway roadblocks can never be sure of their validity, since a jury might later determine that a forbidden purpose exists. Roadblock stops identical to the one that we upheld in *Sitz* 10 years ago, or to the one that we upheld 24 years ago in *Martinez-Fuerte,* may now be challenged on the grounds that they have some concealed forbidden purpose.

Efforts to enforce the law on public highways used by millions of motorists are obviously necessary to our society. The Court's opinion today casts a shadow over what had been assumed, on the basis of *stare decisis,* to be a perfectly lawful activity. Conversely, if the Indianapolis police had assigned a different purpose to their activity here, but in no way changed what was done on the ground to individual motorists, it might well be valid. The Court's non-law-enforcement primary purpose test simply does not serve as a proxy for anything that the Fourth Amendment is, or should be, concerned about in the automobile seizure context.

Petitioners' program complies with our decisions regarding roadblock seizures of automobiles, and the addition of a dog sniff does not add to the length or the intrusion of the stop. Because such stops are consistent with the Fourth Amendment, I would reverse the decision of the Court of Appeals.

JUSTICE THOMAS, dissenting.

Taken together, our decisions in *Michigan Dept. of State Police v. Sitz,* 496 U.S. 444 (1990), and *United States v. Martinez-Fuerte,* 428 U.S. 543 (1976), stand for the proposition that suspicionless roadblock seizures are constitutionally permissible if conducted according to a plan that limits the discretion of the officers conducting the stops. I am not convinced that *Sitz* and *Martinez-Fuerte* were correctly decided. Indeed, I rather doubt that the Framers of the Fourth Amendment would have considered "reasonable" a program of indiscriminate stops of individuals not suspected of wrongdoing.

Respondents did not, however, advocate the overruling of *Sitz* and *Martinez-Fuerte,* and I am reluctant to consider such a step without the benefit of briefing and argument. For the reasons given by the Chief Justice, I believe that those cases compel upholding the program at issue here. I, therefore, join his opinion.

Points for Discussion

1. In invalidating the checkpoints at issue here does the Court conclude that the problem of drug abuse is not as important as the problem of drunk driving? If not, how does the Court distinguish this case from *Sitz*? Isn't preventing or deterring the transport of illegal drugs at least as important as preventing or deterring drunk driving?

2. The Court appears to distinguish *Martinez-Fuerte* and *Sitz* on the ground that "special needs" motivated the checkpoints in those cases but not this one. Yet, as the dissent points out in footnote 2, all three cases involve both the use of law enforcement and the threat of criminal prosecutions. How, then, does the majority conclude that this search has the primary (rather than secondary) purpose of enforcing the criminal laws?

3. Dissenting in *Brinegar v. United States*, Justice Jackson wrote that he would "strive hard to sustain" a suspicionless checkpoint to catch a kidnapper but would "not strain to sustain such a roadblock and universal search to salvage a few bottles of bourbon and catch a bootlegger." 338 U.S. 160, 183 (1949) (JACKSON, J., dissenting). In *Edmond*, Justice O'Connor's majority opinion likewise says (though without citing to Justice Jackson) that a suspicionless checkpoint might be justified "to thwart an imminent terrorist attack or to catch a dangerous criminal who is likely to flee by way of a particular route." Justice Thomas, however, unequivocally states that the Fourth Amendment prohibits "indiscriminate stops of individuals not suspected of wrongdoing." Should the legality of suspicionless searches depend on whether the police are investigating a serious or violent crime? Or is this simply a manifestation of the "hydraulic pressures . . . that bear heavily on the Court to water down constitutional guarantees and give the police the upper hand" that Justice Douglas warned about in *Terry v. Ohio*?

CHAPTER 5

THE PROBLEM OF PRETEXTUAL SEARCHES

■ ■ ■

In his dissent in *Schneckloth v. Bustamonte*, excerpted in chapter 4, Justice Marshall alluded to the problem of pretextual searches when he wrote that "consent [to search] is ordinarily given as acquiescence in an implicit claim of authority to search." This view was echoed years later in Justice Souter's dissent in *United States v. Drayton*, excerpted in chapter 1: "It is very hard to imagine that either Brown or Drayton would have believed that he stood to lose nothing if he refused to cooperate with the police, or that he had any free choice to ignore the police altogether. . . . A police officer who is certain to get his way has no need to shout."

The materials in this chapter show how the Court's decisions over the years have allowed the police to leverage minor intrusions, specifically traffic stops, to conduct mass-scale consensual searches unsupported by probable cause.

WHREN V. UNITED STATES

517 U.S. 806 (1996)

JUSTICE SCALIA delivered the opinion of the court.

In this case we decide whether the temporary detention of a motorist who the police have probable cause to believe has committed a civil traffic violation is inconsistent with the Fourth Amendment's prohibition against unreasonable seizures unless a reasonable officer would have been motivated to stop the car by a desire to enforce the traffic laws.

I

On the evening of June 10, 1993, plainclothes vice-squad officers of the District of Columbia Metropolitan Police Department were patrolling a "high drug area" of the city in an unmarked car. Their suspicions were aroused when they passed a dark Pathfinder truck with temporary license plates and youthful occupants waiting at a stop sign, the driver looking down into the lap of the passenger at his right. The truck remained stopped at the intersection for what seemed an unusually long time-more than 20 seconds. When the police car executed a U-turn in order to head back toward the truck, the Pathfinder turned suddenly to its right, without signaling, and sped off at an "unreasonable" speed. The policemen followed, and in a short while overtook the Pathfinder when it stopped behind other traffic at a red light. They pulled up alongside, and Officer Ephraim Soto stepped out and approached the driver's door, identifying himself as a police officer and directing the driver, petitioner Brown, to put the vehicle in park. When Soto drew up to the driver's window, he immediately observed two large plastic bags of what appeared to be crack cocaine in petitioner Whren's hands. Petitioners were arrested, and quantities of several types of illegal drugs were retrieved from the vehicle.

Petitioners were charged in a four-count indictment with violating various federal drug laws, including 21 U.S.C. §§ 844(a) and 860(a). At a pretrial suppression hearing, they challenged the legality of the stop and the resulting seizure of the drugs. They argued that the stop had not been justified by probable cause to believe, or even reasonable suspicion, that petitioners were engaged in illegal drug-dealing activity; and that Officer Soto's asserted ground for approaching the vehicle—to give the driver a warning concerning traffic violations—was pretextual. The District Court denied the suppression motion, concluding that "the facts of the stop were not controverted," and "[t]here was nothing to really demonstrate that the actions of the officers were contrary to a normal traffic stop."

* * *

II

* * *

Petitioners accept that Officer Soto had probable cause to believe that various provisions of the District of Columbia traffic code had been violated. See 18 D.C. Mun. Regs. §§ 2213.4 (1995) ("An operator shall . . . give full time and attention to the operation of the vehicle"); 2204.3 ("No person shall turn any vehicle . . . without giving an appropriate signal"); 2200.3 ("No person shall drive a vehicle . . . at a speed greater than is reasonable and prudent under the conditions"). They argue, however, that "in the unique context of civil traffic regulations" probable cause is not enough. Since, they contend, the use of automobiles is so heavily and minutely regulated that total compliance with traffic and safety rules is nearly impossible, a police officer will almost invariably be able to catch any given motorist in a technical violation. This creates the temptation to use traffic stops as a means of investigating other law violations, as to which no probable cause or even articulable suspicion exists. Petitioners, who are both black, further contend that police officers might decide which motorists to stop based on decidedly impermissible factors, such as the race of the car's occupants. To avoid this danger, they say, the Fourth Amendment test for traffic stops should be, not the normal one (applied by the Court of Appeals) of whether probable cause existed to justify the stop; but rather, whether a police officer, acting reasonably, would have made the stop for the reason given.

A

Petitioners contend that the standard they propose is consistent with our past cases' disapproval of police attempts to use valid bases of action against citizens as pretexts for pursuing other investigatory agendas. We are reminded that in *Florida v. Wells,* 495 U.S. 1, 4 (1990), we stated that "an inventory search" must not be a ruse for a general rummaging in order to discover incriminating evidence"; that in *Colorado v. Bertine,* 479 U.S. 367, 372 (1987), in approving an inventory search, we apparently thought it significant that there had been "no showing that the police, who were following standardized procedures, acted in bad faith or for the sole purpose of investigation"; and that in *New York v. Burger,* 482 U.S. 691, 716–717, n. 27 (1987), we observed, in upholding the constitutionality of a warrantless administrative inspection, that the search did not appear to be "a 'pretext' for obtaining evidence of . . . violation of . . . penal laws." But only an undiscerning reader would regard these cases as endorsing the principle that ulterior motives can invalidate police conduct that is justifiable on the basis of probable cause to believe that a violation of law has occurred. In each case we were addressing the validity of a search conducted in the *absence* of probable cause. Our quoted statements simply explain that the exemption from the need for probable cause (and warrant), which is accorded to searches made for the purpose of inventory or administrative regulation, is not accorded to searches that are *not* made for those purposes.

Petitioners also rely upon *Colorado v. Bannister,* 449 U.S. 1 (1980) *(per curiam),* a case which, like this one, involved a traffic stop as the prelude to a plain-view sighting and arrest on charges wholly unrelated to the basis for the stop. Petitioners point to our statement that "[t]here was no evidence whatsoever that the officer's presence to issue a traffic citation was a pretext to confirm any other previous suspicion about the occupants" of the car. That dictum *at most* demonstrates that the Court in *Bannister* found no need to inquire into the question now under discussion; not that it was certain of the answer. And it may demonstrate even less than that: If by "pretext" the Court meant that the officer really had not seen the car speeding, the statement would mean only that there was no reason to doubt probable cause for the traffic stop.

It would, moreover, be anomalous, to say the least, to treat a statement in a footnote in the *per curiam Bannister* opinion as indicating a reversal of our prior law. Petitioners' difficulty is not simply a lack of affirmative support for their position. Not only have we never held, outside the context of inventory search or administrative inspection (discussed above), that an officer's motive invalidates objectively justifiable behavior under the Fourth Amendment; but we have repeatedly held and asserted the contrary. In *United States v. Villamonte-Marquez,* 462 U.S. 579, 584, n. 3 (1983), we held that an otherwise valid warrantless boarding of a vessel by customs officials was not rendered invalid "because the customs officers were accompanied by a Louisiana state policeman, and were following an informant's tip that a vessel in the ship channel was thought to be carrying marihuana." We flatly dismissed the idea that an ulterior motive might serve to strip the agents of their legal justification. In *United States v. Robinson,* 414 U.S. 218 (1973), we held that a traffic-violation arrest (of the sort here) would not be rendered invalid by the fact that it was "a mere pretext for a narcotics search," and that a lawful postarrest search of the person would not be rendered invalid by the fact that it was not motivated by the officer-safety concern that justifies such searches. And in *Scott v. United States,* 436 U.S. 128, 138 (1978), in rejecting the contention that wiretap evidence was subject to exclusion because the agents conducting the tap had failed to make any effort to comply with the statutory requirement that unauthorized acquisitions be minimized, we said that "[s]ubjective intent alone . . . does not make otherwise lawful conduct illegal or unconstitutional." We described *Robinson* as having established that "the fact that the officer does not have the state of mind which is hypothecated by the reasons which provide the legal justification for the officer's action does not invalidate the action taken as long as the circumstances, viewed objectively, justify that action."

We think these cases foreclose any argument that the constitutional reasonableness of traffic stops depends on the actual motivations of the individual officers involved. We of course agree with petitioners that the Constitution prohibits selective enforcement of the law based on considerations such as race. But the constitutional basis for objecting to intentionally discriminatory application of laws is the Equal Protection Clause, not the Fourth Amendment. Subjective intentions play no role in ordinary, probable-cause Fourth Amendment analysis.

B

Recognizing that we have been unwilling to entertain Fourth Amendment challenges based on the actual motivations of individual officers, petitioners disavow any intention to make the individual officer's subjective good faith the touchstone of "reasonableness." They insist that the standard they have put forward—whether the officer's conduct deviated materially from usual police practices, so that a reasonable officer in the same circumstances would not have made the stop for the reasons given—is an "objective" one.

But although framed in empirical terms, this approach is plainly and indisputably driven by subjective considerations. Its whole purpose is to prevent the police from doing under the guise of enforcing the traffic code what they would like to do for different reasons. Petitioners' proposed standard may not use the word "pretext," but it is designed to combat nothing other than the perceived "danger" of the pretextual stop, albeit only indirectly and over the run of cases. Instead of asking whether the individual officer had the proper state of mind, the petitioners would have us ask, in effect, whether (based on general police practices) it is plausible to believe that the officer had the proper state of mind.

Why one would frame a test designed to combat pretext in such fashion that the court cannot take into account *actual and admitted pretext* is a curiosity that can only be explained by the fact that our cases have foreclosed the more sensible option. If those cases were based only upon the evidentiary difficulty of establishing subjective intent, petitioners' attempt to root out subjective vices through objective means might make sense. But they were not based only upon that, or indeed even principally upon that. Their principal basis—which applies equally to attempts to reach subjective intent through ostensibly objective means—is simply that the Fourth Amendment's concern with "reasonableness" allows certain actions to be taken in certain circumstances, *whatever* the subjective intent. But even if our concern had been only an evidentiary one, petitioners' proposal would by no means assuage it. Indeed, it seems to us somewhat easier to figure out the intent of an individual officer than to plumb the collective consciousness of law enforcement in order to determine whether a "reasonable officer" would have been moved to act upon the traffic violation. While police manuals and standard procedures may sometimes provide objective assistance, ordinarily one would be reduced to speculating about the hypothetical reaction of a hypothetical constable-an exercise that might be called virtual subjectivity.

Moreover, police enforcement practices, even if they could be practicably assessed by a judge, vary from place to place and from time to time. We cannot accept that the search and seizure protections of the Fourth Amendment are so variable and can be made to turn upon such trivialities. The difficulty is illustrated by petitioners' arguments in this case. Their claim that a reasonable officer would not have made this stop is based largely on District of Columbia police regulations which permit plainclothes officers in unmarked vehicles to enforce traffic laws "only in the case of a violation that is so grave as to pose an *immediate threat* to the safety of others." This basis of invalidation would not apply in jurisdictions that had a different practice. And it would not have applied even in the District of Columbia, if Officer Soto had been wearing a uniform or patrolling in a marked police cruiser.

* * *

III

In what would appear to be an elaboration on the "reasonable officer" test, petitioners argue that the balancing inherent in any Fourth Amendment inquiry requires us to weigh the governmental and individual interests implicated in a traffic stop such as we have here. That balancing, petitioners claim, does not support investigation of minor traffic infractions by plainclothes police in unmarked vehicles; such investigation only minimally advances the government's interest in traffic safety, and may indeed retard it by producing motorist confusion and alarm—a view said to be supported by the Metropolitan Police Department's own regulations generally prohibiting this practice. And as for the Fourth Amendment interests of the individuals concerned, petitioners point out that our cases acknowledge that even ordinary traffic stops entail "a possibly unsettling show of authority"; that they at best "interfere with freedom of movement, are inconvenient, and consume time" and at worst "may create substantial anxiety," [*Delaware v.*] *Prouse,* 440 U.S. 648, 657 (1979). That anxiety is likely to be even more pronounced when the stop is conducted by plainclothes officers in unmarked cars.

It is of course true that in principle every Fourth Amendment case, since it turns upon a "reasonableness" determination, involves a balancing of all relevant factors. With rare exceptions not applicable here, however, the result of that balancing is not in doubt where the search or seizure is based upon probable cause. That is why petitioners must rely upon cases like *Prouse* to provide examples of actual "balancing" analysis. There, the police action in question was a random traffic stop for the purpose of checking a motorist's license and vehicle registration, a practice that—like the practices at issue in the inventory search and administrative inspection cases upon which petitioners rely in making their "pretext" claim—involves police intrusion *without the probable cause that is its traditional justification.* Our opinion in *Prouse* expressly distinguished the case from a stop based on precisely what is at issue here: "probable cause to believe that a driver is violating any one of the multitude of applicable traffic and equipment regulations." It noted approvingly that "[t]he foremost method of enforcing traffic and vehicle safety regulations . . . is acting upon observed violations," which afford the "quantum of individualized suspicion" necessary to ensure that police discretion is sufficiently constrained. What is true of *Prouse* is also true of other cases that engaged in detailed "balancing" to decide the constitutionality of automobile stops, such as *Martinez-Fuerte,* which upheld checkpoint stops, and *Brignoni-Ponce,* which disallowed so-called "roving patrol" stops: The detailed "balancing" analysis was necessary because they involved seizures without probable cause.

Where probable cause has existed, the only cases in which we have found it necessary actually to perform the "balancing" analysis involved searches or seizures conducted in an extraordinary manner, unusually harmful to an individual's privacy or even physical interests—such as, for example, seizure by means of deadly force, unannounced entry into a home, entry into a home without a warrant, or physical penetration of the body. The making of a traffic stop out of uniform does not remotely qualify as such an extreme practice, and so is governed by the usual rule that probable cause to believe the law has been broken "outbalances" private interest in avoiding police contact.

Petitioners urge as an extraordinary factor in this case that the "multitude of applicable traffic and equipment regulations" is so large and so difficult to obey perfectly that virtually everyone is guilty of violation, permitting the police to single out almost whomever they wish for a stop. But we are aware of no principle that would allow us to decide at what point a code of law becomes so expansive and so commonly violated that infraction itself can no longer be the ordinary measure of the lawfulness of enforcement. And even if we could identify such exorbitant codes, we do not know by what standard (or what right) we would decide, as petitioners would have us do, which particular provisions are sufficiently important to merit enforcement.

For the run-of-the-mine case, which this surely is, we think there is no realistic alternative to the traditional common-law rule that probable cause justifies a search and seizure.

* * *

Here the District Court found that the officers had probable cause to believe that petitioners had violated the traffic code. That rendered the stop reasonable under the Fourth Amendment, the evidence thereby discovered admissible, and the upholding of the convictions by the Court of Appeals for the District of Columbia Circuit correct.

Points for Discussion

1. Does the unanimous Court question whether the stop in this case was pretextual? If not, why does the Court seem unbothered by that fact?

2. Is the standard proposed by the defendant—not simply whether probable cause exists for the stop but whether a reasonable officer would have made the stop—a workable one? If not, is there another standard that might avoid the result in this case?

3. Look again at some of the traffic infractions made punishable in the District of Columbia. Isn't the defendant correct that the traffic code is so extensive that the police can pull over whomever they please whenever they please? Does that fact counsel for some standard beyond probable cause for evaluating the reasonableness of traffic stops?

4. The first line of *Whren* acknowledges that this case arose from the enforcement of a civil traffic code, not a criminal code, but this important fact is ignored in the Court's analysis. *New York v. Burger*, 482 U.S. 691 (1987), which *Whren* purports to distinguish, held that police enforcing civil business regulations could search a junkyard without probable cause or a warrant. In dissent, Justice Brennan, joined by Justice Marshall, wrote: "Here the State has used an administrative scheme as a pretext to search without probable cause for evidence of criminal violations." Isn't that exactly what is happening

in *Whren*? *Whren* says *Burger* is inapplicable because in *Whren* the police had "probable cause to believe that a violation of law ha[d] occurred." Is that convincing? Does it make any sense to say that there was "probable cause" to believe that a civil traffic infraction occurred?

With one exception, the Court has steadfastly maintained that "probable cause" means a reasonable ground to suspect *criminal* activity. *See, e.g., Florida v. Harris*, 568 U.S. 237, 243 (2013); *Brinegar v. United States*, 338 U.S. 160, 176 (1949). The Court deviated from the usual definition in *Camara v. Municipal Court of City and County of San Francisco*, 387 U.S. 523, 538–39 (1967), which adopted a different definition of "probable cause" for the housing code context. *Whren*, in contrast, says nothing about deviating from probable cause's usual meaning. The fact that the same police officers who enforce criminal laws also enforce traffic laws cannot make any difference, can it?

OHIO V. ROBINETTE

519 U.S. 33 (1996)

CHIEF JUSTICE REHNQUIST delivered the opinion of the court.

We are here presented with the question whether the Fourth Amendment requires that a lawfully seized defendant must be advised that he is "free to go" before his consent to search will be recognized as voluntary. We hold that it does not.

This case arose on a stretch of Interstate 70 north of Dayton, Ohio, where the posted speed limit was 45 miles per hour because of construction. Respondent Robert D. Robinette was clocked at 69 miles per hour as he drove his car along this stretch of road, and was stopped by Deputy Roger Newsome of the Montgomery County Sheriff's Office. Newsome asked for and was handed Robinette's driver's license, and he ran a computer check which indicated that Robinette had no previous violations. Newsome then asked Robinette to step out of his car, turned on his mounted video camera, issued a verbal warning to Robinette, and returned his license.

At this point, Newsome asked, "One question before you get gone: [A]re you carrying any illegal contraband in your car? Any weapons of any kind, drugs, anything like that?" Robinette answered "no" to these questions, after which Deputy Newsome asked if he could search the car. Robinette consented. In the car, Deputy Newsome discovered a small amount of marijuana and, in a film container, a pill which was later determined to be methylenedioxymethamphetamine. Robinette was then arrested and charged with knowing possession of a controlled substance, MDMA, in violation of Ohio Rev.Code Ann. § 2925.11(A) (1993).

Before trial, Robinette unsuccessfully sought to suppress this evidence. He then pleaded "no contest," and was found guilty. On appeal, the Ohio Court of Appeals reversed, ruling that the search resulted from an unlawful detention. The Supreme Court of Ohio, by a divided vote, affirmed. In its opinion, that court established a bright-line prerequisite for consensual interrogation under these circumstances:

> The right, guaranteed by the federal and Ohio Constitutions, to be secure in one's person and property requires that citizens stopped for traffic offenses be clearly informed by the detaining officer when they are free to go after a valid detention, before an officer attempts to engage in a consensual interrogation. Any attempt at consensual interrogation must be preceded by the phrase "At this time you legally are free to go" or by words of similar import."
>
> We granted certiorari to review this *per se* rule, and we now reverse.

* * *

We think that under our recent decision in *Whren v. United States,* 517 U.S. 806 (1996) (decided after the Supreme Court of Ohio decided the present case), the subjective intentions of the officer did not make the continued detention of respondent illegal under the Fourth Amendment. As we made clear in *Whren,* " 'the fact that [an] officer does not have the state of mind which is hypothecated by the reasons which provide the legal justification for the officer's action does not invalidate the action taken as long as the circumstances, viewed objectively, justify that action.' . . . Subjective intentions play no role in ordinary, probable-cause Fourth Amendment analysis." And there is no question that, in light of the admitted probable cause to stop Robinette for speeding, Deputy Newsome was objectively justified in asking Robinette to get out of the car, subjective thoughts notwithstanding. See *Pennsylvania v. Mimms,* 434 U.S. 106, 111, n. 6 (1977) ("We hold . . . that once a motor vehicle has been lawfully detained for a traffic violation, the police officers may order the driver to get out of the vehicle without violating the Fourth Amendment's proscription of unreasonable searches and seizures").

We now turn to the merits of the question presented. We have long held that the "touchstone of the Fourth Amendment is reasonableness." Reasonableness, in turn, is measured in objective terms by examining the totality of the circumstances.

In applying this test we have consistently eschewed bright-line rules, instead emphasizing the fact-specific nature of the reasonableness inquiry. Thus, in *Florida v. Royer,* 460 U.S. 491 (1983), we expressly disavowed any "litmus-paper test" or single "sentence or . . . paragraph . . . rule," in recognition of the "endless variations in the facts and circumstances" implicating the Fourth Amendment. *Id.,* at 506. Then, in *Michigan v. Chesternut,* 486 U.S. 567 (1988), when both parties urged "bright-line rule[s] applicable to all investigatory pursuits," we rejected both proposed rules as contrary to our "traditional contextual approach." And again, in

Florida v. Bostick, 501 U.S. 429 (1991), when the Florida Supreme Court adopted a *per se* rule that questioning aboard a bus always constitutes a seizure, we reversed, reiterating that the proper inquiry necessitates a consideration of "all the circumstances surrounding the encounter."

We have previously rejected a *per se* rule very similar to that adopted by the Supreme Court of Ohio in determining the validity of a consent to search. In *Schneckloth v. Bustamonte,* 412 U.S. 218 (1973), it was argued that such a consent could not be valid unless the defendant knew that he had a right to refuse the request. We rejected this argument: "While knowledge of the right to refuse consent is one factor to be taken into account, the government need not establish such knowledge as the *sine qua non* of an effective consent." And just as it "would be thoroughly impractical to impose on the normal consent search the detailed requirements of an effective warning," so too would it be unrealistic to require police officers to always inform detainees that they are free to go before a consent to search may be deemed voluntary.

The Fourth Amendment test for a valid consent to search is that the consent be voluntary, and "[v]oluntariness is a question of fact to be determined from all the circumstances." The Supreme Court of Ohio having held otherwise, its judgment is reversed, and the case is remanded for further proceedings not inconsistent with this opinion.

JUSTICE GINSBURG, concurring in the judgment.

Robert Robinette's traffic stop for a speeding violation on an interstate highway in Ohio served as prelude to a search of his automobile for illegal drugs. Robinette's experience was not uncommon in Ohio. As the Ohio Supreme Court related, the sheriff's deputy who detained Robinette for speeding and then asked Robinette for permission to search his vehicle "was on drug interdiction patrol at the time." The deputy testified in Robinette's case that he routinely requested permission to search automobiles he stopped for traffic violations. According to the deputy's testimony in another prosecution, he requested consent to search in 786 traffic stops in 1992, the year of Robinette's arrest.

From their unique vantage point, Ohio's courts observed that traffic stops in the State were regularly giving way to contraband searches, characterized as consensual, even when officers had no reason to suspect illegal activity. One Ohio appellate court noted: "[H]undreds, and perhaps thousands of Ohio citizens are being routinely delayed in their travels and asked to relinquish to uniformed police officers their right to privacy in their automobiles and luggage, sometimes for no better reason than to provide an officer the opportunity to 'practice' his drug interdiction technique."

* * *

Today's opinion reversing the decision of the Ohio Supreme Court does not pass judgment on the wisdom of the first-tell-then-ask rule. This Court's opinion simply clarifies that the Ohio Supreme Court's instruction to police officers in Ohio is not, under this Court's controlling jurisprudence, the command of the Federal Constitution. The Ohio Supreme Court invoked both the Federal Constitution and the Ohio Constitution without clearly indicating whether state law, standing alone, independently justified the court's rule. The ambiguity in the Ohio Supreme Court's decision renders this Court's exercise of jurisdiction proper under *Michigan v. Long,* 463 U.S. 1032, 1040–1042 (1983), and this Court's decision on the merits is consistent with the Court's "totality of the circumstances" Fourth Amendment precedents. I therefore concur in the Court's judgment.

I write separately, however, because it seems to me improbable that the Ohio Supreme Court understood its first-tell-then-ask rule to be the Federal Constitution's mandate for the Nation as a whole. "[A] State is free *as a matter of its own law* to impose greater restrictions on police activity than those this Court holds to be necessary upon federal constitutional standards." But ordinarily, when a state high court grounds a rule of criminal procedure in the Federal Constitution, the court thereby signals its view that the Nation's Constitution would require the rule in all 50 States. Given this Court's decisions in consent-to-search cases such as *Schneckloth v. Bustamonte,* 412 U.S. 218 (1973), and *Florida v. Bostick,* 501 U.S. 429 (1991), however, I suspect that the Ohio Supreme Court may not have homed in on the implication ordinarily to be drawn from a state court's reliance on the Federal Constitution. In other words, I question whether the Ohio court thought of the strict rule it announced as a rule for the governance of police conduct not only in Miami County, Ohio, but also in Miami, Florida.

* * *

On remand, the Ohio Supreme Court may choose to clarify that its instructions to law enforcement officers in Ohio find adequate and independent support in state law, and that in issuing these instructions, the court endeavored to state dispositively only the law applicable in Ohio. To avoid misunderstanding, the Ohio Supreme Court must itself speak with the clarity it sought to require of its State's police officers. The efficacy of its endeavor to safeguard the liberties of Ohioans without disarming the State's police can then be tested in the precise way Our Federalism was designed to work.

JUSTICE STEVENS, dissenting.

The Court's holding today is narrow: The Federal Constitution does not require that a lawfully seized person be advised that he is "free to go" before his consent to search will be recognized as voluntary. I agree with that holding. Given the Court's reading of the opinion of the Supreme Court of Ohio, I also agree that it is appropriate for the Court to limit its review to answering the sole question presented in the State's certiorari petition. As I read the state-court opinion, however, the prophylactic rule announced in the second syllabus was intended as a guide to the decision of future cases rather than an explanation of the decision in this case. I would therefore affirm the judgment of the Supreme Court of Ohio because it correctly held that respondent's consent to the search of his vehicle was the product of an unlawful detention. Moreover, it is important to emphasize that nothing in the Federal Constitution—or in this Court's opinion—prevents a State from requiring its law enforcement officers to give detained motorists the advice mandated by the Ohio court.

I

* * *

Several circumstances support the Ohio courts' conclusion that a reasonable motorist in respondent's shoes would have believed that he had an obligation to answer the "one question" and that he could not simply walk away from the officer, get back in his car, and drive away. The question itself sought an answer "*before* you get gone." In addition, the facts that respondent had been detained, had received no advice that he was free to leave, and was then standing in front of a television camera in response to an official command are all inconsistent with an assumption that he could reasonably believe that he had no duty to respond. The Ohio Supreme Court was surely correct in stating: "Most people believe that they are validly in a police officer's custody as long as the officer continues to interrogate them. The police officer retains the upper hand and the accouterments of authority. That the officer lacks legal license to continue to detain them is unknown to most citizens, and a reasonable person would not feel free to walk away as the officer continues to address him."

Moreover, as an objective matter it is fair to presume that most drivers who have been stopped for speeding are in a hurry to get to their destinations; such drivers have no interest in prolonging the delay occasioned by the stop just to engage in idle conversation with an officer, much less to allow a potentially lengthy search. I also assume that motorists—even those who are not carrying contraband—have an interest in preserving the privacy of their vehicles and possessions from the prying eyes of a curious stranger. The fact that this particular officer successfully used a similar method of obtaining consent to search roughly 786 times in one year, indicates that motorists generally respond in a manner that is contrary to their self-interest. Repeated decisions by ordinary citizens to surrender that interest cannot satisfactorily be explained on any hypothesis other than an assumption that they believed they had a legal duty to do so.

The Ohio Supreme Court was therefore entirely correct to presume in the first syllabus preceding its opinion that a "continued detention" was at issue here. The Ohio Court of Appeals reached a similar conclusion. In response to the State's contention that Robinette "was free to go" at the time consent was sought, that court held—after reviewing the record—that "a reasonable person in Robinette's position would not believe that the investigative stop had been concluded, and that he or she was free to go, so long as the police officer was continuing to ask investigative questions." As I read the Ohio opinions, these determinations were independent of the bright-line rule criticized by the majority. I see no reason to disturb them.

* * *

Notwithstanding that the subjective motivation for the officer's decision to stop respondent related to drug interdiction, the legality of the stop depended entirely on the fact that respondent was speeding. Of course, "[a]s a general matter, the decision to stop an automobile is reasonable where the police have probable cause to believe that a traffic violation has occurred." *Whren v. United States,* 517 U.S. 806, 810 (1996). As noted above, however, by the time Robinette was asked for consent to search his automobile, the lawful traffic stop had come to an end; Robinette had been given his warning, and the speeding violation provided no further justification for detention. The continued detention was therefore only justifiable, if at all, on some other grounds.

At no time prior to the search of respondent's vehicle did any articulable facts give rise to a reasonable suspicion of some separate illegal activity that would justify further detention. As an objective matter, it inexorably follows that when the officer had completed his task of either arresting or reprimanding the driver of the speeding car, his continued detention of that person constituted an illegal seizure. This holding by the Ohio Supreme Court is entirely consistent with federal law.

The proper disposition follows as an application of well-settled law. We held in *Florida v. Royer,* 460 U.S. 491 (1983), that a consent obtained during an illegal detention is ordinarily ineffective to justify an otherwise invalid search. Because Robinette's consent to the search was the product of an unlawful detention, "the consent was tainted by the illegality and was ineffective to justify the search." *Royer,* 460 U.S., at 507–508 (plurality opinion). I would therefore affirm the judgment below.

* * *

RICARDO J. BASCUAS, *FOURTH AMENDMENT LESSONS FROM THE HIGHWAY AND THE SUBWAY: A PRINCIPLED APPROACH TO SUSPICIONLESS SEARCHES*

38 RUTGERS L.J. 719, 761–65 (2007)

It is hardly paranoid to think that police will exploit the ability to stop any car to target minorities and to demand that innocent drivers explain their purpose for being out. In fact, *Whren* fueled the DEA's systematic program to target drivers across the country fitting a drug courier profile (i.e. minorities) for car searches. The DEA's Operation Pipeline, created in 1984 and still operating today, trains state and local law enforcement officers to use traffic stops as pretexts for drug interdiction. Officers learn how to lengthen a routine traffic stop and leverage it into a search for drugs by extorting consent or manufacturing probable cause. The program involves countless municipal and state law enforcement agencies, which make huge profits from the dragnet by splitting seized cash and cars on an 80-20 basis with the DEA. A 2,600-person town near Interstate 85 in Georgia seized well over $2 million in cash and cars in two years. A Louisiana town seized more than $6 million in four years stopping cars along its five miles of Interstate 10. As of 2000, the DEA had trained more than 25,000 officers in forty-eight states in Pipeline tactics.

The DEA claims that it does not train police to use racial profiling, but civil lawsuits against police departments implementing Operation Pipeline suggest otherwise. In 2003, the California Highway Patrol settled a class action suit brought by the American Civil Liberties Union by agreeing to stop making pretextual traffic stops and to extend a ban on consensual car searches through 2006. The lawsuit revealed that Hispanics were three times more likely and blacks twice as likely to be stopped as whites and that Hispanics were stopped and let go with a warning more than any other racial group. The New Jersey State Police settled a similar lawsuit which revealed that Operation Pipeline's profiles singled out Hispanic and black men for searches. A cache of internal documents disclosed by the case showed how New Jersey troopers were trained to target Hispanics and blacks and how management stonewalled a Department of Justice civil rights investigation while the DEA simultaneously praised the troopers' success at interdiction. In July 2006, the Arizona Department of Public Safety settled a similar lawsuit by agreeing to train its officers not to employ racial profiling, not to prolong traffic stops without reasonable suspicion or probable cause, and to videotape all traffic stops and maintain statistics on them.

Operation Pipeline is exactly what the Framers meant to prohibit: a federally-run general search program that targets people without cause for suspicion, particularly those who belong to disfavored groups. The program's efficacy requires stopping "staggering" numbers of people, particularly blacks and Hispanics, in shotgun fashion. A huge number of innocent people fitting the profile must be stopped and searched for every cache of drugs or money that is discovered. In a deposition taken in the ACLU suit, one California Highway Patrol officer said, "It's sheer numbers. . . . You kiss a lot of frogs before you find a prince."

Pipeline officers are trained to check cars for a number of "indicators" (in addition to race) that are supposed hallmarks of drug couriers. Among these are air fresheners, atlases, cellular phones, fast food wrappers, attorney business cards, pre-paid phone cards, rental cars, and borrowed cars. The officers are also trained to have drivers exit their cars and to ask them a series of questions about their origin, travel plans, and destination while looking for signs of nervousness or inconsistencies. After the questioning, the script calls for officers to turn and say, in classic Colombo style, "Just one more thing . . ." and ask whether there are any drugs or guns in the car. That is followed by something along the lines of, "You don't mind if I search your car then, do you?" Most drivers give consent.

Consent searches have been controversial since well before Operation Pipeline. In *Schneckloth v. Bustamonte*, the Court approved a consent search of a car and rejected the argument that police should have to inform drivers that they have the right to refuse the search. The Court's rationale was the same utility argument approved in *Place*—simply that consent searches are helpful to the police because they "may be the only means of obtaining important and reliable evidence." The Court stated that advising drivers of the right to refuse would "be thoroughly impractical" because it would deprive the police of "part of the standard investigatory techniques of law enforcement agencies." Justice Marshall wrote a forceful dissent stating that "consent is ordinarily given as acquiescence in an implicit claim of authority to search" and that the majority failed to make "a realistic assessment of the nature of the interchange between citizens and the police."

Operation Pipeline is far worse than Justice Marshall's darkest fears at the time of *Bustamonte*. Officers not only target minorities and stop anyone they wish, but the federal government trains them in tactics calculated to exploit the imbalance of power between police and motorists and to browbeat them into consenting to a search of their belongings. Moreover, the Court's rulings have supported and encouraged the tactics because the Court repeatedly fails to appreciate the true nature and scope of the issue confronting it.

Just a few months after *Whren*, the Court held in *Ohio v. Robinette* that the Fourth Amendment does not require police officers to advise motorists that they are free to go before asking them whether they have drugs or guns and will consent to a search. *Robinette* arose from an Operation Pipeline stop, though that is not mentioned in the opinions or briefs. Robinette was stopped for speeding and eventually given a verbal warning. The officer then said to him, "One question before you get gone:

are you carrying any illegal contraband in your car? Any weapons of any kind, drugs, anything like that?" Robinette said no but consented to a search of his car. The search turned up a personal-use amount of marijuana and one methamphetamine pill. Relying on *Bustamonte*, the Court held that the consent was valid and that the officer did not have to tell Robinette that he was free to leave before asking to search his car.

Like the majority opinion, neither Justice Ginsburg's concurrence nor Justice Stevens' dissent evinced awareness of Operation Pipeline. Justice Ginsburg noted that the deputy had testified that he routinely asked drivers he stopped for consent to search the car, but she seemed to have the misimpression that this practice was peculiar to Ohio: "From their unique vantage point, Ohio's courts observed that traffic stops in the State were regularly giving way to contraband searches, characterized as consensual, even when officers had no reason to suspect illegal activity." Justice Stevens believed the consent was the product of an unlawful detention and, echoing Justice Marshall's *Bustamonte* dissent, noted that people consent to searches only because they feel they have to.

ILLINOIS V. CABALLES

543 U.S. 405 (2005)

JUSTICE STEVENS delivered the opinion of the court.

Illinois State Trooper Daniel Gillette stopped respondent for speeding on an interstate highway. When Gillette radioed the police dispatcher to report the stop, a second trooper, Craig Graham, a member of the Illinois State Police Drug Interdiction Team, overheard the transmission and immediately headed for the scene with his narcotics-detection dog. When they arrived, respondent's car was on the shoulder of the road and respondent was in Gillette's vehicle. While Gillette was in the process of writing a warning ticket, Graham walked his dog around respondent's car. The dog alerted at the trunk. Based on that alert, the officers searched the trunk, found marijuana, and arrested respondent. The entire incident lasted less than 10 minutes.

Respondent was convicted of a narcotics offense and sentenced to 12 years' imprisonment and a $256,136 fine. The trial judge denied his motion to suppress the seized evidence and to quash his arrest. He held that the officers had not unnecessarily prolonged the stop and that the dog alert was sufficiently reliable to provide probable cause to conduct the search. Although the Appellate Court affirmed, the Illinois Supreme Court reversed, concluding that because the canine sniff was performed without any " 'specific and articulable facts' " to suggest drug activity, the use of the dog "unjustifiably enlarg[ed] the scope of a routine traffic stop into a drug investigation."

The question on which we granted certiorari is narrow: "Whether the Fourth Amendment requires reasonable, articulable suspicion to justify using a drug-detection dog to sniff a vehicle during a legitimate traffic stop." Thus, we proceed on the assumption that the officer conducting the dog sniff had no information about respondent except that he had been stopped for speeding; accordingly, we have omitted any reference to facts about respondent that might have triggered a modicum of suspicion.

Here, the initial seizure of respondent when he was stopped on the highway was based on probable cause and was concededly lawful. It is nevertheless clear that a seizure that is lawful at its inception can violate the Fourth Amendment if its manner of execution unreasonably infringes interests protected by the Constitution. A seizure that is justified solely by the interest in issuing a warning ticket to the driver can become unlawful if it is prolonged beyond the time reasonably required to complete that mission. In an earlier case involving a dog sniff that occurred during an unreasonably prolonged traffic stop, the Illinois Supreme Court held that use of the dog and the subsequent discovery of contraband were the product of an unconstitutional seizure. We may assume that a similar result would be warranted in this case if the dog sniff had been conducted while respondent was being unlawfully detained.

In the state-court proceedings, however, the judges carefully reviewed the details of Officer Gillette's conversations with respondent and the precise timing of his radio transmissions to the dispatcher to determine whether he had improperly extended the duration of the stop to enable the dog sniff to occur. We have not recounted those details because we accept the state court's conclusion that the duration of the stop in this case was entirely justified by the traffic offense and the ordinary inquiries incident to such a stop.

Despite this conclusion, the Illinois Supreme Court held that the initially lawful traffic stop became an unlawful seizure solely as a result of the canine sniff that occurred outside respondent's stopped car. That is, the court characterized the dog sniff as the cause rather than the consequence of a constitutional violation. In its view, the use of the dog converted the citizen-police encounter from a lawful traffic stop into a drug investigation, and because the shift in purpose was not supported by any reasonable suspicion that respondent possessed narcotics, it was unlawful. In our view, conducting a dog sniff would not change the character of a traffic stop that is lawful at its inception and otherwise executed in a reasonable manner, unless the dog sniff itself infringed respondent's constitutionally protected interest in privacy. Our cases hold that it did not.

Official conduct that does not "compromise any legitimate interest in privacy" is not a search subject to the Fourth Amendment. We have held that any interest in possessing contraband cannot be deemed "legitimate," and thus, governmental conduct that *only* reveals the possession of contraband "compromises no legitimate privacy interest." This is because the expectation "that certain facts will not come to the attention of the authorities" is not the same as an interest in "privacy that society is prepared to consider reasonable." In *United States v. Place,* 462 U.S. 696 (1983), we treated a canine sniff by a well-trained narcotics-detection dog as "*sui generis*" because it "discloses only the presence or absence of narcotics, a contraband item." Respondent likewise concedes that "drug sniffs are designed, and if properly conducted are generally likely, to reveal only the presence of contraband." Although respondent argues that the error rates, particularly the existence of false positives, call into question the premise that drug-detection dogs alert only to contraband, the record contains no evidence or findings that support his argument. Moreover, respondent does not suggest that an erroneous alert, in and of itself, reveals any legitimate private information, and, in this case, the trial judge found that the dog sniff was sufficiently reliable to establish probable cause to conduct a full-blown search of the trunk.

Accordingly, the use of a well-trained narcotics-detection dog—one that "does not expose noncontraband items that otherwise would remain hidden from public view,"—during a lawful traffic stop, generally does not implicate legitimate privacy interests. In this case, the dog sniff was performed on the exterior of respondent's car while he was lawfully seized for a traffic violation. Any intrusion on respondent's privacy expectations does not rise to the level of a constitutionally cognizable infringement.

This conclusion is entirely consistent with our recent decision that the use of a thermal-imaging device to detect the growth of marijuana in a home constituted an unlawful search. *Kyllo v. United States,* 533 U.S. 27 (2001). Critical to that decision was the fact that the device was capable of detecting lawful activity-in that case, intimate details in a home, such as "at what hour each night the lady of the house takes her daily sauna and bath." The legitimate expectation that information about perfectly lawful activity will remain private is categorically distinguishable from respondent's hopes or expectations concerning the nondetection of contraband in the trunk of his car. A dog sniff conducted during a concededly lawful traffic stop that reveals no information other than the location of a substance that no individual has any right to possess does not violate the Fourth Amendment.

The judgment of the Illinois Supreme Court is vacated, and the case is remanded for further proceedings not inconsistent with this opinion.

THE CHIEF JUSTICE took no part in the decision of this case.

JUSTICE SOUTER, dissenting.

I would hold that using the dog for the purposes of determining the presence of marijuana in the car's trunk was a search unauthorized as an incident of the speeding stop and unjustified on any other ground. I would accordingly affirm the judgment of the Supreme Court of Illinois, and I respectfully dissent.

In *United States v. Place,* 462 U.S. 696 (1983), we categorized the sniff of the narcotics-seeking dog as *"sui generis"* under the Fourth Amendment and held it was not a search. The classification rests not only upon the limited nature of the intrusion, but on a further premise that experience has shown to be untenable, the assumption that trained sniffing dogs do not err. What we have learned about the fallibility of dogs in the years since *Place* was decided would itself be reason to call for reconsidering *Place's* decision against treating the intentional use of a trained dog as a search. The portent of this very case, however, adds insistence to the call, for an uncritical adherence to *Place* would render the Fourth Amendment indifferent to suspicionless and indiscriminate sweeps of cars in parking garages and pedestrians on sidewalks; if a sniff is not preceded by a seizure subject to Fourth Amendment notice, it escapes Fourth Amendment review entirely unless it is treated as a search. We should not wait for these developments to occur before rethinking *Place's* analysis, which invites such untoward consequences.

At the heart both of *Place* and the Court's opinion today is the proposition that sniffs by a trained dog are *sui generis* because a reaction by the dog in going alert is a response to nothing but the presence of contraband. Hence, the argument goes, because the sniff can only reveal the presence of items devoid of any legal use, the sniff "does not implicate legitimate privacy interests" and is not to be treated as a search.

The infallible dog, however, is a creature of legal fiction. Although the Supreme Court of Illinois did not get into the sniffing averages of drug dogs, their supposed infallibility is belied by judicial opinions describing well-trained animals sniffing and alerting with less than perfect accuracy, whether owing to errors by their handlers, the limitations of the dogs themselves, or even the pervasive contamination of currency by cocaine. Indeed, a study cited by Illinois in this case for the proposition that dog sniffs are "generally reliable" shows that dogs in artificial testing situations return false positives anywhere from 12.5% to 60% of the time, depending on the length of the search. In practical terms, the evidence is clear that the dog that alerts hundreds of times will be wrong dozens of times.

Once the dog's fallibility is recognized, however, that ends the justification claimed in *Place* for treating the sniff as *sui generis* under the Fourth Amendment: the sniff alert does not necessarily signal hidden contraband, and opening the container or enclosed space whose emanations the dog has sensed will not necessarily reveal contraband or any other evidence of crime. This is not, of course, to deny that a dog's reaction may provide reasonable suspicion, or probable cause, to search the container or enclosure; the Fourth Amendment does not demand certainty of success to justify a search for evidence or contraband. The point is simply that the sniff and alert cannot claim the certainty that *Place* assumed, both in treating the deliberate use of sniffing dogs as *sui generis* and then taking that characterization as a reason to say they are not searches subject to Fourth Amendment scrutiny. And when that aura of uniqueness disappears, there is no basis in *Place's* reasoning, and no good reason otherwise, to ignore the actual function that dog sniffs perform. They are conducted to obtain information about the contents of private spaces beyond anything that human senses could perceive, even when conventionally enhanced. The information is not provided by independent third parties beyond the reach of constitutional limitations, but gathered by the government's own officers in order to justify searches of the traditional sort, which may or may not reveal evidence of crime but will disclose anything meant to be kept private in the area searched. Thus in practice the government's use of a trained narcotics dog functions as a limited search to reveal undisclosed facts about private enclosures, to be used to justify a further and complete search of the enclosed area. And given the fallibility of the dog, the sniff is the first step in a process that may disclose "intimate details" without revealing contraband, just as a thermal-imaging device might do, as described in *Kyllo v. United States,* 533 U.S. 27 (2001).[3]

It makes sense, then, to treat a sniff as the search that it amounts to in practice, and to rely on the body of our Fourth Amendment cases, including *Kyllo,* in deciding whether such a search is reasonable. As a general proposition, using a dog to sniff for drugs is subject to the rule that the object of enforcing criminal laws does not, without more, justify suspicionless Fourth Amendment intrusions. See *Indianapolis v. Edmond,* 531 U.S. 32, 41–42 (2000). Since the police claim to have had no particular suspicion that Caballes was violating any drug law,[4] this sniff search must stand or fall on its being ancillary to the traffic stop that led up to it. It is true that the police had probable cause to stop the car for an offense committed in the officer's presence, which Caballes concedes could have justified his arrest. There is no occasion to consider authority incident to arrest, however, for the police did nothing more than detain Caballes long

[3] *Kyllo* was concerned with whether a search occurred when the police used a thermal-imaging device on a house to detect heat emanations associated with high-powered marijuana-growing lamps. In concluding that using the device was a search, the Court stressed that the "Government [may not] us[e] a device . . . to explore details of the home that would previously have been unknowable without physical intrusion." Any difference between the dwelling in *Kyllo* and the trunk of the car here may go to the issue of the reasonableness of the respective searches, but it has no bearing on the question of search or no search. Nor is it significant that *Kyllo*'s imaging device would disclose personal details immediately, whereas they would be revealed only in the further step of opening the enclosed space following the dog's alert reaction; in practical terms the same values protected by the Fourth Amendment are at stake in each case. The justifications required by the Fourth Amendment may or may not differ as between the two practices, but if constitutional scrutiny is in order for the imager, it is in order for the dog.

[4] Despite the remarkable fact that the police pulled over a car for going 71 miles an hour on I-80, the State maintains that excessive speed was the only reason for the stop, and the case comes to us on that assumption.

enough to check his record and write a ticket. As a consequence, the reasonableness of the search must be assessed in relation to the actual delay the police chose to impose, and as Justice Ginsburg points out in her opinion, the Fourth Amendment consequences of stopping for a traffic citation are settled law.

* * *

The Court today does not go so far as to say explicitly that sniff searches by dogs trained to sense contraband always get a free pass under the Fourth Amendment, since it reserves judgment on the constitutional significance of sniffs assumed to be more intrusive than a dog's walk around a stopped car. For this reason, I do not take the Court's reliance on *Jacobsen* as actually signaling recognition of a broad authority to conduct suspicionless sniffs for drugs in any parked car, about which Justice Ginsburg is rightly concerned, or on the person of any pedestrian minding his own business on a sidewalk. But the Court's stated reasoning provides no apparent stopping point short of such excesses. For the sake of providing a workable framework to analyze cases on facts like these, which are certain to come along, I would treat the dog sniff as the familiar search it is in fact, subject to scrutiny under the Fourth Amendment.[7]

JUSTICE GINSBURG, with whom JUSTICE SOUTER joins, dissenting.

Illinois State Police Trooper Daniel Gillette stopped Roy Caballes for driving 71 miles per hour in a zone with a posted speed limit of 65 miles per hour. Trooper Craig Graham of the Drug Interdiction Team heard on the radio that Trooper Gillette was making a traffic stop. Although Gillette requested no aid, Graham decided to come to the scene to conduct a dog sniff. Gillette informed Caballes that he was speeding and asked for the usual documents—driver's license, car registration, and proof of insurance. Caballes promptly provided the requested documents but refused to consent to a search of his vehicle. After calling his dispatcher to check on the validity of Caballes' license and for outstanding warrants, Gillette returned to his vehicle to write Caballes a warning ticket. Interrupted by a radio call on an unrelated matter, Gillette was still writing the ticket when Trooper Graham arrived with his drug-detection dog. Graham walked the dog around the car, the dog alerted at Caballes' trunk, and, after opening the trunk, the troopers found marijuana.

* * *

It is hardly dispositive that the dog sniff in this case may not have lengthened the duration of the stop. *Terry,* it merits repetition, instructs

[7] I should take care myself to reserve judgment about a possible case significantly unlike this one. All of us are concerned not to prejudge a claim of authority to detect explosives and dangerous chemical or biological weapons that might be carried by a terrorist who prompts no individualized suspicion. Suffice it to say here that what is a reasonable search depends in part on demonstrated risk. Unreasonable sniff searches for marijuana are not necessarily unreasonable sniff searches for destructive or deadly material if suicide bombs are a societal risk.

that any investigation must be "reasonably related in *scope* to the circumstances which justified the interference in the first place." The unwarranted and nonconsensual expansion of the seizure here from a routine traffic stop to a drug investigation broadened the scope of the investigation in a manner that, in my judgment, runs afoul of the Fourth Amendment.

* * *

In my view, the Court diminishes the Fourth Amendment's force by abandoning the second *Terry* inquiry (was the police action "reasonably related in scope to the circumstances [justifiying] the [initial] interference"). A drug-detection dog is an intimidating animal. Injecting such an animal into a routine traffic stop changes the character of the encounter between the police and the motorist. The stop becomes broader, more adversarial, and (in at least some cases) longer. Caballes—who, as far as Troopers Gillette and Graham knew, was guilty solely of driving six miles per hour over the speed limit—was exposed to the embarrassment and intimidation of being investigated, on a public thoroughfare, for drugs. Even if the drug sniff is not characterized as a Fourth Amendment "search," the sniff surely broadened the scope of the traffic-violation-related seizure.

The Court has never removed police action from Fourth Amendment control on the ground that the action is well calculated to apprehend the guilty. Under today's decision, every traffic stop could become an occasion to call in the dogs, to the distress and embarrassment of the law-abiding population.

* * *

The dog sniff in this case, it bears emphasis, was for drug detection only. A dog sniff for explosives, involving security interests not presented here, would be an entirely different matter. Detector dogs are ordinarily trained not as all-purpose sniffers, but for discrete purposes. For example, they may be trained for narcotics detection or for explosives detection or for agricultural products detection. There is no indication in this case that the dog accompanying Trooper Graham was trained for anything other than drug detection.

* * *

For the reasons stated, I would hold that the police violated Caballes' Fourth Amendment rights when, without cause to suspect wrongdoing, they conducted a dog sniff of his vehicle. I would therefore affirm the judgment of the Illinois Supreme Court.

Points for Discussion

1. Is the use of a dog during a traffic stop something to which a reasonable, law-abiding citizen would not object? Why does Justice Ginsburg believe that the presence of a narcotics dog changes the dynamic of an otherwise routine traffic stop?

2. What is the import of Justice Souter's statistics about the fallibility of a drug-sniffing dog? Do these statistics go to the reasonableness of the use of drug dogs? To the question of whether the use of a dog is a search at all? Do *Florida v. Harris* or *Florida v. Jardines*, excerpted in chapters 2 and 3 respectively, impact the *Caballes* analysis?

3. Four years after *Whren* and five years before *Caballes*, seven justices agreed in *Edmond* that the Fourth Amendment prohibits police from stopping cars at a checkpoint to have a dog sniff them for drugs. With no change in the Court's membership, six justices held in *Caballes* that a dog sniff during a traffic stop does not violate the Fourth Amendment. The Court failed to recognize that the only difference between *Caballes* and *Edmond* is that in *Edmond* the systematic nature of the stops was obvious while in *Caballes* the DEA's Operation Pipeline functioned as a surreptitious "checkpoint". Why did Caballes fail to raise Pipeline in his appeal?

4. Highlighting the reach of Operation Pipeline and the Supreme Court's failure to grasp the problem of pretextual traffic stops, some state courts have expressed considerable discomfort with Operation Pipeline's implications for the values protected by the Fourth Amendment. They have for that reason found consent searches invalid under the totality-of-the-circumstances test established in *Bustamonte* and affirmed by *Robinette*. In *Robinette* itself, the Ohio Supreme Court held on remand that Robinette's consent was the product of an illegal detention and affirmed the suppression of evidence in his case. *Ohio v. Robinette*, 685 N.E.2d 762, 771 (Ohio 1997). Following Ohio's lead, the Maryland Court of Appeals likewise held that a motorist would not have felt free to leave after receiving a citation and being asked to step out of his car to answer questions. *Ferris v. Maryland*, 735 A.2d 491, 502 (Md. 1999). The Wyoming Supreme Court reached the same conclusion in the case of a man who was stopped for traveling 79 miles per hour in a 75 mile-per-hour zone, given a warning, and then extensively interrogated until a drug-sniffing dog arrived. *O'Boyle v. Wyoming*, 117 P.3d 401, 404, 410–11 (Wyo. 2005). The court noted: "We have previously expressed disapproval of the use of traffic violations as a pretext to conduct narcotics investigations. . . . While we acknowledge the importance of drug interdiction, we are deeply concerned by the resulting intrusion upon the privacy rights of Wyoming citizens." More recently, the Iowa Supreme Court held that a driver's consent to search his car, obtained during a traffic stop, was involuntary under the Iowa Constitution: "In this setting, police plainly have the upper hand and are exerting authority in a fashion that makes it likely that a citizen would not feel free to decline to give consent for a search even though the search is unrelated to the rationale of the original stop." *Iowa v. Pals*, 805 N.W.2d 767, 783 (Iowa

2011). In a footnote, the Iowa Court observed: "Studies in Illinois, Rhode Island, Minnesota, and by the Department of Justice have all shown that minority drivers are the subjects of consent searches at a far higher rate than whites even though consent searches of whites are more likely to produce contraband."

PART II

POLICE QUESTIONING

■ ■ ■

CHAPTER 6

HISTORICAL OVERVIEW

■ ■ ■

The rise of bootlegging and organized crime in reaction to Prohibition in the 1920s led President Herbert Hoover to order a comprehensive national study of crime and law enforcement. Hoover, a graduate of Stanford University's first class and an engineer by profession, believed that social problems should be attacked with technical expertise. In 1929, the president appointed former Attorney General George W. Wickersham chairman of the National Commission on Law Observance and Enforcement. Among the other ten members of the Wickersham Commission, as it became popularly known, were Harvard Law School Dean Roscoe Pound, Radcliffe College President Ada Comstock, and three federal judges.

The Commission published its findings in fourteen separate reports in 1931 and 1932. Despite having extensively catalogued the problems inherent in enforcing Prohibition, the Commission ultimately recommended in its second report that the Eighteenth Amendment not be repealed—a suggestion that was of course ignored. The schizoid report was lampooned by *New York World* columnist Franklin P. Adams with this poem:

Prohibition is an awful flop.

We like it.

It can't stop what it's meant to stop.

We like it.

It's left a trail of graft and slime,

It don't prohibit worth a dime,

It's filled our land with vice and crime.

Nevertheless, we're for it.

The Commission's reports were otherwise highly influential, notably in facilitating the professionalization of federal, state, and local law enforcement agencies. The Supreme Court took particular notice of the Commission's eleventh report, entitled "Lawlessness in Law Enforcement." This volume undertook to investigate "the third degree," which the Commission defined as "the employment of methods which inflict suffering, physical or mental, upon a person in order to obtain information about a crime." The Commission summarized its more than 200 pages of findings on the third degree starkly:

> I. EXISTENCE
>
> The third degree—the inflicting of pain, physical or mental, to extract confessions or statements—is widespread throughout the country.
>
> II. PHYSICAL BRUTALITY
>
> Physical brutality is extensively practiced. The methods are various. They range from beating to harsher forms of torture. The commoner forms are beating with the fists or with some implement, especially the rubber hose, that inflicts pain but is not likely to leave permanent visible scars.
>
> III. PROTRACTED QUESTIONING
>
> The method most commonly employed is protracted questioning. By this we mean questioning—at times by relays of questioners—so protracted that the prisoner's energies are spent and his powers of resistance overcome. At times such questioning is the only method used. At times the questioning is accompanied by blows or by throwing continuous straining light upon the face of the suspect. At times the suspect is kept standing for hours, or deprived of food or sleep, or his sleep periodically interrupted to resume questioning.
>
> IV. THREATS
>
> Methods of intimidation adjusted to the age or mentality of the victim are frequently used alone or in combination with other practices. The threats are usually of bodily injury. They have gone to the extreme of procuring a confession at the point of a pistol or through fear of a mob.
>
> V. ILLEGAL DETENTION
>
> Prolonged illegal detention is a common practice. The law requires prompt production of a prisoner before a magistrate. In a large majority of the cities we have investigated this rule is constantly violated.

These practices threatened the vitality of the adversarial system because police officers' methods for obtaining confessions were, as a practical matter, difficult if not impossible for courts to review: "Difficulties of proof and subtleties of interrogation technique made it impossible in most cases for the judiciary to decide with confidence whether the defendant had voluntarily confessed his guilt or whether his testimony had been unconstitutionally compelled." *New York v. Quarles*, 467 U.S. 649, 683 (1984) (Marshall, J., dissenting). The Supreme Court was concerned that "the secret trial in the police precincts effectively supplants the public trial guaranteed by the Bill of Rights." *Spano v. New York*, 360 U.S. 315, 326 (1959) (Douglas, J., concurring). Police interrogations threatened to "make the trial no more than an appeal from the interrogation." *Escobedo v. Illinois*, 378 U.S. 478, 487 (1964).

As these quotes suggest, concern over the problem that interrogations posed for the criminal justice system permeates the decisions leading up to (and following) *Miranda v. Arizona*, which refers explicitly to the Wickersham Commission's report. In this chapter we examine the build-up to the *Miranda* decision, paying attention to the interplay between the Fifth Amendment privilege against compelled self-incrimination[a] and the Sixth Amendment right to counsel.[b] After concluding with the prophylactic rule created by *Miranda*, we examine each doctrine—Sixth Amendment, Fifth Amendment, and *Miranda*—in its own chapter.

BROWN V. MISSISSIPPI

297 U.S. 278 (1936)

MR. CHIEF JUSTICE HUGHES delivered the opinion of the court.

The question in this case is whether convictions, which rest solely upon confessions shown to have been extorted by officers of the state by brutality and violence, are consistent with the due process of law required by the Fourteenth Amendment of the Constitution of the United States.

Petitioners were indicted for the murder of one Raymond Stewart, whose death occurred on March 30, 1934. They were indicted on April 4, 1934, and were then arraigned and pleaded not guilty. Counsel were appointed by the court to defend them. Trial was begun the next morning and was concluded on the following day, when they were found guilty and sentenced to death.

Aside from the confessions, there was no evidence sufficient to warrant the submission of the case to the jury. After a preliminary inquiry, testimony as to the confessions was received over the objection of defendants' counsel. Defendants then testified that the confessions were false and had been procured by physical torture. The case went to the jury with instructions, upon the request of defendants' counsel, that if the jury had reasonable doubt as to the confessions having resulted from coercion, and that they were not they were not to be considered as evidence. On their to the Supreme Court of the State, defendants assigned as error the inadmissibility of the confessions. The judgment was affirmed.

[a] The Fifth Amendment provides in relevant part: "No person. . . shall be compelled in any criminal case to be a witness against himself."—Eds.

[b] The Sixth Amendment provides in relevant part: "In all criminal prosecutions, the accused shall . . . have the assistance of counsel for his defense."—Eds.

Defendants then moved in the Supreme Court of the State to arrest the judgment and for a new trial on the ground that all the evidence against them was obtained by coercion and brutality known to the court and to the district attorney, and that defendants had been denied the benefit of counsel or opportunity to confer with counsel in a reasonable manner. The motion was supported by affidavits. At about the same time, defendants filed in the Supreme Court a "suggestion of error" explicitly challenging the proceedings of the trial, in the use of the confessions and with respect to the alleged denial of representation by counsel, as violating the due process clause of the Fourteenth Amendment of the Constitution of the United States. The state court entertained the suggestion of error, considered the federal question, and decided it against defendants' contentions. Two judges dissented. We granted a writ of certiorari.

* * *

The opinion of the state court did not set forth the evidence as to the circumstances in which the confessions were procured. That the evidence established that they were procured by coercion was not questioned. The state court said: "After the state closed its case on the merits, the appellants, for the first time, introduced evidence from which it appears that the confessions were not made voluntarily but were coerced." There is no dispute as to the facts upon this point, and as they are clearly and adequately stated in the dissenting opinion of Judge Griffith (with whom Judge Anderson concurred), showing both the extreme brutality of the measures to extort the confessions and the participation of the state authorities, we quote this part of his opinion in full, as follows:

> The crime with which these defendants, all ignorant negroes, are charged, was discovered about 1 o'clock p.m. on Friday, March 30, 1934. On that night one Dial, a deputy sheriff, accompanied by others, came to the home of Ellington, one of the defendants, and requested him to accompany them to the house of the deceased, and there a number of white men were gathered, who began to accuse the defendant of the crime. Upon his denial they seized him, and with the participation of the deputy they hanged him by a rope to the limb of a tree, and, having let him down, they hung him again, and when he was let down the second time, and he still protested his innocence, he was tied to a tree and whipped, and, still declining to accede to the demands that he confess, he was finally released, and he returned with some difficulty to his home, suffering intense pain and agony. The record of the testimony shows that the signs of the rope on his neck were plainly visible during the so-called trial. A day or two thereafter the said deputy, accompanied by another, returned to the home of the said defendant and arrested him, and departed with the prisoner towards the jail in an adjoining county, but went by a route which

> led into the state of Alabama; and while on the way, in that state, the deputy stopped and again severely whipped the defendant, declaring that he would continue the whipping until he confessed, and the defendant then agreed to confess to such a statement as the deputy would dictate, and he did so, after which he was delivered to jail.

The other two defendants, Ed Brown and Henry Shields, were also arrested and taken to the same jail. On Sunday night, April 1, 1934, the same deputy, accompanied by a number of white men, one of whom was also an officer, and by the jailer, came to the jail, and the two last named defendants were made to strip and they were laid over chairs and their backs were cut to pieces with a leather strap with buckles on it, and they were likewise made by the said deputy definitely to understand that the whipping would be continued unless and until they confessed, and not only confessed, but confessed in every matter of detail as demanded by those present; and in this manner the defendants confessed the crime, and, as the whippings progressed and were repeated, they changed or adjusted their confession in all particulars of detail so as to conform to the demands of their torturers. When the confessions had been obtained in the exact form and contents as desired by the mob, they left with the parting admonition and warning that, if the defendants changed their story at any time in any respect from that last stated, the perpetrators of the outrage would administer the same or equally effective treatment.

Further details of the brutal treatment to which these helpless prisoners were subjected need not be pursued. It is sufficient to say that in pertinent respects the transcript reads more like pages torn from some medieval account than a record made within the confines of a modern civilization which aspires to an enlightened constitutional government.

All this having been accomplished, on the next day, that is, on Monday, April 2, when the defendants had been given time to recuperate somewhat from the tortures to which they had been subjected, the two sheriffs, one of the county where the crime was committed, and the other of the county of the jail in which the prisoners were confined, came to the jail, accompanied by eight other persons, some of them deputies, there to hear the free and voluntary confession of these miserable and abject defendants. The sheriff of the county of the crime admitted that he had heard of the whipping, but averred that he had no personal knowledge of it. He admitted that one of the defendants, when brought before him to confess, was limping and did not sit down, and that this particular defendant then and there stated that he had been strapped so severely that he could not sit down, and, as already stated, the signs of the rope on the neck of another of the defendants were plainly visible to all. Nevertheless the solemn farce of hearing the free and voluntary confessions was gone through with, and these two sheriffs and one other person then present were the three witnesses used in court to establish the so-called confessions, which were received by the court and admitted in evidence over the objections of the defendants duly entered of record as each of the said three witnesses delivered their alleged testimony. There was thus enough before the court when these confessions were first offered to make known to the court that they were not, beyond all reasonable doubt, free and voluntary; and the failure of the court then to exclude the confessions is sufficient to reverse the judgment, under every rule of procedure that has heretofore been prescribed, and hence it was not necessary subsequently to renew the objections by motion or otherwise.

The spurious confessions having been obtained—and the farce last mentioned having been gone through with on Monday, April 2d—the court, then in session, on the following day, Tuesday, April 3, 1934, ordered the grand jury to reassemble on the succeeding day, April 4, 1934, at 9 o'clock, and on the morning of the day last mentioned the grand jury returned an indictment against the defendants for murder. Late that afternoon the defendants were brought from the jail in the adjoining county and arraigned, when one or more of them offered to plead guilty, which the court declined to accept, and, upon inquiry whether they had or desired counsel, they stated that they had none, and did not suppose that counsel could be of any assistance to them. The court thereupon appointed counsel, and set the case for trial for the following morning at 9 o'clock, and the defendants were returned to the jail in the adjoining county about thirty miles away.

The defendants were brought to the courthouse of the county on the following morning, April 5th, and the so-called trial was opened, and was concluded on the next day, April 6, 1934, and resulted in a pretended conviction with death sentences. The evidence upon which the conviction was obtained was the so-called confessions. Without this evidence, a peremptory instruction to find for the defendants would have been inescapable. The defendants were put on the stand, and by their testimony the facts and the details thereof as to the manner by which the confessions were extorted from them were fully developed, and it is further disclosed by the record that the same deputy, Dial, under whose guiding hand and active participation the tortures to coerce the confessions were administered, was actively in the performance of the supposed duties of a court deputy in the courthouse and in the presence of the prisoners during what is denominated, in complimentary terms, the trial of these defendants. This deputy was put on the stand by the state in rebuttal, and admitted the whippings. It is interesting to note that in his testimony with reference to the whipping of the defendant Ellington, and in response to the inquiry as to how severely he was whipped, the deputy stated, "Not too much for a negro; not as much as I would have done if it were left to me." Two others who had participated in these whippings were introduced and admitted it—not a single witness was introduced who denied it. The facts are not only undisputed, they are admitted, and admitted to have been done by officers of the state, in conjunction with other participants, and all this was definitely well known to everybody connected with the trial, and during the trial, including the state's prosecuting attorney and the trial judge presiding.[c]

The state stresses the statement in *Twining v. New Jersey*, 211 U.S. 78, 114 (1908), that "exemption from compulsory self-incrimination in the courts of the states is not secured by any part of the Federal Constitution," and the statement in *Snyder v. Massachusetts*, 291 U.S. 97, 105 (1934), that "the privilege against self-incrimination may be withdrawn and the accused put upon the stand as a witness for the state." But the question of the right of the state to withdraw the privilege against self-incrimination is not here involved. The compulsion to which the quoted statements refer is that of the processes of justice by which the accused may be called as a witness and required to testify. Compulsion by torture to extort a confession is a different matter.[d]

The state is free to regulate the procedure of its courts in accordance with its own conceptions of policy, unless in so doing it "offends some principle of justice so rooted in the traditions and conscience of our people as to be ranked as fundamental." The state may abolish trial by jury. It may dispense with indictment by a grand jury and substitute complaint or information. But the freedom of the state in establishing its policy is the freedom of constitutional government and is limited by the requirement of due process of law. Because a state may dispense with a jury trial, it does not follow that it may substitute trial by ordeal. The rack and torture chamber may not be substituted for the witness stand. The state may not permit an accused to be hurried to conviction under mob domination-where the whole proceeding is but a mask-without supplying corrective process. The state may not deny to the accused the aid of counsel. Nor may a state, through the action of its officers, contrive a conviction through the pretense of a trial which in truth is "but used as a means of depriving a defendant of liberty through a deliberate deception of court and jury by the presentation of testimony known to be perjured." And the trial equally is a mere pretense where the state authorities have contrived a conviction resting solely upon confessions obtained by violence. The due process clause requires "that state action, whether through one agency or another, shall be consistent with the fundamental principles of liberty and justice which lie at the base of all our civil and political institutions." It would be difficult to conceive of methods more revolting to the sense of justice than those taken to procure the confessions of these petitioners, and the use of

[c] *Twining* and *Snyder* held that the Due Process Clause of the Fourteenth Amendment did not incorporate the Self-Incrimination Clause of the Fifth Amendment—that is, the Constitution did not forbid the states from forcing a witness to take the stand. These cases would later be overruled. See *Malloy v. Hogan*, 378 U.S. 1 (1964).—Eds.

[d] Although at the time that *Brown* was decided the Sixth Amendment's jury right had not yet been incorporated into the Due Process Clause of the Fourteenth Amendment, it since has been. See *Duncan v. Louisiana*, 391 U.S. 145 (1968).—Eds.

the confessions thus obtained as the basis for conviction and sentence was a clear denial of due process.

* * *

In the instant case, the trial court was fully advised by the undisputed evidence of the way in which the confessions had been procured. The trial court knew that there was no other evidence upon which conviction and sentence could be based. Yet it proceeded to permit conviction and to pronounce sentence. The conviction and sentence were void for want of the essential elements of due process, and the proceeding thus vitiated could be challenged in any appropriate manner. It was challenged before the Supreme Court of the State by the express invocation of the Fourteenth Amendment. That court entertained the challenge, considered the federal question thus presented, but declined to enforce petitioners' constitutional right. The court thus denied a federal right fully established and specially set up and claimed, and the judgment must be reversed.

Points for Discussion

1. Note how casually the perpetrators of Brown's abuse recounted in court the circumstances by which Brown's confession was obtained. Their willingness to admit to their brutality certainly gives credence to the Wickersham Commission's conclusion a few years earlier that the use of torture was widespread in the United States at the time.

2. Why does the Supreme Court overturn the convictions in this case? Because there was no other evidence that these defendants committed this crime? Because there was doubt as to their guilt?

3. In *Watts v. Indiana*, 338 U.S. 49 (1949), the defendant was held for several days in solitary confinement, being interviewed for hours by a relay of officers. In finding the confession eventually obtained to be a violation of the defendant's rights, the Court wrote at some length about where the line between appropriate police work and abuse lies:

> A confession by which life becomes forfeit must be the expression of free choice. A statement to be voluntary of course need not be volunteered. But if it is the product of sustained pressure by the police it does not issue from a free choice. When a suspect speaks because he is overborne, it is immaterial whether he has been subjected to a physical or a mental ordeal. Eventual yielding to questioning under such circumstances is plainly the product of the suction process of interrogation and therefore the reverse of voluntary. We would have to shut our minds to the plain significance of what here transpired to deny that this was a calculated endeavor to secure a confession through the pressure of unrelenting interrogation. The very relentlessness of such interrogation implies that it is better for the prisoner to answer than to persist in the refusal of disclosure which is his constitutional right. To turn the

> detention of an accused into a process of wrenching from him evidence which could not be extorted in open court with all its safeguards, is so grave an abuse of the power of arrest as to offend the procedural standards of due process.
>
> This is so because it violates the underlying principle in our enforcement of the criminal law. Ours is the accusatorial as opposed to the inquisitorial system. Such has been the characteristic of Anglo-American criminal justice since it freed itself from practices borrowed by the Star Chamber from the Continent whereby an accused was interrogated in secret for hours on end. Under our system society carries the burden of proving its charge against the accused not out of his own mouth. It must establish its case, not by interrogation of the accused even under judicial safeguards, but by evidence independently secured through skillful investigation. "The law will not suffer a prisoner to be made the deluded instrument of his own conviction." The requirement of specific charges, their proof beyond a reasonable doubt, the protection of the accused from confessions extorted through whatever form of police pressures, the right to a prompt hearing before a magistrate, the right to assistance of counsel, to be supplied by government when circumstances make it necessary, the duty to advise an accused of his constitutional rights—these are all characteristics of the accusatorial system and manifestations of its demands. Protracted, systematic and uncontrolled subjection of an accused to interrogation by the police for the purpose of eliciting disclosures or confessions is subversive of the accusatorial system. It is the inquisitorial system without its safeguards. For while under that system the accused is subjected to judicial interrogation, he is protected by the disinterestedness of the judge in the presence of counsel.

For years afterward, the Court sought to protect the United States' adversarial system from encroachment by inquisitorial methods.

SPANO V. NEW YORK

360 U.S. 315 (1959)

MR. CHIEF JUSTICE warren delivered the opinion of the court.

This is another in the long line of cases presenting the question whether a confession was properly admitted into evidence under the Fourteenth Amendment. As in all such cases, we are forced to resolve a conflict between two fundamental interests of society; its interest in prompt and efficient law enforcement, and its interest in preventing the rights of its individual members from being abridged by unconstitutional methods of law enforcement. Because of the delicate nature of the constitutional determination which we must make, we cannot escape the responsibility of making our own examination of the record.

The State's evidence reveals the following: Petitioner Vincent Joseph Spano is a derivative citizen of this country, having been born in Messina, Italy. He was 25 years old at the time of the shooting in question and had graduated from junior high school. He had a record of regular employment. The shooting took place on January 22, 1957.

On that day, petitioner was drinking in a bar. The decedent, a former professional boxer weighing almost 200 pounds who had fought in Madison Square Garden, took some of petitioner's money from the bar. Petitioner followed him out of the bar to recover it. A fight ensued, with the decedent knocking petitioner down and then kicking him in the head three or four times. Shock from the force of these blow caused petitioner to vomit. After the bartender applied some ice to his head, petitioner left the bar, walked to his apartment, secured a gun, and walked eight or nine blocks to a candy store where the decedent was frequently to be found. He entered the store in which decedent, three friends of decedent, at least two of whom were ex-convicts, and a boy who was supervising the store were present. He fired five shots, two of which entered the decedent's body, causing his death. The boy was the only eyewitness; the three friends of decedent did not see the person who fired the shot. Petitioner then disappeared for the next week or so.

On February 1, 1957, the Bronx County Grand Jury returned an indictment for first-degree murder against petitioner. Accordingly, a bench warrant was issued for his arrest, commanding that he be forthwith brought before the court to answer the indictment, or, if the court had adjourned for the term, that he be delivered into the custody of the Sheriff of Bronx County.

On February 3, 1957, petitioner called one Gaspar Bruno, a close friend of 8 or 10 years' standing who had attended school with him. Bruno was a fledgling police officer, having at that time not yet finished attending police academy. According to Bruno's testimony, petitioner told him "that he took a terrific beating, that the deceased hurt him real bad and he dropped him a couple of times and he was dazed; he didn't know what he was doing and that he went and shot at him." Petitioner told Bruno that he intended to get a lawyer and give himself up. Bruno relayed this information to his superiors.

The following day, February 4, at 7:10 p.m., petitioner, accompanied by counsel, surrendered himself to the authorities in front of the Bronx County Building, where both the office of the Assistant District Attorney who ultimately prosecuted his case and the court-room in which he was ultimately tried were located. His attorney had cautioned him to answer no questions, and left him in the custody of the officers. He was promptly taken to the office of the Assistant District Attorney and at 7:15 p.m. the questioning began, being conducted by Assistant District Attorney Goldsmith, Lt. Gannon, Detectives Farrell, Lehrer and Motta, and Sgt.

Clarke. The record reveals that the questioning was both persistent and continuous. Petitioner, in accordance with his attorney's instructions, steadfastly refused to answer. Detective Motta testified: "He refused to talk to me." "He just looked up to the ceiling and refused to talk to me." Detective Farrell testified:

> Q. And you started to interrogate him? A. That is right.
>
> Q. What did he say? A. He said "you would have to see my attorney. I tell you nothing but my name."
>
> Q. Did you continue to examine him? A. Verbally, yes, sir.

He asked one officer, Detective Ciccone, if he could speak to his attorney, but that request was denied. Detective Ciccone testified that he could not find the attorney's name in the telephone book. He was given two sandwiches, coffee and cake at 11 p.m.

At 12:15 a.m. on the morning of February 5, after five hours of questioning in which it became evident that petitioner was following his attorney's instructions, on the Assistant District Attorney's orders petitioner was transferred to the 46th Squad, Ryer Avenue Police Station. The Assistant District Attorney also went to the police station and to some extent continued to participate in the interrogation. Petitioner arrived at 12:30 and questioning was resumed at 12:40. The character of the questioning is revealed by the testimony of Detective Farrell:

> Q. Who did you leave him in the room with? A. With Detective Lehrer and Sergeant Clarke came in and Mr. Goldsmith came in or Inspector Halk came in. It was back and forth. People just came in, spoke a few words to the defendant or they listened a few minutes and they left.

But petitioner persisted in his refusal to answer, and again requested permission to see his attorney, this time from Detective Lehrer. His request was again denied.

It was then that those in charge of the investigation decided that petitioner's close friend, Bruno, could be of use. He had been called out on the case around 10 or 11 p.m., although he was not connected with the 46th Squad or Precinct in any way. Although, in fact, his job was in no way threatened, Bruno was told to tell petitioner that petitioner's telephone call had gotten him "in a lot of trouble," and that he should seek to extract sympathy from petitioner for Bruno's pregnant wife and three children. Bruno developed this theme with petitioner without success, and petitioner, also without success, again sought to see his attorney, a request which Bruno relayed unavailingly to his superiors. After this first session with petitioner, Bruno was again directed by Lt. Gannon to play on petitioner's sympathies, but again no confession was forthcoming. But the Lieutenant a third time ordered Bruno falsely to importune his friend to confess but again petitioner clung to his attorney's advice. Inevitably, in the fourth such session directed by the Lieutenant, lasting a full hour, petitioner succumbed to his friend's prevarications and agreed to make a statement. Accordingly, at 3:25 a.m. the Assistant District Attorney, a stenographer, and several other law enforcement officials entered the room where petitioner was being questioned, and took his statement in question and answer form with the Assistant District Attorney asking the questions. The statement was completed at 4:05 a.m.

But this was not the end. At 4:30 a.m. three detectives took petitioner to Police Headquarters in Manhattan. On the way they attempted to find the bridge from which petitioner said he had thrown the murder weapon. They crossed the Triborough Bridge into Manhattan, arriving at Police Headquarters at 5 a.m., and left Manhattan for the Bronx at 5:40 a.m. via the Willis Avenue Bridge. When petitioner recognized neither bridge as the one from which he had thrown the weapon, they re-entered Manhattan via the Third Avenue Bridge, which petitioner stated was the right one, and then returned to the Bronx well after 6 a.m. During that trip the officers also elicited a statement from petitioner that the deceased was always "on (his) back," "always pushing" him and that he was "not sorry" he had shot the deceased. All three detectives testified to that statement at the trial.

Court opened at 10 a.m. that morning, and petitioner was arraigned at 10:15.

At the trial, the confession was introduced in evidence over appropriate objections. The jury was instructed that it could rely on it only if it was found to be voluntary. The jury returned a guilty verdict and petitioner was sentenced to death. The New York Court of Appeals affirmed the conviction over three dissents, and we granted certiorari to resolve the serious problem presented under the Fourteenth Amendment.

Petitioner's first contention is that his absolute right to counsel in a capital case, *Powell v. State of Alabama*, 287 U.S. 45 (1932), became operative on the return of an indictment against him, for at that time he was in every sense a defendant in a criminal case, the grand jury having found sufficient cause to believe that he had committed the crime. He argues accordingly that following indictment no confession obtained in the absence of counsel can be used without violating the Fourteenth Amendment. He seeks to distinguish *Crooker v. State of California*, 357 U.S. 433 (1958), and *Cicenia v. Lagay*, 357 U.S. 504 (1958), on the ground that in those cases no indictment had been returned. We find it unnecessary to reach that contention, for we find use of the confession obtained here inconsistent with the Fourteenth Amendment under traditional principles.

The abhorrence of society to the use of involuntary confessions does not turn alone on their inherent untrustworthiness. It also turns on the deep-rooted feeling that the police must obey the law while enforcing the law; that in the end life and liberty can be as much endangered from illegal methods used to convict those thought to be criminals as from the actual criminals themselves. Accordingly, the actions of police in obtaining confessions have come under scrutiny in a long series of cases. Those cases suggest that in recent years law enforcement officials have become increasingly aware of the burden which they share, along with our courts, in protecting fundamental rights of our citizenry, including that portion of our citizenry suspected of crime. The facts of no case recently in this Court have quite approached the brutal beatings in *Brown v. State of Mississippi*, 297 U.S. 278 (1936), or the 36 consecutive hours of questioning present in *Ashcraft v. State of Tennessee*, 322 U.S. 143 (1944). But as law enforcement officers become more responsible, and the methods used to extract confessions more sophisticated, our duty to enforce federal constitutional protections does not cease. It only becomes more difficult because of the more delicate judgments to be made. Our judgment here is that, on all the facts, this conviction cannot stand.

Petitioner was a foreign-born young man of 25 with no past history of law violation or of subjection to official interrogation, at least insofar as the record shows. He had progressed only one-half year into high school and the record indicates that he had a history of emotional instability.[3] He did not make a narrative statement, but was subject to the leading questions of a skillful prosecutor in a question and answer confession. He was subjected to questioning not by a few men, but by many. They included Assistant District Attorney Goldsmith, one Hyland of the District Attorney's Office, Deputy Inspector Halks, Lieutenant Gannon, Detective Ciccone, Detective Motta, Detective Lehrer, Detective Marshal, Detective Farrell, Detective Leira, Detective Murphy, Detective Murtha, Sergeant Clarke, Patrolman Bruno and Stenographer Baldwin. All played some part, and the effect of such massive official interrogation must have been felt. Petitioner was questioned for virtually eight straight hours before he confessed, with his only respite being a transfer to an arena presumably considered more appropriate by the police for the task at hand. Nor was the questioning conducted during normal business hours, but began in early evening, continued into the night, and did not bear fruition until the not-too-early morning. The drama was not played out, with the final admissions obtained, until almost sunrise. In such circumstances slowly mounting fatigue does, and is calculated to, play its part. The questioners persisted in the face of his repeated refusals to answer on the advice of his attorney, and they ignored his reasonable requests to contact the local

[3] Medical reports from New York City's Fordham Hospital introduced by defendant showed that he had suffered a cerebral concussion in 1955. He was described by a private physician in 1951 as "an extremely nervous tense individual who is emotionally unstable and maladjusted," and was found unacceptable for military service in 1951, primarily because of Psychiatric disorder.' He failed the Army's AFQT-1 intelligence test. His mother had been in mental hospitals on three separate occasions.

attorney whom he had already retained and who had personally delivered him into the custody of these officers in obedience to the bench warrant.

The use of Bruno, characterized in this Court by counsel for the State as a "childhood friend" of petitioner's, is another factor which deserves mention in the totality of the situation. Bruno's was the one face visible to petitioner in which he could put some trust. There was a bond of friendship between them going back a decade into adolescence. It was with this material that the officers felt that they could overcome petitioner's will. They instructed Bruno falsely to state that petitioner's telephone call had gotten him into trouble, that his job was in jeopardy, and that loss of his job would be disastrous to his three children, his wife and his unborn child. And Bruno played this part of a worried father, harried by his superiors, in not one, but four different acts, the final one lasting an hour. Petitioner was apparently unaware of John Gay's famous couplet: "An open foe may prove a curse, But a pretended friend is worse," and he yielded to his false friend's entreaties.

We conclude that petitioner's will was overborne by official pressure, fatigue and sympathy falsely aroused after considering all the facts in their post-indictment setting. Here a grand jury had already found sufficient cause to require petitioner to face trial on a charge of first-degree murder, and the police had an eyewitness to the shooting. The police were not therefore merely trying to solve a crime, or even to absolve a suspect. They were rather concerned primarily with securing a statement from defendant on which they could convict him. The undeviating intent of the officers to extract a confession from petitioner is therefore patent. When such an intent is shown, this Court has held that the confession obtained must be examined with the most careful scrutiny, and has reversed a conviction on facts less compelling than these. Accordingly, we hold that petitioner's conviction cannot stand under the Fourteenth Amendment.

* * *

MR. JUSTICE DOUGLAS, with whom MR. JUSTICE BLACK and MR. JUSTICE BRENNAN join, concurring.

While I join the opinion of the Court, I add what for me is an even more important ground of decision.

* * *

. . . This is a case of an accused, who is scheduled to be tried by a judge and jury, being tried in a preliminary way by the police. This is a kangaroo court procedure whereby the police produce the vital evidence in the form of a confession which is useful or necessary to obtain a conviction. They in effect deny him effective representation by counsel. This seems to me to be a flagrant violation of the principle announced in *Powell v. State of Alabama*, [287 U.S. 45 (1917)], that the right of counsel extends to the preparation for trial, as well as to the trial itself. As Professor Chafee once said, "A person accused of crime needs a lawyer right after his arrest probably more than at any other time." Chafee, *Documents on Fundamental Human Rights*, Pamphlet 2 (1951–1952), p. 541. When he is deprived of that right after indictment and before trial, he may indeed be denied effective representation by counsel at the only stage when legal aid and advice would help him. This *secret inquisition* by the police when defendant asked for and was denied counsel was as serious an invasion of his constitutional rights as the denial of a continuance in order to employ counsel was held to be in *Chandler v. Fretag*, 348 U.S. 3, 10 [(1954)]. What we said in *Avery v. State of Alabama*, 308 U.S. 444, 446 [(1940)], has relevance here:

> The denial of opportunity for appointed counsel to confer, to consult with the accused and to prepare his defense, could convert the appointment of counsel into a sham and nothing more than a formal compliance with the Constitution's requirement that an accused be given the assistance of counsel.

I join with Judges Desmond, Fuld, and Van Voorhis of the New York Court of Appeals, in asking, what use is a defendant's right to effective counsel at every stage of a criminal case if, while he is held awaiting trial, he can be questioned in the absence of counsel until he confesses? In that event the secret trial in the police precincts effectively supplants the public trial guaranteed by the Bill of Rights.

MR. JUSTICE STEWART, whom MR. JUSTICE DOUGLAS and MR. JUSTICE BRENNAN join, concurring.

While I concur in the opinion of the Court, it is my view that the absence of counsel when this confession was elicited was alone enough to render it inadmissible under the Fourteenth Amendment.

Let it be emphasized at the outset that this is not a case where the police were questioning a suspect in the course of investigating an unsolved crime. When the petitioner surrendered to the New York authorities he was under indictment for first degree murder.

Under our system of justice an indictment is supposed to be followed by an arraignment and a trial. At every stage in those proceedings the accused has an absolute right to a lawyer's help if the case is one in which a death sentence may be imposed. Indeed the right to the assistance of counsel whom the accused has himself retained is absolute, whatever the offense for which he is on trial.

What followed the petitioner's surrender in this case was not arraignment in a court of law, but an all-night inquisition in a prosecutor's office, a police station, and an automobile. Throughout the night the petitioner repeatedly asked to be allowed to send for his lawyer, and his requests were repeatedly denied. He finally was induced to make a confession. That confession was used to secure a verdict sending him to the electric chair.

Our Constitution guarantees the assistance of counsel to a man on trial for his life in an orderly courtroom, presided over by a judge, open to the public, and protected by all the procedural safeguards of the law. Surely a Constitution which promises that much can vouchsafe no less to the same man under midnight inquisition in the squad room of a police station.

Points for Discussion

1. What is it, exactly, that the authorities did wrong in this case? Did they question the defendant for too long? Was the use of his friend Bruno the fact that moved the interrogation across the line? How much guidance does this case give law enforcement officials regarding how vigorously they may question a suspect?

2. The majority writes that abusive interrogation practices are forbidden in part because of "the deep-rooted feeling that the police must obey the law while enforcing the law; that in the end life and liberty can be as much endangered from illegal methods used to convict those thought to be criminals as from the actual criminals themselves." This statement suggests that concern about police misconduct in the interrogation room is as much about policing the police as it is about protecting the innocent. Consider how closely the Court hews to that principle in the cases throughout the next four chapters.

3. The majority decides that the introduction of Spano's confession violated the Due Process Clause of the Fourteenth Amendment, passing over Spano's contention that use of the confession violated his right to counsel. The concurring justices would have avoided the amorphous totality of the circumstances test employed under the Fourteenth Amendment and simply held that the police violated Spano's right to counsel.

4. Justice Douglas writes that the police tactics employed in *Spano* threaten the adversarial process because "the secret trial in the police precincts effectively supplants the public trial guaranteed by the Bill of Rights." Echoing that same thought, Justice Stewart writes, "What followed the petitioner's surrender in this case was not arraignment in a court of law, but an all-night inquisition in a prosecutor's office, a police station, and an automobile." With the word "inquisition," Justice Stewart is referring to *inquisitorial* systems of criminal justice, which operate in a fundamentally different way than the *adversarial* system created by British common law. One essential difference between the two systems is that, in an inquisitorial system of criminal justice, the judge actively investigates the case, questioning witnesses and gathering evidence. An adversarial system requires the prosecution (the party with the burden of proof) to gather sufficient evidence to charge and convict the defendant, while the judge presiding over the trial has a more passive, neutral role. The Bill of Rights presupposes an adversarial system of justice in which the accused has aid of counsel and does not have to answer questions put to him. Thus, the Court's concern with secret police interrogations is that they

are inquisitorial in nature and threaten to render the adversarial trial guaranteed by the Bill of Rights an empty formality.

MASSIAH V. UNITED STATES

377 U.S. 201 (1964)

MR. JUSTICE STEWART delivered the opinion of the court.

The petitioner was indicted for violating the federal narcotics laws. He retained a lawyer, pleaded not guilty, and was released on bail. While he was free on bail a federal agent succeeded by surreptitious means in listening to incriminating statements made by him. Evidence of these statements was introduced against the petitioner at his trial over his objection. He was convicted, and the Court of Appeals affirmed. We granted certiorari to consider whether, under the circumstances here presented, the prosecution's use at the trial of evidence of the petitioner's own incriminating statements deprived him of any right secured to him under the Federal Constitution.

The petitioner, a merchant seaman, was in 1958 a member of the crew of the *S.S. Santa Maria*. In April of that year federal customs officials in New York received information that he was going to transport a quantity of narcotics aboard that ship from South America to the United States. As a result of this and other information, the agents searched the Santa Maria upon its arrival in New York and found in the after peak of the vessel five packages containing about three and a half pounds of cocaine. They also learned of circumstances, not here relevant, tending to connect the petitioner with the cocaine. He was arrested, promptly arraigned, and subsequently indicted for possession of narcotics aboard a United States vessel. In July a superseding indictment was returned, charging the petitioner and a man named Colson with the same substantive offense, and in separate counts charging the petitioner, Colson, and others with having conspired to possess narcotics aboard a United States vessel, and to import, conceal, and facilitate the sale of narcotics. The petitioner, who had retained a lawyer, pleaded not guilty and was released on bail, along with Colson.

A few days later, and quite without the petitioner's knowledge, Colson decided to cooperate with the government agents in their continuing investigation of the narcotics activities in which the petitioner, Colson, and others had allegedly been engaged. Colson permitted an agent named Murphy to install a Schmidt radio transmitter under the front seat of Colson's automobile, by means of which Murphy, equipped with an appropriate receiving device, could overhear from some distance away conversations carried on in Colson's car.

On the evening of November 19, 1959, Colson and the petitioner held a lengthy conversation while sitting in Colson's automobile, parked on a

New York street. By prearrangement with Colson, and totally unbeknown to the petitioner, the agent Murphy sat in a car parked out of sight down the street and listened over the radio to the entire conversation. The petitioner made several incriminating statements during the course of this conversation. At the petitioner's trial these incriminating statements were brought before the jury through Murphy's testimony, despite the insistent objection of defense counsel. The jury convicted the petitioner of several related narcotics offenses, and the convictions were affirmed by the Court of Appeals.

The petitioner argues that it was an error of constitutional dimensions to permit the agent Murphy at the trial to testify to the petitioner's incriminating statements which Murphy had overheard under the circumstances disclosed by this record. This argument is based upon two distinct and independent grounds. First, we are told that Murphy's use of the radio equipment violated the petitioner's rights under the Fourth Amendment, and, consequently, that all evidence which Murphy thereby obtained was, under the rule of *Weeks v. United States*, 232 U.S. 383, inadmissible against the petitioner at the trial. Secondly, it is said that the petitioner's Fifth and Sixth Amendment rights were violated by the use in evidence against him of incriminating statements which government agents had deliberately elicited from him after he had been indicted and in the absence of his retained counsel. Because of the way we dispose of the case, we do not reach the Fourth Amendment issue.

* * *

Here we deal not with a state court conviction, but with a federal case, where the specific guarantee of the Sixth Amendment directly applies. We hold that the petitioner was denied the basic protections of that guarantee when there was used against him at his trial evidence of his own incriminating words, which federal agents had deliberately elicited from him after he had been indicted and in the absence of his counsel. It is true that in the *Spano* case the defendant was interrogated in a police station, while here the damaging testimony was elicited from the defendant without his knowledge while he was free on bail. But, as Judge Hays pointed out in his dissent in the Court of Appeals, "if such a rule is to have any efficacy it must apply to indirect and surreptitious interrogations as well as those conducted in the jailhouse. In this case, Massiah was more seriously imposed upon * * * because he did not even know that he was under interrogation by a government agent."

The Solicitor General, in his brief and oral argument, has strenuously contended that the federal law enforcement agents had the right, if not indeed the duty, to continue their investigation of the petitioner and his alleged criminal associates even though the petitioner had been indicted. He points out that the Government was continuing its investigation in order to uncover not only the source of narcotics found on the *S.S. Santa*

Maria, but also their intended buyer. He says that the quantity of narcotics involved was such as to suggest that the petitioner was part of a large and well-organized ring, and indeed that the continuing investigation confirmed this suspicion, since it resulted in criminal charges against many defendants. Under these circumstances the Solicitor General concludes that the Government agents were completely "justified in making use of Colson's cooperation by having Colson continue his normal associations and by surveilling them."

We may accept and, at least for present purposes, completely approve all that this argument implies, Fourth Amendment problems to one side. We do not question that in this case, as in many cases, it was entirely proper to continue an investigation of the suspected criminal activities of the defendant and his alleged confederates, even though the defendant had already been indicted. All that we hold is that the defendant's own incriminating statements, obtained by federal agents under the circumstances here disclosed, could not constitutionally be used by the prosecution as evidence against him at his trial.

MR. JUSTICE WHITE, with whom MR. JUSTICE CLARK and MR. JUSTICE HARLAN join, dissenting.

The current incidence of serious violations of the law represents not only an appalling waste of the potentially happy and useful lives of those who engage in such conduct but also an overhanging, dangerous threat to those unidentified and innocent people who will be the victims of crime today and tomorrow. This is a festering problem for which no adequate cures have yet been devised. At the very least there is much room for discontent with remedial measures so far undertaken. And admittedly there remains much to be settled concerning the disposition to be made of those who violate the law.

But dissatisfaction with preventive programs aimed at eliminating crime and profound dispute about whether we should punish, deter, rehabilitate or cure cannot excuse concealing one of our most menacing problems until the millennium has arrived. In my view, a civilized society must maintain its capacity to discover transgressions of the law and to identify those who flout it. This much is necessary even to know the scope of the problem, much less to formulate intelligent counter-measures. It will just not do to sweep these disagreeable matters under the rug or to pretend they are not there at all.

It is therefore a rather portentous occasion when a constitutional rule is established barring the use of evidence which is relevant, reliable and highly probative of the issue which the trial court has before it—whether the accused committed the act with which he is charged. Without the evidence, the quest for truth may be seriously impeded and in many cases the trial court, although aware of proof showing defendant's guilt, must nevertheless release him because the crucial evidence is deemed inadmissible. This result is entirely justified in some circumstances because exclusion serves other policies of overriding importance, as where evidence seized in an illegal search is excluded, not because of the quality of the proof, but to secure meaningful enforcement of the Fourth Amendment. But this only emphasizes that the soundest of reasons is necessary to warrant the exclusion of evidence otherwise admissible and the creation of another area of privileged testimony. With all due deference, I am not at all convinced that the additional barriers to the pursuit of truth which the Court today erects rest on anything like the solid foundations which decisions of this gravity should require.

The importance of the matter should not be underestimated, for today's rule promises to have wide application well beyond the facts of this case. The reason given for the result here—the admissions were obtained in the absence of counsel—would seem equally pertinent to statements obtained at any time after the right to counsel attaches, whether there has been an indictment or not; to admissions made prior to arraignment, at least where the defendant has counsel or asks for it; to the fruits of admissions improperly obtained under the new rule; to criminal proceedings in state courts; and to defendants long since convicted upon evidence including such admissions. The new rule will immediately do service in a great many cases.

Whatever the content or scope of the rule may prove to be, I am unable to see how this case presents an unconstitutional interference with Massiah's right to counsel. Massiah was not prevented from consulting with counsel as often as he wished. No meetings with counsel were disturbed or spied upon. Preparation for trial was in no way obstructed. It is only a sterile syllogism—an unsound one, besides—to say that because Massiah had a right to counsel's aid before and during the trial, his out-of-court conversations and admissions must be excluded if obtained without counsel's consent or presence. The right to counsel has never meant as much before, and its extension in this case requires some further explanation, so far unarticulated by the Court.

Since the new rule would exclude all admissions made to the police, no matter how voluntary and reliable, the requirement of counsel's presence or approval would seem to rest upon the probability that counsel would foreclose any admissions at all. This is nothing more than a thinly disguised constitutional policy of minimizing or entirely prohibiting the use in evidence of voluntary out-of-court admissions and confessions made by the accused. Carried as far as blind logic may compel some to go, the notion that statements from the mouth of the defendant should not be used in evidence would have a severe and unfortunate impact upon the great bulk of criminal cases.

* * *

The Court presents no facts, no objective evidence, no reasons to warrant scrapping the voluntary-involuntary test for admissibility in this area. Without such evidence I would retain it in its present form.

* * *

Applying the new exclusionary rule is peculiarly inappropriate in this case. At the time of the conversation in question, petitioner was not in custody but free on bail. He was not questioned in what anyone could call an atmosphere of official coercion. What he said was said to his partner in crime who had also been indicted. There was no suggestion or any possibility of coercion. What petitioner did not know was that Colson had decided to report the conversation to the police. Had there been no prior arrangements between Colson and the police, had Colson simply gone to the police after the conversation had occurred, his testimony relating Massiah's statements would be readily admissible at the trial, as would a recording which he might have made of the conversation. In such event, it would simply be said that Massiah risked talking to a friend who decided to disclose what he knew of Massiah's criminal activities. But, if, as occurred here, Colson had been cooperating with the police prior to his meeting with Massiah, both his evidence and the recorded conversation are somehow transformed into inadmissible evidence despite the fact that the hazard to Massiah remains precisely the same—the defection of a confederate in crime.

Reporting criminal behavior is expected or even demanded of the ordinary citizen. Friends may be subpoenaed to testify about friends, relatives about relatives and partners about partners. I therefore question the soundness of insulating Massiah from the apostasy of his partner in crime and of furnishing constitutional sanction for the strict secrecy and discipline of criminal organizations. Neither the ordinary citizen nor the confessed criminal should be discouraged from reporting what he knows to the authorities and from lending his aid to secure evidence of crime. Certainly after this case the Colsons will be few and far between; and the Massiahs can breathe much more easily, secure in the knowledge that the Constitution furnishes an important measure of protection against faithless compatriots and guarantees sporting treatment for sporting peddlers of narcotics.

Meanwhile, of course, the public will again be the loser and law enforcement will be presented with another serious dilemma. The general issue lurking in the background of the Court's opinion is the legitimacy of penetrating or obtaining confederates in criminal organizations. For the law enforcement agency, the answer for the time being can only be in the form of a prediction about the future application of today's new constitutional doctrine. More narrowly, and posed by the precise situation involved here, the question is this: when the police have arrested and released on bail one member of a criminal ring and another member, a confederate, is cooperating with the police, can the confederate be allowed to continue his association with the ring or must he somehow be withdrawn to avoid challenge to trial evidence on the ground that it was acquired after rather than before the arrest, after rather than before the indictment?

* * *

Undoubtedly, the evidence excluded in this case would not have been available but for the conduct of Colson in cooperation with Agent Murphy, but is it this kind of conduct which should be forbidden to those charged with law enforcement? It is one thing to establish safeguards against procedures fraught with the potentiality of coercion and to outlaw "easy but self-defeating ways in which brutality is substituted for brains as an instrument of crime detection." But here there was no substitution of brutality for brains, no inherent danger of police coercion justifying the prophylactic effect of another exclusionary rule. Massiah was not being interrogated in a police station, was not surrounded by numerous officers or questioned in relays, and was not forbidden access to others. Law enforcement may have the elements of a contest about it, but it is not a game. Massiah and those like him receive ample protection from the long line of precedents in this Court holding that confessions may not be introduced unless they are voluntary. In making these determinations the courts must consider the absence of counsel as one of several factors by which voluntariness is to be judged. This is a wiser rule than the automatic rule announced by the Court, which requires courts and juries to disregard voluntary admissions which they might well find to be the best possible evidence in discharging their responsibility for ascertaining truth.

Points for Discussion

1. *Massiah* demonstrates the interrelation of the three constitutional amendments on which we focus in this course: the Fourth, Fifth, and Sixth. Massiah claimed that the use of a wired informant violated each of these. The Court deferred decision of the Fourth Amendment claim (though we saw in chapter 2 how it would rule on such a challenge) and did not squarely resolve the Fifth Amendment question (though the dissent seems quite convinced that this statement was voluntarily given). The Court focused instead on the Sixth Amendment issue, finding this electronic eavesdropping to be a violation of Massiah's right to counsel. As we go through the cases from here forward, it will be useful to consider which claims a defendant might make, not just those covered in the particular section we are reading.

2. What was it that the government did in this case that violated the defendant's right to counsel? As the dissent points out, the government did nothing to keep the defendant from meeting with or speaking with his attorney; the use of the undercover informant did nothing to interfere with the relationship between Massiah and his lawyer. Why then does the Court find the Sixth Amendment violated?

3. Why doesn't the assumption-of-risk doctrine that the Court has applied in the Fourth Amendment context apply here with equal force? Didn't Massiah run the risk that the person he was speaking with might be a police officer, might betray him to a police officer, or might allow a police officer to eavesdrop on their conversation? If so, doesn't that argument apply with equal force to Massiah's Sixth Amendment right?

ESCOBEDO V. ILLINOIS

378 U.S. 478 (1964)

MR. JUSTICE GOLDBERG delivered the opinion of the court.

The critical question in this case is whether, under the circumstances, the refusal by the police to honor petitioner's request to consult with his lawyer during the course of an interrogation constitutes a denial of "the Assistance of Counsel" in violation of the Sixth Amendment to the Constitution as "made obligatory upon the States by the Fourteenth Amendment," *Gideon v. Wainwright*, 372 U.S. 335, 342 [(1963)], and thereby renders inadmissible in a state criminal trial any incriminating statement elicited by the police during the interrogation.

On the night of January 19, 1960, petitioner's brother-in-law was fatally shot. In the early hours of the next morning, at 2:30 a.m., petitioner was arrested without a warrant and interrogated. Petitioner made no statement to the police and was released at 5 that afternoon pursuant to a state court writ of habeas corpus obtained by Mr. Warren Wolfson, a lawyer who had been retained by petitioner.

On January 30, Benedict DiGerlando, who was then in police custody and who was later indicted for the murder along with petitioner, told the police that petitioner had fired the fatal shots. Between 8 and 9 that evening, petitioner and his sister, the widow of the deceased, were arrested and taken to police headquarters. En route to the police station, the police "had handcuffed the defendant behind his back," and "one of the arresting officers told defendant that DiGerlando had named him as the one who shot" the deceased. Petitioner testified, without contradiction, that the "detective said they had us pretty well, up pretty tight, and we might as well admit to this crime," and that he replied, "I am sorry but I would like to have advice from my lawyer." A police officer testified that although petitioner was not formally charged "he was in custody" and "couldn't walk out the door."

Shortly after petitioner reached police headquarters, his retained lawyer arrived. The lawyer described the ensuing events in the following terms:

> On that day I received a phone call (from "the mother of another defendant") and pursuant to that phone call I went to the Detective Bureau at 11th and State. The first person I talked to

> was the Sergeant on duty at the Bureau Desk, Sergeant Pidgeon. I asked Sergeant Pidgeon for permission to speak to my client, Danny Escobedo. . . . Sergeant Pidgeon made a call to the Bureau lockup and informed me that the boy had been taken from the lockup to the Homicide Bureau. This was between 9:30 and 10:00 in the evening. Before I went anywhere, he called the Homicide Bureau and told them there was an attorney waiting to see Escobedo. He told me I could not see him. Then I went upstairs to the Homicide Bureau. There were several Homicide Detectives around and I talked to them. I identified myself as Escobedo's attorney and asked permission to see him. They said I could not. . . . The police officer told me to see Chief Flynn who was on duty. I identified myself to Chief Flynn and asked permission to see my client. He said I could not. . . . I think it was approximately 11:00 o'clock. He said I couldn't see him because they hadn't completed questioning. . . . (F)or a second or two I spotted him in an office in the Homicide Bureau. The door was open and I could see through the office. . . . I waved to him and he waved back and then the door was closed, by one of the officers at Homicide. There were four or five officers milling around the Homicide Detail that night. As to whether I talked to Captain Flynn any later that day, I waited around for another hour or two and went back again and renewed by (sic) request to see my client. He again told me I could not. . . . I filed an official complaint with Commissioner Phelan of the Chicago Police Department. I had a conversation with every police officer I could find. I was told at Homicide that I couldn't see him and I would have to get a writ of habeas corpus. I left the Homicide Bureau and from the Detective Bureau at 11th and State at approximately 1:00 A.M. (Sunday morning) I had no opportunity to talk to my client that night. I quoted to Captain Flynn the Section of the Criminal Code which allows an attorney the right to see his client.

Petitioner testified that during the course of the interrogation he repeatedly asked to speak to his lawyer and that the police said that his lawyer "didn't want to see" him. The testimony of the police officers confirmed these accounts in substantial detail.

Notwithstanding repeated requests by each, petitioner and his retained lawyer were afforded no opportunity to consult during the course of the entire interrogation. At one point, as previously noted, petitioner and his attorney came into each other's view for a few moments but the attorney was quickly ushered away. Petitioner testified "that he heard a detective telling the attorney the latter would not be allowed to talk to (him) 'until they were done' " and that he heard the attorney being refused permission to remain in the adjoining room. A police officer testified that he had told the lawyer that he could not see petitioner until "we were through interrogating" him.

There is testimony by the police that during the interrogation, petitioner, a 22-year-old of Mexican extraction with no record of previous experience with the police, "was handcuffed" in a standing position and that he "was nervous, he had circles under his eyes and he was upset" and was "agitated" because "he had not slept well in over a week."

It is undisputed that during the course of the interrogation Officer Montejano, who "grew up" in petitioner's neighborhood, who knew his family, and who uses "Spanish language in (his) police work," conferred alone with petitioner "for about a quarter of an hour. . . ." Petitioner testified that the officer said to him "in Spanish that my sister and I could go home if I pinned it on Benedict DiGerlando," that "he would see to it that we would go home and be held only as witnesses, if anything, if we had made a statement against DiGerlando . . . that we would be able to go home that night." Petitioner testified that he made the statement in issue because of this assurance. Officer Montejano denied offering any such assurance.

A police officer testified that during the interrogation the following occurred:

> I informed him of what DiGerlando told me and when I did, he told me that DiGerlando was (lying) and I said, "Would you care to tell DiGerlando that?" and he said, "Yes, I will." So, I brought . . . Escobedo in and he confronted DiGerlando and he told him that he was lying and said, "I didn't shoot Manuel, you did it."

In this way, petitioner, for the first time admitted to some knowledge of the crime. After that he made additional statements further implicating himself in the murder plot. At this point an Assistant State's Attorney, Theodore J. Cooper, was summoned "to take" a statement. Mr. Cooper, an experienced lawyer who was assigned to the Homicide Division to take "statements from some defendants and some prisoners that they had in custody," "took" petitioner's statement by asking carefully framed questions apparently designed to assure the admissibility into evidence of the resulting answers. Mr. Cooper testified that he did not advise petitioner of his constitutional rights, and it is undisputed that no one during the course of the interrogation so advised him.

Petitioner moved both before and during trial to suppress the incriminating statement, but the motions were denied. Petitioner was convicted of murder and he appealed the conviction.

* * *

The interrogation here was conducted before petitioner was formally indicted. But in the context of this case, that fact should make no difference. When petitioner requested, and was denied, an opportunity to consult with his lawyer, the investigation had ceased to be a general investigation of "an unsolved crime." *Spano v. New York*, 360 U.S. 315, 327 [(1959)] (Stewart, J., concurring). Petitioner had become the accused, and the purpose of the interrogation was to "get him" to confess his guilt despite his constitutional right not to do so. At the time of his arrest and throughout the course of the interrogation, the police told petitioner that they had convincing evidence that he had fired the fatal shots. Without informing him of his absolute right to remain silent in the face of this accusation, the police urged him to make a statement.[5] As this Court observed many years ago:

> It cannot be doubted that, placed in the position in which the accused was when the statement was made to him that the other suspected person had charged him with crime, the result was to produce upon his mind the fear that, if he remained silent, it would be considered an admission of guilt, and therefore render certain his being committed for trial as the guilty person, and it cannot be conceived that the converse impression would not also have naturally arisen that, by denying, there was hope of removing the suspicion from himself.

Bram v. United States, 168 U.S. 532, 562 (1897).

Petitioner, a layman, was undoubtedly unaware that under Illinois law an admission of "mere" complicity in the murder plot was legally as damaging as an admission of firing of the fatal shots. The "guiding hand of counsel" was essential to advise petitioner of his rights in this delicate situation. This was the "stage when legal aid and advice" were most critical to petitioner. It was a stage surely as critical as was the arraignment in *Hamilton v. Alabama*, 368 U.S. 52 [(1961)], and the preliminary hearing in *White v. Maryland*, 373 U.S. 59 [(1963)]. What happened at this interrogation could certainly "affect the whole trial," since rights "may be as irretrievably lost, if not then and there asserted, as they are when an accused represented by counsel waives a right for strategic purposes." It would exalt form over substance to make the right to counsel, under these circumstances, depend on whether at the time of the interrogation, the authorities had secured a formal indictment. Petitioner had, for all practical purposes, already been charged with murder.

* * *

In *Gideon v. Wainwright*, 372 U.S. 335 [(1963)], we held that every person accused of a crime, whether state or federal, is entitled to a lawyer at trial. The rule sought by the State here, however, would make the trial

---

[5] Although there is testimony in the record that petitioner and his lawyer had previously discussed what petitioner should do in the event of interrogation, there is no evidence that they discussed what petitioner should, or could, do in the face of a false accusation that he had fired the fatal bullets.

no more than an appeal from the interrogation; and the "right to use counsel at the formal trial (would be) a very hollow thing (if), for all practical purposes, the conviction is already assured by pretrial examination." *In re Groban*, 352 U.S. 330, 344 [(1957)] (Black, J., dissenting). "One can imagine a cynical prosecutor saying: 'Let them have the most illustrious counsel, now. They can't escape the noose. There is nothing that counsel can do for them at the trial.' "

It is argued that if the right to counsel is afforded prior to indictment, the number of confessions obtained by the police will diminish significantly, because most confessions are obtained during the period between arrest and indictment, and "any lawyer worth his salt will tell the suspect in no uncertain terms to make no statement to police under any circumstances." *Watts v. Indiana*, 338 U.S. 49, 59 [(1949)] (Jackson, J., concurring in part and dissenting in part). This argument, of course, cuts two ways. The fact that many confessions are obtained during this period points up its critical nature as a "stage when legal aid and advice" are surely needed. *Massiah v. United States*, 377 U.S. at 204. The right to counsel would indeed be hollow if it began at a period when few confessions were obtained. There is necessarily a direct relationship between the importance of a stage to the police in their quest for a confession and the criticalness of that stage to the accused in his need for legal advice. Our Constitution, unlike some others, strikes the balance in favor of the right of the accused to be advised by his lawyer of his privilege against self-incrimination.

We have learned the lesson of history, ancient and modern, that a system of criminal law enforcement which comes to depend on the "confession" will, in the long run, be less reliable and more subject to abuses than a system which depends on extrinsic evidence independently secured through skillful investigation. As Dean Wigmore so wisely said:

> *Any system of administration which permits the prosecution to trust habitually to compulsory self-disclosure as a source of proof must itself suffer morally thereby.* The inclination develops to rely mainly upon such evidence, and to be satisfied with an incomplete investigation of the other sources. The exercise of the power to extract answers begets a forgetfulness of the just limitations of that power. The simple and peaceful process of questioning breeds a readiness to resort to bullying and to physical force and torture. If there is a right to an answer, there soon seems to be a right to the expected answer,—that is, to a confession of guilt. Thus the legitimate use grows into the unjust abuse; ultimately, the innocent are jeopardized by the encroachments of a bad system. Such seems to have been the course of experience in those legal systems where the privilege was not recognized.

8 Wigmore, Evidence (3d ed. 1940), 309. (Emphasis in original.) This Court also has recognized that "history amply shows that confessions have often been extorted to save law enforcement officials the trouble and effort of obtaining valid and independent evidence . . . ." *Haynes v. Washington*, 373 U.S. 503, 519.

We have also learned the companion lesson of history that no system of criminal justice can, or should, survive if it comes to depend for its continued effectiveness on the citizens' abdication through unawareness of their constitutional rights. No system worth preserving should have to fear that if an accused is permitted to consult with a lawyer, he will become aware of, and exercise, these rights. If the exercise of constitutional rights will thwart the effectiveness of a system of law enforcement, then there is something very wrong with that system.[14]

We hold, therefore, that where, as here, the investigation is no longer a general inquiry into an unsolved crime but has begun to focus on a particular suspect, the suspect has been taken into police custody, the police carry out a process of interrogations that lends itself to eliciting incriminating statements, the suspect has requested and been denied an opportunity to consult with his lawyer, and the police have not effectively warned him of his absolute constitutional right to remain silent, the accused has been denied "the Assistance of Counsel" in violation of the Sixth Amendment to the Constitution as "made obligatory upon the States by the Fourteenth Amendment," and that no statement elicited by the police during the interrogation may be used against him at a criminal trial.

* * *

Nothing we have said today affects the powers of the police to investigate "an unsolved crime," by gathering information from witnesses and by other "proper investigative efforts." We hold only that when the process shifts from investigatory to accusatory—when its focus is on the accused and its purpose is to elicit a confession—our adversary system begins to operate, and, under the circumstances here, the accused must be permitted to consult with his lawyer.

The dissenting opinion of MR. JUSTICE HARLAN is omitted.

MR. JUSTICE STEWART, dissenting.

* * *

Massiah v. United States, 377 U.S. 201 [(1964)], is not in point here. In that case a federal grand jury had indicted Massiah. He had retained a lawyer and entered a formal plea of not guilty. Under our system of federal

[14] The accused may, of course, intelligently and knowingly waive his privilege against self-incrimination and his right to counsel either at a pretrial stage or at the trial. But no knowing and intelligent waiver of any constitutional right can be said to have occurred under the circumstances of this case.

justice an indictment and arraignment are followed by a trial, at which the Sixth Amendment guarantees the defendant the assistance of counsel. But Massiah was released on bail, and thereafter agents of the Federal Government deliberately elicited incriminating statements from him in the absence of his lawyer. We held that the use of these statements against him at his trial denied him the basic protections of the Sixth Amendment guarantee. Putting to one side the fact that the case now before us is not a federal case, the vital fact remains that this case does not involve the deliberate interrogation of a defendant after the initiation of judicial proceedings against him. The Court disregards this basic difference between the present case and Massiah's, with the bland assertion that "that fact should make no difference."

It is "that fact," I submit, which makes all the difference. Under our system of criminal justice the institution of formal, meaningful judicial proceedings, by way of indictment, information, or arraignment, marks the point at which a criminal investigation has ended and adversary proceedings have commenced. It is at this point that the constitutional guarantees attach which pertain to a criminal trial. Among those guarantees are the right to a speedy trial, the right of confrontation, and the right to trial by jury. Another is the guarantee of the assistance of counsel.

The confession which the Court today holds inadmissible was a voluntary one. It was given during the course of a perfectly legitimate police investigation of an unsolved murder. The Court says that what happened during this investigation "affected" the trial. I had always supposed that the whole purpose of a police investigation of a murder was to "affect" the trial of the murderer, and that it would be only an incompetent, unsuccessful, or corrupt investigation which would not do so. The Court further says that the Illinois police officers did not advise the petitioner of his "constitutional rights" before he confessed to the murder. This Court has never held that the Constitution requires the police to give any "advice" under circumstances such as these.

Supported by no stronger authority than its own rhetoric, the Court today converts a routine police investigation of an unsolved murder into a distorted analogue of a judicial trial. It imports into this investigation constitutional concepts historically applicable only after the onset of formal prosecutorial proceedings. By doing so, I think the Court perverts those precious constitutional guarantees, and frustrates the vital interests of society in preserving the legitimate and proper function of honest and purposeful police investigation.

Like my Brother Clark, I cannot escape the logic of my Brother White's conclusions as to the extraordinary implications which emanate from the Court's opinion in this case, and I share their views as to the untold and highly unfortunate impact today's decision may have upon the fair administration of criminal justice. I can only hope we have completely misunderstood what the Court has said.

MR. JUSTICE WHITE, with whom MR. JUSTICE CLARK and MR. JUSTICE STEWART join, dissenting.

In *Massiah v. United States,* 377 U.S. 201 [(1964)], the Court held that as of the date of the indictment the prosecution is disentitled to secure admissions from the accused. The Court now moves that date back to the time when the prosecution begins to "focus" on the accused. Although the opinion purports to be limited to the facts of this case, it would be naive to think that the new constitutional right announced will depend upon whether the accused has retained his own counsel or has asked to consult with counsel in the course of interrogation. At the very least the Court holds that once the accused becomes a suspect and, presumably, is arrested, any admission made to the police thereafter is inadmissible in evidence unless the accused has waived his right to counsel. The decision is thus another major step in the direction of the goal which the Court seemingly has in mind-to bar from evidence all admissions obtained from an individual suspected of crime, whether involuntarily made or not. It does of course put us one step "ahead" of the English judges who have had the good sense to leave the matter a discretionary one with the trial court. I reject this step and the invitation to go farther which the Court has now issued.

By abandoning the voluntary-involuntary test for admissibility of confessions, the Court seems driven by the notion that it is uncivilized law enforcement to use an accused's own admissions against him at his trial. It attempts to find a home for this new and nebulous rule of due process by attaching it to the right to counsel guaranteed in the federal system by the Sixth Amendment and binding upon the States by virtue of the due process guarantee of the Fourteenth Amendment. The right to counsel now not only entitles the accused to counsel's advice and aid in preparing for trial but stands as an impenetrable barrier to any interrogation once the accused has become a suspect. From that very moment apparently his right to counsel attaches, a rule wholly unworkable and impossible to administer unless police cars are equipped with public defenders and undercover agents and police informants have defense counsel at their side. I would not abandon the Court's prior cases defining with some care and analysis the circumstances requiring the presence or aid of counsel and substitute the amorphous and wholly unworkable principle that counsel is constitutionally required whenever he would or could be helpful. These cases dealt with the requirement of counsel at proceedings in which definable rights could be won or lost, not with stages where probative evidence might be obtained. Under this new approach one might just as well argue that a potential defendant is constitutionally entitled to a lawyer before, not after, he commits a crime, since it is then that crucial incriminating evidence is put within the reach of the Government by the would-be accused. Until now there simply has been no right guaranteed by the Federal Constitution to be free from the use at trial of a voluntary admission made prior to indictment.

It is incongruous to assume that the provision for counsel in the Sixth Amendment was meant to amend or supersede the self-incrimination provision of the Fifth Amendment, which is now applicable to the States. That amendment addresses itself to the very issue of incriminating admissions of an accused and resolves it by proscribing only compelled statements. Neither the Framers, the constitutional language, a century of decisions of this Court nor Professor Wigmore provides an iota of support for the idea that an accused has an absolute constitutional right not to answer even in the absence of compulsion—the constitutional right not to incriminate himself by making voluntary disclosures.

* * *

The Court may be concerned with a narrower matter: the unknowing defendant who responds to police questioning because he mistakenly believes that he must and that his admissions will not be used against him. But this worry hardly calls for the broadside the Court has now fired. The failure to inform an accused that he need not answer and that his answers may be used against him is very relevant indeed to whether the disclosures are compelled. Cases in this Court, to say the least, have never placed a premium on ignorance of constitutional rights. If an accused is told he must answer and does not know better, it would be very doubtful that the resulting admissions could be used against him. When the accused has not been informed of his rights at all the Court characteristically and properly looks very closely at the surrounding circumstances. I would continue to do so. But, in this case Danny Escobedo knew full well that he did not have to answer and knew full well that his lawyer had advised him not to answer.

* * *

Points for Discussion

1. Relying on the Sixth Amendment, Escobedo holds that an interrogated defendant must be allowed to speak to his lawyer once the investigation has moved from investigatory to accusatory. The Court states that the fact that Escobedo had not yet been formally charged was not dispositive. Why does the dissent disagree with this point so vehemently?

2. Was this confession, as the dissent strongly implies, voluntary under the Fifth and Fourteenth Amendments? How, if at all, should that fact affect the Sixth Amendment analysis in which the Court engages?

3. The majority notes in footnote 5 that Escobedo's lawyer had told him what he "should do in the event of interrogation" but also asserts that a "false accusation" is in some significant way different than mere interrogation.

Escobedo's lawyer undoubtedly told him that "in the event of interrogation" he should say nothing because, as the Court notes, "any lawyer worth his salt will tell the suspect in no uncertain terms to make no statement to police under any circumstances." So, it is not altogether true that Escobedo was unaided by "the guiding hand of counsel" when the police accused him of firing the fatal shot. What problem, then, is the majority attempting to address with the decision in *Escobedo*?

The answer is suggested by *Cicenia v. La Gay*, 357 U.S. 504 (1958), a case that *Escobedo* overruled and that Justice Harlan and Justice Stewart each mentioned in his dissent. The facts were straightforward:

> In the evening of March 17, 1947, Charles Kittuah, the owner of a small dry goods store in Newark, New Jersey, was shot and killed during the course of a robbery. The crime remained unsolved until December 17, 1949, when the Newark police obtained information implicating the petitioner and two others, Armando Corvino and John DeMasi. Petitioner lived with his parents at Orange, New Jersey. Apparently acting at the request of the Newark police, the Orange police sought to locate petitioner at his home. When told that he was out, the police left word that he was to report at the Orange police headquarters the following day. Petitioner sought the advice of Frank A. Palmieri, a lawyer, who advised him to report as requested. Petitioner did so, accompanied by his father and brother. Upon arrival at the Orange police station at 9 a.m. on December 18, petitioner was separated from the others and taken by detectives to the Newark police headquarters. At approximately 2 p.m. the same day petitioner's father, brother and Mr. Palmieri, the lawyer, arrived at the Newark station. Mr. Palmieri immediately asked to see petitioner, but this request was refused by the police. He repeated this request at intervals throughout the afternoon and well into the evening, but without success. During this period petitioner, who was being questioned intermittently by the police, asked to see his lawyer. These requests were also denied. Lawyer and client were not permitted to confer until 9:30 p.m., by which time petitioner had made and signed a written confession to the murder of Kittuah.

The Court held that the police action did not violate due process. Justice Harlan's opinion for a five-justice majority reasoned: "[P]etitioner would have us hold that any state denial of a defendant's request to confer with counsel during police questioning violates due process, irrespective of the particular circumstances involved. Such a holding, in its ultimate reach, would mean that state police could not interrogate a suspect before giving him an opportunity to secure counsel." *Miranda v. Arizona*, which was foreshadowed in Justice Stewart's *Escobedo* dissent, would erect a rule much like the one Justice Harlan resisted.

MIRANDA V. ARIZONA

384 U.S. 436 (1966)

MR. CHIEF JUSTICE WARREN delivered the opinion of the court.

The cases before us raise questions which go to the roots of our concepts of American criminal jurisprudence: the restraints society must observe consistent with the Federal Constitution in prosecuting individuals for crime. More specifically, we deal with the admissibility of statements obtained from an individual who is subjected to custodial police interrogation and the necessity for procedures which assure that the individual is accorded his privilege under the Fifth Amendment to the Constitution not to be compelled to incriminate himself.

We dealt with certain phases of this problem recently in *Escobedo v. State of Illinois*, 378 U.S. 478 (1964). There, as in the four cases before us, law enforcement officials took the defendant into custody and interrogated him in a police station for the purpose of obtaining a confession. The police did not effectively advise him of his right to remain silent or of his right to consult with his attorney. Rather, they confronted him with an alleged accomplice who accused him of having perpetrated a murder. When the defendant denied the accusation and said "I didn't shoot Manuel, you did it," they handcuffed him and took him to an interrogation room. There, while handcuffed and standing, he was questioned for four hours until he confessed. During this interrogation, the police denied his request to speak to his attorney, and they prevented his retained attorney, who had come to the police station, from consulting with him. At his trial, the State, over his objection, introduced the confession against him. We held that the statements thus made were constitutionally inadmissible.

This case has been the subject of judicial interpretation and spirited legal debate since it was decided two years ago. Both state and federal courts, in assessing its implications, have arrived at varying conclusions. A wealth of scholarly material has been written tracing its ramifications and underpinnings. Police and prosecutors have speculated on its range and desirability. We granted certiorari in these cases in order further to explore some facets of the problems, thus exposed, of applying the privilege against self-incrimination to in-custody interrogation, and to give concrete constitutional guidelines for law enforcement agencies and courts to follow.

We start here, as we did in *Escobedo*, with the premise that our holding is not an innovation in our jurisprudence, but is an application of principles long recognized and applied in other settings. We have undertaken a thorough re-examination of the *Escobedo* decision and the principles it announced, and we reaffirm it. That case was but an explication of basic rights that are enshrined in our Constitution—that "No person * * * shall be compelled in any criminal case to be a witness against himself," and that "the accused shall * * * have the Assistance of Counsel"—rights which were put in jeopardy in that case through official overbearing. These precious rights were fixed in our Constitution only after centuries of persecution and struggle. And in the words of Chief Justice Marshall, they were secured "for ages to come, and * * * designed to approach immortality as nearly as human institutions can approach it."

* * *

Our holding will be spelled out with some specificity in the pages which follow but briefly stated it is this: the prosecution may not use statements, whether exculpatory or inculpatory, stemming from custodial interrogation of the defendant unless it demonstrates the use of procedural safeguards effective to secure the privilege against self-incrimination. By custodial interrogation, we mean questioning initiated by law enforcement officers after a person has been taken into custody or otherwise deprived of his freedom of action in any significant way.[4] As for the procedural safeguards to be employed, unless other fully effective means are devised to inform accused persons of their right of silence and to assure a continuous opportunity to exercise it, the following measures are required. Prior to any questioning, the person must be warned that he has a right to remain silent, that any statement he does make may be used as evidence against him, and that he has a right to the presence of an attorney, either retained or appointed. The defendant may waive effectuation of these rights, provided the waiver is made voluntarily, knowingly and intelligently. If, however, he indicates in any manner and at any stage of the process that he wishes to consult with an attorney before speaking there can be no questioning. Likewise, if the individual is alone and indicates in any manner that he does not wish to be interrogated, the police may not question him. The mere fact that he may have answered some questions or volunteered some statements on his own does not deprive him of the right to refrain from answering any further inquiries until he has consulted with an attorney and thereafter consents to be questioned.

I

The constitutional issue we decide in each of these cases is the admissibility of statements obtained from a defendant questioned while in custody or otherwise deprived of his freedom of action in any significant way. In each, the defendant was questioned by police officers, detectives, or a prosecuting attorney in a room in which he was cut off from the outside world. In none of these cases was the defendant given a full and effective warning of his rights at the outset of the interrogation process. In all the cases, the questioning elicited oral admissions, and in three of them, signed statements as well which were admitted at their trials. They all thus share salient features—incommunicado interrogation of individuals in a police-

[4] This is what we meant in *Escobedo* when we spoke of an investigation which had focused on an accused.

dominated atmosphere, resulting in self-incriminating statements without full warnings of constitutional rights.

An understanding of the nature and setting of this in-custody interrogation is essential to our decisions today. The difficulty in depicting what transpires at such interrogations stems from the fact that in this country they have largely taken place incommunicado. From extensive factual studies undertaken in the early 1930's, including the famous Wickersham Report to Congress by a Presidential Commission, it is clear that police violence and the "third degree" flourished at that time. In a series of cases decided by this Court long after these studies, the police resorted to physical brutality—beatings, hanging, whipping—and to sustained and protracted questioning incommunicado in order to extort confessions. The Commission on Civil Rights in 1961 found much evidence to indicate that "some policemen still resort to physical force to obtain confessions." The use of physical brutality and violence is not, unfortunately, relegated to the past or to any part of the country. Only recently in Kings County, New York, the police brutally beat, kicked and placed lighted cigarette butts on the back of a potential witness under interrogation for the purpose of securing a statement incriminating a third party.

* * *

Again we stress that the modern practice of in-custody interrogation is psychologically rather than physically oriented. As we have stated before, "Since *Chambers v. State of Florida*, 309 U.S. 227 [(1940)], this Court has recognized that coercion can be mental as well as physical, and that the blood of the accused is not the only hallmark of an unconstitutional inquisition." *Blackburn v. State of Alabama*, 361 U.S. 199 (1960). Interrogation still takes place in privacy. Privacy results in secrecy and this in turn results in a gap in our knowledge as to what in fact goes on in the interrogation rooms. A valuable source of information about present police practices, however, may be found in various police manuals and texts which document procedures employed with success in the past, and which recommend various other effective tactics. These texts are used by law enforcement agencies themselves as guides. It should be noted that these texts professedly present the most enlightened and effective means presently used to obtain statements through custodial interrogation. By considering these texts and other data, it is possible to describe procedures observed and noted around the country.

The officers are told by the manuals that the "principal psychological factor contributing to a successful interrogation is privacy—being alone with the person under interrogation." The efficacy of this tactic has been explained as follows:

> If at all practicable, the interrogation should take place in the investigator's office or at least in a room of his own choice. The subject should be deprived of every psychological advantage. In his own home he may be confident, indignant, or recalcitrant. He is more keenly aware of his rights and more reluctant to tell of his indiscretions of criminal behavior within the walls of his home. Moreover his family and other friends are nearby, their presence lending moral support. In his office, the investigator possesses all the advantages. The atmosphere suggests the invincibility of the forces of the law.

To highlight the isolation and unfamiliar surroundings, the manuals instruct the police to display an air of confidence in the suspect's guilt and from outward appearance to maintain only an interest in confirming certain details. The guilt of the subject is to be posited as a fact. The interrogator should direct his comments toward the reasons why the subject committed the act, rather than court failure by asking the subject whether he did it. Like other men, perhaps the subject has had a bad family life, had an unhappy childhood, had too much to drink, had an unrequited desire for women. The officers are instructed to minimize the moral seriousness of the offense, to cast blame on the victim or on society. These tactics are designed to put the subject in a psychological state where his story is but an elaboration of what the police purport to know already—that he is guilty. Explanations to the contrary are dismissed and discouraged.

The texts thus stress that the major qualities an interrogator should possess are patience and perseverance. One writer describes the efficacy of these characteristics in this manner:

> In the preceding paragraphs emphasis has been placed on kindness and stratagems. The investigator will, however, encounter many situations where the sheer weight of his personality will be the deciding factor. Where emotional appeals and tricks are employed to no avail, he must rely on an oppressive atmosphere of dogged persistence. He must interrogate steadily and without relent, leaving the subject no prospect of surcease. He must dominate his subject and overwhelm him with his inexorable will to obtain the truth. He should interrogate for a spell of several hours pausing only for the subject's necessities in acknowledgment of the need to avoid a charge of duress that can be technically substantiated. In a serious case, the interrogation may continue for days, with the required intervals for food and sleep, but with no respite from the atmosphere of domination. It is possible in this way to induce the subject to talk without resorting to duress or coercion. The method should be used only when the guilt of the subject appears highly probable.

The manuals suggest that the suspect be offered legal excuses for his actions in order to obtain an initial admission of guilt. Where there is a suspected revenge-killing, for example, the interrogator may say:

> Joe, you probably didn't go out looking for this fellow with the purpose of shooting him. My guess is, however, that you expected something from him and that's why you carried a gun—for your own protection. You knew him for what he was, no good. Then when you met him he probably started using foul, abusive language and he gave some indication that he was about to pull a gun on you, and that's when you had to act to save your own life. That's about it, isn't it, Joe?

Having then obtained the admission of shooting, the interrogator is advised to refer to circumstantial evidence which negates the self-defense explanation. This should enable him to secure the entire story. One text notes that "Even if he fails to do so, the inconsistency between the subject's original denial of the shooting and his present admission of at least doing the shooting will serve to deprive him of a self-defense 'out' at the time of trial."

When the techniques described above prove unavailing, the texts recommend they be alternated with a show of some hostility. One ploy often used has been termed the "friendly-unfriendly" or the "Mutt and Jeff" act:

> In this technique, two agents are employed. Mutt, the relentless investigator, who knows the subject is guilty and is not going to waste any time. He's sent a dozen men away for this crime and he's going to send the subject away for the full term. Jeff, on the other hand, is obviously a kindhearted man. He has a family himself. He has a brother who was involved in a little scrape like this. He disapproves of Mutt and his tactics and will arrange to get him off the case if the subject will cooperate. He can't hold Mutt off for very long. The subject would be wise to make a quick decision. The technique is applied by having both investigators present while Mutt acts out his role. Jeff may stand by quietly and demur at some of Mutt's tactics. When Jeff makes his plea for cooperation, Mutt is not present in the room.

The interrogators sometimes are instructed to induce a confession out of trickery. The technique here is quite effective in crimes which require identification or which run in series. In the identification situation, the interrogator may take a break in his questioning to place the subject among a group of men in a line-up. "The witness or complainant (previously coached, if necessary) studies the line-up and confidently points out the subject as the guilty party." Then the questioning resumes "as though there were now no doubt about the guilt of the subject." A variation on this technique is called the "reverse line-up":

> The accused is placed in a line-up, but this time he is identified by several fictitious witnesses or victims who associated him with different offenses. It is expected that the subject will become desperate and confess to the offense under investigation in order to escape from the false accusations.

The manuals also contain instructions for police on how to handle the individual who refuses to discuss the matter entirely, or who asks for an attorney or relatives. The examiner is to concede him the right to remain silent. "This usually has a very undermining effect. First of all, he is disappointed in his expectation of an unfavorable reaction on the part of the interrogator. Secondly, a concession of this right to remain silent impresses the subject with the apparent fairness of his interrogator." After this psychological conditioning, however, the officer is told to point out the incriminating significance of the suspect's refusal to talk:

> Joe, you have a right to remain silent. That's your privilege and I'm the last person in the world who'll try to take it away from you. If that's the way you want to leave this, O.K. But let me ask you this. Suppose you were in my shoes and I were in yours and you called me in to ask me about this and I told you, "I don't want to answer any of your questions." You'd think I had something to hide, and you'd probably be right in thinking that. That's exactly what I'll have to think about you, and so will everybody else. So let's sit here and talk this whole thing over.

Few will persist in their initial refusal to talk, it is said, if this monologue is employed correctly.

In the event that the subject wishes to speak to a relative or an attorney, the following advice is tendered:

> (T)he interrogator should respond by suggesting that the subject first tell the truth to the interrogator himself rather than get anyone else involved in the matter. If the request is for an attorney, the interrogator may suggest that the subject save himself or his family the expense of any such professional service, particularly if he is innocent of the offense under investigation. The interrogator may also add, "Joe, I'm only looking for the truth, and if you're telling the truth, that's it. You can handle this by yourself."

From these representative samples of interrogation techniques, the setting prescribed by the manuals and observed in practice becomes clear. In essence, it is this: To be alone with the subject is essential to prevent distraction and to deprive him of any outside support. The aura of confidence in his guilt undermines his will to resist. He merely confirms the preconceived story the police seek to have him describe. Patience and persistence, at times relentless questioning, are employed. To obtain a confession, the interrogator must "patiently maneuver himself or his quarry into a position from which the desired objective may be attained." When normal procedures fail to produce the needed result, the police may resort to deceptive stratagems such as giving false legal advice. It is important to keep the subject off balance, for example, by trading on his insecurity about himself or his surroundings. The police then persuade, trick, or cajole him out of exercising his constitutional rights.

Even without employing brutality, the "third degree" or the specific stratagems described above, the very fact of custodial interrogation exacts a heavy toll on individual liberty and trades on the weakness of individuals.[24] This fact may be illustrated simply by referring to three confession cases decided by this Court in the Term immediately preceding our *Escobedo* decision. In *Townsend v. Sain*, 372 U.S. 293 (1963), the defendant was a 19-year-old heroin addict, described as a "near mental defective." The defendant in *Lynumn v. State of Illinois*, 372 U.S. 528 (1963), was a woman who confessed to the arresting officer after being importuned to "cooperate" in order to prevent her children from being taken by relief authorities. This Court as in those cases reversed the conviction of a defendant in *Haynes v. State of Washington*, 373 U.S. 503 (1963), whose persistent request during his interrogation was to phone his wife or attorney. In other settings, these individuals might have exercised their constitutional rights. In the incommunicado police-dominated atmosphere, they succumbed.

In the cases before us today, given this background, we concern ourselves primarily with this interrogation atmosphere and the evils it can bring. In No. 759, *Miranda v. Arizona*, the police arrested the defendant and took him to a special interrogation room where they secured a confession. In No. 760, *Vignera v. New York*, the defendant made oral admissions to the police after interrogation in the afternoon, and then signed an inculpatory statement upon being questioned by an assistant district attorney later the same evening. In No. 761, *Westover v. United States*, the defendant was handed over to the Federal Bureau of Investigation by local authorities after they had detained and interrogated him for a lengthy period, both at night and the following morning. After some two hours of questioning, the federal officers had obtained signed statements from the defendant. Lastly, in No. 584, *California v. Stewart*, the local police held the defendant five days in the station and interrogated him on nine separate occasions before they secured his inculpatory statement.

---

[24] Interrogation procedures may even give rise to a false confession. The most recent conspicuous example occurred in New York, in 1964, when a Negro of limited intelligence confessed to two brutal murders and a rape which he had not committed. When this was discovered, the prosecutor was reported as saying: "Call it what you want—brain-washing, hypnosis, fright. They made him give an untrue confession. The only thing I don't believe is that Whitmore was beaten." N.Y. Times, Jan. 28, 1965, p. 1, col. 5. In two other instances, similar events had occurred.

In these cases, we might not find the defendants' statements to have been involuntary in traditional terms. Our concern for adequate safeguards to protect precious Fifth Amendment rights is, of course, not lessened in the slightest. In each of the cases, the defendant was thrust into an unfamiliar atmosphere and run through menacing police interrogation procedures. The potentiality for compulsion is forcefully apparent, for example, in *Miranda*, where the indigent Mexican defendant was a seriously disturbed individual with pronounced sexual fantasies, and in *Stewart*, in which the defendant was an indigent Los Angeles Negro who had dropped out of school in the sixth grade. To be sure, the records do not evince overt physical coercion or patent psychological ploys. The fact remains that in none of these cases did the officers undertake to afford appropriate safeguards at the outset of the interrogation to insure that the statements were truly the product of free choice.

It is obvious that such an interrogation environment is created for no purpose other than to subjugate the individual to the will of his examiner. This atmosphere carries its own badge of intimidation. To be sure, this is not physical intimidation, but it is equally destructive of human dignity.[26] The current practice of incommunicado interrogation is at odds with one of our Nation's most cherished principles—that the individual may not be compelled to incriminate himself. Unless adequate protective devices are employed to dispel the compulsion inherent in custodial surroundings, no statement obtained from the defendant can truly be the product of his free choice.

* * *

III

Today, then, there can be no doubt that the Fifth Amendment privilege is available outside of criminal court proceedings and serves to protect persons in all settings in which their freedom of action is curtailed in any significant way from being compelled to incriminate themselves. We have concluded that without proper safeguards the process of in-custody interrogation of persons suspected or accused of crime contains inherently compelling pressures which work to undermine the individual's will to

---

[26] The absurdity of denying that a confession obtained under these circumstances is compelled is aptly portrayed by an example in Professor Sutherland's recent article, *Crime and Confession*, 79 HARV. L. REV. 21, 37 (1965):

> Suppose a well-to-do testatrix says she intends to will her property to Elizabeth. John and James want her to bequeath it to them instead. They capture the testatrix, put her in a carefully designed room, out of touch with everyone but themselves and their convenient "witnesses," keep her secluded there for hours while they make insistent demands, weary her with contradictions of her assertions that she wants to leave her money to Elizabeth, and finally induce her to execute the will in their favor. Assume that John and James are deeply and correctly convinced that Elizabeth is unworthy and will make base use of the property if she gets her hands on it, whereas John and James have the noblest and most righteous intentions. Would any judge of probate accept the will so procured as the "voluntary" act of the testatrix?

resist and to compel him to speak where he would not otherwise do so freely. In order to combat these pressures and to permit a full opportunity to exercise the privilege against self-incrimination, the accused must be adequately and effectively apprised of his rights and the exercise of those rights must be fully honored.

It is impossible for us to foresee the potential alternatives for protecting the privilege which might be devised by Congress or the States in the exercise of their creative rule-making capacities. Therefore we cannot say that the Constitution necessarily requires adherence to any particular solution for the inherent compulsions of the interrogation process as it is presently conducted. Our decision in no way creates a constitutional straitjacket which will handicap sound efforts at reform, nor is it intended to have this effect. We encourage Congress and the States to continue their laudable search for increasingly effective ways of protecting the rights of the individual while promoting efficient enforcement of our criminal laws. However, unless we are shown other procedures which are at least as effective in apprising accused persons of their right of silence and in assuring a continuous opportunity to exercise it, the following safeguards must be observed.

At the outset, if a person in custody is to be subjected to interrogation, he must first be informed in clear and unequivocal terms that he has the right to remain silent. For those unaware of the privilege, the warning is needed simply to make them aware of it—the threshold requirement for an intelligent decision as to its exercise. More important, such a warning is an absolute prerequisite in overcoming the inherent pressures of the interrogation atmosphere. It is not just the subnormal or woefully ignorant who succumb to an interrogator's imprecations, whether implied or expressly stated, that the interrogation will continue until a confession is obtained or that silence in the face of accusation is itself damning and will bode ill when presented to a jury. Further, the warning will show the individual that his interrogators are prepared to recognize his privilege should he choose to exercise it.

The Fifth Amendment privilege is so fundamental to our system of constitutional rule and the expedient of giving an adequate warning as to the availability of the privilege so simple, we will not pause to inquire in individual cases whether the defendant was aware of his rights without a warning being given. Assessments of the knowledge the defendant possessed, based on information as to his age, education, intelligence, or prior contact with authorities, can never be more than speculation; a warning is a clearcut fact. More important, whatever the background of the person interrogated, a warning at the time of the interrogation is indispensable to overcome its pressures and to insure that the individual knows he is free to exercise the privilege at that point in time.

The warning of the right to remain silent must be accompanied by the explanation that anything said can and will be used against the individual in court. This warning is needed in order to make him aware not only of the privilege, but also of the consequences of forgoing it. It is only through an awareness of these consequences that there can be any assurance of real understanding and intelligent exercise of the privilege. Moreover, this warning may serve to make the individual more acutely aware that he is faced with a phase of the adversary system—that he is not in the presence of persons acting solely in his interest.

The circumstances surrounding in-custody interrogation can operate very quickly to overbear the will of one merely made aware of his privilege by his interrogators. Therefore, the right to have counsel present at the interrogation is indispensable to the protection of the Fifth Amendment privilege under the system we delineate today. Our aim is to assure that the individual's right to choose between silence and speech remains unfettered throughout the interrogation process. A once-stated warning, delivered by those who will conduct the interrogation, cannot itself suffice to that end among those who most require knowledge of their rights. A mere warning given by the interrogators is not alone sufficient to accomplish that end. Prosecutors themselves claim that the admonishment of the right to remain silent without more "will benefit only the recidivist and the professional." Brief for the National District Attorneys Association as amicus curiae, p. 14. Even preliminary advice given to the accused by his own attorney can be swiftly overcome by the secret interrogation process. Thus, the need for counsel to protect the Fifth Amendment privilege comprehends not merely a right to consult with counsel prior to questioning, but also to have counsel present during any questioning if the defendant so desires.

The presence of counsel at the interrogation may serve several significant subsidiary functions as well. If the accused decides to talk to his interrogators, the assistance of counsel can mitigate the dangers of untrustworthiness. With a lawyer present the likelihood that the police will practice coercion is reduced, and if coercion is nevertheless exercised the lawyer can testify to it in court. The presence of a lawyer can also help to guarantee that the accused gives a fully accurate statement to the police and that the statement is rightly reported by the prosecution at trial.

An individual need not make a pre-interrogation request for a lawyer. While such request affirmatively secures his right to have one, his failure to ask for a lawyer does not constitute a waiver. No effective waiver of the right to counsel during interrogation can be recognized unless specifically made after the warnings we here delineate have been given. The accused who does not know his rights and therefore does not make a request may be the person who most needs counsel. . . .

* * *

Accordingly we hold that an individual held for interrogation must be clearly informed that he has the right to consult with a lawyer and to have the lawyer with him during interrogation under the system for protecting the privilege we delineate today. As with the warnings of the right to remain silent and that anything stated can be used in evidence against him, this warning is an absolute prerequisite to interrogation. No amount of circumstantial evidence that the person may have been aware of this right will suffice to stand in its stead. Only through such a warning is there ascertainable assurance that the accused was aware of this right.

If an individual indicates that he wishes the assistance of counsel before any interrogation occurs, the authorities cannot rationally ignore or deny his request on the basis that the individual does not have or cannot afford a retained attorney. The financial ability of the individual has no relationship to the scope of the rights involved here. The privilege against self-incrimination secured by the Constitution applies to all individuals. The need for counsel in order to protect the privilege exists for the indigent as well as the affluent. In fact, were we to limit these constitutional rights to those who can retain an attorney, our decisions today would be of little significance. The cases before us as well as the vast majority of confession cases with which we have dealt in the past involve those unable to retain counsel. While authorities are not required to relieve the accused of his poverty, they have the obligation not to take advantage of indigence in the administration of justice. Denial of counsel to the indigent at the time of interrogation while allowing an attorney to those who can afford one would be no more supportable by reason or logic than the similar situation at trial and on appeal struck down in *Gideon v. Wainwright*, 372 U.S. 335 (1963), and *Douglas v. People of State of California*, 372 U.S. 353 (1963).

In order fully to apprise a person interrogated of the extent of his rights under this system then, it is necessary to warn him not only that he has the right to consult with an attorney, but also that if he is indigent a lawyer will be appointed to represent him. Without this additional warning, the admonition of the right to consult with counsel would often be understood as meaning only that he can consult with a lawyer if he has one or has the funds to obtain one. The warning of a right to counsel would be hollow if not couched in terms that would convey to the indigent—the person most often subjected to interrogation—the knowledge that he too has a right to have counsel present. As with the warnings of the right to remain silent and of the general right to counsel, only by effective and express explanation to the indigent of this right can there be assurance that he was truly in a position to exercise it.

Once warnings have been given, the subsequent procedure is clear. If the individual indicates in any manner, at any time prior to or during questioning, that he wishes to remain silent, the interrogation must cease. At this point he has shown that he intends to exercise his Fifth Amendment privilege; any statement taken after the person invokes his privilege cannot be other than the product of compulsion, subtle or otherwise. Without the right to cut off questioning, the setting of in-custody interrogation operates on the individual to overcome free choice in producing a statement after the privilege has been once invoked. If the individual states that he wants an attorney, the interrogation must cease until an attorney is present. At that time, the individual must have an opportunity to confer with the attorney and to have him present during any subsequent questioning. If the individual cannot obtain an attorney and he indicates that he wants one before speaking to police, they must respect his decision to remain silent.

This does not mean, as some have suggested, that each police station must have a "station house lawyer" present at all times to advise prisoners. It does mean, however, that if police propose to interrogate a person they must make known to him that he is entitled to a lawyer and that if he cannot afford one, a lawyer will be provided for him prior to any interrogation. If authorities conclude that they will not provide counsel during a reasonable period of time in which investigation in the field is carried out, they may refrain from doing so without violating the person's Fifth Amendment privilege so long as they do not question him during that time.

If the interrogation continues without the presence of an attorney and a statement is taken, a heavy burden rests on the government to demonstrate that the defendant knowingly and intelligently waived his privilege against self-incrimination and his right to retained or appointed counsel. This Court has always set high standards of proof for the waiver of constitutional rights, and we reassert these standards as applied to in-custody interrogation. Since the State is responsible for establishing the isolated circumstances under which the interrogation takes place and has the only means of making available corroborated evidence of warnings given during incommunicado interrogation, the burden is rightly on its shoulders.

An express statement that the individual is willing to make a statement and does not want an attorney followed closely by a statement could constitute a waiver. But a valid waiver will not be presumed simply from the silence of the accused after warnings are given or simply from the fact that a confession was in fact eventually obtained. A statement we made in *Carnley v. Cochran*, 369 U.S. 506, 516 (1962), is applicable here:

> Presuming waiver from a silent record is impermissible. The record must show, or there must be an allegation and evidence which show, that an accused was offered counsel but intelligently and understandingly rejected the offer. Anything less is not waiver.

> Moreover, where in-custody interrogation is involved, there is no room for the contention that the privilege is waived if the individual answers some questions or gives some information on his own prior to invoking his right to remain silent when interrogated.

Whatever the testimony of the authorities as to waiver of rights by an accused, the fact of lengthy interrogation or incommunicado incarceration before a statement is made is strong evidence that the accused did not validly waive his rights. In these circumstances the fact that the individual eventually made a statement is consistent with the conclusion that the compelling influence of the interrogation finally forced him to do so. It is inconsistent with any notion of a voluntary relinquishment of the privilege. Moreover, any evidence that the accused was threatened, tricked, or cajoled into a waiver will, of course, show that the defendant did not voluntarily waive his privilege. The requirement of warnings and waiver of rights is a fundamental with respect to the Fifth Amendment privilege and not simply a preliminary ritual to existing methods of interrogation.

The warnings required and the waiver necessary in accordance with our opinion today are, in the absence of a fully effective equivalent, prerequisites to the admissibility of any statement made by a defendant. No distinction can be drawn between statements which are direct confessions and statements which amount to "admissions" of part or all of an offense. The privilege against self-incrimination protects the individual from being compelled to incriminate himself in any manner; it does not distinguish degrees of incrimination. Similarly, for precisely the same reason, no distinction may be drawn between inculpatory statements and statements alleged to be merely "exculpatory." If a statement made were in fact truly exculpatory it would, of course, never be used by the prosecution. In fact, statements merely intended to be exculpatory by the defendant are often used to impeach his testimony at trial or to demonstrate untruths in the statement given under interrogation and thus to prove guilt by implication. These statements are incriminating in any meaningful sense of the word and may not be used without the full warnings and effective waiver required for any other statement. In *Escobedo* itself, the defendant fully intended his accusation of another as the slayer to be exculpatory as to himself.

The principles announced today deal with the protection which must be given to the privilege against self-incrimination when the individual is first subjected to police interrogation while in custody at the station or otherwise deprived of his freedom of action in any significant way. It is at this point that our adversary system of criminal proceedings commences, distinguishing itself at the outset from the inquisitorial system recognized in some countries. Under the system of warnings we delineate today or under any other system which may be devised and found effective, the safeguards to be erected about the privilege must come into play at this point.

Our decision is not intended to hamper the traditional function of police officers in investigating crime. When an individual is in custody on probable cause, the police may, of course, seek out evidence in the field to be used at trial against him. Such investigation may include inquiry of persons not under restraint. General on-the-scene questioning as to facts surrounding a crime or other general questioning of citizens in the fact-finding process is not affected by our holding. It is an act of responsible citizenship for individuals to give whatever information they may have to aid in law enforcement. In such situations the compelling atmosphere inherent in the process of in-custody interrogation is not necessarily present.

In dealing with statements obtained through interrogation, we do not purport to find all confessions inadmissible. Confessions remain a proper element in law enforcement. Any statement given freely and voluntarily without any compelling influences is, of course, admissible in evidence. The fundamental import of the privilege while an individual is in custody is not whether he is allowed to talk to the police without the benefit of warnings and counsel, but whether he can be interrogated. There is no requirement that police stop a person who enters a police station and states that he wishes to confess to a crime, or a person who calls the police to offer a confession or any other statement he desires to make. Volunteered statements of any kind are not barred by the Fifth Amendment and their admissibility is not affected by our holding today.

To summarize, we hold that when an individual is taken into custody or otherwise deprived of his freedom by the authorities in any significant way and is subjected to questioning, the privilege against self-incrimination is jeopardized. Procedural safeguards must be employed to protect the privilege and unless other fully effective means are adopted to notify the person of his right of silence and to assure that the exercise of the right will be scrupulously honored, the following measures are required. He must be warned prior to any questioning that he has the right to remain silent, that anything he says can be used against him in a court of law, that he has the right to the presence of an attorney, and that if he cannot afford an attorney one will be appointed for him prior to any questioning if he so desires. Opportunity to exercise these rights must be afforded to him throughout the interrogation. After such warnings have been given, and such opportunity afforded him, the individual may knowingly and intelligently waive these rights and agree to answer questions or make a statement. But unless and until such warnings and waiver are demonstrated by the prosecution at trial, no evidence obtained as a result of interrogation can be used against him.

IV

* * *

If the individual desires to exercise his privilege, he has the right to do so. This is not for the authorities to decide. An attorney may advise his client not to talk to police until he has had an opportunity to investigate the case, or he may wish to be present with his client during any police questioning. In doing so an attorney is merely exercising the good professional judgment he has been taught. This is not cause for considering the attorney a menace to law enforcement. He is merely carrying out what he is sworn to do under his oath—to protect to the extent of his ability the rights of his client. In fulfilling this responsibility the attorney plays a vital role in the administration of criminal justice under our Constitution.

In announcing these principles, we are not unmindful of the burdens which law enforcement officials must bear, often under trying circumstances. We also fully recognize the obligation of all citizens to aid in enforcing the criminal laws. This Court, while protecting individual rights, has always given ample latitude to law enforcement agencies in the legitimate exercise of their duties. The limits we have placed on the interrogation process should not constitute an undue interference with a proper system of law enforcement. As we have noted, our decision does not in any way preclude police from carrying out their traditional investigatory functions. Although confessions may play an important role in some convictions, the cases before us present graphic examples of the overstatement of the 'need' for confessions. In each case authorities conducted interrogations ranging up to five days in duration despite the presence, through standard investigating practices, of considerable evidence against each defendant. Further examples are chronicled in our prior cases.

It is also urged that an unfettered right to detention for interrogation should be allowed because it will often redound to the benefit of the person questioned. When police inquiry determines that there is no reason to believe that the person has committed any crime, it is said, he will be released without need for further formal procedures. The person who has committed no offense, however, will be better able to clear himself after warnings with counsel present than without. It can be assumed that in such circumstances a lawyer would advise his client to talk freely to police in order to clear himself.

Custodial interrogation, by contrast, does not necessarily afford the innocent an opportunity to clear themselves. A serious consequence of the present practice of the interrogation alleged to be beneficial for the innocent is that many arrests 'for investigation' subject large numbers of innocent persons to detention and interrogation. In one of the cases before us, No. 584, *California v. Stewart*, police held four persons, who were in the defendant's house at the time of the arrest, in jail for five days until defendant confessed. At that time they were finally released. Police stated that there was "no evidence to connect them with any crime." Available statistics on the extent of this practice where it is condoned indicate that these four are far from alone in being subjected to arrest, prolonged detention, and interrogation without the requisite probable cause.

Over the years the Federal Bureau of Investigation has compiled an exemplary record of effective law enforcement while advising any suspect or arrested person, at the outset of an interview, that he is not required to make a statement, that any statement may be used against him in court, that the individual may obtain the services of an attorney of his own choice and, more recently, that he has a right to free counsel if he is unable to pay. A letter received from the Solicitor General in response to a question from the Bench makes it clear that the present pattern of warnings and respect for the rights of the individual followed as a practice by the FBI is consistent with the procedure which we delineate today. . . .

The practice of the FBI can readily be emulated by state and local enforcement agencies. The argument that the FBI deals with different crimes than are dealt with by state authorities does not mitigate the significance of the FBI experience.

* * *

It is also urged upon us that we withhold decision on this issue until state legislative bodies and advisory groups have had an opportunity to deal with these problems by rule making. We have already pointed out that the Constitution does not require any specific code of procedures for protecting the privilege against self-incrimination during custodial interrogation. Congress and the States are free to develop their own safeguards for the privilege, so long as they are fully as effective as those described above in informing accused persons of their right of silence and in affording a continuous opportunity to exercise it. In any event, however, the issues presented are of constitutional dimensions and must be determined by the courts. The admissibility of a statement in the face of a claim that it was obtained in violation of the defendant's constitutional rights is an issue the resolution of which has long since been undertaken by this Court. Judicial solutions to problems of constitutional dimension have evolved decade by decade. As courts have been presented with the need to enforce constitutional rights, they have found means of doing so. That was our responsibility when *Escobedo* was before us and it is our responsibility today. Where rights secured by the Constitution are involved, there can be no rule making or legislation which would abrogate them.

V

Because of the nature of the problem and because of its recurrent significance in numerous cases, we have to this point discussed the relationship of the Fifth Amendment privilege to police interrogation without specific concentration on the facts of the cases before us. We turn now to these facts to consider the application to these cases of the constitutional principles discussed above. In each instance, we have concluded that statements were obtained from the defendant under circumstances that did not meet constitutional standards for protection of the privilege.

* * *

MR. JUSTICE CLARK, dissenting in Nos. 759, 760, and 761, and concurring in the result in No. 584.

It is with regret that I find it necessary to write in these cases. However, I am unable to join the majority because its opinion goes too far on too little, while my dissenting brethren do not go quite far enough. Nor can I join in the Court's criticism of the present practices of police and investigatory agencies as to custodial interrogation. The materials it refers to as "police manuals" are, as I read them, merely writings in this field by professors and some police officers. Not one is shown by the record here to be the official manual of any police department, much less in universal use in crime detection. Moreover the examples of police brutality mentioned by the Court are rare exceptions to the thousands of cases that appear every year in the law reports. The police agencies—all the way from municipal and state forces to the federal bureaus—are responsible for law enforcement and public safety in this country. I am proud of their efforts, which in my view are not fairly characterized by the Court's opinion.

I

The *ipse dixit* of the majority has no support in our cases. Indeed, the Court admits that "we might not find the defendants' statements (here) to have been involuntary in traditional terms." In short, the Court has added more to the requirements that the accused is entitled to consult with his lawyer and that he must be given the traditional warning that he may remain silent and that anything that he says may be used against him. *Escobedo v. State of Illinois*, 378 U.S. 478, 490–491 (1964). Now, the Court fashions a constitutional rule that the police may engage in no custodial interrogation without additionally advising the accused that he has a right under the Fifth Amendment to the presence of counsel during interrogation and that, if he is without funds, counsel will be furnished him. When at any point during an interrogation the accused seeks affirmatively or impliedly to invoke his rights to silence or counsel, interrogation must be forgone or postponed. The Court further holds that failure to follow the new procedures requires inexorably the exclusion of any statement by the accused, as well as the fruits thereof. Such a strict constitutional specific inserted at the nerve center of crime detection may well kill the patient. Since there is at this time a paucity of information and an almost total lack of empirical knowledge on the practical operation of requirements truly comparable to those announced by the majority, I would be more restrained lest we go too far too fast.

* * *

III

Rather than employing the arbitrary Fifth Amendment rule which the Court lays down I would follow the more pliable dictates of the Due Process Clauses of the Fifth and Fourteenth Amendments which we are accustomed to administering and which we know from our cases are effective instruments in protecting persons in police custody. In this way we would not be acting in the dark nor in one full sweep changing the traditional rules of custodial interrogation which this Court has for so long recognized as a justifiable and proper tool in balancing individual rights against the rights of society. It will be soon enough to go further when we are able to appraise with somewhat better accuracy the effect of such a holding.

* * *

MR. JUSTICE HARLAN, whom MR. JUSTICE STEWART and MR. JUSTICE WHITE join, dissenting.

I believe the decision of the Court represents poor constitutional law and entails harmful consequences for the country at large. How serious these consequences may prove to be only time can tell. But the basic flaws in the Court's justification seem to me readily apparent now once all sides of the problem are considered.

I. INTRODUCTION.

At the outset, it is well to note exactly what is required by the Court's new constitutional code of rules for confessions. The foremost requirement, upon which later admissibility of a confession depends, is that a fourfold warning be given to a person in custody before he is questioned, namely, that he has a right to remain silent, that anything he says may be used against him, that he has a right to have present an attorney during the questioning, and that if indigent he has a right to a lawyer without charge. To forgo these rights, some affirmative statement of rejection is seemingly required, and threats, tricks, or cajolings to obtain this waiver are forbidden. If before or during questioning the suspect seeks to invoke his right to remain silent, interrogation must be forgone or cease; a request for counsel brings about the same result until a lawyer is procured. Finally, there are a miscellany of minor directives, for example, the burden of proof of waiver is on the State, admissions and exculpatory statements are treated just like confessions, withdrawal of a waiver is always permitted, and so forth.

While the fine points of this scheme are far less clear than the Court admits, the tenor is quite apparent. The new rules are not designed to guard against police brutality or other unmistakably banned forms of coercion. Those who use third-degree tactics and deny them in court are equally able and destined to lie as skillfully about warnings and waivers. Rather, the thrust of the new rules is to negate all pressures, to reinforce the nervous or ignorant suspect, and ultimately to discourage any confession at all. The aim in short is toward "voluntariness" in a utopian sense, or to view it from a different angle, voluntariness with a vengeance.

To incorporate this notion into the Constitution requires a strained reading of history and precedent and a disregard of the very pragmatic concerns that alone may on occasion justify such strains. I believe that reasoned examination will show that the Due Process Clauses provide an adequate tool for coping with confessions and that, even if the Fifth Amendment privilege against self-incrimination be invoked, its precedents taken as a whole do not sustain the present rules. Viewed as a choice based on pure policy, these new rules prove to be a highly debatable, if not one-sided, appraisal of the competing interests, imposed over widespread objection, at the very time when judicial restraint is most called for by the circumstances.

II. CONSTITUTIONAL PREMISES.

* * *

I turn now to the Court's asserted reliance on the Fifth Amendment, an approach which I frankly regard as a *trompe l'oeil*. The Court's opinion in my view reveals no adequate basis for extending the Fifth Amendment's privilege against self-incrimination to the police station. Far more important, it fails to show that the Court's new rules are well supported, let alone compelled, by Fifth Amendment precedents. Instead, the new rules actually derive from quotation and analogy drawn from precedents under the Sixth Amendment, which should properly have no bearing on police interrogation.

* * *

Having decided that the Fifth Amendment privilege does apply in the police station, the Court reveals that the privilege imposes more exacting restrictions than does the Fourteenth Amendment's voluntariness test. It then emerges from a discussion of *Escobedo* that the Fifth Amendment requires for an admissible confession that it be given by one distinctly aware of his right not to speak and shielded from "the compelling atmosphere" of interrogation. From these key premises, the Court finally develops the safeguards of warning, counsel, and so forth. I do not believe these premises are sustained by precedents under the Fifth Amendment.

The more important premise is that pressure on the suspect must be eliminated though it be only the subtle influence of the atmosphere and surroundings. The Fifth Amendment, however, has never been thought to forbid all pressure to incriminate one's self in the situations covered by it. On the contrary, it has been held that failure to incriminate one's self can result in denial of removal of one's case from state to federal court, in refusal of a military commission, in denial of a discharge in bankruptcy, and in numerous other adverse consequences. This is not to say that short of jail or torture any sanction is permissible in any case; policy and history alike may impose sharp limits. However, the Court's unspoken assumption that any pressure violates the privilege is not supported by the precedents and it has failed to show why the Fifth Amendment prohibits that relatively mild pressure the Due Process Clause permits.

The Court appears similarly wrong in thinking that precise knowledge of one's rights is a settled prerequisite under the Fifth Amendment to the loss of its protections. A number of lower federal court cases have held that grand jury witnesses need not always be warned of their privilege, and Wigmore states this to be the better rule for trial witnesses. No Fifth Amendment precedent is cited for the Court's contrary view. There might of course be reasons apart from Fifth Amendment precedent for requiring warning or any other safeguard on questioning but that is a different matter entirely.

* * *

The only attempt in this Court to carry the right to counsel into the station house occurred in *Escobedo*, the Court repeating several times that that stage was no less "critical" than trial itself. This is hardly persuasive when we consider that a grand jury inquiry, the filing of a certiorari petition, and certainly the purchase of narcotics by an undercover agent from a prospective defendant may all be equally "critical" yet provision of counsel and advice on the score have never been thought compelled by the Constitution in such cases. The sound reason why this right is so freely extended for a criminal trial is the severe injustice risked by confronting an untrained defendant with a range of technical points of law, evidence, and tactics familiar to the prosecutor but not to himself. This danger shrinks markedly in the police station where indeed the lawyer in fulfilling his professional responsibilities of necessity may become an obstacle to truthfinding. The Court's summary citation of the Sixth Amendment cases here seems to me best described as "the domino method of constitutional adjudication * * * wherein every explanatory statement in a previous opinion is made the basis for extension to a wholly different situation." [Friendly, *The Bill of Rights as a Code of Criminal Procedure*, 53 Calif. L. Rev. 929, 950 (1965)].

III. POLICY CONSIDERATIONS.

* * *

Without at all subscribing to the generally black picture of police conduct painted by the Court, I think it must be frankly recognized at the outset that police questioning allowable under due process precedents may inherently entail some pressure on the suspect and may seek advantage in his ignorance or weaknesses. The atmosphere and questioning techniques, proper and fair though they be, can in themselves exert a tug on the suspect to confess, and in this light "(t)o speak of any confessions of crime made after arrest as being 'voluntary' or 'uncoerced' is somewhat inaccurate, although traditional. A confession is wholly and incontestably voluntary only if a guilty person gives himself up to the law and becomes his own accuser." *Ashcraft v. State of Tennessee*, 322 U.S. 143, 161 (Jackson, J., dissenting). Until today, the role of the Constitution has been only to sift out undue pressure, not to assure spontaneous confessions.

The Court's new rules aim to offset these minor pressures and disadvantages intrinsic to any kind of police interrogation. The rules do not serve due process interests in preventing blatant coercion since, as I noted earlier, they do nothing to contain the policeman who is prepared to lie from the start. The rules work for reliability in confessions almost only in the Pickwickian sense that they can prevent some from being given at all.[12] In short, the benefit of this new regime is simply to lessen or wipe out the inherent compulsion and inequalities to which the Court devotes some nine pages of description.

What the Court largely ignores is that its rules impair, if they will not eventually serve wholly to frustrate, an instrument of law enforcement that has long and quite reasonably been thought worth the price paid for it.[13] There can be little doubt that the Court's new code would markedly decrease the number of confessions. To warn the suspect that he may remain silent and remind him that his confession may be used in court are minor obstructions. To require also an express waiver by the suspect and an end to questioning whenever he demurs must heavily handicap questioning. And to suggest or provide counsel for the suspect simply invites the end of the interrogation.

* * *

[12] The Court's vision of a lawyer "mitigat(ing) the dangers of untrustworthiness" by witnessing coercion and assisting accuracy in the confession is largely a fancy; for if counsel arrives, there is rarely going to be a police station confession.

[13] This need is, of course, what makes so misleading the Court's comparison of a probate judge readily setting aside as involuntary the will of an old lady badgered and beleaguered by the new heirs. With wills, there is no public interest save in a totally free choice; with confessions, the solution of crime is a countervailing gain, however the balance is resolved.

IV. CONCLUSIONS.

* * *

In conclusion: Nothing in the letter or the spirit of the Constitution or in the precedents squares with the heavy-handed and one-sided action that is so precipitously taken by the Court in the name of fulfulling its constitutional responsibilities. The foray which the Court makes today brings to mind the wise and farsighted words of Mr. Justice Jackson in *Douglas v. City of Jeannette*, 319 U.S. 157, 181 (separate opinion): "This Court is forever adding new stories to the temples of constitutional law, and the temples have a way of collapsing when one story too many is added."

MR. JUSTICE WHITE, with whom MR. JUSTICE HARLAN and MR. JUSTICE STEWART join, dissenting.

* * *

II

That the Court's holding today is neither compelled nor even strongly suggested by the language of the Fifth Amendment, is at odds with American and English legal history, and involves a departure from a long line of precedent does not prove either that the Court has exceeded its powers or that the Court is wrong or unwise in its present reinterpretation of the Fifth Amendment. It does, however, underscore the obvious—that the Court has not discovered or found the law in making today's decision, nor has it derived it from some irrefutable sources; what it has done is to make new law and new public policy in much the same way that it has in the course of interpreting other great clauses of the Constitution. This is what the Court historically has done. Indeed, it is what it must do and will continue to do until and unless there is some fundamental change in the constitutional distribution of governmental powers.

But if the Court is here and now to announce new and fundamental policy to govern certain aspects of our affairs, it is wholly legitimate to examine the mode of this or any other constitutional decision in this Court and to inquire into the advisability of its end product in terms of the long-range interest of the country. At the very least, the Court's text and reasoning should withstand analysis and be a fair exposition of the constitutional provision which its opinion interprets. Decisions like these cannot rest alone on syllogism, metaphysics or some ill-defined notions of natural justice, although each will perhaps play its part. In proceeding to such constructions as it now announces, the Court should also duly consider all the factors and interests bearing upon the cases, at least insofar as the relevant materials are available; and if the necessary considerations are not treated in the record or obtainable from some other reliable source, the Court should not proceed to formulate fundamental policies based on speculation alone.

III

First, we may inquire what are the textual and factual bases of this new fundamental rule. To reach the result announced on the grounds it does, the Court must stay within the confines of the Fifth Amendment, which forbids self-incrimination only if compelled. Hence the core of the Court's opinion is that because of the "compulsion inherent in custodial surroundings, no statement obtained from (a) defendant (in custody) can truly be the product of his free choice," absent the use of adequate protective devices as described by the Court. However, the Court does not point to any sudden inrush of new knowledge requiring the rejection of 70 years' experience. Nor does it assert that its novel conclusion reflects a changing consensus among state courts, see *Mapp v. Ohio*, 367 U.S. 643, or that a succession of cases had steadily eroded the old rule and proved it unworkable, see *Gideon v. Wainwright*, 372 U.S. 335. Rather than asserting new knowledge, the Court concedes that it cannot truly know what occurs during custodial questioning, because of the innate secrecy of such proceedings. It extrapolates a picture of what it conceives to be the norm from police investigatorial manuals, published in 1959 and 1962 or earlier, without any attempt to allow for adjustments in police practices that may have occurred in the wake of more recent decisions of state appellate tribunals or this Court. But even if the relentless application of the described procedures could lead to involuntary confessions, it most assuredly does not follow that each and every case will disclose this kind of interrogation or this kind of consequence. Insofar as appears from the Court's opinion, it has not examined a single transcript of any police interrogation, let alone the interrogation that took place in any one of these cases which it decides today. Judged by any of the standards for empirical investigation utilized in the social sciences the factual basis for the Court's premise is patently inadequate.

Although in the Court's view in-custody interrogation is inherently coercive, the Court says that the spontaneous product of the coercion of arrest and detention is still to be deemed voluntary. An accused, arrested on probable cause, may blurt out a confession which will be admissible despite the fact that he is alone and in custody, without any showing that he had any notion of his right to remain silent or of the consequences of his admission. Yet, under the Court's rule, if the police ask him a single question such as "Do you have anything to say?" or "Did you kill your wife?" his response, if there is one, has somehow been compelled, even if the accused has been clearly warned of his right to remain silent. Common sense informs us to the contrary. While one may say that the response was "involuntary" in the sense the question provoked or was the occasion for the response and thus the defendant was induced to speak out when he might have remained silent if not arrested and not questioned, it is patently unsound to say the response is compelled.

Today's result would not follow even if it were agreed that to some extent custodial interrogation is inherently coercive. The test has been whether the totality of circumstances deprived the defendant of a "free choice to admit, to deny, or to refuse to answer," and whether physical or psychological coercion was of such a degree that "the defendant's will was overborne at the time he confessed." The duration and nature of incommunicado custody, the presence or absence of advice concerning the defendant's constitutional rights, and the granting or refusal of requests to communicate with lawyers, relatives or friends have all been rightly regarded as important data bearing on the basic inquiry.[3] But it has never been suggested, until today, that such questioning was so coercive and accused persons so lacking in hardihood that the very first response to the very first question following the commencement of custody must be conclusively presumed to be the product of an overborne will.

If the rule announced today were truly based on a conclusion that all confessions resulting from custodial interrogation are coerced, then it would simply have no rational foundation. *A fortiori* that would be true of the extension of the rule to exculpatory statements, which the Court effects after a brief discussion of why, in the Court's view, they must be deemed incriminatory but without any discussion of why they must be deemed coerced. Even if one were to postulate that the Court's concern is not that all confessions induced by police interrogation are coerced but rather that some such confessions are coerced and present judicial procedures are believed to be inadequate to identify the confessions that are coerced and those that are not, it would still not be essential to impose the rule that the Court has now fashioned. Transcripts or observers could be required, specific time limits, tailored to fit the cause, could be imposed, or other devices could be utilized to reduce the chances that otherwise indiscernible coercion will produce an inadmissible confession.

On the other hand, even if one assumed that there was an adequate factual basis for the conclusion that all confessions obtained during in-custody interrogation are the product of compulsion, the rule propounded by the Court will still be irrational, for, apparently, it is only if the accused is also warned of his right to counsel and waives both that right and the right against self-incrimination that the inherent compulsiveness of interrogation disappears. But if the defendant may not answer without a warning a question such as "Where were you last night?" without having his answer be a compelled one, how can the Court ever accept his negative answer to the question of whether he wants to consult his retained counsel

---

[3] By contrast, the Court indicates that in applying this new rule it "will not pause to inquire in individual cases whether the defendant was aware of his rights without a warning being given." The reason given is that assessment of the knowledge of the defendant based on information as to age, education, intelligence, or prior contact with authorities can never be more than speculation, while a warning is a clear-cut fact. But the officers' claim that they gave the requisite warnings may be disputed, and facts respecting the defendant's prior experience may be undisputed and be of such a nature as to virtually preclude any doubt that the defendant knew of his rights.

or counsel whom the court will appoint? And why if counsel is present and the accused nevertheless confesses, or counsel tells the accused to tell the truth, and that is what the accused does, is the situation any less coercive insofar as the accused is concerned? The Court apparently realizes its dilemma of foreclosing questioning without the necessary warnings but at the same time permitting the accused, sitting in the same chair in front of the same policemen, to waive his right to consult an attorney. It expects, however, that the accused will not often waive the right; and if it is claimed that he has, the State faces a severe, if not impossible burden of proof.

* * *

IV

Criticism of the Court's opinion, however, cannot stop with a demonstration that the factual and textual bases for the rule it propounds are, at best, less than compelling. Equally relevant is an assessment of the rule's consequences measured against community values. The Court's duty to assess the consequences of its action is not satisfied by the utterance of the truth that a value of our system of criminal justice is "to respect the inviolability of the human personality" and to require government to produce the evidence against the accused by its own independent labors. More than the human dignity of the accused is involved; the human personality of others in the society must also be preserved. Thus the values reflected by the privilege are not the sole desideratum; society's interest in the general security is of equal weight.

The obvious underpinning of the Court's decision is a deep-seated distrust of all confessions. As the Court declares that the accused may not be interrogated without counsel present, absent a waiver of the right to counsel, and as the Court all but admonishes the lawyer to advise the accused to remain silent, the result adds up to a judicial judgment that evidence from the accused should not be used against him in any way, whether compelled or not. This is the not so subtle overtone of the opinion—that it is inherently wrong for the police to gather evidence from the accused himself. And this is precisely the nub of this dissent. I see nothing wrong or immoral, and certainly nothing unconstitutional, in the police's asking a suspect whom they have reasonable cause to arrest whether or not he killed his wife or in confronting him with the evidence on which the arrest was based, at least where he has been plainly advised that he may remain completely silent. Until today, "the admissions or confessions of the prisoner, when voluntarily and freely made, have always ranked high in the scale of incriminating evidence." Particularly when corroborated, as where the police have confirmed the accused's disclosure of the hiding place of implements or fruits of the crime, such confessions have the highest reliability and significantly contribute to the certitude with which we may believe the accused is guilty. Moreover, it is by no means certain that the process of confessing is injurious to the accused. To the contrary it may provide psychological relief and enhance the prospects for rehabilitation.

This is not to say that the value of respect for the inviolability of the accused's individual personality should be accorded no weight or that all confessions should be indiscriminately admitted. This Court has long read the Constitution to proscribe compelled confessions, a salutary rule from which there should be no retreat. But I see no sound basis, factual or otherwise, and the Court gives none, for concluding that the present rule against the receipt of coerced confessions is inadequate for the task of sorting out inadmissible evidence and must be replaced by the *per se* rule which is now imposed. Even if the new concept can be said to have advantages of some sort over the present law, they are far outweighed by its likely undesirable impact on other very relevant and important interests.

* * *

In some unknown number of cases the Court's rule will return a killer, a rapist or other criminal to the streets and to the environment which produced him, to repeat his crime whenever it pleases him. As a consequence, there will not be a gain, but a loss, in human dignity. The real concern is not the unfortunate consequences of this new decision on the criminal law as an abstract, disembodied series of authoritative proscriptions, but the impact on those who rely on the public authority for protection and who without it can only engage in violent self-help with guns, knives and the help of their neighbors similarly inclined. There is, of course, a saving factor: the next victims are uncertain, unnamed and unrepresented in this case.

Nor can this decision do other than have a corrosive effect on the criminal laws as an effective device to prevent crime. A major component in its effectiveness in this regard is its swift and sure enforcement. The easier it is to get away with rape and murder, the less the deterrent effect on those who are inclined to attempt it. This is still good common sense. If it were not, we should posthaste liquidate the whole law enforcement establishment as a useless, misguided effort to control human conduct.

And what about the accused who has confessed or would confess in response to simple, noncoercive questioning and whose guilt could not otherwise be proved? Is it so clear that release is the best thing for him in every case? Has it so unquestionably been resolved that in each and every case it would be better for him not to confess and to return to his environment with no attempt whatsoever to help him? I think not. It may well be that in many cases it will be no less than a callous disregard for his own welfare as well as for the interests of his next victim.

There is another aspect to the effect of the Court's rule on the person whom the police have arrested on probable cause. The fact is that he may not be guilty at all and may be able to extricate himself quickly and simply if he were told the circumstances of his arrest and were asked to explain. This effort, and his release, must now await the hiring of a lawyer or his appointment by the court, consultation with counsel and then a session with the police or the prosecutor. Similarly, where probable cause exists to arrest several suspects, as where the body of the victim is discovered in a house having several residents, it will often be true that a suspect may be cleared only through the results of interrogation of other suspects. Here too the release of the innocent may be delayed by the Court's rule.

* * *

Points for Discussion

1. Why is *Miranda* decided under the Fifth Amendment's prohibition on compelled self-incrimination rather than the Sixth Amendment's right to the assistance of counsel? Isn't the latter a more appropriate place to find a right to counsel?

2. Do you find the Court's explanation of the basis for *Escobedo* to be compelling? Why is the Court unwilling to simply overturn that decision?

3. Justice Clark's and Justice White's opinions argue that the Court's totality-of-the-circumstances test for the voluntariness of confessions should be the only standard used to determine their admissibility. In *United States v. Dickerson*, excerpted in Chapter 9, we see the Court take up this argument again, more than 30 years after *Miranda* was decided.

4. Justice White's dissent posits that, even if the problem were that "present judicial procedures are believed to be inadequate to identify the confessions that are coerced and those that are not, it would still not be essential to impose the rule that the Court has now fashioned. Transcripts or observers could be required, specific time limits, tailored to fit the cause, could be imposed or other devices could be utilized . . . ." Whatever the feasibility of taping police interrogations in 1966, it is now indisputably cheap and easy to video and audio record them. Yet few states require recording of interrogations. The Supreme Court of Alaska held, pursuant to the right to due process under Alaska's constitution, that interrogations must be recorded. *Stephan v. Alaska,* 711 P.2d 1156 (Ala. 1985). Other states, such as Minnesota and Wisconsin, have invoked their supervisory powers to mandate that interrogations be recorded. *See Minnesota v. Scales*, 518 N.W.2d 587 (Minn. 1994); *In re Jerrell C.J.*, 699 N.W.2d 110 (Wis. 2005) (limiting holding to interrogations of juveniles). In other jurisdictions, the question is governed by statute. *See, e.g.*, D.C. Code § 5–116.01; 725 Ill. Comp. State. Ann. 5/103–2.1; N.C. Gen. Stat. § 15A–211; N.J. Crim. Prac. R. 3:17.

Indiana added a rule of evidence in 2011 that excludes unrecorded confessions in felony cases (subject to certain exceptions). *See* IND. R. EVID. 617. In 2010, the Uniform Law Commission proposed a Uniform Electronic Recordation of Custodial Interrogations Act, leading the military to also consider recording requirements for some investigations. *See* Andrew E. Taslitz, *High Expectations and Some Wounded Hopes: The Policy and Politics of A Uniform Statute on Videotaping Custodial Interrogations*, 7 NW. J. L. & SOC. POL'Y 400, 408–09 (2012). For an examination of the states' recording requirements, *see* Alan M. Gershel, *A Review of the Law in Jurisdictions Requiring Electronic Recording of Custodial Interrogations*, 16 RICH. J.L. & TECH. 9 (2010).

One rationale for not mandating the recording of interrogations is the chilling effect those recordings will have on obtaining confessions. *See Connecticut v. Lockhart*, 4 A.3d 1176, 1195 (Conn. 2010). *Washington v. Aldrich*, 135 Wash. App. 1017 (Wash. App. Div. 1 2006). Is this reasoning sound? Or does it further support the argument that recording should be required to protect those in custody? As videotaping becomes more ubiquitous, will jurors becomes less accepting of police officers' assertions that they did not tape interrogations because it was not their policy to do so? *See Iowa v. Hajtic*, 724 N.W.2d 449 (Iowa 2006).

FELLERS V. UNITED STATES

540 U.S. 519 (2004)

JUSTICE O'CONNOR delivered the opinion of the court.

* * *

I

On February 24, 2000, after a grand jury indicted petitioner for conspiracy to distribute methamphetamine, Lincoln Police Sergeant Michael Garnett and Lancaster County Deputy Sheriff Jeff Bliemeister went to petitioner's home in Lincoln, Nebraska, to arrest him. The officers knocked on petitioner's door and, when petitioner answered, identified themselves and asked if they could come in. Petitioner invited the officers into his living room.

The officers advised petitioner they had come to discuss his involvement in methamphetamine distribution. They informed petitioner that they had a federal warrant for his arrest and that a grand jury had indicted him for conspiracy to distribute methamphetamine. The officers told petitioner that the indictment referred to his involvement with certain individuals, four of whom they named. Petitioner then told the officers that he knew the four people and had used methamphetamine during his association with them.

After spending about 15 minutes in petitioner's home, the officers transported petitioner to the Lancaster County jail. There, the officers advised petitioner for the first time of his rights under *Miranda v. Arizona,* 384 U.S. 436 (1966), and *Patterson v. Illinois,* 487 U.S. 285 (1988). Petitioner and the two officers signed a *Miranda* waiver form, and petitioner then reiterated the inculpatory statements he had made earlier, admitted to having associated with other individuals implicated in the charged conspiracy and admitted to having loaned money to one of them even though he suspected that she was involved in drug transactions.

* * *

Following a jury trial at which petitioner's jailhouse statements were admitted into evidence, petitioner was convicted of conspiring to possess with intent to distribute methamphetamine. Petitioner appealed, arguing that his jailhouse statements should have been suppressed as fruits of the statements obtained at his home in violation of the Sixth Amendment. . . .

* * *

II

The Sixth Amendment right to counsel is triggered "at or after the time that judicial proceedings have been initiated . . . 'whether by way of formal charge, preliminary hearing, indictment, information, or arraignment.'" *Brewer v. Williams*, 430 U.S. 387, 398 (1977) (quoting *Kirby v. Illinois,* 406 U.S. 682 (1972)). We have held that an accused is denied "the basic protections" of the Sixth Amendment "when there [is] used against him at his trial evidence of his own incriminating words, which federal agents . . . deliberately elicited from him after he had been indicted and in the absence of his counsel." *Massiah v. United States,* 377 U.S. 201, 206 (1964); cf. *Patterson v. Illinois* (holding that the Sixth Amendment does not bar postindictment questioning in the absence of counsel if a defendant waives the right to counsel).

* * *

The Court of Appeals erred in holding that the absence of an "interrogation" foreclosed petitioner's claim that the jailhouse statements should have been suppressed as fruits of the statements taken from petitioner at his home. First, there is no question that the officers in this case "deliberately elicited" information from petitioner. Indeed, the officers, upon arriving at petitioner's house, informed him that their purpose in coming was to discuss his involvement in the distribution of methamphetamine and his association with certain charged co-conspirators. Because the ensuing discussion took place after petitioner had been indicted, outside the presence of counsel, and in the absence of any waiver of petitioner's Sixth Amendment rights, the Court of Appeals erred in holding that the officers' actions did not violate the Sixth Amendment standards established in *Massiah* and its progeny.

Second, because of its erroneous determination that petitioner was not questioned in violation of Sixth Amendment standards, the Court of Appeals improperly conducted its "fruits" analysis under the Fifth Amendment. Specifically, it applied *Elstad* to hold that the admissibility of the jailhouse statements turns solely on whether the statements were

" 'knowingly and voluntarily made.' " The Court of Appeals did not reach the question whether the Sixth Amendment requires suppression of petitioner's jailhouse statements on the ground that they were the fruits of previous questioning conducted in violation of the Sixth Amendment deliberate-elicitation standard. We have not had occasion to decide whether the rationale of *Elstad* applies when a suspect makes incriminating statements after a knowing and voluntary waiver of his right to counsel notwithstanding earlier police questioning in violation of Sixth Amendment standards. We therefore remand to the Court of Appeals to address this issue in the first instance.

Points for Discussion

1. This short unanimous opinion makes clear that the *Massiah* decision provides protection that is different from that afforded by *Miranda*. Why was this still unclear as late as 2004?

CHAPTER 7

THE RIGHT TO COUNSEL

■ ■ ■

The right to counsel guaranteed by the Sixth Amendment has been read to require counsel in any trial in which a sentence of imprisonment is ultimately imposed, *Argersinger v. Hamlin*, 407 U.S. 25 (1972), and any appeal that is afforded by the state as of right, *Douglas v. California*, 372 U.S. 353 (1963). The Amendment guarantees the right not just to have counsel present during these proceedings but to the *effective* assistance of counsel. The Supreme Court has held that a defendant is denied effective assistance when his counsel does not meet a minimum, objective standard of competency and there is a reasonable probability that competent counsel would have obtained a more favorable result. *Strickland v. Washington*, 466 U.S. 668 (1984).

However, as we have already seen, the Sixth Amendment does not guarantee counsel only during trial and appeal. Rather, it states that a defendant shall enjoy the right to counsel in all "criminal prosecutions." The Supreme Court has read this language to guarantee counsel before trial, during the investigative stage of a criminal case. Although the Supreme Court held in *Escobedo* that the Sixth Amendment is triggered when the police focus on a single individual, it has since backed away from this principle. Today, a defendant is entitled to counsel after "the commencement of adversary proceedings" against him. As the Court wrote in *Maine v. Moulton*, 474 U.S. 159 (1985):

> Recognizing that the right to the assistance of counsel is shaped by the need for the assistance of counsel, we have found that the right attaches at earlier, "critical" stages in the criminal justice process "where the results might well settle the accused's fate and reduce the trial itself to a mere formality." And, "[w]hatever else it may mean, the right to counsel granted by the Sixth and Fourteenth Amendments means at least that a person is entitled to the help of a lawyer at or after the time that judicial proceedings have been initiated against him. . . ." This is because, after the initiation of adversary criminal proceedings, " 'the government has committed itself to prosecute, and . . . the adverse positions of government and defendant have solidified. It is then that a defendant finds himself faced with the prosecutorial forces of organized society, and immersed in the intricacies of substantive and procedural criminal law.' "

In this chapter we investigate the scope of this pre-trial right to counsel.

A. "DELIBERATELY ELICITED"

BREWER V. WILLIAMS

430 U.S. 387 (1977)

MR. JUSTICE STEWART delivered the opinion of the court.

An Iowa trial jury found the respondent, Robert Williams, guilty of murder. The judgment of conviction was affirmed in the Iowa Supreme Court by a closely divided vote. In a subsequent habeas corpus proceeding a Federal District Court ruled that under the United States Constitution Williams is entitled to a new trial, and a divided Court of Appeals for the Eighth Circuit agreed. The question before us is whether the District Court and the Court of Appeals were wrong.

I

On the afternoon of December 24, 1968, a 10-year-old girl named Pamela Powers went with her family to the YMCA in Des Moines, Iowa, to watch a wrestling tournament in which her brother was participating. When she failed to return from a trip to the washroom, a search for her began. The search was unsuccessful.

Robert Williams, who had recently escaped from a mental hospital, was a resident of the YMCA. Soon after the girl's disappearance Williams was seen in the YMCA lobby carrying some clothing and a large bundle wrapped in a blanket. He obtained help from a 14-year-old boy in opening the street door of the YMCA and the door to his automobile parked outside. When Williams placed the bundle in the front seat of his car the boy "saw two legs in it and they were skinny and white." Before anyone could see what was in the bundle Williams drove away. His abandoned car was found the following day in Davenport, Iowa, roughly 160 miles east of Des Moines. A warrant was then issued in Des Moines for his arrest on a charge of abduction.

On the morning of December 26, a Des Moines lawyer named Henry McKnight went to the Des Moines police station and informed the officers present that he had just received a long-distance call from Williams, and that he had advised Williams to turn himself in to the Davenport police. Williams did surrender that morning to the police in Davenport, and they booked him on the charge specified in the arrest warrant and gave him the warnings required by *Miranda v. Arizona*. The Davenport police then telephoned their counterparts in Des Moines to inform them that Williams had surrendered. McKnight, the lawyer, was still at the Des Moines police headquarters, and Williams conversed with McKnight on the telephone. In the presence of the Des Moines chief of police and a police detective named Leaming, McKnight advised Williams that Des Moines police officers would be driving to Davenport to pick him up, that the officers would not interrogate him or mistreat him, and that Williams was not to talk to the officers about Pamela Powers until after consulting with McKnight upon his return to Des Moines. As a result of these conversations, it was agreed between McKnight and the Des Moines police officials that Detective Leaming and a fellow officer would drive to Davenport to pick up Williams, that they would bring him directly back to Des Moines, and that they would not question him during the trip.

In the meantime Williams was arraigned before a judge in Davenport on the outstanding arrest warrant. The judge advised him of his Miranda rights and committed him to jail. Before leaving the courtroom, Williams conferred with a lawyer named Kelly, who advised him not to make any statements until consulting with McKnight back in Des Moines.

Detective Leaming and his fellow officer arrived in Davenport about noon to pick up Williams and return him to Des Moines. Soon after their arrival they met with Williams and Kelly, who, they understood, was acting as Williams' lawyer. Detective Leaming repeated the Miranda warnings, and told Williams:

> [W]e both know that you're being represented here by Mr. Kelly and you're being represented by Mr. McKnight in Des Moines, and . . . I want you to remember this because we'll be visiting between here and Des Moines.

Williams then conferred again with Kelly alone, and after this conference Kelly reiterated to Detective Leaming that Williams was not to be questioned about the disappearance of Pamela Powers until after he had consulted with McKnight back in Des Moines. When Leaming expressed some reservations, Kelly firmly stated that the agreement with McKnight was to be carried out that there was to be no interrogation of Williams during the automobile journey to Des Moines. Kelly was denied permission to ride in the police car back to Des Moines with Williams and the two officers.

The two detectives, with Williams in their charge, then set out on the 160-mile drive. At no time during the trip did Williams express a willingness to be interrogated in the absence of an attorney. Instead, he stated several times that "(w)hen I get to Des Moines and see Mr. McKnight, I am going to tell you the whole story." Detective Leaming knew that Williams was a former mental patient, and knew also that he was deeply religious.

The detective and his prisoner soon embarked on a wide-ranging conversation covering a variety of topics, including the subject of religion. Then, not long after leaving Davenport and reaching the interstate highway, Detective Leaming delivered what has been referred to in the briefs and oral arguments as the "Christian burial speech." Addressing Williams as "Reverend," the detective said:

> I want to give you something to think about while we're traveling down the road. . . . Number one, I want you to observe the weather conditions, it's raining, it's sleeting, it's freezing, driving is very treacherous, visibility is poor, it's going to be dark early this evening. They are predicting several inches of snow for tonight, and I feel that you yourself are the only person that knows where this little girl's body is, that you yourself have only been there once, and if you get a snow on top of it you yourself may be unable to find it. And, since we will be going right past the area on the way into Des Moines, I feel that we could stop and locate the body, that the parents of this little girl should be entitled to a Christian burial for the little girl who was snatched away from them on Christmas (E)ve and murdered. And I feel we should stop and locate it on the way in rather than waiting until morning and trying to come back out after a snow storm and possibly not being able to find it at all.

Williams asked Detective Leaming why he thought their route to Des Moines would be taking them past the girl's body, and Leaming responded that he knew the body was in the area of Mitchellville a town they would be passing on the way to Des Moines.[1] Leaming then stated: "I do not want you to answer me. I don't want to discuss it any further. Just think about it as we're riding down the road."

As the car approached Grinnell, a town approximately 100 miles west of Davenport, Williams asked whether the police had found the victim's shoes. When Detective Leaming replied that he was unsure, Williams directed the officers to a service station where he said he had left the shoes; a search for them proved unsuccessful. As they continued towards Des Moines, Williams asked whether the police had found the blanket, and directed the officers to a rest area where he said he had disposed of the blanket. Nothing was found. The car continued towards Des Moines, and as it approached Mitchellville, Williams said that he would show the officers where the body was. He then directed the police to the body of Pamela Powers.

Williams was indicted for first-degree murder. Before trial, his counsel moved to suppress all evidence relating to or resulting from any statements Williams had made during the automobile ride from Davenport to Des Moines. After an evidentiary hearing the trial judge denied the motion. He found that "an agreement was made between defense counsel and the police officials to the effect that the Defendant was not to be questioned on the return trip to Des Moines," and that the evidence in question had been

---

1 The fact of the matter, of course, was that Detective Leaming possessed no such knowledge.

elicited from Williams during "a critical stage in the proceedings requiring the presence of counsel on his request." The judge ruled, however, that Williams had "waived his right to have an attorney present during the giving of such information."

* * *

II

* * *

There can be no doubt in the present case that judicial proceedings had been initiated against Williams before the start of the automobile ride from Davenport to Des Moines. A warrant had been issued for his arrest, he had been arraigned on that warrant before a judge in a Davenport courtroom, and he had been committed by the court to confinement in jail. The State does not contend otherwise.

There can be no serious doubt, either, that Detective Leaming deliberately and designedly set out to elicit information from Williams just as surely as and perhaps more effectively than if he had formally interrogated him. Detective Leaming was fully aware before departing for Des Moines that Williams was being represented in Davenport by Kelly and in Des Moines by McKnight. Yet he purposely sought during Williams' isolation from his lawyers to obtain as much incriminating information as possible. Indeed, Detective Leaming conceded as much when he testified at Williams' trial:

> Q. In fact, Captain, whether he was a mental patient or not, you were trying to get all the information you could before he got to his lawyer, weren't you?
>
> A. I was sure hoping to find out where that little girl was, yes, sir.
>
> Q. Well, I'll put it this way: You was (sic) hoping to get all the information you could before Williams got back to McKnight, weren't you?
>
> A. Yes, sir.

The state courts clearly proceeded upon the hypothesis that Detective Leaming's "Christian burial speech" had been tantamount to interrogation. Both courts recognized that Williams had been entitled to the assistance of counsel at the time he made the incriminating statements. Yet no such constitutional protection would have come into play if there had been no interrogation.

The circumstances of this case are thus constitutionally indistinguishable from those presented in *Massiah v. United States*. The petitioner in that case was indicted for violating the federal narcotics law. He retained a lawyer, pleaded not guilty, and was released on bail. While he was free on bail a federal agent succeeded by surreptitious means in listening to incriminating statements made by him. Evidence of these statements was introduced against the petitioner at his trial, and he was convicted. This Court reversed the conviction, holding "that the petitioner was denied the basic protections of that guarantee (the right to counsel) when there was used against him at his trial evidence of his own incriminating words, which federal agents had deliberately elicited from him after he had been indicted and in the absence of his counsel."

That the incriminating statements were elicited surreptitiously in the *Massiah* case, and otherwise here, is constitutionally irrelevant. Rather, the clear rule of *Massiah* is that once adversary proceedings have commenced against an individual, he has a right to legal representation when the government interrogates him.[8]

It thus requires no wooden or technical application of the *Massiah* doctrine to conclude that Williams was entitled to the assistance of counsel guaranteed to him by the Sixth and Fourteenth Amendments.

III

* * *

The District Court and the Court of Appeals were correct in the view that the question of waiver was not a question of historical fact, but one which, in the words of Mr. Justice Frankfurter, requires "application of constitutional principles to the facts as found . . . ." *Brown v. Allen*, 344 U.S. 443, 507 [(1953)] (separate opinion).

The District Court and the Court of Appeals were also correct in their understanding of the proper standard to be applied in determining the question of waiver as a matter of federal constitutional law—that it was incumbent upon the State to prove "an intentional relinquishment or abandonment of a known right or privilege." *Johnson v. Zerbst*, 304 U.S. [458, 464 (1938)]. That standard has been reiterated in many cases. We have said that the right to counsel does not depend upon a request by the defendant and that courts indulge in every reasonable presumption against waiver. This strict standard applies equally to an alleged waiver of the right to counsel whether at trial or at a critical stage of pretrial proceedings.

---

8 The only other significant factual difference between the present case and *Massiah* is that here the police had agreed that they would not interrogate Williams in the absence of his counsel. This circumstances plainly provides petitioner with no argument for distinguishing away the protection afforded by *Massiah*.

It is argued that this agreement may not have been an enforceable one. But we do not deal here with notions of offer, acceptance, consideration, or other concepts of the law of contracts. We deal with constitutional law. And every court that has looked at this case has found an "agreement" in the sense of a commitment made by the Des Moines police officers that Williams would not be questioned about Pamela Powers in the absence of his counsel.

We conclude, finally that the Court of Appeals was correct in holding that, judged by these standards, the record in this case falls far short of sustaining petitioner's burden. It is true that Williams had been informed of and appeared to understand his right to counsel. But waiver requires not merely comprehension but relinquishment, and Williams' consistent reliance upon the advice of counsel in dealing with the authorities refutes any suggestion that he waived that right. He consulted McKnight by long-distance telephone before turning himself in. He spoke with McKnight by telephone again shortly after being booked. After he was arraigned, Williams sought out and obtained legal advice from Kelly. Williams again consulted with Kelly after Detective Leaming and his fellow officer arrived in Davenport. Throughout, Williams was advised not to make any statements before seeing McKnight in Des Moines, and was assured that the police had agreed not to question him. His statements while in the car that he would tell the whole story after seeing McKnight in Des Moines were the clearest expressions by Williams himself that he desired the presence of an attorney before any interrogation took place. But even before making these statements, Williams had effectively asserted his right to counsel by having secured attorneys at both ends of the automobile trip, both of whom, acting as his agents, had made clear to the police that no interrogation was to occur during the journey. Williams knew of that agreement and, particularly in view of his consistent reliance on counsel, there is no basis for concluding that he disavowed it.

Despite Williams' express and implicit assertions of his right to counsel, Detective Leaming proceeded to elicit incriminating statements from Williams. Leaming did not preface this effort by telling Williams that he had a right to the presence of a lawyer, and made no effort at all to ascertain whether Williams wished to relinquish that right. The circumstances of record in this case thus provide no reasonable basis for finding that Williams waived his right to the assistance of counsel.

The Court of Appeals did not hold, nor do we, that under the circumstances of this case Williams could not, without notice to counsel, have waived his rights under the Sixth and Fourteenth Amendments. It only held, as do we, that he did not.

IV

The crime of which Williams was convicted was senseless and brutal, calling for swift and energetic action by the police to apprehend the perpetrator and gather evidence with which he could be convicted. No mission of law enforcement officials is more important. Yet "(d)isinterested zeal for the public good does not assure either wisdom or right in the methods it pursues." *Haley v. Ohio*, 332 U.S. 596, 605 (Frankfurter, J., concurring in judgment). Although we do not lightly affirm the issuance of a writ of habeas corpus in this case, so clear a violation of the Sixth and Fourteenth Amendments as here occurred cannot be condoned. The pressures on state executive and judicial officers charged with the administration of the criminal law are great, especially when the crime is murder and the victim a small child. But it is precisely the predictability of those pressures that makes imperative a resolute loyalty to the guarantees that the Constitution extends to us all.

The judgment of the Court of Appeals is affirmed.[12]

MR. JUSTICE MARSHALL, concurring.

I concur wholeheartedly in my Brother STEWART's opinion for the Court, but add these words in light of the dissenting opinions filed today. The dissenters have, I believe, lost sight of the fundamental constitutional backbone of our criminal law. They seem to think that Detective Leaming's actions were perfectly proper, indeed laudable, examples of "good police work." In my view, good police work is something far different from catching the criminal at any price. It is equally important that the police, as guardians of the law, fulfill their responsibility to obey its commands scrupulously. For "in the end life and liberty can be as much endangered from illegal methods used to convict those thought to be criminals as from the actual criminals themselves." *Spano v. New York*, 360 U.S. 315, 320–321 (1959).

In this case, there can be no doubt that Detective Leaming consciously and knowingly set out to violate Williams' Sixth Amendment right to counsel and his Fifth Amendment privilege against self-incrimination, as Leaming himself understood those rights. Leaming knew that Williams had been advised by two lawyers not to make any statements to police until he conferred in Des Moines with his attorney there, Mr. McKnight. Leaming surely understood, because he had overheard McKnight tell Williams as much, that the location of the body would be revealed to police. Undoubtedly Leaming realized the way in which that information would be conveyed to the police: McKnight would learn it from his client and then he would lead police to the body. Williams would thereby be protected by the attorney-client privilege from incriminating himself by directly demonstrating his knowledge of the body's location, and the unfortunate Powers child could be given a "Christian burial."

Of course, this scenario would accomplish all that Leaming sought from his investigation except that it would not produce incriminating

[12] The District Court stated that its decision "does not touch upon the issue of what evidence, if any, beyond the incriminating statements themselves must be excluded as 'fruit of the poisonous tree.' " We, too, have no occasion to address this issue, and in the present posture of the case there is no basis for the view of our dissenting Brethren that any attempt to retry the respondent would probably be futile. While neither Williams' incriminating statements themselves nor any testimony describing his having led the police to the victim's body can constitutionally be admitted into evidence, evidence of where the body was found and of its condition might well be admissible on the theory that the body would have been discovered in any event, even had incriminating statements not been elicited from Williams. In the event that a retrial is instituted, it will be for the state courts in the first instance to determine whether particular items of evidence may be admitted.

statements or actions from Williams. Accordingly, Leaming undertook his charade to pry such evidence from Williams. After invoking the no-passengers rule to prevent attorney Kelly from accompanying the prisoner, Leaming had Williams at his mercy: during the three- or four-hour trip he could do anything he wished to elicit a confession. The detective demonstrated once again "that the efficiency of the rack and the thumbscrew can be matched, given the proper subject by more sophisticated modes of 'persuasion.' "

Leaming knowingly isolated Williams from the protection of his lawyers and during that period he intentionally "persuaded" him to give incriminating evidence. It is this intentional police misconduct—not good police practice—that the Court rightly condemns. The heinous nature of the crime is no excuse, as the dissenters would have it, for condoning knowing and intentional police transgression of the constitutional rights of a defendant. If Williams is to go free—and given the ingenuity of Iowa prosecutors on retrial or in a civil commitment proceeding, I doubt very much that there is any chance a dangerous criminal will be loosed on the streets, the bloodcurdling cries of the dissents notwithstanding—it will hardly be because he deserves it. It will be because Detective Leaming, knowing full well that he risked reversal of Williams' conviction, intentionally denied Williams the right of every American under the Sixth Amendment to have the protective shield of a lawyer between himself and the awesome power of the State.

* * *

MR. JUSTICE POWELL, concurring.

* * *

I join the opinion of the Court which also finds that the efforts of Detective Leaming "to elicit information from Williams," as conceded by counsel for petitioner at oral argument, were a skillful and effective form of interrogation. Moreover, the entire setting was conducive to the psychological coercion that was successfully exploited. Williams was known by the police to be a young man with quixotic religious convictions and a history of mental disorders. The date was the day after Christmas, the weather was ominous, and the setting appropriate for Detective Leaming's talk of snow concealing the body and preventing a "Christian burial." Williams was alone in the automobile with two police officers for several hours. It is clear from the record, as both of the federal courts below found, that there was no evidence of a knowing and voluntary waiver of the right to have counsel present beyond the fact that Williams ultimately confessed. It is settled law that an inferred waiver of a constitutional right is disfavored. I find no basis in the record of this case or in the dissenting opinions for disagreeing with the conclusion of the District Court that "the

State has produced no affirmative evidence whatsoever to support its claim of waiver."

The dissenting opinion of the Chief Justice states that the Court's holding today "conclusively presumes a suspect is legally incompetent to change his mind and tell the truth until an attorney is present." I find no justification for this view. On the contrary, the opinion of the Court is explicitly clear that the right to assistance of counsel may be waived, after it has attached, without notice to or consultation with counsel. We would have such a case here if petitioner had proved that the police officers refrained from coercion and interrogation, as they had agreed, and that Williams freely on his own initiative had confessed the crime.

* * *

MR. JUSTICE STEVENS, concurring.

Mr. Justice Stewart, in his opinion for the Court which I join, Mr. Justice Powell, and Mr. Justice Marshall have accurately explained the reasons why the law requires the result we reach today. Nevertheless, the strong language in the dissenting opinions prompts me to add this brief comment about the Court's function in a case such as this.

* * *

Underlying the surface issues in this case is the question whether a fugitive from justice can rely on his lawyer's advice given in connection with a decision to surrender voluntarily. The defendant placed his trust in an experienced Iowa trial lawyer who in turn trusted the Iowa law enforcement authorities to honor a commitment made during negotiations which led to the apprehension of a potentially dangerous person. Under any analysis, this was a critical stage of the proceeding in which the participation of an independent professional was of vital importance to the accused and to society. At this stage as in countless others in which the law profoundly affects the life of the individual the lawyer is the essential medium through which the demands and commitments of the sovereign are communicated to the citizen. If, in the long run, we are seriously concerned about the individual's effective representation by counsel, the State cannot be permitted to dishonor its promise to this lawyer.*

MR. CHIEF JUSTICE BURGER, dissenting.

The result in this case ought to be intolerable in any society which purports to call itself an organized society. It continues the Court by the narrowest margin on the much-criticized course of punishing the public for the mistakes and misdeeds of law enforcement officers, instead of punishing the officer directly, if in fact he is guilty of wrongdoing. It

* The importance of this point is emphasized by the State's refusal to permit counsel to accompany his client on the trip from Davenport to Des Moines.

mechanically and blindly keeps reliable evidence from juries whether the claimed constitutional violation involves gross police misconduct or honest human error.

Williams is guilty of the savage murder of a small child; no member of the Court contends he is not. While in custody, and after no fewer than five warnings of his rights to silence and to counsel, he led police to the concealed body of his victim. The Court concedes Williams was not threatened or coerced and that he spoke and acted voluntarily and with full awareness of his constitutional rights. In the face of all this, the Court now holds that because Williams was prompted by the detective's statement—not interrogation but a statement—the jury must not be told how the police found the body.

Today's holding fulfills Judge (later Mr. Justice) Cardozo's grim prophecy that someday some court might carry the exclusionary rule to the absurd extent that its operative effect would exclude evidence relating to the body of a murder victim because of the means by which it was found. In so ruling the Court regresses to playing a grisly game of "hide and seek," once more exalting the sporting theory of criminal justice which has been experiencing a decline in our jurisprudence. With Justices White, Blackmun, and Rehnquist, I categorically reject the remarkable notion that the police in this case were guilty of unconstitutional misconduct, or any conduct justifying the bizarre result reached by the Court. Apart from a brief comment n the merits, however, I wish to focus on the irrationality of applying the increasingly discredited exclusionary rule to this case.

(1)

The Court Concedes Williams' Disclosures Were Voluntary

* * *

The evidence is uncontradicted that Williams had abundant knowledge of his right to have counsel present and of his right to silence. Since the Court does not question his mental competence, it boggles the mind to suggest that Williams could not understand that leading police to the child's body would have other than the most serious consequences. All of the elements necessary to make out a valid waiver are shown by the record and acknowledged by the Court; we thus are left to guess how the Court reached its holding.

One plausible but unarticulated basis for the result reached is that once a suspect has asserted his right not to talk without the presence of an attorney, it becomes legally impossible for him to waive that right until he has seen an attorney. But constitutional rights are personal, and an otherwise valid waiver should not be brushed aside by judges simply because an attorney was not present. The Court's holding operates to "imprison a man in his privileges;" it conclusively presumes a suspect is legally incompetent to change his mind and tell the truth until an attorney is present. It denigrates an individual to a nonperson whose free will has become hostage to a lawyer so that until the lawyer consents, the suspect is deprived of any legal right or power to decide for himself that he wishes to make a disclosure. It denies that the rights to counsel and silence are personal, nondelegable, and subject to a waiver only by that individual. The opinions in support of the Court's judgment do not enlighten us as to why police conduct whether good or bad should operate to suspend Williams' right to change his mind and "tell all" at once rather than waiting until he reached Des Moines.

In his concurring opinion Mr. Justice Powell suggests that the result in this case turns on whether Detective Leaming's remarks constituted "interrogation," as he views them, or whether they were "statements" intended to prick the conscience of the accused. I find it most remarkable that a murder case should turn on judicial interpretation that a statement becomes a question simply because it is followed by an incriminating disclosure from the suspect. The Court seems to be saying that since Williams said he would "tell the whole story" at Des Moines, the police should have been content and waited; of course, that would have been the wiser course, especially in light of the nuances of constitutional jurisprudence applied by the Court, but a murder case ought no turn on such tenuous strands.

In any case, the Court assures us, this is not at all what it intends, and that a valid waiver was possible in these circumstances, but was not quite made. Here, of course, Williams did not confess to the murder in so many words; it was his conduct in guiding police to the body, not his words, which incriminated him. And the record is replete with evidence that Williams knew precisely what he was doing when he guided police to the body. The human urge to confess wrongdoing is, of course, normal in all save hardened, professional criminals, as psychiatrists and analysts have demonstrated.

(2)

The Exclusionary Rule Should Not be Applied to Non-egregious Police Conduct

Even if there was no waiver, and assuming a technical violation occurred, the Court errs gravely in mechanically applying the exclusionary rule without considering whether that Draconian judicial doctrine should be invoked in these circumstances, or indeed whether any of its conceivable goals will be furthered by its application here.

The obvious flaws of the exclusionary rule as a judicial remedy are familiar. Today's holding interrupts what has been a more rational perception of the constitutional and social utility of excluding reliable evidence from the truth-seeking process. In its Fourth Amendment context, we have now recognized that the exclusionary rule is in no sense a personal constitutional right, but a judicially conceived remedial device designed to safeguard and effectuate guaranteed legal rights generally. We have repeatedly emphasized that deterrence of unconstitutional or otherwise unlawful police conduct is the only valid justification for excluding reliable and probative evidence from the criminal factfinding process.

Accordingly, unlawfully obtained evidence is not automatically excluded from the factfinding process in all circumstances. In a variety of contexts we inquire whether application of the rule will promote its objectives sufficiently to justify the enormous cost it imposes on society. "As with any remedial device, the application of the rule has been restricted to those areas where its remedial objectives are thought most efficaciously served."

* * *

In any event, the fundamental purpose of the Sixth Amendment is to safeguard the fairness of the trial and the integrity of the factfinding process. In this case, where the evidence of how the child's body was found is of unquestioned reliability, and since the Court accepts Williams' disclosures as voluntary and uncoerced, there is no issue either of fairness or evidentiary reliability to justify suppression of truth. It appears suppression is mandated here for no other reason than the Court's general impression that it may have a beneficial effect on future police conduct; indeed, the Court fails to say even that much in defense of its holding.

* * *

MR. JUSTICE WHITE, with whom MR. JUSTICE BLACKMUN and MR. JUSTICE REHNQUIST join, dissenting.

* * *

I

The victim in this case disappeared from a YMCA building in Des Moines, Iowa, on Christmas Eve in 1968. Respondent was seen shortly thereafter carrying a bundle wrapped in a blanket from the YMCA to his car. His car was found in Davenport, Iowa, 160 miles away on Christmas Day. A warrant was then issued for his arrest. On the day after Christmas respondent surrendered himself voluntarily to local police in Davenport where he was arraigned. The Des Moines police, in turn, drove to Davenport, picked respondent up and drove him back to Des Moines. During the trip back to Des Moines respondent made statements evidencing his knowledge of the whereabouts of the victim's clothing and body and leading the police to the body. The statements were, of course, made without the presence of counsel since no counsel was in the police car. The issue in this case is whether respondent who was entitled not to make any statements to the police without consultation with and/or presence of counsel[1] validly waived those rights.

* * *

II

The strictest test of waiver which might be applied to this case is that set forth in *Johnson v. Zerbst*, 304 U.S. 458, 464 (1938), and quoted by the majority. In order to show that a right has been waived under this test, the State must prove "an intentional relinquishment or abandonment of a known right or privilege." The majority creates no new rule preventing an accused who has retained a lawyer from waiving his right to the lawyer's presence during questioning. The majority simply finds that no waiver was proved in this case. I disagree. That respondent knew of his right not to say anything to the officers without advice and presence of counsel is established on this record to a moral certainty. He was advised of the right by three officials of the State telling at least one that he understood the right and by two lawyers. Finally, he further demonstrated his knowledge of the right by informing the police that he would tell them the story in the presence of McKnight when they arrived in Des Moines. The issue in this case, then, is whether respondent relinquished that right intentionally.

Respondent relinquished his right not to talk to the police about his crime when the car approached the place where he had hidden the victim's clothes. Men usually intend to do what they do, and there is nothing in the record to support the proposition that respondent's decision to talk was anything but an exercise of his own free will. Apparently, without any prodding from the officers, respondent—who had earlier said that he would tell the whole story when he arrived in Des Moines—spontaneously changed him mind about the timing of his disclosures when the car approached the places where he had hidden the evidence. However, even if his statements were influenced by Detective Leaming's above-quoted statement, respondent's decision to talk in the absence of counsel can hardly be viewed as the product of an overborne will. The statement by Leaming was not coercive; it was accompanied by a request that respondent not respond to it; and it was delivered hours before respondent decided to make any statement. Respondent's waiver was thus knowing and intentional.

The majority's contrary conclusion seems to rest on the fact that respondent "asserted" his right to counsel by retaining and consulting with one lawyer and by consulting with another. How this supports the conclusion that respondent's later relinquishment of his right not to talk in

[1] It does not matter whether the right not to make statements in the absence of counsel stems from *Massiah v. United States*, 377 U.S. 201 (1964), or *Miranda v. Arizona*, 384 U.S. 436 (1966). In either case the question is one of waiver. Waiver was not addressed in *Massiah* because there the statements were being made to an informant and the defendant had no way of knowing that he had a right not to talk to him without counsel.

the absence of counsel was unintentional is a mystery. The fact that respondent consulted with counsel on the question whether he should talk to the police in counsel's absence makes his later decision to talk in counsel's absence better informed and, if anything, more intelligent.

The majority recognizes that even after this "assertion" of his right to counsel, it would have found that respondent waived his right not to talk in counsel's absence if his waiver had been express—i. e., if the officers had asked him in the car whether he would be willing to answer questions in counsel's absence and if he had answered "yes." But waiver is not a formalistic concept. Waiver is shown whenever the facts establish that an accused knew of a right and intended to relinquish it. Such waiver, even if not express, was plainly shown here. The only other conceivable basis for the majority's holding is the implicit suggestion that the right involved in *Massiah v. United States*, 377 U.S. 201 (1964), as distinguished from the right involved in *Miranda v. Arizona*, 384 U.S. 436 (1966), is a right not to be asked any questions in counsel's absence rather than a right not to answer any questions in counsel's absence, and that the right not to be asked questions must be waived before the questions are asked. Such wafer-thin distinctions cannot determine whether a guilty murderer should go free. The only conceivable purpose for the presence of counsel during questioning is to protect an accused from making incriminating answers. Questions, unanswered, have no significance at all. Absent coercion no matter how the right involved is defined an accused is amply protected by a rule requiring waiver before or simultaneously with the giving by him of an answer or the making by him of a statement.

III

The consequence of the majority's decision is, as the majority recognizes, extremely serious. A mentally disturbed killer whose guilt is not in question may be released. Why? Apparently the answer is that the majority believes that the law enforcement officers acted in a way which involves some risk of injury to society and that such conduct should be deterred. However, the officers' conduct did not, and was not likely to, jeopardize the fairness of respondent's trial or in any way risk the conviction of an innocent man the risk against which the Sixth Amendment guarantee of assistance of counsel is designed to protect. The police did nothing "wrong," let alone anything "unconstitutional." To anyone not lost in the intricacies of the prophylactic rules of *Miranda v. Arizona*, the result in this case seems utterly senseless; and for the reasons stated in Part II, even applying those rules as well as the rule of *Massiah v. United States* the statements made by respondent were properly admitted. In light of these considerations, the majority's protest that the result in this case is justified by a "clear violation" of the Sixth and Fourteenth Amendments has a distressing hollow ring. I respectfully dissent.

MR. JUSTICE BLACKMUN, with whom MR. JUSTICE WHITE and MR. JUSTICE REHNQUIST join, dissenting.

The State of Iowa, and 21 States and others, as amici curiae, strongly urge that this Court's procedural (as distinguished from constitutional) ruling in *Miranda v. Arizona*, 384 U.S. 436 (1966), be re-examined and overruled. I, however, agree with the Court that this is not now the case in which that issue need be considered.

What the Court chooses to do here, and with which I disagree, is to hold that respondent Williams' situation was in the mold of *Massiah v. United States*, 377 U.S. 201 (1964), that is, that it was dominated by a denial to Williams of his Sixth Amendment right to counsel after criminal proceedings had been instituted against him. The Court rules that the Sixth Amendment was violated because Detective Leaming "purposely sought during Williams' isolation from his lawyers to obtain as much incriminating information as possible." I cannot regard that as unconstitutional per se.

* * *

In summary, it seems to me that the Court is holding that *Massiah* is violated whenever police engage in any conduct, in the absence of counsel, with the subjective desire to obtain information from a suspect after arraignment. Such a rule is far too broad. Persons in custody frequently volunteer statements in response to stimuli other than interrogation. When there is no interrogation, such statements should be admissible as long as they are truly voluntary.

The *Massiah* point thus being of no consequence, I would vacate the judgment of the Court of Appeals and remand the case for consideration of the issue of voluntariness, in the constitutional sense, of Williams' statements, an issue the Court of Appeals did not reach when the case was before it.

* * *

Points for Discussion

1. Note that in this case, the Supreme Court defers the Fifth Amendment question (whether the statement was taken from Williams against his will). The Court also declines to decide whether the officers' conduct complies with *Miranda v. Arizona*. We will consider the *Miranda* implications of a fact pattern similar to *Williams* in *Rhode Island v. Innis* in chapter 9.

2. The Court concludes that these facts are indistinguishable from those of *Massiah* and that the conduct of the officer in giving the "Christian burial speech" constituted a violation of Williams' Sixth Amendment rights. Do you agree that the facts of this case are indistinguishable from those of *Massiah*? Didn't Williams, unlike Massiah, know that he was speaking with law

enforcement officials in the absence of his counsel? Doesn't this knowledge make the police conduct in this case more, rather than less, defensible?

3. Having concluded that Williams was entitled to the assistance of counsel and that Detective Leaming deliberately elicited a statement from him in the absence of his lawyer, the Court turns to the question of waiver. That is, the Court considers, but rejects, the possibility that Williams waived his right to counsel by freely choosing to speak with the officers. As the Chief Justice's dissent asks, what was Williams' decision to speak if not a voluntary waiver of the right he clearly knew he had: the right to consult with counsel before speaking with the authorities?

KUHLMANN V. WILSON

477 U.S. 436 (1986)

JUSTICE POWELL announced the judgment of the court and delivered the opinion of the court with respect to Parts I, IV, and V, and an opinion with respect to Parts II and III in which THE CHIEF JUSTICE, JUSTICE REHNQUIST, and JUSTICE O'CONNOR join.

* * *

I

In the early morning of July 4, 1970, respondent and two confederates robbed the Star Taxicab Garage in the Bronx, New York, and fatally shot the night dispatcher. Shortly before, employees of the garage had observed respondent, a former employee there, on the premises conversing with two other men. They also witnessed respondent fleeing after the robbery, carrying loose money in his arms. After eluding the police for four days, respondent turned himself in. Respondent admitted that he had been present when the crimes took place, claimed that he had witnessed the robbery, gave the police a description of the robbers, but denied knowing them. Respondent also denied any involvement in the robbery or murder, claiming that he had fled because he was afraid of being blamed for the crimes.

After his arraignment, respondent was confined in the Bronx House of Detention, where he was placed in a cell with a prisoner named Benny Lee. Unknown to respondent, Lee had agreed to act as a police informant. Respondent made incriminating statements that Lee reported to the police. Prior to trial, respondent moved to suppress the statements on the ground that they were obtained in violation of his right to counsel. The trial court held an evidentiary hearing on the suppression motion, which revealed that the statements were made under the following circumstances.

Before respondent arrived in the jail, Lee had entered into an arrangement with Detective Cullen, according to which Lee agreed to listen to respondent's conversations and report his remarks to Cullen. Since the police had positive evidence of respondent's participation, the purpose of placing Lee in the cell was to determine the identities of respondent's confederates. Cullen instructed Lee not to ask respondent any questions, but simply to "keep his ears open" for the names of the other perpetrators. Respondent first spoke to Lee about the crimes after he looked out the cellblock window at the Star Taxicab Garage, where the crimes had occurred. Respondent said, "someone's messing with me," and began talking to Lee about the robbery, narrating the same story that he had given the police at the time of his arrest. Lee advised respondent that this explanation "didn't sound too good," but respondent did not alter his story. Over the next few days, however, respondent changed details of his original account. Respondent then received a visit from his brother, who mentioned that members of his family were upset because they believed that respondent had murdered the dispatcher. After the visit, respondent again described the crimes to Lee. Respondent now admitted that he and two other men, whom he never identified, had planned and carried out the robbery, and had murdered the dispatcher. Lee informed Cullen of respondent's statements and furnished Cullen with notes that he had written surreptitiously while sharing the cell with respondent.

After hearing the testimony of Cullen and Lee, the trial court found that Cullen had instructed Lee "to ask no questions of [respondent] about the crime but merely to listen as to what [respondent] might say in his presence." The court determined that Lee obeyed these instructions, that he "at no time asked any questions with respect to the crime," and that he "only listened to [respondent] and made notes regarding what [respondent] had to say." The trial court also found that respondent's statements to Lee were "spontaneous" and "unsolicited." Under state precedent, a defendant's volunteered statements to a police agent were admissible in evidence because the police were not required to prevent talkative defendants from making incriminating statements. The trial court accordingly denied the suppression motion.

* * *

IV

* * *

A

* * *

The Court in *Massiah* adopted the reasoning of the concurring opinions in *Spano* and held that, once a defendant's Sixth Amendment right to counsel has attached, he is denied that right when federal agents "deliberately elicit" incriminating statements from him in the absence of his lawyer.

The Court adopted this test, rather than one that turned simply on whether the statements were obtained in an "interrogation," to protect accused persons from "indirect and surreptitious interrogations as well as those conducted in the jailhouse. In this case, Massiah was more seriously imposed upon . . . because he did not even know that he was under interrogation by a government agent." Thus, the Court made clear that it was concerned with interrogation or investigative techniques that were equivalent to interrogation, and that it so viewed the technique in issue in *Massiah*.

In *United States v. Henry,* [447 U.S. 264 (1980),] the Court applied the *Massiah* test to incriminating statements made to a jailhouse informant. The Court of Appeals in that case found a violation of *Massiah* because the informant had engaged the defendant in conversations and "had developed a relationship of trust and confidence with [the defendant] such that [the defendant] revealed incriminating information." This Court affirmed, holding that the Court of Appeals reasonably concluded that the Government informant "deliberately used his position to secure incriminating information from [the defendant] when counsel was not present." Although the informant had not questioned the defendant, the informant had "stimulated" conversations with the defendant in order to "elicit" incriminating information. The Court emphasized that those facts, like the facts of *Massiah,* amounted to "indirect and surreptitious interrogatio[n]" of the defendant.

* * *

As our recent examination of this Sixth Amendment issue in [*Maine v. Moulton,* 474 U.S. 159 (1985),] makes clear, the primary concern of the *Massiah* line of decisions is secret interrogation by investigatory techniques that are the equivalent of direct police interrogation. Since "the Sixth Amendment is not violated whenever—by luck or happenstance—the State obtains incriminating statements from the accused after the right to counsel has attached," a defendant does not make out a violation of that right simply by showing that an informant, either through prior arrangement or voluntarily, reported his incriminating statements to the police. Rather, the defendant must demonstrate that the police and their informant took some action, beyond merely listening, that was designed deliberately to elicit incriminating remarks.

B

It is thus apparent that the Court of Appeals erred in concluding that respondent's right to counsel was violated under the circumstances of this case. Its error did not stem from any disagreement with the District Court over appropriate resolution of the question reserved in *Henry,* but rather from its implicit conclusion that this case did not present that open question. That conclusion was based on a fundamental mistake, namely, the Court of Appeals' failure to accord to the state trial court's factual findings the presumption of correctness expressly required by 28 U.S.C. § 2254(d).[a]

The state court found that Officer Cullen had instructed Lee only to listen to respondent for the purpose of determining the identities of the other participants in the robbery and murder. The police already had solid evidence of respondent's participation. The court further found that Lee followed those instructions, that he "at no time asked any questions" of respondent concerning the pending charges, and that he "only listened" to respondent's "spontaneous" and "unsolicited" statements. The only remark made by Lee that has any support in this record was his comment that respondent's initial version of his participation in the crimes "didn't sound too good." Without holding that any of the state court's findings were not entitled to the presumption of correctness under § 2254(d), the Court of Appeals focused on that one remark and gave a description of Lee's interaction with respondent that is completely at odds with the facts found by the trial court. In the Court of Appeals' view, "[s]ubtly and slowly, but surely, Lee's ongoing verbal intercourse with [respondent] served to exacerbate [respondent's] already troubled state of mind."[24] After thus revising some of the trial court's findings, and ignoring other more relevant findings, the Court of Appeals concluded that the police "deliberately elicited" respondent's incriminating statements. This conclusion conflicts with the decision of every other state and federal judge who reviewed this record, and is clear error in light of the provisions and intent of § 2254(d).

CHIEF JUSTICE BURGER, concurring.

I agree fully with the Court's opinion and judgment. This case is clearly distinguishable from *United States v. Henry,* 447 U.S. 264 (1980). There is a vast difference between placing an "ear" in the suspect's cell and placing a voice in the cell to encourage conversation for the "ear" to record.

* * *

JUSTICE BRENNAN, with whom JUSTICE MARSHALL joins, dissenting.

Because I believe that the Court of Appeals correctly concluded that the "ends of justice" would be served by plenary consideration of respondent's second federal habeas petition and that *United States v. Henry,* 447 U.S. 264 (1980), directly controls the merits of this case, I dissent.

---

[a] The rules for the adjudication of habeas corpus proceedings like this one generally require the federal court to defer to the factual findings of the state court. The current version of § 2254(d)(2) states that a writ of habeas corpus shall not be granted unless the state court opinion "was based on an unreasonable determination of the facts in light of the evidence presented . . . ."—Eds.

[24] Curiously, the Court of Appeals expressed concern that respondent was placed in a cell that overlooked the scene of his crimes. For all the record shows, however, that fact was sheer coincidence. Nor do we perceive any reason to require police to isolate one charged with crime so that he cannot view the scene, whatever it may be, from his cell window.

* * *

II

* * *

The Sixth Amendment guarantees an accused, at least after the initiation of formal charges, the right to rely on counsel as the "medium" between himself and the State. *Maine v. Moulton,* 474 U.S. 159, 176 (1985). Accordingly, the Sixth Amendment "imposes on the State an affirmative obligation to respect and preserve the accused's choice to seek [the assistance of counsel]" and therefore "[t] he determination whether particular action by state agents violates the accused's right to . . . counsel must be made in light of this obligation." To be sure, the Sixth Amendment is not violated whenever, "by luck or happenstance," the State obtains incriminating statements from the accused after the right to counsel has attached. It is violated, however, when "the State obtains incriminating statements by knowingly circumventing the accused's right to have counsel present in a confrontation between the accused and a state agent." As we explained in *Henry,* where the accused has not waived his right to counsel, the government knowingly circumvents the defendant's right to counsel where it "deliberately elicit[s]" inculpatory admissions, that is, "intentionally creat[es] a situation likely to induce [the accused] to make incriminating statements without the assistance of counsel."

In *Henry,* we found that the Federal Government had "deliberately elicited" incriminating statements from Henry based on the following circumstances. The jailhouse informant, Nichols, had apparently followed instructions to obtain information without directly questioning Henry and without initiating conversations concerning the charges pending against Henry. We rejected the Government's argument that because Henry initiated the discussion of his crime, no Sixth Amendment violation had occurred. We pointed out that under *Massiah v. United States,* 377 U.S. 201 (1964), it is irrelevant whether the informant asks pointed questions about the crime or "merely engage[s] in general conversation about it." Nichols, we noted, "was not a passive listener; . . . he had 'some conversations with Mr. Henry' while he was in jail and Henry's incriminatory statements were 'the product of this conversation.' "

In deciding that Nichols' role in these conversations amounted to deliberate elicitation, we also found three other factors important. First, Nichols was to be paid for any information he produced and thus had an incentive to extract inculpatory admissions from Henry. Second, Henry was not aware that Nichols was acting as an informant. "Conversation stimulated in such circumstances," we observed, "may elicit information that an accused would not intentionally reveal to persons known to be Government agents." Third, Henry was in custody at the time he spoke with Nichols. This last fact is significant, we stated, because "custody imposes pressures on the accused [and] confinement may bring into play subtle influences that will make him particularly susceptible to the ploys of undercover Government agents." We concluded that by "intentionally creating a situation likely to induce Henry to make incriminating statements without the assistance of counsel, the Government violated Henry's Sixth Amendment right to counsel."

In the instant case, as in *Henry,* the accused was incarcerated and therefore was "susceptible to the ploys of undercover Government agents." Like Nichols, Lee was a secret informant, usually received consideration for the services he rendered the police, and therefore had an incentive to produce the information which he knew the police hoped to obtain. Just as Nichols had done, Lee obeyed instructions not to question respondent and to report to the police any statements made by the respondent in Lee's presence about the crime in question. And, like Nichols, Lee encouraged respondent to talk about his crime by conversing with him on the subject over the course of several days and by telling respondent that his exculpatory story would not convince anyone without more work. However, unlike the situation in *Henry,* a disturbing visit from respondent's brother, rather than a conversation with the informant, seems to have been the immediate catalyst for respondent's confession to Lee. While it might appear from this sequence of events that Lee's comment regarding respondent's story and his general willingness to converse with respondent about the crime were not the *immediate* causes of respondent's admission, I think that the deliberate-elicitation standard requires consideration of the entire course of government behavior.

The State intentionally created a situation in which it was foreseeable that respondent would make incriminating statements without the assistance of counsel—it assigned respondent to a cell overlooking the scene of the crime and designated a secret informant to be respondent's cellmate. The informant, while avoiding direct questions, nonetheless developed a relationship of cellmate camaraderie with respondent and encouraged him to talk about his crime. While the *coup de grace* was delivered by respondent's brother, the groundwork for respondent's confession was laid by the State. Clearly the State's actions had a sufficient nexus with respondent's admission of guilt to constitute deliberate elicitation within the meaning of *Henry.* I would affirm the judgment of the Court of Appeals.

The dissenting opinion of JUSTICE STEVENS is omitted.

Points for Discussion

1. The majority states that when a defendant whose Sixth Amendment rights have attached—because adversary proceedings have commenced against him—makes incriminating statements to the police through luck or

happenstance, the Sixth Amendment is not violated. Is that a fair description of what happened in this case?

2. Even assuming the correctness of the lower court's factual finding—that Lee was an "ear" and not a "voice"—isn't it still true that the government deliberately elicited incriminating statements from the defendant? Why did they place Lee in the cell if not to obtain information from Wilson? Is it enough, as Justice Brennan writes in dissent, that the state "intentionally created a situation in which it was foreseeable" that Wilson would incriminate himself?

B. "COMMENCEMENT OF ADVERSARIAL PROCEEDINGS"

The cases above allude to the fact that once criminal proceedings have commenced against an individual, the state may not deliberately elicit incriminating statements from him in the absence of his counsel. The following case focuses not on when the Sixth Amendment right is violated but on when it attaches. The case gives greater substance to the often-repeated assertion that the right attaches with the commencement of adversarial proceedings.

ROTHGERY V. GILLESPIE COUNTY, TEXAS

554 U.S. 191 (2008)

JUSTICE SOUTER delivered the opinion of the court.

This Court has held that the right to counsel guaranteed by the Sixth Amendment applies at the first appearance before a judicial officer at which a defendant is told of the formal accusation against him and restrictions are imposed on his liberty. The question here is whether attachment of the right also requires that a public prosecutor (as distinct from a police officer) be aware of that initial proceeding or involved in its conduct. We hold that it does not.

I

A

Although petitioner Walter Rothgery has never been convicted of a felony, a criminal background check disclosed an erroneous record that he had been, and on July 15, 2002, Texas police officers relied on this record to arrest him as a felon in possession of a firearm. The officers lacked a warrant, and so promptly brought Rothgery before a magistrate judge, as required by Tex. Crim. Proc. Code Ann., Art. 14.06(a). Texas law has no formal label for this initial appearance before a magistrate, which is sometimes called the "article 15.17 hearing"; it combines the Fourth Amendment's required probable-cause determination with the setting of bail, and is the point at which the arrestee is formally apprised of the accusation against him.[b]

Rothgery's article 15.17 hearing followed routine. The arresting officer submitted a sworn "Affidavit Of Probable Cause" that described the facts supporting the arrest and "charge[d] that . . . Rothgery . . . commit[ted] the offense of unlawful possession of a firearm by a felon-3rd degree felony [Tex. Penal Code Ann. § 46.04]." After reviewing the affidavit, the magistrate judge "determined that probable cause existed for the arrest." The magistrate judge informed Rothgery of the accusation, set his bail at $5,000, and committed him to jail, from which he was released after posting a surety bond. The bond, which the Gillespie County deputy sheriff signed, stated that "Rothgery stands charged by complaint duly filed . . . with the offense of a . . . felony, to wit: Unlawful Possession of a Firearm by a Felon." The release was conditioned on the defendant's personal appearance in trial court "for any and all subsequent proceedings that may be had relative to the said charge in the course of the criminal action based on said charge."

Rothgery had no money for a lawyer and made several oral and written requests for appointed counsel, which went unheeded. The following January, he was indicted by a Texas grand jury for unlawful possession of a firearm by a felon, resulting in rearrest the next day, and an order increasing bail to $15,000. When he could not post it, he was put in jail and remained there for three weeks.

On January 23, 2003, six months after the article 15.17 hearing, Rothgery was finally assigned a lawyer, who promptly obtained a bail reduction (so Rothgery could get out of jail), and assembled the paperwork confirming that Rothgery had never been convicted of a felony. Counsel relayed this information to the district attorney, who in turn filed a motion to dismiss the indictment, which was granted.

B

Rothgery then brought this 42 U.S.C. § 1983 action against respondent Gillespie County, claiming that if the County had provided a lawyer within a reasonable time after the article 15.17 hearing, he would not have been indicted, rearrested, or jailed for three weeks. The County's failure is said to be owing to its unwritten policy of denying appointed counsel to indigent defendants out on bond until at least the entry of an information or indictment. Rothgery sees this policy as violating his Sixth Amendment right to counsel.

* * *

[b] *Gerstein v. Pugh*, 420 U.S. 103 (1975), held that the Constitution requires that an arrestee be brought promptly (usually within 48 hours) before a magistrate to determine whether probable cause supports the arrest.—Eds.

II

The Sixth Amendment right of the "accused" to assistance of counsel in "all criminal prosecutions" is limited by its terms: "it does not attach until a prosecution is commenced." We have, for purposes of the right to counsel, pegged commencement to " 'the initiation of adversary judicial criminal proceedings—whether by way of formal charge, preliminary hearing, indictment, information, or arraignment.' " The rule is not "mere formalism," but a recognition of the point at which "the government has committed itself to prosecute," "the adverse positions of government and defendant have solidified," and the accused "finds himself faced with the prosecutorial forces of organized society, and immersed in the intricacies of substantive and procedural criminal law." The issue is whether Texas's article 15.17 hearing marks that point, with the consequent state obligation to appoint counsel within a reasonable time once a request for assistance is made.

A

When the Court of Appeals said no, because no prosecutor was aware of Rothgery's article 15.17 hearing or involved in it, the court effectively focused not on the start of adversarial judicial proceedings, but on the activities and knowledge of a particular state official who was presumably otherwise occupied. This was error.

As the Court of Appeals recognized, we have twice held that the right to counsel attaches at the initial appearance before a judicial officer. This first time before a court, also known as the "preliminary arraignment" or "arraignment on the complaint," is generally the hearing at which "the magistrate informs the defendant of the charge in the complaint, and of various rights in further proceedings," and "determine[s] the conditions for pretrial release." Texas's article 15.17 hearing is an initial appearance: Rothgery was taken before a magistrate judge, informed of the formal accusation against him, and sent to jail until he posted bail.[9]

* * *

B

Our latest look at the significance of the initial appearance was *McNeil v. Wisconsin,* 501 U.S. 171 (1991), which is no help to the County. In *McNeil* the State had conceded that the right to counsel attached at the first

---

[9] The Court of Appeals did not resolve whether the arresting officer's formal accusation would count as a "formal complaint" under Texas state law. But it rightly acknowledged (albeit in considering the separate question whether the complaint was a "formal charge") that the constitutional significance of judicial proceedings cannot be allowed to founder on the vagaries of state criminal law, lest the attachment rule be rendered utterly "vague and unpredictable." *Virginia v. Moore,* 553 U.S. 164, 175 (2008). What counts is that the complaint filed with the magistrate judge accused Rothgery of committing a particular crime and prompted the judicial officer to take legal action in response (here, to set the terms of bail and order the defendant locked up).

appearance before a county court commissioner, who set bail and scheduled a preliminary examination. But we did more than just accept the concession; we went on to reaffirm that "[t]he Sixth Amendment right to counsel attaches at the first formal proceeding against an accused," and observed that "in most States, at least with respect to serious offenses, free counsel is made available at that time . . . ."

That was 17 years ago, the same is true today, and the overwhelming consensus practice conforms to the rule that the first formal proceeding is the point of attachment. We are advised without contradiction that not only the Federal Government, including the District of Columbia, but 43 States take the first step toward appointing counsel "before, at, or just after initial appearance." The practice is not free of ambiguity. In any event, to the extent these States have been denying appointed counsel on the heels of the first appearance, they are a distinct minority.

C

The only question is whether there may be some arguable justification for the minority practice. Neither the Court of Appeals in its opinion, nor the County in its briefing to us, has offered an acceptable one.

1

The Court of Appeals thought [*Brewer v. Williams*, 430 U.S. 387 (1977),] and [*Michigan v. Jackson*, 475 U.S. 625 (1986),] could be distinguished on the ground that "neither case addressed the issue of prosecutorial involvement," and the cases were thus "neutral on the point." With *Brewer* and *Jackson* distinguished, the court then found itself bound by Circuit precedent that "an adversary criminal proceeding has not begun in a case where the prosecution officers are unaware of either the charges or the arrest." Under this standard of prosecutorial awareness, attachment depends not on whether a first appearance has begun adversary judicial proceedings, but on whether the prosecutor had a hand in starting it. That standard is wrong.

Neither *Brewer* nor *Jackson* said a word about the prosecutor's involvement as a relevant fact, much less a controlling one. Those cases left no room for the factual enquiry the Court of Appeals would require, and with good reason: an attachment rule that turned on determining the moment of a prosecutor's first involvement would be "wholly unworkable and impossible to administer," *Escobedo v. Illinois,* 378 U.S. 478, 496 (1964) (White, J., dissenting), guaranteed to bog the courts down in prying enquiries into the communication between police (who are routinely present at defendants' first appearances) and the State's attorneys (who are not). And it would have the practical effect of resting attachment on such absurd distinctions as the day of the month an arrest is made, or "the sophistication, or lack thereof, of a jurisdiction's computer intake system."

It is not that the Court of Appeals believed that any such regime would be desirable, but it thought originally that its rule was implied by this Court's statement that the right attaches when the government has "committed itself to prosecute." [*Kirby v. Illinois*, 406 U.S. 682, 689 (1972)]. The Court of Appeals reasoned that because "the decision not to prosecute is the quintessential function of a prosecutor" under Texas law, the State could not commit itself to prosecution until the prosecutor signaled that it had.

But what counts as a commitment to prosecute is an issue of federal law unaffected by allocations of power among state officials under a State's law, and under the federal standard, an accusation filed with a judicial officer is sufficiently formal, and the government's commitment to prosecute it sufficiently concrete, when the accusation prompts arraignment and restrictions on the accused's liberty to facilitate the prosecution. From that point on, the defendant is "faced with the prosecutorial forces of organized society, and immersed in the intricacies of substantive and procedural criminal law" that define his capacity and control his actual ability to defend himself against a formal accusation that he is a criminal. By that point, it is too late to wonder whether he is "accused" within the meaning of the Sixth Amendment, and it makes no practical sense to deny it. All of this is equally true whether the machinery of prosecution was turned on by the local police or the state attorney general. In this case, for example, Rothgery alleges that after the initial appearance, he was "unable to find any employment for wages" because "all of the potential employers he contacted knew or learned of the criminal charge pending against him." One may assume that those potential employers would still have declined to make job offers if advised that the county prosecutor had not filed the complaint.

2

* * *

The County also tries to downplay the significance of the initial appearance by saying that an attachment rule unqualified by prosecutorial involvement would lead to the conclusion "that the State has statutorily committed to prosecute *every* suspect arrested by the police," given that "state law requires [an article 15.17 hearing] for every arrestee." The answer, though, is that the State has done just that, subject to the option to change its official mind later. The State may rethink its commitment at any point: it may choose not to seek indictment in a felony case, say, or the prosecutor may enter *nolle prosequi* after the case gets to the jury room. But without a change of position, a defendant subject to accusation after initial appearance is headed for trial and needs to get a lawyer working, whether to attempt to avoid that trial or to be ready with a defense when the trial date arrives.

3

A third tack on the County's part, slightly different from the one taken by the Fifth Circuit, gets it no further. The County stipulates that "the properly formulated test is not . . . merely whether prosecutors have had any involvement in the case whatsoever, but instead whether the State has objectively committed itself to prosecute." It then informs us that "[p]rosecutorial involvement is merely one form of evidence of such commitment." Other sufficient evidentiary indications are variously described: first (expansively) as "the filing of formal charges . . . by information, indictment or formal complaint, or the holding of an adversarial preliminary hearing to determine probable cause to file such charges;" then (restrictively) as a court appearance following "arrest . . . on an indictment or information." Either version, in any event, runs up against *Brewer* and *Jackson*: an initial appearance following a charge signifies a sufficient commitment to prosecute regardless of a prosecutor's participation, indictment, information, or what the County calls a "formal" complaint.

So the County is reduced to taking aim at those cases. *Brewer* and *Jackson,* we are told, are "vague" and thus of "limited, if any, precedential value." And, according to the County, our cases (*Brewer* and *Jackson* aside) actually establish a "general rule that the right to counsel attaches at the point that [what the County calls] formal charges are filed" with exceptions allowed only in the case of "a very limited set of specific preindictment situations." The County suggests that the latter category should be limited to those appearances at which the aid of counsel is urgent and " 'the dangers to the accused of proceeding without counsel' " are great. Texas's article 15.17 hearing should not count as one of those situations, the County says, because it is not of critical significance, since it "allows no presentation of witness testimony and provides no opportunity to expose weaknesses in the government's evidence, create a basis for later impeachment, or even engage in basic discovery."

We think the County is wrong both about the clarity of our cases and the substance that we find clear. Certainly it is true that the Court in *Brewer* and *Jackson* saw no need for lengthy disquisitions on the significance of the initial appearance, but that was because it found the attachment issue an easy one. The Court's conclusions were not vague; *Brewer* expressed "no doubt" that the right to counsel attached at the initial appearance, and *Jackson* said that the opposite result would be "untenable."

If, indeed, the County had simply taken the cases at face value, it would have avoided the mistake of merging the attachment question (whether formal judicial proceedings have begun) with the distinct "critical stage" question (whether counsel must be present at a postattachment proceeding unless the right to assistance is validly waived). Attachment occurs when the government has used the judicial machinery to signal a commitment to prosecute as spelled out in *Brewer* and *Jackson*. Once attachment occurs, the accused at least is entitled to the presence of appointed counsel during any "critical stage" of the postattachment proceedings; what makes a stage critical is what shows the need for counsel's presence.[16] Thus, counsel must be appointed within a reasonable time after attachment to allow for adequate representation at any critical stage before trial, as well as at trial itself.

* * *

III

Our holding is narrow. We do not decide whether the 6-month delay in appointment of counsel resulted in prejudice to Rothgery's Sixth Amendment rights, and have no occasion to consider what standards should apply in deciding this. We merely reaffirm what we have held before and what an overwhelming majority of American jurisdictions understand in practice: a criminal defendant's initial appearance before a judicial officer, where he learns the charge against him and his liberty is subject to restriction, marks the start of adversary judicial proceedings that trigger attachment of the Sixth Amendment right to counsel. Because the Fifth Circuit came to a different conclusion on this threshold issue, its judgment is vacated, and the case is remanded for further proceedings consistent with this opinion.

CHIEF JUSTICE ROBERTS, with whom JUSTICE SCALIA joins, concurring.

Justice Thomas's analysis of the present issue is compelling, but I believe the result here is controlled by *Brewer v. Williams,* 430 U.S. 387 (1977), and *Michigan v. Jackson,* 475 U.S. 625 (1986). A sufficient case has not been made for revisiting those precedents, and accordingly I join the Court's opinion.

I also join Justice Alito's concurrence, which correctly distinguishes between the time the right to counsel attaches and the circumstances under which counsel must be provided.

JUSTICE ALITO, with whom THE CHIEF JUSTICE and JUSTICE SCALIA join, concurring.

I join the Court's opinion because I do not understand it to hold that a defendant is entitled to the assistance of appointed counsel as soon as his Sixth Amendment right attaches. As I interpret our precedents, the term "attachment" signifies nothing more than the beginning of the defendant's

[16] The cases have defined critical stages as proceedings between an individual and agents of the State (whether "formal or informal, in court or out," see *United States v. Wade,* 388 U.S. 218, 226 (1967)) that amount to "trial-like confrontations," at which counsel would help the accused "in coping with legal problems or . . . meeting his adversary," *United States v. Ash,* 413 U.S. 300, 312–313 (1973); see also *Massiah v. United States,* 377 U.S. 201 (1964).

prosecution. It does not mark the beginning of a substantive entitlement to the assistance of counsel. I write separately to elaborate on my understanding of the term "attachment" and its relationship to the Amendment's substantive guarantee of "the Assistance of Counsel for [the] defence."

* * *

Because pretrial criminal procedures vary substantially from jurisdiction to jurisdiction, there is room for disagreement about when a "prosecution" begins for Sixth Amendment purposes. As the Court, notes, however, we have previously held that "arraignments" that were functionally indistinguishable from the Texas magistration marked the point at which the Sixth Amendment right to counsel "attached."

It does not follow, however, and I do not understand the Court to hold, that the county had an obligation to appoint an attorney to represent petitioner within some specified period after his magistration. To so hold, the Court would need to do more than conclude that petitioner's criminal prosecution had begun. It would also need to conclude that the assistance of counsel in the wake of a Texas magistration is part of the substantive guarantee of the Sixth Amendment. That question lies beyond our reach, petitioner having never sought our review of it. To recall the framework laid out earlier, we have been asked to address only the *when* question, not the *what* question. Whereas the temporal scope of the right is defined by the words "[i]n all criminal prosecutions," the right's substantive guarantee flows from a different textual font: the words "Assistance of Counsel for his defence."

In interpreting this latter phrase, we have held that "defence" means defense at trial, not defense in relation to other objectives that may be important to the accused. We have thus rejected the argument that the Sixth Amendment entitles the criminal defendant to the assistance of appointed counsel at a probable cause hearing. More generally, we have rejected the notion that the right to counsel entitles the defendant to a "preindictment private investigator."

At the same time, we have recognized that certain pretrial events may so prejudice the outcome of the defendant's prosecution that, as a practical matter, the defendant must be represented at those events in order to enjoy genuinely effective assistance at trial. Thus, we have held that an indigent defendant is entitled to the assistance of appointed counsel at a preliminary hearing if "substantial prejudice . . . inheres in the . . . confrontation" and "counsel [may] help avoid that prejudice." *Coleman v. Alabama,* 399 U.S. 1, 9 (1970) (plurality opinion) (internal quotation marks omitted). We have also held that the assistance of counsel is guaranteed at a pretrial lineup, since "the confrontation compelled by the State between the accused and the victim or witnesses to a crime to elicit identification evidence is peculiarly riddled with innumerable dangers and variable factors which might seriously, even crucially, derogate from a fair trial." [*United States v. Wade*, 388 U.S. 218, 228 (1967)] Other "critical stages" of the prosecution include pretrial interrogation, a pretrial psychiatric exam, and certain kinds of arraignments.

Weaving together these strands of authority, I interpret the Sixth Amendment to require the appointment of counsel only after the defendant's prosecution has begun, and then only as necessary to guarantee the defendant effective assistance at trial. It follows that defendants in Texas will not necessarily be entitled to the assistance of counsel within some specified period after their magistrations. Texas counties need only appoint counsel as far in advance of trial, and as far in advance of any pretrial "critical stage," as necessary to guarantee effective assistance at trial.

The Court expresses no opinion on whether Gillespie County satisfied that obligation in this case. Petitioner has asked us to decide only the limited question whether his magistration marked the beginning of his "criminal prosecutio[n]" within the meaning of the Sixth Amendment. Because I agree with the Court's resolution of that limited question, I join its opinion in full.

JUSTICE THOMAS, dissenting.

The Court holds today—for the first time after plenary consideration of the question—that a criminal prosecution begins, and that the Sixth Amendment right to counsel therefore attaches, when an individual who has been placed under arrest makes an initial appearance before a magistrate for a probable-cause determination and the setting of bail. Because the Court's holding is not supported by the original meaning of the Sixth Amendment or any reasonable interpretation of our precedents, I respectfully dissent.

I

* * *

A

There is no better place to begin than with Blackstone, "whose works constituted the preeminent authority on English law for the founding generation." Blackstone devoted more than 100 pages of his Commentaries on the Laws of England to a discussion of the "regular and ordinary method of proceeding in the courts of criminal jurisdiction." 4 W. Blackstone, COMMENTARIES (hereinafter Blackstone).

At the outset of his discussion, Blackstone organized the various stages of a criminal proceeding "under twelve general heads, following each other in a progressive order." The first six relate to pretrial events: "1. Arrest; 2. Commitment and bail; 3. *Prosecution;* 4. Process; 5. Arraignment, and it's incidents; 6. Plea, and issue." Thus, the first significant fact is that Blackstone did not describe the entire criminal process as a "prosecution," but rather listed prosecution as the third step in a list of successive stages. For a more complete understanding of what Blackstone meant by "prosecution," however, we must turn to chapter 23, entitled "Of the Several Modes of Prosecution." There, Blackstone explained that—after arrest and examination by a justice of the peace to determine whether a suspect should be discharged, committed to prison, or admitted to bail—the "next step towards the punishment of offenders is their *prosecution, or the manner of their formal accusation.*"

Blackstone thus provides a definition of "prosecution": the manner of an offender's "formal accusation." The modifier "formal" is significant because it distinguishes "prosecution" from earlier stages of the process involving a different kind of accusation: the allegation of criminal conduct necessary to justify arrest and detention. Blackstone's discussion of arrest, commitment, and bail makes clear that a person could not be arrested and detained without a "charge" or "accusation," *i.e.,* an allegation, supported by probable cause, that the person had committed a crime. But the accusation justifying arrest and detention was clearly preliminary to the "formal accusation" that Blackstone identified with "prosecution."

* * *

From the foregoing, the basic elements of a criminal "prosecution" emerge with reasonable clarity. "Prosecution," as Blackstone used the term, referred to "instituting a criminal suit" by filing a formal charging document—an indictment, presentment, or information—upon which the defendant was to be tried in a court with power to punish the alleged offense. And, significantly, Blackstone's usage appears to have accorded with the ordinary meaning of the term. See 2 N. Webster, AN AMERICAN DICTIONARY OF THE ENGLISH LANGUAGE (1828) (defining "prosecution" as "[t]he institution or commencement and continuance of a criminal suit; the process of exhibiting formal charges against an offender before a legal tribunal, and pursuing them to final judgment," and noting that "*[p]rosecutions* may be by presentment, information or indictment").

* * *

III

It is clear that when [*Kirby v. Illinois*, 406 U.S. 682] was decided in 1972 there was no precedent in this Court for the conclusion that a criminal prosecution begins, and the right to counsel therefore attaches, at an initial appearance before a magistrate. The Court concludes, however, that two subsequent decisions—*Brewer v. Williams,* 430 U.S. 387 (1977), and *Michigan v. Jackson,* 475 U.S. 625 (1986)—stand for that proposition. Those decisions, which relied almost exclusively on *Kirby,* cannot bear the weight the Court puts on them.

In *Brewer,* the defendant challenged his conviction for murdering a 10-year-old girl on the ground that his Sixth Amendment right to counsel had been violated when detectives elicited incriminating statements from him while transporting him from Davenport, Iowa, where he had been arrested on a warrant for abduction and "arraigned before a judge . . . on the outstanding arrest warrant," to Des Moines, where he was to be tried. The principal issue was whether the defendant had waived his right to have counsel present during police questioning when he voluntarily engaged one of the detectives in a "wide-ranging conversation." He subsequently agreed to lead the detectives to the girl's body in response to the so-called " 'Christian burial speech,' " in which one of the detectives told the defendant that " 'the parents of this little girl should be entitled to a Christian burial for the little girl who was snatched away from them on Christmas [E]ve and murdered.' " Not surprisingly, the parties vigorously disputed the waiver issue, and it sharply divided the Court.

In contrast, the question whether the defendant's right to counsel had attached was neither raised in the courts below nor disputed before this Court. Nonetheless, the Court, after quoting *Kirby's* formulation of the test, offered its conclusory observations:

> There can be no doubt in the present case that judicial proceedings had been initiated against Williams before the start of the automobile ride from Davenport to Des Moines. A warrant had been issued for his arrest, he had been arraigned on that warrant before a judge in a Davenport courtroom, and he had been committed by the court to confinement in jail. The State does not contend otherwise.

* * *

Even assuming, however, that the arraignment in *Brewer* was functionally identical to the initial appearance here, *Brewer* offered no reasoning for its conclusion that the right to counsel attached at such a proceeding. One is left with the distinct impression that the Court simply saw the word "arraignment" in *Kirby's* attachment test and concluded that the right must have attached because the defendant had been "arraigned." There is no indication that *Brewer* considered the difference between an arraignment on a warrant and an arraignment at which the defendant pleads to the indictment.

The Court finds it significant that *Brewer* expressed "no doubt" that the right had attached. There was no need for a "lengthy disquisitio[n]," the Court says, because *Brewer* purportedly "found the attachment issue an easy one." What the Court neglects to mention is that *Brewer's* attachment holding is indisputably no longer good law. That is because we have subsequently held that the Sixth Amendment right to counsel is "offense specific," meaning that it attaches only to those offenses for which the defendant has been formally charged, and not to "other offenses 'closely related factually' to the charged offense." *Texas v. Cobb,* 532 U.S. 162, 164 (2001). Because the defendant in *Brewer* had been arraigned only on the abduction warrant, there is no doubt that, under *Cobb,* his right to counsel had not yet attached with respect to the murder charges that were subsequently brought. But the Court in *Cobb* did not consider itself bound by *Brewer's* implicit holding on the attachment question. And here, as in *Cobb, Brewer* did not address the fact that the arraignment on the warrant was not the same type of arraignment at which the right to counsel had previously been held to attach, and the parties did not argue the question. *Brewer* is thus entitled to no more precedential weight here than it was in *Cobb.*

Nor does *Jackson* control. In *Jackson,* as in *Brewer,* the attachment issue was secondary. The question presented was "not whether respondents had a right to counsel at their postarraignment, custodial interrogations," but "whether respondents validly waived their right to counsel." And, as in *Brewer,* the Court's waiver holding was vigorously disputed. Unlike in *Brewer,* however, the attachment question was at least contested in *Jackson*—but barely. With respect to respondent Jackson, the State conceded the issue. And with respect to respondent Bladel, the State had conceded the issue below and raised it for the first time before this Court, devoting only three pages of its brief to the question.

The Court disposed of the issue in a footnote. As in *Brewer,* the Court did not describe the nature of the proceeding. It stated only that the respondents were "arraigned." The Court phrased the question presented in terms of "arraignment," and repeated the words "arraignment" or "postarraignment" no fewer than 35 times in the course of its opinion.

* * *

The only rule that can be derived from the face of the opinion in *Jackson* is that if a proceeding is called an "arraignment," the right to counsel attaches. That rule would not govern this case because petitioner's initial appearance was not called an "arraignment" (the parties refer to it as a "magistration"). And that would, in any case, be a silly rule. The Sixth Amendment consequences of a proceeding should turn on the substance of what happens there, not on what the State chooses to call it. But the Court in *Jackson* did not focus on the substantive distinction between an initial arraignment and an arraignment on the indictment. Instead, the Court simply cited *Kirby* and left it at that. In these circumstances, I would recognize *Jackson* for what it was—a cursory treatment of an issue that was not the primary focus of the Court's opinion. Surely *Jackson's* footnote must yield to our reasoned precedents.

Moreover, even looking behind the opinion, *Jackson* does not support the result the Court reaches today. Respondent Bladel entered a "not guilty" plea at his arraignment and both *Hamilton v. Alabama,* 368 U.S. 52 (1961), and *White v. Maryland,* 373 U.S. 59 (1963) *(per curiam),* had already held that a defendant has a right to counsel when he enters a plea. The Court suggests that this fact is irrelevant because the magistrate in Bladel's case "had no jurisdiction to accept a plea of guilty to a felony charge." But that distinction does not appear in either *Hamilton* or *White.* Thus, the most that *Jackson* can possibly be made to stand for is that the right to counsel attaches at an initial appearance where the defendant enters a plea. And that rule would not govern this case because petitioner did not enter a plea at his initial appearance.

* * *

None of these defining characteristics of a "criminal prosecution" applies to petitioner's initial appearance before the magistrate. The initial appearance was not an "adversary" proceeding, and petitioner was not "faced with the prosecutorial forces of organized society." Instead, he stood in front of a "little glass window," filled out various forms, and was read his *Miranda* rights. The State had not committed itself to prosecute—only a prosecutor may file felony charges in Texas, and there is no evidence that any prosecutor was even aware of petitioner's arrest or appearance. The adverse positions of government and defendant had not yet solidified—the State's prosecutorial officers had not yet decided whether to press charges and, if so, which charges to press. And petitioner was not immersed in the intricacies of substantive and procedural criminal law—shortly after the proceeding he was free on bail, and no further proceedings occurred until six months later when he was indicted.

* * *

Neither petitioner nor the Court identifies any way in which petitioner's ability to receive a fair trial was undermined by the absence of counsel during the period between his initial appearance and his indictment. Nothing during that period exposed petitioner to the risk that he would be convicted as the result of ignorance of his rights. Instead, the gravamen of petitioner's complaint is that if counsel had been appointed earlier, he would have been able to stave off indictment by convincing the prosecutor that petitioner was not guilty of the crime alleged. But the Sixth Amendment protects against the risk of erroneous *conviction,* not the risk of unwarranted *prosecution.*

Petitioner argues that the right to counsel is implicated here because restrictions were imposed on his liberty when he was required to post bail. But we have never suggested that the accused's right to the assistance of counsel "for his defence" entails a right to use counsel as a sword to contest pretrial detention. To the contrary, we have flatly rejected that notion, reasoning that a defendant's liberty interests are protected by other constitutional guarantees.

* * *

Points for Discussion

1. Justice Alito argues in his concurrence that the Court does not hold that there was a Sixth Amendment violation here, merely that the right to counsel "attached" at the defendant's article 15.17 hearing. He points out that it does not necessarily follow from the fact that the right to counsel has "attached" that the defendant was denied the right to counsel. The initial appearance may simply not have been a critical stage of the prosecution. The Court did not reach this issue.

2. Justice Thomas cites historical evidence for the proposition that the founders envisioned the prosecution as commencing significantly after the initial appearance before a magistrate. Would such a reading leave a defendant without any protections until the trial begins?

CHAPTER 8

THE PRIVILEGE AGAINST COMPELLED SELF-INCRIMINATION

■ ■ ■

The Fifth Amendment provides that no person shall be "compelled in any criminal case to be a witness against himself." Despite the categorical language of the Amendment, the Supreme Court has consistently held that some evidence can be compelled from a defendant. The police may, without violating the prohibition against compelled self-incrimination, draw blood, *Schmerber v. California*, 384 U.S. 757 (1966); obtain a handwriting sample, *Gilbert v. California*, 388 U.S. 263 (1967); or demand a voice exemplar, *United States v. Dionisio*, 410 U.S. 1 (1971). This is so because the Amendment has been read to prohibit only the compulsion of testimonial communications.

In *Holt v. United States*, 218 U.S. 245, 252–53 (1910), the Court explained the distinction between evidence that could be compelled from a defendant and evidence that could not:

> [T]he prohibition of compelling a man in a criminal court to be witness against himself is a prohibition of the use of physical or moral compulsion to extort communications from him, not an exclusion of his body as evidence when it may be material. The objection in principle would forbid a jury to look at a prisoner and compare his features with a photograph in proof.

In other words, the defendant can be compelled to give evidence against himself; he simply cannot be compelled to *testify* against himself. In this chapter, we investigate both parts of this prohibition: what it means to be compelled and what it means to testify.

A. "COMPELLED"

We have already seen two cases of police interrogation held to violate the prohibition on compelled testimony. In *Brown v. Mississippi*, the use of torture was held to violate the Fourteenth Amendment's requirement that the states provide a criminal defendant with due process of law. In *Spano v. New York*, the Court came to the same conclusion with regard to the subtler coercion employed by the police in that case. The cases below provide a modern view of when police behavior compels a defendant to give testimony against himself.

COLORADO V. CONNELLY

479 U.S. 157 (1986)

CHIEF JUSTICE REHNQUIST delivered the opinion of the court.

In this case, the Supreme Court of Colorado held that the United States Constitution requires a court to suppress a confession when the mental state of the defendant, at the time he made the confession, interfered with his "rational intellect" and his "free will." Because this decision seemed to conflict with prior holdings of this Court, we granted certiorari. We conclude that the admissibility of this kind of statement is governed by state rules of evidence, rather than by our previous decisions regarding coerced confessions and *Miranda* waivers. We therefore reverse.

I

On August 18, 1983, Officer Patrick Anderson of the Denver Police Department was in uniform, working in an off-duty capacity in downtown Denver. Respondent Francis Connelly approached Officer Anderson and, without any prompting, stated that he had murdered someone and wanted to talk about it. Anderson immediately advised respondent that he had the right to remain silent, that anything he said could be used against him in court, and that he had the right to an attorney prior to any police questioning. Respondent stated that he understood these rights but he still wanted to talk about the murder. Understandably bewildered by this confession, Officer Anderson asked respondent several questions. Connelly denied that he had been drinking, denied that he had been taking any drugs, and stated that, in the past, he had been a patient in several mental hospitals. Officer Anderson again told Connelly that he was under no obligation to say anything. Connelly replied that it was "all right," and that he would talk to Officer Anderson because his conscience had been bothering him. To Officer Anderson, respondent appeared to understand fully the nature of his acts.

Shortly thereafter, Homicide Detective Stephen Antuna arrived. Respondent was again advised of his rights, and Detective Antuna asked him "what he had on his mind." Respondent answered that he had come all the way from Boston to confess to the murder of Mary Ann Junta, a young girl whom he had killed in Denver sometime during November 1982. Respondent was taken to police headquarters, and a search of police records revealed that the body of an unidentified female had been found in April 1983. Respondent openly detailed his story to Detective Antuna and Sergeant Thomas Haney, and readily agreed to take the officers to the scene of the killing. Under Connelly's sole direction, the two officers and respondent proceeded in a police vehicle to the location of the crime. Respondent pointed out the exact location of the murder. Throughout this episode, Detective Antuna perceived no indication whatsoever that respondent was suffering from any kind of mental illness.

Respondent was held overnight. During an interview with the public defender's office the following morning, he became visibly disoriented. He began giving confused answers to questions, and for the first time, stated that "voices" had told him to come to Denver and that he had followed the directions of these voices in confessing. Respondent was sent to a state hospital for evaluation. He was initially found incompetent to assist in his own defense. By March 1984, however, the doctors evaluating respondent determined that he was competent to proceed to trial.

At a preliminary hearing, respondent moved to suppress all of his statements. Dr. Jeffrey Metzner, a psychiatrist employed by the state hospital, testified that respondent was suffering from chronic schizophrenia and was in a psychotic state at least as of August 17, 1983, the day before he confessed. Metzner's interviews with respondent revealed that respondent was following the "voice of God." This voice instructed respondent to withdraw money from the bank, to buy an airplane ticket, and to fly from Boston to Denver. When respondent arrived from Boston, God's voice became stronger and told respondent either to confess to the killing or to commit suicide. Reluctantly following the command of the voices, respondent approached Officer Anderson and confessed.

Dr. Metzner testified that, in his expert opinion, respondent was experiencing "command hallucinations." This condition interfered with respondent's "volitional abilities; that is, his ability to make free and rational choices." Dr. Metzner further testified that Connelly's illness did not significantly impair his cognitive abilities. Thus, respondent understood the rights he had when Officer Anderson and Detective Antuna advised him that he need not speak. Dr. Metzner admitted that the "voices" could in reality be Connelly's interpretation of his own guilt, but explained that in his opinion, Connelly's psychosis motivated his confession.

* * *

II

The Due Process Clause of the Fourteenth Amendment provides that no State shall "deprive any person of life, liberty, or property, without due process of law." Just last Term, in *Miller v. Fenton,* 474 U.S. 104, 109 (1985), we held that by virtue of the Due Process Clause "certain interrogation techniques, either in isolation or as applied to the unique characteristics of a particular suspect, are so offensive to a civilized system of justice that they must be condemned."

Indeed, coercive government misconduct was the catalyst for this Court's seminal confession case, *Brown v. Mississippi,* 297 U.S. 278 (1936). In that case, police officers extracted confessions from the accused through brutal torture. The Court had little difficulty concluding that even though the Fifth Amendment did not at that time apply to the States, the actions of the police were "revolting to the sense of justice." The Court has retained this due process focus, even after holding, in *Malloy v. Hogan,* 378 U.S. 1 (1964), that the Fifth Amendment privilege against compulsory self-incrimination applies to the States.

Thus the cases considered by this Court over the 50 years since *Brown v. Mississippi* have focused upon the crucial element of police overreaching. While each confession case has turned on its own set of factors justifying the conclusion that police conduct was oppressive, all have contained a substantial element of coercive police conduct. Absent police conduct causally related to the confession, there is simply no basis for concluding that any state actor has deprived a criminal defendant of due process of law. Respondent correctly notes that as interrogators have turned to more subtle forms of psychological persuasion, courts have found the mental condition of the defendant a more significant factor in the "voluntariness" calculus. See *Spano v. New York,* 360 U.S. 315 (1959). But this fact does not justify a conclusion that a defendant's mental condition, by itself and apart from its relation to official coercion, should ever dispose of the inquiry into constitutional "voluntariness."

* * *

Our "involuntary confession" jurisprudence is entirely consistent with the settled law requiring some sort of "state action" to support a claim of violation of the Due Process Clause of the Fourteenth Amendment. The Colorado trial court, of course, found that the police committed no wrongful acts, and that finding has been neither challenged by respondent nor disturbed by the Supreme Court of Colorado. The latter court, however, concluded that sufficient state action was present by virtue of the admission of the confession into evidence in a court of the State.[a]

The difficulty with the approach of the Supreme Court of Colorado is that it fails to recognize the essential link between coercive activity of the State, on the one hand, and a resulting confession by a defendant, on the other. The flaw in respondent's constitutional argument is that it would expand our previous line of "voluntariness" cases into a far-ranging requirement that courts must divine a defendant's motivation for speaking or acting as he did even though there be no claim that governmental conduct coerced his decision.

The most outrageous behavior by a private party seeking to secure evidence against a defendant does not make that evidence inadmissible under the Due Process Clause. We have also observed that "[j]urists and

[a] Although the Fifth Amendment now applies with equal force against the states as against the federal government, the Court often analyzes claims of police coercion under the Due Process Clause of the Fourteenth Amendment rather than under the Compelled Self-Incrimination Clause of the Fifth Amendment. One distinction between the two is that the Fifth Amendment privilege is fundamentally a trial right; it is not violated until a defendant is compelled *in a criminal case* to testify. By contrast, the Fourteenth Amendment's Due Process provision is a restraint on police overreaching; government officials may deprive an individual of due process even if she is never ultimately prosecuted for a crime. *See, e.g., Chavez v. Martinez,* 538 U.S. 760 (2003).—Eds.

scholars uniformly have recognized that the exclusionary rule imposes a substantial cost on the societal interest in law enforcement by its proscription of what concededly is relevant evidence." *United States v. Janis,* 428 U.S. 433, 448–449 (1976). Moreover, suppressing respondent's statements would serve absolutely no purpose in enforcing constitutional guarantees. The purpose of excluding evidence seized in violation of the Constitution is to substantially deter future violations of the Constitution. See *United States v. Leon,* 468 U.S. 897, 906–913 (1984). Only if we were to establish a brand new constitutional right—the right of a criminal defendant to confess to his crime only when totally rational and properly motivated—could respondent's present claim be sustained.

We have previously cautioned against expanding "currently applicable exclusionary rules by erecting additional barriers to placing truthful and probative evidence before state juries. . . ." We abide by that counsel now. "[T]he central purpose of a criminal trial is to decide the factual question of the defendant's guilt or innocence," and while we have previously held that exclusion of evidence may be necessary to protect constitutional guarantees, both the necessity for the collateral inquiry and the exclusion of evidence deflect a criminal trial from its basic purpose. Respondent would now have us require sweeping inquiries into the state of mind of a criminal defendant who has confessed, inquiries quite divorced from any coercion brought to bear on the defendant by the State. We think the Constitution rightly leaves this sort of inquiry to be resolved by state laws governing the admission of evidence and erects no standard of its own in this area. A statement rendered by one in the condition of respondent might be proved to be quite unreliable, but this is a matter to be governed by the evidentiary laws of the forum and not by the Due Process Clause of the Fourteenth Amendment. "The aim of the requirement of due process is not to exclude presumptively false evidence, but to prevent fundamental unfairness in the use of evidence, whether true or false."

We hold that coercive police activity is a necessary predicate to the finding that a confession is not "voluntary" within the meaning of the Due Process Clause of the Fourteenth Amendment. We also conclude that the taking of respondent's statements, and their admission into evidence, constitute no violation of that Clause.

* * *

The opinion of JUSTICE BLACKMUN, concurring in part and concurring in the judgment, is omitted.

JUSTICE STEVENS, concurring in the judgment in part and dissenting in part.

Respondent made incriminatory statements both before and after he was handcuffed and taken into custody. The only question presented by the Colorado District Attorney in his certiorari petition concerned the admissibility of respondent's precustodial statements. I agree with the State of Colorado that the United States Constitution does not require suppression of those statements, but in reaching that conclusion, unlike the Court, I am perfectly willing to accept the state trial court's finding that the statements were involuntary.

The state trial court found that, in view of the "overwhelming evidence presented by the Defense," the prosecution did not meet its burden of demonstrating that respondent's initial statements to Officer Anderson were voluntary. Nevertheless, in my opinion, the use of these involuntary precustodial statements does not violate the Fifth Amendment because they were not the product of state compulsion. Although they may well be so unreliable that they could not support a conviction, at this stage of the proceeding I could not say that they have no probative force whatever. The fact that the statements were involuntary—just as the product of Lady Macbeth's nightmare was involuntary—does not mean that their use for whatever evidentiary value they may have is fundamentally unfair or a denial of due process.

The postcustodial statements raise an entirely distinct question. When the officer whom respondent approached elected to handcuff him and to take him into custody, the police assumed a fundamentally different relationship with him. Prior to that moment, the police had no duty to give respondent *Miranda* warnings and had every right to continue their exploratory conversation with him. Once the custodial relationship was established, however, the questioning assumed a presumptively coercive character. In my opinion the questioning could not thereafter go forward in the absence of a valid waiver of respondent's constitutional rights unless he was provided with counsel. Since it is undisputed that respondent was not then competent to stand trial, I would also conclude that he was not competent to waive his constitutional right to remain silent.

The Court seems to believe that a waiver can be voluntary even if it is not the product of an exercise of the defendant's "free will." The Court's position is not only incomprehensible to me; it is also foreclosed by the Court's recent pronouncement in *Moran v. Burbine,* 475 U.S. 412, 421 (1986), that "the relinquishment of the right must have been voluntary in the sense that it was the product of a free and deliberate choice . . . ." Because respondent's waiver was not voluntary in that sense, his custodial interrogation was presumptively coercive. The Colorado Supreme Court was unquestionably correct in concluding that his post-custodial incriminatory statements were inadmissible.

Accordingly, I concur in the judgment insofar as it applies to respondent's precustodial statements but respectfully dissent from the Court's disposition of the question that was not presented by the certiorari petition.

JUSTICE BRENNAN, with whom JUSTICE MARSHALL joins, dissenting.

Today the Court denies Mr. Connelly his fundamental right to make a vital choice with a sane mind, involving a determination that could allow the State to deprive him of liberty or even life. This holding is unprecedented: "Surely in the present stage of our civilization a most basic sense of justice is affronted by the spectacle of incarcerating a human being upon the basis of a statement he made while insane. . . ." Because I believe that the use of a mentally ill person's involuntary confession is antithetical to the notion of fundamental fairness embodied in the Due Process Clause, I dissent.

I

* * *

At the time of his confession, Mr. Connelly's mental problems included "grandiose and delusional thinking." He had a known history of "thought withdrawal and insertion." Although physicians had treated Mr. Connelly "with a wide variety of medications in the past including antipsychotic medications," he had not taken any antipsychotic medications for at least six months prior to his confession. Following his arrest, Mr. Connelly initially was found incompetent to stand trial because the court-appointed psychiatrist, Dr. Metzner, "wasn't very confident that he could consistently relate accurate information." Dr. Metzner testified that Mr. Connelly was unable "to make free and rational choices" due to auditory hallucinations: "[W]hen he was read his *Miranda* rights, he probably had the capacity to know that he was being read his *Miranda* rights [but] he wasn't able to use that information because of the command hallucinations that he had experienced." He achieved competency to stand trial only after six months of hospitalization and treatment with antipsychotic and sedative medications.

* * *

II

The absence of police wrongdoing should not, by itself, determine the voluntariness of a confession by a mentally ill person. The requirement that a confession be voluntary reflects a recognition of the importance of free will and of reliability in determining the admissibility of a confession, and thus demands an inquiry into the totality of the circumstances surrounding the confession.

A

Today's decision restricts the application of the term "involuntary" to those confessions obtained by police coercion. Confessions by mentally ill individuals or by persons coerced by parties other than police officers are now considered "voluntary." The Court's failure to recognize all forms of involuntariness or coercion as antithetical to due process reflects a refusal to acknowledge free will as a value of constitutional consequence. But due process derives much of its meaning from a conception of fundamental fairness that emphasizes the right to make vital choices voluntarily: "The Fourteenth Amendment secures against state invasion . . . the right of a person to remain silent unless he chooses to speak in the unfettered exercise of his own will. . . ." *Malloy v. Hogan,* 378 U.S. 1, 8 (1964). This right requires vigilant protection if we are to safeguard the values of private conscience and human dignity.

* * *

We have never confined our focus to police coercion, because the value of freedom of will has demanded a broader inquiry. The confession cases decided by this Court over the 50 years since *Brown v. Mississippi,* 297 U.S. 278 (1936), have focused upon both police overreaching and free will. While it is true that police overreaching has been an element of every confession case to date, it is also true that in every case the Court has made clear that ensuring that a confession is a product of free will is an independent concern. The fact that involuntary confessions have always been excluded in part because of police overreaching signifies only that this is a case of first impression. Until today, we have never upheld the admission of a confession that does not reflect the exercise of free will.

* * *

This Court abandons this precedent in favor of the view that only confessions rendered involuntary by some state action are inadmissible, and that the only relevant form of state action is police conduct. But even if state action is required, police overreaching is not its only relevant form. The Colorado Supreme Court held that the trial court's admission of the involuntary confession into evidence is also state action. The state court's analysis is consistent with *Brown v. Mississippi,* 297 U.S. 278 (1936), on which this Court so heavily relies. *Brown,* a case involving the use of confessions at trial, makes clear that "[t]he due process clause requires 'that state action, *whether through one agency or another,* shall be consistent with the fundamental principles of liberty and justice which lie at the base of all our civil and political institutions.'" Police conduct constitutes but one form of state action. "The objective of deterring improper police conduct is only part of the larger objective of safeguarding the integrity of our adversary system." *Harris v. New York,* 401 U.S. 222, 231 (1971) (Brennan, J., dissenting).[3]

[3] Even if police knowledge of the defendant's insanity is required to exclude an involuntary confession, the record supports a finding of police knowledge in this case. The Court accepts the trial court's finding of no police wrongdoing since, in the trial judge's view, none of the police officers knew that Mr. Connelly was insane. After plenary review of the record, I conclude that this finding is clearly erroneous.

When the defendant confessed to Officer Anderson, the officer's first thought was that Mr. Connelly was a "crackpot." Today's Court describes Officer Anderson as "[u]nderstandably bewildered." After giving *Miranda* warnings, the officer questioned the defendant about whether

The only logical "flaw" which the Court detects in this argument is that it would require courts to "divine a defendant's motivation for speaking or acting as he did even though there be no claim that governmental conduct coerced his decision." Such a criticism, however, ignores the fact that we have traditionally examined the totality of the circumstances, including the motivation and competence of the defendant, in determining whether a confession is voluntary. Even today's Court admits that "as interrogators have turned to more subtle forms of psychological persuasion, courts have found the mental condition of the defendant a more significant factor in the 'voluntariness' calculus." The Court's holding that involuntary confessions are only those procured through police misconduct is thus inconsistent with the Court's historical insistence that only confessions reflecting an exercise of free will be admitted into evidence.

B

Since the Court redefines voluntary confessions to include confessions by mentally ill individuals, the reliability of these confessions becomes a central concern. A concern for reliability is inherent in our criminal justice system, which relies upon accusatorial rather than inquisitorial practices. While an inquisitorial system prefers obtaining confessions from criminal defendants, an accusatorial system must place its faith in determinations of "guilt by evidence independently and freely secured." In *Escobedo v. Illinois,* 378 U.S. 478 (1964), we justified our reliance upon accusatorial practices:

> We have learned the lesson of history, ancient and modern, that a system of criminal law enforcement which comes to depend on the "confession" will, in the long run, be less reliable and more subject to abuses than a system which depends on extrinsic evidence independently secured through skillful investigation.

Our interpretation of the Due Process Clause has been shaped by this preference for accusatorial practices and by a concern for reliability.

Our distrust for reliance on confessions is due, in part, to their decisive impact upon the adversarial process. Triers of fact accord confessions such heavy weight in their determinations that "the introduction of a confession makes the other aspects of a trial in court superfluous, and the real trial, for all practical purposes, occurs when the confession is obtained." No other class of evidence is so profoundly prejudicial. "Thus the decision to confess

---

he used drugs or alcohol. He also asked Mr. Connelly if he had been treated for any mental disorders, and the defendant responded that he had been treated in five different mental hospitals. While this Court concludes that "Detective Antuna perceived no indication whatsoever that respondent was suffering from any kind of mental illness," the record indicates that Officer Anderson informed the detective about the defendant's five hospitalizations in mental institutions. Thus, even under this Court's test requiring police wrongdoing, the record indicates that the officers here had sufficient knowledge about the defendant's mental incapacity to render the confession "involuntary."

before trial amounts in effect to a waiver of the right to require the state at trial to meet its heavy burden of proof."

Because the admission of a confession so strongly tips the balance against the defendant in the adversarial process, we must be especially careful about a confession's reliability. We have to date not required a finding of reliability for involuntary confessions only because *all* such confessions have been excluded upon a finding of involuntariness, regardless of reliability. The Court's adoption today of a restrictive definition of an "involuntary" confession will require heightened scrutiny of a confession's reliability.

* * *

Moreover, the record is barren of any corroboration of the mentally ill defendant's confession. No physical evidence links the defendant to the alleged crime. Police did not identify the alleged victim's body as the woman named by the defendant. Mr. Connelly identified the alleged scene of the crime, but it has not been verified that the unidentified body was found there or that a crime actually occurred there. There is not a shred of competent evidence in this record linking the defendant to the charged homicide. There is only Mr. Connelly's confession.

Minimum standards of due process should require that the trial court find substantial indicia of reliability, on the basis of evidence extrinsic to the confession itself, before admitting the confession of a mentally ill person into evidence. I would require the trial court to make such a finding on remand. To hold otherwise allows the State to imprison and possibly to execute a mentally ill defendant based solely upon an inherently unreliable confession.

* * *

Points for Discussion

1. If the central inquiry of the Fifth and Fourteenth Amendments is one of voluntariness, then it is relatively clear that Connelly's confession must be suppressed. If, by contrast, the admissibility of a confession depends on the absence of official coercion, then the statements likely ought to be admitted. Which seems a more appropriate measure of a confession's admissibility?

2. The majority holds that even the worst conduct of private actors cannot violate the Fifth Amendment. Does that mean that the statements obtained in *Brown* would be admissible were it not for the participation of the sheriff's deputies in Brown's torture?

3. The Court cites to *United States v. Leon* for the proposition that exclusionary rules are meant only to deter police misconduct. Justice Brennan's dissent takes a broader view of the purpose of exclusionary rules. What is his position? Did *Miranda v. Arizona* and *Massiah v. United States*

give a deterrence rationale for excluding evidence? Does it make sense to cite *Leon*, a Fourth Amendment case, in this context?

4. Justice Rehnquist's majority opinion states that Connelly did not "bec[o]me visibly disoriented" until he met with a public defender after his confession. According to that opinion, Connelly "appeared to understand fully the nature of his acts" while he was talking with the police. Footnote 3 of Justice Brennan's dissent casts some doubt on that. Does it matter whether the police had reason to believe that Connelly was mentally ill?

5. The majority mentions early in its opinion that "the body of an unidentified female had been found," suggesting that the body is that of Connelly's confessed victim. However, deep into Justice Brennan's opinion, the reader learns that "[p]olice did not identify the alleged victim's body as the woman named by the defendant." Do these facts go to the admissibility of the confession or merely the weight a jury should accord it? For a discussion of the facts of *Connelly*, see William T. Pizzi, Colorado v. Connelly: *What Really Happened*, 7 OHIO ST. J. CRIM. L. 377 (2009).

ARIZONA V. FULMINANTE

499 U.S. 279 (1991)

JUSTICE WHITE delivered an opinion, Parts I, II, and IV of which are the opinion of the court, and Part III of which is a dissenting opinion.†

The Arizona Supreme Court ruled in this case that respondent Oreste Fulminante's confession, received in evidence at his trial for murder, had been coerced and that its use against him was barred by the Fifth and Fourteenth Amendments to the United States Constitution. The court also held that the harmless-error rule could not be used to save the conviction. We affirm the judgment of the Arizona court, although for different reasons than those upon which that court relied.

I

Early in the morning of September 14, 1982, Fulminante called the Mesa, Arizona, Police Department to report that his 11-year-old stepdaughter, Jeneane Michelle Hunt, was missing. He had been caring for Jeneane while his wife, Jeneane's mother, was in the hospital. Two days later, Jeneane's body was found in the desert east of Mesa. She had been shot twice in the head at close range with a large caliber weapon, and a ligature was around her neck. Because of the decomposed condition of the body, it was impossible to tell whether she had been sexually assaulted.

Fulminante's statements to police concerning Jeneane's disappearance and his relationship with her contained a number of inconsistencies, and he became a suspect in her killing. When no charges

† JUSTICE MARSHALL, JUSTICE BLACKMUN AND JUSTICE STEVENS JOIN THIS OPINION IN ITS ENTIRETY; JUSTICE SCALIA JOINS PARTS I AND II; AND JUSTICE KENNEDY JOINS PARTS I AND IV.

were filed against him, Fulminante left Arizona for New Jersey. Fulminante was later convicted in New Jersey on federal charges of possession of a firearm by a felon.

Fulminante was incarcerated in the Ray Brook Federal Correctional Institution in New York. There he became friends with another inmate, Anthony Sarivola, then serving a 60-day sentence for extortion. The two men came to spend several hours a day together. Sarivola, a former police officer, had been involved in loansharking for organized crime but then became a paid informant for the Federal Bureau of Investigation. While at Ray Brook, he masqueraded as an organized crime figure. After becoming friends with Fulminante, Sarivola heard a rumor that Fulminante was suspected of killing a child in Arizona. Sarivola then raised the subject with Fulminante in several conversations, but Fulminante repeatedly denied any involvement in Jeneane's death. During one conversation, he told Sarivola that Jeneane had been killed by bikers looking for drugs; on another occasion, he said he did not know what had happened. Sarivola passed this information on to an agent of the Federal Bureau of Investigation, who instructed Sarivola to find out more.

Sarivola learned more one evening in October 1983, as he and Fulminante walked together around the prison track. Sarivola said that he knew Fulminante was "starting to get some tough treatment and whatnot" from other inmates because of the rumor. Sarivola offered to protect Fulminante from his fellow inmates, but told him, " 'You have to tell me about it,' you know. I mean, in other words, 'For me to give you any help.' " Fulminante then admitted to Sarivola that he had driven Jeneane to the desert on his motorcycle, where he choked her, sexually assaulted her, and made her beg for her life, before shooting her twice in the head.

Sarivola was released from prison in November 1983. Fulminante was released the following May, only to be arrested the next month for another weapons violation. On September 4, 1984, Fulminante was indicted in Arizona for the first-degree murder of Jeneane.

Prior to trial, Fulminante moved to suppress the statement he had given Sarivola in prison, as well as a second confession he had given to Donna Sarivola, then Anthony Sarivola's fiancée and later his wife, following his May 1984 release from prison. He asserted that the confession to Sarivola was coerced, and that the second confession was the "fruit" of the first. Following the hearing, the trial court denied the motion to suppress, specifically finding that, based on the stipulated facts, the confessions were voluntary. The State introduced both confessions as evidence at trial, and on December 19, 1985, Fulminante was convicted of Jeneane's murder. He was subsequently sentenced to death.

Fulminante appealed, arguing, among other things, that his confession to Sarivola was the product of coercion and that its admission at trial violated his rights to due process under the Fifth and Fourteenth

Amendments to the United States Constitution. After considering the evidence at trial as well as the stipulated facts before the trial court on the motion to suppress, the Arizona Supreme Court held that the confession was coerced, but initially determined that the admission of the confession at trial was harmless error, because of the overwhelming nature of the evidence against Fulminante. Upon Fulminante's motion for reconsideration, however, the court ruled that this Court's precedent precluded the use of the harmless-error analysis in the case of a coerced confession. The court therefore reversed the conviction and ordered that Fulminante be retried without the use of the confession to Sarivola. Because of differing views in the state and federal courts over whether the admission at trial of a coerced confession is subject to a harmless-error analysis, we granted the State's petition for certiorari. Although a majority of this Court finds that such a confession is subject to a harmless-error analysis, for the reasons set forth below, we affirm the judgment of the Arizona court.

II

* * *

In applying the totality of the circumstances test to determine that the confession to Sarivola was coerced, the Arizona Supreme Court focused on a number of relevant facts. First, the court noted that "because [Fulminante] was an alleged child murderer, he was in danger of physical harm at the hands of other inmates." In addition, Sarivola was aware that Fulminante had been receiving "rough treatment from the guys." Using his knowledge of these threats, Sarivola offered to protect Fulminante in exchange for a confession to Jeneane's murder and "[i]n response to Sarivola's offer of protection, [Fulminante] confessed." Agreeing with Fulminante that "Sarivola's promise was 'extremely coercive,' " the Arizona court declared: "[T]he confession was obtained as a direct result of extreme coercion and was tendered in the belief that the defendant's life was in jeopardy if he did not confess. This is a true coerced confession in every sense of the word."[2]

* * *

Although the question is a close one, we agree with the Arizona Supreme Court's conclusion that Fulminante's confession was coerced. The

[2] There are additional facts in the record, not relied upon by the Arizona Supreme Court, which also support a finding of coercion. Fulminante possesses low average to average intelligence; he dropped out of school in the fourth grade. He is short in stature and slight in build. Although he had been in prison before, he had not always adapted well to the stress of prison life. While incarcerated at the age of 26, he had "felt threatened by the [prison] population," and he therefore requested that he be placed in protective custody. Once there, however, he was unable to cope with the isolation and was admitted to a psychiatric hospital. The Court has previously recognized that factors such as these are relevant in determining whether a defendant's will has been overborne. In addition, we note that Sarivola's position as Fulminante's friend might well have made the latter particularly susceptible to the former's entreaties.

Arizona Supreme Court found a credible threat of physical violence unless Fulminante confessed. Our cases have made clear that a finding of coercion need not depend upon actual violence by a government agent;[4] a credible threat is sufficient. As we have said, "coercion can be mental as well as physical, and . . . the blood of the accused is not the only hallmark of an unconstitutional inquisition." As in *Payne v. Arkansas,* 356 U.S. 560 (1958), where the Court found that a confession was coerced because the interrogating police officer had promised that if the accused confessed, the officer would protect the accused from an angry mob outside the jailhouse door, so too here, the Arizona Supreme Court found that it was fear of physical violence, absent protection from his friend (and Government agent) Sarivola, which motivated Fulminante to confess. Accepting the Arizona court's finding, permissible on this record, that there was a credible threat of physical violence, we agree with its conclusion that Fulminante's will was overborne in such a way as to render his confession the product of coercion.

III

Four of us, Justices Marshall, Blackmun, Stevens, and myself, would affirm the judgment of the Arizona Supreme Court on the ground that the harmless-error rule is inapplicable to erroneously admitted coerced confessions. We thus disagree with the Justices who have a contrary view.

In extending to coerced confessions the harmless-error rule of *Chapman v. California,* the majority declares that because the Court has applied that analysis to numerous other "trial errors," there is no reason that it should not apply to an error of this nature as well. The four of us remain convinced, however, that we should abide by our cases that have refused to apply the harmless-error rule to coerced confessions, for a coerced confession is fundamentally different from other types of erroneously admitted evidence to which the rule has been applied. Indeed, as the majority concedes, *Chapman* itself recognized that prior cases "have indicated that there are some constitutional rights so basic to a fair trial that their infraction can *never* be treated as harmless error," and it placed in that category the constitutional rule against using a defendant's coerced confession against him at his criminal trial. Moreover, cases since *Chapman* have reiterated the rule that using a defendant's coerced confession against him is a denial of due process of law regardless of the other evidence in the record aside from the confession.

* * *

As the majority concedes, there are other constitutional errors that invalidate a conviction even though there may be no reasonable doubt that

[4] The parties agree that Sarivola acted as an agent of the Government when he questioned Fulminante about the murder and elicited the confession.

the defendant is guilty and would be convicted absent the trial error. For example, a judge in a criminal trial "is prohibited from entering a judgment of conviction or directing the jury to come forward with such a verdict, regardless of how overwhelmingly the evidence may point in that direction." A defendant is entitled to counsel at trial, and as *Chapman* recognized, violating this right can never be harmless error. In *Vasquez v. Hillery,* 474 U.S. 254 (1986), a defendant was found guilty beyond reasonable doubt, but the conviction had been set aside because of the unlawful exclusion of members of the defendant's race from the grand jury that indicted him, despite overwhelming evidence of his guilt. The error at the grand jury stage struck at fundamental values of our society and "undermine[d] the structural integrity of the criminal tribunal itself, and [was] not amenable to harmless-error review." *Vasquez,* like *Chapman,* also noted that rule of automatic reversal when a defendant is tried before a judge with a financial interest in the outcome, despite a lack of any indication that bias influenced the decision. *Waller v. Georgia,* 467 U.S. 39, 49 (1984), recognized that violation of the guarantee of a public trial required reversal without any showing of prejudice and even though the values of a public trial may be intangible and unprovable in any particular case.

The search for truth is indeed central to our system of justice, but "certain constitutional rights are not, and should not be, subject to harmless-error analysis because those rights protect important values that are unrelated to the truth-seeking function of the trial." The right of a defendant not to have his coerced confession used against him is among those rights, for using a coerced confession "abort[s] the basic trial process" and "render[s] a trial fundamentally unfair."

* * *

IV

Since five Justices have determined that harmless-error analysis applies to coerced confessions, it becomes necessary to evaluate under that ruling the admissibility of Fulminante's confession to Sarivola. *Chapman v. California,* 386 U.S., at 24, made clear that "before a federal constitutional error can be held harmless, the court must be able to declare a belief that it was harmless beyond a reasonable doubt." The Court has the power to review the record *de novo* in order to determine an error's harmlessness. In so doing, it must be determined whether the State has met its burden of demonstrating that the admission of the confession to Sarivola did not contribute to Fulminante's conviction. Five of us are of the view that the State has not carried its burden and accordingly affirm the judgment of the court below reversing respondent's conviction.

A confession is like no other evidence. Indeed, "the defendant's own confession is probably the most probative and damaging evidence that can be admitted against him. . . . [T]he admissions of a defendant come from the actor himself, the most knowledgeable and unimpeachable source of information about his past conduct. Certainly, confessions have profound impact on the jury, so much so that we may justifiably doubt its ability to put them out of mind even if told to do so." *Bruton v. United States,* 391 U.S. [123], 139–140 [(1968)] (White, J., dissenting). While some statements by a defendant may concern isolated aspects of the crime or may be incriminating only when linked to other evidence, a full confession in which the defendant discloses the motive for and means of the crime may tempt the jury to rely upon that evidence alone in reaching its decision. In the case of a coerced confession such as that given by Fulminante to Sarivola, the risk that the confession is unreliable, coupled with the profound impact that the confession has upon the jury, requires a reviewing court to exercise extreme caution before determining that the admission of the confession at trial was harmless.

In the Arizona Supreme Court's initial opinion, in which it determined that harmless-error analysis could be applied to the confession, the court found that the admissible second confession to Donna Sarivola rendered the first confession to Anthony Sarivola cumulative. The court also noted that circumstantial physical evidence concerning the wounds, the ligature around Jeneane's neck, the location of the body, and the presence of motorcycle tracks at the scene corroborated the second confession. The court concluded that "due to the overwhelming evidence adduced from the second confession, if there had not been a first confession, the jury would still have had the same basic evidence to convict" Fulminante.

We have a quite different evaluation of the evidence. Our review of the record leads us to conclude that the State has failed to meet its burden of establishing, beyond a reasonable doubt, that the admission of Fulminante's confession to Anthony Sarivola was harmless error. . . .

* * *

Because a majority of the Court has determined that Fulminante's confession to Anthony Sarivola was coerced and because a majority has determined that admitting this confession was not harmless beyond a reasonable doubt, we agree with the Arizona Supreme Court's conclusion that Fulminante is entitled to a new trial at which the confession is not admitted.

CHIEF JUSTICE REHNQUIST, with whom JUSTICE O'CONNOR joins, JUSTICE KENNEDY and JUSTICE SOUTER join as to Parts I and II, and JUSTICE SCALIA joins as to Parts II and III, delivered the opinion of the court with respect to Part II, and a dissenting opinion with respect to Parts I and III.

The Court today properly concludes that the admission of an "involuntary" confession at trial is subject to harmless error analysis.

Nonetheless, the independent review of the record which we are required to make shows that respondent Fulminante's confession was not in fact involuntary. And even if the confession were deemed to be involuntary, the evidence offered at trial, including a second, untainted confession by Fulminante, supports the conclusion that any error here was certainly harmless.

I

* * *

The admissibility of a confession such as that made by respondent Fulminante depends upon whether it was voluntarily made. "The ultimate test remains that which has been the only clearly established test in Anglo-American courts for two hundred years: the test of voluntariness. Is the confession the product of an essentially free and unconstrained choice by its maker? If it is, if he has willed to confess, it may be used against him. If it is not, if his will has been overborne and his capacity for self-determination critically impaired, the use of his confession offends due process."

* * *

Exercising our responsibility to make the independent examination of the record necessary to decide this federal question, I am at a loss to see how the Supreme Court of Arizona reached the conclusion that it did. Fulminante offered no evidence that he believed that his life was in danger or that he in fact confessed to Sarivola in order to obtain the proffered protection. Indeed, he had stipulated that "[a]t no time did the defendant indicate he was in fear of other inmates nor did he ever seek Mr. Sarivola's 'protection.'" Sarivola's testimony that he told Fulminante that "if [he] would tell the truth, he could be protected," adds little if anything to the substance of the parties' stipulation. The decision of the Supreme Court of Arizona rests on an assumption that is squarely contrary to this stipulation, and one that is not supported by any testimony of Fulminante.

The facts of record in the present case are quite different from those present in cases where we have found confessions to be coerced and involuntary. Since Fulminante was unaware that Sarivola was an FBI informant, there existed none of "the danger of coercion result[ing] from the interaction of custody and official interrogation." *Illinois v. Perkins,* 496 U.S. 292, 297 (1990). The fact that Sarivola was a Government informant does not by itself render Fulminante's confession involuntary, since we have consistently accepted the use of informants in the discovery of evidence of a crime as a legitimate investigatory procedure consistent with the Constitution. The conversations between Sarivola and Fulminante were not lengthy, and the defendant was free at all times to leave Sarivola's company. Sarivola at no time threatened him or demanded that he confess; he simply requested that he speak the truth about the matter. Fulminante was an experienced habitue of prisons, and presumably able to fend for himself. In concluding on these facts that Fulminante's confession was involuntary, the Court today embraces a more expansive definition of that term than is warranted by any of our decided cases.

II

Since this Court's landmark decision in *Chapman* v. *California,* 386 U.S. 18 (1967), in which we adopted the general rule that a constitutional error does not automatically require reversal of a conviction, the Court has applied harmless error analysis to a wide range of errors and has recognized that most constitutional errors can be harmless.

The common thread connecting these cases is that each involved "trial error"—error which occurred during the presentation of the case to the jury, and which may therefore be quantitatively assessed in the context of other evidence presented in order to determine whether its admission was harmless beyond a reasonable doubt. In applying harmless-error analysis to these many different constitutional violations, the Court has been faithful to the belief that the harmless-error doctrine is essential to preserve the "principle that the central purpose of a criminal trial is to decide the factual question of the defendant's guilt or innocence, and promotes public respect for the criminal process by focusing on the underlying fairness of the trial rather than on the virtually inevitable presence of immaterial error."

* * *

It is evident from a comparison of the constitutional violations which we have held subject to harmless error, and those which we have held not, that involuntary statements or confessions belong in the former category. The admission of an involuntary confession is a "trial error," similar in both degree and kind to the erroneous admission of other types of evidence. The evidentiary impact of an involuntary confession, and its effect upon the composition of the record, is indistinguishable from that of a confession obtained in violation of the Sixth Amendment—of evidence seized in violation of the Fourth Amendment—or of a prosecutor's improper comment on a defendant's silence at trial in violation of the Fifth Amendment. When reviewing the erroneous admission of an involuntary confession, the appellate court, as it does with the admission of other forms of improperly admitted evidence, simply reviews the remainder of the evidence against the defendant to determine whether the admission of the confession was harmless beyond a reasonable doubt.

* * *

Of course an involuntary confession may have a more dramatic effect on the course of a trial than do other trial errors—in particular cases it may be devastating to a defendant—but this simply means that a reviewing court will conclude in such a case that its admission was not harmless error; it is not a reason for eschewing the harmless-error test entirely. The Supreme Court of Arizona, in its first opinion in the present case, concluded that the admission of Fulminante's confession *was* harmless error. That court concluded that a second and more explicit confession of the crime made by Fulminante after he was released from prison was not tainted by the first confession, and that the second confession, together with physical evidence from the wounds (the victim had been shot twice in the head with a large calibre weapon at close range and a ligature was found around her neck) and other evidence introduced at trial rendered the admission of the first confession harmless beyond a reasonable doubt.

* * *

JUSTICE KENNEDY, concurring in the judgment.

For the reasons stated by the Chief Justice, I agree that Fulminante's confession to Anthony Sarivola was not coerced. In my view, the trial court did not err in admitting this testimony. A majority of the Court, however, finds the confession coerced and proceeds to consider whether harmless-error analysis may be used when a coerced confession has been admitted at trial. With the case in this posture, it is appropriate for me to address the harmless-error issue.

* * *

Points for Discussion

1. A shifting majority of the Court makes three holdings in this case:

   a. that the confession in this case was coerced,

   b. that the introduction of coerced confessions is subject to the harmless error doctrine, and

   c. that the introduction of the confession in this case was not harmless.

With regard to each of these conclusions, who has the better argument, the majority or the dissent?

2. Part of the coercion in this case had to do with the fear that Fulminante felt while in prison. Should that fear be considered in determining whether his confession was voluntary? Is such consideration consistent with *Colorado v. Connelly*?

B. "WITNESS"

SCHMERBER V. CALIFORNIA

384 U.S. 757 (1966)

MR. JUSTICE BRENNAN delivered the opinion of the court.

Petitioner was convicted in Los Angeles Municipal Court of the criminal offense of driving an automobile while under the influence of intoxicating liquor. He had been arrested at a hospital while receiving treatment for injuries suffered in an accident involving the automobile that he had apparently been driving. At the direction of a police officer, a blood sample was then withdrawn from petitioner's body by a physician at the hospital. The chemical analysis of this sample revealed a percent by weight of alcohol in his blood at the time of the offense which indicated intoxication, and the report of this analysis was admitted in evidence at the trial. Petitioner objected to receipt of this evidence of the analysis on the ground that the blood had been withdrawn despite his refusal, on the advice of his counsel, to consent to the test. He contended that in that circumstance the withdrawal of the blood and the admission of the analysis in evidence denied him due process of law under the Fourteenth Amendment, as well as specific guarantees of the Bill of Rights secured against the States by that Amendment: his privilege against self-incrimination under the Fifth Amendment; his right to counsel under the Sixth Amendment; and his right not to be subjected to unreasonable searches and seizures in violation of the Fourth Amendment. The Appellate Department of the California Superior Court rejected these contentions and affirmed the conviction. In view of constitutional decisions since we last considered these issues in *Breithaupt v. Abram*, 352 U.S. 432—see *Escobedo v. State of Illinois*, 378 U.S. 478; *Malloy v. Hogan*, 378 U.S. 1, and *Mapp v. State of Ohio*, 367 U.S. 643—we granted certiorari. We affirm.

* * *

II

THE PRIVILEGE AGAINST SELF-INCRIMINATION CLAIM

* * *

It could not be denied that in requiring petitioner to submit to the withdrawal and chemical analysis of his blood the State compelled him to submit to an attempt to discover evidence that might be used to prosecute him for a criminal offense. He submitted only after the police officer rejected his objection and directed the physician to proceed. The officer's direction to the physician to administer the test over petitioner's objection constituted compulsion for the purposes of the privilege. The critical question, then, is whether petitioner was thus compelled 'to be a witness against himself.'

If the scope of the privilege coincided with the complex of values it helps to protect, we might be obliged to conclude that the privilege was violated. In *Miranda v. Arizona*, 384 U.S. 436, the Court said of the interests protected by the privilege: "All these policies point to one overriding thought: the constitutional foundation underlying the privilege is the respect a government—state or federal—must accord to the dignity and integrity of its citizens. To maintain a 'fair state-individual balance,' to require the government 'to shoulder the entire load,' * * * to respect the inviolability of the human personality, our accusatory system of criminal justice demands that the government seeking to punish an individual produce the evidence against him by its own independent labors, rather than by the cruel, simple expedient of compelling it from his own mouth." The withdrawal of blood necessarily involves puncturing the skin for extraction, and the percent by weight of alcohol in that blood, as established by chemical analysis, is evidence of criminal guilt. Compelled submission fails on one view to respect the "inviolability of the human personality." Moreover, since it enables the State to rely on evidence forced from the accused, the compulsion violates at least one meaning of the requirement that the State procure the evidence against an accused "by its own independent labors."

As the passage in *Miranda* implicitly recognizes, however, the privilege has never been given the full scope which the values it helps to protect suggest. History and a long line of authorities in lower courts have consistently limited its protection to situations in which the State seeks to submerge those values by obtaining the evidence against an accused through 'the cruel, simple expedient of compelling it from his own mouth. * * * In sum, the privilege is fulfilled only when the person is guaranteed the right 'to remain silent unless he chooses to speak in the unfettered exercise of his own will." The leading case in this Court is *Holt v. United States*, 218 U.S. 245 [(1910)]. There the question was whether evidence was admissible that the accused, prior to trial and over his protest, put on a blouse that fitted him. It was contended that compelling the accused to submit to the demand that he model the blouse violated the privilege. Mr. Justice Holmes, speaking for the Court, rejected the argument as "based upon an extravagant extension of the 5th Amendment," and went on to say: "(T)he prohibition of compelling a man in a criminal court to be witness against himself is a prohibition of the use of physical or moral compulsion to extort communications from him, not an exclusion of his body as evidence when it may be material. The objection in principle would forbid a jury to look at a prisoner and compare his features with a photograph in proof."

It is clear that the protection of the privilege reaches an accused's communications, whatever form they might take, and the compulsion of responses which are also communications, for example, compliance with a subpoena to produce one's papers. On the other hand, both federal and state courts have usually held that it offers no protection against compulsion to submit to fingerprinting, photographing, or measurements, to write or speak for identification, to appear in court, to stand, to assume a stance, to walk, or to make a particular gesture. The distinction which has emerged, often expressed in different ways, is that the privilege is a bar against compelling "communications" or "testimony", but that compulsion which makes a suspect or accused the source of "real or physical evidence" does not violate it.

Although we agree that this distinction is a helpful framework for analysis, we are not to be understood to agree with past applications in all instances. There will be many cases in which such a distinction is not readily drawn. Some tests seemingly directed to obtain "physical evidence," for example, lie detector tests measuring changes in body function during interrogation, may actually be directed to eliciting responses which are essentially testimonial. To compel a person to submit to testing in which an effort will be made to determine his guilt or innocence on the basis of physiological responses, whether willed or not, is to evoke the spirit and history of the Fifth Amendment. Such situations call to mind the principle that the protection of the privilege "is as broad as the mischief against which it seeks to guard."

In the present case, however, no such problem of application is presented. Not even a shadow of testimonial compulsion upon or enforced communication by the accused was involved either in the extraction or in the chemical analysis. Petitioner's testimonial capacities were in no way implicated; indeed, his participation, except as a donor, was irrelevant to the results of the test, which depend on chemical analysis and on that alone.[9] Since the blood test evidence, although an incriminating product of compulsion, was neither petitioner's testimony nor evidence relating to some communicative act or writing by the petitioner, it was not inadmissible on privilege grounds.

Petitioner has raised a similar issue in this case, in connection with a police request that he submit to a "breathalyzer" test of air expelled from

[9] This conclusion would not necessarily govern had the State tried to show that the accused had incriminated himself when told that he would have to be tested. Such incriminating evidence may be an unavoidable by-product of the compulsion to take the test, especially for an individual who fears the extraction or opposes it on religious grounds. If it wishes to compel persons to submit to such attempts to discover evidence, the State may have to forgo the advantage of any testimonial products of administering the test—products which would fall within the privilege. Indeed, there may be circumstances in which the pain, danger, or severity of an operation would almost inevitably cause a person to prefer confession to undergoing the 'search,' and nothing we say today should be taken as establishing the permissibility of compulsion in that case. But no such situation is presented in this case.

his lungs for alcohol content. He refused the request, and evidence of his refusal was admitted in evidence without objection. He argues that the introduction of this evidence and a comment by the prosecutor in closing argument upon his refusal is ground for reversal under *Griffin v. State of California*, 380 U.S. 609, [(1965)]. We think general Fifth Amendment principles, rather than the particular holding of *Griffin*, would be applicable in these circumstances. Since trial here was conducted after our decision in *Malloy v. Hogan* making those principles applicable to the States, we think petitioner's contention is foreclosed by his failure to object on this ground to the prosecutor's question and statements.

* * *

IV

THE SEARCH AND SEIZURE CLAIM

* * *

Because we are dealing with intrusions into the human body rather than with state interferences with property relationships or private papers—"houses, papers, and effects"—we write on a clean slate. Limitations on the kinds of property which may be seized under warrant, as distinct from the procedures for search and the permissible scope of search, are not instructive in this context. We begin with the assumption that once the privilege against self-incrimination has been found not to bar compelled intrusions into the body for blood to be analyzed for alcohol content, the Fourth Amendment's proper function is to constrain, not against all intrusions as such, but against intrusions which are not justified in the circumstances, or which are made in an improper manner. In other words, the questions we must decide in this case are whether the police were justified in requiring petitioner to submit to the blood test, and whether the means and procedures employed in taking his blood respected relevant Fourth Amendment standards of reasonableness.

In this case, as will often be true when charges of driving under the influence of alcohol are pressed, these questions arise in the context of an arrest made by an officer without a warrant. Here, there was plainly probable cause for the officer to arrest petitioner and charge him with driving an automobile while under the influence of intoxicating liquor. The police officer who arrived at the scene shortly after the accident smelled liquor on petitioner's breath, and testified that petitioner's eyes were "bloodshot, watery, sort of a glassy appearance." The officer saw petitioner again at the hospital, within two hours of the accident. There he noticed similar symptoms of drunkenness. He thereupon informed petitioner "that he was under arrest and that he was entitled to the services of an attorney, and that he could remain silent, and that anything that he told me would be used against him in evidence."

* * *

Although the facts which established probable cause to arrest in this case also suggested the required relevance and likely success of a test of petitioner's blood for alcohol, the question remains whether the arresting officer was permitted to draw these inferences himself, or was required instead to procure a warrant before proceeding with the test. Search warrants are ordinarily required for searches of dwellings, and absent an emergency, no less could be required where intrusions into the human body are concerned. The requirement that a warrant be obtained is a requirement that inferences to support the search "be drawn by a neutral and detached magistrate instead of being judged by the officer engaged in the often competitive enterprise of ferreting out crime." *Johnson v. United States*, 333 U.S. 10, 13–14 [(1948)]. The importance of informed, detached and deliberate determinations of the issue whether or not to invade another's body in search of evidence of guilt is indisputable and great.

The officer in the present case, however, might reasonably have believed that he was confronted with an emergency, in which the delay necessary to obtain a warrant, under the circumstances, threatened "the destruction of evidence." We are told that the percentage of alcohol in the blood begins to diminish shortly after drinking stops, as the body functions to eliminate it from the system. Particularly in a case such as this, where time had to be taken to bring the accused to a hospital and to investigate the scene of the accident, there was no time to seek out a magistrate and secure a warrant. Given these special facts, we conclude that the attempt to secure evidence of blood-alcohol content in this case was an appropriate incident to petitioner's arrest.

Similarly, we are satisfied that the test chosen to measure petitioner's blood-alcohol level was a reasonable one. Extraction of blood samples for testing is a highly effective means of determining the degree to which a person is under the influence of alcohol. Such tests are a commonplace in these days of periodic physical examination and experience with them teaches that the quantity of blood extracted is minimal, and that for most people the procedure involves virtually no risk, trauma, or pain. Petitioner is not one of the few who on grounds of fear, concern for health, or religious scruple might prefer some other means of testing, such as the 'Breathalyzer' test petitioner refused. We need not decide whether such wishes would have to be respected.

Finally, the record shows that the test was performed in a reasonable manner. Petitioner's blood was taken by a physician in a hospital environment according to accepted medical practices. We are thus not presented with the serious questions which would arise if a search involving use of a medical technique, even of the most rudimentary sort, were made by other than medical personnel or in other than a medical environment—for example, if it were administered by police in the privacy of the stationhouse. To tolerate searches under these conditions might be to invite an unjustified element of personal risk of infection and pain.

We thus conclude that the present record shows no violation of petitioner's right under the Fourth and Fourteenth Amendments to be free of unreasonable searches and seizures. It bears repeating, however, that we reach this judgment only on the facts of the present record. The integrity of an individual's person is a cherished value of our society. That we today told that the Constitution does not forbid the States minor intrusions into an individual's body under stringently limited conditions in no way indicates that it permits more substantial intrusions, or intrusions under other conditions.

MR. JUSTICE HARLAN, whom MR. JUSTICE STEWART joins, concurring.

In joining the Court's opinion I desire to add the following comment. While agreeing with the Court that the taking of this blood test involved no testimonial compulsion, I would go further and hold that apart from this consideration the case in no way implicates the Fifth Amendment.

The dissenting opinion of MR. CHIEF JUSTICE WARREN is omitted.

MR. JUSTICE BLACK with whom MR. JUSTICE DOUGLAS joins, dissenting.

* * *

The Court admits that "the State compelled (petitioner) to submit to an attempt to discover evidence (in his blood) that might be (and was) used to prosecute him for a criminal offense." To reach the conclusion that compelling a person to give his blood to help the State convict him is not equivalent to compelling him to be a witness against himself strikes me as quite an extraordinary feat. The Court, however, overcomes what had seemed to me to be an insuperable obstacle to its conclusion by holding that "the privilege protects an accused only from being compelled to testify against himself, or otherwise provide the State with evidence of a testimonial or communicative nature, and that the withdrawal of blood and use of the analysis in question in this case did not involve compulsion to these ends." I cannot agree that this distinction and reasoning of the Court justify denying petitioner his Bill of Rights' guarantee that he must not be compelled to be a witness against himself.

In the first place it seems to me that the compulsory extraction of petitioner's blood for analysis so that the person who analyzed it could give evidence to convict him had both a "testimonial" and a "communicative nature." The sole purpose of this project which proved to be successful was to obtain "testimony" from some person to prove that petitioner had alcohol in his blood at the time he was arrested. And the purpose of the project was certainly 'communicative' in that the analysis of the blood was to supply information to enable a witness to communicate to the court and jury that petitioner was more or less drunk.

I think it unfortunate that the Court rests so heavily for its very restrictive reading of the Fifth Amendment's privilege against self-incrimination on the words "testimonial" and "communicative." These words are not models of clarity and precision as the Court's rather labored explication shows. Nor can the Court, so far as I know, find precedent in the former opinions of this Court for using these particular words to limit the scope of the Fifth Amendment's protection. There is a scholarly precedent, however, in the late Professor Wigmore's learned treatise on evidence. He used "testimonial" which, according to the latest edition of his treatise revised by McNaughton, means "communicative" (8 Wigmore, Evidence § 2263 (McNaughton rev. 1961), p. 378), as a key word in his vigorous and extensive campaign designed to keep the privilege against self-incrimination "within limits the strictest possible." Though my admiration for Professor Wigmore's scholarship is great, I regret to see the word he used to narrow the Fifth Amendment's protection play such a major part in any of this Court's opinions.

* * *

The Court apparently, for a reason I cannot understand, finds some comfort for its narrow construction of the Fifth Amendment in this Court's decision in *Miranda v. Arizona*, 384 U.S. 436. I find nothing whatever in the majority opinion in that case which either directly or indirectly supports the holding in this case. In fact I think the interpretive constitutional philosophy used in *Miranda*, unlike that used in this case, gives the Fifth Amendment's prohibition against compelled self-incrimination a broad and liberal construction in line with the wholesome admonitions in [*Boyd v. United States*, 116 U.S. 616 (1886)]. The closing sentence in the Fifth Amendment section of the Court's opinion in the present case is enough by itself, I think, to expose the unsoundness of what the Court here holds. That sentence reads:

> Since the blood test evidence, although an incriminating product of compulsion, was neither petitioner's testimony nor evidence relating to some communicative act or writing by the petitioner, it was not inadmissible on privilege grounds.

How can it reasonably be doubted that the blood test evidence was not in all respects the actual equivalent of 'testimony' taken from petitioner when the result of the test was offered as testimony, was considered by the jury as testimony, and the jury's verdict of guilt rests in part on that testimony? The refined, subtle reasoning and balancing process used here to narrow the scope of the Bill of Rights' safeguard against self-incrimination provides a handy instrument for further narrowing of that constitutional protection, as well as others, in the future. Believing with the Framers that these constitutional safeguards broadly construed by independent tribunals of justice provide our best hope for keeping our people free from governmental oppression, I deeply regret the Court's holding.

MR. JUSTICE DOUGLAS, dissenting.

I adhere to the views of the Chief Justice in his dissent in *Breithaupt v. Abram*, 352 U.S. 432, 440, and to the views I stated in my dissent in that case and add only a word.

We are dealing with the right of privacy which, since the *Breithaupt* case, we have held to be within the penumbra of some specific guarantees of the Bill of Rights. Thus, the Fifth Amendment marks "a zone of privacy" which the Government may not force a person to surrender. Likewise the Fourth Amendment recognizes that right when it guarantees the right of the people to be secure "in their persons." No clearer invasion of this right of privacy can be imagined than forcible bloodletting of the kind involved here.

MR. JUSTICE FORTAS, dissenting.

I would reverse. In my view, petitioner's privilege against self-incrimination applies. I would add that, under the Due Process Clause, the State, in its role as prosecutor, has no right to extract blood from an accused or anyone else, over his protest. As prosecutor, the State has no right to commit any kind of violence upon the person, or to utilize the results of such a tort, and the extraction of blood, over protest, is an act of violence.

Points for Discussion

1. *Schmerber* highlights once again the interaction between the Fourth and Fifth Amendments. The Court holds that withdrawing blood from an unwilling defendant may be compulsion, but that it doesn't violate the Fifth Amendment because the evidence obtained is not testimonial. It then holds that the taking of blood is a search, but one that is reasonable under the Fourth Amendment. Why does the Court limit the Fifth Amendment to testimonial communications? Isn't the core of the privilege against compelled self-incrimination the idea that the state may not compel the defendant's assistance in convicting him of a crime?

2. In *Pennsylvania v. Muniz*, 496 U.S. 582 (1990), the Court described the difference between testimonial and non-testimonial communications thusly:

> After canvassing the purposes of the privilege recognized in prior cases, we concluded that "[t]hese policies are served when the privilege is asserted to spare the accused from having to reveal, directly or indirectly, his knowledge of facts relating him to the offense or from having to share his thoughts and beliefs with the Government."

> This definition of testimonial evidence reflects an awareness of the historical abuses against which the privilege against self-incrimination was aimed. "Historically, the privilege was intended to prevent the use of legal compulsion to extract from the accused a sworn communication of facts which would incriminate him. Such was the process of the ecclesiastical courts and the Star Chamber—the inquisitorial method of putting the accused upon his oath and compelling him to answer questions designed to uncover uncharged offenses, without evidence from another source. The major thrust of the policies undergirding the privilege is to prevent such compulsion." At its core, the privilege reflects our fierce "unwillingness to subject those suspected of crime to the cruel trilemma of self-accusation, perjury or contempt," that defined the operation of the Star Chamber, wherein suspects were forced to choose between revealing incriminating private thoughts and forsaking their oath by committing perjury.
>
> We need not explore the outer boundaries of what is "testimonial" today, for our decision flows from the concept's core meaning. Because the privilege was designed primarily to prevent "a recurrence of the Inquisition and the Star Chamber, even if not in their stark brutality," it is evident that a suspect is "compelled . . . to be a witness against himself" at least whenever he must face the modern-day analog of the historic trilemma—either during a criminal trial where a sworn witness faces the identical three choices, or during custodial interrogation where, as we explained in *Miranda,* the choices are analogous and hence raise similar concerns. Whatever else it may include, therefore, the definition of "testimonial" evidence articulated in *Doe* must encompass all responses to questions that, if asked of a sworn suspect during a criminal trial, could place the suspect in the "cruel trilemma." This conclusion is consistent with our recognition in *Doe* that "[t]he vast majority of verbal statements thus will be testimonial" because "[t]here are very few instances in which a verbal statement, either oral or written, will not convey information or assert facts." Whenever a suspect is asked for a response requiring him to communicate an express or implied assertion of fact or belief, the suspect confronts the "trilemma" of truth, falsity, or silence, and hence the response (whether based on truth or falsity) contains a testimonial component.

The Court then applied this test to the facts:

> During the early morning hours of November 30, 1986, a patrol officer spotted respondent Inocencio Muniz and a passenger parked in a car on the shoulder of a highway. When the officer inquired whether Muniz needed assistance, Muniz replied that he had stopped the car so he could urinate. The officer smelled alcohol on Muniz's breath and observed that Muniz's eyes were glazed and bloodshot and his face was flushed. The officer then directed Muniz to remain parked until

> his condition improved, and Muniz gave assurances that he would do so. But as the officer returned to his vehicle, Muniz drove off. After the officer pursued Muniz down the highway and pulled him over, the officer asked Muniz to perform three standard field sobriety tests: a "horizontal gaze nystagmus" test, a "walk and turn" test, and a "one leg stand" test. Muniz performed these tests poorly, and he informed the officer that he had failed the tests because he had been drinking.
>
> The patrol officer arrested Muniz and transported him to the West Shore facility of the Cumberland County Central Booking Center. Following its routine practice for receiving persons suspected of driving while intoxicated, the booking center videotaped the ensuing proceedings. Muniz was informed that his actions and voice were being recorded, but he was not at this time (nor had he been previously) advised of his rights under *Miranda v. Arizona,* 384 U.S. 436 (1966). Officer Hosterman first asked Muniz his name, address, height, weight, eye color, date of birth, and current age. He responded to each of these questions, stumbling over his address and age. The officer then asked Muniz, "Do you know what the date was of your sixth birthday?" After Muniz offered an inaudible reply, the officer repeated, "When you turned six years old, do you remember what the date was?" Muniz responded, "No, I don't."

Was Muniz's performance in the sobriety tests testimonial? Was his answer (or non-answer) to the sixth-birthday question testimonial?

There is no majority opinion in *Muniz.* Justice Brennan, joined by Justices O'Connor, Scalia, and Kennedy, reasoned that the questions were asked "for recordkeeping purposes only" and therefore came within a "routine booking question" exception to *Miranda's* exclusionary rule. Chief Justice Rehnquist, joined by Justices White, Blackmun, and Stevens, would have held that the question about Muniz's sixth birthday was not testimonial because it was only "an effort on the part of the police to check how well Muniz was able to do a simple mathematical exercise." Only Justice Marshall believed that the questioning violated *Miranda's* rule: "I disagree, however, with the plurality's recognition . . . of a 'routine booking question' exception to *Miranda.* Moreover, even were such an exception warranted, it should not extend to booking questions that the police should know are reasonably likely to elicit incriminating responses."

C. LIMITS ON THE PRIVILEGE

KASTIGAR V. UNITED STATES

406 U.S. 441 (1972)

MR. JUSTICE POWELL delivered the opinion of the court.

This case presents the question whether the United States Government may compel testimony from an unwilling witness, who invokes the Fifth Amendment privilege against compulsory self-incrimination, by conferring on the witness immunity from use of the compelled testimony in subsequent criminal proceedings, as well as immunity from use of evidence derived from the testimony.

Petitioners were subpoenaed to appear before a United States grand jury in the Central District of California on February 4, 1971. The Government believed that petitioners were likely to assert their Fifth Amendment privilege. Prior to the scheduled appearances, the Government applied to the District Court for an order directing petitioners to answer questions and produce evidence before the grand jury under a grant of immunity conferred pursuant to 18 U.S.C. §§ 6002, 6003. Petitioners opposed issuance of the order, contending primarily that the scope of the immunity provided by the statute was not coextensive with the scope of the privilege against self-incrimination, and therefore was not sufficient to supplant the privilege and compel their testimony. The District Court rejected this contention, and ordered petitioners to appear before the grand jury and answer its questions under the grant of immunity.

Petitioners appeared but refused to answer questions, asserting their privilege against compulsory self-incrimination. They were brought before the District Court, and each persisted in his refusal to answer the grand jury's questions, notwithstanding the grant of immunity. The court found both in contempt, and committed them to the custody of the Attorney General until either they answered the grand jury's questions or the term of the grand jury expired. The Court of Appeals for the Ninth Circuit affirmed. This Court granted certiorari to resolve the important question whether testimony may be compelled by granting immunity from the use of compelled testimony and evidence derived therefrom ('use and derivative use' immunity), or whether it is necessary to grant immunity from prosecution for offenses to which compelled testimony relates ('transactional' immunity).

I

The power of government to compel persons to testify in court or before grand juries and other governmental agencies is firmly established in Anglo-American jurisprudence. The power with respect to courts was established by statute in England as early as 1562, and Lord Bacon observed in 1612 that all subjects owed the King their "knowledge and discovery." While it is not clear when grand juries first resorted to compulsory process to secure the attendance and testimony of witnesses, the general common-law principle that 'the public has a right to every man's evidence" was considered an "indubitable certainty" that "cannot be denied" by 1742. The power to compel testimony, and the corresponding duty to testify, are recognized in the Sixth Amendment requirements that an accused be confronted with the witnesses against him, and have compulsory process for obtaining witnesses in his favor. The first Congress recognized the testimonial duty in the Judiciary Act of 1789, which provided for compulsory attendance of witnesses in the federal courts. Mr. Justice White noted the importance of this essential power of government in his concurring opinion in *Murphy v. Waterfront Comm'n*, 378 U.S. 52, 93–94 (1964):

> Among the necessary and most important of the powers of the States as well as the Federal Government to assure the effective functioning of government in an ordered society is the broad power to compel residents to testify in court or before grand juries or agencies. Such testimony constitutes one of the Government's primary sources of information.

But the power to compel testimony is not absolute. There are a number of exemptions from the testimonial duty, the most important of which is the Fifth Amendment privilege against compulsory self-incrimination. The privilege reflects a complex of our fundamental values and aspirations, and marks an important advance in the development of our liberty. It can be asserted in any proceeding, civil or criminal, administrative or judicial, investigatory or adjudicatory; and it protects against any disclosures which the witness reasonably believes could be used in a criminal prosecution or could lead to other evidence that might be so used. This Court has been zealous to safeguard the values which underlie the privilege.

Immunity statutes, which have historical roots deep in Anglo-American jurisprudence, are not incompatible with these values. Rather, they seek a rational accommodation between the imperatives of the privilege and the legitimate demands of government to compel citizens to testify. The existence of these statutes reflects the importance of testimony, and the fact that many offenses are of such a character that the only persons capable of giving useful testimony are those implicated in the crime. Indeed, their origins were in the context of such offenses, and their primary use has been to investigate such offenses. Congress included immunity statutes in many of the regulatory measures adopted in the first half of this century. Indeed, prior to the enactment of the statute under consideration in this case, there were in force over 50 federal immunity statutes. In addition, every State in the Union, as well as the District of Columbia and Puerto Rico, has one or more such statutes. The commentators, and this Court on several occasions, have characterized immunity statutes as essential to the effective enforcement of various criminal statutes. As Mr. Justice Frankfurter observed, speaking for the Court in *Ullmann v. United States*, 350 U.S. 422 (1956), such statutes have "become part of our constitutional fabric."

II

Petitioners contend, first, that the Fifth Amendment's privilege against compulsory self-incrimination, which is that "(n)o person . . . shall be compelled in any criminal case to be a witness against himself," deprives Congress of power to enact laws that compel self-incrimination, even if complete immunity from prosecution is granted prior to the compulsion of the incriminatory testimony. In other words, petitioners assert that no immunity statute, however drawn, can afford a lawful basis for compelling incriminatory testimony. . . .

We find no merit to this contention . . . .

III

Petitioners' second contention is that the scope of immunity provided by the federal witness immunity statute, 18 U.S.C. § 6002, is not coextensive with the scope of the Fifth Amendment privilege against compulsory self-incrimination, and therefore is not sufficient to supplant the privilege and compel testimony over a claim of the privilege. The statute provides that when a witness is compelled by district court order to testify over a claim of the privilege:

> the witness may not refuse to comply with the order on the basis of his privilege against self-incrimination; but no testimony or other information compelled under the order (or any information directly or indirectly derived from such testimony or other information) may be used against the witness in any criminal case, except a prosecution for perjury, giving a false statement, or otherwise failing to comply with the order.

The constitutional inquiry, rooted in logic and history, as well as in the decisions of this Court, is whether the immunity granted under this statute is coextensive with the scope of the privilege. If so, petitioners' refusals to answer based on the privilege were unjustified, and the judgments of contempt were proper, for the grant of immunity has removed the dangers against which the privilege protects. If, on the other hand, the immunity granted is not as comprehensive as the protection afforded by the privilege, petitioners were justified in refusing to answer, and the judgments of contempt must be vacated.

Petitioners draw a distinction between statutes that provide transactional immunity and those that provide, as does the statute before us, immunity from use and derivative use. They contend that a statute must at a minimum grant full transactional immunity in order to be coextensive with the scope of the privilege. In support of this contention, they rely on *Counselman v. Hitchcock*, 142 U.S. 547 (1892), the first case in which this Court considered a constitutional challenge to an immunity statute. The statute, a reenactment of the Immunity Act of 1868, provided that no "evidence obtained from a party or witness by means of a judicial proceeding . . . shall be given in evidence, or in any manner used against him . . . in any court of the United States . . ." Notwithstanding a grant of immunity and order to testify under the revised 1868 Act, the witness, asserting his privilege against compulsory self-incrimination, refused to testify before a federal grand jury. He was consequently adjudged in contempt of court. On appeal, this Court construed the statute as affording a witness protection only against the use of the specific testimony compelled from him under the grant of immunity. This construction meant that the statute "could not, and would not, prevent the use of his testimony to search out other testimony to be used in evidence against him." Since the revised 1868 Act, as construed by the Court, would permit the use against the immunized witness of evidence derived from his compelled testimony, it did not protect the witness to the same extent that a claim of the privilege would protect him. Accordingly, under the principle that a grant of immunity cannot supplant the privilege, and is not sufficient to compel testimony over a claim of the privilege, unless the scope of the grant of immunity is coextensive with the scope of the privilege, the witness' refusal to testify was held proper. In the course of its opinion, the Court made the following statement, on which petitioners heavily rely:

> We are clearly of opinion that no statute which leaves the party or witness subject to prosecution after he answers the criminating question put to him, can have the effect of supplanting the privilege conferred by the Constitution of the United States. (The immunity statute under consideration) does not supply a complete protection from all the perils against which the constitutional prohibition was designed to guard, and is not a full substitute for that prohibition. In view of the constitutional provision, a statutory enactment, to be valid, must afford absolute immunity against future prosecution for the offence to which the question relates.

Sixteen days after the *Counselman* decision, a new immunity bill was introduced by Senator Cullom, who urged that enforcement of the Interstate Commerce Act would be impossible in the absence of an effective immunity statute. The bill, which became the Compulsory Testimony Act of 1893, was drafted specifically to meet the broad language in *Counselman* set forth above. The new Act removed the privilege against self-incrimination in hearings before the Interstate Commerce Commission and provided that:

> no person shall be prosecuted or subjected to any penalty or forfeiture for or on account of any transaction, matter or thing, concerning which he may testify, or produce evidence, documentary or otherwise . . .

This transactional immunity statute became the basic form for the numerous federal immunity statutes until 1970, when, after re-examining applicable constitutional principles and the adequacy of existing law, Congress enacted the statute here under consideration. The new statute, which does not "afford (the) absolute immunity against future prosecution" referred to in *Counselman*, was drafted to meet what Congress judged to be the conceptual basis of *Counselman*, as elaborated in subsequent decisions of the Court, namely, that immunity from the use of compelled testimony and evidence derived therefrom is coextensive with the scope of the privilege.

The statute's explicit proscription of the use in any criminal case of "testimony or other information compelled under the order (or any information directly or indirectly derived from such testimony or other information)" is consonant with Fifth Amendment standards. We hold that such immunity from use and derivative use is coextensive with the scope of the privilege against self-incrimination, and therefore is sufficient to compel testimony over a claim of the privilege. While a grant of immunity must afford protection commensurate with that afforded by the privilege, it need not be broader. Transactional immunity, which accords full immunity from prosecution for the offense to which the compelled testimony relates, affords the witness considerably broader protection than does the Fifth Amendment privilege. The privilege has never been construed to mean that one who invokes it cannot subsequently be prosecuted. Its sole concern is to afford protection against being "forced to give testimony leading to the infliction of 'penalties affixed to . . . criminal acts.' " Immunity from the use of compelled testimony, as well as evidence derived directly and indirectly therefrom, affords this protection. It prohibits the prosecutorial authorities from using the compelled testimony in any respect, and it therefore insures that the testimony cannot lead to the infliction of criminal penalties on the witness.

Our holding is consistent with the conceptual basis of *Counselman*. The *Counselman* statute, as construed by the Court, was plainly deficient in its failure to prohibit the use against the immunized witness of evidence derived from his compelled testimony. The Court repeatedly emphasized this deficiency, noting that the statute:

> could not, and would not, prevent the use of his testimony to search out other testimony to be used in evidence against him or his property, in a criminal proceeding . . .;

that it:

> could not prevent the obtaining and the use of witnesses and evidence which should be attributable directly to the testimony he might give under compulsion and on which he might be convicted, when otherwise, and if he had refused to answer, he could not possibly have been convicted;

and that it:

> affords no protection against that use of compelled testimony which consists in gaining therefrom a knowledge of the details of

> a crime, and of sources of information which may supply other means of convicting the witness or party.

The basis of the Court's decision was recognized in *Ullmann v. United States*, 350 U.S. 422 (1956), in which the Court reiterated that the *Counselman* statute was insufficient:

> because the immunity granted was incomplete, in that it merely forbade the use of the testimony given and failed to protect a witness from future prosecution based on knowledge and sources of information obtained from the compelled testimony.'

The broad language in *Counselman* relied upon by petitioners was unnecessary to the Court's decision, and cannot be considered binding authority.

In *Murphy v. Waterfront Comm'n*, 378 U.S. 52 (1964), the Court carefully considered immunity from use of compelled testimony and evidence derived therefrom. The *Murphy* petitioners were subpoenaed to testify at a hearing conducted by the Waterfront Commission of New York Harbor. After refusing to answer certain questions on the ground that the answers might tend to incriminate them, petitioners were granted immunity from prosecution under the laws of New Jersey and New York. They continued to refuse to testify, however, on the ground that their answers might tend to incriminate them under federal law, to which the immunity did not purport to extend. They were adjudged in civil contempt, and that judgment was affirmed by the New Jersey Supreme Court.

The issue before the Court in *Murphy* was whether New Jersey and New York could compel the witnesses, whom these States had immunized from prosecution under their laws, to give testimony that might then be used to convict them of a federal crime. Since New Jersey and New York had not purported to confer immunity from federal prosecution, the Court was faced with the question what limitations the Fifth Amendment privilege imposed on the prosecutorial powers of the Federal Government, a nonimmunizing sovereign. After undertaking an examination of the policies and purposes of the privilege, the Court overturned the rule that one jurisdiction within our federal structure may compel a witness to give testimony which could be used to convict him of a crime in another jurisdiction. The Court held that the privilege protects state witnesses against incrimination under federal as well as state law, and federal witnesses against incrimination under state as well as federal law. Applying this principle to the state immunity legislation before it, the Court held the constitutional rule to be that:

> (A) state witness may not be compelled to give testimony which may be incriminating under federal law unless the compelled testimony and its fruits cannot be used in any manner by federal officials in connection with a criminal prosecution against him.

> We conclude, moreover, that in order to implement this constitutional rule and accommodate the interests of the State and Federal Government in investigating and prosecuting crime, the Federal Government must be prohibited from making any such use of compelled testimony and its fruits.

The Court emphasized that this rule left the state witness and the Federal Government, against which the witness had immunity only from the use of the compelled testimony and evidence derived therefrom, "in substantially the same position as if the witness had claimed his privilege in the absence of a state grant of immunity."

It is true that in *Murphy* the Court was not presented with the precise question presented by this case, whether a jurisdiction seeking to compel testimony may do so by granting only use and derivative-use immunity, for New Jersey and New York had granted petitioners transactional immunity. The Court heretofore has not squarely confronted this question, because post-*Counselman* immunity statutes reaching the Court either have followed the pattern of the 1893 Act in providing transactional immunity, or have been found deficient for failure to prohibit the use of all evidence derived from compelled testimony. But both the reasoning of the Court in *Murphy* and the result reached compel the conclusion that use and derivative-use immunity is constitutionally sufficient to compel testimony over a claim of the privilege. Since the privilege is fully applicable and its scope is the same whether invoked in a state or in a federal jurisdiction, the *Murphy* conclusion that a prohibition on use and derivative use secures a witness' Fifth Amendment privilege against infringement by the Federal Government demonstrates that immunity from use and derivative use is coextensive with the scope of the privilege. As the *Murphy* Court noted, immunity from use and derivative use "leaves the witness and the Federal Government in substantially the same position as if the witness had claimed his privilege" in the absence of a grant of immunity. The *Murphy* Court was concerned solely with the danger of incrimination under federal law, and held that immunity from use and derivative use was sufficient to displace the danger. This protection coextensive with the privilege is the degree of protection that the Constitution requires, and is all that the Constitution requires even against the jurisdiction compelling testimony by granting immunity.

IV

Although an analysis of prior decisions and the purpose of the Fifth Amendment privilege indicates that use and derivative-use immunity is coextensive with the privilege, we must consider additional arguments advanced by petitioners against the sufficiency of such immunity. We start from the premise, repeatedly affirmed by this Court, that an appropriately broad immunity grant is compatible with the Constitution.

Petitioners argue that use and derivative-use immunity will not adequately protect a witness from various possible incriminating uses of the compelled testimony: for example, the prosecutor or other law enforcement officials may obtain leads, names of witnesses, or other information not otherwise available that might result in a prosecution. It will be difficult and perhaps impossible, the argument goes, to identify, by testimony or cross-examination, the subtle ways in which the compelled testimony may disadvantage a witness, especially in the jurisdiction granting the immunity.

This argument presupposes that the statute's prohibition will prove impossible to enforce. The statute provides a sweeping proscription of any use, direct or indirect, of the compelled testimony and any information derived therefrom:

> '(N)o testimony or other information compelled under the order (or any information directly or indirectly derived from such testimony or other information) may be used against the witness in any criminal case . . .' 18 U.S.C. § 6002.

This total prohibition on use provides a comprehensive safeguard, barring the use of compelled testimony as an "investigatory lead," and also barring the use of any evidence obtained by focusing investigation on a witness as a result of his compelled disclosures.

A person accorded this immunity under 18 U.S.C. § 6002, and subsequently prosecuted, is not dependent for the preservation of his rights upon the integrity and good faith of the prosecuting authorities. As stated in *Murphy*:

> Once a defendant demonstrates that he has testified, under a state grant of immunity, to matters related to the federal prosecution, the federal authorities have the burden of showing that their evidence is not tainted by establishing that they had an independent, legitimate source for the disputed evidence.

This burden of proof, which we reaffirm as appropriate, is not limited to a negation of taint; rather, it imposes on the prosecution the affirmative duty to prove that the evidence it proposes to use is derived from a legitimate source wholly independent of the compelled testimony.

* * *

The statutory proscription is analogous to the Fifth Amendment requirement in cases of coerced confessions. A coerced confession, as revealing of leads as testimony given in exchange for immunity, is inadmissible in a criminal trial, but it does not bar prosecution. Moreover, a defendant against whom incriminating evidence has been obtained through a grant of immunity may be in a stronger position at trial than a defendant who asserts a Fifth Amendment coerced-confession claim. One raising a claim under this statute need only show that he testified under a grant of immunity in order to shift to the government the heavy burden of proving that all of the evidence it proposes to use was derived from legitimate independent sources. On the other hand, a defendant raising a coerced-confession claim under the Fifth Amendment must first prevail in a voluntariness hearing before his confession and evidence derived from it become inadmissible.

There can be no justification in reason or policy for holding that the Constitution requires an amnesty grant where, acting pursuant to statute and accompanying safeguards, testimony is compelled in exchange for immunity from use and derivative use when no such amnesty is required where the government, acting without colorable right, coerces a defendant into incriminating himself.

We conclude that the immunity provided by 18 U.S.C. § 6002 leaves the witness and the prosecutorial authorities in substantially the same position as if the witness had claimed the Fifth Amendment privilege. The immunity therefore is coextensive with the privilege and suffices to supplant it. The judgment of the Court of Appeals for the Ninth Circuit accordingly is affirmed.

MR. JUSTICE BRENNAN and MR. JUSTICE REHNQUIST took no part in the consideration or decision of this case.

MR. JUSTICE DOUGLAS, dissenting.

The Self-Incrimination Clause says: "No person . . . shall be compelled in any criminal case to be a witness against himself." I see no answer to the proposition that he is such a witness when only 'use' immunity is granted.

* * *

If, as some have thought, the Bill of Rights contained only 'counsels of moderation' from which courts and legislatures could deviate according to their conscience or discretion, then today's contraction of the Self-Incrimination Clause of the Fifth Amendment would be understandable. But that has not been true, starting with Chief Justice Marshall's opinion in *United States v. Burr*, 25 F.Cas. p. 38 (No. 14,692e) (CC Va.), where he ruled that the reach of the Fifth Amendment was so broad as to make the privilege applicable when there was a mere possibility of a criminal charge being made.

The Court said in *Hale v. Henkel*, 201 U.S. 43, 67 (1906), that "if the criminality has already been taken away, the Amendment ceases to apply." In other words, the immunity granted is adequate if it operates as a complete pardon for the offense. That is the true measure of the Self-Incrimination Clause. As Mr. Justice Brennan has stated: "(U)se immunity literally misses half the point of the privilege, for it permits the compulsion without removing the criminality."

As Mr. Justice Brennan has also said:

> Transactional immunity . . . provides the individual with an assurance that he is not testifying about matters for which he may later be prosecuted. No question arises of tracing the use or non-use of information gleaned from the witness' compelled testimony. The sole question presented to a court is whether the subsequent prosecution is related to the substance of the compelled testimony. Both witness and government know precisely where they stand. Respect for law is furthered when the individual knows his position and is not left suspicious that a later prosecution was actually the fruit of his compelled testimony.

When we allow the prosecution to offer only "use" immunity we allow it to grant far less than it has taken away. For while the precise testimony that is compelled may not be used, leads from that testimony may be pursued and used to convict the witness. My view is that the framers put it beyond the power of Congress to compel anyone to confess his crimes. The Self-Incrimination Clause creates, as I have said before, "the federally protected right of silence," making it unconstitutional to use a law "to pry open one's lips and make him a witness against himself." That is indeed one of the chief procedural guarantees in our accusatorial system. Government acts in an ignoble way when it stoops to the end which we authorize today.

I would adhere to *Counselman v. Hitchcock* and hold that this attempt to dilute the Self-Incrimination Clause is unconstitutional.

MR. JUSTICE MARSHALL, dissenting.

Today the Court holds that the United States may compel a witness to give incriminating testimony, and subsequently prosecute him for crimes to which that testimony relates. I cannot believe the Fifth Amendment permits that result.

The Fifth Amendment gives a witness an absolute right to resist interrogation, if the testimony sought would tend to incriminate him. A grant of immunity may strip the witness of the right to refuse to testify, but only if it is broad enough to eliminate all possibility that the testimony will in fact operate to incriminate him. It must put him in precisely the same position, vis-a-vis the government that has compelled his testimony, as he would have been in had he remained silent in reliance on the privilege.

The Court recognizes that an immunity statute must be tested by that standard, that the relevant inquiry is whether it "leaves the witness and the prosecutorial authorities in substantially the same position as if the witness had claimed the Fifth Amendment privilege." I assume, moreover, that in theory that test would be met by a complete ban on the use of the compelled testimony, including all derivative, use, however remote and indirect. But I cannot agree that a ban on use will in practice be total, if it remains open for the government to convict the witness on the basis of evidence derived from a legitimate independent source. The Court asserts that the witness is adequately protected by a rule imposing on the government a heavy burden of proof if it would establish the independent character of evidence to be used against the witness. But in light of the inevitable uncertainties of the fact-finding process, a greater margin of protection is required in order to provide a reliable guarantee that the witness is in exactly the same position as if he had not testified. That margin can be provided only by immunity from prosecution for the offenses to which the testimony relates, i.e., transactional immunity.

I do not see how it can suffice merely to put the burden of proof on the government. First, contrary to the Court's assertion, the Court's rule does leave the witness "dependent for the preservation of his rights upon the integrity and good faith of the prosecuting authorities." For the information relevant to the question of taint is uniquely within the knowledge of the prosecuting authorities. They alone are in a position to trace the chains of information and investigation that lead to the evidence to be used in a criminal prosecution. A witness who suspects that his compelled testimony was used to develop a lead will be hard pressed indeed to ferret out the evidence necessary to prove it. And of course it is no answer to say he need not prove it, for though the Court puts the burden of proof on the government, the government will have no difficulty in meeting its burden by mere assertion if the witness produces no contrary evidence. The good faith of the prosecuting authorities is thus the sole safeguard of the witness' rights. Second, even their good faith is not a sufficient safeguard. For the paths of information through the investigative bureaucracy may well be long and winding, and even a prosecutor acting in the best of faith cannot be certain that somewhere in the depths of his investigative apparatus, often including hundreds of employees, there was not some prohibited use of the compelled testimony. The Court today sets out a loose net to trap tainted evidence and prevent its use against the witness, but it accepts an intolerably great risk that tainted evidence will in fact slip through that net.

In my view the Court turns reason on its head when it compares a statutory grant of immunity to the "immunity" that is inadvertently conferred by an unconstitutional interrogation. The exclusionary rule of evidence that applies in that situation has nothing whatever to do with this case. Evidence obtained through a coercive interrogation, like evidence obtained through an illegal search, is excluded at trial because the Constitution prohibits such methods of gathering evidence. The exclusionary rules provide a partial and inadequate remedy to some victims of illegal police conduct, and a similarly partial and inadequate deterrent to police officers. An immunity statute, on the other hand, is much more ambitious than any exclusionary rule. It does not merely attempt to provide a remedy for past police misconduct, which never should have occurred. An immunity statute operates in advance of the event, and it authorizes—even encourages—interrogation that would otherwise be prohibited by the Fifth Amendment. An immunity statute thus differs from an exclusionary rule of evidence in at least two critical respects.

First, because an immunity statute gives constitutional approval to the resulting interrogation, the government is under an obligation here to remove the danger of incrimination completely and absolutely, whereas in the case of the exclusionary rules it may be sufficient to shield the witness from the fruits of the illegal search or interrogation in a partial and reasonably adequate manner. For when illegal police conduct has occurred, the exclusion of evidence does not purport to purge the conduct of its unconstitutional character. The constitutional violation remains, and may provide the basis for other relief, such as a civil action for damages or a criminal prosecution of the responsible officers. The Constitution does not authorize police officers to coerce confessions or to invade privacy without cause, so long as no use is made of the evidence they obtain. But this Court has held that the Constitution does authorize the government to compel a witness to give potentially incriminating testimony, so long as no incriminating use is made of the resulting evidence. Before the government puts its seal of approval on such an interrogation, it must provide an absolutely reliable guarantee that it will not use the testimony in any way at all in aid of prosecution of the witness. The only way to provide that guarantee is to give the witness immunity from prosecution for crimes to which his testimony relates.

Second, because an immunity statute operates in advance of the interrogation, there is room to require a broad grant of transactional immunity without imperiling large numbers of otherwise valid convictions. An exclusionary rule comes into play after the interrogation or search has occurred; and the decision to question or to search is often made in haste, under pressure, by an officer who is not a lawyer. If an unconstitutional interrogation or search were held to create transactional immunity, that might well be regarded as an excessively high price to pay for the "constable's blunder." An immunity statute, on the other hand, creates a framework in which the prosecuting attorney can make a calm and reasoned decision whether to compel testimony and suffer the resulting ban on prosecution, or to forgo the testimony.

For both these reasons it is clear to me that an immunity statute must be tested by a standard far more demanding than that appropriate for an exclusionary rule fashioned to deal with past constitutional violations. Measured by that standard, the statute approved today by the Court fails miserably. I respectfully dissent.

Points for Discussion

1. It is important to be able to differentiate the three types of immunity the Court discusses in this case: use, derivative use, and transactional immunity. It is likewise important to see why the Court has held that derivative use but not use immunity serves as the "equivalent" of the privilege against compelled self-incrimination and what the consequences of that conclusion are. Finally, it is important to understand why the Court rejects Kastigar's assertion that only transactional immunity will suffice to stand in for the privilege.

2. The majority writes that a grant of immunity should be treated like a coerced confession. It holds that neither a grant of immunity nor a wrongfully obtained confession should bar a future prosecution, so long as the government can demonstrate to a preponderance that it did not use the tainted information or evidence derived from it. Why does Justice Marshall object so strongly to this proposition?

3. In his dissent, Justice Marshall writes that "an immunity statute must be tested by a standard far more demanding than that appropriate for an exclusionary rule fashioned to deal with past constitutional violations . . . ." Why should that be so?

BALTIMORE CITY DEPT. OF SOCIAL SERVICES V. BOUKNIGHT

493 U.S. 549 (1990)

JUSTICE O'CONNOR delivered the opinion of the court.

In this action, we must decide whether a mother, the custodian of a child pursuant to a court order, may invoke the Fifth Amendment privilege against self-incrimination to resist an order of the juvenile court to produce the child. We hold that she may not.

I

Petitioner Maurice M. is an abused child. When he was three months old, he was hospitalized with a fractured left femur, and examination revealed several partially healed bone fractures and other indications of severe physical abuse. In the hospital, respondent Bouknight, Maurice's mother, was observed shaking Maurice, dropping him in his crib despite his spica cast, and otherwise handling him in a manner inconsistent with his recovery and continued health. Hospital personnel notified the Baltimore City Department of Social Services (BCDSS), petitioner in No. 88-1182, of suspected child abuse. In February 1987, BCDSS secured a court order removing Maurice from Bouknight's control and placing him in shelter care. Several months later, the shelter care order was inexplicably modified to return Maurice to Bouknight's custody temporarily. Following a hearing held shortly thereafter, the juvenile court declared Maurice to be a "child in need of assistance," thus asserting jurisdiction over Maurice and placing him under BCDSS' continuing oversight. BCDSS agreed that

Bouknight could continue as custodian of the child, but only pursuant to extensive conditions set forth in a court-approved protective supervision order. The order required Bouknight to "cooperate with BCDSS," "continue in therapy," participate in parental aid and training programs, and "refrain from physically punishing [Maurice]." The order's terms were "all subject to the further Order of the Court." Bouknight's attorney signed the order, and Bouknight in a separate form set forth her agreement to each term.

Eight months later, fearing for Maurice's safety, BCDSS returned to juvenile court. BCDSS caseworkers related that Bouknight would not cooperate with them and had in nearly every respect violated the terms of the protective order. BCDSS stated that Maurice's father had recently died in a shooting incident and that Bouknight, in light of the results of a psychological examination and her history of drug use, could not provide adequate care for the child. On April 20, 1988, the court granted BCDSS' petition to remove Maurice from Bouknight's control for placement in foster care. BCDSS officials also petitioned for judicial relief from Bouknight's failure to produce Maurice or reveal where he could be found. The petition recounted that on two recent visits by BCDSS officials to Bouknight's home, she had refused to reveal the location of the child or had indicated that the child was with an aunt whom she would not identify. The petition further asserted that inquiries of Bouknight's known relatives had revealed that none of them had recently seen Maurice and that BCDSS had prompted the police to issue a missing persons report and referred the case for investigation by the police homicide division. Also on April 20, the juvenile court, upon a hearing on the petition, cited Bouknight for violating the protective custody order and for failing to appear at the hearing. Bouknight had indicated to her attorney that she would appear with the child, but also expressed fear that if she appeared the State would "snatch the child." The court issued an order to show cause why Bouknight should not be held in civil contempt for failure to produce the child. Expressing concern that Maurice was endangered or perhaps dead, the court issued a bench warrant for Bouknight's appearance.

Maurice was not produced at subsequent hearings. At a hearing one week later, Bouknight claimed that Maurice was with a relative in Dallas. Investigation revealed that the relative had not seen Maurice. The next day, following another hearing at which Bouknight again declined to produce Maurice, the juvenile court found Bouknight in contempt for failure to produce the child as ordered. There was and has been no indication that she was unable to comply with the order. The court directed that Bouknight be imprisoned until she "purge[d] herself of contempt by either producing [Maurice] before the court or revealing to the court his exact whereabouts."

The juvenile court rejected Bouknight's subsequent claim that the contempt order violated the Fifth Amendment's guarantee against self-incrimination. The court stated that the production of Maurice would purge the contempt and that "[t]he contempt is issued not because she refuse[d] to testify in any proceeding . . . [but] because she has failed to abide by the Order of this Court, mainly [for] the production of Maurice M." While that decision was being appealed, Bouknight was convicted of theft and sentenced to 18 months' imprisonment in separate proceedings. The Court of Appeals of Maryland vacated the juvenile court's judgment upholding the contempt order. The Court of Appeals found that the contempt order unconstitutionally compelled Bouknight to admit through the act of production "a measure of continuing control and dominion over Maurice's person" in circumstances in which "Bouknight has a reasonable apprehension that she will be prosecuted." Chief Justice Rehnquist granted BCDSS' application for a stay of the judgment and mandate of the Maryland Court of Appeals, pending disposition of the petition for a writ of certiorari. We granted certiorari and we now reverse.

II

The Fifth Amendment provides that "No person . . . shall be compelled in any criminal case to be a witness against himself." The Fifth Amendment's protection "applies only when the accused is compelled to make a *testimonial* communication that is incriminating." *Fisher v. United States,* 425 U.S. 391, 408 (1976). The juvenile court concluded that Bouknight could comply with the order through the unadorned act of producing the child, and we thus address that aspect of the order. When the government demands that an item be produced, "the only thing compelled is the act of producing the [item]." The Fifth Amendment's protection may nonetheless be implicated because the act of complying with the government's demand testifies to the existence, possession, or authenticity of the things produced. But a person may not claim the Amendment's protections based upon the incrimination that may result from the contents or nature of the thing demanded. Bouknight therefore cannot claim the privilege based upon anything that examination of Maurice might reveal, nor can she assert the privilege upon the theory that compliance would assert that the child produced is in fact Maurice (a fact the State could readily establish, rendering any testimony regarding existence or authenticity insufficiently incriminating). Rather, Bouknight claims the benefit of the privilege because the act of production would amount to testimony regarding her control over, and possession of, Maurice. Although the State could readily introduce evidence of Bouknight's continuing control over the child—*e.g.,* the custody order, testimony of relatives, and Bouknight's own statements to Maryland officials before invoking the privilege—her implicit communication of control over Maurice at the moment of production might aid the State in prosecuting Bouknight.[b]

The possibility that a production order will compel testimonial assertions that may prove incriminating does not, in all contexts, justify invoking the privilege to resist production. Even assuming that this limited testimonial assertion is sufficiently incriminating and "sufficiently testimonial for purposes of the privilege," Bouknight may not invoke the privilege to resist the production order because she has assumed custodial duties related to production and because production is required as part of a noncriminal regulatory regime.

The Court has on several occasions recognized that the Fifth Amendment privilege may not be invoked to resist compliance with a regulatory regime constructed to effect the State's public purposes unrelated to the enforcement of its criminal laws. In *Shapiro v. United States,* 335 U.S. 1 (1948), the Court considered an application of the Emergency Price Control Act of 1942 and a regulation issued thereunder which required licensed businesses to maintain records and make them available for inspection by administrators. The Court indicated that no Fifth Amendment protection attached to production of the "required records," which the "defendant was required to keep, not for his private uses, but for the benefit of the public, and for public inspection." The Court's discussion of the constitutional implications of the scheme focused upon the relation between the Government's regulatory objectives and the Government's interest in gaining access to the records in Shapiro's possession:

> It may be assumed at the outset that there are limits which the Government cannot constitutionally exceed in requiring the keeping of records which may be inspected by an administrative agency and may be used in prosecuting statutory violations committed by the recordkeeper himself. But no serious misgiving that those bounds have been overstepped would appear to be evoked when there is a sufficient relation between the activity sought to be regulated and the public concern so that the Government can constitutionally regulate or forbid the basic activity concerned, and can constitutionally require the keeping of particular records, subject to inspection by the Administrator.

The Court has since refined those limits to the government's authority to gain access to items or information vested with this public character. The Court has noted that "the requirements at issue in *Shapiro* were imposed in 'an essentially non-criminal and regulatory area of inquiry,' "

[b] *Fisher* held that the government can enforce a subpoena requiring a person to produce a document that he has created. Although there is compulsion in such a demand, what is compelled is not testimonial unless the government also compelled the defendant to create the document in the first place.—Eds.

and that *Shapiro*'s reach is limited where requirements "are directed to a 'selective group inherently suspect of criminal activities.' "

California v. Byers, 402 U.S. 424 (1971), confirms that the ability to invoke the privilege may be greatly diminished when invocation would interfere with the effective operation of a generally applicable, civil regulatory requirement. In *Byers,* the Court upheld enforcement of California's statutory requirement that drivers of cars involved in accidents stop and provide their names and addresses. A plurality found the risk of incrimination too insubstantial to implicate the Fifth Amendment, and noted that the statute "was not intended to facilitate criminal convictions but to promote the satisfaction of civil liabilities," was "directed at the public at large," and required disclosure of no inherently illegal activity. . . .

* * *

These principles readily apply to this case. Once Maurice was adjudicated a child in need of assistance, his care and safety became the particular object of the State's regulatory interests. Maryland first placed Maurice in shelter care, authorized placement in foster care, and then entrusted responsibility for Maurice's care to Bouknight. By accepting care of Maurice subject to the custodial order's conditions (including requirements that she cooperate with BCDSS, follow a prescribed training regime, and be subject to further court orders), Bouknight submitted to the routine operation of the regulatory system and agreed to hold Maurice in a manner consonant with the State's regulatory interests and subject to inspection by BCDSS. In assuming the obligations attending custody, Bouknight "has accepted the incident obligation to permit inspection." The State imposes and enforces that obligation as part of a broadly directed, noncriminal regulatory regime governing children cared for pursuant to custodial orders.

Persons who care for children pursuant to a custody order, and who may be subject to a request for access to the child, are hardly a "selective group inherently suspect of criminal activities." The juvenile court may place a child within its jurisdiction with social service officials or "under supervision in his own home or in the custody or under the guardianship of a relative or other fit person, upon terms the court deems appropriate." Children may be placed, for example, in foster care, in homes of relatives, or in the care of state officials. Even when the court allows a parent to retain control of a child within the court's jurisdiction, that parent is not one singled out for criminal conduct, but rather has been deemed to be, without the State's assistance, simply "unable or unwilling to give proper care and attention to the child and his problems." The provision that authorized the juvenile court's efforts to gain production of Maurice reflects this broad applicability. This provision "fairly may be said to be directed at

. . . parents, guardians, and custodians who accept placement of juveniles in custody."

Similarly, BCDSS' efforts to gain access to children, as well as judicial efforts to the same effect, do not "focu[s] almost exclusively on conduct which was criminal." *Byers,* 402 U.S., at 454 (Harlan, J., concurring in judgment). Many orders will arise in circumstances entirely devoid of criminal conduct. Even when criminal conduct may exist, the court may properly request production and return of the child, and enforce that request through exercise of the contempt power, for reasons related entirely to the child's well-being and through measures unrelated to criminal law enforcement or investigation. This case provides an illustration: concern for the child's safety underlay the efforts to gain access to and then compel production of Maurice. Finally, production in the vast majority of cases will embody no incriminating testimony, even if in particular cases the act of production may incriminate the custodian through an assertion of possession or the existence, or the identity, of the child. These orders to produce children cannot be characterized as efforts to gain some testimonial component of the act of production. The government demands production of the very public charge entrusted to a custodian, and makes the demand for compelling reasons unrelated to criminal law enforcement and as part of a broadly applied regulatory regime. In these circumstances, Bouknight cannot invoke the privilege to resist the order to produce Maurice.

We are not called upon to define the precise limitations that may exist upon the State's ability to use the testimonial aspects of Bouknight's act of production in subsequent criminal proceedings. But we note that imposition of such limitations is not foreclosed. The same custodial role that limited the ability to resist the production order may give rise to corresponding limitations upon the direct and indirect use of that testimony. The State's regulatory requirement in the usual case may neither compel incriminating testimony nor aid a criminal prosecution, but the Fifth Amendment protections are not thereby necessarily unavailable to the person who complies with the regulatory requirement after invoking the privilege and subsequently faces prosecution. In a broad range of contexts, the Fifth Amendment limits prosecutors' ability to use testimony that has been compelled.

JUSTICE MARSHALL, with whom JUSTICE BRENNAN joins, dissenting.

Although the Court assumes that respondent's act of producing her child would be testimonial and could be incriminating, it nonetheless concludes that she cannot invoke her privilege against self-incrimination and refuse to reveal her son's current location. Neither of the reasons the Court articulates to support its refusal to permit respondent to invoke her constitutional privilege justifies its decision. I therefore dissent.

I

The Court correctly assumes that Bouknight's production of her son to the Maryland court would be testimonial because it would amount to an admission of Bouknight's physical control over her son. See *Fisher v. United States,* 425 U.S. 391, 410 (1976) (acts of production are testimonial if they contain implicit statement of fact). The Court also assumes that Bouknight's act of production would be self-incriminating. I would not hesitate to hold explicitly that Bouknight's admission of possession or control presents a "real and appreciable" threat of self-incrimination. Bouknight's ability to produce the child would conclusively establish her actual and present physical control over him, and thus might "prove a significant 'link in a chain' of evidence tending to establish [her] guilt."

Indeed, the stakes for Bouknight are much greater than the Court suggests. Not only could she face criminal abuse and neglect charges for her alleged mistreatment of Maurice, but she could also be charged with causing his death. The State acknowledges that it suspects that Maurice is dead, and the police are investigating his case as a possible homicide. In these circumstances, the potentially incriminating aspects to Bouknight's act of production are undoubtedly significant.

II

Notwithstanding the real threat of self-incrimination, the Court holds that "Bouknight may not invoke the privilege to resist the production order because she has assumed custodial duties related to production and because production is required as part of a noncriminal regulatory regime." In characterizing Bouknight as Maurice's "custodian," and in describing the relevant Maryland juvenile statutes as part of a noncriminal regulatory regime, the Court relies on two distinct lines of Fifth Amendment precedent, neither of which applies to this litigation.

A

The Court's first line of reasoning turns on its view that Bouknight has agreed to exercise on behalf of the State certain custodial obligations with respect to her son, obligations that the Court analogizes to those of a custodian of the records of a collective entity. This characterization is baffling, both because it is contrary to the facts of this case and because this Court has never relied on such a characterization to override the privilege against self-incrimination except in the context of a claim of privilege by an agent of a collective entity.

Jacqueline Bouknight is Maurice's mother; she is not, and in fact could not be, his "custodian" whose rights and duties are determined solely by the Maryland juvenile protection law. Although Bouknight surrendered physical custody of her child during the pendency of the proceedings to determine whether Maurice was a "child in need of assistance" (CINA) within the meaning of the Maryland Code, § 3–801(e), Maurice's placement in shelter care was only temporary and did not extinguish her legal right to custody of her son. When the CINA proceedings were settled, Bouknight regained physical custody of Maurice and entered into an agreement with the Baltimore City Department of Social Services. In that agreement, which was approved by the juvenile court, Bouknight promised, among other things, to "cooperate with BCDSS," but she retained legal custody of Maurice.

A finding that a child is in need of assistance does not by itself divest a parent of legal or physical custody, nor does it transform such custody to something conferred by the State. Thus, the parent of a CINA continues to exercise custody because she is the child's parent, not because the State has delegated that responsibility to her. Although the State has obligations "[t]o provide for the care, protection, and wholesome mental and physical development of children" who are in need of assistance, these duties do not eliminate or override a parent's continuing legal obligations similarly to provide for her child.

In light of the statutory structure governing a parent's relationship to a CINA, Bouknight is not acting as a custodian in the traditional sense of that word because she is not acting *on behalf of the State*. In reality, she continues to exercise her parental duties, constrained by an agreement between her and the State. That agreement, which includes a stipulation that Maurice was a CINA, allows the State, in certain circumstances, to intercede in Bouknight's relationship with her child. It does not, however, confer custodial rights and obligations on Bouknight in the same way corporate law creates the custodial status of a corporate agent.

Moreover, the rationale for denying a corporate custodian Fifth Amendment protection for acts done in her representative capacity does not apply to this case. The rule for a custodian of corporate records rests on the well-established principle that a collective entity, unlike a natural person, has no Fifth Amendment privilege against self-incrimination. Because an artificial entity can act only through its agents, a custodian of such an entity's documents may not invoke her personal privilege to resist producing documents that may incriminate the entity, even if the documents may also incriminate the custodian. As we explained in *United States v. White:*

> [I]ndividuals, when acting as representatives of a collective group, cannot be said to be exercising their personal rights and duties nor to be entitled to their purely personal privileges. Rather they assume the rights, duties and privileges of the artificial entity or association of which they are agents or officers and they are bound by its obligations. . . . And the official records and documents of the organization that are held by them *in a representative rather than in a personal capacity* cannot be the subject of the personal

> privilege against self-incrimination, even though production of the papers might tend to incriminate them personally.

322 U.S., [694, 699 (1944)] (emphasis added).

Jacqueline Bouknight is not the agent for an artificial entity that possesses no Fifth Amendment privilege. Her role as Maurice's parent is very different from the role of a corporate custodian who is merely the instrumentality through whom the corporation acts. I am unwilling to extend the collective entity doctrine into a context where it denies individuals, acting in their personal rather than representative capacities, their constitutional privilege against self-incrimination.

B

The Court's decision rests as well on cases holding that "the ability to invoke the privilege may be greatly diminished when invocation would interfere with the effective operation of a generally applicable, civil regulatory requirement." The cases the Court cites have two common features: they concern civil regulatory systems not primarily intended to facilitate criminal investigations, and they target the general public. In contrast, regulatory regimes that are directed at a " 'selective group inherently suspect of criminal activities,' " do not result in a similar diminution of the Fifth Amendment privilege.

1

Applying the first feature to this case, the Court describes Maryland's juvenile protection scheme as "a broadly directed, noncriminal regulatory regime governing children cared for pursuant to custodial orders." The Court concludes that Bouknight cannot resist an order necessary for the functioning of that system. The Court's characterization of Maryland's system is dubious and highlights the flaws inherent in the Court's formulation of the appropriate Fifth Amendment inquiry. Virtually any civil regulatory scheme could be characterized as essentially noncriminal by looking narrowly or, as in this case, *solely* to the avowed non-criminal purpose of the regulations. If one focuses instead on the practical effects, the same scheme could be seen as facilitating criminal investigations. The fact that the Court holds Maryland's juvenile statute to be essentially noncriminal, notwithstanding the overlapping purposes underlying that statute and Maryland's criminal child abuse statutes, proves that the Court's test will never be used to find a relationship between the civil scheme and law enforcement goals significant enough to implicate the Fifth Amendment.

* * *

I would apply a different analysis, one that is more faithful to the concerns underlying the Fifth Amendment. This approach would target respondent's particular claim of privilege, the precise nature of the testimony sought, and the likelihood of self-incrimination caused by this respondent's compliance. "To sustain the privilege, it need only be evident from the implications of the question, in the setting in which it is asked, that a responsive answer to the question or an explanation of why it cannot be answered might be dangerous because injurious disclosure could result." This analysis unambiguously indicates that Bouknight's Fifth Amendment privilege must be respected to protect her from the serious risk of self-incrimination.

An individualized inquiry is preferable to the Court's analysis because it allows the privilege to turn on the concrete facts of a particular case, rather than on abstract characterizations concerning the nature of a regulatory scheme. Moreover, this particularized analysis would not undermine any appropriate goals of civil regulatory schemes that may intersect with criminal prohibitions. Instead, the ability of a State to provide immunity from criminal prosecution permits it to gather information necessary for civil regulation, while also preserving the integrity of the privilege against self-incrimination. The fact that the State throws a wide net in seeking information does not mean that it can demand from the few persons whose Fifth Amendment rights are implicated that they participate in their own criminal prosecutions. Rather, when the State demands testimony from its citizens, it should do so with an explicit grant of immunity.

2

The Court's approach includes a second element; it holds that a civil regulatory scheme cannot override Fifth Amendment protection unless it is targeted at the general public. Such an analysis would not be necessary under the particularized approach I advocate. Even under the Court's test, however, Bouknight's right against self-incrimination should not be diminished because Maryland's juvenile welfare scheme clearly is *not* generally applicable. A child is considered in need of assistance because "[h]e is mentally handicapped or is not receiving ordinary and proper care and attention, and . . . [h]is parents . . . are unable or unwilling to give proper care and attention to the child and his problems." The juvenile court has jurisdiction only over children who are alleged to be in need of assistance, not over all children in the State. It thus has power to compel testimony only from those parents whose children are alleged to be CINA's. In other words, the regulatory scheme that the Court describes as "broadly directed" is actually narrowly targeted at parents who through abuse or neglect deny their children the minimal reasonable level of care and attention. Not all such abuse or neglect rises to the level of criminal child abuse, but parents of children who have been so seriously neglected or abused as to warrant allegations that the children are in need of state assistance are clearly "a selective group inherently suspect of criminal activities."

III

* * *

Although I am disturbed by the Court's willingness to apply inapposite precedent to deny Bouknight her constitutional right against self-incrimination, especially in light of the serious allegations of homicide that accompany this civil proceeding, I take some comfort in the Court's recognition that the State may be prohibited from using any testimony given by Bouknight in subsequent criminal proceedings.[2] Because I am not content to deny Bouknight the constitutional protection required by the Fifth Amendment *now* in the hope that she will not be convicted *later* on the basis of her own testimony, I dissent.

Points for Discussion

1. The Court here invokes the oft-repeated distinction between the act of production and the act of creation. That is, while the government cannot compel an individual to create a document (a confession, say) it may require him to turn over a document (a business record, say) that he has previously created. The theory underlying the distinction is that the act of production is not testimonial and therefore does not implicate the Fifth Amendment. If the government seeks to make use, however, not of the documents' contents but of the fact that the defendant was in possession of them, his act of production becomes testimonial and the government is prohibited from using his production of the documents as proof of their existence or authenticity.

2. Why does the Court concede here that the Fifth Amendment privilege would likely be implicated by Bouknight's production of the child? If, as seems clear, Bouknight could have avoided contempt by simply bringing the child to Court (rather than saying anything) why is the privilege relevant to this case at all?

3. At the end of his dissent Justice Marshall expresses skepticism about the sincerity of the state's interest in Maurice's well-being. Because, he argues, Maryland law provides for the provision of use immunity to witnesses unwilling to testify, the state could demonstrate its concern for Maurice by giving his mother immunity and compelling her to testify. Does the Maryland statute serve as an adequate substitute for the Fifth Amendment privilege?

[2] I note, with both exasperation and skepticism about the bona fide nature of the State's intentions, that the State may be able to grant Bouknight use immunity under a recently enacted immunity statute, even though it has thus far failed to do so. See 1989 Md.Laws, ch. 288 (amending § 9–123). Although the statute applies only to testimony "in a criminal prosecution or a proceeding before a grand jury of the State," Md.Cts. & Jud.Proc.Code Ann. § 9–123(b)(1) (Supp.1989), the State represented to this Court that "[a]s a matter of law, [granting limited use immunity for the testimonial aspects of Bouknight's compliance with the production order] would now be possible." If such a grant of immunity has been possible since July 1989 and the State has refused to invoke it so that it can litigate Bouknight's claim of privilege, I have difficulty believing that the State is sincere in its protestations of concern for Maurice's well-being.

4. In *United States v. Hubbell*, 530 U.S. 27 (2000), Independent Counsel Kenneth Starr compelled Webster Hubbell, a former law partner of Hillary Clinton, to produce 11 broad categories of documents that might be within his possession. Hubbell refused to do so and was then granted immunity compelling him to produce the records. He was then indicted based on information contained within the documents. The district court dismissed the charges on the grounds that Hubbell's production of the documents was testimonial and thus protected by the grant of immunity. The Supreme Court began by reviewing when an act of production is testimonial:

> [A] person may be required to produce specific documents even though they contain incriminating assertions of fact or belief because the creation of those documents was not "compelled" within the meaning of the privilege. Our decision in *Fisher* v. *United States,* 425 U.S. 391 (1976), dealt with summonses issued by the Internal Revenue Service seeking working papers used in the preparation of tax returns. Because the papers had been voluntarily prepared prior to the issuance of the summonses, they could not be "said to contain compelled testimonial evidence, either of the taxpayers or of anyone else." Accordingly, the taxpayer could not "avoid compliance with the subpoena merely by asserting that the item of evidence which he is required to produce contains incriminating writing, whether his own or that of someone else." It is clear, therefore, that respondent Hubbell could not avoid compliance with the subpoena served on him merely because the demanded documents contained incriminating evidence, whether written by others or voluntarily prepared by himself.
>
> On the other hand, we have also made it clear that the act of producing documents in response to a subpoena may have a compelled testimonial aspect. We have held that "the act of production" itself may implicitly communicate "statements of fact." By "producing documents in compliance with a subpoena, the witness would admit that the papers existed, were in his possession or control, and were authentic." Moreover, as was true in this case, when the custodian of documents responds to a subpoena, he may be compelled to take the witness stand and answer questions designed to determine whether he has produced everything demanded by the subpoena. The answers to those questions, as well as the act of production itself, may certainly communicate information about the existence, custody, and authenticity of the documents. Whether the constitutional privilege protects the answers to such questions, or protects the act of production itself, is a question that is distinct from the question whether the unprotected contents of the documents themselves are incriminating.

The Court concluded that Hubbell's production of the documents was testimonial because, unlike in *Fisher*, "here the Government has not shown that it had any prior knowledge of either the existence or the whereabouts of the 13,120 pages of documents ultimately produced by the respondent." In determining that the production was testimonial, Justice Stevens' opinion on behalf of an eight-justice majority reasoned: "It was unquestionably necessary for respondent to make extensive use of 'the contents of his own mind' in identifying the hundreds of documents responsive to the requests in the subpoena. The assembly of those documents was like telling an inquisitor the combination to a wall safe, not like being forced to surrender the key to a strongbox."

CHAPTER 9

ADMINISTERING *MIRANDA*

■ ■ ■

In chapter 6 we saw that *Miranda v. Arizona* arose out of a concern that police interrogation practices were undermining the adversarial system. Although the Supreme Court created an extensive regulatory regime in *Miranda*, its rules are hardly self-enforcing. In this chapter we look at how the Court has interpreted the *Miranda* decision over the last five decades.

A. CUSTODY, INTERROGATION, AND INCRIMINATION

BERKEMER V. MCCARTY

468 U.S. 420 (1984)

JUSTICE MARSHALL delivered the opinion of the court.

This case presents two related questions: First, does our decision in *Miranda v. Arizona*, 384 U.S. 436 (1966), govern the admissibility of statements made during custodial interrogation by a suspect accused of a misdemeanor traffic offense? Second, does the roadside questioning of a motorist detained pursuant to a traffic stop constitute custodial interrogation for the purposes of the doctrine enunciated in *Miranda*?

I

The parties have stipulated to the essential facts. On the evening of March 31, 1980, Trooper Williams of the Ohio State Highway Patrol observed respondent's car weaving in and out of a lane on Interstate Highway 270. After following the car for two miles, Williams forced respondent to stop and asked him to get out of the vehicle. When respondent complied, Williams noticed that he was having difficulty standing. At that point, "Williams concluded that [respondent] would be charged with a traffic offense and, therefore, his freedom to leave the scene was terminated." However, respondent was not told that he would be taken into custody. Williams then asked respondent to perform a field sobriety test, commonly known as a "balancing test." Respondent could not do so without falling.

While still at the scene of the traffic stop, Williams asked respondent whether he had been using intoxicants. Respondent replied that "he had consumed two beers and had smoked several joints of marijuana a short time before." Respondent's speech was slurred, and Williams had difficulty understanding him. Williams thereupon formally placed respondent under arrest and transported him in the patrol car to the Franklin County Jail.

At the jail, respondent was given an intoxilyzer test to determine the concentration of alcohol in his blood. The test did not detect any alcohol whatsoever in respondent's system. Williams then resumed questioning respondent in order to obtain information for inclusion in the State Highway Patrol Alcohol Influence Report. Respondent answered affirmatively a question whether he had been drinking. When then asked if he was under the influence of alcohol, he said, "I guess, barely." Williams next asked respondent to indicate on the form whether the marihuana he had smoked had been treated with any chemicals. In the section of the report headed "Remarks," respondent wrote, "No ang[el] dust or PCP in the pot. Rick McCarty."

At no point in this sequence of events did Williams or anyone else tell respondent that he had a right to remain silent, to consult with an attorney, and to have an attorney appointed for him if he could not afford one.

* * *

II

* * *

In the years since the decision in *Miranda*, we have frequently reaffirmed the central principle established by that case: if the police take a suspect into custody and then ask him questions without informing him of the rights enumerated above, his responses cannot be introduced into evidence to establish his guilt.

Petitioner asks us to carve an exception out of the foregoing principle. When the police arrest a person for allegedly committing a misdemeanor traffic offense and then ask him questions without telling him his constitutional rights, petitioner argues, his responses should be admissible against him. We cannot agree.

One of the principal advantages of the doctrine that suspects must be given warnings before being interrogated while in custody is the clarity of that rule.

* * *

The exception to *Miranda* proposed by petitioner would substantially undermine this crucial advantage of the doctrine. The police often are unaware when they arrest a person whether he may have committed a misdemeanor or a felony. Consider, for example, the reasonably common situation in which the driver of a car involved in an accident is taken into custody. Under Ohio law, both driving while under the influence of intoxicants and negligent vehicular homicide are misdemeanors, while reckless vehicular homicide is a felony. When arresting a person for causing a collision, the police may not know which of these offenses he may have committed. Indeed, the nature of his offense may depend upon circumstances unknowable to the police, such as whether the suspect has previously committed a similar offense or has a criminal record of some other kind. It may even turn upon events yet to happen, such as whether a victim of the accident dies. It would be unreasonable to expect the police to make guesses as to the nature of the criminal conduct at issue before deciding how they may interrogate the suspect.

It might be argued that the police would not need to make such guesses; whenever in doubt, they could ensure compliance with the law by giving the full *Miranda* warnings. It cannot be doubted, however, that in some cases a desire to induce a suspect to reveal information he might withhold if informed of his rights would induce the police not to take the cautious course.

Equally importantly, the doctrinal complexities that would confront the courts if we accepted petitioner's proposal would be Byzantine. Difficult questions quickly spring to mind: For instance, investigations into seemingly minor offenses sometimes escalate gradually into investigations into more serious matters; at what point in the evolution of an affair of this sort would the police be obliged to give *Miranda* warnings to a suspect in custody? What evidence would be necessary to establish that an arrest for a misdemeanor offense was merely a pretext to enable the police to interrogate the suspect (in hopes of obtaining information about a felony) without providing him the safeguards prescribed by *Miranda*? The litigation necessary to resolve such matters would be time-consuming and disruptive of law enforcement. And the end result would be an elaborate set of rules, interlaced with exceptions and subtle distinctions, discriminating between different kinds of custodial interrogations. Neither the police nor criminal defendants would benefit from such a development.

Absent a compelling justification we surely would be unwilling so seriously to impair the simplicity and clarity of the holding of *Miranda*. Neither of the two arguments proffered by petitioner constitutes such a justification. Petitioner first contends that *Miranda* warnings are unnecessary when a suspect is questioned about a misdemeanor traffic offense, because the police have no reason to subject such a suspect to the sort of interrogation that most troubled the Court in *Miranda*. We cannot agree that the dangers of police abuse are so slight in this context. For example, the offense of driving while intoxicated is increasingly regarded in many jurisdictions as a very serious matter. Especially when the intoxicant at issue is a narcotic drug rather than alcohol, the police sometimes have difficulty obtaining evidence of this crime. Under such circumstances, the incentive for the police to try to induce the defendant to incriminate himself may well be substantial. Similar incentives are likely to be present when a person is arrested for a minor offense but the police suspect that a more serious crime may have been committed.

* * *

We do not suggest that compliance with *Miranda* conclusively establishes the voluntariness of a subsequent confession. But cases in which a defendant can make a colorable argument that a self-incriminating statement was "compelled" despite the fact that the law enforcement authorities adhered to the dictates of *Miranda* are rare.

Petitioner's second argument is that law enforcement would be more expeditious and effective in the absence of a requirement that persons arrested for traffic offenses be informed of their rights. Again, we are unpersuaded. The occasions on which the police arrest and then interrogate someone suspected only of a misdemeanor traffic offense are rare. The police are already well accustomed to giving *Miranda* warnings to persons taken into custody. Adherence to the principle that all suspects must be given such warnings will not significantly hamper the efforts of the police to investigate crimes.

We hold therefore that a person subjected to custodial interrogation is entitled to the benefit of the procedural safeguards enunciated in *Miranda*, regardless of the nature or severity of the offense of which he is suspected or for which he was arrested.

The implication of this holding is that the Court of Appeals was correct in ruling that the statements made by respondent at the County Jail were inadmissible. There can be no question that respondent was "in custody" at least as of the moment he was formally placed under arrest and instructed to get into the police car. Because he was not informed of his constitutional rights at that juncture, respondent's subsequent admissions should not have been used against him.

III

To assess the admissibility of the self-incriminating statements made by respondent prior to his formal arrest, we are obliged to address a second issue concerning the scope of our decision in *Miranda*: whether the roadside questioning of a motorist detained pursuant to a routine traffic stop should be considered "custodial interrogation." Respondent urges that it should, on the ground that *Miranda* by its terms applies whenever "a person has been taken into custody or otherwise deprived of his freedom of action *in any significant way*." Petitioner contends that a holding that every detained motorist must be advised of his rights before being questioned would constitute an unwarranted extension of the Miranda doctrine.

It must be acknowledged at the outset that a traffic stop significantly curtails the "freedom of action" of the driver and the passengers, if any, of the detained vehicle. Under the law of most States, it is a crime either to ignore a policeman's signal to stop one's car or, once having stopped, to drive away without permission. Certainly few motorists would feel free either to disobey a directive to pull over or to leave the scene of a traffic stop without being told they might do so. Partly for these reasons, we have long acknowledged that "stopping an automobile and detaining its occupants constitute a 'seizure' within the meaning of [the Fourth] Amendmen[t], even though the purpose of the stop is limited and the resulting detention quite brief."

However, we decline to accord talismanic power to the phrase in the *Miranda* opinion emphasized by respondent. Fidelity to the doctrine announced in *Miranda* requires that it be enforced strictly, but only in those types of situations in which the concerns that powered the decision are implicated. Thus, we must decide whether a traffic stop exerts upon a detained person pressures that sufficiently impair his free exercise of his privilege against self-incrimination to require that he be warned of his constitutional rights.

Two features of an ordinary traffic stop mitigate the danger that a person questioned will be induced "to speak where he would not otherwise do so freely," *Miranda v. Arizona*, 384 U.S., at 467. First, detention of a motorist pursuant to a traffic stop is presumptively temporary and brief. The vast majority of roadside detentions last only a few minutes. A motorist's expectations, when he sees a policeman's light flashing behind him, are that he will be obliged to spend a short period of time answering questions and waiting while the officer checks his license and registration, that he may then be given a citation, but that in the end he most likely will be allowed to continue on his way. In this respect, questioning incident to an ordinary traffic stop is quite different from stationhouse interrogation, which frequently is prolonged, and in which the detainee often is aware that questioning will continue until he provides his interrogators the answers they seek.

Second, circumstances associated with the typical traffic stop are not such that the motorist feels completely at the mercy of the police. To be sure, the aura of authority surrounding an armed, uniformed officer and the knowledge that the officer has some discretion in deciding whether to issue a citation, in combination, exert some pressure on the detainee to respond to questions. But other aspects of the situation substantially offset these forces. Perhaps most importantly, the typical traffic stop is public, at least to some degree. Passersby, on foot or in other cars, witness the interaction of officer and motorist. This exposure to public view both reduces the ability of an unscrupulous policeman to use illegitimate means to elicit self-incriminating statements and diminishes the motorist's fear that, if he does not cooperate, he will be subjected to abuse. The fact that the detained motorist typically is confronted by only one or at most two policemen further mutes his sense of vulnerability. In short, the atmosphere surrounding an ordinary traffic stop is substantially less "police dominated" than that surrounding the kinds of interrogation at issue in *Miranda* itself and in the subsequent cases in which we have applied *Miranda*.

* * *

Respondent contends that to "exempt" traffic stops from the coverage of *Miranda* will open the way to widespread abuse. Policemen will simply delay formally arresting detained motorists, and will subject them to sustained and intimidating interrogation at the scene of their initial detention. The net result, respondent contends, will be a serious threat to the rights that the *Miranda* doctrine is designed to protect.

We are confident that the state of affairs projected by respondent will not come to pass. It is settled that the safeguards prescribed by *Miranda* become applicable as soon as a suspect's freedom of action is curtailed to a "degree associated with formal arrest." If a motorist who has been detained pursuant to a traffic stop thereafter is subjected to treatment that renders him "in custody" for practical purposes, he will be entitled to the full panoply of protections prescribed by *Miranda*.

Admittedly, our adherence to the doctrine just recounted will mean that the police and lower courts will continue occasionally to have difficulty deciding exactly when a suspect has been taken into custody. Either a rule that *Miranda* applies to all traffic stops or a rule that a suspect need not be advised of his rights until he is formally placed under arrest would provide a clearer, more easily administered line. However, each of these two alternatives has drawbacks that make it unacceptable. The first would substantially impede the enforcement of the Nation's traffic laws—by compelling the police either to take the time to warn all detained motorists of their constitutional rights or to forgo use of self-incriminating statements made by those motorists—while doing little to protect citizens' Fifth Amendment rights. The second would enable the police to circumvent the constraints on custodial interrogations established by *Miranda*.

Turning to the case before us, we find nothing in the record that indicates that respondent should have been given *Miranda* warnings at any point prior to the time Trooper Williams placed him under arrest. For the reasons indicated above, we reject the contention that the initial stop of respondent's car, by itself, rendered him "in custody." And respondent has failed to demonstrate that, at any time between the initial stop and the arrest, he was subjected to restraints comparable to those associated with a formal arrest. Only a short period of time elapsed between the stop and the arrest. At no point during that interval was respondent informed that his detention would not be temporary. Although Trooper Williams apparently decided as soon as respondent stepped out of his car that respondent would be taken into custody and charged with a traffic offense, Williams never communicated his intention to respondent. A policeman's unarticulated plan has no bearing on the question whether a suspect was "in custody" at a particular time; the only relevant inquiry is how a reasonable man in the suspect's position would have understood his situation. Nor do other aspects of the interaction of Williams and respondent support the contention that respondent was exposed to "custodial interrogation" at the scene of the stop. From aught that appears in the stipulation of facts, a single police officer asked respondent a modest number of questions and requested him to perform a simple balancing test at a location visible to passing motorists. Treatment of this sort cannot fairly be characterized as the functional equivalent of formal arrest.

We conclude, in short, that respondent was not taken into custody for the purposes of *Miranda* until Williams arrested him. Consequently, the statements respondent made prior to that point were admissible against him.

* * *

JUSTICE STEVENS, concurring in part and concurring in the judgment.

The only question presented by the petition for certiorari reads as follows: "Whether law enforcement officers must give 'Miranda warnings' to individuals arrested for misdemeanor traffic offenses."

In Parts I, II, and IV of its opinion, the Court answers that question in the affirmative and explains why that answer requires that the judgment of the Court of Appeals be affirmed. Part III of the Court's opinion is written for the purpose of discussing the admissibility of statements made by respondent "prior to his formal arrest." That discussion is not necessary to the disposition of the case, nor necessary to answer the only question presented by the certiorari petition. Indeed, the Court of Appeals quite properly did not pass on the question answered in Part III since it was entirely unnecessary to the judgment in this case. It thus wisely followed the cardinal rule that a court should not pass on a constitutional question in advance of the necessity of deciding it.

* * *

Points for Discussion

1. The Court clarifies in this case that the terms "seizure" and "custody" are not synonymous for constitutional purposes. Do you agree that the respondent here was not in custody for *Miranda* purposes?

2. Is the Court's first holding—that *Miranda* applies to misdemeanors as well as to felonies—undercut by its second holding—that the warnings of *Miranda* are not triggered by a *Terry*-type stop?

3. Justice Marshall dissents from many of the important opinions in this book. Why do you think he was the author of this essentially unanimous opinion limiting *Miranda* rights in the oft-recurring context of traffic stops?

J.D.B. v. NORTH CAROLINA

564 U.S. 261 (2011)

JUSTICE SOTOMAYOR delivered the opinion of the court.

This case presents the question whether the age of a child subjected to police questioning is relevant to the custody analysis of *Miranda v. Arizona,* 384 U.S. 436 (1966). It is beyond dispute that children will often feel bound to submit to police questioning when an adult in the same circumstances would feel free to leave. Seeing no reason for police officers or courts to blind themselves to that commonsense reality, we hold that a child's age properly informs the *Miranda* custody analysis.

I

A

Petitioner J.D.B. was a 13-year-old, seventh-grade student attending class at Smith Middle School in Chapel Hill, North Carolina when he was removed from his classroom by a uniformed police officer, escorted to a closed-door conference room, and questioned by police for at least half an hour.

This was the second time that police questioned J.D.B. in the span of a week. Five days earlier, two home break-ins occurred, and various items were stolen. Police stopped and questioned J.D.B. after he was seen behind a residence in the neighborhood where the crimes occurred. That same day, police also spoke to J.D.B.'s grandmother—his legal guardian—as well as his aunt.

Police later learned that a digital camera matching the description of one of the stolen items had been found at J.D.B.'s middle school and seen in J.D.B.'s possession. Investigator DiCostanzo, the juvenile investigator with the local police force who had been assigned to the case, went to the school to question J.D.B. Upon arrival, DiCostanzo informed the uniformed police officer on detail to the school (a so-called school resource officer), the assistant principal, and an administrative intern that he was there to question J.D.B. about the break-ins. Although DiCostanzo asked the school administrators to verify J.D.B.'s date of birth, address, and parent contact information from school records, neither the police officers nor the school administrators contacted J.D.B.'s grandmother.

The uniformed officer interrupted J.D.B.'s afternoon social studies class, removed J.D.B. from the classroom, and escorted him to a school conference room. There, J.D.B. was met by DiCostanzo, the assistant principal, and the administrative intern. The door to the conference room was closed. With the two police officers and the two administrators present, J.D.B. was questioned for the next 30 to 45 minutes. Prior to the commencement of questioning, J.D.B. was given neither *Miranda* warnings nor the opportunity to speak to his grandmother. Nor was he informed that he was free to leave the room.

Questioning began with small talk—discussion of sports and J.D.B.'s family life. DiCostanzo asked, and J.D.B. agreed, to discuss the events of the prior weekend. Denying any wrongdoing, J.D.B. explained that he had been in the neighborhood where the crimes occurred because he was seeking work mowing lawns. DiCostanzo pressed J.D.B. for additional detail about his efforts to obtain work; asked J.D.B. to explain a prior incident, when one of the victims returned home to find J.D.B. behind her house; and confronted J.D.B. with the stolen camera. The assistant principal urged J.D.B. to "do the right thing," warning J.D.B. that "the truth always comes out in the end."

Eventually, J.D.B. asked whether he would "still be in trouble" if he returned the "stuff." In response, DiCostanzo explained that return of the stolen items would be helpful, but "this thing is going to court" regardless. DiCostanzo then warned that he may need to seek a secure custody order if he believed that J.D.B. would continue to break into other homes. When J.D.B. asked what a secure custody order was, DiCostanzo explained that "it's where you get sent to juvenile detention before court."

After learning of the prospect of juvenile detention, J.D.B. confessed that he and a friend were responsible for the break-ins. DiCostanzo only then informed J.D.B. that he could refuse to answer the investigator's questions and that he was free to leave. Asked whether he understood, J.D.B. nodded and provided further detail, including information about the location of the stolen items. Eventually J.D.B. wrote a statement, at DiCostanzo's request. When the bell rang indicating the end of the schoolday, J.D.B. was allowed to leave to catch the bus home.

Nonetheless, both parties' submissions to this Court suggest that the warnings came after DiCostanzo raised the possibility of a secure custody order but before J.D.B. confessed for the first time. Because we remand for a determination whether J.D.B. was in custody under the proper analysis, the state courts remain free to revisit whether the trial court made a conclusive finding of fact in this respect.

* * *

II

A

* * *

By its very nature, custodial police interrogation entails "inherently compelling pressures." *Miranda,* 384 U.S., at 467. Even for an adult, the physical and psychological isolation of custodial interrogation can "undermine the individual's will to resist and . . . compel him to speak where he would not otherwise do so freely." Indeed, the pressure of custodial interrogation is so immense that it "can induce a frighteningly high percentage of people to confess to crimes they never committed." *Corley v. United States,* 556 U.S. 303 (2009). That risk is all the more troubling—and recent studies suggest, all the more acute—when the subject of custodial interrogation is a juvenile.

Recognizing that the inherently coercive nature of custodial interrogation "blurs the line between voluntary and involuntary statements," *Dickerson*, 530 U.S., at 435, this Court in *Miranda* adopted a set of prophylactic measures designed to safeguard the constitutional guarantee against self-incrimination. Prior to questioning, a suspect "must be warned that he has a right to remain silent, that any statement he does make may be used as evidence against him, and that he has a right to the presence of an attorney, either retained or appointed." And, if a suspect makes a statement during custodial interrogation, the burden is on the Government to show, as a "prerequisit[e]" to the statement's admissibility as evidence in the Government's case in chief, that the defendant "voluntarily, knowingly and intelligently" waived his rights.

Because these measures protect the individual against the coercive nature of custodial interrogation, they are required "only where there has been such a restriction on a person's freedom as to render him 'in custody.' " As we have repeatedly emphasized, whether a suspect is "in custody" is an objective inquiry.

> Two discrete inquiries are essential to the determination: first, what were the circumstances surrounding the interrogation; and second, given those circumstances, would a reasonable person have felt he or she was at liberty to terminate the interrogation and leave. Once the scene is set and the players' lines and actions are reconstructed, the court must apply an objective test to resolve the ultimate inquiry: was there a formal arrest or restraint on freedom of movement of the degree associated with formal arrest.

Thompson v. Keohane, 516 U.S. 99, 112 (1995). Rather than demarcate a limited set of relevant circumstances, we have required police officers and courts to "examine all of the circumstances surrounding the interrogation," including any circumstance that "would have affected how a reasonable person" in the suspect's position "would perceive his or her freedom to leave." On the other hand, the "subjective views harbored by either the interrogating officers or the person being questioned" are irrelevant. The test, in other words, involves no consideration of the "actual mindset" of the particular suspect subjected to police questioning.

The benefit of the objective custody analysis is that it is "designed to give clear guidance to the police." Police must make in-the-moment judgments as to when to administer *Miranda* warnings. By limiting analysis to the objective circumstances of the interrogation, and asking how a reasonable person in the suspect's position would understand his freedom to terminate questioning and leave, the objective test avoids burdening police with the task of anticipating the idiosyncrasies of every individual suspect and divining how those particular traits affect each person's subjective state of mind.

B

The State and its *amici* contend that a child's age has no place in the custody analysis, no matter how young the child subjected to police questioning. We cannot agree. In some circumstances, a child's age "would have affected how a reasonable person" in the suspect's position "would perceive his or her freedom to leave." That is, a reasonable child subjected to police questioning will sometimes feel pressured to submit when a reasonable adult would feel free to go. We think it clear that courts can account for that reality without doing any damage to the objective nature of the custody analysis.

* * *

Time and again, this Court has drawn these commonsense conclusions for itself. We have observed that children "generally are less mature and responsible than adults," that they "often lack the experience, perspective, and judgment to recognize and avoid choices that could be detrimental to them," that they "are more vulnerable or susceptible to . . . outside pressures" than adults, and so on. Addressing the specific context of police interrogation, we have observed that events that "would leave a man cold and unimpressed can overawe and overwhelm a lad in his early teens." Describing no one child in particular, these observations restate what "any parent knows"—indeed, what any person knows—about children generally.

Our various statements to this effect are far from unique. The law has historically reflected the same assumption that children characteristically lack the capacity to exercise mature judgment and possess only an incomplete ability to understand the world around them. See, *e.g.,* 1 W. BLACKSTONE, COMMENTARIES ON THE LAWS OF ENGLAND 464–465 (explaining that limits on children's legal capacity under the common law "secure them from hurting themselves by their own improvident acts"). Like this Court's own generalizations, the legal disqualifications placed on children as a class—*e.g.,* limitations on their ability to alienate property, enter a binding contract enforceable against them, and marry without parental consent—exhibit the settled understanding that the differentiating characteristics of youth are universal.

Indeed, even where a "reasonable person" standard otherwise applies, the common law has reflected the reality that children are not adults. In negligence suits, for instance, where liability turns on what an objectively reasonable person would do in the circumstances, "[a]ll American jurisdictions accept the idea that a person's childhood is a relevant circumstance" to be considered. RESTATEMENT (THIRD) OF TORTS § 10, Comment *b,* p. 117 (2005).

As this discussion establishes, "[o]ur history is replete with laws and judicial recognition" that children cannot be viewed simply as miniature adults. We see no justification for taking a different course here. So long as the child's age was known to the officer at the time of the interview, or would have been objectively apparent to any reasonable officer, including age as part of the custody analysis requires officers neither to consider circumstances "unknowable" to them, [*Berkemer v. McCarty,* 468 U.S. 420, 430 (1984)], nor to "anticipat[e] the frailties or idiosyncrasies" of the particular suspect whom they question, [*Yarborough v. Alvarado,* 541 U.S. 652, 662 (2004)]. The same "wide basis of community experience" that makes it possible, as an objective matter, "to determine what is to be expected" of children in other contexts, RESTATEMENT (SECOND) OF TORTS § 283A, at 15, likewise makes it possible to know what to expect of children subjected to police questioning.

In other words, a child's age differs from other personal characteristics that, even when known to police, have no objectively discernible relationship to a reasonable person's understanding of his freedom of action. *Alvarado,* holds, for instance, that a suspect's prior interrogation history with law enforcement has no role to play in the custody analysis because such experience could just as easily lead a reasonable person to feel free to walk away as to feel compelled to stay in place. Because the effect in any given case would be "contingent [on the] psycholog[y]" of the individual suspect, the Court explained, such experience cannot be considered without compromising the objective nature of the custody analysis. A child's age, however, is different. Precisely because childhood yields objective conclusions like those we have drawn ourselves—among others, that children are "most susceptible to influence" and "outside pressures"—considering age in the custody analysis in no way involves a determination of how youth "subjectively affect[s] the mindset" of any particular child.

In fact, in many cases involving juvenile suspects, the custody analysis would be nonsensical absent some consideration of the suspect's age. This case is a prime example. Were the court precluded from taking J.D.B.'s youth into account, it would be forced to evaluate the circumstances present here through the eyes of a reasonable person of average years. In other words, how would a reasonable adult understand his situation, after being removed from a seventh-grade social studies class by a uniformed school resource officer; being encouraged by his assistant principal to "do the right thing"; and being warned by a police investigator of the prospect of juvenile detention and separation from his guardian and primary caretaker? To describe such an inquiry is to demonstrate its absurdity. Neither officers nor courts can reasonably evaluate the effect of objective circumstances that, by their nature, are specific to children without accounting for the age of the child subjected to those circumstances.

Indeed, although the dissent suggests that concerns "regarding the application of the *Miranda* custody rule to minors can be accommodated by considering the unique circumstances present when minors are questioned in school," the effect of the schoolhouse setting cannot be disentangled from the identity of the person questioned. A student—whose presence at school is compulsory and whose disobedience at school is cause for disciplinary action—is in a far different position than, say, a parent volunteer on school grounds to chaperone an event, or an adult from the community on school grounds to attend a basketball game. Without asking whether the person "questioned in school" is a "minor," the coercive effect of the schoolhouse setting is unknowable.

* * *

Reviewing the question *de novo* today, we hold that so long as the child's age was known to the officer at the time of police questioning, or would have been objectively apparent to a reasonable officer, its inclusion in the custody analysis is consistent with the objective nature of that test. This is not to say that a child's age will be a determinative, or even a significant, factor in every case. It is, however, a reality that courts cannot simply ignore.

III

The State and its *amici* offer numerous reasons that courts must blind themselves to a juvenile defendant's age. None is persuasive.

* * *

The State further argues that age is irrelevant to the custody analysis because it "go[es] to how a suspect may internalize and perceive the circumstances of an interrogation." But the same can be said of every objective circumstance that the State agrees is relevant to the custody analysis: Each circumstance goes to how a reasonable person would "internalize and perceive" every other. Indeed, this is the very reason that we ask whether the objective circumstances "add up to custody," instead of evaluating the circumstances one by one.

In the same vein, the State and its *amici* protest that the "effect of . . . age on [the] perception of custody is internal" or "psychological." But the whole point of the custody analysis is to determine whether, given the circumstances, "a reasonable person [would] have felt he or she was . . . at liberty to terminate the interrogation and leave." Because the *Miranda* custody inquiry turns on the mindset of a reasonable person in the suspect's position, it cannot be the case that a circumstance is subjective simply because it has an "internal" or "psychological" impact on perception. Were that so, there would be no objective circumstances to consider at all.

Relying on our statements that the objective custody test is "designed to give clear guidance to the police," *Alvarado,* 541 U.S., at 668, the State next argues that a child's age must be excluded from the analysis in order to preserve clarity. Similarly, the dissent insists that the clarity of the custody analysis will be destroyed unless a "one-size-fits-all reasonable-person test" applies. In reality, however, ignoring a juvenile defendant's age will often make the inquiry more artificial, and thus only add confusion. And in any event, a child's age, when known or apparent, is hardly an obscure factor to assess. Though the State and the dissent worry about gradations among children of different ages, that concern cannot justify ignoring a child's age altogether. Just as police officers are competent to account for other objective circumstances that are a matter of degree such as the length of questioning or the number of officers present, so too are they competent to evaluate the effect of relative age. Indeed, they are competent to do so even though an interrogation room lacks the "reflective atmosphere of a [jury] deliberation room." The same is true of judges, including those whose childhoods have long since passed. In short, officers and judges need no imaginative powers, knowledge of developmental psychology, training in cognitive science, or expertise in social and cultural anthropology to account for a child's age. They simply need the common sense to know that a 7-year-old is not a 13-year-old and neither is an adult.

There is, however, an even more fundamental flaw with the State's plea for clarity and the dissent's singular focus on simplifying the analysis: Not once have we excluded from the custody analysis a circumstance that we determined was relevant and objective, simply to make the fault line between custodial and noncustodial "brighter." Indeed, were the guiding concern clarity and nothing else, the custody test would presumably ask only whether the suspect had been placed under formal arrest. But we have rejected that "more easily administered line," recognizing that it would simply "enable the police to circumvent the constraints on custodial interrogations established by *Miranda*."

Finally, the State and the dissent suggest that excluding age from the custody analysis comes at no cost to juveniles' constitutional rights because the due process voluntariness test independently accounts for a child's youth. To be sure, that test permits consideration of a child's age, and it erects its own barrier to admission of a defendant's inculpatory statements at trial. But *Miranda*'s procedural safeguards exist precisely because the voluntariness test is an inadequate barrier when custodial interrogation is at stake. To hold, as the State requests, that a child's age is never relevant to whether a suspect has been taken into custody—and thus to ignore the very real differences between children and adults—would be to deny children the full scope of the procedural safeguards that *Miranda* guarantees to adults.

* * *

The question remains whether J.D.B. was in custody when police interrogated him. We remand for the state courts to address that question, this time taking account of all of the relevant circumstances of the interrogation, including J.D.B.'s age at the time.

JUSTICE ALITO, with whom THE CHIEF JUSTICE, JUSTICE SCALIA, and JUSTICE THOMAS join, dissenting.

The Court's decision in this case may seem on first consideration to be modest and sensible, but in truth it is neither. It is fundamentally inconsistent with one of the main justifications for the *Miranda* rule: the perceived need for a clear rule that can be easily applied in all cases. And today's holding is not needed to protect the constitutional rights of minors who are questioned by the police.

Miranda's prophylactic regime places a high value on clarity and certainty. Dissatisfied with the highly fact-specific constitutional rule against the admission of involuntary confessions, the *Miranda* Court set down rigid standards that often require courts to ignore personal characteristics that may be highly relevant to a particular suspect's actual susceptibility to police pressure. This rigidity, however, has brought with it one of *Miranda*'s principal strengths—"the ease and clarity of its application" by law enforcement officials and courts. A key contributor to this clarity, at least up until now, has been *Miranda*'s objective reasonable-person test for determining custody.

Miranda's custody requirement is based on the proposition that the risk of unconstitutional coercion is heightened when a suspect is placed under formal arrest or is subjected to some functionally equivalent limitation on freedom of movement. When this custodial threshold is reached, *Miranda* warnings must precede police questioning. But in the interest of simplicity, the custody analysis considers only whether, under the circumstances, a hypothetical reasonable person would consider himself to be confined.

Many suspects, of course, will differ from this hypothetical reasonable person. Some, including those who have been hardened by past interrogations, may have no need for *Miranda* warnings at all. And for other suspects—those who are unusually sensitive to the pressures of police questioning—*Miranda* warnings may come too late to be of any use. That is a necessary consequence of *Miranda*'s rigid standards, but it does not mean that the constitutional rights of these especially sensitive suspects are left unprotected. A vulnerable defendant can still turn to the constitutional rule against *actual* coercion and contend that that his confession was extracted against his will.

Today's decision shifts the *Miranda* custody determination from a one-size-fits-all reasonable-person test into an inquiry that must account for at least one individualized characteristic—age—that is thought to correlate with susceptibility to coercive pressures. Age, however, is in no way the only personal characteristic that may correlate with pliability, and in future cases the Court will be forced to choose between two unpalatable alternatives. It may choose to limit today's decision by arbitrarily distinguishing a suspect's age from other personal characteristics—such as intelligence, education, occupation, or prior experience with law enforcement—that may also correlate with susceptibility to coercive pressures. Or, if the Court is unwilling to draw these arbitrary lines, it will be forced to effect a fundamental transformation of the *Miranda* custody test—from a clear, easily applied prophylactic rule into a highly fact-intensive standard resembling the voluntariness test that the *Miranda* Court found to be unsatisfactory.

For at least three reasons, there is no need to go down this road. First, many minors subjected to police interrogation are near the age of majority, and for these suspects the one-size-fits-all *Miranda* custody rule may not be a bad fit. Second, many of the difficulties in applying the *Miranda* custody rule to minors arise because of the unique circumstances present when the police conduct interrogations at school. The *Miranda* custody rule has always taken into account the setting in which questioning occurs, and accounting for the school setting in such cases will address many of these problems. Third, in cases like the one now before us, where the suspect is especially young, courts applying the constitutional voluntariness standard can take special care to ensure that incriminating statements were not obtained through coercion.

Safeguarding the constitutional rights of minors does not require the extreme makeover of *Miranda* that today's decision may portend.

I

In the days before *Miranda,* this Court's sole metric for evaluating the admissibility of confessions was a voluntariness standard rooted in both the Fifth Amendment's Self-Incrimination Clause and the Due Process Clause of the Fourteenth Amendment. The question in these voluntariness cases was whether the particular "defendant's will" had been "overborne." Courts took into account both "the details of the interrogation" *and* "the characteristics of the accused," and then "weigh[ed] . . . the circumstances of pressure against the power of resistance of the person confessing."

All manner of individualized, personal characteristics were relevant in this voluntariness inquiry. Among the most frequently mentioned factors were the defendant's education, physical condition, intelligence, and mental health. The suspect's age also received prominent attention in several cases, especially when the suspect was a "mere child." The weight assigned to any one consideration varied from case to case. But all of these factors, along with anything else that might have affected the "individual's . . . capacity for effective choice," were relevant in determining whether the confession was coerced or compelled.

* * *

In *Miranda,* the Court supplemented the voluntariness inquiry with a "set of prophylactic measures" designed to ward off the " 'inherently compelling pressures' of custodial interrogation." *Miranda* greatly simplified matters by requiring police to give suspects standard warnings before commencing any custodial interrogation. Its requirements are no doubt "rigid," and they often require courts to suppress "trustworthy and highly probative" statements that may be perfectly "voluntary under a traditional Fifth Amendment analysis." But with this rigidity comes increased clarity. *Miranda* provides "a workable rule to guide police officers," and an administrable standard for the courts. As has often been recognized, this gain in clarity and administrability is one of *Miranda*'s "principal advantages."

* * *

Until today, the Court's cases applying this test have focused solely on the "objective circumstances of the interrogation," not the personal characteristics of the interrogated. Relevant factors have included such things as where the questioning occurred, how long it lasted, what was said, any physical restraints placed on the suspect's movement, and whether the suspect was allowed to leave when the questioning was through. The totality of *these* circumstances—the external circumstances, that is, of the interrogation itself—is what has mattered in this Court's cases. Personal characteristics of suspects have consistently been rejected or ignored as irrelevant under a one-size-fits-all reasonable-person standard.

* * *

II

* * *

In its present form, *Miranda*'s prophylactic regime already imposes "high cost[s]" by requiring suppression of confessions that are often "highly probative" and "voluntary" by any traditional standard. *Oregon v. Elstad,* 470 U.S. 298, 312 (1985). Nonetheless, a "core virtue" of *Miranda* has been the clarity and precision of its guidance to "police and courts." This increased clarity "has been thought to outweigh the burdens" that *Miranda* imposes. The Court has, however, repeatedly cautioned against upsetting the careful "balance" that *Miranda* struck, and it has "refused to sanction attempts to expand [the] *Miranda* holding" in ways that would reduce its "clarity." Given this practice, there should be a "strong presumption" against the Court's new departure from the established custody test. In my judgment, that presumption cannot be overcome here.

A

The Court's rationale for importing age into the custody standard is that minors tend to lack adults' "capacity to exercise mature judgment" and that failing to account for that "reality" will leave some minors unprotected under *Miranda* in situations where they perceive themselves to be confined. I do not dispute that many suspects who are under 18 will be more susceptible to police pressure than the average adult. As the Court notes, our pre-*Miranda* cases were particularly attuned to this "reality" in applying the constitutional requirement of voluntariness in fact. It is no less a "reality," however, that many persons *over* the age of 18 are also more susceptible to police pressure than the hypothetical reasonable person. Yet the *Miranda* custody standard has never accounted for the personal characteristics of these or any other individual defendants.

* * *

That is undoubtedly why this Court's *Miranda* cases have never before mentioned "the suspect's age" or any other individualized consideration in applying the custody standard. And unless the *Miranda* custody rule is now to be radically transformed into one that takes into account the wide range of individual characteristics that are relevant in determining whether a confession is voluntary, the Court must shoulder the burden of explaining why age is different from these other personal characteristics.

Why, for example, is age different from intelligence? Suppose that an officer, upon going to a school to question a student, is told by the principal that the student has an I.Q. of 75 and is in a special-education class. Are those facts more or less important than the student's age in determining whether he or she "felt . . . at liberty to terminate the interrogation and leave"? An I.Q. score, like age, is more than just a number. And an individual's intelligence can also yield "conclusions" similar to those "we have drawn ourselves" in cases far afield of *Miranda.*

How about the suspect's cultural background? Suppose the police learn (or should have learned) that a suspect they wish to question is a recent immigrant from a country in which dire consequences often befall any person who dares to attempt to cut short any meeting with the police. Is this really less relevant than the fact that a suspect is a month or so away from his 18th birthday?

The defendant's education is another personal characteristic that may generate "conclusions about behavior and perception." Under today's decision, why should police officers and courts "blind themselves," to the fact that a suspect has "only a fifth-grade education"? Alternatively, what if the police know or should know that the suspect is "a college-educated man with law school training"? How are these individual considerations meaningfully different from age in their "relationship to a reasonable person's understanding of his freedom of action"? The Court proclaims that "[a] child's age . . . is different," but the basis for this *ipse dixit* is dubious.

* * *

B

* * *

The Court holds that age must be taken into account when it "was known to the officer at the time of the interview," or when it "would have been objectively apparent" to a reasonable officer. The first half of this test overturns the rule that the "initial determination of custody" does not depend on the "subjective views harbored by . . . interrogating officers." The second half will generate time-consuming satellite litigation over a reasonable officer's perceptions. When, as here, the interrogation takes place in school, the inquiry may be relatively simple. But not all police questioning of minors takes place in schools. In many cases, courts will presumably have to make findings as to whether a particular suspect had a sufficiently youthful look to alert a reasonable officer to the possibility that the suspect was under 18, or whether a reasonable officer would have recognized that a suspect's I.D. was a fake. The inquiry will be both "time-consuming and disruptive" for the police and the courts. It will also be made all the more complicated by the fact that a suspect's dress and manner will often be different when the issue is litigated in court than it was at the time of the interrogation.

Even after courts clear this initial hurdle, further problems will likely emerge as judges attempt to put themselves in the shoes of the average 16-year-old, or 15-year-old, or 13-year-old, as the case may be. Consider, for example, a 60-year-old judge attempting to make a custody determination through the eyes of a hypothetical, average 15-year-old. Forty-five years of personal experience and societal change separate this judge from the days when he or she was 15 years old. And this judge may or may not have been an average 15-year-old. The Court's answer to these difficulties is to state that "no imaginative powers, knowledge of developmental psychology, [or] training in cognitive science" will be necessary. Judges "simply need the common sense," the Court assures, "to know that a 7-year-old is not a 13-

year-old and neither is an adult." It is obvious, however, that application of the Court's new rule demands much more than this.

Take a fairly typical case in which today's holding may make a difference. A 16½-year-old moves to suppress incriminating statements made prior to the administration of *Miranda* warnings. The circumstances are such that, if the defendant were at least 18, the court would not find that he or she was in custody, but the defendant argues that a reasonable 16½-year-old would view the situation differently. The judge will not have the luxury of merely saying: "It is common sense that a 16½-year-old is not an 18-year-old. Motion granted." Rather, the judge will be required to determine whether the differences between a typical 16½-year-old and a typical 18-year-old with respect to susceptibility to the pressures of interrogation are sufficient to change the outcome of the custody determination. Today's opinion contains not a word of actual guidance as to how judges are supposed to go about making that determination.

C

Petitioner and the Court attempt to show that this task is not unmanageable by pointing out that age is taken into account in other legal contexts. In particular, the Court relies on the fact that the age of a defendant is a relevant factor under the reasonable-person standard applicable in negligence suits. But negligence is generally a question for the jury, the members of which can draw on their varied experiences with persons of different ages. It also involves a *post hoc* determination, in the reflective atmosphere of a deliberation room, about whether the defendant conformed to a standard of care. The *Miranda* custody determination, by contrast, must be made in the first instance by police officers in the course of an investigation that may require quick decisionmaking.

* * *

III

The Court's decision greatly diminishes the clarity and administrability that have long been recognized as "principal advantages" of *Miranda*'s prophylactic requirements. But what is worse, the Court takes this step unnecessarily, as there are other, less disruptive tools available to ensure that minors are not coerced into confessing.

As an initial matter, the difficulties that the Court's standard introduces will likely yield little added protection for most juvenile defendants. Most juveniles who are subjected to police interrogation are teenagers nearing the age of majority. These defendants' reactions to police pressure are unlikely to be much different from the reaction of a typical 18-year-old in similar circumstances. A one-size-fits-all *Miranda* custody rule thus provides a roughly reasonable fit for these defendants.

In addition, many of the concerns that petitioner raises regarding the application of the *Miranda* custody rule to minors can be accommodated by considering the unique circumstances present when minors are questioned in school. The *Miranda* custody rule has always taken into account the setting in which questioning occurs, restrictions on a suspect's freedom of movement, and the presence of police officers or other authority figures. It can do so here as well.

Finally, in cases like the one now before us, where the suspect is much younger than the typical juvenile defendant, courts should be instructed to take particular care to ensure that incriminating statements were not obtained involuntarily. The voluntariness inquiry is flexible and accommodating by nature, and the Court's precedents already make clear that "special care" must be exercised in applying the voluntariness test where the confession of a "mere child" is at issue. If *Miranda*'s rigid, one-size-fits-all standards fail to account for the unique needs of juveniles, the response should be to rigorously apply the constitutional rule against coercion to ensure that the rights of minors are protected. There is no need to run *Miranda* off the rails.

* * *

The Court rests its decision to inject personal characteristics into the *Miranda* custody inquiry on the principle that judges applying *Miranda* cannot "blind themselves to . . . commonsense reality." But the Court's shift is fundamentally at odds with the clear prophylactic rules that *Miranda* has long enforced. *Miranda* frequently requires judges to blind themselves to the reality that many un-Mirandized custodial confessions are "by no means involuntary" or coerced. It also requires police to provide a rote recitation of *Miranda* warnings that many suspects already know and could likely recite from memory. Under today's new, "reality"-based approach to the doctrine, perhaps these and other principles of our *Miranda* jurisprudence will, like the custody standard, now be ripe for modification. Then, bit by bit, *Miranda* will lose the clarity and ease of application that has long been viewed as one of its chief justifications.

Points for Discussion

1. In a footnote omitted from this excerpted version of *J.D.B.*, the majority noted that an amicus brief filed in support of J.D.B. "question[ed] whether children of all ages can comprehend *Miranda* warnings and suggest[ed] that additional procedural safeguards may be necessary to protect their *Miranda* rights. Whatever the merit of that contention, it has no relevance here, where no *Miranda* warnings were administered at all." The brief mentioned that some states have laws requiring that parents be present for any interrogation of a child and other states require that parents be notified before a child's interrogation. Regardless of whether the statutes embody good or bad policy, is there a good argument to be made that the Fifth Amendment

requires this? See Barry C. Feld, *Real Interrogation: What Actually Happens When Cops Question Kids*, 47 L. & SOC. REV. 1 (2013).

2. If the test of custody is truly objective and if a child's age is relevant to that determination, what difference does it make whether "the child's age was known to the officer at the time of the interview or would have been objectively apparent to any reasonable officer"? Doesn't this limitation make this purportedly "objective" test dependent on what the officer knew (or should have known) and isn't that a subjective test, as the dissent argues? Did *Miranda* itself consider the question of custody to be objective or subjective?

RHODE ISLAND V. INNIS

446 U.S. 291 (1980)

MR. JUSTICE STEWART delivered the opinion of the court.

In *Miranda v. Arizona*, 384 U.S. 436, 474, the Court held that, once a defendant in custody asks to speak with a lawyer, all interrogation must cease until a lawyer is present. The issue in this case is whether the respondent was "interrogated" in violation of the standards promulgated in the *Miranda* opinion.

I

On the night of January 12, 1975, John Mulvaney, a Providence, R.I., taxicab driver, disappeared after being dispatched to pick up a customer. His body was discovered four days later buried in a shallow grave in Coventry, R.I. He had died from a shotgun blast aimed at the back of his head.

On January 17, 1975, shortly after midnight, the Providence police received a telephone call from Gerald Aubin, also a taxicab driver, who reported that he had just been robbed by a man wielding a sawed-off shotgun. Aubin further reported that he had dropped off his assailant near Rhode Island College in a section of Providence known as Mount Pleasant. While at the Providence police station waiting to give a statement, Aubin noticed a picture of his assailant on a bulletin board. Aubin so informed one of the police officers present. The officer prepared a photo array, and again Aubin identified a picture of the same person. That person was the respondent. Shortly thereafter, the Providence police began a search of the Mount Pleasant area.

At approximately 4:30 a. m. on the same date, Patrolman Lovell, while cruising the streets of Mount Pleasant in a patrol car, spotted the respondent standing in the street facing him. When Patrolman Lovell stopped his car, the respondent walked towards it. Patrolman Lovell then arrested the respondent, who was unarmed, and advised him of his so-called *Miranda* rights. While the two men waited in the patrol car for other police officers to arrive, Patrolman Lovell did not converse with the respondent other than to respond to the latter's request for a cigarette.

Within minutes, Sergeant Sears arrived at the scene of the arrest, and he also gave the respondent the *Miranda* warnings. Immediately thereafter, Captain Leyden and other police officers arrived. Captain Leyden advised the respondent of his *Miranda* rights. The respondent stated that he understood those rights and wanted to speak with a lawyer. Captain Leyden then directed that the respondent be placed in a "caged wagon," a four-door police car with a wire screen mesh between the front and rear seats, and be driven to the central police station. Three officers, Patrolmen Gleckman, Williams, and McKenna, were assigned to accompany the respondent to the central station. They placed the respondent in the vehicle and shut the doors. Captain Leyden then instructed the officers not to question the respondent or intimidate or coerce him in any way. The three officers then entered the vehicle, and it departed.

While en route to the central station, Patrolman Gleckman initiated a conversation with Patrolman McKenna concerning the missing shotgun. As Patrolman Gleckman later testified:

> At this point, I was talking back and forth with Patrolman McKenna stating that I frequent this area while on patrol and [that because a school for handicapped children is located nearby,] there's a lot of handicapped children running around in this area, and God forbid one of them might find a weapon with shells and they might hurt themselves.

Patrolman McKenna apparently shared his fellow officer's concern:

> I more or less concurred with him [Gleckman] that it was a safety factor and that we should, you know, continue to search for the weapon and try to find it.

While Patrolman Williams said nothing, he overheard the conversation between the two officers:

> He [Gleckman] said it would be too bad if the little—I believe he said a girl—would pick up the gun, maybe kill herself.

The respondent then interrupted the conversation, stating that the officers should turn the car around so he could show them where the gun was located. At this point, Patrolman McKenna radioed back to Captain Leyden that they were returning to the scene of the arrest and that the respondent would inform them of the location of the gun. At the time the respondent indicated that the officers should turn back, they had traveled no more than a mile, a trip encompassing only a few minutes.

The police vehicle then returned to the scene of the arrest where a search for the shotgun was in progress. There, Captain Leyden again advised the respondent of his *Miranda* rights. The respondent replied that he understood those rights but that he "wanted to get the gun out of the way because of the kids in the area in the school." The respondent then led the police to a nearby field, where he pointed out the shotgun under some rocks by the side of the road.

On March 20, 1975, a grand jury returned an indictment charging the respondent with the kidnapping, robbery, and murder of John Mulvaney. Before trial, the respondent moved to suppress the shotgun and the statements he had made to the police regarding it. After an evidentiary hearing at which the respondent elected not to testify, the trial judge found that the respondent had been "repeatedly and completely advised of his *Miranda* rights." He further found that it was "entirely understandable that [the officers in the police vehicle] would voice their concern [for the safety of the handicapped children] to each other." The judge then concluded that the respondent's decision to inform the police of the location of the shotgun was "a waiver, clearly, and on the basis of the evidence that I have heard, and [*sic*] intelligent waiver, of his [*Miranda*] right to remain silent." Thus, without passing on whether the police officers had in fact "interrogated" the respondent, the trial court sustained the admissibility of the shotgun and testimony related to its discovery. That evidence was later introduced at the respondent's trial, and the jury returned a verdict of guilty on all counts.

* * *

II

* * *

In the present case, the parties are in agreement that the respondent was fully informed of his *Miranda* rights and that he invoked his *Miranda* right to counsel when he told Captain Leyden that he wished to consult with a lawyer. It is also uncontested that the respondent was "in custody" while being transported to the police station.

The issue, therefore, is whether the respondent was "interrogated" by the police officers in violation of the respondent's undisputed right under *Miranda* to remain silent until he had consulted with a lawyer. In resolving this issue, we first define the term "interrogation" under *Miranda* before turning to a consideration of the facts of this case.

A

The starting point for defining "interrogation" in this context is, of course, the Court's *Miranda* opinion. There the Court observed that "[b]y custodial interrogation, we mean *questioning* initiated by law enforcement officers after a person has been taken into custody or otherwise deprived of his freedom of action in any significant way." (emphasis added). This passage and other references throughout the opinion to "questioning" might suggest that the *Miranda* rules were to apply only to those police interrogation practices that involve express questioning of a defendant while in custody.

We do not, however, construe the *Miranda* opinion so narrowly. The concern of the Court in *Miranda* was that the "interrogation environment" created by the interplay of interrogation and custody would "subjugate the individual to the will of his examiner" and thereby undermine the privilege against compulsory self-incrimination. The police practices that evoked this concern included several that did not involve express questioning. For example, one of the practices discussed in *Miranda* was the use of line-ups in which a coached witness would pick the defendant as the perpetrator. This was designed to establish that the defendant was in fact guilty as a predicate for further interrogation. A variation on this theme discussed in *Miranda* was the so-called "reverse line-up" in which a defendant would be identified by coached witnesses as the perpetrator of a fictitious crime, with the object of inducing him to confess to the actual crime of which he was suspected in order to escape the false prosecution. The Court in *Miranda* also included in its survey of interrogation practices the use of psychological ploys, such as to "posi[t]" "the guilt of the subject," to "minimize the moral seriousness of the offense," and "to cast blame on the victim or on society." It is clear that these techniques of persuasion, no less than express questioning, were thought, in a custodial setting, to amount to interrogation.

* * *

It is clear therefore that the special procedural safeguards outlined in *Miranda* are required not where a suspect is simply taken into custody, but rather where a suspect in custody is subjected to interrogation. "Interrogation," as conceptualized in the *Miranda* opinion, must reflect a measure of compulsion above and beyond that inherent in custody itself.[4]

We conclude that the *Miranda* safeguards come into play whenever a person in custody is subjected to either express questioning or its functional equivalent. That is to say, the term "interrogation" under *Miranda* refers not only to express questioning, but also to any words or actions on the part of the police (other than those normally attendant to arrest and custody) that the police should know are reasonably likely to elicit an incriminating

[4] There is language in the opinion of the Rhode Island Supreme Court in this case suggesting that the definition of "interrogation" under *Miranda* is informed by this Court's decision in *Brewer v. Williams*, 430 U.S. 387. This suggestion is erroneous. Our decision in *Brewer* rested solely on the Sixth and Fourteenth Amendment right to counsel. That right, as we held in *Massiah v. United States*, 377 U.S. 201, 206, prohibits law enforcement officers from "deliberately elicit[ing]" incriminating information from a defendant in the absence of counsel after a formal charge against the defendant has been filed. Custody in such a case is not controlling; indeed, the petitioner in *Massiah* was not in custody. By contrast, the right to counsel at issue in the present case is based not on the Sixth and Fourteenth Amendments, but rather on the Fifth and Fourteenth Amendments as interpreted in the *Miranda* opinion. The definitions of "interrogation" under the Fifth and Sixth Amendments, if indeed the term "interrogation" is even apt in the Sixth Amendment context, are not necessarily interchangeable, since the policies underlying the two constitutional protections are quite distinct.

response from the suspect. The latter portion of this definition focuses primarily upon the perceptions of the suspect, rather than the intent of the police. This focus reflects the fact that the *Miranda* safeguards were designed to vest a suspect in custody with an added measure of protection against coercive police practices, without regard to objective proof of the underlying intent of the police. A practice that the police should know is reasonably likely to evoke an incriminating response from a suspect thus amounts to interrogation.[7] But, since the police surely cannot be held accountable for the unforeseeable results of their words or actions, the definition of interrogation can extend only to words or actions on the part of police officers that they *should have known* were reasonably likely to elicit an incriminating response.[8]

B

Turning to the facts of the present case, we conclude that the respondent was not "interrogated" within the meaning of *Miranda*. It is undisputed that the first prong of the definition of "interrogation" was not satisfied, for the conversation between Patrolmen Gleckman and McKenna included no express questioning of the respondent. Rather, that conversation was, at least in form, nothing more than a dialogue between the two officers to which no response from the respondent was invited.

Moreover, it cannot be fairly concluded that the respondent was subjected to the "functional equivalent" of questioning. It cannot be said, in short, that Patrolmen Gleckman and McKenna should have known that their conversation was reasonably likely to elicit an incriminating response from the respondent. There is nothing in the record to suggest that the officers were aware that the respondent was peculiarly susceptible to an appeal to his conscience concerning the safety of handicapped children. Nor is there anything in the record to suggest that the police knew that the respondent was unusually disoriented or upset at the time of his arrest.[9]

The case thus boils down to whether, in the context of a brief conversation, the officers should have known that the respondent would suddenly be moved to make a self-incriminating response. Given the fact that the entire conversation appears to have consisted of no more than a

---

[7] This is not to say that the intent of the police is irrelevant, for it may well have a bearing on whether the police should have known that their words or actions were reasonably likely to evoke an incriminating response. In particular, where a police practice is designed to elicit an incriminating response from the accused, it is unlikely that the practice will not also be one which the police should have known was reasonably likely to have that effect.

[8] Any knowledge the police may have had concerning the unusual susceptibility of a defendant to a particular form of persuasion might be an important factor in determining whether the police should have known that their words or actions were reasonably likely to elicit an incriminating response from the suspect.

[9] The record in no way suggests that the officers' remarks were *designed* to elicit a response. See n.7. It is significant that the trial judge, after hearing the officers' testimony, concluded that it was "entirely understandable that [the officers] would voice their concern [for the safety of the handicapped children] to each other."

few off hand remarks, we cannot say that the officers should have known that it was reasonably likely that Innis would so respond. This is not a case where the police carried on a lengthy harangue in the presence of the suspect. Nor does the record support the respondent's contention that, under the circumstances, the officers' comments were particularly "evocative." It is our view, therefore, that the respondent was not subjected by the police to words or actions that the police should have known were reasonably likely to elicit an incriminating response from him.

The Rhode Island Supreme Court erred, in short, in equating "subtle compulsion" with interrogation. That the officers' comments struck a responsive chord is readily apparent. Thus, it may be said, as the Rhode Island Supreme Court did say, that the respondent was subjected to "subtle compulsion." But that is not the end of the inquiry. It must also be established that a suspect's incriminating response was the product of words or actions on the part of the police that they should have known were reasonably likely to elicit an incriminating response. This was not established in the present case.[10]

For the reasons stated, the judgment of the Supreme Court of Rhode Island is vacated, and the case is remanded to that court for further proceedings not inconsistent with this opinion.

MR. JUSTICE WHITE, concurring.

I would prefer to reverse the judgment for the reasons stated in my dissenting opinion in *Brewer v. Williams*, 430 U.S. 387 (1977); but given that judgment and the Court's opinion in *Brewer*, I join the opinion of the Court in the present case.

MR. CHIEF JUSTICE BURGER, concurring in the judgment.

Since the result is not inconsistent with *Miranda v. Arizona*, 384 U.S. 436 (1966), I concur in the judgment.

The meaning of *Miranda* has become reasonably clear and law enforcement practices have adjusted to its strictures; I would neither overrule *Miranda*, disparage it, nor extend it at this late date. I fear, however, that the rationale in Parts II-A and II-B, of the Court's opinion will not clarify the tension between this holding and *Brewer v. Williams*, 430 U.S. 387 (1977), and our other cases. It may introduce new elements of uncertainty; under the Court's test, a police officer, in the brief time available, apparently must evaluate the suggestibility and susceptibility of an accused. Few, if any, police officers are competent to make the kind of evaluation seemingly contemplated; even a psychiatrist asked to express

[10] By way of example, if the police had done no more than to drive past the site of the concealed weapon while taking the most direct route to the police station, and if the respondent, upon noticing for the first time the proximity of the school for handicapped children, had blurted out that he would show the officers where the gun was located, it could not seriously be argued that this "subtle compulsion" would have constituted "interrogation" within the meaning of the *Miranda* opinion.

an expert opinion on these aspects of a suspect in custody would very likely employ extensive questioning and observation to make the judgment now charged to police officers.

Trial judges have enough difficulty discerning the boundaries and nuances flowing from post-*Miranda* opinions, and we do not clarify that situation today.

MR. JUSTICE MARSHALL, with whom MR. JUSTICE BRENNAN joins, dissenting.

I am substantially in agreement with the Court's definition of "interrogation" within the meaning of *Miranda v. Arizona*, 384 U.S. 436 (1966). In my view, the *Miranda* safeguards apply whenever police conduct is intended or likely to produce a response from a suspect in custody. As I read the Court's opinion, its definition of "interrogation" for *Miranda* purposes is equivalent, for practical purposes, to my formulation, since it contemplates that "where a police practice is designed to elicit an incriminating response from the accused, it is unlikely that the practice will not also be one which the police should have known was reasonably likely to have that effect." Thus, the Court requires an objective inquiry into the likely effect of police conduct on a typical individual, taking into account any special susceptibility of the suspect to certain kinds of pressure of which the police know or have reason to know.

I am utterly at a loss, however, to understand how this objective standard as applied to the facts before us can rationally lead to the conclusion that there was no interrogation. Innis was arrested at 4:30 a. m., handcuffed, searched, advised of his rights, and placed in the back seat of a patrol car. Within a short time he had been twice more advised of his rights and driven away in a four-door sedan with three police officers. Two officers sat in the front seat and one sat beside Innis in the back seat. Since the car traveled no more than a mile before Innis agreed to point out the location of the murder weapon, Officer Gleckman must have begun almost immediately to talk about the search for the shotgun.

The Court attempts to characterize Gleckman's statements as "no more than a few off hand remarks" which could not reasonably have been expected to elicit a response. If the statements had been addressed to respondent, it would be impossible to draw such a conclusion. The simple message of the "talking back and forth" between Gleckman and McKenna was that they had to find the shotgun to avert a child's death.

One can scarcely imagine a stronger appeal to the conscience of a suspect—*any* suspect—than the assertion that if the weapon is not found an innocent person will be hurt or killed. And not just any innocent person, but an innocent child-a little girl-a helpless, handicapped little girl on her way to school. The notion that such an appeal could not be expected to have any effect unless the suspect were known to have some special interest in handicapped children verges on the ludicrous. As a matter of fact, the appeal to a suspect to confess for the sake of others, to "display some evidence of decency and honor," is a classic interrogation technique. See, *e. g.*, F. Inbau & J. Reid, CRIMINAL INTERROGATION AND CONFESSIONS 60–62 (2d ed. 1967).

Gleckman's remarks would obviously have constituted interrogation if they had been explicitly directed to respondent, and the result should not be different because they were nominally addressed to McKenna. This is not a case where police officers speaking among themselves are accidentally overheard by a suspect. These officers were "talking back and forth" in close quarters with the handcuffed suspect, traveling past the very place where they believed the weapon was located. They knew respondent would hear and attend to their conversation, and they are chargeable with knowledge of and responsibility for the pressures to speak which they created.

I firmly believe that this case is simply an aberration, and that in future cases the Court will apply the standard adopted today in accordance with its plain meaning.

MR. JUSTICE STEVENS, dissenting.

* * *

I

* * *

In limiting its test to police statements "likely to elicit an incriminating response," the Court confuses the scope of the exclusionary rule with the definition of "interrogation." Of course, any incriminating statement as defined in *Miranda* must be excluded from evidence if it is the product of impermissible interrogation. But I fail to see how this rule helps in deciding whether a particular statement or tactic constitutes "interrogation." After all, *Miranda* protects a suspect in Innis' position not simply from interrogation that is likely to be successful, but from any interrogation at all.

In *Miranda* the Court required the now-familiar warnings to be given to suspects prior to custodial interrogation in order to dispel the atmosphere of coercion that necessarily accompanies such interrogations. In order to perform that function effectively, the warnings must be viewed by both the police and the suspect as a correct and binding statement of their respective rights. Thus, if, after being told that he has a right to have an attorney present during interrogation, a suspect chooses to cut off questioning until counsel can be obtained, his choice must be "scrupulously honored" by the police. At the least this must mean that the police are prohibited from making deliberate attempts to elicit statements from the suspect.[7] Yet the Court is unwilling to characterize all such attempts as "interrogation," noting only that "where a police practice is designed to elicit an incriminating response from the accused, it is unlikely that the practice will not also be one which the police should have known was reasonable likely to have that effect."

From the suspect's, point of view, the effectiveness of the warnings depends on whether it appears that the police are scrupulously honoring his rights. Apparent attempts to elicit information from a suspect after he has invoked his right to cut off questioning necessarily demean that right and tend to reinstate the imbalance between police and suspect that the *Miranda* warnings are designed to correct. Thus, if the rationale for requiring those warnings in the first place is to be respected, any police conduct or statements that would appear to a reasonable person in the suspect's position to call for a response must be considered "interrogation."[10]

In short, in order to give full protection to a suspect's right to be free from any interrogation at all, the definition of "interrogation" must include any police statement or conduct that has the same purpose or effect as a direct question. Statements that appear to call for a response from the suspect, as well as those that are designed to do so, should be considered interrogation. By prohibiting only those relatively few statements or actions that a police officer should know are likely to elicit an incriminating response, the Court today accords a suspect considerably less protection. Indeed, since I suppose most suspects are unlikely to incriminate themselves even when questioned directly, this new definition will almost certainly exclude every statement that is not punctuated with a question mark from the concept of "interrogation."

The difference between the approach required by a faithful adherence to *Miranda* and the stinted test applied by the Court today can be illustrated by comparing three different ways in which Officer Gleckman could have communicated his fears about the possible dangers posed by the shotgun to handicapped children. He could have:

> (1) directly asked Innis: Will you please tell me where the shotgun is so we can protect handicapped school children from danger?

---

[7] In *Brewer v. Williams*, 430 U.S. 387, 398–399, the Court applied the "deliberately elicited" standard in determining that statements were extracted from Williams in violation of his Sixth Amendment right to counsel. Although this case involves Fifth Amendment rights and the *Miranda* rules designed to safeguard those rights, respondent's invocation of his right to counsel makes the two cases indistinguishable. In both cases the police had an unqualified obligation to refrain from trying to elicit a response from the suspect in the absence of his attorney.

[10] I would use an objective standard both to avoid the difficulties of proof inherent in a subjective standard and to give police adequate guidance in their dealings with suspects who have requested counsel.

(2) announced to the other officers in the wagon: If the man sitting in the back seat with me should decide to tell us where the gun is, we can protect handicapped children from danger.

or (3) stated to the other officers: It would be too bad if a little handicapped girl would pick up the gun that this man left in the area and maybe kill herself.

In my opinion, all three of these statements should be considered interrogation because all three appear to be designed to elicit a response from anyone who in fact knew where the gun was located. Under the Court's test, on the other hand, the form of the statements would be critical. The third statement would not be interrogation because in the Court's view there was no reason for Officer Gleckman to believe that Innis was susceptible to this type of an implied appeal; therefore, the statement would not be reasonably likely to elicit an incriminating response. Assuming that this is true, then it seems to me that the first two statements, which would be just as unlikely to elicit such a response, should also not be considered interrogation. But, because the first statement is clearly an express question, it *would* be considered interrogation under the Court's test. The second statement, although just as clearly a deliberate appeal to Innis to reveal the location of the gun, would presumably not be interrogation because (a) it was not in form a direct question and (b) it does not fit within the "reasonably likely to elicit an incriminating response" category that applies to indirect interrogation.

As this example illustrates, the Court's test creates an incentive for police to ignore a suspect's invocation of his rights in order to make continued attempts to extract information from him. If a suspect does not appear to be susceptible to a particular type of psychological pressure, the police are apparently free to exert that pressure on him despite his request for counsel, so long as they are careful not to punctuate their statements with question marks. And if, contrary to all reasonable expectations, the suspect makes an incriminating statement, that statement can be used against him at trial. The Court thus turns *Miranda's* unequivocal rule against any interrogation at all into a trap in which unwary suspects may be caught by police deception.

II

* * *

The Court's assumption that criminal suspects are not susceptible to appeals to conscience is directly contrary to the teachings of police interrogation manuals, which recommend appealing to a suspect's sense of morality as a standard and often successful interrogation technique. Surely the practical experience embodied in such manuals should not be ignored in a case such as this in which the record is devoid of any evidence—one way or the other—as to the susceptibility of suspects in general or of Innis in particular.

Moreover, there is evidence in the record to support the view that Officer Gleckman's statement was intended to elicit a response from Innis. Officer Gleckman, who was not regularly assigned to the caged wagon, was directed by a police captain to ride with respondent to the police station. Although there is a dispute in the testimony, it appears that Gleckman may well have been riding in the back seat with Innis. The record does not explain why, notwithstanding the fact that respondent was handcuffed, unarmed, and had offered no resistance when arrested by an officer acting alone, the captain ordered Officer Gleckman to ride with respondent. It is not inconceivable that two professionally trained police officers concluded that a few well-chosen remarks might induce respondent to disclose the whereabouts of the shotgun. This conclusion becomes even more plausible in light of the emotionally charged words chosen by Officer Gleckman ("God forbid" that a "little girl" should find the gun and hurt herself).

* * *

Points for Discussion

1. The Court here adopts an objective test for interrogation—whether a reasonable officer would know that his words or actions were likely to elicit an incriminating response. How often will this test and the subjective, deliberate-elicitation test of *Brewer v. Williams* produce different results?

2. How compelling is the majority's application of the test it develops in this case? If these words were not likely to elicit an incriminating response, what words, short of direct questioning, are likely to? The dissent criticizes the majority's view of the susceptibility of criminal defendants as lacking in empirical support. What evidence does the dissent refer to for support?

3. Justice Stevens writes that this case and *Williams* are "indistinguishable." Does he argue, therefore, that Innis was entitled to the right to counsel at the time that he was being driven to the police station? Would such an argument be consistent with the Court's Sixth Amendment jurisprudence?

NEW YORK V. QUARLES

467 U.S. 649 (1984)

JUSTICE REHNQUIST delivered the opinion of the court.

Respondent Benjamin Quarles was charged in the New York trial court with criminal possession of a weapon. The trial court suppressed the gun in question, and a statement made by respondent, because the statement was obtained by police before they read respondent his "*Miranda* rights." That ruling was affirmed on appeal through the New

York Court of Appeals. We granted certiorari and we now reverse. We conclude that under the circumstances involved in this case, overriding considerations of public safety justify the officer's failure to provide *Miranda* warnings before he asked questions devoted to locating the abandoned weapon.

On September 11, 1980, at approximately 12:30 a.m., Officer Frank Kraft and Officer Sal Scarring were on road patrol in Queens, N.Y., when a young woman approached their car. She told them that she had just been raped by a black male, approximately six feet tall, who was wearing a black jacket with the name "Big Ben" printed in yellow letters on the back. She told the officers that the man had just entered an A & P supermarket located nearby and that the man was carrying a gun.

The officers drove the woman to the supermarket, and Officer Kraft entered the store while Officer Scarring radioed for assistance. Officer Kraft quickly spotted respondent, who matched the description given by the woman, approaching a checkout counter. Apparently upon seeing the officer, respondent turned and ran toward the rear of the store, and Officer Kraft pursued him with a drawn gun. When respondent turned the corner at the end of an aisle, Officer Kraft lost sight of him for several seconds, and upon regaining sight of respondent, ordered him to stop and put his hands over his head.

Although more than three other officers had arrived on the scene by that time, Officer Kraft was the first to reach respondent. He frisked him and discovered that he was wearing a shoulder holster which was then empty. After handcuffing him, Officer Kraft asked him where the gun was. Respondent nodded in the direction of some empty cartons and responded, "the gun is over there." Officer Kraft thereafter retrieved a loaded .38-caliber revolver from one of the cartons, formally placed respondent under arrest, and read him his *Miranda* rights from a printed card. Respondent indicated that he would be willing to answer questions without an attorney present. Officer Kraft then asked respondent if he owned the gun and where he had purchased it. Respondent answered that he did own it and that he had purchased it in Miami, Fla.

* * *

In this case we have before us no claim that respondent's statements were actually compelled by police conduct which overcame his will to resist. Thus the only issue before us is whether Officer Kraft was justified in failing to make available to respondent the procedural safeguards associated with the privilege against compulsory self-incrimination since *Miranda*.[5]

---

[5] The dissent curiously takes us to task for "endors[ing] the introduction of coerced self-incriminating statements in criminal prosecutions," and for "sanction[ing] sub silentio criminal prosecutions based on compelled self-incriminating statements." Of course our decision today does

The New York Court of Appeals was undoubtedly correct in deciding that the facts of this case come within the ambit of the *Miranda* decision as we have subsequently interpreted it. We agree that respondent was in police custody because we have noted that "the ultimate inquiry is simply whether there is a 'formal arrest or restraint on freedom of movement' of the degree associated with a formal arrest." Here Quarles was surrounded by at least four police officers and was handcuffed when the questioning at issue took place. As the New York Court of Appeals observed, there was nothing to suggest that any of the officers were any longer concerned for their own physical safety. The New York Court of Appeals' majority declined to express an opinion as to whether there might be an exception to the *Miranda* rule if the police had been acting to protect the public, because the lower courts in New York had made no factual determination that the police had acted with that motive.

We hold that on these facts there is a "public safety" exception to the requirement that *Miranda* warnings be given before a suspect's answers may be admitted into evidence, and that the availability of that exception does not depend upon the motivation of the individual officers involved. In a kaleidoscopic situation such as the one confronting these officers, where spontaneity rather than adherence to a police manual is necessarily the order of the day, the application of the exception which we recognize today should not be made to depend on post hoc findings at a suppression hearing concerning the subjective motivation of the arresting officer. Undoubtedly most police officers, if placed in Officer Kraft's position, would act out of a host of different, instinctive, and largely unverifiable motives—their own safety, the safety of others, and perhaps as well the desire to obtain incriminating evidence from the suspect.

Whatever the motivation of individual officers in such a situation, we do not believe that the doctrinal underpinnings of *Miranda* require that it be applied in all its rigor to a situation in which police officers ask questions reasonably prompted by a concern for the public safety. The *Miranda* decision was based in large part on this Court's view that the warnings which it required police to give to suspects in custody would reduce the likelihood that the suspects would fall victim to constitutionally impermissible practices of police interrogation in the presumptively coercive environment of the station house. The dissenters warned that the requirement of *Miranda* warnings would have the effect of decreasing the number of suspects who respond to police questioning. The *Miranda* majority, however, apparently felt that whatever the cost to society in terms of fewer convictions of guilty suspects, that cost would simply have

---

nothing of the kind. As the *Miranda* Court itself recognized, the failure to provide *Miranda* warnings in and of itself does not render a confession involuntary, and respondent is certainly free on remand to argue that his statement was coerced under traditional due process standards. Today we merely reject the only argument that respondent has raised to support the exclusion of his statement, that the statement must be presumed compelled because of Officer Kraft's failure to read him his *Miranda* warnings.

to be borne in the interest of enlarged protection for the Fifth Amendment privilege.

The police in this case, in the very act of apprehending a suspect, were confronted with the immediate necessity of ascertaining the whereabouts of a gun which they had every reason to believe the suspect had just removed from his empty holster and discarded in the supermarket. So long as the gun was concealed somewhere in the supermarket, with its actual whereabouts unknown, it obviously posed more than one danger to the public safety: an accomplice might make use of it, a customer or employee might later come upon it.

In such a situation, if the police are required to recite the familiar *Miranda* warnings before asking the whereabouts of the gun, suspects in Quarles' position might well be deterred from responding. Procedural safeguards which deter a suspect from responding were deemed acceptable in *Miranda* in order to protect the Fifth Amendment privilege; when the primary social cost of those added protections is the possibility of fewer convictions, the *Miranda* majority was willing to bear that cost. Here, had *Miranda* warnings deterred Quarles from responding to Officer Kraft's question about the whereabouts of the gun, the cost would have been something more than merely the failure to obtain evidence useful in convicting Quarles. Officer Kraft needed an answer to his question not simply to make his case against Quarles but to insure that further danger to the public did not result from the concealment of the gun in a public area.

We conclude that the need for answers to questions in a situation posing a threat to the public safety outweighs the need for the prophylactic rule protecting the Fifth Amendment's privilege against self-incrimination. We decline to place officers such as Officer Kraft in the untenable position of having to consider, often in a matter of seconds, whether it best serves society for them to ask the necessary questions without the Miranda warnings and render whatever probative evidence they uncover inadmissible, or for them to give the warnings in order to preserve the admissibility of evidence they might uncover but possibly damage or destroy their ability to obtain that evidence and neutralize the volatile situation confronting them.[7]

In recognizing a narrow exception to the *Miranda* rule in this case, we acknowledge that to some degree we lessen the desirable clarity of that

[7] The dissent argues that a public safety exception to *Miranda* is unnecessary because in every case an officer can simply ask the necessary questions to protect himself or the public, and then the prosecution can decline to introduce any incriminating responses at a subsequent trial. But absent actual coercion by the officer, there is no constitutional imperative requiring the exclusion of the evidence that results from police inquiry of this kind; and we do not believe that the doctrinal underpinnings of *Miranda* require us to exclude the evidence, thus penalizing officers for asking the very questions which are the most crucial to their efforts to protect themselves and the public.

rule. At least in part in order to preserve its clarity, we have over the years refused to sanction attempts to expand our *Miranda* holding. As we have in other contexts, we recognize here the importance of a workable rule "to guide police officers, who have only limited time and expertise to reflect on and balance the social and individual interests involved in the specific circumstances they confront." But as we have pointed out, we believe that the exception which we recognize today lessens the necessity of that on-the-scene balancing process. The exception will not be difficult for police officers to apply because in each case it will be circumscribed by the exigency which justifies it. We think police officers can and will distinguish almost instinctively between questions necessary to secure their own safety or the safety of the public and questions designed solely to elicit testimonial evidence from a suspect.

The facts of this case clearly demonstrate that distinction and an officer's ability to recognize it. Officer Kraft asked only the question necessary to locate the missing gun before advising respondent of his rights. It was only after securing the loaded revolver and giving the warnings that he continued with investigatory questions about the ownership and place of purchase of the gun. The exception which we recognize today, far from complicating the thought processes and the on-the-scene judgments of police officers, will simply free them to follow their legitimate instincts when confronting situations presenting a danger to the public safety.

* * *

JUSTICE O'CONNOR, concurring in the judgment in part and dissenting in part.

In *Miranda v. Arizona*, 384 U.S. 436 (1966), the Court held unconstitutional, because inherently compelled, the admission of statements derived from in-custody questioning not preceded by an explanation of the privilege against self-incrimination and the consequences of forgoing it. Today, the Court concludes that overriding considerations of public safety justify the admission of evidence-oral statements and a gun-secured without the benefit of such warnings. In so holding, the Court acknowledges that it is departing from prior precedent and that it is "lessen[ing] the desirable clarity of [the *Miranda*] rule." Were the Court writing from a clean slate, I could agree with its holding. But *Miranda* is now the law and, in my view, the Court has not provided sufficient justification for departing from it or for blurring its now clear strictures. Accordingly, I would require suppression of the initial statement taken from respondent in this case. On the other hand, nothing in *Miranda* or the privilege itself requires exclusion of nontestimonial evidence derived from informal custodial interrogation, and I therefore agree with the Court that admission of the gun in evidence is proper.

I

* * *

In my view, a "public safety" exception unnecessarily blurs the edges of the clear line heretofore established and makes *Miranda*'s requirements more difficult to understand. In some cases, police will benefit because a reviewing court will find that an exigency excused their failure to administer the required warnings. But in other cases, police will suffer because, though they thought an exigency excused their noncompliance, a reviewing court will view the "objective" circumstances differently and require exclusion of admissions thereby obtained. The end result will be a finespun new doctrine on public safety exigencies incident to custodial interrogation, complete with the hair-splitting distinctions that currently plague our Fourth Amendment jurisprudence. "While the rigidity of the prophylactic rules was a principal weakness in the view of dissenters and critics outside the Court, . . . that rigidity [has also been called a] strength of the decision. It [has] afforded police and courts clear guidance on the manner in which to conduct a custodial investigation: if it was rigid, it was also precise. . . . [T]his core virtue of *Miranda* would be eviscerated if the prophylactic rules were freely [ignored] by . . . courts under the guise of [reinterpreting] *Miranda*. . . ."

The justification the Court provides for upsetting the equilibrium that has finally been achieved—that police cannot and should not balance considerations of public safety against the individual's interest in avoiding compulsory testimonial self-incrimination—really misses the critical question to be decided. *Miranda* has never been read to prohibit the police from asking questions to secure the public safety. Rather, the critical question *Miranda* addresses is who shall bear the cost of securing the public safety when such questions are asked and answered: the defendant or the State. *Miranda*, for better or worse, found the resolution of that question implicit in the prohibition against compulsory self-incrimination and placed the burden on the State. When police ask custodial questions without administering the required warnings, *Miranda* quite clearly requires that the answers received be presumed compelled and that they be excluded from evidence at trial.

The Court concedes, as it must, both that respondent was in "custody" and subject to "interrogation" and that his statement "the gun is over there" was compelled within the meaning of our precedent. In my view, since there is nothing about an exigency that makes custodial interrogation any less compelling, a principled application of *Miranda* requires that respondent's statement be suppressed.

II

The court below assumed, without discussion, that the privilege against self-incrimination required that the gun derived from respondent's statement also be suppressed, whether or not the State could independently link it to him. That conclusion was, in my view, incorrect.

* * *

JUSTICE MARSHALL, with whom JUSTICE BRENNAN and JUSTICE STEVENS join, dissenting.

The police in this case arrested a man suspected of possessing a firearm in violation of New York law. Once the suspect was in custody and found to be unarmed, the arresting officer initiated an interrogation. Without being advised of his right not to respond, the suspect incriminated himself by locating the gun. The majority concludes that the State may rely on this incriminating statement to convict the suspect of possessing a weapon. I disagree. The arresting officers had no legitimate reason to interrogate the suspect without advising him of his rights to remain silent and to obtain assistance of counsel. By finding on these facts justification for unconsented interrogation, the majority abandons the clear guidelines enunciated in *Miranda v. Arizona*, 384 U.S. 436 (1966), and condemns the American judiciary to a new era of post hoc inquiry into the propriety of custodial interrogations. More significantly and in direct conflict with this Court's longstanding interpretation of the Fifth Amendment, the majority has endorsed the introduction of coerced self-incriminating statements in criminal prosecutions. I dissent.

I

* * *

The majority's entire analysis rests on the factual assumption that the public was at risk during Quarles' interrogation. This assumption is completely in conflict with the facts as found by New York's highest court. Before the interrogation began, Quarles had been "reduced to a condition of physical powerlessness." Contrary to the majority's speculations, Quarles was not believed to have, nor did he in fact have, an accomplice to come to his rescue. When the questioning began, the arresting officers were sufficiently confident of their safety to put away their guns. As Officer Kraft acknowledged at the suppression hearing, "the situation was under control." Based on Officer Kraft's own testimony, the New York Court of Appeals found: "Nothing suggests that any of the officers was by that time concerned for his own physical safety." The Court of Appeals also determined that there was no evidence that the interrogation was prompted by the arresting officers' concern for the public's safety.

The majority attempts to slip away from these unambiguous findings of New York's highest court by proposing that danger be measured by objective facts rather than the subjective intentions of arresting officers. Though clever, this ploy was anticipated by the New York Court of Appeals: "[T]here is no evidence in the record before us that there were exigent circumstances posing a risk to the public safety. . . ."

The New York court's conclusion that neither Quarles nor his missing gun posed a threat to the public's safety is amply supported by the evidence presented at the suppression hearing. Again contrary to the majority's intimations, no customers or employees were wandering about the store in danger of coming across Quarles' discarded weapon. Although the supermarket was open to the public, Quarles' arrest took place during the middle of the night when the store was apparently deserted except for the clerks at the checkout counter. The police could easily have cordoned off the store and searched for the missing gun. Had they done so, they would have found the gun forthwith. The police were well aware that Quarles had discarded his weapon somewhere near the scene of the arrest. As the State acknowledged before the New York Court of Appeals: "After Officer Kraft had handcuffed and frisked the defendant in the supermarket, he knew with a high degree of certainty that the defendant's gun was within the immediate vicinity of the encounter. He undoubtedly would have searched for it in the carton a few feet away without the defendant having looked in that direction and saying that it was there."

* * *

II

The majority's treatment of the legal issues presented in this case is no less troubling than its abuse of the facts. Before today's opinion, the Court had twice concluded that, under *Miranda* v. Arizona, 384 U.S. 436 (1966), police officers conducting custodial interrogations must advise suspects of their rights before any questions concerning the whereabouts of incriminating weapons can be asked. *Rhode Island v. Innis*, 446 U.S. 291, 298–302 (1980) (dicta); *Orozco v. Texas*, 394 U.S. 324 (1969) (holding). Now the majority departs from these cases and rules that police may withhold *Miranda* warnings whenever custodial interrogations concern matters of public safety.

* * *

Before today's opinion, the procedures established in *Miranda v. Arizona* had "the virtue of informing police and prosecutors with specificity as to what they may do in conducting custodial interrogation, and of informing courts under what circumstances statements obtained during such interrogation are not admissible." In a chimerical quest for public safety, the majority has abandoned the rule that brought 18 years of doctrinal tranquility to the field of custodial interrogations. As the majority candidly concedes, a public-safety exception destroys forever the clarity of *Miranda* for both law enforcement officers and members of the judiciary. The Court's candor cannot mask what a serious loss the administration of justice has incurred.

This case is illustrative of the chaos the "public-safety" exception will unleash. The circumstances of Quarles' arrest have never been in dispute.

After the benefit of briefing and oral argument, the New York Court of Appeals, as previously noted, concluded that there was "no evidence in the record before us that there were exigent circumstances posing a risk to the public safety." Upon reviewing the same facts and hearing the same arguments, a majority of this Court has come to precisely the opposite conclusion: "So long as the gun was concealed somewhere in the supermarket, with its actual whereabouts unknown, it obviously posed more than one danger to the public safety. . . ."

If after plenary review two appellate courts so fundamentally differ over the threat to public safety presented by the simple and uncontested facts of this case, one must seriously question how law enforcement officers will respond to the majority's new rule in the confusion and haste of the real world. As the Chief Justice wrote in a similar context: "Few, if any, police officers are competent to make the kind of evaluation seemingly contemplated. . . ." *Rhode Island v. Innis*, 446 U.S., at 304 (concurring in judgment). Not only will police officers have to decide whether the objective facts of an arrest justify an unconsented custodial interrogation; they will also have to remember to interrupt the interrogation and read the suspect his *Miranda* warnings once the focus of the inquiry shifts from protecting the public's safety to ascertaining the suspect's guilt. Disagreements of the scope of the "public-safety" exception and mistakes in its application are inevitable.

The end result, as Justice O'Connor predicts, will be "a finespun new doctrine on public safety exigencies incident to custodial interrogation, complete with the hairsplitting distinctions that currently plague our Fourth Amendment jurisprudence." In the meantime, the courts will have to dedicate themselves to spinning this new web of doctrines, and the country's law enforcement agencies will have to suffer patiently through the frustations of another period of constitutional uncertainty.

III

Though unfortunate, the difficulty of administering the "public-safety" exception is not the most profound flaw in the majority's decision. The majority has lost sight of the fact that *Miranda v. Arizona* and our earlier custodial-interrogation cases all implemented a constitutional privilege against self-incrimination. The rules established in these cases were designed to protect criminal defendants against prosecutions based on coerced self-incriminating statements. The majority today turns its back on these constitutional considerations, and invites the government to prosecute through the use of what necessarily are coerced statements.

A

The majority's error stems from a serious misunderstanding of *Miranda v. Arizona* and of the Fifth Amendment upon which that decision was based. The majority implies that *Miranda* consisted of no more than a judicial balancing act in which the benefits of "enlarged protection for the Fifth Amendment privilege" were weighed against "the cost to society in terms of fewer convictions of guilty suspects." Supposedly because the scales tipped in favor of the privilege against self-incrimination, the *Miranda* Court erected a prophylactic barrier around statements made during custodial interrogations. The majority now proposes to return to the scales of social utility to calculate whether *Miranda*'s prophylactic rule remains cost-effective when threats to the public's safety are added to the balance. The results of the majority's "test" are announced with pseudoscientific precision: "We conclude that the need for answers to questions in a situation posing a threat to the public safety outweighs the need for the prophylactic rule protecting the Fifth Amendment's privilege against self-incrimination."

* * *

Whether society would be better off if the police warned suspects of their rights before beginning an interrogation or whether the advantages of giving such warnings would outweigh their costs did not inform the *Miranda* decision. On the contrary, the *Miranda* Court was concerned with the proscriptions of the Fifth Amendment, and, in particular, whether the Self-Incrimination Clause permits the government to prosecute individuals based on statements made in the course of custodial interrogations.

Miranda v. Arizona was the culmination of a century-long inquiry into how this Court should deal with confessions made during custodial interrogations. Long before *Miranda*, the Court had recognized that the Federal Government was prohibited from introducing at criminal trials compelled confessions, including confessions compelled in the course of custodial interrogations. In 1924, Justice Brandeis was reciting settled law when he wrote: "[A] confession obtained by compulsion must be excluded whatever may have been the character of the compulsion, and whether the compulsion was applied in a judicial proceeding or otherwise."

* * *

When *Miranda* reached this Court, it was undisputed that both the States and the Federal Government were constitutionally prohibited from prosecuting defendants with confessions coerced during custodial interrogations.[5] As a theoretical matter, the law was clear. In practice, however, the courts found it exceedingly difficult to determine whether a given confession had been coerced. Difficulties of proof and subtleties of interrogation technique made it impossible in most cases for the judiciary to decide with confidence whether the defendant had voluntarily confessed his guilt or whether his testimony had been unconstitutionally compelled.

[5] There was, of course, still considerable confusion over whether the Sixth Amendment or the Fifth Amendment provided the basis for this prohibition. See *Escobedo v. Illinois*, 378 U.S. 478 (1964). But the matter was undeniably of constitutional magnitude.

Courts around the country were spending countless hours reviewing the facts of individual custodial interrogations.

Miranda dealt with these practical problems. After a detailed examination of police practices and a review of its previous decisions in the area, the Court in *Miranda* determined that custodial interrogations are inherently coercive. The Court therefore created a constitutional presumption that statements made during custodial interrogations are compelled in violation of the Fifth Amendment and are thus inadmissible in criminal prosecutions. As a result of the Court's decision in *Miranda*, a statement made during a custodial interrogation may be introduced as proof of a defendant's guilt only if the prosecution demonstrates that the defendant knowingly and intelligently waived his constitutional rights before making the statement. The now-familiar *Miranda* warnings offer law enforcement authorities a clear, easily administered device for ensuring that criminal suspects understand their constitutional rights well enough to waive them and to engage in consensual custodial interrogation.

In fashioning its "public-safety" exception to *Miranda*, the majority makes no attempt to deal with the constitutional presumption established by that case. The majority does not argue that police questioning about issues of public safety is any less coercive than custodial interrogations into other matters. The majority's only contention is that police officers could more easily protect the public if *Miranda* did not apply to custodial interrogations concerning the public's safety. But *Miranda* was not a decision about public safety; it was a decision about coerced confessions. Without establishing that interrogations concerning the public's safety are less likely to be coercive than other interrogations, the majority cannot endorse the "public-safety" exception and remain faithful to the logic of *Miranda v. Arizona*.

B

The majority's avoidance of the issue of coercion may not have been inadvertent. It would strain credulity to contend that Officer Kraft's questioning of respondent Quarles was not coercive. In the middle of the night and in the back of an empty supermarket, Quarles was surrounded by four armed police officers. His hands were handcuffed behind his back. The first words out of the mouth of the arresting officer were: "Where is the gun?" In the majority's phrase, the situation was "kaleidoscopic." Police and suspect were acting on instinct. Officer Kraft's abrupt and pointed question pressured Quarles in precisely the way that the *Miranda* Court feared the custodial interrogations would coerce self-incriminating testimony.

That the application of the "public-safety" exception in this case entailed coercion is no happenstance. The majority's *ratio decidendi* is that interrogating suspects about matters of public safety will be coercive. In its cost-benefit analysis, the Court's strongest argument in favor of a "public-safety" exception to *Miranda* is that the police would be better able to protect the public's safety if they were not always required to give suspects their *Miranda* warnings. The crux of this argument is that, by deliberately withholding *Miranda* warnings, the police can get information out of suspects who would refuse to respond to police questioning were they advised of their constitutional rights. The "public-safety" exception is efficacious precisely because it permits police officers to coerce criminal defendants into making involuntary statements.

* * *

The irony of the majority's decision is that the public's safety can be perfectly well protected without abridging the Fifth Amendment. If a bomb is about to explode or the public is otherwise imminently imperiled, the police are free to interrogate suspects without advising them of their constitutional rights. Such unconsented questioning may take place not only when police officers act on instinct but also when higher faculties lead them to believe that advising a suspect of his constitutional rights might decrease the likelihood that the suspect would reveal life-saving information. If trickery is necessary to protect the public, then the police may trick a suspect into confessing. While the Fourteenth Amendment sets limits on such behavior, nothing in the Fifth Amendment or our decision in *Miranda v. Arizona* proscribes this sort of emergency questioning. All the Fifth Amendment forbids is the introduction of coerced statements at trial.

* * *

IV

* * *

Accordingly, I would affirm the order of the Court of Appeals to the extent that it found Quarles' incriminating statement inadmissible under the Fifth Amendment, would vacate the order to the extent that it suppressed Quarles' gun, and would remand the matter for reconsideration in light of *Nix v. Williams*.

Points for Discussion

1. The majority here holds that, although Quarles was in custody and subject to interrogation when he incriminated himself, *Miranda* warnings were not necessary. On what basis does the Court create the public safety exception that justifies this result?

2. The dissenters argue that the statement here was obtained through a violation, not just of the prophylactic rule of *Miranda* but of the Fifth Amendment itself. Do you agree with the dissenters' assertion that Quarles, isolated and surrounded by four armed officers, gave up the location of the gun as a result of coercion rather than free will?

3. What do you make of the dissenters' argument that, if the officers were so concerned about public safety, they were free to question the defendant about the whereabouts of the gun but that his answers could not be used against him in court? What is the majority's view about the relevance of the officers' subjective motivation?

ILLINOIS V. PERKINS

496 U.S. 292 (1990)

JUSTICE KENNEDY **delivered the opinion of the court.**

An undercover government agent was placed in the cell of respondent Perkins, who was incarcerated on charges unrelated to the subject of the agent's investigation. Respondent made statements that implicated him in the crime that the agent sought to solve. Respondent claims that the statements should be inadmissible because he had not been given *Miranda* warnings by the agent. We hold that the statements are admissible. *Miranda* warnings are not required when the suspect is unaware that he is speaking to a law enforcement officer and gives a voluntary statement.

I

In November 1984, Richard Stephenson was murdered in a suburb of East St. Louis, Illinois. The murder remained unsolved until March 1986, when one Donald Charlton told police that he had learned about a homicide from a fellow inmate at the Graham Correctional Facility, where Charlton had been serving a sentence for burglary. The fellow inmate was Lloyd Perkins, who is the respondent here. Charlton told police that, while at Graham, he had befriended respondent, who told him in detail about a murder that respondent had committed in East St. Louis. On hearing Charlton's account, the police recognized details of the Stephenson murder that were not well known, and so they treated Charlton's story as a credible one.

By the time the police heard Charlton's account, respondent had been released from Graham, but police traced him to a jail in Montgomery County, Illinois, where he was being held pending trial on a charge of aggravated battery, unrelated to the Stephenson murder. The police wanted to investigate further respondent's connection to the Stephenson murder, but feared that the use of an eavesdropping device would prove impracticable and unsafe. They decided instead to place an undercover agent in the cellblock with respondent and Charlton. The plan was for Charlton and undercover agent John Parisi to pose as escapees from a work release program who had been arrested in the course of a burglary. Parisi and Charlton were instructed to engage respondent in casual conversation and report anything he said about the Stephenson murder.

Parisi, using the alias "Vito Bianco," and Charlton, both clothed in jail garb, were placed in the cellblock with respondent at the Montgomery

County jail. The cellblock consisted of 12 separate cells that opened onto a common room. Respondent greeted Charlton who, after a brief conversation with respondent, introduced Parisi by his alias. Parisi told respondent that he "wasn't going to do any more time" and suggested that the three of them escape. Respondent replied that the Montgomery County jail was "rinky-dink" and that they could "break out." The trio met in respondent's cell later that evening, after the other inmates were asleep, to refine their plan. Respondent said that his girlfriend could smuggle in a pistol. Charlton said: "Hey, I'm not a murderer, I'm a burglar. That's your guys' profession." After telling Charlton that he would be responsible for any murder that occurred, Parisi asked respondent if he had ever "done" anybody. Respondent said that he had and proceeded to describe at length the events of the Stephenson murder. Parisi and respondent then engaged in some casual conversation before respondent went to sleep. Parisi did not give respondent *Miranda* warnings before the conversations.

* * *

We granted certiorari to decide whether an undercover law enforcement officer must give *Miranda* warnings to an incarcerated suspect before asking him questions that may elicit an incriminating response. We now reverse.

II

* * *

Conversations between suspects and undercover agents do not implicate the concerns underlying *Miranda*. The essential ingredients of a "police-dominated atmosphere" and compulsion are not present when an incarcerated person speaks freely to someone whom he believes to be a fellow inmate. Coercion is determined from the perspective of the suspect. When a suspect considers himself in the company of cellmates and not officers, the coercive atmosphere is lacking. There is no empirical basis for the assumption that a suspect speaking to those whom he assumes are not officers will feel compelled to speak by the fear of reprisal for remaining silent or in the hope of more lenient treatment should he confess.

It is the premise of *Miranda* that the danger of coercion results from the interaction of custody and official interrogation. We reject the argument that *Miranda* warnings are required whenever a suspect is in custody in a technical sense and converses with someone who happens to be a government agent. Questioning by captors, who appear to control the suspect's fate, may create mutually reinforcing pressures that the Court has assumed will weaken the suspect's will, but where a suspect does not know that he is conversing with a government agent, these pressures do not exist. The state court here mistakenly assumed that because the suspect was in custody, no undercover questioning could take place. When the suspect has no reason to think that the listeners have official power over him, it should not be assumed that his words are motivated by the reaction he expects from his listeners. "[W]hen the agent carries neither badge nor gun and wears not 'police blue,' but the same prison gray" as the suspect, there is no "*interplay* between police interrogation and police custody." Kamisar, Brewer v. Williams, Massiah *and* Miranda*: What is "Interrogation"? When Does it Matter*?, 67 GEO.L.J. 1, 67, 63 (1978).

Miranda forbids coercion, not mere strategic deception by taking advantage of a suspect's misplaced trust in one he supposes to be a fellow prisoner. As we recognized in *Miranda:* "[C]onfessions remain a proper element in law enforcement. Any statement given freely and voluntarily without any compelling influences is, of course, admissible in evidence." Ploys to mislead a suspect or lull him into a false sense of security that do not rise to the level of compulsion or coercion to speak are not within *Miranda*'s concerns.

Miranda was not meant to protect suspects from boasting about their criminal activities in front of persons whom they believe to be their cellmates. This case is illustrative. Respondent had no reason to feel that undercover agent Parisi had any legal authority to force him to answer questions or that Parisi could affect respondent's future treatment. Respondent viewed the cellmate-agent as an equal and showed no hint of being intimidated by the atmosphere of the jail. In recounting the details of the Stephenson murder, respondent was motivated solely by the desire to impress his fellow inmates. He spoke at his own peril.

The tactic employed here to elicit a voluntary confession from a suspect does not violate the Self-Incrimination Clause. We held in *Hoffa v. United States,* 385 U.S. 293 (1966), that placing an undercover agent near a suspect in order to gather incriminating information was permissible under the Fifth Amendment. In *Hoffa,* while petitioner Hoffa was on trial, he met often with one Partin, who, unbeknownst to Hoffa, was cooperating with law enforcement officials. Partin reported to officials that Hoffa had divulged his attempts to bribe jury members. We approved using Hoffa's statements at his subsequent trial for jury tampering, on the rationale that "no claim ha[d] been or could [have been] made that [Hoffa's] incriminating statements were the product of any sort of coercion, legal or factual." In addition, we found that the fact that Partin had fooled Hoffa into thinking that Partin was a sympathetic colleague did not affect the voluntariness of the statements. The only difference between this case and *Hoffa* is that the suspect here was incarcerated, but detention, whether or not for the crime in question, does not warrant a presumption that the use of an undercover agent to speak with an incarcerated suspect makes any confession thus obtained involuntary.

Our decision in *Mathis v. United States,* 391 U.S. 1 (1968), is distinguishable. In *Mathis,* an inmate in a state prison was interviewed by an Internal Revenue Service agent about possible tax violations. No

Miranda warning was given before questioning. The Court held that the suspect's incriminating statements were not admissible at his subsequent trial on tax fraud charges. The suspect in *Mathis* was aware that the agent was a Government official, investigating the possibility of noncompliance with the tax laws. The case before us now is different. Where the suspect does not know that he is speaking to a government agent there is no reason to assume the possibility that the suspect might feel coerced. (The bare fact of custody may not in every instance require a warning even when the suspect is aware that he is speaking to an official, but we do not have occasion to explore that issue here.)

This Court's Sixth Amendment decisions in *Massiah v. United States,* 377 U.S. 201 (1964), *United States v. Henry,* 447 U.S. 264 (1980), and *Maine v. Moulton,* 474 U.S. 159 (1985), also do not avail respondent. We held in those cases that the government may not use an undercover agent to circumvent the Sixth Amendment right to counsel once a suspect has been charged with the crime. After charges have been filed, the Sixth Amendment prevents the government from interfering with the accused's right to counsel. In the instant case no charges had been filed on the subject of the interrogation, and our Sixth Amendment precedents are not applicable.

Respondent can seek no help from his argument that a bright-line rule for the application of *Miranda* is desirable. Law enforcement officers will have little difficulty putting into practice our holding that undercover agents need not give *Miranda* warnings to incarcerated suspects. The use of undercover agents is a recognized law enforcement technique, often employed in the prison context to detect violence against correctional officials or inmates, as well as for the purposes served here. The interests protected by *Miranda* are not implicated in these cases, and the warnings are not required to safeguard the constitutional rights of inmates who make voluntary statements to undercover agents.

* * *

JUSTICE BRENNAN, concurring in the judgment.

The Court holds that *Miranda v. Arizona,* 384 U.S. 436 (1966), does not require suppression of a statement made by an incarcerated suspect to an undercover agent. Although I do not subscribe to the majority's characterization of *Miranda* in its entirety, I do agree that when a suspect does not know that his questioner is a police agent, such questioning does not amount to "interrogation" in an "inherently coercive" environment so as to require application of *Miranda.* Since the only issue raised at this stage of the litigation is the applicability of *Miranda,* I concur in the judgment of the Court.

* * *

The method used to elicit the confession in this case deserves close scrutiny. The police devised a ruse to lure respondent into incriminating himself when he was in jail on an unrelated charge. A police agent, posing as a fellow inmate and proposing a sham escape plot, tricked respondent into confessing that he had once committed a murder, as a way of proving that he would be willing to do so again should the need arise during the escape. The testimony of the undercover officer and a police informant at the suppression hearing reveal the deliberate manner in which the two elicited incriminating statements from respondent. We have recognized that "the mere fact of custody imposes pressures on the accused; confinement may bring into play subtle influences that will make him particularly susceptible to the ploys of undercover Government agents." As Justice Marshall points out, the pressures of custody make a suspect more likely to confide in others and to engage in "jailhouse bravado." The State is in a unique position to exploit this vulnerability because it has virtually complete control over the suspect's environment. Thus, the State can ensure that a suspect is barraged with questions from an undercover agent until the suspect confesses. The testimony in this case suggests the State did just that.

The deliberate use of deception and manipulation by the police appears to be incompatible "with a system that presumes innocence and assures that a conviction will not be secured by inquisitorial means," and raises serious concerns that respondent's will was overborne. It is open to the lower court on remand to determine whether, under the totality of the circumstances, respondent's confession was elicited in a manner that violated the Due Process Clause. That the confession was not elicited through means of physical torture or overt psychological pressure does not end the inquiry. "[A]s law enforcement officers become more responsible, and the methods used to extract confessions more sophisticated, [a court's] duty to enforce federal constitutional protections does not cease. It only becomes more difficult because of the more delicate judgments to be made."

JUSTICE MARSHALL, dissenting.

* * *

The Court does not dispute that the police officer here conducted a custodial interrogation of a criminal suspect. Perkins was incarcerated in county jail during the questioning at issue here; under these circumstances, he was in custody as that term is defined in *Miranda*. The United States argues that Perkins was not in custody for purpose of *Miranda* because he was familiar with the custodial environment as a result of being in jail for two days and previously spending time in prison. Perkins' familiarity with confinement, however, does not transform his incarceration into some sort of noncustodial arrangement.

While Perkins was confined, an undercover police officer, with the help of a police informant, questioned him about a serious crime. Although the Court does not dispute that Perkins was interrogated, it downplays the nature of the 35-minute questioning by disingenuously referring to it as a "conversatio[n]." The officer's narration of the "conversation" at Perkins' suppression hearing however, reveals that it clearly was an interrogation.

> [Agent:] You ever do anyone?
>
> [Perkins:] Yeah, once in East St. Louis, in a rich white neighborhood.
>
> Informant: I didn't know they had any rich white neighborhoods in East St. Louis.
>
> Perkins: It wasn't in East St. Louis, it was by a race track in Fairview Heights. . . .
>
> [Agent]: You did a guy in Fairview Heights?
>
> Perkins: Yeah in a rich white section where most of the houses look the same.
>
> [Informant]: If all the houses look the same, how did you know you had the right house?
>
> Perkins: Me and two guys cased the house for about a week. I knew exactly which house, the second house on the left from the corner.
>
> [Agent]: How long ago did this happen?
>
> Perkins: Approximately about two years ago. I got paid $5,000 for that job.
>
> [Agent]: How did it go down?
>
> Perkins: I walked up [to] this guy['s] house with a sawed-off under my trench coat.
>
> [Agent]: What type gun[?]
>
> Perkins: A .12 gauge Remmington *[sic]* Automatic Model 1100 sawed-off.

The police officer continued the inquiry, asking a series of questions designed to elicit specific information about the victim, the crime scene, the weapon, Perkins' motive, and his actions during and after the shooting. This interaction was not a "conversation"; Perkins, the officer, and the informant were not equal participants in a free-ranging discussion, with each man offering his views on different topics. Rather, it was an interrogation: Perkins was subjected to express questioning likely to evoke an incriminating response.

Because Perkins was interrogated by police while he was in custody, *Miranda* required that the officer inform him of his rights. In rejecting that conclusion, the Court finds that "conversations" between undercover agents and suspects are devoid of the coercion inherent in station house interrogations conducted by law enforcement officials who openly represent the State. *Miranda* was not, however, concerned solely with police *coercion*. It dealt with *any* police tactics that may operate to compel a suspect in custody to make incriminating statements without full awareness of his constitutional rights. Thus, when a law enforcement agent structures a custodial interrogation so that a suspect feels compelled to reveal incriminating information, he must inform the suspect of his constitutional rights and give him an opportunity to decide whether or not to talk.

The compulsion proscribed by *Miranda* includes deception by the police. Although the Court did not find trickery by itself sufficient to constitute compulsion in *Hoffa v. United States,* 385 U.S. 293 (1966), the defendant in that case was not in custody. Perkins, however, was interrogated while incarcerated. As the Court has acknowledged in the Sixth Amendment context: "[T]he mere fact of custody imposes pressures on the accused; confinement may bring into play subtle influences that will make him particularly susceptible to the ploys of undercover Government agents."

Custody works to the State's advantage in obtaining incriminating information. The psychological pressures inherent in confinement increase the suspect's anxiety, making him likely to seek relief by talking with others. The inmate is thus more susceptible to efforts by undercover agents to elicit information from him. Similarly, where the suspect is incarcerated, the constant threat of physical danger peculiar to the prison environment may make him demonstrate his toughness to other inmates by recounting or inventing past violent acts. "Because the suspect's ability to select people with whom he can confide is completely within their control, the police have a unique opportunity to exploit the suspect's vulnerability. In short, the police can insure that if the pressures of confinement lead the suspect to confide in anyone, it will be a police agent." White, *Police Trickery in Inducing Confessions*, 127 U.PA.L.REV. 581, 605 (1979). In this case, the police deceptively took advantage of Perkins' psychological vulnerability by including him in a sham escape plot, a situation in which he would feel compelled to demonstrate his willingness to shoot a prison guard by revealing his past involvement in a murder.

Thus, the pressures unique to custody allow the police to use deceptive interrogation tactics to compel a suspect to make an incriminating statement. The compulsion is not eliminated by the suspect's ignorance of his interrogator's true identity. The Court therefore need not inquire past the bare facts of custody and interrogation to determine whether *Miranda* warnings are required.

* * *

The Court's holding today complicates a previously clear and straightforward doctrine. The Court opines that "[l]aw enforcement officers will have little difficulty putting into practice our holding that undercover agents need not give *Miranda* warnings to incarcerated suspects." Perhaps this prediction is true with respect to fact patterns virtually identical to the one before the Court today. But the outer boundaries of the exception created by the Court are by no means clear. Would *Miranda* be violated, for instance, if an undercover police officer beat a confession out of a suspect, but the suspect thought the officer was another prisoner who wanted the information for his own purposes?

Even if *Miranda,* as interpreted by the Court, would not permit such obviously compelled confessions, the ramifications of today's opinion are still disturbing. The exception carved out of the *Miranda* doctrine today may well result in a proliferation of departmental policies to encourage police officers to conduct interrogations of confined suspects through undercover agents, thereby circumventing the need to administer *Miranda* warnings. Indeed, if *Miranda* now requires a police officer to issue warnings only in those situations in which the suspect might feel compelled "to speak by the fear of reprisal for remaining silent or in the hope of more lenient treatment should he confess," presumably it allows custodial interrogation by an undercover officer posing as a member of the clergy or a suspect's defense attorney. Although such abhorrent tricks would play on a suspect's need to confide in a trusted adviser, neither would cause the suspect to "think that the listeners have official power over him." The Court's adoption of the "undercover agent" exception to the *Miranda* rule thus is necessarily also the adoption of a substantial loophole in our jurisprudence protecting suspects' Fifth Amendment rights.

Points for Discussion

1. Why were *Miranda* warnings not required here? Because the suspect was not in custody? That cannot be the answer, as the suspect was, at all relevant times, incarcerated. Because he was not subject to interrogation? Surely the direct questions quoted by the dissent constitute interrogation under any definition of the term. So how does the Court arrive at the conclusion that *Miranda* warnings were not required on these facts?

2. Justice Marshall, alone in dissent, argues that *Miranda* applies to this situation. Would he really have had Parisi Mirandize Perkins before asking him questions about prior crimes? If not, what does Justice Marshall imagine, exactly?

3. Why is this case not governed by *Kuhlmann v. Wilson's* holding that the use of an undercover agent to question (as opposed to just observe) violates a defendant's Sixth Amendment rights?

4. Do Justice Marshall's concerns about the reliability of Perkins' statements to Parisi go to those statements' admissibility or to the weight they ought to be afforded by the jury? If the latter, is his objection really one of constitutional dimension?

B. INVOCATION AND WAIVER

MICHIGAN V. MOSLEY

423 U.S. 96 (1975)

MR. JUSTICE STEWART delivered the opinion of the court.

The respondent, Richard Bert Mosley, was arrested in Detroit, Mich., in the early afternoon of April 8, 1971, in connection with robberies that had recently occurred at the Blue Goose Bar and the White Tower Restaurant on that city's lower east side. The arresting officer, Detective James Cowie of the Armed Robbery Section of the Detroit Police Department, was acting on a tip implicating Mosley and three other men in the robberies. After effecting the arrest, Detective Cowie brought Mosley to the Robbery, Breaking and Entering Bureau of the Police Department, located on the fourth floor of the departmental headquarters building. The officer advised Mosley of his rights under this Court's decision in *Miranda v. Arizona*, 384 U.S. 436, and had him read and sign the department's constitutional rights notification certificate. After filling out the necessary arrest papers, Cowie began questioning Mosley about the robbery of the White Tower Restaurant. When Mosley said he did not want to answer any questions about the robberies, Cowie promptly ceased the interrogation. The completion of the arrest papers and the questioning of Mosley together took approximately 20 minutes. At no time during the questioning did Mosley indicate a desire to consult with a lawyer, and there is no claim that the procedures followed to this point did not fully comply with the strictures of the *Miranda* opinion. Mosley was then taken to a ninth-floor cell block.

Shortly after 6 p.m., Detective Hill of the Detroit Police Department Homicide Bureau brought Mosley from the cell block to the fifth-floor office of the Homicide Bureau for questioning about the fatal shooting of a man named Leroy Williams. Williams had been killed on January 9, 1971, during a holdup attempt outside the 101 Ranch Bar in Detroit. Mosley had not been arrested on this charge or interrogated about it by Detective Cowie. Before questioning Mosley about this homicide, Detective Hill carefully advised him of his "*Miranda* rights." Mosley read the notification form both silently and aloud, and Detective Hill then read and explained the warnings to him and had him sign the form. Mosley at first denied any involvement in the Williams murder, but after the officer told him that Anthony Smith had confessed to participating in the slaying and had named him as the "shooter," Mosley made a statement implicating himself in the homicide. The interrogation by Detective Hill lasted approximately 15 minutes, and at no time during its course did Mosley ask to consult with a lawyer or indicate that he did not want to discuss the homicide. In short, there is no claim that the procedures followed during Detective Hill's interrogation of Mosley, standing alone, did not fully comply with the strictures of the *Miranda* opinion.

Mosley was subsequently charged in a one-count information with first-degree murder. Before the trial he moved to suppress his incriminating statement on a number of grounds, among them the claim that under the doctrine of the *Miranda* case it was constitutionally impermissible for Detective Hill to question him about the Williams murder after he had told Detective Cowie that he did not want to answer any questions about the robberies. The trial court denied the motion to suppress after an evidentiary hearing, and the incriminating statement was subsequently introduced in evidence against Mosley at his trial. The jury convicted Mosley of first-degree murder, and the court imposed a mandatory sentence of life imprisonment.

* * *

Neither party in the present case challenges the continuing validity of the *Miranda* decision, or of any of the so-called guidelines it established to protect what the Court there said was a person's constitutional privilege against compulsory self-incrimination. The issue in this case, rather, is whether the conduct of the Detroit police that led to Mosley's incriminating statement did in fact violate the *Miranda* "guidelines," so as to render the statement inadmissible in evidence against Mosley at his trial. Resolution of the question turns almost entirely on the interpretation of a single passage in the *Miranda* opinion, upon which the Michigan appellate court relied in finding a per se violation of *Miranda*:

> Once warnings have been given, the subsequent procedure is clear. If the individual indicates in any manner, at any time prior to or during questioning, that he wishes to remain silent, the interrogation must cease. At this point he has shown that he intends to exercise his Fifth Amendment privilege; any statement taken after the person invokes his privilege cannot be other than the product of compulsion, subtle or otherwise. Without the right to cut off questioning, the setting of in-custody interrogation operates on the individual to overcome free choice in producing a statement after the privilege has been once invoked.[7]

This passage states that "the interrogation must cease" when the person in custody indicates that "he wishes to remain silent." It does not state under what circumstances, if any, a resumption of questioning is

[7] The present case does not involve the procedures to be followed if the person in custody asks to consult with a lawyer, since Mosley made no such request at any time. . . .

permissible. The passage could be literally read to mean that a person who has invoked his "right to silence" can never again be subjected to custodial interrogation by any police officer at any time or place on any subject. Another possible construction of the passage would characterize "any statement taken after the person invokes his privilege" as "the product of compulsion" and would therefore mandate its exclusion from evidence, even if it were volunteered by the person in custody without any further interrogation whatever. Or the passage could be interpreted to require only the immediate cessation of questioning, and to permit a resumption of interrogation after a momentary respite.

It is evident that any of these possible literal interpretations would lead to absurd and unintended results. To permit the continuation of custodial interrogation after a momentary cessation would clearly frustrate the purposes of *Miranda* by allowing repeated rounds of questioning to undermine the will of the person being questioned. At the other extreme, a blanket prohibition against the taking of voluntary statements or a permanent immunity from further interrogation, regardless of the circumstances, would transform the *Miranda* safeguards into wholly irrational obstacles to legitimate police investigative activity, and deprive suspects of an opportunity to make informed and intelligent assessments of their interests. Clearly, therefore, neither this passage nor any other passage in the Miranda opinion can sensibly be read to create a per se proscription of indefinite duration upon any further questioning by any police officer on any subject, once the person in custody has indicated a desire to remain silent.

A reasonable and faithful interpretation of the *Miranda* opinion must rest on the intention of the Court in that case to adopt "fully effective means . . . to notify the person of his right of silence and to assure that the exercise of the right will be scrupulously honored . . . ." The critical safeguard identified in the passage at issue is a person's "right to cut off questioning." Through the exercise of his option to terminate questioning he can control the time at which questioning occurs, the subjects discussed, and the duration of the interrogation. The requirement that law enforcement authorities must respect a person's exercise of that option counteracts the coercive pressures of the custodial setting. We therefore conclude that the admissibility of statements obtained after the person in custody has decided to remain silent depends under *Miranda* on whether his "right to cut off questioning" was "scrupulously honored."

A review of the circumstances leading to Mosley's confession reveals that his "right to cut off questioning" was fully respected in this case. Before his initial interrogation, Mosley was carefully advised that he was under no obligation to answer any questions and could remain silent if he wished. He orally acknowledged that he understood the *Miranda* warnings and then signed a printed notification-of-rights form. When Mosley stated that he did not want to discuss the robberies, Detective Cowie immediately ceased the interrogation and did not try either to resume the questioning or in any way to persuade Mosley to reconsider his position. After an interval of more than two hours, Mosley was questioned by another police officer at another location about an unrelated holdup murder. He was given full and complete *Miranda* warnings at the outset of the second interrogation. He was thus reminded again that he could remain silent and could consult with a lawyer, and was carefully given a full and fair opportunity to exercise these options. The subsequent questioning did not undercut Mosley's previous decision not to answer Detective Cowie's inquiries. Detective Hill did not resume the interrogation about the White Tower Restaurant robbery or inquire about the Blue Goose Bar robbery, but instead focused exclusively on the Leroy Williams homicide, a crime different in nature and in time and place of occurrence from the robberies for which Mosley had been arrested and interrogated by Detective Cowie. Although it is not clear from the record how much Detective Hill knew about the earlier interrogation, his questioning of Mosley about an unrelated homicide was quite consistent with a reasonable interpretation of Mosley's earlier refusal to answer any questions about the robberies.

This is not a case, therefore, where the police failed to honor a decision of a person in custody to cut off questioning, either by refusing to discontinue the interrogation upon request or by persisting in repeated efforts to wear down his resistance and make him change his mind. In contrast to such practices, the police here immediately ceased the interrogation, resumed questioning only after the passage of a significant period of time and the provision of a fresh set of warnings, and restricted the second interrogation to a crime that had not been a subject of the earlier interrogation.

* * *

MR. JUSTICE WHITE, concurring.

I concur in the result and in much of the majority's reasoning. However, it appears to me that in an effort to make only a limited holding in this case, the majority has implied that some custodial confessions will be suppressed even though they follow an informed and voluntary waiver of the defendant's rights. The majority seems to say that a statement obtained within some unspecified time after an assertion by an individual of his "right to silence" is always inadmissible, even if it was the result of an informed and voluntary decision following, for example, a disclosure to such an individual of a piece of information bearing on his waiver decision which the police had failed to give him prior to his assertion of the privilege but which they gave him immediately thereafter. Indeed, the majority characterizes as "absurd" any contrary rule. I disagree. I do not think the majority's conclusion is compelled by *Miranda v. Arizona*, 384 U.S. 436 (1966), and I suspect that in the final analysis the majority will adopt voluntariness as the standard by which to judge the waiver of the right to silence by a properly informed defendant. I think the Court should say so now.

* * *

In justifying the implication that questioning must inevitably cease for some unspecified period of time following an exercise of the "right to silence," the majority says only that such a requirement would be necessary to avoid "undermining" "the will of the person being questioned." Yet, surely a waiver of the "right to silence" obtained by "undermining the will" of the person being questioned would be considered an involuntary waiver. Thus, in order to achieve the majority's only stated purpose, it is sufficient to exclude all confessions which are the result of involuntary waivers. To exclude any others is to deprive the factfinding process of highly probative information for no reason at all. The "repeated rounds" of questioning following an assertion of the privilege, which the majority is worried about, would, of course, count heavily against the State in any determination of voluntariness particularly if no reason (such as new facts communicated to the accused or a new incident being inquired about) appeared for repeated questioning. There is no reason, however, to rob the accused of the choice to answer questions voluntarily for some unspecified period of time following his own previous contrary decision. The Court should now so state.

MR. JUSTICE BRENNAN, with whom MR. JUSTICE MARSHALL joins, dissenting.

* * *

I agree that *Miranda* is not to be read, on the one hand, to impose an absolute ban on resumption of questioning "at any time or place on any subject," or on the other hand, "to permit a resumption of interrogation after a momentary respite." But this surely cannot justify adoption of a vague and ineffective procedural standard that falls somewhere between those absurd extremes, for *Miranda* in flat and unambiguous terms requires that questioning "cease" when a suspect exercises the right to remain silent. *Miranda*'s terms, however, are not so uncompromising as to preclude the fashioning of guidelines to govern this case. Those guidelines must, of course, necessarily be sensitive to the reality that "(a)s a practical matter, the compulsion to speak in the isolated setting of the police station may well be greater than in courts or other official investigations, where there are often impartial observers to guard against intimidation or trickery."

The fashioning of guidelines for this case is an easy task. Adequate procedures are readily available. Michigan law requires that the suspect be arraigned before a judicial officer "without unnecessary delay," certainly not a burdensome requirement. Alternatively, a requirement that resumption of questioning should await appointment and arrival of counsel for the suspect would be an acceptable and readily satisfied precondition to resumption. *Miranda* expressly held that "(t) he presence of counsel . . . would be the adequate protective device necessary to make the process of police interrogation conform to the dictates of the privilege (against self-incrimination)." The Court expediently bypasses this alternative in its search for circumstances where renewed questioning would be permissible.

* * *

These procedures would be wholly consistent with the Court's rejection of a "per se proscription of indefinite duration," a rejection to which I fully subscribe. Today's decision, however, virtually empties *Miranda* of principle, for plainly the decision encourages police asked to cease interrogation to continue the suspect's detention until the police station's coercive atmosphere does its work and the suspect responds to resumed questioning. Today's rejection of that reality of life contrasts sharply with the Court's acceptance only two years ago that "(i)n *Miranda* the Court found that the techniques of police questioning and the nature of custodial surroundings produce an inherently coercive situation." *Schneckloth v. Bustamonte*, 412 U.S. 218, 247 (1973). I can only conclude that today's decision signals rejection of *Miranda*'s basic premise.

* * *

Points for Discussion

1. The Court states in *Mosley* that the officers were permitted to re-Mirandize the defendant and obtain a waiver and confession from him, even though he had asserted his right to remain silent. Is that finding consistent with *Miranda*'s requirement that when the defendant invokes his rights, questioning must cease?

2. The Court notes in footnote 7 that it does not decide whether the same rule—scrupulously honoring the defendant's invocation—would apply to an invocation of the right to counsel. In the next case, the Court considers that very question.

EDWARDS V. ARIZONA

451 U.S. 477 (1981)

JUSTICE WHITE delivered the opinion of the court.

* * *

I

On January 19, 1976, a sworn complaint was filed against Edwards in Arizona state court charging him with robbery, burglary, and first-degree murder. An arrest warrant was issued pursuant to the complaint, and

Edwards was arrested at his home later that same day. At the police station, he was informed of his rights as required by *Miranda v. Arizona*, 384 U.S. 436 (1966). Petitioner stated that he understood his rights, and was willing to submit to questioning. After being told that another suspect already in custody had implicated him in the crime, Edwards denied involvement and gave a taped statement presenting an alibi defense. He then sought to "make a deal." The interrogating officer told him that he wanted a statement, but that he did not have the authority to negotiate a deal. The officer provided Edwards with the telephone number of a county attorney. Petitioner made the call, but hung up after a few moments. Edwards then said: "I want an attorney before making a deal." At that point, questioning ceased and Edwards was taken to county jail.

At 9:15 the next morning, two detectives, colleagues of the officer who had interrogated Edwards the previous night, came to the jail and asked to see Edwards. When the detention officer informed Edwards that the detectives wished to speak with him, he replied that he did not want to talk to anyone. The guard told him that "he had" to talk and then took him to meet with the detectives. The officers identified themselves, stated they wanted to talk to him, and informed him of his *Miranda* rights. Edwards was willing to talk, but he first wanted to hear the taped statement of the alleged accomplice who had implicated him. After listening to the tape for several minutes, petitioner said that he would make a statement so long as it was not tape-recorded. The detectives informed him that the recording was irrelevant since they could testify in court concerning whatever he said. Edwards replied: "I'll tell you anything you want to know, but I don't want it on tape." He thereupon implicated himself in the crime.

II

In *Miranda v. Arizona*, the Court determined that the Fifth and Fourteenth Amendments' prohibition against compelled self-incrimination required that custodial interrogation be preceded by advice to the putative defendant that he has the right to remain silent and also the right to the presence of an attorney. The Court also indicated the procedures to be followed subsequent to the warnings. If the accused indicates that he wishes to remain silent, "the interrogation must cease." If he requests counsel, "the interrogation must cease until an attorney is present."

Miranda thus declared that an accused has a Fifth and Fourteenth Amendment right to have counsel present during custodial interrogation. Here, the critical facts as found by the Arizona Supreme Court are that Edwards asserted his right to counsel and his right to remain silent on January 19, but that the police, without furnishing him counsel, returned the next morning to confront him and as a result of the meeting secured incriminating oral admissions. Contrary to the holdings of the state courts, Edwards insists that having exercised his right on the 19th to have counsel present during interrogation, he did not validly waive that right on the 20th. For the following reasons, we agree.

First, the Arizona Supreme Court applied an erroneous standard for determining waiver where the accused has specifically invoked his right to counsel. It is reasonably clear under our cases that waivers of counsel must not only be voluntary, but must also constitute a knowing and intelligent relinquishment or abandonment of a known right or privilege, a matter which depends in each case "upon the particular facts and circumstances surrounding that case, including the background, experience, and conduct of the accused."

* * *

In referring to the necessity to find Edwards' confession knowing and intelligent, the State Supreme Court cited *Schneckloth v. Bustamonte*, 412 U.S. 218, 226 (1973). Yet, it is clear that *Schneckloth* does not control the issue presented in this case. The issue in *Schneckloth* was under what conditions an individual could be found to have consented to a search and thereby waived his Fourth Amendment rights. The Court declined to impose the "intentional relinquishment or abandonment of a known right or privilege" standard and required only that the consent be voluntary under the totality of the circumstances. The Court specifically noted that the right to counsel was a prime example of those rights requiring the special protection of the knowing and intelligent waiver standard but held that "[t]he considerations that informed the Court's holding in *Miranda* are simply inapplicable in the present case." *Schneckloth* itself thus emphasized that the voluntariness of a consent or an admission on the one hand, and a knowing and intelligent waiver on the other, are discrete inquiries. Here, however sound the conclusion of the state courts as to the voluntariness of Edwards' admission may be, neither the trial court nor the Arizona Supreme Court undertook to focus on whether Edwards understood his right to counsel and intelligently and knowingly relinquished it. It is thus apparent that the decision below misunderstood the requirement for finding a valid waiver of the right to counsel, once invoked.

Second, although we have held that after initially being advised of his *Miranda* rights, the accused may himself validly waive his rights and respond to interrogation, the Court has strongly indicated that additional safeguards are necessary when the accused asks for counsel; and we now hold that when an accused has invoked his right to have counsel present during custodial interrogation, a valid waiver of that right cannot be established by showing only that he responded to further police-initiated custodial interrogation even if he has been advised of his rights. We further hold that an accused, such as Edwards, having expressed his desire to deal with the police only through counsel, is not subject to further interrogation by the authorities until counsel has been made available to him, unless the accused himself initiates further communication, exchanges, or conversations with the police.

* * *

In concluding that the fruits of the interrogation initiated by the police on January 20 could not be used against Edwards, we do not hold or imply that Edwards was powerless to countermand his election or that the authorities could in no event use any incriminating statements made by Edwards prior to his having access to counsel. Had Edwards initiated the meeting on January 20, nothing in the Fifth and Fourteenth Amendments would prohibit the police from merely listening to his voluntary, volunteered statements and using them against him at the trial. The Fifth Amendment right identified in *Miranda* is the right to have counsel present at any custodial interrogation. Absent such interrogation, there would have been no infringement of the right that Edwards invoked and there would be no occasion to determine whether there had been a valid waiver. *Rhode Island v. Innis* makes this sufficiently clear.[9]

* * *

But this is not what the facts of this case show. Here, the officers conducting the interrogation on the evening of January 19 ceased interrogation when Edwards requested counsel as he had been advised he had the right to do. The Arizona Supreme Court was of the opinion that this was a sufficient invocation of his *Miranda* rights, and we are in accord. It is also clear that without making counsel available to Edwards, the police returned to him the next day. This was not at his suggestion or request. Indeed, Edwards informed the detention officer that he did not want to talk to anyone. At the meeting, the detectives told Edwards that they wanted to talk to him and again advised him of his *Miranda* rights. Edwards stated that he would talk, but what prompted this action does not appear. He listened at his own request to part of the taped statement made by one of his alleged accomplices and then made an incriminating statement, which was used against him at his trial. We think it is clear that Edwards was subjected to custodial interrogation on January 20 within the meaning of *Rhode Island v. Innis*, and that this occurred at the instance of the authorities. His statement made without having had access to counsel, did not amount to a valid waiver and hence was inadmissible.

CHIEF JUSTICE BURGER, concurring in the judgment.

I concur only in the judgment because I do not agree that either any constitutional standard or the holding of *Miranda v. Arizona*, 384 U.S. 436

[9] If, as frequently would occur in the course of a meeting initiated by the accused, the conversation is not wholly one-sided, it is likely that the officers will say or do something that clearly would be "interrogation." In that event, the question would be whether a valid waiver of the right to counsel and the right to silence had occurred, that is, whether the purported waiver was knowing and intelligent and found to be so under the totality of the circumstances, including the necessary fact that the accused, not the police, reopened the dialogue with the authorities.

(1966)—as distinguished from its dicta—calls for a special rule as to how an accused in custody may waive the right to be free from interrogation. The extraordinary protections afforded a person in custody suspected of criminal conduct are not without a valid basis, but as with all "good" things they can be carried too far. The notion that any "prompting" of a person in custody is somehow evil *per se* has been rejected. *Rhode Island v. Innis*, 446 U.S. 291 (1980). For me, the inquiry in this setting is whether resumption of interrogation is a result of a voluntary waiver, and that inquiry should be resolved under the traditional standards established in *Johnson v. Zerbst*, 304 U.S. 458, 464 (1938):

> A waiver is ordinarily an intentional relinquishment or abandonment of a known right or privilege. The determination of whether there has been an intelligent waiver . . . must depend, in each case, upon the particular facts and circumstances surrounding that case, including the background, experience, and conduct of the accused.

In this case, the Supreme Court of Arizona described the situation as follows:

> When the detention officer told Edwards that the detectives were there to see him, he told the officer that he did not wish to speak to anyone. The officer told him *that he had to.*

This is enough for me, and on this record the Supreme Court of Arizona erred in holding that the resumption of interrogation was the product of a voluntary waiver, such as I found to be the situation in both *Innis,* 446 U.S., at 304 (concurring opinion), and *Brewer v. Williams*, 430 U.S. 387, 417–418 (1977) (dissenting opinion).

JUSTICE POWELL, with whom JUSTICE REHNQUIST joins, concurring in the result.

Although I agree that the judgment of the Arizona Supreme Court must be reversed, I do not join the Court's opinion because I am not sure what it means.

* * *

I have thought it settled law, as these cases tell us, that one accused of crime may waive *any* of the constitutional safeguards—including the right to remain silent, to jury trial, to call witnesses, to cross-examine one's accusers, to testify in one's own behalf, and—of course—to have counsel. Whatever the right, the standard for waiver is whether the actor fully understands the right in question and voluntarily intends to relinquish it.

* * *

In view of the emphasis placed on "initiation," I find the Court's opinion unclear. If read to create a new *per se* rule, requiring a threshold inquiry as to precisely who opened any conversation between an accused and state officials, I cannot agree. I would not superimpose a new element of proof on the established doctrine of waiver of counsel.

* * *

In sum, once warnings have been given and the right to counsel has been invoked, the relevant inquiry—whether the suspect now desires to talk to police without counsel—is a question of fact to be determined in light of all of the circumstances. Who "initiated" a conversation may be relevant to the question of waiver, but it is not the *sine qua non* to the inquiry. The ultimate question is whether there was a free and knowing waiver of counsel before interrogation commenced.

* * *

Points for Discussion

1. Why does the Court conclude that an invocation of the right to counsel should be treated differently for *Miranda* purposes than an invocation of the right to remain silent? Is there any language in *Miranda* that would support such a distinction?

2. Justice Powell argues in his concurrence that who initiated a post-invocation discussion should be relevant to, but not dispositive of, the validity of a waiver. How convincing do you find his argument? Why did the Court reject this flexible approach in favor of a bright line rule?

MARYLAND V. SHATZER

559 U.S. 98 (2010)

JUSTICE SCALIA delivered the opinion of the court.

We consider whether a break in custody ends the presumption of involuntariness established in *Edwards v. Arizona,* 451 U.S. 477 (1981).

I

In August 2003, a social worker assigned to the Child Advocacy Center in the Criminal Investigation Division of the Hagerstown Police Department referred to the department allegations that respondent Michael Shatzer, Sr., had sexually abused his 3-year-old son. At that time, Shatzer was incarcerated at the Maryland Correctional Institution-Hagerstown, serving a sentence for an unrelated child-sexual-abuse offense. Detective Shane Blankenship was assigned to the investigation and interviewed Shatzer at the correctional institution on August 7, 2003. Before asking any questions, Blankenship reviewed Shatzer's *Miranda* rights with him, and obtained a written waiver of those rights. When Blankenship explained that he was there to question Shatzer about sexually abusing his son, Shatzer expressed confusion—he had thought

Blankenship was an attorney there to discuss the prior crime for which he was incarcerated. Blankenship clarified the purpose of his visit, and Shatzer declined to speak without an attorney. Accordingly, Blankenship ended the interview, and Shatzer was released back into the general prison population. Shortly thereafter, Blankenship closed the investigation.

Two years and six months later, the same social worker referred more specific allegations to the department about the same incident involving Shatzer. Detective Paul Hoover, from the same division, was assigned to the investigation. He and the social worker interviewed the victim, then eight years old, who described the incident in more detail. With this new information in hand, on March 2, 2006, they went to the Roxbury Correctional Institute, to which Shatzer had since been transferred, and interviewed Shatzer in a maintenance room outfitted with a desk and three chairs. Hoover explained that he wanted to ask Shatzer about the alleged incident involving Shatzer's son. Shatzer was surprised because he thought that the investigation had been closed, but Hoover explained they had opened a new file. Hoover then read Shatzer his *Miranda* rights and obtained a written waiver on a standard department form.

Hoover interrogated Shatzer about the incident for approximately 30 minutes. Shatzer denied ordering his son to perform fellatio on him, but admitted to masturbating in front of his son from a distance of less than three feet. Before the interview ended, Shatzer agreed to Hoover's request that he submit to a polygraph examination. At no point during the interrogation did Shatzer request to speak with an attorney or refer to his prior refusal to answer questions without one.

Five days later, on March 7, 2006, Hoover and another detective met with Shatzer at the correctional facility to administer the polygraph examination. After reading Shatzer his *Miranda* rights and obtaining a written waiver, the other detective administered the test and concluded that Shatzer had failed. When the detectives then questioned Shatzer, he became upset, started to cry, and incriminated himself by saying, "I didn't force him. I didn't force him." After making this inculpatory statement, Shatzer requested an attorney, and Hoover promptly ended the interrogation.

* * *

II

* * *

The rationale of *Edwards* is that once a suspect indicates that "he is not capable of undergoing [custodial] questioning without advice of counsel," "any subsequent waiver that has come at the authorities' behest, and not at the suspect's own instigation, is itself the product of the 'inherently compelling pressures' and not the purely voluntary choice of the suspect." *Arizona v. Roberson,* 486 U.S. 675, 681 (1988). Under this rule, a voluntary *Miranda* waiver is sufficient at the time of an initial attempted interrogation to protect a suspect's right to have counsel present, but it is not sufficient at the time of subsequent attempts if the suspect initially requested the presence of counsel. The implicit assumption, of course, is that the subsequent requests for interrogation pose a significantly greater risk of coercion. That increased risk results not only from the police's persistence in trying to get the suspect to talk, but also from the continued pressure that begins when the individual is taken into custody as a suspect and sought to be interrogated—pressure likely to "increase as custody is prolonged," *Minnick v. Mississippi,* 498 U.S. 146, 153 (1990). The *Edwards* presumption of involuntariness ensures that police will not take advantage of the mounting coercive pressures of "prolonged police custody," by repeatedly attempting to question a suspect who previously requested counsel until the suspect is "badgered into submission."

We have frequently emphasized that the *Edwards* rule is not a constitutional mandate, but judicially prescribed prophylaxis. Because *Edwards* is "our rule, not a constitutional command," "it is our obligation to justify its expansion." Lower courts have uniformly held that a break in custody ends the *Edwards* presumption but we have previously addressed the issue only in dicta.

A judicially crafted rule is "justified only by reference to its prophylactic purpose," and applies only where its benefits outweigh its costs. We begin with the benefits. *Edwards'* presumption of involuntariness has the incidental effect of "conserv[ing] judicial resources which would otherwise be expended in making difficult determinations of voluntariness." Its fundamental purpose, however, is to "[p]reserv[e] the integrity of an accused's choice to communicate with police only through counsel," by "prevent[ing] police from badgering a defendant into waiving his previously asserted *Miranda* rights." Thus, the benefits of the rule are measured by the number of coerced confessions it suppresses that otherwise would have been admitted.

It is easy to believe that a suspect may be coerced or badgered into abandoning his earlier refusal to be questioned without counsel in the paradigm *Edwards* case. That is a case in which the suspect has been arrested for a particular crime and is held in uninterrupted pretrial custody while that crime is being actively investigated. After the initial interrogation, and up to and including the second one, he remains cut off from his normal life and companions, "thrust into" and isolated in an "unfamiliar," "police-dominated atmosphere," where his captors "appear to control [his] fate." That was the situation confronted by the suspects in *Edwards, Roberson,* and *Minnick,* the three cases in which we have held the *Edwards* rule applicable. Edwards was arrested pursuant to a warrant and taken to a police station, where he was interrogated until he requested counsel. The officer ended the interrogation and took him to the county jail, but at 9:15 the next morning, two of the officer's colleagues reinterrogated Edwards at the jail. Roberson was arrested "at the scene of a just-completed burglary" and interrogated there until he requested a lawyer. A different officer interrogated him three days later while he "was still in custody pursuant to the arrest." Minnick was arrested by local police and taken to the San Diego jail, where two FBI agents interrogated him the next morning until he requested counsel. Two days later a Mississippi Deputy Sheriff reinterrogated him at the jail. None of these suspects regained a sense of control or normalcy after they were initially taken into custody for the crime under investigation.

When, unlike what happened in these three cases, a suspect has been released from his pretrial custody and has returned to his normal life for some time before the later attempted interrogation, there is little reason to think that his change of heart regarding interrogation without counsel has been coerced. He has no longer been isolated. He has likely been able to seek advice from an attorney, family members, and friends. And he knows from his earlier experience that he need only demand counsel to bring the interrogation to a halt; and that investigative custody does not last indefinitely. In these circumstances, it is far fetched to think that a police officer's asking the suspect whether he would like to waive his *Miranda* rights will any more "wear down the accused," than did the first such request at the original attempted interrogation—which is of course not deemed coercive. His change of heart is less likely attributable to "badgering" than it is to the fact that further deliberation in familiar surroundings has caused him to believe (rightly or wrongly) that cooperating with the investigation is in his interest. Uncritical extension of *Edwards* to this situation would not significantly increase the number of genuinely coerced confessions excluded. The "justification for a conclusive presumption disappears when application of the presumption will not reach the correct result most of the time."

At the same time that extending the *Edwards* rule yields diminished benefits, extending the rule also increases its costs: the in-fact voluntary confessions it excludes from trial, and the voluntary confessions it deters law enforcement officers from even trying to obtain. Voluntary confessions are not merely "a proper element in law enforcement," they are an "unmitigated good," " 'essential to society's compelling interest in finding, convicting, and punishing those who violate the law.' "

The only logical endpoint of *Edwards* disability is termination of *Miranda* custody and any of its lingering effects. Without that limitation—and barring some purely arbitrary time-limit[4]—every *Edwards* prohibition of custodial interrogation of a particular suspect would be eternal. The

[4] The State's alternative argument in the present case is that the substantial lapse in time between the 2003 and 2006 attempts at interrogation independently ended the *Edwards* presumption. Our disposition makes it unnecessary to address that argument.

prohibition applies, of course, when the subsequent interrogation pertains to a different crime, when it is conducted by a different law enforcement authority, and even when the suspect has met with an attorney after the first interrogation. And it not only prevents questioning *ex ante*; it would render invalid *ex post,* confessions invited and obtained from suspects who (unbeknownst to the interrogators) have acquired *Edwards* immunity previously in connection with any offense in any jurisdiction. In a country that harbors a large number of repeat offenders, this consequence is disastrous.

We conclude that such an extension of *Edwards* is not justified; we have opened its "protective umbrella," far enough. The protections offered by *Miranda,* which we have deemed sufficient to ensure that the police respect the suspect's desire to have an attorney present the first time police interrogate him, adequately ensure that result when a suspect who initially requested counsel is reinterrogated after a break in custody that is of sufficient duration to dissipate its coercive effects.

If Shatzer's return to the general prison population qualified as a break in custody (a question we address in Part III, *infra*), there is no doubt that it lasted long enough (2½ years) to meet that durational requirement. But what about a break that has lasted only one year? Or only one week? It is impractical to leave the answer to that question for clarification in future case-by-case adjudication; law enforcement officers need to know, with certainty and beforehand, when renewed interrogation is lawful. And while it is certainly unusual for this Court to set forth precise time limits governing police action, it is not unheard-of. In *County of Riverside v. McLaughlin,* 500 U.S. 44 (1991), we specified 48 hours as the time within which the police must comply with the requirement of *Gerstein v. Pugh,* 420 U.S. 103 (1975), that a person arrested without a warrant be brought before a magistrate to establish probable cause for continued detention.

Like *McLaughlin,* this is a case in which the requisite police action (there, presentation to a magistrate; here, abstention from further interrogation) has not been prescribed by statute but has been established by opinion of this Court. We think it appropriate to specify a period of time to avoid the consequence that continuation of the *Edwards* presumption "will not reach the correct result most of the time." It seems to us that period is 14 days. That provides plenty of time for the suspect to get reacclimated to his normal life, to consult with friends and counsel, and to shake off any residual coercive effects of his prior custody.

The 14-day limitation meets Shatzer's concern that a break-in-custody rule lends itself to police abuse. He envisions that once a suspect invokes his *Miranda* right to counsel, the police will release the suspect briefly (to end the *Edwards* presumption) and then promptly bring him back into custody for reinterrogation. But once the suspect has been out of custody long enough (14 days) to eliminate its coercive effect, there will be nothing to gain by such gamesmanship—nothing, that is, except the entirely appropriate gain of being able to interrogate a suspect who has made a valid waiver of his *Miranda* rights.[7]

* * *

III

The facts of this case present an additional issue. No one questions that Shatzer was in custody for *Miranda* purposes during the interviews with Detective Blankenship in 2003 and Detective Hoover in 2006. Likewise, no one questions that Shatzer triggered the *Edwards* protections when, according to Detective Blankenship's notes of the 2003 interview, he stated that "he would not talk about this case without having an attorney present." After the 2003 interview, Shatzer was released back into the general prison population where he was serving an unrelated sentence. The issue is whether that constitutes a break in *Miranda* custody.

We have never decided whether incarceration constitutes custody for *Miranda* purposes, and have indeed explicitly declined to address the issue. Whether it does depends upon whether it exerts the coercive pressure that *Miranda* was designed to guard against—the "danger of coercion [that] results from the *interaction* of custody and official interrogation." To determine whether a suspect was in *Miranda* custody we have asked whether "there is a 'formal arrest or restraint on freedom of movement' of the degree associated with a formal arrest." *New York v. Quarles,* 467 U.S. 649, 655 (1984). This test, no doubt, is satisfied by all forms of incarceration. Our cases make clear, however, that the freedom-of-movement test identifies only a necessary and not a sufficient condition for *Miranda* custody. We have declined to accord it "talismanic power," because *Miranda* is to be enforced "only in those types of situations in which the concerns that powered the decision are implicated." Thus, the temporary and relatively nonthreatening detention involved in a traffic stop or *Terry* stop does not constitute *Miranda* custody.

Here, we are addressing the interim period during which a suspect was not interrogated, but was subject to a baseline set of restraints imposed pursuant to a prior conviction. Without minimizing the harsh realities of incarceration, we think lawful imprisonment imposed upon conviction of a crime does not create the coercive pressures identified in *Miranda*.

Interrogated suspects who have previously been convicted of crime live in prison. When they are released back into the general prison population, they return to their accustomed surroundings and daily routine—they

---

[7] A defendant who experiences a 14-day break in custody after invoking the *Miranda* right to counsel is not left without protection. *Edwards* establishes a *presumption* that a suspect's waiver of *Miranda* rights is involuntary. Even without this "second layer of prophylaxis," *McNeil v. Wisconsin,* 501 U.S. 171, 176 (1991), a defendant is still free to claim the prophylactic protection of *Miranda*—arguing that his waiver of *Miranda* rights was in fact involuntary under *Johnson v. Zerbst,* 304 U.S. 458 (1938).

regain the degree of control they had over their lives prior to the interrogation. Sentenced prisoners, in contrast to the *Miranda* paradigm, are not isolated with their accusers. They live among other inmates, guards, and workers, and often can receive visitors and communicate with people on the outside by mail or telephone.

Their detention, moreover, is relatively disconnected from their prior unwillingness to cooperate in an investigation. The former interrogator has no power to increase the duration of incarceration, which was determined at sentencing.[8] And even where the possibility of parole exists, the former interrogator has no apparent power to decrease the time served. This is in stark contrast to the circumstances faced by the defendants in *Edwards, Roberson,* and *Minnick,* whose continued detention as suspects rested with those controlling their interrogation, and who confronted the uncertainties of what final charges they would face, whether they would be convicted, and what sentence they would receive.

Shatzer's experience illustrates the vast differences between *Miranda* custody and incarceration pursuant to conviction. At the time of the 2003 attempted interrogation, Shatzer was already serving a sentence for a prior conviction. After that, he returned to the general prison population in the Maryland Correctional Institution-Hagerstown and was later transferred, for unrelated reasons, down the street to the Roxbury Correctional Institute. Both are medium-security state correctional facilities. Inmates in these facilities generally can visit the library each week; have regular exercise and recreation periods; can participate in basic adult education and occupational training; are able to send and receive mail; and are allowed to receive visitors twice a week. His continued detention after the 2003 interrogation did not depend on what he said (or did not say) to Detective Blankenship, and he has not alleged that he was placed in a higher level of security or faced any continuing restraints as a result of the 2003 interrogation. The "inherently compelling pressures" of custodial interrogation ended when he returned to his normal life.

* * *

JUSTICE THOMAS, concurring in part and concurring in the judgment.

* * *

Our precedents insist that judicially created prophylactic rules like those in *Edwards* and *Miranda v. Arizona,* 384 U.S. 436 (1966), maintain "the closest possible fit" between the rule and the Fifth Amendment

---

[8] We distinguish the duration of incarceration from the duration of what might be termed interrogative custody. When a prisoner is removed from the general prison population and taken to a separate location for questioning, the duration of *that separation* is assuredly dependent upon his interrogators. For which reason once he has asserted a refusal to speak without assistance of counsel *Edwards* prevents any efforts to get him to change his mind during that interrogative custody.

interests they seek to protect. *United States v. Patane,* 542 U.S. 630, 640–641 (2004) (plurality opinion). The Court's 14-day rule does not satisfy this test. The Court relates its 14-day rule to the Fifth Amendment simply by asserting that 14 days between release and recapture should provide "plenty of time for the suspect . . . to shake off any residual coercive effects of his prior custody."

This *ipse dixit* does not explain why extending the *Edwards* presumption for 14 days following a break in custody—as opposed to 0, 10, or 100 days—provides the "closest possible fit" with the Self-Incrimination Clause. Nor does it explain how the benefits of a prophylactic 14-day rule (either on its own terms or compared with other possible rules) "outweigh its costs" (which would include the loss of law enforcement information as well as the exclusion of confessions that are in fact voluntary).

To be sure, the Court's rule has the benefit of providing a bright line. But bright-line rules are not necessary to prevent Fifth Amendment violations, as the Court has made clear when refusing to adopt such rules in cases involving other *Miranda* rights. And an otherwise arbitrary rule is not justifiable merely because it gives clear instruction to law enforcement officers.

As the Court concedes, "clarity and certainty are not goals in themselves. They are valuable only when they reasonably further the achievement of some substantive end—here, the exclusion of compelled confessions" that the Fifth Amendment prohibits. The Court's arbitrary 14-day rule fails this test, even under the relatively permissive criteria set forth in our precedents. Accordingly, I do not join that portion of the Court's opinion.

JUSTICE STEVENS, concurring in the judgment.

* * *

II

The Court never explains why its rule cannot depend on, in addition to a break in custody and passage of time, a concrete event or state of affairs, such as the police having honored their commitment to provide counsel. Instead, the Court simply decides to create a time-based rule, and in so doing, disregards much of the analysis upon which *Edwards* and subsequent decisions were based. "[T]he assertion of the right to counsel" "[i]s a significant event." As the Court today acknowledges, the right to counsel, like the right to remain silent, is one that police may "coerc[e] or badge[r]," a suspect into abandoning. However, as discussed above, the Court ignores the effects not of badgering but of reinterrogating a suspect who took the police at their word that he need not answer questions without an attorney present. The Court, moreover, ignores that when a suspect asks for counsel, until his request is answered, there are still the same "inherently compelling" pressures of custodial interrogation on which the *Miranda* line of cases is based, and that the concern about compulsion is especially serious for a detainee who has requested a lawyer, an act that signals his "inability to cope with the pressures of custodial interrogation."

Instead of deferring to these well-settled understandings of the *Edwards* rule, the Court engages in its own speculation that a 14-day break in custody eliminates the compulsion that animated *Edwards*. But its opinion gives no strong basis for believing that this is the case. A 14-day break in custody does not eliminate the rationale for the initial *Edwards* rule: The detainee has been told that he may remain silent and speak only through a lawyer and that if he cannot afford an attorney, one will be provided for him. He has asked for a lawyer. He does not have one. He is in custody. And police are still questioning him. A 14-day break in custody does not change the fact that custodial interrogation is inherently compelling. It is unlikely to change the fact that a detainee "considers himself unable to deal with the pressures of custodial interrogation without legal assistance." And in some instances, a 14-day break in custody may make matters worse "[w]hen a suspect understands his (expressed) wishes to have been ignored" and thus "may well see further objection as futile and confession (true or not) as the only way to end his interrogation."

The Court ignores these understandings from the *Edwards* line of cases and instead speculates that if a suspect is reinterrogated and eventually talks, it must be that "further deliberation in familiar surroundings has caused him to believe (rightly or wrongly) that cooperating with the investigation is in his interest." But it is not apparent why that is the case. The answer, we are told, is that once a suspect has been out of *Miranda* custody for 14 days, "[h]e has likely been able to seek advice from an attorney, family members, and friends." This speculation, however, is overconfident and only questionably relevant. As a factual matter, we do not know whether the defendant has been able to seek advice: First of all, suspects are told that if they cannot afford a lawyer, one will be provided for them. Yet under the majority's rule, an indigent suspect who took the police at their word when he asked for a lawyer will nonetheless be assumed to have "been able to seek advice from an attorney." Second, even suspects who are not indigent cannot necessarily access legal advice (or social advice as the Court presumes) within 14 days. Third, suspects may not realize that they *need* to seek advice from an attorney. Unless police warn suspects that the interrogation will resume in 14 days, why contact a lawyer? When a suspect is let go, he may assume that the police were satisfied. In any event, it is not apparent why interim advice matters. In *Minnick v. Mississippi,* 498 U.S. 146, 153 (1990), we held that it is not sufficient that a detainee happened to speak at some point with a lawyer. If the actual interim advice of an attorney is not sufficient, the hypothetical, interim advice of "an attorney, family members, and friends," is not enough.

The many problems with the Court's new rule are exacerbated in the very situation in this case: a suspect who is in prison. Even if, as the Court assumes, a trip to one's home significantly changes the *Edwards* calculus, a trip to one's prison cell is not the same. A prisoner's freedom is severely limited, and his entire life remains subject to government control. Such an environment is not conducive to "shak[ing] off any residual coercive effects of his prior custody." Nor can a prisoner easily "seek advice from an attorney, family members, and friends," especially not within 14 days; prisoners are frequently subject to restrictions on communications. Nor, in most cases, can he live comfortably knowing that he cannot be badgered by police; prison is not like a normal situation in which a suspect "is in control, and need only shut his door or walk away to avoid police badgering." Indeed, for a person whose every move is controlled by the State, it is likely that "his sense of dependence on, and trust in, counsel as the guardian of his interests in dealing with government officials intensified." The Court ignores these realities of prison, and instead rests its argument on the supposition that a prisoner's "detention . . . is relatively disconnected from their prior unwillingness to cooperate in an investigation." But that is not necessarily the case. Prisoners are uniquely vulnerable to the officials who control every aspect of their lives; prison guards may not look kindly upon a prisoner who refuses to cooperate with police. And cooperation frequently is relevant to whether the prisoner can obtain parole. Moreover, even if it is true as a factual matter that a prisoner's fate is not controlled by the police who come to interrogate him, how is the prisoner supposed to know that? As the Court itself admits, compulsion is likely when a suspect's "captors appear to control [his] fate," (internal quotation marks omitted). But when a guard informs a suspect that he must go speak with police, it will "appear" to the prisoner that the guard and police are not independent. "Questioning by captors, who *appear* to control the suspect's fate, may create mutually reinforcing pressures that the Court has assumed will weaken the suspect's will."

III

Because, at the very least, we do not know whether Shatzer could obtain a lawyer, and thus would have felt that police had lied about providing one, I cannot join the Court's opinion. I concur in today's judgment, however, on another ground: Even if Shatzer could not consult a lawyer and the police never provided him one, the 2½-year break in custody is a basis for treating the second interrogation as no more coercive than the first. Neither a break in custody nor the passage of time has an inherent, curative power. But certain things change over time. An indigent suspect who took police at their word that they would provide an attorney probably will feel that he has "been denied the counsel he has clearly requested," when police begin to question him, without a lawyer, only 14 days later. But, when a suspect has been left alone for a significant period of time, he is not as likely to draw such conclusions when the police interrogate him again. It is concededly "impossible to determine with precision" where to draw such a line. In the case before us, however, the suspect was returned to the general prison population for 2½ years. I am convinced that this period of time is sufficient. I therefore concur in the judgment.

Points for Discussion

1. All of the Justices agreed that the *Edwards* rule was inapplicable on these facts. They disagreed, largely, on the majority's decision to create a bright-line rule that an interrogation conducted more than 14 days after a request for counsel does not automatically render the defendant's waiver of his *Miranda* rights invalid. Is the Court's creation of this standard a rule or dicta? Is that standard necessary to the resolution of the case?

2. If, as the Court holds, being in the general prison population is not custody for *Miranda* purposes, doesn't that change a number of the Court's holdings? Couldn't the Court in *Perkins*, for example, simply have held that Perkins was not in custody and that no *Miranda* warnings were therefore necessary?

BERGHUIS V. THOMPKINS

560 U.S. 370 (2010)

JUSTICE KENNEDY delivered the opinion of the court.

* * *

I

A

On January 10, 2000, a shooting occurred outside a mall in Southfield, Michigan. Among the victims was Samuel Morris, who died from multiple gunshot wounds. The other victim, Frederick France, recovered from his injuries and later testified. Thompkins, who was a suspect, fled. About one year later he was found in Ohio and arrested there.

Two Southfield police officers traveled to Ohio to interrogate Thompkins, then awaiting transfer to Michigan. The interrogation began around 1:30 p.m. and lasted about three hours. The interrogation was conducted in a room that was 8 by 10 feet, and Thompkins sat in a chair that resembled a school desk (it had an arm on it that swings around to provide a surface to write on). At the beginning of the interrogation, one of the officers, Detective Helgert, presented Thompkins with a form derived from the *Miranda* rule. It stated:

NOTIFICATION OF CONSTITUTIONAL RIGHTS AND STATEMENT

1. You have the right to remain silent.

2. Anything you say can and will be used against you in a court of law.

3. You have a right to talk to a lawyer before answering any questions and you have the right to have a lawyer present with you while you are answering any questions.

4. If you cannot afford to hire a lawyer, one will be appointed to represent you before any questioning, if you wish one.

5. You have the right to decide at any time before or during questioning to use your right to remain silent and your right to talk with a lawyer while you are being questioned.

Helgert asked Thompkins to read the fifth warning out loud. Thompkins complied. Helgert later said this was to ensure that Thompkins could read, and Helgert concluded that Thompkins understood English. Helgert then read the other four *Miranda* warnings out loud and asked Thompkins to sign the form to demonstrate that he understood his rights. Thompkins declined to sign the form. The record contains conflicting evidence about whether Thompkins then verbally confirmed that he understood the rights listed on the form.

Officers began an interrogation. At no point during the interrogation did Thompkins say that he wanted to remain silent, that he did not want to talk with the police, or that he wanted an attorney. Thompkins was "[l]argely" silent during the interrogation, which lasted about three hours. He did give a few limited verbal responses, however, such as "yeah," "no," or "I don't know." And on occasion he communicated by nodding his head. Thompkins also said that he "didn't want a peppermint" that was offered to him by the police and that the chair he was "sitting in was hard."

About 2 hours and 45 minutes into the interrogation, Helgert asked Thompkins, "Do you believe in God?" Thompkins made eye contact with Helgert and said "Yes," as his eyes "well[ed] up with tears." Helgert asked, "Do you pray to God?" Thompkins said "Yes." Helgert asked, "Do you pray to God to forgive you for shooting that boy down?" Thompkins answered "Yes" and looked away. Thompkins refused to make a written confession, and the interrogation ended about 15 minutes later.

Thompkins was charged with first-degree murder, assault with intent to commit murder, and certain firearms-related offenses. He moved to suppress the statements made during the interrogation. He argued that he had invoked his Fifth Amendment right to remain silent, requiring police to end the interrogation at once that he had not waived his right to remain silent, and that his inculpatory statements were involuntary. The trial court denied the motion.

* * *

The jury found Thompkins guilty on all counts. He was sentenced to life in prison without parole.

* * *

III

The *Miranda* Court formulated a warning that must be given to suspects before they can be subjected to custodial interrogation. The substance of the warning still must be given to suspects today. A suspect in custody must be advised as follows:

> He must be warned prior to any questioning that he has the right to remain silent, that anything he says can be used against him in a court of law, that he has the right to the presence of an attorney, and that if he cannot afford an attorney one will be appointed for him prior to any questioning if he so desires.

All concede that the warning given in this case was in full compliance with these requirements. The dispute centers on the response—or nonresponse—from the suspect.

A

Thompkins makes various arguments that his answers to questions from the detectives were inadmissible. He first contends that he "invoke[d] his privilege" to remain silent by not saying anything for a sufficient period of time, so the interrogation should have "cease[d]" before he made his inculpatory statements.

This argument is unpersuasive. In the context of invoking the *Miranda* right to counsel, the Court in *Davis v. United States,* 512 U.S. 452, 459 (1994), held that a suspect must do so "unambiguously." If an accused makes a statement concerning the right to counsel "that is ambiguous or equivocal" or makes no statement, the police are not required to end the interrogation, or ask questions to clarify whether the accused wants to invoke his or her *Miranda* rights.

The Court has not yet stated whether an invocation of the right to remain silent can be ambiguous or equivocal, but there is no principled reason to adopt different standards for determining when an accused has invoked the *Miranda* right to remain silent and the *Miranda* right to counsel at issue in *Davis*. Both protect the privilege against compulsory self-incrimination by requiring an interrogation to cease when either right is invoked.

There is good reason to require an accused who wants to invoke his or her right to remain silent to do so unambiguously. A requirement of an unambiguous invocation of *Miranda* rights results in an objective inquiry that "avoid[s] difficulties of proof and . . . provide[s] guidance to officers" on how to proceed in the face of ambiguity. If an ambiguous act, omission, or statement could require police to end the interrogation, police would be required to make difficult decisions about an accused's unclear intent and face the consequence of suppression "if they guess wrong." Suppression of a voluntary confession in these circumstances would place a significant burden on society's interest in prosecuting criminal activity. Treating an ambiguous or equivocal act, omission, or statement as an invocation of *Miranda* rights "might add marginally to *Miranda*'s goal of dispelling the compulsion inherent in custodial interrogation." But "as *Miranda* holds, full comprehension of the rights to remain silent and request an attorney are sufficient to dispel whatever coercion is inherent in the interrogation process."

Thompkins did not say that he wanted to remain silent or that he did not want to talk with the police. Had he made either of these simple, unambiguous statements, he would have invoked his "right to cut off questioning." Here he did neither, so he did not invoke his right to remain silent.

B

We next consider whether Thompkins waived his right to remain silent. Even absent the accused's invocation of the right to remain silent, the accused's statement during a custodial interrogation is inadmissible at trial unless the prosecution can establish that the accused "in fact knowingly and voluntarily waived *[Miranda]* rights" when making the statement. The waiver inquiry "has two distinct dimensions": waiver must be "voluntary in the sense that it was the product of a free and deliberate choice rather than intimidation, coercion, or deception," and "made with a full awareness of both the nature of the right being abandoned and the consequences of the decision to abandon it."

Some language in *Miranda* could be read to indicate that waivers are difficult to establish absent an explicit written waiver or a formal, express oral statement. *Miranda* said "a valid waiver will not be presumed simply from the silence of the accused after warnings are given or simply from the fact that a confession was in fact eventually obtained." In addition, the *Miranda* Court stated that "a heavy burden rests on the government to demonstrate that the defendant knowingly and intelligently waived his privilege against self-incrimination and his right to retained or appointed counsel."

The course of decisions since *Miranda,* informed by the application of *Miranda* warnings in the whole course of law enforcement, demonstrates that waivers can be established even absent formal or express statements of waiver that would be expected in, say, a judicial hearing to determine if a guilty plea has been properly entered. The main purpose of *Miranda* is to ensure that an accused is advised of and understands the right to remain silent and the right to counsel. Thus, "[i] f anything, our subsequent cases have reduced the impact of the *Miranda* rule on legitimate law enforcement while reaffirming the decision's core ruling that unwarned statements may not be used as evidence in the prosecution's case in chief." *Dickerson v. United States,* 530 U.S. 428, 443–444 (2000).

One of the first cases to decide the meaning and import of *Miranda* with respect to the question of waiver was *North Carolina v. Butler*. The *Butler* Court, after discussing some of the problems created by the language in *Miranda,* established certain important propositions. *Butler* interpreted the *Miranda* language concerning the "heavy burden" to show waiver, in accord with usual principles of determining waiver, which can include waiver implied from all the circumstances. And in a later case, the Court stated that this "heavy burden" is not more than the burden to establish waiver by a preponderance of the evidence.

The prosecution therefore does not need to show that a waiver of *Miranda* rights was express. An "implicit waiver" of the "right to remain silent" is sufficient to admit a suspect's statement into evidence. *Butler* made clear that a waiver of *Miranda* rights may be implied through "the defendant's silence, coupled with an understanding of his rights and a course of conduct indicating waiver." The Court in *Butler* therefore "retreated" from the "language and tenor of the *Miranda* opinion," which "suggested that the Court would require that a waiver . . . be 'specifically made.' "

If the State establishes that a *Miranda* warning was given and the accused made an uncoerced statement, this showing, standing alone, is insufficient to demonstrate "a valid waiver" of *Miranda* rights. The prosecution must make the additional showing that the accused understood these rights. Where the prosecution shows that a *Miranda* warning was given and that it was understood by the accused, an accused's uncoerced statement establishes an implied waiver of the right to remain silent.

* * *

The record in this case shows that Thompkins waived his right to remain silent. There is no basis in this case to conclude that he did not understand his rights; and on these facts it follows that he chose not to invoke or rely on those rights when he did speak. First, there is no contention that Thompkins did not understand his rights; and from this it follows that he knew what he gave up when he spoke. There was more than enough evidence in the record to conclude that Thompkins understood his *Miranda* rights. Thompkins received a written copy of the *Miranda* warnings; Detective Helgert determined that Thompkins could read and understand English; and Thompkins was given time to read the warnings. Thompkins, furthermore, read aloud the fifth warning, which stated that "you have the right to decide at any time before or during questioning to use your right to remain silent and your right to talk with a lawyer while you are being questioned." He was thus aware that his right to remain silent would not dissipate after a certain amount of time and that police would have to honor his right to be silent and his right to counsel during the whole course of interrogation. Those rights, the warning made clear, could be asserted at any time. Helgert, moreover, read the warnings aloud.

Second, Thompkins's answer to Detective Helgert's question about whether Thompkins prayed to God for forgiveness for shooting the victim is a "course of conduct indicating waiver" of the right to remain silent. If Thompkins wanted to remain silent, he could have said nothing in response to Helgert's questions, or he could have unambiguously invoked his *Miranda* rights and ended the interrogation. The fact that Thompkins made a statement about three hours after receiving a *Miranda* warning does not overcome the fact that he engaged in a course of conduct indicating waiver. Police are not required to rewarn suspects from time to time. Thompkins's answer to Helgert's question about praying to God for forgiveness for shooting the victim was sufficient to show a course of conduct indicating waiver. This is confirmed by the fact that before then Thompkins had given sporadic answers to questions throughout the interrogation.

Third, there is no evidence that Thompkins's statement was coerced. Thompkins does not claim that police threatened or injured him during the interrogation or that he was in any way fearful. The interrogation was conducted in a standard-sized room in the middle of the afternoon. It is true that apparently he was in a straight-backed chair for three hours, but there is no authority for the proposition that an interrogation of this length is inherently coercive. Indeed, even where interrogations of greater duration were held to be improper, they were accompanied, as this one was not, by other facts indicating coercion, such as an incapacitated and sedated suspect, sleep and food deprivation, and threats. The fact that Helgert's question referred to Thompkins's religious beliefs also did not render Thompkins's statement involuntary. "[T]he Fifth Amendment privilege is not concerned with moral and psychological pressures to confess emanating from sources other than official coercion." In these circumstances, Thompkins knowingly and voluntarily made a statement to police, so he waived his right to remain silent.

C

Thompkins next argues that, even if his answer to Detective Helgert could constitute a waiver of his right to remain silent, the police were not allowed to question him until they obtained a waiver first.

Butler forecloses this argument. The *Butler* Court held that courts can infer a waiver of *Miranda* rights "from the actions and words of the person interrogated." This principle would be inconsistent with a rule that requires a waiver at the outset. The *Butler* Court thus rejected the rule proposed by the *Butler* dissent, which would have "requir[ed] the police to obtain an express waiver of [*Miranda* rights] before proceeding with interrogation." This holding also makes sense given that "the primary protection afforded suspects subject[ed] to custodial interrogation is the *Miranda* warnings themselves." The *Miranda* rule and its requirements are met if a suspect receives adequate *Miranda* warnings, understands them, and has an opportunity to invoke the rights before giving any answers or admissions. Any waiver, express or implied, may be contradicted by an invocation at any time. If the right to counsel or the right to remain silent is invoked at any point during questioning, further interrogation must cease.

* * *

In order for an accused's statement to be admissible at trial, police must have given the accused a *Miranda* warning. If that condition is established, the court can proceed to consider whether there has been an express or implied waiver of *Miranda* rights. In making its ruling on the admissibility of a statement made during custodial questioning, the trial court, of course, considers whether there is evidence to support the conclusion that, from the whole course of questioning, an express or implied waiver has been established. Thus, after giving a *Miranda* warning, police may interrogate a suspect who has neither invoked nor waived his or her *Miranda* rights. On these premises, it follows the police were not required to obtain a waiver of Thompkins's *Miranda* rights before commencing the interrogation.

D

In sum, a suspect who has received and understood the *Miranda* warnings, and has not invoked his *Miranda* rights, waives the right to remain silent by making an uncoerced statement to the police. Thompkins did not invoke his right to remain silent and stop the questioning. Understanding his rights in full, he waived his right to remain silent by making a voluntary statement to the police. The police, moreover, were not required to obtain a waiver of Thompkins's right to remain silent before interrogating him. The state court's decision rejecting Thompkins's *Miranda* claim was thus correct under *de novo* review and therefore necessarily reasonable under the more deferential AEDPA standard of review.

* * *

JUSTICE SOTOMAYOR, with whom JUSTICE STEVENS, JUSTICE GINSBURG, and JUSTICE BREYER join, dissenting.

* * *

II

A

Like the Sixth Circuit, I begin with the question whether Thompkins waived his right to remain silent. Even if Thompkins did not invoke that right, he is entitled to relief because Michigan did not satisfy its burden of establishing waiver.

Miranda's discussion of the prosecution's burden in proving waiver speaks with particular clarity to the facts of this case and therefore merits reproducing at length:

> If [an] interrogation continues without the presence of an attorney and a statement is taken, a heavy burden rests on the government to demonstrate that the defendant knowingly and intelligently waived his privilege against self-incrimination and his right to retained or appointed counsel . . . . Since the State is responsible for establishing the isolated circumstances under which [an] interrogation takes place and has the only means of making available corroborated evidence of warnings given during incommunicado interrogation, the burden is rightly on its shoulders.
>
> An express statement that the individual is willing to make a statement and does not want an attorney followed closely by a statement could constitute a waiver. But a valid waiver will not be presumed simply from the silence of the accused after warnings are given or simply from the fact that a confession was in fact eventually obtained.

Miranda went further in describing the facts likely to satisfy the prosecution's burden of establishing the admissibility of statements obtained after a lengthy interrogation:

> Whatever the testimony of the authorities as to waiver of rights by an accused, the fact of lengthy interrogation or incommunicado incarceration before a statement is made is strong evidence that the accused did not validly waive his rights. In these circumstances the fact that the individual eventually made a statement is consistent with the conclusion that the compelling influence of the interrogation finally forced him to do so. It is inconsistent with any notion of a voluntary relinquishment of the privilege.

This Court's decisions subsequent to *Miranda* have emphasized the prosecution's "heavy burden" in proving waiver. We have also reaffirmed that a court may not presume waiver from a suspect's silence or from the mere fact that a confession was eventually obtained.

Even in concluding that *Miranda* does not invariably require an express waiver of the right to silence or the right to counsel, this Court in *Butler* made clear that the prosecution bears a substantial burden in establishing an implied waiver. The Federal Bureau of Investigation had obtained statements after advising Butler of his rights and confirming that he understood them. When presented with a written waiver-of-rights form, Butler told the agents, "I will talk to you but I am not signing any form." He then made inculpatory statements, which he later sought to suppress on the ground that he had not expressly waived his right to counsel.

Although this Court reversed the state-court judgment concluding that the statements were inadmissible, we quoted at length portions of the *Miranda* opinion reproduced above. We cautioned that even an "express written or oral statement of waiver of the right to remain silent or of the right to counsel" is not "inevitably . . . sufficient to establish waiver," emphasizing that "[t]he question is . . . whether the defendant in fact knowingly and voluntarily waived the rights delineated in the *Miranda* case." In *Miranda,* we observed, "unequivocally said . . . mere silence is not enough." While we stopped short in *Butler* of announcing a *per se* rule that "the defendant's silence, coupled with an understanding of his rights and a course of conduct indicating waiver, may never support a conclusion that a defendant has waived his rights," we reiterated that "courts must presume that a defendant did not waive his rights; the prosecution's burden is great."

Rarely do this Court's precedents provide clearly established law so closely on point with the facts of a particular case. Together, *Miranda* and *Butler* establish that a court "must presume that a defendant did not waive his right[s]"; the prosecution bears a "heavy burden" in attempting to demonstrate waiver; the fact of a "lengthy interrogation" prior to obtaining statements is "strong evidence" against a finding of valid waiver; "mere silence" in response to questioning is "not enough"; and waiver may not be presumed "simply from the fact that a confession was in fact eventually obtained."

It is undisputed here that Thompkins never expressly waived his right to remain silent. His refusal to sign even an acknowledgment that he understood his *Miranda* rights evinces, if anything, an intent not to waive those rights. That Thompkins did not make the inculpatory statements at issue until after approximately 2 hours and 45 minutes of interrogation serves as "strong evidence" against waiver. *Miranda* and *Butler* expressly preclude the possibility that the inculpatory statements themselves are sufficient to establish waiver.

In these circumstances, Thompkins' "actions and words" preceding the inculpatory statements simply do not evidence a "course of conduct indicating waiver" sufficient to carry the prosecution's burden. Although the Michigan court stated that Thompkins "sporadically" participated in the interview, that court's opinion and the record before us are silent as to the subject matter or context of even a single question to which Thompkins purportedly responded, other than the exchange about God and the statements respecting the peppermint and the chair. Unlike in *Butler,* Thompkins made no initial declaration akin to "I will talk to you." Indeed, Michigan and the United States concede that no waiver occurred in this case until Thompkins responded "yes" to the questions about God. I believe it is objectively unreasonable under our clearly established precedents to conclude the prosecution met its "heavy burden" of proof on a record consisting of three one-word answers, following 2 hours and 45 minutes of silence punctuated by a few largely nonverbal responses to unidentified questions.

B

* * *

Today's dilution of the prosecution's burden of proof to the bare fact that a suspect made inculpatory statements after *Miranda* warnings were given and understood takes an unprecedented step away from the "high standards of proof for the waiver of constitutional rights" this Court has long demanded. When waiver is to be inferred during a custodial interrogation, there are sound reasons to require evidence beyond inculpatory statements themselves. *Miranda* and our subsequent cases are premised on the idea that custodial interrogation is inherently coercive. Requiring proof of a course of conduct beyond the inculpatory statements themselves is critical to ensuring that those statements are voluntary admissions and not the dubious product of an overborne will.

Today's decision thus ignores the important interests *Miranda* safeguards. The underlying constitutional guarantee against self-incrimination reflects "many of our fundamental values and most noble aspirations," our society's "preference for an accusatorial rather than an inquisitorial system of criminal justice"; a "fear that self-incriminating statements will be elicited by inhumane treatment and abuses" and a resulting "distrust of self-deprecatory statements"; and a realization that while the privilege is "sometimes a shelter to the guilty, [it] is often a protection to the innocent." For these reasons, we have observed, a criminal law system "which comes to depend on the 'confession' will, in the long run, be less reliable and more subject to abuses than a system relying on independent investigation." "By bracing against 'the possibility of unreliable statements in every instance of in-custody interrogation,'" *Miranda*'s prophylactic rules serve to "'protect the fairness of the trial itself.'" Today's decision bodes poorly for the fundamental principles that *Miranda* protects.

III

Thompkins separately argues that his conduct during the interrogation invoked his right to remain silent, requiring police to terminate questioning. Like the Sixth Circuit, I would not reach this question because Thompkins is in any case entitled to relief as to waiver. But even if Thompkins would not prevail on his invocation claim under AEDPA's deferential standard of review, I cannot agree with the Court's much broader ruling that a suspect must clearly invoke his right to silence by speaking. Taken together with the Court's reformulation of the prosecution's burden of proof as to waiver, today's novel clear-statement rule for invocation invites police to question a suspect at length—notwithstanding his persistent refusal to answer questions—in the hope of eventually obtaining a single inculpatory response which will suffice to prove waiver of rights. Such a result bears little semblance to the "fully effective" prophylaxis that *Miranda* requires.

A

* * *

Thompkins contends that in refusing to respond to questions he effectively invoked his right to remain silent, such that police were required to terminate the interrogation prior to his inculpatory statements. In Michigan's view, Thompkins cannot prevail under AEDPA because this Court's precedents have not previously established whether a suspect's ambiguous statements or actions require the police to stop questioning. We have held that a suspect who has " 'invoked his right to have counsel present . . . is not subject to further interrogation by the authorities until counsel has been made available to him, unless [he] initiates further communication, exchanges, or conversations with the police.' " *Maryland v. Shatzer,* 559 U.S. 98, 104 (2010). Notwithstanding *Miranda*'s statement that "there can be no questioning" if a suspect "indicates in any manner . . . that he wishes to consult with an attorney," the Court in *Davis v. United States,* 512 U.S. 452, 461 (1994) established a clear-statement rule for invoking the right to counsel. After a suspect has knowingly and voluntarily waived his *Miranda* rights, *Davis* held, police may continue questioning "until and unless the suspect *clearly* requests an attorney."

* * *

B

The Court [extends] *Davis* to hold that police may continue questioning a suspect until he unambiguously invokes his right to remain silent. Because Thompkins neither said "he wanted to remain silent" nor said "he did not want to talk with the police," the Court concludes, he did not clearly invoke his right to silence.

I disagree with this novel application of *Davis*. Neither the rationale nor holding of that case compels today's result. *Davis* involved the right to counsel, not the right to silence. The Court in *Davis* reasoned that extending *Edwards*' "rigid" prophylactic rule to ambiguous requests for a lawyer would transform *Miranda* into a " 'wholly irrational obstacl[e] to legitimate police investigative activity' " by "needlessly prevent[ing] the police from questioning a suspect in the absence of counsel even if [he] did not wish to have a lawyer present." But *Miranda* itself "distinguished between the procedural safeguards triggered by a request to remain silent and a request for an attorney." [*Michigan v. Mosley*, 423 U.S. 96 (1975)] upheld the admission of statements when police immediately stopped interrogating a suspect who invoked his right to silence, but reapproached him after a 2-hour delay and obtained inculpatory responses relating to a different crime after administering fresh *Miranda* warnings. The different effects of invoking the rights are consistent with distinct standards for invocation. To the extent *Mosley* contemplates a more flexible form of prophylaxis than *Edwards*—and, in particular, does not categorically bar police from reapproaching a suspect who has invoked his right to remain silent—*Davis*' concern about "wholly irrational obstacles" to police investigation applies with less force.

* * *

In my mind, a more appropriate standard for addressing a suspect's ambiguous invocation of the right to remain silent is the constraint *Mosley* places on questioning a suspect who has invoked that right: The suspect's "right to cut off questioning" must be "scrupulously honored." Such a standard is necessarily precautionary and fact specific. The rule would acknowledge that some statements or conduct are so equivocal that police may scrupulously honor a suspect's rights without terminating questioning-for instance, if a suspect's actions are reasonably understood to indicate a willingness to listen before deciding whether to respond. But other statements or actions—in particular, when a suspect sits silent throughout prolonged interrogation, long past the point when he could be deciding whether to respond—cannot reasonably be understood other than as an invocation of the right to remain silent. Under such circumstances, "scrupulous" respect for the suspect's rights will require police to terminate questioning under *Mosley*.

To be sure, such a standard does not provide police with a bright-line rule. But, as we have previously recognized, *Mosley* itself does not offer clear guidance to police about when and how interrogation may continue after a suspect invokes his rights. Given that police have for nearly 35 years applied *Mosley*'s fact-specific standard in questioning suspects who have invoked their right to remain silent; that our cases did not during that time resolve what statements or actions suffice to invoke that right; and that neither Michigan nor the Solicitor General have provided evidence in this case that the status quo has proved unworkable, I see little reason to believe today's clear-statement rule is necessary to ensure effective law enforcement.

* * *

Points for Discussion

1. Thompkins makes several arguments against the admission of his confession—that he invoked his right to remain silent by remaining silent, that he never waived his right to remain silent, and that, in any event, police should not have begun questioning him until they understood that he wished to waive these rights. Why does the Court reject each of these arguments?

2. Isn't the Court correct when it writes that people who have been informed of the right to remain silent and choose to speak should generally be held to have waived the right to silence? How does the dissent counter this common-sense presumption?

3. Is there support in *Miranda* for the Court's conclusion that silence may suffice as a waiver of *Miranda* rights? What do you make of the Court's quotation of *Dickerson* (discussed at the end of this chapter) for the proposition that whatever *Miranda* may have meant when decided, subsequent decisions have weakened much of its categorical language?

4. In 2013 the Supreme Court decided *Salinas v. Texas*, 570 U.S. 178. In *Salinas* the Court held that it was not a violation of the Fifth Amendment for a prosecutor to comment at trial on the silence of a defendant in response to police questioning during a voluntary pretrial meeting. A plurality of three Justices cited *Berghuis v. Thompkins* for the proposition that the Fifth Amendment must be asserted expressly and that mere silence is not enough to invoke the right to silence. Is that a fair reading of *Thompkins*?

C. TRICKERY

MORAN V. BURBINE

475 U.S. 412 (1986)

JUSTICE O'CONNOR delivered the opinion of the court.

After being informed of his rights pursuant to *Miranda v. Arizona,* 384 U.S. 436 (1966), and after executing a series of written waivers, respondent confessed to the murder of a young woman. At no point during the course of the interrogation, which occurred prior to arraignment, did he request an attorney. While he was in police custody, his sister attempted to retain a lawyer to represent him. The attorney telephoned the police station and received assurances that respondent would not be questioned further until the next day. In fact, the interrogation session that yielded the inculpatory statements began later that evening. The question presented is whether either the conduct of the police or respondent's ignorance of the attorney's efforts to reach him taints the validity of the waivers and therefore requires exclusion of the confessions.

I

On the morning of March 3, 1977, Mary Jo Hickey was found unconscious in a factory parking lot in Providence, Rhode Island. Suffering from injuries to her skull apparently inflicted by a metal pipe found at the scene, she was rushed to a nearby hospital. Three weeks later she died from her wounds.

Several months after her death, the Cranston, Rhode Island, police arrested respondent and two others in connection with a local burglary. Shortly before the arrest, Detective Ferranti of the Cranston police force had learned from a confidential informant that the man responsible for Ms. Hickey's death lived at a certain address and went by the name of "Butch." Upon discovering that respondent lived at that address and was known by that name, Detective Ferranti informed respondent of his *Miranda* rights. When respondent refused to execute a written waiver, Detective Ferranti spoke separately with the two other suspects arrested on the breaking and entering charge and obtained statements further implicating respondent in Ms. Hickey's murder. At approximately 6 p.m., Detective Ferranti telephoned the police in Providence to convey the information he had uncovered. An hour later, three officers from that department arrived at the Cranston headquarters for the purpose of questioning respondent about the murder.

That same evening, at about 7:45 p.m., respondent's sister telephoned the Public Defender's Office to obtain legal assistance for her brother. Her sole concern was the breaking and entering charge, as she was unaware that respondent was then under suspicion for murder. She asked for Richard Casparian who had been scheduled to meet with respondent earlier that afternoon to discuss another charge unrelated to either the break-in or the murder. As soon as the conversation ended, the attorney who took the call attempted to reach Mr. Casparian. When those efforts were unsuccessful, she telephoned Allegra Munson, another Assistant Public Defender, and told her about respondent's arrest and his sister's subsequent request that the office represent him.

At 8:15 p.m., Ms. Munson telephoned the Cranston police station and asked that her call be transferred to the detective division. In the words of the Supreme Court of Rhode Island, whose factual findings we treat as presumptively correct, 28 U.S.C. § 2254(d), the conversation proceeded as follows:

> A male voice responded with the word "Detectives." Ms. Munson identified herself and asked if Brian Burbine was being held; the person responded affirmatively. Ms. Munson explained to the

> person that Burbine was represented by attorney Casparian who was not available; she further stated that she would act as Burbine's legal counsel in the event that the police intended to place him in a lineup or question him. The unidentified person told Ms. Munson that the police would not be questioning Burbine or putting him in a lineup and that they were through with him for the night. Ms. Munson was not informed that the Providence Police were at the Cranston police station or that Burbine was a suspect in Mary's murder.

At all relevant times, respondent was unaware of his sister's efforts to retain counsel and of the fact and contents of Ms. Munson's telephone conversation.

Less than an hour later, the police brought respondent to an interrogation room and conducted the first of a series of interviews concerning the murder. Prior to each session, respondent was informed of his *Miranda* rights, and on three separate occasions he signed a written form acknowledging that he understood his right to the presence of an attorney and explicitly indicating that he "[did] not want an attorney called or appointed for [him]" before he gave a statement. Uncontradicted evidence at the suppression hearing indicated that at least twice during the course of the evening, respondent was left in a room where he had access to a telephone, which he apparently declined to use. Eventually, respondent signed three written statements fully admitting to the murder.

* * *

We granted certiorari to decide whether a prearraignment confession preceded by an otherwise valid waiver must be suppressed either because the police misinformed an inquiring attorney about their plans concerning the suspect or because they failed to inform the suspect of the attorney's efforts to reach him. We now reverse.

II

* * *

A

Echoing the standard first articulated in *Johnson v. Zerbst,* 304 U.S. 458, 464 (1938), *Miranda* holds that "[t]he defendant may waive effectuation" of the rights conveyed in the warnings "provided the waiver is made voluntarily, knowingly and intelligently." The inquiry has two distinct dimensions. First, the relinquishment of the right must have been voluntary in the sense that it was the product of a free and deliberate choice rather than intimidation, coercion, or deception. Second, the waiver must have been made with a full awareness of both the nature of the right being abandoned and the consequences of the decision to abandon it. Only if the "totality of the circumstances surrounding the interrogation" reveal both an uncoerced choice and the requisite level of comprehension may a court properly conclude that the *Miranda* rights have been waived.

Under this standard, we have no doubt that respondent validly waived his right to remain silent and to the presence of counsel. The voluntariness of the waiver is not at issue. As the Court of Appeals correctly acknowledged, the record is devoid of any suggestion that police resorted to physical or psychological pressure to elicit the statements. Indeed it appears that it was respondent, and not the police, who spontaneously initiated the conversation that led to the first and most damaging confession. Nor is there any question about respondent's comprehension of the full panoply of rights set out in the *Miranda* warnings and of the potential consequences of a decision to relinquish them. Nonetheless, the Court of Appeals believed that the "[d]eliberate or reckless" conduct of the police, in particular their failure to inform respondent of the telephone call, fatally undermined the validity of the otherwise proper waiver. We find this conclusion untenable as a matter of both logic and precedent.

Events occurring outside of the presence of the suspect and entirely unknown to him surely can have no bearing on the capacity to comprehend and knowingly relinquish a constitutional right. Under the analysis of the Court of Appeals, the same defendant, armed with the same information and confronted with precisely the same police conduct, would have knowingly waived his *Miranda* rights had a lawyer not telephoned the police station to inquire about his status. Nothing in any of our waiver decisions or in our understanding of the essential components of a valid waiver requires so incongruous a result. No doubt the additional information would have been useful to respondent; perhaps even it might have affected his decision to confess. But we have never read the Constitution to require that the police supply a suspect with a flow of information to help him calibrate his self-interest in deciding whether to speak or stand by his rights. Once it is determined that a suspect's decision not to rely on his rights was uncoerced, that he at all times knew he could stand mute and request a lawyer, and that he was aware of the State's intention to use his statements to secure a conviction, the analysis is complete and the waiver is valid as a matter of law.[1] The Court of Appeals' conclusion to the contrary was in error.

---

[1] The dissent incorrectly reads our analysis of the components of a valid waiver to be inconsistent with the Court's holding in *Edwards v. Arizona,* 451 U.S. 477 (1981). When a suspect *has* requested counsel, the interrogation must cease, regardless of any question of waiver, unless the suspect himself initiates the conversation. In the course of its lengthy exposition, however, the dissent never comes to grips with the crucial distinguishing feature of this case—that Burbine at no point requested the presence of counsel, as was his right under *Miranda* to do. We do not quarrel with the dissent's characterization of police interrogation as a "privilege terminable at the will of the suspect." We reject, however, the dissent's entirely undefended suggestion that the Fifth Amendment "right to counsel" requires anything more than that the police inform the suspect of his right to representation and honor his request that the interrogation cease until his attorney is present.

Nor do we believe that the level of the police's culpability in failing to inform respondent of the telephone call has any bearing on the validity of the waivers. In light of the state-court findings that there was no "conspiracy or collusion" on the part of the police, we have serious doubts about whether the Court of Appeals was free to conclude that their conduct constituted "deliberate or reckless irresponsibility." But whether intentional or inadvertent, the state of mind of the police is irrelevant to the question of the intelligence and voluntariness of respondent's election to abandon his rights. Although highly inappropriate, even deliberate deception of an attorney could not possibly affect a suspect's decision to waive his *Miranda* rights unless he were at least aware of the incident. Nor was the failure to inform respondent of the telephone call the kind of "trick[ery]" that can vitiate the validity of a waiver. Granting that the "deliberate or reckless" withholding of information is objectionable as a matter of ethics, such conduct is only relevant to the constitutional validity of a waiver if it deprives a defendant of knowledge essential to his ability to understand the nature of his rights and the consequences of abandoning them. Because respondent's voluntary decision to speak was made with full awareness and comprehension of all the information *Miranda* requires the police to convey, the waivers were valid.

B

At oral argument respondent acknowledged that a constitutional rule requiring the police to inform a suspect of an attorney's efforts to reach him would represent a significant extension of our precedents. He contends, however, that the conduct of the Providence police was so inimical to the Fifth Amendment values *Miranda* seeks to protect that we should read that decision to condemn their behavior. Regardless of any issue of waiver, he urges, the Fifth Amendment requires the reversal of a conviction if the police are less than forthright in their dealings with an attorney or if they fail to tell a suspect of a lawyer's unilateral efforts to contact him. Because the proposed modification ignores the underlying purposes of the *Miranda* rules and because we think that the decision as written strikes the proper balance between society's legitimate law enforcement interests and the protection of the defendant's Fifth Amendment rights, we decline the invitation to further extend *Miranda*'s reach.

At the outset, while we share respondent's distaste for the deliberate misleading of an officer of the court, reading *Miranda* to forbid police deception of an *attorney* "would cut [the decision] completely loose from its own explicitly stated rationale." As is now well established, "[t]he . . . *Miranda* warnings are 'not themselves rights protected by the Constitution but [are] instead measures to insure that the [suspect's] right against compulsory self-incrimination [is] protected.' " Their objective is not to mold police conduct for its own sake. Nothing in the Constitution vests in us the authority to mandate a code of behavior for state officials wholly unconnected to any federal right or privilege. The purpose of the *Miranda* warnings instead is to dissipate the compulsion inherent in custodial interrogation and, in so doing, guard against abridgment of the suspect's Fifth Amendment rights. Clearly, a rule that focuses on how the police treat an attorney—conduct that has no relevance at all to the degree of compulsion experienced by the defendant during interrogation—would ignore both *Miranda*'s mission and its only source of legitimacy.

Nor are we prepared to adopt a rule requiring that the police inform a suspect of an attorney's efforts to reach him. While such a rule might add marginally to *Miranda*'s goal of dispelling the compulsion inherent in custodial interrogation, overriding practical considerations counsel against its adoption. As we have stressed on numerous occasions, "[o]ne of the principal advantages" of *Miranda* is the ease and clarity of its application. We have little doubt that the approach urged by respondent and endorsed by the Court of Appeals would have the inevitable consequence of muddying *Miranda*'s otherwise relatively clear waters. The legal questions it would spawn are legion: To what extent should the police be held accountable for knowing that the accused has counsel? Is it enough that someone in the station house knows, or must the interrogating officer himself know of counsel's efforts to contact the suspect? Do counsel's efforts to talk to the suspect concerning one criminal investigation trigger the obligation to inform the defendant before interrogation may proceed on a wholly separate matter? We are unwilling to modify *Miranda* in a manner that would so clearly undermine the decision's central "virtue of informing police and prosecutors with specificity . . . what they may do in conducting [a] custodial interrogation, and of informing courts under what circumstances statements obtained during such interrogation are not admissible."

Moreover, problems of clarity to one side, reading *Miranda* to require the police in each instance to inform a suspect of an attorney's efforts to reach him would work a substantial and, we think, inappropriate shift in the subtle balance struck in that decision. Custodial interrogations implicate two competing concerns. On the one hand, "the need for police questioning as a tool for effective enforcement of criminal laws" cannot be doubted. Admissions of guilt are more than merely "desirable," they are essential to society's compelling interest in finding, convicting, and punishing those who violate the law. On the other hand, the Court has recognized that the interrogation process is "inherently coercive" and that, as a consequence, there exists a substantial risk that the police will inadvertently traverse the fine line between legitimate efforts to elicit admissions and constitutionally impermissible compulsion. *Miranda* attempted to reconcile these opposing concerns by giving the *defendant* the power to exert some control over the course of the interrogation. Declining to adopt the more extreme position that the actual presence of a lawyer was necessary to dispel the coercion inherent in custodial interrogation, the Court found that the suspect's Fifth Amendment rights could be adequately protected by less intrusive means. Police questioning, often an essential part of the investigatory process, could continue in its traditional form, the Court held, but only if the suspect clearly understood that, at any time, he could bring the proceeding to a halt or, short of that, call in an attorney to give advice and monitor the conduct of his interrogators.

The position urged by respondent would upset this carefully drawn approach in a manner that is both unnecessary for the protection of the Fifth Amendment privilege and injurious to legitimate law enforcement. Because, as *Miranda* holds, full comprehension of the rights to remain silent and request an attorney are sufficient to dispel whatever coercion is inherent in the interrogation process, a rule requiring the police to inform the suspect of an attorney's efforts to contact him would contribute to the protection of the Fifth Amendment privilege only incidentally, if at all. This minimal benefit, however, would come at a substantial cost to society's legitimate and substantial interest in securing admissions of guilt. Indeed, the very premise of the Court of Appeals was not that awareness of Ms. Munson's phone call would have dissipated the coercion of the interrogation room, but that it might have convinced respondent not to speak at all. Because neither the letter nor purposes of *Miranda* require this additional handicap on otherwise permissible investigatory efforts, we are unwilling to expand the *Miranda* rules to require the police to keep the suspect abreast of the status of his legal representation.

* * *

III

Respondent also contends that the Sixth Amendment requires exclusion of his three confessions.[2] It is clear, of course, that, absent a valid waiver, the defendant has the right to the presence of an attorney during any interrogation occurring after the first formal charging proceeding, the point at which the Sixth Amendment right to counsel initially attaches. And we readily agree that once the right *has* attached, it follows that the police may not interfere with the efforts of a defendant's attorney to act as a " 'medium' between [the suspect] and the State" during the interrogation. The difficulty for respondent is that the interrogation sessions that yielded the inculpatory statements took place *before* the initiation of "adversary judicial proceedings." He contends, however, that this circumstance is not fatal to his Sixth Amendment claim. At least in some situations, he argues, the Sixth Amendment protects the integrity of the attorney-client relationship[3] regardless of whether the prosecution has in fact commenced

[2] Petitioner does not argue that respondent's valid waiver of his Fifth Amendment right to counsel necessarily served to waive his parallel rights under the Sixth Amendment. Accordingly, we have no occasion to consider whether a waiver for one purpose necessarily operates as a general waiver of the right to counsel for all purposes.

[3] Notwithstanding the Rhode Island Supreme Court's finding that, as a matter of state law, no attorney-client relationship existed between respondent and Ms. Munson, the Sixth

"by way of formal charge, preliminary hearing, indictment, information or arraignment." Placing principal reliance on a footnote in *Miranda,* 384 U.S., at 465, n. 35, and on *Escobedo v. Illinois,* 378 U.S. 478 (1964), he maintains that [*United States v. Gouveia,* 467 U.S. 180 (1984), *Kirby v. Illinois,* 406 U.S. 682 (1972),] and our other "critical stage" cases, concern only the narrow question of when the right *to* counsel—that is, to the appointment or presence of counsel—attaches. The right to noninterference with an attorney's dealings with a criminal suspect, he asserts, arises the moment that the relationship is formed, or, at the very least, once the defendant is placed in custodial interrogation.

We are not persuaded. At the outset, subsequent decisions foreclose any reliance on *Escobedo* and *Miranda* for the proposition that the Sixth Amendment right, in any of its manifestations, applies prior to the initiation of adversary judicial proceedings. Although *Escobedo* was originally decided as a Sixth Amendment case, "the Court in retrospect perceived that the 'prime purpose' of *Escobedo* was not to vindicate the constitutional right to counsel as such, but, like *Miranda,* 'to guarantee full effectuation of the privilege against self-incrimination. . . .' " Clearly then, *Escobedo* provides no support for respondent's argument. Nor, of course, does *Miranda,* the holding of which rested exclusively on the Fifth Amendment. Thus, the decision's brief observation about the reach of *Escobedo*'s Sixth Amendment analysis is not only dictum, but reflects an understanding of the case that the Court has expressly disavowed.

Questions of precedent to one side, we find respondent's understanding of the Sixth Amendment both practically and theoretically unsound. As a practical matter, it makes little sense to say that the Sixth Amendment right to counsel attaches at different times depending on the fortuity of whether the suspect or his family happens to have retained counsel prior to interrogation. More importantly, the suggestion that the existence of an attorney-client relationship itself triggers the protections of the Sixth Amendment misconceives the underlying purposes of the right to counsel. The Sixth Amendment's intended function is not to wrap a protective cloak around the attorney-client relationship for its own sake any more than it is to protect a suspect from the consequences of his own candor. Its purpose, rather, is to assure that in any "criminal prosecutio[n]," U.S. Const., Amdt. 6, the accused shall not be left to his own devices in facing the " 'prosecutorial forces of organized society.' " By its

Amendment issue is properly before us. Petitioner now concedes that such a relationship existed and invites us to decide the Sixth Amendment question based on that concession. Of course, a litigant's concession cannot be used to circumvent the rule that this Court may not disregard a state court's interpretation of state law. Respondent's argument, however, does not focus on whether an attorney-client relationship actually existed as a formal matter of state law. He argues instead that, on the particular facts of this case, the Sixth Amendment right to counsel has been violated. In any event, even if the existence of an attorney-client relationship could somehow independently trigger the Sixth Amendment right to counsel, a position we reject, the type of circumstances that would give rise to the right would certainly have a federal definition.

very terms, it becomes applicable only when the government's role shifts from investigation to accusation. For it is only then that the assistance of one versed in the "intricacies . . . of law," is needed to assure that the prosecution's case encounters "the crucible of meaningful adversarial testing."

* * *

Because, as respondent acknowledges, the events that led to the inculpatory statements preceded the formal initiation of adversary judicial proceedings, we reject the contention that the conduct of the police violated his rights under the Sixth Amendment.

IV

Finally, respondent contends that the conduct of the police was so offensive as to deprive him of the fundamental fairness guaranteed by the Due Process Clause of the Fourteenth Amendment. Focusing primarily on the impropriety of conveying false information to an attorney, he invites us to declare that such behavior should be condemned as violative of canons fundamental to the "traditions and conscience of our people." *Rochin v. California,* 342 U.S. 165, 169 (1952). We do not question that on facts more egregious than those presented here police deception might rise to a level of a due process violation. Accordingly, Justice Stevens' apocalyptic suggestion that we have approved any and all forms of police misconduct is demonstrably incorrect. We hold only that, on these facts, the challenged conduct falls short of the kind of misbehavior that so shocks the sensibilities of civilized society as to warrant a federal intrusion into the criminal processes of the States.

JUSTICE STEVENS, with whom JUSTICE BRENNAN and JUSTICE MARSHALL join, dissenting.

This case poses fundamental questions about our system of justice. As this Court has long recognized, and reaffirmed only weeks ago, "ours is an accusatorial and not an inquisitorial system." *Miller v. Fenton,* 474 U.S. 104, 110 (1985). The Court's opinion today represents a startling departure from that basic insight.

The Court concludes that the police may deceive an attorney by giving her false information about whether her client will be questioned, and that the police may deceive a suspect by failing to inform him of his attorney's communications and efforts to represent him. For the majority, this conclusion, though "distaste[ful]," is not even debatable. The deception of the attorney is irrelevant because the attorney has no right to information, accuracy, honesty, or fairness in the police response to her questions about her client. The deception of the client is acceptable, because, although the information would affect the client's assertion of his rights, the client's actions in ignorance of the availability of his attorney are voluntary, knowing, and intelligent; additionally, society's interest in apprehending, prosecuting, and punishing criminals outweighs the suspect's interest in information regarding his attorney's efforts to communicate with him. Finally, even mendacious police interference in the communications between a suspect and his lawyer does not violate any notion of fundamental fairness because it does not shock the conscience of the majority.

* * *

The Court's holding focuses on the period after a suspect has been taken into custody and before he has been charged with an offense. The core of the Court's holding is that police interference with an attorney's access to her client during that period is not unconstitutional. The Court reasons that a State has a compelling interest, not simply in custodial interrogation, but in lawyer-free, incommunicado custodial interrogation. Such incommunicado interrogation is so important that a lawyer may be given false information that prevents her presence and representation; it is so important that police may refuse to inform a suspect of his attorney's communications and immediate availability. This conclusion flies in the face of this Court's repeated expressions of deep concern about incommunicado questioning. Until today, incommunicado questioning has been viewed with the strictest scrutiny by this Court; today, incommunicado questioning is embraced as a societal goal of the highest order that justifies police deception of the shabbiest kind.

* * *

It is not only the Court's ultimate conclusion that is deeply disturbing; it is also its manner of reaching that conclusion. The Court completely rejects an entire body of law on the subject—the many carefully reasoned state decisions that have come to precisely the opposite conclusion. The Court similarly dismisses the fact that the police deception which it sanctions quite clearly violates the American Bar Association's Standards for Criminal Justice—standards which the Chief Justice has described as "the single most comprehensive and probably the most monumental undertaking in the field of criminal justice ever attempted by the American legal profession in our national history," and which this Court frequently finds helpful. And, of course, the Court dismisses the fact that the American Bar Association has emphatically endorsed the prevailing state-court position and expressed its serious concern about the effect that a contrary view—a view, such as the Court's, that exalts incommunicado interrogation, sanctions police deception, and demeans the right to consult with an attorney—will have in police stations and courtrooms throughout this Nation. Of greatest importance, the Court misapprehends or rejects the central principles that have, for several decades, animated this Court's decisions concerning incommunicado interrogation.

Police interference with communications between an attorney and his client is a recurrent problem. The factual variations in the many state-court opinions condemning this interference as a violation of the Federal Constitution suggest the variety of contexts in which the problem emerges. In Oklahoma, police led a lawyer to several different locations while they interrogated the suspect; in Oregon, police moved a suspect to a new location when they learned that his lawyer was on his way; in Illinois, authorities failed to tell a suspect that his lawyer had arrived at the jail and asked to see him; in Massachusetts, police did not tell suspects that their lawyers were at or near the police station. In all these cases, the police not only failed to inform the suspect, but also misled the attorneys. The scenarios vary, but the core problem of police interference remains. "Its recurrence suggests that it has roots in some condition fundamental and general to our criminal system." *Watts v. Indiana,* 338 U.S. 49, 57 (1949) (Jackson, J., concurring in result).

The near-consensus of state courts and the legal profession's standards about this recurrent problem lends powerful support to the conclusion that police may not interfere with communications between an attorney and the client whom they are questioning. Indeed, at least two opinions from this Court seemed to express precisely that view. The Court today flatly rejects that widely held view and responds to this recurrent problem by adopting the most restrictive interpretation of the federal constitutional restraints on police deception, misinformation, and interference in attorney-client communications.

* * *

II

Well-settled principles of law lead inexorably to the conclusion that the failure to inform Burbine of the call from his attorney makes the subsequent waiver of his constitutional rights invalid. Analysis should begin with an acknowledgment that the burden of proving the validity of a waiver of constitutional rights is always on the *government*. When such a waiver occurs in a custodial setting, that burden is an especially heavy one because custodial interrogation is inherently coercive, because disinterested witnesses are seldom available to describe what actually happened, and because history has taught us that the danger of overreaching during incommunicado interrogation is so real.

In applying this heavy presumption against the validity of waivers, this Court has sometimes relied on a case-by-case totality of the circumstances analysis. We have found, however, that some custodial interrogation situations require strict presumptions against the validity of a waiver. *Miranda* established that a waiver is not valid in the absence of certain warnings. *Edwards v. Arizona,* 451 U.S. 477 (1981), similarly established that a waiver is not valid if police initiate questioning after the defendant has invoked his right to counsel. In these circumstances, the waiver is invalid as a matter of law even if the evidence overwhelmingly establishes, as a matter of fact, that "a suspect's decision not to rely on his rights was uncoerced, that he at all times knew that he could stand mute and request a lawyer, and that he was aware of the State's intention to use his statements to secure a conviction." In light of our decision in *Edwards,* the Court is simply wrong in stating that "the analysis is complete and the waiver is valid as a matter of law" when these facts have been established. Like the failure to give warnings and like police initiation of interrogation after a request for counsel, police deception of a suspect through omission of information regarding attorney communications greatly exacerbates the inherent problems of incommunicado interrogation and requires a clear principle to safeguard the presumption against the waiver of constitutional rights. As in those situations, the police deception should render a subsequent waiver invalid.

Indeed, as *Miranda* itself makes clear, proof that the required warnings have been given is a necessary, but by no means sufficient, condition for establishing a valid waiver. As the Court plainly stated in *Miranda,* "any evidence that the accused was threatened, tricked, or cajoled into a waiver will, of course, show that the defendant did not voluntarily waive his privilege. The requirement of warnings and waiver of rights is a fundamental with respect to the Fifth Amendment privilege and not simply a preliminary ritual to existing methods of interrogation."

In this case it would be perfectly clear that Burbine's waiver was invalid if, for example, Detective Ferranti had "threatened, tricked, or cajoled" Burbine in their private preconfession meeting—perhaps by misdescribing the statements obtained from DiOrio and Sparks—even though, under the Court's truncated analysis of the issue, Burbine fully understood his rights. For *Miranda* clearly condemns threats or trickery that cause a suspect to make an unwise waiver of his rights even though he fully understands those rights. In my opinion there can be no constitutional distinction—as the Court appears to draw—between a deceptive misstatement and the concealment by the police of the critical fact that an attorney retained by the accused or his family has offered assistance, either by telephone or in person.

* * *

III

The Court makes the alternative argument that requiring police to inform a suspect of his attorney's communications to and about him is not required because it would upset the careful "balance" of *Miranda.* Despite its earlier notion that the attorney's call is an "outside event" that has "no bearing" on a knowing and intelligent waiver, the majority does acknowledge that information of attorney Munson's call "would have been useful to respondent" and "might have affected his decision to confess." Thus, a rule requiring the police to inform a suspect of an attorney's call would have two predictable effects. It would serve "*Miranda's* goal of dispelling the compulsion inherent in custodial interrogation," and it would disserve the goal of custodial interrogation because it would result in fewer confessions. By a process of balancing these two concerns, the Court finds the benefit to the individual outweighed by the "substantial cost to society's legitimate and substantial interest in securing admissions of guilt."

The Court's balancing approach is profoundly misguided. The cost of suppressing evidence of guilt will always make the value of a procedural safeguard appear "minimal," "marginal," or "incremental." Indeed, the value of any trial at all seems like a "procedural technicality" when balanced against the interest in administering prompt justice to a murderer or a rapist caught redhanded. The individual interest in procedural safeguards that minimize the risk of error is easily discounted when the fact of guilt appears certain beyond doubt.

* * *

If the Court's cost-benefit analysis were sound, it would justify a repudiation of the right to a warning about counsel itself. There is only a difference in degree between a presumption that advice about the immediate availability of a lawyer would not affect the voluntariness of a decision to confess, and a presumption that every citizen knows that he has a right to remain silent and therefore no warnings of any kind are needed. In either case, the withholding of information serves precisely the same law enforcement interests. And in both cases, the cost can be described as nothing more than an incremental increase in the risk that an individual will make an unintelligent waiver of his rights.

In cases like *Escobedo, Miranda,* and *Dunaway,* the Court has viewed the balance from a much broader perspective. In all these cases—indeed, whenever the distinction between an inquisitorial and an accusatorial system of justice is implicated—the law enforcement interest served by incommunicado interrogation has been weighed against the interest in individual liberty that is threatened by such practices. The balance has never been struck by an evaluation of empirical data of the kind submitted to legislative decisionmakers—indeed, the Court relies on no such data today. Rather, the Court has evaluated the quality of the conflicting rights and interests. In the past, that kind of balancing process has led to the conclusion that the police have *no right* to compel an individual to respond to custodial interrogation, and that the interest in liberty that is threatened by incommunicado interrogation is so precious that special procedures must be followed to protect it. The Court's contrary conclusion today can only be explained by its failure to appreciate the value of the liberty that an accusatorial system seeks to protect.

IV

The Court also argues that a rule requiring the police to inform a suspect of an attorney's efforts to reach him would have an additional cost: it would undermine the "clarity" of the rule of the *Miranda* case. This argument is not supported by any reference to the experience in the States that have adopted such a rule. The Court merely professes concern about its ability to answer three quite simple questions.

Moreover, the Court's evaluation of the interest in "clarity" is rather one-sided. For a police officer with a printed card containing the exact text he is supposed to recite, perhaps the rule is clear. But the interest in clarity that the *Miranda* decision was intended to serve is not merely for the benefit of the police. Rather, the decision was also, and primarily, intended to provide adequate guidance to the person in custody who is being asked to waive the protections afforded by the Constitution. Inevitably, the *Miranda* decision also serves the judicial interest in clarifying the inquiry into what actually transpired during a custodial interrogation. Under the Court's conception of the interest in clarity, however, the police would presumably prevail whenever they could convince the trier of fact that a required ritual was performed before the confession was obtained.

V

At the time attorney Munson made her call to the Cranston police station, she was acting as Burbine's attorney. Under ordinary principles of agency law the deliberate deception of Munson was tantamount to deliberate deception of her client. If an attorney makes a mistake in the course of her representation of her client, the client must accept the consequences of that mistake. It is equally clear that when an attorney makes an inquiry on behalf of her client, the client is entitled to a truthful answer. Surely the client must have the same remedy for a false representation to his lawyer that he would have if he were acting *pro se* and had propounded the question himself.

* * *

The possible reach of the Court's opinion is stunning. For the majority seems to suggest that police may deny counsel all access to a client who is being held. At least since *Escobedo v. Illinois,* it has been widely accepted that police may not simply deny attorneys access to their clients who are in custody. This view has survived the recasting of *Escobedo* from a Sixth Amendment to a Fifth Amendment case that the majority finds so critically important. That this prevailing view is shared *by the police* can be seen in the state-court opinions detailing various forms of police deception of attorneys. For, if there were no obligation to give attorneys access, there would be no need to take elaborate steps to avoid access, such as shuttling the suspect to a different location, or taking the lawyer to different locations; police could simply refuse to allow the attorneys to see the suspects. But the law enforcement profession has apparently believed, quite rightly in my view, that denying lawyers access to their clients is impermissible. The Court today seems to assume that this view was error—that, from the federal constitutional perspective, the lawyer's access is, as a question from the Court put it in oral argument, merely "a matter of prosecutorial grace." Certainly, nothing in the Court's Fifth and Sixth Amendments analysis acknowledges that there is *any* federal constitutional bar to an absolute denial of lawyer access to a suspect who is in police custody.

In sharp contrast to the majority, I firmly believe that the right to counsel at custodial interrogation is infringed by police treatment of an attorney that prevents or impedes the attorney's representation of the suspect at that interrogation.

VI

The Court devotes precisely five sentences to its conclusion that the police interference in the attorney's representation of Burbine did not violate the Due Process Clause. In the majority's view, the due process analysis is a simple "shock the conscience" test. Finding its conscience troubled, but not shocked, the majority rejects the due process challenge.

* * *

Police interference with communications between an attorney and his client violates the due process requirement of fundamental fairness. Burbine's attorney was given completely false information about the lack of questioning; moreover, she was not told that her client would be questioned regarding a murder charge about which she was unaware. Burbine, in turn, was not told that his attorney had phoned and that she had been informed that he would not be questioned. Quite simply, the Rhode Island police effectively drove a wedge between an attorney and a suspect through misinformation and omissions.

The majority does not "question that on facts more egregious than those presented here police deception might rise to a level of a due process violation." In my view, the police deception disclosed by this record plainly does rise to that level.

VII

This case turns on a proper appraisal of the role of the lawyer in our society. If a lawyer is seen as a nettlesome obstacle to the pursuit of wrongdoers—as in an inquisitorial society—then the Court's decision today makes a good deal of sense. If a lawyer is seen as an aid to the understanding and protection of constitutional rights—as in an accusatorial society—then today's decision makes no sense at all.

Like the conduct of the police in the Cranston station on the evening of June 29, 1977, the Court's opinion today serves the goal of insuring that the perpetrator of a vile crime is punished. Like the police on that June night as well, however, the Court has trampled on well-established legal principles and flouted the spirit of our accusatorial system of justice.

Points for Discussion

1. The Court concludes that it was the attorney and not the client who was deceived here and that, as a result, Burbine was still able to give a voluntary, knowing, and intelligent waiver of his *Miranda* rights. The dissent, by contrast, would treat deception of the attorney as deception of the client himself. Which side has the better of the argument?

2. What role should state-law agency conceptions play in this case? Should it matter that there was not a contractual relationship between Burbine and his attorney? Would the case have come out differently if Burbine or his family had paid Munson for her services prior to the events of March 3, 1977?

3. The dissent raises the specter of inquisition to describe the police conduct in this case. Isn't the conduct here—isolating the defendant, keeping him from his attorney, etc.—exactly what the Court meant to curtail with *Miranda*? If so, what is the appropriate constitutional provision for checking such police over-reaching?

COLORADO V. SPRING

479 U.S. 564 (1987)

JUSTICE POWELL delivered the opinion of the court.

In *Miranda v. Arizona,* 384 U.S. 436 (1966), the Court held that a suspect's waiver of the Fifth Amendment privilege against self-incrimination is valid only if it is made voluntarily, knowingly, and intelligently. This case presents the question whether the suspect's awareness of all the crimes about which he may be questioned is relevant to determining the validity of his decision to waive the Fifth Amendment privilege.

I

In February 1979, respondent John Leroy Spring and a companion shot and killed Donald Walker during a hunting trip in Colorado. Shortly thereafter, an informant told agents of the Bureau of Alcohol, Tobacco, and Firearms (ATF) that Spring was engaged in the interstate transportation of stolen firearms. The informant also told the agents that Spring had discussed his participation in the Colorado killing. At the time the ATF agents received this information, Walker's body had not been found and the police had received no report of his disappearance. Based on the information received from the informant relating to the firearms violations, the ATF agents set up an undercover operation to purchase firearms from

Spring. On March 30, 1979, ATF agents arrested Spring in Kansas City, Missouri, during the undercover purchase.

An ATF agent on the scene of the arrest advised Spring of his *Miranda* rights. Spring was advised of his *Miranda* rights a second time after he was transported to the ATF office in Kansas City. At the ATF office, the agents also advised Spring that he had the right to stop the questioning at any time or to stop the questioning until the presence of an attorney could be secured. Spring then signed a written form stating that he understood and waived his rights, and that he was willing to make a statement and answer questions.

ATF agents first questioned Spring about the firearms transactions that led to his arrest. They then asked Spring if he had a criminal record. He admitted that he had a juvenile record for shooting his aunt when he was 10 years old. The agents asked if Spring had ever shot anyone else. Spring ducked his head and mumbled, "I shot another guy once." The agents asked Spring if he had ever been to Colorado. Spring said no. The agents asked Spring whether he had shot a man named Walker in Colorado and thrown his body into a snowbank. Spring paused and then ducked his head again and said no. The interview ended at this point.

On May 26, 1979, Colorado law enforcement officials visited Spring while he was in jail in Kansas City pursuant to his arrest on the firearms offenses. The officers gave Spring the *Miranda* warnings, and Spring again signed a written form indicating that he understood his rights and was willing to waive them. The officers informed Spring that they wanted to question him about the Colorado homicide. Spring indicated that he "wanted to get it off his chest." In an interview that lasted approximately 1½ hours, Spring confessed to the Colorado murder. During that time, Spring talked freely to the officers, did not indicate a desire to terminate the questioning, and never requested counsel. The officers prepared a written statement summarizing the interview. Spring read, edited, and signed the statement.

* * *

We granted certiorari to resolve an arguable Circuit conflict and to review the Colorado Supreme Court's determination that a suspect's awareness of the possible subjects of questioning is a relevant and sometimes determinative consideration in assessing whether a waiver of the Fifth Amendment privilege is valid. We now reverse.

II

There is no dispute that the police obtained the May 26 confession after complete *Miranda* warnings and after informing Spring that he would be questioned about the Colorado homicide. The Colorado Supreme Court nevertheless held that the confession should have been suppressed because it was the illegal "fruit" of the March 30 statement. A confession cannot be "fruit of the poisonous tree" if the tree itself is not poisonous.

Our inquiry, therefore, centers on the validity of the March 30 statement.[4]

* * *

There is no doubt that Spring's decision to waive his Fifth Amendment privilege was voluntary. He alleges no "coercion of a confession by physical violence or other deliberate means calculated to break [his] will," and the trial court found none. His allegation that the police failed to supply him with certain information does not relate to any of the traditional indicia of coercion: "the duration and conditions of detention . . ., the manifest attitude of the police toward him, his physical and mental state, the diverse pressures which sap or sustain his powers of resistance and self-control." Absent evidence that Spring's "will [was] overborne and his capacity for self-determination critically impaired" because of coercive police conduct, his waiver of his Fifth Amendment privilege was voluntary under this Court's decision in *Miranda*.

There also is no doubt that Spring's waiver of his Fifth Amendment privilege was knowingly and intelligently made: that is, that Spring understood that he had the right to remain silent and that anything he said could be used as evidence against him. The Constitution does not require that a criminal suspect know and understand every possible consequence of a waiver of the Fifth Amendment privilege. The Fifth Amendment's guarantee is both simpler and more fundamental: A defendant may not be compelled to be a witness against himself in any respect. The *Miranda* warnings protect this privilege by ensuring that a suspect knows that he may choose not to talk to law enforcement officers, to talk only with counsel present, or to discontinue talking at any time. The *Miranda* warnings ensure that a waiver of these rights is knowing and intelligent by requiring that the suspect be fully advised of this constitutional privilege, including the critical advice that whatever he chooses to say may be used as evidence against him.

In this case there is no allegation that Spring failed to understand the basic privilege guaranteed by the Fifth Amendment. Nor is there any allegation that he misunderstood the consequences of speaking freely to the law enforcement officials. In sum, we think that the trial court was indisputably correct in finding that Spring's waiver was made knowingly and intelligently within the meaning of *Miranda*.

---

[4] The State argued for the first time in its petition for rehearing to the Colorado Supreme Court that this Court's decision in *Oregon v. Elstad*, 470 U.S. 298 (1985), renders the May 26 statement admissible without regard to the validity of the March 30 waiver. The Colorado Supreme Court noted that the State would be free to make this argument to the trial court on remand. The question whether our decision in *Oregon v. Elstad* provides an independent basis for admitting the May 26 statement therefore is not before us in this case.

III

A

Spring relies on this Court's statement in *Miranda* that "any evidence that the accused was threatened, tricked, or cajoled into a waiver will . . . show that the defendant did not voluntarily waive his privilege." He contends that the failure to inform him of the potential subjects of interrogation constitutes the police trickery and deception condemned in *Miranda,* thus rendering his waiver of *Miranda* rights invalid. Spring, however, reads this statement in *Miranda* out of context and without due regard to the constitutional privilege the *Miranda* warnings were designed to protect.

We note first that the Colorado courts made no finding of official trickery. In fact, as noted above, the trial court expressly found that "there was no element of duress or coercion used to induce Spring's statements." Spring nevertheless insists that the failure of the ATF agents to inform him that he would be questioned about the murder constituted official "trickery" sufficient to invalidate his waiver of his Fifth Amendment privilege, even if the official conduct did not amount to "coercion." Even assuming that Spring's proposed distinction has merit, we reject his conclusion. This Court has never held that mere silence by law enforcement officials as to the subject matter of an interrogation is "trickery" sufficient to invalidate a suspect's waiver of *Miranda* rights, and we expressly decline so to hold today.[8]

Once *Miranda* warnings are given, it is difficult to see how official silence could cause a suspect to misunderstand the nature of his constitutional right—"his right to refuse to answer any question which might incriminate him." "Indeed, it seems self-evident that one who is told he is free to refuse to answer questions is in a curious posture to later complain that his answers were compelled." We have held that a valid waiver does not require that an individual be informed of all information "useful" in making his decision or all information that "might . . . affec[t] his decision to confess." "[W]e have never read the Constitution to require that the police supply a suspect with a flow of information to help him calibrate his self-interest in deciding whether to speak or stand by his rights." Here, the additional information could affect only the wisdom of a *Miranda* waiver, not its essentially voluntary and knowing nature.

---

[8] In certain circumstances, the Court has found affirmative misrepresentations by the police sufficient to invalidate a suspect's waiver of the Fifth Amendment privilege. See, *e.g., Lynumn v. Illinois,* 372 U.S. 528 (1963) (misrepresentation by police officers that a suspect would be deprived of state financial aid for her dependent child if she failed to cooperate with authorities rendered the subsequent confession involuntary); *Spano v. New York,* 360 U.S. 315 (1959) (misrepresentation by the suspect's friend that the friend would lose his job as a police officer if the suspect failed to cooperate rendered his statement involuntary). In this case, we are not confronted with an affirmative misrepresentation by law enforcement officials as to the scope of the interrogation and do not reach the question whether a waiver of *Miranda* rights would be valid in such a circumstance.

Accordingly, the failure of the law enforcement officials to inform Spring of the subject matter of the interrogation could not affect Spring's decision to waive his Fifth Amendment privilege in a constitutionally significant manner.

B

This Court's holding in *Miranda* specifically required that the police inform a criminal suspect that he has the right to remain silent and that *anything* he says may be used against him. There is no qualification of this broad and explicit warning. The warning, as formulated in *Miranda,* conveys to a suspect the nature of his constitutional privilege and the consequences of abandoning it. Accordingly, we hold that a suspect's awareness of all the possible subjects of questioning in advance of interrogation is not relevant to determining whether the suspect voluntarily, knowingly, and intelligently waived his Fifth Amendment privilege.

* * *

JUSTICE MARSHALL, with whom JUSTICE BRENNAN joins, dissenting.

* * *

Consistent with our prior decisions, the Court acknowledges that a suspect's waiver of fundamental constitutional rights, such as *Miranda*'s protections against self-incrimination during a custodial interrogation, must be examined in light of the "totality of the circumstances." Nonetheless, the Court proceeds to hold that the specific crimes and topics of investigation known to the interrogating officers before questioning begins are "not relevant" to, and in this case "could not affect," the validity of the suspect's decision to waive his Fifth Amendment privilege. It seems to me self-evident that a suspect's decision to waive this privilege will necessarily be influenced by his awareness of the scope and seriousness of the matters under investigation.

To attempt to minimize the relevance of such information by saying that it "could affect only the wisdom of" the suspect's waiver, as opposed to the validity of that waiver, ventures an inapposite distinction. Wisdom and validity in this context are overlapping concepts, as circumstances relevant to assessing the validity of a waiver may also be highly relevant to its wisdom in any given context. Indeed, the admittedly "critical" piece of advice the Court recognizes today—that the suspect be informed that whatever he says may be used as evidence against him—is certainly relevant to the wisdom of any suspect's decision to submit to custodial interrogation without first consulting his lawyer. The Court offers no principled basis for concluding that this is a relevant factor for determining the validity of a waiver but that, under what it calls a *totality* of the circumstances analysis, a suspect's knowledge of the specific crimes and other topics previously identified for questioning can never be.

The Court quotes *Moran v. Burbine,* as holding that "a valid waiver does not require that an individual be informed of *all* information 'useful' in making his decision or *all* information that 'might . . . affec[t] his decision to confess.' " Noticeably similar is the Court's holding today: "[A] suspect's awareness of *all* the possible subjects of questioning in advance of interrogation is not relevant to determining" the validity of his waiver. This careful phraseology avoids the important question whether the lack of *any* indication of the identified subjects for questioning *is* relevant to determining the validity of the suspect's waiver.

I would include among the relevant factors for consideration whether before waiving his Fifth Amendment rights the suspect was aware, either through the circumstances surrounding his arrest or through a specific advisement from the arresting or interrogating officers, of the crime or crimes he was suspected of committing and about which they intended to ask questions. To hold that such knowledge is relevant would not undermine the " 'virtue of informing police and prosecutors with specificity' as to how a pretrial questioning of a suspect must be conducted," nor would it interfere with the use of legitimate interrogation techniques. Indeed, requiring the officers to articulate at a minimum the crime or crimes for which the suspect has been arrested could contribute significantly toward ensuring that the arrest was in fact lawful and the suspect's statement not compelled because of an error at this stage alone, a problem we addressed in *Brown v. Illinois,* 422 U.S. 590, 601 (1975), under the Fourth Amendment on the assumption that the defendant's waiver of his Fifth Amendment rights in that case had been voluntary.

The interrogation tactics utilized in this case demonstrate the relevance of the information Spring did not receive. The agents evidently hoped to obtain from Spring a valid confession to the federal firearms charge for which he was arrested and then parlay this admission into an additional confession of first-degree murder. Spring could not have expected questions about the latter, separate offense when he agreed to waive his rights, as it occurred in a different State and was a violation of state law outside the normal investigative focus of federal Alcohol, Tobacco, and Firearms agents.

"Interrogators describe the point of the first admission as the 'breakthrough' and the 'beachhead,' which once obtained will give them enormous 'tactical advantages.' " *Oregon v. Elstad,* 470 U.S. 298, 328 (1985) (Brennan, J., dissenting). The coercive aspects of the psychological ploy intended in this case, when combined with an element of surprise which may far too easily rise to a level of deception, cannot be justified in light of *Miranda*'s strict requirements that the suspect's waiver and confession be voluntary, knowing, and intelligent. If a suspect has signed a waiver form with the intention of making a statement regarding a specifically alleged crime, the Court today would hold this waiver valid with respect to questioning about any other crime, regardless of its relation to the charges the suspect believes he will be asked to address. Yet once this waiver is given and the intended statement made, the protections afforded by *Miranda* against the "inherently compelling pressures" of the custodial interrogation have effectively dissipated. Additional questioning about entirely separate and more serious suspicions of criminal activity can take unfair advantage of the suspect's psychological state, as the unexpected questions cause the compulsive pressures suddenly to reappear. Given this technique of interrogation, a suspect's understanding of the topics planned for questioning is, therefore, at the very least "relevant" to assessing whether his decision to talk to the officers was voluntarily, knowingly, and intelligently made.

Not only is the suspect's awareness of the suspected criminal conduct relevant, its absence may be determinative in a given case. The State's burden of proving that a suspect's waiver was voluntary, knowing, and intelligent is a "heavy" one. We are to " 'indulge every reasonable presumption against waiver' of fundamental constitutional rights" and we shall " 'not presume acquiescence in the loss of fundamental rights.' " It is reasonable to conclude that, had Spring known of the federal agents' intent to ask questions about a murder unrelated to the offense for which he was arrested, he would not have consented to interrogation without first consulting his attorney. In this case, I would therefore accept the determination of the Colorado Supreme Court that Spring did not voluntarily, knowingly, and intelligently waive his Fifth Amendment rights.

Points for Discussion

1. The Court in *Burbine* permitted police deception partly because it was not directed at the defendant himself. Here, it seems clear that Springs believed he was being interrogated about one crime while the investigators were actually interested in a more serious one. How, then, does the Court conclude that Springs' waiver of his *Miranda* rights was voluntary, intelligent, and *knowing*?

MISSOURI V. SEIBERT

542 U.S. 600 (2004)

JUSTICE SOUTER announced the judgment of the court and delivered an opinion, in which JUSTICE STEVENS, JUSTICE GINSBURG, and JUSTICE BREYER join.

This case tests a police protocol for custodial interrogation that calls for giving no warnings of the rights to silence and counsel until interrogation has produced a confession. Although such a statement is generally inadmissible, since taken in violation of *Miranda v. Arizona,* 384

U.S. 436 (1966), the interrogating officer follows it with *Miranda* warnings and then leads the suspect to cover the same ground a second time. The question here is the admissibility of the repeated statement. Because this midstream recitation of warnings after interrogation and unwarned confession could not effectively comply with *Miranda's* constitutional requirement, we hold that a statement repeated after a warning in such circumstances is inadmissible.

I

Respondent Patrice Seibert's 12-year-old son Jonathan had cerebral palsy, and when he died in his sleep she feared charges of neglect because of bedsores on his body. In her presence, two of her teenage sons and two of their friends devised a plan to conceal the facts surrounding Jonathan's death by incinerating his body in the course of burning the family's mobile home, in which they planned to leave Donald Rector, a mentally ill teenager living with the family, to avoid any appearance that Jonathan had been unattended. Seibert's son Darian and a friend set the fire, and Donald died.

Five days later, the police awakened Seibert at 3 a.m. at a hospital where Darian was being treated for burns. In arresting her, Officer Kevin Clinton followed instructions from Rolla, Missouri, Officer Richard Hanrahan that he refrain from giving *Miranda* warnings. After Seibert had been taken to the police station and left alone in an interview room for 15 to 20 minutes, Officer Hanrahan questioned her without *Miranda* warnings for 30 to 40 minutes, squeezing her arm and repeating "Donald was also to die in his sleep." App. 59 (internal quotation marks omitted). After Seibert finally admitted she knew Donald was meant to die in the fire, she was given a 20-minute coffee and cigarette break. Officer Hanrahan then turned on a tape recorder, gave Seibert the *Miranda* warnings, and obtained a signed waiver of rights from her. He resumed the questioning with "Ok, 'trice, we've been talking for a little while about what happened on Wednesday the twelfth, haven't we?" and confronted her with her prewarning statements:

> Hanrahan: "Now, in discussion you told us, you told us that there was a[n] understanding about Donald."
>
> Seibert: "Yes."
>
> Hanrahan: "Did that take place earlier that morning?"
>
> Seibert: "Yes."
>
> Hanrahan: "And what was the understanding about Donald?"
>
> Seibert: "If they could get him out of the trailer, to take him out of the trailer."
>
> Hanrahan: "And if they couldn't?"

Seibert: "I, I never even thought about it. I just figured they would."

Hanrahan: " 'Trice, didn't you tell me that he was supposed to die in his sleep?"

Seibert: "If that would happen, 'cause he was on that new medicine, you know . . . ."

Hanrahan: "The Prozac? And it makes him sleepy. So he was supposed to die in his sleep?"

Seibert: "Yes."

After being charged with first-degree murder for her role in Donald's death, Seibert sought to exclude both her prewarning and postwarning statements. At the suppression hearing, Officer Hanrahan testified that he made a "conscious decision" to withhold *Miranda* warnings, thus resorting to an interrogation technique he had been taught: question first, then give the warnings, and then repeat the question "until I get the answer that she's already provided once." He acknowledged that Seibert's ultimate statement was "largely a repeat of information . . . obtained" prior to the warning.

* * *

III

* * *

The technique of interrogating in successive, unwarned and warned phases raises a new challenge to *Miranda*. Although we have no statistics on the frequency of this practice, it is not confined to Rolla, Missouri. An officer of that police department testified that the strategy of withholding *Miranda* warnings until after interrogating and drawing out a confession was promoted not only by his own department, but by a national police training organization and other departments in which he had worked. Consistently with the officer's testimony, the Police Law Institute, for example, instructs that "officers may conduct a two-stage interrogation. . . . At any point during the pre-*Miranda* interrogation, usually after arrestees have confessed, officers may then read the *Miranda* warnings and ask for a waiver. If the arrestees waive their *Miranda* rights, officers will be able to repeat any *subsequent* incriminating statements later in court." The upshot of all this advice is a question-first practice of some popularity, as one can see from the reported cases describing its use, sometimes in obedience to departmental policy.

It is not the case, of course, that law enforcement educators en masse are urging that *Miranda* be honored only in the breach. Most police manuals do not advocate the question-first tactic, because they understand that *Oregon v. Elstad,* 470 U.S. 298 (1985), involved an officer's good-faith failure to warn.

IV[a]

When a confession so obtained is offered and challenged, attention must be paid to the conflicting objects of *Miranda* and question-first. *Miranda* addressed "interrogation practices . . . likely . . . to disable [an individual] from making a free and rational choice" about speaking and held that a suspect must be "adequately and effectively" advised of the choice the Constitution guarantees. The object of question-first is to render *Miranda* warnings ineffective by waiting for a particularly opportune time to give them, after the suspect has already confessed.[b]

Just as "no talismanic incantation [is] required to satisfy [*Miranda's*] strictures," *California v. Prysock,* 453 U.S. 355, 359 (1981) *(per curiam),* it would be absurd to think that mere recitation of the litany suffices to satisfy *Miranda* in every conceivable circumstance. "The inquiry is simply whether the warnings reasonably 'conve[y] to [a suspect] his rights as required by *Miranda.*'" *Duckworth v. Eagan,* 492 U.S. 195, 203 (1989) (quoting *Prysock,* at 361). The threshold issue when interrogators question first and warn later is thus whether it would be reasonable to find that in these circumstances the warnings could function "effectively" as *Miranda* requires. Could the warnings effectively advise the suspect that he had a real choice about giving an admissible statement at that juncture? Could they reasonably convey that he could choose to stop talking even if he had talked earlier? For unless the warnings could place a suspect who has just been interrogated in a position to make such an informed choice, there is no practical justification for accepting the formal warnings as compliance with *Miranda,* or for treating the second stage of interrogation as distinct from the first, unwarned and inadmissible segment.[4]

---

[a] In *Elstad,* the officers questioned the defendant in his parents' living room before taking him to the station house. The officers believed, apparently in good faith, that Elstad was not yet in custody and that there was no reason to Mirandize him. Their subsequent questioning of the defendant, which took place at the station, was preceded by appropriate warnings. The Court rejected the assertion that a Mirandized confession that follows an un-Mirandized confession is always inadmissible in the government's case in chief.—Eds.

[b] The Court notes in note 4 that *Elstad* refused to apply the fruit of the poisonous tree doctrine to a Mirandized confession that followed an un-Mirandized one. *United States v. Patane,* decided the same day as *Seibert,* held the fruit of the poisonous tree doctrine inapplicable to the tangible fruits of a *Miranda* violation.—Eds.

[4] Respondent Seibert argues that her second confession should be excluded from evidence under the doctrine known by the metaphor of the "fruit of the poisonous tree," developed in the Fourth Amendment context in *Wong Sun v. United States,* 371 U.S. 471 (1963): evidence otherwise admissible but discovered as a result of an earlier violation is excluded as tainted, lest the law encourage future violations. But the Court in *Elstad* rejected the *Wong Sun* fruits doctrine for analyzing the admissibility of a subsequent warned confession following "an initial failure . . . to administer the warnings required by *Miranda.*" In *Elstad,* "a simple failure to administer the warnings, unaccompanied by any actual coercion or other circumstances calculated to undermine the suspect's ability to exercise his free will," did not "so tain[t] the investigatory process that a subsequent voluntary and informed waiver is ineffective for some indeterminate period. Though *Miranda* requires that the unwarned admission must be suppressed, the admissibility of any

There is no doubt about the answer that proponents of question-first give to this question about the effectiveness of warnings given only after successful interrogation, and we think their answer is correct. By any objective measure, applied to circumstances exemplified here, it is likely that if the interrogators employ the technique of withholding warnings until after interrogation succeeds in eliciting a confession, the warnings will be ineffective in preparing the suspect for successive interrogation, close in time and similar in content. After all, the reason that question-first is catching on is as obvious as its manifest purpose, which is to get a confession the suspect would not make if he understood his rights at the outset; the sensible underlying assumption is that with one confession in hand before the warnings, the interrogator can count on getting its duplicate, with trifling additional trouble. Upon hearing warnings only in the aftermath of interrogation and just after making a confession, a suspect would hardly think he had a genuine right to remain silent, let alone persist in so believing once the police began to lead him over the same ground again.[5]

A more likely reaction on a suspect's part would be perplexity about the reason for discussing rights at that point, bewilderment being an unpromising frame of mind for knowledgeable decision. What is worse, telling a suspect that "anything you say can and will be used against you," without expressly excepting the statement just given, could lead to an entirely reasonable inference that what he has just said will be used, with subsequent silence being of no avail. Thus, when *Miranda* warnings are inserted in the midst of coordinated and continuing interrogation, they are likely to mislead and "depriv[e] a defendant of knowledge essential to his ability to understand the nature of his rights and the consequences of abandoning them." *Moran v. Burbine,* 475 U.S. 412, 424 (1986). By the same token, it would ordinarily be unrealistic to treat two spates of integrated and proximately conducted questioning as independent interrogations subject to independent evaluation simply because *Miranda* warnings formally punctuate them in the middle.

---

subsequent statement should turn in these circumstances solely on whether it is knowingly and voluntarily made." *Elstad* held that "a suspect who has once responded to unwarned yet uncoercive questioning is not thereby disabled from waiving his rights and confessing after he has been given the requisite *Miranda* warnings." In a sequential confession case, clarity is served if the later confession is approached by asking whether in the circumstances the *Miranda* warnings given could reasonably be found effective. If yes, a court can take up the standard issues of voluntary waiver and voluntary statement; if no, the subsequent statement is inadmissible for want of adequate *Miranda* warnings, because the earlier and later statements are realistically seen as parts of a single, unwarned sequence of questioning.

[5] It bears emphasizing that the effectiveness *Miranda* assumes the warnings can have must potentially extend through the repeated interrogation, since a suspect has a right to stop at any time. It seems highly unlikely that a suspect could retain any such understanding when the interrogator leads him a second time through a line of questioning the suspect has already answered fully. The point is not that a later unknowing or involuntary confession cancels out an earlier, adequate warning; the point is that the warning is unlikely to be effective in the question-first sequence we have described.

V

* * *

The contrast between *Elstad* and this case reveals a series of relevant facts that bear on whether *Miranda* warnings delivered midstream could be effective enough to accomplish their object: the completeness and detail of the questions and answers in the first round of interrogation, the overlapping content of the two statements, the timing and setting of the first and the second, the continuity of police personnel, and the degree to which the interrogator's questions treated the second round as continuous with the first. In *Elstad,* it was not unreasonable to see the occasion for questioning at the station house as presenting a markedly different experience from the short conversation at home; since a reasonable person in the suspect's shoes could have seen the station house questioning as a new and distinct experience, the *Miranda* warnings could have made sense as presenting a genuine choice whether to follow up on the earlier admission.

At the opposite extreme are the facts here, which by any objective measure reveal a police strategy adapted to undermine the *Miranda* warnings.[6] The unwarned interrogation was conducted in the station house, and the questioning was systematic, exhaustive, and managed with psychological skill. When the police were finished there was little, if anything, of incriminating potential left unsaid. The warned phase of questioning proceeded after a pause of only 15 to 20 minutes, in the same place as the unwarned segment. When the same officer who had conducted the first phase recited the *Miranda* warnings, he said nothing to counter the probable misimpression that the advice that anything Seibert said could be used against her also applied to the details of the inculpatory statement previously elicited. In particular, the police did not advise that her prior statement could not be used.[7]

Nothing was said or done to dispel the oddity of warning about legal rights to silence and counsel right after the police had led her through a systematic interrogation, and any uncertainty on her part about a right to stop talking about matters previously discussed would only have been aggravated by the way Officer Hanrahan set the scene by saying "we've been talking for a little while about what happened on Wednesday the twelfth, haven't we?" The impression that the further questioning was a mere continuation of the earlier questions and responses was fostered by references back to the confession already given. It would have been

[6] Because the intent of the officer will rarely be as candidly admitted as it was here (even as it is likely to determine the conduct of the interrogation), the focus is on facts apart from intent that show the question-first tactic at work.

[7] We do not hold that a formal addendum warning that a previous statement could not be used would be sufficient to change the character of the question-first procedure to the point of rendering an ensuing statement admissible, but its absence is clearly a factor that blunts the efficacy of the warnings and points to a continuing, not a new, interrogation.

reasonable to regard the two sessions as parts of a continuum, in which it would have been unnatural to refuse to repeat at the second stage what had been said before. These circumstances must be seen as challenging the comprehensibility and efficacy of the *Miranda* warnings to the point that a reasonable person in the suspect's shoes would not have understood them to convey a message that she retained a choice about continuing to talk.

VI

Strategists dedicated to draining the substance out of *Miranda* cannot accomplish by training instructions what *Dickerson* held Congress could not do by statute. Because the question-first tactic effectively threatens to thwart *Miranda's* purpose of reducing the risk that a coerced confession would be admitted, and because the facts here do not reasonably support a conclusion that the warnings given could have served their purpose, Seibert's postwarning statements are inadmissible. The judgment of the Supreme Court of Missouri is affirmed.

JUSTICE BREYER, concurring.

In my view, the following simple rule should apply to the two-stage interrogation technique: Courts should exclude the "fruits" of the initial unwarned questioning unless the failure to warn was in good faith. I believe this is a sound and workable approach to the problem this case presents. Prosecutors and judges have long understood how to apply the "fruits" approach, which they use in other areas of law. And in the workaday world of criminal law enforcement the administrative simplicity of the familiar has significant advantages over a more complex exclusionary rule.

I believe the plurality's approach in practice will function as a "fruits" test. The truly "effective" *Miranda* warnings on which the plurality insists will occur only when certain circumstances—a lapse in time, a change in location or interrogating officer, or a shift in the focus of the questioning—intervene between the unwarned questioning and any postwarning statement.

I consequently join the plurality's opinion in full. I also agree with Justice KENNEDY's opinion insofar as it is consistent with this approach and makes clear that a good-faith exception applies.

JUSTICE KENNEDY, concurring in the judgment.

* * *

The technique used in this case distorts the meaning of *Miranda* and furthers no legitimate countervailing interest. The *Miranda* rule would be frustrated were we to allow police to undermine its meaning and effect. The technique simply creates too high a risk that postwarning statements will be obtained when a suspect was deprived of "knowledge essential to his ability to understand the nature of his rights and the consequences of abandoning them." When an interrogator uses this deliberate, two-step strategy, predicated upon violating *Miranda* during an extended interview, postwarning statements that are related to the substance of prewarning statements must be excluded absent specific, curative steps.

The plurality concludes that whenever a two-stage interview occurs, admissibility of the postwarning statement should depend on "whether [the] *Miranda* warnings delivered midstream could have been effective enough to accomplish their object" given the specific facts of the case. This test envisions an objective inquiry from the perspective of the suspect, and applies in the case of both intentional and unintentional two-stage interrogations. In my view, this test cuts too broadly. *Miranda's* clarity is one of its strengths, and a multifactor test that applies to every two-stage interrogation may serve to undermine that clarity. I would apply a narrower test applicable only in the infrequent case, such as we have here, in which the two-step interrogation technique was used in a calculated way to undermine the *Miranda* warning.

The admissibility of postwarning statements should continue to be governed by the principles of *Elstad* unless the deliberate two-step strategy was employed. If the deliberate two-step strategy has been used, postwarning statements that are related to the substance of prewarning statements must be excluded unless curative measures are taken before the postwarning statement is made. Curative measures should be designed to ensure that a reasonable person in the suspect's situation would understand the import and effect of the *Miranda* warning and of the *Miranda* waiver. For example, a substantial break in time and circumstances between the prewarning statement and the *Miranda* warning may suffice in most circumstances, as it allows the accused to distinguish the two contexts and appreciate that the interrogation has taken a new turn. Alternatively, an additional warning that explains the likely inadmissibility of the prewarning custodial statement may be sufficient. No curative steps were taken in this case, however, so the postwarning statements are inadmissible and the conviction cannot stand.

JUSTICE O'CONNOR, with whom THE CHIEF JUSTICE, JUSTICE SCALIA, and JUSTICE THOMAS join, dissenting.

The plurality devours *Oregon v. Elstad,* 470 U.S. 298 (1985), even as it accuses petitioner's argument of "disfigur[ing]" that decision. I believe that we are bound by *Elstad* to reach a different result, and I would vacate the judgment of the Supreme Court of Missouri.

I

On two preliminary questions I am in full agreement with the plurality. First, the plurality appropriately follows *Elstad* in concluding that Seibert's statement cannot be held inadmissible under a "fruit of the poisonous tree" theory. Second, the plurality correctly declines to focus its analysis on the subjective intent of the interrogating officer.

A

* * *

Although the analysis the plurality ultimately espouses examines the same facts and circumstances that a "fruits" analysis would consider (such as the lapse of time between the two interrogations and change of questioner or location), it does so for entirely different reasons. The fruits analysis would examine those factors because they are relevant to the balance of deterrence value versus the "drastic and socially costly course" of excluding reliable evidence. The plurality, by contrast, looks to those factors to inform the *psychological* judgment regarding whether the suspect has been informed effectively of her right to remain silent. The analytical underpinnings of the two approaches are thus entirely distinct, and they should not be conflated just because they function similarly in practice.

B

The plurality's rejection of an intent-based test is also, in my view, correct. Freedom from compulsion lies at the heart of the Fifth Amendment, and requires us to assess whether a suspect's decision to speak truly was voluntary. Because voluntariness is a matter of the suspect's state of mind, we focus our analysis on the way in which suspects experience interrogation.

* * *

Because the isolated fact of Officer Hanrahan's intent could not have had any bearing on Seibert's "capacity to comprehend and knowingly relinquish" her right to remain silent, it could not by itself affect the voluntariness of her confession. Moreover, recognizing an exception to *Elstad* for intentional violations would require focusing constitutional analysis on a police officer's subjective intent, an unattractive proposition that we all but uniformly avoid. In general, "we believe that 'sending state and federal courts on an expedition into the minds of police officers would produce a grave and fruitless misallocation of judicial resources.'" *United States v. Leon,* 468 U.S. 897, 922, n. 23 (1984). This case presents the uncommonly straightforward circumstance of an officer openly admitting that the violation was intentional. But the inquiry will be complicated in other situations probably more likely to occur. For example, different officers involved in an interrogation might claim different states of mind regarding the failure to give *Miranda* warnings. Even in the simple case of a single officer who claims that a failure to give *Miranda* warnings was inadvertent, the likelihood of error will be high.

* * *

For these reasons, I believe that the approach espoused by Justice KENNEDY is ill advised. Justice KENNEDY would extend *Miranda's* exclusionary rule to any case in which the use of the "two-step interrogation technique" was "deliberate" or "calculated." This approach untethers the analysis from facts knowable to, and therefore having any potential directly to affect, the suspect. Far from promoting "clarity," the approach will add a third step to the suppression inquiry. In virtually every two-stage interrogation case, in addition to addressing the standard *Miranda* and voluntariness questions, courts will be forced to conduct the kind of difficult, state-of-mind inquiry that we normally take pains to avoid.

II

The plurality's adherence to *Elstad,* and mine to the plurality, end there. Our decision in *Elstad* rejected two lines of argument advanced in favor of suppression. The first was based on the "fruit of the poisonous tree" doctrine, discussed above. The second was the argument that the "lingering compulsion" inherent in a defendant's having let the "cat out of the bag" required suppression. The Court of Appeals of Oregon, in accepting the latter argument, had endorsed a theory indistinguishable from the one today's plurality adopts: "[T]he coercive impact of the unconstitutionally obtained statement remains, because in a defendant's mind it has sealed his fate. It is this impact that must be dissipated in order to make a subsequent confession admissible."

We rejected this theory outright. We did so not because we refused to recognize the "psychological impact of the suspect's conviction that he has let the cat out of the bag," but because we refused to "endo[w]" those "psychological effects" with "constitutional implications." To do so, we said, would "effectively immuniz[e] a suspect who responds to pre-*Miranda* warning questions from the consequences of his subsequent informed waiver," an immunity that "comes at a high cost to legitimate law enforcement activity, while adding little desirable protection to the individual's interest in not being *compelled* to testify against himself." The plurality might very well think that we struck the balance between Fifth Amendment rights and law enforcement interests incorrectly in *Elstad;* but that is not normally a sufficient reason for ignoring the dictates of *stare decisis.*

I would analyze the two-step interrogation procedure under the voluntariness standards central to the Fifth Amendment and reiterated in *Elstad. Elstad* commands that if Seibert's first statement is shown to have been involuntary, the court must examine whether the taint dissipated through the passing of time or a change in circumstances: "When a prior statement is actually coerced, the time that passes between confessions, the change in place of interrogations, and the change in identity of the interrogators all bear on whether that coercion has carried over into the second confession." In addition, Seibert's second statement should be suppressed if she showed that it was involuntary despite the *Miranda* warnings. Although I would leave this analysis for the Missouri courts to conduct on remand, I note that, unlike the officers in *Elstad,* Officer Hanrahan referred to Seibert's unwarned statement during the second part of the interrogation when she made a statement at odds with her unwarned confession. Such a tactic may bear on the voluntariness inquiry.

* * *

Because I believe that the plurality gives insufficient deference to *Elstad* and that Justice KENNEDY places improper weight on subjective intent, I respectfully dissent.

Points for Discussion

1. *Oregon v. Elstad*, cited in *Siebert*, held that a Mirandized statement that follows an un-Mirandized statement can be admissible if the defendant's waiver of *Miranda* is voluntary. Why did the Court not simply follow that rule in this case? What result would have obtained in this case under that analysis?

2. Note that the Justice Souter's opinion is joined by only three other justices. What, in the end, does *Seibert* stand for?

3. The officers in this case admitted that they set out systematically to obtain a confession, then read the *Miranda* warnings, then obtain a second confession. How might the Court have ruled if the evidence of malfeasance had been less clear? What incentives does that create for law enforcement officers in future cases?

D. CONTINUING VALIDITY

DICKERSON V. UNITED STATES

530 U.S. 428 (2000)

CHIEF JUSTICE REHNQUIST delivered the opinion of the court.

In *Miranda v. Arizona,* 384 U.S. 436 (1966), we held that certain warnings must be given before a suspect's statement made during custodial interrogation could be admitted in evidence. In the wake of that decision, Congress enacted 18 U.S.C. § 3501, which in essence laid down a rule that the admissibility of such statements should turn only on whether or not they were voluntarily made. We hold that *Miranda,* being a constitutional decision of this Court, may not be in effect overruled by an Act of Congress, and we decline to overrule *Miranda* ourselves. We therefore hold that *Miranda* and its progeny in this Court govern the admissibility of statements made during custodial interrogation in both state and federal courts.

Petitioner Dickerson was indicted for bank robbery, conspiracy to commit bank robbery, and using a firearm in the course of committing a crime of violence, all in violation of the applicable provisions of Title 18 of the United States Code. Before trial, Dickerson moved to suppress a statement he had made at a Federal Bureau of Investigation field office, on the grounds that he had not received "*Miranda* warnings" before being interrogated. The District Court granted his motion to suppress, and the Government took an interlocutory appeal to the United States Court of Appeals for the Fourth Circuit. That court, by a divided vote, reversed the District Court's suppression order. It agreed with the District Court's conclusion that petitioner had not received *Miranda* warnings before making his statement. But it went on to hold that § 3501, which in effect makes the admissibility of statements such as Dickerson's turn solely on whether they were made voluntarily, was satisfied in this case. It then concluded that our decision in *Miranda* was not a constitutional holding, and that, therefore, Congress could by statute have the final say on the question of admissibility.

Because of the importance of the questions raised by the Court of Appeals' decision, we granted certiorari and now reverse.

We begin with a brief historical account of the law governing the admission of confessions. Prior to *Miranda,* we evaluated the admissibility of a suspect's confession under a voluntariness test. The roots of this test developed in the common law, as the courts of England and then the United States recognized that coerced confessions are inherently untrustworthy. Over time, our cases recognized two constitutional bases for the requirement that a confession be voluntary to be admitted into evidence: the Fifth Amendment right against self-incrimination and the Due Process Clause of the Fourteenth Amendment.

* * *

We have never abandoned this due process jurisprudence, and thus continue to exclude confessions that were obtained involuntarily. But our decisions in *Malloy v. Hogan,* 378 U.S. 1 (1964), and *Miranda* changed the focus of much of the inquiry in determining the admissibility of suspects' incriminating statements. In *Malloy,* we held that the Fifth Amendment's Self-Incrimination Clause is incorporated in the Due Process Clause of the Fourteenth Amendment and thus applies to the States. We decided *Miranda* on the heels of *Malloy.*

In *Miranda,* we noted that the advent of modern custodial police interrogation brought with it an increased concern about confessions obtained by coercion. Because custodial police interrogation, by its very nature, isolates and pressures the individual, we stated that "[e]ven without employing brutality, the 'third degree' or [other] specific stratagems, . . . custodial interrogation exacts a heavy toll on individual liberty and trades on the weakness of individuals." We concluded that the coercion inherent in custodial interrogation blurs the line between voluntary and involuntary statements, and thus heightens the risk that an individual will not be "accorded his privilege under the Fifth Amendment . . . not to be compelled to incriminate himself." Accordingly, we laid down "concrete constitutional guidelines for law enforcement agencies and courts to follow." Those guidelines established that the admissibility in evidence of any statement given during custodial interrogation of a suspect would depend on whether the police provided the suspect with four warnings. These warnings (which have come to be known colloquially as "*Miranda* rights") are: a suspect "has the right to remain silent, that anything he says can be used against him in a court of law, that he has the right to the presence of an attorney, and that if he cannot afford an attorney one will be appointed for him prior to any questioning if he so desires."

Two years after *Miranda* was decided, Congress enacted § 3501. That section provides, in relevant part:

> (a) In any criminal prosecution brought by the United States or by the District of Columbia, a confession . . . shall be admissible in evidence if it is voluntarily given. Before such confession is received in evidence, the trial judge shall, out of the presence of the jury, determine any issue as to voluntariness. If the trial judge determines that the confession was voluntarily made it shall be admitted in evidence and the trial judge shall permit the jury to hear relevant evidence on the issue of voluntariness and shall instruct the jury to give such weight to the confession as the jury feels it deserves under all the circumstances.
>
> (b) The trial judge in determining the issue of voluntariness shall take into consideration all the circumstances surrounding the giving of the confession, including (1) the time elapsing between arrest and arraignment of the defendant making the confession, if it was made after arrest and before arraignment, (2) whether such defendant knew the nature of the offense with which he was charged or of which he was suspected at the time of making the confession, (3) whether or not such defendant was advised or knew that he was not required to make any statement and that any such statement could be used against him, (4) whether or not such defendant had been advised prior to questioning of his right to the assistance of counsel; and (5) whether or not such defendant was without the assistance of counsel when questioned and when giving such confession.
>
> The presence or absence of any of the above-mentioned factors to be taken into consideration by the judge need not be conclusive on the issue of voluntariness of the confession.

Given § 3501's express designation of voluntariness as the touchstone of admissibility, its omission of any warning requirement, and the instruction for trial courts to consider a nonexclusive list of factors relevant to the circumstances of a confession, we agree with the Court of Appeals that Congress intended by its enactment to overrule *Miranda*. Because of the obvious conflict between our decision in *Miranda* and § 3501, we must address whether Congress has constitutional authority to thus supersede *Miranda*. If Congress has such authority, § 3501's totality-of-the-circumstances approach must prevail over *Miranda's* requirement of warnings; if not, that section must yield to *Miranda's* more specific requirements.

The law in this area is clear. This Court has supervisory authority over the federal courts, and we may use that authority to prescribe rules of evidence and procedure that are binding in those tribunals. However, the power to judicially create and enforce nonconstitutional "rules of procedure and evidence for the federal courts exists only in the absence of a relevant Act of Congress." Congress retains the ultimate authority to modify or set aside any judicially created rules of evidence and procedure that are not required by the Constitution.

But Congress may not legislatively supersede our decisions interpreting and applying the Constitution. This case therefore turns on whether the *Miranda* Court announced a constitutional rule or merely exercised its supervisory authority to regulate evidence in the absence of congressional direction. Recognizing this point, the Court of Appeals surveyed *Miranda* and its progeny to determine the constitutional status of the *Miranda* decision. Relying on the fact that we have created several exceptions to *Miranda's* warnings requirement and that we have repeatedly referred to the *Miranda* warnings as "prophylactic," and "not themselves rights protected by the Constitution," *Michigan v. Tucker,* 417 U.S. 433, 444 (1974), the Court of Appeals concluded that the protections announced in *Miranda* are not constitutionally required.

We disagree with the Court of Appeals' conclusion, although we concede that there is language in some of our opinions that supports the view taken by that court. But first and foremost of the factors on the other side—that *Miranda* is a constitutional decision—is that both *Miranda* and two of its companion cases applied the rule to proceedings in state courts—to wit, Arizona, California, and New York. Since that time, we have consistently applied *Miranda*'s rule to prosecutions arising in state courts. It is beyond dispute that we do not hold a supervisory power over the courts of the several States. With respect to proceedings in state courts, our "authority is limited to enforcing the commands of the United States Constitution."

The *Miranda* opinion itself begins by stating that the Court granted certiorari "to explore some facets of the problems . . . of applying the privilege against self-incrimination to in-custody interrogation, *and to give concrete constitutional guidelines for law enforcement agencies and courts to follow.*" (emphasis added). In fact, the majority opinion is replete with statements indicating that the majority thought it was announcing a constitutional rule. Indeed, the Court's ultimate conclusion was that the unwarned confessions obtained in the four cases before the Court in *Miranda* "were obtained from the defendant under circumstances that did not meet constitutional standards for protection of the privilege."

Additional support for our conclusion that *Miranda* is constitutionally based is found in the *Miranda* Court's invitation for legislative action to protect the constitutional right against coerced self-incrimination. After discussing the "compelling pressures" inherent in custodial police interrogation, the *Miranda* Court concluded that, "[i]n order to combat these pressures and to permit a full opportunity to exercise the privilege against self-incrimination, the accused must be adequately and effectively apprised of his rights and the exercise of those rights must be fully honored." However, the Court emphasized that it could not foresee "the potential alternatives for protecting the privilege which might be devised by Congress or the States," and it accordingly opined that the Constitution would not preclude legislative solutions that differed from the prescribed *Miranda* warnings but which were "at least as effective in apprising accused persons of their right of silence and in assuring a continuous opportunity to exercise it."

The Court of Appeals also relied on the fact that we have, after our *Miranda* decision, made exceptions from its rule in cases such as *New York v. Quarles,* 467 U.S. 649 (1984), and *Harris v. New York,* 401 U.S. 222 (1971). But we have also broadened the application of the *Miranda* doctrine in cases such as *Doyle v. Ohio,* 426 U.S. 610 (1976), and *Arizona v. Roberson,* 486 U.S. 675 (1988). These decisions illustrate the principle—not that *Miranda* is not a constitutional rule—but that no constitutional rule is immutable. No court laying down a general rule can possibly foresee the various circumstances in which counsel will seek to apply it, and the sort of modifications represented by these cases are as much a normal part of constitutional law as the original decision.

* * *

As an alternative argument for sustaining the Court of Appeals' decision, the court-invited *amicus curiae*[7] contends that the section complies with the requirement that a legislative alternative to *Miranda* be equally as effective in preventing coerced confessions. We agree with the *amicus*' contention that there are more remedies available for abusive police conduct than there were at the time *Miranda* was decided. But we do not agree that these additional measures supplement § 3501's protections sufficiently to meet the constitutional minimum. *Miranda* requires procedures that will warn a suspect in custody of his right to

---

[7] Because no party to the underlying litigation argued in favor of § 3501's constitutionality in this Court, we invited Professor Paul Cassell to assist our deliberations by arguing in support of the judgment below.

remain silent and which will assure the suspect that the exercise of that right will be honored. As discussed above, § 3501 explicitly eschews a requirement of preinterrogation warnings in favor of an approach that looks to the administration of such warnings as only one factor in determining the voluntariness of a suspect's confession. The additional remedies cited by *amicus* do not, in our view, render them, together with § 3501, an adequate substitute for the warnings required by *Miranda*.

The dissent argues that it is judicial overreaching for this Court to hold § 3501 unconstitutional unless we hold that the *Miranda* warnings are required by the Constitution, in the sense that nothing else will suffice to satisfy constitutional requirements. But we need not go further than *Miranda* to decide this case. In *Miranda,* the Court noted that reliance on the traditional totality-of-the-circumstances test raised a risk of overlooking an involuntary custodial confession, a risk that the Court found unacceptably great when the confession is offered in the case in chief to prove guilt. The Court therefore concluded that something more than the totality test was necessary. As discussed above, § 3501 reinstates the totality test as sufficient. Section 3501 therefore cannot be sustained if *Miranda* is to remain the law.

Whether or not we would agree with *Miranda's* reasoning and its resulting rule were we addressing the issue in the first instance, the principles of *stare decisis* weigh heavily against overruling it now. While "*stare decisis* is not an inexorable command," particularly when we are interpreting the Constitution, "even in constitutional cases, the doctrine carries such persuasive force that we have always required a departure from precedent to be supported by some 'special justification.' "

We do not think there is such justification for overruling *Miranda*. *Miranda* has become embedded in routine police practice to the point where the warnings have become part of our national culture. While we have overruled our precedents when subsequent cases have undermined their doctrinal underpinnings, we do not believe that this has happened to the *Miranda* decision. If anything, our subsequent cases have reduced the impact of the *Miranda* rule on legitimate law enforcement while reaffirming the decision's core ruling that unwarned statements may not be used as evidence in the prosecution's case in chief.

The disadvantage of the *Miranda* rule is that statements which may be by no means involuntary, made by a defendant who is aware of his "rights," may nonetheless be excluded and a guilty defendant go free as a result. But experience suggests that the totality-of-the-circumstances test which § 3501 seeks to revive is more difficult than *Miranda* for law enforcement officers to conform to, and for courts to apply in a consistent manner. The requirement that *Miranda* warnings be given does not, of course, dispense with the voluntariness inquiry. But as we said in *Berkemer v. McCarty,* 468 U.S. 420 (1984), "[c]ases in which a defendant can make a colorable argument that a self-incriminating statement was 'compelled' despite the fact that the law enforcement authorities adhered to the dictates of *Miranda* are rare."

* * *

JUSTICE SCALIA, with whom JUSTICE THOMAS joins, dissenting.

Those to whom judicial decisions are an unconnected series of judgments that produce either favored or disfavored results will doubtless greet today's decision as a paragon of moderation, since it declines to overrule *Miranda v. Arizona,* 384 U.S. 436 (1966). Those who understand the judicial process will appreciate that today's decision is not a reaffirmation of *Miranda,* but a radical revision of the most significant element of *Miranda* (as of all cases): the rationale that gives it a permanent place in our jurisprudence.

Marbury v. Madison, 1 Cranch 137 (1803), held that an Act of Congress will not be enforced by the courts if what it prescribes violates the Constitution of the United States. That was the basis on which *Miranda* was decided. One will search today's opinion in vain, however, for a statement (surely simple enough to make) that what 18 U.S.C. § 3501 prescribes—the use at trial of a voluntary confession, even when a *Miranda* warning or its equivalent has failed to be given—violates the Constitution. The reason the statement does not appear is not only (and perhaps not so much) that it would be absurd, inasmuch as § 3501 excludes from trial precisely what the Constitution excludes from trial, viz., compelled confessions; but also that Justices whose votes are needed to compose today's majority are on record as believing that a violation of *Miranda* is *not* a violation of the Constitution. And so, to justify today's agreed-upon result, the Court must adopt a significant *new,* if not entirely comprehensible, principle of constitutional law. As the Court chooses to describe that principle, statutes of Congress can be disregarded, not only when what they prescribe violates the Constitution, but when what they prescribe contradicts a decision of this Court that "announced a constitutional rule." As I shall discuss in some detail, the only thing that can possibly mean in the context of this case is that this Court has the power, not merely to apply the Constitution but to expand it, imposing what it regards as useful "prophylactic" restrictions upon Congress and the States. That is an immense and frightening antidemocratic power, and it does not exist.

It takes only a small step to bring today's opinion out of the realm of power-judging and into the mainstream of legal reasoning: The Court need only go beyond its carefully couched iterations that "*Miranda* is a constitutional decision," that "*Miranda* is constitutionally based," that *Miranda* has "constitutional underpinnings," and come out and say quite clearly: "We reaffirm today that custodial interrogation that is not preceded by *Miranda* warnings or their equivalent violates the Constitution of the United States." It cannot say that, because a majority of the Court does not believe it. The Court therefore acts in plain violation of the Constitution when it denies effect to this Act of Congress.

I

* * *

It was once possible to characterize the so-called *Miranda* rule as resting (however implausibly) upon the proposition that what the statute here before us permits—the admission at trial of un-Mirandized confessions—violates the Constitution. That is the fairest reading of the *Miranda* case itself. The Court began by announcing that the Fifth Amendment privilege against self-incrimination applied in the context of extrajudicial custodial interrogation—itself a doubtful proposition as a matter both of history and precedent. Having extended the privilege into the confines of the station house, the Court liberally sprinkled throughout its sprawling 60-page opinion suggestions that, because of the compulsion inherent in custodial interrogation, the privilege was violated by any statement thus obtained that did not conform to the rules set forth in *Miranda,* or some functional equivalent.

The dissenters, for their part, also understood *Miranda's* holding to be based on the "premise . . . that pressure on the suspect must be eliminated though it be only the subtle influence of the atmosphere and surroundings." And at least one case decided shortly after *Miranda* explicitly confirmed the view. See *Orozco v. Texas,* 394 U.S. 324, 326 (1969) ("[T]he use of these admissions obtained in the absence of the required warnings was a flat violation of the Self-Incrimination Clause of the Fifth Amendment as construed in *Miranda*").

So understood, *Miranda* was objectionable for innumerable reasons, not least the fact that cases spanning more than 70 years had rejected its core premise that, absent the warnings and an effective waiver of the right to remain silent and of the (thitherto unknown) right to have an attorney present, a statement obtained pursuant to custodial interrogation was necessarily the product of compulsion. Moreover, history and precedent aside, the decision in *Miranda,* if read as an explication of what the Constitution *requires,* is preposterous. There is, for example, simply no basis in reason for concluding that a response to the very first question asked, by a suspect who already *knows* all of the rights described in the *Miranda* warning, is anything other than a volitional act. And even if one assumes that the elimination of compulsion absolutely requires informing even the most knowledgeable suspect of his right to remain silent, it cannot conceivably require the right to have *counsel* present. There is a world of difference, which the Court recognized under the traditional voluntariness test but ignored in *Miranda,* between compelling a suspect to incriminate himself and preventing him from foolishly doing so of his own accord. Only the latter (which is *not* required by the Constitution) could explain the Court's inclusion of a right to counsel and the requirement that it, too, be knowingly and intelligently waived. Counsel's presence is not required to tell the suspect that he *need* not speak; the interrogators can do that. The only good reason for having counsel there is that he can be counted on to advise the suspect that he *should* not speak.

Preventing foolish (rather than compelled) confessions is likewise the only conceivable basis for the rules (suggested in *Miranda*), that courts must exclude any confession elicited by questioning conducted, without interruption, after the suspect has indicated a desire to stand on his right to remain silent, see *Michigan v. Mosley,* 423 U.S. 96, 105–106 (1975), or initiated by police after the suspect has expressed a desire to have counsel present, see *Edwards v. Arizona,* 451 U.S. 477, 484–485 (1981). Nonthreatening attempts to persuade the suspect to reconsider that initial decision are not, without more, enough to render a change of heart the product of anything other than the suspect's free will. Thus, what is most remarkable about the *Miranda* decision—and what made it unacceptable as a matter of straightforward constitutional interpretation in the *Marbury* tradition—is its palpable hostility toward the act of confession *per se,* rather than toward what the Constitution abhors, *compelled* confession.

For these reasons, and others more than adequately developed in the *Miranda* dissents and in the subsequent works of the decision's many critics, any conclusion that a violation of the *Miranda* rules *necessarily* amounts to a violation of the privilege against compelled self-incrimination can claim no support in history, precedent, or common sense, and as a result would at least presumptively be worth reconsidering even at this late date. But that is unnecessary, since the Court has (thankfully) long since abandoned the notion that failure to comply with *Miranda's* rules is itself a violation of the Constitution.

II

As the Court today acknowledges, since *Miranda* we have explicitly, and repeatedly, interpreted that decision as having announced, not the circumstances in which custodial interrogation runs afoul of the Fifth or Fourteenth Amendment, but rather only "prophylactic" rules that go beyond the right against compelled self-incrimination. Of course the seeds of this "prophylactic" interpretation of *Miranda* were present in the decision itself. In subsequent cases, the seeds have sprouted and borne fruit: The Court has squarely concluded that it is possible—indeed not uncommon—for the police to violate *Miranda* without also violating the Constitution.

Michigan v. Tucker, 417 U.S. 433 (1974), an opinion for the Court written by then-Justice Rehnquist, rejected the true-to-*Marbury,* failure-to-warn-as-constitutional-violation interpretation of *Miranda.* It held that exclusion of the "fruits" of a *Miranda* violation—the statement of a witness whose identity the defendant had revealed while in custody—was not required. The opinion explained that the question whether the "police conduct complained of directly infringed upon respondent's right against compulsory self-incrimination" was a "separate question" from "whether it instead violated only the prophylactic rules developed to protect that right." The "procedural safeguards" adopted in *Miranda,* the Court said, "were not themselves rights protected by the Constitution but were instead measures to insure that the right against compulsory self-incrimination was protected," and to "provide practical reinforcement for the right." Comparing the particular facts of the custodial interrogation with the "historical circumstances underlying the privilege," the Court concluded, unequivocally, that the defendant's statement could not be termed "involuntary as that term has been defined in the decisions of this Court," and thus that there had been no constitutional violation, notwithstanding the clear violation of the "procedural rules later established in *Miranda*." Lest there be any confusion on the point, the Court reiterated that the "police conduct at issue here did not abridge respondent's constitutional privilege against compulsory self-incrimination, but departed only from the prophylactic standards later laid down by this Court in *Miranda* to safeguard that privilege." It is clear from our cases, of course, that if the statement in *Tucker had* been obtained in violation of the Fifth Amendment, the statement and its fruits would have been excluded.

The next year, in *Oregon v. Hass,* 420 U.S. 714 (1975), the Court held that a defendant's statement taken in violation of *Miranda* that was nonetheless *voluntary* could be used at trial for impeachment purposes. This holding turned upon the recognition that violation of *Miranda* is not unconstitutional compulsion, since statements obtained in actual violation of the privilege against compelled self-incrimination, "as opposed to . . . taken in violation of *Miranda*," quite simply "may not be put to any testimonial use whatever against [the defendant] in a criminal trial," including as impeachment evidence.

Nearly a decade later, in *New York v. Quarles,* 467 U.S. 649 (1984), the Court relied upon the fact that "[t]he prophylactic *Miranda* warnings . . . are 'not themselves rights protected by the Constitution,' " to create a "public safety" exception. In that case, police apprehended, after a chase in a grocery store, a rape suspect known to be carrying a gun. After handcuffing and searching him (and finding no gun)—but before reading him his *Miranda* warnings—the police demanded to know where the gun was. The defendant nodded in the direction of some empty cartons and responded that "the gun is over there." The Court held that both the unwarned statement—"the gun is over there"—and the recovered weapon were admissible in the prosecution's case in chief under a "public safety exception" to the "prophylactic rules enunciated in *Miranda*." It explicitly acknowledged that if the *Miranda* warnings were an imperative of the Fifth Amendment itself, such an exigency exception would be impossible, since the Fifth Amendment's bar on compelled self-incrimination is absolute, and its "strictures, unlike the Fourth's are not removed by showing reasonableness."(For the latter reason, the Court found it necessary to note that respondent did not "claim that [his] statements were actually compelled by police conduct which overcame his will to resist.")

The next year, the Court again declined to apply the "fruit of the poisonous tree" doctrine to a *Miranda* violation, this time allowing the admission of a suspect's properly warned statement even though it had been preceded (and, arguably, induced) by an earlier inculpatory statement taken in violation of *Miranda. Oregon v. Elstad,* 470 U.S. 298 (1985). As in *Tucker,* the Court distinguished the case from those holding that a confession obtained as a result of an unconstitutional search is inadmissible, on the ground that the violation of *Miranda* does not involve an "actual infringement of the suspect's constitutional rights." *Miranda,* the Court explained, "sweeps more broadly than the Fifth Amendment itself," and "*Miranda*'s preventive medicine provides a remedy even to the defendant who has suffered no identifiable constitutional harm." "[E]rrors [that] are made by law enforcement officers in administering the prophylactic *Miranda* procedures . . . should not breed the same irremediable consequences as police infringement of the Fifth Amendment itself."

In light of these cases, and our statements to the same effect in others, it is simply no longer possible for the Court to conclude, even if it wanted to, that a violation of *Miranda's* rules is a violation of the Constitution. But as I explained at the outset, that is what is required before the Court may disregard a law of Congress governing the admissibility of evidence in federal court. The Court today insists that the *decision* in *Miranda* is a "constitutional" one, that it has "constitutional underpinnings," a "constitutional basis" and a "constitutional origin," that it was "constitutionally based," and that it announced a "constitutional rule." It is fine to play these word games; but what makes a decision "constitutional" in the only sense relevant here—in the sense that renders it impervious to supersession by congressional legislation such as § 3501—is the determination that the Constitution *requires* the result that the decision announces and the statute ignores. By disregarding congressional action that concededly does not violate the Constitution, the Court flagrantly offends fundamental principles of separation of powers, and arrogates to itself prerogatives reserved to the representatives of the people.

The Court seeks to avoid this conclusion in two ways: First, by misdescribing these post-*Miranda* cases as mere dicta. The Court concedes only "that there is language in some of our opinions that supports the view" that *Miranda's* protections are not "constitutionally required." It is not a matter of *language*; it is a matter of *holdings*. The proposition that failure to comply with *Miranda*'s rules does not establish a constitutional violation was central to the *holdings* of *Tucker, Hass, Quarles,* and *Elstad*.

The second way the Court seeks to avoid the impact of these cases is simply to disclaim responsibility for reasoned decisionmaking. It says:

> These decisions illustrate the principle—not that *Miranda* is not a constitutional rule—but that no constitutional rule is immutable. No court laying down a general rule can possibly foresee the various circumstances in which counsel will seek to apply it, and the sort of modifications represented by these cases are as much a normal part of constitutional law as the original decision.

The issue, however, is not whether court rules are "mutable"; they assuredly are. It is not whether, in the light of "various circumstances," they can be "modifi[ed]"; they assuredly can. The issue is whether, *as mutated and modified,* they must *make sense*. The requirement that they do so is the only thing that prevents this Court from being some sort of nine-headed Caesar, giving thumbs—up or thumbs—down to whatever outcome, case by case, suits or offends its collective fancy. And if confessions procured in violation of *Miranda* are confessions "compelled" in violation of the Constitution, the post-*Miranda* decisions I have discussed do not make sense. The only reasoned basis for their outcome was that a violation of *Miranda* is *not* a violation of the Constitution. If, for example, as the Court acknowledges was the holding of *Elstad,* "the traditional 'fruits' doctrine developed in Fourth Amendment cases" (that the fruits of evidence obtained unconstitutionally must be excluded from trial) does *not* apply to the fruits of *Miranda* violations, and if the reason for the difference is *not* that *Miranda* violations are not constitutional violations (which is plainly and flatly what *Elstad* said), then the Court must come up with some *other* explanation for the difference. (That will take quite a bit of doing, by the way, since it is *not* clear on the face of the Fourth Amendment that evidence obtained in violation of that guarantee must be excluded from trial, whereas it *is* clear on the face of the Fifth Amendment that unconstitutionally compelled confessions cannot be used.) To say simply that "unreasonable searches under the Fourth Amendment are different from unwarned interrogation under the Fifth Amendment," is true but supremely unhelpful.

Finally, the Court asserts that *Miranda* must be a "constitutional decision" announcing a "constitutional rule," and thus immune to congressional modification, because we have since its inception applied it to the States. If this argument is meant as an invocation of *stare decisis,* it fails because, though it is true that our cases applying *Miranda* against the States must be reconsidered if *Miranda* is not required by the Constitution, it is likewise true that our cases (discussed above) based on the principle that *Miranda* is *not* required by the Constitution will have to be reconsidered if it *is*. So the *stare decisis* argument is a wash. If, on the other hand, the argument is meant as an appeal to logic rather than *stare decisis,* it is a classic example of begging the question: Congress's attempt to set aside *Miranda,* since it represents an assertion that violation of *Miranda* is not a violation of the Constitution, *also* represents an assertion that the Court has no power to impose *Miranda* on the States. To answer this assertion—not by showing why violation of *Miranda is* a violation of the Constitution—but by asserting that *Miranda does* apply against the States, is to assume precisely the point at issue. In my view, our continued application of the *Miranda* code to the States despite our consistent statements that running afoul of its dictates does not necessarily—or even usually—result in an actual constitutional violation, represents not the source of *Miranda's* salvation but rather evidence of its ultimate illegitimacy. As Justice Stevens has elsewhere explained: "This Court's power to require state courts to exclude probative self-incriminatory statements rests entirely on the premise that the use of such evidence violates the Federal Constitution. . . . If the Court does not accept that premise, it must regard the holding in the *Miranda* case itself, as well as all of the federal jurisprudence that has evolved from that decision, as nothing more than an illegitimate exercise of raw judicial power." Quite so.

III

There was available to the Court a means of reconciling the established proposition that a violation of *Miranda* does not itself offend the Fifth Amendment with the Court's assertion of a right to ignore the present statute. That means of reconciliation was argued strenuously by both petitioner and the United States, who were evidently more concerned than the Court is with maintaining the coherence of our jurisprudence. It is not mentioned in the Court's opinion because, I assume, a majority of the Justices intent on reversing believes that incoherence is the lesser evil. They may be right.

Petitioner and the United States contend that there is nothing at all exceptional, much less unconstitutional, about the Court's adopting prophylactic rules to buttress constitutional rights, and enforcing them against Congress and the States. Indeed, the United States argues that "[p]rophylactic rules are now and have been for many years a feature of this Court's constitutional adjudication." That statement is not wholly inaccurate, if by "many years" one means since the mid-1960's. However, in their zeal to validate what is in my view a lawless practice, the United States and petitioner greatly overstate the frequency with which we have engaged in it. For instance, petitioner cites several cases in which the Court quite simply exercised its traditional judicial power to define the scope of constitutional protections and, relatedly, the circumstances in which they are violated.

* * *

The foregoing demonstrates that, petitioner's and the United States' suggestions to the contrary notwithstanding, what the Court did in *Miranda* (assuming, as later cases hold, that *Miranda* went beyond what the Constitution actually requires) is in fact extraordinary. That the Court has, on rare and recent occasion, repeated the mistake does not transform error into truth, but illustrates the potential for future mischief that the error entails. Where the Constitution has wished to lodge in one of the branches of the Federal Government some limited power to supplement its guarantees, it has said so. The power with which the Court would endow itself under a "prophylactic" justification for *Miranda* goes far beyond what it has permitted Congress to do under authority of that text. Whereas we have insisted that congressional action under § 5 of the Fourteenth Amendment must be "congruent" with, and "proportional" to, a *constitutional violation,* the *Miranda* nontextual power to embellish confers authority to prescribe preventive measures against not only constitutionally prohibited compelled confessions, but also (as discussed earlier) foolhardy ones.

I applaud, therefore, the refusal of the Justices in the majority to enunciate this boundless doctrine of judicial empowerment as a means of rendering today's decision rational. In nonetheless joining the Court's judgment, however, they overlook two truisms: that actions speak louder than silence, and that (in judge-made law at least) logic will out. Since there is in fact no other principle that can reconcile today's judgment with the post-*Miranda* cases that the Court refuses to abandon, what today's decision will stand for, whether the Justices can bring themselves to say it or not, is the power of the Supreme Court to write a prophylactic, extraconstitutional Constitution, binding on Congress and the States.

IV

Thus, while I agree with the Court that § 3501 cannot be upheld without also concluding that *Miranda* represents an illegitimate exercise of our authority to review state-court judgments, I do not share the Court's hesitation in reaching that conclusion. For while the Court is also correct that the doctrine of *stare decisis* demands some "special justification" for a departure from longstanding precedent—even precedent of the constitutional variety—that criterion is more than met here. To repeat Justice Stevens' cogent observation, it is "[o]bviou[s]" that "the Court's power to reverse Miranda's conviction rested *entirely* on the determination that a violation of the Federal Constitution had occurred." Despite the Court's Orwellian assertion to the contrary, it is undeniable that later cases (discussed above) have "undermined [*Miranda's*] doctrinal underpinnings," denying constitutional violation and thus stripping the holding of its only constitutionally legitimate support. *Miranda's* critics and supporters alike have long made this point.

* * *

Neither am I persuaded by the argument for retaining *Miranda* that touts its supposed workability as compared with the totality-of-the-circumstances test it purported to replace. *Miranda's* proponents cite *ad nauseam* the fact that the Court was called upon to make difficult and subtle distinctions in applying the "voluntariness" test in some 30-odd due process "coerced confessions" cases in the 30 years between *Brown v. Mississippi,* 297 U.S. 278 (1936), and *Miranda.* It is not immediately apparent, however, that the judicial burden has been eased by the "bright-line" rules adopted in *Miranda.* In fact, in the 34 years since *Miranda* was decided, this Court has been called upon to decide nearly *60* cases involving a host of *Miranda* issues, most of them predicted with remarkable prescience by Justice White in his *Miranda* dissent.

* * *

But even were I to agree that the old totality-of-the-circumstances test was more cumbersome, it is simply not true that *Miranda* has banished it from the law and replaced it with a new test. Under the current regime, which the Court today retains in its entirety, courts are frequently called upon to undertake *both* inquiries. That is because, as explained earlier, voluntariness remains the *constitutional* standard, and as such continues to govern the admissibility for impeachment purposes of statements taken in violation of *Miranda,* the admissibility of the "fruits" of such statements, and the admissibility of statements challenged as unconstitutionally obtained *despite* the interrogator's compliance with *Miranda,* see, *e.g., Colorado v. Connelly,* 479 U.S. 157 (1986).

Finally, I am not convinced by petitioner's argument that *Miranda* should be preserved because the decision occupies a special place in the "public's consciousness." As far as I am aware, the public is not under the illusion that we are infallible. I see little harm in admitting that we made a mistake in taking away from the people the ability to decide for themselves what protections (beyond those required by the Constitution) are reasonably affordable in the criminal investigatory process. And I see much to be gained by reaffirming for the people the wonderful reality that they govern themselves—which means that "[t]he powers not delegated to the United States by the Constitution" that the people adopted, "nor prohibited . . . to the States" by that Constitution, "are reserved to the States respectively, or to the people," U.S. Const., Amdt. 10.[2]

[2] The Court cites my dissenting opinion in *Mitchell v. United States,* 526 U.S. 314, 331–332 (1999), for the proposition that "the fact that a rule has found 'wide acceptance in the legal culture' is 'adequate reason not to overrule' it." But the legal culture is not the same as the "public's consciousness"; and unlike the rule at issue in *Mitchell* (prohibiting comment on a defendant's refusal to testify), *Miranda* has been continually criticized by lawyers, law enforcement officials, and scholars since its pronouncement (not to mention by Congress, as § 3501 shows). In *Mitchell,* moreover, the constitutional underpinnings of the earlier rule had not been demolished by subsequent cases.

* * *

Today's judgment converts *Miranda* from a milestone of judicial overreaching into the very Cheops' Pyramid (or perhaps the Sphinx would be a better analogue) of judicial arrogance. In imposing its Court-made code upon the States, the original opinion at least *asserted* that it was demanded by the Constitution. Today's decision does not pretend that it is—and yet *still* asserts the right to impose it against the will of the people's representatives in Congress. Far from believing that *stare decisis* compels this result, I believe we cannot allow to remain on the books even a celebrated decision—*especially* a celebrated decision—that has come to stand for the proposition that the Supreme Court has power to impose extraconstitutional constraints upon Congress and the States. This is not the system that was established by the Framers, or that would be established by any sane supporter of government by the people.

* * *

Points for Discussion

1. The dissent points out that the majority is unwilling to say, because it does not believe, that the *Miranda* warnings are required by the Constitution. In fact, at least twice in *Miranda* the Court says explicitly that the warnings are not constitutionally required. So how can the Court assert that *Miranda* is a "constitutional decision" that Congress cannot amend?

2. After the district court decision in *Dickerson*, the new Clinton Justice Department sided with the defendant and refused to argue for § 3501's constitutionality. This led several senators and congressmen as well as various organizations to file amicus briefs in support of the statute and to the appointment of Professor Paul Cassell to argue for its constitutionality. Should the Court have simply ruled in this case that because neither of the parties would argue for the statute's constitutionality that the issue was not properly before the Court?

3. Justice Scalia argues in dissent that the Court has not treated *Miranda* as a constitutional decision, creating exception after exception to its holding over the years. The majority responds that "[t]hese decisions illustrate the principle—not that *Miranda* is not a constitutional rule—but that no constitutional rule is immutable." Who has the better of the argument here?

4. The majority writes that it is strong evidence of *Miranda*'s constitutional nature that *Miranda* and the cases with which it was consolidated arose from state rather than federal prosecutions. Because the Court's authority with respect to the state courts is limited to "enforcing the commands of the United States Constitution" the Court argues, *Miranda* must have been a constitutional command. Is that persuasive legal argumentation?

PART III

REMEDY

CHAPTER 10

THE REMEDY OF EXCLUSION

■ ■ ■

In criminal trials, the principal remedy for a constitutional violation is the suppression of all evidence that derives from that constitutional violation. However, the consistency with which the Supreme Court applies this rule varies greatly across time and context. While the Supreme Court long treated exclusion as an automatic result of a proven constitutional violation, it now evaluates whether exclusion is appropriate in every case. Not surprisingly, the appropriate scope of the exclusion remedy has been the subject of pointed debate for decades.

A. THE EXCLUSIONARY RULE AND THE FRUIT OF THE POISONOUS TREE DOCTRINE

Although tainted evidence had been held inadmissible in federal court since 1914, in 1949 in *Wolf v. Colorado*, the Supreme Court refused to apply the Fourth Amendment exclusionary rule to state court prosecutions. The Court noted that the rule had been almost universally rejected in the English-speaking world, which remains true to this day. *Mapp v. Ohio*, decided just twelve years later, reversed *Wolf* and required the states to apply the rule in all criminal prosecutions. *Mapp*, incorporated the exclusionary rule into the Due Process Clause of the Fourteenth Amendment, requiring the states to apply a remedy not mentioned anywhere in the Constitution's text.

MAPP V. OHIO

367 U.S. 643 (1961)

MR. JUSTICE CLARK delivered the opinion of the court.

Appellant stands convicted of knowingly having had in her possession and under her control certain lewd and lascivious books, pictures, and photographs in violation of § 2905.34 of Ohio's Revised Code. As officially stated in the syllabus to its opinion, the Supreme Court of Ohio found that her conviction was valid though "based primarily upon the introduction in evidence of lewd and lascivious books and pictures unlawfully seized during an unlawful search of defendant's home * * *."

On May 23, 1957, three Cleveland police officers arrived at appellant's residence in that city pursuant to information that "a person (was) hiding out in the home, who was wanted for questioning in connection with a recent bombing, and that there was a large amount of policy paraphernalia being hidden in the home." Miss Mapp and her daughter by a former marriage lived on the top floor of the two-family dwelling. Upon their arrival at that house, the officers knocked on the door and demanded entrance but appellant, after telephoning her attorney, refused to admit them without a search warrant. They advised their headquarters of the situation and undertook a surveillance of the house.

The officers again sought entrance some three hours later when four or more additional officers arrived on the scene. When Miss Mapp did not come to the door immediately, at least one of the several doors to the house was forcibly opened and the policemen gained admittance. Meanwhile Miss Mapp's attorney arrived, but the officers, having secured their own entry, and continuing in their defiance of the law, would permit him neither to see Miss Mapp nor to enter the house. It appears that Miss Mapp was halfway down the stairs from the upper floor to the front door when the officers, in this highhanded manner, broke into the hall. She demanded to see the search warrant. A paper, claimed to be a warrant, was held up by one of the officers. She grabbed the "warrant" and placed it in her bosom. A struggle ensued in which the officers recovered the piece of paper and as a result of which they handcuffed appellant because she had been "belligerent" in resisting their official rescue of the "warrant" from her person. Running roughshod over appellant, a policeman "grabbed" her, "twisted (her) hand," and she "yelled (and) pleaded with him" because "it was hurting." Appellant, in handcuffs, was then forcibly taken upstairs to her bedroom where the officers searched a dresser, a chest of drawers, a closet and some suitcases. They also looked into a photo album and through personal papers belonging to the appellant. The search spread to the rest of the second floor including the child's bedroom, the living room, the kitchen and a dinette. The basement of the building and a trunk found therein were also searched. The obscene materials for possession of which she was ultimately convicted were discovered in the course of that widespread search.

At the trial no search warrant was produced by the prosecution, nor was the failure to produce one explained or accounted for. At best, "There is, in the record, considerable doubt as to whether there ever was any warrant for the search of defendant's home." The Ohio Supreme Court believed a "reasonable argument" could be made that the conviction should be reversed "because the 'methods' employed to obtain the (evidence) were such as to 'offend' 'a sense of justice,' " but the court found determinative the fact that the evidence had not been taken "from defendant's person by the use of brutal or offensive physical force against defendant."

* * *

II

* * *

. . . [I]n the year 1914, in [*Weeks v. United States*, 232 U.S. 383], this Court "for the first time" held that, "in a federal prosecution, the Fourth Amendment barred the use of evidence secured through an illegal search and seizure." This Court has ever since required of federal law officers a strict adherence to that command which this Court has held to be a clear, specific, and constitutionally required—even if judicially implied—deterrent safeguard without insistence upon which the Fourth Amendment would have been reduced to "a form of words." Holmes, J., *Silverthorne Lumber Co. v. United States,* 251 U.S. 385, 392 (1920). It meant, quite simply, that "conviction by means of unlawful seizures and enforced confessions . . . should find no sanction in the judgments of the courts . . .," and that such evidence "shall not be used at all."

* * *

In 1949, 35 years after *Weeks* was announced, this Court, in *Wolf v. Colorado*, [338 U.S. 25], again for the first time, discussed the effect of the Fourth Amendment upon the States through the operation of the Due Process Clause of the Fourteenth Amendment. It said:

> [W]e have no hesitation in saying that, were a State affirmatively to sanction such police incursion into privacy, it would run counter to the guaranty of the Fourteenth Amendment.

Nevertheless, after declaring that the "security of one's privacy against arbitrary intrusion by the police" is "implicit in 'the concept of ordered liberty' and, as such, enforceable against the States through the Due Process Clause," cf. *Palko v. Connecticut*, 302 U.S. 319 (1937), and announcing that it "stoutly adhere[d]" to the *Weeks* decision, the Court decided that the *Weeks* exclusionary rule would not then be imposed upon the States as "an essential ingredient of the right." The Court's reasons for not considering essential to the right to privacy, as a curb imposed upon the States by the Due Process Clause, that which decades before had been posited as part and parcel of the Fourth Amendment's limitation upon federal encroachment of individual privacy, were bottomed on factual considerations.

While they are not basically relevant to a decision that the exclusionary rule is an essential ingredient of the Fourth Amendment as the right it embodies is vouchsafed against the States by the Due Process Clause, we will consider the current validity of the factual grounds upon which *Wolf* was based.

The Court in *Wolf* first stated that "(t)he contrariety of views of the States" on the adoption of the exclusionary rule of *Weeks* was "particularly impressive"; and, in this connection that it could not "brush aside the experience of States which deem the incidence of such conduct by the police too slight to call for a deterrent remedy * * * by overriding the (States') relevant rules of evidence." While in 1949, prior to the *Wolf* case, almost two-thirds of the States were opposed to the use of the exclusionary rule, now, despite the *Wolf* case, more than half of those since passing upon it, by their own legislative or judicial decision, have wholly or partly adopted or adhered to the *Weeks* rule. Significantly, among those now following the rule is California, which, according to its highest court, was "compelled to reach that conclusion because other remedies have completely failed to secure compliance with the constitutional provisions * * *." In connection with this California case, we note that the second basis elaborated in *Wolf* in support of its failure to enforce the exclusionary doctrine against the States was that "other means of protection" have been afforded "the right to privacy." The experience of California that such other remedies have been worthless and futile is buttressed by the experience of other States. The obvious futility of relegating the Fourth Amendment of the protection of other remedies has, moreover, been recognized by this Court since *Wolf*.

Likewise, time has set its face against what *Wolf* called the "weighty testimony" of *People v. Defore*, 1926, 150 N.E. 585. There Justice (then Judge) Cardozo, rejecting adoption of the *Weeks* exclusionary rule in New York, had said that "(t) he Federal rule as it stands is either too strict or too lax." However, the force of that reasoning has been largely vitiated by later decisions of this Court. These include the recent discarding of the "silver platter" doctrine which allowed federal judicial use of evidence seized in violation of the Constitution by state agents; the relaxation of the formerly strict requirements as to standing to challenge the use of evidence thus seized, so that now the procedure of exclusion, "ultimately referable to constitutional safeguards," is available to anyone even "legitimately on (the) premises" unlawfully searched; and finally, the formulation of a method to prevent state use of evidence unconstitutionally seized by federal agents. Because there can be no fixed formula, we are admittedly met with "recurring questions of the reasonableness of searches," but less is not to be expected when dealing with a Constitution, and, at any rate, "(r)easonableness is in the first instance for the (trial court) to determine."

It, therefore, plainly appears that the factual considerations supporting the failure of the *Wolf* Court to include the *Weeks* exclusionary rule when it recognized the enforceability of the right to privacy against the States in 1949, while not basically relevant to the constitutional consideration, could not, in any analysis, now be deemed controlling.

* * *

IV

Since the Fourth Amendment's right of privacy has been declared enforceable against the States through the Due Process Clause of the

Fourteenth, it is enforceable against them by the same sanction of exclusion as is used against the Federal Government. Were it otherwise, then just as without the *Weeks* rule the assurance against unreasonable federal searches and seizures would be "a form of words", valueless and undeserving of mention in a perpetual charter of inestimable human liberties, so too, without that rule the freedom from state invasions of privacy would be so ephemeral and so neatly severed from its conceptual nexus with the freedom from all brutish means of coercing evidence as not to merit this Court's high regard as a freedom "implicit in 'the concept of ordered liberty.'" At the time that the Court held in Wolf that the Amendment was applicable to the States through the Due Process Clause, the cases of this Court, as we have seen, had steadfastly held that as to federal officers the Fourth Amendment included the exclusion of the evidence seized in violation of its provisions. Even *Wolf* "stoutly adhered" to that proposition. The right to privacy, when conceded operatively enforceable against the States, was not susceptible of destruction by avulsion of the sanction upon which its protection and enjoyment had always been deemed dependent under the *Boyd*, *Weeks* and *Silverthorne* cases. Therefore, in extending the substantive protections of due process to all constitutionally unreasonable searches—state or federal—it was logically and constitutionally necessary that the exclusion doctrine—an essential part of the right to privacy—be also insisted upon as an essential ingredient of the right newly recognized by the *Wolf* case. In short, the admission of the new constitutional right by *Wolf* could not consistently tolerate denial of its most important constitutional privilege, namely, the exclusion of the evidence which an accused had been forced to give by reason of the unlawful seizure. To hold otherwise is to grant the right but in reality to withhold its privilege and enjoyment. Only last year the Court itself recognized that the purpose of the exclusionary rule "is to deter—to compel respect for the constitutional guaranty in the only effectively available way—by removing the incentive to disregard it."

Indeed, we are aware of no restraint, similar to that rejected today, conditioning the enforcement of any other basic constitutional right. The right to privacy, no less important than any other right carefully and particularly reserved to the people, would stand in marked contrast to all other rights declared as "basic to a free society." *Wolf*, 338 U.S. at 27. This Court has not hesitated to enforce as strictly against the States as it does against the Federal Government the rights of free speech and of a free press, the rights to notice and to a fair, public trial, including, as it does, the right not to be convicted by use of a coerced confession, however logically relevant it be, and without regard to its reliability. And nothing could be more certain that that when a coerced confession is involved, "the relevant rules of evidence" are overridden without regard to "the incidence of such conduct by the police," slight or frequent. Why should not the same rule apply to what is tantamount to coerced testimony by way of unconstitutional seizure of goods, papers, effect, documents, etc.? We find that, as to the Federal Government, the Fourth and Fifth Amendments and, as to the States, the freedom from unconscionable invasions of privacy and the freedom from convictions based upon coerced confessions do enjoy an "intimate relation" in their perpetuation of "principles of humanity and civil liberty (secured) * * * only after years of struggle." They express "supplementing phases of the same constitutional purpose—to maintain inviolate large areas of personal privacy." The philosophy of each Amendment and of each freedom is complementary to, although not dependent upon, that of the other in its sphere of influence—the very least that together they assure in either sphere is that no man is to be convicted on unconstitutional evidence.

V

Moreover, our holding that the exclusionary rule is an essential part of both the Fourth and Fourteenth Amendments is not only the logical dictate of prior cases, but it also makes very good sense. There is no war between the Constitution and common sense. Presently, a federal prosecutor may make no use of evidence illegally seized, but a State's attorney across the street may, although he supposedly is operating under the enforceable prohibitions of the same Amendment. Thus the State, by admitting evidence unlawfully seized, serves to encourage disobedience to the Federal Constitution which it is bound to uphold. Moreover, as was said in *Elkins*, "(t)he very essence of a healthy federalism depends upon the avoidance of needless conflict between state and federal courts." Such a conflict, hereafter needless, arose this very Term, in *Wilson v. Schnettler*, 1961, 365 U.S. 381, in which . . . we gave full recognition to our practice in this regard by refusing to restrain a federal officer from testifying in a state court as to evidence unconstitutionally seized by him in the performance of his duties. Yet the double standard recognized until today hardly put such a thesis into practice. In non-exclusionary States, federal officers, being human, were by it invited to and did, as our cases indicate, step across the street to the State's attorney with their unconstitutionally seized evidence. Prosecution on the basis of that evidence was then had in a state court in utter disregard of the enforceable Fourth Amendment. If the fruits of an unconstitutional search had been inadmissible in both state and federal courts, this inducement to evasion would have been sooner eliminated. . . .

Federal-state cooperation in the solution of crime under constitutional standards will be promoted, if only by recognition of their now mutual obligation to respect the same fundamental criteria in their approaches. "However much in a particular case insistence upon such rules may appear as a technicality that inures to the benefit of a guilty person, the history of the criminal law proves that tolerance of shortcut methods in law enforcement impairs its enduring effectiveness." Denying shortcuts to only one of two cooperating law enforcement agencies tends naturally to breed legitimate suspicion of "working arrangements" whose results are equally tainted.

There are those who say, as did Justice (then Judge) Cardozo, that under our constitutional exclusionary doctrine "(t)he criminal is to go free because the constable has blundered." In some cases this will undoubtedly be the result. But, as was said in *Elkins*, "there is another consideration—the imperative of judicial integrity." The criminal goes free, if he must, but it is the law that sets him free. Nothing can destroy a government more quickly than its failure to observe its own laws, or worse, its disregard of the charter of its own existence. As Mr. Justice Brandeis, dissenting, said in *Olmstead v. United States*, 1928, 277 U.S. 438, 485: "Our government is the potent, the omnipresent teacher. For good or for ill, it teaches the whole people by its example. * * * If the government becomes a lawbreaker, it breeds contempt for law; it invites every man to become a law unto himself; it invites anarchy." Nor can it lightly be assumed that, as a practical matter, adoption of the exclusionary rule fetters law enforcement. Only last year this Court expressly considered that contention and found that "pragmatic evidence of a sort" to the contrary was not wanting. The Court noted that

> The federal courts themselves have operated under the exclusionary rule of *Weeks* for almost half a century; yet it has not been suggested either that the Federal Bureau of Investigation has thereby been rendered ineffective, or that the administration of criminal justice in the federal courts has thereby been disrupted. Moreover, the experience of the states is impressive * * *. The movement towards the rule of exclusion has been halting but seemingly inexorable.

The ignoble shortcut to conviction left open to the State tends to destroy the entire system of constitutional restraints on which the liberties of the people rest. Having once recognized that the right to privacy embodied in the Fourth Amendment is enforceable against the States, and that the right to be secure against rude invasions of privacy by state officers is, therefore, constitutional in origin, we can no longer permit that right to remain an empty promise. Because it is enforceable in the same manner and to like effect as other basic rights secured by the Due Process Clause, we can no longer permit it to be revocable at the whim of any police officer who, in the name of law enforcement itself, chooses to suspend its enjoyment. Our decision, founded on reason and truth, gives to the individual no more than that which the Constitution guarantees him, to the police officer no less than that to which honest law enforcement is entitled, and, to the courts, that judicial integrity so necessary in the true administration of justice.

MR. JUSTICE BLACK, concurring.

* * *

I am still not persuaded that the Fourth Amendment, standing alone, would be enough to bar the introduction into evidence against an accused of papers and effects seized from him in violation of its commands. For the Fourth Amendment does not itself contain any provision expressly precluding the use of such evidence, and I am extremely doubtful that such a provision could properly be inferred from nothing more than the basic command against unreasonable searches and seizures. Reflection on the problem, however, in the light of cases coming before the Court since *Wolf*, has led me to conclude that when the Fourth Amendment's ban against unreasonable searches and seizures is considered together with the Fifth Amendment's ban against compelled self-incrimination, a constitutional basis emerges which not only justifies but actually requires the exclusionary rule.

The close interrelationship between the Fourth and Fifth Amendments, as they apply to this problem, has long been recognized and, indeed, was expressly made the ground for this Court's holding in *Boyd v. United States*, [116 U.S. 616 (1861)]. There the Court fully discussed this relationship and declared itself "unable to perceive that the seizure of a man's private books and papers to be used in evidence against him is substantially different from compelling him to be a witness against himself." It was upon this ground that Mr. Justice Rutledge largely relied in his dissenting opinion in the *Wolf* case. And, although I rejected the argument at that time, its force has, for me at least, become compelling with the more thorough understanding of the problem brought on by recent cases. In the final analysis, it seems to me that the *Boyd* doctrine, though perhaps not required by the express language of the Constitution strictly construed, is amply justified from an historical standpoint, soundly based in reason, and entirely consistent with what I regard to be the proper approach to interpretation of our Bill of Rights—an approach well set out by Mr. Justice Bradley in the *Boyd* case:

> (C)onstitutional provisions for the security of person and property should be liberally construed. A close and literal construction deprives them of half their efficacy, and leads to gradual depreciation of the right, as if it consisted more in sound than in substance. It is the duty of (the) courts to be watchful for the constitutional rights of the citizen, and against any stealthy encroachments thereon.

* * *

MR. JUSTICE DOUGLAS, concurring.

* * *

We held in *Wolf v. People of State of Colorado*, 338 U.S. 25, that the Fourth Amendment was applicable to the States by reason of the Due Process Clause of the Fourteenth Amendment. But a majority held that the exclusionary rule of the *Weeks* case was not required of the States, that they could apply such sanctions as they chose. That position had the necessary votes to carry the day. But with all respect it was not the voice of reason or principle. As stated in the *Weeks* case, if evidence seized in violation of the Fourth Amendment can be used against an accused, "his right to be secure against such searches and seizures, is of no value, and * * * might as well be stricken from the Constitution."

When we allowed States to give constitutional sanction to the "shabby business" of unlawful entry into a home (to use an expression of Mr. Justice Murphy, *Wolf v. People of State of Colorado*, 338 U.S. at page 46), we did indeed rob the Fourth Amendment of much meaningful force. There are, of course, other theoretical remedies. One is disciplinary action within the hierarchy of the police system, including prosecution of the police officer for a crime. Yet as Mr. Justice Murphy said in *Wolf v. People of State of Colorado*, "Self-scrutiny is a lofty ideal, but its exaltation reaches new heights if we expect a District Attorney to prosecute himself or his associates for well-meaning violations of the search and seizure clause during a raid the District Attorney or his associates have ordered."

The only remaining remedy, if exclusion of the evidence is not required, is an action of trespass by the homeowner against the offending officer. Mr. Justice Murphy showed how onerous and difficult it would be for the citizen to maintain that action and how meagre the relief even if the citizen prevails. The truth is that trespass actions against officers who make unlawful searches and seizures are mainly illusory remedies.

* * *

Memorandum of MR. JUSTICE STEWART.

Agreeing fully with Part I of Mr. Justice Harlan's dissenting opinion, I express no view as to the merits of the constitutional issue which the Court today decides. I would, however, reverse the judgment in this case, because I am persuaded that the provision of § 2905.34 of the Ohio Revised Code, upon which the petitioner's conviction was based, is, in the words of Mr. Justice Harlan, not "consistent with the rights of free thought and expression assured against state action by the Fourteenth Amendment."

MR. JUSTICE HARLAN, whom MR. JUSTICE FRANKFURTER and MR. JUSTICE WHITTAKER join, dissenting.

In overruling the *Wolf* case the Court, in my opinion, has forgotten the sense of judicial restraint which, with due regard for *stare decisis*, is one element that should enter into deciding whether a past decision of this Court should be overruled. Apart from that I also believe that the *Wolf* rule represents sounder Constitutional doctrine than the new rule which now replaces it.

I

From the Court's statement of the case one would gather that the central, if not controlling, issue on this appeal is whether illegally state-seized evidence is Constitutionally admissible in a state prosecution, an issue which would of course face us with the need for re-examining *Wolf*. However, such is not the situation. For, although that question was indeed raised here and below among appellant's subordinate points, the new and pivotal issue brought to the Court by this appeal is whether § 2905.34 of the Ohio Revised Code making criminal the mere knowing possession or control of obscene material, and under which appellant has been convicted, is consistent with the rights of free thought and expression assured against state action by the Fourteenth Amendment. That was the principal issue which was decided by the Ohio Supreme Court, which was tendered by appellant's Jurisdictional Statement, and which was briefed and argued in this Court.

In this posture of things, I think it fair to say that five members of this Court have simply "reached out" to overrule Wolf. With all respect for the views of the majority, and recognizing that *stare decisis* carries different weight in Constitutional adjudication than it does in nonconstitutional decision, I can perceive no justification for regarding this case as an appropriate occasion for re-examining *Wolf*.

* * *

The occasion which the Court has taken here is in the context of a case where the question was briefed not at all and argued only extremely tangentially. The unwisdom of overruling *Wolf* without full-dress argument is aggravated by the circumstance that that decision is a comparatively recent one (1949) to which three members of the present majority have at one time or other expressly subscribed, one to be sure with explicit misgivings. I would think that our obligation to the States, on whom we impose this new rule, as well as the obligation of orderly adherence to our own processes would demand that we seek that aid which adequate briefing and argument lends to the determination of an important issue. It certainly has never been a postulate of judicial power that mere altered disposition, or subsequent membership on the Court, is sufficient warrant for overturning a deliberately decided rule of Constitutional law.

Thus, if the Court were bent on reconsidering *Wolf*, I think that there would soon have presented itself an appropriate opportunity in which we could have had the benefit of full briefing and argument. In any event, at the very least, the present case should have been set down for reargument, in view of the inadequate briefing and argument we have received on the *Wolf* point. To all intents and purposes the Court's present action amounts to a summary reversal of *Wolf*, without argument.

I am bound to say that what has been done is not likely to promote respect either for the Court's adjudicatory process or for the stability of its decisions. Having been unable, however, to persuade any of the majority to a different procedural course, I now turn to the merits of the present decision.

II

* * *

At the heart of the majority's opinion in this case is the following syllogism: (1) the rule excluding in federal criminal trials evidence which is the product of all illegal search and seizure is a "part and parcel" of the Fourth Amendment; (2) *Wolf* held that the "privacy" assured against federal action by the Fourth Amendment is also protected against state action by the Fourteenth Amendment; and (3) it is therefore "logically and constitutionally necessary" that the Weeks exclusionary rule should also be enforced against the States.

This reasoning ultimately rests on the unsound premise that because *Wolf* carried into the States, as part of "the concept of ordered liberty" embodied in the Fourteenth Amendment, the principle of "privacy" underlying the Fourth Amendment, it must follow that whatever configurations of the Fourth Amendment have been developed in the particularizing federal precedents are likewise to be deemed a part of "ordered liberty," and as such are enforceable against the States. For me, this does not follow at all.

It cannot be too much emphasized that what was recognized in *Wolf* was not that the Fourth Amendment as such is enforceable against the States as a facet of due process, a view of the Fourteenth Amendment which, as *Wolf* itself pointed out, has long since been discredited, but the principle of privacy "which is at the core of the Fourth Amendment." It would not be proper to expect or impose any precise equivalence, either as regards the scope of the right or the means of its implementation, between the requirements of the Fourth and Fourteenth Amendments. For the Fourth, unlike what was said in *Wolf* of the Fourteenth, does not state a general principle only; it is a particular command, having its setting in a pre-existing legal context on which both interpreting decisions and enabling statutes must at least build.

Thus, even in a case which presented simply the question of whether a particular search and seizure was constitutionally "unreasonable"—say in a tort action against state officers—we would not be true to the Fourteenth Amendment were we merely to stretch the general principle of individual privacy on a Procrustean bed of federal precedents under the Fourth Amendment. But in this instance more than that is involved, for here we are reviewing not a determination that what the state police did was Constitutionally permissible (since the state court quite evidently assumed that it was not), but a determination that appellant was properly found guilty of conduct which, for present purposes, it is to be assumed the State could Constitutionally punish. Since there is not the slightest suggestion that Ohio's policy is "affirmatively to sanction * * * police incursion into privacy" what the Court is now doing is to impose upon the States not only federal substantive standards of "search and seizure" but also the basic federal remedy for violation of those standards. For I think it entirely clear that the *Weeks* exclusionary rule is but a remedy which, by penalizing past official misconduct, is aimed at deterring such conduct in the future.

I would not impose upon the States this federal exclusionary remedy. The reasons given by the majority for now suddenly turning its back on *Wolf* seem to me notably unconvincing.

First, it is said that "the factual grounds upon which *Wolf* was based" have since changed, in that more States now follow the Weeks exclusionary rule than was so at the time *Wolf* was decided. While that is true, a recent survey indicates that at present one-half of the States still adhere to the common-law non-exclusionary rule, and one, Maryland, retains the rule as to felonies. But in any case surely all this is beside the point, as the majority itself indeed seems to recognize. Our concern here, as it was in *Wolf*, is not with the desirability of that rule but only with the question whether the States are Constitutionally free to follow it or not as they may themselves determine, and the relevance of the disparity of views among the States on this point lies simply in the fact that the judgment involved is a debatable one. Moreover, the very fact on which the majority relies, instead of lending support to what is now being done, points away from the need of replacing voluntary state action with federal compulsion.

The preservation of a proper balance between state and federal responsibility in the administration of criminal justice demands patience on the part of those who might like to see things move faster among the States in this respect. Problems of criminal law enforcement vary widely from State of State. One State, in considering the totality of its legal picture, may conclude that the need for embracing the Weeks rule is pressing because other remedies are unavailable or inadequate to secure compliance with the substantive Constitutional principle involved. Another, though equally solicitous of Constitutional rights, may choose to pursue one purpose at a time, allowing all evidence relevant to guilt to be brought into a criminal trial, and dealing with Constitutional infractions by other means. Still another may consider the exclusionary rule too rough-and-ready a remedy, in that it reaches only unconstitutional intrusions which eventuate in criminal prosecution of the victims. Further, a State after experimenting with the *Weeks* rule for a time may, because of unsatisfactory experience with it, decide to revert to a non-exclusionary rule. And so on. From the standpoint of Constitutional permissibility in pointing a State in one direction or another, I do not see at all why "time has set its face against" the considerations which led Mr. Justice Cardozo, then chief judge of the New York Court of Appeals, to reject for New York in *People v. Defore*, 150 N.E. 585, the *Weeks* exclusionary rule. For us the question remains, as it has always been, one of state power, not one of passing judgment on the wisdom of one state course or another. In my view this Court should continue to forbear from fettering the States with an adamant rule which may embarrass them in coping with their own peculiar problems in criminal law enforcement.

Further, we are told that imposition of the *Weeks* rule on the States makes "very good sense," in that it will promote recognition by state and federal officials of their "mutual obligation to respect the same fundamental criteria" in their approach to law enforcement, and will avoid "needless conflict between state and federal courts." Indeed the majority now finds an incongruity in *Wolf*'s discriminating perception between the demands of "ordered liberty" as respects the basic right of "privacy" and the means of securing it among the States. That perception, resting both on a sensitive regard for our federal system and a sound recognition of this Court's remoteness from particular state problems, is for me the strength of that decision.

* * *

A state conviction comes to us as the complete product of a sovereign judicial system. Typically a case will have been tried in a trial court, tested in some final appellate court, and will go no further. In the comparatively rare instance when a conviction is reviewed by us on due process grounds we deal then with a finished product in the creation of which we are allowed no hand, and our task, far from being one of over-all supervision, is, speaking generally, restricted to a determination of whether the prosecution was Constitutionally fair. The specifics of trial procedure, which in every mature legal system will vary greatly in detail, are within the sole competence of the States. I do not see how it can be said that a trial becomes unfair simply because a State determines that evidence may be considered by the trier of fact, regardless of how it was obtained, if it is relevant to the one issue with which the trial is concerned, the guilt or innocence of the accused. Of course, a court may use its procedures as an incidental means of pursuing other ends than the correct resolution of the controversies before it. Such indeed is the *Weeks* rule, but if a State does not choose to use its courts in this way, I do not believe that this Court is empowered to impose this much-debated procedure on local courts, however efficacious we may consider the *Weeks* rule to be as a means of securing Constitutional rights.

Finally, it is said that the overruling of *Wolf* is supported by the established doctrine that the admission in evidence of an involuntary confession renders a state conviction Constitutionally invalid. Since such a confession may often be entirely reliable, and therefore of the greatest relevance to the issue of the trial, the argument continues, this doctrine is ample warrant in precedent that the way evidence was obtained, and not just its relevance, is Constitutionally significant to the fairness of a trial. I believe this analogy is not a true one. The "coerced confession" rule is certainly not a rule that any illegally obtained statements may not be used in evidence. I would suppose that a statement which is procured during a period of illegal detention, is, as much as unlawfully seized evidence, illegally obtained, but this Court has consistently refused to reverse state convictions resting on the use of such statements. . . .

The point, then, must be that in requiring exclusion of an involuntary statement of an accused, we are concerned not with an appropriate remedy for what the police have done, but with something which is regarded as going to the heart of our concepts of fairness in judicial procedure. The operative assumption of our procedural system is that "Ours is the accusatorial as opposed to the inquisitorial system. Such has been the characteristic of Anglo-American criminal justice since it freed itself from practices borrowed by the Star Chamber from the Continent whereby an accused was interrogated in secret for hours on end." *Watts v. State of Indiana*, 338 U.S. 49, 54. The pressures brought to bear against an accused leading to a confession, unlike an unconstitutional violation of privacy, do not, apart from the use of the confession at trial, necessarily involve independent Constitutional violations. What is crucial is that the trial defense to which an accused is entitled should not be rendered an empty formality by reason of statements wrung from him, for then "a prisoner * * * (has been) made the deluded instrument of his own conviction." 2 Hawkins, PLEAS OF THE CROWN (8th ed., 1824), c. 46, § 34. That this is a procedural right, and that its violation occurs at the time his improperly obtained statement is admitted at trial, is manifest. For without this right all the careful safeguards erected around the giving of testimony, whether by an accused or any other witness, would become empty formalities in a procedure where the most compelling possible evidence of guilt, a confession, would have already been obtained at the unsupervised pleasure of the police.

This, and not the disciplining of the police, as with illegally seized evidence, is surely the true basis for excluding a statement of the accused which was unconstitutionally obtained. In sum, I think the coerced confession analogy works strongly against what the Court does today.

In conclusion, it should be noted that the majority opinion in this case is in fact an opinion only for the judgment overruling *Wolf*, and not for the basic rationale by which four members of the majority have reached that result. For my Brother Black is unwilling to subscribe to their view that the *Weeks* exclusionary rule derives from the Fourth Amendment itself, but joins the majority opinion on the premise that its end result can be achieved by bringing the Fifth Amendment to the aid of the Fourth.[12] On that score I need only say that whatever the validity of the "Fourth-Fifth Amendment" correlation which the *Boyd* case found, we have only very recently again reiterated the long-established doctrine of this Court that the Fifth Amendment privilege against self-incrimination is not applicable to the States.

I regret that I find so unwise in principle and so inexpedient in policy a decision motivated by the high purpose of increasing respect for Constitutional rights. But in the last analysis I think this Court can increase respect for the Constitution only if it rigidly respects the limitations which the Constitution places upon it, and respects as well the principles inherent in its own processes. In the present case I think we exceed both, and that our voice becomes only a voice of power, not of reason.

Points for Discussion

1. Having concluded in *Weeks v. United States* that the exclusionary rule is required in federal courts and in *Wolf v. Colorado* that the Fourth Amendment applies to the states, the Supreme Court here concludes that the exclusionary rule is required in the state court as well. Is this decision grounded in the text or history of the Constitution? If not how does the Court justify imposing this obligation on the states?

2. What are the alternatives to exclusion as a remedy for law enforcement violations of the Constitution? Is any of these a remedies suitable alternative to the exclusionary rule?

3. Is there a distinction between Justice Cardozo's famous maxim that the criminal should not go free because the constable blundered and the Court's assertion that if the criminal goes free it is the law (not the constable) that frees him?

4. Justice Harlan's dissent notes that only four justices argue that the Fourth Amendment of its own force requires the exclusion of evidence. Justice Black believes that the Fourth and Fifth Amendments, considered together,

[12] My Brother Stewart concurs in the Court's judgment on grounds which have nothing to do with *Wolf*.

require that result, and Justice Stewart concurs in the result on First Amendment grounds. Justice Harlan does not challenge Justice Black's " 'Fourth-Fifth Amendment' correlation" but notes that the Fifth Amendment had not yet been applied to the states, and Justice Stewart agrees. What, then, does *Mapp* hold?

SILVERTHORNE LUMBER CO. V. UNITED STATES

251 U.S. 385 (1920)

MR. JUSTICE HOLMES delivered the opinion of the court.

This is a writ of error brought to reverse a judgment of the District Court fining the Silverthorne Lumber Company two hundred and fifty dollars for contempt of court and ordering Frederick W. Silverthorne to be imprisoned until he should purge himself of a similar contempt. The contempt in question was a refusal to obey subpoenas and an order of Court to produce books and documents of the company before the grand jury to be used in regard to alleged violation of the statutes of the United States by the said Silverthorne and his father. One ground of the refusal was that the order of the Court infringed the rights of the parties under the Fourth Amendment of the Constitution of the United States.

The facts are simple. An indictment upon a single specific charge having been brought against the two Silverthornes mentioned, they both were arrested at their homes early in the morning of February 25, and were detained in custody a number of hours. While they were thus detained representatives of the Department of Justice and the United States marshal without a shadow of authority went to the office of their company and made a clean sweep of all the books, papers and documents found there. All the employees were taken or directed to go to the office of the District Attorney of the United States to which also the books, &c., were taken at once. An application was made as soon as might be to the District Court for a return of what thus had been taken unlawfully. It was opposed by the District Attorney so far as he had found evidence against the plaintiffs in error, and it was stated that the evidence so obtained was before the grand jury. Color had been given by the District Attorney to the approach of those concerned in the act by an invalid subpoena for certain documents relating to the charge in the indictment then on file. Thus the case is not that of knowledge acquired through the wrongful act of a stranger, but it must be assumed that the Government planned or at all events ratified the whole performance. Photographs and copies of material papers were made and a new indictment was framed based upon the knowledge thus obtained. The District Court ordered a return of the originals but impounded the photographs and copies. Subpoenas to produce the originals then were served and on the refusal of the plaintiffs in error to produce them the Court made an order that the subpoenas should be complied with, although it had found that all the papers had been seized in violation of the parties' constitutional rights. The refusal to obey this order is the contempt alleged. The Government now, while in form repudiating and condemning the illegal seizure, seeks to maintain its right to avail itself of the knowledge obtained by that means which otherwise it would not have had.

The proposition could not be presented more nakedly. It is that although of course its seizure was an outrage which the Government now regrets, it may study the papers before it returns them, copy them, and then may use the knowledge that it has gained to call upon the owners in a more regular form to produce them; that the protection of the Constitution covers the physical possession but not any advantages that the Government can gain over the object of its pursuit by doing the forbidden act. *Weeks v. United States*, 232 U. S. 383, to be sure, had established that laying the papers directly before the grand jury was unwarranted, but it is taken to mean only that two steps are required instead of one. In our opinion such is not the law. It reduces the Fourth Amendment to a form of words. The essence of a provision forbidding the acquisition of evidence in a certain way is that not merely evidence so acquired shall not be used before the Court but that it shall not be used at all. Of course this does not mean that the facts thus obtained become sacred and inaccessible. If knowledge of them is gained from an independent source they may be proved like any others, but the knowledge gained by the Government's own wrong cannot be used by it in the way proposed. . . .

THE CHIEF JUSTICE and MR. JUSTICE PITNEY dissent.

Points for Discussion

1. The Court's opinion in *Silverthorne*, reproduced here in its entirety, underpins two important corollaries of the exclusionary rule. It stands first for the proposition that not only evidence seized in violation of the Fourth Amendment but also any evidence that *derives* from such a violation cannot be used in the government's case-in-chief. Second, the opinion states that evidence obtained in violation of the Fourth Amendment is not necessarily irretrievably tainted; rather, evidence discovered through a violation of the Fourth Amendment may be used "[i]f knowledge of them is gained from an independent source. . . ." These two ideas—the fruit-of-the-poisonous-tree and independent-source doctrines—would become cornerstones of the Court's exclusionary rule jurisprudence over the next century.

2. What rationale does Justice Holmes' brief opinion give for excluding evidence? Is that the rationale that modern cases critical of the exclusionary rule generally give?

B. RETRENCHMENT OF THE RULE

1. STANDING

WONG SUN V. UNITED STATES

371 U.S. 471 (1963)

MR. JUSTICE BRENNAN delivered the opinion of the court.

The petitioners were tried without a jury in the District Court for the Northern District of California under a two-count indictment for violation of the Federal Narcotics Laws. They were acquitted under the first count which charged a conspiracy, but convicted under the second count which charged the substantive offense of fraudulent and knowing transportation and concealment of illegally imported heroin. The Court of Appeals for the Ninth Circuit, one judge dissenting, affirmed the convictions. We granted certiorari. We heard argument in the 1961 Term and reargument this Term.

About 2 a.m. on the morning of June 4, 1959, federal narcotics agents in San Francisco, after having had one Hom Way under surveillance for six weeks, arrested him and found heroin in his possession. Hom Way, who had not before been an informant, stated after his arrest that he had bought an ounce of heroin the night before from one known to him only as "Blackie Toy," proprietor of a laundry on Leavenworth Street.

About 6 a.m. that morning six or seven federal agents went to a laundry at 1733 Leavenworth Street. The sign above the door of this establishment said "Oye's Laundry." It was operated by the petitioner James Wah Toy. There is, however, nothing in the record which identifies James Wah Toy and "Blackie Toy" as the same person. The other federal officers remained nearby out of sight while Agent Alton Wong, who was of Chinese ancestry, rang the bell. When petitioner Toy appeared and opened the door, Agent Wong told him that he was calling for laundry and dry cleaning. Toy replied that he didn't open until 8 o'clock and told the agent to come back at that time. Toy started to close the door. Agent Wong thereupon took his badge from his pocket and said, "I am a federal narcotics agent." Toy immediately "slammed the door and started running" down the hallway through the laundry to his living quarters at the back where his wife and child were sleeping in a bedroom. Agent Wong and the other federal officers broke open the door and followed Toy down the hallway to the living quarters and into the bedroom. Toy reached into a nightstand drawer. Agent Wong thereupon drew his pistol, pulled Toy's hand out of the drawer, placed him under arrest and handcuffed him. There was nothing in the drawer and a search of the premises uncovered no narcotics.

One of the agents said to Toy "* * * (Hom Way) says he got narcotics from you." Toy responded, "No, I haven't been selling any narcotics at all.

However, I do know somebody who has." When asked who that was, Toy said, "I only know him as Johnny. I don't know his last name." However, Toy described a house on Eleventh Avenue where he said Johnny lived; he also described a bedroom in the house where he said "Johnny kept about a piece"[2] of heroin, and where he and Johnny had smoked some of the drug the night before. The agents left immediately for Eleventh Avenue and located the house. They entered and found one Johnny Yee in the bedroom. After a discussion with the agents, Yee took from a bureau drawer several tubes containing in all just less than one ounce of heroin, and surrendered them. Within the hour Yee and Toy were taken to the Office of the Bureau of Narcotics. Yee there stated that the heroin had been brought to him some four days earlier by petitioner Toy and another Chinese known to him only as "Sea Dog."

Toy was questioned as to the identity of "Sea Dog" and said that "Sea Dog" was Wong Sun. Some agents, including Agent Alton Wong, took Toy to Wong Sun's neighborhood where Toy pointed out a multifamily dwelling where he said Wong Sun lived. Agent Wong rang a downstairs door bell and a buzzer sounded, opening the door. The officer identified himself as a narcotics agent to a woman on the landing and asked "for Mr. Wong." The woman was the wife of petitioner Wong Sun. She said that Wong Sun was "in the back room sleeping." Alton Wong and some six other officers climbed the stairs and entered the apartment. One of the officers went into the back room and brought petitioner Wong Sun from the bedroom in handcuffs. A thorough search of the apartment followed, but no narcotics were discovered.

Petitioner Toy and Johnny Yee were arraigned before a United States Commissioner on June 4 on a complaint charging a violation of 21 U.S.C. § 174. Later that day, each was released on his own recognizance. Petitioner Wong Sun was arraigned on a similar complaint filed the next day and was also released on his own recognizance. Within a few days, both petitioners and Yee were interrogated at the office of the Narcotics Bureau by Agent William Wong, also of Chinese ancestry. The agent advised each of the three of his right to withhold information which might be used against him, and stated to each that he was entitled to the advice of counsel, though it does not appear that any attorney was present during the questioning of any of the three. The officer also explained to each that no promises or offers of immunity or leniency were being or could be made.

The agent interrogated each of the three separately. After each had been interrogated the agent prepared a statement in English from rough notes. The agent read petitioner Toy's statement to him in English and interpreted certain portions of it for him in Chinese. Toy also read the statement in English aloud to the agent, said there were corrections to be made, and made the corrections in his own hand. Toy would not sign the

[2] A "piece" is approximately one ounce.

statement, however; in the agent's words "he wanted to know first if the other persons involved in the case had signed theirs." Wong Sun had considerable difficulty understanding the statement in English and the agent restated its substance in Chinese. Wong Sun refused to sign the statement although he admitted the accuracy of its contents.

Hom Way did not testify at petitioners' trial. The Government offered Johnny Yee as its principal witness but excused him after he invoked the privilege against self-incrimination and flatly repudiated the statement he had given to Agent William Wong. That statement was not offered in evidence nor was any testimony elicited from him identifying either petitioner as the source of the heroin in his possession, or otherwise tending to support the charges against the petitioners.

The statute expressly provides that proof of the accused's possession of the drug will support a conviction under the statute unless the accused satisfactorily explains the possession. The Government's evidence tending to prove the petitioners' possession (the petitioners offered no exculpatory testimony) consisted of four items which the trial court admitted over timely objections that they were inadmissible as "fruits" of unlawful arrests or of attendant searches: (1) the statements made orally by petitioner Toy in his bedroom at the time of his arrest; (2) the heroin surrendered to the agents by Johnny Yee; (3) petitioner Toy's pretrial unsigned statement; and (4) petitioner Wong Sun's similar statement. The dispute below and here has centered around the correctness of the rulings of the trial judge allowing these items in evidence.

* * *

We believe that significant differences between the cases of the two petitioners require separate discussion of each. We shall first consider the case of petitioner Toy.

I

The Court of Appeals found there was neither reasonable grounds nor probable cause for Toy's arrest. Giving due weight to that finding, we think it is amply justified by the facts clearly shown on this record. It is basic that an arrest with or without a warrant must stand upon firmer ground than mere suspicion, though the arresting officer need not have in hand evidence which would suffice to convict. The quantum of information which constitutes probable cause—evidence which would "warrant a man of reasonable caution in the belief" that a felony has been committed—must be measured by the facts of the particular case. The history of the use, and not infrequent abuse, of the power to arrest cautions that a relaxation of the fundamental requirements of probable cause would "leave law-abiding citizens at the mercy of the officers' whim or caprice." *Brinegar v. United States*, 338 U.S. 160, 176 (1949).

Whether or not the requirements of reliability and particularity of the information on which an officer may act are more stringent where an arrest warrant is absent, they surely cannot be less stringent then where an arrest warrant is obtained. Otherwise, a principal incentive now existing for the procurement of arrest warrants would be destroyed. The threshold question in this case, therefore, is whether the officers could, on the information which impelled them to act, have procured a warrant for the arrest of Toy. We think that no warrant would have issued on evidence then available.

The narcotics agents had no basis in experience for confidence in the reliability of Hom Way's information; he had never before given information. And yet they acted upon his imprecise suggestion that a person described only as "Blackie Toy," the proprietor of a laundry somewhere on Leavenworth Street, had sold one ounce of heroin. We have held that identification of the suspect by a reliable informant may constitute probable cause for arrest where the information given is sufficiently accurate to lead the officers directly to the suspect. *Draper v. United States*, 358 U.S. 307. That rule does not, however, fit this case. For aught that the record discloses, Hom Way's accusation merely invited the officers to roam the length of Leavenworth Street (some 30 blocks) in search of one "Blackie Toy's" laundry—and whether by chance or other means (the record does not say) they came upon petitioner Toy's laundry, which bore not his name over the door, but the unrevealing label "Oye's." Not the slightest intimation appears on the record, or was made on oral argument, to suggest that the agents had information giving them reason to equate "Blackie" Toy and James Wah Toy—e.g., that they had the criminal record of a Toy, or that they had consulted some other kind of official record or list, or had some information of some kind which had narrowed the scope of their search to this particular Toy.

* * *

The Government contends, however, that any defects in the information which somehow took the officers to petitioner Toy's laundry were remedied by events which occurred after they arrived. Specifically, it is urged that Toy's flight down the hall when the supposed customer at the door revealed that he was a narcotics agent adequately corroborates the suspicion generated by Hom Way's accusation. Our holding in *Miller v. United States*, 357 U.S. 301, is relevant here, and exposes the fallacy of this contention. We noted in that case that the lawfulness of an officer's entry to arrest without a warrant "must be tested by criteria identical with those embodied in 18 U.S.C. § 3109, which deals with entry to execute a search warrant." That statute requires that an officer must state his authority and his purpose at the threshold, and be refused admittance, before he may break open the door. We held that when an officer insufficiently or unclearly identifies his office or his mission, the occupant's flight from the door must be regarded as ambiguous conduct. We expressly reserved the question "whether the unqualified requirements of the rule admit of an exception justifying noncompliance in exigent circumstances." In the instant case, Toy's flight from the door afforded no surer an inference of guilty knowledge than did the suspect's conduct in the *Miller* case. Agent Wong did eventually disclose that he was a narcotics officer. However, he affirmatively misrepresented his mission at the outset, by stating that he had come for laundry and dry cleaning. And before Toy fled, the officer never adequately dispelled the misimpression engendered by his own ruse.

* * *

A contrary holding here would mean that a vague suspicion could be transformed into probable cause for arrest by reason of ambiguous conduct which the arresting officers themselves have provoked. That result would have the same essential vice as a proposition we have consistently rejected—that a search unlawful at its inception may be validated by what it turns up. Thus we conclude that the Court of Appeals' finding that the officers' uninvited entry into Toy's living quarters was unlawful and that the bedroom arrest which followed was likewise unlawful, was fully justified on the evidence. It remains to be seen what consequences flow from this conclusion.

II

It is conceded that Toy's declarations in his bedroom are to be excluded if they are held to be "fruits" of the agents' unlawful action.

* * *

The exclusionary rule has traditionally barred from trial physical, tangible materials obtained either during or as a direct result of an unlawful invasion. It follows from our holding in *Silverman v. United States*, 365 U.S. 505, that the Fourth Amendment may protect against the overhearing of verbal statements as well as against the more traditional seizure of "papers and effects." Similarly, testimony as to matters observed during an unlawful invasion has been excluded in order to enforce the basic constitutional policies. Thus, verbal evidence which derives so immediately from an unlawful entry and an unauthorized arrest as the officers' action in the present case is no less the "fruit" of official illegality than the more common tangible fruits of the unwarranted intrusion. Nor do the policies underlying the exclusionary rule invite any logical distinction between physical and verbal evidence. Either in terms of deterring lawless conduct by federal officers or of closing the doors of the federal courts to any use of evidence unconstitutionally obtained, the danger in relaxing the exclusionary rules in the case of verbal evidence would seem too great to warrant introducing such a distinction.

The Government argues that Toy's statements to the officers in his bedroom, although closely consequent upon the invasion which we hold unlawful, were nevertheless admissible because they resulted from "an intervening independent act of a free will." This contention, however, takes insufficient account of the circumstances. Six or seven officers had broken the door and followed on Toy's heels into the bedroom where his wife and child were sleeping. He had been almost immediately handcuffed and arrested. Under such circumstances it is unreasonable to infer that Toy's response was sufficiently an act of free will to purge the primary taint of the unlawful invasion.

The Government also contends that Toy's declarations should be admissible because they were ostensibly exculpatory rather than incriminating. There are two answers to this argument. First, the statements soon turned out to be incriminating, for they led directly to the evidence which implicated Toy. Second, when circumstances are shown such as those which induced these declarations, it is immaterial whether the declarations be termed "exculpatory." Thus we find no substantial reason to omit Toy's declarations from the protection of the exclusionary rule.

III

We now consider whether the exclusion of Toy's declarations requires also the exclusion of the narcotics taken from Yee, to which those declarations led the police. The prosecutor candidly told the trial court that "we wouldn't have found those drugs except that Mr. Toy helped us to." Hence this is not the case envisioned by this Court where the exclusionary rule has no application because the Government learned of the evidence "from an independent source," *Silverthorne Lumber Co. v. United States*, 251 U.S. 385, 392; nor is this a case in which the connection between the lawless conduct of the police and the discovery of the challenged evidence has "become so attenuated as to dissipate the taint." We need not hold that all evidence is "fruit of the poisonous tree" simply because it would not have come to light but for the illegal actions of the police. Rather, the more apt question in such a case is "whether, granting establishment of the primary illegality, the evidence to which instant objection is made has been come at by exploitation of that illegality or instead by means sufficiently distinguishable to be purged of the primary taint." We think it clear that the narcotics were "come at by the exploitation of that illegality" and hence that they may not be used against Toy.

IV

It remains only to consider Toy's unsigned statement. We need not decide whether, in light of the fact that Toy was free on his own recognizance when he made the statement, that statement was a fruit of the illegal arrest. Since we have concluded that his declarations in the bedroom and the narcotics surrendered by Yee should not have been admitted in evidence against him, the only proofs remaining to sustain his conviction are his and Wong Sun's unsigned statements. Without scrutinizing the contents of Toy's ambiguous recitals, we conclude that no reference to Toy in Wong Sun's statement constitutes admissible evidence corroborating any admission by Toy. We arrive at this conclusion upon two clear lines of decisions which converge to require it. One line of our decisions establishes that criminal confessions and admissions of guilt require extrinsic corroboration; the other line of precedents holds that an out-of-court declaration made after arrest may not be used at trial against one of the declarant's partners in crime.

* * *

V

We turn now to the case of the other petitioner, Wong Sun. We have no occasion to disagree with the finding of the Court of Appeals that his arrest, also, was without probable cause or reasonable grounds. At all events no evidentiary consequences turn upon that question. For Wong Sun's unsigned confession was not the fruit of that arrest, and was therefore properly admitted at trial. On the evidence that Wong Sun had been released on his own recognizance after a lawful arraignment, and had returned voluntarily several days later to make the statement, we hold that the connection between the arrest and the statement had "become so attenuated as to dissipate the taint." *Nardone v. United States*, 308 U.S. 338, 341 [(1939)]. The fact that the statement was unsigned, whatever bearing this may have upon its weight and credibility, does not render it inadmissible; Wong Sun understood and adopted its substance, though he could not comprehend the English words. The petitioner has never suggested any impropriety in the interrogation itself which would require the exclusion of this statement.

We must then consider the admissibility of the narcotics surrendered by Yee. Our holding that this ounce of heroin was inadmissible against Toy does not compel a like result with respect to Wong Sun. The exclusion of the narcotics as to Toy was required solely by their tainted relationship to information unlawfully obtained from Toy, and not by any official impropriety connected with their surrender by Yee. The seizure of this heroin invaded no right of privacy of person or premises which would entitle Wong Sun to object to its use at his trial.

However, for the reasons that Wong Sun's statement was incompetent to corroborate Toy's admissions contained in Toy's own statement, any references to Wong Sun in Toy's statement were incompetent to corroborate Wong Sun's admissions. Thus, the only competent source of corroboration for Wong Sun's statement was the heroin itself. We cannot be certain, however, on this state of the record, that the trial judge may not also have considered the contents of Toy's statement as a source of corroboration. Petitioners raised as one ground of objection to the introduction of the statements the claim that each statement, "even if it were a purported admission or confession or declaration against interest of a defendant * * * would not be binding upon the other defendant." The trial judge, in allowing the statements in, apparently overruled all of petitioners' objections, including this one. Thus we presume that he considered all portions of both statements as hearing upon the guilt of both petitioners.

We intimate no view one way or the other as to whether the trial judge might have found in the narcotics alone sufficient evidence to corroborate Wong Sun's admissions that he delivered heroin to Yee and smoked heroin at Yee's house around the date in question. But because he might, as the factfinder, have found insufficient corroboration from the narcotics alone, we cannot be sure that the scales were not tipped in favor of conviction by reliance upon the inadmissible Toy statement. This is particularly important because of the nature of the offense involved here.

Surely, under the narcotics statute, the discovery of heroin raises a presumption that someone—generally the possessor—violated the law. As to him, once possession alone is proved, the other elements of the offense—transportation and concealment with knowledge of the illegal importation of the drug—need not be separately demonstrated, much less corroborated. Thus particular care ought to be taken in this area, when the crucial element of the accused's possession is proved solely by his own admissions, that the requisite corroboration be found among the evidence which is properly before the trier of facts. We therefore hold that petitioner Wong Sun is also entitled to a new trial.

MR. JUSTICE DOUGLAS, concurring.

While I join the Court's opinion I do so because nothing the Court holds is inconsistent with my belief that there having been time to get a warrant, probable cause alone could not have justified the arrest of petitioner Toy without a warrant.

* * *

MR. JUSTICE CLARK, with whom MR. JUSTICE HARLAN, MR. JUSTICE STEWART and MR. JUSTICE WHITE join, dissenting.

The Court has made a Chinese puzzle out of this simple case involving four participants: Hom Way, Blackie Toy, Johnny Yee and "Sea Dog" Sun. In setting aside the convictions of Toy and Sun it has dashed to pieces the heretofore recognized standards of probable cause necessary to secure an arrest warrant or to make an arrest without one. Instead of dealing with probable cause as involving "probabilities," "the factual and practical considerations of everyday life on which reasonable and prudent men, not legal technicians, act," *Brinegar v. United States*, 338 U.S. 160, 175 (1949), the Court sets up rigid, mechanical standards, applying the 20-20 vision of hind-sight in an area where the ambiguity and immediacy inherent in unexpected arrest are present. While probable cause must be based on more than mere suspicion, it does not require proof sufficient to establish guilt. The sole requirement heretofore has been that the knowledge in the hands of the officers at the time of arrest must support a "man of reasonable caution in the belief" that the subject had committed narcotic offenses. That decision is faced initially not in the courtroom but at the scene of arrest where the totality of the circumstances facing the officer is weighed against his split-second decision to make the arrest. This is an everyday occurrence facing law enforcement officers, and the unrealistic, enlarged standards announced here place an unnecessarily heavy hand upon them. I therefore dissent.

I

The first character in this affair is Hom Way, who was arrested in possession of narcotics and told the officers early that morning that he had purchased an ounce of heroin on the previous night from Blackie Toy, who operated a laundry on Leavenworth Street. Narcotics agents, armed with this information from a person they had known for six weeks and who was under arrest for possession of narcotics, immediately sought out Blackie Toy, the second character. The laundry was located without difficulty (as far as the record shows) from the information furnished by Hom Way. The Court gratuitously reads into the record its supposition that Hom Way "merely invited the officers to roam the length of Leavenworth Street (some 30 blocks) in search of one "Blackie Toy's' laundry * * *." On the contrary, the identification of "Blackie" and the directions to his laundry were sufficiently accurate for the officers—two of whom were of Chinese ancestry—to find Blackie at his laundry within an hour. I cannot say in the face of this record that this was a 'roaming' performance up and down Leavenworth Street. To me it was efficient police work by officers familiar with San Francisco and the habits and practices of its Chinese-American inhabitants. Indeed, the information was much more explicit than that approved by this Court in *Draper v. United States.*

* * *

But even assuming there was no probable cause at this point, the Government produced additional evidence to support the lawfulness of Blackie's arrest. In broad daylight, about 6:30 on the same morning that Hom Way was arrested, one of the officers of Chinese ancestry, Agent Alton Wong, knocked on Blackie Toy's laundry door. When Wong told him that he wanted laundry, Blackie opened the door and advised him to return at 8 a.m. Wong testified that he then "pulled out (his) badge" and announced that he was a narcotics agent. Blackie slammed the door in Wong's face and ran down the hall of the laundry. Wong broke through the door after him—calling again that he was "a narcotics Treasury agent." Only when Blackie reached the family bedroom was Wong able to arrest him, as he reached into a nightstand drawer, apparently looking for narcotics. Agent Wong immediately confronted him with Hom Way's accusation that Blackie Toy had sold him narcotics. Blackie denied selling narcotics, but he did not deny knowing Hom Way and later admitted knowing him. There is no basis in *Miller v. United States*, 357 U.S. 301 (1958), for the Court's conclusion that Blackie's flight "signified * * * a natural desire (by Toy) to repel an apparently unauthorized intrusion. * * *" As I see it this is incredible in the light of the record. Nor is there any support in the record that "before Toy fled, the officer never adequately dispelled the misimpression engendered by his own ruse." On the contrary the officer's showing of his badge and announcement that he was a narcotics agent immediately put Blackie in flight behind the slamming door. To conclude otherwise takes all prizes as a non sequitur. As he pursued, Wong continued to identify himself as a narcotics agent. I ask, how could he more clearly announce himself and his purpose?

* * *

The information from Hom Way and Blackie Toy's unexplained flight cannot be viewed "in two separate, logic-tight compartments. * * * (T)ogether they composed a picture meaningful to a trained, experienced observer." *Christensen v. United States*, 259 F.2d 192, 193 (1958). I submit that the officers as reasonable men properly concluded that the petitioner was the "Blackie Toy" who Hom Way informed them had committed a felony and that his immediate arrest—as he ran through his hall—was lawful and was imperative in order to prevent his escape. In view of this there is no "poisonous tree" whose fruits we must evaluate, and Blackie's declaration at the time of the arrest and the narcotics found in Yee's possession are admissible in evidence. The trial court found that evidence sufficiently corroborative of Toy's confession, and the Court of Appeals affirmed. For the same reasons discussed, infra, as to Wong Sun, I see no occasion to overturn these consistent findings of two courts.

II

As to "Sea Dog," Wong Sun, there is no disagreement that his confession and the narcotics found in Yee's possession were admissible in evidence against him. The question remains as to whether there was sufficient independent evidence to corroborate the confession. Such evidence "does not have to prove the offense beyond a reasonable doubt, or even by a preponderance * * *." *Smith v. United States*, 348 U.S. 147, 156 (1954). The requirement is satisfied "if the corroboration merely fortifies the truth of the confession, without independently establishing the crime charged * * *." Wong Sun's confession stated in part that about four days before his arrest he and Toy delivered an ounce of heroin to Yee and that on the night before his arrest—the night of June 3, 1959—he and Toy smoked some heroin at Yee's house. On June 4, 1959, the officers found at Yee's residence quantities of heroin totaling "just less than one ounce." In light of this evidence, I am unable to say that the trial court and the Court of Appeals erred in holding that Wong Sun's confession was sufficiently corroborated.

The Court does not reach a contrary conclusion as to corroboration, but it grants Wong Sun a new trial on the ground that the trial court "may" also "have considered the contents of Toy's statement as a source of corroboration" of it. This point was not raised as a question here nor was it discussed in the briefs. Despite this the Court goes to some lengths to develop a chain of inferences in finding prejudicial error. This might be plausible where the case was tried to a jury, as were all the cases cited by the Court. Indeed, I find no case where such presumption of error was applied, as here, to a trial before a judge. The Court admits that the heroin found in Johnny Yee's possession might itself be sufficient corroboration, but it reverses on the excuse that the judge "may" have considered Toy's confession as well. I see no reason for this assumption where a federal judge is the trier of the fact, and I would therefore affirm the judgment as to both petitioners.

Points for Discussion

1. As *Wong Sun* shows, a piece of evidence may be admissible against one defendant but not against another. Why should this be? If the evidence directly derived from a violation of the Constitution, why should it not be suppressed against all defendants?

2. The approach that the Supreme Court takes in *Wong Sun*—asking of each defendant what evidence is admissible against him—is one that students should take in every case. It is tempting to assume that if a piece of evidence was obtained in violation of the constitution then it must be excluded as to each defendant. As both *Wong Sun* and many of the cases that follow indicate, however, this temptation can lead to incorrect results.

RAKAS V. ILLINOIS

439 U.S. 128 (1978)

MR. JUSTICE REHNQUIST delivered the opinion of the court.

Petitioners were convicted of armed robbery in the Circuit Court of Kankakee County, Ill., and their convictions were affirmed on appeal. At their trial, the prosecution offered into evidence a sawed-off rifle and rifle shells that had been seized by police during a search of an automobile in which petitioners had been passengers. Neither petitioner is the owner of the automobile and neither has ever asserted that he owned the rifle or shells seized. The Illinois Appellate Court held that petitioners lacked standing to object to the allegedly unlawful search and seizure and denied their motion to suppress the evidence. We granted certiorari in light of the obvious importance of the issues raised to the administration of criminal justice and now affirm.

I

Because we are not here concerned with the issue of probable cause, a brief description of the events leading to the search of the automobile will suffice. A police officer on a routine patrol received a radio call notifying him of a robbery of a clothing store in Bourbonnais, Ill., and describing the getaway car. Shortly thereafter, the officer spotted an automobile which he thought might be the getaway car. After following the car for some time and after the arrival of assistance, he and several other officers stopped the vehicle. The occupants of the automobile, petitioners and two female companions, were ordered out of the car and, after the occupants had left the car, two officers searched the interior of the vehicle. They discovered a box of rifle shells in the glove compartment, which had been locked, and a sawed-off rifle under the front passenger seat. After discovering the rifle and the shells, the officers took petitioners to the station and placed them under arrest.

* * *

II

Petitioners first urge us to relax or broaden the rule of standing enunciated in *Jones v. United States*, 362 U.S. 257 (1960), so that any criminal defendant at whom a search was "directed" would have standing to contest the legality of that search and object to the admission at trial of evidence obtained as a result of the search. Alternatively, petitioners argue that they have standing to object to the search under *Jones* because they were "legitimately on [the] premises" at the time of the search.

The concept of standing discussed in *Jones* focuses on whether the person seeking to challenge the legality of a search as a basis for suppressing evidence was himself the "victim" of the search or seizure. Adoption of the so-called "target" theory advanced by petitioners would in effect permit a defendant to assert that a violation of the Fourth Amendment rights of a third party entitled him to have evidence suppressed at his trial. If we reject petitioners' request for a broadened rule of standing such as this, and reaffirm the holding of *Jones* and other cases that Fourth Amendment rights are personal rights that may not be asserted vicariously, we will have occasion to re-examine the "standing" terminology emphasized in *Jones*. For we are not at all sure that the determination of a motion to suppress is materially aided by labeling the inquiry identified in *Jones* as one of standing, rather than simply recognizing it as one involving the substantive question of whether or not the proponent of the motion to suppress has had his own Fourth Amendment rights infringed by the search and seizure which he seeks to challenge. We shall therefore consider in turn petitioners' target theory, the necessity for continued adherence to the notion of standing discussed in *Jones* as a concept that is theoretically distinct from the merits of a defendant's Fourth Amendment claim, and, finally, the proper disposition of petitioners' ultimate claim in this case.

There is an aspect of traditional standing doctrine that was not considered in *Jones* and which we do not question. It is the proposition that a party seeking relief must allege such a personal stake or interest in the outcome of the controversy as to assure the concrete adverseness which Art. III requires. Thus, a person whose Fourth Amendment rights were violated by a search or seizure, but who is not a defendant in a criminal action in which the illegally seized evidence is sought to be introduced, would not have standing to invoke the exclusionary rule to prevent use of that evidence in that action.

A

We decline to extend the rule of standing in Fourth Amendment cases in the manner suggested by petitioners. As we stated in *Alderman v. United States*, 394 U.S. 165, 174 (1969), "Fourth Amendment rights are personal rights which, like some other constitutional rights, may not be vicariously asserted." A person who is aggrieved by an illegal search and seizure only through the introduction of damaging evidence secured by a search of a third person's premises or property has not had any of his Fourth Amendment rights infringed. And since the exclusionary rule is an attempt to effectuate the guarantees of the Fourth Amendment, it is proper to permit only defendants whose Fourth Amendment rights have been violated to benefit from the rule's protections. There is no reason to think that a party whose rights have been infringed will not, if evidence is used against him, have ample motivation to move to suppress it. Even if such a person is not a defendant in the action, he may be able to recover damages for the violation of his Fourth Amendment rights or seek redress under state law for invasion of privacy or trespass.

* * *

Each time the exclusionary rule is applied it exacts a substantial social cost for the vindication of Fourth Amendment rights. Relevant and reliable evidence is kept from the trier of fact and the search for truth at trial is deflected. Since our cases generally have held that one whose Fourth Amendment rights are violated may successfully suppress evidence obtained in the course of an illegal search and seizure, misgivings as to the benefit of enlarging the class of persons who may invoke that rule are properly considered when deciding whether to expand standing to assert Fourth Amendment violations.

B

Had we accepted petitioners' request to allow persons other than those whose own Fourth Amendment rights were violated by a challenged search and seizure to suppress evidence obtained in the course of such police activity, it would be appropriate to retain *Jones'* use of standing in Fourth

Amendment analysis. Under petitioners' target theory, a court could determine that a defendant had standing to invoke the exclusionary rule without having to inquire into the substantive question of whether the challenged search or seizure violated the Fourth Amendment rights of that particular defendant. However, having rejected petitioners' target theory and reaffirmed the principle that the "rights assured by the Fourth Amendment are personal rights, [which] . . . may be enforced by exclusion of evidence only at the instance of one whose own protection was infringed by the search and seizure," the question necessarily arises whether it serves any useful analytical purpose to consider this principle a matter of standing, distinct from the merits of a defendant's Fourth Amendment claim. We can think of no decided cases of this Court that would have come out differently had we concluded, as we do now, that the type of standing requirement discussed in *Jones* and reaffirmed today is more properly subsumed under substantive Fourth Amendment doctrine. Rigorous application of the principle that the rights secured by this Amendment are personal, in place of a notion of "standing," will produce no additional situations in which evidence must be excluded. The inquiry under either approach is the same. But we think the better analysis forthrightly focuses on the extent of a particular defendant's rights under the Fourth Amendment, rather than on any theoretically separate, but invariably intertwined concept of standing. The Court in *Jones* also may have been aware that there was a certain artificiality in analyzing this question in terms of standing because in at least three separate places in its opinion the Court placed that term within quotation marks.

It should be emphasized that nothing we say here casts the least doubt on cases which recognize that, as a general proposition, the issue of standing involves two inquiries: first, whether the proponent of a particular legal right has alleged "injury in fact," and, second, whether the proponent is asserting his own legal rights and interests rather than basing his claim for relief upon the rights of third parties. But this Court's long history of insistence that Fourth Amendment rights are personal in nature has already answered many of these traditional standing inquiries, and we think that definition of those rights is more properly placed within the purview of substantive Fourth Amendment law than within that of standing.

Analyzed in these terms, the question is whether the challenged search or seizure violated the Fourth Amendment rights of a criminal defendant who seeks to exclude the evidence obtained during it. That inquiry in turn requires a determination of whether the disputed search and seizure has infringed an interest of the defendant which the Fourth Amendment was designed to protect. We are under no illusion that by dispensing with the rubric of standing used in *Jones* we have rendered any simpler the determination of whether the proponent of a motion to suppress is entitled to contest the legality of a search and seizure. But by frankly recognizing that this aspect of the analysis belongs more properly under the heading of substantive Fourth Amendment doctrine than under the heading of standing, we think the decision of this issue will rest on sounder logical footing.

C

Here petitioners, who were passengers occupying a car which they neither owned nor leased, seek to analogize their position to that of the defendant in *Jones v. United States*. In *Jones,* petitioner was present at the time of the search of an apartment which was owned by a friend. The friend had given Jones permission to use the apartment and a key to it, with which Jones had admitted himself on the day of the search. He had a suit and shirt at the apartment and had slept there "maybe a night," but his home was elsewhere. At the time of the search, Jones was the only occupant of the apartment because the lessee was away for a period of several days. Under these circumstances, this Court stated that while one wrongfully on the premises could not move to suppress evidence obtained as a result of searching them, "anyone legitimately on premises where a search occurs may challenge its legality." Petitioners argue that their occupancy of the automobile in question was comparable to that of Jones in the apartment and that they therefore have standing to contest the legality of the search—or as we have rephrased the inquiry, that they, like Jones, had their Fourth Amendment rights violated by the search.

We do not question the conclusion in *Jones* that the defendant in that case suffered a violation of his personal Fourth Amendment rights if the search in question was unlawful. Nonetheless, we believe that the phrase "legitimately on premises" coined in *Jones* creates too broad a gauge for measurement of Fourth Amendment rights. For example, applied literally, this statement would permit a casual visitor who has never seen, or been permitted to visit, the basement of another's house to object to a search of the basement if the visitor happened to be in the kitchen of the house at the time of the search. Likewise, a casual visitor who walks into a house one minute before a search of the house commences and leaves one minute after the search ends would be able to contest the legality of the search. The first visitor would have absolutely no interest or legitimate expectation of privacy in the basement, the second would have none in the house, and it advances no purpose served by the Fourth Amendment to permit either of them to object to the lawfulness of the search.[11]

We think that *Jones* on its facts merely stands for the unremarkable proposition that a person can have a legally sufficient interest in a place other than his own home so that the Fourth Amendment protects him from unreasonable governmental intrusion into that place. In defining the scope of that interest, we adhere to the view expressed in *Jones* and echoed in

[11] This is not to say that such visitors could not contest the lawfulness of the seizure of evidence or the search if their own property were seized during the search.

later cases that arcane distinctions developed in property and tort law between guests, licensees, invitees, and the like, ought not to control. But the *Jones* statement that a person need only be "legitimately on premises" in order to challenge the validity of the search of a dwelling place cannot be taken in its full sweep beyond the facts of that case.

Katz v. United States, 389 U.S. 347 (1967), provides guidance in defining the scope of the interest protected by the Fourth Amendment. In the course of repudiating the doctrine derived from *Olmstead v. United States,* 277 U.S. 438 (1928), and *Goldman v. United States,* 316 U.S. 129 (1942), that if police officers had not been guilty of a common-law trespass they were not prohibited by the Fourth Amendment from eavesdropping, the Court in *Katz* held that capacity to claim the protection of the Fourth Amendment depends not upon a property right in the invaded place but upon whether the person who claims the protection of the Amendment has a legitimate expectation of privacy in the invaded place. Viewed in this manner, the holding in *Jones* can best be explained by the fact that Jones had a legitimate expectation of privacy in the premises he was using and therefore could claim the protection of the Fourth Amendment with respect to a governmental invasion of those premises, even though his "interest" in those premises might not have been a recognized property interest at common law.[12]

* * *

D

Judged by the foregoing analysis, petitioners' claims must fail. They asserted neither a property nor a possessory interest in the automobile, nor

[12] Obviously, however, a "legitimate" expectation of privacy by definition means more than a subjective expectation of not being discovered. A burglar plying his trade in a summer cabin during the off season may have a thoroughly justified subjective expectation of privacy, but it is not one which the law recognizes as "legitimate." His presence, in the words of *Jones,* is "wrongful"; his expectation is not "one that society is prepared to recognize as 'reasonable.' " *Katz v. United States,* 389 U.S., at 361 (Harlan, J., concurring). And it would, of course, be merely tautological to fall back on the notion that those expectations of privacy which are legitimate depend primarily on cases deciding exclusionary-rule issues in criminal cases. Legitimation of expectations of privacy by law must have a source outside of the Fourth Amendment, either by reference to concepts of real or personal property law or to understandings that are recognized and permitted by society. One of the main rights attaching to property is the right to exclude others, see W. Blackstone, Commentaries, Book 2, ch. 1, and one who owns or lawfully possesses or controls property will in all likelihood have a legitimate expectation of privacy by virtue of this right to exclude. Expectations of privacy protected by the Fourth Amendment, of course, need not be based on a common-law interest in real or personal property, or on the invasion of such an interest. These ideas were rejected both in *Jones* and *Katz.* But by focusing on legitimate expectations of privacy in Fourth Amendment jurisprudence, the Court has not altogether abandoned use of property concepts in determining the presence or absence of the privacy interests protected by that Amendment. No better demonstration of this proposition exists than the decision in *Alderman v. United States,* 394 U.S. 165 (1969), where the Court held that an individual's property interest in his own home was so great as to allow him to object to electronic surveillance of conversations emanating from his home, even though he himself was not a party to the conversations. On the other hand, even a property interest in premises may not be sufficient to establish a legitimate expectation of privacy with respect to particular items located on the premises or activity conducted thereon.

an interest in the property seized. And as we have previously indicated, the fact that they were "legitimately on [the] premises" in the sense that they were in the car with the permission of its owner is not determinative of whether they had a legitimate expectation of privacy in the particular areas of the automobile searched. It is unnecessary for us to decide here whether the same expectations of privacy are warranted in a car as would be justified in a dwelling place in analogous circumstances. We have on numerous occasions pointed out that cars are not to be treated identically with houses or Apartments for Fourth Amendment purposes. But here petitioners' claim is one which would fail even in an analogous situation in a dwelling place, since they made no showing that they had any legitimate expectation of privacy in the glove compartment or area under the seat of the car in which they were merely passengers. Like the trunk of an automobile, these are areas in which a passenger *qua* passenger simply would not normally have a legitimate expectation of privacy.

* * *

III

The Illinois courts were therefore correct in concluding that it was unnecessary to decide whether the search of the car might have violated the rights secured to someone else by the Fourth and Fourteenth Amendments to the United States Constitution. Since it did not violate any rights of these petitioners, their judgment of conviction is affirmed.

MR. JUSTICE POWELL, with whom THE CHIEF JUSTICE joins, concurring.

* * *

The petitioners do not challenge the constitutionality of the police action in stopping the automobile in which they were riding; nor do they complain of being made to get out of the vehicle. Rather, petitioners assert that their constitutionally protected interest in privacy was violated when the police, after stopping the automobile and making them get out, searched the vehicle's interior, where they discovered a sawed-off rifle under the front seat and rifle shells in the locked glove compartment. The question before the Court, therefore, is a narrow one: Did the search of their friend's automobile after they had left it violate any Fourth Amendment right of the petitioners?

The dissenting opinion urges the Court to answer this question by considering only the talisman of legitimate presence on the premises. To be sure, one of the two alternative reasons given by the Court for its ruling in *Jones v. United States*, 362 U.S. 257 (1960), was that the defendant had been legitimately on the premises searched. Since *Jones*, however, the view that mere legitimate presence is enough to create a Fourth Amendment right has been questioned. There also has been a signal absence of uniformity in the application of this theory.

This Court's decisions since *Jones* have emphasized a sounder standard for determining the scope of a person's Fourth Amendment rights: Only legitimate expectations of privacy are protected by the Constitution. In *Katz v. United States*, 389 U.S. 347 (1967), the Court rejected the notion that the Fourth Amendment protects places or property, ruling that the scope of the Amendment must be determined by the scope of privacy that a free people legitimately may expect. As Mr. Justice Harlan pointed out in his concurrence, however, it is not enough that an individual desired or anticipated that he would be free from governmental intrusion. Rather, for an expectation to deserve the protection of the Fourth Amendment, it must "be one that society is prepared to recognize as 'reasonable.' "

The ultimate question, therefore, is whether one's claim to privacy from government intrusion is reasonable in light of all the surrounding circumstances. As the dissenting opinion states, this standard "will not provide law enforcement officials with a bright line between the protected and the unprotected." Whatever the application of this standard may lack in ready administration, it is more faithful to the purposes of the Fourth Amendment than a test focusing solely or primarily on whether the defendant was legitimately present during the search.

* * *

MR. JUSTICE WHITE, with whom MR. JUSTICE BRENNAN, MR. JUSTICE MARSHALL, and MR. JUSTICE STEVENS join, dissenting.

The Court today holds that the Fourth Amendment protects property, not people, and specifically that a legitimate occupant of an automobile may not invoke the exclusionary rule and challenge a search of that vehicle unless he happens to own or have a possessory interest in it. Though professing to acknowledge that the primary purpose of the Fourth Amendment's prohibition of unreasonable searches is the protection of privacy—not property—the Court nonetheless effectively ties the application of the Fourth Amendment and the exclusionary rule in this situation to property law concepts. Insofar as passengers are concerned, the Court's opinion today declares an "open season" on automobiles. However unlawful stopping and searching a car may be, absent a possessory or ownership interest, no "mere" passenger may object, regardless of his relationship to the owner. Because the majority's conclusion has no support in the Court's controlling decisions, in the logic of the Fourth Amendment, or in common sense, I must respectfully dissent. If the Court is troubled by the practical impact of the exclusionary rule, it should face the issue of that rule's continued validity squarely instead of distorting other doctrines in an attempt to reach what are perceived as the correct results in specific cases.

I

Two intersecting doctrines long established in this Court's opinions control here. The first is the recognition of some cognizable level of privacy in the interior of an automobile. Though the reasonableness of the expectation of privacy in a vehicle may be somewhat weaker than that in a home, "[a] search even of an automobile, is a substantial invasion of privacy. To protect that privacy from official arbitrariness, the Court always has regarded probable cause as the minimum requirement for a lawful search." So far, the Court has not strayed from this application of the Fourth Amendment.

The second tenet is that when a person is legitimately present in a private place, his right to privacy is protected from unreasonable governmental interference even if he does not own the premises. Just a few years ago, the Chief Justice, for a unanimous Court, wrote that the "[p]resence of the defendant at the search and seizure was held, in *Jones,* to be a sufficient source of standing in itself." *Brown v. United States,* 411 U.S. 223, 227 n. 2 (1973). *Brown* was not the first time we had recognized that *Jones* established the rights of one legitimately in a private area against unreasonable governmental intrusion. The Court in *Jones* itself was unanimous in this regard, and its holding is not the less binding because it was an alternative one.

These two fundamental aspects of Fourth Amendment law demand that petitioners be permitted to challenge the search and seizure of the automobile in this case. It is of no significance that a car is different for Fourth Amendment purposes from a house, for if there is some protection for the privacy of an automobile then the only relevant analogy is between a person legitimately in someone else's vehicle and a person legitimately in someone else's home. If both strands of the Fourth Amendment doctrine adumbrated above are valid, the Court must reach a different result. Instead, it chooses to eviscerate the *Jones* principle, an action in which I am unwilling to participate.

* * *

IV

The Court's holding is contrary not only to our past decisions and the logic of the Fourth Amendment but also to the everyday expectations of privacy that we all share. Because of that, it is unworkable in all the various situations that arise in real life. If the owner of the car had not only invited petitioners to join her but had said to them, "I give you a temporary possessory interest in my vehicle so that you will share the right to privacy that the Supreme Court says that I own," then apparently the majority would reverse. But people seldom say such things, though they may mean their invitation to encompass them if only they had thought of the problem. If the nonowner were the spouse or child of the owner, would the Court recognize a sufficient interest? If so, would distant relatives somehow have more of an expectation of privacy than close friends? What if the nonowner were driving with the owner's permission? Would nonowning drivers have more of an expectation of privacy than mere passengers? What about a passenger in a taxicab? *Katz* expressly recognized protection for such passengers. Why should Fourth Amendment rights be present when one pays a cabdriver for a ride but be absent when one is given a ride by a friend?

The distinctions the Court would draw are based on relationships between private parties, but the Fourth Amendment is concerned with the relationship of one of those parties to the government. Divorced as it is from the purpose of the Fourth Amendment, the Court's essentially property-based rationale can satisfactorily answer none of the questions posed above. That is reason enough to reject it. The *Jones* rule is relatively easily applied by police and courts; the rule announced today will not provide law enforcement officials with a bright line between the protected and the unprotected. Only rarely will police know whether one private party has or has not been granted a sufficient possessory or other interest by another private party. Surely in this case the officers had no such knowledge. The Court's rule will ensnare defendants and police in needless litigation over factors that should not be determinative of Fourth Amendment rights.

More importantly, the ruling today undercuts the force of the exclusionary rule in the one area in which its use is most certainly justified—the deterrence of bad-faith violations of the Fourth Amendment. This decision invites police to engage in patently unreasonable searches every time an automobile contains more than one occupant. Should something be found, only the owner of the vehicle, or of the item, will have standing to seek suppression, and the evidence will presumably be usable against the other occupants. The danger of such bad faith is especially high in cases such as this one where the officers are only after the passengers and can usually infer accurately that the driver is the owner. The suppression remedy for those owners in whose vehicles something is found and who are charged with crime is small consolation for all those owners *and* occupants whose privacy will be needlessly invaded by officers following mistaken hunches not rising to the level of probable cause but operated on in the knowledge that someone in a crowded car will probably be unprotected if contraband or incriminating evidence happens to be found. After this decision, police will have little to lose by unreasonably searching vehicles occupied by more than one person.

Of course, most police officers will decline the Court's invitation and will continue to do their jobs as best they can in accord with the Fourth Amendment. But the very purpose of the Bill of Rights was to answer the justified fear that governmental agents cannot be left totally to their own devices, and the Bill of Rights is enforceable in the courts because human experience teaches that not all such officials will otherwise adhere to the stated precepts. Some policemen simply do act in bad faith, even if for understandable ends, and some deterrent is needed. In the rush to limit the applicability of the exclusionary rule somewhere, anywhere, the Court ignores precedent, logic, and common sense to exclude the rule's operation from situations in which, paradoxically, it is justified and needed.

Points for Discussion

1. The Court begins its opinion by rejecting the "target theory" of standing—the idea that a defendant may challenge the seizure of any evidence to be offered against him. Why does the Court reject this bright-line rule?

2. The test that the Court in fact adopts here—whether the defendant is able to assert that the evidence in question was seized in violation of his own Fourth Amendment rights—is certainly more complicated than the one it rejects. How does the Court attempt to guide lower courts in the application the *Rakas* standard? Is the guidance that it provides here likely to prove effective?

3. The dissent complains that the majority revives the notion that property rights determine the extent of constitutional rights. How fair is that charge?

4. In *Byrd v. United States,* 138 S.Ct. 1518 (2018), the Supreme Court unanimously held that the driver of a rental car can have a reasonable expectation of privacy in it even if he is not named as an authorized driver on the rental agreement. The holding reaffirmed that Fourth Amendment rights do not depend solely on legalistic notions of property law, rejecting the government's argument for a categorical holding that it claimed *Rakas* supported:

> Stripped to its essentials, the Government's position is that only authorized drivers of rental cars have expectations of privacy in those vehicles. This position is based on the following syllogism: Under *Rakas*, passengers do not have an expectation of privacy in an automobile glove compartment or like places; an unauthorized driver like Byrd would have been the passenger had the renter been driving; and the unauthorized driver cannot obtain greater protection when he takes the wheel and leaves the renter behind. The flaw in this syllogism is its major premise, for it is a misreading of *Rakas*.
>
> The Court in *Rakas* did not hold that passengers cannot have an expectation of privacy in automobiles. To the contrary, the Court disclaimed any intent to hold "that a passenger lawfully in an automobile may not invoke the exclusionary rule and challenge a search of that vehicle unless he happens to own or have a possessory interest in it." The Court instead rejected the argument that legitimate presence alone was sufficient to assert a Fourth Amendment interest, which was fatal to the petitioners' case there

> because they had "claimed only that they were 'legitimately on [the] premises' and did not claim that they had any legitimate expectation of privacy in the areas of the car which were searched."
>
> What is more, the Government's syllogism is beside the point, because this case does not involve a passenger at all but instead the driver and sole occupant of a rental car. As Justice Powell observed in his concurring opinion in *Rakas,* a "distinction . . . may be made in some circumstances between the Fourth Amendment rights of passengers and the rights of an individual who has exclusive control of an automobile or of its locked compartments." This situation would be similar to the defendant in *Jones v. United States,* 362 U.S. 257, 259 (1960), who, as *Rakas* notes, had a reasonable expectation of privacy in his friend's apartment because he "had complete dominion and control over the apartment and could exclude others from it." Justice Powell's observation was also consistent with the majority's explanation that "one who owns or lawfully possesses or controls property will in all likelihood have a legitimate expectation of privacy by virtue of [the] right to exclude," *id.,* at 144, n. 12, an explanation tied to the majority's discussion of *Jones.*

However, the Court also rejected Byrd's proposed categorical rule—"that the sole occupant of a rental car always has an expectation of privacy in it based on mere possession and control"—because "without qualification, it would include within its ambit thieves and others who, not least because of their lack of any property-based justification, would not have a reasonable expectation of privacy." The Court remanded the case for further fact-finding regarding whether Byrd's alleged "fraudulent scheme" to obtain the car through an acquaintance vitiated any expectation of privacy or, alternatively, whether the police had probable cause to pull him over.

MINNESOTA V. CARTER

525 U.S. 83 (1998)

CHIEF JUSTICE REHNQUIST delivered the opinion of the court.

Respondents and the lessee of an apartment were sitting in one of its rooms, bagging cocaine. While so engaged they were observed by a police officer, who looked through a drawn window blind. The Supreme Court of Minnesota held that the officer's viewing was a search that violated respondents' Fourth Amendment rights. We hold that no such violation occurred.

James Thielen, a police officer in the Twin Cities' suburb of Eagan, Minnesota, went to an apartment building to investigate a tip from a confidential informant. The informant said that he had walked by the window of a ground-floor apartment and had seen people putting a white powder into bags. The officer looked in the same window through a gap in the closed blind and observed the bagging operation for several minutes.

He then notified headquarters, which began preparing affidavits for a search warrant while he returned to the apartment building. When two men left the building in a previously identified Cadillac, the police stopped the car. Inside were respondents Carter and Johns. As the police opened the door of the car to let Johns out, they observed a black, zippered pouch and a handgun, later determined to be loaded, on the vehicle's floor. Carter and Johns were arrested, and a later police search of the vehicle the next day discovered pagers, a scale, and 47 grams of cocaine in plastic sandwich bags.

After seizing the car, the police returned to Apartment 103 and arrested the occupant, Kimberly Thompson, who is not a party to this appeal. A search of the apartment pursuant to a warrant revealed cocaine residue on the kitchen table and plastic baggies similar to those found in the Cadillac. Thielen identified Carter, Johns, and Thompson as the three people he had observed placing the powder into baggies. The police later learned that while Thompson was the lessee of the apartment, Carter and Johns lived in Chicago and had come to the apartment for the sole purpose of packaging the cocaine. Carter and Johns had never been to the apartment before and were only in the apartment for approximately 2½ hours. In return for the use of the apartment, Carter and Johns had given Thompson one-eighth of an ounce of the cocaine.

* * *

The text of the [Fourth] Amendment suggests that its protections extend only to people in "their" houses. But we have held that in some circumstances a person may have a legitimate expectation of privacy in the house of someone else. In *Minnesota v. Olson,* 495 U.S. 91 (1990), for example, we decided that an overnight guest in a house had the sort of expectation of privacy that the Fourth Amendment protects.

* * *

In *Jones v. United States,* 362 U.S. 257, 259 (1960), the defendant seeking to exclude evidence resulting from a search of an apartment had been given the use of the apartment by a friend. He had clothing in the apartment, had slept there "maybe a night," and at the time was the sole occupant of the apartment. But while the holding of *Jones*—that a search of the apartment violated the defendant's Fourth Amendment rights—is still valid, its statement that "anyone legitimately on the premises where a search occurs may challenge its legality" was expressly repudiated in *Rakas v. Illinois,* 439 U.S. 128 (1978). Thus, an overnight guest in a home may claim the protection of the Fourth Amendment, but one who is merely present with the consent of the householder may not.

Respondents here were obviously not overnight guests, but were essentially present for a business transaction and were only in the home a matter of hours. There is no suggestion that they had a previous relationship with Thompson, or that there was any other purpose to their visit. Nor was there anything similar to the overnight guest relationship in *Olson* to suggest a degree of acceptance into the household. While the apartment was a dwelling place for Thompson, it was for these respondents simply a place to do business.

Property used for commercial purposes is treated differently for Fourth Amendment purposes from residential property. "An expectation of privacy in commercial premises, however, is different from, and indeed less than, a similar expectation in an individual's home." *New York v. Burger,* 482 U.S. 691, 700 (1987). And while it was a "home" in which respondents were present, it was not their home. Similarly, the Court has held that in some circumstances a worker can claim Fourth Amendment protection over his own workplace. *See e.g., O'Connor v. Ortega,* 480 U.S. 709 (1987). But there is no indication that respondents in this case had nearly as significant a connection to Thompson's apartment as the worker in *O'Connor* had to his own private office.

If we regard the overnight guest in *Minnesota v. Olson* as typifying those who may claim the protection of the Fourth Amendment in the home of another, and one merely "legitimately on the premises" as typifying those who may not do so, the present case is obviously somewhere in between. But the purely commercial nature of the transaction engaged in here, the relatively short period of time on the premises, and the lack of any previous connection between respondents and the householder, all lead us to conclude that respondents' situation is closer to that of one simply permitted on the premises. We therefore hold that any search which may have occurred did not violate their Fourth Amendment rights.

Because we conclude that respondents had no legitimate expectation of privacy in the apartment, we need not decide whether the police officer's observation constituted a "search." The judgments of the Supreme Court of Minnesota are accordingly reversed, and the cause is remanded for proceedings not inconsistent with this opinion.

JUSTICE SCALIA, with whom JUSTICE THOMAS joins, concurring.

I join the opinion of the Court because I believe it accurately applies our recent case law, including *Minnesota v. Olson,* 495 U.S. 91 (1990). I write separately to express my view that that case law—like the submissions of the parties in this case—gives short shrift to the text of the Fourth Amendment, and to the well and long understood meaning of that text. Specifically, it leaps to apply the fuzzy standard of "legitimate expectation of privacy"—a consideration that is often relevant to whether a search or seizure covered by the Fourth Amendment is "unreasonable"—to the threshold question whether a search or seizure covered by the Fourth Amendment *has occurred.* If that latter question is addressed first and analyzed under the text of the Constitution as traditionally understood, the present case is not remotely difficult.

The Fourth Amendment protects "[t]he right of the people to be secure in *their* persons, houses, papers, and effects, against unreasonable searches and seizures . . . ." U.S. Const., Amdt. 4 (emphasis added). It must be acknowledged that the phrase "their . . . houses" in this provision is, in isolation, ambiguous. It could mean "their respective houses," so that the protection extends to each person only in his *own* house. But it could also mean "their respective and each other's houses," so that each person would be protected even when visiting the house of someone else. As today's opinion for the Court suggests, however, it is not linguistically possible to give the provision the latter, expansive interpretation with respect to "houses" without giving it the same interpretation with respect to the nouns that are parallel to "houses"—"persons, . . . papers, and effects"—which would give me a constitutional right not to have your person unreasonably searched. This is so absurd that it has to my knowledge never been contemplated. The obvious meaning of the provision is that *each* person has the right to be secure against unreasonable searches and seizures in *his own* person, house, papers, and effects.

* * *

That "their . . . houses" was understood to mean "their respective houses" would have been clear to anyone who knew the English and early American law of arrest and trespass that underlay the Fourth Amendment. The people's protection against unreasonable search and seizure in their "houses" was drawn from the English common-law maxim, "A man's home is *his* castle." As far back as *Semayne's Case* of 1604, the leading English case for that proposition (and a case cited by Coke in his discussion of the proposition that Magna Carta outlawed general warrants based on mere surmise), the King's Bench proclaimed that "the house of any one is not a castle or privilege but for himself, and shall not extend to protect any person who flies to his house." Thus Cooley, in discussing Blackstone's statement that a bailiff could not break into a house to conduct an arrest because "every man's house is looked upon by the law to be his castle," 3 W. Blackstone, COMMENTARIES ON THE LAWS OF ENGLAND 288 (1768), added the explanation: "[I] t is the defendant's own dwelling which by law is said to be his castle; for if he be in the house of another, the bailiff or sheriff may break and enter it to effect his purpose . . . ." 3 W. Blackstone, COMMENTARIES ON THE LAWS OF ENGLAND 287, n. 5 (T. Cooley 2d rev. ed. 1872).

Of course this is not to say that the Fourth Amendment protects only the Lord of the Manor who holds his estate in fee simple. People call a house "their" home when legal title is in the bank, when they rent it, and even when they merely occupy it rent free—*so long as they actually live there.* That this is the criterion of the people's protection against government intrusion into "their" houses is established by the leading American case of *Oystead v. Shed,* 13 Mass. 520 (1816), which held it a trespass for the sheriff to break into a dwelling to capture a boarder who lived there. The court reasoned that the "inviolability of dwelling-houses" described by Foster, Hale, and Coke extends to "the occupier or any of his family . . . who have their domicile or ordinary residence there," including "a boarder or a servant" "who have made the house *their* home." But, it added, "the house shall not be made a sanctuary" for one such as "a stranger, or perhaps a visitor," who "upon a pursuit, take[s] refuge in the house of another," for "the house is not *his* castle; and the officer may break open the doors or windows in order to execute his process."

Thus, in deciding the question presented today we write upon a slate that is far from clean. The text of the Fourth Amendment, the common-law background against which it was adopted, and the understandings consistently displayed after its adoption make the answer clear. We were right to hold in *Chapman v. United States,* 365 U.S. 610 (1961), that the Fourth Amendment protects an apartment tenant against an unreasonable search of his dwelling, even though he is only a leaseholder. And we were right to hold in *Bumper v. North Carolina,* 391 U.S. 543 (1968), that an unreasonable search of a grandmother's house violated her resident grandson's Fourth Amendment rights because the area searched "was *his* home." We went to the absolute limit of what text and tradition permit in *Minnesota v. Olson,* 495 U.S. 91 (1990), when we protected a mere overnight guest against an unreasonable search of his hosts' apartment. But whereas it is plausible to regard a person's overnight lodging as at least his "temporary" residence, it is entirely impossible to give that characterization to an apartment that he uses to package cocaine. Respondents here were not searched in "their . . . hous[e]" under any interpretation of the phrase that bears the remotest relationship to the well-understood meaning of the Fourth Amendment.

The dissent believes that "[o]ur obligation to produce coherent results" requires that we ignore this clear text and 4-century-old tradition, and apply instead the notoriously unhelpful test adopted in a "benchmar[k]" decision that is 31 years old. In my view, the only thing the past three decades have established about the *Katz* test (which has come to mean the test enunciated by Justice Harlan's separate concurrence in *Katz*) is that, unsurprisingly, those "actual (subjective) expectation[s] of privacy" " that society is prepared to recognize as 'reasonable,' " bear an uncanny resemblance to those expectations of privacy that this Court considers reasonable. When that self-indulgent test is employed (as the dissent would employ it here) to determine whether a "search or seizure" within the meaning of the Constitution has *occurred* (as opposed to whether that "search or seizure" is an "unreasonable" one), it has no plausible foundation in the text of the Fourth Amendment. That provision did not guarantee some generalized "right of privacy" and leave it to this Court to determine which particular manifestations of the value of privacy "society is prepared to recognize as 'reasonable.' " Rather, it enumerated ("persons, houses, papers, and effects") the objects of privacy protection to which the *Constitution* would extend, leaving further expansion to the good judgment, not of this Court, but of the people through their representatives in the legislature.

The dissent may be correct that a person invited into someone else's house to engage in a common business (even common monkey business, so to speak) *ought* to be protected against government searches of the room in which that business is conducted; and that persons invited in to deliver milk or pizza (whom the dissent dismisses as "classroom hypotheticals," as opposed, presumably, to flesh-and-blood hypotheticals) ought *not* to be protected against government searches of the rooms that they occupy. I am not sure of the answer to those policy questions. But I am sure that the answer is not remotely contained in the Constitution, which means that it is left—as *many,* indeed *most,* important questions are left—to the judgment of state and federal legislators. We go beyond our proper role as judges in a democratic society when we restrict the people's power to govern themselves over the full range of policy choices that the Constitution has left available to them.

JUSTICE KENNEDY, concurring.

I join the Court's opinion, for its reasoning is consistent with my view that almost all social guests have a legitimate expectation of privacy, and hence protection against unreasonable searches, in their host's home.

* * *

The settled rule is that the requisite connection is an expectation of privacy that society recognizes as reasonable. *Katz v. United States,* 389 U.S. 347, 361 (1967) (Harlan, J., concurring). The application of that rule involves consideration of the kind of place in which the individual claims the privacy interest and what expectations of privacy are traditional and well recognized. I would expect that most, if not all, social guests legitimately expect that, in accordance with social custom, the homeowner will exercise her discretion to include or exclude others for the guests' benefit. As we recognized in *Minnesota v. Olson,* 495 U.S. 91 (1990), where these social expectations exist—as in the case of an overnight guest—they are sufficient to create a legitimate expectation of privacy, even in the absence of any property right to exclude others. In this respect, the dissent must be correct that reasonable expectations of the owner are shared, to some extent, by the guest. This analysis suggests that, as a general rule, social guests will have an expectation of privacy in their host's home. That is not the case before us, however.

In this case respondents have established nothing more than a fleeting and insubstantial connection with Thompson's home. For all that appears in the record, respondents used Thompson's house simply as a convenient processing station, their purpose involving nothing more than the mechanical act of chopping and packing a substance for distribution. There is no suggestion that respondents engaged in confidential communications with Thompson about their transaction. Respondents had not been to Thompson's apartment before, and they left it even before their arrest. The Minnesota Supreme Court, which overturned respondents' convictions, acknowledged that respondents could not be fairly characterized as Thompson's "guests."

* * *

JUSTICE BREYER, concurring in the judgment.

I agree with Justice Ginsburg that respondents can claim the Fourth Amendment's protection. Petitioner, however, raises a second question, whether under the circumstances Officer Thielen's observation made "from a public area outside the curtilage of the residence" violated respondents' Fourth Amendment rights. In my view, it did not.

I would answer the question on the basis of the following factual assumptions, derived from the evidentiary record presented here: (1) On the evening of May 15, 1994, an anonymous individual approached Officer Thielen, telling him that he had just walked by a nearby apartment window through which he had seen some people bagging drugs; (2) the apartment in question was a garden apartment that was partly below ground level; (3) families frequently used the grassy area just outside the apartment's window for walking or for playing; (4) members of the public also used the area just outside the apartment's window to store bicycles; (5) in an effort to verify the tipster's information, Officer Thielen walked to a position about 1 to 1½ feet in front of the window; (6) Officer Thielen stood there for about 15 minutes looking down through a set of venetian blinds; (7) what he saw, namely, people putting white powder in bags, verified the account he had heard; and (8) he then used that information to help obtain a search warrant.

* * *

Officer Thielen, then, stood at a place used by the public and from which one could see through the window into the kitchen. The precautions that the apartment's dwellers took to maintain their privacy would have failed in respect to an ordinary passerby standing in that place. Given this Court's well-established case law, I cannot say that the officer engaged in what the Constitution forbids, namely, an "unreasonable search."

* * *

Neither can the matter turn upon "gaps" in drawn blinds. Whether there were holes in the blinds or they were simply pulled the "wrong way" makes no difference. One who lives in a basement apartment that fronts a publicly traveled street, or similar space, ordinarily understands the need for care lest a member of the public simply direct his gaze downward.

* * *

JUSTICE GINSBURG, with whom JUSTICE STEVENS and JUSTICE SOUTER join, dissenting.

The Court's decision undermines not only the security of short-term guests, but also the security of the home resident herself. In my view, when a homeowner or lessee personally invites a guest into her home to share in a common endeavor, whether it be for conversation, to engage in leisure activities, or for business purposes licit or illicit, that guest should share his host's shelter against unreasonable searches and seizures.

I do not here propose restoration of the "legitimately on the premises" criterion stated in *Jones v. United States,* 362 U.S. 257, 267 (1960), for the Court rejected that formulation in *Rakas v. Illinois,* 439 U.S. 128, 142 (1978), as it did the "automatic standing rule" in *United States v. Salvucci,* 448 U.S. 83, 95 (1980). First, the disposition I would reach in this case responds to the unique importance of the home—the most essential bastion of privacy recognized by the law. Second, even within the home itself, the position to which I would adhere would not permit "a casual visitor who has never seen, or been permitted to visit, the basement of another's house to object to a search of the basement if the visitor happened to be in the kitchen of the house at the time of the search." *Rakas,* 439 U.S., at 142. Further, I would here decide only the case of the homeowner who chooses to share the privacy of her home and her company with a guest, and would not reach classroom hypotheticals like the milkman or pizza deliverer.

* * *

Through the host's invitation, the guest gains a reasonable expectation of privacy in the home. *Minnesota v. Olson,* 495 U.S. 91 (1990), so held with respect to an overnight guest. The logic of that decision extends to shorter term guests as well. Visiting the home of a friend, relative, or business associate, whatever the time of day, "serves functions recognized as valuable by society." One need not remain overnight to anticipate privacy in another's home, "a place where [the guest] and his possessions will not be disturbed by anyone but his host and those his host allows inside." In sum, when a homeowner chooses to share the privacy of her home and her company with a short-term guest, the twofold requirement "emerg[ing] from prior decisions" has been satisfied: Both host and guest "have exhibited an actual (subjective) expectation of privacy"; that "expectation [is] one [our] society is prepared to recognize as 'reasonable.'" *Katz v. United States,* 389 U.S. 347, 361 (1967) (Harlan, J., concurring).

As the Solicitor General acknowledged, the illegality of the host-guest conduct, the fact that they were partners in crime, would not alter the analysis. In *Olson,* for example, the guest whose security this Court's decision shielded stayed overnight while the police searched for him. The Court held that the guest had Fourth Amendment protection against a warrantless arrest in his host's home despite the guest's involvement in grave crimes (first-degree murder, armed robbery, and assault). Other decisions have similarly sustained Fourth Amendment pleas despite the criminality of the defendants' activities. Indeed, it must be this way. If the illegality of the activity made constitutional an otherwise unconstitutional search, such Fourth Amendment protection, reserved for the innocent only, would have little force in regulating police behavior toward either the innocent or the guilty.

* * *

Points for Discussion

1. Do you find the Court's distinguishing of *Minnesota v. Olson* convincing? What if Carter had brought a toothbrush and an overnight bag with him when packaging drugs at another's house? Would that entitle him to object to a search of that house?

2. Why shouldn't the Fourth Amendment be read to protect "the people" in each others' homes? Wouldn't that bright-line rule obviate the need for the kind of fact-based, case-by-case adjudication that the Court undertakes in these cases?

3. Contrary to what the majority opinion might suggest, the case holds that social guests do have an expectation of privacy in the homes of their hosts. The dissent certainly states that. Plus, Justice Kennedy's and Justice Breyer's separate concurrences both say so from their starts. So, there are five votes for that principle, making it a precedential holding of the Court even though it is not in a majority opinion. Why, then, do the respondents lose?

4. Justice Scalia, who was in the majority in *Olson*, chides the Court for sidestepping the question of whether what the officer did in *Carter* was a Fourth Amendment "search." Specifically, the Court's holding is that "any search *which may have occurred* did not violate their Fourth Amendment rights." Why does Justice Scalia think it is important for the Court to decide first whether there was a "search" rather than simply assuming there was and concluding that Carter could not object to it?

2. COST-BENEFIT ANALYSIS

HUDSON V. MICHIGAN

547 U.S. 586 (2006)

JUSTICE SCALIA delivered the opinion of the court, except as to Part IV.

We decide whether violation of the "knock-and-announce" rule requires the suppression of all evidence found in the search.

I

Police obtained a warrant authorizing a search for drugs and firearms at the home of petitioner Booker Hudson. They discovered both. Large quantities of drugs were found, including cocaine rocks in Hudson's pocket. A loaded gun was lodged between the cushion and armrest of the chair in which he was sitting. Hudson was charged under Michigan law with unlawful drug and firearm possession.

This case is before us only because of the method of entry into the house. When the police arrived to execute the warrant, they announced their presence, but waited only a short time—perhaps "three to five seconds,"—before turning the knob of the unlocked front door and entering Hudson's home. Hudson moved to suppress all the inculpatory evidence, arguing that the premature entry violated his Fourth Amendment rights.

* * *

II

The common-law principle that law enforcement officers must announce their presence and provide residents an opportunity to open the door is an ancient one. Since 1917, when Congress passed the Espionage Act, this traditional protection has been part of federal statutory law, and is currently codified at 18 U.S.C. § 3109. We applied that statute in *Miller v. United States,* 357 U.S. 301 (1958), and again in *Sabbath v. United States,* 391 U.S. 585 (1968). Finally, in *Wilson* [*v. Arkansas*, 514 U.S. 927 (1995)], we were asked whether the rule was also a command of the Fourth Amendment. Tracing its origins in our English legal heritage, we concluded that it was.

We recognized that the new constitutional rule we had announced is not easily applied. *Wilson* and cases following it have noted the many situations in which it is not necessary to knock and announce. It is not necessary when "circumstances presen[t] a threat of physical violence," or if there is "reason to believe that evidence would likely be destroyed if advance notice were given," or if knocking and announcing would be "futile." We require only that police "have a reasonable suspicion . . . under the particular circumstances" that one of these grounds for failing to knock and announce exists, and we have acknowledged that "[t]his showing is not high."

When the knock-and-announce rule does apply, it is not easy to determine precisely what officers must do. How many seconds' wait are too few? Our "reasonable wait time" standard, see *United States v. Banks,* 540 U.S. 31, 41 (2003), is necessarily vague. *Banks* (a drug case, like this one) held that the proper measure was not how long it would take the resident to reach the door, but how long it would take to dispose of the suspected drugs—but that such a time (15 to 20 seconds in that case) would necessarily be extended when, for instance, the suspected contraband was not easily concealed. If our *ex post* evaluation is subject to such calculations, it is unsurprising that, *ex ante,* police officers about to encounter someone who may try to harm them will be uncertain how long to wait.

Happily, these issues do not confront us here. From the trial level onward, Michigan has conceded that the entry was a knock-and-announce violation. The issue here is remedy. *Wilson* specifically declined to decide whether the exclusionary rule is appropriate for violation of the knock-and-announce requirement. That question is squarely before us now.

III

A

In *Weeks v. United States,* 232 U.S. 383 (1914), we adopted the federal exclusionary rule for evidence that was unlawfully seized from a home without a warrant in violation of the Fourth Amendment. We began applying the same rule to the States, through the Fourteenth Amendment, in *Mapp v. Ohio,* 367 U.S. 643 (1961).

Suppression of evidence, however, has always been our last resort, not our first impulse. The exclusionary rule generates "substantial social costs," which sometimes include setting the guilty free and the dangerous at large. We have therefore been "cautio[us] against expanding" it, and "have repeatedly emphasized that the rule's 'costly toll' upon truth-seeking and law enforcement objectives presents a high obstacle for those urging [its] application." We have rejected "[i]ndiscriminate application" of the rule, and have held it to be applicable only "where its remedial objectives are thought most efficaciously served"—that is, "where its deterrence benefits outweigh its 'substantial social costs.' "

* * *

In other words, exclusion may not be premised on the mere fact that a constitutional violation was a "but-for" cause of obtaining evidence. Our cases show that but-for causality is only a necessary, not a sufficient, condition for suppression. In this case, of course, the constitutional violation of an illegal *manner* of entry was *not* a but-for cause of obtaining the evidence. Whether that preliminary misstep had occurred *or not,* the police would have executed the warrant they had obtained, and would have discovered the gun and drugs inside the house. But even if the illegal entry here could be characterized as a but-for cause of discovering what was inside, we have "never held that evidence is 'fruit of the poisonous tree' simply because 'it would not have come to light but for the illegal actions of the police.' " Rather, but-for cause, or "causation in the logical sense alone," can be too attenuated to justify exclusion. Even in the early days of the exclusionary rule, we declined to

> hold that all evidence is "fruit of the poisonous tree" simply because it would not have come to light *but for* the illegal actions

> of the police. Rather, the more apt question in such a case is "whether, granting establishment of the primary illegality, the evidence to which instant objection is made has been come at by exploitation of that illegality or instead by means sufficiently distinguishable to be purged of the primary taint."

Wong Sun v. United States, 371 U.S. 471, 487–88 (1959) (emphasis added).

Attenuation can occur, of course, when the causal connection is remote. Attenuation also occurs when, even given a direct causal connection, the interest protected by the constitutional guarantee that has been violated would not be served by suppression of the evidence obtained. . . .

* * *

For this reason, cases excluding the fruits of unlawful warrantless searches say nothing about the appropriateness of exclusion to vindicate the interests protected by the knock-and-announce requirement. Until a valid warrant has issued, citizens are entitled to shield "their persons, houses, papers, and effects," U.S. Const., Amdt. 4, from the government's scrutiny. Exclusion of the evidence obtained by a warrantless search vindicates that entitlement. The interests protected by the knock-and-announce requirement are quite different—and do not include the shielding of potential evidence from the government's eyes.

One of those interests is the protection of human life and limb, because an unannounced entry may provoke violence in supposed self-defense by the surprised resident. Another interest is the protection of property. Breaking a house (as the old cases typically put it) absent an announcement would penalize someone who "did not know of the process, of which, if he had notice, it is to be presumed that he would obey it . . . ." The knock-and-announce rule gives individuals "the opportunity to comply with the law and to avoid the destruction of property occasioned by a forcible entry." And thirdly, the knock-and-announce rule protects those elements of privacy and dignity that can be destroyed by a sudden entrance. It gives residents the "opportunity to prepare themselves for" the entry of the police. "The brief interlude between announcement and entry with a warrant may be the opportunity that an individual has to pull on clothes or get out of bed." In other words, it assures the opportunity to collect oneself before answering the door.

What the knock-and-announce rule has never protected, however, is one's interest in preventing the government from seeing or taking evidence described in a warrant. Since the interests that *were* violated in this case have nothing to do with the seizure of the evidence, the exclusionary rule is inapplicable.

B

Quite apart from the requirement of unattenuated causation, the exclusionary rule has never been applied except "where its deterrence benefits outweigh its 'substantial social costs.'" The costs here are considerable. In addition to the grave adverse consequence that exclusion of relevant incriminating evidence always entails (viz., the risk of releasing dangerous criminals into society), imposing that massive remedy for a knock-and-announce violation would generate a constant flood of alleged failures to observe the rule. . . . The cost of entering this lottery would be small, but the jackpot enormous: suppression of all evidence, amounting in many cases to a get-out-of-jail-free card. Courts would experience as never before the reality that "[t]he exclusionary rule frequently requires extensive litigation to determine whether particular evidence must be excluded." Unlike the warrant or *Miranda* requirements, compliance with which is readily determined (either there was or was not a warrant; either the *Miranda* warning was given, or it was not), what constituted a "reasonable wait time" in a particular case (or, for that matter, how many seconds the police in fact waited), or whether there was "reasonable suspicion" of the sort that would invoke the *Richards* exceptions, is difficult for the trial court to determine and even more difficult for an appellate court to review.

Another consequence of the incongruent remedy Hudson proposes would be police officers' refraining from timely entry after knocking and announcing. As we have observed, the amount of time they must wait is necessarily uncertain. If the consequences of running afoul of the rule were so massive, officers would be inclined to wait longer than the law requires—producing preventable violence against officers in some cases, and the destruction of evidence in many others. We deemed these consequences severe enough to produce our unanimous agreement that a mere "reasonable suspicion" that knocking and announcing "under the particular circumstances, would be dangerous or futile, or that it would inhibit the effective investigation of the crime," will cause the requirement to yield.

Next to these "substantial social costs" we must consider the deterrence benefits, existence of which is a necessary condition for exclusion. (It is not, of course, a sufficient condition: "[I]t does not follow that the Fourth Amendment requires adoption of every proposal that might deter police misconduct.") To begin with, the value of deterrence depends upon the strength of the incentive to commit the forbidden act. Viewed from this perspective, deterrence of knock-and-announce violations is not worth a lot. Violation of the warrant requirement sometimes produces incriminating evidence that could not otherwise be obtained. But ignoring knock-and-announce can realistically be expected to achieve absolutely nothing except the prevention of destruction of evidence and the avoidance of life-threatening resistance by occupants of the premises—dangers which, if there is even "reasonable suspicion" of their existence, *suspend the knock-and-announce requirement anyway*. Massive deterrence is hardly required.

It seems to us not even true, as Hudson contends, that without suppression there will be no deterrence of knock-and-announce violations at all. Of course even if this assertion were accurate, it would not necessarily justify suppression. Assuming (as the assertion must) that civil suit is not an effective deterrent, one can think of many forms of police misconduct that are similarly "undeterred." When, for example, a confessed suspect in the killing of a police officer, arrested (along with incriminating evidence) in a lawful warranted search, is subjected to physical abuse at the station house, would it seriously be suggested that the evidence must be excluded, since that is the only "effective deterrent"? And what, other than civil suit, is the "effective deterrent" of police violation of an already-confessed suspect's Sixth Amendment rights by denying him prompt access to counsel? Many would regard these violated rights as more significant than the right not to be intruded upon in one's nightclothes—and yet nothing but "ineffective" civil suit is available as a deterrent. And the police incentive for those violations is arguably greater than the incentive for disregarding the knock-and-announce rule.

We cannot assume that exclusion in this context is necessary deterrence simply because we found that it was necessary deterrence in different contexts and long ago. That would be forcing the public today to pay for the sins and inadequacies of a legal regime that existed almost half a century ago. Dollree Mapp could not turn to Rev.Stat. § 1979, 42 U.S.C. § 1983, for meaningful relief; *Monroe v. Pape*, 365 U.S. 167 (1961), which began the slow but steady expansion of that remedy, was decided the same Term as *Mapp*. It would be another 17 years before the § 1983 remedy was extended to reach the deep pocket of municipalities. Citizens whose Fourth Amendment rights were violated by federal officers could not bring suit until 10 years after Mapp, with this Court's decision in *Bivens v. Six Unknown Fed. Narcotics Agents*, 403 U.S. 388 (1971).

Hudson complains that "it would be very hard to find a lawyer to take a case such as this," but 42 U.S.C. § 1988(b) answers this objection. Since some civil-rights violations would yield damages too small to justify the expense of litigation, Congress has authorized attorney's fees for civil-rights plaintiffs. This remedy was unavailable in the heydays of our exclusionary-rule jurisprudence, because it is tied to the availability of a cause of action. For years after *Mapp*, "very few lawyers would even consider representation of persons who had civil rights claims against the police," but now "much has changed. Citizens and lawyers are much more willing to seek relief in the courts for police misconduct." M. Avery, D. Rudovsky, & K. Blum, POLICE MISCONDUCT: LAW AND LITIGATION, p. v (3d ed. 2005). The number of public-interest law firms and lawyers who specialize in civil-rights grievances has greatly expanded.

Another development over the past half-century that deters civil-rights violations is the increasing professionalism of police forces, including a new emphasis on internal police discipline. Even as long ago as 1980 we felt it proper to "assume" that unlawful police behavior would "be dealt with appropriately" by the authorities, but we now have increasing evidence that police forces across the United States take the constitutional rights of citizens seriously. There have been "wide-ranging reforms in the education, training, and supervision of police officers." Numerous sources are now available to teach officers and their supervisors what is required of them under this Court's cases, how to respect constitutional guarantees in various situations, and how to craft an effective regime for internal discipline. Failure to teach and enforce constitutional requirements exposes municipalities to financial liability. Moreover, modern police forces are staffed with professionals; it is not credible to assert that internal discipline, which can limit successful careers, will not have a deterrent effect. There is also evidence that the increasing use of various forms of citizen review can enhance police accountability.

In sum, the social costs of applying the exclusionary rule to knock-and-announce violations are considerable; the incentive to such violations is minimal to begin with, and the extant deterrences against them are substantial-incomparably greater than the factors deterring warrantless entries when *Mapp* was decided. Resort to the massive remedy of suppressing evidence of guilt is unjustified.

IV

A trio of cases—*Segura v. United States,* 468 U.S. 796 (1984); *New York v. Harris,* 495 U.S. 14 (1990); and *United States v. Ramirez,* 523 U.S. 65 (1998)—confirms our conclusion that suppression is unwarranted in this case.

Like today's case, *Segura* involved a concededly illegal entry. Police conducting a drug crime investigation waited for Segura outside an apartment building; when he arrived, he denied living there. The police arrested him and brought him to the apartment where they suspected illegal activity. An officer knocked. When someone inside opened the door, the police entered, taking Segura with them. They had neither a warrant nor consent to enter, and they did not announce themselves as police—an entry as illegal as can be. Officers then stayed in the apartment for *19 hours* awaiting a search warrant. Once alerted that the search warrant had been obtained, the police—still inside, having secured the premises so that no evidence could be removed—conducted a search. We refused to exclude the resulting evidence. We recognized that only the evidence gained from the particular violation could be excluded, and therefore distinguished the effects of the illegal entry from the effects of the legal search: "None of the information on which the warrant was secured was derived from or related in any way to the initial entry into petitioners' apartment. . . ." It was therefore "beyond dispute that the information possessed by the agents before they entered the apartment constituted an independent source for the discovery and seizure of the evidence now challenged."

If the search in *Segura* could be "wholly unrelated to the prior entry" when the only entry was warrantless, it would be bizarre to treat more harshly the actions in this case, where the only entry was *with* a warrant. If the probable cause backing a warrant that was issued *later in time* could be an "independent source" for a search that proceeded after the officers illegally entered and waited, a search warrant obtained *before* going in must have at least this much effect.

In the second case, *Harris,* the police violated the defendant's Fourth Amendment rights by arresting him at home without a warrant, contrary to *Payton v. New York,* 445 U.S. 573 (1980). Once taken to the station house, he gave an incriminating statement. We refused to exclude it. Like the illegal entry which led to discovery of the evidence in today's case, the illegal arrest in *Harris* began a process that culminated in acquisition of the evidence sought to be excluded. While Harris's statement was "the product of an arrest and being in custody," it "was not the fruit of the fact that the arrest was made in the house rather than someplace else." Likewise here: While acquisition of the gun and drugs was the product of a search pursuant to warrant, it was not the fruit of the fact that the entry was not preceded by knock and announce.

United States v. Ramirez involved a claim that police entry violated the Fourth Amendment because it was effected by breaking a window. We ultimately concluded that the property destruction was, under all the circumstances, reasonable, but in the course of our discussion we unanimously said the following: "[D]estruction of property in the course of a search may violate the Fourth Amendment, even though the entry itself is lawful and the fruits of the search are not subject to suppression." Had the breaking of the window been unreasonable, the Court said, it would have been necessary to determine whether there had been a "sufficient causal relationship between the breaking of the window and the discovery of the guns to warrant suppression of the evidence." What clearer expression could there be of the proposition that an impermissible manner of entry does not necessarily trigger the exclusionary rule?

JUSTICE KENNEDY, concurring in part and concurring in the judgment.

Two points should be underscored with respect to today's decision. First, the knock-and-announce requirement protects rights and expectations linked to ancient principles in our constitutional order. The Court's decision should not be interpreted as suggesting that violations of the requirement are trivial or beyond the law's concern. Second, the continued operation of the exclusionary rule, as settled and defined by our precedents, is not in doubt. Today's decision determines only that in the specific context of the knock-and-announce requirement, a violation is not sufficiently related to the later discovery of evidence to justify suppression.

* * *

Our system, as the Court explains, has developed procedures for training police officers and imposing discipline for failures to act competently and lawfully. If those measures prove ineffective, they can be fortified with more detailed regulations or legislation. Supplementing these safeguards are civil remedies, such as those available under 42 U.S.C. § 1983, that provide restitution for discrete harms. These remedies apply to all violations, including, of course, exceptional cases in which unannounced entries cause severe fright and humiliation.

Suppression is another matter. Under our precedents the causal link between a violation of the knock-and-announce requirement and a later search is too attenuated to allow suppression. When, for example, a violation results from want of a 20-second pause but an ensuing, lawful search lasting five hours discloses evidence of criminality, the failure to wait at the door cannot properly be described as having caused the discovery of evidence.

Today's decision does not address any demonstrated pattern of knock-and-announce violations. If a widespread pattern of violations were shown, and particularly if those violations were committed against persons who lacked the means or voice to mount an effective protest, there would be reason for grave concern. Even then, however, the Court would have to acknowledge that extending the remedy of exclusion to all the evidence seized following a knock-and-announce violation would mean revising the requirement of causation that limits our discretion in applying the exclusionary rule. That type of extension also would have significant practical implications, adding to the list of issues requiring resolution at the criminal trial questions such as whether police officers entered a home after waiting 10 seconds or 20.

In this case the relevant evidence was discovered not because of a failure to knock-and-announce, but because of a subsequent search pursuant to a lawful warrant. The Court in my view is correct to hold that suppression was not required. While I am not convinced that *Segura v. United States,* 468 U.S. 796 (1984), and *New York v. Harris,* 495 U.S. 14 (1990), have as much relevance here as Justice Scalia appears to conclude, the Court's holding is fully supported by Parts I through III of its opinion. I accordingly join those Parts and concur in the judgment.

JUSTICE BREYER, with whom JUSTICE STEVENS, JUSTICE SOUTER, and JUSTICE GINSBURG join, dissenting.

* * *

II

Reading our knock-and-announce cases in light of [our] foundational Fourth Amendment case law, it is clear that the exclusionary rule should apply. For one thing, elementary logic leads to that conclusion. We have held that a court must "conside[r]" whether officers complied with the knock-and-announce requirement "in assessing the reasonableness of a search or seizure." The Fourth Amendment insists that an unreasonable search or seizure is, constitutionally speaking, an illegal search or seizure. And ever since *Weeks* (in respect to federal prosecutions) and *Mapp* (in respect to state prosecutions), "the use of evidence secured through an illegal search and seizure" is "barred" in criminal trials.

For another thing, the driving legal purpose underlying the exclusionary rule, namely, the deterrence of unlawful government behavior, argues strongly for suppression. In *Weeks, Silverthorne,* and *Mapp,* the Court based its holdings requiring suppression of unlawfully obtained evidence upon the recognition that admission of that evidence would seriously undermine the Fourth Amendment's promise. All three cases recognized that failure to apply the exclusionary rule would make that promise a hollow one, reducing it to "a form of words," "of no value" to those whom it seeks to protect. Indeed, this Court in *Mapp* held that the exclusionary rule applies to the States in large part due to its belief that alternative state mechanisms for enforcing the Fourth Amendment's guarantees had proved "worthless and futile."

Why is application of the exclusionary rule any the less necessary here? Without such a rule, as in *Mapp,* police know that they can ignore the Constitution's requirements without risking suppression of evidence discovered after an unreasonable entry. As in *Mapp,* some government officers will find it easier, or believe it less risky, to proceed with what they consider a necessary search immediately and without the requisite constitutional (say, warrant or knock-and-announce) compliance.

Of course, the State or the Federal Government may provide alternative remedies for knock-and-announce violations. But that circumstance was true of *Mapp* as well. What reason is there to believe that those remedies (such as private damages actions under 42 U.S.C. § 1983), which the Court found inadequate in *Mapp,* can adequately deter unconstitutional police behavior here?

The cases reporting knock-and-announce violations are legion. Indeed, these cases of reported violations seem sufficiently frequent and serious as to indicate "a widespread pattern." Yet the majority, like Michigan and the United States, has failed to cite a single reported case in which a plaintiff has collected more than nominal damages solely as a result of a knock-and-announce violation. Even Michigan concedes that, "in cases like the present one . . ., damages may be virtually non-existent." And Michigan's *amici* further concede that civil immunities prevent tort law from being an effective substitute for the exclusionary rule at this time.

As Justice Stewart, the author of a number of significant Fourth Amendment opinions, explained, the deterrent effect of damage actions "can hardly be said to be great," as such actions are "expensive, time-consuming, not readily available, and rarely successful." The upshot is that the need for deterrence—the critical factor driving this Court's Fourth Amendment cases for close to a century—argues with at least comparable strength for evidentiary exclusion here.

To argue, as the majority does, that new remedies, such as 42 U.S.C. § 1983 actions or better trained police, make suppression unnecessary is to argue that *Wolf,* not *Mapp,* is now the law. (The Court recently rejected a similar argument in *Dickerson v. United States,* 530 U.S. 428, 441–442 (2000).) To argue that there may be few civil suits because violations may produce nothing "more than nominal injury" is to confirm, not to deny, the inability of civil suits to deter violations. And to argue without evidence (and despite myriad reported cases of violations, no reported case of civil damages, and Michigan's concession of their nonexistence) that civil suits may provide deterrence because claims *may* "have been settled" is, perhaps, to search in desperation for an argument. Rather, the majority, as it candidly admits, has simply "assumed" that, "[a]s far as [it] know[s], civil liability is an effective deterrent," a support-free assumption that *Mapp* and subsequent cases make clear does not embody the Court's normal approach to difficult questions of Fourth Amendment law.

It is not surprising, then, that after looking at virtually every pertinent Supreme Court case decided since *Weeks,* I can find no precedent that might offer the majority support for its contrary conclusion. The Court has, of course, recognized that not every Fourth Amendment violation necessarily triggers the exclusionary rule. But the class of Fourth Amendment violations that do not result in suppression of the evidence seized, however, is limited.

The Court has declined to apply the exclusionary rule only:

(1) where there is a specific reason to believe that application of the rule would "not result in appreciable deterrence," or

(2) where admissibility in proceedings other than criminal trials was at issue.

Neither of these two exceptions applies here. . . .

I am aware of no other basis for an exception. The Court has decided more than 300 Fourth Amendment cases since *Weeks.* The Court has found constitutional violations in nearly a third of them. The nature of the constitutional violation varies. In most instances officers lacked a warrant; in others, officers possessed a warrant based on false affidavits; in still others, the officers executed the search in an unconstitutional manner. But in every case involving evidence seized during an illegal search of a home (federally since *Weeks,* nationally since *Mapp*), the Court, with the exceptions mentioned, has either explicitly or implicitly upheld (or required) the suppression of the evidence at trial. In not one of those cases did the Court "questio[n], in the absence of a more efficacious sanction, the continued application of the [exclusionary] rule to suppress evidence from the State's case" in a criminal trial.

* * *

Neither can the majority justify its failure to respect the need for deterrence, as set forth consistently in the Court's prior case law, through its claim of "substantial social costs"—at least if it means that those "social costs" are somehow special here. The only costs it mentions are those that typically accompany *any* use of the Fourth Amendment's exclusionary principle: (1) that where the constable blunders, a guilty defendant may be set free (consider *Mapp* itself); (2) that defendants may assert claims where Fourth Amendment rights are uncertain (consider the Court's qualified immunity jurisprudence), and (3) that sometimes it is difficult to decide the merits of those uncertain claims. In fact, the "no-knock" warrants that are provided by many States, by diminishing uncertainty, may make application of the knock-and-announce principle less "cost[ly]" on the whole than application of comparable Fourth Amendment principles, such as determining whether a particular warrantless search was justified by exigency. The majority's "substantial social costs" argument is an argument against the Fourth Amendment's exclusionary principle itself. And it is an argument that this Court, until now, has consistently rejected.

III

The majority, Michigan, and the United States make several additional arguments. In my view, those arguments rest upon misunderstandings of the principles underlying this Court's precedents.

A

The majority first argues that "the constitutional violation of an illegal *manner* of entry was *not* a but-for cause of obtaining the evidence." But taking causation as it is commonly understood in the law, I do not see how that can be so. Although the police might have entered Hudson's home lawfully, they did not in fact do so. Their unlawful behavior inseparably characterizes their actual entry; that entry was a necessary condition of their presence in Hudson's home; and their presence in Hudson's home was a necessary condition of their finding and seizing the evidence. At the same time, their discovery of evidence in Hudson's home was a readily foreseeable consequence of their entry and their unlawful presence within the home.

* * *

The Court nonetheless accepts Michigan's argument that the requisite but-for-causation is not satisfied in this case because, whether or not the constitutional violation occurred (what the Court refers to as a "preliminary misstep"), "the police would have executed the warrant they had obtained, and would have discovered the gun and drugs inside the house." As support for this proposition, Michigan rests on this Court's inevitable discovery cases.

This claim, however, misunderstands the inevitable discovery doctrine. Justice Holmes in *Silverthorne,* in discussing an "independent source" exception, set forth the principles underlying the inevitable discovery rule. That rule does not refer to discovery that would have taken place if the police behavior in question had (contrary to fact) been lawful. The doctrine does not treat as critical what *hypothetically could* have happened had the police acted lawfully in the first place. Rather, "independent" or "inevitable" discovery refers to discovery that did occur or that would have occurred (1) *despite* (not simply *in the absence of*) the unlawful behavior and (2) *independently* of that unlawful behavior. The government cannot, for example, avoid suppression of evidence seized without a warrant (or pursuant to a defective warrant) simply by showing that it could have obtained a valid warrant had it sought one. Instead, it must show that the same evidence "inevitably *would* have been discovered *by lawful means.*" *Nix v. Williams,* 467 U.S., at 444 (emphasis added). "What a man *could* do is not at all the same as what he *would* do." Austin, *Ifs And Cans,* 42 PROCEEDINGS OF THE BRITISH ACADEMY 109, 111–112 (1956).

* * *

Of course, had the police entered the house lawfully, they would have found the gun and drugs. But that fact is beside the point. The question is not what police might have done had they not behaved unlawfully. The question is what they did do. Was there set in motion an independent chain of events that would have inevitably led to the discovery and seizure of the evidence despite, and independent of, that behavior? The answer here is "no."

B

The majority, Michigan, and the United States point out that the officers here possessed a warrant authorizing a search. That fact, they argue, means that the evidence would have been discovered independently or somehow diminishes the need to suppress the evidence. But I do not see why that is so. The warrant in question was not a "no-knock" warrant, which many States (but not Michigan) issue to assure police that a prior knock is not necessary. It did not authorize a search that fails to comply with knock-and-announce requirements. Rather, it was an ordinary search warrant. It authorized a search that *complied with,* not a search that *disregarded,* the Constitution's knock-and-announce rule.

* * *

C

The majority and the United States set forth a policy-related variant of the causal connection theme: The United States argues that the law should suppress evidence only insofar as a Fourth Amendment violation causes the kind of harm that the particular Fourth Amendment rule seeks to protect against. It adds that the constitutional purpose of the knock-and-announce rule is to prevent needless destruction of property (such as breaking down a door) and to avoid unpleasant surprise. And it concludes that the exclusionary rule should suppress evidence of, say, damage to property, the discovery of a defendant in an "intimate or compromising moment," or an excited utterance from the occupant caught by surprise, but nothing more.

The majority makes a similar argument. It says that evidence should not be suppressed once the causal connection between unlawful behavior and discovery of the evidence becomes too "attenuated." But the majority then makes clear that it is not using the word "attenuated" to mean what this Court's precedents have typically used that word to mean, namely, that the discovery of the evidence has come about long after the unlawful behavior took place or in an independent way, *i.e.,* through "means sufficiently distinguishable to be purged of the primary taint." *Wong Sun v. United States,* 371 U.S. 471, 487–488 (1963).

Rather, the majority gives the word "attenuation" a new meaning (thereby, in effect, making the same argument as the United States). "Attenuation," it says, "also occurs when, even given a direct causal connection, the interest protected by the constitutional guarantee that has been violated would not be served by suppression of the evidence obtained." The interests the knock-and-announce rule seeks to protect, the Court adds, are "human life" (at stake when a householder is "surprised"), "property" (such as the front door), and "those elements of privacy and dignity that can be destroyed by a sudden entrance," namely, "the opportunity to collect oneself before answering the door." Since none of those interests led to the discovery of the evidence seized here, there is no reason to suppress it.

There are three serious problems with this argument. First, it does not fully describe the constitutional values, purposes, and objectives underlying the knock-and-announce requirement. That rule does help to protect homeowners from damaged doors; it does help to protect occupants from surprise. But it does more than that. It protects the occupants' privacy by assuring them that government agents will not enter their home without complying with those requirements (among others) that diminish the offensive nature of any such intrusion. . . .

* * *

Second, whether the interests underlying the knock-and-announce rule are implicated in any given case is, in a sense, beside the point. As we have explained, failure to comply with the knock-and-announce rule renders the related search unlawful. And where a search is unlawful, the law insists upon suppression of the evidence consequently discovered, even if that evidence or its possession has little or nothing to do with the reasons underlying the unconstitutionality of a search. The Fourth Amendment does not seek to protect contraband, yet we have required suppression of contraband seized in an unlawful search. That is because the exclusionary rule protects more general "privacy values through deterrence of future police misconduct." The same is true here.

Third, the majority's interest-based approach departs from prior law. Ordinarily a court will simply look to see if the unconstitutional search produced the evidence. The majority does not refer to any relevant case in which, beyond that, suppression turned on the far more detailed relation between, say, (1) a particular materially false statement made to the magistrate who issued a (consequently) invalid warrant and (2) evidence found after a search with that warrant. And the majority's failure does not surprise me, for such efforts to trace causal connections at retail could well complicate Fourth Amendment suppression law, threatening its workability.

* * *

IV

There is perhaps one additional argument implicit in the majority's approach. The majority says, for example, that the "cost" to a defendant of "entering this lottery," *i.e.,* of claiming a "knock-and-announce" violation, "would be small, but the jackpot enormous"—namely, a potential "get-out-of-jail-free card." It adds that the "social costs" of applying the exclusionary rule here are not worth the deterrence benefits. Leaving aside what I believe are invalid arguments based on precedent or the majority's own estimate that suppression is not necessary to deter constitutional violations, one is left with a simple unvarnished conclusion, namely, that in this kind of case, a knock-and-announce case, "[r]esort to the massive remedy of suppressing evidence of guilt is unjustified." Why is that judicial judgment, taken on its own, inappropriate? Could it not be argued that the knock-and-announce rule, a subsidiary Fourth Amendment rule, is simply not important enough to warrant a suppression remedy? Could the majority not simply claim that the suppression game is not worth the candle?

The answer, I believe, is "no." That "no" reflects history, a history that shows the knock-and-announce rule is important. That "no" reflects precedent, precedent that shows there is no pre-existing legal category of exceptions to the exclusionary rule into which the knock-and-announce cases might fit. That "no" reflects empirical fact, experience that provides confirmation of what common sense suggests: without suppression there is little to deter knock-and-announce violations.

There may be instances in the law where text or history or tradition leaves room for a judicial decision that rests upon little more than an unvarnished judicial instinct. But this is not one of them. Rather, our Fourth Amendment traditions place high value upon protecting privacy in the home. They emphasize the need to assure that its constitutional protections are effective, lest the Amendment "sound the word of promise to the ear but break it to the hope." They include an exclusionary principle, which since *Weeks* has formed the centerpiece of the criminal law's effort to ensure the practical reality of those promises. That is why the Court should assure itself that any departure from that principle is firmly grounded in logic, in history, in precedent, and in empirical fact. It has not done so. That is why, with respect, I dissent.

Points for Discussion

1. The majority argues that the exclusion of evidence has always been a last resort rather than a default assumption. How much is this assertion undercut by the dissent's empirical showing that *Hudson* was the *first* case since *Mapp* in which evidence found in a home in violation of the Fourth Amendment was not excluded?

2. Justice Kennedy makes a point of stating in his concurrence that "the continued operation of the exclusionary rule, as settled and defined by our precedents, is not in doubt." This, of course, is because Justice Scalia's opinion puts the vitality of the exclusionary rule very much into doubt. Justice Scalia makes a series of assertions to support his suggestion that the exclusionary rule is not as necessary today as it was at the time of *Mapp*. Are these assertions as indubitable as Justice Scalia claims?

3. In Part III-A of its opinion, the Court finds that the discovery of the evidence was not caused by a constitutional violation and that causation is a necessary, but not a sufficient, requirement of exclusion. Is Part III-B (describing the balancing test for whether exclusion is appropriate in any particular case) necessary to the result in this case? If not, what is its precedential value?

4. In *Frisbie v. Collins*, 342 U.S. 519 (1952), the defendant was assaulted in Illinois by Michigan police officers and taken against his will to Michigan to stand trial for murder. He brought a habeas corpus action in Michigan, arguing that his kidnapping and illegal transportation across state lines precluded his prosecution. The Supreme Court disagreed. The

exclusionary rule requires the suppression of illegally seized evidence; it does not forbid the trial of a defendant who is before the court solely because of the illegal conduct of state officials.

3. ATTENUATION

UTAH V. STRIEFF

136 S.Ct. 2056 (2016)

JUSTICE THOMAS delivered the opinion of the court.

To enforce the Fourth Amendment's prohibition against "unreasonable searches and seizures," this Court has at times required courts to exclude evidence obtained by unconstitutional police conduct. But the Court has also held that, even when there is a Fourth Amendment violation, this exclusionary rule does not apply when the costs of exclusion outweigh its deterrent benefits. In some cases, for example, the link between the unconstitutional conduct and the discovery of the evidence is too attenuated to justify suppression. The question in this case is whether this attenuation doctrine applies when an officer makes an unconstitutional investigatory stop; learns during that stop that the suspect is subject to a valid arrest warrant; and proceeds to arrest the suspect and seize incriminating evidence during a search incident to that arrest. We hold that the evidence the officer seized as part of the search incident to arrest is admissible because the officer's discovery of the arrest warrant attenuated the connection between the unlawful stop and the evidence seized incident to arrest.

I

This case began with an anonymous tip. In December 2006, someone called the South Salt Lake City police's drug-tip line to report "narcotics activity" at a particular residence. Narcotics detective Douglas Fackrell investigated the tip. Over the course of about a week, Officer Fackrell conducted intermittent surveillance of the home. He observed visitors who left a few minutes after arriving at the house. These visits were sufficiently frequent to raise his suspicion that the occupants were dealing drugs.

One of those visitors was respondent Edward Strieff. Officer Fackrell observed Strieff exit the house and walk toward a nearby convenience store. In the store's parking lot, Officer Fackrell detained Strieff, identified himself, and asked Strieff what he was doing at the residence.

As part of the stop, Officer Fackrell requested Strieff's identification, and Strieff produced his Utah identification card. Officer Fackrell relayed Strieff's information to a police dispatcher, who reported that Strieff had an outstanding arrest warrant for a traffic violation. Officer Fackrell then arrested Strieff pursuant to that warrant. When Officer Fackrell searched

Strieff incident to the arrest, he discovered a baggie of methamphetamine and drug paraphernalia.

The State charged Strieff with unlawful possession of methamphetamine and drug paraphernalia. Strieff moved to suppress the evidence, arguing that the evidence was inadmissible because it was derived from an unlawful investigatory stop. At the suppression hearing, the prosecutor conceded that Officer Fackrell lacked reasonable suspicion for the stop but argued that the evidence should not be suppressed because the existence of a valid arrest warrant attenuated the connection between the unlawful stop and the discovery of the contraband.

* * *

We granted certiorari to resolve disagreement about how the attenuation doctrine applies where an unconstitutional detention leads to the discovery of a valid arrest warrant. We now reverse.

II

A

* * *

Under the Court's precedents, the exclusionary rule encompasses both the "primary evidence obtained as a direct result of an illegal search or seizure" and, relevant here, "evidence later discovered and found to be derivative of an illegality," the so-called " 'fruit of the poisonous tree.' " *Segura v. United States,* 468 U.S. 796, 804 (1984). But the significant costs of this rule have led us to deem it "applicable only . . . where its deterrence benefits outweigh its substantial social costs." *Hudson v. Michigan,* 547 U.S. 586, 591 (2006) (internal quotation marks omitted). "Suppression of evidence . . . has always been our last resort, not our first impulse." *Ibid.*

We have accordingly recognized several exceptions to the rule. Three of these exceptions involve the causal relationship between the unconstitutional act and the discovery of evidence. First, the independent source doctrine allows trial courts to admit evidence obtained in an unlawful search if officers independently acquired it from a separate, independent source. See *Murray v. United States,* 487 U.S. 533, 537 (1988). Second, the inevitable discovery doctrine allows for the admission of evidence that would have been discovered even without the unconstitutional source. See *Nix v. Williams,* 467 U.S. 431, 443–444 (1984). Third, and at issue here, is the attenuation doctrine: Evidence is admissible when the connection between unconstitutional police conduct and the evidence is remote or has been interrupted by some intervening circumstance, so that "the interest protected by the constitutional guarantee that has been violated would not be served by suppression of the evidence obtained." *Hudson, supra,* at 593.

B

Turning to the application of the attenuation doctrine to this case, we first address a threshold question: whether this doctrine applies at all to a case like this, where the intervening circumstance that the State relies on is the discovery of a valid, pre-existing, and untainted arrest warrant. The Utah Supreme Court declined to apply the attenuation doctrine because it read our precedents as applying the doctrine only "to circumstances involving an independent act of a defendant's 'free will' in confessing to a crime or consenting to a search." In this Court, Strieff has not defended this argument, and we disagree with it, as well. The attenuation doctrine evaluates the causal link between the government's unlawful act and the discovery of evidence, which often has nothing to do with a defendant's actions. And the logic of our prior attenuation cases is not limited to independent acts by the defendant.

It remains for us to address whether the discovery of a valid arrest warrant was a sufficient intervening event to break the causal chain between the unlawful stop and the discovery of drug-related evidence on Strieff's person. The three factors articulated in *Brown v. Illinois,* 422 U.S. 590 (1975), guide our analysis. First, we look to the "temporal proximity" between the unconstitutional conduct and the discovery of evidence to determine how closely the discovery of evidence followed the unconstitutional search. Second, we consider "the presence of intervening circumstances." Third, and "particularly" significant, we examine "the purpose and flagrancy of the official misconduct." In evaluating these factors, we assume without deciding (because the State conceded the point) that Officer Fackrell lacked reasonable suspicion to initially stop Strieff. And, because we ultimately conclude that the warrant breaks the causal chain, we also have no need to decide whether the warrant's existence alone would make the initial stop constitutional even if Officer Fackrell was unaware of its existence.

1

The first factor, temporal proximity between the initially unlawful stop and the search, favors suppressing the evidence. Our precedents have declined to find that this factor favors attenuation unless "substantial time" elapses between an unlawful act and when the evidence is obtained. *Kaupp v. Texas,* 538 U.S. 626, 633 (2003) (*per curiam*). Here, however, Officer Fackrell discovered drug contraband on Strieff's person only minutes after the illegal stop. As the Court explained in *Brown,* such a short time interval counsels in favor of suppression; there, we found that the confession should be suppressed, relying in part on the "less than two hours" that separated the unconstitutional arrest and the confession.

In contrast, the second factor, the presence of intervening circumstances, strongly favors the State. In *Segura,* the Court addressed similar facts to those here and found sufficient intervening circumstances to allow the admission of evidence. There, agents had probable cause to believe that apartment occupants were dealing cocaine. They sought a warrant. In the meantime, they entered the apartment, arrested an occupant, and discovered evidence of drug activity during a limited search for security reasons. The next evening, the Magistrate Judge issued the search warrant. This Court deemed the evidence admissible notwithstanding the illegal search because the information supporting the warrant was "wholly unconnected with the [arguably illegal] entry and was known to the agents well before the initial entry."

Segura, of course, applied the independent source doctrine because the unlawful entry "did not contribute in any way to discovery of the evidence seized under the warrant." But the *Segura* Court suggested that the existence of a valid warrant favors finding that the connection between unlawful conduct and the discovery of evidence is "sufficiently attenuated to dissipate the taint." That principle applies here.

In this case, the warrant was valid, it predated Officer Fackrell's investigation, and it was entirely unconnected with the stop. And once Officer Fackrell discovered the warrant, he had an obligation to arrest Strieff. "A warrant is a judicial mandate to an officer to conduct a search or make an arrest, and the officer has a sworn duty to carry out its provisions." *United States v. Leon,* 468 U.S. 897, 920, n. 21 (1984) (internal quotation marks omitted). Officer Fackrell's arrest of Strieff thus was a ministerial act that was independently compelled by the pre-existing warrant. And once Officer Fackrell was authorized to arrest Strieff, it was undisputedly lawful to search Strieff as an incident of his arrest to protect Officer Fackrell's safety. See *Arizona v. Gant,* 556 U.S. 332, 339 (2009) (explaining the permissible scope of searches incident to arrest).

Finally, the third factor, "the purpose and flagrancy of the official misconduct," also strongly favors the State. The exclusionary rule exists to deter police misconduct. *Davis v. United States,* 564 U.S. 229, 236–237 (2011). The third factor of the attenuation doctrine reflects that rationale by favoring exclusion only when the police misconduct is most in need of deterrence—that is, when it is purposeful or flagrant.

Officer Fackrell was at most negligent. In stopping Strieff, Officer Fackrell made two good-faith mistakes. First, he had not observed what time Strieff entered the suspected drug house, so he did not know how long Strieff had been there. Officer Fackrell thus lacked a sufficient basis to conclude that Strieff was a short-term visitor who may have been consummating a drug transaction. Second, because he lacked confirmation that Strieff was a short-term visitor, Officer Fackrell should have asked Strieff whether he would speak with him, instead of demanding that Strieff do so. Officer Fackrell's stated purpose was to "find out what was going on in the house." Nothing prevented him from approaching Strieff simply to ask. See *Florida v. Bostick,* 501 U.S. 429, 434 (1991) ("A seizure does not occur simply because a police officer approaches an individual and asks a few questions"). But these errors in judgment hardly rise to a purposeful or flagrant violation of Strieff's Fourth Amendment rights.

While Officer Fackrell's decision to initiate the stop was mistaken, his conduct thereafter was lawful. The officer's decision to run the warrant check was a "negligibly burdensome precaution" for officer safety. *Rodriguez v. United States,* 575 U.S. ___, ___ (2015). And Officer Fackrell's actual search of Strieff was a lawful search incident to arrest.

Moreover, there is no indication that this unlawful stop was part of any systemic or recurrent police misconduct. To the contrary, all the evidence suggests that the stop was an isolated instance of negligence that occurred in connection with a bona fide investigation of a suspected drug house. Officer Fackrell saw Strieff leave a suspected drug house. And his suspicion about the house was based on an anonymous tip and his personal observations.

Applying these factors, we hold that the evidence discovered on Strieff's person was admissible because the unlawful stop was sufficiently attenuated by the pre-existing arrest warrant. Although the illegal stop was close in time to Strieff's arrest, that consideration is outweighed by two factors supporting the State. The outstanding arrest warrant for Strieff's arrest is a critical intervening circumstance that is wholly independent of the illegal stop. The discovery of that warrant broke the causal chain between the unconstitutional stop and the discovery of evidence by compelling Officer Fackrell to arrest Strieff. And, it is especially significant that there is no evidence that Officer Fackrell's illegal stop reflected flagrantly unlawful police misconduct.

2

We find Strieff's counterarguments unpersuasive.

First, he argues that the attenuation doctrine should not apply because the officer's stop was purposeful and flagrant. He asserts that Officer Fackrell stopped him solely to fish for evidence of suspected wrongdoing. But Officer Fackrell sought information from Strieff to find out what was happening inside a house whose occupants were legitimately suspected of dealing drugs. This was not a suspicionless fishing expedition "in the hope that something would turn up." *Taylor v. Alabama,* 457 U.S. 687, 691 (1982).

Strieff argues, moreover, that Officer Fackrell's conduct was flagrant because he detained Strieff without the necessary level of cause (here, reasonable suspicion). But that conflates the standard for an illegal stop with the standard for flagrancy. For the violation to be flagrant, more severe police misconduct is required than the mere absence of proper cause for the seizure. Neither the officer's alleged purpose nor the flagrancy of the violation rise to a level of misconduct to warrant suppression.

Second, Strieff argues that, because of the prevalence of outstanding arrest warrants in many jurisdictions, police will engage in dragnet searches if the exclusionary rule is not applied. We think that this outcome is unlikely. Such wanton conduct would expose police to civil liability. See 42 U.S.C. § 1983; *Monell v. New York City Dept. of Social Servs.,* 436 U.S. 658, 690 (1978); see also *Segura,* 468 U.S., at 812. And in any event, the *Brown* factors take account of the purpose and flagrancy of police misconduct. Were evidence of a dragnet search presented here, the application of the *Brown* factors could be different. But there is no evidence that the concerns that Strieff raises with the criminal justice system are present in South Salt Lake City, Utah.

* * *

JUSTICE SOTOMAYOR, with whom JUSTICE GINSBURG joins as to Parts I, II, and III, dissenting.

The Court today holds that the discovery of a warrant for an unpaid parking ticket will forgive a police officer's violation of your Fourth Amendment rights. Do not be soothed by the opinion's technical language: This case allows the police to stop you on the street, demand your identification, and check it for outstanding traffic warrants—even if you are doing nothing wrong. If the officer discovers a warrant for a fine you forgot to pay, courts will now excuse his illegal stop and will admit into evidence anything he happens to find by searching you after arresting you on the warrant. Because the Fourth Amendment should prohibit, not permit, such misconduct, I dissent.

I

Minutes after Edward Strieff walked out of a South Salt Lake City home, an officer stopped him, questioned him, and took his identification to run it through a police database. The officer did not suspect that Strieff had done anything wrong. Strieff just happened to be the first person to leave a house that the officer thought might contain "drug activity."

As the State of Utah concedes, this stop was illegal. The Fourth Amendment protects people from "unreasonable searches and seizures." An officer breaches that protection when he detains a pedestrian to check his license without any evidence that the person is engaged in a crime. *Delaware v. Prouse,* 440 U.S. 648, 663 (1979); *Terry v. Ohio,* 392 U.S. 1, 21 (1968). The officer deepens the breach when he prolongs the detention just to fish further for evidence of wrongdoing. *Rodriguez v. United States,* 575 U.S. ___, ___–___ (2015). In his search for lawbreaking, the officer in this case himself broke the law.

The officer learned that Strieff had a "small traffic warrant." Pursuant to that warrant, he arrested Strieff and, conducting a search incident to the arrest, discovered methamphetamine in Strieff's pockets.

* * *

II

It is tempting in a case like this, where illegal conduct by an officer uncovers illegal conduct by a civilian, to forgive the officer. After all, his instincts, although unconstitutional, were correct. But a basic principle lies at the heart of the Fourth Amendment: Two wrongs don't make a right. When "lawless police conduct" uncovers evidence of lawless civilian conduct, this Court has long required later criminal trials to exclude the illegally obtained evidence. *Terry,* 392 U.S., at 12; *Mapp v. Ohio,* 367 U.S. 643, 655 (1961). For example, if an officer breaks into a home and finds a forged check lying around, that check may not be used to prosecute the homeowner for bank fraud. We would describe the check as " 'fruit of the poisonous tree.' " *Wong Sun v. United States,* 371 U.S. 471, 488 (1963). Fruit that must be cast aside includes not only evidence directly found by an illegal search but also evidence "come at by exploitation of that illegality." *Ibid.*

This "exclusionary rule" removes an incentive for officers to search us without proper justification. It also keeps courts from being "made party to lawless invasions of the constitutional rights of citizens by permitting unhindered governmental use of the fruits of such invasions." When courts admit only lawfully obtained evidence, they encourage "those who formulate law enforcement polices, and the officers who implement them, to incorporate Fourth Amendment ideals into their value system." *Stone v. Powell,* 428 U.S. 465, 492 (1976). But when courts admit illegally obtained evidence as well, they reward "manifest neglect if not an open defiance of the prohibitions of the Constitution." *Weeks,* 232 U.S., at 394.

Applying the exclusionary rule, the Utah Supreme Court correctly decided that Strieff's drugs must be excluded because the officer exploited his illegal stop to discover them. The officer found the drugs only after learning of Strieff's traffic violation; and he learned of Strieff's traffic violation only because he unlawfully stopped Strieff to check his driver's license.

* * *

The warrant check, in other words, was not an "intervening circumstance" separating the stop from the search for drugs. It was part and parcel of the officer's illegal "expedition for evidence in the hope that something might turn up." *Brown,* 422 U.S., at 605. Under our precedents, because the officer found Strieff's drugs by exploiting his own constitutional violation, the drugs should be excluded.

III

A

The Court sees things differently. To the Court, the fact that a warrant gives an officer cause to arrest a person severs the connection between illegal policing and the resulting discovery of evidence. This is a remarkable proposition: The mere existence of a warrant not only gives an officer legal cause to arrest and search a person, it also forgives an officer who, with no knowledge of the warrant at all, unlawfully stops that person on a whim or hunch.

To explain its reasoning, the Court relies on *Segura v. United States,* 468 U.S. 796 (1984). There, federal agents applied for a warrant to search an apartment but illegally entered the apartment to secure it before the judge issued the warrant. After receiving the warrant, the agents then searched the apartment for drugs. The question before us was what to do with the evidence the agents then discovered. We declined to suppress it because "the illegal entry into petitioners' apartment did not contribute in any way to discovery of the evidence seized under the warrant." *Id.,* at 815.

According to the majority, *Segura* involves facts "similar" to this case and "suggest[s]" that a valid warrant will clean up whatever illegal conduct uncovered it. It is difficult to understand this interpretation. In *Segura,* the agents' illegal conduct in entering the apartment had nothing to do with their procurement of a search warrant. Here, the officer's illegal conduct in stopping Strieff was essential to his discovery of an arrest warrant. *Segura* would be similar only if the agents used information they illegally obtained from the apartment to procure a search warrant or discover an arrest warrant. Precisely because that was not the case, the Court admitted the untainted evidence.

The majority likewise misses the point when it calls the warrant check here a " 'negligibly burdensome precaution' " taken for the officer's "safety." Remember, the officer stopped Strieff without suspecting him of committing any crime. By his own account, the officer did not fear Strieff. Moreover, the safety rationale we discussed in *Rodriguez,* an opinion about highway patrols, is conspicuously absent here. A warrant check on a highway "ensures that vehicles on the road are operated safely and responsibly." We allow such checks during legal traffic stops because the legitimacy of a person's driver's license has a "close connection to roadway safety." A warrant check of a pedestrian on a sidewalk, "by contrast, is a measure aimed at 'detecting evidence of ordinary criminal wrongdoing.' " *Ibid.* (quoting *Indianapolis v. Edmond,* 531 U.S. 32, 40–41 (2000)). Surely we would not allow officers to warrant-check random joggers, dog walkers, and lemonade vendors just to ensure they pose no threat to anyone else.

The majority also posits that the officer could not have exploited his illegal conduct because he did not violate the Fourth Amendment on purpose. Rather, he made "good-faith mistakes." Never mind that the officer's sole purpose was to fish for evidence. The majority casts his unconstitutional actions as "negligent" and therefore incapable of being deterred by the exclusionary rule.

But the Fourth Amendment does not tolerate an officer's unreasonable searches and seizures just because he did not know any better. Even officers prone to negligence can learn from courts that exclude illegally obtained evidence. Indeed, they are perhaps the most in need of the education, whether by the judge's opinion, the prosecutor's future guidance, or an updated manual on criminal procedure. If the officers are in doubt about what the law requires, exclusion gives them an "incentive to err on the side of constitutional behavior." *United States v. Johnson,* 457 U.S. 537, 561 (1982).

B

Most striking about the Court's opinion is its insistence that the event here was "isolated," with "no indication that this unlawful stop was part of any systemic or recurrent police misconduct." Respectfully, nothing about this case is isolated.

Outstanding warrants are surprisingly common. When a person with a traffic ticket misses a fine payment or court appearance, a court will issue a warrant. When a person on probation drinks alcohol or breaks curfew, a court will issue a warrant. The States and Federal Government maintain databases with over 7.8 million outstanding warrants, the vast majority of which appear to be for minor offenses. Even these sources may not track the "staggering" numbers of warrants, " 'drawers and drawers' " full, that many cities issue for traffic violations and ordinance infractions. Dept. of Justice, Civil Rights Div., *Investigation of the Ferguson Police Department* 47, 55 (2015) (Ferguson Report). The county in this case has had a "backlog" of such warrants. The Department of Justice recently reported that in the town of Ferguson, Missouri, with a population of 21,000, 16,000 people had outstanding warrants against them. Ferguson Report, at 6, 55.

Justice Department investigations across the country have illustrated how these astounding numbers of warrants can be used by police to stop people without cause. In a single year in New Orleans, officers "made nearly 60,000 arrests, of which about 20,000 were of people with outstanding traffic or misdemeanor warrants from neighboring parishes for such infractions as unpaid tickets." Dept. of Justice, Civil Rights Div., *Investigation of the New Orleans Police Department* 29 (2011). In the St. Louis metropolitan area, officers "routinely" stop people—on the street, at bus stops, or even in court—for no reason other than "an officer's desire to check whether the subject had a municipal arrest warrant pending." Ferguson Report, at 49, 57. In Newark, New Jersey, officers stopped 52,235 pedestrians within a 4-year period and ran warrant checks on 39,308 of them. Dept. of Justice, Civil Rights Div., *Investigation of the Newark Police*

Department 8, 19, n. 15 (2014). The Justice Department analyzed these warrant-checked stops and reported that "approximately 93% of the stops would have been considered unsupported by articulated reasonable suspicion." *Id.*, at 9, n. 7.

I do not doubt that most officers act in "good faith" and do not set out to break the law. That does not mean these stops are "isolated instance[s] of negligence," however. Many are the product of institutionalized training procedures. The New York City Police Department long trained officers to, in the words of a District Judge, "stop and question first, develop reasonable suspicion later." *Ligon v. New York,* 925 F.Supp.2d 478, 537–538 (S.D.N.Y.), *stay granted on other grounds*, 736 F.3d 118 (C.A.2 2013). The Utah Supreme Court described as " 'routine procedure' or 'common practice' " the decision of Salt Lake City police officers to run warrant checks on pedestrians they detained without reasonable suspicion. In the related context of traffic stops, one widely followed police manual instructs officers looking for drugs to "run at least a warrants check on all drivers you stop. Statistically, narcotics offenders are . . . more likely to fail to appear on simple citations, such as traffic or trespass violations, leading to the issuance of bench warrants. Discovery of an outstanding warrant gives you cause for an immediate custodial arrest and search of the suspect." C. Remsberg, *Tactics for Criminal Patrol* 205–206 (1995).

The majority does not suggest what makes this case "isolated" from these and countless other examples. Nor does it offer guidance for how a defendant can prove that his arrest was the result of "widespread" misconduct. Surely it should not take a federal investigation of Salt Lake County before the Court would protect someone in Strieff's position.

IV

Writing only for myself, and drawing on my professional experiences, I would add that unlawful "stops" have severe consequences much greater than the inconvenience suggested by the name. This Court has given officers an array of instruments to probe and examine you. When we condone officers' use of these devices without adequate cause, we give them reason to target pedestrians in an arbitrary manner. We also risk treating members of our communities as second-class citizens.

Although many Americans have been stopped for speeding or jaywalking, few may realize how degrading a stop can be when the officer is looking for more. This Court has allowed an officer to stop you for whatever reason he wants—so long as he can point to a pretextual justification after the fact. *Whren v. United States,* 517 U.S. 806, 813 (1996). That justification must provide specific reasons why the officer suspected you were breaking the law, *Terry,* 392 U.S., at 21, but it may factor in your ethnicity, *United States v. Brignoni-Ponce,* 422 U.S. 873, 886–887 (1975), where you live, *Adams v. Williams,* 407 U.S. 143, 147 (1972), what you were wearing, *United States v. Sokolow,* 490 U.S. 1, 4–5

(1989), and how you behaved, *Illinois v. Wardlow,* 528 U.S. 119, 124–125 (2000). The officer does not even need to know which law you might have broken so long as he can later point to any possible infraction—even one that is minor, unrelated, or ambiguous. *Devenpeck v. Alford,* 543 U.S. 146, 154–155 (2004); *Heien v. North Carolina,* 574 U.S. 54 (2014).

The indignity of the stop is not limited to an officer telling you that you look like a criminal. The officer may next ask for your "consent" to inspect your bag or purse without telling you that you can decline. See *Florida v. Bostick,* 501 U.S. 429, 438 (1991). Regardless of your answer, he may order you to stand "helpless, perhaps facing a wall with [your] hands raised." *Terry,* 392 U.S., at 17. If the officer thinks you might be dangerous, he may then "frisk" you for weapons. This involves more than just a pat down. As onlookers pass by, the officer may " 'feel with sensitive fingers every portion of [your] body. A thorough search [may] be made of [your] arms and armpits, waistline and back, the groin and area about the testicles, and entire surface of the legs down to the feet.' " *Id.,* at 17, n. 13.

The officer's control over you does not end with the stop. If the officer chooses, he may handcuff you and take you to jail for doing nothing more than speeding, jaywalking, or "driving [your] pickup truck . . . with [your] 3-year-old son and 5-year-old daughter . . . without [your] seatbelt fastened." *Atwater v. Lago Vista,* 532 U.S. 318, 323–324 (2001). At the jail, he can fingerprint you, swab DNA from the inside of your mouth, and force you to "shower with a delousing agent" while you "lift [your] tongue, hold out [your] arms, turn around, and lift [your] genitals." *Florence v. Board of Chosen Freeholders of County of Burlington,* 566 U.S. 318, 323 (2012); *Maryland v. King,* 569 U.S. 435, 462 (2013). Even if you are innocent, you will now join the 65 million Americans with an arrest record and experience the "civil death" of discrimination by employers, landlords, and whoever else conducts a background check. Chin, *The New Civil Death,* 160 U. PA. L. REV. 1789, 1805 (2012). And, of course, if you fail to pay bail or appear for court, a judge will issue a warrant to render you "arrestable on sight" in the future.

* * *

By legitimizing the conduct that produces this double consciousness, this case tells everyone, white and black, guilty and innocent, that an officer can verify your legal status at any time. It says that your body is subject to invasion while courts excuse the violation of your rights. It implies that you are not a citizen of a democracy but the subject of a carceral state, just waiting to be cataloged.

We must not pretend that the countless people who are routinely targeted by police are "isolated." They are the canaries in the coal mine whose deaths, civil and literal, warn us that no one can breathe in this atmosphere. They are the ones who recognize that unlawful police stops corrode all our civil liberties and threaten all our lives. Until their voices matter too, our justice system will continue to be anything but.

I dissent.

JUSTICE KAGAN, with whom JUSTICE GINSBURG joins, dissenting.

If a police officer stops a person on the street without reasonable suspicion, that seizure violates the Fourth Amendment. And if the officer pats down the unlawfully detained individual and finds drugs in his pocket, the State may not use the contraband as evidence in a criminal prosecution. That much is beyond dispute. The question here is whether the prohibition on admitting evidence dissolves if the officer discovers, after making the stop but before finding the drugs, that the person has an outstanding arrest warrant. Because that added wrinkle makes no difference under the Constitution, I respectfully dissent.

* * *

This case thus requires the Court to determine whether excluding the fruits of Officer Douglas Fackrell's unjustified stop of Edward Strieff would significantly deter police from committing similar constitutional violations in the future. And as the Court states, that inquiry turns on application of the "attenuation doctrine,"—our effort to "mark the point" at which the discovery of evidence "becomes so attenuated" from the police misconduct that the deterrent benefit of exclusion drops below its cost. *United States v. Leon,* 468 U.S. 897, 911 (1984). Since *Brown v. Illinois,* 422 U.S. 590, 604–605 (1975), three factors have guided that analysis. First, the closer the "temporal proximity" between the unlawful act and the discovery of evidence, the greater the deterrent value of suppression. Second, the more "purposeful" or "flagrant" the police illegality, the clearer the necessity, and better the chance, of preventing similar misbehavior. And third, the presence (or absence) of "intervening circumstances" makes a difference: The stronger the causal chain between the misconduct and the evidence, the more exclusion will curb future constitutional violations. Here, as shown below, each of those considerations points toward suppression: Nothing in Fackrell's discovery of an outstanding warrant so attenuated the connection between his wrongful behavior and his detection of drugs as to diminish the exclusionary rule's deterrent benefits.

Start where the majority does: The temporal proximity factor, it forthrightly admits, "favors suppressing the evidence." After all, Fackrell's discovery of drugs came just minutes after the unconstitutional stop. And in prior decisions, this Court has made clear that only the lapse of "substantial time" between the two could favor admission. *Kaupp v. Texas,* 538 U.S. 626, 633 (2003) (*per curiam*). So the State, by all accounts, takes strike one.

Move on to the purposefulness of Fackrell's conduct, where the majority is less willing to see a problem for what it is. The majority chalks up Fackrell's Fourth Amendment violation to a couple of innocent "mistakes." But far from a Barney Fife-type mishap, Fackrell's seizure of Strieff was a calculated decision, taken with so little justification that the State has never tried to defend its legality. At the suppression hearing, Fackrell acknowledged that the stop was designed for investigatory purposes—*i.e.,* to "find out what was going on in the house" he had been watching, and to figure out "what Strieff was doing there." And Fackrell frankly admitted that he had no basis for his action except that Strieff "was coming out of the house." Plug in Fackrell's and Strieff's names, substitute "stop" for "arrest" and "reasonable suspicion" for "probable cause," and this Court's decision in *Brown* perfectly describes this case:

> It is not disputed that [Fackrell stopped Strieff] without [reasonable suspicion]. [He] later testified that [he] made the [stop] for the purpose of questioning [Strieff] as part of [his] investigation. . . . The illegality here . . . had a quality of purposefulness. The impropriety of the [stop] was obvious. [A]wareness of that fact was virtually conceded by [Fackrell] when [he] repeatedly acknowledged, in [his] testimony, that the purpose of [his] action was 'for investigation': [Fackrell] embarked upon this expedition for evidence in the hope that something might turn up.

422 U.S., at 592 (some internal punctuation altered; footnote, citation, and paragraph break omitted).

In *Brown,* the Court held those facts to support suppression—and they do here as well. Swing and a miss for strike two.

Finally, consider whether any intervening circumstance "broke the causal chain" between the stop and the evidence. The notion of such a disrupting event comes from the tort law doctrine of proximate causation. And as in the tort context, a circumstance counts as intervening only when it is unforeseeable—not when it can be seen coming from miles away. See W. Keeton, D. Dobbs, B. Keeton, & D. Owen, PROSSER AND KEETON ON LAW OF TORTS 312 (5th ed. 1984). For rather than breaking the causal chain, **predictable effects** (*e.g.,* X leads naturally to Y leads naturally to Z) are its very links.

And Fackrell's discovery of an arrest warrant—the only event the majority thinks intervened—was an eminently foreseeable consequence of stopping Strieff. As Fackrell testified, checking for outstanding warrants during a stop is the "normal" practice of South Salt Lake City police. In other words, the department's standard detention procedures—stop, ask for identification, run a check—are partly designed to find outstanding warrants. And find them they will, given the staggering number of such warrants on the books. To take just a few examples: The State of California has 2.5 million outstanding arrest warrants (a number corresponding to about 9% of its adult population); Pennsylvania (with a population of about

12.8 million) contributes 1.4 million more; and New York City (population 8.4 million) adds another 1.2 million. So outstanding warrants do not appear as bolts from the blue. They are the run-of-the-mill results of police stops—what officers look for when they run a routine check of a person's identification and what they know will turn up with fair regularity. In short, they are nothing like what intervening circumstances are supposed to be. Strike three.

The majority's misapplication of *Brown*'s three-part inquiry creates unfortunate incentives for the police—indeed, practically invites them to do what Fackrell did here. Consider an officer who, like Fackrell, wishes to stop someone for investigative reasons, but does not have what a court would view as reasonable suspicion. If the officer believes that any evidence he discovers will be inadmissible, he is likely to think the unlawful stop not worth making—precisely the deterrence the exclusionary rule is meant to achieve. But when he is told of today's decision? Now the officer knows that the stop may well yield admissible evidence: So long as the target is one of the many millions of people in this country with an outstanding arrest warrant, anything the officer finds in a search is fair game for use in a criminal prosecution. The officer's incentive to violate the Constitution thus increases: From here on, he sees potential advantage in stopping individuals without reasonable suspicion—exactly the temptation the exclusionary rule is supposed to remove. Because the majority thus places Fourth Amendment protections at risk, I respectfully dissent.

Points for Discussion

1. The majority claims that the officer's arrest of Strieff "was a ministerial act that was independently compelled by the pre-existing warrant." A ministerial act, as many cases including *Marbury v. Madison* have held, is one that leaves nothing to the discretion of the government agent charged with performing it. The act must be performed because the law requires it. In the very next sentence, however, the majority apparently retreats from this characterization and says that the officer "was authorized to arrest Strieff." To authorize is to give permission, not to command. Which of these two better describes the legal effect of an arrest warrant issued at the request of prosecutors or police?

2. Is the majority correct to conclude that the stop of Strieff "was not a suspicionless fishing expedition" because the police wanted to know "what was happening inside a house whose occupants were legitimately suspected of dealing drugs"? Given the fact that both the majority and the State of Utah conceded that the officer lacked even reasonable suspicion for a stop, why does the majority feel the need to defend the officer's actions?

3. The majority posits that the *only* purpose of the Fourth Amendment exclusionary rule is to deter police misconduct. Justice Sotomayor's dissent gives an additional rationale for the rule. What is it?

4. The last point in Justice Kagan's dissent is that this decision invites officers to violate people's civil rights because a stop "may well yield admissible evidence." If an officer seizes an individual solely to determine whether they have outstanding warrants and a search shows that they do not, what remedies are available to the person whose rights were violated by the unconstitutional seizure?

UNITED STATES V. PATANE

542 U.S. 630 (2004)

JUSTICE THOMAS announced the judgment of the court and delivered an opinion, in which THE CHIEF JUSTICE and JUSTICE SCALIA join.

In this case we must decide whether a failure to give a suspect the warnings prescribed by *Miranda v. Arizona,* 384 U.S. 436 (1966), requires suppression of the physical fruits of the suspect's unwarned but voluntary statements. The Court has previously addressed this question but has not reached a definitive conclusion. Although we believe that the Court's decisions in *Oregon v. Elstad,* 470 U.S. 298 (1985), and *Michigan v. Tucker,* 417 U.S. 433 (1974), are instructive, the Courts of Appeals have split on the question after our decision in *Dickerson v. United States,* 530 U.S. 428 (2000). Because the *Miranda* rule protects against violations of the Self-Incrimination Clause, which, in turn, is not implicated by the introduction at trial of physical evidence resulting from voluntary statements, we answer the question presented in the negative.

I

In June 2001, respondent, Samuel Francis Patane, was arrested for harassing his ex-girlfriend, Linda O'Donnell. He was released on bond, subject to a temporary restraining order that prohibited him from contacting O'Donnell. Respondent apparently violated the restraining order by attempting to telephone O'Donnell. On June 6, 2001, Officer Tracy Fox of the Colorado Springs Police Department began to investigate the matter. On the same day, a county probation officer informed an agent of the Bureau of Alcohol, Tobacco and Firearms, that respondent, a convicted felon, illegally possessed a .40 Glock pistol. The ATF relayed this information to Detective Josh Benner, who worked closely with the ATF. Together, Detective Benner and Officer Fox proceeded to respondent's residence.

After reaching the residence and inquiring into respondent's attempts to contact O'Donnell, Officer Fox arrested respondent for violating the restraining order. Detective Benner attempted to advise respondent of his *Miranda* rights but got no further than the right to remain silent. At that point, respondent interrupted, asserting that he knew his rights, and neither officer attempted to complete the warning.[1]

Detective Benner then asked respondent about the Glock. Respondent was initially reluctant to discuss the matter, stating: "I am not sure I should tell you anything about the Glock because I don't want you to take it away from me." Detective Benner persisted, and respondent told him that the pistol was in his bedroom. Respondent then gave Detective Benner permission to retrieve the pistol. Detective Benner found the pistol and seized it.

* * *

As we explain below, the *Miranda* rule is a prophylactic employed to protect against violations of the Self-Incrimination Clause. The Self-Incrimination Clause, however, is not implicated by the admission into evidence of the physical fruit of a voluntary statement. Accordingly, there is no justification for extending the *Miranda* rule to this context. And just as the Self-Incrimination Clause primarily focuses on the criminal trial, so too does the *Miranda* rule. The *Miranda* rule is not a code of police conduct, and police do not violate the Constitution (or even the *Miranda* rule, for that matter) by mere failures to warn. For this reason, the exclusionary rule articulated in cases such as *Wong Sun* does not apply. Accordingly, we reverse the judgment of the Court of Appeals and remand the case for further proceedings.

II

* * *

To be sure, the Court has recognized and applied several prophylactic rules designed to protect the core privilege against self-incrimination. For example, although the text of the Self-Incrimination Clause at least suggests that "its coverage [is limited to] compelled testimony that is used against the defendant in the trial itself," potential suspects may, at times, assert the privilege in proceedings in which answers might be used to incriminate them in a subsequent criminal case. We have explained that "[t]he natural concern which underlies [these] decisions is that an inability to protect the right at one stage of a proceeding may make its invocation useless at a later stage." [*Michigan v. Tucker,* 417 U.S. 433, 440–41 (1974)].

Similarly, in *Miranda,* the Court concluded that the possibility of coercion inherent in custodial interrogations unacceptably raises the risk that a suspect's privilege against self-incrimination might be violated. To protect against this danger, the *Miranda* rule creates a presumption of

[1] The Government concedes that respondent's answers to subsequent on-the-scene questioning are inadmissible at trial under *Miranda v. Arizona,* 384 U.S. 436 (1966), despite the partial warning and respondent's assertions that he knew his rights.

coercion, in the absence of specific warnings, that is generally irrebuttable for purposes of the prosecution's case in chief.

But because these prophylactic rules (including the *Miranda* rule) necessarily sweep beyond the actual protections of the Self-Incrimination Clause, any further extension of these rules must be justified by its necessity for the protection of the actual right against compelled self-incrimination. Indeed, at times the Court has declined to extend *Miranda* even where it has perceived a need to protect the privilege against self-incrimination.

It is for these reasons that statements taken without *Miranda* warnings (though not actually compelled) can be used to impeach a defendant's testimony at trial, though the fruits of actually compelled testimony cannot. More generally, the *Miranda* rule "does not require that the statements [taken without complying with the rule] and their fruits be discarded as inherently tainted," [*Oregon v. Elstad,* 470 U.S. 298, 307 (1985)]. Such a blanket suppression rule could not be justified by reference to the "Fifth Amendment goal of assuring trustworthy evidence" or by any deterrence rationale and would therefore fail our close-fit requirement.

Furthermore, the Self-Incrimination Clause contains its own exclusionary rule. It provides that "[n]o person . . . shall be compelled in any criminal case to be a witness against himself." Amdt. 5. Unlike the Fourth Amendment's bar on unreasonable searches, the Self-Incrimination Clause is self-executing. We have repeatedly explained "that those subjected to coercive police interrogations have an *automatic* protection from the use of their involuntary statements (or evidence derived from their statements) in any subsequent criminal trial." This explicit textual protection supports a strong presumption against expanding the *Miranda* rule any further.

Finally, nothing in *Dickerson,* including its characterization of *Miranda* as announcing a constitutional rule changes any of these observations. Indeed, in *Dickerson,* the Court specifically noted that the Court's "subsequent cases have reduced the impact of the *Miranda* rule on legitimate law enforcement while reaffirming *[Miranda]*'s core ruling that unwarned statements may not be used as evidence in the prosecution's case in chief." This description of *Miranda,* especially the emphasis on the use of "unwarned statements . . . in the prosecution's case in chief," makes clear our continued focus on the protections of the Self-Incrimination Clause. The Court's reliance on our *Miranda* precedents, including both *Tucker* and *Elstad,* further demonstrates the continuing validity of those decisions. In short, nothing in *Dickerson* calls into question our continued insistence that the closest possible fit be maintained between the Self-Incrimination Clause and any rule designed to protect it.

III

Our cases also make clear the related point that a mere failure to give *Miranda* warnings does not, by itself, violate a suspect's constitutional rights or even the *Miranda* rule. So much was evident in many of our pre-*Dickerson* cases, and we have adhered to this view since *Dickerson*. This, of course, follows from the nature of the right protected by the Self-Incrimination Clause, which the *Miranda* rule, in turn, protects. It is "a fundamental *trial* right."

It follows that police do not violate a suspect's constitutional rights (or the *Miranda* rule) by negligent or even deliberate failures to provide the suspect with the full panoply of warnings prescribed by *Miranda*. Potential violations occur, if at all, only upon the admission of unwarned statements into evidence at trial. And, at that point, "[t]he exclusion of unwarned statements . . . is a complete and sufficient remedy" for any perceived *Miranda* violation.

Thus, unlike unreasonable searches under the Fourth Amendment or actual violations of the Due Process Clause or the Self-Incrimination Clause, there is, with respect to mere failures to warn, nothing to deter. There is therefore no reason to apply the "fruit of the poisonous tree" doctrine of *Wong Sun*. It is not for this Court to impose its preferred police practices on either federal law enforcement officials or their state counterparts.

IV

In the present case, the Court of Appeals, relying on *Dickerson,* wholly adopted the position that the taking of unwarned statements violates a suspect's constitutional rights. And, of course, if this were so, a strong deterrence-based argument could be made for suppression of the fruits.

But *Dickerson's* characterization of *Miranda* as a constitutional rule does not lessen the need to maintain the closest possible fit between the Self-Incrimination Clause and any judge-made rule designed to protect it. And there is no such fit here. Introduction of the nontestimonial fruit of a voluntary statement, such as respondent's Glock, does not implicate the Self-Incrimination Clause. The admission of such fruit presents no risk that a defendant's coerced statements (however defined) will be used against him at a criminal trial. In any case, "[t]he exclusion of unwarned statements . . . is a complete and sufficient remedy" for any perceived *Miranda* violation. There is simply no need to extend (and therefore no justification for extending) the prophylactic rule of *Miranda* to this context.

Similarly, because police cannot violate the Self-Incrimination Clause by taking unwarned though voluntary statements, an exclusionary rule cannot be justified by reference to a deterrence effect on law enforcement, as the Court of Appeals believed. Our decision not to apply *Wong Sun* to mere failures to give *Miranda* warnings was sound at the time *Tucker* and

Elstad were decided, and we decline to apply *Wong Sun* to such failures now.

* * *

JUSTICE KENNEDY, with whom JUSTICE O'CONNOR joins, concurring in the judgment.

In *Oregon v. Elstad,* 470 U.S. 298 (1985), *New York v. Quarles,* 467 U.S. 649 (1984), and *Harris v. New York,* 401 U.S. 222 (1971), evidence obtained following an unwarned interrogation was held admissible. This result was based in large part on our recognition that the concerns underlying the *Miranda v. Arizona,* 384 U.S. 436 (1966), rule must be accommodated to other objectives of the criminal justice system. I agree with the plurality that *Dickerson v. United States,* 530 U.S. 428 (2000), did not undermine these precedents and, in fact, cited them in support. Here, it is sufficient to note that the Government presents an even stronger case for admitting the evidence obtained as the result of Patane's unwarned statement. Admission of nontestimonial physical fruits (the Glock in this case), even more so than the postwarning statements to the police in *Elstad* and *Michigan v. Tucker,* 417 U.S. 433 (1974), does not run the risk of admitting into trial an accused's coerced incriminating statements against himself. In light of the important probative value of reliable physical evidence, it is doubtful that exclusion can be justified by a deterrence rationale sensitive to both law enforcement interests and a suspect's rights during an in-custody interrogation. Unlike the plurality, however, I find it unnecessary to decide whether the detective's failure to give Patane the full *Miranda* warnings should be characterized as a violation of the *Miranda* rule itself, or whether there is "[any]thing to deter" so long as the unwarned statements are not later introduced at trial.

JUSTICE SOUTER, with whom JUSTICE STEVENS and JUSTICE GINSBURG join, dissenting.

The plurality repeatedly says that the Fifth Amendment does not address the admissibility of nontestimonial evidence, an overstatement that is beside the point. The issue actually presented today is whether courts should apply the fruit of the poisonous tree doctrine lest we create an incentive for the police to omit *Miranda* warnings before custodial interrogation. In closing their eyes to the consequences of giving an evidentiary advantage to those who ignore *Miranda,* the plurality adds an important inducement for interrogators to ignore the rule in that case.

Miranda rested on insight into the inherently coercive character of custodial interrogation and the inherently difficult exercise of assessing the voluntariness of any confession resulting from it. Unless the police give the prescribed warnings meant to counter the coercive atmosphere, a custodial confession is inadmissible, there being no need for the previous time-consuming and difficult enquiry into voluntariness. That inducement to forestall involuntary statements and troublesome issues of fact can only atrophy if we turn around and recognize an evidentiary benefit when an unwarned statement leads investigators to tangible evidence. There is, of course, a price for excluding evidence, but the Fifth Amendment is worth a price, and in the absence of a very good reason, the logic of *Miranda* should be followed: a *Miranda* violation raises a presumption of coercion, and the Fifth Amendment privilege against compelled self-incrimination extends to the exclusion of derivative evidence, see *United States v. Hubbell,* 530 U.S. 27, 37–38 (2000) (recognizing "the Fifth Amendment's protection against the prosecutor's use of incriminating information derived directly or indirectly from . . . [actually] compelled testimony"); *Kastigar v. United States,* 406 U.S. 441, 453 (1972). That should be the end of this case.

* * *

JUSTICE BREYER, dissenting.

For reasons similar to those set forth in Justice Souter's dissent and in my concurring opinion in *Missouri v. Seibert,* 542 U.S., at 617, I would extend to this context the "fruit of the poisonous tree" approach, which I believe the Court has come close to adopting in *Seibert.* Under that approach, courts would exclude physical evidence derived from unwarned questioning unless the failure to provide *Miranda v. Arizona*, 384 U.S. 436 (1966), warnings was in good faith. Because the courts below made no explicit finding as to good or bad faith, I would remand for such a determination.

Points for Discussion

1. The Court holds in *Patane* that the fruit-of-the-poisonous-tree doctrine, which plays such a fundamental role in the Court's Fourth Amendment jurisprudence, is inapplicable to violations of *Miranda*. How does it arrive at that conclusion?

2. The plurality writes that the Self-Incrimination Clause is not even implicated by the introduction of tangible evidence in court because the Fifth Amendment is concerned only with compelled testimonial communications. Does this mean that the Fifth Amendment is not violated if a suspect is tortured into a confession and that confession leads to physical evidence which is ultimately introduced against the defendant at trial?

3. Footnote 1 of the plurality opinion suggests that the categorical rule that a failure to read the *Miranda* warnings gives rise to an irrebutable presumption of coercion may be open to question. Where else in the majority opinion does hostility toward *Miranda* manifest? How does the dissent respond to this hostility?

4. INDEPENDENT SOURCE AND INEVITABLE DISCOVERY

Justice Holmes' very brief majority opinion in *Silverthorne Lumber Co. v. United States* noted that information discovered through a constitutional violation can be presented at trial if it also comes to light independently of the violation, i.e., if the authorities have another, untainted source for the same information. The Court has since extended the independent-source rationale to also apply when the circumstances demonstrate that the authorities were likely to discover the information in another, legal way at the time the violation occurred. This section discusses both rationales.

NIX V. WILLIAMS

467 U.S. 431 (1984)

CHIEF JUSTICE BURGER delivered the opinion of the court.

We granted certiorari to consider whether, at respondent Williams' second murder trial in state court, evidence pertaining to the discovery and condition of the victim's body was properly admitted on the ground that it would ultimately or inevitably have been discovered even if no violation of any constitutional or statutory provision had taken place.

I

A

On December 24, 1968, 10-year-old Pamela Powers disappeared from a YMCA building in Des Moines, Iowa, where she had accompanied her parents to watch an athletic contest. Shortly after she disappeared, Williams was seen leaving the YMCA carrying a large bundle wrapped in a blanket; a 14-year-old boy who had helped Williams open his car door reported that he had seen "two legs in it and they were skinny and white."

Williams' car was found the next day 160 miles east of Des Moines in Davenport, Iowa. Later several items of clothing belonging to the child, some of Williams' clothing, and an army blanket like the one used to wrap the bundle that Williams carried out of the YMCA were found at a rest stop on Interstate 80 near Grinnell, between Des Moines and Davenport. A warrant was issued for Williams' arrest.

Police surmised that Williams had left Pamela Powers or her body somewhere between Des Moines and the Grinnell rest stop where some of the young girl's clothing had been found. On December 26, the Iowa Bureau of Criminal Investigation initiated a large-scale search. Two hundred volunteers divided into teams began the search 21 miles east of Grinnell, covering an area several miles to the north and south of Interstate 80. They moved westward from Poweshiek County, in which Grinnell was located, into Jasper County. Searchers were instructed to check all roads, abandoned farm buildings, ditches, culverts, and any other place in which the body of a small child could be hidden.

Meanwhile, Williams surrendered to local police in Davenport, where he was promptly arraigned. Williams contacted a Des Moines attorney who arranged for an attorney in Davenport to meet Williams at the Davenport police station. Des Moines police informed counsel they would pick Williams up in Davenport and return him to Des Moines without questioning him. Two Des Moines detectives then drove to Davenport, took Williams into custody, and proceeded to drive him back to Des Moines.

During the return trip, one of the policemen, Detective Leaming, began a conversation with Williams, saying:

> I want to give you something to think about while we're traveling down the road. . . . They are predicting several inches of snow for tonight, and I feel that you yourself are the only person that knows where this little girl's body is . . . and if you get a snow on top of it you yourself may be unable to find it. And since we will be going right past the area [where the body is] on the way into Des Moines, I feel that we could stop and locate the body, that the parents of this little girl should be entitled to a Christian burial for the little girl who was snatched away from them on Christmas [E]ve and murdered. . . . [A]fter a snow storm [we may not be] able to find it at all.

Leaming told Williams he knew the body was in the area of Mitchellville—a town they would be passing on the way to Des Moines. He concluded the conversation by saying "I do not want you to answer me. . . . Just think about it. . . ."

Later, as the police car approached Grinnell, Williams asked Leaming whether the police had found the young girl's shoes. After Leaming replied that he was unsure, Williams directed the police to a point near a service station where he said he had left the shoes; they were not found. As they continued to drive to Des Moines, Williams asked whether the blanket had been found and then directed the officers to a rest area in Grinnell where he said he had disposed of the blanket; they did not find the blanket. At this point Leaming and his party were joined by the officers in charge of the search. As they approached Mitchellville, Williams, without any further conversation, agreed to direct the officers to the child's body.

The officers directing the search had called off the search at 3 p.m., when they left the Grinnell Police Department to join Leaming at the rest area. At that time, one search team near the Jasper County-Polk County line was only two and one-half miles from where Williams soon guided Leaming and his party to the body. The child's body was found next to a culvert in a ditch beside a gravel road in Polk County, about two miles south of Interstate 80, and essentially within the area to be searched.

B

FIRST TRIAL

In February 1969 Williams was indicted for first-degree murder. Before trial in the Iowa court, his counsel moved to suppress evidence of the body and all related evidence including the condition of the body as shown by the autopsy. The ground for the motion was that such evidence was the "fruit" or product of Williams' statements made during the automobile ride from Davenport to Des Moines and prompted by Leaming's statements. The motion to suppress was denied.

The jury found Williams guilty of first-degree murder; the judgment of conviction was affirmed by the Iowa Supreme Court. Williams then sought release on habeas corpus in the United States District Court for the Southern District of Iowa. That court concluded that the evidence in question had been wrongly admitted at Williams' trial; a divided panel of the Court of Appeals for the Eighth Circuit agreed.

We granted certiorari, and a divided Court affirmed, holding that Detective Leaming had obtained incriminating statements from Williams by what was viewed as interrogation in violation of his right to counsel. *Brewer v. Williams*, 430 U.S. 387 (1977). This Court's opinion noted, however, that although Williams' incriminating statements could not be introduced into evidence at a second trial, evidence of the body's location and condition "might well be admissible on the theory that the body would have been discovered in any event, even had incriminating statements not been elicited from Williams."

C

SECOND TRIAL

At Williams' second trial in 1977 in the Iowa court, the prosecution did not offer Williams' statements into evidence, nor did it seek to show that Williams had directed the police to the child's body. However, evidence of the condition of her body as it was found, articles and photographs of her clothing, and the results of post mortem medical and chemical tests on the body were admitted. The trial court concluded that the State had proved by a preponderance of the evidence that, if the search had not been suspended and Williams had not led the police to the victim, her body would have been discovered "within a short time" in essentially the same condition as it was actually found. The trial court also ruled that if the police had not located the body, "the search would clearly have been taken up again where it left off, given the extreme circumstances of this case and the body would [have] been found in short order."

In finding that the body would have been discovered in essentially the same condition as it was actually found, the court noted that freezing temperatures had prevailed and tissue deterioration would have been suspended. The challenged evidence was admitted and the jury again found Williams guilty of first-degree murder; he was sentenced to life in prison.

* * *

II

A

The Iowa Supreme Court correctly stated that the "vast majority" of all courts, both state and federal, recognize an inevitable discovery exception to the exclusionary rule. We are now urged to adopt and apply the so-called ultimate or inevitable discovery exception to the exclusionary rule.

Williams contends that evidence of the body's location and condition is "fruit of the poisonous tree," *i.e.*, the "fruit" or product of Detective Leaming's plea to help the child's parents give her "a Christian burial," which this Court had already held equated to interrogation. He contends that admitting the challenged evidence violated the Sixth Amendment whether it would have been inevitably discovered or not. Williams also contends that, if the inevitable discovery doctrine is constitutionally permissible, it must include a threshold showing of police good faith.

B

* * *

The core rationale consistently advanced by this Court for extending the exclusionary rule to evidence that is the fruit of unlawful police conduct has been that this admittedly drastic and socially costly course is needed to deter police from violations of constitutional and statutory protections. This Court has accepted the argument that the way to ensure such protections is to exclude evidence seized as a result of such violations notwithstanding the high social cost of letting persons obviously guilty go unpunished for their crimes. On this rationale, the prosecution is not to be put in a better position than it would have been in if no illegality had transpired.

By contrast, the derivative evidence analysis ensures that the prosecution is not put in a worse position simply because of some earlier police error or misconduct. The independent source doctrine allows admission of evidence that has been discovered by means wholly independent of any constitutional violation. That doctrine, although closely related to the inevitable discovery doctrine, does not apply here; Williams' statements to Leaming indeed led police to the child's body, but that is not the whole story. The independent source doctrine teaches us that the interest of society in deterring unlawful police conduct and the public interest in having juries receive all probative evidence of a crime are properly balanced by putting the police in the same, not a worse, position that they would have been in if no police error or misconduct had occurred.[4] When the challenged evidence has an independent source, exclusion of such evidence would put the police in a worse position than they would have been in absent any error or violation. There is a functional similarity between these two doctrines in that exclusion of evidence that would inevitably have been discovered would also put the government in a worse position, because the police would have obtained that evidence if no misconduct had taken place. Thus, while the independent source exception would not justify admission of evidence in this case, its rationale is wholly consistent with and justifies our adoption of the ultimate or inevitable discovery exception to the exclusionary rule.

It is clear that the cases implementing the exclusionary rule "begin with the premise that the challenged evidence is in some sense the product of illegal governmental activity." Of course, this does not end the inquiry. If the prosecution can establish by a preponderance of the evidence that the information ultimately or inevitably would have been discovered by lawful means—here the volunteers' search—then the deterrence rationale has so little basis that the evidence should be received. Anything less would reject logic, experience, and common sense.

* * *

Williams contends that because he did not waive his right to the assistance of counsel, the Court may not balance competing values in deciding whether the challenged evidence was properly admitted. He argues that, unlike the exclusionary rule in the Fourth Amendment context, the essential purpose of which is to deter police misconduct, the Sixth Amendment exclusionary rule is designed to protect the right to a fair trial and the integrity of the factfinding process. Williams contends that, when those interests are at stake, the societal costs of excluding evidence obtained from responses presumed involuntary are irrelevant in determining whether such evidence should be excluded. We disagree.

Exclusion of physical evidence that would inevitably have been discovered adds nothing to either the integrity or fairness of a criminal trial. The Sixth Amendment right to counsel protects against unfairness by preserving the adversary process in which the reliability of proffered evidence may be tested in cross-examination. Here, however, Detective Leaming's conduct did nothing to impugn the reliability of the evidence in question—the body of the child and its condition as it was found, articles of clothing found on the body, and the autopsy. No one would seriously contend that the presence of counsel in the police car when Leaming

[4] The ultimate or inevitable discovery exception to the exclusionary rule is closely related in purpose to the harmless-error rule of *Chapman v. California*, 386 U.S. 18, 22 (1967). The harmless-constitutional-error rule "serve[s] a very useful purpose insofar as [it] block[s] setting aside convictions for small errors or defects that have little, if any, likelihood of having changed the result of the trial." The purpose of the inevitable discovery rule is to block setting aside convictions that would have been obtained without police misconduct.

appealed to Williams' decent human instincts would have had any bearing on the reliability of the body as evidence. Suppression, in these circumstances, would do nothing whatever to promote the integrity of the trial process, but would inflict a wholly unacceptable burden on the administration of criminal justice.

Nor would suppression ensure fairness on the theory that it tends to safeguard the adversary system of justice. To assure the fairness of trial proceedings, this Court has held that assistance of counsel must be available at pretrial confrontations where "the subsequent trial [cannot] cure a[n otherwise] one-sided confrontation between prosecuting authorities and the uncounseled defendant." Fairness can be assured by placing the State and the accused in the same positions they would have been in had the impermissible conduct not taken place. However, if the government can prove that the evidence would have been obtained inevitably and, therefore, would have been admitted regardless of any overreaching by the police, there is no rational basis to keep that evidence from the jury in order to ensure the fairness of the trial proceedings. In that situation, the State has gained no advantage at trial and the defendant has suffered no prejudice. Indeed, suppression of the evidence would operate to undermine the adversary system by putting the State in a worse position than it would have occupied without any police misconduct. Williams' argument that inevitable discovery constitutes impermissible balancing of values is without merit.

* * *

C

The Court of Appeals did not find it necessary to consider whether the record fairly supported the finding that the volunteer search party would ultimately or inevitably have discovered the victim's body. However, three courts independently reviewing the evidence have found that the body of the child inevitably would have been found by the searchers. Williams challenges these findings, asserting that the record contains only the "post hoc rationalization" that the search efforts would have proceeded two and one-half miles into Polk County where Williams had led police to the body.

When that challenge was made at the suppression hearing preceding Williams' second trial, the prosecution offered the testimony of Agent Ruxlow of the Iowa Bureau of Criminal Investigation. Ruxlow had organized and directed some 200 volunteers who were searching for the child's body. The searchers were instructed "to check all the roads, the ditches, any culverts. . . . If they came upon any abandoned farm buildings, they were instructed to go onto the property and search those abandoned farm buildings or any other places where a small child could be secreted." Ruxlow testified that he marked off highway maps of Poweshiek and Jasper Counties in grid fashion, divided the volunteers into teams of four to six persons, and assigned each team to search specific grid areas. Ruxlow also testified that, if the search had not been suspended because of Williams' promised cooperation, it would have continued into Polk County, using the same grid system. Although he had previously marked off into grids only the highway maps of Poweshiek and Jasper Counties, Ruxlow had obtained a map of Polk County, which he said he would have marked off in the same manner had it been necessary for the search to continue.

The search had commenced at approximately 10 a.m. and moved westward through Poweshiek County into Jasper County. At approximately 3 p.m., after Williams had volunteered to cooperate with the police, Detective Leaming, who was in the police car with Williams, sent word to Ruxlow and the other Special Agent directing the search to meet him at the Grinnell truck stop and the search was suspended at that time. Ruxlow also stated that he was "under the impression that there was a possibility" that Williams would lead them to the child's body at that time. The search was not resumed once it was learned that Williams had led the police to the body, which was found two and one-half miles from where the search had stopped in what would have been the easternmost grid to be searched in Polk County. There was testimony that it would have taken an additional three to five hours to discover the body if the search had continued; the body was found near a culvert, one of the kinds of places the teams had been specifically directed to search.

On this record it is clear that the search parties were approaching the actual location of the body, and we are satisfied, along with three courts earlier, that the volunteer search teams would have resumed the search had Williams not earlier led the police to the body and the body inevitably would have been found. The evidence asserted by Williams as newly discovered, *i.e.*, certain photographs of the body and deposition testimony of Agent Ruxlow made in connection with the federal habeas proceeding, does not demonstrate that the material facts were inadequately developed in the suppression hearing in state court or that Williams was denied a full, fair, and adequate opportunity to present all relevant facts at the suppression hearing.

JUSTICE WHITE, concurring.

I join fully in the opinion of the Court. I write separately only to point out that many of Justice Stevens' remarks are beside the point when it is recalled that *Brewer v. Williams*, 430 U.S. 387 (1977), was a 5–4 decision and that four Members of the Court, including myself, were of the view that Detective Leaming had done nothing wrong at all, let alone anything unconstitutional. Three of us observed: "To anyone not lost in the intricacies of the prophylactic rules of *Miranda v. Arizona*, the result in this case seems utterly senseless . . . ." It is thus an unjustified reflection on Detective Leaming to say that he "decide[d] to dispense with the requirements of law," or that he decided "to take procedural short-cuts instead of complying with the law." He was no doubt acting as many competent police officers would have acted under similar circumstances and in light of the then-existing law. That five Justices later thought he was mistaken does not call for making him out to be a villain or for a lecture on deliberate police misconduct and its resulting costs to society.

JUSTICE STEVENS, concurring in the judgment.

This litigation is exceptional for at least three reasons. The facts are unusually tragic; it involves an unusually clear violation of constitutional rights; and it graphically illustrates the societal costs that may be incurred when police officers decide to dispense with the requirements of law. Because the Court does not adequately discuss any of these aspects of the case, I am unable to join its opinion.

* * *

II

The constitutional violation that gave rise to the decision in *Williams I* is neither acknowledged nor fairly explained in the Court's opinion. Yet the propriety of admitting evidence relating to the victim's body can only be evaluated if that constitutional violation is properly identified.

Before he was taken into custody, Williams, as a recent escapee from a mental hospital who had just abducted and murdered a small child, posed a special threat to public safety. Acting on his lawyer's advice, Williams surrendered to the Davenport police. The lawyer notified the Des Moines police of Williams' imminent surrender, and police officials, in the presence of Detective Leaming, agreed that Williams would not be questioned while being brought back from Davenport. Williams was advised of this agreement by his attorney. After he was arraigned in Davenport, Williams conferred with another lawyer who was acting as local counsel. This lawyer reminded Williams that he would not be questioned. When Detective Leaming arrived in Davenport, local counsel stressed that the agreement was to be carried out and that Williams was not to be questioned. Detective Leaming then took custody of respondent, and denied counsel's request to ride to Des Moines in the police car with Williams. The "Christian burial speech" occurred during the ensuing trip. As Justice Powell succinctly observed, this was a case "in which the police deliberately took advantage of an inherently coercive setting in the absence of counsel, contrary to their express agreement." (concurring opinion).

The Sixth Amendment guarantees that the conviction of the accused will be the product of an adversarial process, rather than the *ex parte* investigation and determination by the prosecutor. *Williams I* grew out of a line of cases in which this Court made it clear that the adversarial process protected by the Sixth Amendment may not be undermined by the strategems of the police.

* * *

This view ripened into a holding in *Massiah v. United States*, 377 U.S. 201 (1964): "We hold that the petitioner was denied the basic protections of [the Sixth Amendment] when there was used against him at his trial evidence of his own incriminating words, which federal agents had deliberately elicited from him after he had been indicted and in the absence of his counsel." *Williams I* held that Detective Leaming had violated "the clear rule of *Massiah*" by deliberately eliciting incriminating statements from respondent during the pendency of the adversarial process and outside of that process. The violation was aggravated by the fact that Detective Leaming had breached a promise to counsel, an act which can only undermine the role of counsel in the adversarial process. The "Christian burial speech" was nothing less than an attempt to substitute an *ex parte*, inquisitorial process for the clash of adversaries commanded by the Constitution. Thus the now-familiar plaint that " '[t]he criminal is to go free because the constable has blundered,' " is entirely beside the point. More pertinent is what the Chief Justice wrote for the Court on another occasion: "This is not a case where, in Justice Cardozo's words, 'the constable . . . blundered,' rather, it is one where the 'constable' planned an impermissible interference with the right to the assistance of counsel."

III

Once the constitutional violation is properly identified, the answers to the questions presented in this case follow readily. Admission of the victim's body, if it would have been discovered anyway, means that the trial in this case was not the product of an inquisitorial process; that process was untainted by illegality. The good or bad faith of Detective Leaming is therefore simply irrelevant. If the trial process was not tainted as a result of his conduct, this defendant received the type of trial that the Sixth Amendment envisions. Generalizations about the exclusionary rule employed by the majority simply do not address the primary question in the case.

The majority is correct to insist that any rule of exclusion not provide the authorities with an incentive to commit violations of the Constitution. If the inevitable discovery rule provided such an incentive by permitting the prosecution to avoid the uncertainties inherent in its search for evidence, it would undermine the constitutional guarantee itself, and therefore be inconsistent with the deterrent purposes of the exclusionary rule. But when the burden of proof on the inevitable discovery question is placed on the prosecution, it must bear the risk of error in the determination made necessary by its constitutional violation. The uncertainty as to whether the body would have been discovered can be resolved in its favor here only because, as the Court explains *ante* petitioner adduced evidence demonstrating that at the time of the constitutional violation an investigation was already under way which, in the natural and probable course of events, would have soon discovered the body. This is not a case in which the prosecution can escape responsibility for a constitutional violation through speculation; to the extent uncertainty was created by the constitutional violation the prosecution was required to resolve that uncertainty through proof. Even if Detective Leaming acted in bad faith in the sense that he deliberately violated the Constitution in order to avoid the possibility that the body would not be discovered, the prosecution ultimately does not avoid that risk; its burden of proof forces it to assume the risk. The need to adduce proof sufficient to discharge its burden, and the difficulty in predicting whether such proof will be available or sufficient, means that the inevitable discovery rule does not permit state officials to avoid the uncertainty they would have faced but for the constitutional violation.

The majority refers to the "societal cost" of excluding probative evidence. In my view, the more relevant cost is that imposed on society by police officers who decide to take procedural shortcuts instead of complying with the law. What is the consequence of the shortcut that Detective Leaming took when he decided to question Williams in this case and not to wait an hour or so until he arrived in Des Moines?[9] The answer is years and years of unnecessary but costly litigation. Instead of having a 1969 conviction affirmed in routine fashion, the case is still alive 15 years later. Thanks to Detective Leaming, the State of Iowa has expended vast sums of money and countless hours of professional labor in his defense. That expenditure surely provides an adequate deterrent to similar violations; the responsibility for that expenditure lies not with the Constitution, but rather with the constable.

JUSTICE BRENNAN, with whom JUSTICE MARSHALL joins, dissenting.

In *Brewer v. Williams*, 430 U.S. 387 (1977), we held that the respondent's state conviction for first-degree murder had to be set aside because it was based in part on statements obtained from the respondent in violation of his right to the assistance of counsel guaranteed by the Sixth and Fourteenth Amendments. At the same time, we noted that, "[w]hile neither Williams' incriminating statements themselves nor any testimony describing his having led the police to the victim's body can constitutionally be admitted into evidence, evidence of where the body was found and of its condition might well be admissible on the theory that the body would have been discovered in any event."

To the extent that today's decision adopts this "inevitable discovery" exception to the exclusionary rule, it simply acknowledges a doctrine that is akin to the "independent source" exception first recognized by the Court

[9] In this connection, it is worth noting, as Justice Marshall did in *Williams I*, that in light of the assistance that respondent's attorney had provided to the Des Moines police, it seems apparent that the lawyer intended to learn the location of the body from his client and then reveal it to the police. Thus, the need for a shortcut was practically non-existent.

in *Silverthorne Lumber Co. v. United States*, 251 U.S. 385, 392 (1920). In particular, the Court concludes that unconstitutionally obtained evidence may be admitted at trial if it inevitably would have been discovered in the same condition by an independent line of investigation that was already being pursued when the constitutional violation occurred. As has every Federal Court of Appeals previously addressing this issue, I agree that in these circumstances the "inevitable discovery" exception to the exclusionary rule is consistent with the requirements of the Constitution.

In its zealous efforts to emasculate the exclusionary rule, however, the Court loses sight of the crucial difference between the "inevitable discovery" doctrine and the "independent source" exception from which it is derived. When properly applied, the "independent source" exception allows the prosecution to use evidence only if it was, in fact, obtained by fully lawful means. It therefore does no violence to the constitutional protections that the exclusionary rule is meant to enforce. The "inevitable discovery" exception is likewise compatible with the Constitution, though it differs in one key respect from its next of kin: specifically, the evidence sought to be introduced at trial has not actually been obtained from an independent source, but rather would have been discovered as a matter of course if independent investigations were allowed to proceed.

In my view, this distinction should require that the government satisfy a heightened burden of proof before it is allowed to use such evidence. The inevitable discovery exception necessarily implicates a hypothetical finding that differs in kind from the factual finding that precedes application of the independent source rule. To ensure that this hypothetical finding is narrowly confined to circumstances that are functionally equivalent to an independent source, and to protect fully the fundamental rights served by the exclusionary rule, I would require clear and convincing evidence before concluding that the government had met its burden of proof on this issue. Increasing the burden of proof serves to impress the factfinder with the importance of the decision and thereby reduces the risk that illegally obtained evidence will be admitted. Because the lower courts did not impose such a requirement, I would remand this case for application of this heightened burden of proof by the lower courts in the first instance. I am therefore unable to join either the Court's opinion or its judgment.

Points for Discussion

1. In *Nix*, the Court expands its earlier independent source rule by endorsing the inevitable discovery rule that most lower courts had by then accepted. What is the difference between the two rules?

2. Why does the Supreme Court reject a good faith requirement for the inevitable discovery rule? If Detective Leaming had known that a search was ongoing, what reason would he have had *not* to violate Williams' Sixth Amendment rights by deliberately eliciting incriminating statements?

3. The Court unanimously holds that evidence obtained from the body of the victim should have been admitted at Williams' second trial. (As the Court notes, the jury was not told that Williams had led police to the body.) Justice Stevens writes that the inevitable discovery doctrine eliminates the taint of the inquisitorial interrogation of Williams because the prosecution had to prove that the body would have been found "in the natural and probable course of events." Justices Brennan and Marshall argue for a "heightened burden of proof" but do not disagree in principle.

MURRAY V. UNITED STATES

487 U.S. 533 (1988)

JUSTICE SCALIA delivered the opinion of the court.

In *Segura v. United States,* 468 U.S. 796 (1984), we held that police officers' illegal entry upon private premises did not require suppression of evidence subsequently discovered at those premises when executing a search warrant obtained on the basis of information wholly unconnected with the initial entry. In these consolidated cases we are faced with the question whether, again assuming evidence obtained pursuant to an independently obtained search warrant, the portion of such evidence that had been observed in plain view at the time of a prior illegal entry must be suppressed.

I

Both cases arise out of the conviction of petitioner Michael F. Murray, petitioner James D. Carter, and others for conspiracy to possess and distribute illegal drugs. Insofar as relevant for our purposes, the facts are as follows: Based on information received from informants, federal law enforcement agents had been surveilling petitioner Murray and several of his co-conspirators. At about 1:45 p.m. on April 6, 1983, they observed Murray drive a truck and Carter drive a green camper, into a warehouse in South Boston. When the petitioners drove the vehicles out about 20 minutes later, the surveilling agents saw within the warehouse two individuals and a tractor-trailer rig bearing a long, dark container. Murray and Carter later turned over the truck and camper to other drivers, who were in turn followed and ultimately arrested, and the vehicles lawfully seized. Both vehicles were found to contain marijuana.

After receiving this information, several of the agents converged on the South Boston warehouse and forced entry. They found the warehouse unoccupied, but observed in plain view numerous burlap-wrapped bales that were later found to contain marijuana. They left without disturbing the bales, kept the warehouse under surveillance, and did not reenter it until they had a search warrant. In applying for the warrant, the agents did not mention the prior entry, and did not rely on any observations made during that entry. When the warrant was issued—at 10:40 p.m., approximately eight hours after the initial entry—the agents immediately reentered the warehouse and seized 270 bales of marijuana and notebooks listing customers for whom the bales were destined.

Before trial, petitioners moved to suppress the evidence found in the warehouse. The District Court denied the motion, rejecting petitioners' arguments that the warrant was invalid because the agents did not inform the Magistrate about their prior warrantless entry, and that the warrant was tainted by that entry. The First Circuit affirmed, assuming for purposes of its decision that the first entry into the warehouse was unlawful. Murray and Carter then separately filed petitions for certiorari, which we granted, and have consolidated here.

II

* * *

Almost simultaneously with our development of the exclusionary rule, in the first quarter of this century, we also announced what has come to be known as the "independent source" doctrine. See *Silverthorne Lumber Co. v. United States,* 251 U.S. 385, 392 (1920). That doctrine, which has been applied to evidence acquired not only through Fourth Amendment violations but also through Fifth and Sixth Amendment violations, has recently been described as follows:

> [T]he interest of society in deterring unlawful police conduct and the public interest in having juries receive all probative evidence of a crime are properly balanced by putting the police in the same, not a *worse,* position that they would have been in if no police error or misconduct had occurred. . . . When the challenged evidence has an independent source, exclusion of such evidence would put the police in a worse position than they would have been in absent any error or violation.

Nix v. Williams, 467 U.S. 431, 443 (1984)

The dispute here is over the scope of this doctrine. Petitioners contend that it applies only to evidence obtained for the first time during an independent lawful search. The Government argues that it applies also to evidence initially discovered during, or as a consequence of, an unlawful search, but later obtained independently from activities untainted by the initial illegality. We think the Government's view has better support in both precedent and policy.

* * *

Petitioners' asserted policy basis for excluding evidence which is initially discovered during an illegal search, but is subsequently acquired through an independent and lawful source, is that a contrary rule will remove all deterrence to, and indeed positively encourage, unlawful police searches. As petitioners see the incentives, law enforcement officers will routinely enter without a warrant to make sure that what they expect to be on the premises is in fact there. If it is not, they will have spared themselves the time and trouble of getting a warrant; if it is, they can get the warrant and use the evidence despite the unlawful entry. We see the incentives differently. An officer with probable cause sufficient to obtain a search warrant would be foolish to enter the premises first in an unlawful manner. By doing so, he would risk suppression of all evidence on the premises, both seen and unseen, since his action would add to the normal burden of convincing a magistrate that there is probable cause the much more onerous burden of convincing a trial court that no information gained from the illegal entry affected either the law enforcement officers' decision to seek a warrant or the magistrate's decision to grant it. Nor would the officer *without* sufficient probable cause to obtain a search warrant have any added incentive to conduct an unlawful entry, since whatever he finds cannot be used to establish probable cause before a magistrate.[2]

* * *

III

To apply what we have said to the present cases: Knowledge that the marijuana was in the warehouse was assuredly acquired at the time of the unlawful entry. But it was also acquired at the time of entry pursuant to the warrant, and if that later acquisition was not the result of the earlier entry there is no reason why the independent source doctrine should not apply. Invoking the exclusionary rule would put the police (and society) not in the *same* position they would have occupied if no violation occurred, but in a *worse* one.

We think this is also true with respect to the tangible evidence, the bales of marijuana. It would make no more sense to exclude that than it would to exclude tangible evidence found upon the corpse in *Nix,* if the search in that case had not been abandoned and had in fact come upon the body. The First Circuit has discerned a difference between tangible and intangible evidence that has been tainted, in that objects "once seized cannot be cleanly reseized without returning the objects to private control." It seems to us, however, that reseizure of tangible evidence already seized is no more impossible than rediscovery of intangible evidence already discovered. The independent source doctrine does not rest upon such metaphysical analysis, but upon the policy that, while the government should not profit from its illegal activity, neither should it be placed in a

[2] Justice Marshall argues, in effect, that where the police cannot point to some historically verifiable fact demonstrating that the subsequent search pursuant to a warrant was wholly unaffected by the prior illegal search—*e.g.,* that they had already sought the warrant before entering the premises—we should adopt a *per se* rule of inadmissibility. We do not believe that such a prophylatic exception to the independent source rule is necessary. To say that a district court must be satisfied that a warrant would have been sought without the illegal entry is not to give dispositive effect to police officers' assurances on the point. Where the facts render those assurances implausible, the independent source doctrine will not apply.

worse position than it would otherwise have occupied. So long as a later, lawful seizure is genuinely independent of an earlier, tainted one (which may well be difficult to establish where the seized goods are kept in the police's possession) there is no reason why the independent source doctrine should not apply.

The ultimate question, therefore, is whether the search pursuant to warrant was in fact a genuinely independent source of the information and tangible evidence at issue here. This would not have been the case if the agents' decision to seek the warrant was prompted by what they had seen during the initial entry,[3] or if information obtained during that entry was presented to the Magistrate and affected his decision to issue the warrant. On this point the Court of Appeals said the following:

> [W]e can be absolutely certain that the warrantless entry in no way contributed in the slightest either to the issuance of a warrant or to the discovery of the evidence during the lawful search that occurred pursuant to the warrant.
>
> This is as clear a case as can be imagined where the discovery of the contraband in plain view was totally irrelevant to the later securing of a warrant and the successful search that ensued. As there was no causal link whatever between the illegal entry and the discovery of the challenged evidence, we find no error in the court's refusal to suppress.

United States v. Moscatiello, 771 F.2d, at 603, 604.

Although these statements can be read to provide emphatic support for the Government's position, it is the function of the District Court rather than the Court of Appeals to determine the facts, and we do not think the Court of Appeals' conclusions are supported by adequate findings. The District Court found that the agents did not reveal their warrantless entry to the Magistrate and that they did not include in their application for a warrant any recitation of their observations in the warehouse. It did not, however, explicitly find that the agents would have sought a warrant if they had not earlier entered the warehouse. The Government concedes this in its brief. To be sure, the District Court did determine that the purpose of the warrantless entry was in part "to guard against the destruction of possibly critical evidence," and one could perhaps infer from this that the agents who made the entry already planned to obtain that "critical

[3] Justice Marshall argues that "the relevant question [is] whether, even if the initial entry uncovered no evidence, the officers would return immediately with a warrant to conduct a second search." We do not see how this is "relevant" at all. To determine whether the warrant was independent of the illegal entry, one must ask whether it would have been sought even if what actually happened had not occurred—not whether it would have been sought if something else had happened. That is to say, what counts is whether the actual illegal search had any effect in producing the warrant, not whether some hypothetical illegal search would have aborted the warrant. Only that much is needed to assure that what comes before the court is not the product of illegality; to go further than that would be to expand our existing exclusionary rule.

evidence" through a warrant-authorized search. That inference is not, however, clear enough to justify the conclusion that the District Court's findings amounted to a determination of independent source.

Accordingly, we vacate the judgment and remand these cases to the Court of Appeals with instructions that it remand to the District Court for determination whether the warrant-authorized search of the warehouse was an independent source of the challenged evidence in the sense we have described.

JUSTICE BRENNAN and JUSTICE KENNEDY took no part in the consideration or decision of these cases.

JUSTICE MARSHALL, with whom JUSTICE STEVENS and JUSTICE O'CONNOR join, dissenting.

The Court today holds that the "independent source" exception to the exclusionary rule may justify admitting evidence discovered during an illegal warrantless search that is later "rediscovered" by the same team of investigators during a search pursuant to a warrant obtained immediately after the illegal search. I believe the Court's decision, by failing to provide sufficient guarantees that the subsequent search was, in fact, independent of the illegal search, emasculates the Warrant Clause and undermines the deterrence function of the exclusionary rule. I therefore dissent.

. . . The independent source exception, like the inevitable discovery exception, is primarily based on a practical view that under certain circumstances the beneficial deterrent effect that exclusion will have on future constitutional violations is too slight to justify the social cost of excluding probative evidence from a criminal trial. When the seizure of the evidence at issue is "wholly independent of" the constitutional violation, then exclusion arguably will have no effect on a law enforcement officer's incentive to commit an unlawful search.

Given the underlying justification for the independent source exception, any inquiry into the exception's application must keep sight of the practical effect admission will have on the incentives facing law enforcement officers to engage in unlawful conduct. The proper scope of the independent source exception, and guidelines for its application, cannot be divined in a factual vacuum; instead, they must be informed by the nature of the constitutional violation and the deterrent effect of exclusion in particular circumstances. In holding that the independent source exception may apply to the facts of these cases, I believe the Court loses sight of the practical moorings of the independent source exception and creates an affirmative incentive for unconstitutional searches. This holding can find no justification in the purposes underlying both the exclusionary rule and the independent source exception.

The factual setting of the instant case is straightforward. Federal Bureau of Investigation (FBI) and Drug Enforcement Agency (DEA) agents stopped two vehicles after they left a warehouse and discovered bales of marijuana. DEA Supervisor Garibotto and an assistant United States attorney then returned to the warehouse, which had been under surveillance for several hours. After demands that the warehouse door be opened went unanswered, Supervisor Garibotto forced open the door with a tire iron. A number of agents entered the warehouse. No persons were found inside, but the agents saw numerous bales of marijuana in plain view. Supervisor Garibotto then ordered everyone out of the warehouse. Agents did not reenter the warehouse until a warrant was obtained some eight hours later. The warehouse was kept under surveillance during the interim.

It is undisputed that the agents made no effort to obtain a warrant prior to the initial entry. The agents had not begun to prepare a warrant affidavit, and according to FBI Agent Cleary, who supervised the FBI's involvement, they had not even engaged in any discussions of obtaining a warrant. The affidavit in support of the warrant obtained after the initial search was prepared by DEA Agent Keaney, who had tactical control over the DEA agents, and who had participated in the initial search of the warehouse. The affidavit did not mention the warrantless search of the warehouse, nor did it cite information obtained from that search. In determining that the challenged evidence was admissible, the Court of Appeals assumed that the initial warrantless entry was not justified by exigent circumstances and that the search therefore violated the Warrant Clause of the Fourth Amendment.

Under the circumstances of these cases, the admission of the evidence "reseized" during the second search severely undermines the deterrence function of the exclusionary rule. Indeed, admission in these cases affirmatively encourages illegal searches. The incentives for such illegal conduct are clear. Obtaining a warrant is inconvenient and time consuming. Even when officers have probable cause to support a warrant application, therefore, they have an incentive first to determine whether it is worthwhile to obtain a warrant. Probable cause is much less than certainty, and many "confirmatory" searches will result in the discovery that no evidence is present, thus saving the police the time and trouble of getting a warrant. If contraband is discovered, however, the officers may later seek a warrant to shield the evidence from the taint of the illegal search. The police thus know in advance that they have little to lose and much to gain by forgoing the bother of obtaining a warrant and undertaking an illegal search.

The Court, however, "see[s] the incentives differently." Under the Court's view, today's decision does not provide an incentive for unlawful searches, because the officer undertaking the search would know that "his action would add to the normal burden of convincing a magistrate that there is probable cause the much more onerous burden of convincing a trial court that no information gained from the illegal entry affected either the law enforcement officers' decision to seek a warrant or the magistrate's decision to grant it." The Court, however, provides no hint of why this risk would actually seem significant to the officers. Under the circumstances of these cases, the officers committing the illegal search have both knowledge and control of the factors central to the trial court's determination. First, it is a simple matter, as was done in these cases, to exclude from the warrant application any information gained from the initial entry so that the magistrate's determination of probable cause is not influenced by the prior illegal search. Second, today's decision makes the application of the independent source exception turn entirely on an evaluation of the officers' intent. It normally will be difficult for the trial court to verify, or the defendant to rebut, an assertion by officers that they always intended to obtain a warrant, regardless of the results of the illegal search. The testimony of the officers conducting the illegal search is the only direct evidence of intent, and the defendant will be relegated simply to arguing that the officers should not be believed. Under these circumstances, the litigation risk described by the Court seems hardly a risk at all; it does not significantly dampen the incentive to conduct the initial illegal search.

The strong Fourth Amendment interest in eliminating these incentives for illegal entry should cause this Court to scrutinize closely the application of the independent source exception to evidence obtained under the circumstances of the instant cases; respect for the constitutional guarantee requires a rule that does not undermine the deterrence function of the exclusionary rule. When, as here, the same team of investigators is involved in both the first and second search, there is a significant danger that the "independence" of the source will in fact be illusory, and that the initial search will have affected the decision to obtain a warrant notwithstanding the officers' subsequent assertions to the contrary. It is therefore crucial that the factual premise of the exception—complete independence—be clearly established before the exception can justify admission of the evidence. I believe the Court's reliance on the intent of the law enforcement officers who conducted the warrantless search provides insufficient guarantees that the subsequent legal search was unaffected by the prior illegal search.

To ensure that the source of the evidence is genuinely independent, the basis for a finding that a search was untainted by a prior illegal search must focus, as with the inevitable discovery doctrine, on "demonstrated historical facts capable of ready verification or impeachment." In the instant cases, there are no "demonstrated historical facts" capable of supporting a finding that the subsequent warrant search was wholly unaffected by the prior illegal search. The same team of investigators was involved in both searches. The warrant was obtained immediately after the illegal search, and no effort was made to obtain a warrant prior to the discovery of the marijuana during the illegal search. The only evidence available that the warrant search was wholly independent is the testimony of the agents who conducted the illegal search. Under these circumstances, the threat that the subsequent search was tainted by the illegal search is too great to allow for the application of the independent source exception.[4] The Court's contrary holding lends itself to easy abuse, and offers an incentive to bypass the constitutional requirement that probable cause be assessed by a neutral and detached magistrate before the police invade an individual's privacy.

* * *

In sum, under circumstances as are presented in these cases, when the very law enforcement officers who participate in an illegal search immediately thereafter obtain a warrant to search the same premises, I believe the evidence discovered during the initial illegal entry must be suppressed. Any other result emasculates the Warrant Clause and provides an intolerable incentive for warrantless searches. I respectfully dissent.

JUSTICE STEVENS, dissenting.

While I join Justice Marshall's opinion explaining why the majority's extension of the Court's holding in *Segura v. United States,* 468 U.S. 796 (1984), "emasculates the Warrant Clause and provides an intolerable incentive for warrantless searches," I remain convinced that the *Segura* decision itself was unacceptable because, even then, it was obvious that it would "provide government agents with an affirmative incentive to engage in unconstitutional violations of the privacy of the home," 468 U.S., at 817 (dissenting opinion). I fear that the Court has taken another unfortunate step down the path to a system of "law enforcement unfettered by process concerns." *Patterson v. Illinois,* 487 U.S. 285, 305 (Stevens, J., dissenting). In due course, I trust it will pause long enough to remember that "the efforts of the courts and their officials to bring the guilty to punishment, praiseworthy as they are, are not to be aided by the sacrifice of those great principles established by years of endeavor and suffering which have resulted in their embodiment in the fundamental law of the land." *Weeks v. United States,* 232 U.S. 383, 393–394 (1914).

[4] To conclude that the initial search had no effect on the decision to obtain a warrant, and thus that the warrant search was an "independent source" of the challenged evidence, one would have to assume that even if the officers entered the premises and discovered no contraband, they nonetheless would have gone to the Magistrate, sworn that they had probable cause to believe that contraband was in the building, and then returned to conduct another search. Although such a scenario is possible, I believe it is more plausible to believe that the officers would not have chosen to return immediately to the premises with a warrant to search for evidence had they not discovered evidence during the initial search.

Points for Discussion

1. The point in Justice Stevens' dissent—that the *Murray* decision undermines basic constitutional guarantees—may seem melodramatic, but consider this:

> Consider the position of the rational police officer. Assume that it is true, as the Court avers, that if he has ample probable cause and ample time, he will go ahead and get a warrant in order to avoid the additional explanations that a warrantless search will entail. But suppose, as is frequently the case, that his probable cause is shaky or nonexistent. *Murray* positively encourages him to proceed with an illegal search. If he finds nothing, he simply shrugs his shoulders and walks away. If he finds evidence, he leaves his partner to watch over it, repairs to the magistrate, and reports that "an anonymous reliable informant who has given information on three occasions in the past that has led to convictions called to tell me that he had just seen bales of marijuana stored at a warehouse at 123 Elm Street." The warrant issues and the marijuana is seized. Before trial (assuming that the defense has found out about the illegal search), the officer admits it, chalks it up to a fear that the evidence would be lost if the warehouse were not immediately secured, apologizes for being wrong in this assessment, and introduces the warrant affidavit to demonstrate an independent source. The Court, in allowing such behavior, has missed the point of the warrant requirement and the exclusionary rule—that it "reduces the Fourth Amendment to a nullity" to allow warrantless searches to go unpunished.
>
> But the majority might argue that "there's not much that we can do about police lying. If police chose to lie, even before *Murray* and *Segura*, they could beat the system." This is only partially true.
>
> Of course, it has always been the case that the police could make up the existence of "Old Reliable," the informant, and use his fictitious "tip" as the basis for a search warrant. The problem with this tactic is that, if the police are wrong and no evidence is found, they are forced to return to the magistrate empty-handed. This is embarrassing to the police department and would only have to happen a few times before the magistrates and defense attorneys would realize that the police were liars. After *Murray*, there is no such fear, because the fictitious "Old Reliable" will always be right! His "tip" will always lead to evidence because the police will have found it in advance.
>
> It is generally difficult for the police to cover up an illegal search—the defendant will usually be aware of it. If the rule is that evidence found in such a search will never be admissible unless it would have been inevitably discovered by a wholly independent third party (as in *Nix*), the police, fearing the disclosure of the search, will

> not perform it. The *Murray* rule, by encouraging warrantless searches, is flatly inconsistent with the warrant requirement.

Craig M. Bradley, *Murray v. United States: The Bell Tolls for the Search Warrant Requirement*, 64 IND. L.J. 907, 917–18 (1989).

5. GOOD FAITH

The rationale for excluding evidence matters. If, as some cases state, illegally obtained evidence must be excluded to uphold judicial integrity, then more evidence will need to be excluded than if the only purpose of the exclusionary rule is to deter police misconduct. Furthermore, if the aim is only to deter deliberate, as opposed to inadvertent, constitutional violations, then even less evidence need be excluded. The "good-faith" exception to the exclusionary rule takes as a given that the exclusionary rule is meant only to deter deliberate constitutional violations. As you read the cases in this section, consider the arguments deployed against that premise in these and earlier cases

UNITED STATES V. LEON

468 U.S. 897 (1984)

JUSTICE WHITE delivered the opinion of the court.

This case presents the question whether the Fourth Amendment exclusionary rule should be modified so as not to bar the use in the prosecution's case in chief of evidence obtained by officers acting in reasonable reliance on a search warrant issued by a detached and neutral magistrate but ultimately found to be unsupported by probable cause. To resolve this question, we must consider once again the tension between the sometimes competing goals of, on the one hand, deterring official misconduct and removing inducements to unreasonable invasions of privacy and, on the other, establishing procedures under which criminal defendants are "acquitted or convicted on the basis of all the evidence which exposes the truth."

I

In August 1981, a confidential informant of unproven reliability informed an officer of the Burbank Police Department that two persons known to him as "Armando" and "Patsy" were selling large quantities of cocaine and methaqualone from their residence at 620 Price Drive in Burbank, Cal. The informant also indicated that he had witnessed a sale of methaqualone by "Patsy" at the residence approximately five months earlier and had observed at that time a shoebox containing a large amount of cash that belonged to "Patsy." He further declared that "Armando" and "Patsy" generally kept only small quantities of drugs at their residence and stored the remainder at another location in Burbank.

On the basis of this information, the Burbank police initiated an extensive investigation focusing first on the Price Drive residence and later on two other residences as well. Cars parked at the Price Drive residence were determined to belong to respondents Armando Sanchez, who had previously been arrested for possession of marihuana, and Patsy Stewart, who had no criminal record. During the course of the investigation, officers observed an automobile belonging to respondent Ricardo Del Castillo, who had previously been arrested for possession of 50 pounds of marihuana, arrive at the Price Drive residence. The driver of that car entered the house, exited shortly thereafter carrying a small paper sack, and drove away. A check of Del Castillo's probation records led the officers to respondent Alberto Leon, whose telephone number Del Castillo had listed as his employer's. Leon had been arrested in 1980 on drug charges, and a companion had informed the police at that time that Leon was heavily involved in the importation of drugs into this country. Before the current investigation began, the Burbank officers had learned that an informant had told a Glendale police officer that Leon stored a large quantity of methaqualone at his residence in Glendale. During the course of this investigation, the Burbank officers learned that Leon was living at 716 South Sunset Canyon in Burbank.

Subsequently, the officers observed several persons, at least one of whom had prior drug involvement, arriving at the Price Drive residence and leaving with small packages; observed a variety of other material activity at the two residences as well as at a condominium at 7902 Via Magdalena; and witnessed a variety of relevant activity involving respondents' automobiles. The officers also observed respondents Sanchez and Stewart board separate flights for Miami. The pair later returned to Los Angeles together, consented to a search of their luggage that revealed only a small amount of marihuana, and left the airport. Based on these and other observations summarized in the affidavit, Officer Cyril Rombach of the Burbank Police Department, an experienced and well-trained narcotics investigator, prepared an application for a warrant to search 620 Price Drive, 716 South Sunset Canyon, 7902 Via Magdalena, and automobiles registered to each of the respondents for an extensive list of items believed to be related to respondents' drug-trafficking activities. Officer Rombach's extensive application was reviewed by several Deputy District Attorneys.

A facially valid search warrant was issued in September 1981 by a State Superior Court Judge. The ensuing searches produced large quantities of drugs at the Via Magdalena and Sunset Canyon addresses and a small quantity at the Price Drive residence. Other evidence was discovered at each of the residences and in Stewart's and Del Castillo's automobiles. Respondents were indicted by a grand jury in the District Court for the Central District of California and charged with conspiracy to possess and distribute cocaine and a variety of substantive counts.

The respondents then filed motions to suppress the evidence seized pursuant to the warrant. The District Court held an evidentiary hearing and, while recognizing that the case was a close one, granted the motions to suppress in part. It concluded that the affidavit was insufficient to establish probable cause, but did not suppress all of the evidence as to all of the respondents because none of the respondents had standing to challenge all of the searches. In response to a request from the Government, the court made clear that Officer Rombach had acted in good faith, but it rejected the Government's suggestion that the Fourth Amendment exclusionary rule should not apply where evidence is seized in reasonable, good-faith reliance on a search warrant.

* * *

The Government's petition for certiorari expressly declined to seek review of the lower courts' determinations that the search warrant was unsupported by probable cause and presented only the question "[w]hether the Fourth Amendment exclusionary rule should be modified so as not to bar the admission of evidence seized in reasonable, good-faith reliance on a search warrant that is subsequently held to be defective." We granted certiorari to consider the propriety of such a modification. Although it undoubtedly is within our power to consider the question whether probable cause existed under the "totality of the circumstances" test announced last Term in *Illinois v. Gates*, 462 U.S. 213 (1983), that question has not been briefed or argued; and it is also within our authority, which we choose to exercise, to take the case as it comes to us, accepting the Court of Appeals' conclusion that probable cause was lacking under the prevailing legal standards.

We have concluded that, in the Fourth Amendment context, the exclusionary rule can be modified somewhat without jeopardizing its ability to perform its intended functions. Accordingly, we reverse the judgment of the Court of Appeals.

II

Language in opinions of this Court and of individual Justices has sometimes implied that the exclusionary rule is a necessary corollary of the Fourth Amendment, *Mapp v. Ohio*, 367 U.S. 643, 651, 655–657 (1961); *Olmstead v. United States*, 277 U.S. 438, 462–463 (1928), or that the rule is required by the conjunction of the Fourth and Fifth Amendments. *Mapp v. Ohio*, 367 U.S., at 661–662 (Black, J., concurring). These implications need not detain us long. The Fifth Amendment theory has not withstood critical analysis or the test of time, and the Fourth Amendment "has never been interpreted to proscribe the introduction of illegally seized evidence in all proceedings or against all persons."

A

* * *

Whether the exclusionary sanction is appropriately imposed in a particular case, our decisions make clear, is "an issue separate from the question whether the Fourth Amendment rights of the party seeking to invoke the rule were violated by police conduct." Only the former question is currently before us, and it must be resolved by weighing the costs and benefits of preventing the use in the prosecution's case in chief of inherently trustworthy tangible evidence obtained in reliance on a search warrant issued by a detached and neutral magistrate that ultimately is found to be defective.

The substantial social costs exacted by the exclusionary rule for the vindication of Fourth Amendment rights have long been a source of concern. "Our cases have consistently recognized that unbending application of the exclusionary sanction to enforce ideals of governmental rectitude would impede unacceptably the truth-finding functions of judge and jury." An objectionable collateral consequence of this interference with the criminal justice system's truth-finding function is that some guilty defendants may go free or receive reduced sentences as a result of favorable plea bargains. Particularly when law enforcement officers have acted in objective good faith or their transgressions have been minor, the magnitude of the benefit conferred on such guilty defendants offends basic concepts of the criminal justice system. Indiscriminate application of the exclusionary rule, therefore, may well "generat[e] disrespect for the law and administration of justice." Accordingly, "[a]s with any remedial device, the application of the rule has been restricted to those areas where its remedial objectives are thought most efficaciously served."

B

* * *

As cases considering the use of unlawfully obtained evidence in criminal trials themselves make clear, it does not follow from the emphasis on the exclusionary rule's deterrent value that "anything which deters illegal searches is thereby commanded by the Fourth Amendment." In determining whether persons aggrieved solely by the introduction of damaging evidence unlawfully obtained from their co-conspirators or co-defendants could seek suppression, for example, we found that the additional benefits of such an extension of the exclusionary rule would not outweigh its costs. Standing to invoke the rule has thus been limited to cases in which the prosecution seeks to use the fruits of an illegal search or seizure against the victim of police misconduct. *Rakas v. Illinois*, 439 U.S. 128 (1978).

* * *

When considering the use of evidence obtained in violation of the Fourth Amendment in the prosecution's case in chief, moreover, we have declined to adopt a per se or "but for" rule that would render inadmissible any evidence that came to light through a chain of causation that began with an illegal arrest. We also have held that a witness' testimony may be admitted even when his identity was discovered in an unconstitutional search. *United States v. Ceccolini*, 435 U.S. 268 (1978). The perception underlying these decisions—that the connection between police misconduct and evidence of crime may be sufficiently attenuated to permit the use of that evidence at trial—is a product of considerations relating to the exclusionary rule and the constitutional principles it is designed to protect. In short, the "dissipation of the taint" concept that the Court has applied in deciding whether exclusion is appropriate in a particular case "attempts to mark the point at which the detrimental consequences of illegal police action become so attenuated that the deterrent effect of the exclusionary rule no longer justifies its cost." Not surprisingly in view of this purpose, an assessment of the flagrancy of the police misconduct constitutes an important step in the calculus.

* * *

As yet, we have not recognized any form of good-faith exception to the Fourth Amendment exclusionary rule. But the balancing approach that has evolved during the years of experience with the rule provides strong support for the modification currently urged upon us. As we discuss below, our evaluation of the costs and benefits of suppressing reliable physical evidence seized by officers reasonably relying on a warrant issued by a detached and neutral magistrate leads to the conclusion that such evidence should be admissible in the prosecution's case in chief.

III

A

Because a search warrant "provides the detached scrutiny of a neutral magistrate, which is a more reliable safeguard against improper searches than the hurried judgment of a law enforcement officer 'engaged in the often competitive enterprise of ferreting out crime,' " we have expressed a strong preference for warrants and declared that "in a doubtful or marginal case a search under a warrant may be sustainable where without one it would fall." Reasonable minds frequently may differ on the question whether a particular affidavit establishes probable cause, and we have thus concluded that the preference for warrants is most appropriately effectuated by according "great deference" to a magistrate's determination.

Deference to the magistrate, however, is not boundless. It is clear, first, that the deference accorded to a magistrate's finding of probable cause does not preclude inquiry into the knowing or reckless falsity of the affidavit on which that determination was based. Second, the courts must also insist that the magistrate purport to "perform his 'neutral and detached' function and not serve merely as a rubber stamp for the police." A magistrate failing to "manifest that neutrality and detachment demanded of a judicial officer when presented with a warrant application" and who acts instead as "an adjunct law enforcement officer" cannot provide valid authorization for an otherwise unconstitutional search.

Third, reviewing courts will not defer to a warrant based on an affidavit that does not "provide the magistrate with a substantial basis for determining the existence of probable cause." "Sufficient information must be presented to the magistrate to allow that official to determine probable cause; his action cannot be a mere ratification of the bare conclusions of others." Even if the warrant application was supported by more than a "bare bones" affidavit, a reviewing court may properly conclude that, notwithstanding the deference that magistrates deserve, the warrant was invalid because the magistrate's probable-cause determination reflected an improper analysis of the totality of the circumstances or because the form of the warrant was improper in some respect.

Only in the first of these three situations, however, has the Court set forth a rationale for suppressing evidence obtained pursuant to a search warrant; in the other areas, it has simply excluded such evidence without considering whether Fourth Amendment interests will be advanced. To the extent that proponents of exclusion rely on its behavioral effects on judges and magistrates in these areas, their reliance is misplaced. First, the exclusionary rule is designed to deter police misconduct rather than to punish the errors of judges and magistrates. Second, there exists no evidence suggesting that judges and magistrates are inclined to ignore or subvert the Fourth Amendment or that lawlessness among these actors requires application of the extreme sanction of exclusion.[14]

Third, and most important, we discern no basis, and are offered none, for believing that exclusion of evidence seized pursuant to a warrant will have a significant deterrent effect on the issuing judge or magistrate. Many of the factors that indicate that the exclusionary rule cannot provide an effective "special" or "general" deterrent for individual offending law enforcement officers apply as well to judges or magistrates. And, to the extent that the rule is thought to operate as a "systemic" deterrent on a wider audience, it clearly can have no such effect on individuals empowered to issue search warrants. Judges and magistrates are not adjuncts to the law enforcement team; as neutral judicial officers, they have no stake in the outcome of particular criminal prosecutions. The threat of exclusion thus cannot be expected significantly to deter them. Imposition of the exclusionary sanction is not necessary meaningfully to inform judicial

[14] Although there are assertions that some magistrates become rubber stamps for the police and others may be unable effectively to screen police conduct, we are not convinced that this is a problem of major proportions.

officers of their errors, and we cannot conclude that admitting evidence obtained pursuant to a warrant while at the same time declaring that the warrant was somehow defective will in any way reduce judicial officers' professional incentives to comply with the Fourth Amendment, encourage them to repeat their mistakes, or lead to the granting of all colorable warrant requests.[18]

Federal magistrates, moreover, are subject to the direct supervision of district courts. They may be removed for "incompetency, misconduct, neglect of duty, or physical or mental disability." 28 U.S.C. § 631(i). If a magistrate serves merely as a "rubber stamp" for the police or is unable to exercise mature judgment, closer supervision or removal provides a more effective remedy than the exclusionary rule.

B

If exclusion of evidence obtained pursuant to a subsequently invalidated warrant is to have any deterrent effect, therefore, it must alter the behavior of individual law enforcement officers or the policies of their departments. One could argue that applying the exclusionary rule in cases where the police failed to demonstrate probable cause in the warrant application deters future inadequate presentations or "magistrate shopping" and thus promotes the ends of the Fourth Amendment. Suppressing evidence obtained pursuant to a technically defective warrant supported by probable cause also might encourage officers to scrutinize more closely the form of the warrant and to point out suspected judicial errors. We find such arguments speculative and conclude that suppression of evidence obtained pursuant to a warrant should be ordered only on a case-by-case basis and only in those unusual cases in which exclusion will further the purposes of the exclusionary rule.[19]

We have frequently questioned whether the exclusionary rule can have any deterrent effect when the offending officers acted in the objectively reasonable belief that their conduct did not violate the Fourth Amendment. "No empirical researcher, proponent or opponent of the rule, has yet been able to establish with any assurance whether the rule has a deterrent effect . . . ." But even assuming that the rule effectively deters some police misconduct and provides incentives for the law enforcement profession as a whole to conduct itself in accord with the Fourth Amendment, it cannot be expected, and should not be applied, to deter objectively reasonable law enforcement activity.

---

[18] Limiting the application of the exclusionary sanction may well increase the care with which magistrates scrutinize warrant applications. We doubt that magistrates are more desirous of avoiding the exclusion of evidence obtained pursuant to warrants they have issued than of avoiding invasions of privacy.

[19] Our discussion of the deterrent effect of excluding evidence obtained in reasonable reliance on a subsequently invalidated warrant assumes, of course, that the officers properly executed the warrant and searched only those places and for those objects that it was reasonable to believe were covered by the warrant.

* * *

This is particularly true, we believe, when an officer acting with objective good faith has obtained a search warrant from a judge or magistrate and acted within its scope. In most such cases, there is no police illegality and thus nothing to deter. It is the magistrate's responsibility to determine whether the officer's allegations establish probable cause and, if so, to issue a warrant comporting in form with the requirements of the Fourth Amendment. In the ordinary case, an officer cannot be expected to question the magistrate's probable-cause determination or his judgment that the form of the warrant is technically sufficient. "[O]nce the warrant issues, there is literally nothing more the policeman can do in seeking to comply with the law." Penalizing the officer for the magistrate's error, rather than his own, cannot logically contribute to the deterrence of Fourth Amendment violations.[22]

C

We conclude that the marginal or nonexistent benefits produced by suppressing evidence obtained in objectively reasonable reliance on a subsequently invalidated search warrant cannot justify the substantial costs of exclusion. We do not suggest, however, that exclusion is always inappropriate in cases where an officer has obtained a warrant and abided by its terms. "[S]earches pursuant to a warrant will rarely require any deep inquiry into reasonableness," for "a warrant issued by a magistrate normally suffices to establish" that a law enforcement officer has "acted in good faith in conducting the search." Nevertheless, the officer's reliance on the magistrate's probable-cause determination and on the technical sufficiency of the warrant he issues must be objectively reasonable and it is clear that in some circumstances the officer[24] will have no reasonable grounds for believing that the warrant was properly issued.

---

[22] To the extent that Justice Stevens' conclusions concerning the integrity of the courts rest on a foundation other than his judgment, which we reject, concerning the effects of our decision on the deterrence of police illegality, we find his argument unpersuasive. "Judicial integrity clearly does not mean that the courts must never admit evidence obtained in violation of the Fourth Amendment." *United States v. Janis*, 428 U.S. 433, 458, n. 35 (1976). "While courts, of course, must ever be concerned with preserving the integrity of the judicial process, this concern has limited force as a justification for the exclusion of highly probative evidence." *Stone v. Powell*, 428 U.S., at 485.Our cases establish that the question whether the use of illegally obtained evidence in judicial proceedings represents judicial participation in a Fourth Amendment violation and offends the integrity of the courts

> "is essentially the same as the inquiry into whether exclusion would serve a deterrent purpose. . . . The analysis showing that exclusion in this case has no demonstrated deterrent effect and is unlikely to have any significant such effect shows, by the same reasoning, that the admission of the evidence is unlikely to encourage violations of the Fourth Amendment." *United States v. Janis,* 428 U.S., at 459, n. 35.

Absent unusual circumstances, when a Fourth Amendment violation has occurred because the police have reasonably relied on a warrant issued by a detached and neutral magistrate but ultimately found to be defective, "the integrity of the courts is not implicated." *Illinois v. Gates,* 462 U.S., at 259, n. 14 (White, J., concurring in judgment).

[24] References to "officer" throughout this opinion should not be read too narrowly. It is necessary to consider the objective reasonableness, not only of the officers who eventually executed

Suppression therefore remains an appropriate remedy if the magistrate or judge in issuing a warrant was misled by information in an affidavit that the affiant knew was false or would have known was false except for his reckless disregard of the truth. The exception we recognize today will also not apply in cases where the issuing magistrate wholly abandoned his judicial role in the manner condemned in *Lo-Ji Sales, Inc. v. New York*, 442 U.S. 319 (1979); in such circumstances, no reasonably well trained officer should rely on the warrant. Nor would an officer manifest objective good faith in relying on a warrant based on an affidavit "so lacking in indicia of probable cause as to render official belief in its existence entirely unreasonable." Finally, depending on the circumstances of the particular case, a warrant may be so facially deficient—i.e., in failing to particularize the place to be searched or the things to be seized—that the executing officers cannot reasonably presume it to be valid.

In so limiting the suppression remedy, we leave untouched the probable-cause standard and the various requirements for a valid warrant. Other objections to the modification of the Fourth Amendment exclusionary rule we consider to be insubstantial. The good-faith exception for searches conducted pursuant to warrants is not intended to signal our unwillingness strictly to enforce the requirements of the Fourth Amendment, and we do not believe that it will have this effect. As we have already suggested, the good-faith exception, turning as it does on objective reasonableness, should not be difficult to apply in practice. When officers have acted pursuant to a warrant, the prosecution should ordinarily be able to establish objective good faith without a substantial expenditure of judicial time.

Nor are we persuaded that application of a good-faith exception to searches conducted pursuant to warrants will preclude review of the constitutionality of the search or seizure, deny needed guidance from the courts, or freeze Fourth Amendment law in its present state.[25] There is no need for courts to adopt the inflexible practice of always deciding whether the officers' conduct manifested objective good faith before turning to the question whether the Fourth Amendment has been violated. Defendants seeking suppression of the fruits of allegedly unconstitutional searches or seizures undoubtedly raise live controversies which Art. III empowers federal courts to adjudicate. As cases addressing questions of good-faith immunity under 42 U.S.C. § 1983 and cases involving the harmless-error

a warrant, but also of the officers who originally obtained it or who provided information material to the probable-cause determination. Nothing in our opinion suggests, for example, that an officer could obtain a warrant on the basis of a "bare bones" affidavit and then rely on colleagues who are ignorant of the circumstances under which the warrant was obtained to conduct the search.

[25] The argument that defendants will lose their incentive to litigate meritorious Fourth Amendment claims as a result of the good-faith exception we adopt today is unpersuasive. Although the exception might discourage presentation of insubstantial suppression motions, the magnitude of the benefit conferred on defendants by a successful motion makes it unlikely that litigation of colorable claims will be substantially diminished.

doctrine make clear, courts have considerable discretion in conforming their decisionmaking processes to the exigencies of particular cases.

If the resolution of a particular Fourth Amendment question is necessary to guide future action by law enforcement officers and magistrates, nothing will prevent reviewing courts from deciding that question before turning to the good-faith issue. Indeed, it frequently will be difficult to determine whether the officers acted reasonably without resolving the Fourth Amendment issue. Even if the Fourth Amendment question is not one of broad import, reviewing courts could decide in particular cases that magistrates under their supervision need to be informed of their errors and so evaluate the officers' good faith only after finding a violation. In other circumstances, those courts could reject suppression motions posing no important Fourth Amendment questions by turning immediately to a consideration of the officers' good faith. We have no reason to believe that our Fourth Amendment jurisprudence would suffer by allowing reviewing courts to exercise an informed discretion in making this choice.

IV

When the principles we have enunciated today are applied to the facts of this case, it is apparent that the judgment of the Court of Appeals cannot stand. The Court of Appeals applied the prevailing legal standards to Officer Rombach's warrant application and concluded that the application could not support the magistrate's probable-cause determination. In so doing, the court clearly informed the magistrate that he had erred in issuing the challenged warrant. This aspect of the court's judgment is not under attack in this proceeding.

Having determined that the warrant should not have issued, the Court of Appeals understandably declined to adopt a modification of the Fourth Amendment exclusionary rule that this Court had not previously sanctioned. Although the modification finds strong support in our previous cases, the Court of Appeals' commendable self-restraint is not to be criticized. We have now reexamined the purposes of the exclusionary rule and the propriety of its application in cases where officers have relied on a subsequently invalidated search warrant. Our conclusion is that the rule's purposes will only rarely be served by applying it in such circumstances.

In the absence of an allegation that the magistrate abandoned his detached and neutral role, suppression is appropriate only if the officers were dishonest or reckless in preparing their affidavit or could not have harbored an objectively reasonable belief in the existence of probable cause. Only respondent Leon has contended that no reasonably well trained police officer could have believed that there existed probable cause to search his house; significantly, the other respondents advance no comparable argument. Officer Rombach's application for a warrant clearly was supported by much more than a "bare bones" affidavit. The affidavit related the results of an extensive investigation and, as the opinions of the divided panel of the Court of Appeals make clear, provided evidence sufficient to create disagreement among thoughtful and competent judges as to the existence of probable cause. Under these circumstances, the officers' reliance on the magistrate's determination of probable cause was objectively reasonable, and application of the extreme sanction of exclusion is inappropriate.

JUSTICE BLACKMUN, concurring.

* * *

As the Court's opinion in this case makes clear, the Court has narrowed the scope of the exclusionary rule because of an empirical judgment that the rule has little appreciable effect in cases where officers act in objectively reasonable reliance on search warrants. Because I share the view that the exclusionary rule is not a constitutionally compelled corollary of the Fourth Amendment itself, I see no way to avoid making an empirical judgment of this sort, and I am satisfied that the Court has made the correct one on the information before it. Like all courts, we face institutional limitations on our ability to gather information about "legislative facts," and the exclusionary rule itself has exacerbated the shortage of hard data concerning the behavior of police officers in the absence of such a rule. Nonetheless, we cannot escape the responsibility to decide the question before us, however imperfect our information may be, and I am prepared to join the Court on the information now at hand.

What must be stressed, however, is that any empirical judgment about the effect of the exclusionary rule in a particular class of cases necessarily is a provisional one. By their very nature, the assumptions on which we proceed today cannot be cast in stone. To the contrary, they now will be tested in the real world of state and federal law enforcement, and this Court will attend to the results. If it should emerge from experience that, contrary to our expectations, the good-faith exception to the exclusionary rule results in a material change in police compliance with the Fourth Amendment, we shall have to reconsider what we have undertaken here. The logic of a decision that rests on untested predictions about police conduct demands no less.

If a single principle may be drawn from this Court's exclusionary rule decisions, from *Weeks* through *Mapp v. Ohio*, 367 U.S. 643 (1961), to the decisions handed down today, it is that the scope of the exclusionary rule is subject to change in light of changing judicial understanding about the effects of the rule outside the confines of the courtroom. It is incumbent on the Nation's law enforcement officers, who must continue to observe the Fourth Amendment in the wake of today's decisions, to recognize the double-edged nature of that principle.

JUSTICE BRENNAN, with whom JUSTICE MARSHALL joins, dissenting.

Ten years ago in *United States v. Calandra*, 414 U.S. 338 (1974), I expressed the fear that the Court's decision "may signal that a majority of my colleagues have positioned themselves to reopen the door [to evidence secured by official lawlessness] still further and abandon altogether the exclusionary rule in search-and-seizure cases." Since then, in case after case, I have witnessed the Court's gradual but determined strangulation of the rule. It now appears that the Court's victory over the Fourth Amendment is complete. That today's decisions represent the *pièce de résistance* of the Court's past efforts cannot be doubted, for today the Court sanctions the use in the prosecution's case in chief of illegally obtained evidence against the individual whose rights have been violated—a result that had previously been thought to be foreclosed.

The Court seeks to justify this result on the ground that the "costs" of adhering to the exclusionary rule in cases like those before us exceed the "benefits." But the language of deterrence and of cost/benefit analysis, if used indiscriminately, can have a narcotic effect. It creates an illusion of technical precision and ineluctability. It suggests that not only constitutional principle but also empirical data support the majority's result. When the Court's analysis is examined carefully, however, it is clear that we have not been treated to an honest assessment of the merits of the exclusionary rule, but have instead been drawn into a curious world where the "costs" of excluding illegally obtained evidence loom to exaggerated heights and where the "benefits" of such exclusion are made to disappear with a mere wave of the hand.

* * *

I

* * *

A

At bottom, the Court's decision turns on the proposition that the exclusionary rule is merely a " 'judicially created remedy designed to safeguard Fourth Amendment rights generally through its deterrent effect, rather than a personal constitutional right.' " The germ of that idea is found in *Wolf v. Colorado*, 338 U.S. 25 (1949), and although I had thought that such a narrow conception of the rule had been forever put to rest by our decision in *Mapp v. Ohio*, 367 U.S. 643 (1961), it has been revived by the present Court and reaches full flower with today's decision. The essence of this view, as expressed initially in the *Calandra* opinion and as reiterated today, is that the sole "purpose of the Fourth Amendment is to prevent unreasonable governmental intrusions into the privacy of one's person, house, papers, or effects. The wrong condemned is the unjustified governmental invasion of these areas of an individual's life. That wrong . . . is fully accomplished by the original search without probable cause." 414

U.S., at 354 (emphasis added). This reading of the Amendment implies that its proscriptions are directed solely at those government agents who may actually invade an individual's constitutionally protected privacy. The courts are not subject to any direct constitutional duty to exclude illegally obtained evidence, because the question of the admissibility of such evidence is not addressed by the Amendment. This view of the scope of the Amendment relegates the judiciary to the periphery. Because the only constitutionally cognizable injury has already been "fully accomplished" by the police by the time a case comes before the courts, the Constitution is not itself violated if the judge decides to admit the tainted evidence. Indeed, the most the judge can do is wring his hands and hope that perhaps by excluding such evidence he can deter future transgressions by the police.

Such a reading appears plausible, because, as critics of the exclusionary rule never tire of repeating, the Fourth Amendment makes no express provision for the exclusion of evidence secured in violation of its commands. A short answer to this claim, of course, is that many of the Constitution's most vital imperatives are stated in general terms and the task of giving meaning to these precepts is therefore left to subsequent judicial decisionmaking in the context of concrete cases. The nature of our Constitution, as Chief Justice Marshall long ago explained, "requires that only its great outlines should be marked, its important objects designated, and the minor ingredients which compose those objects be deduced from the nature of the objects themselves." *McCulloch v. Maryland*, 4 Wheat. 316, 407 (1819).

A more direct answer may be supplied by recognizing that the Amendment, like other provisions of the Bill of Rights, restrains the power of the government as a whole; it does not specify only a particular agency and exempt all others. The judiciary is responsible, no less than the executive, for ensuring that constitutional rights are respected.

When that fact is kept in mind, the role of the courts and their possible involvement in the concerns of the Fourth Amendment comes into sharper focus. Because seizures are executed principally to secure evidence, and because such evidence generally has utility in our legal system only in the context of a trial supervised by a judge, it is apparent that the admission of illegally obtained evidence implicates the same constitutional concerns as the initial seizure of that evidence. Indeed, by admitting unlawfully seized evidence, the judiciary becomes a part of what is in fact a single governmental action prohibited by the terms of the Amendment. Once that connection between the evidence-gathering role of the police and the evidence-admitting function of the courts is acknowledged, the plausibility of the Court's interpretation becomes more suspect. Certainly nothing in the language or history of the Fourth Amendment suggests that a recognition of this evidentiary link between the police and the courts was meant to be foreclosed. It is difficult to give any meaning at all to the limitations imposed by the Amendment if they are read to proscribe only certain conduct by the police but to allow other agents of the same government to take advantage of evidence secured by the police in violation of its requirements. The Amendment therefore must be read to condemn not only the initial unconstitutional invasion of privacy—which is done, after all, for the purpose of securing evidence—but also the subsequent use of any evidence so obtained.

The Court evades this principle by drawing an artificial line between the constitutional rights and responsibilities that are engaged by actions of the police and those that are engaged when a defendant appears before the courts. According to the Court, the substantive protections of the Fourth Amendment are wholly exhausted at the moment when police unlawfully invade an individual's privacy and thus no substantive force remains to those protections at the time of trial when the government seeks to use evidence obtained by the police.

I submit that such a crabbed reading of the Fourth Amendment casts aside the teaching of those Justices who first formulated the exclusionary rule, and rests ultimately on an impoverished understanding of judicial responsibility in our constitutional scheme. For my part, "[t]he right of the people to be secure in their persons, houses, papers, and effects, against unreasonable searches and seizures" comprises a personal right to exclude all evidence secured by means of unreasonable searches and seizures. The right to be free from the initial invasion of privacy and the right of exclusion are coordinate components of the central embracing right to be free from unreasonable searches and seizures.

* * *

B

* * *

By remaining within its redoubt of empiricism and by basing the rule solely on the deterrence rationale, the Court has robbed the rule of legitimacy. A doctrine that is explained as if it were an empirical proposition but for which there is only limited empirical support is both inherently unstable and an easy mark for critics. The extent of this Court's fidelity to Fourth Amendment requirements, however, should not turn on such statistical uncertainties. I share the view, expressed by Justice Stewart for the Court in *Faretta v. California*, 422 U.S. 806 (1975), that "[p]ersonal liberties are not rooted in the law of averages." Rather than seeking to give effect to the liberties secured by the Fourth Amendment through guesswork about deterrence, the Court should restore to its proper place the principle framed 70 years ago in *Weeks* that an individual whose privacy has been invaded in violation of the Fourth Amendment has a right grounded in that Amendment to prevent the government from subsequently making use of any evidence so obtained.

II

Application of that principle clearly requires affirmance in the two cases decided today. In the first, *United States v. Leon*, 468 U.S. 897, it is conceded by the Government and accepted by the Court that the affidavit filed by the police officers in support of their application for a search warrant failed to provide a sufficient basis on which a neutral and detached magistrate could conclude that there was probable cause to issue the warrant. Specifically, it is conceded that the officers' application for a warrant was based in part on information supplied by a confidential informant of unproven reliability that was over five months old by the time it was relayed to the police. Although the police conducted an independent investigation on the basis of this tip, both the District Court and the Court of Appeals concluded that the additional information gathered by the officers failed to corroborate the details of the informant's tip and was "as consistent with innocence as . . . with guilt." The warrant, therefore, should never have issued. Stripped of the authority of the warrant, the conduct of these officers was plainly unconstitutional-it amounted to nothing less than a naked invasion of the privacy of respondents' homes without the requisite justification demanded by the Fourth Amendment. In order to restore the Government to the position it would have occupied had this unconstitutional search not occurred, therefore, it was necessary that the evidence be suppressed. As we said in *Coolidge v. New Hampshire*, 403 U.S. 443 (1971), the Warrant Clause is not "an inconvenience to be somehow 'weighed' against the claims of police efficiency. It is, or should be, an important working part of our machinery of government, operating as a matter of course to check the 'well-intentioned but mistakenly overzealous executive officers' who are part of any system of law enforcement."

A close examination of the facts of this case reveals that this is neither an extraordinary nor indeed a very costly step. The warrant had authorized a search for cocaine, methaqualone tablets, and miscellaneous narcotics paraphernalia at several locations: a condominium at 7902 Via Magdalena in Los Angeles; a residence at 620 Price Drive in Burbank; a residence at 716 South Sunset Canyon in Burbank; and four automobiles owned respectively by respondents Leon, Sanchez, Stewart, and Del Castillo. Pursuant to this warrant, the officers seized approximately four pounds of cocaine and over 1,000 methaqualone tablets from the Via Magdalena condominium, nearly one pound of cocaine from the Sunset Canyon residence, about an ounce of cocaine from the Price Drive residence, and certain paraphernalia from Del Castillo's and Stewart's automobiles. On the basis of this and other evidence, the four respondents were charged with violating 21 U.S.C. § 846 for conspiring to possess and distribute cocaine, and § 841(a)(1) for possessing methaqualone and cocaine with intent to distribute. The indictment specifically alleged that respondents had maintained the Via Magdalena condominium as a storage area for controlled substances which they distributed to prospective purchasers.

At the suppression hearing, the District Court determined that none of the respondents had a sufficient expectation of privacy to contest the search of the Via Magdalena condominium, that respondents Stewart and Sanchez could challenge the search of their home at Price Drive, that respondent Leon was entitled to challenge the search of his home at Sunset Canyon, and that respondents Del Castillo and Stewart could contest the search of their cars. Given its finding that probable cause to issue the warrant was lacking, the District Court ruled that the evidence from the Price Drive residence could not be used against respondents Stewart and Sanchez, that evidence from the Sunset Canyon residence could not be used against Leon, and that evidence obtained from both Del Castillo's and Stewart's automobiles could not be used against them.

The tenor of the Court's opinion suggests that this order somehow imposed a grave and presumably unjustifiable cost on society. Such a suggestion, however, is a gross exaggeration. Since the indictment focused upon a conspiracy among all respondents to use the Via Magdalena condominium as a storage area for controlled substances, and since the bulk of the evidence seized was from that condominium and was plainly admissible under the District Court's order, the Government would clearly still be able to present a strong case to the jury following the court's suppression order. I emphasize these details not to suggest how the Government's case would fare before the jury but rather to clarify a point that is lost in the Court's rhetorical excesses over the costs of the exclusionary rule-namely, that the suppression of evidence will certainly tend to weaken the Government's position but it will rarely force the Government to abandon a prosecution. In my view, a doctrine that preserves intact the constitutional rights of the accused, and, at the same time, is sufficiently limited to permit society's legitimate and pressing interest in criminal law enforcement to be served should not be so recklessly discarded. It is a doctrine that gives life to the "very heart of the Fourth Amendment directive: that . . . a governmental search and seizure should represent both the efforts of the officer to gather evidence of wrongful acts and the judgment of the magistrate that the collected evidence is sufficient to justify invasion of a citizen's private premises."

* * *

What the Framers of the Bill of Rights sought to accomplish through the express requirements of the Fourth Amendment was to define precisely the conditions under which government agents could search private property so that citizens would not have to depend solely upon the discretion and restraint of those agents for the protection of their privacy. Although the self-restraint and care exhibited by the officers in this case is commendable, that alone can never be a sufficient protection for constitutional liberties. I am convinced that it is not too much to ask that an attentive magistrate take those minimum steps necessary to ensure that every warrant he issues describes with particularity the things that his independent review of the warrant application convinces him are likely to be found in the premises. And I am equally convinced that it is not too much to ask that well-trained and experienced police officers take a moment to check that the warrant they have been issued at least describes those things for which they have sought leave to search. These convictions spring not from my own view of sound criminal law enforcement policy, but are instead compelled by the language of the Fourth Amendment and the history that led to its adoption.

III

* * *

At the outset, the Court suggests that society has been asked to pay a high price—in terms either of setting guilty persons free or of impeding the proper functioning of trials—as a result of excluding relevant physical evidence in cases where the police, in conducting searches and seizing evidence, have made only an "objectively reasonable" mistake concerning the constitutionality of their actions. But what evidence is there to support such a claim?

Significantly, the Court points to none, and, indeed, as the Court acknowledges, recent studies have demonstrated that the "costs" of the exclusionary rule—calculated in terms of dropped prosecutions and lost convictions—are quite low. Contrary to the claims of the rule's critics that exclusion leads to "the release of countless guilty criminals," these studies have demonstrated that federal and state prosecutors very rarely drop cases because of potential search and seizure problems. For example, a 1979 study prepared at the request of Congress by the General Accounting Office reported that only 0.4% of all cases actually declined for prosecution by federal prosecutors were declined primarily because of illegal search problems. If the GAO data are restated as a percentage of all arrests, the study shows that only 0.2% of all felony arrests are declined for prosecution because of potential exclusionary rule problems. Of course, these data describe only the costs attributable to the exclusion of evidence in all cases; the costs due to the exclusion of evidence in the narrower category of cases where police have made objectively reasonable mistakes must necessarily be even smaller. The Court, however, ignores this distinction and mistakenly weighs the aggregated costs of exclusion in all cases, irrespective of the circumstances that led to exclusion against the potential benefits associated with only those cases in which evidence is excluded because police reasonably but mistakenly believe that their conduct does not violate the Fourth Amendment. When such faulty scales are used, it is little wonder that the balance tips in favor of restricting the application of the rule.

In another measure of the rule's impact—the number of prosecutions that are dismissed or result in acquittals in cases where evidence has been excluded—the available data again show that the Court's past assessment of the rule's costs has generally been exaggerated. For example, a study based on data from nine mid-sized counties in Illinois, Michigan, and Pennsylvania reveals that motions to suppress physical evidence were filed in approximately 5% of the 7,500 cases studied, but that such motions were successful in only 0.7% of all these cases. The study also shows that only 0.6% of all cases resulted in acquittals because evidence had been excluded. In the GAO study, suppression motions were filed in 10.5% of all federal criminal cases surveyed, but of the motions filed, approximately 80–90% were denied. Evidence was actually excluded in only 1.3% of the cases studied, and only 0.7% of all cases resulted in acquittals or dismissals after evidence was excluded. And in another study based on data from cases during 1978 and 1979 in San Diego and Jacksonville, it was shown that only 1% of all cases resulting in nonconviction were caused by illegal searches.

* * *

If the overall educational effect of the exclusionary rule is considered, application of the rule to even those situations in which individual police officers have acted on the basis of a reasonable but mistaken belief that their conduct was authorized can still be expected to have a considerable long-term deterrent effect. If evidence is consistently excluded in these circumstances, police departments will surely be prompted to instruct their officers to devote greater care and attention to providing sufficient information to establish probable cause when applying for a warrant, and to review with some attention the form of the warrant that they have been issued, rather than automatically assuming that whatever document the magistrate has signed will necessarily comport with Fourth Amendment requirements.

After today's decisions, however, that institutional incentive will be lost. Indeed, the Court's "reasonable mistake" exception to the exclusionary rule will tend to put a premium on police ignorance of the law. Armed with the assurance provided by today's decisions that evidence will always be admissible whenever an officer has "reasonably" relied upon a warrant, police departments will be encouraged to train officers that if a warrant has simply been signed, it is reasonable, without more, to rely on it. Since in close cases there will no longer be any incentive to err on the side of constitutional behavior, police would have every reason to adopt a "let's-wait-until-it's-decided" approach in situations in which there is a question about a warrant's validity or the basis for its issuance.

Although the Court brushes these concerns aside, a host of grave consequences can be expected to result from its decision to carve this new exception out of the exclusionary rule. A chief consequence of today's decisions will be to convey a clear and unambiguous message to magistrates that their decisions to issue warrants are now insulated from subsequent judicial review. Creation of this new exception for good-faith reliance upon a warrant implicitly tells magistrates that they need not take much care in reviewing warrant applications, since their mistakes will from now on have virtually no consequence: If their decision to issue a warrant was correct, the evidence will be admitted; if their decision was incorrect but the police relied in good faith on the warrant, the evidence will also be admitted. Inevitably, the care and attention devoted to such an inconsequential chore will dwindle. Although the Court is correct to note that magistrates do not share the same stake in the outcome of a criminal case as the police, they nevertheless need to appreciate that their role is of some moment in order to continue performing the important task of carefully reviewing warrant applications. Today's decisions effectively remove that incentive.

After today's decisions, there will little reason for reviewing courts to conduct such a conscientious review; rather, these courts will be more likely to focus simply on the question of police good faith. Despite the Court's confident prediction that such review will continue to be conducted, it is difficult to believe that busy courts faced with heavy dockets will take the time to render essentially advisory opinions concerning the constitutionality of the magistrate's decision before considering the officer's good faith.

* * *

IV

When the public, as it quite properly has done in the past as well as in the present, demands that those in government increase their efforts to combat crime, it is all too easy for those government officials to seek expedient solutions. In contrast to such costly and difficult measures as building more prisons, improving law enforcement methods, or hiring more prosecutors and judges to relieve the overburdened court systems in the country's metropolitan areas, the relaxation of Fourth Amendment standards seems a tempting, costless means of meeting the public's demand for better law enforcement. In the long run, however, we as a society pay a heavy price for such expediency, because as Justice Jackson observed, the rights guaranteed in the Fourth Amendment "are not mere second-class rights but belong in the catalog of indispensable freedoms." Once lost, such rights are difficult to recover. There is hope, however, that in time this or some later Court will restore these precious freedoms to their rightful place as a primary protection for our citizens against overreaching officialdom.

JUSTICE STEVENS, concurring in the judgment in No. 82-963 and dissenting in No. 82-1771.

* * *

The Court assumes that the searches in these cases violated the Fourth Amendment, yet refuses to apply the exclusionary rule because the Court concludes that it was "reasonable" for the police to conduct them. In my opinion an official search and seizure cannot be both "unreasonable" and "reasonable" at the same time. The doctrinal vice in the Court's holding is its failure to consider the separate purposes of the two prohibitory Clauses in the Fourth Amendment.

The first Clause prohibits unreasonable searches and seizures and the second prohibits the issuance of warrants that are not supported by probable cause or that do not particularly describe the place to be searched and the persons or things to be seized. We have, of course, repeatedly held that warrantless searches are presumptively unreasonable, and that there are only a few carefully delineated exceptions to that basic presumption. But when such an exception has been recognized, analytically we have necessarily concluded that the warrantless activity was not "unreasonable" within the meaning of the first Clause. Thus, any Fourth Amendment case may present two separate questions: whether the search was conducted pursuant to a warrant issued in accordance with the second Clause, and, if not, whether it was nevertheless "reasonable" within the meaning of the first. On these questions, the constitutional text requires that we speak with one voice. We cannot intelligibly assume, arguendo, that a search was constitutionally unreasonable but that the seized evidence is admissible because the same search was reasonable.

I

In No. 82-963, the Supreme Judicial Court of Massachusetts determined that a warrant which purported to authorize a search of respondent's home had been issued in violation of the Warrant Clause. In its haste to make new law, this Court does not tarry to consider this holding. Yet, as I will demonstrate, this holding is clearly wrong; I would reverse the judgment on that ground alone.

In No. 82-1771, there is also a substantial question whether the warrant complied with the Fourth Amendment. There was a strong dissent on the probable-cause issue when *Leon* was before the Court of Appeals, and that dissent has been given added force by this Court's intervening decision in *Illinois v. Gates*, 462 U.S. 213 (1983), which constituted a significant development in the law. It is probable, though admittedly not certain, that the Court of Appeals would now conclude that the warrant in *Leon* satisfied the Fourth Amendment if it were given the opportunity to reconsider the issue in the light of *Gates*. Adherence to our normal practice following the announcement of a new rule would therefore postpone, and probably obviate, the need for the promulgation of the broad new rule the Court announces today.

* * *

Judges, more than most, should understand the value of adherence to settled procedures. By adopting a set of fair procedures, and then adhering to them, courts of law ensure that justice is administered with an even hand. "These are subtle matters, for they concern the ingredients of what constitutes justice. Therefore, justice must satisfy the appearance of justice." Of course, this Court has a duty to face questions of constitutional law when necessary to the disposition of an actual case or controversy. *Marbury v. Madison*, 1 Cranch 137, 177 (1803). But when the Court goes beyond what is necessary to decide the case before it, it can only encourage the perception that it is pursuing its own notions of wise social policy, rather than adhering to its judicial role. I do not believe the Court should reach out to decide what is undoubtedly a profound question concerning the administration of criminal justice before assuring itself that this question is actually and of necessity presented by the concrete facts before the Court. Although it may appear that the Court's broad holding will serve the public interest in enforcing obedience to the rule of law, for my part, I remain firmly convinced that "the preservation of order in our communities will be best ensured by adherence to established and respected procedures."

* * *

III

Even if it be assumed that there was a technical violation of the particularity requirement in No. 82-963, it by no means follows that the "warrantless" search in that case was "unreasonable" within the meaning of the Fourth Amendment. For this search posed none of the dangers to which the Fourth Amendment is addressed. It was justified by a neutral magistrate's determination of probable cause and created no risk of a general search. It was eminently "reasonable."

In No. 82-1771, however, the Government now admits—at least for the tactical purpose of achieving what it regards as a greater benefit—that the substance, as well as the letter, of the Fourth Amendment was violated. The Court therefore assumes that the warrant in that case was not supported by probable cause, but refuses to suppress the evidence obtained thereby because it considers the police conduct to satisfy a "newfangled" nonconstitutional standard of reasonableness. Yet if the Court's assumption is correct—if there was no probable cause—it must follow that it was "unreasonable" for the authorities to make unheralded entries into and searches of private dwellings and automobiles. The Court's conclusion that such searches undertaken without probable cause can nevertheless be "reasonable" is totally without support in our Fourth Amendment jurisprudence.

* * *

The notion that a police officer's reliance on a magistrate's warrant is automatically appropriate is one the Framers of the Fourth Amendment would have vehemently rejected. The precise problem that the Amendment was intended to address was the unreasonable issuance of warrants. As we have often observed, the Amendment was actually motivated by the practice of issuing general warrants—warrants which did not satisfy the particularity and probable-cause requirements. The resentments which led to the Amendment were directed at the issuance of warrants unjustified by particularized evidence of wrongdoing. Those who sought to amend the Constitution to include a Bill of Rights repeatedly voiced the view that the evil which had to be addressed was the issuance of warrants on insufficient evidence. As Professor Taylor has written:

> [O]ur constitutional fathers were not concerned about warrantless searches, but about overreaching warrants. It is perhaps too much to say that they feared the warrant more than the search, but it is plain enough that the warrant was the prime object of their concern. Far from looking at the warrant as a protection against unreasonable searches, they saw it as an authority for unreasonable and oppressive searches . . . ."

In short, the Framers of the Fourth Amendment were deeply suspicious of warrants; in their minds the paradigm of an abusive search was the execution of a warrant not based on probable cause. The fact that colonial officers had magisterial authorization for their conduct when they engaged in general searches surely did not make their conduct "reasonable." The Court's view that it is consistent with our Constitution to adopt a rule that it is presumptively reasonable to rely on a defective warrant is the product of constitutional amnesia.

IV

* * *

The Court is of course correct that the exclusionary rule cannot deter when the authorities have no reason to know that their conduct is unconstitutional. But when probable cause is lacking, then by definition a reasonable person under the circumstances would not believe there is a fair likelihood that a search will produce evidence of a crime. Under such circumstances well-trained professionals must know that they are violating the Constitution. The Court's approach—which, in effect, encourages the police to seek a warrant even if they know the existence of probable cause is doubtful—can only lead to an increased number of constitutional violations.

* * *

Thus, "Courts which sit under our Constitution cannot and will not be made party to lawless invasions of the constitutional rights of citizens by permitting unhindered governmental use of the fruits of such invasions . . . ." As the Court correctly notes, we have refused to apply the exclusionary rule to collateral contexts in which its marginal efficacy is questionable; until today, however, every time the police have violated the applicable commands of the Fourth Amendment a court has been prepared to vindicate that Amendment by preventing the use of evidence so obtained in the prosecution's case in chief against those whose rights have been violated. Today, for the first time, this Court holds that although the Constitution has been violated, no court should do anything about it at any time and in any proceeding. In my judgment, the Constitution requires more. Courts simply cannot escape their responsibility for redressing constitutional violations if they admit evidence obtained through unreasonable searches and seizures, since the entire point of police conduct that violates the Fourth Amendment is to obtain evidence for use at trial. If such evidence is admitted, then the courts become not merely the final and necessary link in an unconstitutional chain of events, but its actual motivating force. "If the existing code does not permit district attorneys to have a hand in such dirty business it does not permit the judge to allow such iniquities to succeed." *Olmstead v. United States*, 277 U.S. 438, 470 (1928) (Holmes, J., dissenting). Nor should we so easily concede the existence of a constitutional violation for which there is no remedy. To do so is to convert a bill of Rights into an unenforced honor code that the police may follow in their discretion. The Constitution requires more; it requires a remedy. If the Court's new rule is to be followed, the Bill of Rights should be renamed.

It is of course true that the exclusionary rule exerts a high price—the loss of probative evidence of guilt. But that price is one courts have often been required to pay to serve important social goals. That price is also one the Fourth Amendment requires us to pay, assuming as we must that the Framers intended that its strictures "shall not be violated." For in all such cases, as Justice Stewart has observed, "the same extremely relevant evidence would not have been obtained had the police officer complied with the commands of the fourth amendment in the first place."

* * *

Points for Discussion

1. The Court holds here that when an officer acts in good-faith reliance on a facially valid warrant, application of the exclusionary rule is not appropriate. Part of the Court's reasoning is that magistrates, who are required by law to be neutral and detached from the process of law

enforcement, cannot be deterred by the threat of exclusion. How do the dissenters respond? Who has the better of the argument?

2. Issues of deterrence to one side, why do the dissenters believe that exclusion is appropriate in a case like this?

3. Prior to *Leon*, a defendant's right to be free from unreasonable searches was protected, first, at an *ex parte* proceeding at which a magistrate determined whether the police had probable cause to effect a search or seizure, and, second, at an adversary proceeding where a judge determined whether the magistrate's initial probable-cause determination was correct. After *Leon*, the second, adversarial proceeding is far less important because the search may be deemed constitutionally "reasonable" even if the magistrate's probable cause determination is overturned. After *Leon*, whom do warrants protect?

HERRING V. UNITED STATES

555 U.S. 135 (2009)

CHIEF JUSTICE ROBERTS delivered the opinion of the court.

The Fourth Amendment forbids "unreasonable searches and seizures," and this usually requires the police to have probable cause or a warrant before making an arrest. What if an officer reasonably believes there is an outstanding arrest warrant, but that belief turns out to be wrong because of a negligent bookkeeping error by another police employee? The parties here agree that the ensuing arrest is still a violation of the Fourth Amendment, but dispute whether contraband found during a search incident to that arrest must be excluded in a later prosecution.

Our cases establish that such suppression is not an automatic consequence of a Fourth Amendment violation. Instead, the question turns on the culpability of the police and the potential of exclusion to deter wrongful police conduct. Here the error was the result of isolated negligence attenuated from the arrest. We hold that in these circumstances the jury should not be barred from considering all the evidence.

I

On July 7, 2004, Investigator Mark Anderson learned that Bennie Dean Herring had driven to the Coffee County Sheriff's Department to retrieve something from his impounded truck. Herring was no stranger to law enforcement, and Anderson asked the county's warrant clerk, Sandy Pope, to check for any outstanding warrants for Herring's arrest. When she found none, Anderson asked Pope to check with Sharon Morgan, her counterpart in neighboring Dale County. After checking Dale County's computer database, Morgan replied that there was an active arrest warrant for Herring's failure to appear on a felony charge. Pope relayed the information to Anderson and asked Morgan to fax over a copy of the warrant as confirmation. Anderson and a deputy followed Herring as he left the impound lot, pulled him over, and arrested him. A search incident to the arrest revealed methamphetamine in Herring's pocket, and a pistol (which as a felon he could not possess) in his vehicle.

Herring was indicted in the District Court for the Middle District of Alabama for illegally possessing the gun and drugs, violations of 18 U.S.C. § 922(g)(1) and 21 U.S.C. § 844(a). He moved to suppress the evidence on the ground that his initial arrest had been illegal because the warrant had been rescinded. The Magistrate Judge recommended denying the motion because the arresting officers had acted in a good-faith belief that the warrant was still outstanding. Thus, even if there were a Fourth Amendment violation, there was "no reason to believe that application of the exclusionary rule here would deter the occurrence of any future mistakes." The District Court adopted the Magistrate Judge's recommendation and the Court of Appeals for the Eleventh Circuit affirmed.

There had, however, been a mistake about the warrant. The Dale County sheriff's computer records are supposed to correspond to actual arrest warrants, which the office also maintains. But when Morgan went to the files to retrieve the actual warrant to fax to Pope, Morgan was unable to find it. She called a court clerk and learned that the warrant had been recalled five months earlier. Normally when a warrant is recalled the court clerk's office or a judge's chambers calls Morgan, who enters the information in the sheriff's computer database and disposes of the physical copy. For whatever reason, the information about the recall of the warrant for Herring did not appear in the database. Morgan immediately called Pope to alert her to the mixup, and Pope contacted Anderson over a secure radio. This all unfolded in 10 to 15 minutes, but Herring had already been arrested and found with the gun and drugs, just a few hundred yards from the sheriff's office.

* * *

II

When a probable-cause determination was based on reasonable but mistaken assumptions, the person subjected to a search or seizure has not necessarily been the victim of a constitutional violation. The very phrase "probable cause" confirms that the Fourth Amendment does not demand all possible precision. And whether the error can be traced to a mistake by a state actor or some other source may bear on the analysis. For purposes of deciding this case, however, we accept the parties' assumption that there was a Fourth Amendment violation. The issue is whether the exclusionary rule should be applied.

* * *

B

1. The fact that a Fourth Amendment violation occurred—*i.e.,* that a search or arrest was unreasonable—does not necessarily mean that the exclusionary rule applies. Indeed, exclusion "has always been our last resort, not our first impulse," *Hudson v. Michigan,* 547 U.S. 586, 591 (2006), and our precedents establish important principles that constrain application of the exclusionary rule.

First, the exclusionary rule is not an individual right and applies only where it "result[s] in appreciable deterrence." We have repeatedly rejected the argument that exclusion is a necessary consequence of a Fourth Amendment violation. Instead we have focused on the efficacy of the rule in deterring Fourth Amendment violations in the future.

In addition, the benefits of deterrence must outweigh the costs. "We have never suggested that the exclusionary rule must apply in every circumstance in which it might provide marginal deterrence." "[T]o the extent that application of the exclusionary rule could provide some incremental deterrent, that possible benefit must be weighed against [its] substantial social costs." *Illinois v. Krull,* 480 U.S. 340, 352–353 (1987). The principal cost of applying the rule is, of course, letting guilty and possibly dangerous defendants go free—something that "offends basic concepts of the criminal justice system." "[T]he rule's costly toll upon truth-seeking and law enforcement objectives presents a high obstacle for those urging [its] application."

* * *

2. The extent to which the exclusionary rule is justified by these deterrence principles varies with the culpability of the law enforcement conduct. As we said in *Leon,* "an assessment of the flagrancy of the police misconduct constitutes an important step in the calculus" of applying the exclusionary rule. 468 U.S., at 911. Similarly, in *Krull* we elaborated that "evidence should be suppressed 'only if it can be said that the law enforcement officer had knowledge, or may properly be charged with knowledge, that the search was unconstitutional under the Fourth Amendment.' "

* * *

Indeed, the abuses that gave rise to the exclusionary rule featured intentional conduct that was patently unconstitutional. In *Weeks,* 232 U.S. 383, a foundational exclusionary rule case, the officers had broken into the defendant's home (using a key shown to them by a neighbor), confiscated incriminating papers, then returned again with a U.S. Marshal to confiscate even more. Not only did they have no search warrant, which the Court held was required, but they could not have gotten one had they tried. They were so lacking in sworn and particularized information that "not even an order of court would have justified such procedure." *Silverthorne*

Lumber Co. v. United States, 251 U.S. 385 (1920), on which petitioner repeatedly relies, was similar; federal officials "without a shadow of authority" went to the defendants' office and "made a clean sweep" of every paper they could find. Even the Government seemed to acknowledge that the "seizure was an outrage."

Equally flagrant conduct was at issue in *Mapp v. Ohio,* 367 U.S. 643 (1961), which overruled *Wolf v. Colorado,* 338 U.S. 25 (1949), and extended the exclusionary rule to the States. Officers forced open a door to Ms. Mapp's house, kept her lawyer from entering, brandished what the court concluded was a false warrant, then forced her into handcuffs and canvassed the house for obscenity. An error that arises from nonrecurring and attenuated negligence is thus far removed from the core concerns that led us to adopt the rule in the first place. And in fact since *Leon,* we have never applied the rule to exclude evidence obtained in violation of the Fourth Amendment, where the police conduct was no more intentional or culpable than this.

3. To trigger the exclusionary rule, police conduct must be sufficiently deliberate that exclusion can meaningfully deter it, and sufficiently culpable that such deterrence is worth the price paid by the justice system. As laid out in our cases, the exclusionary rule serves to deter deliberate, reckless, or grossly negligent conduct, or in some circumstances recurring or systemic negligence. The error in this case does not rise to that level.

Our decision in *Franks v. Delaware,* 438 U.S. 154 (1978), provides an analogy. In *Franks,* we held that police negligence in obtaining a warrant did not even rise to the level of a Fourth Amendment violation, let alone meet the more stringent test for triggering the exclusionary rule. We held that the Constitution allowed defendants, in some circumstances, "to challenge the truthfulness of factual statements made in an affidavit supporting the warrant," even after the warrant had issued. If those false statements were necessary to the Magistrate Judge's probable-cause determination, the warrant would be "voided." But we did not find all false statements relevant: "There must be allegations of deliberate falsehood or of reckless disregard for the truth," and "[a]llegations of negligence or innocent mistake are insufficient."

Both this case and *Franks* concern false information provided by police. Under *Franks,* negligent police miscommunications in the course of acquiring a warrant do not provide a basis to rescind a warrant and render a search or arrest invalid. Here, the miscommunications occurred in a different context—after the warrant had been issued and recalled-but that fact should not require excluding the evidence obtained.

The pertinent analysis of deterrence and culpability is objective, not an "inquiry into the subjective awareness of arresting officers." We have already held that "our good-faith inquiry is confined to the objectively ascertainable question whether a reasonably well trained officer would have known that the search was illegal" in light of "all of the circumstances." These circumstances frequently include a particular officer's knowledge and experience, but that does not make the test any more subjective than the one for probable cause, which looks to an officer's knowledge and experience but not his subjective intent.

4. We do not suggest that all recordkeeping errors by the police are immune from the exclusionary rule. In this case, however, the conduct at issue was not so objectively culpable as to require exclusion. In *Leon* we held that "the marginal or nonexistent benefits produced by suppressing evidence obtained in objectively reasonable reliance on a subsequently invalidated search warrant cannot justify the substantial costs of exclusion." The same is true when evidence is obtained in objectively reasonable reliance on a subsequently recalled warrant.

If the police have been shown to be reckless in maintaining a warrant system, or to have knowingly made false entries to lay the groundwork for future false arrests, exclusion would certainly be justified under our cases should such misconduct cause a Fourth Amendment violation. We said as much in *Leon,* explaining that an officer could not "obtain a warrant on the basis of a 'bare bones' affidavit and then rely on colleagues who are ignorant of the circumstances under which the warrant was obtained to conduct the search." Petitioner's fears that our decision will cause police departments to deliberately keep their officers ignorant are thus unfounded.

* * *

Petitioner's claim that police negligence automatically triggers suppression cannot be squared with the principles underlying the exclusionary rule, as they have been explained in our cases. In light of our repeated holdings that the deterrent effect of suppression must be substantial and outweigh any harm to the justice system, we conclude that when police mistakes are the result of negligence such as that described here, rather than systemic error or reckless disregard of constitutional requirements, any marginal deterrence does not "pay its way." In such a case, the criminal should not "go free because the constable has blundered."

JUSTICE GINSBURG, with whom JUSTICE STEVENS, JUSTICE SOUTER, and JUSTICE BREYER join, dissenting.

Petitioner Bennie Dean Herring was arrested, and subjected to a search incident to his arrest, although no warrant was outstanding against him, and the police lacked probable cause to believe he was engaged in criminal activity. The arrest and ensuing search therefore violated Herring's Fourth Amendment right "to be secure . . . against unreasonable searches and seizures." The Court of Appeals so determined, and the Government does not contend otherwise. The exclusionary rule provides redress for Fourth Amendment violations by placing the government in the position it would have been in had there been no unconstitutional arrest and search. The rule thus strongly encourages police compliance with the Fourth Amendment in the future. The Court, however, holds the rule inapplicable because careless recordkeeping by the police—not flagrant or deliberate misconduct—accounts for Herring's arrest.

I would not so constrict the domain of the exclusionary rule and would hold the rule dispositive of this case: "[I]f courts are to have any power to discourage [police] error of [the kind here at issue], it must be through the application of the exclusionary rule." The unlawful search in this case was contested in court because the police found methamphetamine in Herring's pocket and a pistol in his truck. But the "most serious impact" of the Court's holding will be on innocent persons "wrongfully arrested based on erroneous information [carelessly maintained] in a computer data base."

I

A warrant for Herring's arrest was recalled in February 2004, apparently because it had been issued in error. The warrant database for the Dale County Sheriff's Department, however, does not automatically update to reflect such changes. A member of the Dale County Sheriff's Department—whom the parties have not identified—returned the hard copy of the warrant to the County Circuit Clerk's office, but did not correct the Department's database to show that the warrant had been recalled. The erroneous entry for the warrant remained in the database, undetected, for five months.

On a July afternoon in 2004, Herring came to the Coffee County Sheriff's Department to retrieve his belongings from a vehicle impounded in the Department's lot. Investigator Mark Anderson, who was at the Department that day, knew Herring from prior interactions: Herring had told the district attorney, among others, of his suspicion that Anderson had been involved in the killing of a local teenager, and Anderson had pursued Herring to get him to drop the accusations. Informed that Herring was in the impoundment lot, Anderson asked the Coffee County warrant clerk whether there was an outstanding warrant for Herring's arrest. The clerk, Sandy Pope, found no warrant.

Anderson then asked Pope to call the neighboring Dale County Sheriff's Department to inquire whether a warrant to arrest Herring was outstanding there. Upon receiving Pope's phone call, Sharon Morgan, the warrant clerk for the Dale County Department, checked her computer database. As just recounted, that Department's database preserved an error. Morgan's check therefore showed—incorrectly—an active warrant for Herring's arrest. Morgan gave the misinformation to Pope, who relayed it to Investigator Anderson. Armed with the report that a warrant existed, Anderson promptly arrested Herring and performed an incident search minutes before detection of the error.

* * *

II

A

* * *

The Court's discussion invokes a view of the exclusionary rule famously held by renowned jurists Henry J. Friendly and Benjamin Nathan Cardozo. Over 80 years ago, Cardozo, then seated on the New York Court of Appeals, commented critically on the federal exclusionary rule, which had not yet been applied to the States. He suggested that in at least some cases the rule exacted too high a price from the criminal justice system. In words often quoted, Cardozo questioned whether the criminal should "go free because the constable has blundered."

Judge Friendly later elaborated on Cardozo's query. "The sole reason for exclusion," Friendly wrote, "is that experience has demonstrated this to be the only effective method for deterring the police from violating the Constitution." He thought it excessive, in light of the rule's aim to deter police conduct, to require exclusion when the constable had merely "blundered"—when a police officer committed a technical error in an on-the-spot judgment or made a "slight and unintentional miscalculation." As the Court recounts, Judge Friendly suggested that deterrence of police improprieties could be "sufficiently accomplished" by confining the rule to "evidence obtained by flagrant or deliberate violation of rights."

B

Others have described "a more majestic conception" of the Fourth Amendment and its adjunct, the exclusionary rule. Protective of the fundamental "right of the people to be secure in their persons, houses, papers, and effects," the Amendment "is a constraint on the power of the sovereign, not merely on some of its agents." I share that vision of the Amendment.

* * *

Beyond doubt, a main objective of the rule "is to deter—to compel respect for the constitutional guaranty in the only effectively available way—by removing the incentive to disregard it." But the rule also serves other important purposes: It "enabl[es] the judiciary to avoid the taint of partnership in official lawlessness," and it "assur[es] the people—all potential victims of unlawful government conduct—that the government would not profit from its lawless behavior, thus minimizing the risk of seriously undermining popular trust in government."

The exclusionary rule, it bears emphasis, is often the only remedy effective to redress a Fourth Amendment violation. Civil liability will not lie for "the vast majority of [F]ourth [A]mendment violations—the frequent infringements motivated by commendable zeal, not condemnable malice." Criminal prosecutions or administrative sanctions against the offending officers and injunctive relief against widespread violations are an even farther cry.

III

The Court maintains that Herring's case is one in which the exclusionary rule could have scant deterrent effect and therefore would not "pay its way." I disagree.

A

The exclusionary rule, the Court suggests, is capable of only marginal deterrence when the misconduct at issue is merely careless, not intentional or reckless. The suggestion runs counter to a foundational premise of tort law—that liability for negligence, *i.e.*, lack of due care, creates an incentive to act with greater care. The Government so acknowledges.

That the mistake here involved the failure to make a computer entry hardly means that application of the exclusionary rule would have minimal value. "Just as the risk of *respondeat superior* liability encourages employers to supervise . . . their employees' conduct [more carefully], so the risk of exclusion of evidence encourages policymakers and systems managers to monitor the performance of the systems they install and the personnel employed to operate those systems."

Consider the potential impact of a decision applying the exclusionary rule in this case. As earlier observed, the record indicates that there is no electronic connection between the warrant database of the Dale County Sheriff's Department and that of the County Circuit Clerk's office, which is located in the basement of the same building. When a warrant is recalled, one of the "many different people that have access to th[e] warrants," must find the hard copy of the warrant in the "two or three different places" where the department houses warrants, return it to the Clerk's office, and manually update the Department's database. The record reflects no routine practice of checking the database for accuracy, and the failure to remove the entry for Herring's warrant was not discovered until Investigator Anderson sought to pursue Herring five months later. Is it not altogether obvious that the Department could take further precautions to ensure the integrity of its database? The Sheriff's Department "is in a position to remedy the situation and might well do so if the exclusionary rule is there to remove the incentive to do otherwise."

B

Is the potential deterrence here worth the costs it imposes? In light of the paramount importance of accurate recordkeeping in law enforcement, I would answer yes, and next explain why, as I see it, Herring's motion presents a particularly strong case for suppression.

Electronic databases form the nervous system of contemporary criminal justice operations. In recent years, their breadth and influence have dramatically expanded. Police today can access databases that include not only the updated National Crime Information Center (NCIC), but also terrorist watchlists, the Federal Government's employee eligibility system, and various commercial databases. Moreover, States are actively expanding information sharing between jurisdictions. As a result, law enforcement has an increasing supply of information within its easy electronic reach.

The risk of error stemming from these databases is not slim. Herring's *amici* warn that law enforcement databases are insufficiently monitored and often out of date. Government reports describe, for example, flaws in NCIC databases, terrorist watchlist databases, and databases associated with the Federal Government's employment eligibility verification system.

Inaccuracies in expansive, interconnected collections of electronic information raise grave concerns for individual liberty. "The offense to the dignity of the citizen who is arrested, handcuffed, and searched on a public street simply because some bureaucrat has failed to maintain an accurate computer data base" is evocative of the use of general warrants that so outraged the authors of our Bill of Rights.

C

The Court assures that "exclusion would certainly be justified" if "the police have been shown to be reckless in maintaining a warrant system, or to have knowingly made false entries to lay the groundwork for future false arrests." This concession provides little comfort.

First, by restricting suppression to bookkeeping errors that are deliberate or reckless, the majority leaves Herring, and others like him, with no remedy for violations of their constitutional rights. There can be no serious assertion that relief is available under 42 U.S.C. § 1983. The arresting officer would be sheltered by qualified immunity, and the police department itself is not liable for the negligent acts of its employees. Moreover, identifying the department employee who committed the error may be impossible.

Second, I doubt that police forces already possess sufficient incentives to maintain up-to-date records. The Government argues that police have no desire to send officers out on arrests unnecessarily, because arrests consume resources and place officers in danger. The facts of this case do not fit that description of police motivation. Here the officer wanted to arrest Herring and consulted the Department's records to legitimate his predisposition.[6]

---

[6] It has been asserted that police departments have become sufficiently "professional" that they do not need external deterrence to avoid Fourth Amendment violations. But professionalism is a sign of the exclusionary rule's efficacy—not of its superfluity.

Third, even when deliberate or reckless conduct is afoot, the Court's assurance will often be an empty promise: How is an impecunious defendant to make the required showing? If the answer is that a defendant is entitled to discovery (and if necessary, an audit of police databases), then the Court has imposed a considerable administrative burden on courts and law enforcement.[7]

IV

Negligent recordkeeping errors by law enforcement threaten individual liberty, are susceptible to deterrence by the exclusionary rule, and cannot be remedied effectively through other means. Such errors present no occasion to further erode the exclusionary rule. The rule "is needed to make the Fourth Amendment something real; a guarantee that does not carry with it the exclusion of evidence obtained by its violation is a chimera." In keeping with the rule's "core concerns," suppression should have attended the unconstitutional search in this case.

JUSTICE BREYER, with whom JUSTICE SOUTER joins, dissenting.

I agree with Justice Ginsburg and join her dissent. I write separately to note one additional supporting factor that I believe important. In *Arizona v. Evans,* 514 U.S. 1 (1995), we held that recordkeeping errors made by a court clerk do not trigger the exclusionary rule, so long as the police reasonably relied upon the court clerk's recordkeeping. The rationale for our decision was premised on a distinction between judicial errors and police errors, and we gave several reasons for recognizing that distinction.

* * *

Points for Discussion

1. How much does *Herring* change the state of the law? The Court had already held that exclusion is inappropriate when officers rely in good faith on a facially valid warrant, on a court clerk's representations, or on a properly enacted statute later found to be unconstitutional.

2. The majority at least implies that—unlike intentional misconduct, recklessness, or systemic negligence—"simple" negligence cannot be deterred through the threat of exclusion. As the dissent notes, this idea "runs counter to a fundamental premise of tort law—that liability for negligence, i.e., lack of due care, creates an incentive to act with greater care."

3. Justice Ginsburg's dissent resurrects rationales for the exclusionary rule that had not been seriously entertained by the Court for years. Why was

[7] It is not clear how the Court squares its focus on deliberate conduct with its recognition that application of the exclusionary rule does not require inquiry into the mental state of the police. See *Whren v. United States,* 517 U.S. 806, 812–813 (1996).

it necessary for the dissent to invoke purposes other than police deterrence in this case?

4. Justice Ginsburg's dissent also speaks of providing incentives for agencies to maintain accurate databases. Deterrence, however, is frequently used to refer only to preventing deliberate constitutional violations by individual officers. Which conception of "deterrence" is more faithful to the purpose of the Fourth Amendment?

DAVIS V. UNITED STATES

564 U.S. 229 (2011)

JUSTICE ALITO delivered the opinion of the court.

The Fourth Amendment protects the right to be free from "unreasonable searches and seizures," but it is silent about how this right is to be enforced. To supplement the bare text, this Court created the exclusionary rule, a deterrent sanction that bars the prosecution from introducing evidence obtained by way of a Fourth Amendment violation. The question here is whether to apply this sanction when the police conduct a search in compliance with binding precedent that is later overruled. Because suppression would do nothing to deter police misconduct in these circumstances, and because it would come at a high cost to both the truth and the public safety, we hold that searches conducted in objectively reasonable reliance on binding appellate precedent are not subject to the exclusionary rule.

I

* * *

B

The search at issue in this case took place a full two years before this Court announced its new rule in [*Arizona v. Gant*, 556 U.S. 332 (2009)]. On an April evening in 2007, police officers in Greenville, Alabama, conducted a routine traffic stop that eventually resulted in the arrests of driver Stella Owens (for driving while intoxicated) and passenger Willie Davis (for giving a false name to police). The police handcuffed both Owens and Davis, and they placed the arrestees in the back of separate patrol cars. The police then searched the passenger compartment of Owens's vehicle and found a revolver inside Davis's jacket pocket.

* * *

While Davis's appeal was pending, this Court decided *Gant*. The Eleventh Circuit, in the opinion below, applied *Gant*'s new rule and held that the vehicle search incident to Davis's arrest "violated [his] Fourth Amendment rights." As for whether this constitutional violation warranted suppression, the Eleventh Circuit viewed that as a separate issue that turned on "the potential of exclusion to deter wrongful police conduct." The court concluded that "penalizing the arresting officer" for following binding appellate precedent would do nothing to "deter . . . Fourth Amendment violations." It therefore declined to apply the exclusionary rule and affirmed Davis's conviction. We granted certiorari.

II

The Fourth Amendment protects the "right of the people to be secure in their persons, houses, papers, and effects, against unreasonable searches and seizures." The Amendment says nothing about suppressing evidence obtained in violation of this command. That rule—the exclusionary rule—is a "prudential" doctrine, created by this Court to "compel respect for the constitutional guaranty." *Elkins v. United States,* 364 U.S. 206, 217 (1960). Exclusion is "not a personal constitutional right," nor is it designed to "redress the injury" occasioned by an unconstitutional search. *Stone v. Powell,* 428 U.S. 465, 486 (1976). The rule's sole purpose, we have repeatedly held, is to deter future Fourth Amendment violations. Our cases have thus limited the rule's operation to situations in which this purpose is "thought most efficaciously served." Where suppression fails to yield "appreciable deterrence," exclusion is "clearly . . . unwarranted."

Real deterrent value is a "necessary condition for exclusion," but it is not "a sufficient" one. *Hudson v. Michigan,* 547 U.S. 586, 596 (2006). The analysis must also account for the "substantial social costs" generated by the rule. [*United States v. Leon,* 468 U.S. 897, 907 (1984)]. Exclusion exacts a heavy toll on both the judicial system and society at large. It almost always requires courts to ignore reliable, trustworthy evidence bearing on guilt or innocence. And its bottom-line effect, in many cases, is to suppress the truth and set the criminal loose in the community without punishment. Our cases hold that society must swallow this bitter pill when necessary, but only as a "last resort." For exclusion to be appropriate, the deterrence benefits of suppression must outweigh its heavy costs.

Admittedly, there was a time when our exclusionary-rule cases were not nearly so discriminating in their approach to the doctrine. "Expansive dicta" in several decisions suggested that the rule was a self-executing mandate implicit in the Fourth Amendment itself. As late as our 1971 decision in *Whiteley v. Warden, Wyo. State Penitentiary,* 401 U.S. 560, 568–569, the Court "treated identification of a Fourth Amendment violation as synonymous with application of the exclusionary rule." *Arizona v. Evans,* 514 U.S. 1, 13 (1995). In time, however, we came to acknowledge the exclusionary rule for what it undoubtedly is—a "judicially created remedy" of this Court's own making. We abandoned the old, "reflexive" application of the doctrine, and imposed a more rigorous weighing of its costs and deterrence benefits. In a line of cases beginning with *United States v. Leon,* we also recalibrated our cost-benefit analysis in exclusion cases to focus the inquiry on the "flagrancy of the police misconduct" at issue.

The basic insight of the *Leon* line of cases is that the deterrence benefits of exclusion "var[y] with the culpability of the law enforcement conduct" at issue. *Herring,* 555 U.S., at 143. When the police exhibit "deliberate," "reckless," or "grossly negligent" disregard for Fourth Amendment rights, the deterrent value of exclusion is strong and tends to outweigh the resulting costs. But when the police act with an objectively "reasonable good-faith belief" that their conduct is lawful, or when their conduct involves only simple, "isolated" negligence, the " 'deterrence rationale loses much of its force,' " and exclusion cannot "pay its way."

The Court has over time applied this "good-faith" exception across a range of cases. *Leon* itself, for example, held that the exclusionary rule does not apply when the police conduct a search in "objectively reasonable reliance" on a warrant later held invalid. The error in such a case rests with the issuing magistrate, not the police officer, and "punish[ing] the errors of judges" is not the office of the exclusionary rule.

Other good-faith cases have sounded a similar theme. *Illinois v. Krull,* 480 U.S. 340 (1987), extended the good-faith exception to searches conducted in reasonable reliance on subsequently invalidated statutes. In *Arizona v. Evans*, the Court applied the good-faith exception in a case where the police reasonably relied on erroneous information concerning an arrest warrant in a database maintained by judicial employees. Most recently, in *Herring v. United States,* we extended *Evans* in a case where *police* employees erred in maintaining records in a warrant database. "[I]solated," "nonrecurring" police negligence, we determined, lacks the culpability required to justify the harsh sanction of exclusion.

III

The question in this case is whether to apply the exclusionary rule when the police conduct a search in objectively reasonable reliance on binding judicial precedent. At the time of the search at issue here, we had not yet decided *Arizona v. Gant*, and the Eleventh Circuit had interpreted our decision in *New York v. Belton,* 453 U.S. 454 [(1981)], to establish a bright-line rule authorizing the search of a vehicle's passenger compartment incident to a recent occupant's arrest. . . .

Under our exclusionary-rule precedents, this acknowledged absence of police culpability dooms Davis's claim. Police practices trigger the harsh sanction of exclusion only when they are deliberate enough to yield "meaningful" deterrence, and culpable enough to be "worth the price paid by the justice system." *Herring,* 555 U.S., at 144. The conduct of the officers here was neither of these things. The officers who conducted the search did not violate Davis's Fourth Amendment rights deliberately, recklessly, or with gross negligence. Nor does this case involve any "recurring or systemic negligence" on the part of law enforcement. The police acted in strict compliance with binding precedent, and their behavior was not wrongful.

Unless the exclusionary rule is to become a strict-liability regime, it can have no application in this case.

* * *

About all that exclusion would deter in this case is conscientious police work. Responsible law-enforcement officers will take care to learn "what is required of them" under Fourth Amendment precedent and will conform their conduct to these rules. But by the same token, when binding appellate precedent specifically *authorizes* a particular police practice, well-trained officers will and should use that tool to fulfill their crime-detection and public-safety responsibilities. An officer who conducts a search in reliance on binding appellate precedent does no more than " 'act as a reasonable officer would and should act' " under the circumstances. *Leon,* 468 U.S., at 920. The deterrent effect of exclusion in such a case can only be to discourage the officer from " 'doing his duty.' "

That is not the kind of deterrence the exclusionary rule seeks to foster. We have stated before, and we reaffirm today, that the harsh sanction of exclusion "should not be applied to deter objectively reasonable law enforcement activity." Evidence obtained during a search conducted in reasonable reliance on binding precedent is not subject to the exclusionary rule.

IV

* * *

A

* * *

The dissent and Davis argue that applying the good-faith exception in this case is "incompatible" with our retroactivity precedent under [*Griffith v. Kentucky,* 479 U.S. 314 (1987)]. We think this argument conflates what are two distinct doctrines.

Our retroactivity jurisprudence is concerned with whether, as a categorical matter, a new rule is available on direct review as a *potential* ground for relief. Retroactive application under *Griffith* lifts what would otherwise be a categorical bar to obtaining redress for the government's violation of a newly announced constitutional rule. Retroactive application does not, however, determine what "appropriate remedy" (if any) the defendant should obtain. Remedy is a separate, analytically distinct issue. As a result, the retroactive application of a new rule of substantive Fourth Amendment law *raises* the question whether a suppression remedy applies; it does not answer that question.

When this Court announced its decision in *Gant,* Davis's conviction had not yet become final on direct review. *Gant* therefore applies retroactively to this case. Davis may invoke its newly announced rule of substantive Fourth Amendment law as a basis for seeking relief. The question, then, becomes one of remedy, and on that issue Davis seeks application of the exclusionary rule. But exclusion of evidence does not automatically follow from the fact that a Fourth Amendment violation occurred. The remedy is subject to exceptions and applies only where its "purpose is effectively advanced."

The dissent and Davis recognize that at least some of the established exceptions to the exclusionary rule limit its availability in cases involving new Fourth Amendment rules. Suppression would thus be inappropriate, the dissent and Davis acknowledge, if the inevitable-discovery exception were applicable in this case. The good-faith exception, however, is no less an established limit on the *remedy* of exclusion than is inevitable discovery. Its application here neither contravenes *Griffith* nor denies retroactive effect to *Gant*.

* * *

B

Davis also contends that applying the good-faith exception to searches conducted in reliance on binding precedent will stunt the development of Fourth Amendment law. With no possibility of suppression, criminal defendants will have no incentive, Davis maintains, to request that courts overrule precedent.

1

This argument is difficult to reconcile with our modern understanding of the role of the exclusionary rule. We have never held that facilitating the overruling of precedent is a relevant consideration in an exclusionary-rule case. Rather, we have said time and again that the *sole* purpose of the exclusionary rule is to deter misconduct by law enforcement.

* * *

2

And in any event, applying the good-faith exception in this context will not prevent judicial reconsideration of prior Fourth Amendment precedents. In most instances, as in this case, the precedent sought to be challenged will be a decision of a Federal Court of Appeals or State Supreme Court. But a good-faith exception for objectively reasonable reliance on binding precedent will not prevent review and correction of such decisions. This Court reviews criminal convictions from 12 Federal Courts of Appeals, 50 state courts of last resort, and the District of Columbia Court of Appeals. If one or even many of these courts uphold a particular type of search or seizure, defendants in jurisdictions in which the question remains open will still have an undiminished incentive to litigate the issue. This Court can then grant certiorari, and the development of Fourth Amendment law will in no way be stunted.

Davis argues that Fourth Amendment precedents of *this* Court will be effectively insulated from challenge under a good-faith exception for reliance on appellate precedent. But this argument is overblown. For one thing, it is important to keep in mind that this argument applies to an exceedingly small set of cases. Decisions overruling this Court's Fourth Amendment precedents are rare. Indeed, it has been more than 40 years since the Court last handed down a decision of the type to which Davis refers. *Chimel v. California,* 395 U.S. 752 [(1969)] (overruling *United States v. Rabinowitz,* 339 U.S. 56 (1950), and *Harris v. United States,* 331 U.S. 145 (1947)). And even in those cases, Davis points out that no fewer than eight separate doctrines may preclude a defendant who successfully challenges an existing precedent from getting any relief. Moreover, as a practical matter, defense counsel in many cases will test this Court's Fourth Amendment precedents in the same way that *Belton* was tested in *Gant*—by arguing that the precedent is distinguishable.

At most, Davis's argument might suggest that—to prevent Fourth Amendment law from becoming ossified—the petitioner in a case that results in the overruling of one of this Court's Fourth Amendment precedents should be given the benefit of the victory by permitting the suppression of evidence in that one case. Such a result would undoubtedly be a windfall to this one random litigant. But the exclusionary rule is "not a personal constitutional right." *Stone,* 428 U.S., at 486. It is a "judicially created" sanction, specifically designed as a "windfall" remedy to deter future Fourth Amendment violations. The good-faith exception is a judicially created exception to this judicially created rule. Therefore, in a future case, we could, if necessary, recognize a limited exception to the good-faith exception for a defendant who obtains a judgment over-ruling one of our Fourth Amendment precedents.

In any event, even if some criminal defendants will be unable to challenge some precedents for the reason that Davis suggests, that provides no good reason for refusing to apply the good-faith exception. As noted, the exclusionary rule is not a personal right, and therefore the rights of these defendants will not be impaired. And because (at least in almost all instances) the precedent can be challenged by others, Fourth Amendment case law will not be insulated from reconsideration.

But this is not such a case. Davis did not secure a decision overturning a Supreme Court precedent; the police in his case reasonably relied on binding Circuit precedent. That sort of blameless police conduct, we hold, comes within the good-faith exception and is not properly subject to the exclusionary rule.

* * *

JUSTICE SOTOMAYOR, concurring in the judgment.

Under our precedents, the primary purpose of the exclusionary rule is "to deter future Fourth Amendment violations." Accordingly, we have held, application of the exclusionary rule is unwarranted when it " 'does not result in appreciable deterrence.' " *Arizona v. Evans,* 514 U.S. 1, 11, (1995). In the circumstances of this case, where "binding appellate precedent specifically *authorized* a particular police practice," in accord with the holdings of nearly every other court in the country—application of the exclusionary rule cannot reasonably be expected to yield appreciable deterrence. I am thus compelled to conclude that the exclusionary rule does not apply in this case and to agree with the Court's disposition.

This case does not present the markedly different question whether the exclusionary rule applies when the law governing the constitutionality of a particular search is unsettled. As we previously recognized in deciding whether to apply a Fourth Amendment holding retroactively, when police decide to conduct a search or seizure in the absence of case law (or other authority) specifically sanctioning such action, exclusion of the evidence obtained may deter Fourth Amendment violations:

> If, as the Government argues, all rulings resolving unsettled Fourth Amendment questions should be nonretroactive, then, in close cases, law enforcement officials would have little incentive to err on the side of constitutional behavior. Official awareness of the dubious constitutionality of a practice would be counterbalanced by official certainty that, so long as the Fourth Amendment law in the area remained unsettled, evidence obtained through the questionable practice would be excluded only in the one case definitively resolving the unsettled question.

United States v. Johnson, 457 U.S. 537, 561 (1982).

* * *

The dissent suggests that today's decision essentially answers those questions, noting that an officer who conducts a search in the face of unsettled precedent "is no more culpable than an officer who follows erroneous 'binding precedent.' " The Court does not address this issue. In my view, whether an officer's conduct can be characterized as "culpable" is not itself dispositive. We have never refused to apply the exclusionary rule where its application would appreciably deter Fourth Amendment violations on the mere ground that the officer's conduct could be characterized as nonculpable. Rather, an officer's culpability is relevant because it may inform the overarching inquiry whether exclusion would result in appreciable deterrence. Whatever we have said about culpability, the ultimate questions have always been, one, whether exclusion would result in appreciable deterrence and, two, whether the benefits of exclusion outweigh its costs.

As stated, whether exclusion would result in appreciable deterrence in the circumstances of this case is a different question from whether exclusion would appreciably deter Fourth Amendment violations when the governing law is unsettled. The Court's answer to the former question in this case thus does not resolve the latter one.

JUSTICE BREYER, with whom JUSTICE GINSBURG joins, dissenting.

In 2009, in *Arizona v. Gant,* 556 U.S. 332, this Court held that a police search of an automobile without a warrant violates the Fourth Amendment if the police have previously removed the automobile's occupants and placed them securely in a squad car. The present case involves these same circumstances, and it was pending on appeal when this Court decided *Gant*. Because *Gant* represents a "shift" in the Court's Fourth Amendment jurisprudence, we must decide *whether* and *how Gant*'s new rule applies here.

I

I agree with the Court about *whether Gant*'s new rule applies. It does apply. . . .

* * *

II

The Court goes on, however, to decide *how Gant*'s new rule will apply. And here it adds a fatal twist. While conceding that, like the search in *Gant,* this search violated the Fourth Amendment, it holds that, unlike Gant, this defendant is not entitled to a remedy. That is because the Court finds a new "good faith" exception which prevents application of the normal remedy for a Fourth Amendment violation, namely, suppression of the illegally seized evidence. Leaving Davis with a right but not a remedy, the Court "keep[s] the word of promise to our ear" but "break[s] it to our hope."

A

At this point I can no longer agree with the Court. A new "good faith" exception and this Court's retroactivity decisions are incompatible. For one thing, the Court's distinction between (1) retroactive application of a new rule and (2) availability of a remedy is highly artificial and runs counter to precedent. To determine that a new rule is retroactive *is* to determine that, at least in the normal case, there is a remedy. As we have previously said, the "source of a 'new rule' is the Constitution itself, not any judicial power to create new rules of law"; hence, "[w]hat we are actually determining when we assess the 'retroactivity' of a new rule is not the temporal scope of a newly announced right, but whether a violation of the right that occurred prior to the announcement of the new rule will entitle a criminal defendant to the relief sought." *Danforth v. Minnesota,* 552 U.S. 264, 271 (2008). The Court's "good faith" exception (unlike, say, inevitable discovery, a remedial doctrine that applies only upon occasion) creates "a categorical bar to obtaining redress" in *every* case pending when a precedent is overturned.

* * *

Of course, the Court may, as it suggests, avoid this unfairness by refusing to apply the exclusionary rule even to the defendant in the very case in which it announces a "new rule." But that approach would make matters worse. What would then happen in the lower courts? How would courts of appeals, for example, come to reconsider their prior decisions when other circuits' cases lead them to believe those decisions may be wrong? Why would a defendant seek to overturn any such decision? After all, if the (incorrect) circuit precedent is clear, then even if the defendant wins (on the constitutional question), he loses (on relief). To what extent then could this Court rely upon lower courts to work out Fourth Amendment differences among themselves—through circuit reconsideration of a precedent that other circuits have criticized?

B

Perhaps more important, the Court's rationale for creating its new "good faith" exception threatens to undermine well-settled Fourth Amendment law. The Court correctly says that pre-*Gant* Eleventh Circuit precedent had held that a *Gant*-type search was constitutional; hence the police conduct in this case, consistent with that precedent, was "innocent." But the Court then finds this fact sufficient to create a new "good faith" exception to the exclusionary rule. It reasons that the "sole purpose" of the exclusionary rule "is to deter future Fourth Amendment violations." Those benefits are sufficient to justify exclusion where "police exhibit deliberate, reckless, or grossly negligent disregard for Fourth Amendment rights." But those benefits do not justify exclusion where, as here, the police act with "simple, isolated negligence" or an "objectively reasonable good-faith belief that their conduct is lawful."

If the Court means what it says, what will happen to the exclusionary rule, a rule that the Court adopted nearly a century ago for federal courts and made applicable to state courts a half century ago through the Fourteenth Amendment? The Court has thought of that rule not as punishment for the individual officer or as reparation for the individual defendant but more generally as an effective way to secure enforcement of the Fourth Amendment's commands. This Court has deviated from the "suppression" norm in the name of "good faith" only a handful of times and in limited, atypical circumstances: where a magistrate has erroneously issued a warrant, *United States v. Leon,* 468 U.S. 897 (1984); where a database has erroneously informed police that they have a warrant, *Arizona v. Evans,* 514 U.S. 1 (1995), *Herring v. United States,* 555 U.S. 135 (2009); and where an unconstitutional statute purported to authorize the search, *Illinois v. Krull,* 480 U.S. 340 (1987).

The fact that such exceptions are few and far between is understandable. Defendants frequently move to suppress evidence on Fourth Amendment grounds. In many, perhaps most, of these instances the police, uncertain of how the Fourth Amendment applied to the particular factual circumstances they faced, will have acted in objective good faith. Yet, in a significant percentage of these instances, courts will find that the police were wrong. And, unless the police conduct falls into one of the exceptions previously noted, courts have required the suppression of the evidence seized.

But an officer who conducts a search that he believes complies with the Constitution but which, it ultimately turns out, falls just outside the Fourth Amendment's bounds is no more culpable than an officer who follows erroneous "binding precedent." Nor is an officer more culpable where circuit precedent is simply suggestive rather than "binding," where it only describes how to treat roughly analogous instances, or where it just does not exist. Thus, if the Court means what it now says, if it would place determinative weight upon the culpability of an individual officer's conduct, and if it would apply the exclusionary rule only where a Fourth Amendment violation was "deliberate, reckless, or grossly negligent," then the "good faith" exception will swallow the exclusionary rule. Indeed, our broad dicta in *Herring*—dicta the Court repeats and expands upon today—may already be leading lower courts in this direction. Today's decision will doubtless accelerate this trend.

Any such change (which may already be underway) would affect not "an exceedingly small set of cases," but a very large number of cases, potentially many thousands each year. And since the exclusionary rule is often the only sanction available for a Fourth Amendment violation, the Fourth Amendment would no longer protect ordinary Americans from "unreasonable searches and seizures." It would become a watered-down Fourth Amendment, offering its protection against only those searches and seizures that are *egregiously* unreasonable.

* * *

Points for Discussion

1. The majority insists that deterring police misconduct is the sole purpose for the Fourth Amendment exclusionary rule. Justice Sotomayor begins her concurrence by carefully noting that police deterrence is merely the "primary purpose of the exclusionary rule". Who is right? What other purposes might the exclusionary rule serve? What purposes does excluding evidence for Fifth and Sixth Amendment violations serve?

2. In the first paragraph of Section II of his dissent, Justice Breyer quotes (without citation) from *Macbeth*, act V, scene VII. At that moment in the play, Macduff has just informed Macbeth that Macduff was not "of woman

born" because he was delivered by Caesarian section. Macbeth realizes that the Three Witches' prophesy that "none of woman born / Shall harm Macbeth" was a bit of trickery, and he is annoyed that the Witches toyed with him:

> And be these juggling fiends no more believ'd,
>
> That palter with us in a double sense;
>
> That keep the word of promise to our ear,
>
> And break it to our hope.

In Shakespeare's time, the word "juggler" (which also appears in *A Midsummer Night's Dream* and *Hamlet*) referred to someone who prevaricates. Comparing the Justices in the majority to the Shakespeare's Witches allows Justice Breyer to indirectly but pointedly criticize their reasoning. Why might a judge in particular find this comparison to the Three Witches insulting? How fair is Justice Breyer's intimation?

6. USING SUPPRESSED EVIDENCE TO IMPEACH

When evidence is excluded, the federal government or the state must prove its case without so much as alluding to the existence of the tainted evidence. If the defendant chooses to testify during the defense case, however, he may offer an explanation of events that is inconsistent with or perhaps even contradicted by the suppressed physical evidence or statements. In that situation, the prosecution typically seeks to impeach the defendant with the suppressed evidence. Impeachment refers to the goal of any cross-examination—to show that the jury should not credit the witness's testimony because the witness is mistaken, distorting, misremembering, or lying. Whether excluded evidence can be used to impeach a defendant who chooses to testify depends on the rationale for excluding the evidence in the first place.

HARRIS V. NEW YORK

401 U.S. 222 (1971)

MR. CHIEF JUSTICE BURGER delivered the opinion of the court.

We granted the writ in this case to consider petitioner's claim that a statement made by him to police under circumstances rendering it inadmissible to establish the prosecution's case in chief under *Miranda v. Arizona*, 384 U.S. 436 (1966), may not be used to impeach his credibility.

The State of New York charged petitioner in a two-count indictment with twice selling heroin to an undercover police officer. At a subsequent jury trial the officer was the State's chief witness, and he testified as to details of the two sales. A second officer verified collateral details of the sales, and a third offered testimony about the chemical analysis of the heroin.

Petitioner took the stand in his own defense. He admitted knowing the undercover police officer but denied a sale on January 4, 1966. He admitted making a sale of contents of a glassine bag to the officer on January 6 but claimed it was baking powder and part of a scheme to defraud the purchaser.

On cross-examination petitioner was asked seriatim whether he had made specified statements to the police immediately following his arrest on January 7—statements that partially contradicted petitioner's direct testimony at trial. In response to the cross-examination, petitioner testified that he could not remember virtually any of the questions or answers recited by the prosecutor. At the request of petitioner's counsel the written statement from which the prosecutor had read questions and answers in his impeaching process was placed in the record for possible use on appeal; the statement was not shown to the jury.

The trial judge instructed the jury that the statements attributed to petitioner by the prosecution could be considered only in passing on petitioner's credibility and not as evidence of guilt. In closing summations both counsel argued the substance of the impeaching statements. The jury then found petitioner guilty on the second count of the indictment. The New York Court of Appeals affirmed in a per curiam opinion.

At trial the prosecution made no effort in its case in chief to use the statements allegedly made by petitioner, conceding that they were inadmissible under *Miranda v. Arizona*, 384 U.S. 436 (1966). The transcript of the interrogation used in the impeachment, but not given to the jury, shows that no warning of a right to appointed counsel was given before questions were put to petitioner when he was taken into custody. Petitioner makes no claim that the statements made to the police were coerced or involuntary.

* * *

Petitioner's testimony in his own behalf concerning the events of January 7 contrasted sharply with what he told the police shortly after his arrest. The impeachment process here undoubtedly provided valuable aid to the jury in assessing petitioner's credibility, and the benefits of this process should not be lost, in our view, because of the speculative possibility that impermissible police conduct will be encouraged thereby. Assuming that the exclusionary rule has a deterrent effect on proscribed police conduct, sufficient deterrence flows when the evidence in question is made unavailable to the prosecution in its case in chief.

Every criminal defendant is privileged to testify in his own defense, or to refuse to do so. But that privilege cannot be construed to include the right to commit perjury. Having voluntarily taken the stand, petitioner was under an obligation to speak truthfully and accurately, and the prosecution here did no more than utilize the traditional truth-testing devices of the adversary process. Had inconsistent statements been made by the accused to some third person, it could hardly be contended that the conflict could not be laid before the jury by way of cross-examination and impeachment.

The shield provided by *Miranda* cannot be perverted into a license to use perjury by way of a defense, free from the risk of confrontation with prior inconsistent utterances. We hold, therefore, that petitioner's credibility was appropriately impeached by use of his earlier conflicting statements.

MR. JUSTICE BLACK dissents.

MR. JUSTICE BRENNAN, with whom MR. JUSTICE DOUGLAS and MR. JUSTICE MARSHALL, join, dissenting.

It is conceded that the question-and-answer statement used to impeach petitioner's direct testimony was, under *Miranda v. Arizona*, 384 U.S. 436 (1966), constitutionally inadmissible as part of the State's direct case against petitioner. I think that the Constitution also denied the State the use of the statement on cross-examination to impeach the credibility of petitioner's testimony given in his own defense. . . .

* * *

The objective of deterring improper police conduct is only part of the larger objective of safeguarding the integrity of our adversary system. The "essential mainstay" of that system, *Miranda v. Arizona*, 384 U.S., at 460, is the privilege against self-incrimination, which for that reason has occupied a central place in our jurisprudence since before the Nation's birth. Moreover, "we may view the historical development of the privilege as one which groped for the proper scope of governmental power over the citizen. * * * All these policies point to one overriding thought: the constitutional foundation underlying the privilege is the respect a government * * * must accord to the dignity and integrity of its citizens." These values are plainly jeopardized if an exception against admission of tainted statements is made for those used for impeachment purposes. Moreover, it is monstrous that courts should aid or abet the law-breaking police officer. It is abiding truth that "(n)othing can destroy a government more quickly than its failure to observe its own laws, or worse, its disregard of the charter of its own existence." *Mapp v. Ohio*, 367 U.S. 643 (1961). Thus even to the extent that *Miranda* was aimed at deterring police practices in disregard of the Constitution, I fear that today's holding will seriously undermine the achievement of that objective. The Court today tells the police that they may freely interrogate an accused incommunicado and without counsel and know that although any statement they obtain in violation of Miranda cannot be used on the State's direct case, it may be introduced if the defendant has the temerity to testify in his own defense. This goes far toward undoing much of the progress made in conforming police methods to the Constitution.

Points for Discussion

1. *Harris* illustrates how every exclusionary rule creates a risk that the party benefitting from exclusion can then attempt to subvert the trial by presenting a defense that would be vitiated by the excluded evidence. In other words, exclusion opens the door for a defendant to mislead the jury. Just as with evidence excluded as violative of *Miranda*, evidence excluded under the Fourth Amendment can also be used to impeach. *See United States v. Havens*, 446 U.S. 620 (1980). The majority in *Harris* declares that *Miranda*'s shield cannot be wielded as a sword. What countervailing value is the Court protecting?

2. In *Doyle v. Ohio*, 426 U.S. 610 (1976), the Court considered whether a defendant's post-*Miranda* silence (as opposed to his statements) could be used to impeach him. Doyle took the stand and testified to an alternative explanation for his conduct that he had not given after being Mirandized upon arrest. The Court held by a vote of 6–3 that it violated due process for the prosecutor to impeach Doyle with the fact that he had not given this alternate explanation at the time. How is this conclusion consistent with *Harris*? If statements obtained in violation of *Miranda* can be used to impeach, why shouldn't a defendant's silence in the face of *Miranda*'s warnings be treated the same way?

KANSAS V. VENTRIS

556 U.S. 586 (2009)

JUSTICE SCALIA delivered the opinion of the court.

We address in this case the question whether a defendant's incriminating statement to a jailhouse informant, concededly elicited in violation of Sixth Amendment strictures, is admissible at trial to impeach the defendant's conflicting statement.

I

In the early hours of January 7, 2004, after two days of no sleep and some drug use, Rhonda Theel and respondent Donnie Ray Ventris reached an ill-conceived agreement to confront Ernest Hicks in his home. The couple testified that the aim of the visit was simply to investigate rumors that Hicks abused children, but the couple may have been inspired by the potential for financial gain: Theel had recently learned that Hicks carried large amounts of cash.

The encounter did not end well. One or both of the pair shot and killed Hicks with shots from a .38-caliber revolver, and the companions drove off in Hicks's truck with approximately $300 of his money and his cell phone. On receiving a tip from two friends of the couple who had helped transport them to Hicks's home, officers arrested Ventris and Theel and charged them with various crimes, chief among them murder and aggravated robbery. The State dropped the murder charge against Theel in exchange for her guilty plea to the robbery charge and her testimony identifying Ventris as the shooter.

Prior to trial, officers planted an informant in Ventris's holding cell, instructing him to "keep [his] ear open and listen" for incriminating statements. According to the informant, in response to his statement that Ventris appeared to have "something more serious weighing in on his mind," Ventris divulged that "[h]e'd shot this man in his head and in his chest" and taken "his keys, his wallet, about $350.00, and . . . a vehicle."

At trial, Ventris took the stand and blamed the robbery and shooting entirely on Theel. The government sought to call the informant, to testify to Ventris's prior contradictory statement; Ventris objected. The State conceded that there was "probably a violation" of Ventris's Sixth Amendment right to counsel but nonetheless argued that the statement was admissible for impeachment purposes because the violation "doesn't give the Defendant . . . a license to just get on the stand and lie." The trial court agreed and allowed the informant's testimony, but instructed the jury to "consider with caution" all testimony given in exchange for benefits from the State. The jury ultimately acquitted Ventris of felony murder and misdemeanor theft but returned a guilty verdict on the aggravated burglary and aggravated robbery counts.

* * *

II

* * *

A

Whether otherwise excluded evidence can be admitted for purposes of impeachment depends upon the nature of the constitutional guarantee that is violated. Sometimes that explicitly mandates exclusion from trial, and sometimes it does not. The Fifth Amendment guarantees that no person shall be compelled to give evidence against himself, and so is violated whenever a truly coerced confession is introduced at trial, whether by way of impeachment or otherwise. The Fourth Amendment, on the other hand, guarantees that no person shall be subjected to unreasonable searches or seizures, and says nothing about excluding their fruits from evidence; exclusion comes by way of deterrent sanction rather than to avoid violation of the substantive guarantee. Inadmissibility has not been automatic, therefore, but we have instead applied an exclusionary-rule balancing test. The same is true for violations of the Fifth and Sixth Amendment prophylactic rules forbidding certain pretrial police conduct.

Respondent argues that the Sixth Amendment's right to counsel is a "right an accused is to enjoy a[t] trial." The core of the right to counsel is indeed a trial right, ensuring that the prosecution's case is subjected to "the crucible of meaningful adversarial testing." But our opinions under the

Sixth Amendment, as under the Fifth, have held that the right covers pretrial interrogations to ensure that police manipulation does not render counsel entirely impotent—depriving the defendant of "effective representation by counsel at the only stage when legal aid and advice would help him."

Our opinion in *Massiah,* to be sure, was equivocal on what precisely constituted the violation. It quoted various authorities indicating that the violation occurred at the moment of the postindictment interrogation because such questioning "contravenes the basic dictates of fairness in the conduct of criminal causes." But the opinion later suggested that the violation occurred only when the improperly obtained evidence was "used against [the defendant] at his trial." That question was irrelevant to the decision in *Massiah* in any event. Now that we are confronted with the question, we conclude that the *Massiah* right is a right to be free of uncounseled interrogation, and is infringed at the time of the interrogation. That, we think, is when the "Assistance of Counsel" is denied.

It is illogical to say that the right is not violated until trial counsel's task of opposing conviction has been undermined by the statement's admission into evidence. A defendant is not denied counsel merely because the prosecution has been permitted to introduce evidence of guilt—even evidence so overwhelming that the attorney's job of gaining an acquittal is rendered impossible. In such circumstances the accused continues to enjoy the assistance of counsel; the assistance is simply not worth much. The assistance of counsel has been denied, however, at the prior critical stage which produced the inculpatory evidence. Our cases acknowledge that reality in holding that the stringency of the warnings necessary for a waiver of the assistance of counsel varies according to "the usefulness of counsel to the accused at the particular [pretrial] proceeding." It is *that* deprivation which demands a remedy.

The United States insists that "post-charge deliberate elicitation of statements without the defendant's counsel or a valid waiver of counsel is not intrinsically unlawful." That is true when the questioning is unrelated to charged crimes—the Sixth Amendment right is "offense specific." We have never said, however, that officers may badger counseled defendants about charged crimes so long as they do not use information they gain. The constitutional violation occurs when the uncounseled interrogation is conducted.

B

This case does not involve, therefore, the prevention of a constitutional violation, but rather the scope of the remedy for a violation that has already occurred. Our precedents make clear that the game of excluding tainted evidence for impeachment purposes is not worth the candle. The interests safeguarded by such exclusion are "outweighed by the need to prevent perjury and to assure the integrity of the trial process." *Stone v. Powell,*

428 U.S. 465, 488 (1976). "It is one thing to say that the Government cannot make an affirmative use of evidence unlawfully obtained. It is quite another to say that the defendant can . . . provide himself with a shield against contradiction of his untruths." Once the defendant testifies in a way that contradicts prior statements, denying the prosecution use of "the traditional truth-testing devices of the adversary process" is a high price to pay for vindication of the right to counsel at the prior stage.

On the other side of the scale, preventing impeachment use of statements taken in violation of *Massiah* would add little appreciable deterrence. Officers have significant incentive to ensure that they and their informants comply with the Constitution's demands, since statements lawfully obtained can be used for all purposes rather than simply for impeachment. And the *ex ante* probability that evidence gained in violation of *Massiah* would be of use for impeachment is exceedingly small. An investigator would have to anticipate both that the defendant would choose to testify at trial (an unusual occurrence to begin with) *and* that he would testify inconsistently despite the admissibility of his prior statement for impeachment. Not likely to happen—or at least not likely enough to risk squandering the opportunity of using a properly obtained statement for the prosecution's case in chief.

In any event, even if "the officer may be said to have little to lose and perhaps something to gain by way of possibly uncovering impeachment material," we have multiple times rejected the argument that this "speculative possibility" can trump the costs of allowing perjurious statements to go unchallenged. *Oregon v. Hass,* 420 U.S. 714, 723 (1975). We have held in every other context that tainted evidence—evidence whose very introduction does not constitute the constitutional violation, but whose obtaining was constitutionally invalid—is admissible for impeachment. We see no distinction that would alter the balance here.*

* * *

We hold that the informant's testimony, concededly elicited in violation of the Sixth Amendment, was admissible to challenge Ventris's inconsistent testimony at trial.

JUSTICE STEVENS, with whom JUSTICE GINSBURG joins, dissenting.

In *Michigan v. Harvey,* 494 U.S. 344 (1990), the Court held that a statement obtained from a defendant in violation of the Sixth Amendment

* Respondent's *amicus* insists that jailhouse snitches are so inherently unreliable that this Court should craft a broader exclusionary rule for uncorroborated statements obtained by that means. Our legal system, however, is built on the premise that it is the province of the jury to weigh the credibility of competing witnesses, and we have long purported to avoid "establish[ing] this Court as a rule-making organ for the promulgation of state rules of criminal procedure." *Spencer v. Texas,* 385 U.S. 554, 564 (1967). It would be especially inappropriate to fabricate such a rule in this case, where it appears the jury took to heart the trial judge's cautionary instruction on the unreliability of rewarded informant testimony by acquitting Ventris of felony murder.

could be used to impeach his testimony at trial. As I explained in a dissent joined by three other Members of the Court, that holding eroded the principle that "those who are entrusted with the power of government have the same duty to respect and obey the law as the ordinary citizen." It was my view then, as it is now, that "the Sixth Amendment is violated when the fruits of the State's impermissible encounter with the represented defendant are used for impeachment just as it is when the fruits are used in the prosecutor's case in chief."

In this case, the State has conceded that it violated the Sixth Amendment as interpreted in *Massiah v. United States,* 377 U.S. 201 (1964), when it used a jailhouse informant to elicit a statement from the defendant. No *Miranda* warnings were given to the defendant, nor was he otherwise alerted to the fact that he was speaking to a state agent. Even though the jury apparently did not credit the informant's testimony, the Kansas Supreme Court correctly concluded that the prosecution should not be allowed to exploit its pretrial constitutional violation during the trial itself. The Kansas Court's judgment should be affirmed.

This Court's contrary holding relies on the view that a defendant's pretrial right to counsel is merely "prophylactic" in nature. The majority argues that any violation of this prophylactic right occurs solely at the time the State subjects a counseled defendant to an uncounseled interrogation, not when the fruits of the encounter are used against the defendant at trial. This reasoning is deeply flawed.

* * *

Treating the State's actions in this case as a violation of a prophylactic right, the Court concludes that introducing the illegally obtained evidence at trial does not itself violate the Constitution. I strongly disagree. While the constitutional breach began at the time of interrogation, the State's use of that evidence at trial compounded the violation. The logic that compels the exclusion of the evidence during the State's case in chief extends to any attempt by the State to rely on the evidence, even for impeachment. The use of ill-gotten evidence during any phase of criminal prosecution does damage to the adversarial process—the fairness of which the Sixth Amendment was designed to protect.

When counsel is excluded from a critical pretrial interaction between the defendant and the State, she may be unable to effectively counter the potentially devastating, and potentially false,[2] evidence subsequently introduced at trial. Inexplicably, today's Court refuses to recognize that this is a constitutional harm. Yet in *Massiah,* the Court forcefully explained that a defendant is "denied the basic protections of the [Sixth

---

[2] The likelihood that evidence gathered by self-interested jailhouse informants may be false cannot be ignored. Indeed, by deciding to acquit respondent of felony murder, the jury seems to have dismissed the informant's trial testimony as unreliable.

Amendment] guarantee when there [is] used against him at his trial evidence of his own incriminating words" that were "deliberately elicited from him after he had been indicted and in the absence of counsel." Sadly, the majority has retreated from this robust understanding of the right to counsel.

Today's decision is lamentable not only because of its flawed underpinnings, but also because it is another occasion in which the Court has privileged the prosecution at the expense of the Constitution. Permitting the State to cut corners in criminal proceedings taxes the legitimacy of the entire criminal process. "The State's interest in truthseeking is congruent with the defendant's interest in representation by counsel, for it is an elementary premise of our system of criminal justice that partisan advocacy on both sides of a case will best promote the ultimate objective that the guilty be convicted and the innocent go free." Although the Court may not be concerned with the use of ill-gotten evidence in derogation of the right to counsel, I remain convinced that such shabby tactics are intolerable in all cases. I respectfully dissent.

Points for Discussion

1. In *Nix v. Williams*, Justice Stevens asserted in his dissent, "The 'Christian burial speech' was nothing less than an attempt to substitute an *ex parte*, inquisitorial process for the clash of adversaries commanded by the Constitution." This concern with the process by which the government gathers evidence harkens back to the concerns that animated *Massiah*, *Escobedo*, and *Miranda*. Nonetheless, Justice Stevens concluded that the inevitable discovery of the body "means that the trial in this case was not the product of an inquisitorial process." Fifteen years later in *Ventris*, Justice Stevens again reiterates the importance of enforcing the adversarial aspects of the criminal justice system. How important is it to Justice Stevens' reasoning in *Ventris* that jailhouse informants are notoriously prone to lying, as he notes in footnote 2?

2. In *Mincey v. Arizona*, 437 U.S. 385 (1978), the defendant was interrogated in his hospital room while attached to numerous tubes; he repeatedly asked to stop the interview and speak to a lawyer but was refused. At trial, the government sought to use the statements obtained from the hospital interview to impeach the defendant's testimony on the stand. The Supreme Court held that, as opposed to evidence obtained in violation of *Miranda*, evidence obtained through a violation of the Fifth Amendment itself may not be used "for any trial purpose". Why does the Court come to a different conclusion regarding violations of the Sixth Amendment in *Ventris*?

INDEX

References are to Pages